2nd Edition

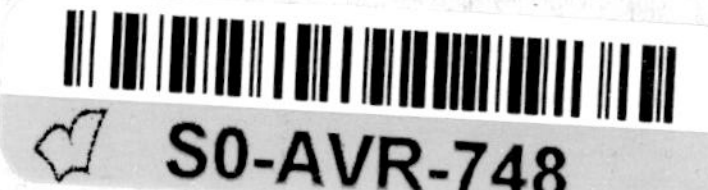

Guitar Tab White Pages

Volume 1

Also Available!

HL00699557

HL00690791

HL00699590

HL00690508

ISBN-13: 978-0-634-02611-9
ISBN-10: 0-634-02611-9

HAL•LEONARD®
CORPORATION
7777 W. BLUEMOUND RD. P.O. BOX 13819 MILWAUKEE, WI 53213

Visit Hal Leonard Online at
www.halleonard.com

Contents

Aerials

Words and Music by Daron Malakian and Serj Tankian

Gtrs. 1, 2 & 3: Drop D tuning, down 1 step:
(low to high) C–G–C–F–A–D

Gtr. 4: DADGAD tuning, down 1 step:
(low to high) C–G–C–F–G–C

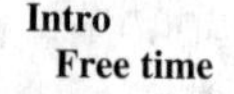

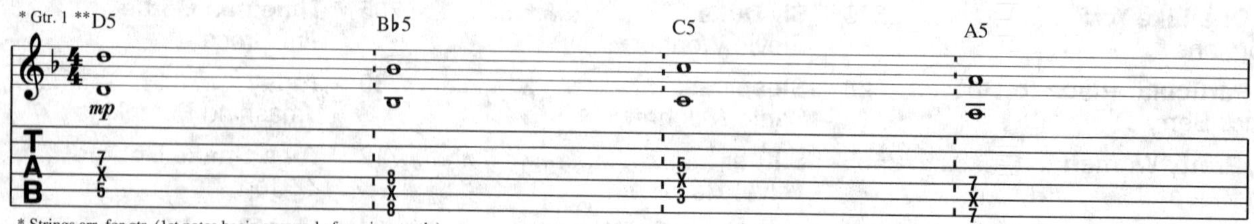

* Strings arr. for gtr. (1st notes begin over end of previous track.)

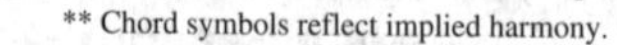

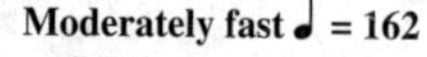

Dsus2/A
D7(no3rd)/A
D5/A
Dsus2/A
Dm/A
w/ bar
Dsus4/A
Dm/A
Dsus2/A
D5
D7(no3rd)/A
D5/A
D5
w/ bar
Verse
Half-time feel
Gtrs. 1 & 2 tacet
2nd time, Gtr. 4 tacet
B♭5
1., 2.Life is a wa - ter - fall,
we're one in the riv - er and one a - gain af - ter the fall.
we drink from the riv - er, then we turn a - round and put up our walls.
* Gtr. 3
(elec.) Rhy. Fig. 1
f
w/ dist.
* Doubled throughout

D5
G5
D5
F5
D5
E5
D5
End Rhy. Fig. 1
P.M.
P.M.
P.M.
P.M.

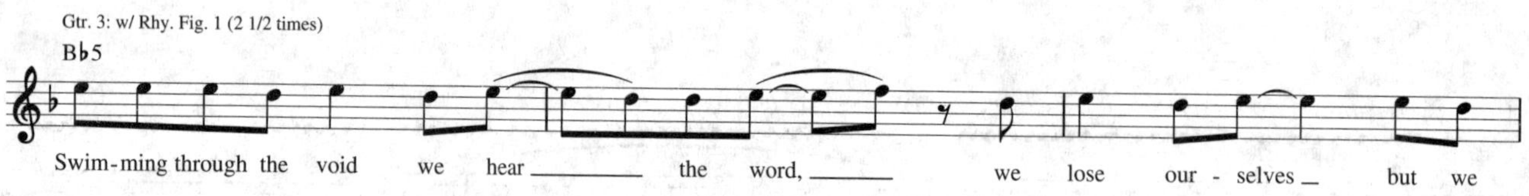
Gtr. 3: w/ Rhy. Fig. 1 (2 1/2 times)
B♭5
Swim-ming through the void we hear the word, we lose our - selves but we

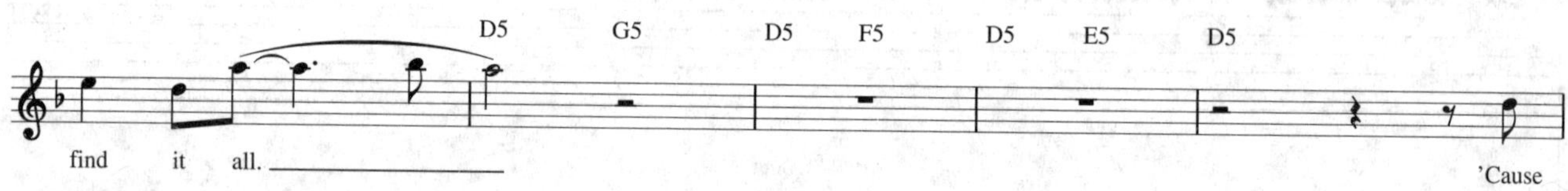
D5
G5
D5
F5
D5
E5
D5
find it all.
'Cause

B♭5
we are the ones that wan - na play, al - ways wan - na go but you

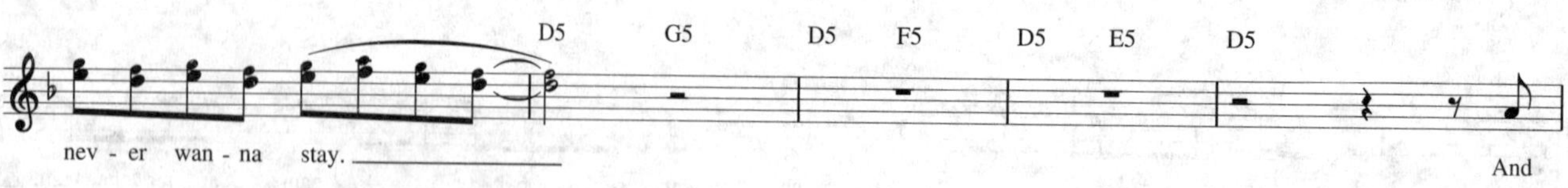
D5
G5
D5
F5
D5
E5
D5
nev - er wan - na stay.
And

To Coda
B♭5
we are the ones that wan - na choose, al - ways wan - na play but you nev - er wan - na lose.

Interlude
Gtr. 2: w/ Riff A
Gtr. 3 tacet
D5/F D5/E D5
D5/G D5/F D5/E
Gtr. 4 (acous.)
Riff B
mp
let ring throughout
Gtr. 3
P.M.
D5/F D5/G D5/A D5/B♭ D5/A D5/G D5/F D5/E D5
Gtr. 4
End Riff B
Chorus
Gtrs. 2 & 4: w/ Riffs A & B (1st 4 meas.)
D5/F D5/E D5
D5/G D5/F D5/E
Aer - i - als
in the sky.
D.S. al Coda
D5/F D5/G D5/A D5/B♭ D5/A D5/G D5/F D5/E D5
When you lose small mind, you free your life.
Gtr. 4
Gtr. 2
let ring

Coda

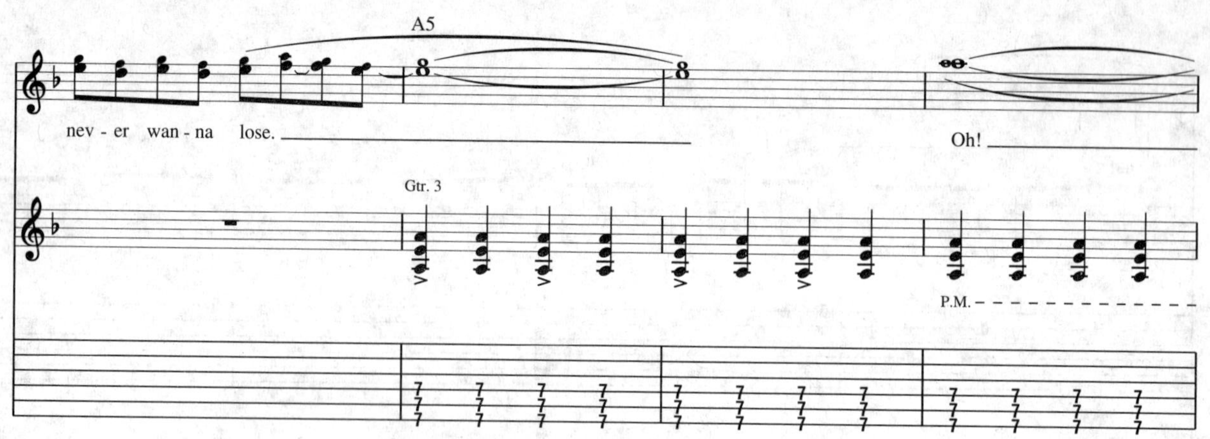
A5
nev - er wan - na lose.
Oh!
Gtr. 3
P.M.

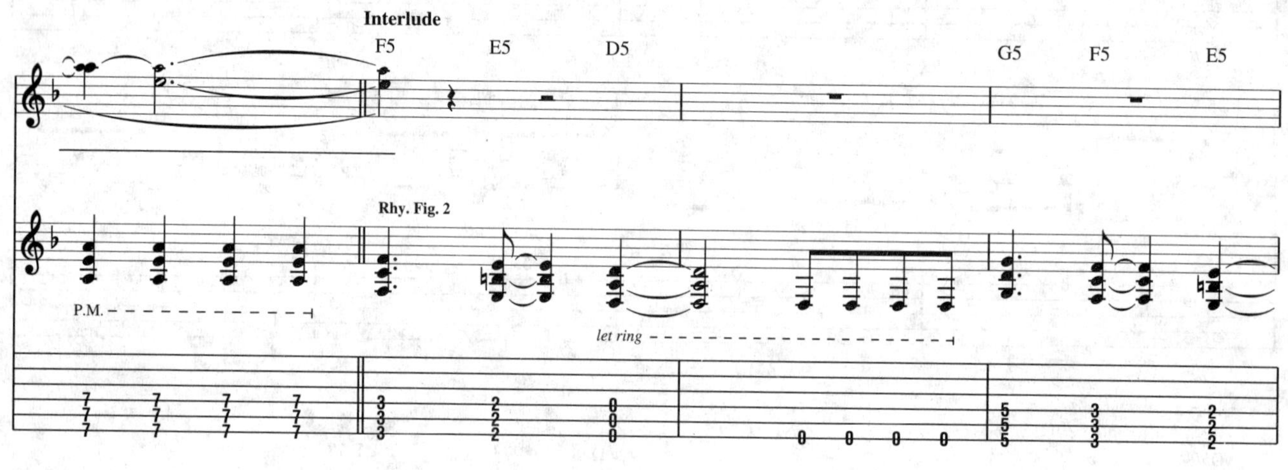
Interlude
F5
E5
D5
G5
F5
E5
Rhy. Fig. 2
P.M.
let ring

F5
G5
A5
B♭5
A5
G5
F5
E5
D5
End Rhy. Fig. 2

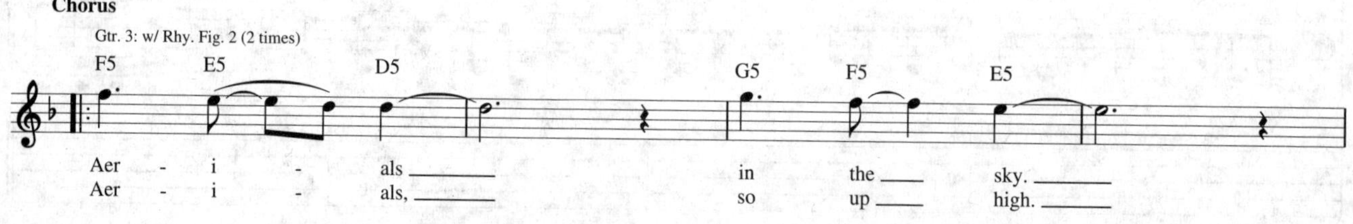
Chorus
Gtr. 3: w/ Rhy. Fig. 2 (2 times)
F5
E5
D5
G5
F5
E5
Aer - i - als in the sky.
Aer - i - als, so up high.

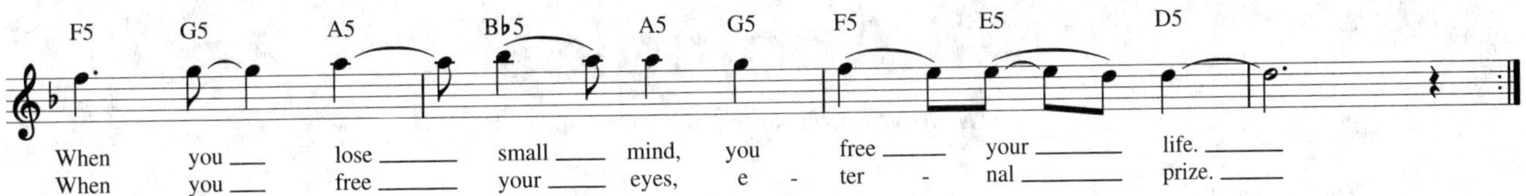
F5 G5 A5 B♭5 A5 G5 F5 E5 D5
When you lose small mind, you free your life.
When you free your eyes, e - ter - nal prize.

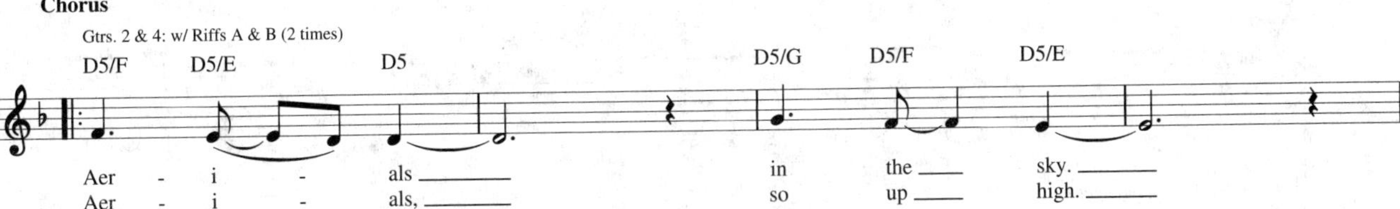
Chorus
Gtrs. 2 & 4: w/ Riffs A & B (2 times)
D5/F D5/E D5 D5/G D5/F D5/E
Aer - i - als in the sky.
Aer - i - als, so up high.

D5/F D5/G D5/A D5/B♭ D5/A D5/G D5/F D5/E D5
When you lose small mind, you free your life.
When you free your eyes, e - ter - nal prize.

Outro
Gtrs. 2 & 4: w/ Riffs A & B (1 3/4 times)
D5/F D5/E D5 D5/G D5/F D5/E D5/F D5/G D5/A D5/B♭ D5/A D5/G
Ah, ah. Ah.

1.
D5/F D5/E D5
2.
D5/F D5/E D5
Gtr. 4
Gtr. 2
let ring

All Apologies

Words and Music by Kurt Cobain

What else should I say?
Find my nest of salt.
Ev - 'ry - one is gay.
Ev - 'ry - thing is my fault.
What else should I write?
I'll take all the blame,
I don't have the right.
a - qua sea - foam shame.
What else should I be?
Sun - burn, freez - er - burn.
All a - pol - o - gies.
Chok - ing on the ash - es of her en - e - my.
0 0 0 0 0 0 0 0
0 0 0 9 0 0 0 0
0 0 0 0 0 0 0 0
0 0 0 9 0 9 0 0
0 0 0 9 0 0 0 9
0 9 0 0 0 9 0 0
0 0 0 0 0 0 0 0
0 0 9 0 0 0 0
0 0 0 0 0 0 0 0
0 0 0 9 0 0 0 9
0 0 0 9 0 0 0 9
0 9 9 9

Chorus

*Composite arrangement

Mar - ried,
bur - ied,
yeah,
yeah,
yeah,
yeah.
Outro
Gtr. 1: w/ Riff A
Gtr. 2: w/ Riff B
N.C.(D)
*Gtrs. 1 & 2: w/ Riffs A & B (4 times)
All a - lone is all
*Gtr. 2 fades out 4th time.
Play 4 times
we all are. All a - lone is all we all are.
All a - lone is all we all, are. All a - lone is all we all are.
Gtr. 1
mp
p
All a - lone is all we all...
All a - lone is all we all are.
Gtr. 1 tacet
All a - lone is all we all are.

All Day and All of the Night

Words and Music by Ray Davies

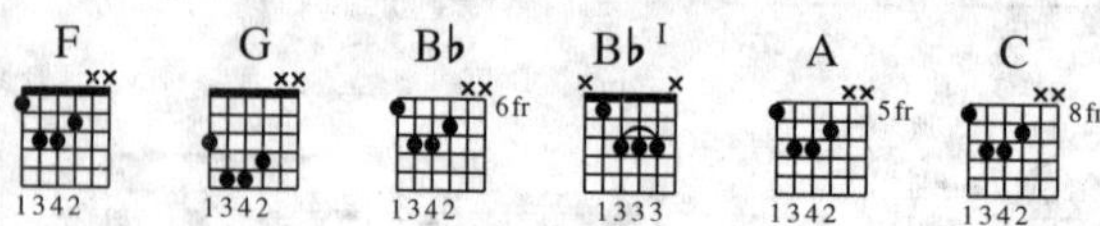

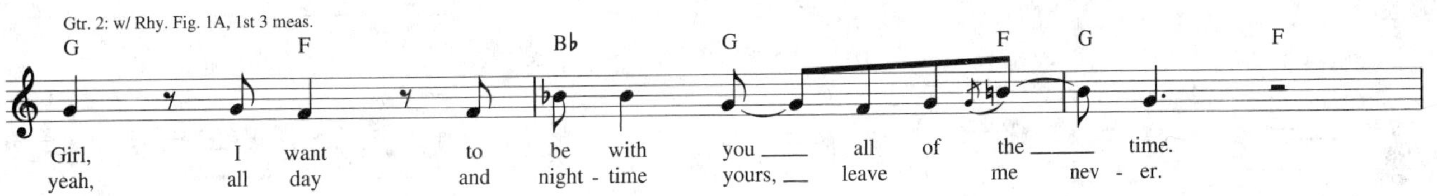
Gtr. 2: w/ Rhy. Fig. 1A, 1st 3 meas.
G F B♭ G F G F
Girl, I want to be with you all of the time.
yeah, all day and night - time yours, leave me nev - er.

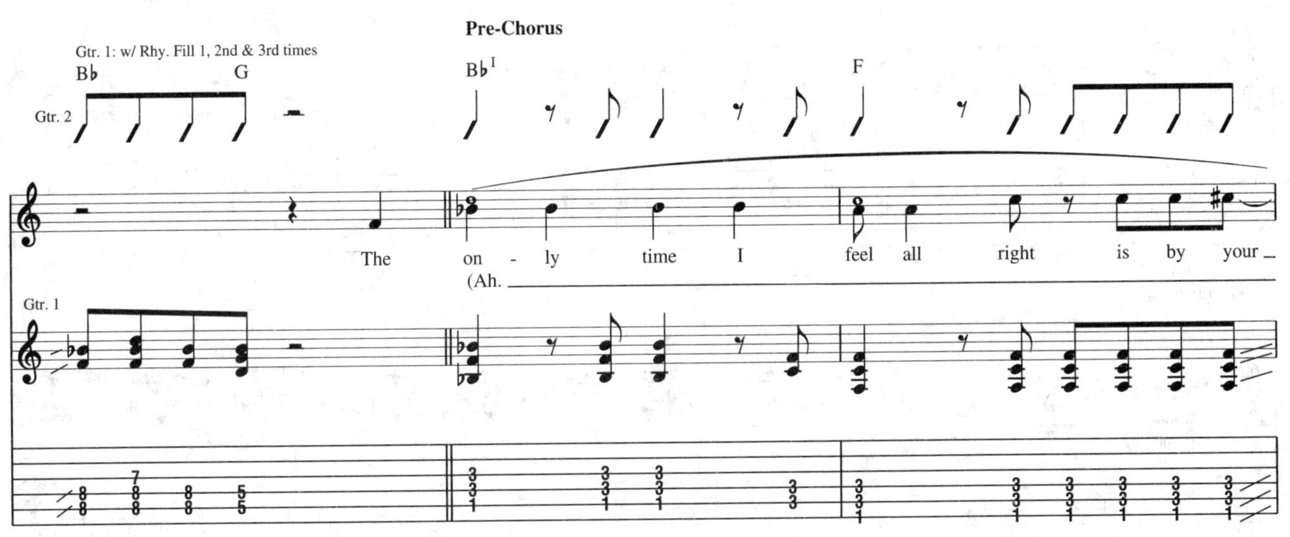
Pre-Chorus
Gtr. 1: w/ Rhy. Fill 1, 2nd & 3rd times
B♭ G B♭ F
Gtr. 2
The on - ly time I feel all right is by your
(Ah.
Gtr. 1

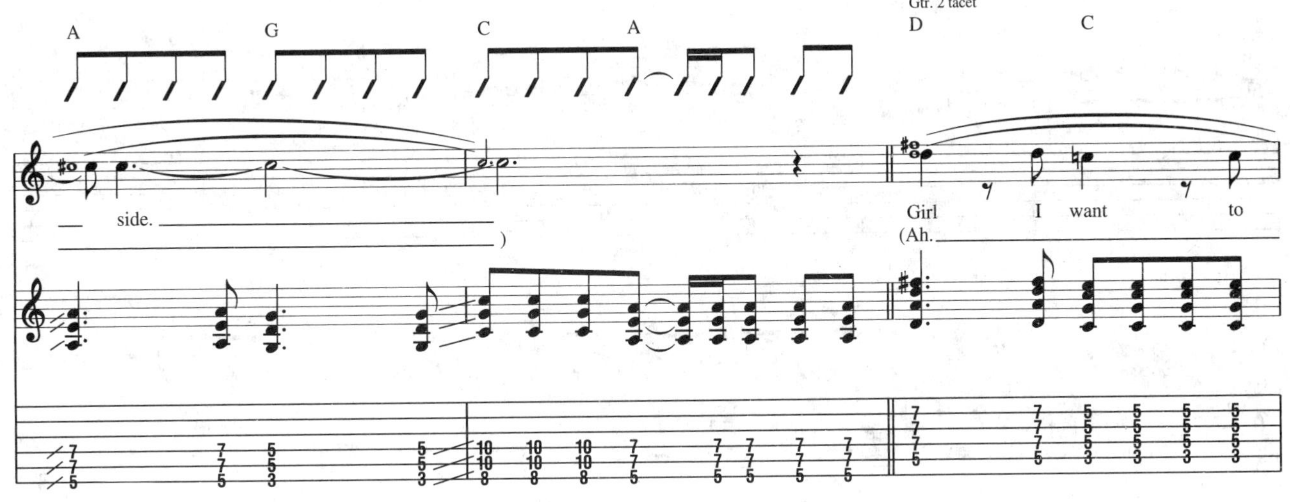
Chorus
Gtr. 2 tacet
A G C A D C
side.
)
Girl I want to
(Ah.

F D C F D C
be with you all of the time. All day and all of the night.
)
Rhy. Fig. 2
End Rhy. Fig. 2

To Coda
1.
Gtr. 1: w/ Rhy. Fig. 2, simile
All day and all of the night.
2.
Gtr. 1
N.C.
Oh, come on!
Guitar Solo
Gtr. 2:/w/ Rhy. Fig. 1A, 1 1/2 times, simile
let ring
Gtr. 2
D.S. al Coda
Coda
All day and all of the night.

All the Small Things

Words and Music by Tom De Longe and Mark Hoppus

Pre-Chorus
C5
Say it ain't so. I will not go. Turn the lights off. Car - ry me
Chorus
C5
G5
F5
home.
Na, na, na, na, na, na, na, na, na, na. Na, na, na, na, na, na, na, na, na, na.
Gtr. 2 Riff A
(dist.)
End Riff A
mf
let ring throughout
Gtr. 1 Rhy. Fig. 4
End Rhy. Fig. 4
To Coda
Gtr. 1: w/ Rhy. Fig. 4
Gtr. 2: w/ Riff A
C5
G5
F5
Na, na, na, na, na, na, na, na, na, na. Na, na, na, na, na, na, na, na, na, na.
Interlude
Gtr. 1: w/ Rhy. Fig. 1, 2 times
Gtr. 2
C5
F5
G5
N.C.
F5
P.M.

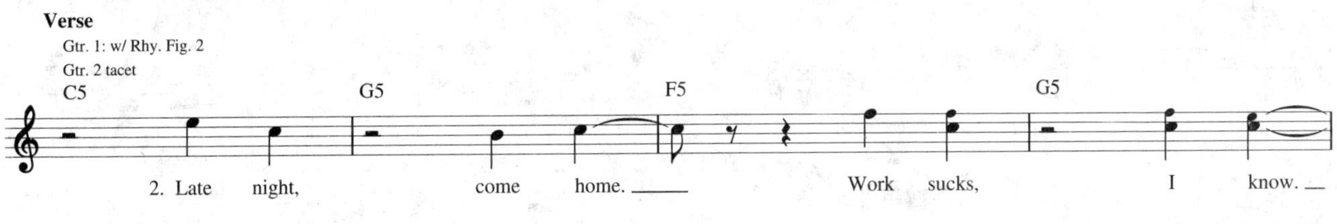
Verse
Gtr. 1: w/ Rhy. Fig. 2
Gtr. 2 tacet
C5 G5 F5 G5
2. Late night, come home. Work sucks, I know.

D.S. al Coda
Gtr. 1: w/ Rhy. Fig. 3
C5 G5 F5 G5 C5
She left me ros - es by the stairs. Sur - pris - es let me know she cares.

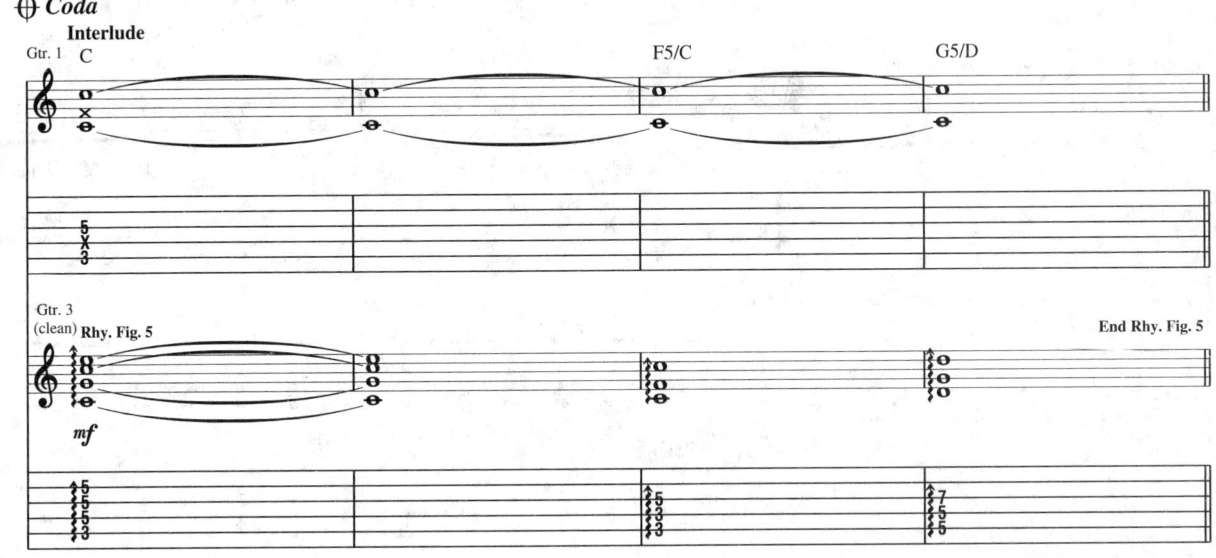
Coda
Interlude
Gtr. 1
C F5/C G5/D
Gtr. 3
(clean)
Rhy. Fig. 5
End Rhy. Fig. 5
mf

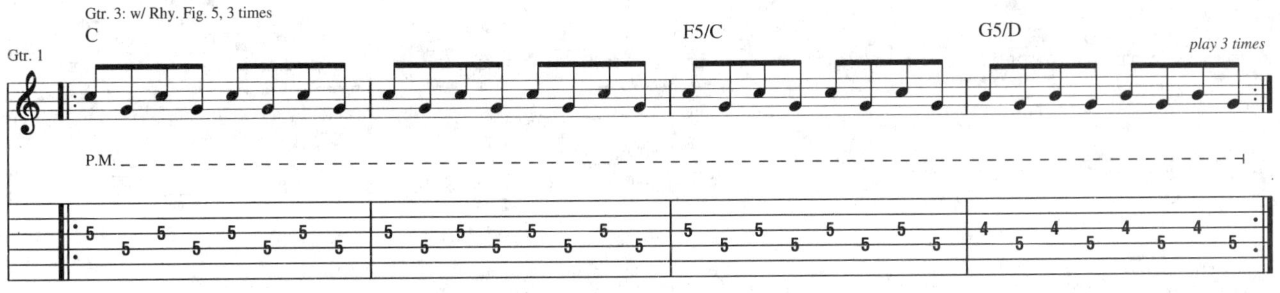
Gtr. 3: w/ Rhy. Fig. 5, 3 times
C F5/C G5/D
Gtr. 1
play 3 times
P.M.

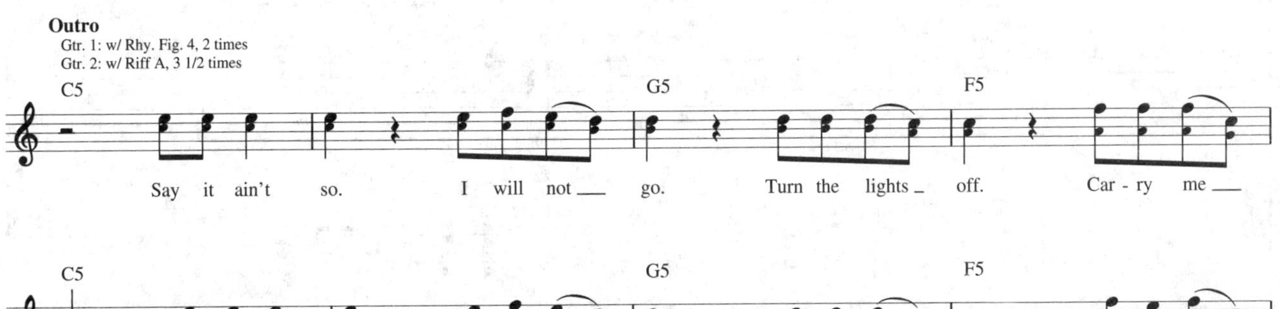
Outro
Gtr. 1: w/ Rhy. Fig. 4, 2 times
Gtr. 2: w/ Riff A, 3 1/2 times
C5 G5 F5
Say it ain't so. I will not go. Turn the lights off. Car - ry me
C5 G5 F5
home. Keep your head still. I'll be your thrill. The night will go on, my lit - tle wind -

C5
G5
mill. Say it ain't so. I will not go. Turn the lights
(Na, na, na, na, na, na, na, na, na, na. Na, na, na, na, na, na,
Gtr. 1
F5
C5
off. Car - ry me home. Keep your head still. I'll be your
na, na, na, na. Na, na, na, na, na, na, na, na, na, na.
P.M.
P.M.
G5
F5
C5
thrill. The night will go on, the night will go on, my lit - tle wind - mill.
Na, na, na, na, na, na, na, na, na, na, na, na, na, na.)
Gtr. 2
Gtr. 1
P.M.
P.M.
P.M.
P.M.

All Your Love (I Miss Loving)

Words and Music by Otis Rush

Verse
F#m
1. All the love I miss lov-in', all the kiss-es I miss kiss-in'.
ba-by, I have in store for you.
simile on repeat
Rhy. Fig. 1

Bm
All the love I miss lov-in', all the kiss-es I miss
All the love, pret-ty ba-by, I have in store for

F#m
C#m
kiss - in'.
you.
Be - fore I met you, ba - by,
The way I love you, ba - by,
End Rhy. Fig. 1

1.
Bm
F#m
I did - n't know what I was miss - in'.
2. All the love, pret - ty

2.
Bm
F♯m
I know you love me, too.
f
w/ dist.
let ring
*Gtr. 1 plays w/ triplet feel till Outro.
Interlude
Gtr. 2 tacet
F♯m
Gtr. 1
let ring
Bm
F♯m
C♯m
Bm
F♯m
8va

Guitar Solo
Triplet Feel
F#7
8va
Gtr. 1
1/2
full
Gtr. 2
Rhy. Fig. 2
B7
loco
*Played slightly behind the beat.
F#7
C#7

B7
F#7
Whoa,
full
End Rhy. Fig. 2

Chorus

Gtr. 2: w/ Rhy. Fig. 2, simile
F#7
whoa, whoa, ba - by.
You know I love you, ba - by.
Yeah,
Gtr. 1
w/ clean tone

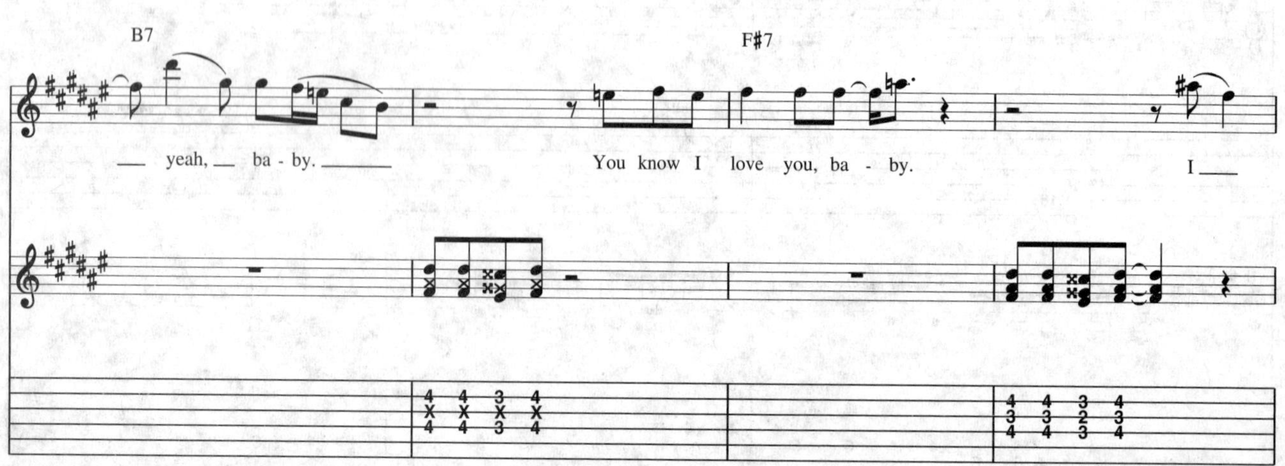
B7
F#7
yeah, ba - by.
You know I love you, ba - by.
I

Outro

Straight Eighths Feel 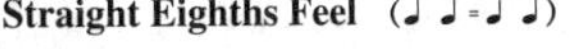

Gtr. 2: w/ Rhy. Fig. 1

F#m

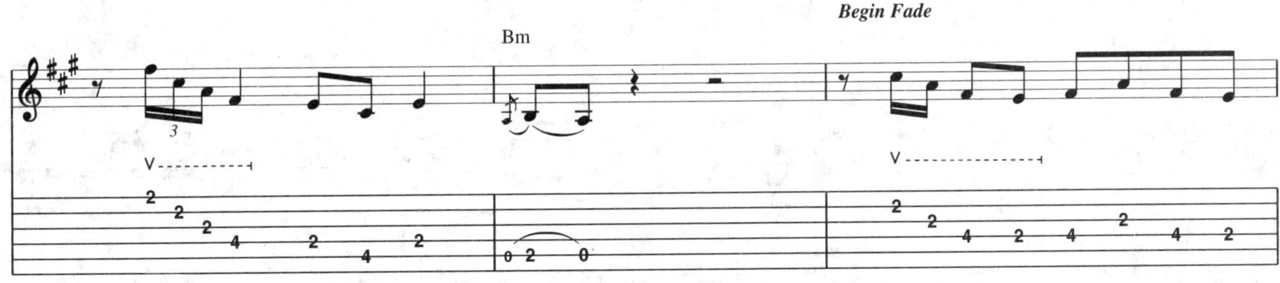

American Woman

Written by Burton Cummings, Randy Bachman, Gary Peterson and Jim Kale

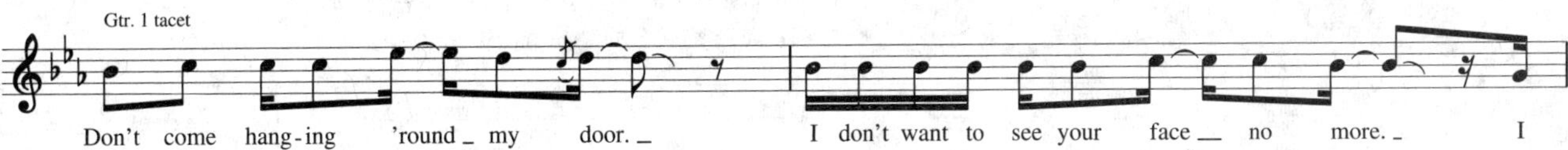
Gtr. 1 tacet
Don't come hang-ing 'round my door. I don't want to see your face no more. I

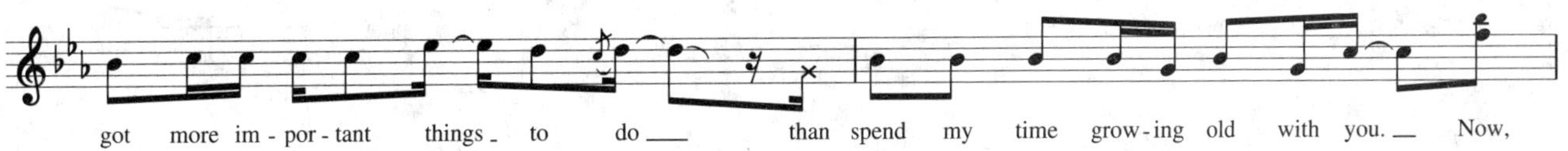
got more im-por-tant things to do than spend my time grow-ing old with you. Now,

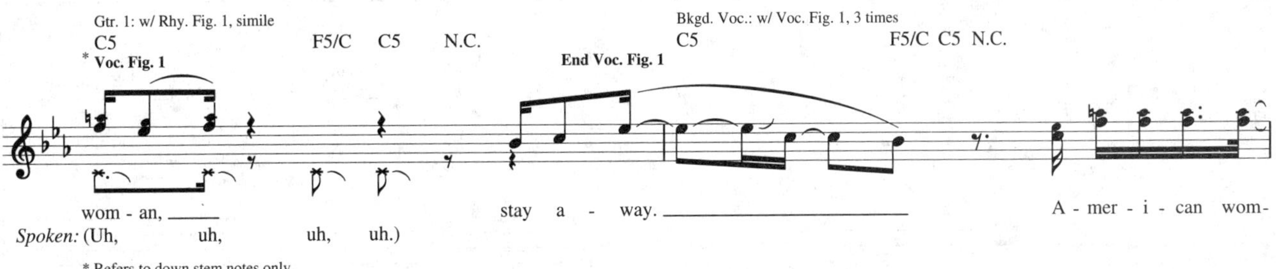
Gtr. 1: w/ Rhy. Fig. 1, simile
C5 F5/C C5 N.C.
* Voc. Fig. 1
End Voc. Fig. 1
Bkgd. Voc.: w/ Voc. Fig. 1, 3 times
C5 F5/C C5 N.C.
wom - an, stay a - way. A - mer - i - can wom-
Spoken: (Uh, uh, uh, uh.)
* Refers to down stem notes only.

C5 F5/C C5 N.C. C5 F5/C C5 N.C.
- an lis - ten what I say.

Bb5 C5 Bb5 C5 Bb5 C5 Bb5 C5 N.C.
Voc. Fig. 2
End Voc. Fig. 2
(Bow, ka, dow, ka, dow, ka, dow, dow. Bow, ka, dow, ka, dow, ka, dow, dow.)
Gtr. 2
(dist.)
Rhy. Fig. 2
mp
Gtr. 3
(dist.)
Rhy. Fig. 2A
mp

Bkgd. Voc.: w/ Voc. Fig. 2, simile
Bb5 C5 Bb5 C5 Bb5 C5 Bb5 C5 N.C.
2. A - mer - i - can wom-
End Rhy. Fig. 2
End Rhy. Fig. 2A

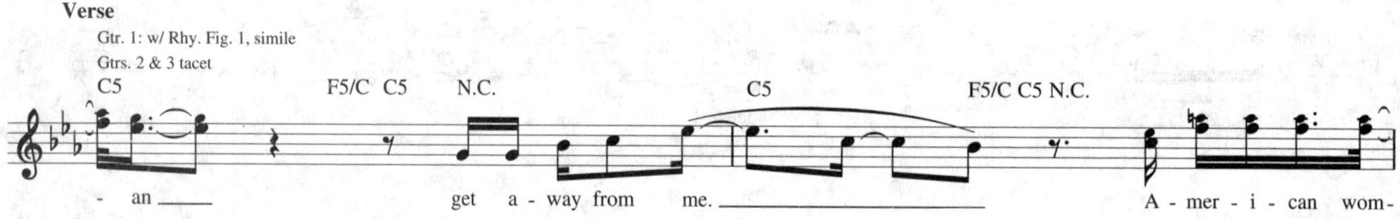
Verse
Gtr. 1: w/ Rhy. Fig. 1, simile
Gtrs. 2 & 3 tacet
C5 F5/C C5 N.C. C5 F5/C C5 N.C.
- an get a - way from me. A - mer - i - can wom-

C5 F5/C C5 N.C. C5 F5/C C5 N.C.
Gtr. 1 tacet
- an, ma-ma, let me be. Don't come knock-ing 'round my door.

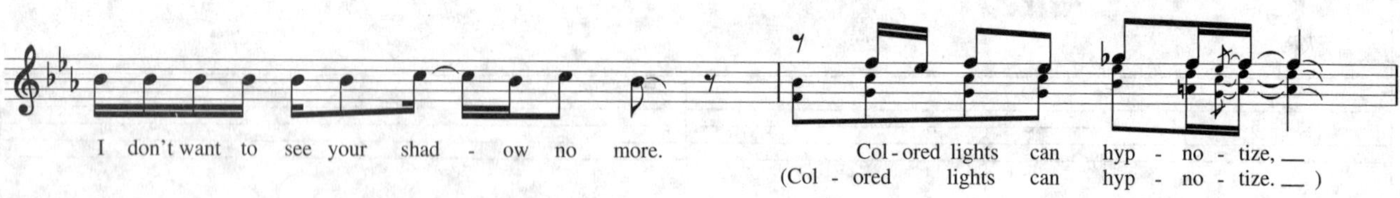
I don't want to see your shad - ow no more. Col-ored lights can hyp - no - tize,
(Col - ored lights can hyp - no - tize.)

Bkgd. Voc.: w/ Voc. Fig. 1, 4 times
Gtr. 1: w/ Rhy. Fig. 1, simile
C5 F5/C C5 N.C.
spark - le some-one el - se's eyes. Now, wom - an, get a - way.

C5
F5/C C5 N.C.
C5
F5/C C5
N.C.
C5
F5/C C5 N.C.
A-mer-i-can wom - an
lis-ten what I say.

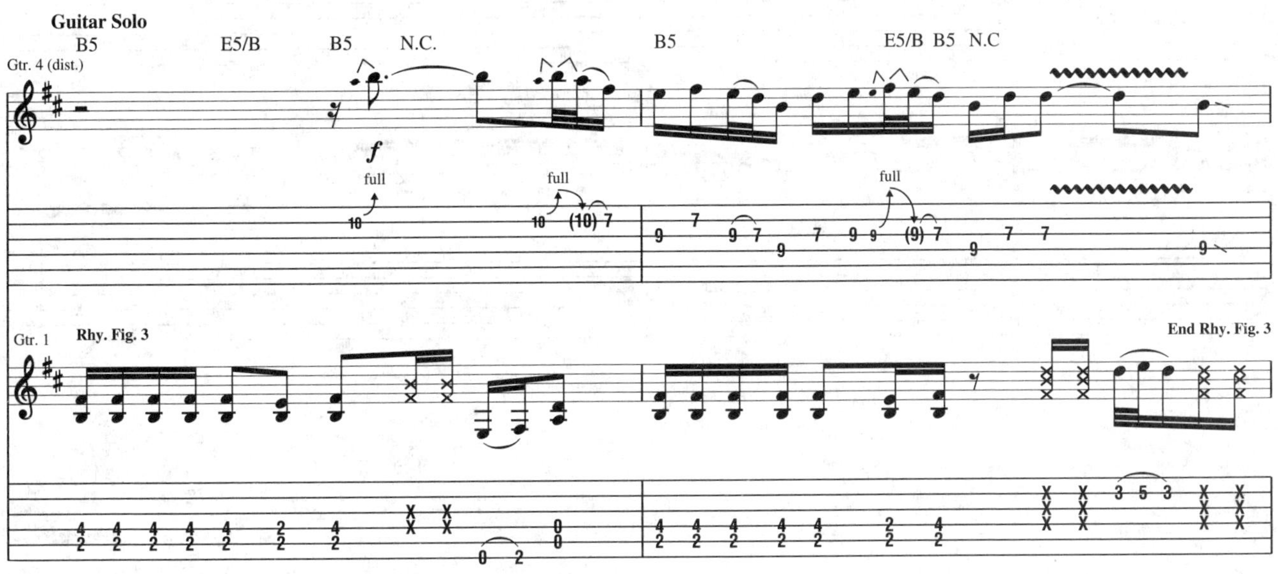
Guitar Solo
B5
E5/B
B5 N.C.
B5
E5/B B5 N.C
Gtr. 4 (dist.)
f
full
full
full
Gtr. 1
Rhy. Fig. 3
End Rhy. Fig. 3

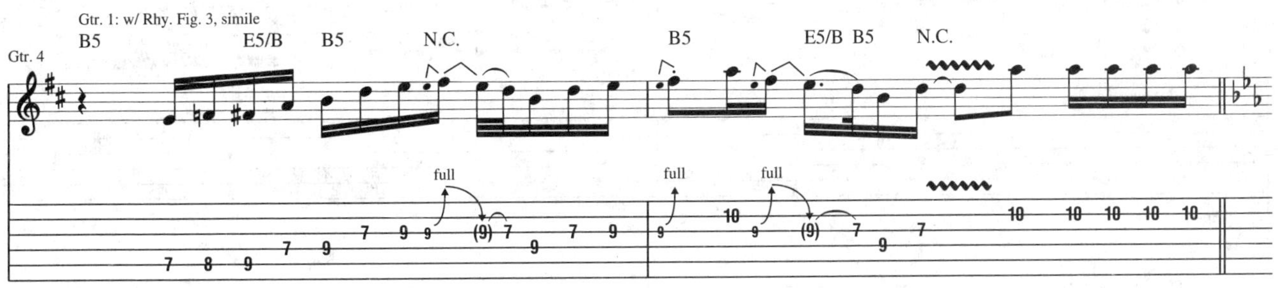
Gtr. 1: w/ Rhy. Fig. 3, simile
B5
E5/B
B5
N.C.
B5
E5/B B5
N.C.
Gtr. 4
full
full
full

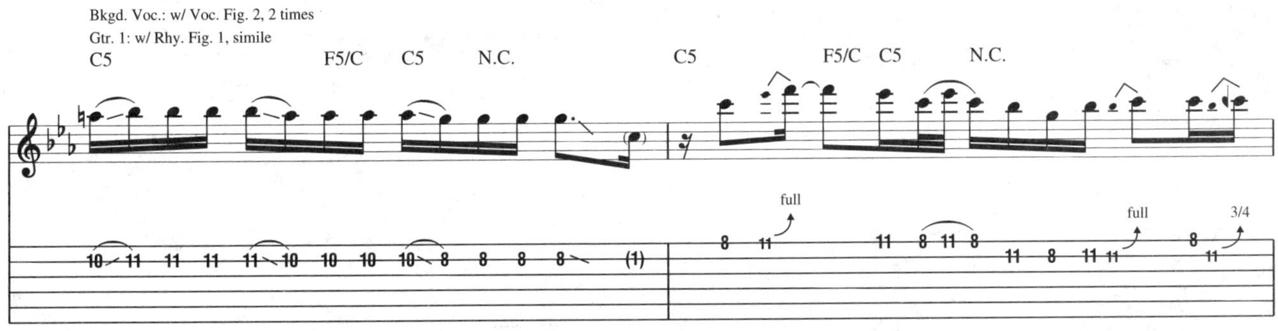
Bkgd. Voc.: w/ Voc. Fig. 2, 2 times
Gtr. 1: w/ Rhy. Fig. 1, simile
C5
F5/C
C5
N.C.
C5
F5/C C5
N.C.
full
full
3/4

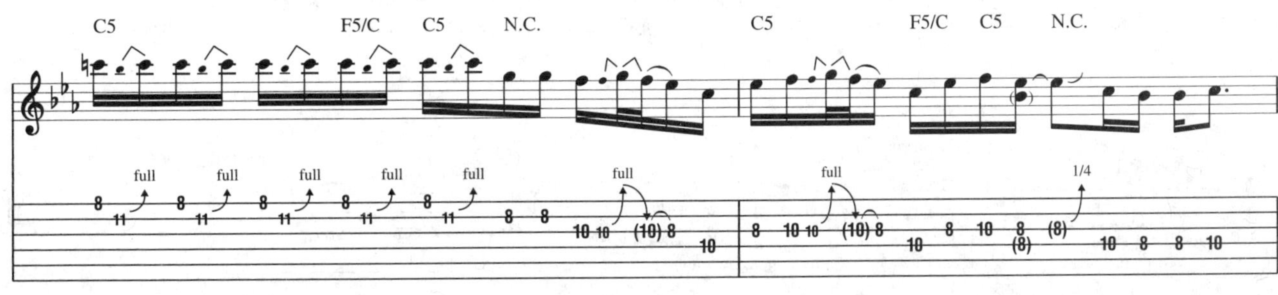
C5
F5/C
C5
N.C.
C5
F5/C
C5
N.C.
full
full
full
full
full
full
full
1/4

Gtr. 4 tacet
Uh.
Gtr. 4
C5
F5/C C5 N.C.
C5
F5/C C5 N.C.
w/ delay
Gtr. 1

C5
F5/C C5 N.C.
C5
F5/C C5 N.C.
A - mer - i - can wom -
Gtr. 1
Gtr. 3

Verse

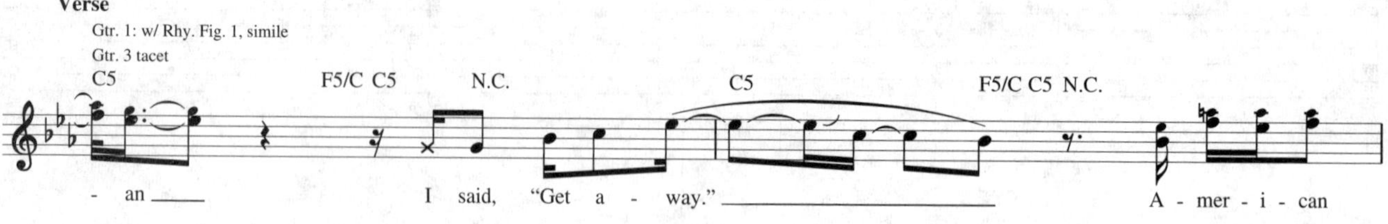
Gtr. 1: w/ Rhy. Fig. 1, simile
Gtr. 3 tacet
C5
F5/C C5
N.C.
C5
F5/C C5 N.C.
- an
I said, "Get a - way."
A - mer - i - can

C5
F5/C C5
N.C.
C5
F5/C C5 N.C.
wom - an
lis - ten what I say.

N.C.
C5
F5/C C5 N.C.
Don't come hang-ing 'round my door.
Don't want to see your face no more.
Gtr. 1
Rhy. Fig. 4
End Rhy. Fig. 4
Gtr. 1: w/ Rhy. Fig. 4, 2 times
I don't need your war ma - chines.
I don't need your ghet - to scenes.
Col-ored lights can hyp - no - tize.
Spar-kle some-one el - se's eyes. Now
Bkgd. Voc.: w/ Voc. Fig. 1, 8 times
Gtr. 1: w/ Rhy. Fig. 1, 2 times, simile
Gtrs. 2 & 3: w/ Rhy. Figs. 2 & 2A, 2 times, simile
wom - an get a - way. A - mer - i - can
wom-an lis-ten what I say. A-mer-i-can wom-an stay a-way from me.
A-mer-i-can wom-an, ma-ma let me be. I got to
* Increased gain causes dist. in vocal
Outro
Gtrs. 2 & 3: w/ Rhy. Figs. 2 & 2A, 5 1/2 times, simile
B♭5 C5
go. I got to get a - way. Babe, I got to
Gtr. 5 (dist.)
Rhy. Fig. 5
End Rhy. Fig. 5
mp

Gtr. 5: w/ Rhy. Fig. 5, 10 times, simile
Bb5 C5
go. I want to fly a - way. I'm gon - na
leave you wom - an. I'm gon - na leave you, wom - an. I'm gon - na
leave you wom - an. I'm gon - na leave you, wom - an. A, bye,
bye, a, bye, bye. A, bye, bye, a, bye,
Voc. Fig. 3
End Voc. Fig. 3
bye. You're no good for me, and
(A - mer - i - can wom - an.)
Bkgd. Voc.: w/ Voc. Fig. 3, 4 times, simile
I'm no good for you. I look you right straight in the eye, I
tell you what I'm gon - na do. I'm gon - na leave you, wom - an. You know I got to
go. I'm gon - na leave you, wom - an. I got to
go. I got to go.
N.C.
Spoken: I got to go, A-mer-i-can wom-an. Yeah.
(drums & synth.)
Begin Fade
Fade Out

Badge

Words and Music by Eric Clapton and George Harrison

2.
C
Am
Bm
Am(add9)
Then I told you 'bout our kid now he's mar-ried to Ma - ble.
Gtr. 1 tacet
* D
Cmaj7(sus2)
G/B
G
Rhy. Fig. 2
Gtr. 1
Gtr. 2
Gtr. 2
divisi
mf w/ chorus & delay
let ring
* Chord symbols reflect implied tonality.
Bridge
Gtr. 2: w/ Rhy. Fig. 2, 2 1/2 times, simile
Yes, I told you that the light goes up and down. Don't you no -
End Rhy. Fig. 2
- tice how the wheel goes 'round. And you bet - ter pick your-self up from the ground be - fore
Rhy. Fig. 3
End Rhy. Fig. 3

G/B G D Cmaj7(sus2) G/B G
they bring the cur - tain down. Yes, be - fore they bring the cur - tain down.
P.M.
Guitar Solo
Gtr. 2: w/ Rhy. Fig. 2, 3 1/4 times, simile
Gtr. 1: w/ Rhy. Fig. 3, 3 1/4 times, simile
D Cmaj7(sus2) G/B G D Cmaj7(sus2)
Woo.
Gtr. 3 (dist.)
Gtr. 1
G/B G D Cmaj7 G/B G
Gtr. 3
D Cmaj7(sus2) G/B G D Cmaj7(sus2)
Yea, yea, yea.
8va

G/B
G
D
Cmaj7(sus2)
G/B
G
8va
hold bend
1/4
full
full
1/2
Gtr. 2: w/ Rhy. Fill 3
Gtr. 1: w/ Rhy. Fill 4
D
Cmaj7(sus2)
G/B
G
D
Yeah, yeah, yeah.
8va
loco
let ring
full
3/4
1/2
1/2
1/2
Verse
Gtr. 1: w/ Rhy. Fig. 1, last 3 meas., simile
Am
D
Esus2
Em
3. Talk - in' 'bout a girl that looks quite like you.
let ring
full
full
Rhy. Fill 3
Gtr. 2
let ring
Rhy. Fill 4
Gtr. 1
P.M.
P.M.

Gtr. 1: w/ Rhy. Fig. 1, 1st 3 meas., simile
Am
D
Esus2
She did - n't have the time to wait in the queue.
full
full
Em
Gtr. 1: w/ Rhy. Fill 2
C
Am
She cried a - way her
Gtr. 3
full
full
Gtr. 1
P.M.
P.M.
P.M.
Bm7
Am(add9)
life since she fell off the cra - dle.

Best of You

Words and Music by Dave Grohl, Taylor Hawkins, Chris Shiflett and Nate Mendel

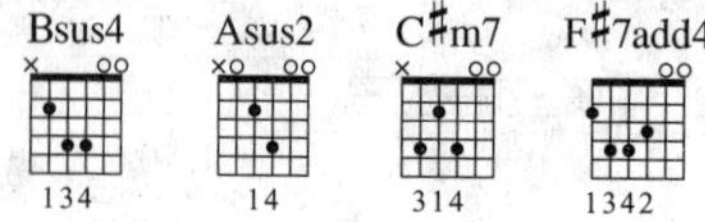

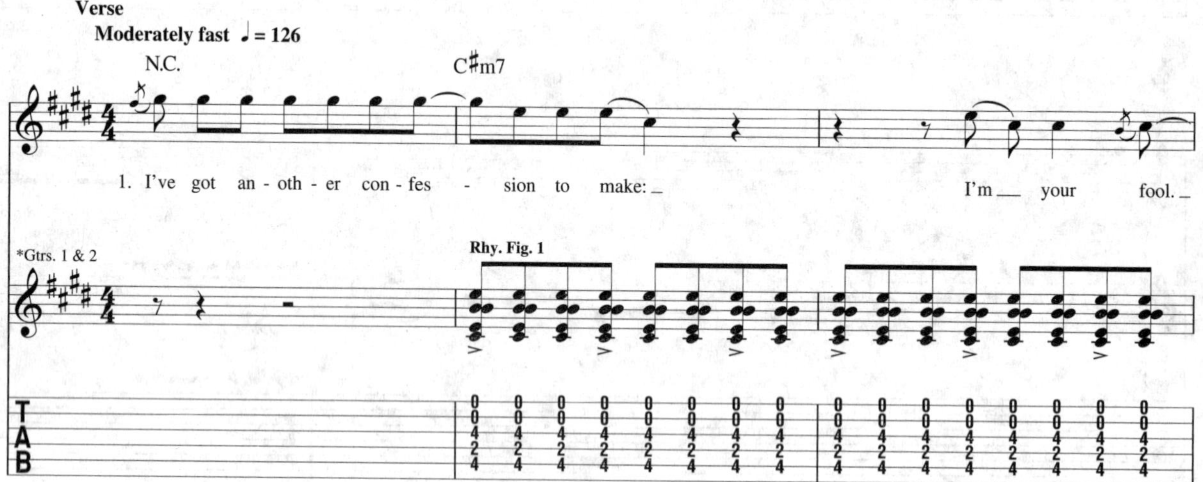

*Gtr. 1 (acous.) played *p*. Gtr. 2 (elec.) w/ slight dist. played *mf*. Composite arrangement

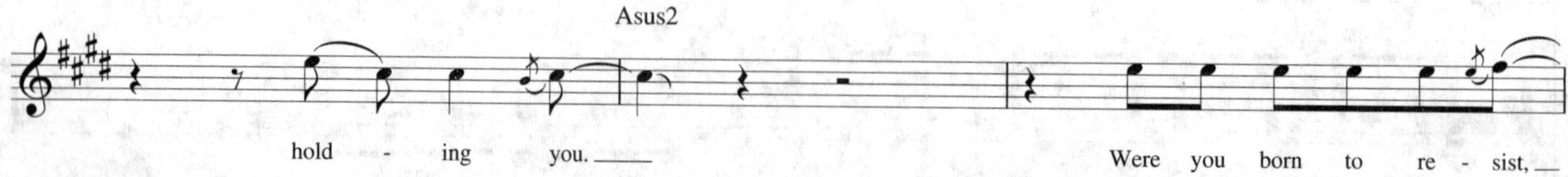

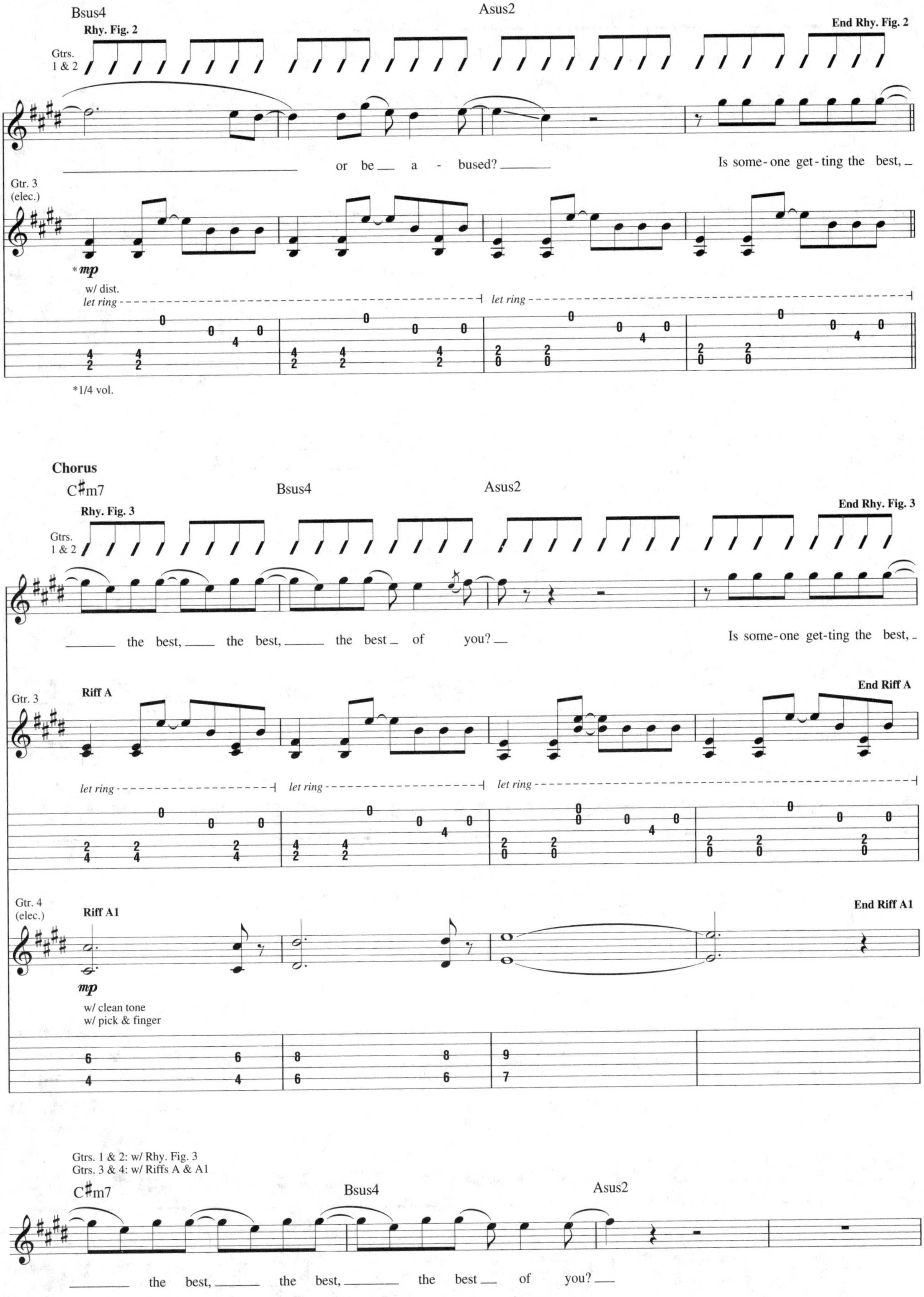

Chorus

C♯m7 Bsus4 Asus2

Rhy. Fig. 3 End Rhy. Fig. 3

Gtrs. 1 & 2

the best, the best, the best of you?

Is some-one get-ting the best,

Gtr. 3

Riff A End Riff A

let ring let ring let ring

Gtr. 4 (elec.)

Riff A1 End Riff A1

mp

w/ clean tone
w/ pick & finger

C#m7
Bsus4
Asus2
Gtrs. 1 & 2
Are you gone and on to some - one new?
2. I need-ed some-where to hang
Gtr. 3
let ring
let ring
let ring
*Vol. swell to full vol.
Gtr. 4
Verse
Gtrs. 1, 2 & 4 tacet
Gtr. 3: w/ Rhy. Fig. 1 (2 times)
C#m7
Asus2
my head with-out your noose.
a - gain, but I break loose.
You gave me some-thing that I
My head is giv - ing me life
Gtr. 5 (elec.)
w/ dist.
C#m7
Asus2
did-n't have, but had no use.
or death, but I can't choose.
I was too weak to give in,
I swear I'll nev - er give in,

Gtr. 3: w/ Rhy. Fig. 2
Bsus4
1.
Asus2
too strong to lose.
I re - fuse.
3. My heart is un-der ar - rest
2.
Asus2
Chorus
C♯m7
Rhy. Fig. 4
Gtr. 3
Is some-one get-ting the best, the best, the best,
Gtr. 5
Riff B
Bsus4
Asus2
F♯7add4
End Rhy. Fig. 4
the best of you?
Is some-one get-ting the best,
Gtr. 3: w/ Rhy. Fig. 4 (3 times)
C♯m7
Bsus4
Asus2
F♯7add4
the best, the best, the best of you?
Has some-one tak-en your faith?
Gtr. 5
End Riff B

*Composite arrangement

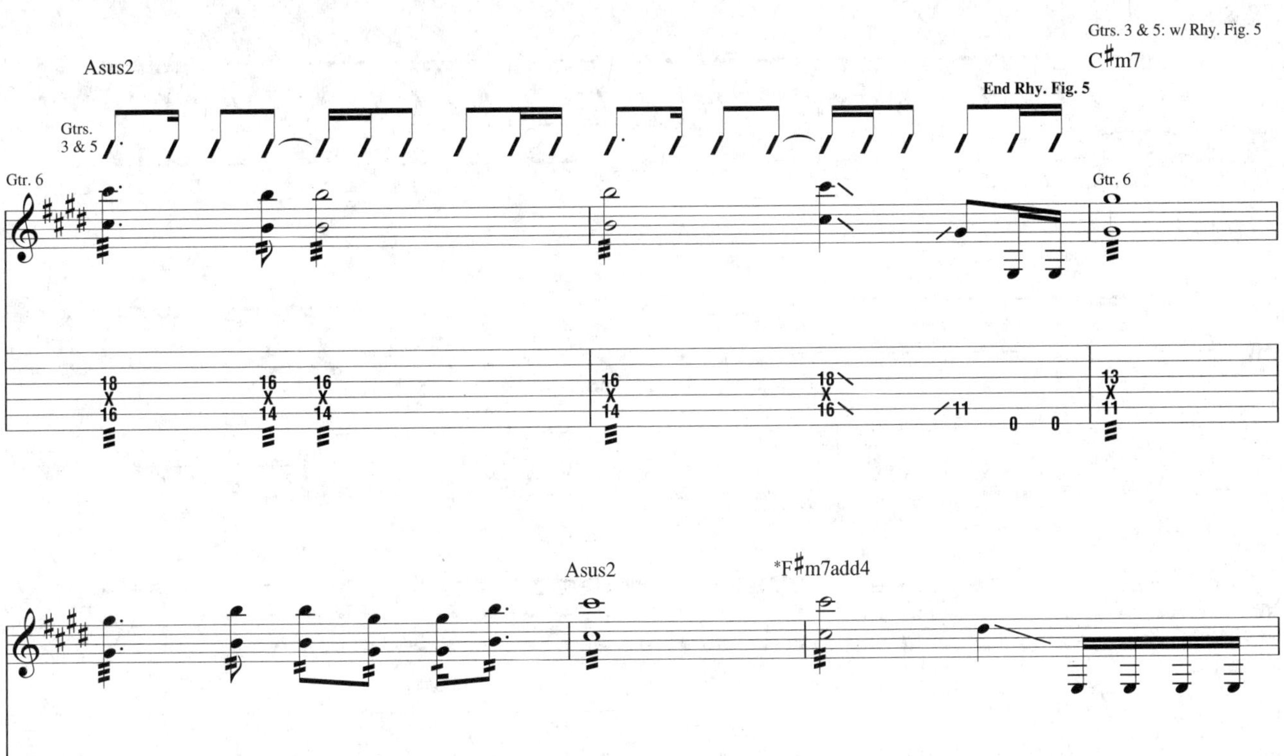

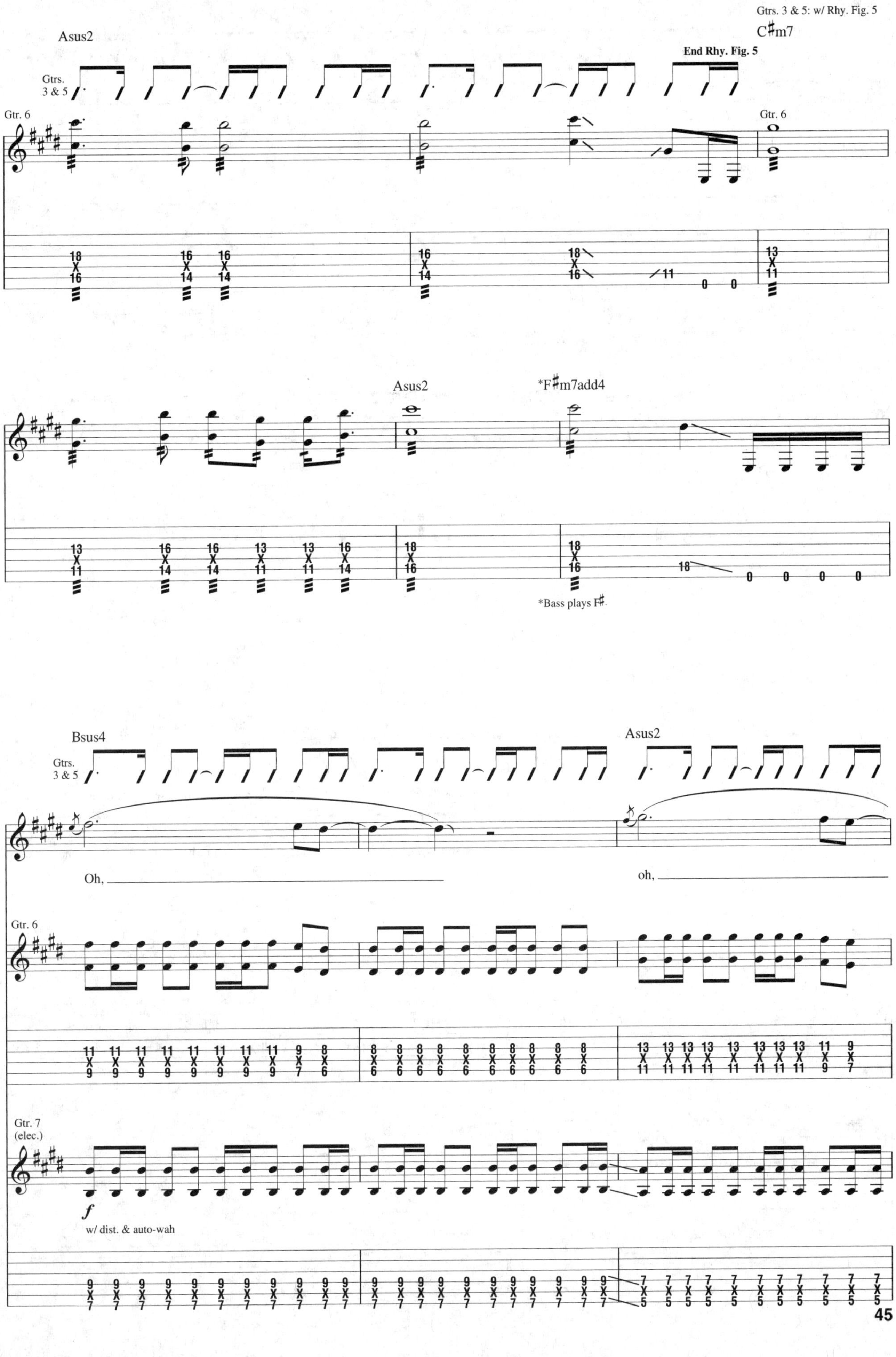
Gtrs. 3 & 5: w/ Rhy. Fig. 5
Asus2
C♯m7
End Rhy. Fig. 5
Gtrs. 3 & 5
Gtr. 6
Gtr. 6
Asus2
*F♯m7add4
*Bass plays F♯.
Bsus4
Asus2
Gtrs. 3 & 5
Oh,
oh,
Gtr. 6
Gtr. 7 (elec.)
f
w/ dist. & auto-wah

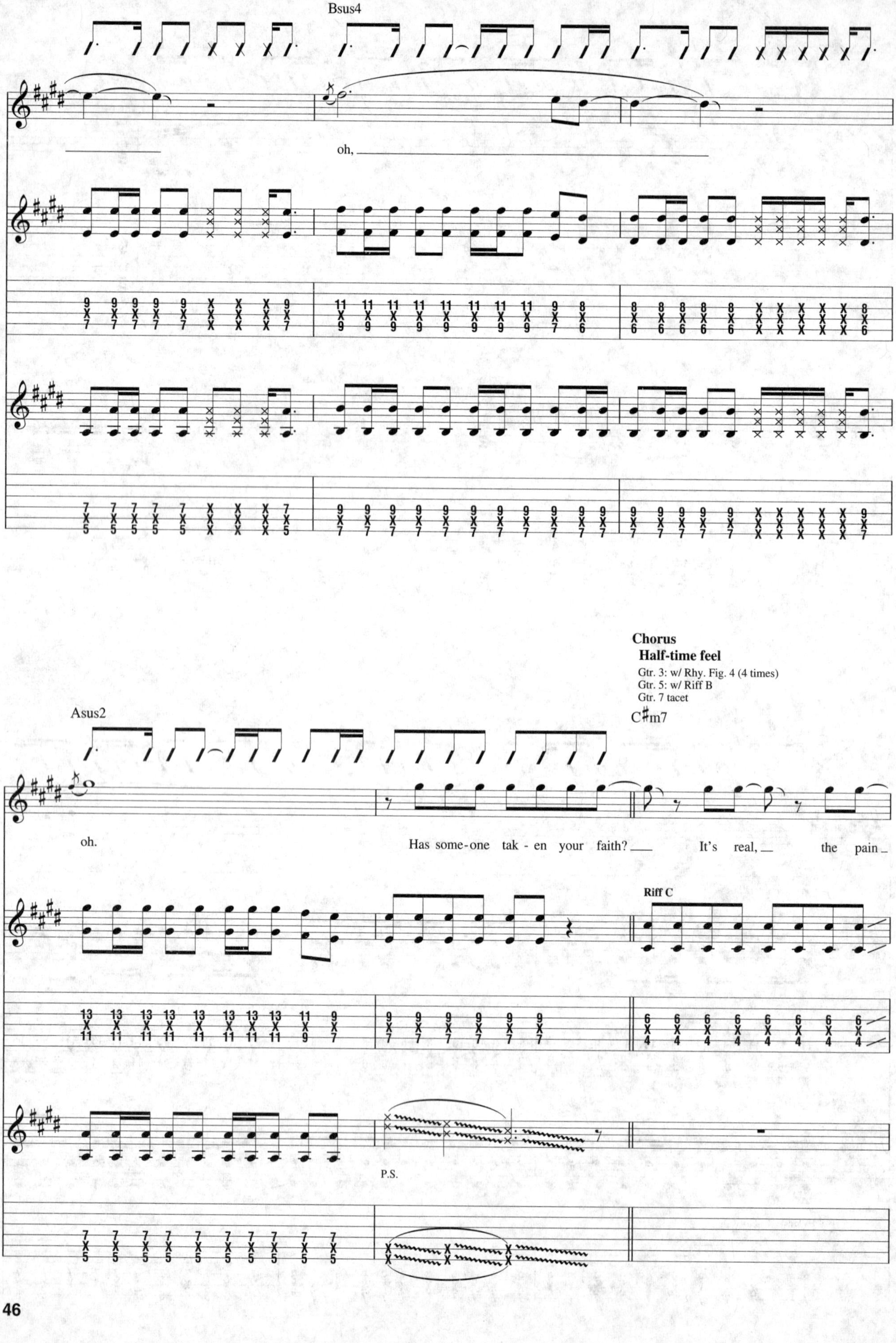

Asus2

oh.

Has some-one tak - en your faith?

Chorus

Half-time feel

Gtr. 3: w/ Rhy. Fig. 4 (4 times)
Gtr. 5: w/ Riff B
Gtr. 7 tacet

C♯m7

It's real, the pain

Riff C

P.S.

Bsus4
Asus2
F#7add4
you feel. The life, the love you thought you healed. The hope
Gtr. 6
End Riff C
Gtr. 6: w/ Riff C (2 times)
C#m7
Bsus4
Asus2
F#7add4
that stops the bro - ken hearts. Your trust, you must con - fess. Is some - one get - ting the best,
C#m7
Bsus4
Asus2
F#7add4
the best, the best, the best of you? Is some - one get - ting the best,
Gtr. 5
End half-time feel
C#m7
Bsus4
Asus2
F#7add4
the best, the best, the best of you? 4. I've got an - oth - er con - fes -
Gtr. 5
Gtr. 6

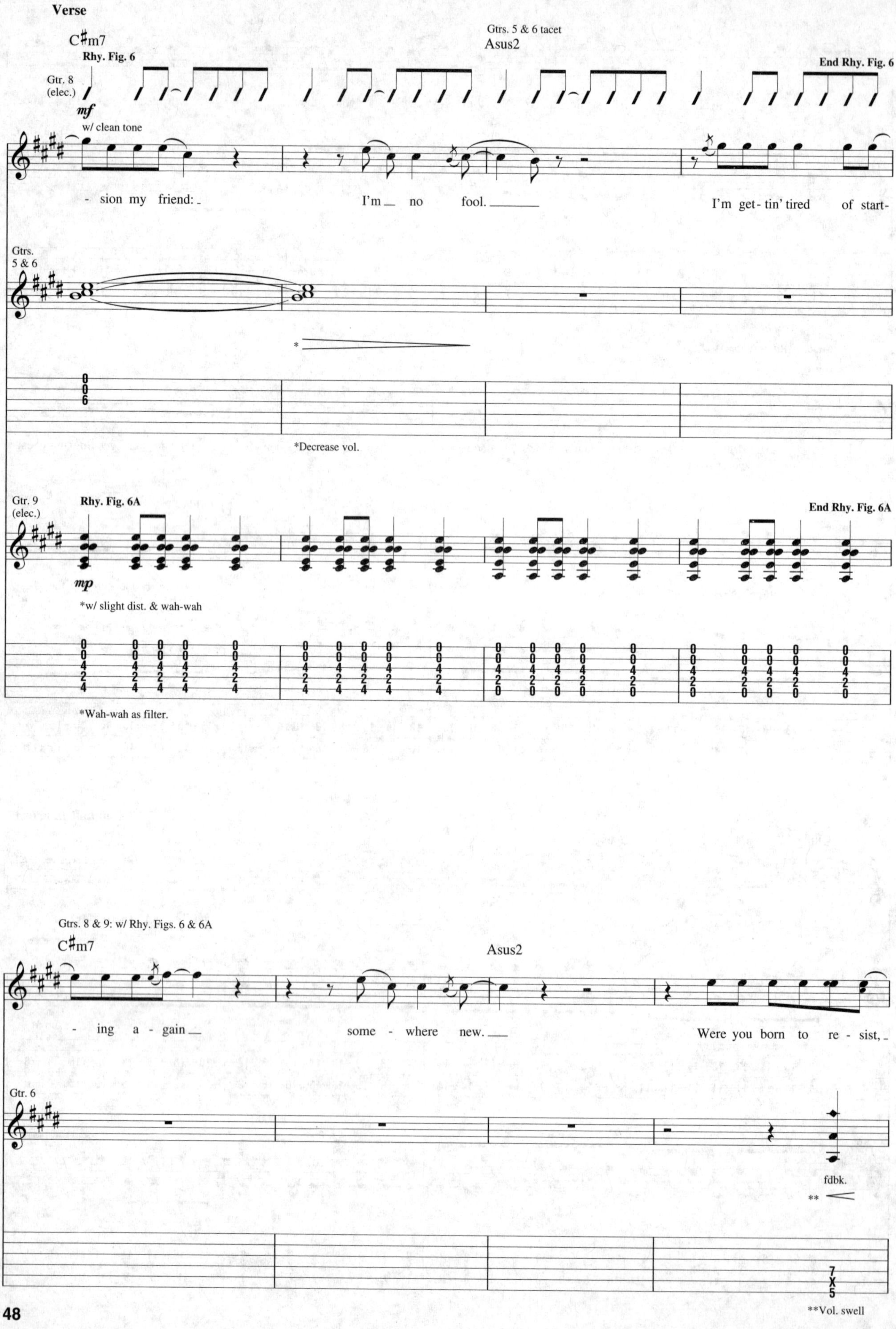

Verse

C♯m7

Rhy. Fig. 6

Gtr. 8 (elec.)

mf

w/ clean tone

Gtrs. 5 & 6 tacet

Asus2

End Rhy. Fig. 6

- sion my friend: _ I'm _ no fool. _ I'm get - tin' tired of start-

Gtrs. 5 & 6

*Decrease vol.

Gtr. 9 (elec.)

Rhy. Fig. 6A

End Rhy. Fig. 6A

mp

*w/ slight dist. & wah-wah

*Wah-wah as filter.

Bsus4
Asus2
or be a - bused?
I swear I'll nev - er give in,
Gtr. 5
Gtr. 3
slight P.M.
Gtr. 6
Bsus4
Asus2
N.C.
I re - fuse.
Is some - one get - ting the best,
slight P.M.

Chorus

Gtr. 3: w/ Rhy. Fig. 4
Gtr. 5: w/ Riff C (2 times)
Gtr. 6: w/ Riff C (4 times)

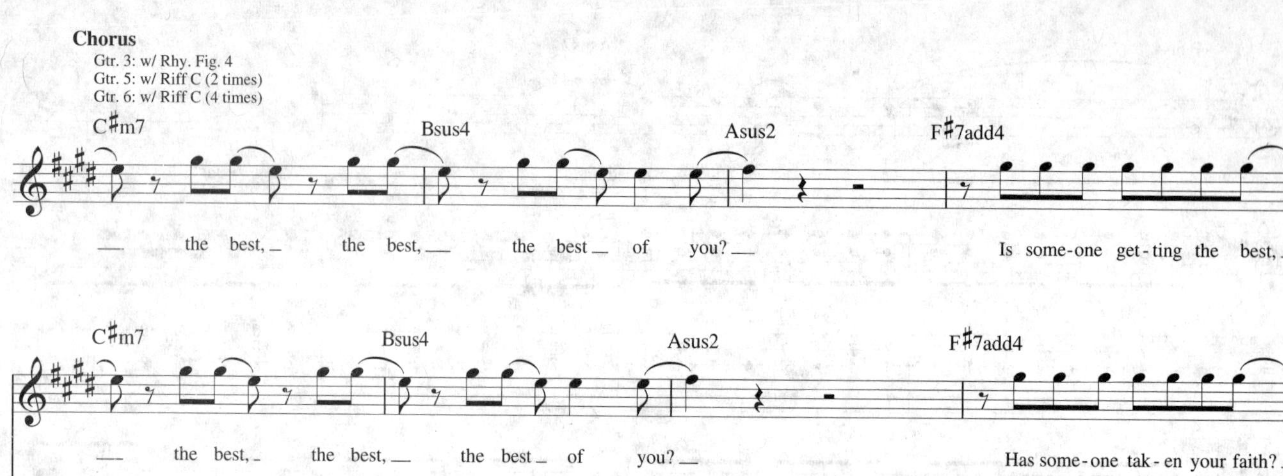

Gtr. 3: w/ Rhy. Fig. 7 (2 times)

Outro
C#m
Gtrs. 3 & 5: w/ Riffs D & D1 (2 times)
Gtr. 6
Gtr. 5
Riff D1
End Riff D1
P.M.
Gtr. 3
Riff D
End Riff D
N.C.

Birthday

Words and Music by John Lennon and Paul McCartney

Verse
Gtr. 2: w/ Riff A
A7
1. They say it's your birth - day.
Well, it's my birth-day too, _ yeah.
Gtr. 1
1/2
D7
They say it's your birth - day.
A7
We're gon-na have a good time.
E7
I'm glad it's your birth - day.
A7
Hap-py birth - day to ___ you.
(drums) 8
Bridge
Yes, we're go - in' to a
Gtrs. 1 & 2
let ring

par - ty, par - ty.
Yes, we're go - in' to a
par - ty, par - ty.
Yes, we're go - in' to a
let ring
let ring
let ring
let ring
Chorus
C
G7
par - ty, par - ty.
I would like you to dance.
Gtrs. 1 & 2
Gtr. 1
Gtr. 2
C
G7
C
G7
Take a cha-cha-cha - chance.
(Birth - day.
I would like you to dance.
Birth - day.

To Coda

Gtr. 1: w/ Fill 1, 2nd time

Gtr. 2 tacet, 2nd time

C G7 N.C. (E)

Birth - day. _) Dance! ______ Yeah!

full full full

full full

Interlude

w/ Lead Voc. ad lib

Gtr. 2: w/ Riff A

Gtr. 1 A7

1/2 1/2

D7 A7

1/2 1/2

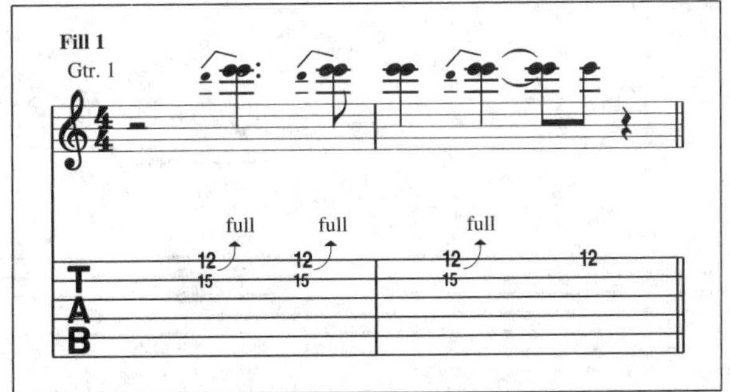

E7
A7
1/2
1/2

Gtr. 1
N.C.
D.S. al Coda
full
full
Gtr. 2
full

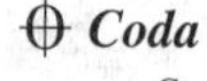
Coda

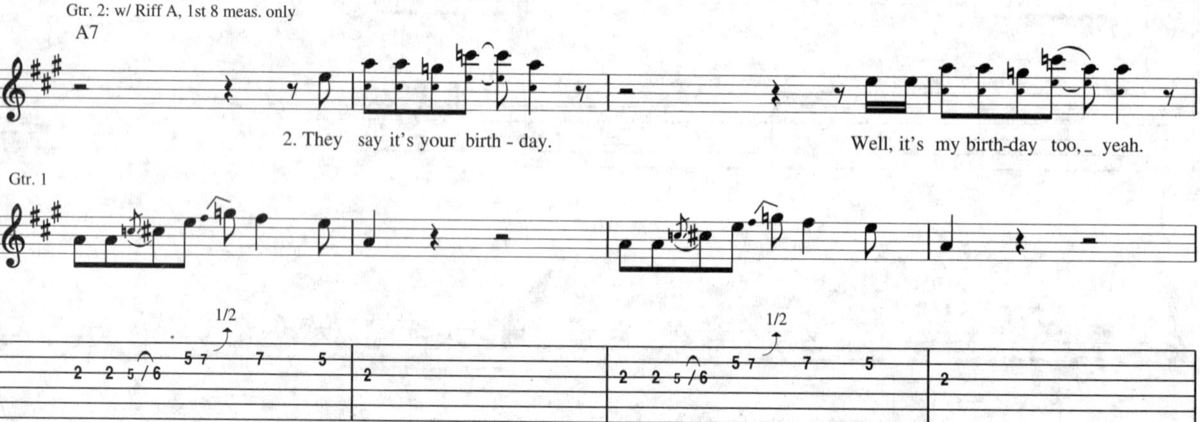
Gtr. 2: w/ Riff A, 1st 8 meas. only
A7
2. They say it's your birth - day.
Well, it's my birth-day too, _ yeah.
Gtr. 1
1/2
1/2

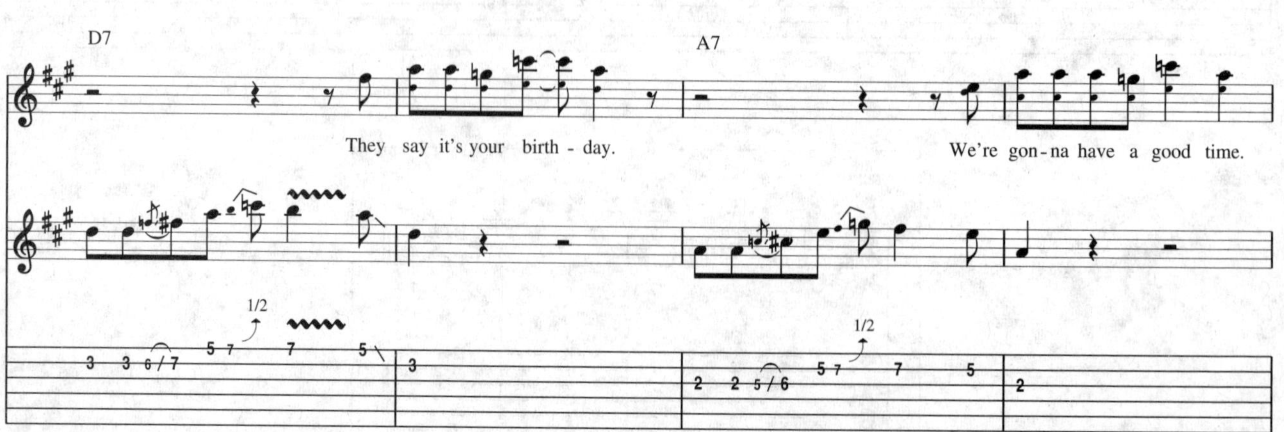
D7
A7
They say it's your birth - day.
We're gon - na have a good time.
1/2
1/2

E7

A7

I'm glad it's your birth - day. Hap - py

Gtr. 1

1/2

1/2

Gtr. 2

birth - day to you.

1/2

1/2

Blue Suede Shoes

Words and Music by Carl Lee Perkins

Verse
A
knock me down, step in my face, slan-der my name all o-ver the place.
burn my house, steal my car, drink my li-quor from an old fruit jar.
Well,
simile on repeat
do an-y-thing that you wan-na do, but, uh-uh, hon-ey, lay off them my shoes. And don't
1/2
Chorus
Gtr. 1: w/ Rhy. Fig. 1
D
even
you step on my blue suede shoes. Well, you can
Gtr. 2
E
A
do an-y-thing, but stay off of my blue suede shoes. Let's go cats!
2nd time: Rock it!
1.
f

Guitar Solo
w/ Voc. ad lib.
A
Rhy. Fig. 2
Gtr. 1
Gtr. 2
D
A
E
A
End Rhy. Fig. 2
3. Well, you can
2.
Guitar Solo
Gtr. 1: w/ Rhy. Fig. 2, simile
A
D
full
A

D.S. al Coda
E
A
4. Well, it's a
Coda
Outro
Gtr. 1: w/ Rhy. Fig. 2, 1st 10 meas., simile
A
Well, it's blue, blue, blue suede shoes. Blue, blue, blue suede shoes, yeah.
D
A
Blue, blue, blue suede shoes, ba - by. Blue, blue, blue suede shoes. Well, you can
E
A
Gtr. 1
do an - y - thing, but stay off of my blue suede shoes.
Gtr. 2

Brass in Pocket

Words and Music by Chrissie Hynde and James Honeyman-Scott

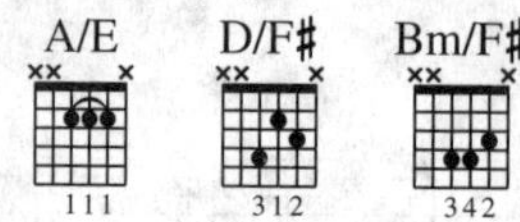

*Chord symbols reflect overall tonality.

Asus4/F# Aadd9/F# Aadd9/D Aadd9/E
I feel in - ven - tive. Gon-na make you, make you, make you no - tice.
End Riff A
P.M.
End Rhy. Fig. 1
let ring
Verse
Gtr. 1: w/ Rhy. Fig. 1
Gtr. 2: w/ Riff A
A* Asus2 Asus4 A Asus2 Asus4 A
2. Got mo-tion, re-strained e-mo - tion. Been driv-in', De - troit lean - in'.
3. I got rhy-thm, I can't miss a beat. I got new skank, so reet.
* Sing 1st time only.
A/F# Asus2/F# Asus4/F# Aadd9/F# Aadd9/D Aadd9/E
No rea - son, just seems so pleas - in'.
Got some - thing; I'm wink-in' at you.
Gon-na make you, make you, make you no - tice.
Pre-Chorus
E6 E5 Esus4 E E6 E5 Esus4 E
Gon-na use my arms. Gon-na use my legs. Gon-na use my style. Gon-na use my
Gtr. 2
Riff B
End Riff B
P.M.
Gtr. 1
Rhy. Fig. 2
End Rhy. Fig. 2

Gtr. 1: w/ Rhy. Fig. 2
Gtr. 2: w/ Riff B
Gtr. 3: w/ Rhy. Fill 1, 2nd time
E6
E5
Esus4
E
side-step. Gon-na use my fin - gers. Gon-na use my, my, my, 'mag - i - na - tion, oh. 'Cause
Chorus
A/E
D/F#
Bm/F#
Gtr. 2
I gon-na make you see there's no - bod - y else here, no one like
Gtr. 1
let ring throughout
me. I'm spe - cial, so spe - cial, I got - ta
(Spe - cial, spe - cial.)
To Coda
1.
2.
D.S. al Coda
have some of your at - ten - tion. Give it to me. ten - tion. Give it to me. 'Cause
Rhy. Fill 1
Gtr. 3 (dist.)
8va
mf
T
A
B

Coda
Outro
Gtr. 1: w/ Rhy. Fig. 1, 1st 2 meas., simile
A
Asus2
Asus4
A
(cont. in notation)
ten - tion.
Give it to me.
Gtr. 2
P.M.
Asus2
Asus4
A
Asus2
Oh.
And when you walk.
Gtr. 2
P.M.
Gtr. 1
Asus4
A
Asus2
sus4
Aadd9
Aadd9
P.M.
let ring
let ring

Brick House

Words and Music by Lionel Richie, Ronald LaPread, Walter Orange, Milan Williams, Thomas McClary and William King

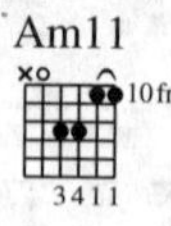

Intro

Moderately ♩ = 102

N.C.

Gtr. 1 (clean)

* (drums)

p

sim.

Uh.

*Key signature denotes A Dorian.

**Tap body of gtr. near pickup w/ pick.

Uh, mm, mm.

(cont. in notation)

Whistle:

Ow, she's a

Chorus

*Am Bm Am Bm Am

brick house.

Gtr. 1

Rhy. Fig. 1

End Rhy. Fig. 1

mf mp mf

P.M. P.M. P.M. P.M.

Gtr. 2 (clean)

Rhy. Fig. 1A

mp

P.M. P.M. let ring

*Chord symbols reflect tonality of gtr. 1

Gtr. 1: w/ Rhy. Fig. 1, 5 times, simile
Bm Am Bm Am
She's might - y, might - y just let - tin' it all hang out. Ah, she's a
Gtr. 2
P.M.
Am Bm Am Bm Am Bm Am
brick house. I like la - dies stacked and that's a fact.
let ring
Bm Am Am Bm Am Bm Am
Ain't hold - in' no - thin' back. Ow, she's a brick house. Well,
Bm Am Bm Am
we're to - geth - er ev - 'ry - bod - y knows this is how the sto - ry goes.
End Rhy. Fig. 1A

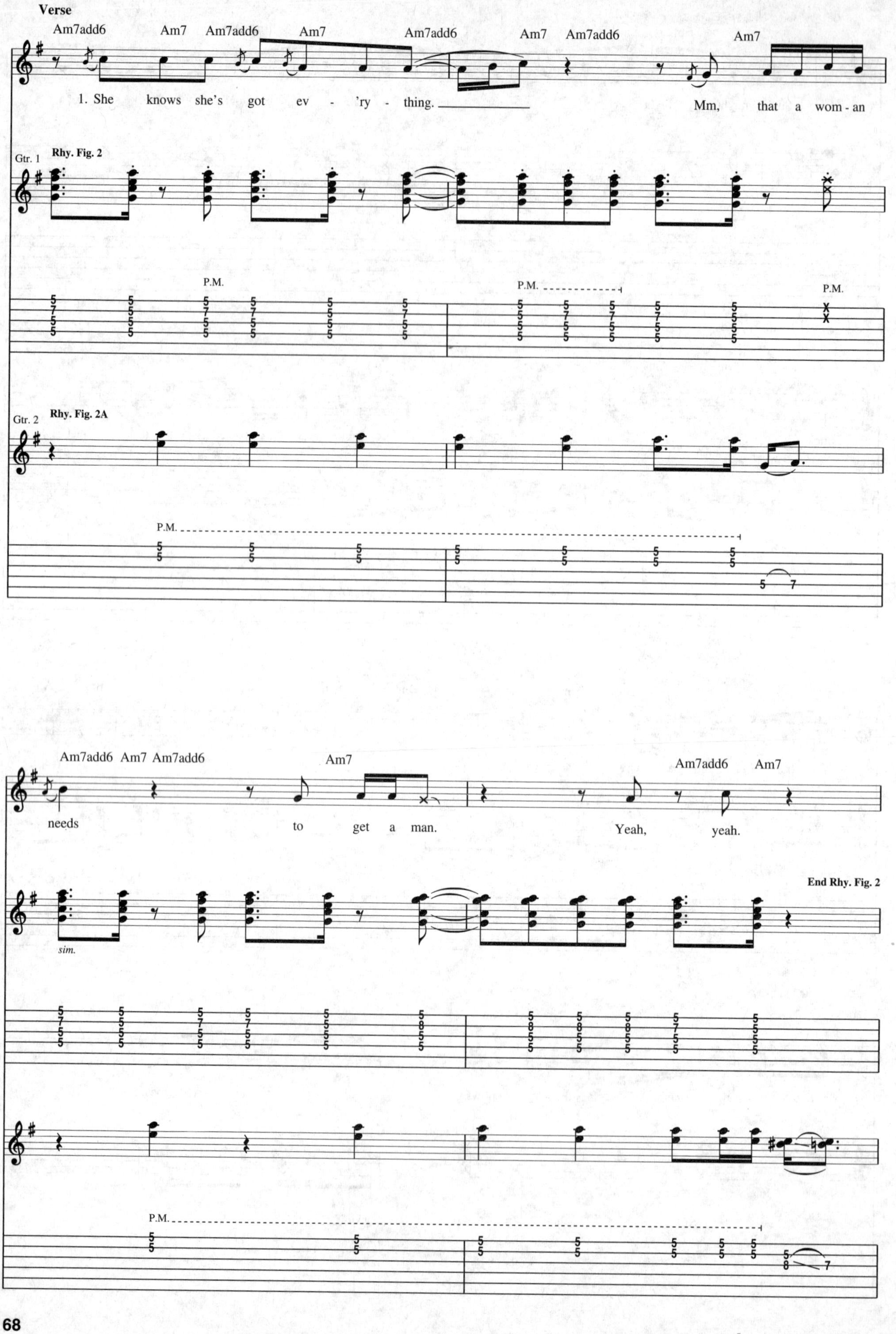

Verse

Am7add6 Am7 Am7add6 Am7 Am7add6 Am7 Am7add6 Am7

1. She knows she's got ev - 'ry - thing. Mm, that a wom - an

Gtr. 1 **Rhy. Fig. 2**

P.M. P.M. P.M.

Gtr. 2 **Rhy. Fig. 2A**

P.M.

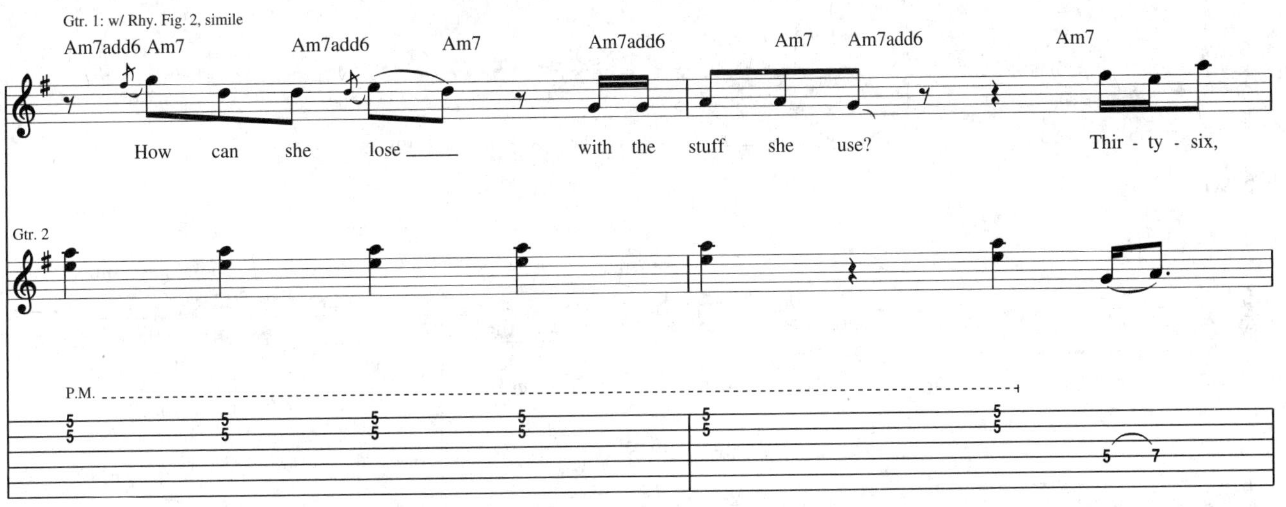

Gtr. 1: w/ Rhy. Fig. 2, simile
Am7add6 Am7 Am7add6 Am7 Am7add6 Am7 Am7add6 Am7
How can she lose with the stuff she use? Thir - ty - six,
Gtr. 2
P.M.

Am7add6 Am7 Am7add6 Am7 Am7add6 Am7
twen - ty - four, thir - ty - six. Ow, what a win - ning hand - ful. She's a
End Rhy. Fig. 2A
P.M.

Chorus
Gtr. 1: w/ Rhy. Fig. 1, 6 times, simile
Gtr. 2: w/ Rhy. Fig. 1A, simile
Am Bm Am Bm Am Bm Am Bm Am
brick house. She's might-y, might - y just let-tin' it all hang out. Ah, she's a
Am Bm Am Bm Am Bm Am
brick house. Oh, I like la - dies stacked and that's a fact.
Bm Am Am Bm Am Bm Am
Ain't hold - in' noth - in' back. Oh, she's a brick house. Yeah,

Gtr. 2: w/ Rhy. Fill 1
Bm
Am
she's the one, the on - ly one
built like an Am - a - zon.
2. Mm,
Verse
Gtr. 1: w/ Rhy. Fig. 2, 2 times, simile
Gtr. 2: w/ Rhy. Fig. 2A, simile
Am7add6 Am7
the clothes she wear, her sex - y ways make an old man wish for
young - er days yeah, yeah. She knows she's built and knows how to please.
Sure 'nough can knock a strong man to his knees. 'Cause she's a brick house. Yeah.
Chorus
Gtr. 1: w/ Rhy. Fig. 1, 4 times, simile
Gtr. 1: w/ Rhy. Fig. 1A, 1st 7 meas., simile
she's might - y, might - y just let-tin' it all hang out. Hey brick house.
Gtr. 2: w/ Rhy. Fill 2
I like la - dies stacked and that's a fact. Ain't hold - in noth - in' back. Ow.
Rhy. Fill 1
Gtr. 2
Rhy. Fill 2
Gtr. 2
P.M.

Bridge
Am11
Gtr. 1
A shake it down, shake it down now.
A shake it down, shake it down now.
Gtr. 2
A shake it down, shake it down now.
A shake it down, shake it down, down, down.
A shake it down say, "Ow."
sim.
1/2
Chorus
Gtr. 1: w/ Rhy. Fig. 1, 4 times, simile
Gtr. 2: w/ Rhy. Fig. 1A, 1st 3 meas., simile
Am Bm Am Bm Am Bm Am
Brick house. Yeah, she's might - y, might - y a just
Gtr. 2: w/ Rhy. Fill 1
Gtr. 2: w/ Rhy. Fig. 1A, 1st 4 meas., simile
let-tin' it all hang out. Ow, a brick house. Yeah she's the one, the on - ly one
Bridge
Gtr. 1: w/ Rhy. Fig. 1, 2 times, simile
Gtr. 2: w/ Rhy. Fig. 1A, 1st 4 meas., simile
built like an Am - a - zon. Yeah. Shake it down, shake it down, shake it now, now.
Shake it down, shake it down, shake it now, now. Shake it down, shake it down, shake it now, now.
Shake it down, shake it down, shake it, shake it. Shake it down, shake it down. Shake it.

Interlude

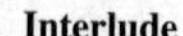

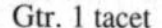

Outro

Begin Fade

*Chord symbols reflect implied tonality.

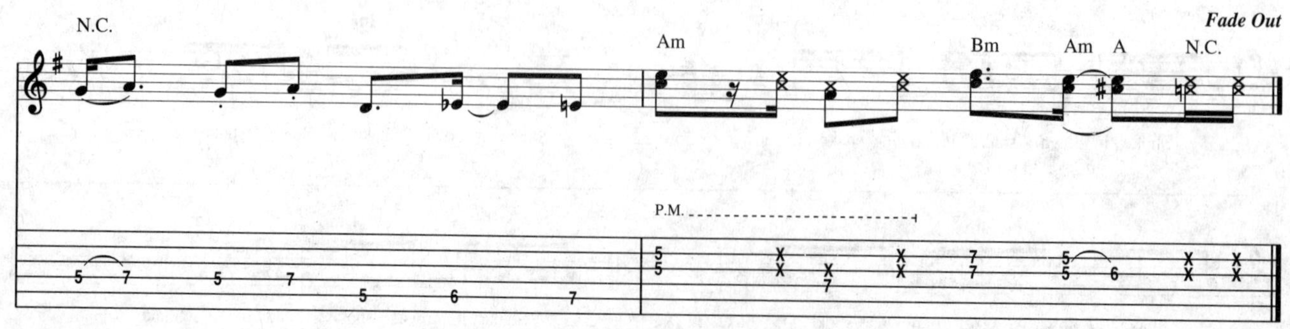

Bulls on Parade

Written and Arranged by Rage Against The Machine

That rot-ten sore on tha face of Moth-er Earth gets big-ger. Tha trig-ger's cold, emp-ty ya purse._
arms ware - hous-es fill as quick as tha cells. Ral - ly 'round tha fam-'ly, pock-et full of shells.
Chorus
N.C.
Ral - ly 'round tha __ fam-'ly with a pock-et full of shells. They
Gtr. 1
Rhy. Fig. 2
wah-wah off
ral - ly 'round the __ fam-'ly with a pock-et full of shells. They
End Rhy. Fig. 2
Gtr. 1: w/ Rhy. Fig. 2
ral - ly 'round the __ fam-'ly with a pock-et full of shells. They
ral - ly 'round the _ fam-'ly with a pock-et full of shells. pock-et full of shells.
Interlude
B5
Play 3 times
Bulls on pa-rade!
Gtrs. 1 & 2
w/ wah-wah

Guitar Solo
Gtr. 2 tacet
N.C.
15ma
Gtr. 1
wah-wah off
*
*Without picking, slide left hand fingers up & down strings near neck pickup while switching toggle switch with right hand in the rhythm indicated.
(Set neck pickup at 0 & bridge pickup at 10.)
Outro
Gtr. 1: w/ Rhy. Fig. 1
F#5
Gtrs. 1 & 2: w/ Rhy. Fig. 1 (2 times)
Quit it now!
Quit it now!
Bulls on pa - rade!
Gtrs. 1 & 2: w/ Riff A (2 times)
N.C.(F#5)
1., 2., 3.
4.
Bulls on pa - rade!
Bulls on pa - rade!

Can't You See

Words and Music by Toy Caldwell

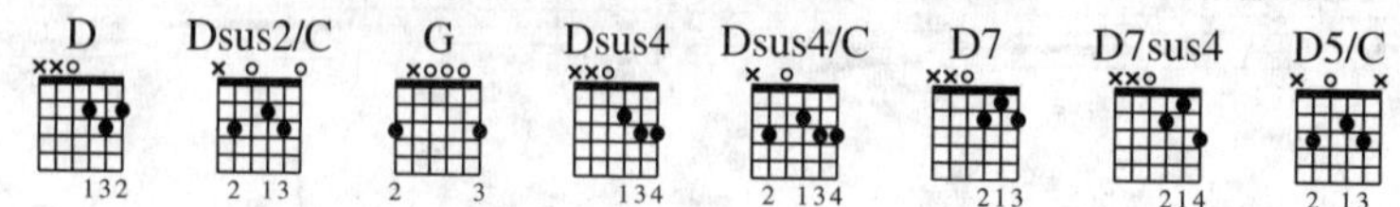

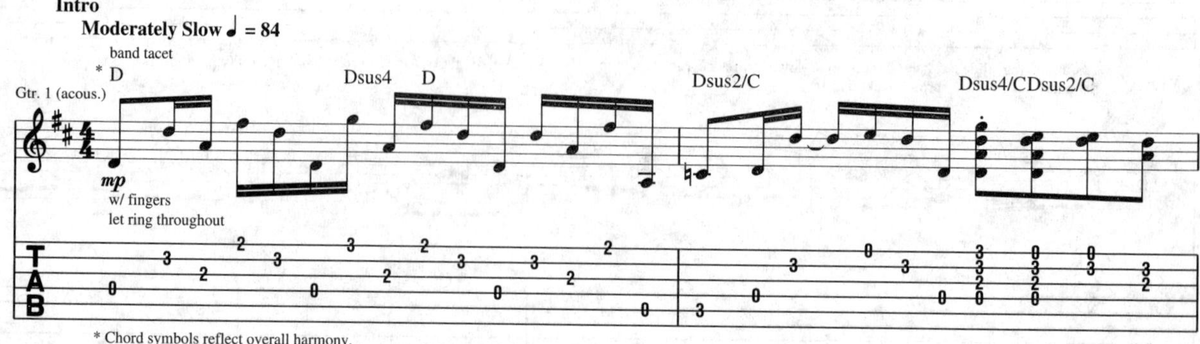

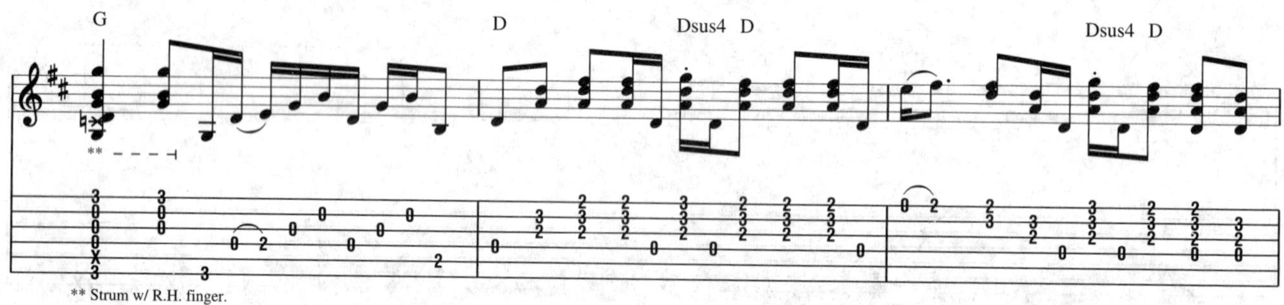

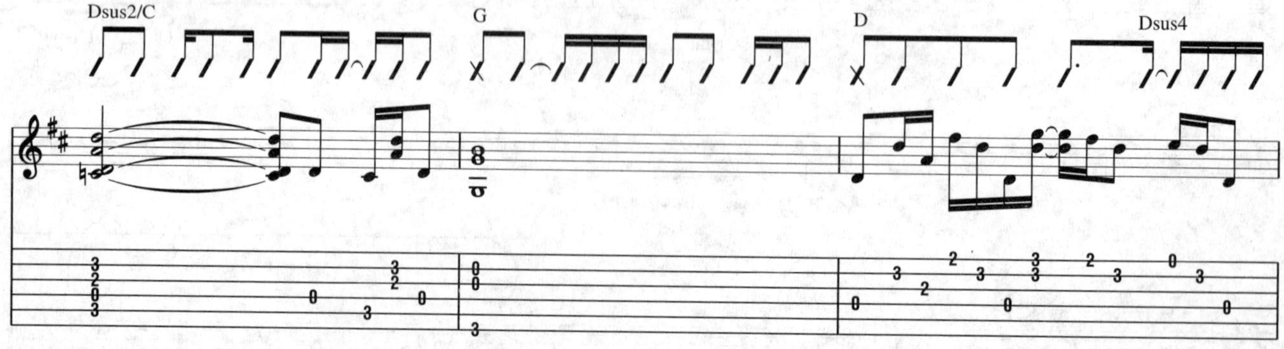

D
Rhy. Fig. 1
Gtr. 2
Dsus2/C
Dsus4/C Dsus2/C
Gtr. 3 (elec.)
mf
w/ slight dist.
full
Gtr. 1
* played w/ thumb
G
D
Dsus4
1/2
full
D
Dsus2/C
Dsus4/C Dsus2/C
full
full

G
D
Dsus4 D
Dsus4
End Rhy. Fig. 1
full
Verse
Gtr. 3 tacet
D
Rhy. Fig. 2A
Gtr. 2
* D7
D7sus4
D7
1. Gon-na take a freight train
down at the sta - tion, Lord.
Rhy. Fig. 2
Gtr. 1
* bass plays C
G
Gtr. 2
D
Dsus4
D
I don't care where it goes.
Gon-na climb a moun-tain,
Gtr. 3
full
Gtr. 1

Gtr. 3 tacet
*D7
D7sus4 D7
G
Gtr. 2
the high-est moun - tain.
I jump off, no-bod - y gon-na know.
Gtr. 1
* bass plays C
Chorus
Gtr. 2: w/ Rhy. Fig. 1, simile
D
Dsus4
D
Dsus4 D
End Rhy. Fig. 2A
Can't you see,
whoa,
Gtr. 3
End Rhy. Fig. 2
Rhy. Fig. 3
Gtr. 3 tacet
Dsus2/C
Dsus4/C Dsus2/C
G
can't you see what that wom - an, Lord, she been do - in' to me?

D
Dsus4
Dsus 2/4
D
Can't you see, can't you see
Gtr. 3
full
Gtr. 1
Dsus2/C
Dsus4/C Dsus2/C G
D
Dsus4 D
what that woman, she been do-in' to me?
1/2
End Rhy. Fig. 3
Verse
Gtr. 2: w/ Rhy. Fig. 2A, simile
D
*D7
D7sus4 D7
G
2. I'm gon-na find me a hole in the wall. I'm gon-na crawl in-side and die.
Gtr. 1
* bass plays C

D
Dsus4
D
Dsus2
D
* D7
D7sus4 D7
Come lat - er now,
a mean old wom-an, Lord,
Gtr. 3
full
full
1/2
Gtr. 1
* bass plays C
Chorus
Gtr. 2: w/ Rhy. Fig. 1, simile
G
D
Dsus4
D
Dsus4
D
nev-er told
me good-bye.
Can't you see,
whoa,
Rhy. Fig. 4
Dsus2/C
Dsus4/C Dsus2/C
G
can't you see
what that
wom - an, Lord,
she been do - in' to me?
full
full

D
Dsus4
D
Can't you see,
can't you see
mp
End Rhy. Fig. 4
Dsus2/C
Dsus4/C
Dsus2/C
G
D
Dsus4
D
what that woman, she been do-in' to me?
mf
f
full
Guitar Solo
Gtr. 1: w/ Rhy. Fig. 4, 1 1/2 times, simile
Gtr. 2: w/ Rhy. Fig. 1, simile
Gtr. 3
D
Dsus4
D
Dsus2/C
Dsus4/C
Dsus2/C
full
full
full

G
D
Dsus4
D
full
full

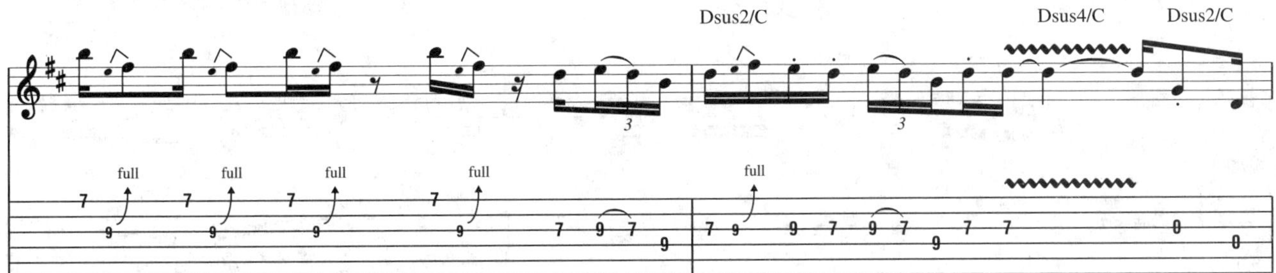
Dsus2/C
Dsus4/C
Dsus2/C
full
full
full
full
full

Gtr. 3
G
D
Dsus4
D
full
full
Gtr. 1
w/ pick
w/ fingers

Verse
Gtrs. 1 & 2: w/ Rhy. Figs. 2 & 2A, simile
D
* D7
D7sus4
D7
G
3. I'm gon-na buy a tick-et, now,
as far as I can.
Ain't nev-er com-in' back.
Gtr. 3
mf
full
full
* bass plays C

D
Dsus4
D
* D7
D7sus4
D7
Grab me a south bound
all the way to Geor - gia now,
full
17
17
(17)
15 17 15
16
15
15
14 16 14
full
9
7
* bass plays C
G
D
Dsus4
till the train,
it run out of
track.
Can't
you see,
full
9
7
3 2
3
2 0
4 2 0
0 2
0
**Sung behind the beat.
Chorus
Gtr. 2: w/ Rhy. Fig. 1, simile
D
Dsus4
D
Dsus2/C
Dsus4/C Dsus2/C
whoa,
can't you see
what that
Gtr. 3
7
7
Gtr. 1
Gtr. 3 tacet
G
D
Dsus4 D
Gtr. 1: w/ Rhy. Fig. 3, last 4 meas., simile
wom - an, Lord,
she been
do - in' to me?
Can't you
see,
can't you see
Gtr. 1
Rhy. Fig. 5
End Rhy. Fig. 5
Gtr. 3
w/ pick
w/ fingers
7 7 8 7
7

Dsus2/C
Dsus4/C Dsus2/C G
D
Dsus4 D
what that wom-an, she been do-in' to me? Oh, Lord.
full
Guitar Solo
Gtr. 1: w/ Rhy. Fig. 4, simile
Gtr. 2: w/ Rhy. Fig. 1, simile
D
Dsus4 D
Dsus2/C
Dsus4/C Dsus2/C
G
D
Dsus4 D
Dsus4 D Dsus4 D
Dsus2/C
G
D
Dsus4 D
Can't you
Gtr. 3
1/2
Gtr. 1
Rhy. Fig. 6
End Rhy. Fig. 6
w/ pick
w/ fingers

*Played ahead of the beat.

band enters
Gtr. 1: w/ Rhy. Fig. 3, 1st 3 meas., simile
Gtr. 2: w/ Rhy. Fig. 1, 2 times, simile
D
Dsus4 D
Dsus2/C
Dsus4/C Dsus2/C
Voc. Fig. 1
Oh, she's such a cra - zy la - dy.
can't you see what that
Gtr. 3
mf
full

G
D
Dsus4
End Voc. Fig. 1
What that wom-an, she been do - in' to me.
wom - an, she been do - in' to me?
Can't you see,
Gtr. 3
Gtr. 1
w/ pick
1/2

Bkgd. Voc.: w/ Voc. Fig. 1, 2 3/4 times
Gtr. 1: w/ Rhy. Fig. 3, last 4 meas., simile
D
Dsus2/C
Dsus4/C Dsus2/C G
Lord, I can't stand it no more.
Oh, she been do-in' to me.
Gtr. 3
full
full

Gtr. 1: w/ Rhy. Fig. 3, 1st 6 meas., simile
D
Dsus4 D
Dsus4 D
Dsus2/C
Dsus4/C Dsus2/C
I'm gon-na take a freight train
down at the sta - tion, Lord.
full
G
D
Dsus4
Dsus 2/4
D
Ain't nev - er com-in' back, oh, no.
Gon-na ride me a south bound, now,
1/2
Gtr. 1: w/ Rhy. Fig. 5, simile
Dsus2/C
Dsus4/C Dsus2/C
G
all the way to Geor - gia, Lord,
till the train, it run out
full
full
Guitar Solo
Gtr. 1: w/ Rhy. Fig. 6, 1 1/2 times, simile
Gtr. 2: w/ Rhy. Fig. 1, simile
D
Dsus4 D
Dsus4 D Dsus4 D
Dsus2/C
of track.
Oh, Lord.
full
full
full
full

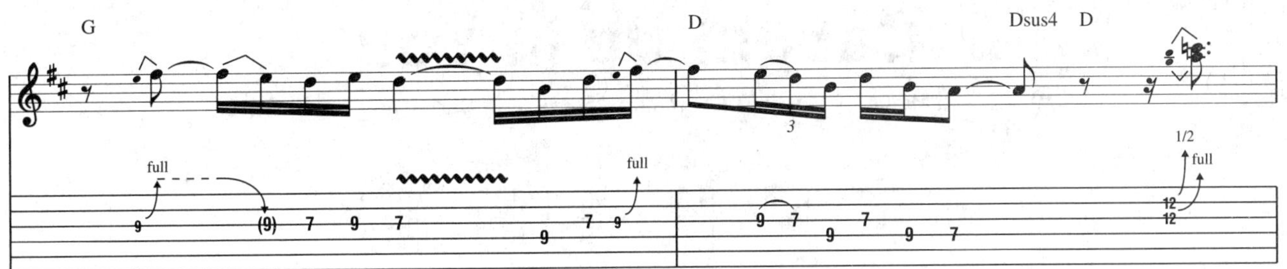
G
D
Dsus4 D
full
full
1/2
full
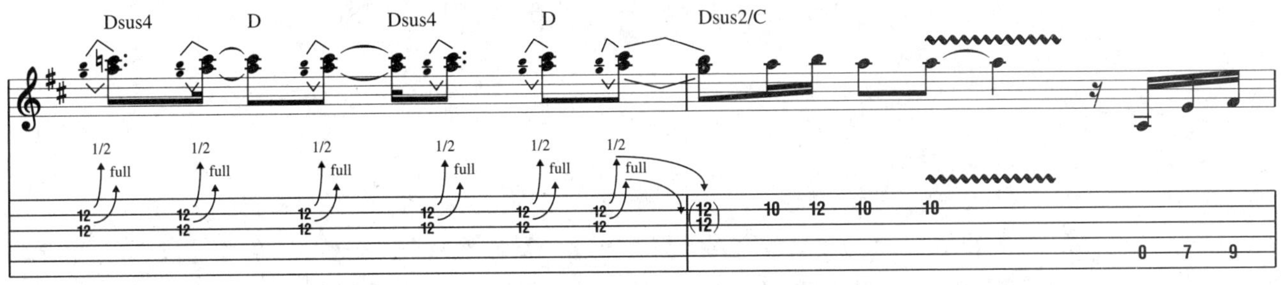
Dsus4
D
Dsus4
D
Dsus2/C
1/2
full
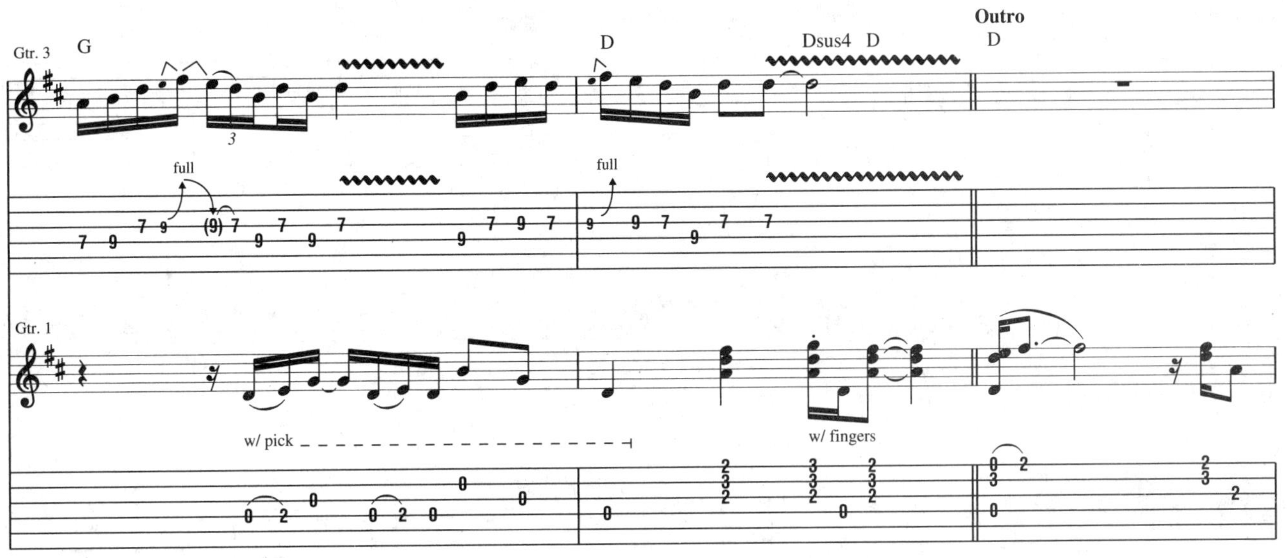
Outro
Gtr. 3
G
D
Dsus4 D
D
full
full
Gtr. 1
w/ pick
w/ fingers
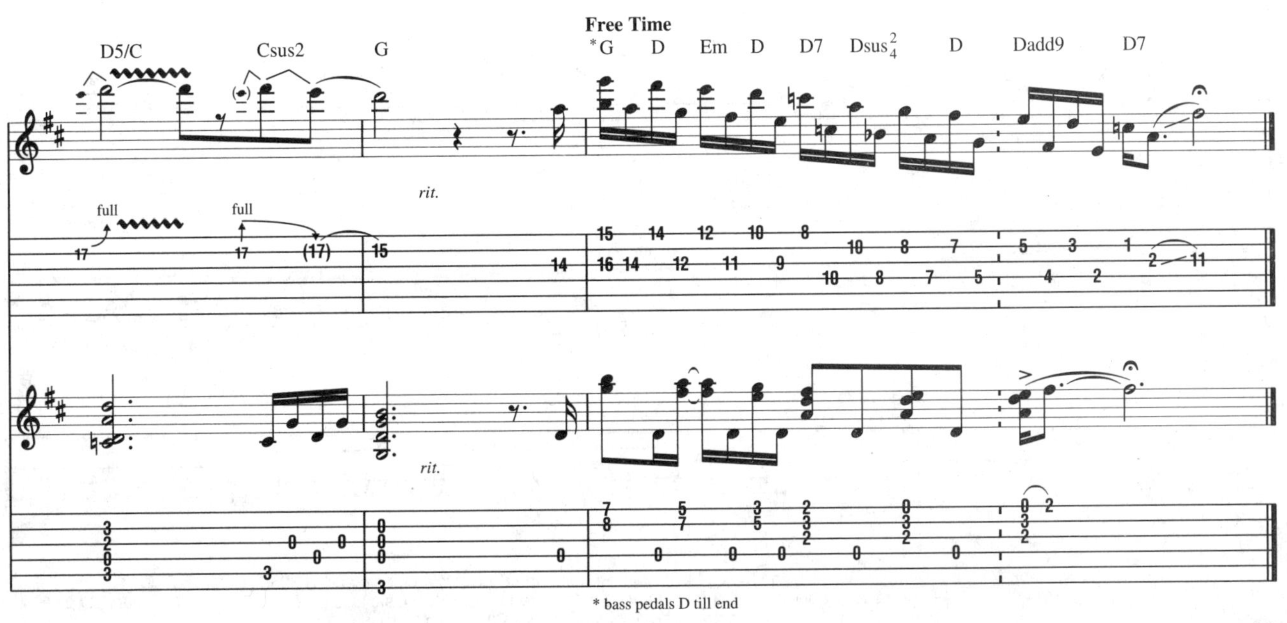
Free Time
D5/C
Csus2
G
*G
D
Em
D
D7
Dsus2/4
D
Dadd9
D7
rit.
full
full
rit.
* bass pedals D till end

Caught Up in You

Words and Music by Frank Sullivan, Jim Peterik, Jeff Carlisi and Don Barnes

C#m7
4fr
13121
F#m
133111
B
13331
E
231
F#m9
131114
E5
7fr
1 3
B/D#
6fr
14
B5
134
G#5
4fr
134
A5
11
E/G#
3 14
F#5
134
C#5
4fr
134

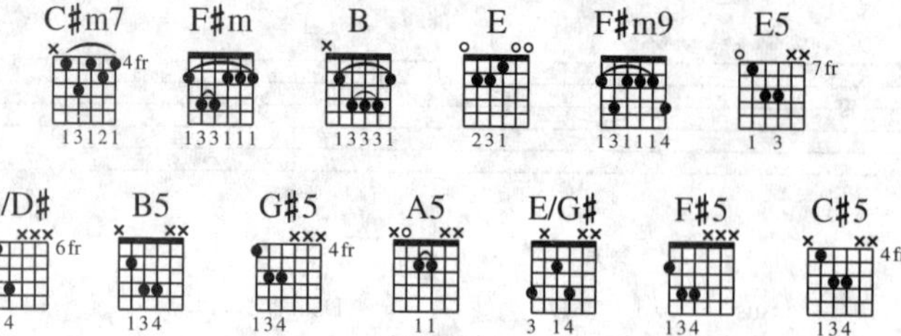

Intro
Moderately Fast ♩ = 128
Gtr. 1
(slight dist.)
*E5
B
E5
B
E5
B
E5
B
mf
slight P.M. throughout

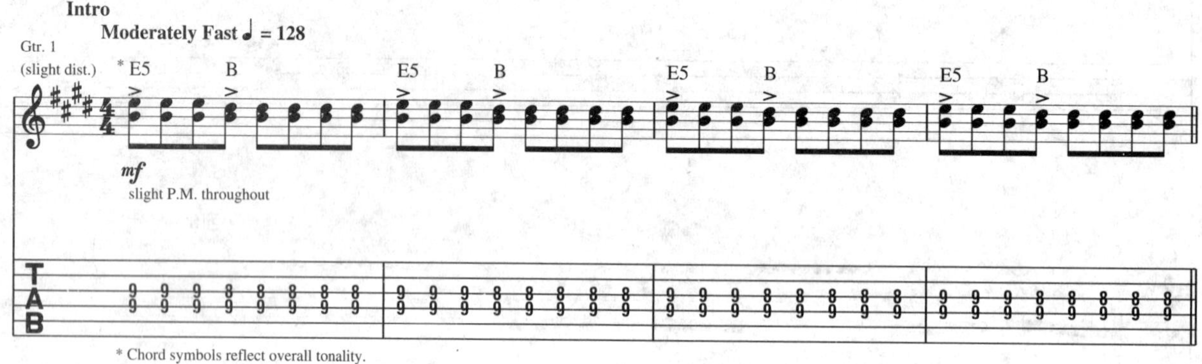

* Chord symbols reflect overall tonality.

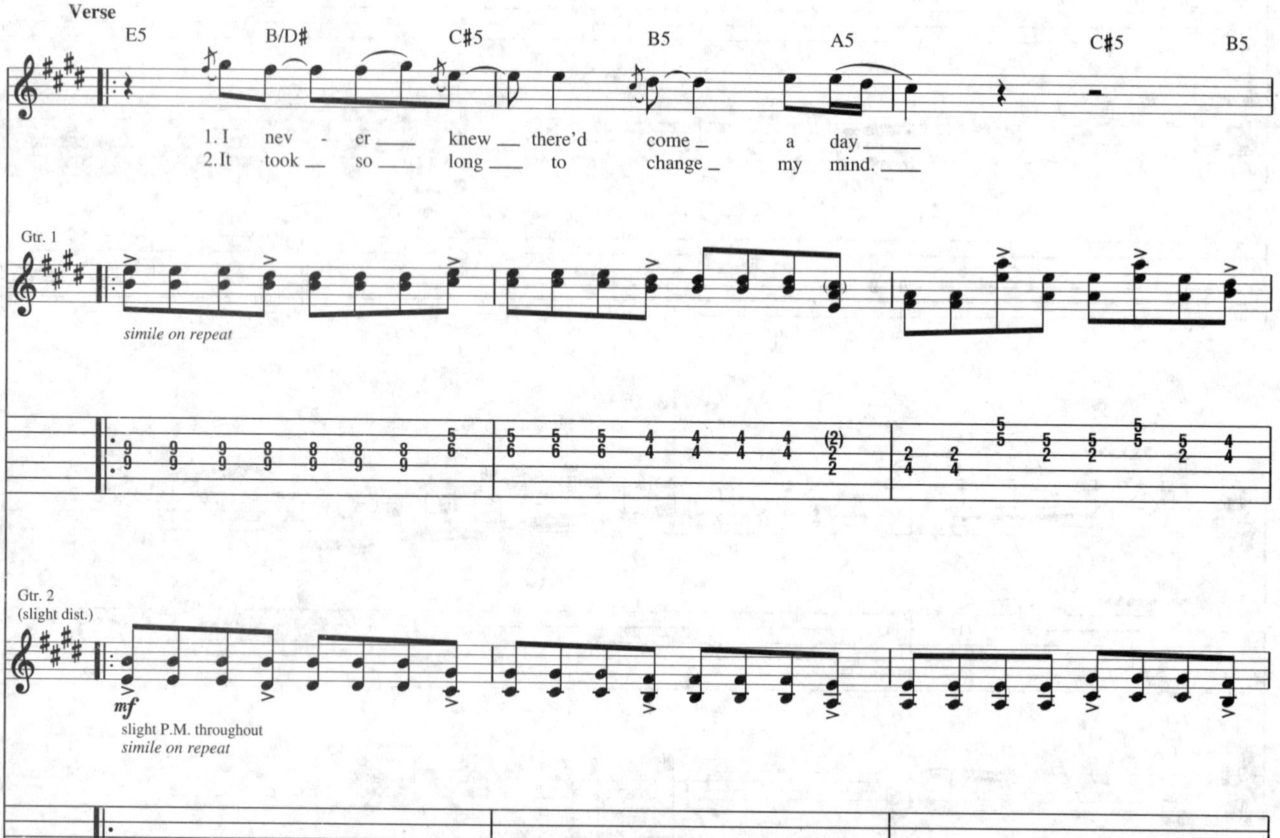
Verse
E5
B/D#
C#5
B5
A5
C#5
B5
1. I nev - er knew there'd come a day
2. It took so long to change my mind.
Gtr. 1
simile on repeat
Gtr. 2
(slight dist.)
mf
slight P.M. throughout
simile on repeat

E5 B/D# C#5 B5 A5

when I'd be say - in' to you, "Don't let this good ___ love slip ___ a - way, ___
I thought that love was a game. I played a - round ___ e - nough _ to find ___

C#5 B5 A5 C#5 B5

Gtr. 1 tacet

now that we know that it's true." Don't, don't you know _ the kind of man I ___ am? ___
no two are ev - er the same. You made me re - al - ize the love I'd ___ missed. _

Gtr. 1

Gtr. 3 (dist.)
divisi

mf

Gtr. 3

Gtr. 2

A5
C#5
B5
A5
F#5
E/G#
A5
No, said I'd nev - er fall in love a - gain. But it's real and the feel -
So hot, love I could - n't quite re - sist. When it's right the light
Gtr. 1
* Gtrs. 1 & 3
Gtr. 3
divisi
Gtr. 2
* composite arrangement
A#°
B5
- ing comes shin - ing through.
just comes shin - ing through.
I'm so caught up in you,
I'm so caught up in you,
let ring
1/2
1/2

Chorus

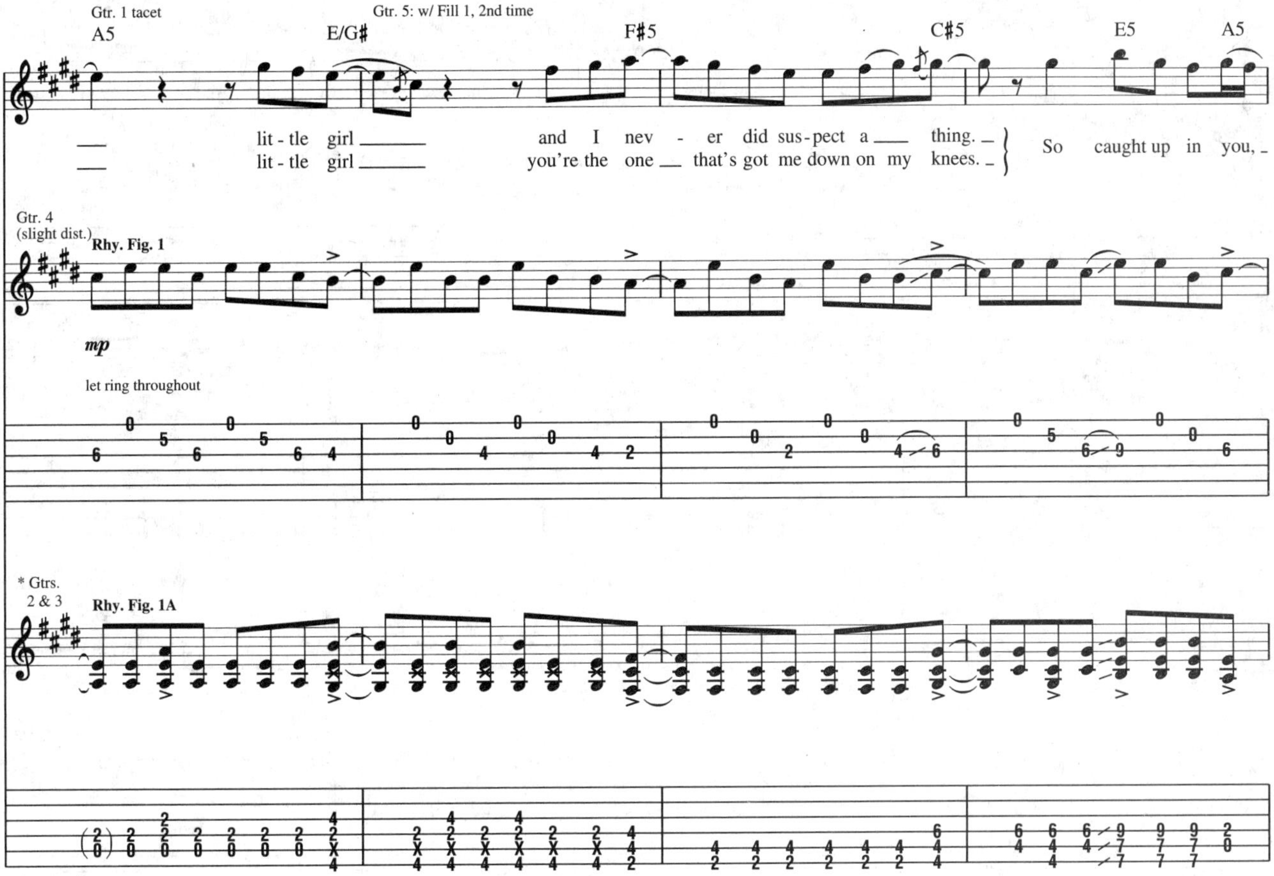
Gtr. 1 tacet
Gtr. 5: w/ Fill 1, 2nd time
A5
E/G#
F#5
C#5
E5
A5
lit - tle girl and I nev - er did sus-pect a thing.
lit - tle girl you're the one that's got me down on my knees.
So caught up in you,
Gtr. 4
(slight dist.)
Rhy. Fig. 1
mp
let ring throughout
* Gtrs.
2 & 3
Rhy. Fig. 1A

* composite arrangement

Fill 1
Gtr. 5 (dist.)
mp
mp
mf
T
A
B

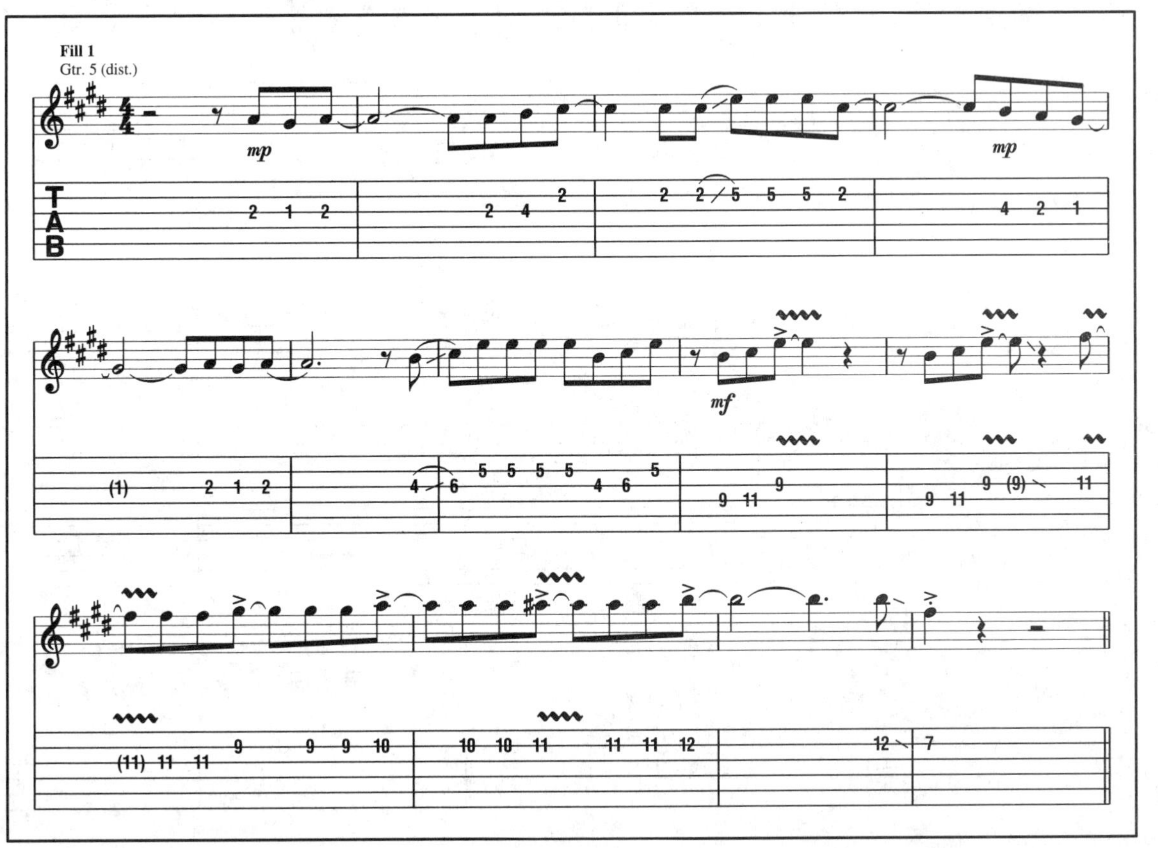

E/G#
F#5
C#5
E5
A5
lit - tle girl that I nev - er wan-na get my-self free. And ba - by, it's true.
E/G#
F#5
E/G#
A5
A#°
B
You're the one who caught me, ba - by, you taught me how good it could be.
End Rhy. Fig. 1
End Rhy. Fig. 1A
1.
2.
Bridge
C#m7
F#m
Gtr. 4
Fill your days and your nights, no need to
(cont. in slash)
Gtrs. 2 & 3
mp
P.M.

B E C#m7 F#m9

Gtr. 4

ev - er ask me twice, oh, no, when - ev - er you want

* Gtr. 5

mp

Gtrs. 2 & 3

P.M.

* Multiple gtrs. arr. for one gtr.

Interlude

B C#m7 F#m B

Gtr. 5 tacet

Rhy. Fig. 2

w/ dist.

me. And if ev - er comes a day when you should turn and walk a - way,

Rhy. Fig. 2A

**P.M.

f

**Gradually release P.M.

E5 B/D# C#m7 F#m B5

End Rhy. Fig. 2

oh, no, I can't live with-out you. I'm so caught up in you.

mf

End Rhy. Fig. 2A

P.M.

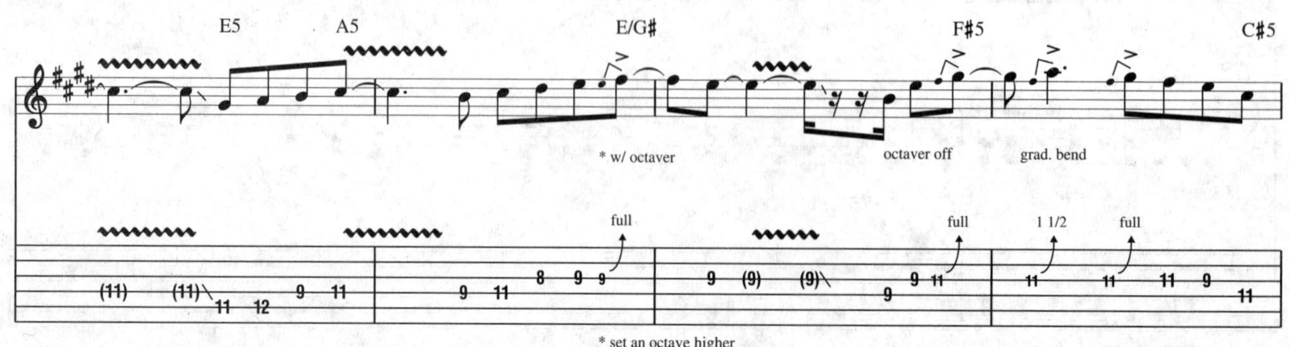

E5
A5
E/G#
F#5
P.H.
full
1/2
E/G#
A5
A#°
B
B5
Gtrs. 2, 3 & 4
G#5 B5
And if ev -
Gtr. 5
P.H.
rake
full
full
Gtr. 6 (dist.)
mf
full
full
Interlude
Gtrs. 2, 3 & 4: w/ Rhy. Figs. 2 & 2A, simile
Gtrs. 5 & 6 tacet
C#m7
F#m
B
E5
B/D#
- er comes a day when you should turn and walk a - way, oh,
C#m7
F#m
B5
Gtrs. 2 & 3
A5
no, I can't live with - out you. I'm so caught up in you.

Chorus
A5
Rhy. Fig. 3
E/G#
F#5
C#5
E5
A5
Gtrs. 2 & 3
lit - tle girl.
You're the one that's got me down on my knees.
So caught up in you,
Gtr. 5
Gtr. 6
divisi
mp
Gtr. 4
Rhy. Fig. 3A
mp
let ring throughout
E/G#
Gtr. 6 tacet
F#5
C#5
E5
A5
lit - tle girl
that I nev - er wan-na get my-self free.
And ba-by, it's true.
Gtr. 5

E/G# F#5 E/G# A5 B5 A5
End Rhy. Fig. 3
you're the one who caught me, ba - by, you taught me how good it could be.
Gtr. 6
Gtr. 5
divisi
mf
End Rhy. Fig. 3A
Gtr. 6 tacet
Gtrs. 2, 3, & 4: w/ Rhy. Figs. 3 & 3A, simile
A5 E/G# F#5 C#5 E5 A5
Lit-tle girl, you're the one that's got me down on my knees. So caught up in you
Gtr. 6
Gtr. 5
Gtr. 5
divisi
P.H.
1/2
1/2
E/G# F#5 C#5 E5 A5
lit-tle girl that I nev - er wan-na get my-self free. And ba-by, it's true,
full
full
full
full

E/G#
F#5
E/G#
A5
B5
A5
you're the one
who caught me, an' taught me,
an' got me so caught up in you.
1/2
1/2
full
Outro-Guitar Solo
Gtrs. 2, 3 & 4: w/ Rhy. Figs. 3 & 3A, simile, till fade
A5
E/G#
F#5
C#5
E5
A5
full
let ring

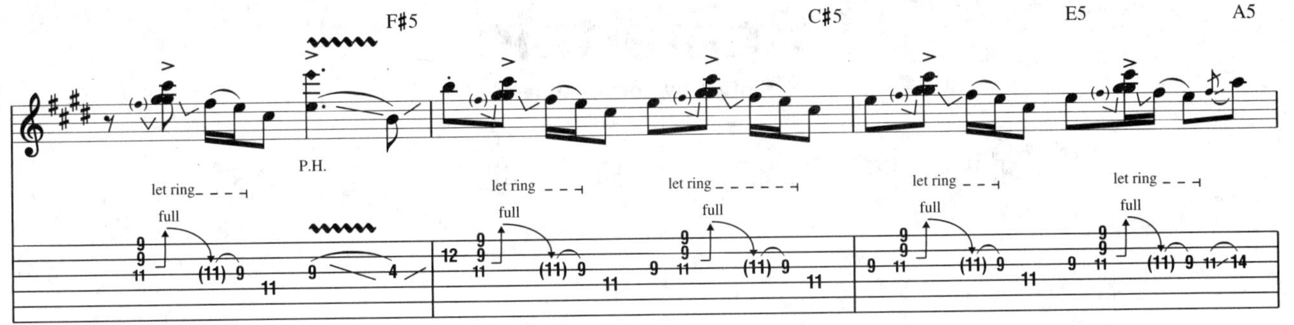
F#5
C#5
E5
A5
P.H.
let ring
full
let ring
let ring
full
full
let ring
let ring
full
full

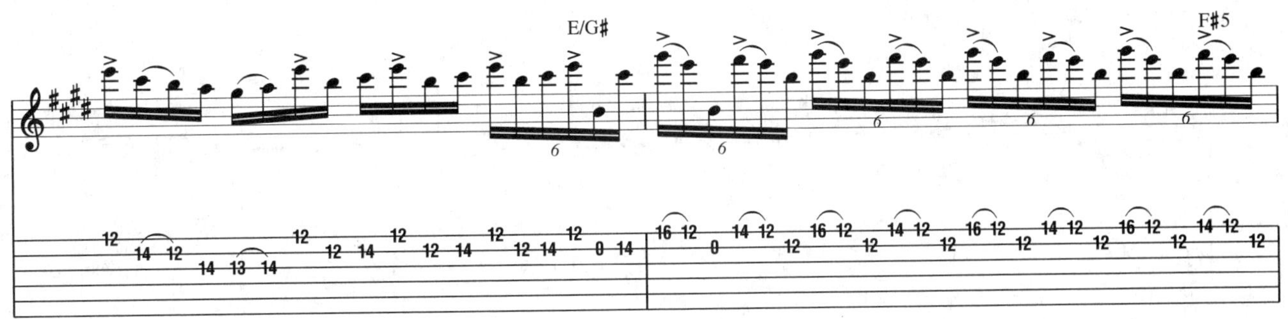
E/G#
F#5

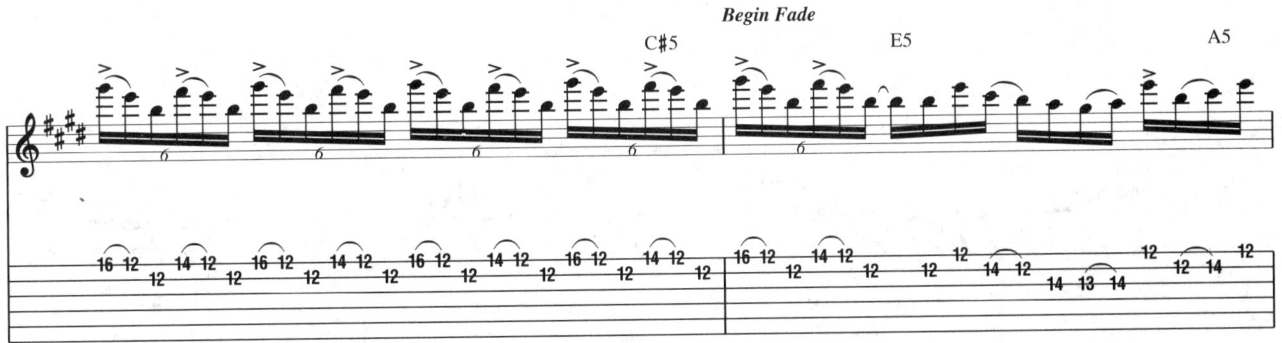
Begin Fade
C#5
E5
A5

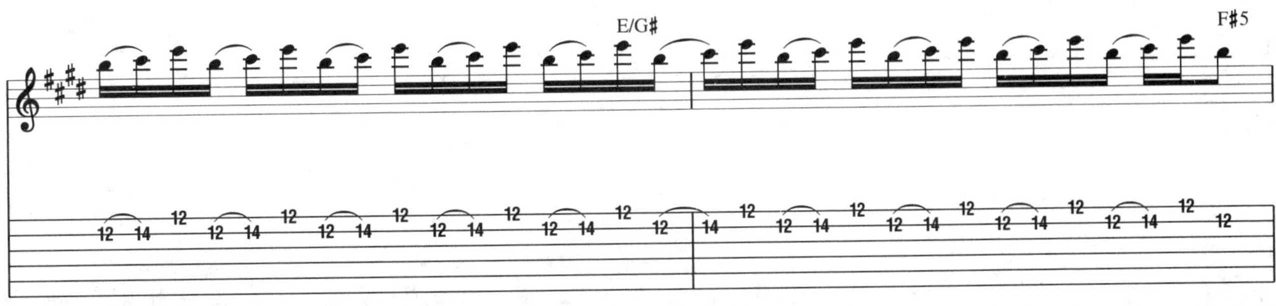
E/G#
F#5

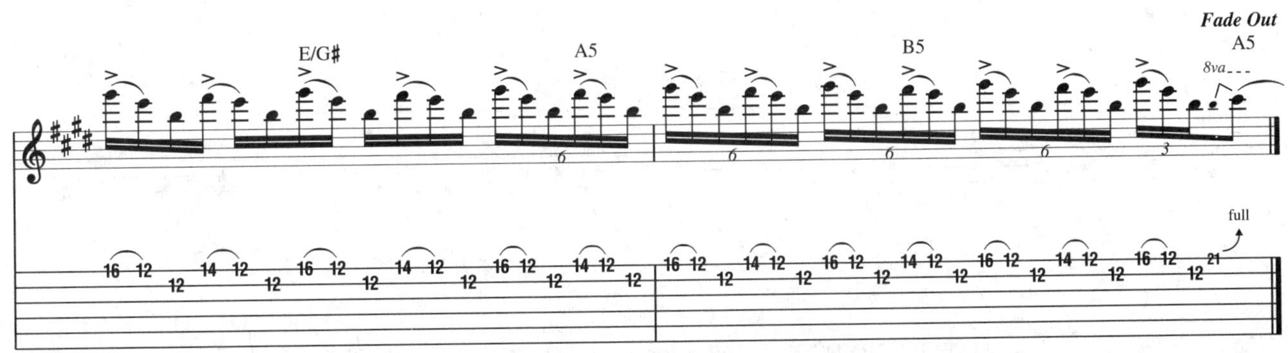
Fade Out
E/G#
A5
B5
A5
8va
full

Centerfold

Written by Seth Justman

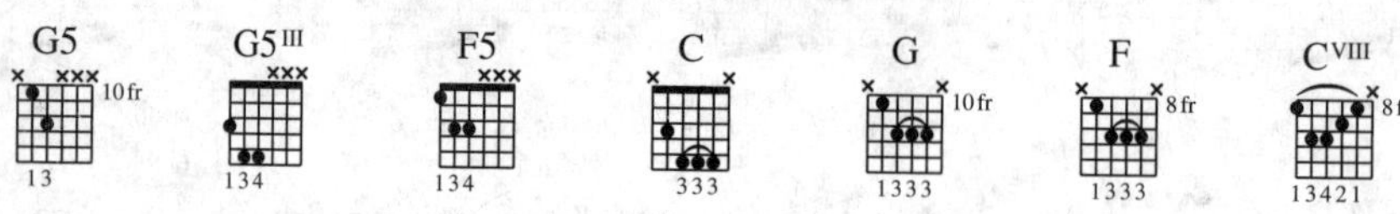

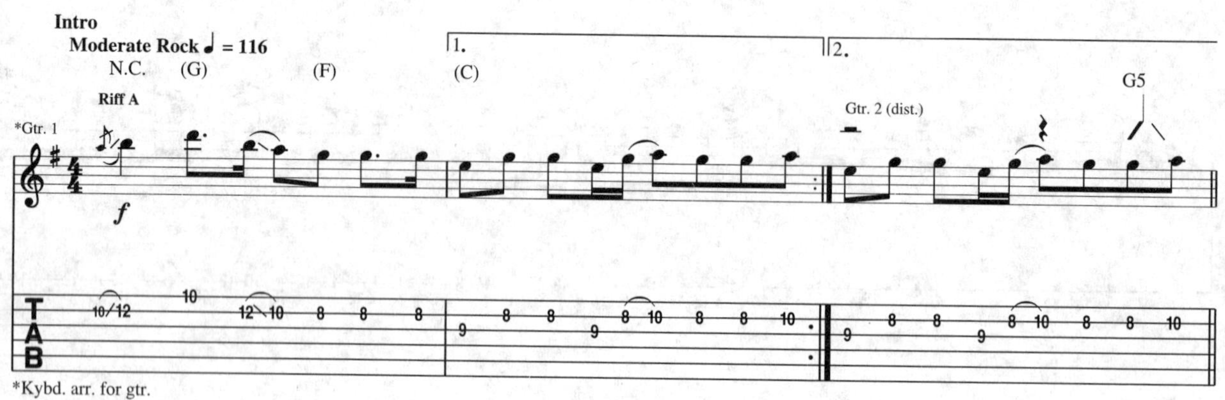

Verse
Gtrs. 1 & 2 tacet
Bkgd. Voc.: w/ Voc. Fill 1, 3 times, 2nd time
G5 F5 C F5 C
1. Does she walk, does she talk, does she come com - plete? My
2. Slipped me notes un - der the desk while I was think-ing a - bout her dress.
Gtr. 3 Rhy. Fig. 2
End Rhy. Fig. 2
simile on repeat
Gtr. 3: w/ Rhy. Fig. 2, 3 times
G5 F5 C F5 C G5 F5
home-room, home-room An - gel love has pulled me from my seat. She was pure like snow-flakes no
I was shy, I turned a-way, be - fore she caught my eye. I was shak-ing in my shoes when -
C F5 C G5 F5 C F5 C
one could ev - er stain. The mem - o - ry of my An - gel could nev - er cause me pain. Years
ev - er she flashed those ba - by blues. Some - thing had a hold on me when An - gel passed close by. Those
Pre-Chorus
Gtr. 5: w/ Fill 1, 3rd time
*Em Am C D
go by I'm look - ing through a girl - ie mag - a - zine, and
soft and fuz - zy sweat - ers, too mag - i - cal to touch. To
part of me has just been ripped, the pag - es from my mind are stripped.
Gtr. 4 (slight dist.)
Riff B
End Riff B
w/ amp tremolo
*Chord symbols reflect overall tonality, next 4 meas.
Gtr. 4: w/ Riff B
Em Am C D
there's my home - room An - gel on the pag - es in be - tween.
see her in that neg - li - gee is real - ly just too much. My
Oh no, I can't de - ny it. Oh yeah, I guess I got - ta buy it.
Voc. Fill 1
Do, do, do, do, wah.
Fill 1

Chorus
Gtrs. 2&3: w/ Rhy. Figs. 1&1A, 4 times
G5 F5 C F5 C G5 F5 C F5 C
blood runs cold. My mem-o-ry has just been sold. My An-gel is the cen-ter-fold. An-gel is the cen-ter-fold. My
Bkgd. Voc. Fill 2, 2nd time
To Coda
G5 F5 C F5 C G5 F5 C F5 C
blood runs cold. My mem-o-ry has just been sold. An-gel is the cen-ter-fold.
Gtr. 4
amp tremolo off
w/ bar
Interlude
Gtr. 1: w/ Riff A
Gtrs. 2 & 3: w/ Rhy. Figs. 1 & 1A, 4 times, simile
1., 2., 3.
4.
G5 F5 C F5 C C F5 C
Voc. Fig. 1
End Voc. Fig. 1
(Na, na, na, na, na, na, na, na, na, na, na, na, na, na, na, na. na, na, na, na, na, na, na, na.)
Spoken: Now listen.
Verse
Gtr. 3: w/ Rhy. Fig. 2, 4 times
Bkgd. Voc.: w/ Voc. Fill 1, 3 times
G5 F5 C F5 C
3. It's O. K. I un-der-stand this ain't no Nev-er Nev-er-land. I
G5 F5 C F5 C G5 F5
hope that when this is-sue's gone I'll see you when your clothes are on. Take your car, yes we will, we'll
Gtr. 5 (dist.)
mf
D.S. al Coda
C F5 C G5 F5 C F5 C
take your car and drive it. We'll take it to a mo-tel room and take 'em off in pri-vate. A
full
full
1/4
Voc. Fill 2
(Oh, yeah.)

Coda
Gtr. 1: w/ Riff A, last 2 meas., simile
G F C G
Gtr. 3
Spoken: Al-right, al-right. One, two, three, four.
(Na, na, na, na, na, na, na, na, na, na, na, na, na, na, na, na.)
Gtr. 2
1. 2.
Outro-Chorus
Bkgd. Voc.: w/ Voc. Fig. 1 till fade
Gtr. 1: w/ Riff A, 1st 2 meas., till fade
Gtr. 3: w/ Rhy. Fig. 1A, 2 times
G5 F5 C F5 C C F5 C
Voc. Fig. 2
End Voc. Fig. 2
(Whistle)
Gtr. 2
Riff C
End Riff C
1/2 1/2
Bkgd. Voc.: w/ Voc. Fig. 2, 6 times
Gtr. 2: w/ Riff C, till fade
Gtr. 3: w/ Rhy. Fig. 2, till fade
Na, na, na, na, na, na, na, na, na, na, na, na, na, na, na, na, na, na, na. Na, na, na, na, na, na, na,
na, na, na, na, na, na. My blood runs cold. My mem-o-ry has just been sold. My
An-gel is the cen-ter-fold. An-gel is the cen-ter-fold. Huh. Blood runs cold. Oh, yeah. My
mem-o-ry has just been sold. My An-gel is the cen-ter-fold. An-gel is the cen-ter-fold.
*Begin Fade
(Whistle)
*all instruments and vocals except for Voc. Fig. 2 (Whistle)

Change the World

Words and Music by Wayne Kirkpatrick, Gordon Kennedy and Tommy Sims

Verse
Gtr. 3 tacet
E
A/E
E7(no3rd)
1. If I could reach the stars,
A/E
E
pull one down for you.
Rhy. Fig. 2
A/E
E7(no3rd)
Shine it on my heart
A/E
E
so you could see the truth.
A
D/A
A7(no3rd)
Then this love I have in - side

D/A
A
E
A/E
E7(no3rd)
is ev - 'ry - thing it seems.
But for now I find
1/2
1/4
A/E
G#7
it's on - ly in my dreams.
And I can
End Rhy. Fig. 2
(cont. in slash)
Chorus
Gtr. 2 tacet
F#m7
G#7
C#m7
D#m7♭5
G#7
Rhy. Fig. 3
Gtr. 1
change the world.
(Change the world.
I will be the sun - light in your
I will be the sun - light in your
C#m7
D#m7♭5
G#7
u - ni - verse.
u - ni - verse.
You would think my love was real - ly
You would think my love,
Gtr. 2

C♯m7
Cm7
Bm7
A
Eadd2/G♯
End Rhy. Fig. 3
some - thing good, ba - by, if I could
some - thing good.)
E/G♯
E°/G
F♯m7type2
Gtr. 1
change
the world.
Gtr. 2
Gtr. 3
Rhy. Fill 1
End Rhy. Fill 1
*vol. knob swell
Interlude
Gtr. 1: w/ Rhy Fig. 1, simile
Gtr. 3 tacet
E
F♯m7
Gadd2
F♯m7
E
Verse
Gtr. 1: w/ Rhy. Fig. 2, simile
E
A/E
E7(no3rd)
A/E
E
2. If I could be king, e - ven for a day,
1/2

A/E
E7(no3rd)
I'd take you as my queen,
A/E
E
I'd have it no oth - er way.
1/2
1/4
A
D/A
A7(no3rd)
And our love would rule in this
D/A
A
king - dom we have made.
E
A/E
E7(no3rd)
Till then I'd be a fool,
1/4
A/E
G#7
wish - ing for the day.
And I can
Chorus
Gtr. 1: w/ Rhy. Fig. 3
Gtr. 2 tacet, 1st time; w/ Fill 1, 2nd time
F#m7
G#7
C#m7
change the world.
(Change the, change the world.
Fill 1
Gtr. 2
T
A
B

Gtr. 2: Fill 2, 2nd time
D♯m7♭5
G♯7
C♯m7
I will be the sun - light in your u - ni - verse.
I will be the sun - light in your u - ni - verse.
To Coda
D♯m7♭5
G♯7
C♯m7
Cm7
Bm7
You would think my love was real - ly some - thing good, ba - by,
You would think my love, some - thing good, oh,
A
Eadd2/G♯
E/G♯
E°/G
F♯m7
E
Gtr. 3
if I could change the world, ba - by,
if I could, yeah.)
Gtr. 2
Gtr. 1
Fill 2
Gtr. 2
T
A
B

Gtr. 2 & 3 tacet
A7
Eadd2/G#
Gtr. 3: w/ Rhy. Fill 1
E/G#
E°/G
F#m7
if I could change the world.
Gtr. 1
Guitar Solo
Gtr. 1: w/ Rhy. Fig. 1 1½ times, simile
E
F#m7
Gadd2
F#m7
E
Gtr. 2
1/2
full
1/4
F#m7
Gadd2
full
D.S. al Coda
F#m7
G#7
I can
Gtr. 2
1/2
1/4
Gtr. 1

Coda
Bkgd. Voc.: w/ Voc. Fig. 1
A
Eadd2/G#
E/G#
E°/G
F#m7type2
Gtr. 1
if I could change the world, ba - by,
if I could, yeah.)
Gtr. 2
A
Eadd2/G#
E/G#
E°/G
F#m7type2
if I could change the world, ba - by,
A
Eadd2/G#
E/G#
E°/G
if I could change
Voc. Fig. 1
(Change.)

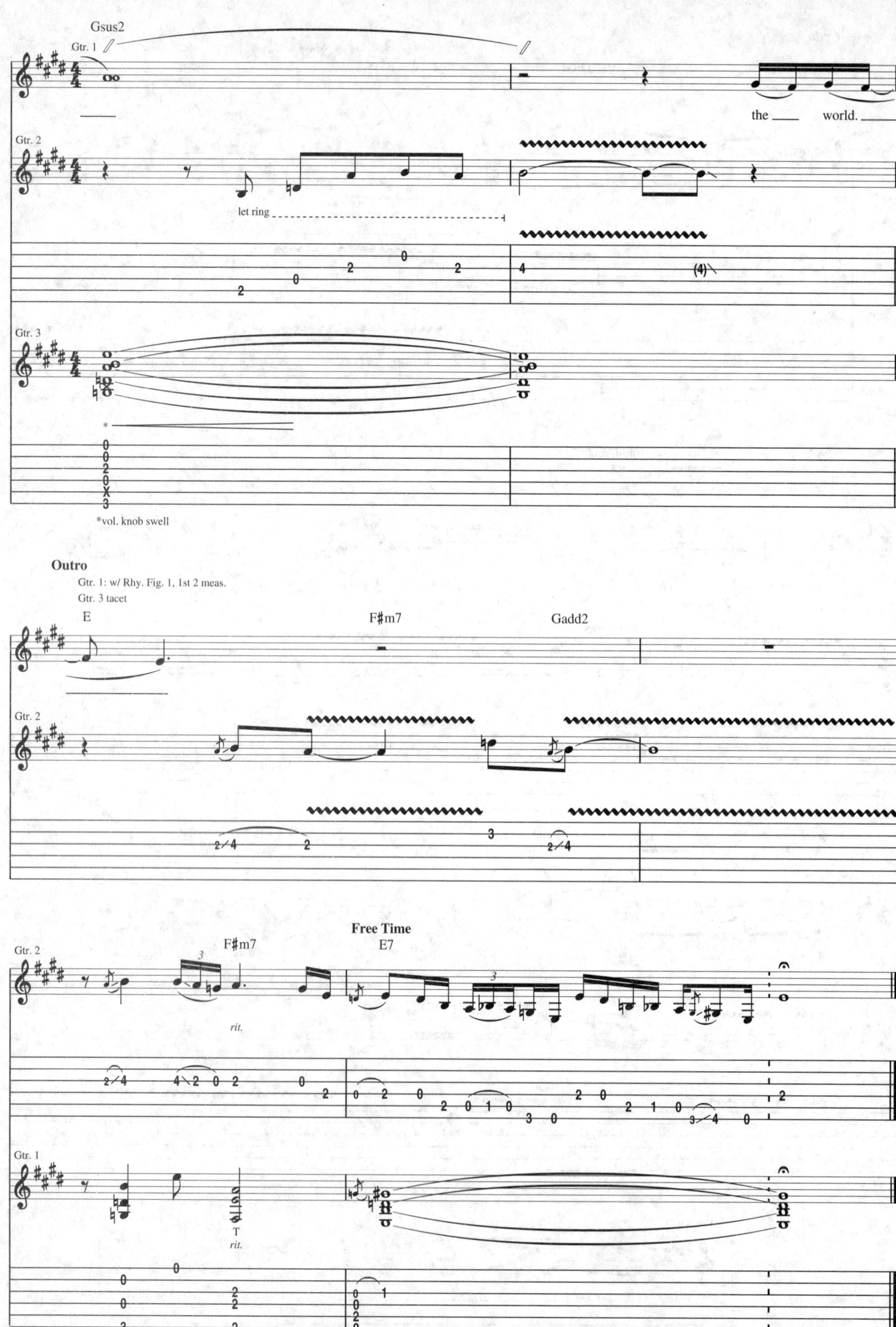

Gsus2
Gtr. 1
the world.
Gtr. 2
let ring
Gtr. 3
*vol. knob swell
Outro
Gtr. 1: w/ Rhy. Fig. 1, 1st 2 meas.
Gtr. 3 tacet
E
F#m7
Gadd2
Free Time
E7
rit.
T

Chinatown, My Chinatown

Arranged by Chet Atkins

* To play artificial harmonics, fret string as shown in tab, touch string 12 frets higher with tip of right index-finger, and sound harmonic with thumbpick.

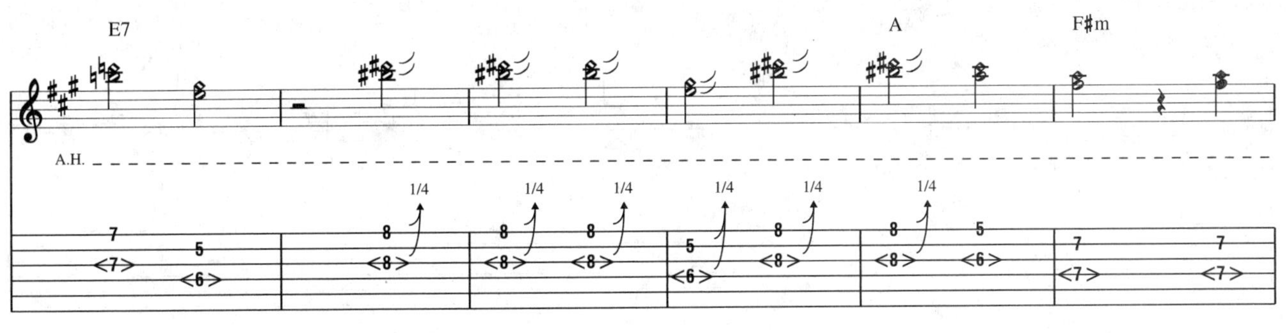
E7
A
F♯m
A.H.
1/4
1/4
1/4
1/4
1/4
1/4

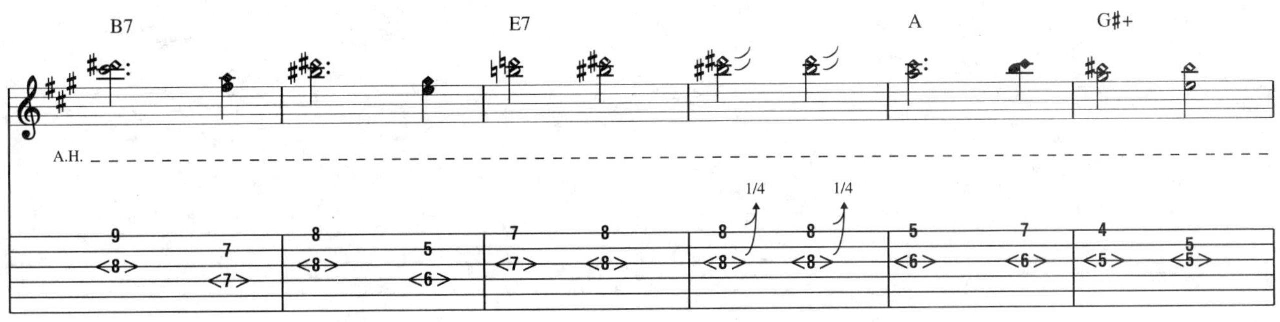
B7
E7
A
G♯+
A.H.
1/4
1/4

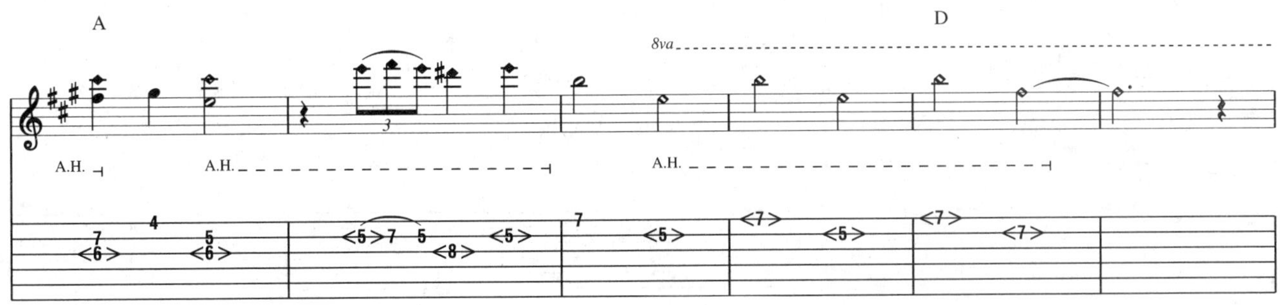
A
D
8va
A.H.
A.H.
A.H.
3

8va
Dm
A
F♯7
B7
E7
A.H.
1/2

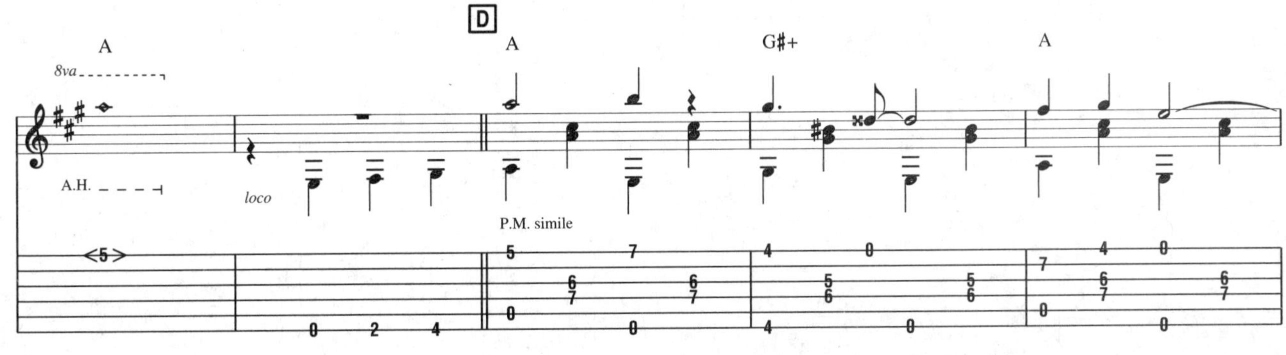
A
D
A
G♯+
A
8va
A.H.
loco
P.M. simile

Amaj7/C♯
F9/C
E9/B
C♯7
F♯m
B7
E6
F9
E9
A
G♯+
A
A9
D6
w/ bar
-1/2

Dm
A
F#7
B7
E7
A
E
A
E7
C#7

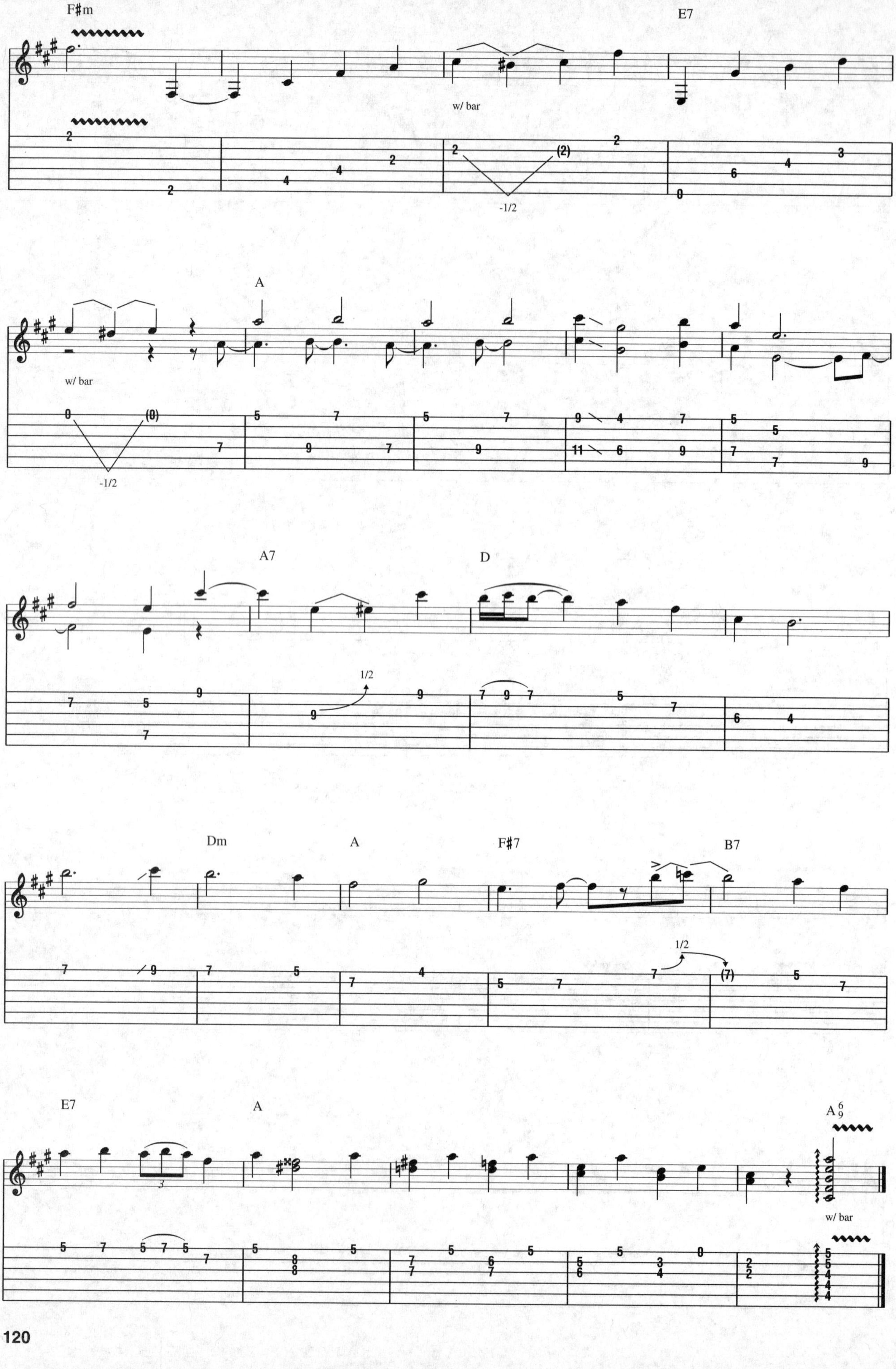
F#m
E7
w/ bar
-1/2
A
w/ bar
-1/2
A7
D
1/2
Dm
A
F#7
B7
1/2
E7
A
A 6/9
w/ bar

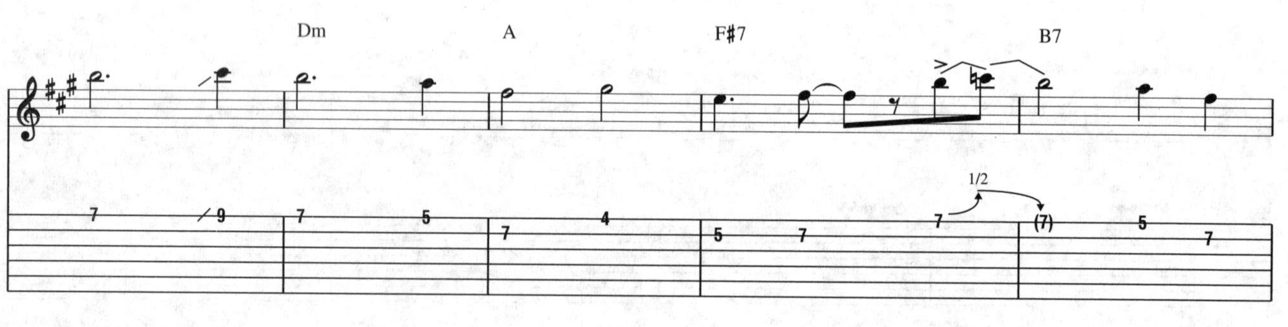

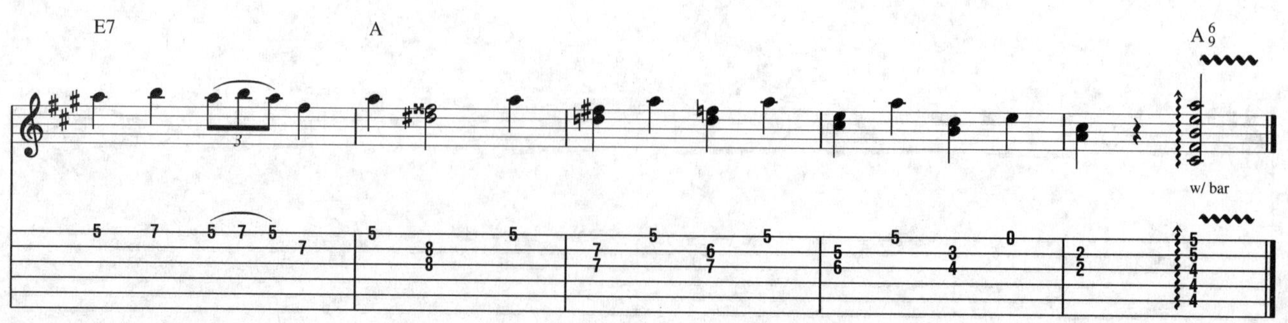

Cliffs of Dover

By Eric Johnson

Medium-Fast Shuffle ♩. = 190
N.C.
play 3 times
P.M.
B
G5
C5
N.C.(D)
(G)
(C)
full
let ring
(D)
G5
8va
N.C.(C)
P.H.
(D)
(G)
C
C5
D5
N.C.(Am)
(D)

(G)
(Em)
(Am)
(D)
(G)
(Em)
(Am)
(D)
full
(G)
(Em)
(Am)
(D)
(G)
(Em)
N.C.
P.M.
P.M.
P.M.
D
G5
N.C.(C5)
(D)
(G)
1/2
P.M.
P.M.
P.M.

(C)
(D)
P.M.
(G)
8va
(C)
full
full
(D)
(G)
C5
D5
E
N.C.(Am)
(D)
(G)
(Em)
(Am)
(D)
(G)
(Em)
8va
loco
P.H.
(Am)
(D)
(G)
(Em)
(Am)
(D)
(G)

F Half-Time Feel
(Em)
(D)
G5
Gsus4
let ring
* T
* Thumb on 6
8va
full
let ring
N.C.
G
N.C.(Em)
P.M.
1/2

G5
C5
Cadd9
1/2
H Guitar Solo
End Half-Time Feel
Dsus2
D5
N.C.(Am)
(D)
full
(G)
(Em)
(Am)
8va
(D)
8va
(G)
1/2
(Em)
loco
(Am)
(D)
(G)
(Em)
(Am)
(D)
(G)
(Em)
8va
(Am)

(D)
8va
(G)
loco
(Em)
(Am)
(D)
(G)
(Em)
8va
(Am)
8va
(D)
(G)
(Em)
8va
loco
(Am)
(B/D#)
8va
H
(E)
8va
(D)
loco
full
(Am)
(D)
(G)
(Em)
(Am)
(D)
full
1 1/2

(G)
(Em)
(Am)
(D)
8va
1/2
full
loco
Guitar Cadenza
Freely
G5

Close My Eyes Forever

Words and Music by Lita Ford and Ozzy Osbourne

Am(add9)
G6
Heav-en is in the palm of my hand, and it's wait - in' here for you. What am
dag-ger, and stick me in the heart, and taste the blood from my blade. And

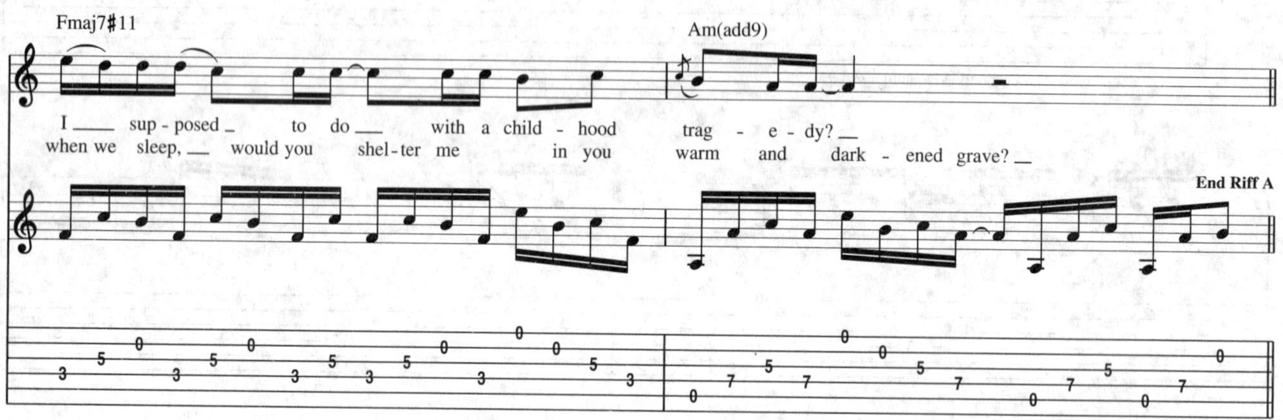
Fmaj7♯11
Am(add9)
I sup - posed to do with a child - hood trag - e - dy?
when we sleep, would you shel-ter me in you warm and dark - ened grave?
End Riff A

𝄋 Chorus
Fadd♯4/C
Asus2
Asus4
Am
G
If I close my eyes for-ev - er

Fadd♯4/C
Asus2
Asus4
Am
G
will it all re - main un - changed?

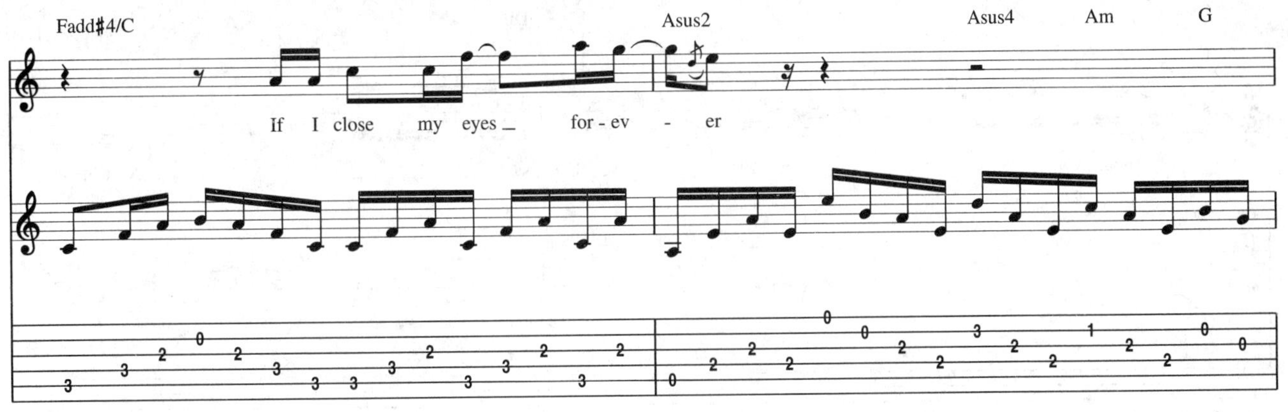

Fadd♯4/C
Asus2
Asus4
Am
G
If I close my eyes_ for-ev - er

1.
Fadd♯4/C
G5
G6
will it all_ re-main_ the same?
*T
T
T
T
*T = Thumb on ⑥

2.
To Coda
G
Em
T

Bridge

band enters
Gtr. 1 tacet
B♭
Rhy. Fig. 1
Gm
Dm
C
*Gtr. 2
mf
Will you ev - er take_ me?
No, I just can't take the pain.
*Synth arr. for gtr.

B♭
Gm
Dm
A
End Rhy. Fig. 1
Would you ev - er trust me?
No, I'll nev - er feel the
same.
Oh!
Gtr. 3 (elec.)
w/ dist.

Guitar Solo

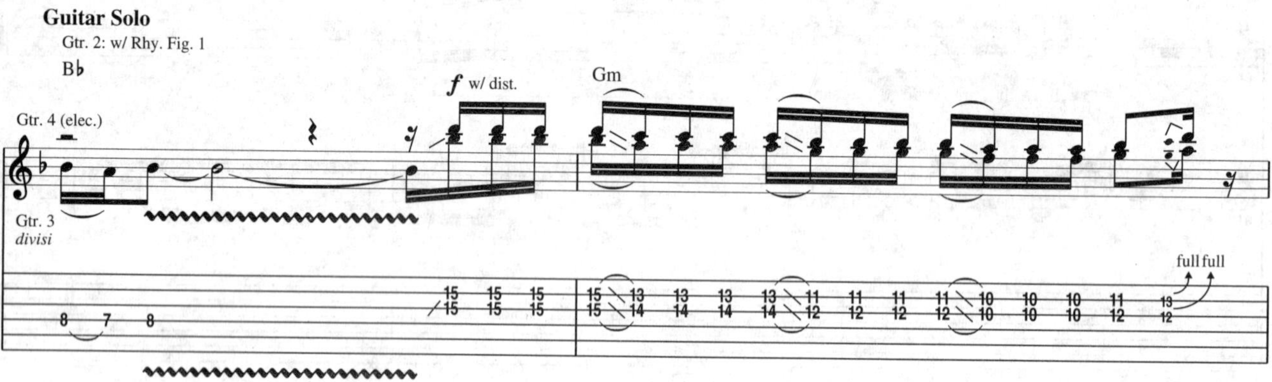
Gtr. 2: w/ Rhy. Fig. 1
B♭
Gm
w/ dist.
Gtr. 4 (elec.)
Gtr. 3
divisi
full full

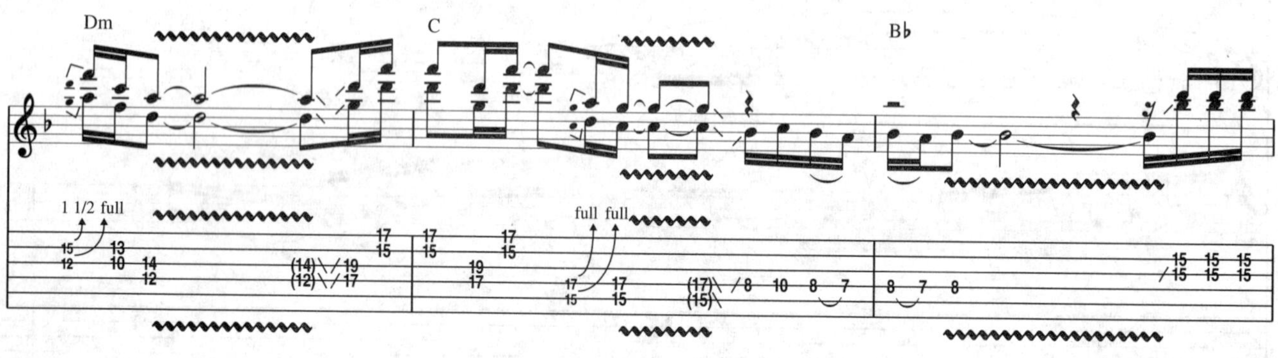
Dm
C
B♭
1 1/2 full
full full

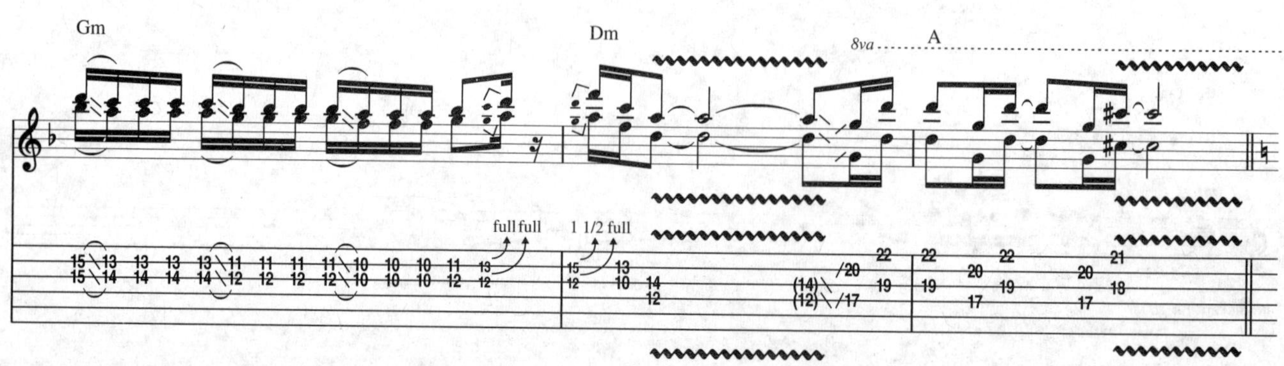
Gm
Dm
8va
A
full full
1 1/2 full

D.S. al Coda
(take 2nd ending)

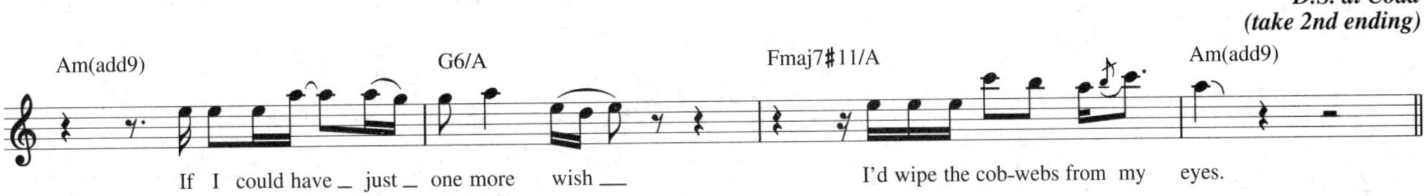

Couldn't Stand the Weather

Written by Stevie Ray Vaughan

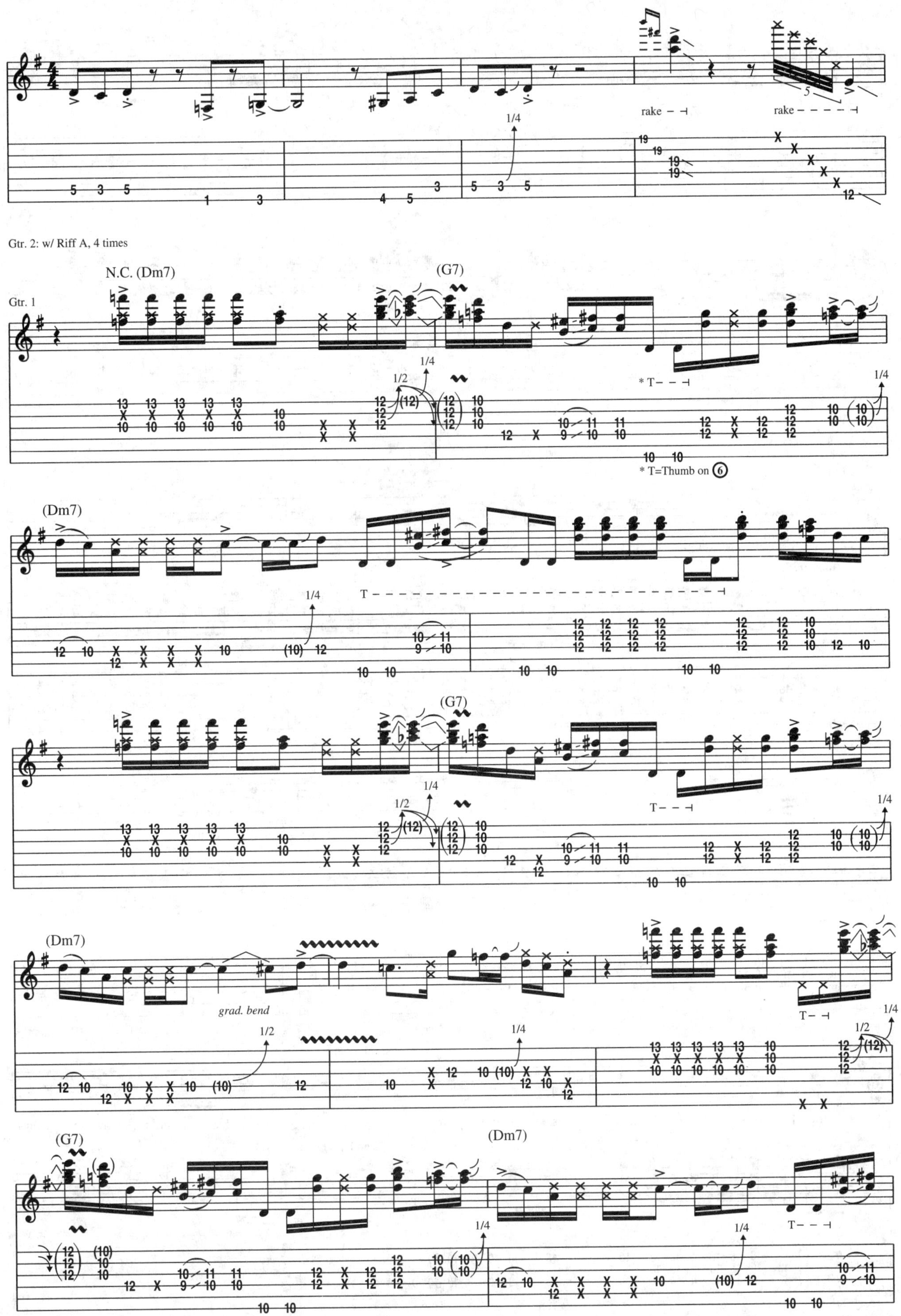

rake
rake
1/4
Gtr. 2: w/ Riff A, 4 times
N.C. (Dm7)
(G7)
Gtr. 1
1/2
1/4
* T
1/4
* T=Thumb on ⑥
(Dm7)
1/4
T
(G7)
1/2
1/4
T
1/4
(Dm7)
grad. bend
1/2
1/4
T
1/2
1/4
(G7)
(Dm7)
1/4
1/4
T

(G7)
1/4
1/2
(Dm7)
Verse
Gtr. 1 tacet
Dm7
1. Com-in' through_ this ah bus-'ness of life,__ rare-ly time_ if I'm
Gtr. 2
Rhy. Fig. 1
need - ed to.___ Ain't so fun-ny when things__ ain't feel-in' right,_
then Dad-dy's hand_ helps to see me through._ Sweet as sug-ar, love won't_
End Rhy. Fig. 1
Rhy. Fig. 2
Bm
let ring

A7
G7
wash a - way.
Rain or shine, it's al - ways here to stay.
All these years, you 'n' I've
let ring
let ring
1/4

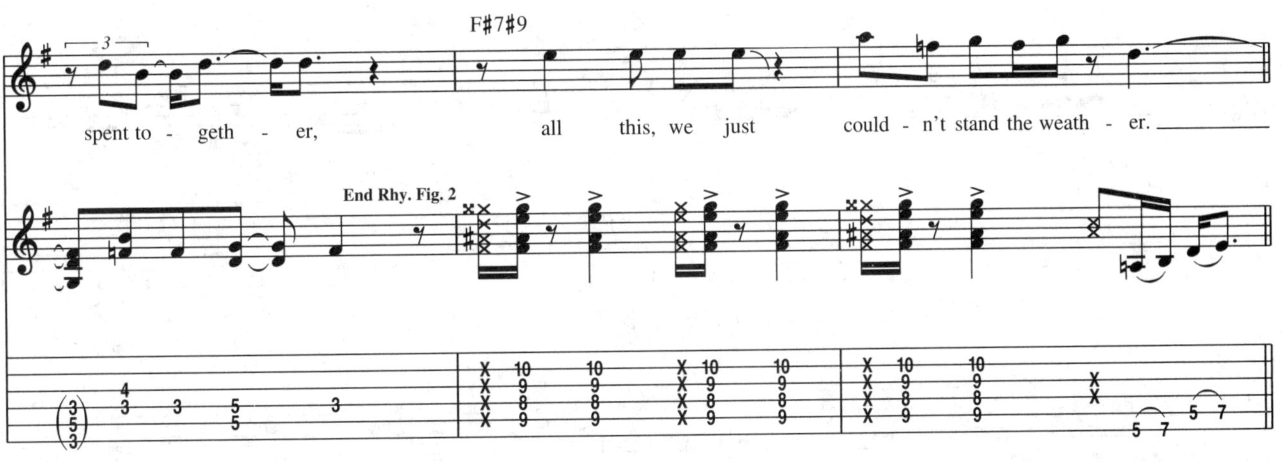
F#7#9
spent to - geth - er,
all this, we just
could - n't stand the weath - er.
End Rhy. Fig. 2

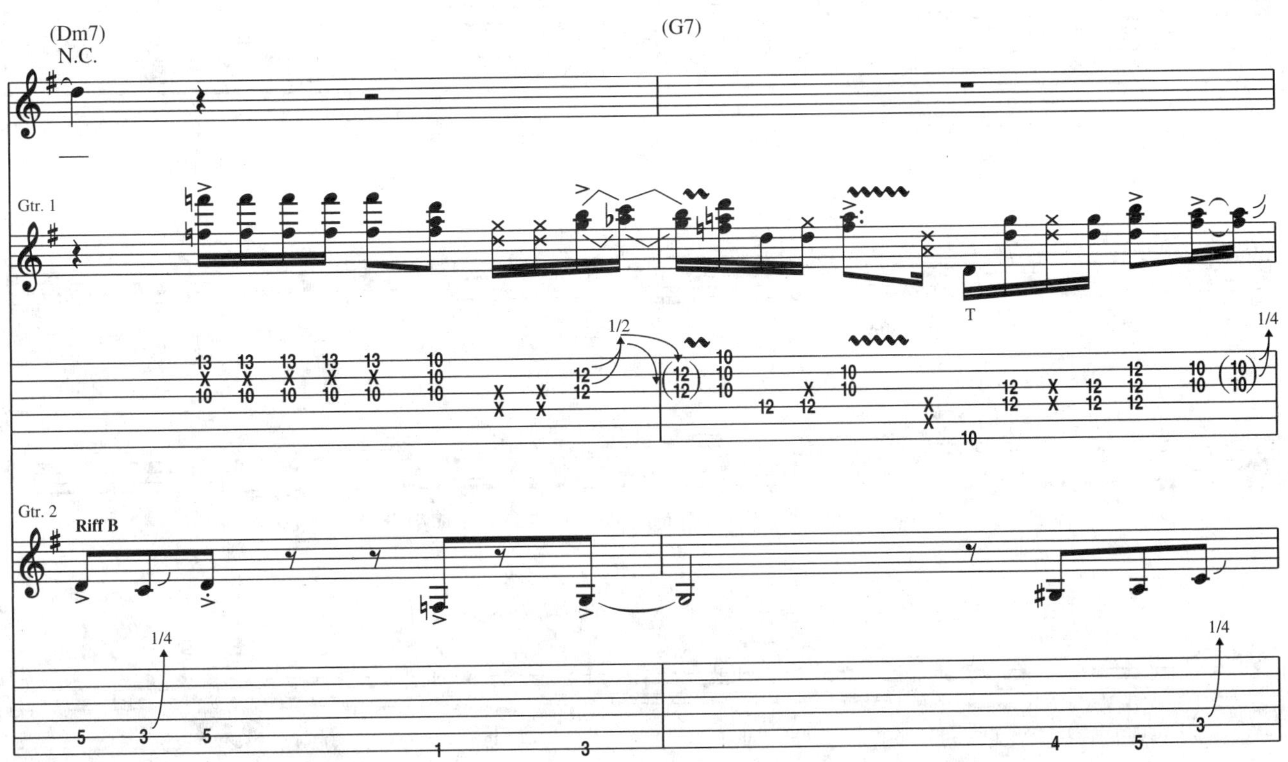
(Dm7)
N.C.
(G7)
Gtr. 1
Gtr. 2
Riff B
1/2
1/4
T

(Dm7)
End Riff B
Gtr. 2: w/ Riff B
Gtr. 1
(G7)
1/2
T
(Dm7)
1/4
P.M.
Verse
Gtr. 1 tacet
Gtr. 2: w/ Rhy. Fig. 1
Dm7
2. Like a train that stops at ev-'ry sta-tion, we all deal with trials
and trib-u-la-tions. Fear hangs the fel-low that ties up his years,
Gtr. 2: w/ Rhy. Fig. 2
Bm
en-tan-gled in yel-low and cries all his tears. Chang-es come be-fore we can go.

A9
G9
Learn to see them be - fore we're too old.
Don't just take me for
Gtr. 1
let ring

F#7#9
Gtr. 2
try'n' to be heav - y. Un-der-stand, it's time to get r-ead-y for the storm.
string noise
w/ flanger & dist.

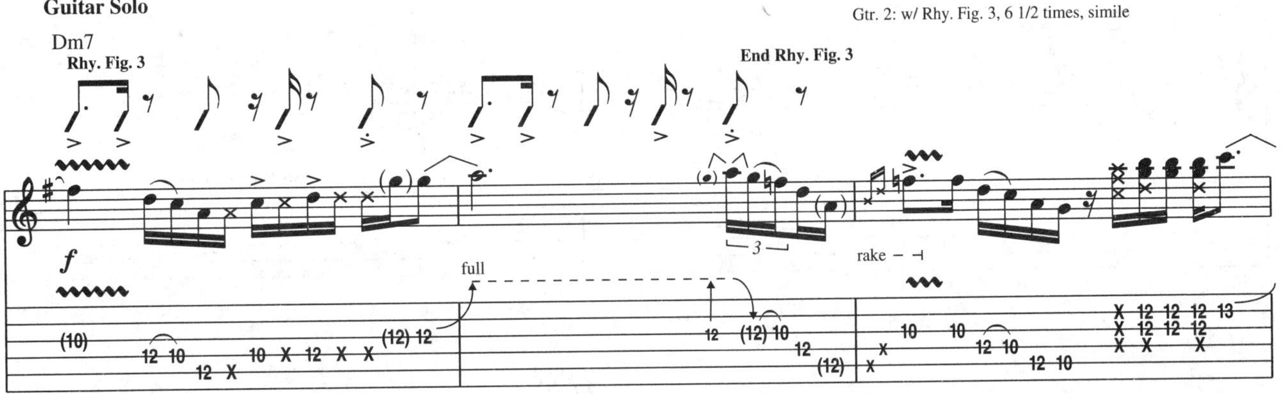
Guitar Solo
Gtr. 2: w/ Rhy. Fig. 3, 6 1/2 times, simile
Dm7
Rhy. Fig. 3
End Rhy. Fig. 3
full
rake

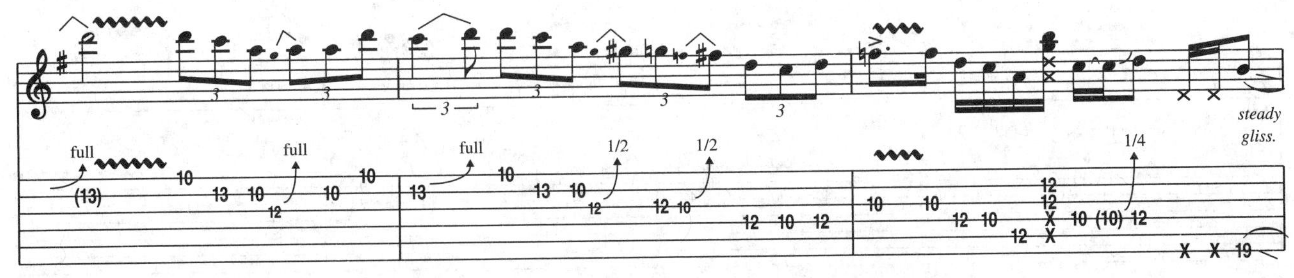
full
full
full
1/2
1/2
1/4
steady gliss.

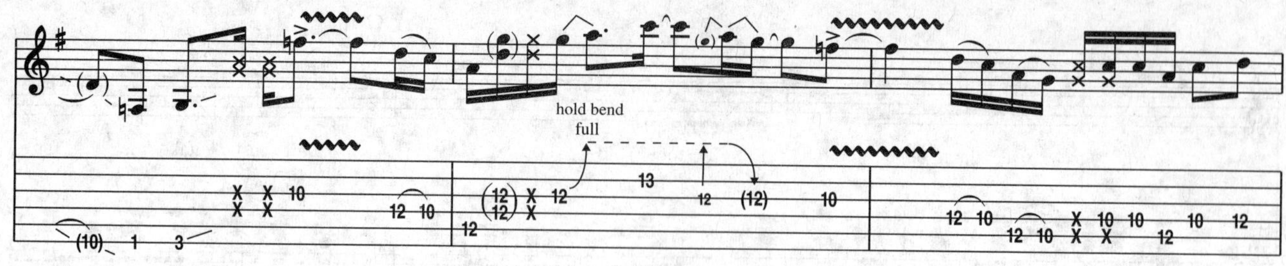
hold bend
full

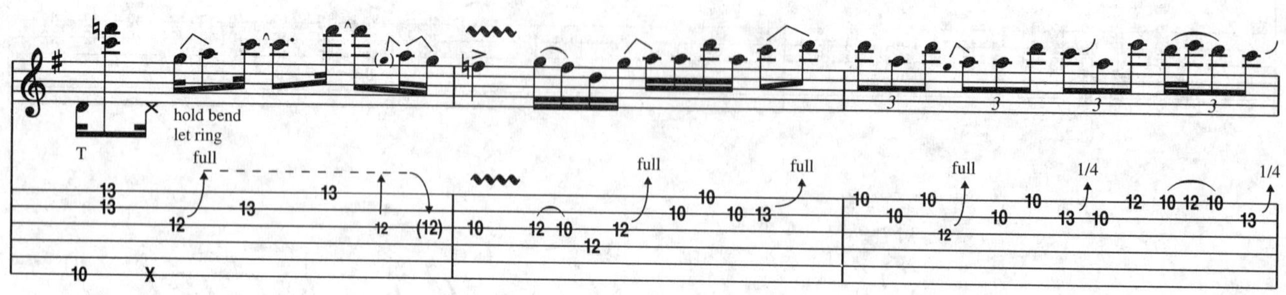
hold bend
let ring
T
full
full
full
full
1/4
1/4

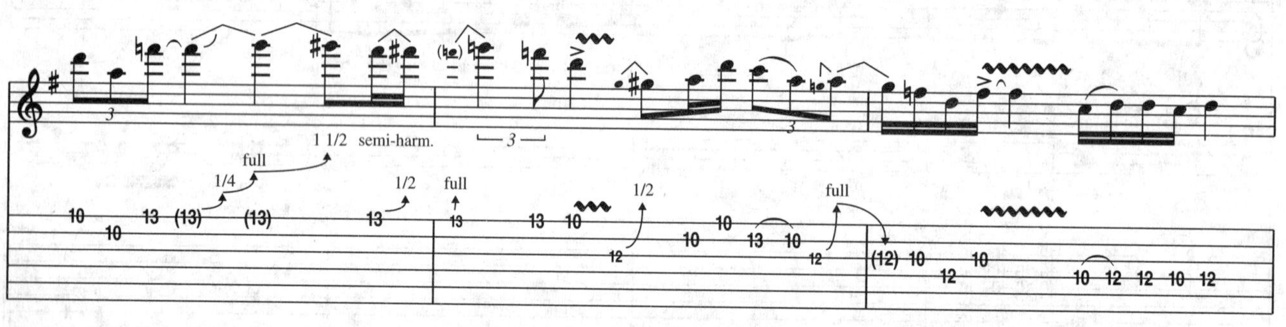
1/4
full
1 1/2 semi-harm.
1/2
full
1/2
full

Gtr. 2: w/ Rhy. Fig. 2, simile
Bm
A7
1/2
full
1/2
1/4
steady
gliss.

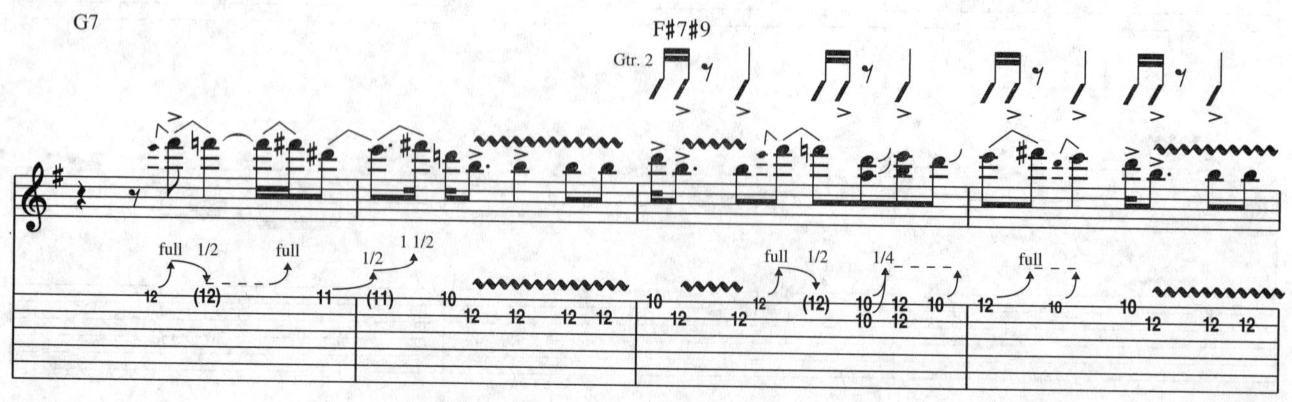
G7
F#7#9
Gtr. 2
full
1/2
full
1/2
1 1/2
full
1/2
1/4
full

Gtr. 2: w/ Rhy. Fig. 2, simile
Bm
A7
full
1/2
G7
1/4
F#7#9
Gtrs. 1 & 2
Outro
Gtr. 2: w/ Riff A, 4 1/4 times
(Dm7)
N.C.
Gtr. 1
mf clean tone
(G7)
(Dm7)
T

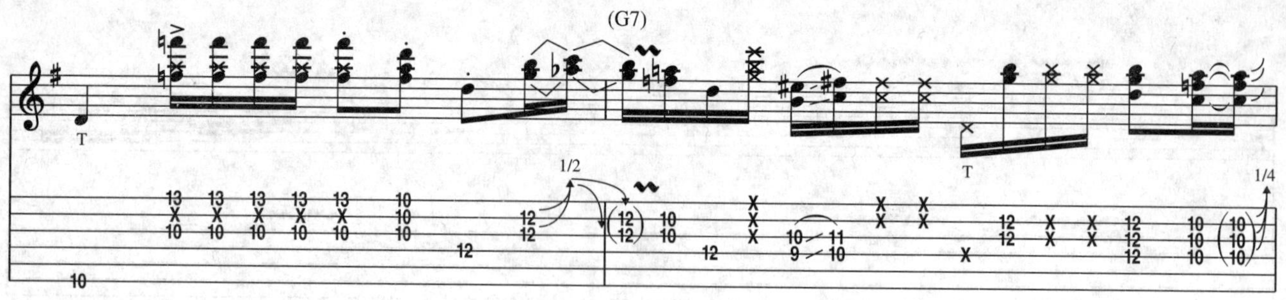
(G7)
T
1/2
T
1/4

(Dm7)
T
1/4
1/4
1/2

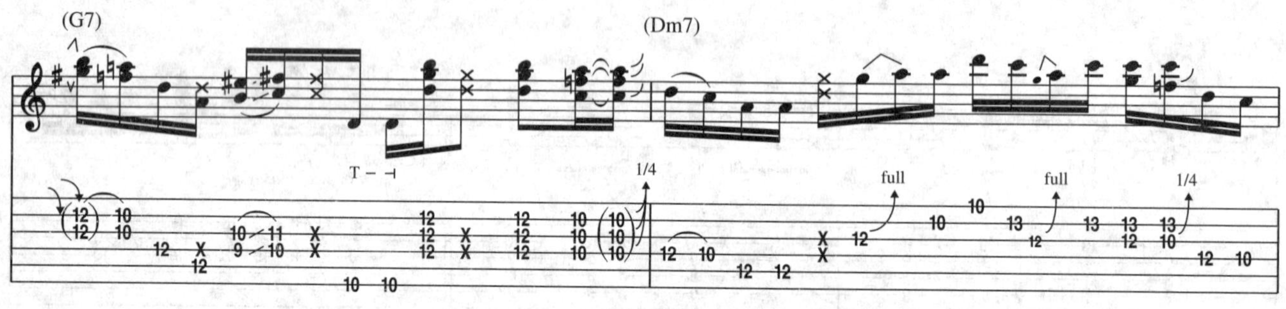
(G7)
(Dm7)
T
1/4
full
full
1/4

G
G7
3 fr.
Gtr. 2
T

Free Time Cadenza
Dm7
F
rake
rake
dim.

Cradle of Love

Words and Music by David Werner and Billy Idol

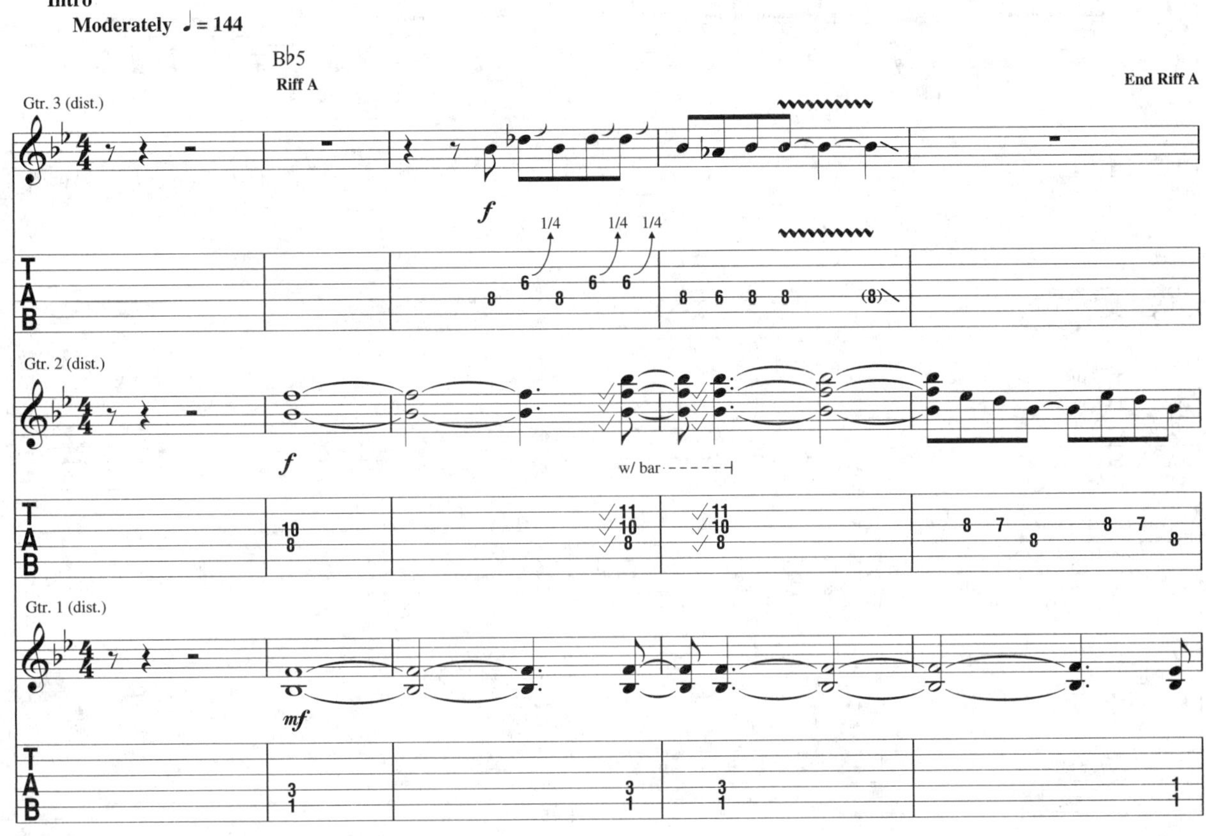

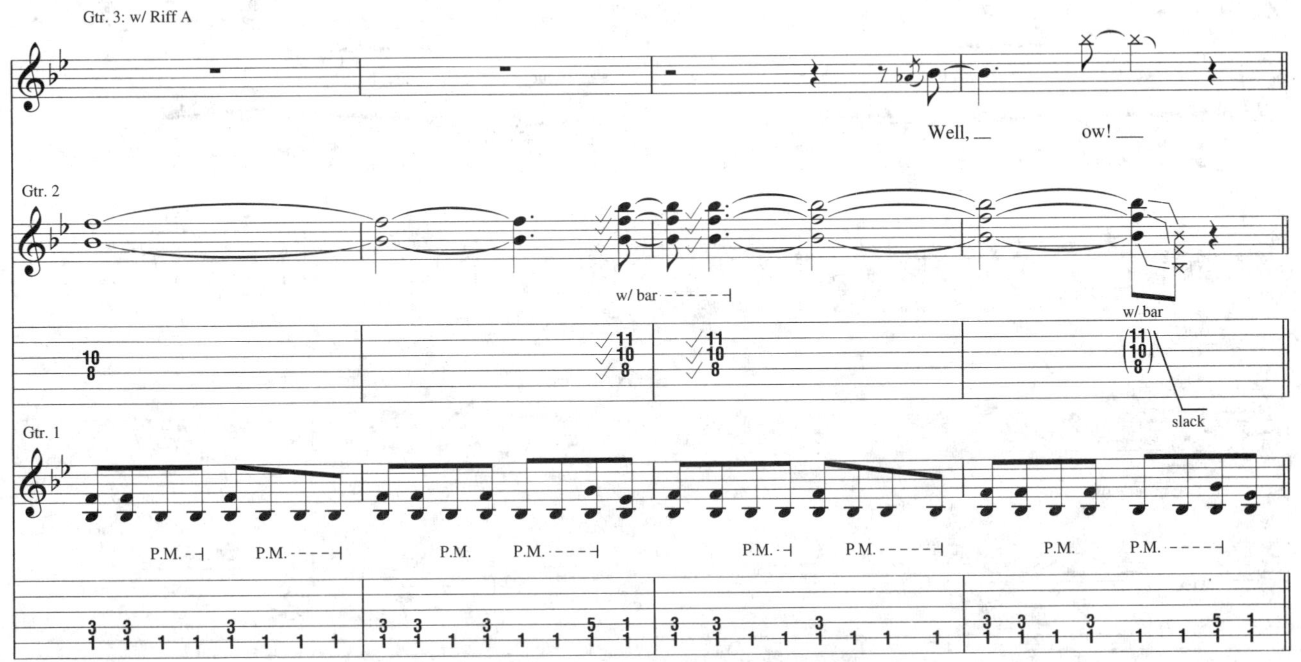

Chorus
Gtr. 2 tacet
Rock the cra - dle of love. Oh, rock the cra - dle of love. Yes, the
Gtr. 1
Rhy. Fig. 1
P.M.
G5
F5
G5
F5
B♭5
cra - dle of love don't rock eas - i - ly, it's true. Well, and
Gtr. 2
Rhy. Fig. 2
End Rhy. Fig. 2
Gtr. 1
Gtr. 2 tacet
rock the cra - dle of love. I rocked the cra - dle of love. Yes, the
Gtr. 1
P.M.
Gtr. 2: w/ Rhy. Fig. 2
G5
F5
G5
F5
cra - dle of love don't rock eas - i - ly, it's true. 1. Well, now,
End Rhy. Fig. 1

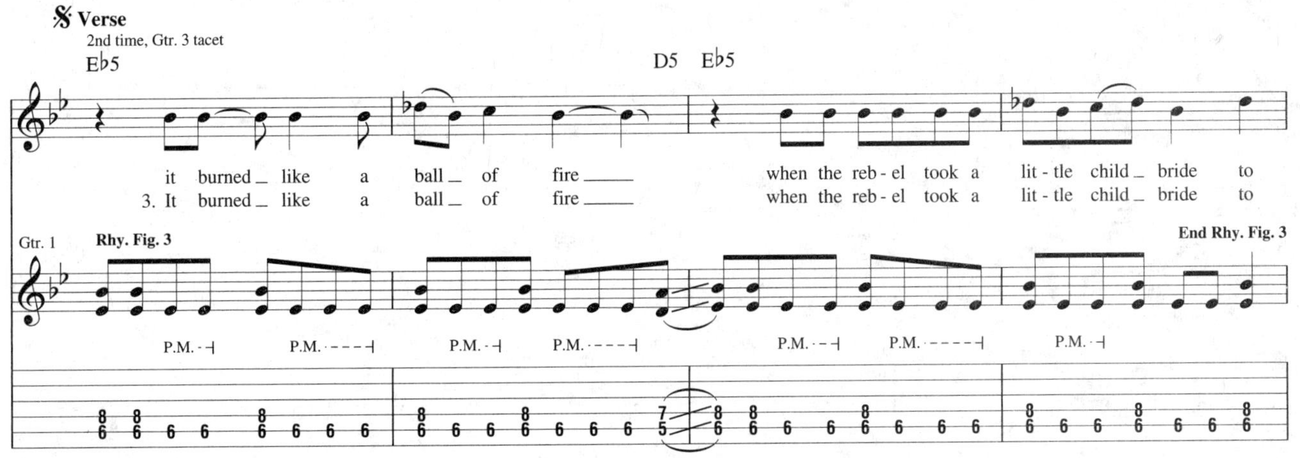
Verse
2nd time, Gtr. 3 tacet
Eb5
D5 Eb5
it burned like a ball of fire when the reb - el took a lit - tle child bride to
3. It burned like a ball of fire when the reb - el took a lit - tle child bride to
Gtr. 1
Rhy. Fig. 3
End Rhy. Fig. 3
P.M.

2nd time, Gtr. 2: w/ Rhy. Fill 1
Gm
F/G
Gm
F/G
tease, yeah. So go eas - y, yeah. Ow!
tease, yeah. 'Cause I know how to please you, yeah. Ow!
Gtr. 2
let ring
w/ bar
-1/2
slack
Gtr. 1
Rhy. Fig. 4
End Rhy. Fig. 4
P.M.

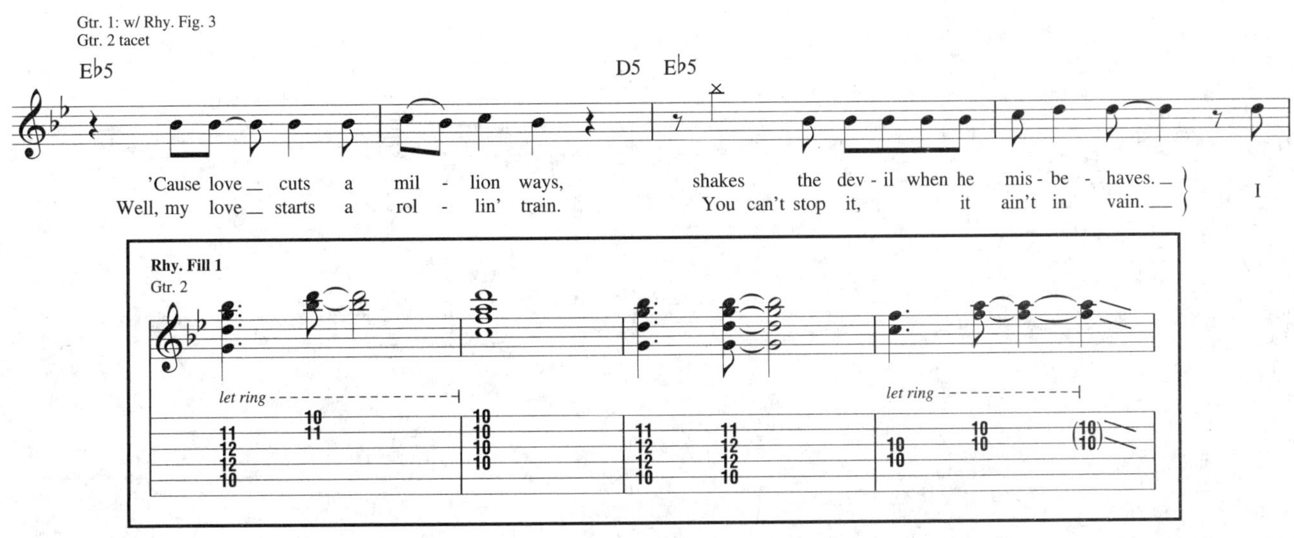
Gtr. 1: w/ Rhy. Fig. 3
Gtr. 2 tacet
Eb5
D5 Eb5
'Cause love cuts a mil - lion ways, shakes the dev - il when he mis - be - haves.
Well, my love starts a rol - lin' train. You can't stop it, it ain't in vain.
I
Rhy. Fill 1
Gtr. 2
let ring

To Coda

Chorus

Gtr. 2 tacet
Gtr. 3 tacet
Sent from heav-en a-bove, that's right, oo, to rob the cra-dle of love. Yes, the
Gtr. 3
1/4 mf 1/4 1/4
8 6 8 6 8 6 8
(8)

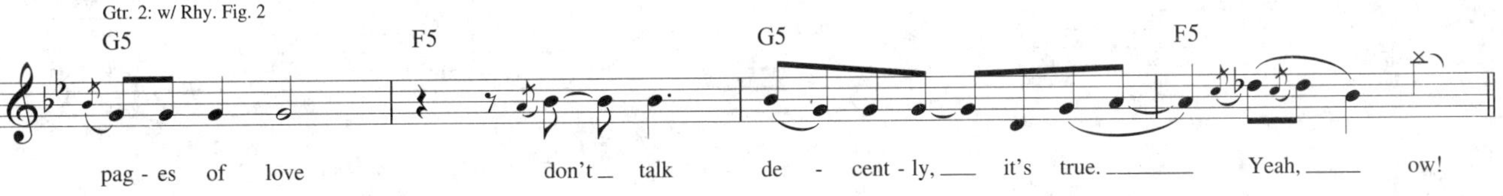
Gtr. 2: w/ Rhy. Fig. 2
G5 F5 G5 F5
pag-es of love don't talk de-cent-ly, it's true. Yeah, ow!

Verse

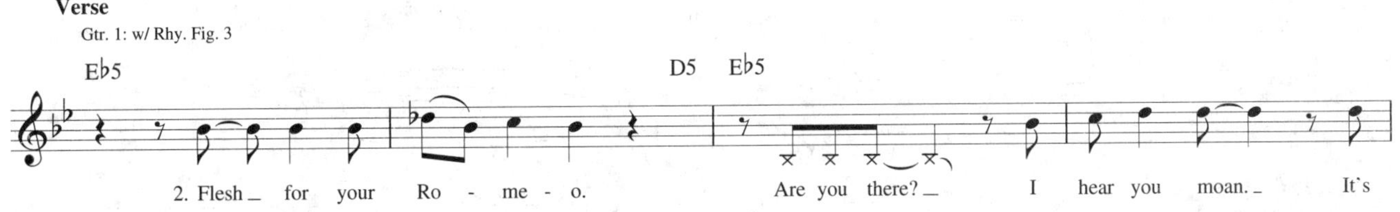
Gtr. 1: w/ Rhy. Fig. 3
E♭5 D5 E♭5
2. Flesh for your Ro-me-o. Are you there? I hear you moan. It's

Gtr. 1: w/ Rhy. Fig. 4
Gm F/G Gm F/G
eas-y, you know how to please me, yeah, ow!
Gtr. 2
10 11 12 12 10
10 10
10 11 12 12 10
10 10
(10) (10)

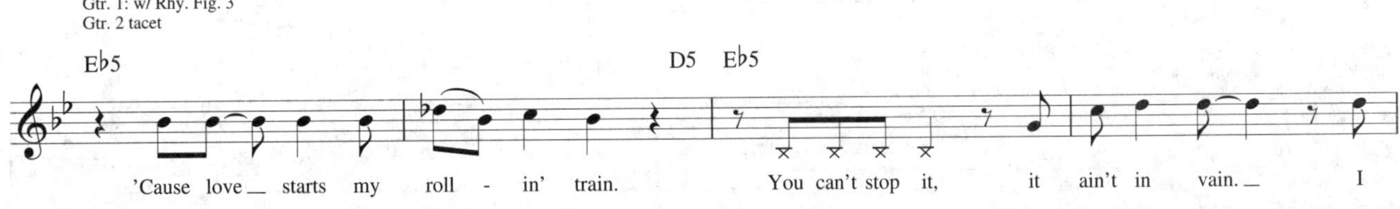
Gtr. 1: w/ Rhy. Fig. 3
Gtr. 2 tacet
E♭5 D5 E♭5
'Cause love starts my roll-in' train. You can't stop it, it ain't in vain. I

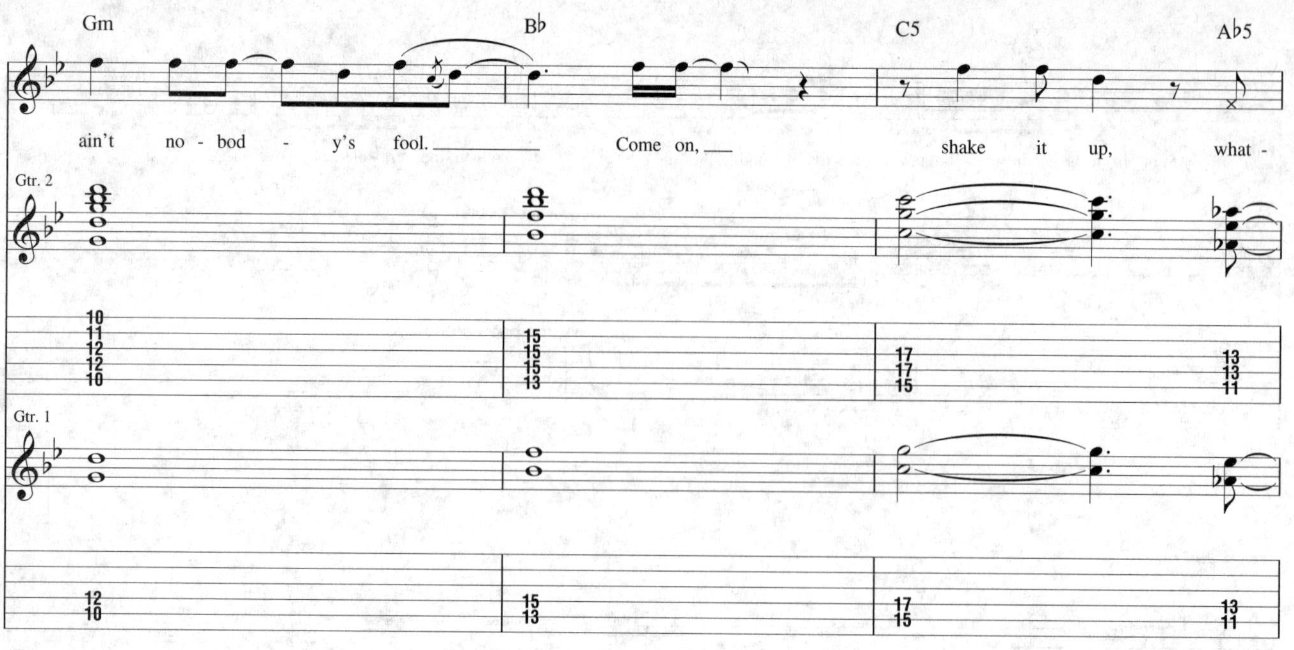
Gm
B♭
C5
A♭5
ain't no - bod - y's fool.
Come on,
shake it up, what -
Gtr. 2
Gtr. 1

ev - er I do.
Ha, how!
Woo!
Oh.
w/ bar
-1 1/2

Bridge

Gtrs. 1 & 2 tacet
Fm
D♭maj7
A♭
Cm
Uh, these are the wag - es of love.
Gtr. 4 (clean)
mf
w/ heavy reverb
let ring throughout

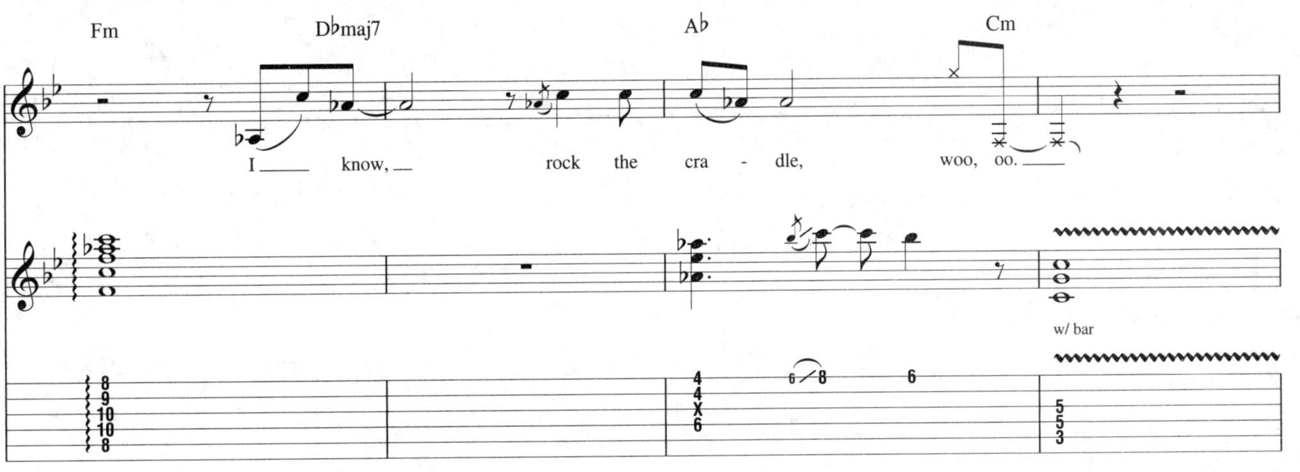

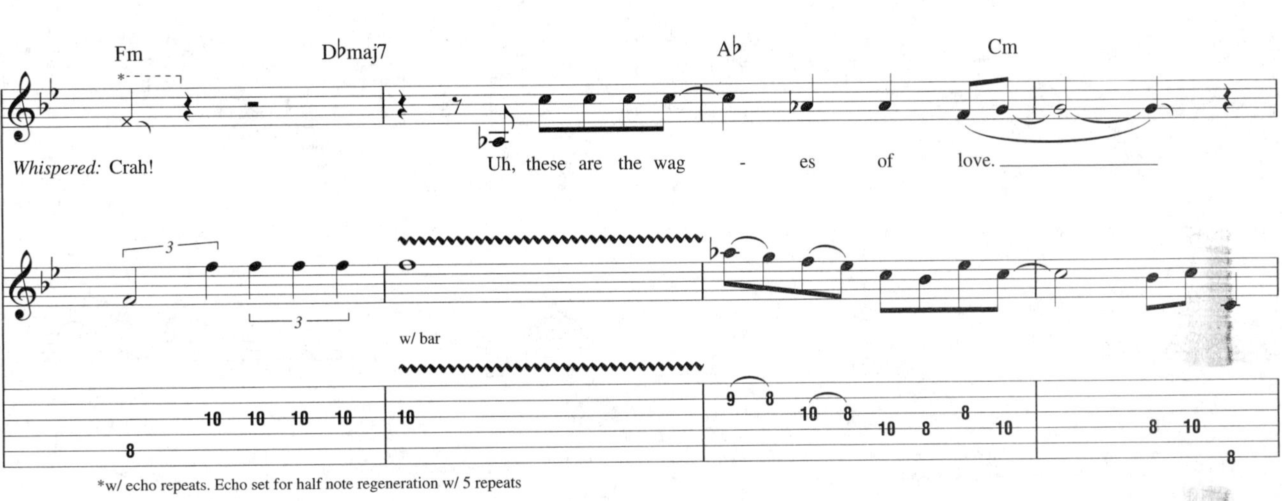

*w/ echo repeats. Echo set for half note regeneration w/ 5 repeats

Gtr. 4 tacet
Yeah, yeah, yeah, yeah, yeah, yeah, yeah!
Gtr. 3
P.M.
P.M.
P.M.
P.M.

Guitar Solo

Gtr. 1: w. Rhy. Fig. 1 (1st 6 meas.)
B♭5
Ow!
Woo!
Yeah, come on!
Gtr. 3

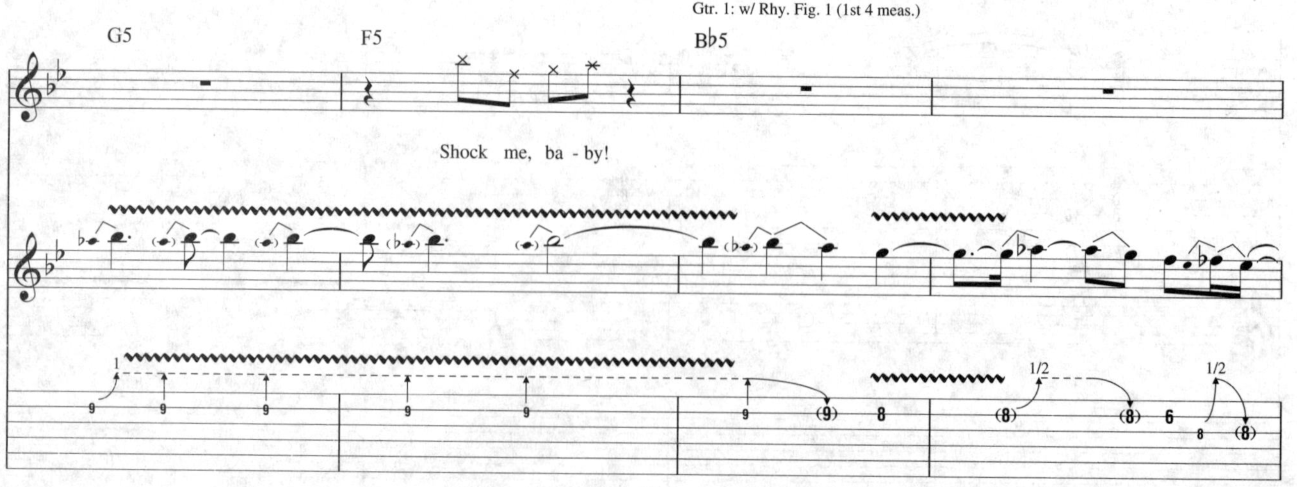
Gtr. 1: w/ Rhy. Fig. 1 (1st 4 meas.)
G5
F5
B♭5
Shock me, ba - by!

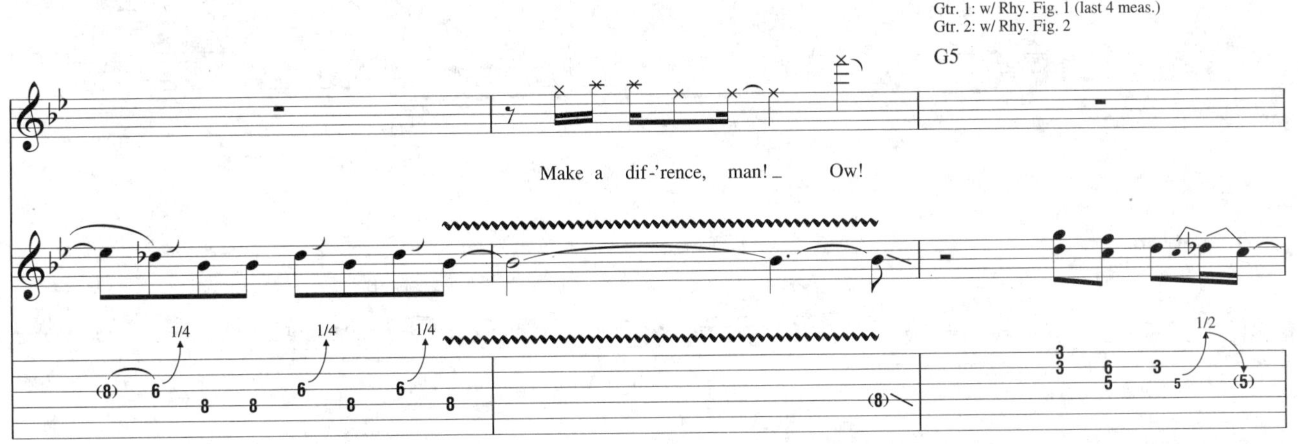
Gtr. 1: w/ Rhy. Fig. 1 (last 4 meas.)
Gtr. 2: w/ Rhy. Fig. 2
G5
Make a dif-'rence, man! Ow!
1/4
1/4
1/4
1/2

D.S. al Coda
F5
G5
F5
1/2

Coda
Chorus
Gtr. 2 tacet
B♭5
Rock the cra - dle of love, yeah.
Gtr. 1
P.M.
P.M.
P.M.
P.M.

Gtr. 1: w/ Rhy. Fig. 1 (1st 4 meas.)
Rock the cra - dle of love, oo. Sent from heav - en a - bove,
P.M.
P.M.
P.M.
P.M.

Outro-Chorus

Bkgd. Voc: w/ Voc. Fig. 1 (4 times)
E♭/B♭
A♭/B♭
B♭5
A♭/B♭
- dle of love. Ow! If you tease me to - night, then you must sleaze
End Voc. Fig. 1
- dle of love.)
E♭/B♭
A♭/B♭
B♭5
A♭/B♭
me, all right. If you ap - pease me to - night, and let me ease
E♭/B♭
A♭/B♭
B♭5
A♭/B♭
E♭/B♭
A♭/B♭
you, yeah, ow! Oo, yeah. All right.
B♭5
A♭/B♭
E♭/B♭
A♭/B♭
I'll snatch your bod - y and sal - vage your soul, ma - ma. Ha! Yeah, wow!
Begin fade
Gtr. 2
B♭5
B♭sus4
let ring
let ring
B♭5
B♭sus4
let ring
Fade out
B♭5
B♭sus4

Crush 'Em

Words and Music by Dave Mustaine, Marty Friedman and Bud Prager

Ab5
N.C.(Ab5)
Gb5
G5
N.C.(B5)
You bet - ter not mess us a - round. _ The stakes are rich, take a
Hear us scream, _ and shout all night. _ Down on the floor and

A5
Bb5
B5
N.C.(B5)
hit or stay. _ The price is high, some - one's gon - na pay.
eat the grit. _ This is gon - na hurt a lit - tle bit.
(cont. in slash)
(cont. in slash)

Chorus
F#5
A5
F#5
B5
D5
Rhy. Fig. 1
* Gtrs. 1 & 2
(cont. in notation)
Heads, I win, _ tails, you lose. _ Out of my way, I'm com-in' through. _
Gtr. 3 (dist.)
Riff B
mp
* composite arrangement

E5
F#5
N.C.(C#5) B5
To Coda
Roll the dice, don't think twice. And we crush, crush 'em.
(Crush! Crush 'em!)
Gtr. 3
End Riff B
Gtrs. 1 & 2
End Rhy. Fig. 1
(Gtr. 2 cont. in slash)
Interlude
F5
Gtr. 2
Gtr. 3 tacet
Gtr. 1 tacet
(cont. in notation)
Verse
N.C.(F5)
2. Look - in' for trou - ble,
Gtr. 3
Gtr. 1
divisi
w/ bar
slack
Riff C
Gtr. 2
End Riff C
P.M.
Gtr. 2: w/ Riff C, 7 times
Now you've found it.
Gtr. 1
Gtr. 4 (dist.)
mf
w/ wah-wah
(cont. in slash)

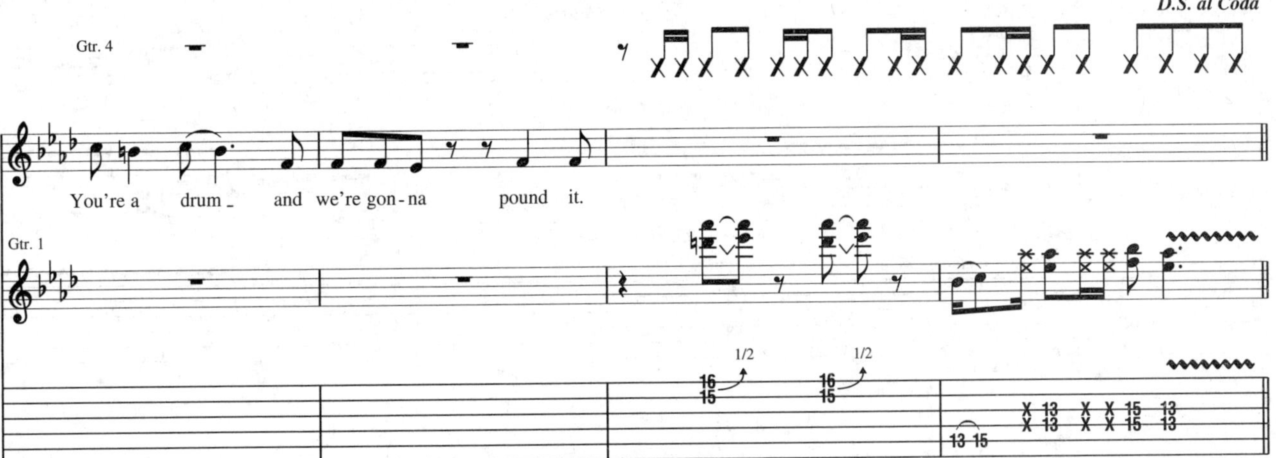
D.S. al Coda
Gtr. 4
You're a drum _ and we're gon-na pound it.
Gtr. 1
1/2
1/2

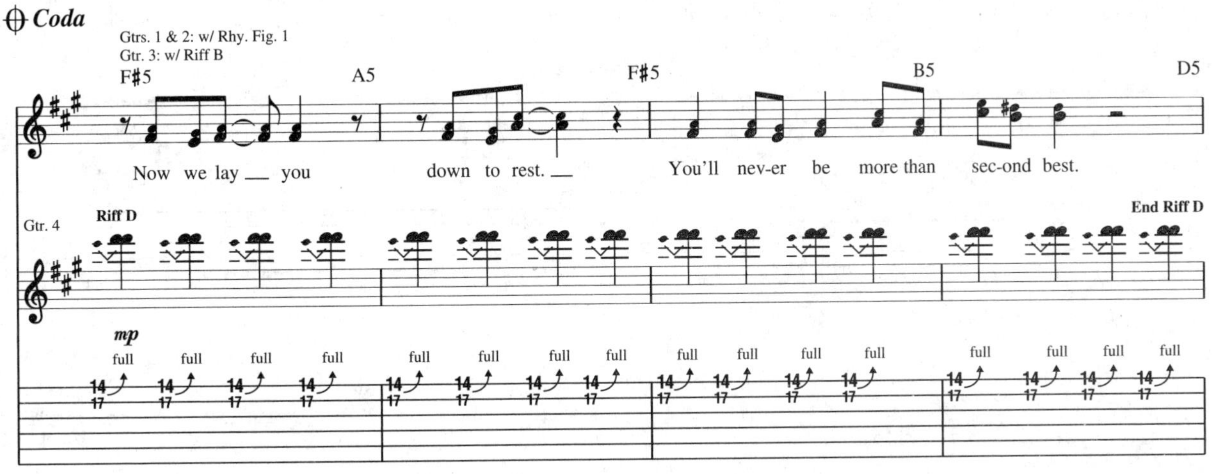
Coda
Gtrs. 1 & 2: w/ Rhy. Fig. 1
Gtr. 3: w/ Riff B
F♯5
A5
F♯5
B5
D5
Now we lay _ you down to rest. _ You'll nev-er be more than sec-ond best.
Gtr. 4
Riff D
End Riff D
mp
full

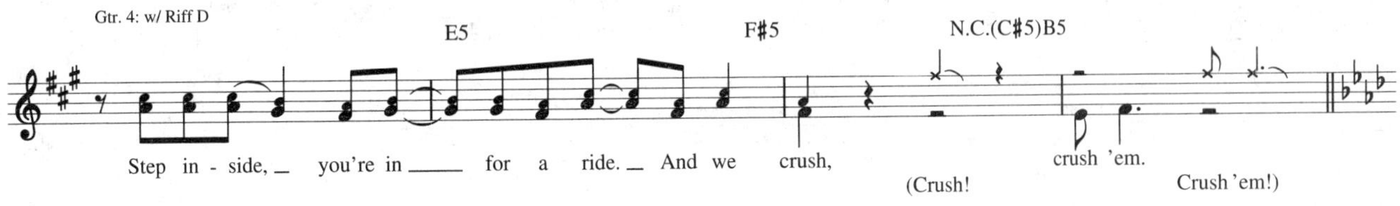
Gtr. 4: w/ Riff D
E5
F♯5
N.C.(C♯5)B5
Step in - side, _ you're in _ for a ride. _ And we crush, crush 'em.
(Crush! Crush 'em!)

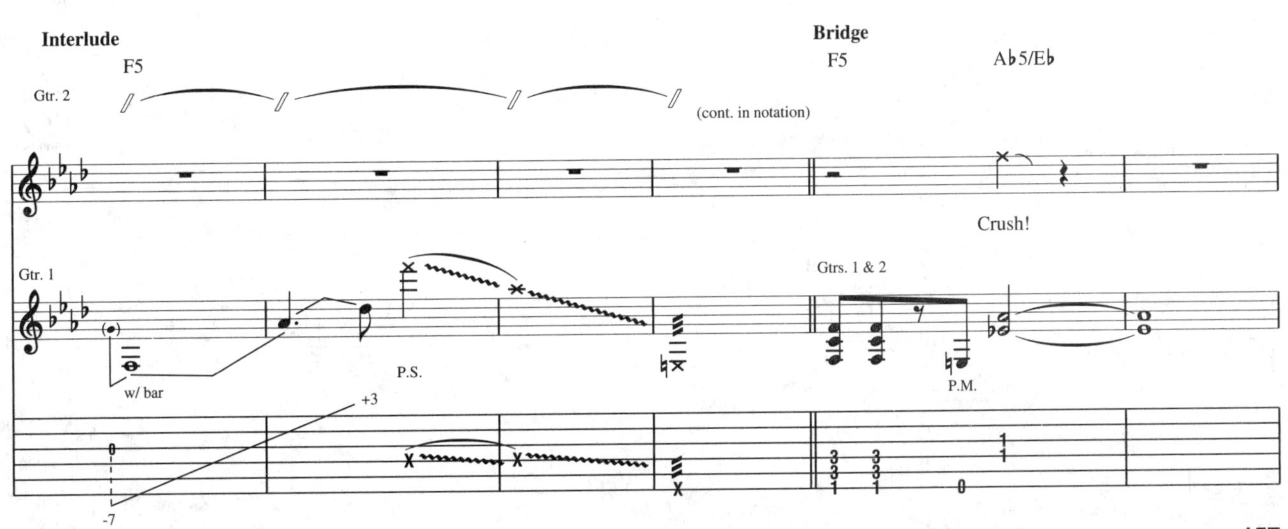
Interlude
F5
Bridge
F5
A♭5/E♭
Gtr. 2
(cont. in notation)
Crush!
Gtr. 1
Gtrs. 1 & 2
w/ bar
P.S.
P.M.
+3
-7

F5
Bb5/F
Ab5/Eb
Crush!
P.M.
Db5/Ab Eb5/Bb
Crush 'em!
Spoken: Don't need reason, don't want names just a John Doe to put to shame. Step aside and let me explain the name of the game is pain. Now we've
found you, we're gonna pound you. We're gonna beat you, gonna defeat you. We're gonna bust you, we're gonna crush you, we're gonna...crush 'em.
Eb5/Bb F5/C
(cont. in slash)
Chorus
G5
Rhy. Fig. 3
Gtrs. 1 & 2
Bb5
C5
Eb5
(cont. in notation)
Heads, I win. Tails, you lose. Out-ta my way, I'm com-in' through.
Gtr. 3
Riff E

F5 G5 N.C.(D5) C5 G5
Roll the dice, don't think twice. And we crush, crush 'em.
(Crush! Crush 'em!)
Gtr. 3
End Riff E
Gtrs. 1 & 2
End Rhy. Fig. 3
Gtrs. 1 & 2: w/ Rhy. Fig. 3
Gtr. 3: w/ Riff E
G5 B♭5 G5 C5 E♭5
Now I lay you down to rest. You'll nev-er, nev-er be more than sec-ond best.
Riff F
Gtr. 4
End Riff F
full
Gtr. 4: w/ Riff F
F5 G5 N.C.(D5) C5 G5
Step in-side, you're in for a ride. And we crush, crush 'em.
(Crush! Crush 'em!)
G5 B♭5/F G5 C5/G G5 B♭5/F G5 E♭5/B♭ F5/C
Crush! Crush! Crush! Crush 'em!
Gtr. 4
P.S.
Gtrs. 1 & 2
Rhy. Fig. 4
P.M.

G5 Bb5/F G5 C5/G G5 Bb5/F G5 Eb5/Bb F5/C
Crush! Crush! Crush! Crush 'em!
w/ wah-wah
steady gliss.
End Rhy. Fig. 4
P.M.
Outro-Guitar Solo
Gtrs. 1 & 2: w/ Rhy. Fig. 4, till fade
Spoken: Don't worry. And here we go. It's time to crush 'em. Yeah,
Gtr. 4
full
and you shed some tears. It's gotta hurt.
G5 Bb5 G5 C5 G5 Bb5/F
Crush 'em. Not here, not tonight. It's our town and we'll
let ring

G5
Eb5/Bb
F5/C
Bb5/F
C5/G
crush 'em.
Crush 'em!
Crush.
Crush!
8va
loco
P.H.
full
Begin Fade
Crush 'em.
let ring
1/2
Fade Out
5:4

Cult of Personality

Words and Music by William Calhoun, Corey Glover, Muzz Skillings and Vernon Reid

Spoken: "And during the few moments that we have left, we want to talk right down to earth in a language that everybody here can easily understand."

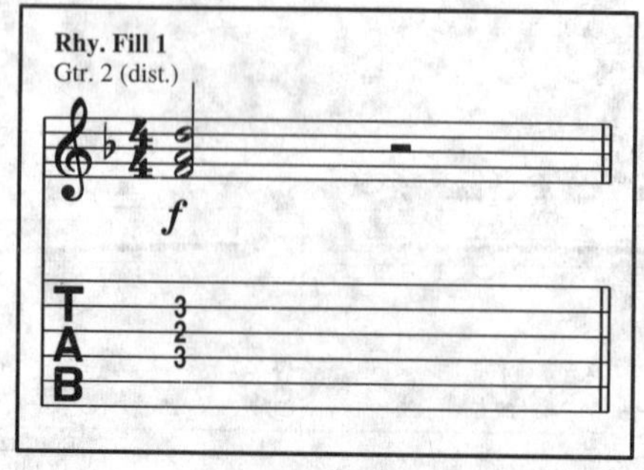

Gtr. 2: w/ Rhy. Fill 1, 1st time
G9
N.C.
1. Look in my eyes, what do you see?
I'm the smil - in' face on your T V.
Bb5
F5
The cult of per - son - al - i - ty.
Oh, I'm the
End Rhy. Fig. 1
N.C.
I know your an - ger, I know your dreams.
I ex - ploit you, still you love
I've been ev - 'ry-thing you wan - na be.
me.
I tell you one an' one makes

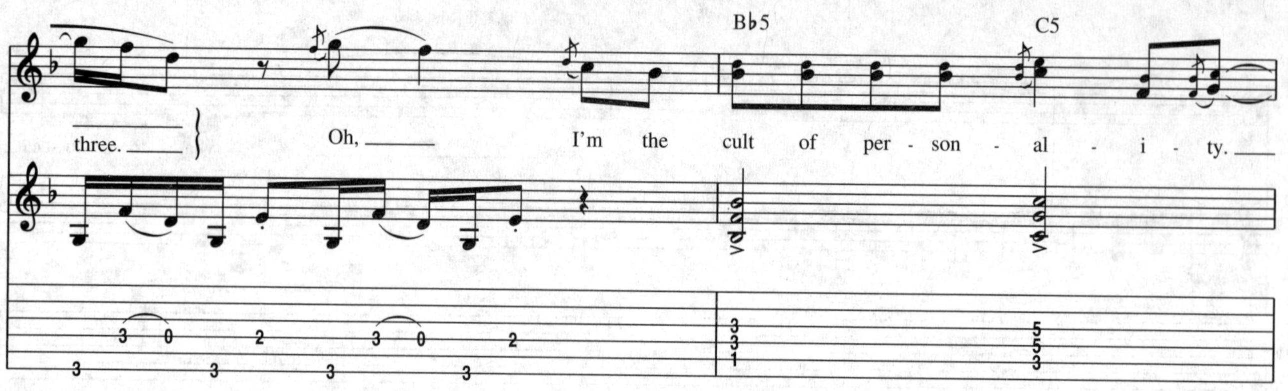
Bb5
C5
three.
Oh,
I'm the cult of per - son - al - i - ty.

N.C.
Like Mus - sol - i - ni an' Ken - ne - dy,
Like Jo - seph Stal - in and Ghand - i,

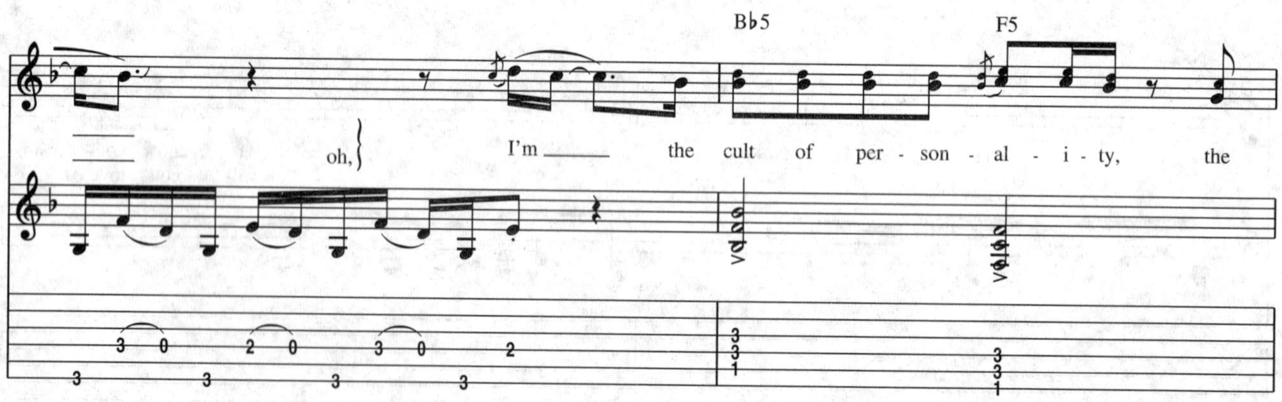
Bb5
F5
oh,
I'm the cult of per - son - al - i - ty, the

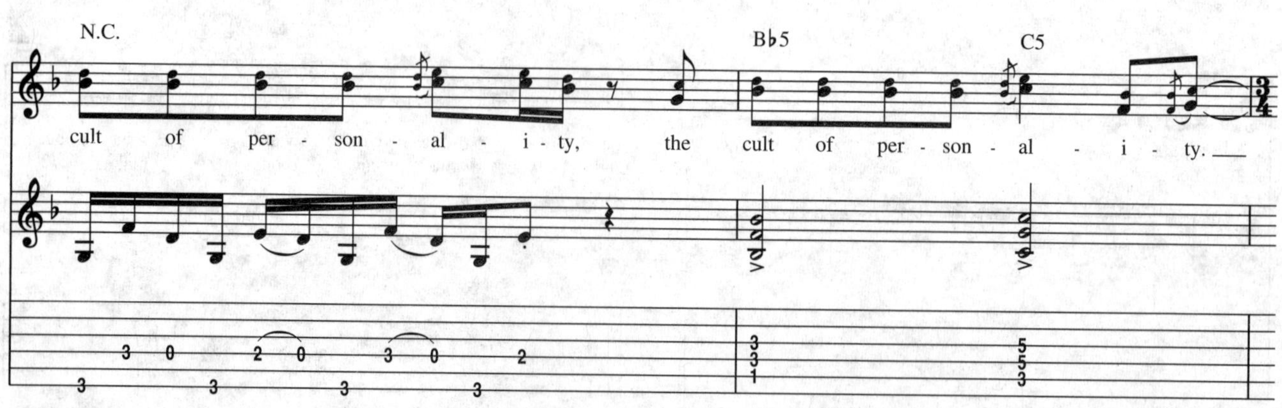
N.C.
Bb5
C5
cult of per - son - al - i - ty, the cult of per - son - al - i - ty.

* Chord symbols reflect implied tonality.

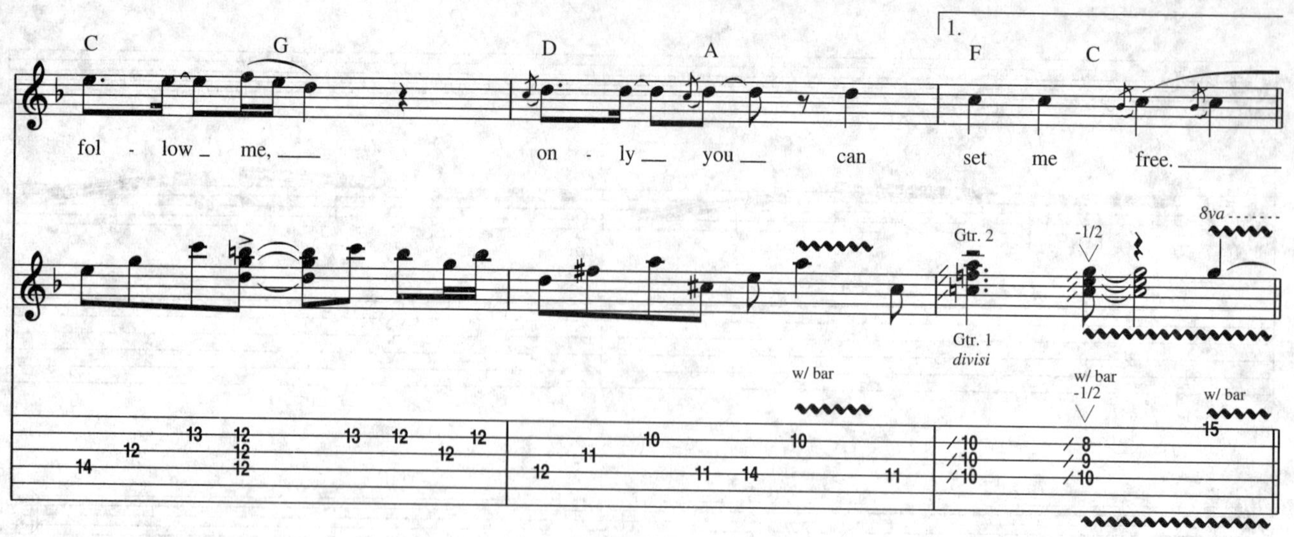
1.
C G D A F C
fol - low _ me, ___ on - ly __ you __ can set me free. ___
Gtr. 2
Gtr. 1
divisi
w/ bar
8va

Guitar Solo

Gtr. 1: w/ Rhy. Fig. 1
N.C.
Gtr. 2
8va
full
w/ bar

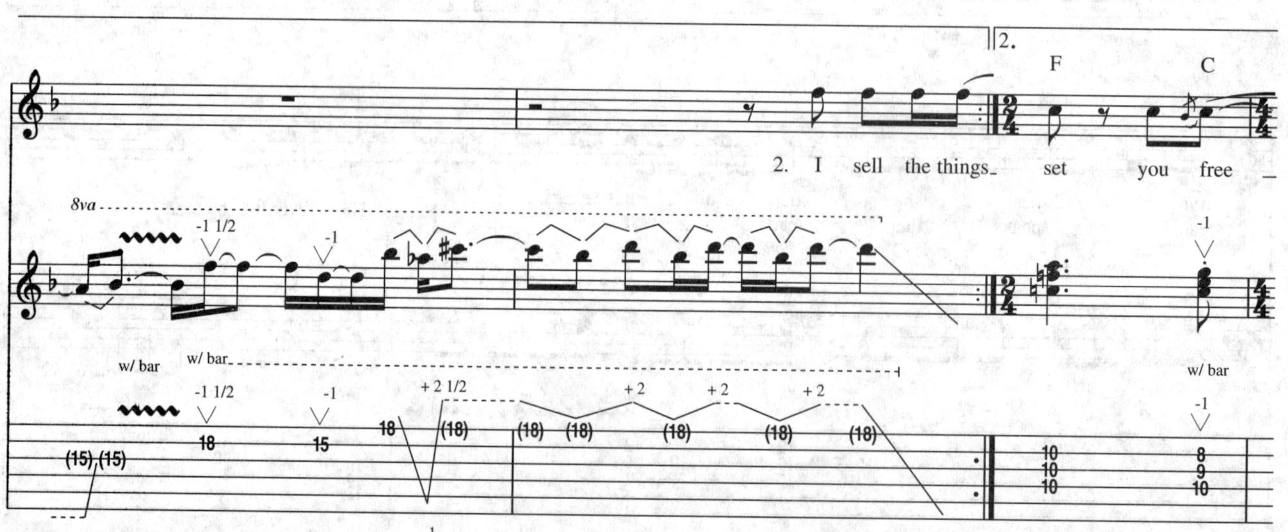
2.
F C
2. I sell the things _ set you free _
8va
w/ bar

w/ Voc. ad Lib.

Gtr. 1

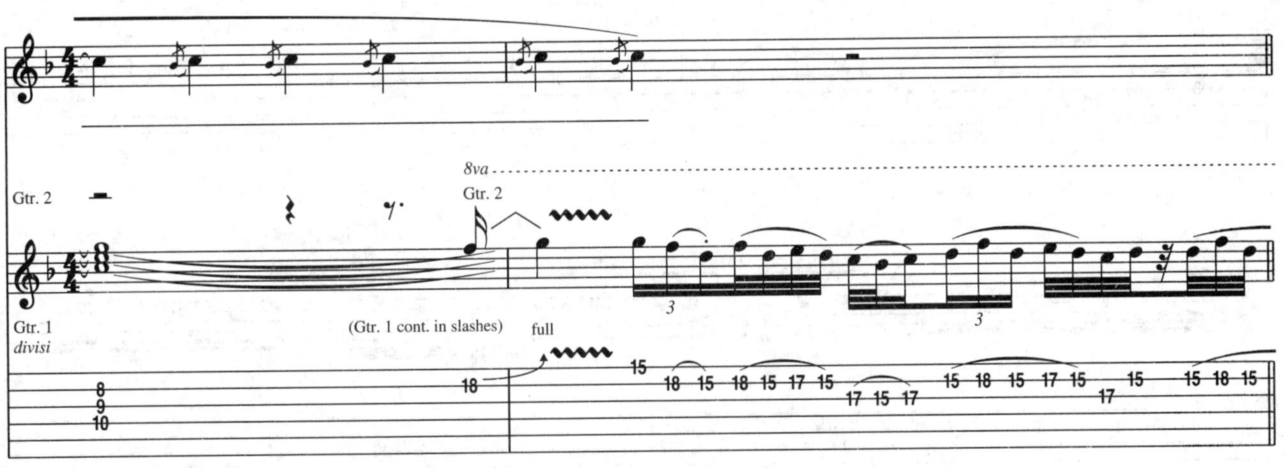

Guitar Solo

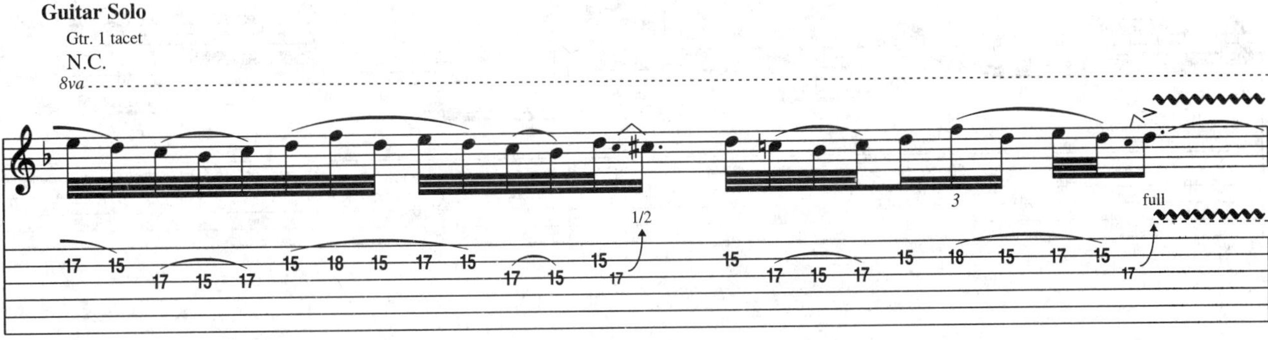

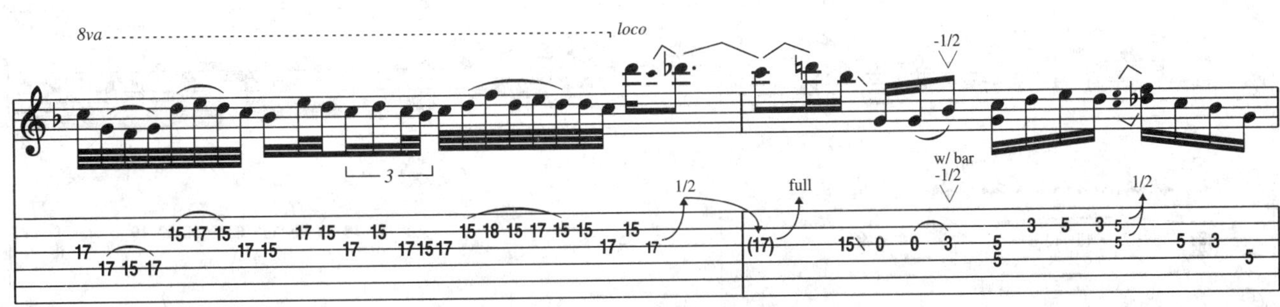

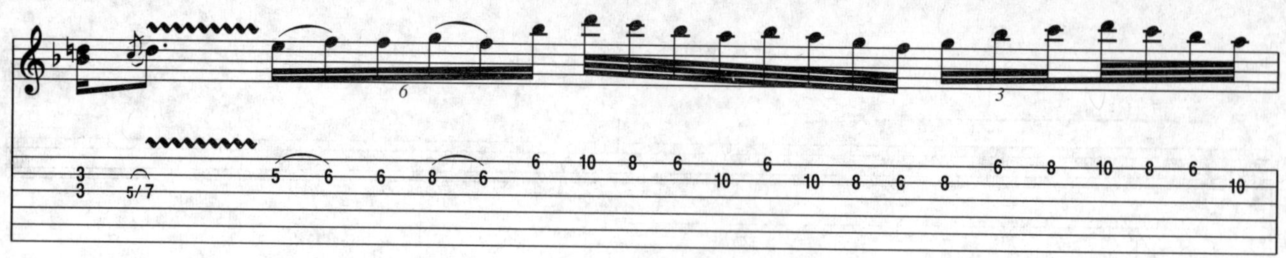

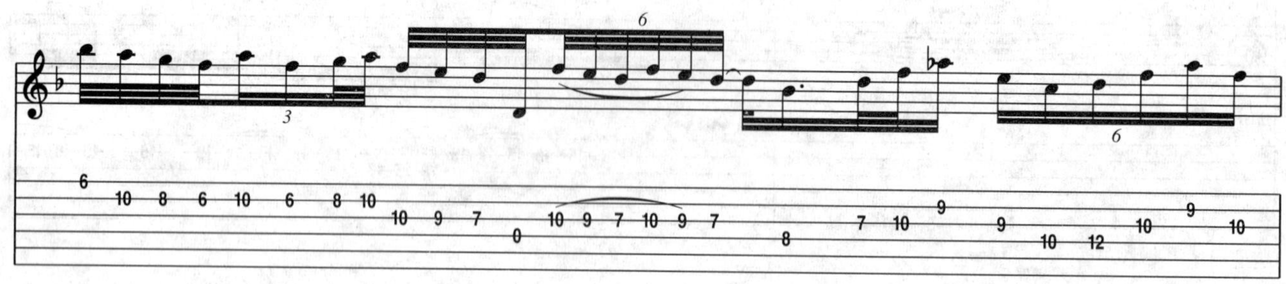

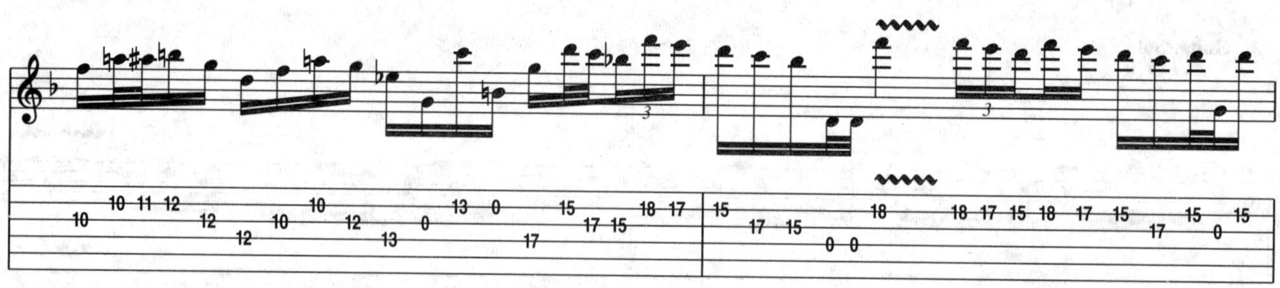

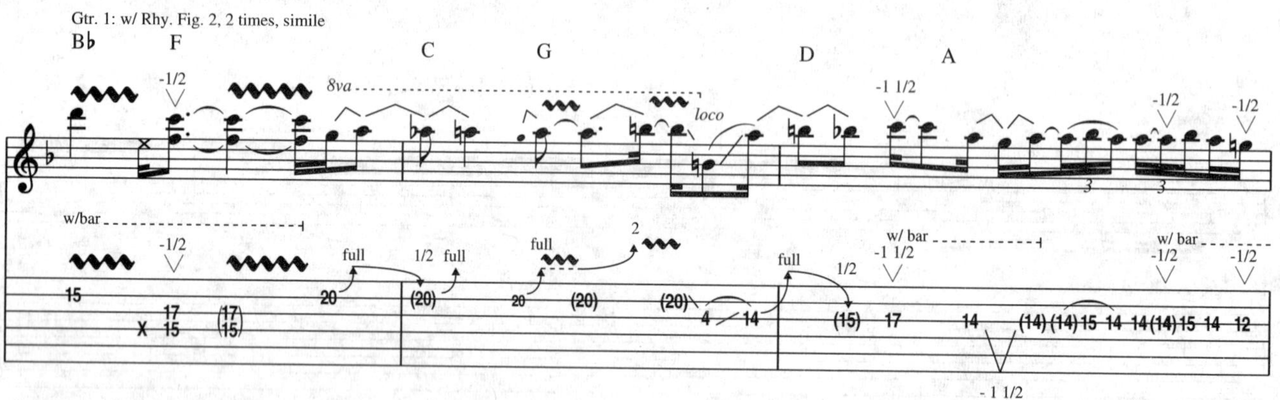
Gtr. 1: w/ Rhy. Fig. 2, 2 times, simile
B♭
F
C
G
D
A
8va
loco
w/bar
w/ bar
full
1/2
-1/2
-1 1/2

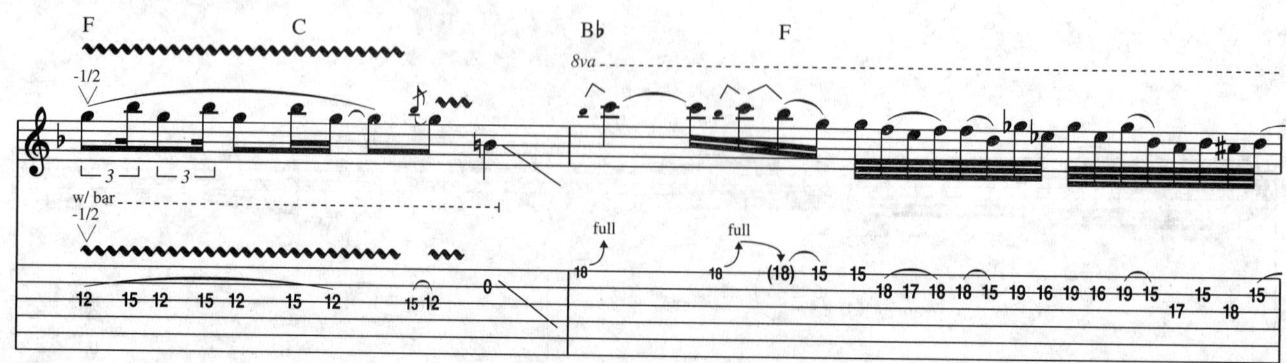
F
C
B♭
F
8va
w/ bar
-1/2
full

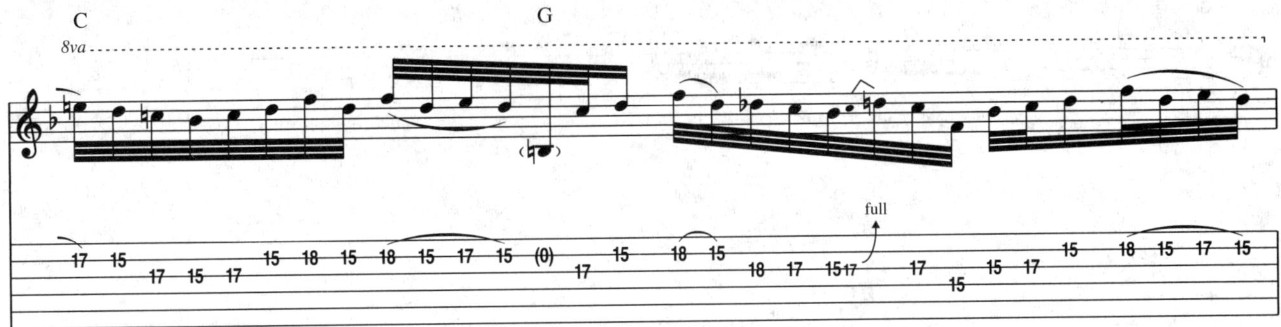
C
G
8va
full

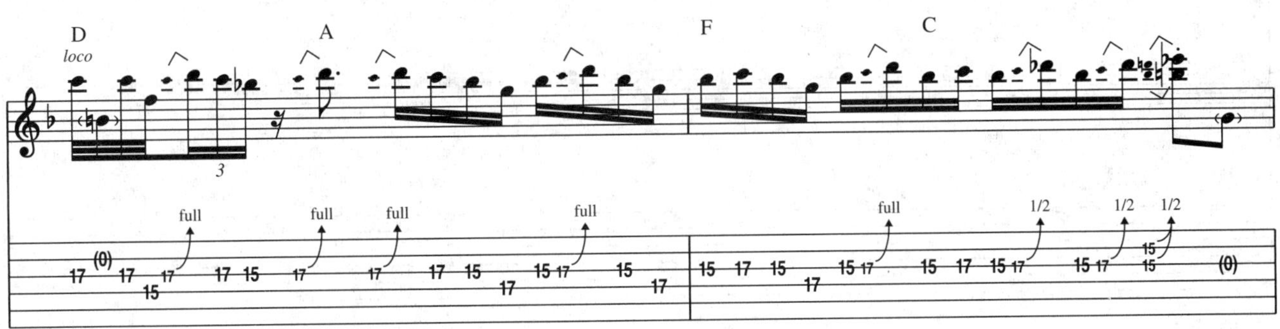
D
loco
A
F
C
full
1/2

Gtr. 1 tacet
N.C.
1/2

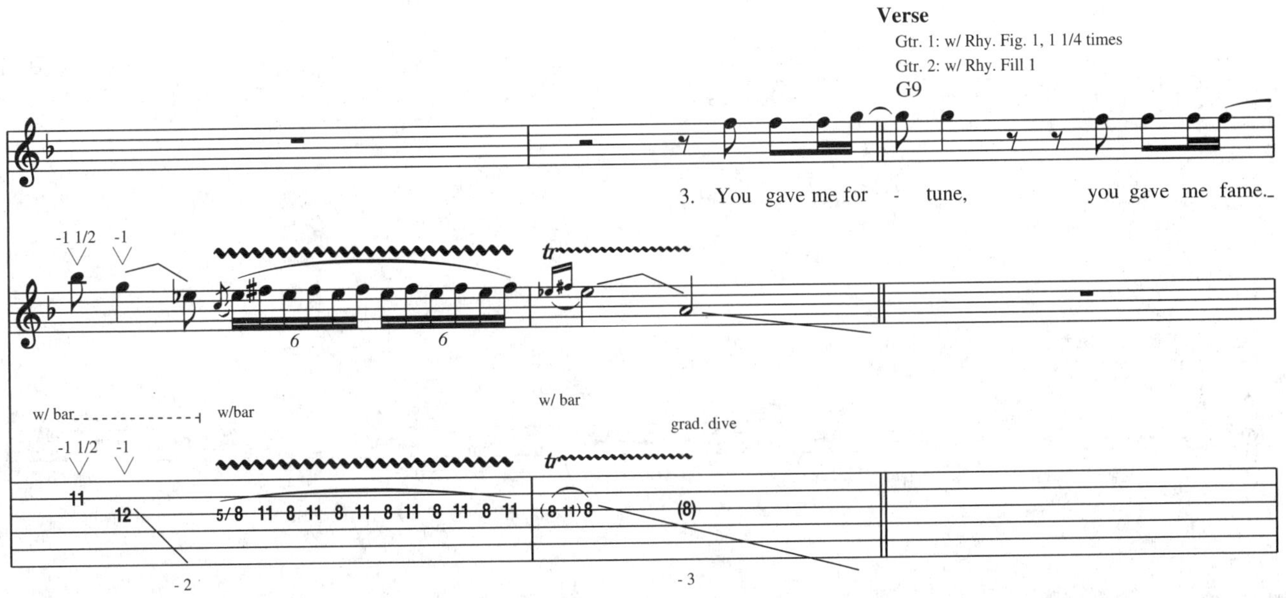
Verse
Gtr. 1: w/ Rhy. Fig. 1, 1 1/4 times
Gtr. 2: w/ Rhy. Fill 1
G9
3. You gave me for - tune, you gave me fame.
w/ bar
w/bar
w/ bar
grad. dive

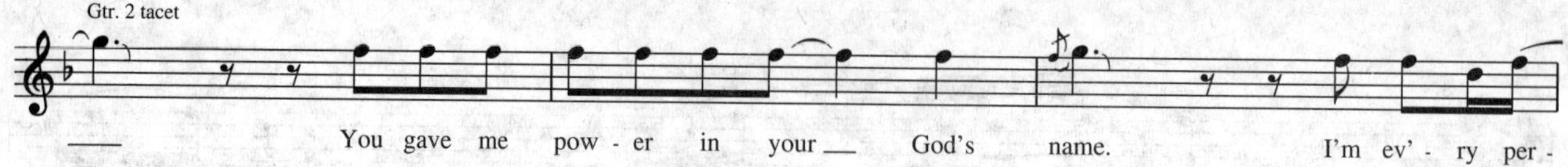
Gtr. 2 tacet
You gave me pow - er in your God's name. I'm ev' - ry per -

- son you need to be. Oh,
Rhy. Fig. 3
Gtr. 1

Chorus
B♭5 F5 N.C. B♭5 C
Voc. Fig. 1
I'm the cult of per - son
(I'm the cult of, I'm the
End Rhy. Fig. 3

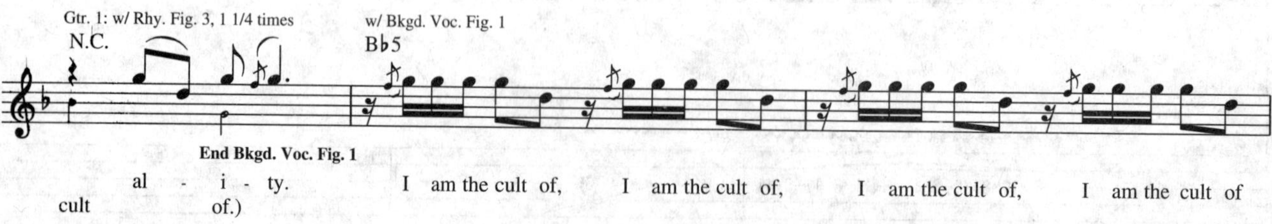
Gtr. 1: w/ Rhy. Fig. 3, 1 1/4 times
N.C.
w/ Bkgd. Voc. Fig. 1
B♭5
End Bkgd. Voc. Fig. 1
al - i - ty. I am the cult of, I am the cult of, I am the cult of, I am the cult of
cult of.)

B♭5
C
N.C.
I am the cult of, I am the cult of, I am the cult of, I am the cult of per - son - al - i - ty.
Spoken: "Ask
Gtr. 1
Outro
Double-Time Feel
N.C.
not what your coun - try can do for you..."
Spoken: "The only thing we have to fear, is fear itself."

Dani California

Words and Music by Anthony Kiedis, Flea, John Frusciante and Chad Smith

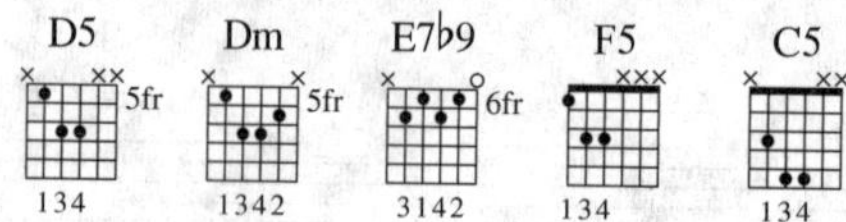

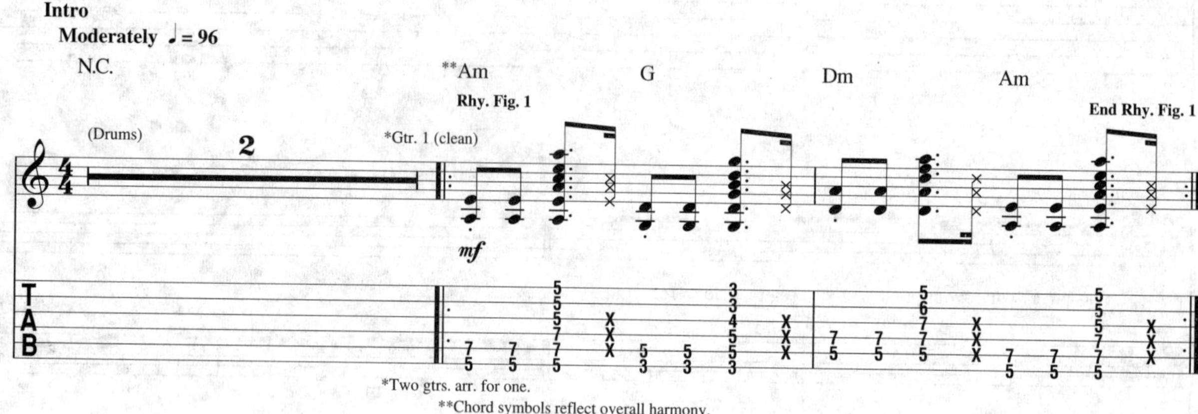

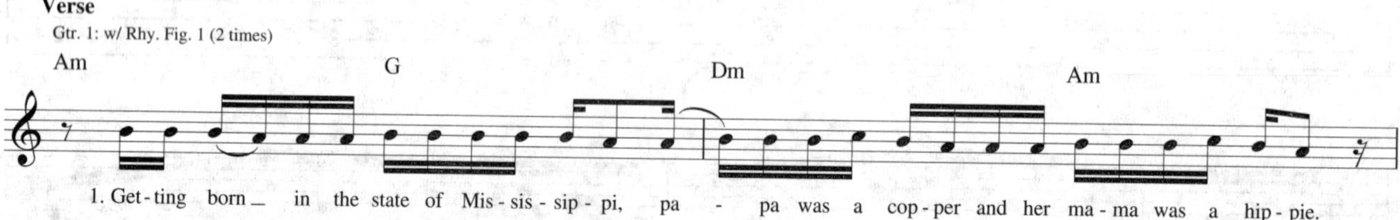

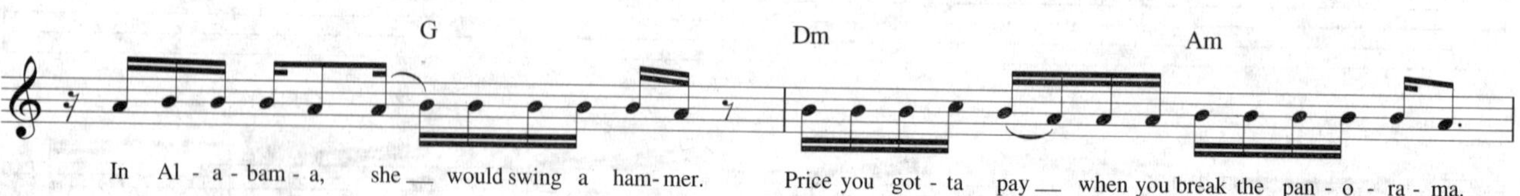

G
Dm
Am
What in the world does your com - pa - ny take ___ me for?

Verse

*Gtr. 1: w/ Rhy. Fig. 1 (2 times)
Gtr. 2 tacet
Am
G
Dm
Am
2. Black ban - dan - na, sweet _ Lou - i - si - an - a, rob - bin' on a bank _ in the state of In - di - an - a.
*Modular filter off

G
Dm
Am
She's a run - ner, reb - el, and a stun - ner, on her mer - ry way, _ say - in', "Ba - by, what-cha gon - na?"

G
Dm
Am
G
Look-ing down the bar - rel of a hot met - al for - ty - five. Just an - oth - er way to sur - vive. _
Riff A
**Gtrs. 1 & 2
End Riff A
w/ modular filter
**Composite arrangement

Gtr. 2 tacet

Dm

D5

E ⑥ open

Gtr. 3 (dist.)

(cont. in notation)

Cal - i - for -

Rhy. Fig. 2

Gtr. 1

End Rhy. Fig. 2

modular filter off

*Vol. swell

𝄋 Chorus

Gtr. 1 tacet
3rd time, Gtrs. 7 & 8 tacet

F5 C5 D5 G5

- nia, rest in peace. Si - mul - ta -

Gtr. 1 Rhy. Fig. 3

End Rhy. Fig. 3

Gtr. 3: w/ Rhy. Fig. 3 (2 times)

F5 C5 D5 G5 F5 C5 D5 G5

- ne - ous re - lease. Cal - i - for - nia, show your teeth. She's my priest-

To Coda 1 𝄌

To Coda 2 𝄌

F5 C5 D5 D5

Gtr. 3

- ess, I'm your priest, yeah, yeah.

Gtr. 3

**Gtr. 4 (slight dist.)

(1st time, cont. in slashes)

mf

**Doubled throughout

Interlude
Gtr. 3 tacet
Am G Dm Am G Dm Am
Gtr. 5 (dist.)
f
w/ wah-wah
Gtr. 6 (dist.)
f
w/ wah-wah
Gtr. 4
w/ Leslie
Verse
Gtr. 1: w/ Rhy. Fig. 1 (2 times)
Gtrs. 5 & 6 tacet
Gtr. 4 tacet
Am G Dm Am
3. She's a lov - er, ba - by, and a fight - er. Should - a seen her com - in' when it got a lit - tle bright - er.
Riff B
End Riff B
Gtr. 2
Gtr. 4
divisi
wah-wah off
Gtr. 2: w/ Riff B
G Dm Am
With a name like Dan - i Cal - i - for - nia, (the) day was gon - na come when I was gon - na mourne ya.

*Gtrs. 1 & 2: w/ Riff A
**Gtr. 1: w/ Rhy. Fig. 2
G
Dm
Am
A lit - tle load - ed, she was steal - in' an - oth - er breath.
I love my ba - by to death.
*w/ modular filter
**Modular filter off
Coda 1
D.S. al Coda 1
D5
Cal - i - for -
Gtr. 3
***Vol. swell
Bridge
Gtr. 3 tacet
Bm
†D/F#
††F#5/C#
Gtr. 4: w/ Rhy. Fig. 4 (2 times)
Who knew the oth - er side of you?
Who know what
Rhy. Fig. 4
Gtr. 4
End Rhy. Fig. 4
w/ fast phase shifter
†Bass plays F♯.
††Bass plays C♯.
D/F#
F#5/C#
oth - ers died to prove?
Too true to
say good - bye to you.
Gtr. 2
modular filter off

Gtr. 2 tacet
Bm
Too true to say, say, say...
Gtr. 2
Gtr. 4
Verse
Gtr. 1: w/ Rhy. Fig. 1 (2 times)
Gtr. 4 tacet
Am G Dm Am
4. Push the fad - er, gift - ed an - i - ma - tor one for the now and e - lev - en for the lat - er.
Gtr. 2
Gtr. 4 divisi
phase shifter off
G Dm Am
Nev - er made it up to Min - ne - so - ta, North Da - ko - ta man was a gun - nin' for the quo - ta.

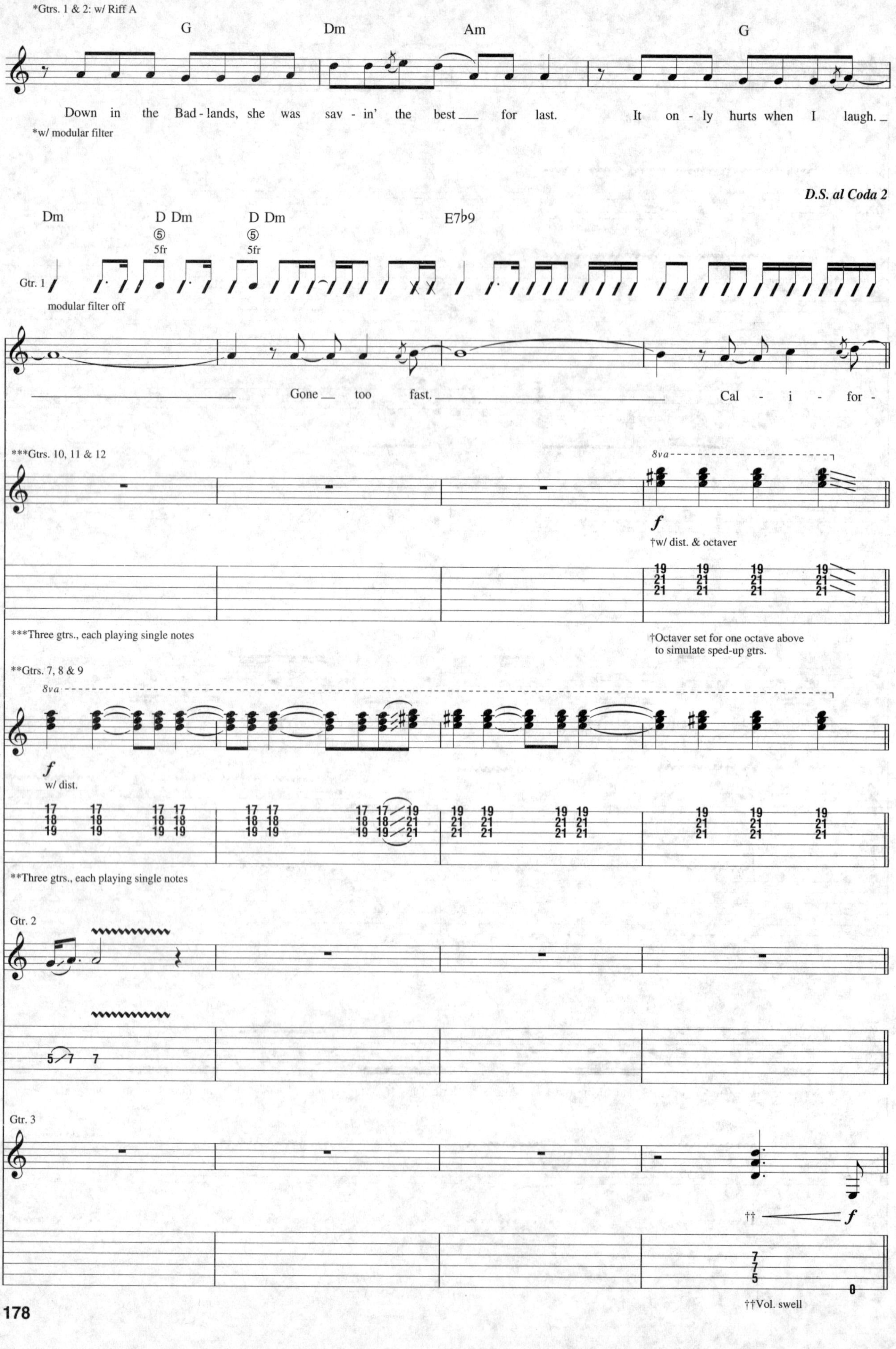

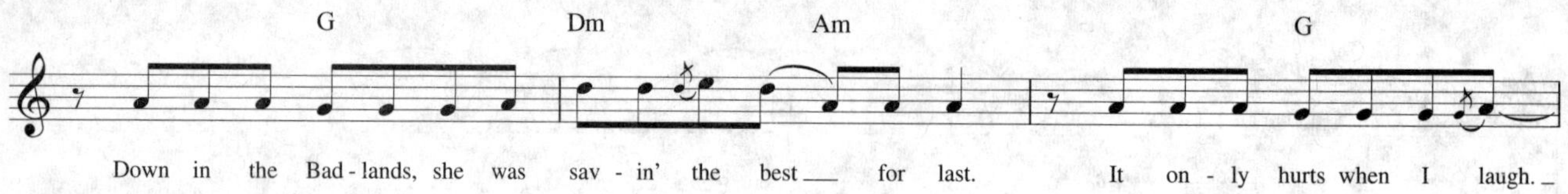

*w/ modular filter

D.S. al Coda 2

Dm D Dm D Dm E7♭9

⑤ 5fr ⑤ 5fr

Gtr. 1

modular filter off

___ Gone ___ too fast. ___ Cal - i - for -

***Gtrs. 10, 11 & 12

8va

f

†w/ dist. & octaver

***Three gtrs., each playing single notes

†Octaver set for one octave above to simulate sped-up gtrs.

**Gtrs. 7, 8 & 9

8va

f

w/ dist.

**Three gtrs., each playing single notes

Gtr. 2

Gtr. 3

†† *f*

††Vol. swell

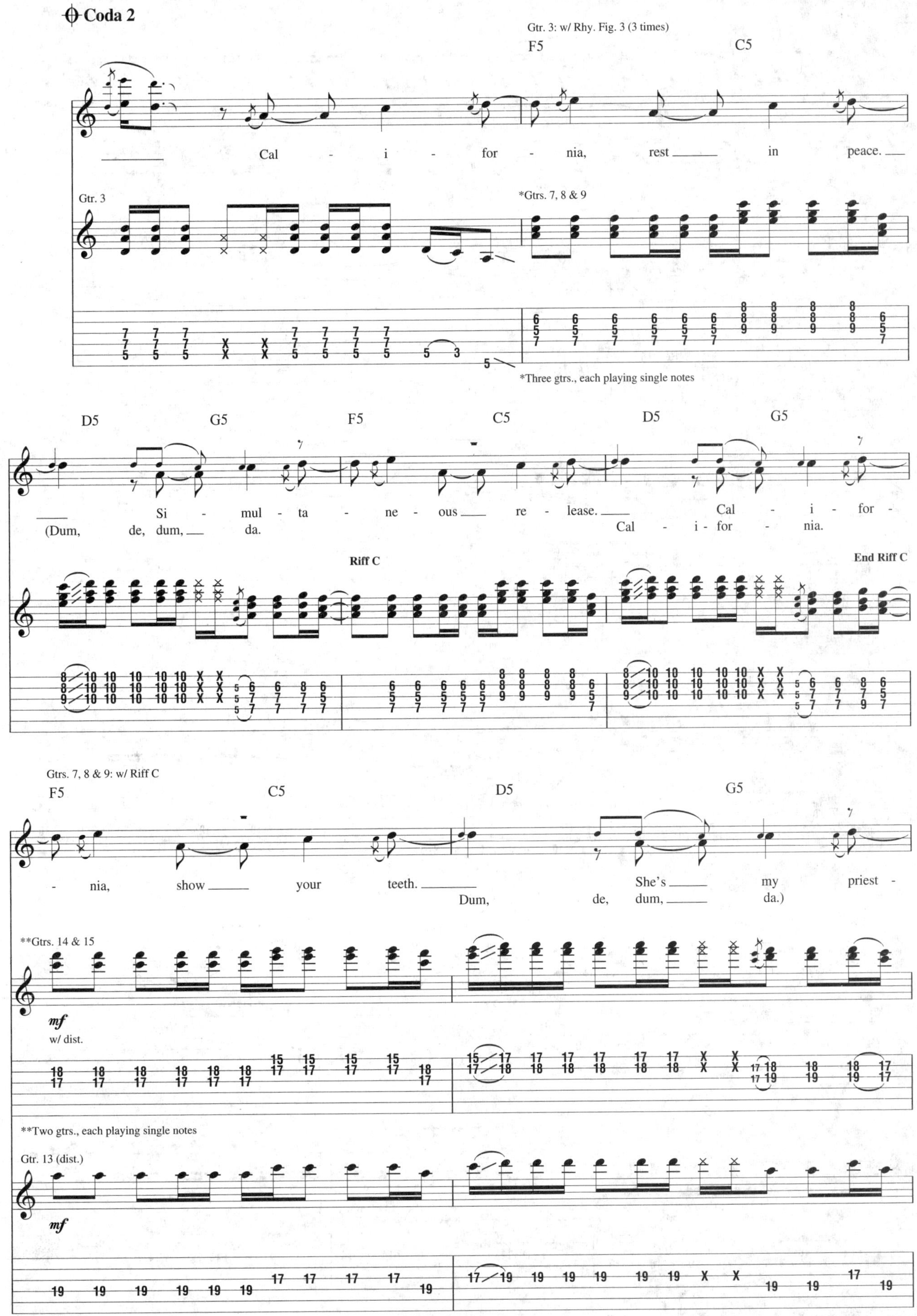
Coda 2
Gtr. 3: w/ Rhy. Fig. 3 (3 times)
F5
C5
Cal - i - for - nia, rest in peace.
Gtr. 3
*Gtrs. 7, 8 & 9
*Three gtrs., each playing single notes
D5
G5
F5
C5
D5
G5
Si - mul - ta - ne - ous re - lease. Cal - i - for -
(Dum, de, dum, da. Cal - i - for - nia.
Riff C
End Riff C
Gtrs. 7, 8 & 9: w/ Riff C
F5
C5
D5
G5
- nia, show your teeth. She's my priest -
Dum, de, dum, da.)
**Gtrs. 14 & 15
mf
w/ dist.
**Two gtrs., each playing single notes
Gtr. 13 (dist.)
mf

F5
C5
A
open
C5 D5
A
17fr
Gtr. 3
(cont. in notation)
- ess, I'm your priest, yeah, yeah.
Gtrs. 13, 14 & 15
Gtrs. 10, 11 & 12
Gtrs. 13, 14 & 15
divisi
Gtrs. 7, 8 & 9
*w/ flanger on entire mix
Outro-Guitar Solo
Gtrs. 7 - 15 tacet
F5
C5
D5
G5
F5
C5
Gtr. 3
D5
G5
F5
C5
D5
G5
F5
C5
D5

F5
C5
D5
G5
F5
C5
D5
G5
F5
C5
D5
G5
F5
w/ wah-wah
C5
D5
N.C.
w/ bar

Day Tripper

Words and Music by John Lennon and Paul McCartney

A7 A7^II F♯7 A7^type2 G♯7 C♯7 B7
E A7^V B7sus4 B7^type2 B7^VII B7♯9

Intro

Moderate Rock ♩ = 138

Gtr. 1 N.C.(E7)

mf

Gtr. 1 E E7 E E7 E E7

Gtr. 2 **Rhy. Fig. 1** *p* *let ring* **End Rhy. Fig. 1**

Gtr. 2: w/ Rhy. Fig. 1, 2 times

Gtr. 1 E E7 E E7 E E7 (drums enter) E E7 E E7 E E7

𝄋 **Verse**

Gtr. 2: w/ Rhy. Fig. 1, 2 times

E E7 E E7 E E7 E E7 E E7 E E7

1. Got a good rea - son for tak - ing the ea - sy way out.
2. She's a big tea - ser. She took me half the way there.
3. Tried to please her, she on - ly played one night stands.

Gtr. 1

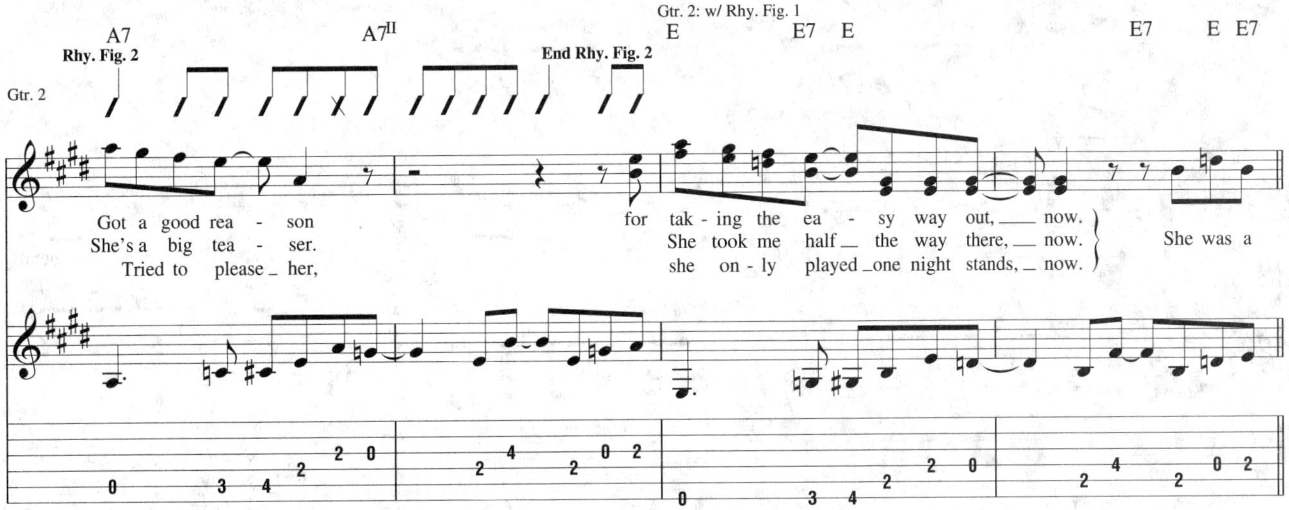
Gtr. 2: w/ Rhy. Fig. 1
A7
A7II
E
E7 E
E7
E E7
Rhy. Fig. 2
End Rhy. Fig. 2
Gtr. 2
Got a good rea - son for tak - ing the ea - sy way out, now.
She's a big tea - ser. She took me half the way there, now.
Tried to please her, she on - ly played one night stands, now.
She was a

Chorus

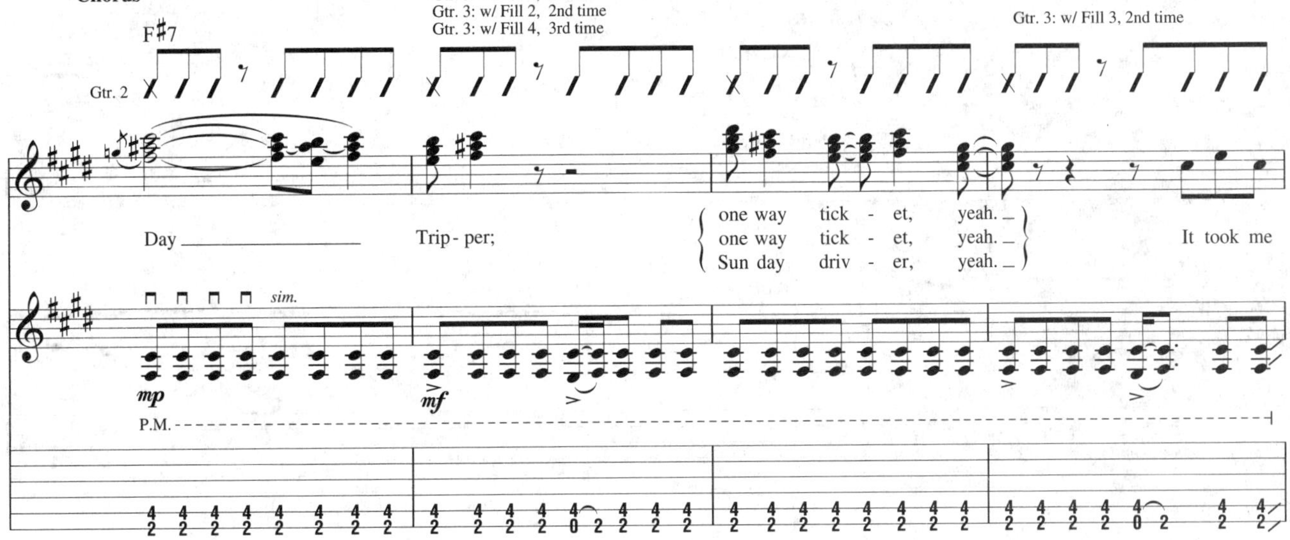
Gtr. 3: w/ Fill 1, 1st time
Gtr. 3: w/ Fill 2, 2nd time
Gtr. 3: w/ Fill 4, 3rd time
Gtr. 3: w/ Fill 3, 2nd time
F♯7
Gtr. 2
Day Trip - per;
one way tick - et, yeah.
one way tick - et, yeah.
Sun day driv - er, yeah.
It took me
sim.
mp
mf
P.M.

Fill 1
Gtr. 3
p
Fill 2
Gtr. 3
Fill 3
Gtr. 3

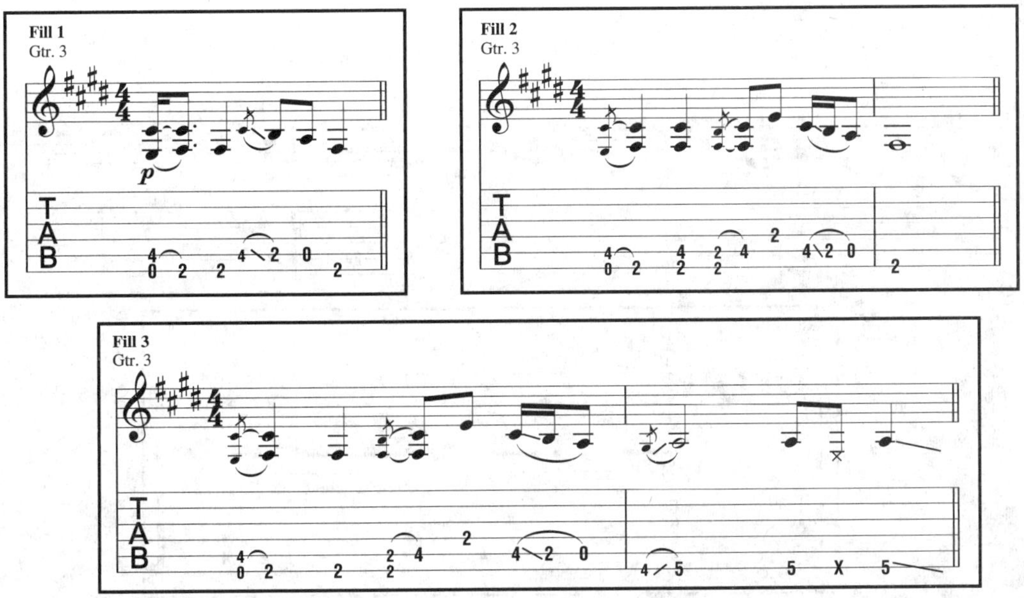

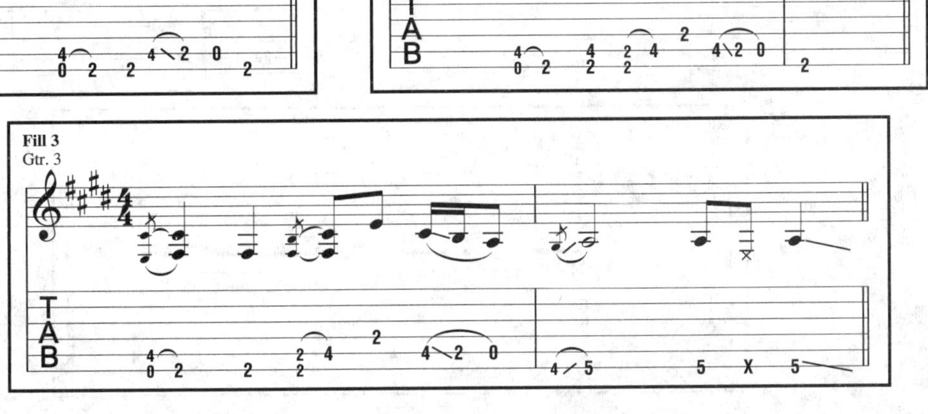

Gtr. 1: w/ Rhy. Fill 1, 2nd time
A7type2
G♯7
C♯7
so
long
to find out,
and I found
P.M.
P.M.
1.
To Coda
B7
N.C.(E7)
E
Gtr. 2
(cont. in notation)
out.
Gtrs. 1 & 2
Gtr. 1
Gtr. 2: w/ Rhy. Fig. 1
E7 E
E7 E E7
2.
B7
A7V
out.
Rhy. Fill 1
Gtr. 1
P.M.
T
A
B

Interlude
Gtr. 3: w/ Riff A
B7
B7sus4
cont. strum simile

B7type2
B7

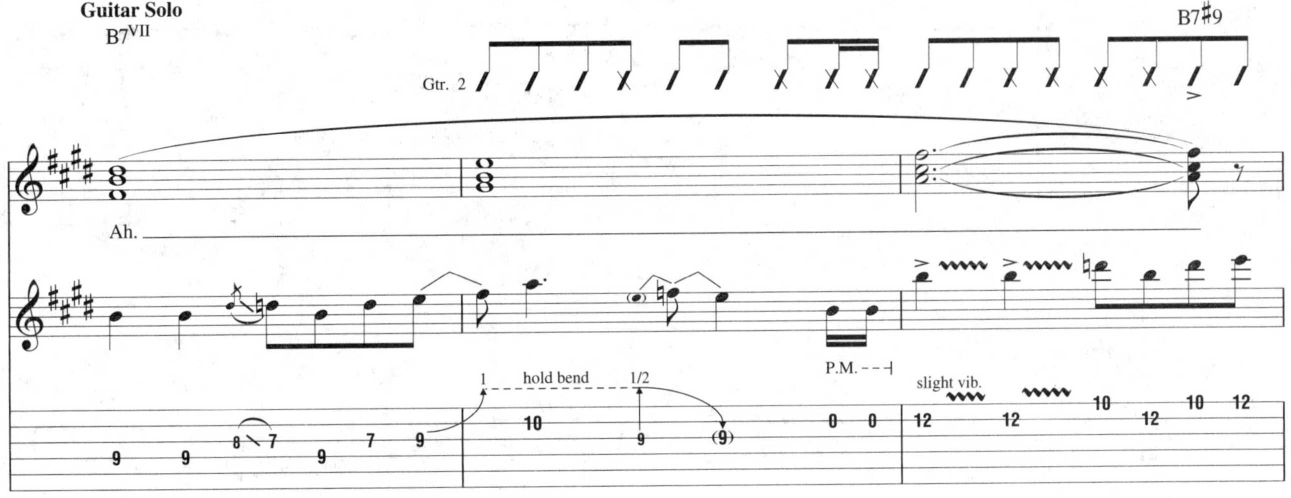
Guitar Solo
B7VII
B7♯9
Gtr. 2
Ah.
hold bend
1/2
P.M.
slight vib.

Riff A
Gtr. 3

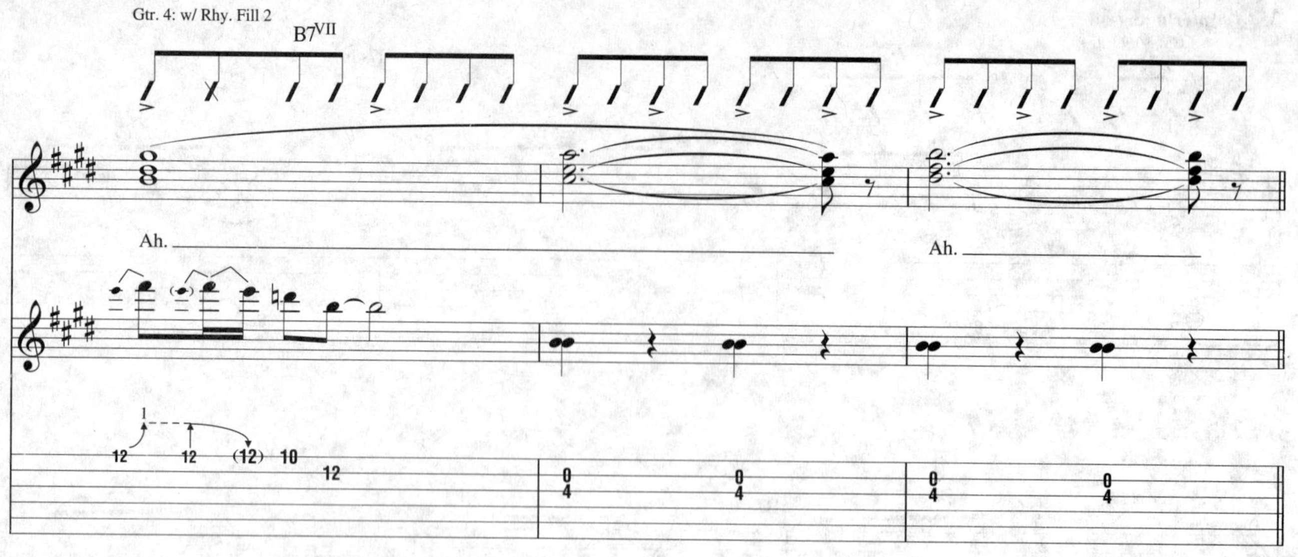

D.S. al Coda
(take 1st ending)

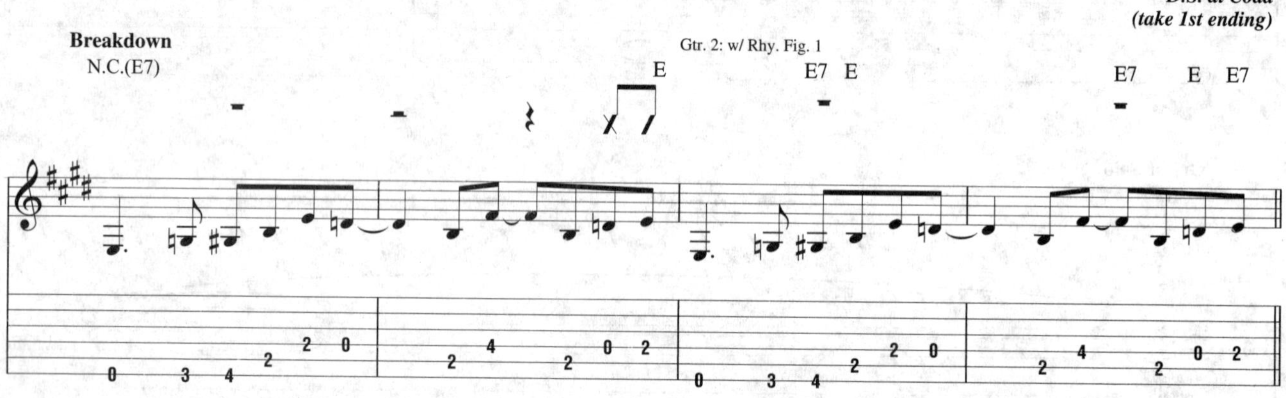

Gtr. 2: w/ Rhy. Fig. 1, 2 times
E
E7
E
E7
E
E7
Gtr. 2
Gtr. 1

Outro - Chorus
Gtr. 2: w/ Rhy. Fig. 1, till fade
E
E7
E
E7
E
E7
E
E7
E
Day
Trip - per,

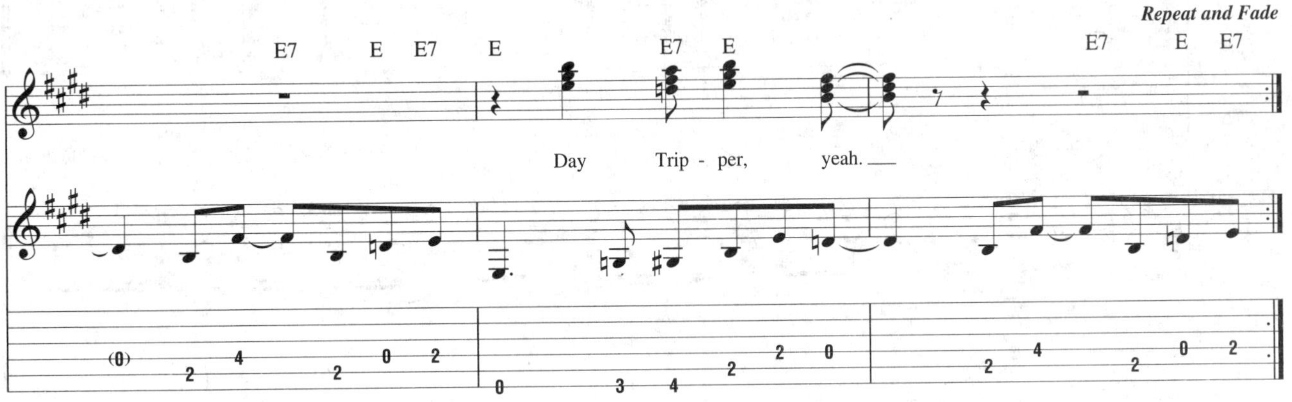
Repeat and Fade
E7
E
E7
E
E7
E
E7
E
E7
Day
Trip - per,
yeah.

Fill 4
Gtr. 3

Dissident

Words and Music by Stone Gossard, Jeffrey Ament, Eddie Vedder, Michael McCready and David Abbruzzese

Intro

Moderately slow ♩ = 78

G5 G5/F♯ G5/F G5/E G5

Riff A

Gtr. 1 (dist.)

End Riff A

f

1

14 14 (14) 12 14

1

14 14 (14) 12

Rhy. Fig. 1A

*Gtr. 3 (slight dist.)

End Rhy. Fig. 1A

p

*Two gtrs. arr. for one.

Rhy. Fig. 1

Gtr. 2 (dist.)

End Rhy. Fig. 1

f

let ring throughout

Gtrs. 2 & 3: w/ Rhy. Figs. 1 & 1A (1 1/2 times)

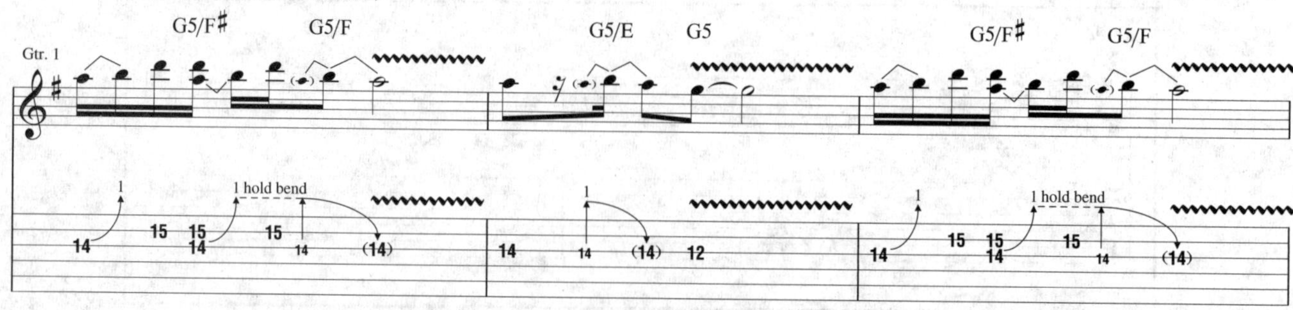

Verse
Gtr. 1 tacet
G5/E G5
*C
C7sus2
C7sus4 C7 C7sus2 C7
Csus2
1. She nursed him there, oo, o - ver a night.
Gtr. 1
Gtr. 3
mf
let ring
Rhy. Fill 1
End Rhy. Fill 1
Rhy. Fig. 2
Gtr. 2
mf
*Chord symbols reflect implied harmony.
C
C7sus2
C7sus4 C7 C7sus2 Csus2
C
C7sus2
I was n't so sure she want - ed him to stay, what to say, what to say.
But soon she was down,
Gtr. 3
w/ pick & fingers
let ring
Gtr. 2

C7sus4 C7 C7sus2 C7 Csus2 Csus4 C C7sus2 C7sus4 C7sus2 C7 Csus2
soon he was low. At a quarter past, ah, ho-ly, no, she had to turn a-round.
Gtr. 1
Gtr. 3
*T
let ring
*T = Thumb on 6th string
Gtr. 2
End Rhy. Fig. 2
Chorus
Gtr. 1: w/ Riff A (1 1/2 times)
Gtr. 2: w/ Rhy. Fig. 1 (3 1/2 times)
Gtr. 3: w/ Rhy. Fig. 1A (3 times)
G5 G5/F♯ G5/F G5/E G5 G5/F♯ G5/F
When she could-n't hold, oh, she fold - ed. A dis - si - dent is
G5/E G5 G5/F♯ G5/F G5/E G5
here. Es - cape is nev - er the saf - est path. Oh, a
Gtr. 1

Gtr. 2: w/ Rhy. Fill 1
G5/F♯ G5/F G5/E G5
dis - si - dent, a dis - si - dent is here.
Gtr. 1
Gtr. 3
Verse
Gtr. 1 tacet
Gtr. 2: w/ Rhy. Fig. 2
C C7sus2 C7sus4 C7 C7sus2 C7 Csus2 C C7sus2
2. And to this day, she's glid - ed on, al - ways home but so far a - way like a
mf
let ring
C7sus4 C7 C7sus2 Csus2 C C7sus2 C7sus4 C7 C7sus2 C7 Csus2
word mis - placed. Noth - ing said, what a waste. And when she had con - tact with the con - flict, there was mean -
let ring
let ring
let ring

C
C7sus2
C7sus4 C7sus2
C7
Csus2
ing, but she sold him to the state.
She had to turn a - round.
Gtr. 1
Gtr. 3
let ring
Chorus
Gtr. 1: w/ Riff A (1 1/2 times)
Gtr. 2: w/ Rhy. Fig. 1 (3 1/2 times)
Gtr. 3: w/ Rhy. Fig. 1A (4 times)
G5 G5/F♯ G5/F
G5/E
G5
A, when she could-n't hold,
she fold - ed.
A dis - si - dent is
here.
Es - cape is nev - er the saf - est path.
Oh, a
Gtr. 1: w/ Riff A
Gtr. 2: w/ Rhy. Fill 1
dis - si - dent, a dis - si - dent is here.
Oh.

Interlude
w/ Voc. ad lib.
G5 B♭ C
*Gtrs. 1 & 3
Play 3 times
let ring
*Composite arrangement
Gtr. 2
Play 3 times
G5 B♭ C
Csus4 C
Csus4 C
She
let ring
Chorus
Gtrs. 2 & 3: w/ Rhy. Figs. 1 & 1A (7 times)
G5 G5/F♯ G5/F
G5/E G5
gave him a - way. When she could - n't hold, no, she fold -
Gtr. 1

G5/F♯
G5/F
G5/E
G5
- ed. A dis - si - dent is here. Es -
cape is nev - er the saf - est path. Oh. A
dis - si - dent, a dis - si - dent is here, oh.
Could - n't hold on, she could - n't hold, no, she fold -

G5/F♯
G5/F
G5/E
G5
-ed. A dis-si-dent is here. Es-
cape is nev-er the saf-est place. Oh, a
G/E
rit.
dis-si-dent is here.
Gtr. 1
Gtr. 3
mf
*w/ amp tremolo
*Set for sixteenth-note regeneration.
Gtr. 2

Divorce Me C.O.D.

Words and Music by Cliff Stone and Merle Travis

C
thought your lit - tle ro - mance was on the strict Q. T. If you
mp
P.M.
Eb E°7 Bb/F G7 C F Bb
want your free-dom P. D. - Q.; di - vorce me C. O. D. I won't be a -
p
P.M.
Eb7 Bb
round to hear you cry, I'm Tex - as bound
P.M.
C6 F7
and bye and bye. You can
mp
P.M.

Bb
C7
reach me down in Dal-las. gen-er-al de-liv-er-y. So if you
P.M.
Eb
E°7
Bb/F
G
C
F
want your free-dom P. D. Q. di-vorce me C. O. D.
Guitar Solo
P.M. ⑥ - ④
Eb
G7/B
let ring

Steel Guitar Solo
C7
F
B♭
E♭
B♭
mp
mf
f
mp
let ring
let ring
P.M.
C
F7
p
mp
mp
p
P.M. ⑥ - ④ throughout
Interlude
B♭
C
C7
let ring
E♭
E°7
B♭/F
G7
C7
F
B♭
2. Now
Verse
B♭
C
C9
there's gon-na come a day, gal, when you'll be feel-in' blue. You're gon-na
P.M.
P.M.

F
Bb
find that you can't pay ___ your bills ___ with a lit - tle ol' I. O. U. This
P.M.
dy - na - mite ___ that you're a - mes-sin' with
C7
may be T. N. T. ___ So if you
P.M. ⑥ - ③ throughout
Eb
E°7
Bb/F
G7
C7
F7
Bb
want your free-dom P. ___ D. Q., ___ di - vorce me C. O. D. ___ When the win - ter
Eb
Bb
comes, I hope you freeze. While I ___ twid - dle my
mp
p

C7
F9
thumbs lay-in' a-round in my B. V. D.'s
Well, now I

B♭
C7
ain't no col-lege pro-fes-sor. I ain't got no P. H. D. but if you

E♭
E°7
B♭/F
G7
C7
F9
F7
B♭
want your free-dom P. D. Q. di-vorce me C. O. D.

E♭
E°7
B♭/F
G7
C
F7
B♭
mp
mf

Don't Fear the Reaper

Words and Music by Donald Roeser

F6/9 no3rd
G
A5
G
F6/9 no3rd
G
A5
G
- er. Ba - by take my hand. Don't fear the reap - er. We'll be a - ble to fly. Don't fear the reap -

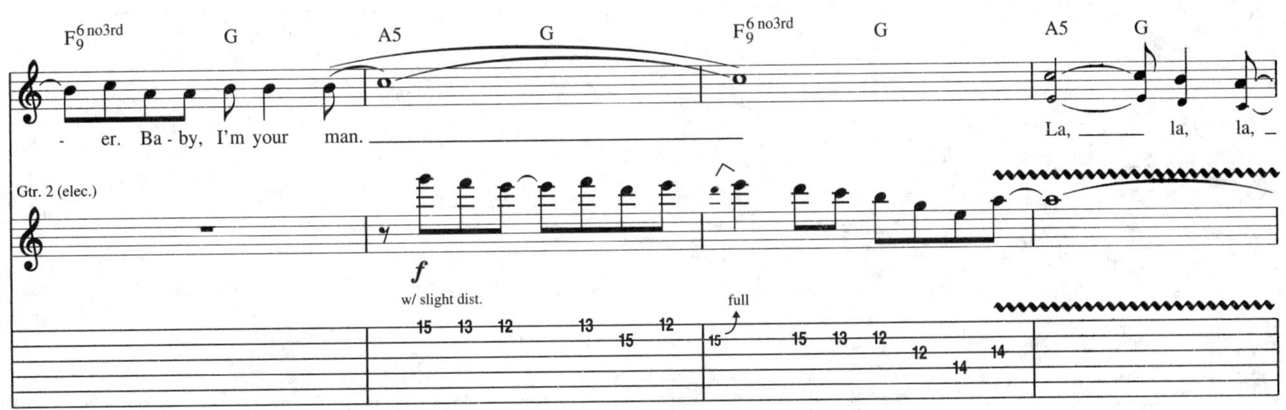
F6/9 no3rd
G
A5
G
F6/9 no3rd
G
A5
G
- er. Ba - by, I'm your man.
La, la, la,
Gtr. 2 (elec.)
f
w/ slight dist.
full
15 13 12 13 15 12
15 15 13 12 12 14 14

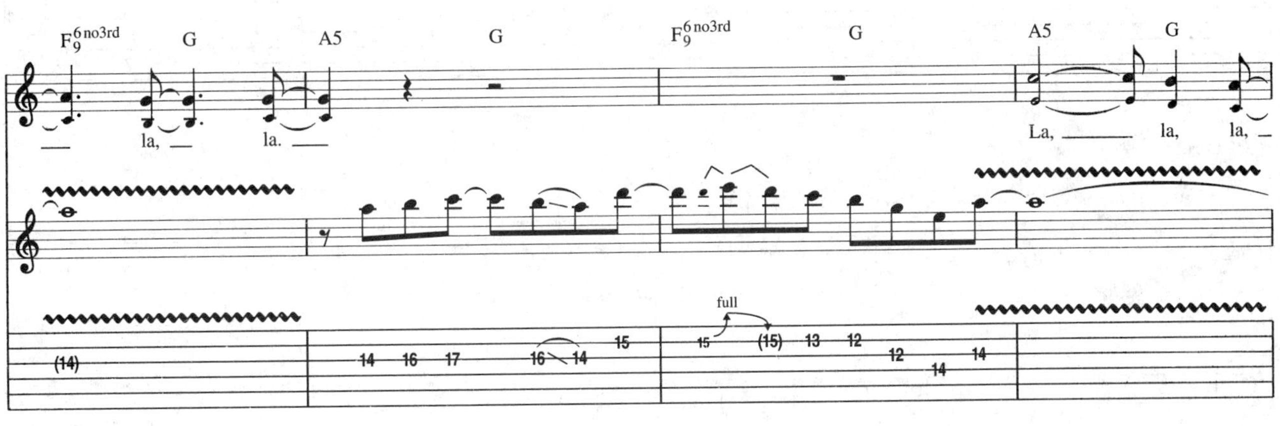
F6/9 no3rd
G
A5
G
F6/9 no3rd
G
A5
G
la, la.
La, la, la,
full
(14)
14 16 17 16 14 15
15 (15) 13 12 12 14 14

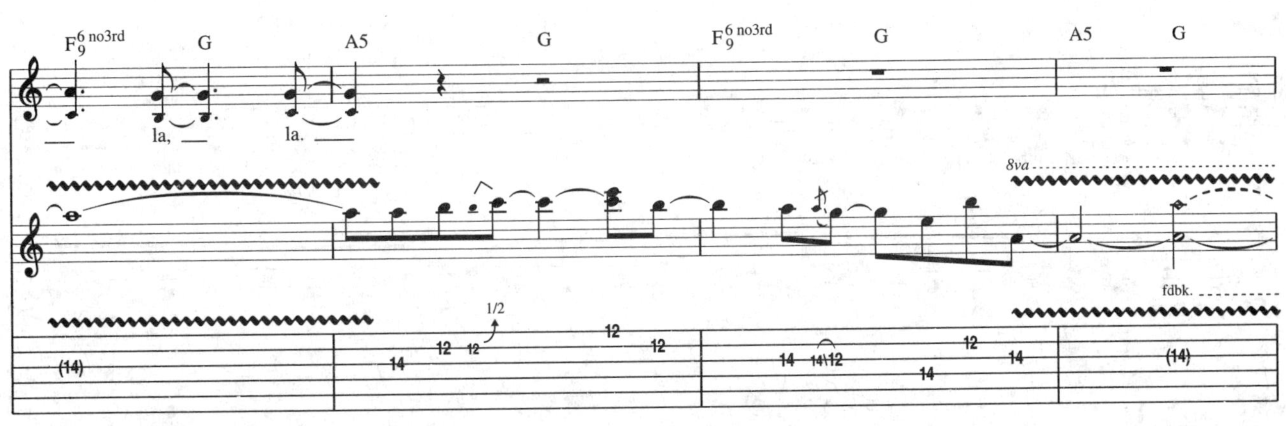
F6/9 no3rd
G
A5
G
F6/9 no3rd
G
A5
G
la, la.
8va
fdbk.
1/2
(14)
14 12 12 12 12
14 14\12 14 12 14
(14)

F6/9 no3rd G
8va
fdbk.
Gtr. 2 tacet
Am
loco
Gtr. 1
Gtr. 1: w/ Riff A, 4 times
Verse
Gtr. 1: w/ Riff A, 4 times
A5 G F6/9 no3rd G A5 G F6/9 no3rd G
2. Val - en - tine is done.
A5 G F6/9 no3rd G A5 G F6/9 no3rd G
Here but now they're gone.
Gtr. 2
Chorus
N.C.(F) (G) (A5) (F) (E5) (A5) (G) G5
Gtr. 2 tacet
Ro-me-o and Ju - li-et are to-geth-er in e-ter-ni - ty.
(Rom-e - o and Ju -
Gtr. 2
Gtr. 1
Gtr. 1 divisi
P.M.
F5 G5 A5 G5 F5 G5
For - ty thou-sand men and wom-en ev - 'ry day. For - ty thou-sand men and wom-en ev -
- li - et.) (Like Rom-e - o and Ju - li - et.)
P.M.

A5
G5
F5
G5
A5
G5
- 'ry day. A - noth-er for - ty thou-sand com-ing ev - 'ry day.
(Re - de-fine hap - pi-ness.)
(We can be like they
P.M.
7 5 5 5 7 5 3 3 3 3 5 3 3 1 1 1 1 3 3 5 3 3 3 5 3 5 7 5 5 5 7 5 3 3 3 3 0

Gtr. 1: w/ Riff A, 9 times
F6/9 no3rd
G
A5
G
F6/9 no3rd
G
Come on ba - by.
Ba - by, take my hand.
are.)
(Don't fear the reap - er.)
let ring
1 3 0 0 3 2 0 0

A5
G
F6/9 no3rd
G
A5
G
We'll be a - ble to fly.
(Don't fear the reap - er.)
(Don't fear the reap -

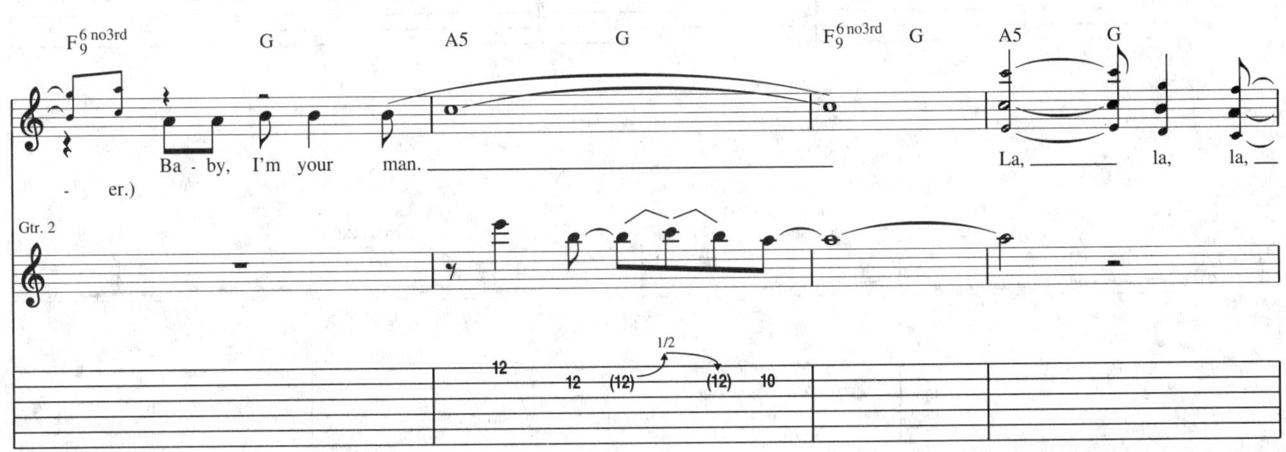
F6/9 no3rd
G
A5
G
F6/9 no3rd
G
A5
G
Ba - by, I'm your man.
La, la, la,
- er.)
Gtr. 2
1/2
12 12 (12) (12) 10

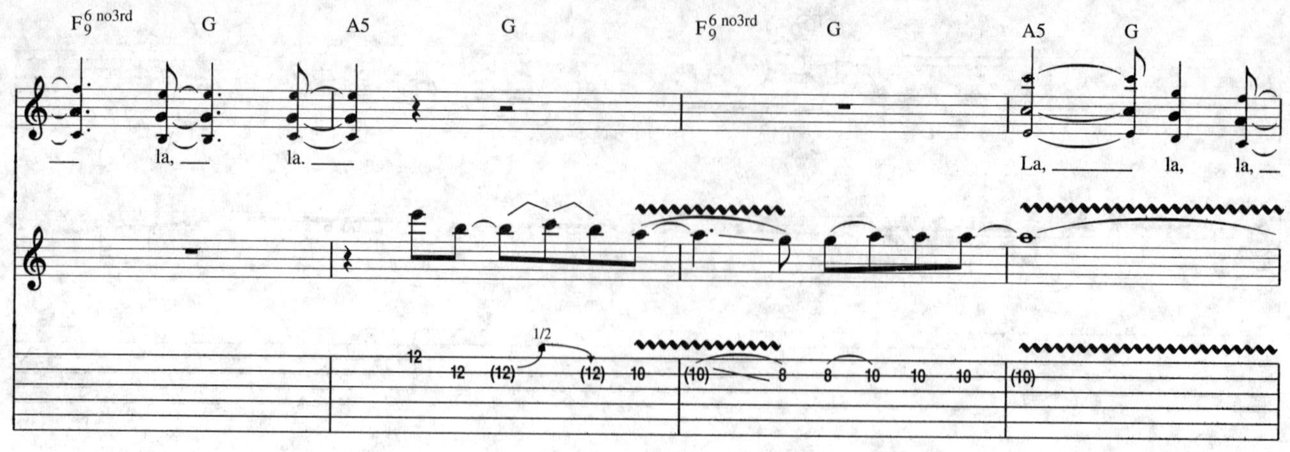
F6/9 no3rd
G
A5
G
F6/9 no3rd
G
A5
G
la,
la.
La,
la,
la,
1/2

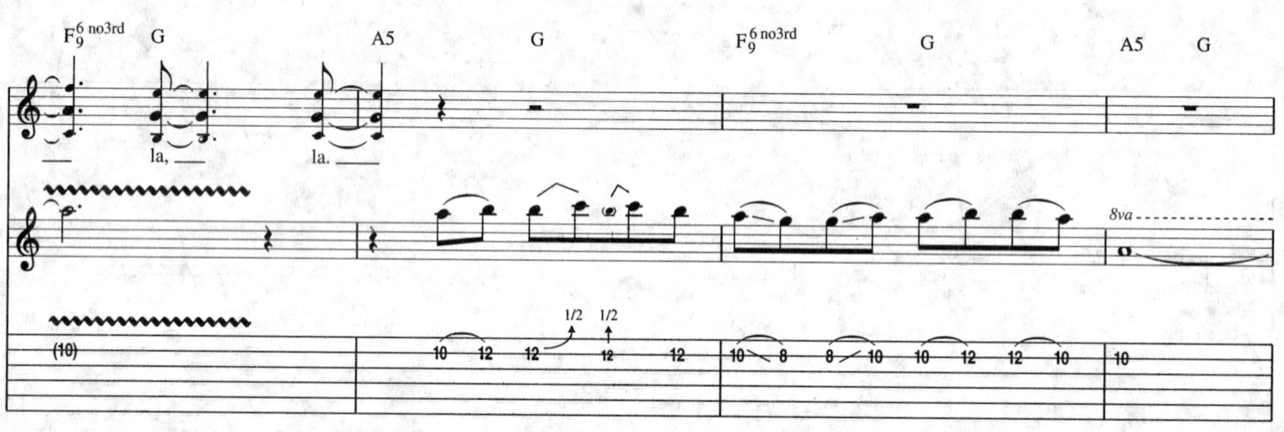
F6/9 no3rd
G
A5
G
F6/9 no3rd
G
A5
G
la,
la.
8va
1/2
1/2

Interlude

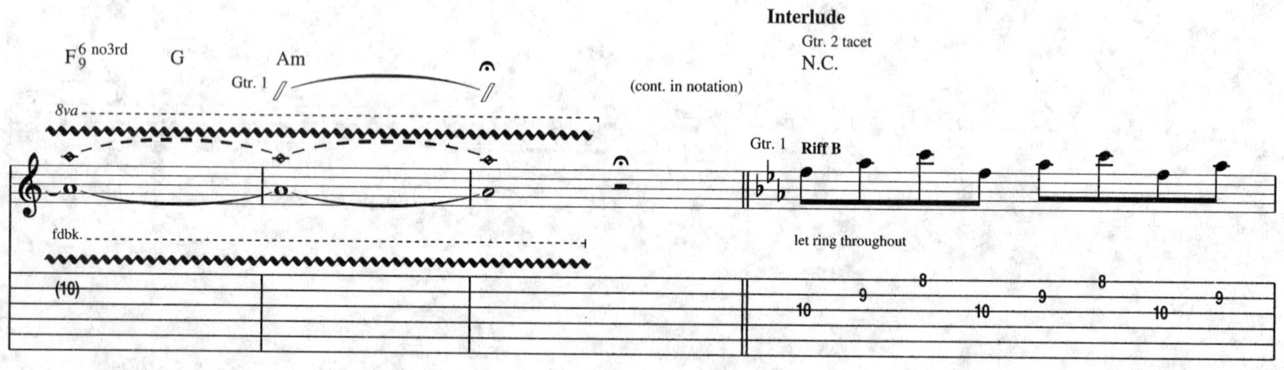
F6/9 no3rd
G
Am
Gtr. 1
(cont. in notation)
Gtr. 2 tacet
N.C.
8va
fdbk.
Gtr. 1
Riff B
let ring throughout

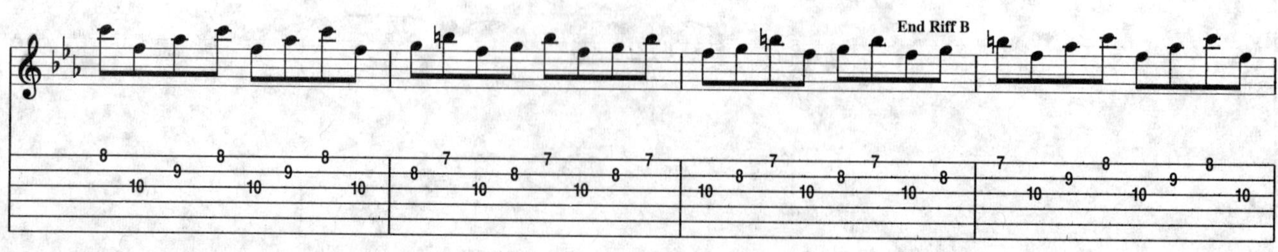
End Riff B

Guitar Solo
Gtr. 1: w/ Riff B
N.C.
Gtr. 2
Rhy. Fig. 1
End Rhy. Fig. 1
Gtr. 2: w/ Rhy. Fig. 1, 2 1/2 times
Gtr. 1
Gtr. 3 (dist.)
8va

F5
Gtr. 1
Gtr. 2
divisi
8va
loco
G5
F5
let ring
1/2
8va
fdbk.
pitch: C
G5
8va
loco
fdbk.
fdbk.

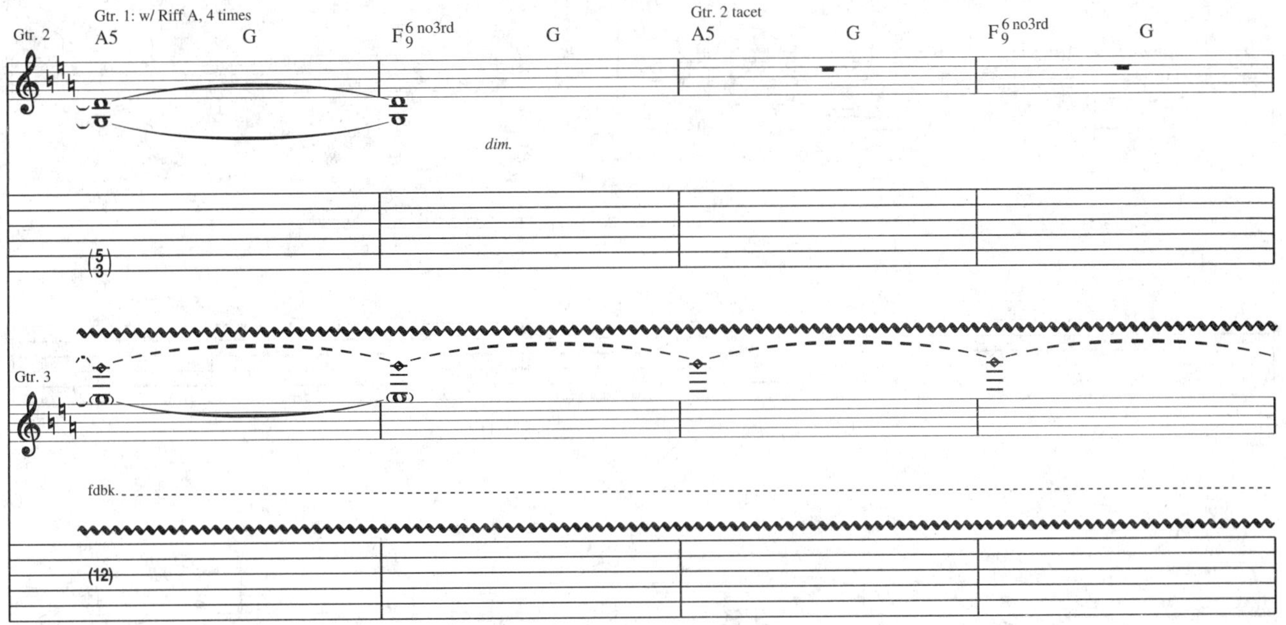
Gtr. 1: w/ Riff A, 4 times
Gtr. 2 tacet
Gtr. 2
A5
G
F6 no3rd 9
G
A5
G
F6 no3rd 9
G
dim.
Gtr. 3
fdbk.

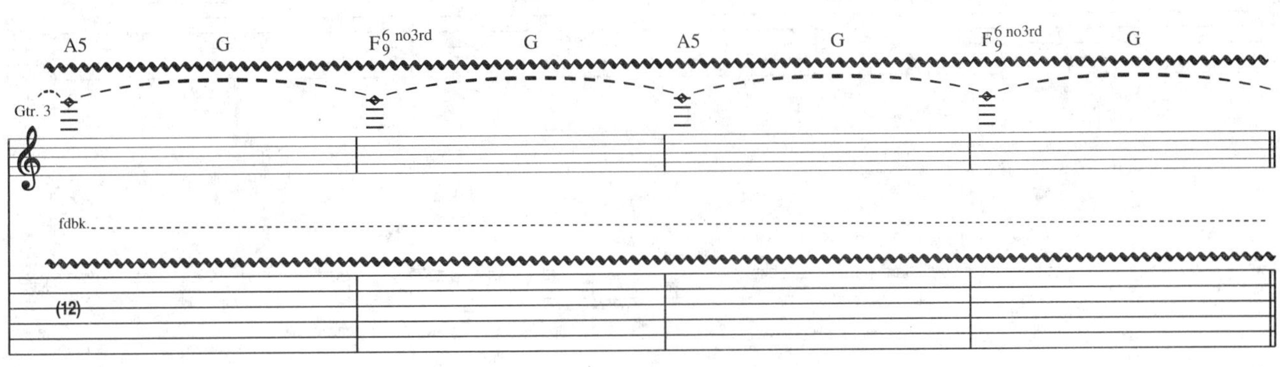
A5
G
F6 no3rd 9
G
A5
G
F6 no3rd 9
G
Gtr. 3
fdbk.

Verse

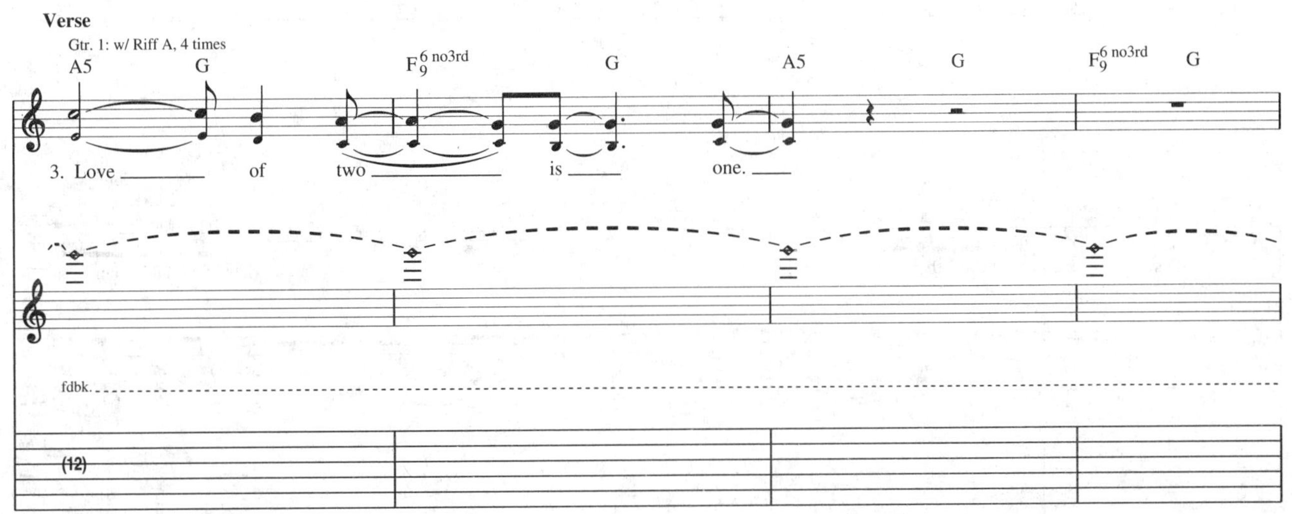
Gtr. 1: w/ Riff A, 4 times
A5
G
F6 no3rd 9
G
A5
G
F6 no3rd 9
G
3. Love of two is one.
fdbk.

A5
G
F9 6 no3rd
G
A5
G
F9 6 no3rd
G
Here but now they're gone.
8va
fdbk.
full
(12)
20
(20)

Chorus

Gtr. 3 tacet
F5
G5
A5
F5
G5
Came the last night of sad - ness, and it was clear she could - n't go on.
Gtr. 1

A5
G5
F5
G5
A5
G5
And the door was o - pen and the wind a'peared. The

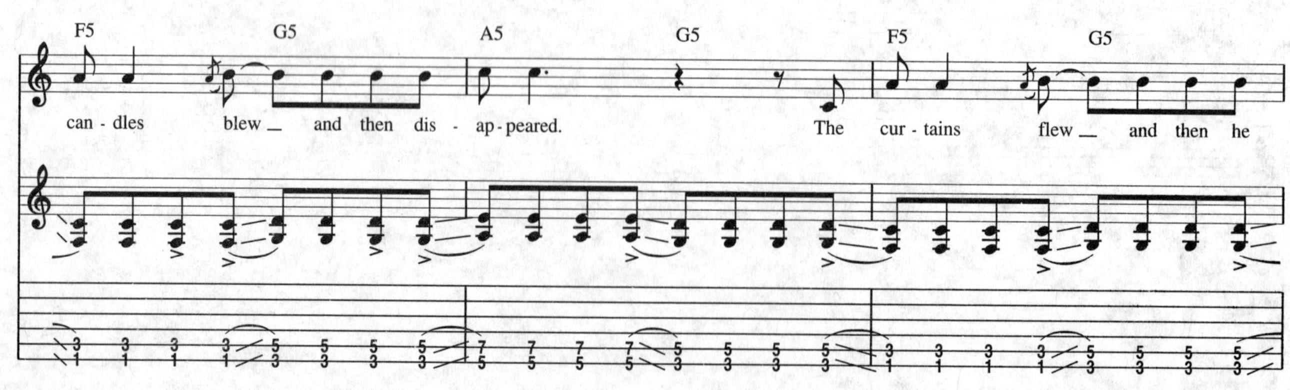
F5
G5
A5
G5
F5
G5
can - dles blew and then dis - ap - peared. The cur - tains flew and then he

A5 G5 F G Am V G
Rhy. Fig. 2A
End Rhy. Fig. 2A
Gtr. 2
ap - peared. Said don't be a - fraid. Come on ba - by. And she had no fear.
Rhy. Fig. 2
End Rhy. Fig. 2
let ring

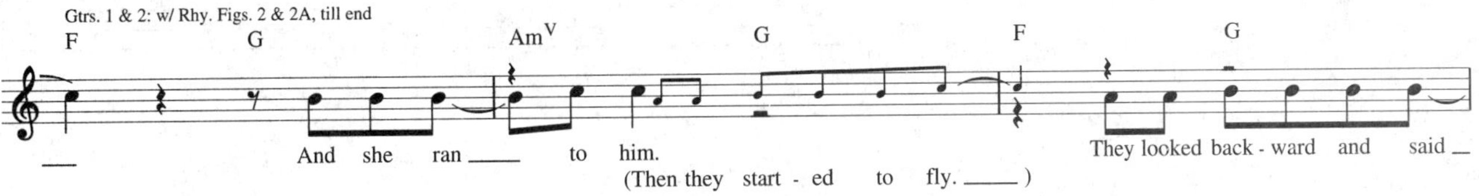
Gtrs. 1 & 2: w/ Rhy. Figs. 2 & 2A, till end
F G Am V G F G
And she ran to him. They looked back - ward and said
(Then they start - ed to fly.)

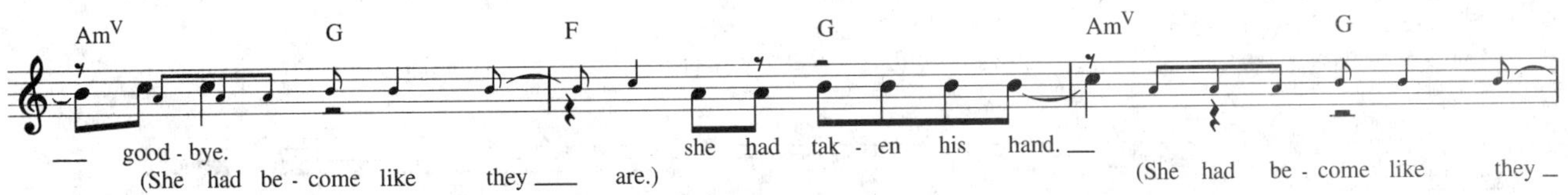
Am V G F G Am V G
good - bye. she had tak - en his hand.
(She had be - come like they are.) (She had be - come like they

F G Am V G F G
Come on ba - by.
are.) (Don't fear the reap - er.)
*Gtr. 3
8va
full
1/2
*Two gtrs. arr. for one.

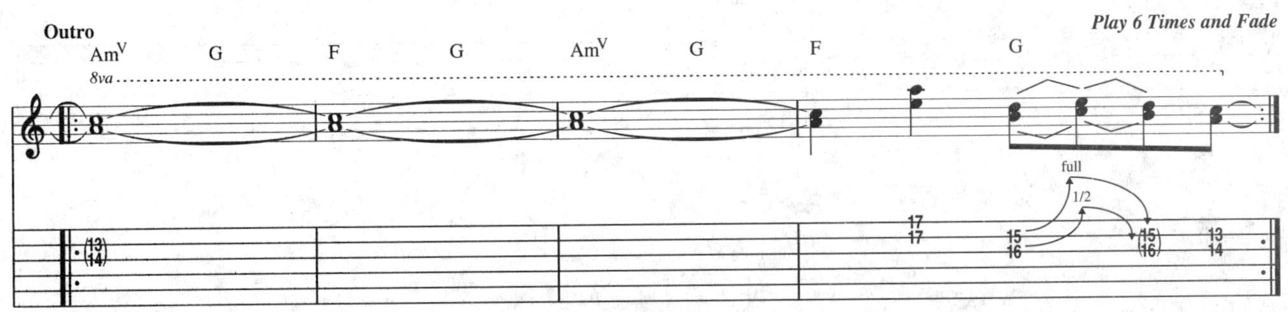
Outro
Play 6 Times and Fade
Am V G F G Am V G F G
8va
full
1/2

Drive My Car

Words and Music by John Lennon and Paul McCartney

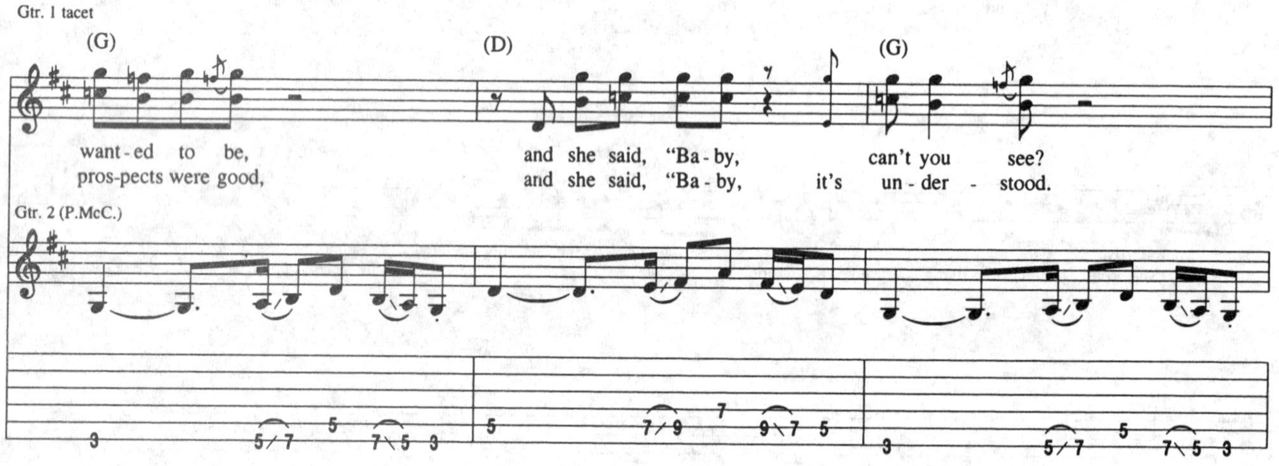

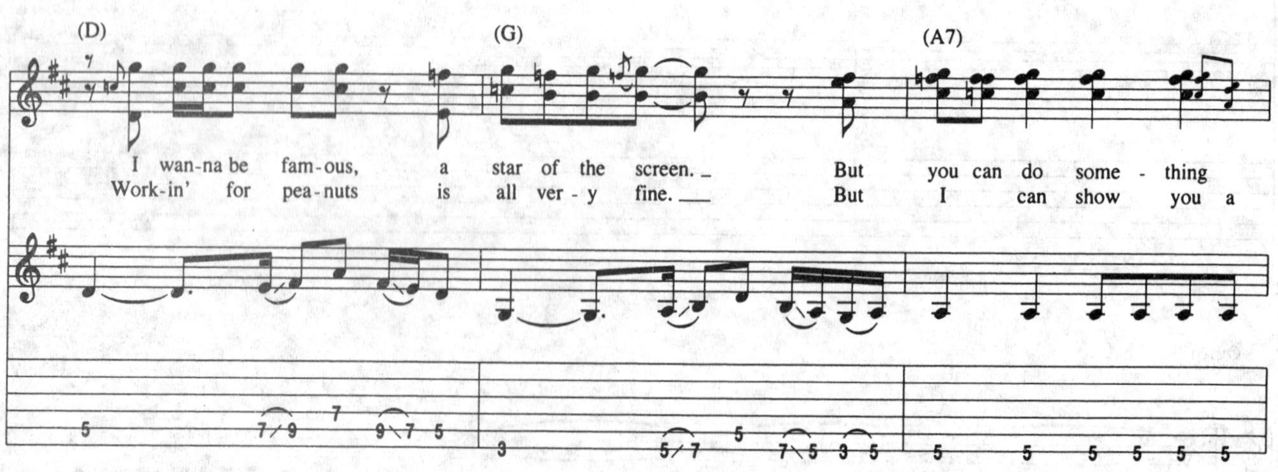

Chorus
(Bm)
(G)
in be - tween."
bet - ter time."
"Ba - by, you can drive my car.
(Bm)
(G)
(Bm)
Yes, I'm gon - na be a star.
Ba - by, you can drive my car,
1.
(E)
(A)
(D)
(A)
and may - be I'll love you."
2.
(D)
(A) N.C.
you."
Beep, beep, mm, beep, beep, yeah!
Gtr. 1 (P.McC.)
Gtr. 1

Guitar Solo

(D) (G) (D)

Gtr. 1

mf w/ slide w/ slide

1/2 1/2 1/2 1/2

Gtr. 2

Chorus
(A7)
(Bm)
"Ba - by, you can drive my car.
w/ slide
Gtr. 1 tacet
(G)
(Bm)
(G)
Yes, I'm gon - na be a star.
Gtr. 2
(Bm)
(E)
(A)
(D)
(G)
To Coda
Ba - by, you can drive my car, and may - be I'll love you."

Verse
(A)
(D)
(G)
3. I told that girl I could start right a - way,
(D)
(G)
(D)
and she said, "Lis-ten babe, I got some-thin' to say.
I got no car an' it's
(G)
(A7)
D.S. al Coda
break-in' my heart, but I found a driv - er, and that's a start."
Coda
(A) N.C.
(D)
Beep, beep, mm, beep, beep, yeah!

(A)
(D)
(A)
Beep, beep, mm, beep, beep, yeah!
Beep, beep, mm, beep, beep, yeah!
5 5 5 7 9 7 9 7 9
5 5 5 7 5 7 5 3
5 5 5 7 9 7 9 7 9
Begin Fade
(D)
(A)
Beep, beep, mm, beep, beep, yeah!
Gtr. 2
5 5 5 7 5 7 5 3
5 5 5 7 9 7 9 7 9
Gtr. 1
w/ slide
10 12 (12) 10 12 (12) 10 12 (12) 10 12
Fade Out
(D)
(A)
(D)
Beep, beep, mm, beep, beep, yeah!
5 5 5 7 5 7 5 3
5 5 5 7 9 7 9 7 9
5
10 12 (12) 10 12 (12) 10 12 (12) 10 12

Dust in the Wind

Words and Music by Kerry Livgren

C
G/B
Am
G
Dm7
All my dreams pass be - fore my eyes, a cu - ri - os - i - ty.
All we do crum-bles to the ground though we re - fuse to see.
slips a - way and all your mon - ey won't an - oth - er min - ute buy.
Am
Chorus
D/F#
G
Am
Am/G
To Coda
Dust in the wind
1.
D/F#
G
Am
G/B
All they are is dust in the wind.
(we)
2.
Am(add9)
wind.
G/A
F(#11)/A
F6(#11)/A
Oh, ho, ho.

Instrumental Bridge
Am(add9)
G/A
F(♯11)/A
F6(♯11)/A
D.C. al Coda
Coda
D/F♯
G
Am
Am/G
All we are is dust in the wind.
(All we are is dust in the
wind.
Dust in the wind.
Ev - 'ry-thing is dust in the wind.)
Ev - 'ry-thing is dust in the
Outro
Am
Asus2
Asus4(♭13)
*Play 4 Times and Fade
wind.
The wind.
*ad lib. voc. on repeat

Eye of the Tiger

Theme from ROCKY III

Words and Music by Frank Sullivan and Jim Peterik

Verse
Gtr. 2 tacet
Gtr. 1: w/ Riff A, 2 times
Cm
Ab/C
Bb/C
Cm
1. Ris - in' up, back on the street, did my time, took my chanc - es.

Ab/C
Bb/C
Cm
Went the dis - tance, now I'm back on my feet, just a man and his will to sur-vive.

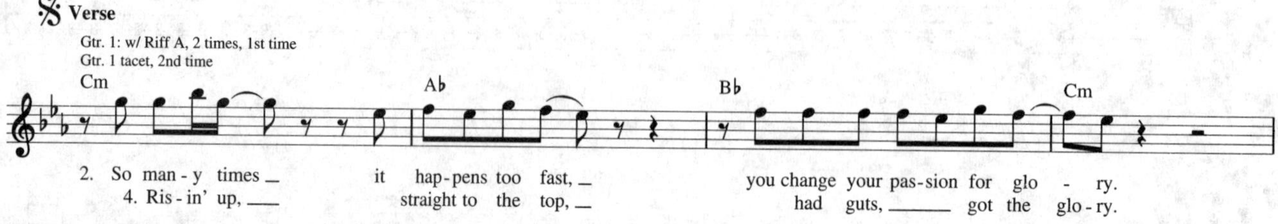
Verse
Gtr. 1: w/ Riff A, 2 times, 1st time
Gtr. 1 tacet, 2nd time
Cm
Ab
Bb
Cm
2. So man - y times it hap-pens too fast, you change your pas-sion for glo - ry.
4. Ris - in' up, straight to the top, had guts, got the glo - ry.

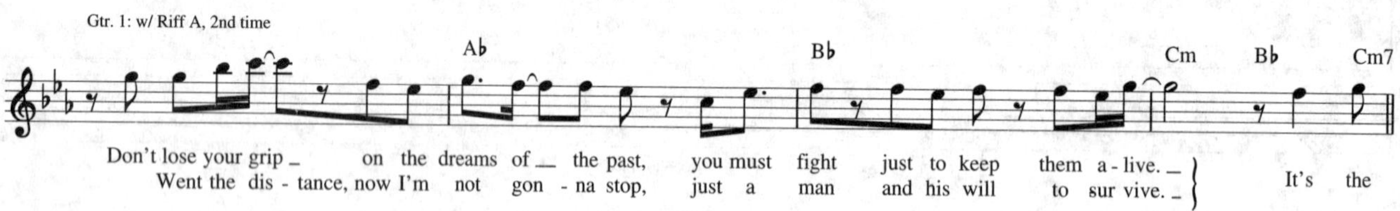
Gtr. 1: w/ Riff A, 2nd time
Ab
Bb
Cm
Bb
Cm7
Don't lose your grip on the dreams of the past, you must fight just to keep them a - live.
Went the dis - tance, now I'm not gon - na stop, just a man and his will to sur vive.
It's the

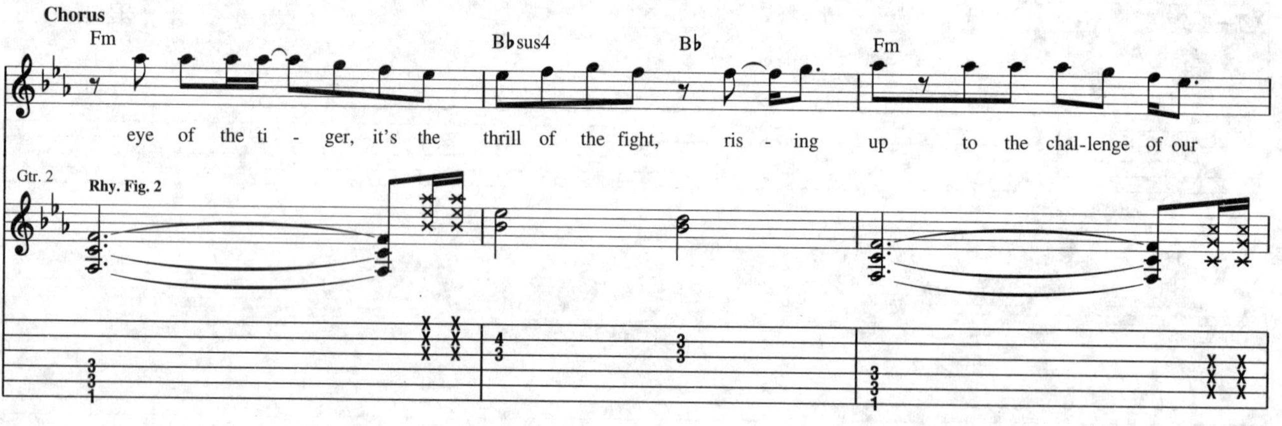
Chorus
Fm
Bbsus4
Bb
Fm
eye of the ti - ger, it's the thrill of the fight, ris - ing up to the chal-lenge of our
Gtr. 2
Rhy. Fig. 2

C5
Bb5
Fm
Bbsus4
Bb
ri - val. And the last known sur - vi - vor stalks his prey in the night, and he's

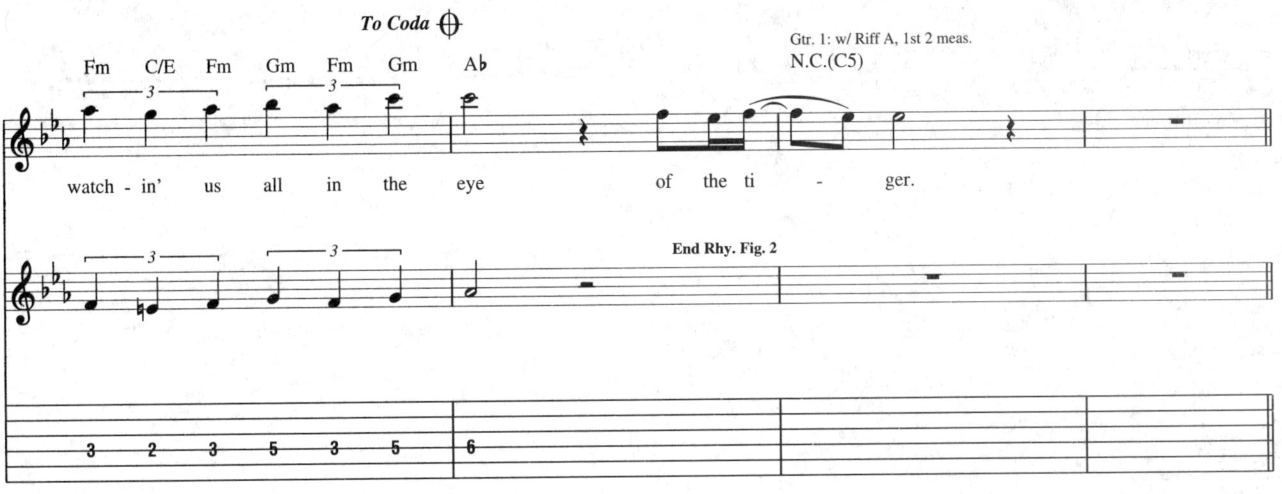

Verse

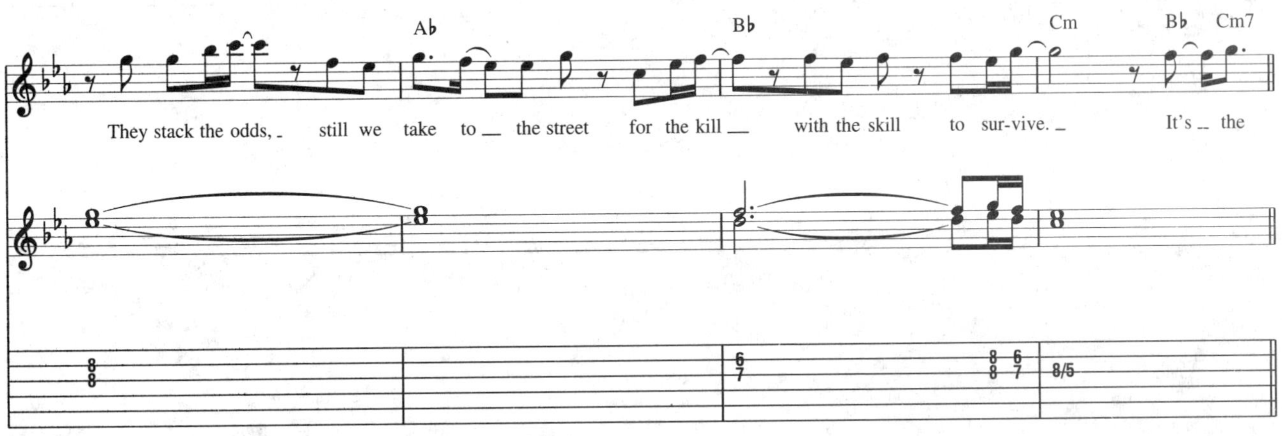

Chorus

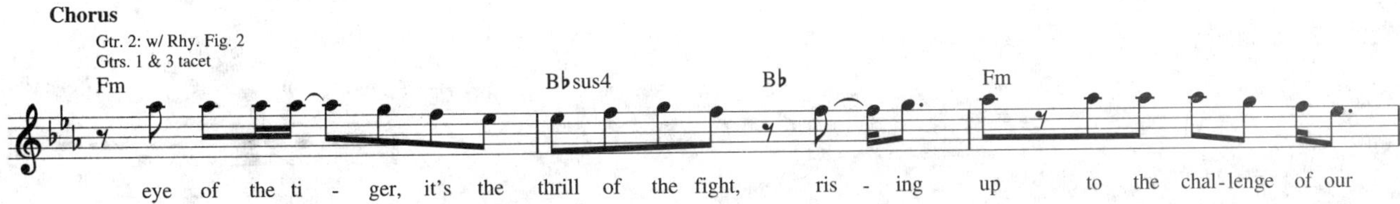

C5 B♭5 Fm B♭sus4 B♭
ri - val. And the last known sur - vi - vor stalks his prey in the night, and he's

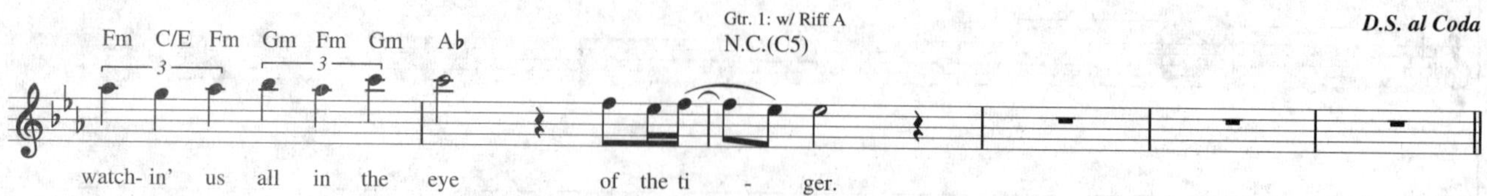
Fm C/E Fm Gm Fm Gm A♭
Gtr. 1: w/ Riff A
N.C.(C5)
D.S. al Coda
watch- in' us all in the eye of the ti - ger.

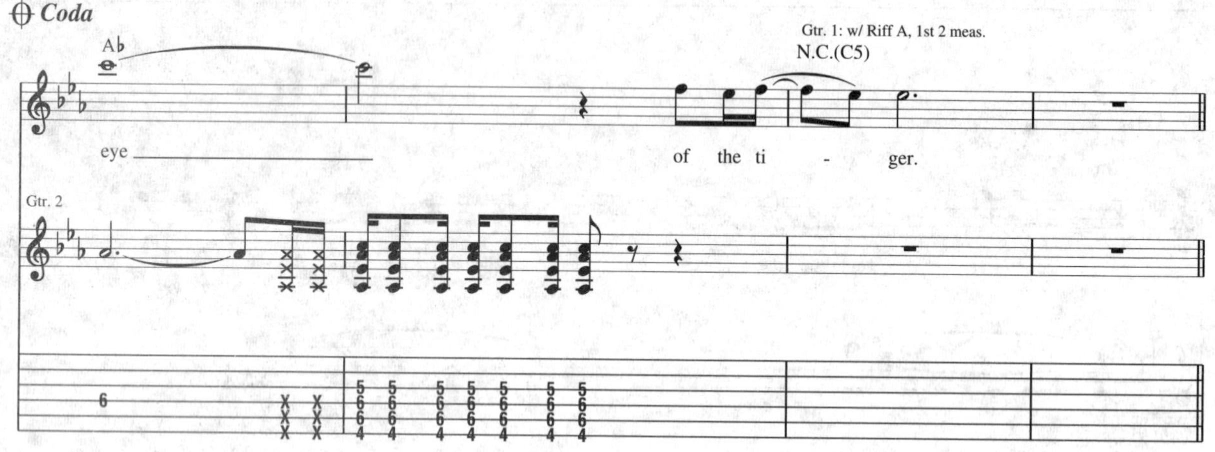
Coda
A♭
Gtr. 1: w/ Riff A, 1st 2 meas.
N.C.(C5)
eye of the ti - ger.
Gtr. 2

Outro

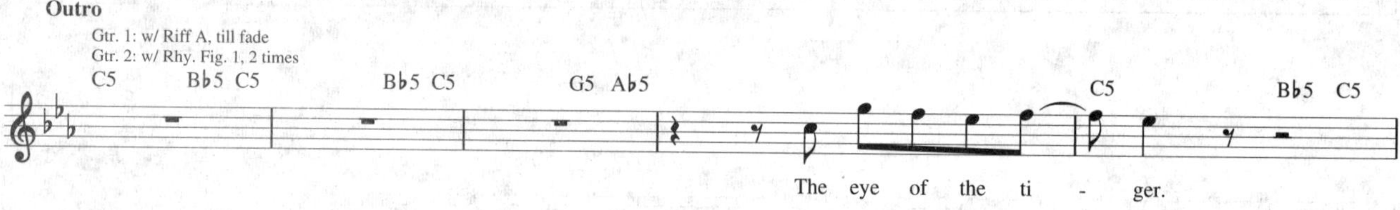
Gtr. 1: w/ Riff A, till fade
Gtr. 2: w/ Rhy. Fig. 1, 2 times
C5 B♭5 C5 B♭5 C5 G5 A♭5 C5 B♭5 C5
The eye of the ti - ger.

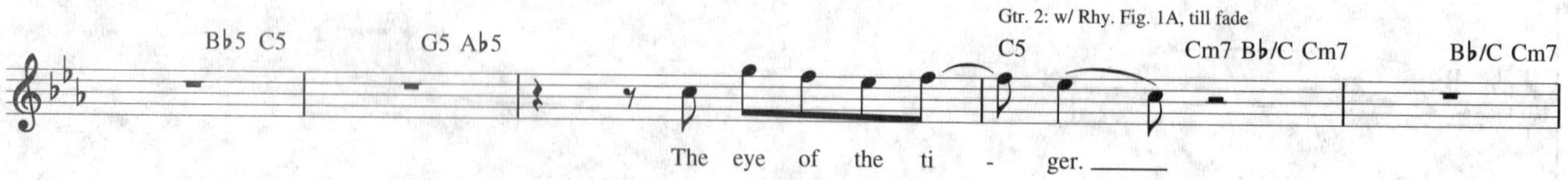
B♭5 C5 G5 A♭5
Gtr. 2: w/ Rhy. Fig. 1A, till fade
C5 Cm7 B♭/C Cm7 B♭/C Cm7
The eye of the ti - ger.

Begin Fade
C5 G5 A♭5 C5 Cm7 B♭/C Cm7 B♭/C Cm7 C5 G5 A♭5
The eye of the ti - ger.

C5 Cm7 B♭/C Cm7
Fade Out
The eye of the ti - ger.

Fly Like an Eagle

Words and Music by Steve Miller

Verse
Am7
1. Time keeps on slip-pin', slip-pin', slip-pin' in-to the fu-ture.
Time keeps on slip-pin', slip-pin', slip-pin' in-to the fu - ture.
I wan-na fly
P.M.
Chorus
Am
D/A
Dm/A
Am
D/A
like an ea - gle to the sea.
Fly like an ea - gle, let my

Dm/A
Am
D/A
Dm/A
Am
spir-it car - ry me. I want to fly like an ea - gle till I'm free.
D/A
Dm
Am
Verse
Am7
Oh, Lord, through the rev - o - lu - tion. 2. Feed the ba - bies who
P.M.
D/A
Dm/A
Am
don't have e - nough to eat. Shoe the chil - dren with no shoes on their feet. House the peo-
P.M.
P.M.
Am7
D/A
Dm/A
- ple liv - in' in the street. Oh, there's a so - lu -
P.M.

Chorus
Am7
Am
D/A
Dm/A
Am
- tion. I want to fly like an ea - gle to the sea.
P.M.
D/A
Dm/A
Am
Fly like an ea - gle, let my spir - it car - ry me. I want to fly
D/A
Dm/A
Am
D/A
like an ea - gle till I'm free, right through the rev - o -
Gtr. 1 tacet
Dm/A
Am
Verse
Am7
lu - tion. 3. Time keeps on slip - pin', slip - pin', slip - pin' in - to the fu -
- ture. Time keeps on slip - pin', slip - pin',
Gtr. 1
P.M.
P.M.
P.M.

1.,2.
3.
slip-pin' in-to the fu - ture.
P.M.
P.M.
P.M.
P.M.
3 5 0 3 5 0 3 5 0 3 5 5 3

Bridge
Am7

Do, doot - n', do, do.
Do, doot - n', do, do.
Do, doot - n', do, do.
P.M.
P.M.
P.M.
P.M.
5 X X 5 5 X X X X X X X X 3 5 X X X X X X X X X X X X 3 5 5 5 5 5 X X X X X X X X

Do, doot - n', do, do.
Do, doot - n', do, do.
Do, doot - n', do, do.
P.M.
P.M.
P.M.
P.M.
3 5 5 5 5 5 X X X X X X X X 3 5 5 5 X X X X X X X X X X 0 3 5 5 X X X X X X X X X X X X

Do, doot - n', do, do.
Do, doot - n', do, do.
I want to
P.M.
P.M.
3 5 X X X X X X X X X X X X 3 5 5 7 5 7 5 7

Chorus
Am
D/A
Dm/A
Am
fly like an ea - gle
to the sea.
P.M.
Fly like an ea - gle, let my spir - it car - ry me. I want to fly
like a ea - gle till I'm free,
right through the rev - o - lu - tion.
Interlude

D/A
Dm/A
Am
P.M.
*Played behind the beat.
D/A
Dm/A
Am
P.M.
Am7
1. Tick, tock, tick. Doot, doot, do, do. Tick, tock, tick.
2. Tick, tock, tick. Doot, doot, do, do.
P.M.
Outro
Am7
Tick, tock, tick. Doot, doot, do, do.
Tick, tock, tick. Doot, doot, do, do.
Time keeps on slip - pin', slip - pin',
P.M.
P.M.
Repeat & fade
slip - pin' in - to the fu - ture.
P.M.

For Your Love

Words and Music by Graham Gouldman

To Coda
Em
G
A
Am
There'll be days I will ex - cite to make you dream of me at night.
(For your love.
Chorus
Gtr. 1: w/ Rhy. Fig. 1, 3 times, simile
For your
love.
For your
love.
)
Slower ♩ = 132
Bridge
N.C.
(drums)
B
For your love, for your love,
Gtr. 1
*w/ slight P.M.
*Vocals doubled throughout bridge.
*next 7 meas.
E
I would give the stars a - bove. For your love, for your love,

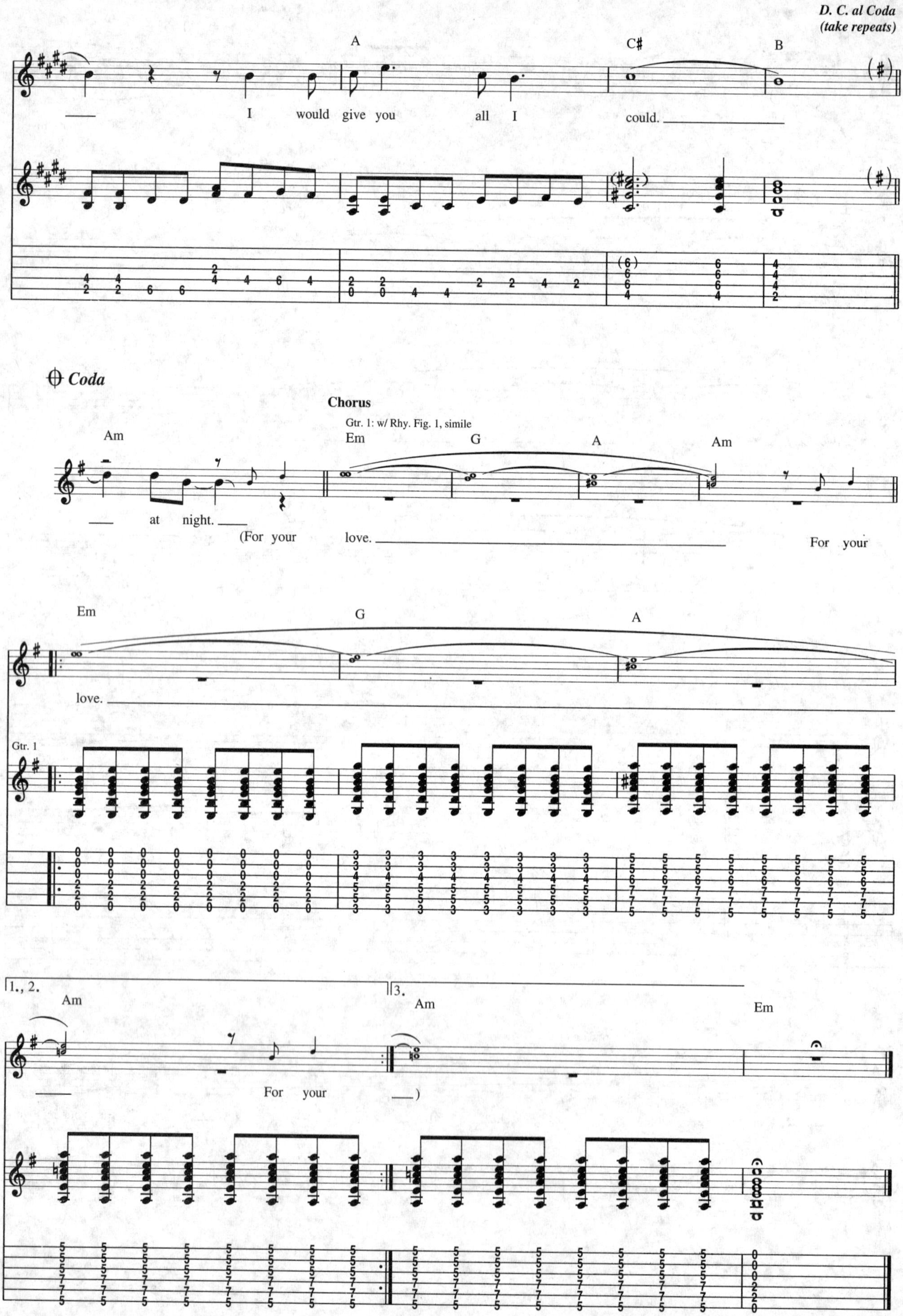

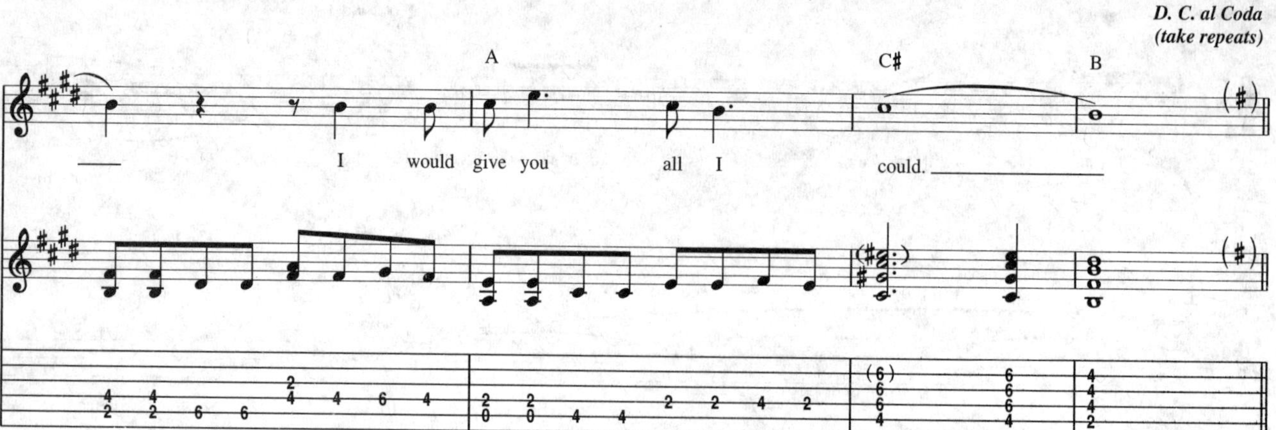

Coda

Chorus

Gtr. 1: w/ Rhy. Fig. 1, simile

Am Em G A Am

at night.

(For your love.

For your

Em G A

love.

Gtr. 1

1., 2.

Am

For your

3.

Am Em

)

Fortunate Son

Words and Music by John Fogerty

A5
G5
D5
E5
5fr
11
133
113
11

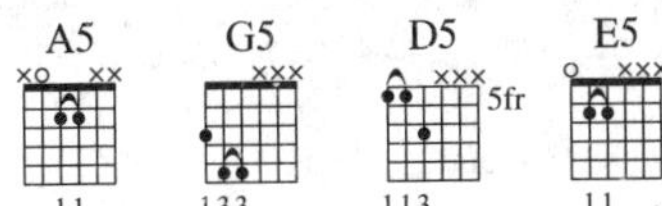

Tune down 1 step:
(low to high) D-G-C-F-A-D

Intro

Moderately ♩ = 128

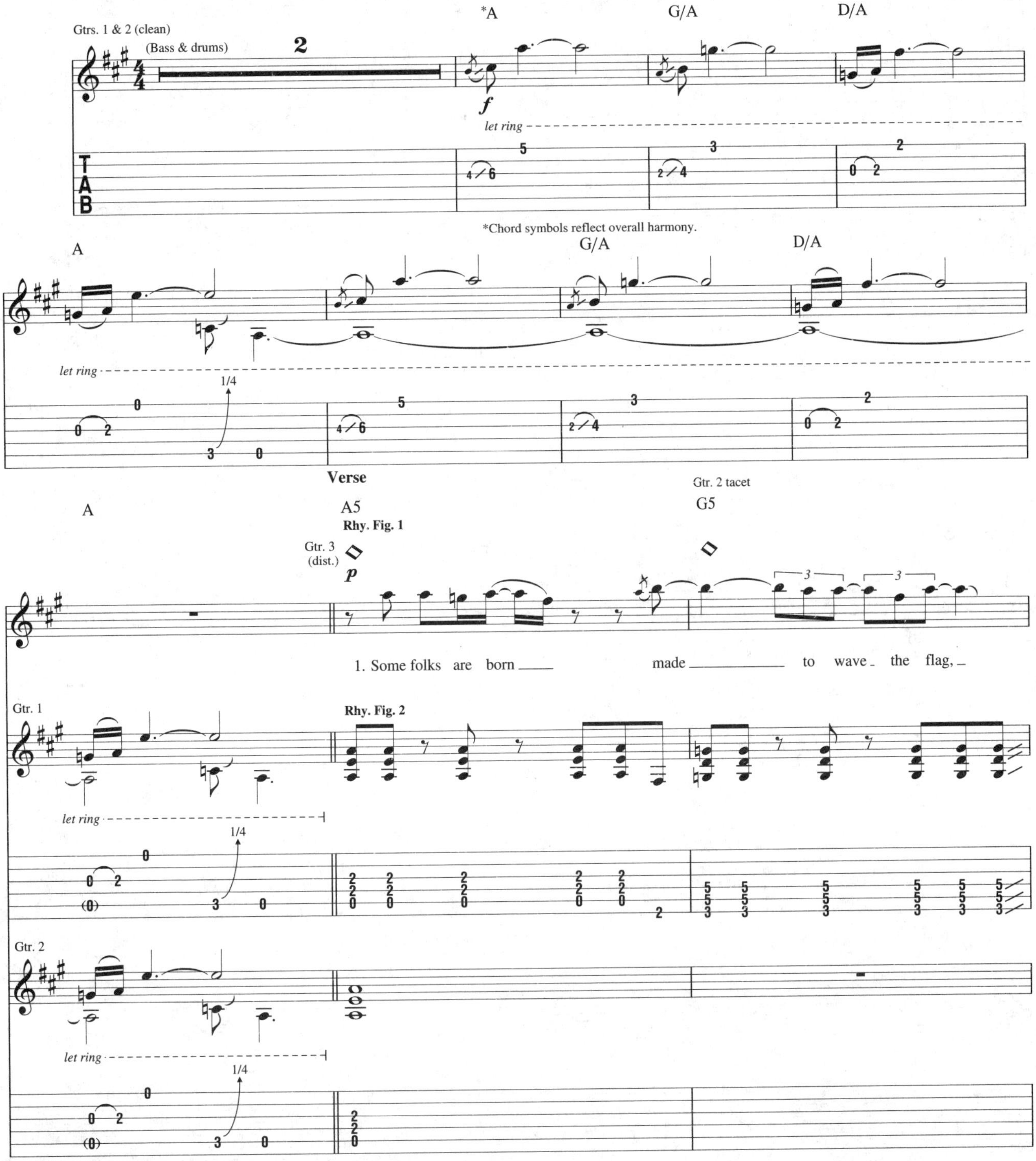
*A
G/A
D/A
Gtrs. 1 & 2 (clean)
(Bass & drums)
2
let ring
*Chord symbols reflect overall harmony.
A
G/A
D/A
let ring
1/4
A
Verse
A5
Rhy. Fig. 1
Gtr. 3
(dist.)
Gtr. 2 tacet
G5
1. Some folks are born made to wave the flag,
Gtr. 1
Rhy. Fig. 2
let ring
1/4
Gtr. 2
let ring
1/4

D5 A5

End Rhy. Fig. 1

ooh, their red, white and blue.

Gtr. 1

Gtr. 4 (dist.)

f

1/2

G5 D5

And when the band plays "Hail to the Chief," ooh, they point the can - non at

Chorus
A5
A5
E5
Rhy. Fig. 3A
you, Lord.
But it ain't me,
it ain't me;
End Rhy. Fig. 2
Rhy. Fig. 3
1/4
1/4
D5
A5
End Rhy. Fig. 3A
I ain't no sen - a - tor's son,
son.
End Rhy. Fig. 3
1
1/2
1/2

Gtrs. 1 & 3: w/ Rhy. Figs. 3 & 3A
E5
D5
It ain't me,
it ain't me;
I ain't no for - tu - nate one,
Gtr. 4
1/4
1
Verse
Gtr. 1: w/ Rhy. Fig. 2
Gtr. 3: w/ Rhy. Fig. 1 (2 times)
A5
A5
G5
no.
2. Some folks are born sil - ver spoon in hand.
3. Some folks in - her - it star - span - gled eyes.
1/2
D5
A5
Lord, don't they help them - selves, y'all?
Oo, they send you down to war, y'all.
But when the tax man come
And when you ask 'em, "How
1/2
1/2
G5
D5
A5
to the door,
much should we give?"
Lord, the house look, a, like a rum - mage sale, yeah, now.
Oo, they on - ly an - swer, "More, more, more," y'all.
1/2

Chorus

Interlude

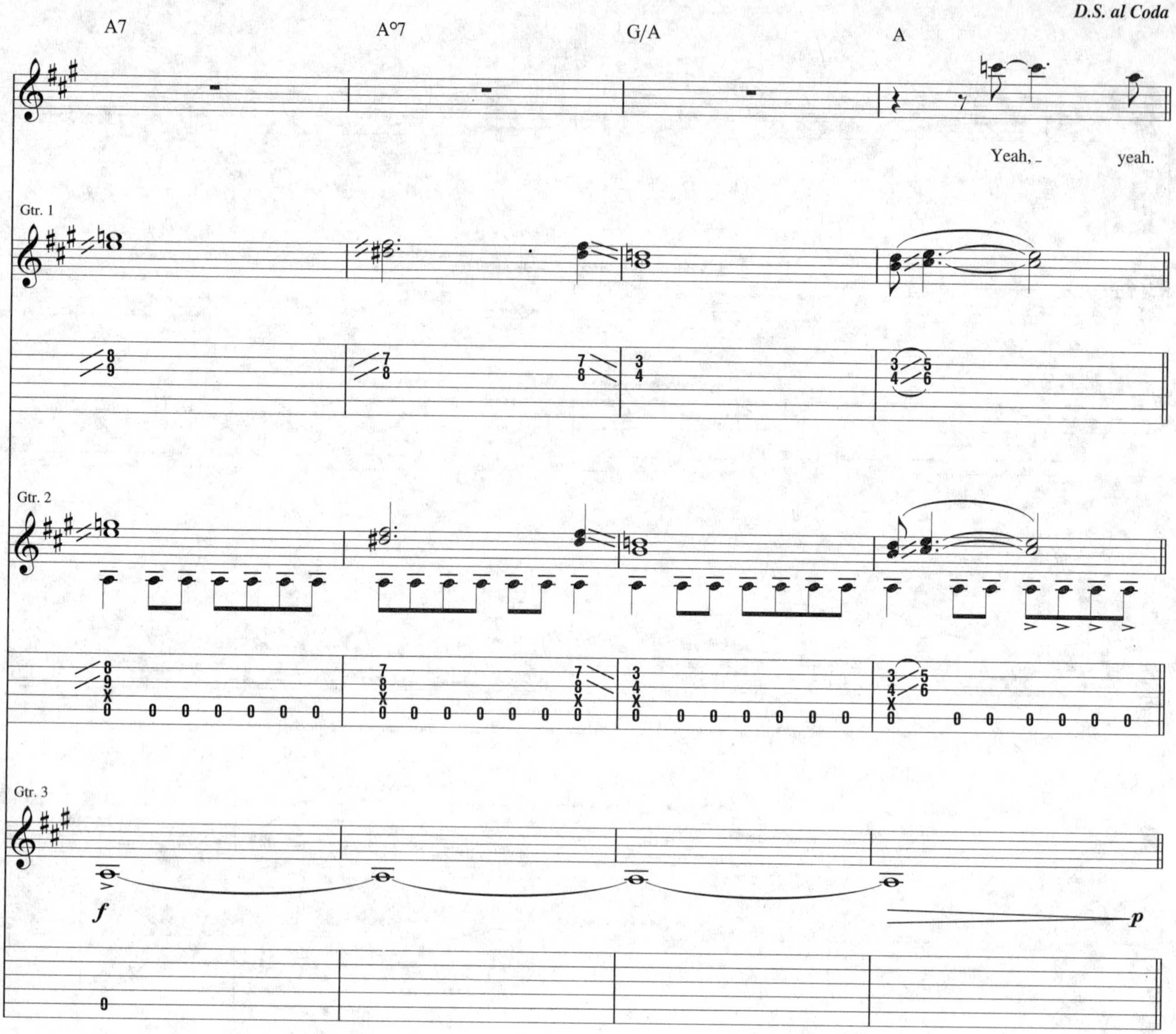
D.S. al Coda
A7
A°7
G/A
A
Yeah, _ yeah.
Gtr. 1
Gtr. 2
Gtr. 3
f
p

Coda
Gtr. 1: w/ Rhy. Fig. 3 (till fade)
Gtr. 3: w/ Rhy. Fig. 3A
A5
no. ___
It ain't me, ___

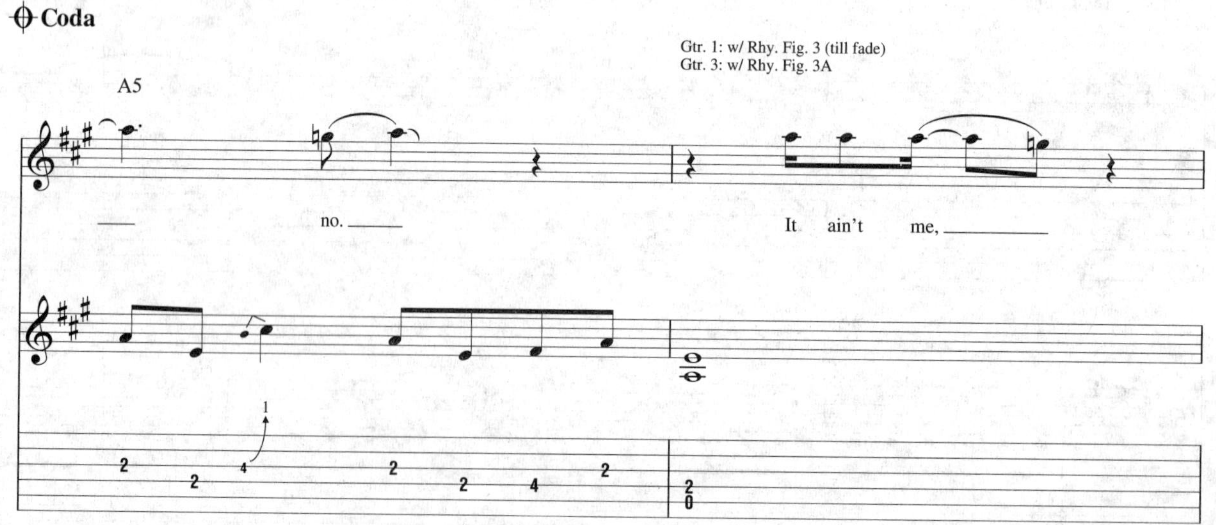

E5
D5
A5
it ain't me;
I ain't no for - tu - nate one,
no,
no,
no.
Begin fade
It ain't me,
it ain't me;
I ain't no for - tu - nate son,
Gtr. 4
Gtr. 2
Fade out
son,
son,
y'all.
But it ain't me,
it ain't me;

Free Ride

Words and Music by Dan Hartman

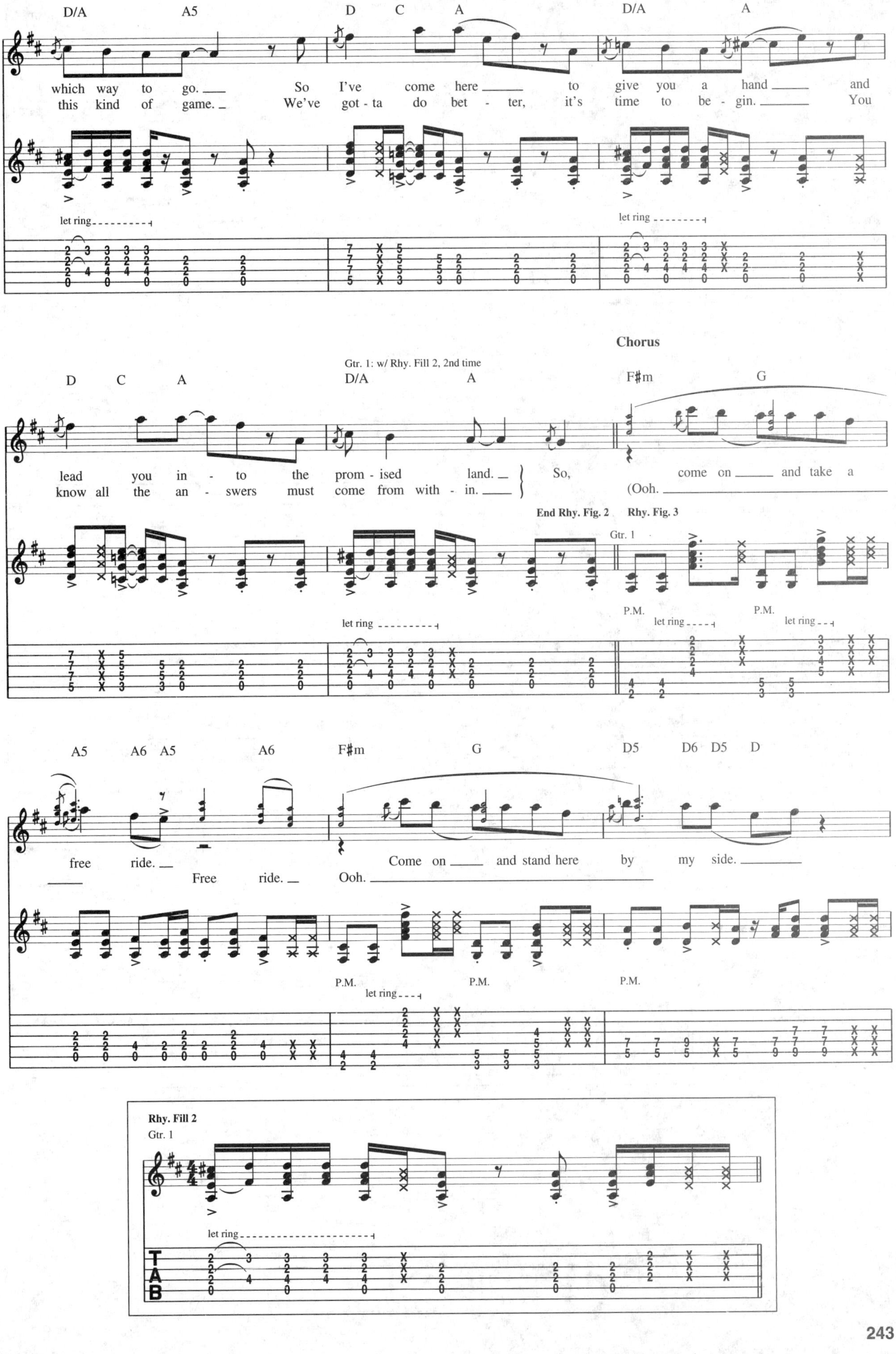

Chorus

Gtr. 1: w/ Rhy. Fill 2, 2nd time

D C A D/A A F#m G

lead you in - to the prom - ised land. So, come on and take a
know all the an - swers must come from with - in. (Ooh.

End Rhy. Fig. 2 Rhy. Fig. 3

Gtr. 1

let ring P.M. let ring P.M. let ring

A5 A6 A5 A6 F#m G D5 D6 D5 D

free ride. Come on and stand here by my side.
Free ride. Ooh.

P.M. let ring P.M. P.M.

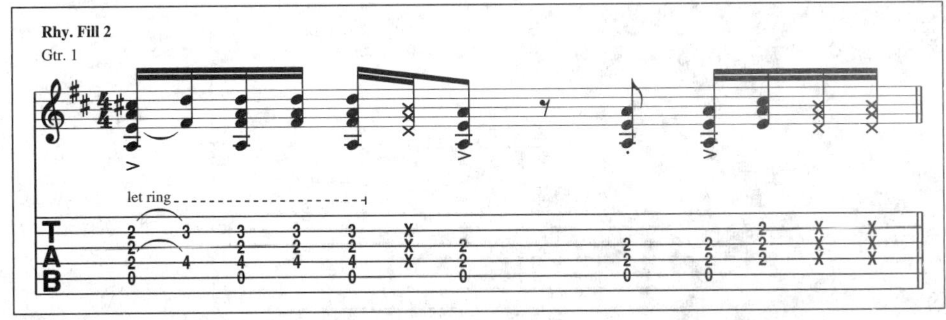

To Coda ⊕

Gtr. 2: w/ Rhy. Fill 1

F♯m G D5

Come on ___ and take a free ride.

Ooh. ___)

*Gtr. 3 (dist.)

Gtr. 1

End Rhy. Fig. 3

P.M. let ring P.M. let ring

*Two gtrs. arr. for one.

Guitar Solo

Gtrs. 1 & 2: w/ Rhy. Fig. 1, simile

G A G D G D A D G A G D G D A D

full full

D. S. al Coda

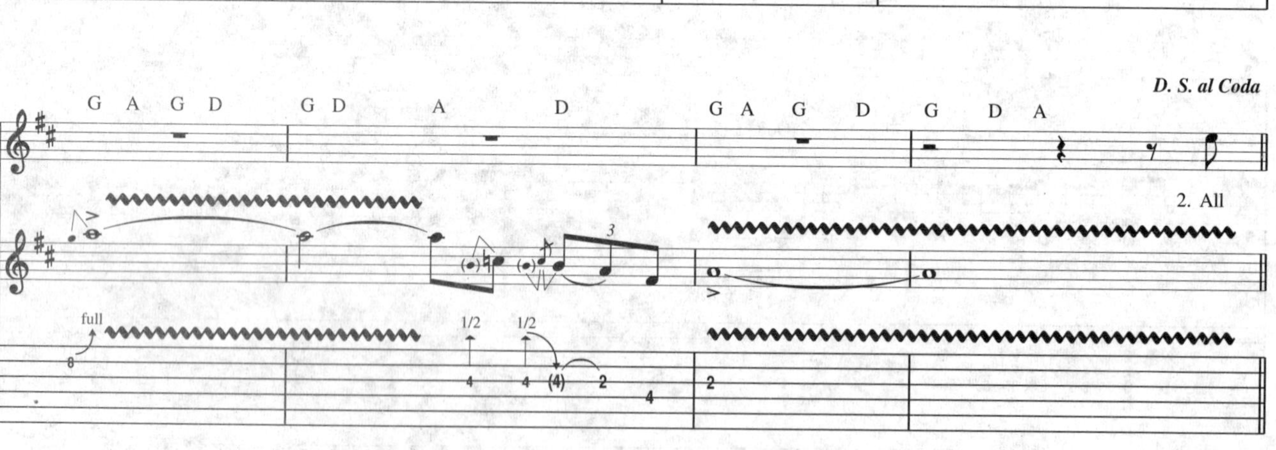

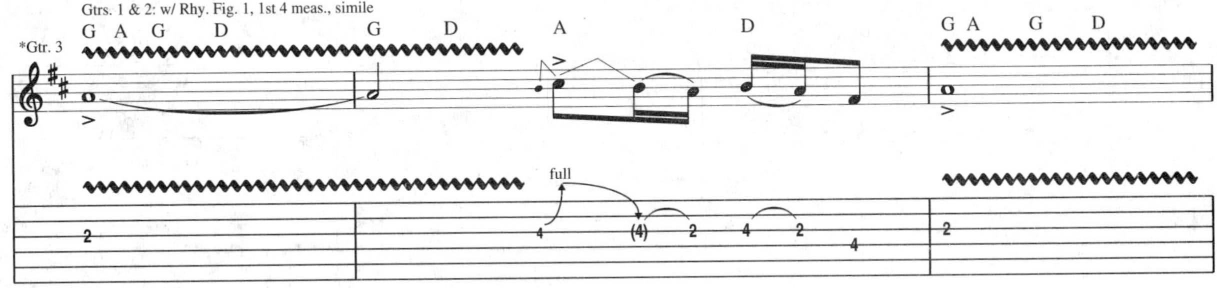

*Two gtrs. arr. for one.

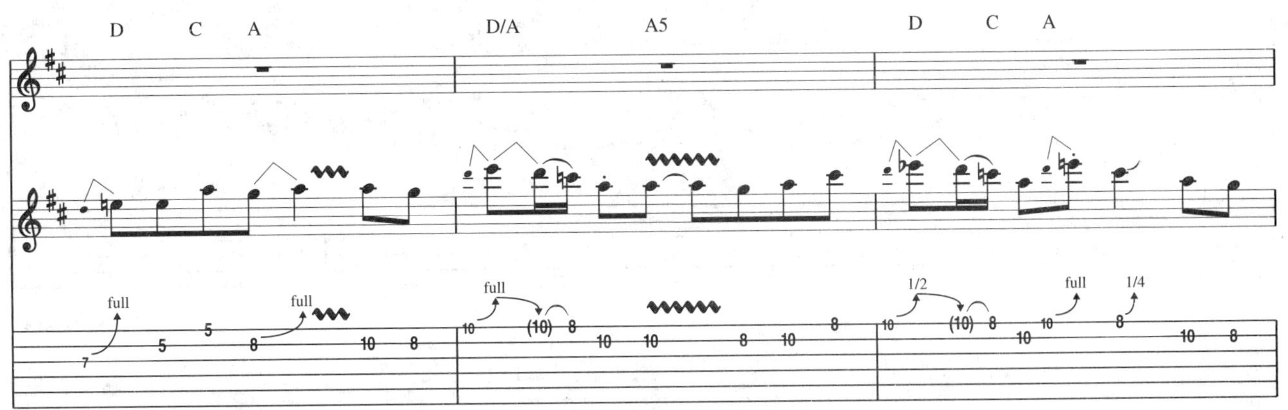

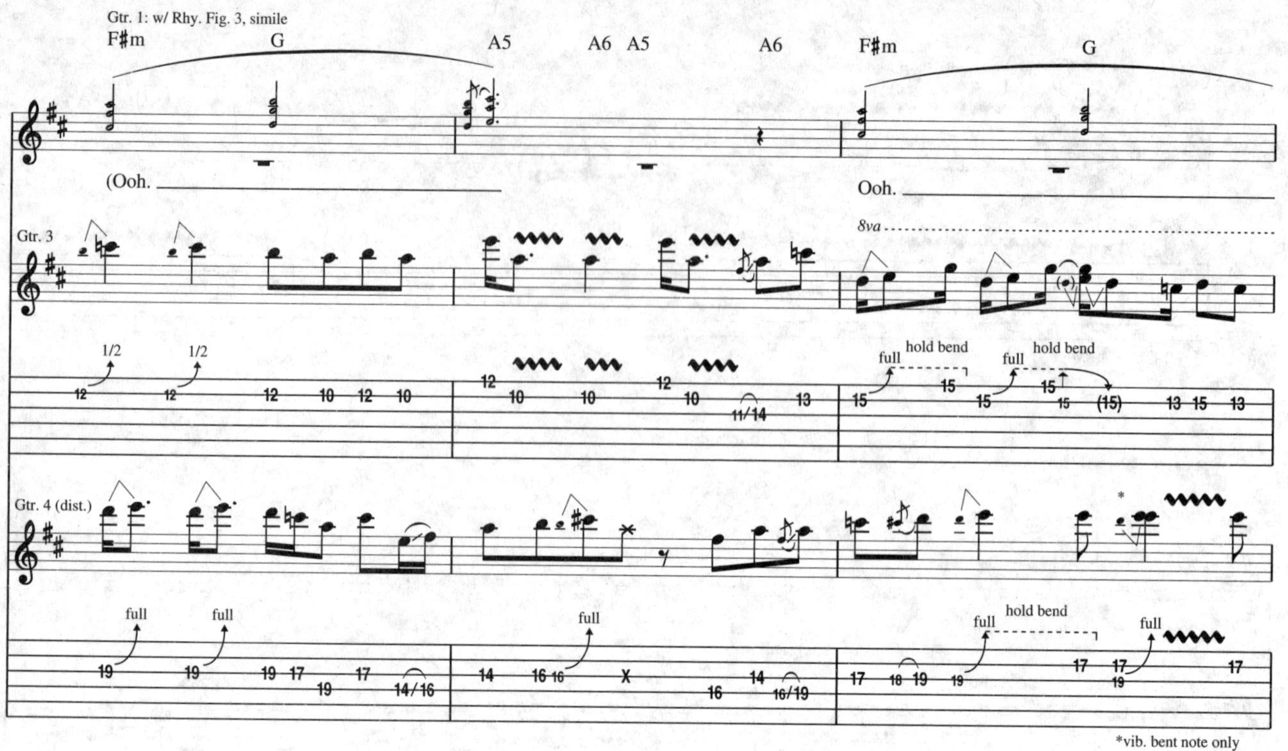
Gtr. 1: w/ Rhy. Fig. 3, simile
F#m
G
A5
A6
A5
A6
F#m
G
(Ooh.
Ooh.
Gtr. 3
8va
1/2
1/2
full
hold bend
full
hold bend
Gtr. 4 (dist.)
full
full
full
full
hold bend
full
*vib. bent note only

D5
D6
D5
F#m
G
Gtr. 1: w/ Rhy. Fill 3
D
Ooh.
Free
ride.)
8va
full
full
1/2
1/4
full
1/4
full
full
full
full
hold bend
full
full
full

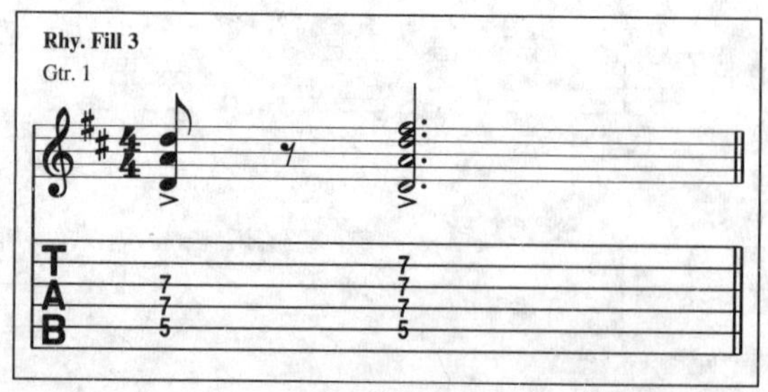
Rhy. Fill 3
Gtr. 1
T
A
B

Interlude
Gtrs. 1, 3 & 4 tacet
N.C.
Gtr. 1: w/ Rhy. Fill 1
Gtr. 2: w/ Rhy. Fill 4
D
Outro
Gtrs. 1 & 2: w/ Rhy. Fig. 1, till fade, simile
w/ Voc. ad lib, throughout
G A G D
Voc. Fig. 1
Come on and take a
G D A D G A G D G D A D
End Voc. Fig. 1
free ride.
Yeah, yeah, yeah, yeah.
Gtr. 4
full
hold bend
1/2
Gtr. 3
1/2
w/ Voc. Fig. 1, till fade, simile
G A G D G D A D G A G D
let ring
1/2
Rhy. Fill 4
Gtr. 1

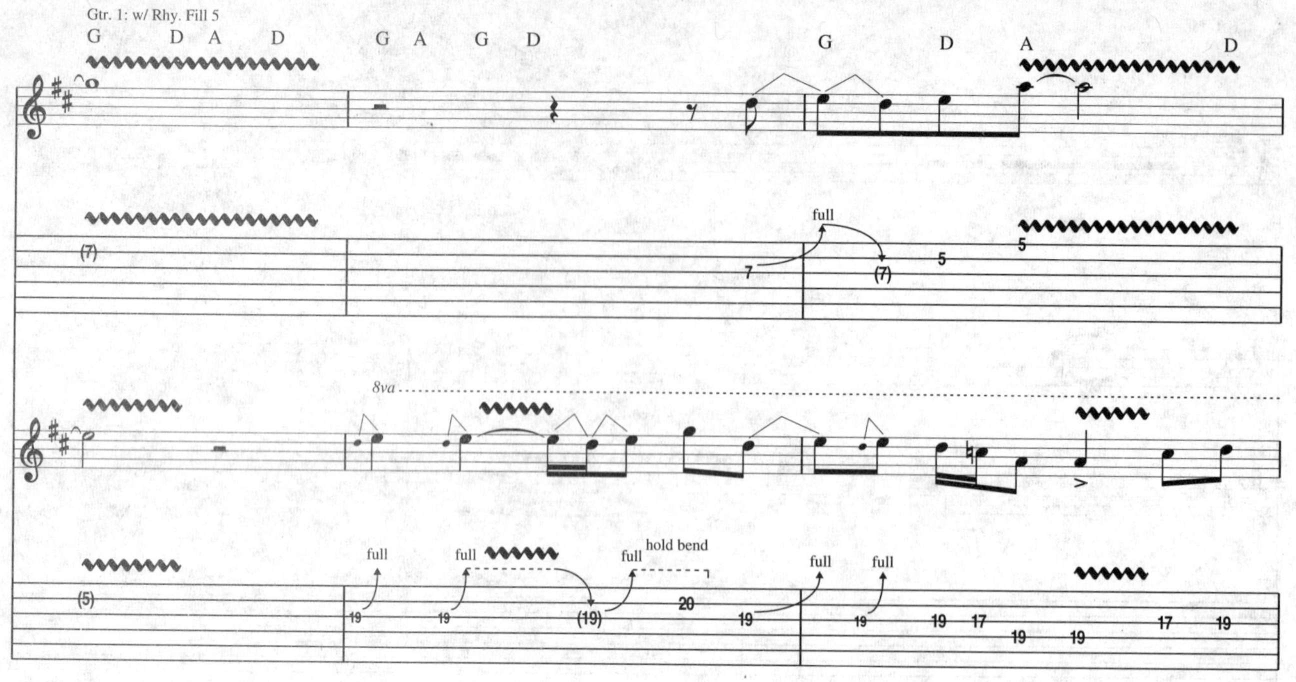

Gtr. 1: w/ Rhy. Fill 5
G D A D G A G D G D A D
full
8va
full full full hold bend full full

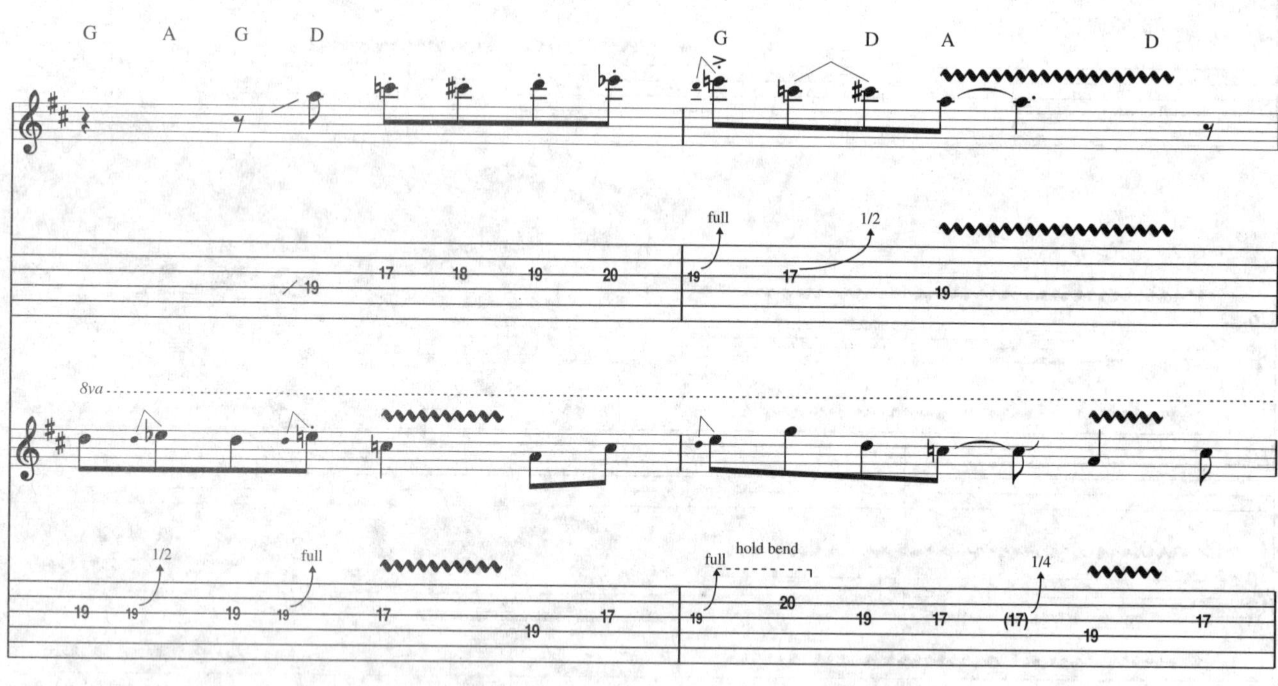

G A G D G D A D
full 1/2
8va
1/2 full full hold bend 1/4

Rhy. Fill 5
Gtr. 1
let ring

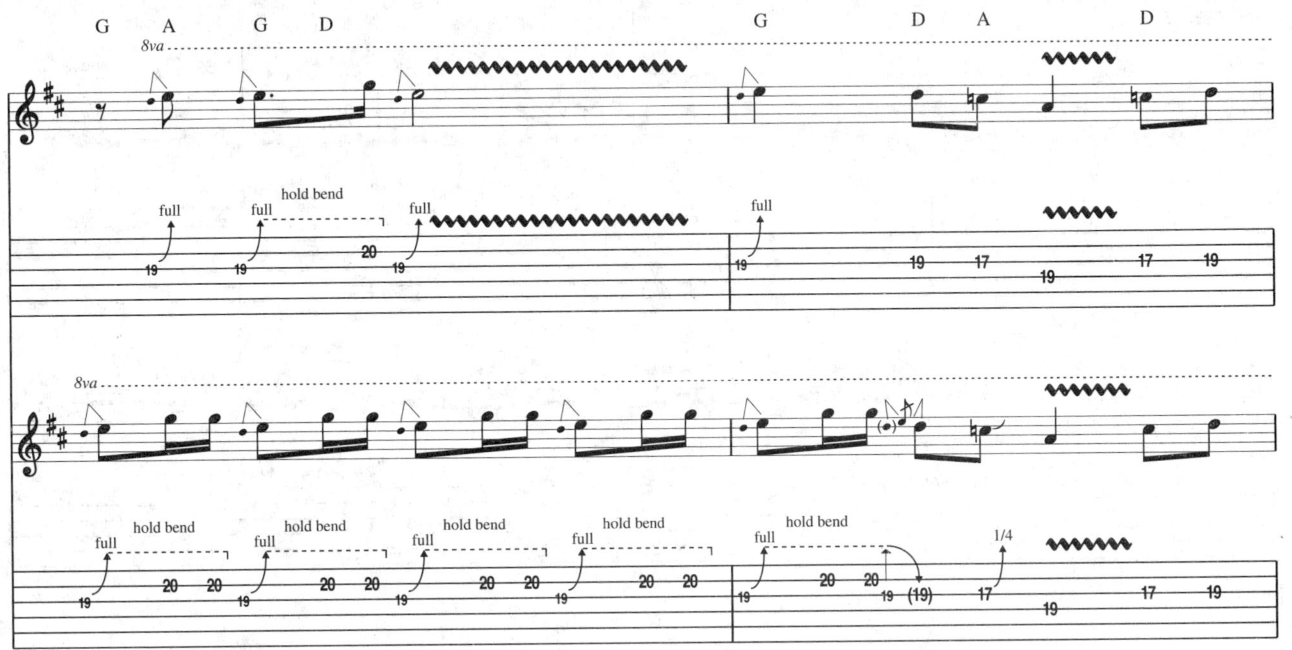
G A G D G D A D
8va
full
full
hold bend
full
full
hold bend
hold bend
hold bend
hold bend
hold bend
1/4

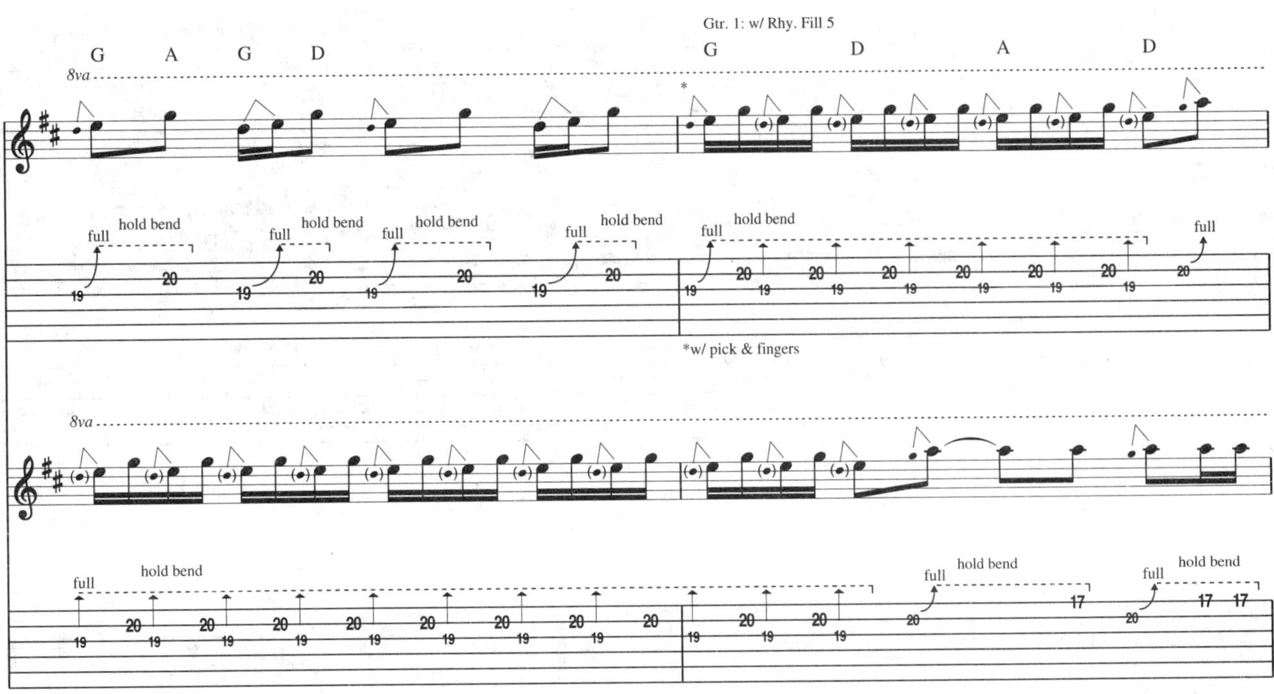
Gtr. 1: w/ Rhy. Fill 5
G A G D G D A D
8va
full
hold bend
*w/ pick & fingers

Rhy. Fill 5
Gtr. 1
let ring

Begin Fade

Fade Out

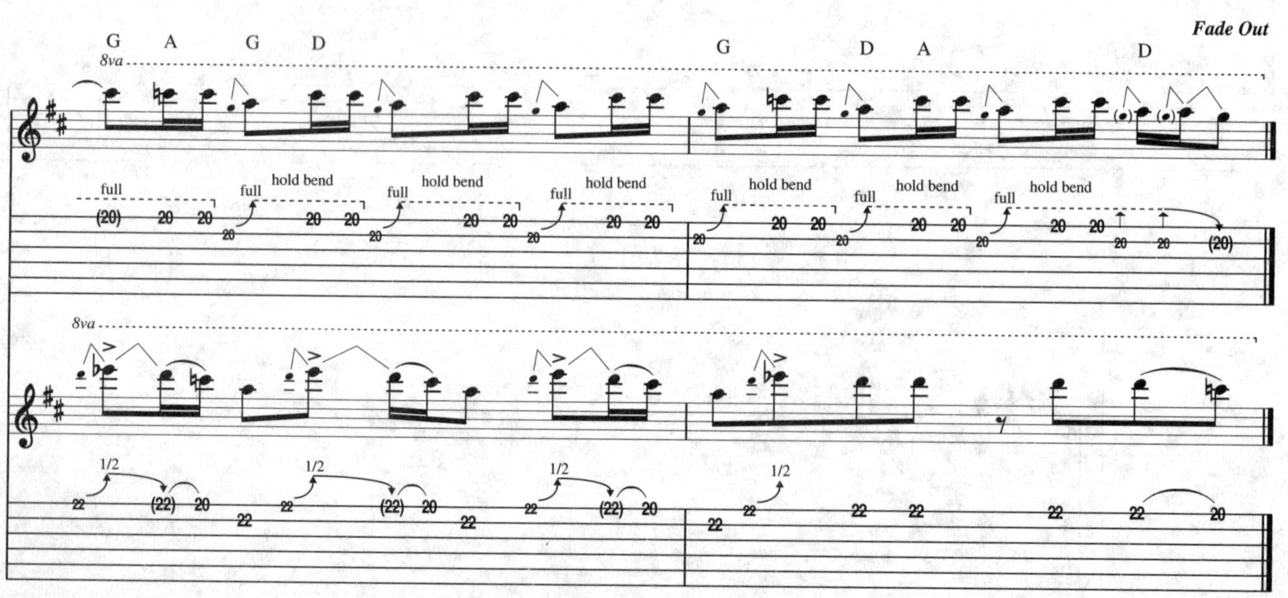

Full House

By John L. (Wes) Montgomery

A♭maj9
Gm9
Fm9
Gm9
A♭maj9
1.
Fm9
2.
Fm9
C
B♭m9
E♭13
A♭maj9
D♭7
G♭maj9
C♭maj9
Gmin7♭5
C7♭9(♯11)
D
Fm9
Gm9
A♭maj7
Gm9
Fm9
Gm9
Fm9
C7♯9
Fm9
Gm9
A♭maj9
Gm9
Fm9
Gm9
Fm9
To Coda

E Guitar Solo
Fm9
B♭13♯11
Fm9
B♭13♯11
Fm9
B♭13♯11
D♭9
C7♯9
Fm9
B♭13♯11
Fm9
B♭13♯11
Fm9
B♭13♯11
D♭7
C7♯9
Fm9
B♭13♯11
Fm9
B♭13♯11
Fm9
B♭13♯11
D♭11
C7♭9
Fm9
B♭13
Fm9
B♭13♯11
Fm9

Bb13
Db13
C7#9
Fm9
Bbm9
Eb13b9
Abmaj9
Db9
Gbmaj7
Cbmaj9
Gm7b5
C7#9
Fm9
Bb13
Fm9
Bb13#11
Fm9
Bb13#11
Db13
C7#9
Fm9
Bb13#11
Fm9
Bb13
Fm9
Bb13#11
Db7
C7b9
Fm9
Bb13#11
Fm9
1/2

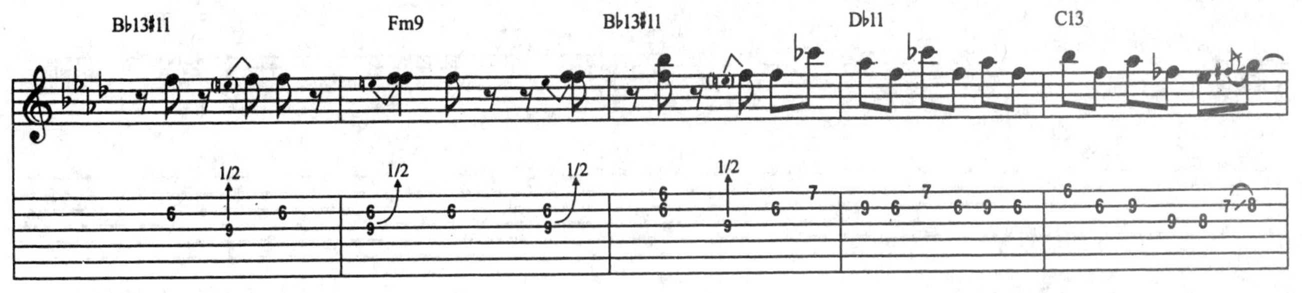
B♭13♯11
Fm9
B♭13♯11
D♭11
C13
1/2
1/2
1/2
1/2

Fm9
B♭13♯11
Fm9
B♭13
Fm9

B♭13♯11
D♭9
C7♯9
Fm9
B♭13♯11

Fm9
B♭13♯11
Fm9
B♭13♯11
D♭13

C13
Fm9
B♭13♯11
Fm9
B♭13♯11

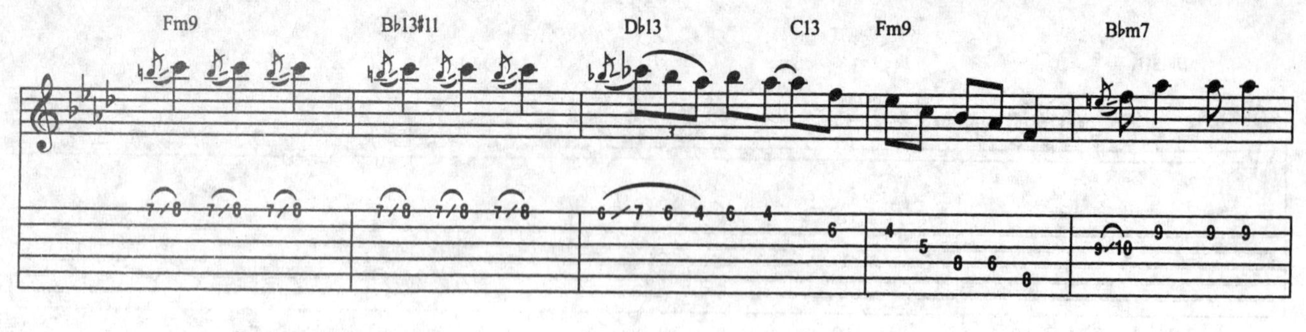
Fm9
B♭13♯11
D♭13
C13
Fm9
B♭m7

E♭7♭9
A♭maj7
D♭9
G♭maj7
C♭maj7

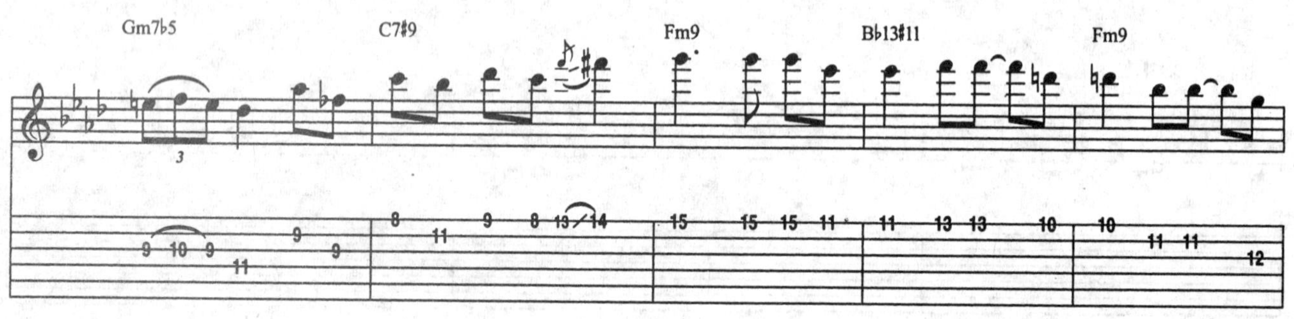
Gm7♭5
C7♯9
Fm9
B♭13♯11
Fm9

B♭13♯11
Fm9
B♭13♯11
D♭13
C13

Fm9
B♭13♯11
Fm9
B♭13♯11
Fm9

B♭13
D♭13
C13♯9
Fm9
B♭13♯11

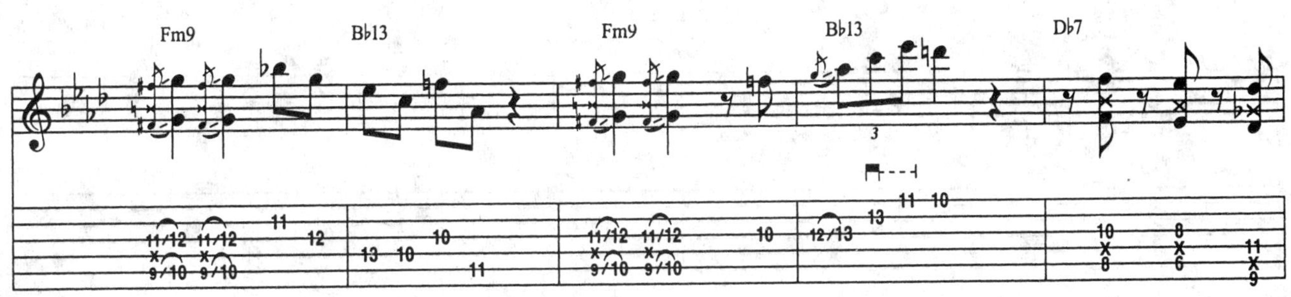
Fm9
B♭13
Fm9
B♭13
D♭7

C7
Fm9
B♭13
Fm9
B♭13

Fm9
B♭13
D♭13
C7
Fm9

B♭13♯11
Fm9
B♭13
Fm9
B♭13♯11

D♭13 C7♭13 Fm9 B♭13♯11 Fm9

B♭13♯11 Fm9 B♭13♯11 D♭9 C7♯9 Fm9

B♭m9 E♭13♭9 A♭maj9 D♭9 G♭maj7

C♭maj7 Gm7♭5 C7♯9 Fm9 B♭13♯11

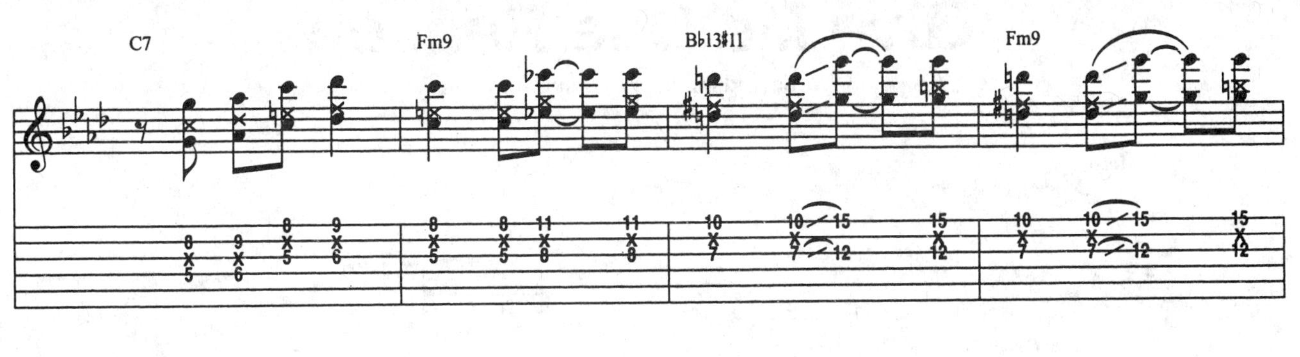
C7
Fm9
B♭13♯11
Fm9

B♭13♯11
Fm9
B♭13♯11
D♭9
C7♯9

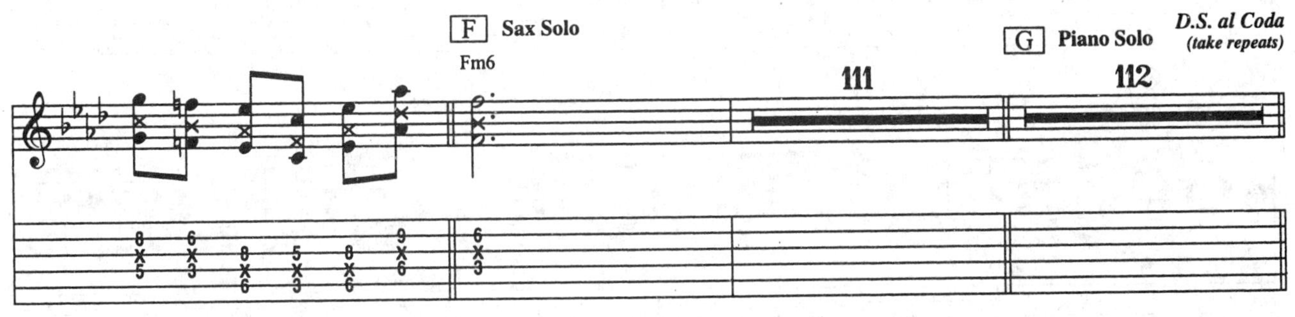
F Sax Solo
Fm6
111
G Piano Solo
D.S. al Coda
(take repeats)
112

Coda
H Outro
Fm9

1.
2.
16

Give Me One Reason

Words and Music by Tracy Chapman

Verse
band enters
Gtr. 1: w/ Rhy. Fig. 1
F♯
B
C♯
F♯
2. Ba - by, I got your num - ber,
oh,
and I know that a you got
mine.
Gtr. 2 (dist.)
mf
B
You know that I called you,
C♯
I call too man - y times.
F♯
C♯
You can call me, ba - by, you can
full
1/2
* Played ahead of the beat.
B
F♯
call me an - y - time.
You got to call me.
1/2
1/4

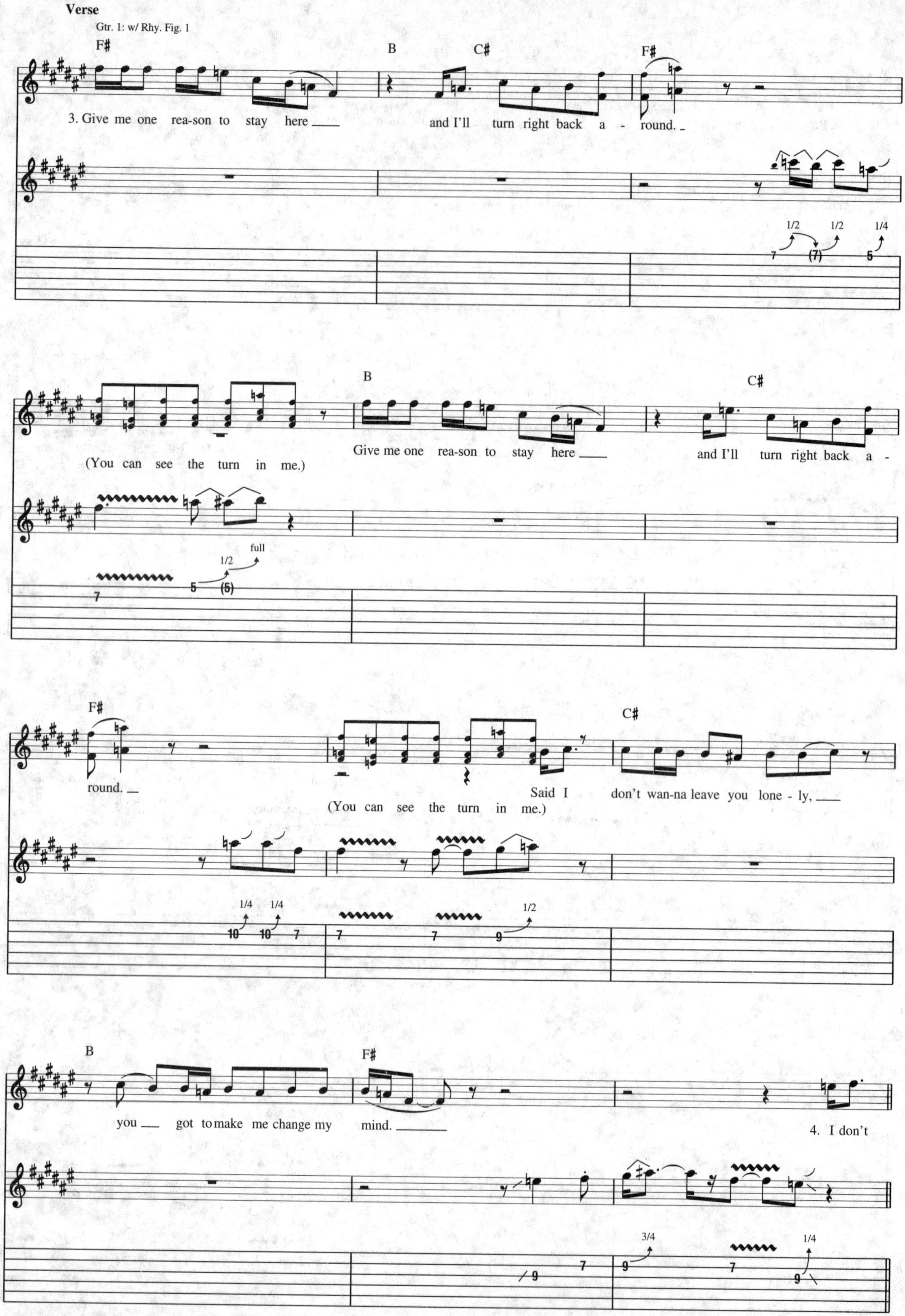

Verse

Gtr. 1: w/ Rhy. Fig. 1

F♯ B C♯ F♯

3. Give me one rea-son to stay here ___ and I'll turn right back a - round. _

1/2 1/2 1/4

7 (7) 5

B C♯

(You can see the turn in me.) Give me one rea-son to stay here ___ and I'll turn right back a -

1/2 full

7 5 (5)

F♯ C♯

round. _ (You can see the turn in me.) Said I don't wan-na leave you lone - ly, ___

1/4 1/4 1/2

10 10 7 7 7 9

Verse
Gtr. 1: w/ Rhy. Fig. 1
F♯
B
C♯
F♯
want no one to squeeze me,
they might take a - way my
life.
hold bend
let ring
full
12
B
C♯
I don't want no one to squeeze me,
they might take a - way my
let ring
full
12
12
(12)
10
12
10
11
* Played behind the beat.
F♯
C♯
life.
I just want some - one to hold me,
9
11
9
8
B
F♯
oh, and rock me through the night.
1/2
1/4
(8)
6
4
4
4
4
2
4
4
6
5
7
7

Guitar Solo
Gtr. 1: w/ Rhy. Fig. 1
F♯
B
C♯
F♯
1/4
full
full
1/4
1/4
B
C♯
F♯
full
1/2
1/2
1/2
1/4
1/4
1/2
C♯
B
F♯
hold bend
full
full
1/4
Verse
Gtr. 1: w/ Rhy. Fig. 1
F♯
B
C♯
F♯
5. This youth-ful heart can love you, yes, and give you what you need.
B
C♯
F♯
I said this youth-ful heart can love you, ho, and give you what you need.

C♯
C♯7 B7
F♯
But I'm too old to go chas-in' you a-round, wast-in' my pre-cious en-er-gy.
1/4
Verse
Gtr. 1: w/ Rhy. Fig. 1
F♯
B
C♯
6. Give me one rea-son to stay here, yes, now turn right back a-round.
(A - round.
You can see the turn in me.)
1/4
F♯
B
Give me one rea-son to stay here
full
1/2
1/2
full
C♯
F♯
oh, I'll turn right back a - round.
Said I
(You can see the turn in me.)
full
Gtr. 2 tacet
C♯
B
don't wan-na leave you lone - ly, you got to make me change my

F#
mind.
Verse
Gtr. 1: w/ Rhy. Fig. 1, 1st 8 meas.
F#
7. Ba-by, just give me one rea - son,
Gtr. 2
full
full
1/4
1/2
B
C#
F#
B
oh, give me just one rea-son why.
Ba-by, just give me one rea - son,
1/2
1/2
C#
F#
oh, give me just one rea - son why, I should stay.
Said I
1/4
1/2
C#
B
rit.
told you that I loved you,
and there ain't no more to say.
Gtr. 2
1/2
rit.
Gtr. 1
rit.

Gloria

Words and Music by Van Morrison

Em D A E Em D A E Em D A E Em D A E
L, O, R, I.
Chorus
Gtr. 1: w/ Rhy. Fig. 1, 2 times, simile
Em D A E Em D A E Em D A E Em D A E
G, L, O, R, I, A. G, L, O, R, I, A.
(Glo - ri - a.
Em D A E Em D A E Em D A E
Glo - ri - a. I'm gon - na shout it all night. Glo - ri - a.
To Coda
Em D A E Em D A E Em D A E
I'm gon - na shout it ev - 'ry day. Yeah, yeah, yeah, yeah, yeah, yeah, yeah.
Glo - ri - a.)
Interlude
Gtr. 1
Em D A E Em D A E D A D E D A D
f
E D A D E D A D E D A D E D A D
E D A E D A E D A E D A
mf

Verse
E
2. She comes a-round here. Just a-bout mid-night.
Rhy. Fig. 2
End Rhy. Fig. 2
mp
p
Gtr. 1: w/ Rhy. Fig. 2, 8 times
Ha, she make me feel so good, Lord. I wan-na say she make me feel al-right.
Comes walk-in' down my street. Watch her come up to my house.
You knock up-on my door. And then she comes to my room.
D.S. al Coda
Then she make me feel al-right. G, L, O, R, I, A.
Coda
Gtr. 1: w/ Rhy. Fig. 1, 1 1/2 times, simile
E Em D A E Em D A E Em D A E
yeah, yeah, yeah, so good. Al-right. Just so good.
(Glo-ri-a.
Em D A E Em D A E Em D A E Em D A E
Al-right. Yeah.
Glo-ri-a.)
Outro
E D A D E D A D E D A D E
Gtr. 1

Godzilla

Words and Music by Donald Roeser

F♯5 B5 C♯5 G♯5 A5 D♯5 E5 B5^VII E5 open E7sus4 F♯7sus4

134 134 134 4fr 134 4fr 134 5fr 134 6fr 134 7fr 134 7fr 23 111

Intro

Moderately ♩ = 90

Gtr. 1: w/ Rhy. Fig. 1, 2 times, simile

F♯5 B5 C♯5 G♯5 A5 D♯5 E5 B5^VII F♯5 B5 C♯5 G♯5 A5 D♯5 E5 B5^VII

Rhy. Fig. 1 **End Rhy. Fig. 1**

*Gtr. 1 (dist.)

w/ panned delay

mf

Gtr. 2 (dist.)

Riff A

mf

full 12 (12) (12) full 12 (12)

Gtr. 3 (dist.)

Riff A1

mf

full 9 (9) (9) full 9 (9)

*Two gtrs. arr. for one.

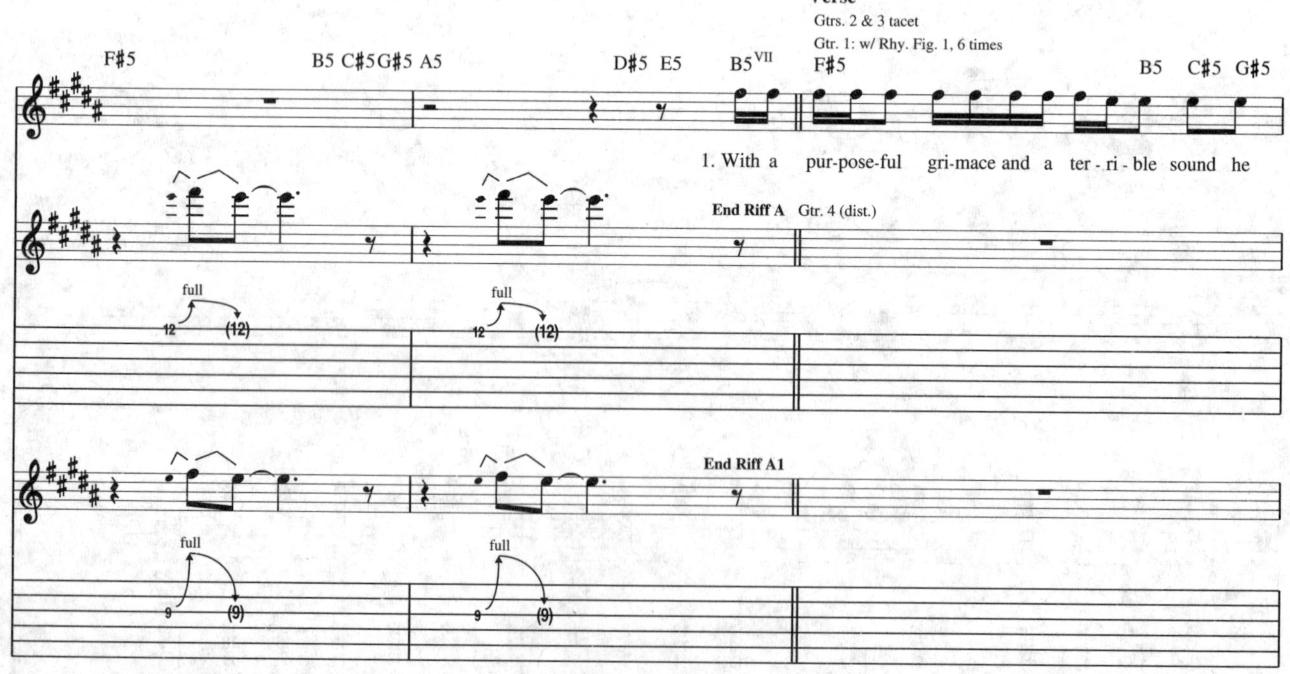

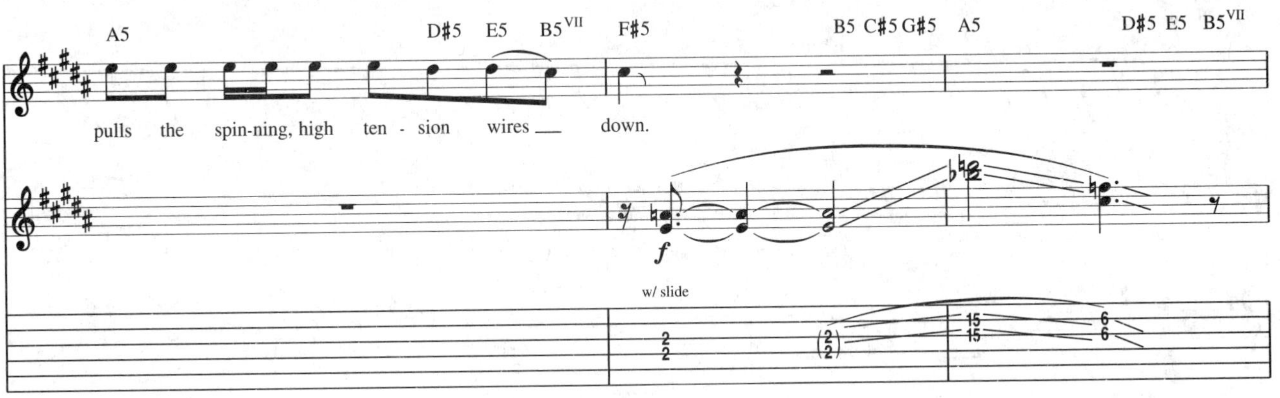
A5
D♯5 E5 B5VII
F♯5
B5 C♯5 G♯5 A5
D♯5 E5 B5VII
pulls the spin-ning, high ten - sion wires down.
f
w/ slide

F♯5
B5 C♯5 G♯5 A5
D♯5 E5 B5VII
F♯5
B5 C♯5 G♯5
Help-less peo-ple on sub-way trains scream bug-eyed as he looks in on them.
w/ o slide
full
full
hold bend

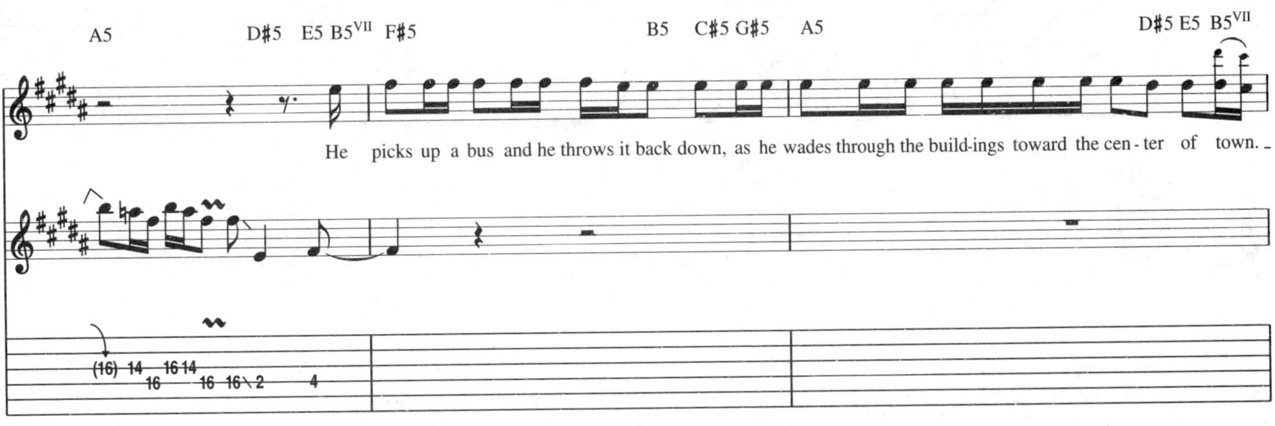
A5
D♯5 E5 B5VII
F♯5
B5 C♯5 G♯5 A5
D♯5 E5 B5VII
He picks up a bus and he throws it back down, as he wades through the build-ings toward the cen - ter of town.

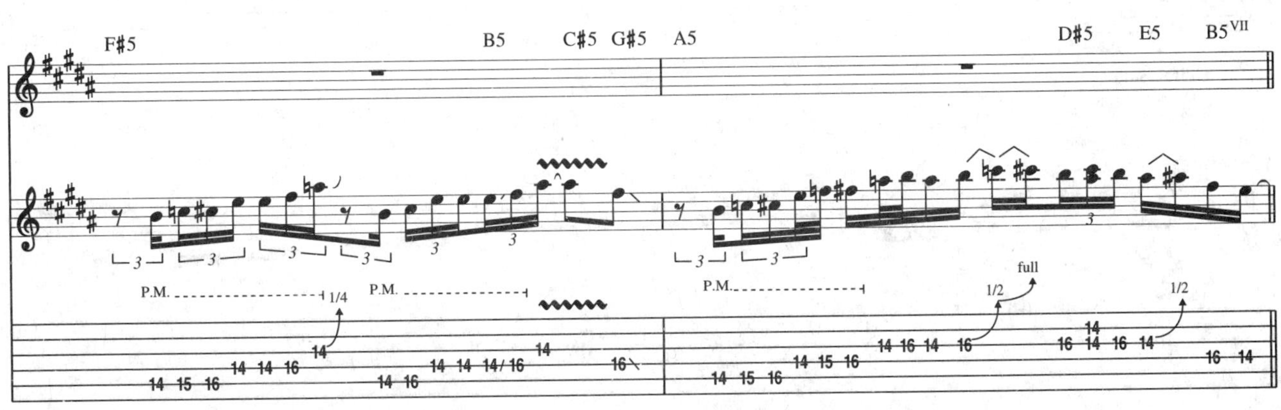
F♯5
B5 C♯5 G♯5 A5
D♯5 E5 B5VII
P.M.
1/4
P.M.
P.M.
full
1/2
1/2

Chorus
E5open
E7sus4
F#5
F#7sus4
Gtr. 1
Oh, no, they say he's got to go. Go, go God - zil-la. Whoo.
full
P.M.
1/2
hold bend
Oh, no there goes To-kyo. Go, go God -
zil - la. Whoo.
Guitar Solo
Gtr. 1: w/ Rhy. Fig. 1, 4 times
B5
C#5
G#5
A5
D#5
E5
B5VII
8va
loco

F#5
B5
C#5 G#5
A5
D#5
E5
B5VII
full
G#5
Chorus
E5open
E7sus4
F#5
F#7sus4
Gtr. 1
Oh no, they say he's got to go. Go, go God - zil-la. Whoo.
8va
loco
1 1/2
P.M.
Oh no, there goes To-kyo. Go, go God -

F#5
F#7sus4 F#5
F#7sus4 F#5
F#7sus4 F#5
Interlude
E
2fr
F#
4fr
zil - la.
Whoo.
full
1/2
Gtrs. 1 & 4 tacet
w/ Vocal ad Lib.
N.C. (F#7)
8
Gtr. 1
E5
Oh
1/2
1/4
(cont. in slash)
Chorus
Gtr. 1
E5open
E7sus4 E5open
E7sus4
E5open
E7sus4 E5open
E7sus4
F#5
F#7sus4 F#5
F#7sus4
no,
they
say
he's got
to go.
Go,
go God
-
zil-la.
Whoo.
Gtr. 4
full
F#5
F#7sus4
F#5
F#7sus4
E5open
E7sus4
E5open
E7sus4
Oh
no,

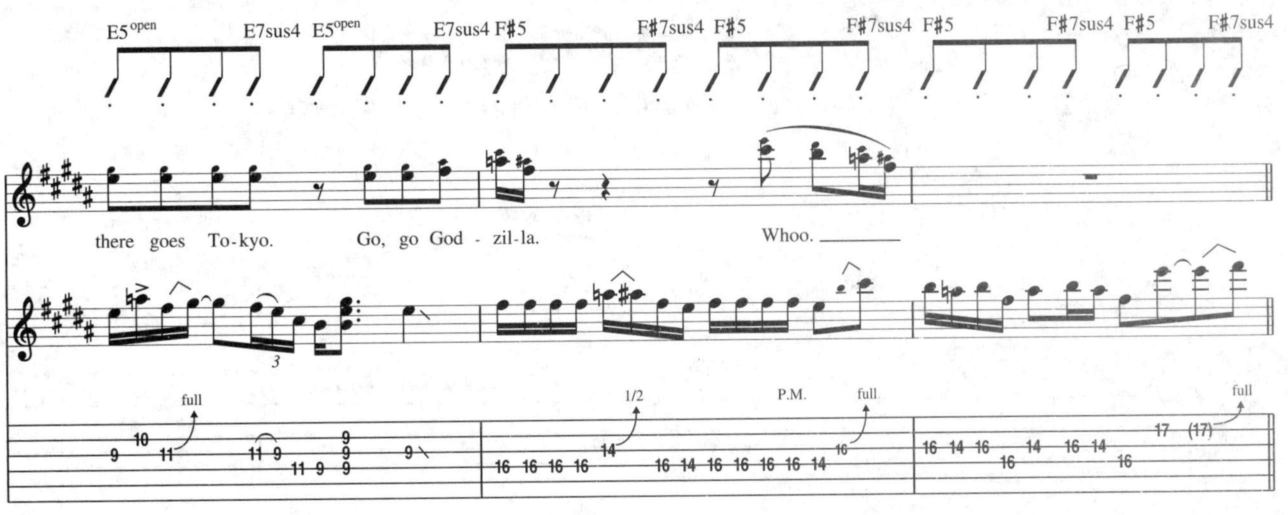
E5open E7sus4 E5open E7sus4 F#5 F#7sus4 F#5 F#7sus4 F#5 F#7sus4 F#5 F#7sus4
there goes To-kyo. Go, go God - zil-la. Whoo.
full
1/2
P.M.
full
full

Outro

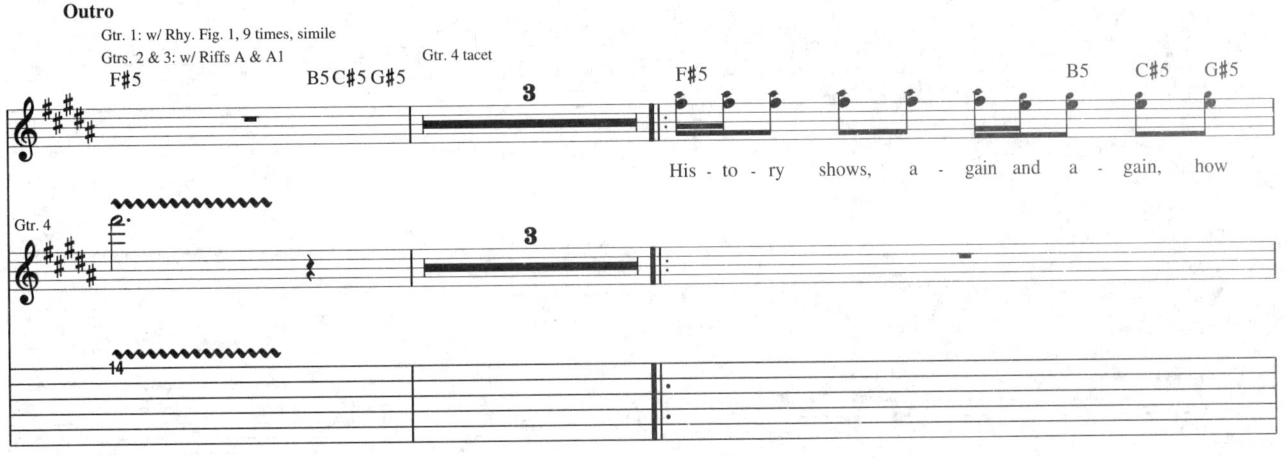
Gtr. 1: w/ Rhy. Fig. 1, 9 times, simile
Gtrs. 2 & 3: w/ Riffs A & A1
Gtr. 4 tacet
F#5 B5 C#5 G#5 F#5 B5 C#5 G#5
His - to - ry shows, a - gain and a - gain, how
Gtr. 4

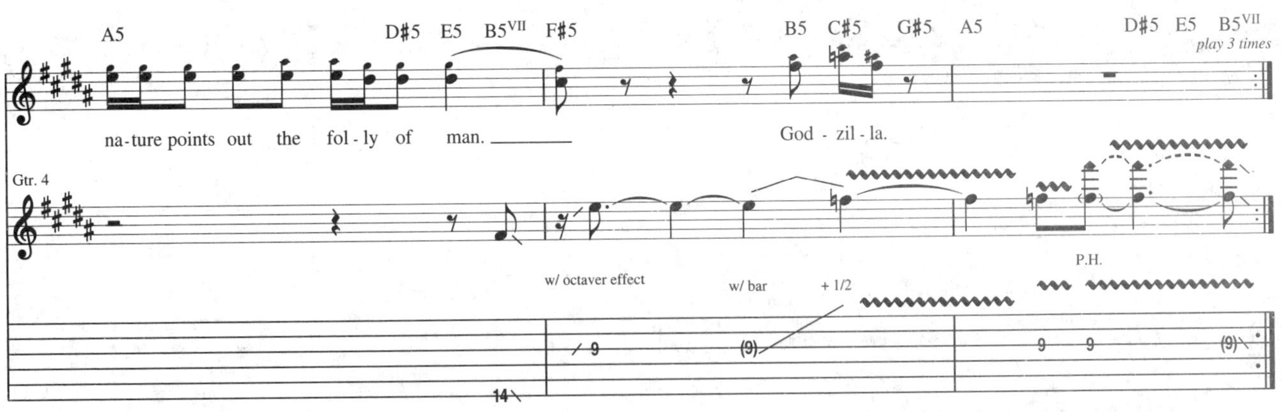
A5 D#5 E5 B5VII F#5 B5 C#5 G#5 A5 D#5 E5 B5VII
play 3 times
na-ture points out the fol - ly of man. God - zil - la.
Gtr. 4
w/ octaver effect
w/ bar
+ 1/2
P.H.

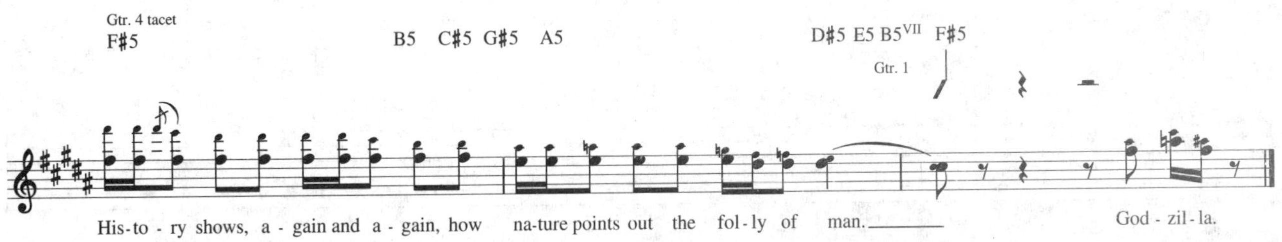
Gtr. 4 tacet
F#5 B5 C#5 G#5 A5 D#5 E5 B5VII F#5
Gtr. 1
His-to - ry shows, a - gain and a - gain, how na-ture points out the fol-ly of man. God - zil - la.

Green-Eyed Lady

Words and Music by Jerry Corbetta, J.C. Phillips and David Riordan

* Two gtrs. arr. for one.

** Key signature denotes E Dorian.

*** Keyboard arr. for gtr.

† Chord symbols reflect overall tonality.

† Delay set for quarter-note triplet regeneration with multiple repeats.

Am7/E
Em7
Stroll - ing slow - ly to - wards the sun.
Rules the night, the waves, the sand.
End Riff A
Gtr. 1: w/ Riff A, 3 times
A7/E
Green-eyed la - dy, o - cean la - dy.
Sooth - ing
Child of na -
ev - 'ry rag - ing wave that comes.
- ture, friend of man.
Green - eyed la - dy pas - sions la - dy.
Dressed in love, she lives for life to be.
Green-eyed la - dy feels life, I nev - er see
set - ting suns and lone - ly lov - ers free.
To Coda
Em9(maj7)
Gtr. 1
Organ Solo
F#m7
Gmaj7
w/ clean tone
simile on repeats

1.- 4.
5.
Guitar Solo
N.C.(Em7)
F♯m7
Gmaj7
F♯m7
w/ slight dist.
full
(B/E)
(B7/E)
8va
full
full
full
Interlude
Em(maj7)
loco
N.C.
Am7/E
Em7
D.S. al Coda
Coda
Outro
Gtr. 1: w/ Riff A, 1 1/4 times
Begin Fade
Em7
Fade Out
6

Hair of the Dog

Words and Music by Dan McCafferty, Darrell Sweet, Pete Agnew and Manuel Charlton

Gtr. 2
Gtr. 1: w/ Riff A, simile
P.M.
1/4
(cont. in slash)
Chorus
E5
G5
A5
E5
D5
E5
Rhy. Fig. 1A
End Rhy. Fig. 1A
Gtr. 2
mf
Now you're mess-in' with a...
Now you're mess-in' with a son of a bitch.
Voc. Fig. 1
End Voc. Fig. 1
(A son of a bitch.)
Gtr. 1
Rhy. Fig. 1
End Rhy. Fig. 1
simile on repeats
3rd time, To Coda
Bkgd. Voc.: w/ Voc. Fig. 1
E5
G5
A5
E5
D5
E5
E
7fr
Now you're mess-in' with a...
Now you're mess-in' with a son of a bitch.
let ring
Interlude
Gtrs. 1 & 2: w/ Riff A, simile
E5
Gtrs. 1 & 2
(cont. in notation)
Bop, bop, bop, bop, ba, bu, ba, bu, ba, bu, bow.
Gtr. 3 (fuzz)
Riff B
End Riff B
mf
w/ talk box
P.M.
P.M.
P.M.
P.M.

Gtr. 3: w/ Riff B
Gtr. 3: w/ Riff B, 8 times
Gtr. 4: w/ Riff C, 2nd time
E5
G5
A5
E5
Gtrs. 1 & 2
D.S. al Coda
Gtrs. 1 & 2: w/ Riff A
G5
A5
E5
D5
C5
B5
4
Coda
Outro
Gtrs. 1 & 2: w/ Rhy. Fig. 1, till fade
Gtr. 3: w/ Riff B, till fade, simile
Bkgd. Voc.: w/ Voc. Fig. 1
E5
G5
A5
Now you're mess - in' with a...
Gtr. 5 (clean)
Rhy. Fig. 2
End Rhy. Fig. 2
p
Gtr. 5: w/ Rhy. Fig. 2, till fade
E5
D5
E5
E5
G5
Now you're mess - in' with a son of a bitch.
(Spoken: Son of a bitch.)
Now you're mess - in' with a...
Play 4 Times & Fade
Bkgd. Voc.: w/ Voc. Fig. 1
A5
E5
D5
E5
Now you're mess - in' with a son of a bitch.
Riff C
Gtr. 4 (dist.)
play 4 times
mp
w/ wah-wah

Heartache Tonight

Words and Music by John David Souther, Don Henley, Glenn Frey and Bob Seger

E5
F#5 G5
B5 C5
F#5 G5
C#5
Ev - 'ry - bod - y wants to take a lit - tle chance,
make it come out right.

Chorus

Gtr. 3: w/ Fill 1, 2nd time
D5
C7
There's gon - na be a heart - ache to - night, a heart - ache to - night I know
Gtr. 3 (dist.)
mf w/ slide
Gtrs. 1 & 2
Rhy. Fig. 1
slight P.M.

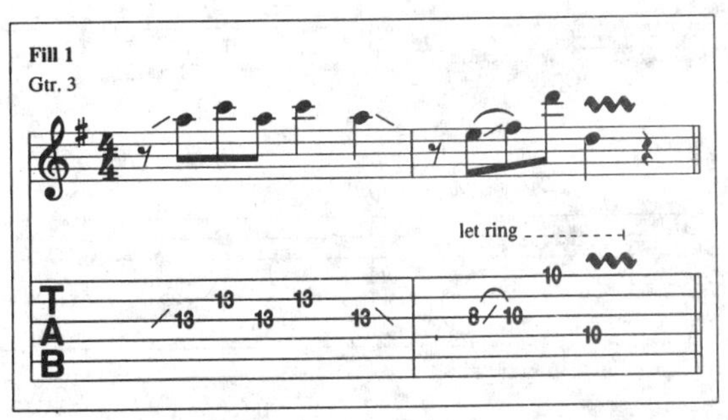
Fill 1
Gtr. 3
let ring

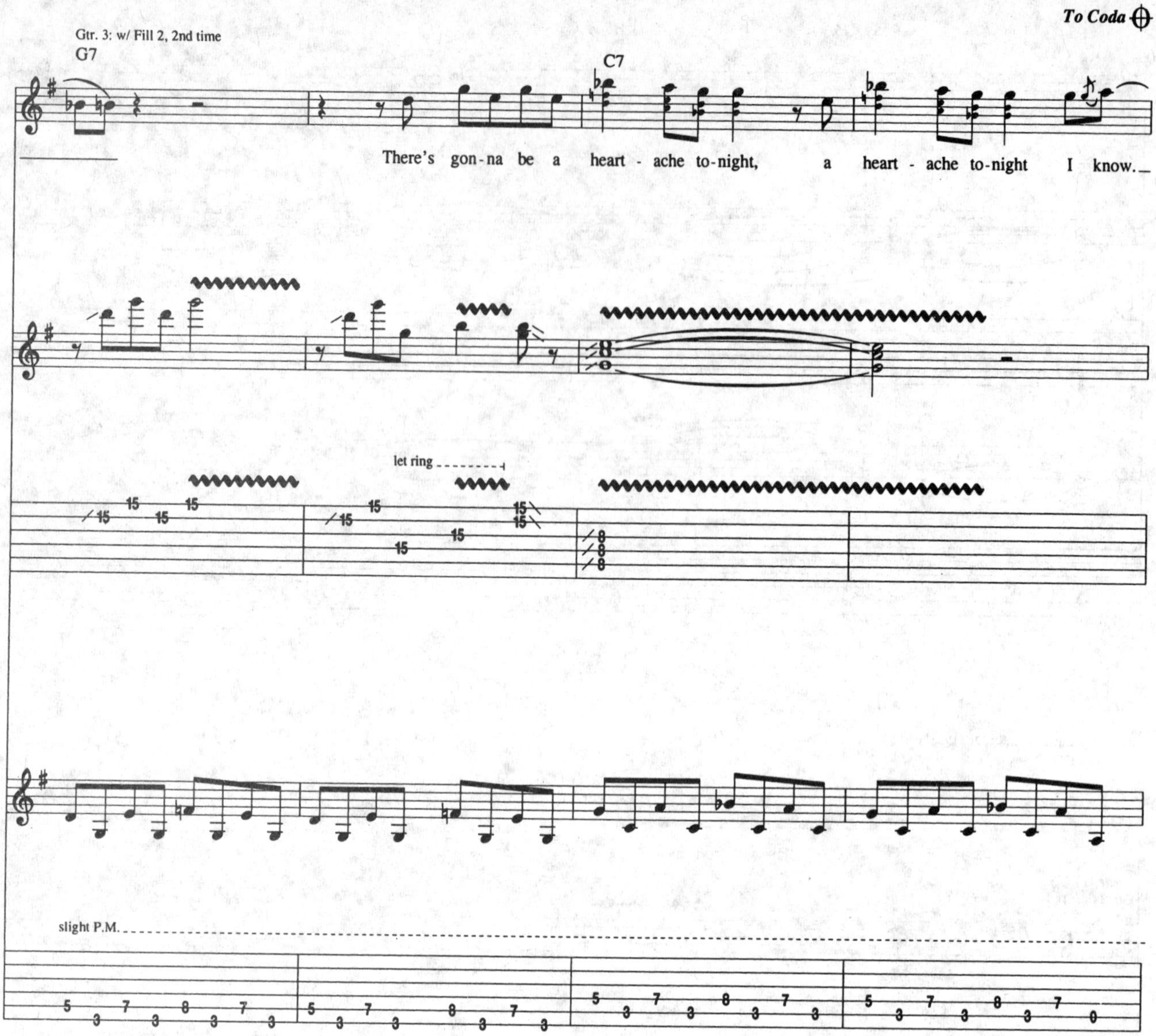

To Coda ⊕

Gtr. 3: w/ Fill 2, 2nd time

G7 C7

There's gon-na be a heart - ache to-night, a heart - ache to-night I know.

let ring

slight P.M.

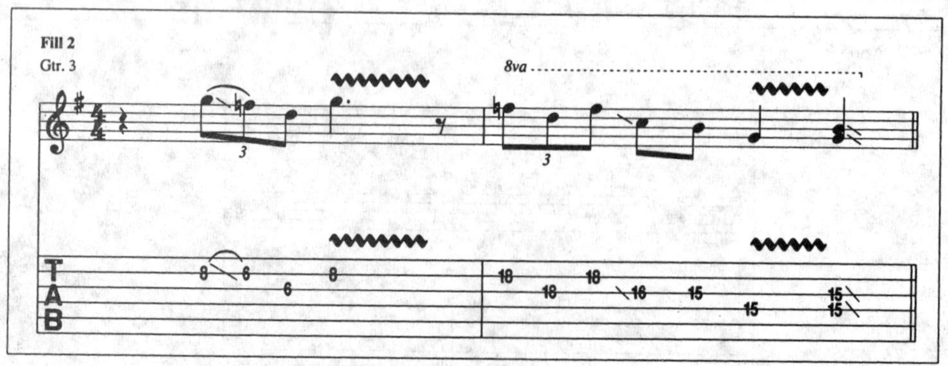

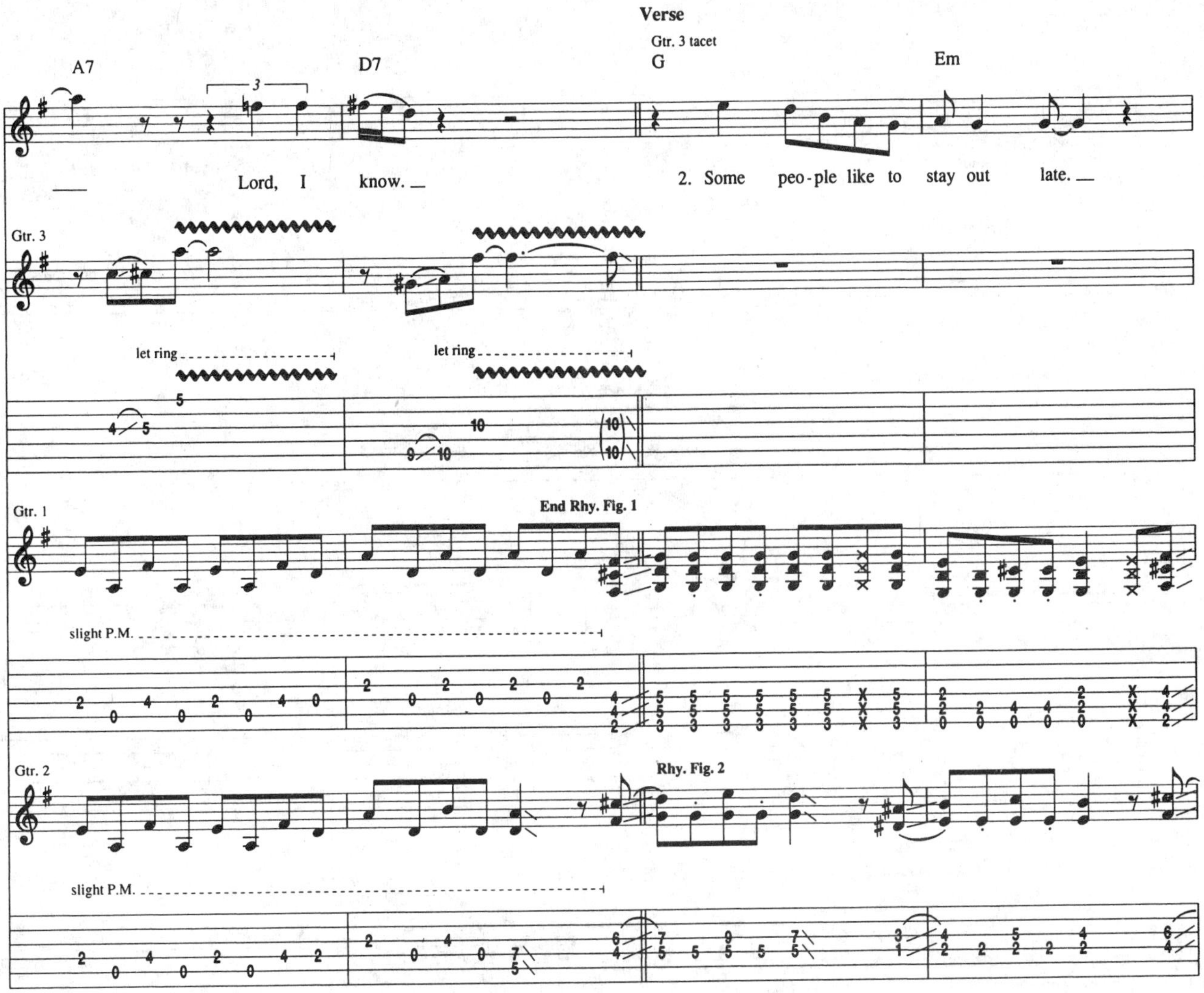
Verse
Gtr. 3 tacet
A7
D7
G
Em
Lord, I know.
2. Some peo-ple like to stay out late.
Gtr. 3
let ring
let ring
Gtr. 1
End Rhy. Fig. 1
slight P.M.
Gtr. 2
Rhy. Fig. 2
slight P.M.

G
Em
G
C
Some folks can't hold out that long.
But no - bod - y wants to go home now;
Gtr. 1
Gtr. 2

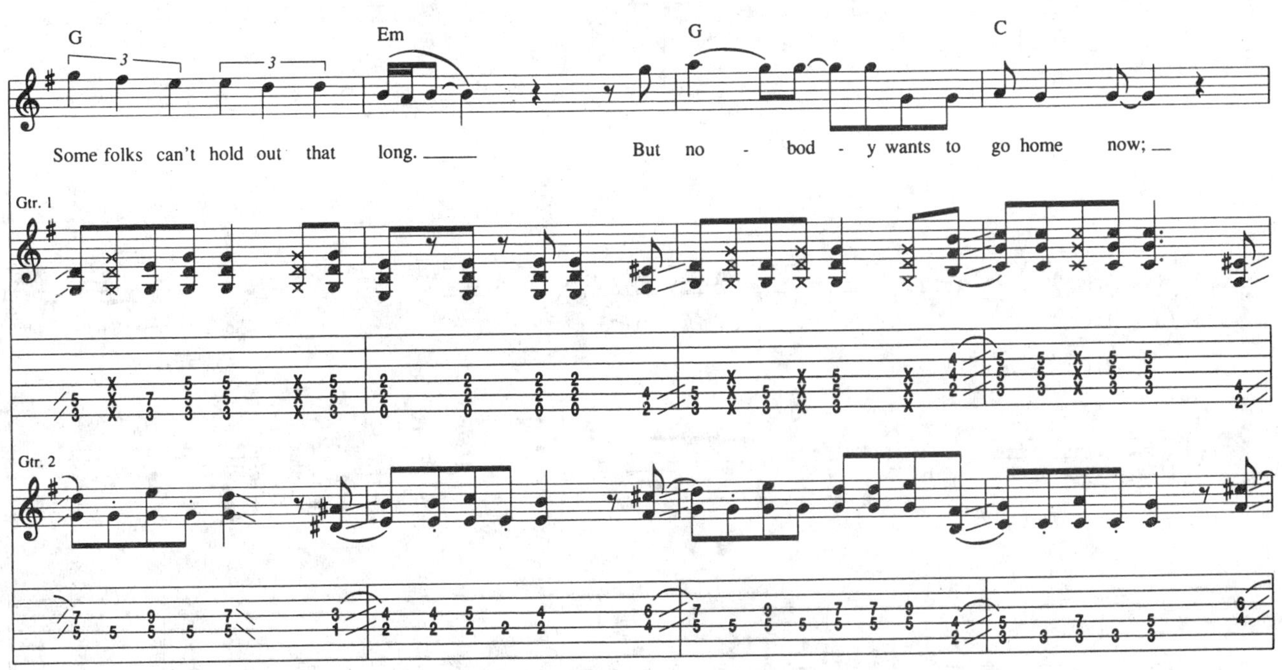

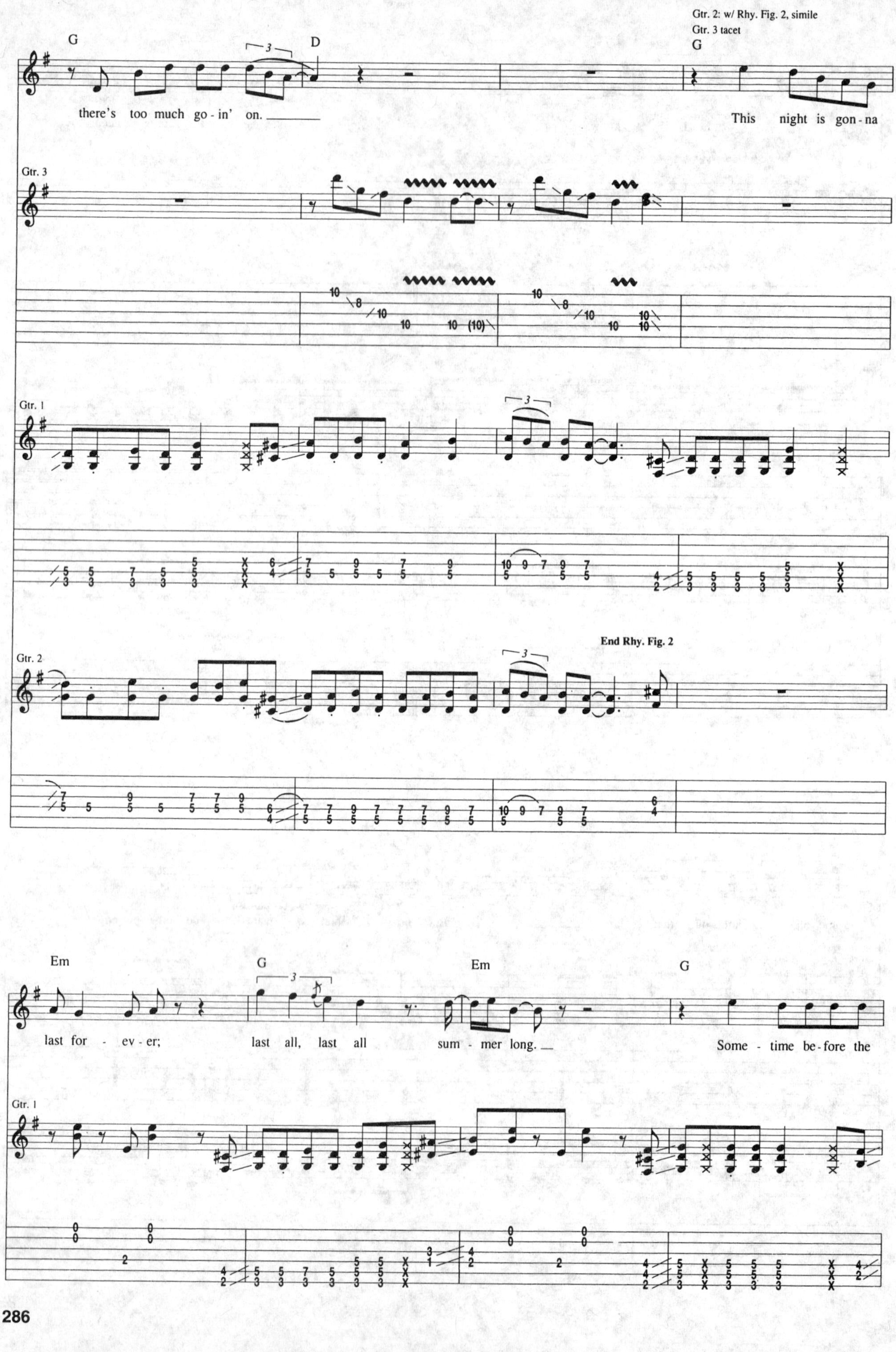

Gtr. 2: w/ Rhy. Fig. 2, simile
Gtr. 3 tacet

G D G

there's too much go - in' on. This night is gon - na

Gtr. 3

Gtr. 1

End Rhy. Fig. 2

Gtr. 2

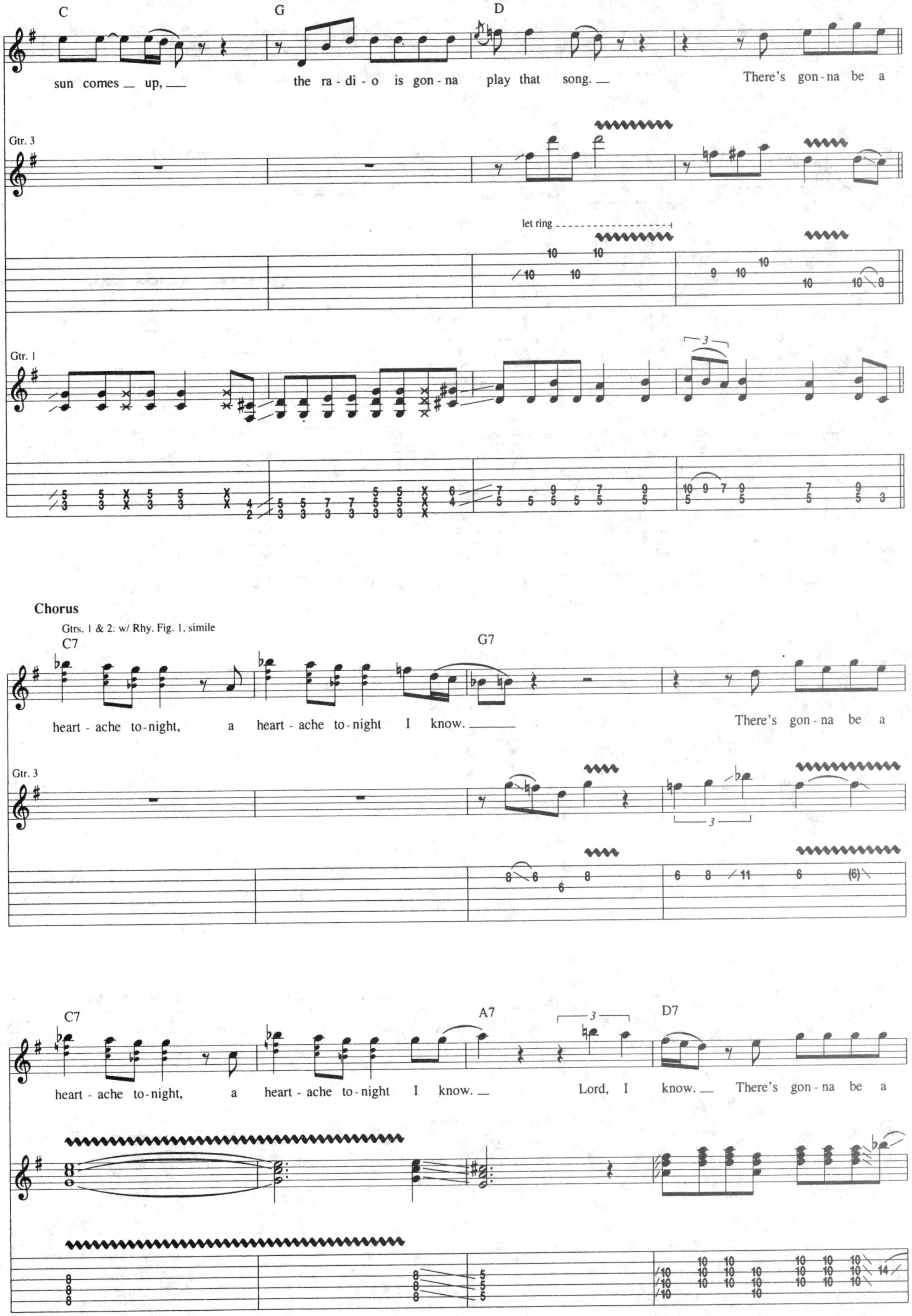

C G D

sun comes up, the ra-di-o is gon-na play that song. There's gon-na be a

Gtr. 3

let ring

Gtr. 1

G G7 C C#°

heart - ache to-night, the moon's shin - ing bright so turn out the light, _ and we'll get it right._ There's gon - na be a

Gtr. 3

8va

loco

let ring

Gtrs. 1 & 2

G D G

heart - ache to - night, _ a heart - ache to-night I know. _ *Spoken: Heartache, baby.*

let ring

Guitar Solo
Bb F
C
G
grad. slide
Rhy. Fig. 3
D.S. al Coda
8va
loco
End Rhy. Fig. 3
Coda
A7
D7
Let's go.
We can beat a - round the bush - es we can
Gtr. 3
let ring
Gtrs. 1 & 2

G7 C C#°

get down to the bone. We can leave it in the par - king lot, but ei - ther way there's gon - na be a

8va loco

G D G C

heart - ache to - night, ___ a heart - ache to - night I know. ___ Oh, I know. ___ There'll be a heart -

G
D
G
ache to - night, a heart - ache to-night I know. Woo.
Outro-Guitar Solo
Gtrs. 1 & 2: w/ Rhy. Fig. 3
B♭ F
C
G
B♭ F
C
G
Spoken: Break my heart.
Gtr. 3
8va
loco
grad. slide
grad. slide
B♭ F
C
G
8va
loco
B♭ F
C
G
Gtr. 3
Gtrs. 1 & 2
fdbk.
pitch: F♯

Heaven Beside You

Lyrics by Jerry Cantrell
Music by Jerry Cantrell and Mike Inez

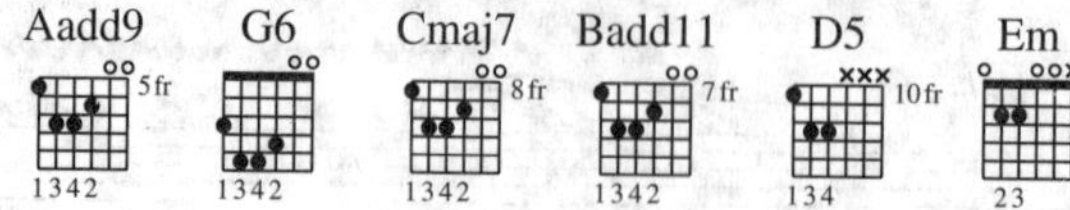

Tune Down 1/2 Step:
① = E♭ ④ = D♭
② = B♭ ⑤ = A♭
③ = G♭ ⑥ = E♭

Intro
Moderately ♩ = 110

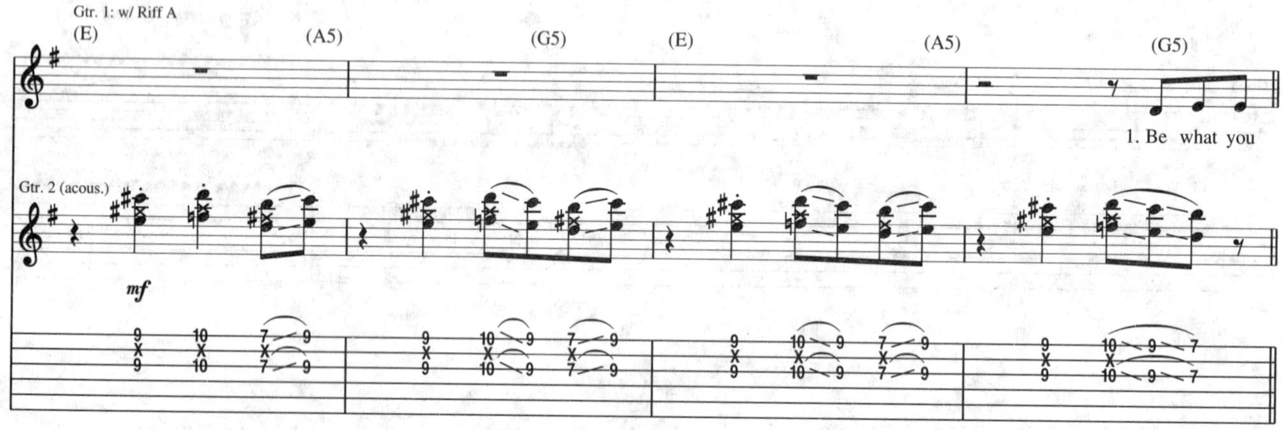

Verse

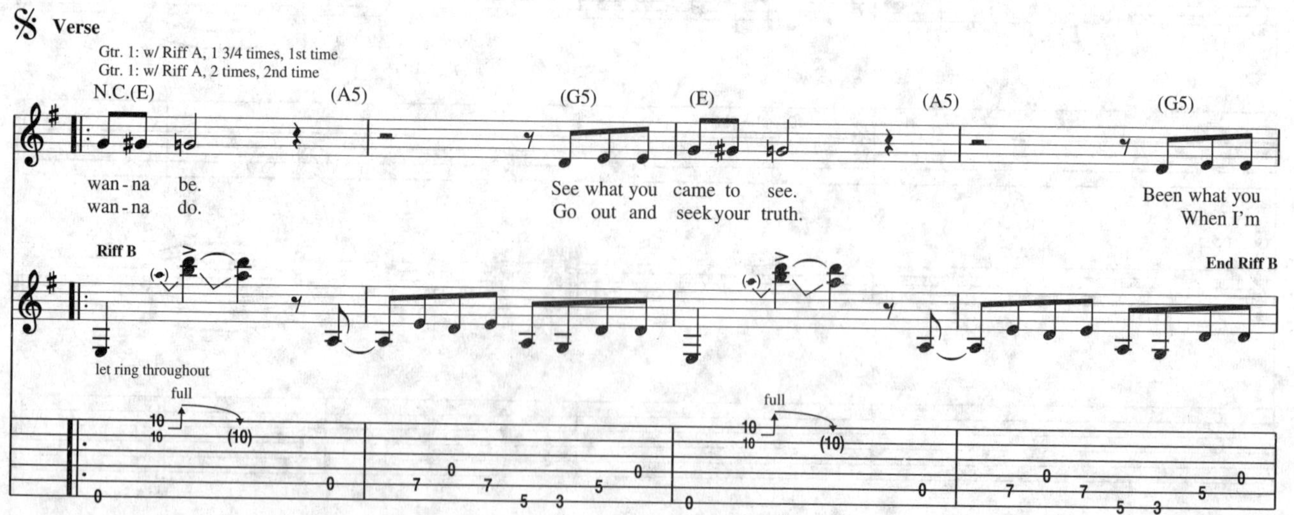

Gtr. 2: w/ Riff B, 1st 3 meas., 1st time
Gtr. 2: w/ Riff B, 2nd time
Gtrs. 1 & 2: w/ Fill 1, 1st time
(E) (A5) (G5) (E) (A5) (G5)
wan - na be. I don't like what I see.
down and blue, rath - er be me than you.
Chorus
A Aadd9 G6 Cmaj7
5fr
* Gtrs. 1 & 2
Rhy. Fig. 1
simile on repeats
Like the cold - est win - ter chill; heav - en be - side
* composite arrangement
Gtrs. 1 & 2: w/ Rhy. Fig. 1, 2 3/4 times, simile
Badd11 Aadd9 G6
End Rhy. Fig. 1
you, hell with - in. Like the cold - est win - ter chill;
Cmaj7 Badd11 Aadd9
heav - en be - side you, hell with - in. Like the
G6 Cmaj7 Badd11
cold - est win - ter will; heav - en be - side you, hell with - in.
Aadd9 G6 Cmaj7 Badd11 D5 E
open
Gtrs. 1 & 2
(cont. in notation)
And you think wish know you have had have it still; heav - en in - side you.
Fill 1
Gtrs. 1 & 2
T
A
B

Bridge
G♯ A B♭ B
So, there's prob - lems in your life. That's fucked up, and I'm not blind.
3rd time: but you're not blind.
Gtr. 1
Riff C
End Riff C
Gtr. 2
Rhy. Fig. 2
End Rhy. Fig. 2
Gtr. 1: w/ Riff C
Gtr. 2: w/ Rhy. Fig. 2
G♯ A B♭
Gtr. 2: w/ Rhy. Fill 1
B
I'm just see through fad - ed, su - per jad - ed, out of my
You're just see through fad - ed, o - ver - rat - ed, out of your
To Coda 1
To Coda 2
Interlude
Em N.C. (G) (F♯+) Em N.C.
mind.
mind.
Gtrs. 1 & 2
Riff D
End Riff D
1/2
Rhy. Fill 1
Gtr. 2
T
A
B

(G)
(F#+)
Em
N.C.
1/2
N.C.
Interlude
Gtr. 1: w/ Riff A, 2 times
N.C.(E)
(A5)
Gtr. 2
(G5)
(E)
D.S. al Coda 1
3. Do what you
Coda 1
Guitar Solo
Gtr. 2: w/ Riff D, 7 times
Gtr. 1

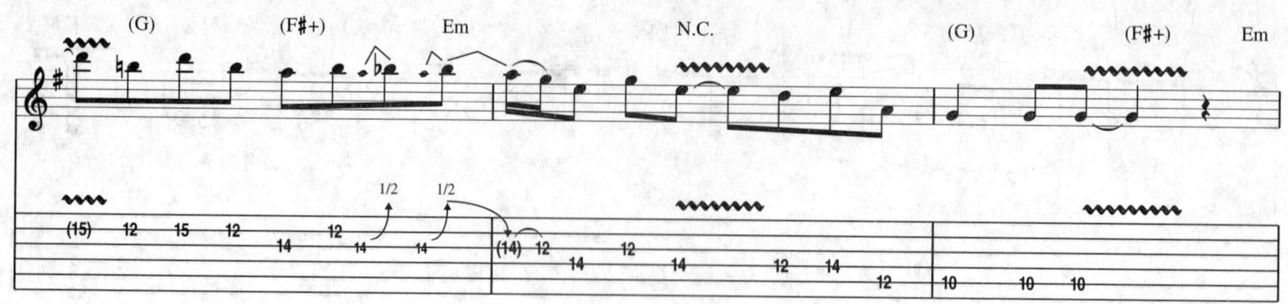
(G)
(F#+)
Em
N.C.
(G)
(F#+)
Em
1/2
1/2

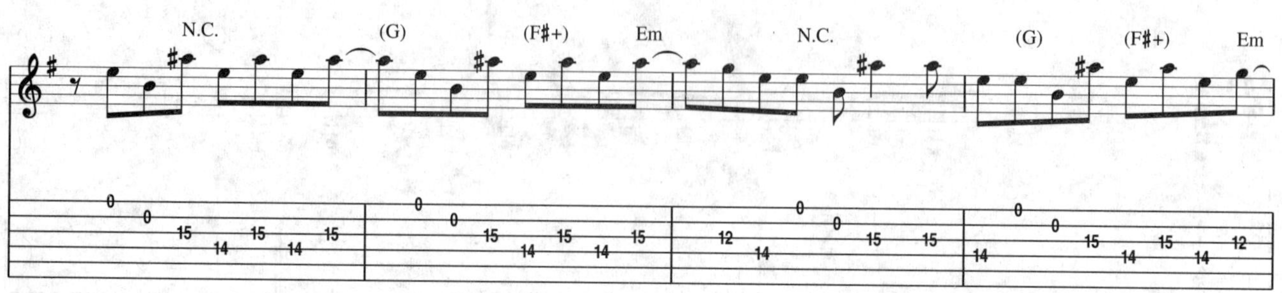
N.C.
(G)
(F#+)
Em
N.C.
(G)
(F#+)
Em

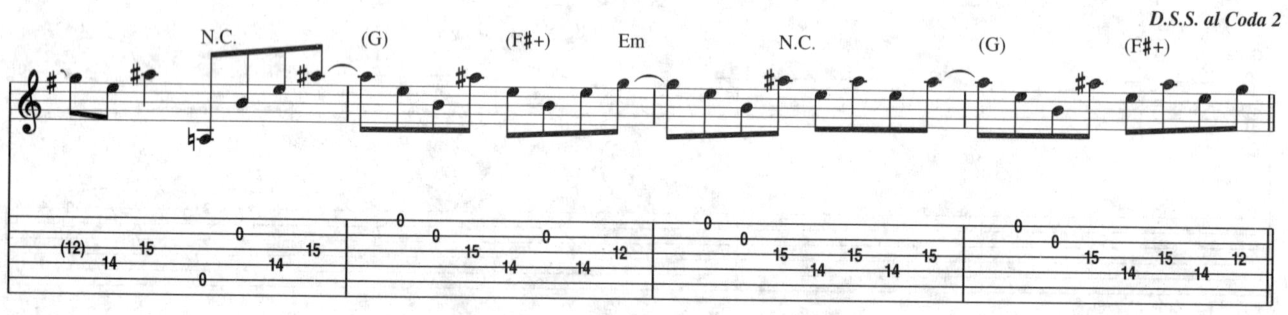
D.S.S. al Coda 2
N.C.
(G)
(F#+)
Em
N.C.
(G)
(F#+)

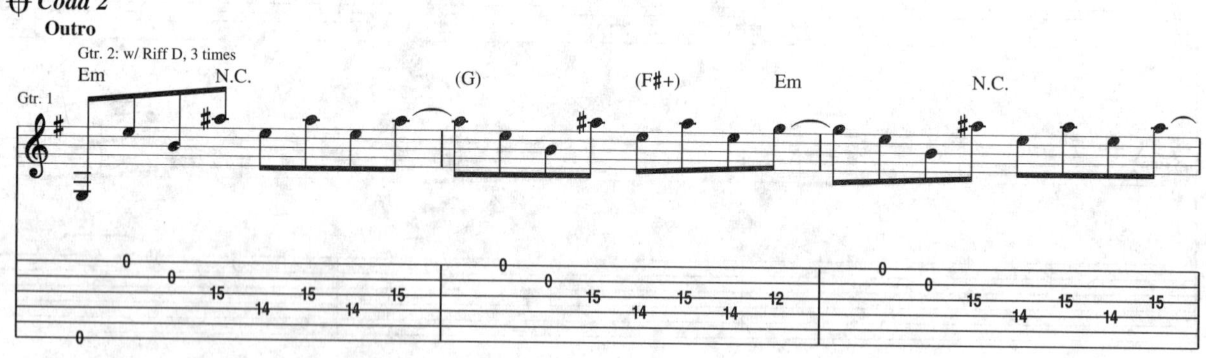
Coda 2
Outro
Gtr. 2: w/ Riff D, 3 times
Em
N.C.
Gtr. 1
(G)
(F#+)
Em
N.C.

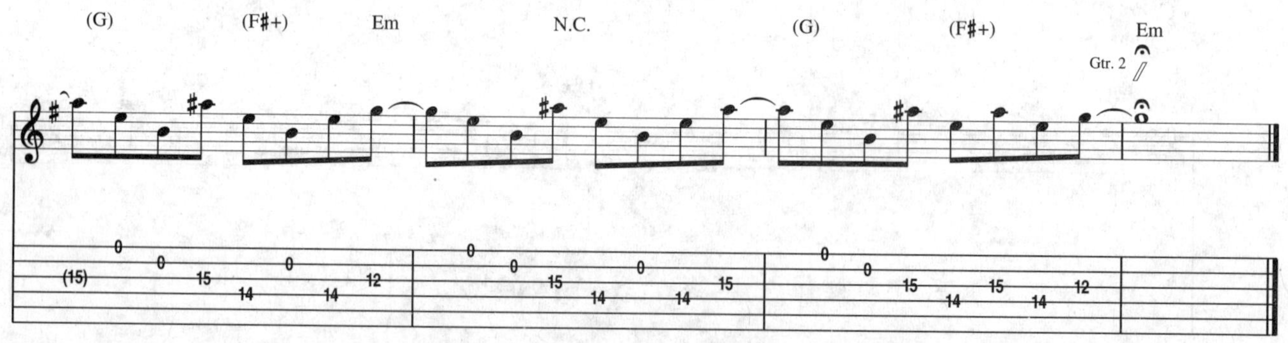
(G)
(F#+)
Em
N.C.
(G)
(F#+)
Em
Gtr. 2

Hey Joe

Words and Music by Billy Roberts

D
A
E
I said where you go - in' with that gun in your hand? Al - right.
C
G
I'm go - in' down to shoot my old la - dy,
D
A
E
you know I caught her mess - in' 'round with an - oth - er man.
let ring
Yeah!
C
G
I'm go - in' down to shoot my old la - dy.

D
A
E
you know I caught her mess - in' 'round with an - oth - er man.
Huh!
And that ain't
too cool.
Verse
C
G
2. Uh, hey Joe,
D
A
E
I heard you shot your wom - an down, you shot her down now.
C
G
Uh, hey Joe,

D
A
E
I heard you shot your old la - dy down, you shot her down in the ground.
C
G
Yeah!
Yes, I did, I shot her,
D
A
E
you know I caught her mess - in' 'round, mess - in' 'round town.
C
G
Uh, yes I did, I shot her,

D
A
E
you know I caught my old la - dy mess - in' 'round town.
And I gave her the
T
Guitar Solo
C
G
gun.
I shot her.
f
hold bend
1/2

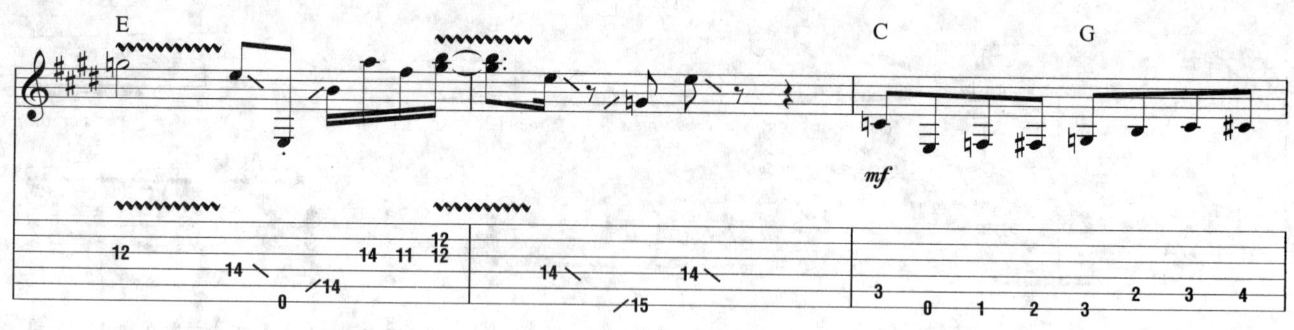
E
C
G
mf

D
A
E

Verse
C
G
D
A
3. Hey Joe,
uh, where you gon - na run

E
to now?
let ring

C
G
D
A
Hey Joe, I said, where you gon - na run
E
to now, where you, where you gon - na go?
Well dig it!
1/4
C
G
D
A
I'm goin' way down south, way down to
E
Mex - i - co way.
tr

Outro
C
G
D
A
I'm goin' way down south, way down where I
E
can be free.
C
G
D
A
Ain't no hang - man gon - na, he ain't gon - na put a rope a - round
E
Repeat and fade
me.

Hit Me With Your Best Shot

Words and Music by Eddie Schwartz

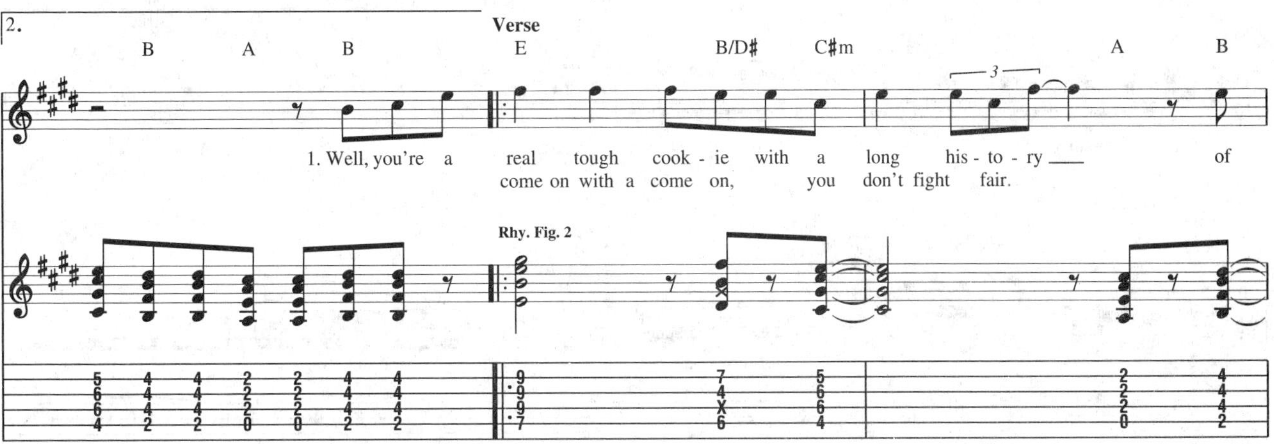

A B
how you do it. Put up your dukes, let's get down to it.
in vain. I'll get right back on my feet a - gain.
End Rhy. Fig. 2
*P.M.
*grad. release
Chorus
Gtrs. 1 & 2: w/ Rhy. Fig. 1, 2 times, simile
E A C#m B E A C#m B A B
Hit me with your best shot. Why don't you hit me with your best shot?
E A C#m B E A C#m B A B B A B
Hit me with your best shot. Fire a - way.
2. You
Guitar Solo
Gtrs. 1 & 2: w/ Rhy. Fig. 2
E B/D# C#m A B
Gtr. 3 (dist.)
slight P.M.
Gtr. 1: w/ Fill 1
E B/D# C#m A B
Gtrs. 1 & 2: w/ Rhy. Fig. 1, 2 times, simile
E A C#m
semi-harm.
P.M.
full
B E A C#m B A B E A C#m
full

* Chord symbols reflect implied tonality.

Chorus
Gtrs. 1 & 3: w/ Rhy. Fig. 1, 2 times, simile
Gtr. 2: w/ Fill 2, 1st time
E A C#m B E A C#m B A B
Hit me with your best shot. Come on, hit me with your best shot.
E A C#m B
1.
E A C#m B A B
Hit me with your best shot. Fire a - way.
2.
Outro
1., 2.
E A C#m B A B E A C#m B A B E
Gtrs. 1 & 3
3.
Freely
B A B E E7
Gtr. 1
1/4 1/4 1/4
let ring
Gtr. 3
Fill 2
Gtr. 2
play 7 times

Hold My Hand

Words and Music by Darius Carlos Rucker, Everett Dean Felber, Mark William Bryan and James George Sonefeld

Bsus2
E
take the world to-geth-er, we'll take 'em by the hand.
let ring
(cont. in slash)
Pre-Chorus
drums enter
F♯
E
B
Rhy. Fig. 3
Gtrs. 1 & 2
End Rhy. Fig. 3
Gtrs. 1 & 2: w/ Rhy. Fig. 3
'Cause I got a hand for you. Oh. I wan-na run with you.
Verse
Gtr. 1: w/ Rhy. Fig. 2, 3 times
Gtr. 2: w/ Fill 1
2. Yes-ter-day I saw you stand-ing there. Your
-ed and I was wast-ing time, 'til I
Gtr. 2: w/ Fill 2
head was down, your eyes were red, no comb had touched your hair. I said, "Get
thought a-bout your prob-lems, I thought a-bout your crimes. Then I stood
Gtr. 1
Fill 2
Gtr. 2

Gtr. 1: w/ Rhy. Fig. 2, 2 times
Gtr. 2: w/ Fill 1
Bsus2
E
up and let me see you smile. We'll
up, and then I screamed a - loud. I don't wan-na
Gtr. 2: w/ Fill 2
take a walk to - geth - er, walk the road a - while." 'Cause,
be part of your prob - lems, don't wan-na be part of your crowd, no.
Gtr. 1
let ring
Pre-Chorus
Gtrs. 1 & 2: w/ Rhy. Fig. 3, 2 times
F♯
B
I got a hand for you.
('Cause, I got a hand for you.)
*Lead harmony 2nd time.
Won't you let me run with you.
(I wan - na run with you.)
Chorus
Rhy. Fig. 4A
End Rhy. Fig. 4A
Gtr. 3 (clean elec.)
mp
F♯sus4
1. Want you to hold my hand.
2. Want you to hold my hand.
(Hold my hand.)
Gtr. 1 & 2
Rhy. Fig. 4
End Rhy. Fig. 4

Gtr. 3: w/ Rhy. Fig. 4A, 2 times
B
E
F#
F#sus4
F#
F#sus4
I'll take you to a place where you
I'll take you to the prom - ised
(Hold my hand)
Rhy. Fig. 5
End Rhy. Fig. 5

Gtrs. 1 & 2: w/ Rhy. Fig. 4
B
E
F#
F#sus4
F#
F#sus4
can be
land.
(Hold my hand.)
an - y - thing you wan - na be, be-cause
May-be we can change the world but

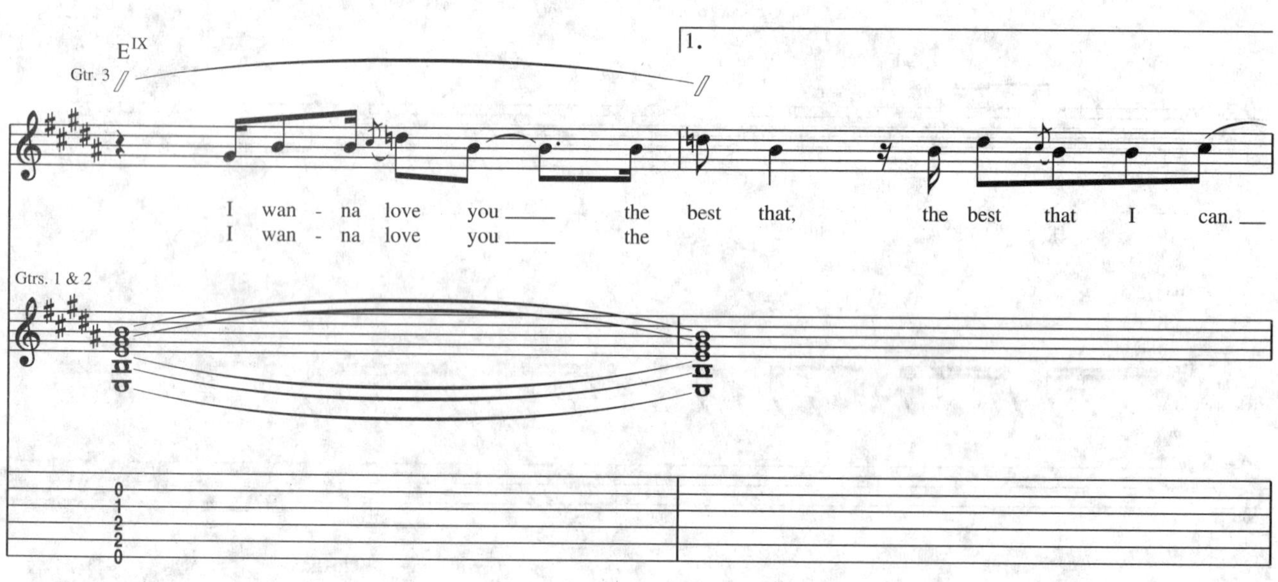
E IX
Gtr. 3
1.
I wan - na love you the best that, the best that I can.
I wan - na love you the
Gtrs. 1 & 2

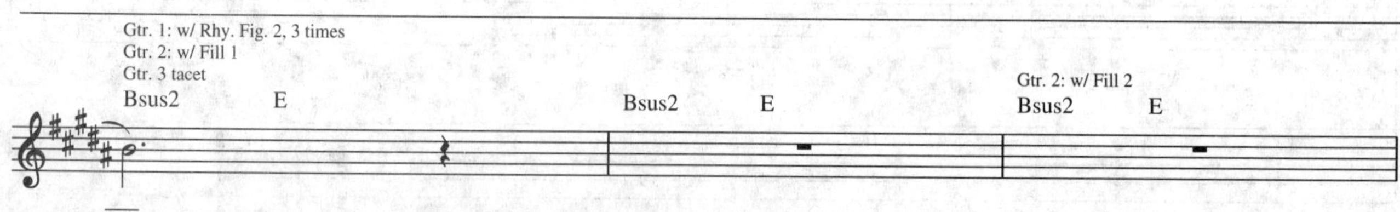
Gtr. 1: w/ Rhy. Fig. 2, 3 times
Gtr. 2: w/ Fill 1
Gtr. 3 tacet
Bsus2
E
Bsus2
E
Gtr. 2: w/ Fill 2
Bsus2
E

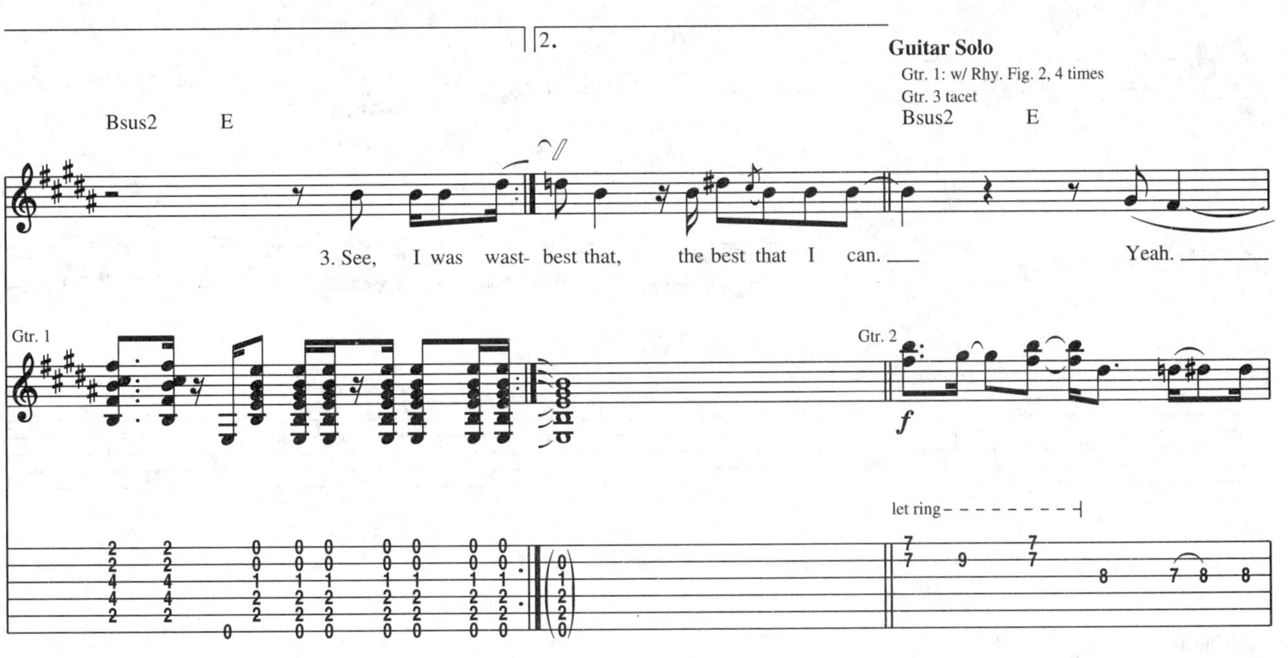
2.
Guitar Solo
Gtr. 1: w/ Rhy. Fig. 2, 4 times
Gtr. 3 tacet
Bsus2
E
3. See, I was wast- best that, the best that I can.
Yeah.
Gtr. 1
Gtr. 2
let ring

Bsus2
E

Gtrs. 1 & 3: w/ Rhy. Fig. 3, 2 times
F♯
E
B
Oh.
full
hold bend

F♯
E
B
Let me run, won't you let me run with you.
hold bend
full

Chorus
*Gtrs. 1 & 2: w/ Rhy. Fig. 4
Gtr. 3: w/ Rhy. Fig. 4A, 3 times
B
E
F♯
Gtrs. 1 & 2: w/ Rhy. Fig. 5
B
E
F♯
Want you to hold my hand.
(Hold my hand.)
(Hold my hand.
* Gtr. 2 holds notes from end of solo for two beats, then resumes with Rhy. Fig. 4

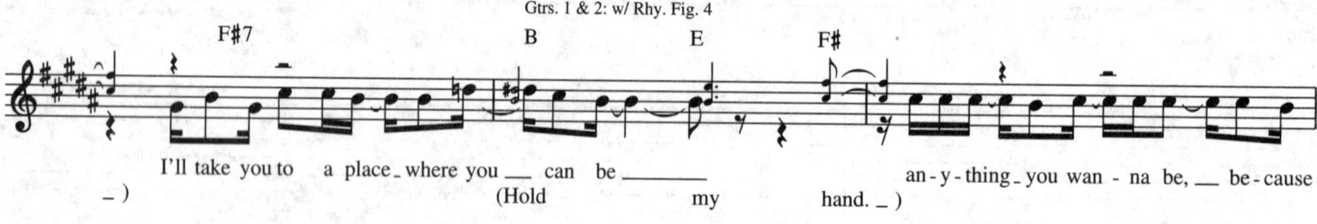
F♯7
Gtrs. 1 & 2: w/ Rhy. Fig. 4
B
E
F♯
)
I'll take you to a place where you can be
(Hold my hand.)
an-y-thing you wan-na be, be-cause

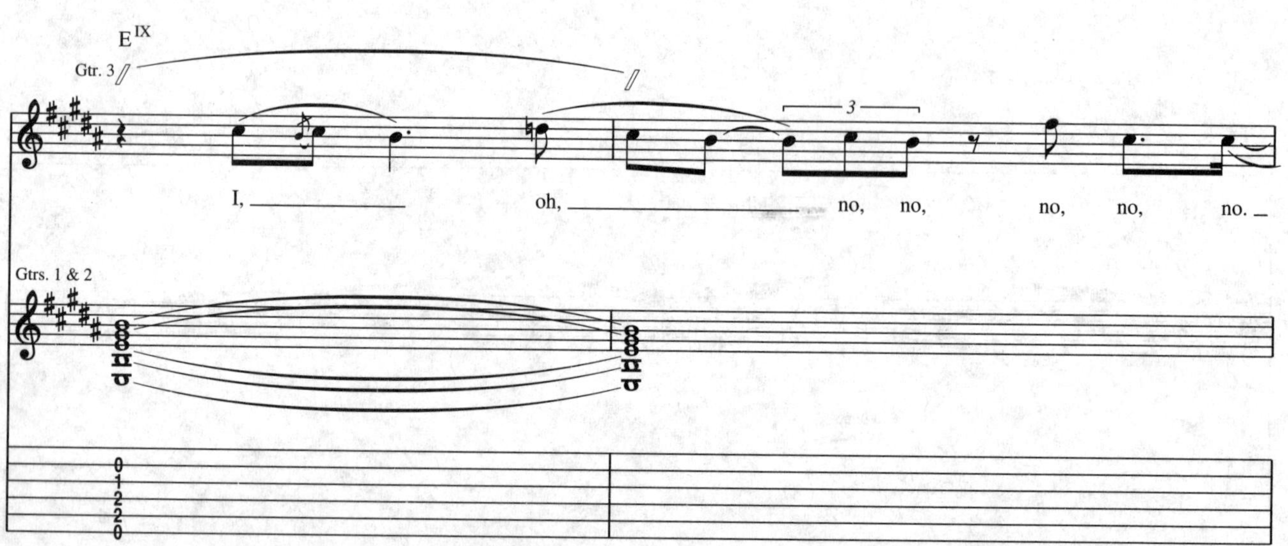
E IX
Gtr. 3
I, oh, no, no, no, no, no.
Gtrs. 1 & 2

Gtrs. 1 & 2: w/ Rhy. Fig. 4
Gtr. 3: w/ Rhy. Fig. 4A, 3 times
B
E
F#
Want you to hold my hand.
(Hold my hand.)
Gtrs. 1 & 2: w/ Rhy. Fig. 5
B
E
F#
(Hold my hand.
F#7
I'll take you to the prom - ised land.
)
Gtrs. 1 & 2: w/ Rhy. Fig. 4
B
E
F#
(Hold my hand.)
May-be we can't change the world, but
E[IX]
Gtr. 3
I wan - na love you the best that, the best that I can.
Gtrs. 1 & 2
Gtr. 1: w/ Rhy. Fig. 2, 2 times, simile
Gtr. 2: w/ Fill 1
Gtr. 3: tacet
Bsus2
E
Bsus2
E
Oh.
Best that I can.
Bsus2
E
E
open
Bsus2
E
E
open
Gtr. 3
Gtrs. 1 & 2

Honeysuckle Rose

Words by Andy Razaf
Music by Thomas "Fats" Waller

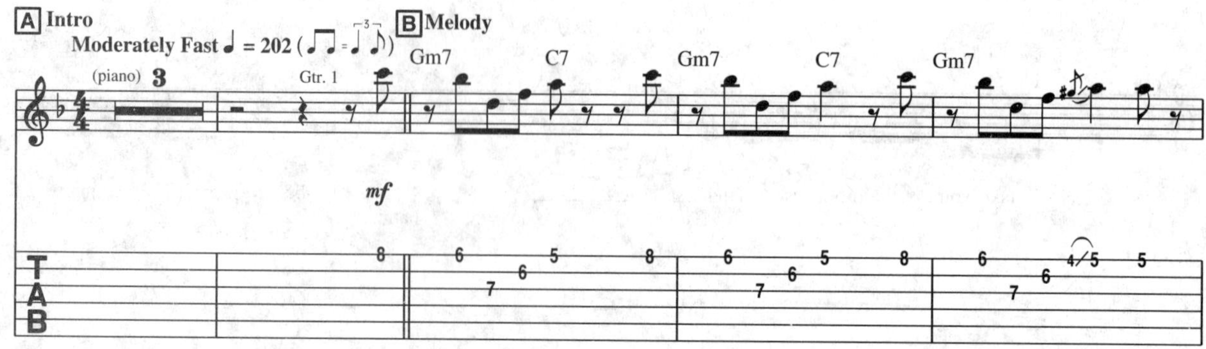

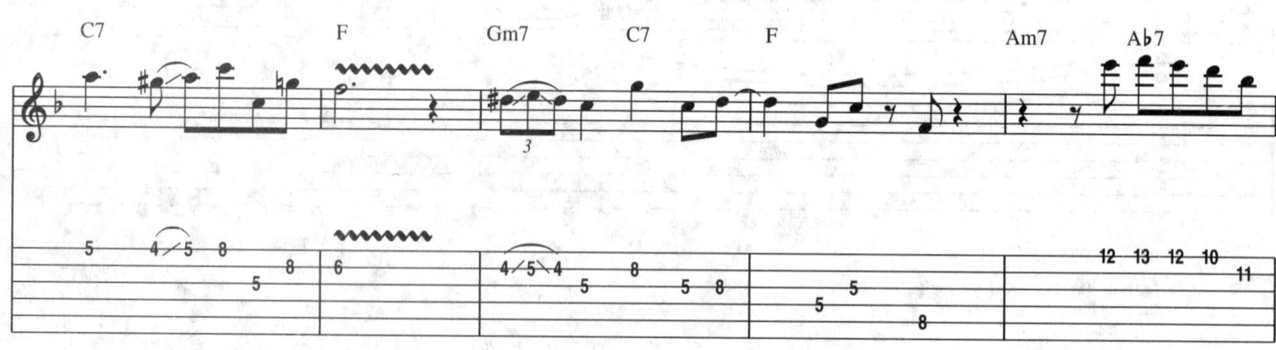

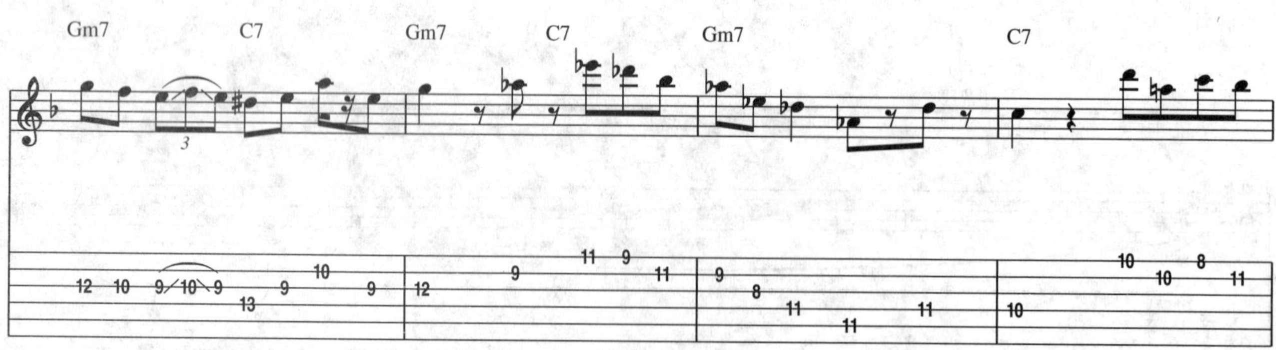

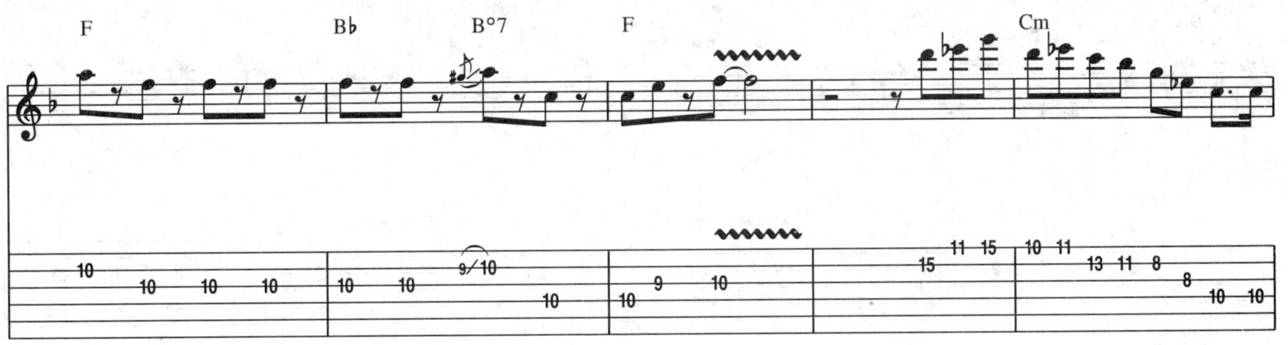
F
B♭
B°7
F
Cm

B♭
G7

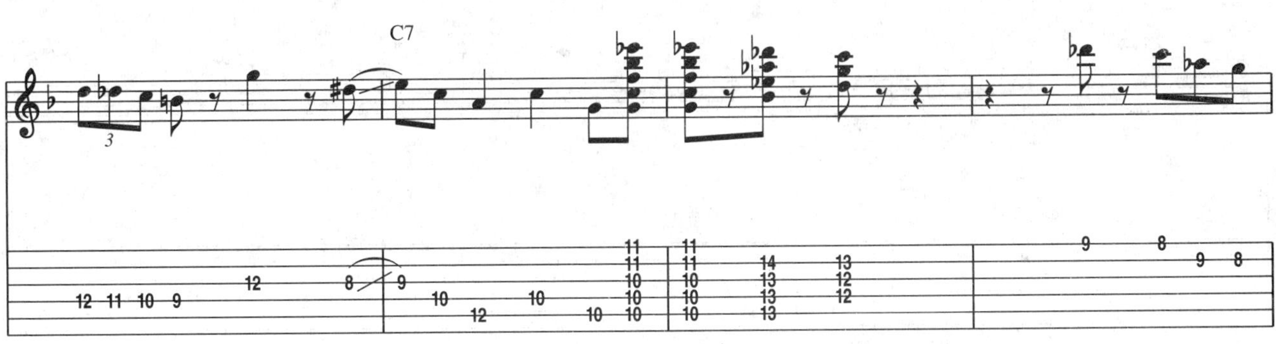
C7

F

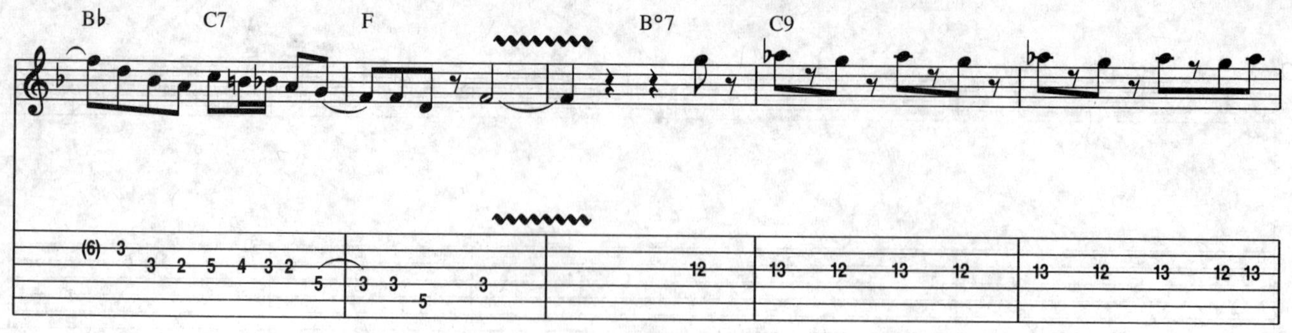
B♭
C7
F
B°7
C9

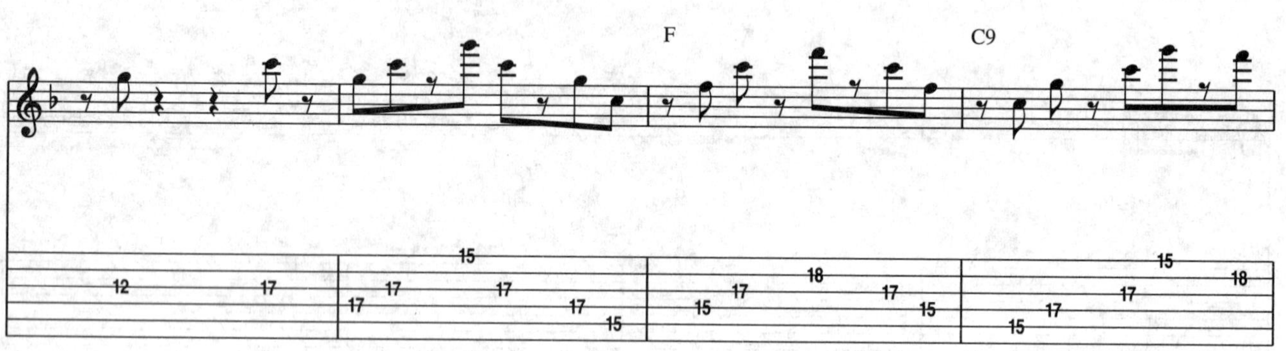
F
C9

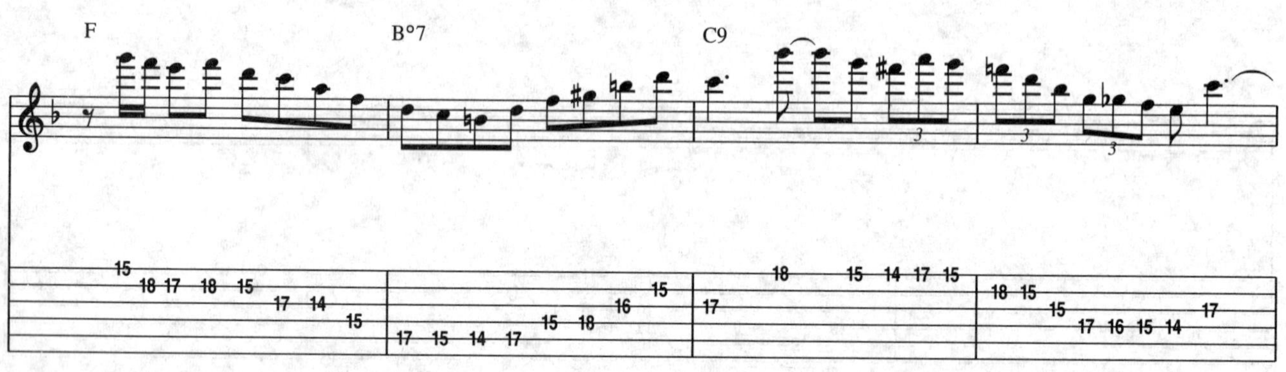
F
B°7
C9

F
Gm7
C13
F

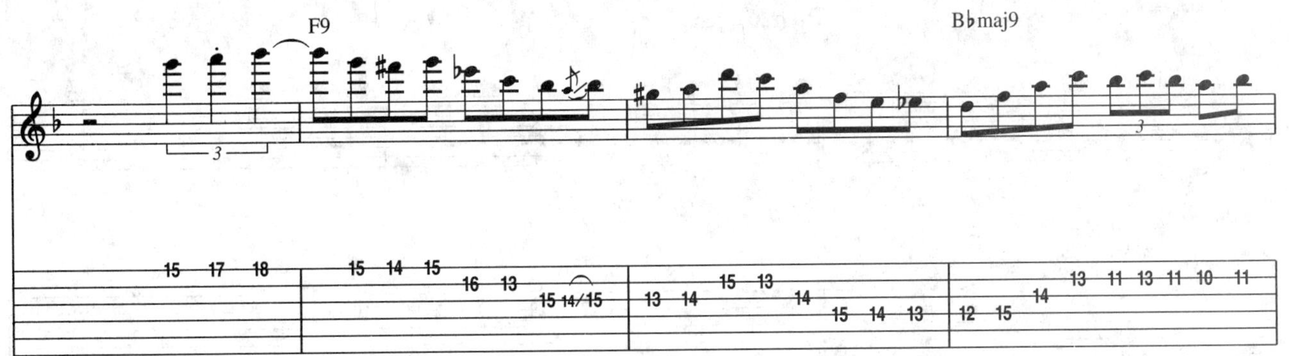
F9
B♭maj9
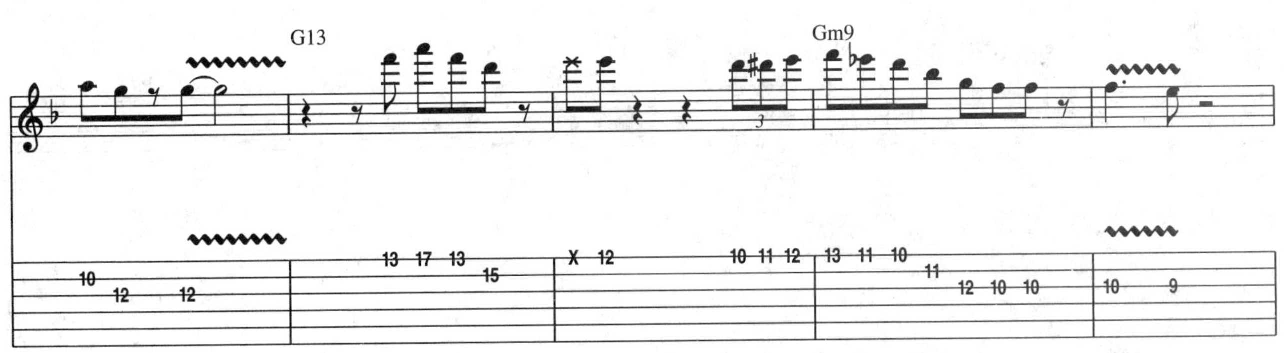
G13
Gm9

C7
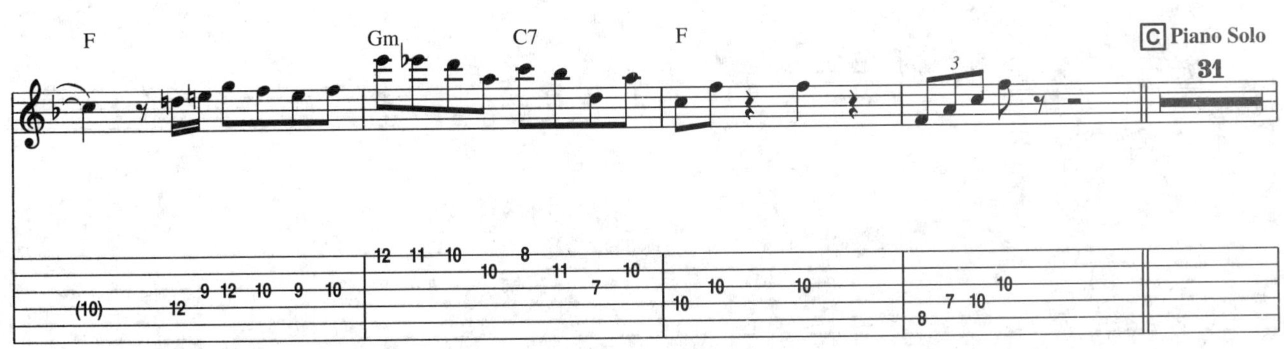
F
Gm
C7
F
C Piano Solo
31

D Guitar Solo

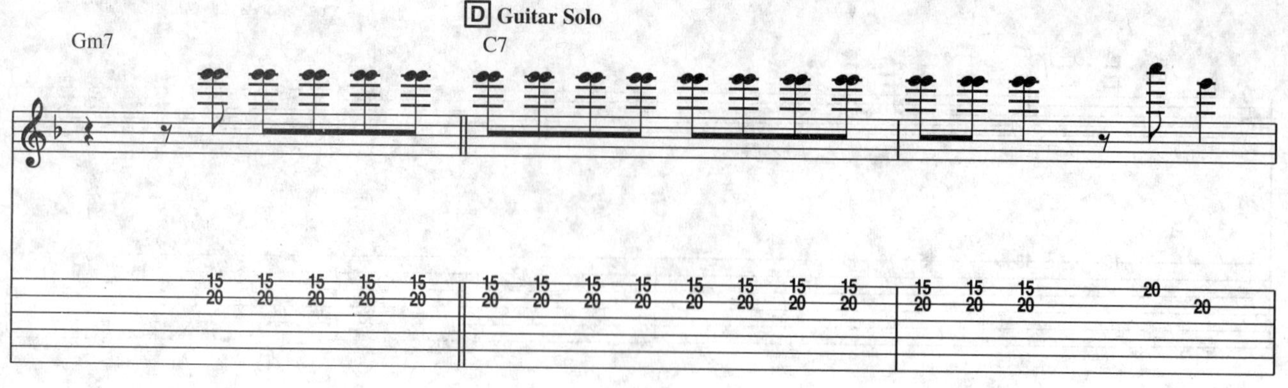

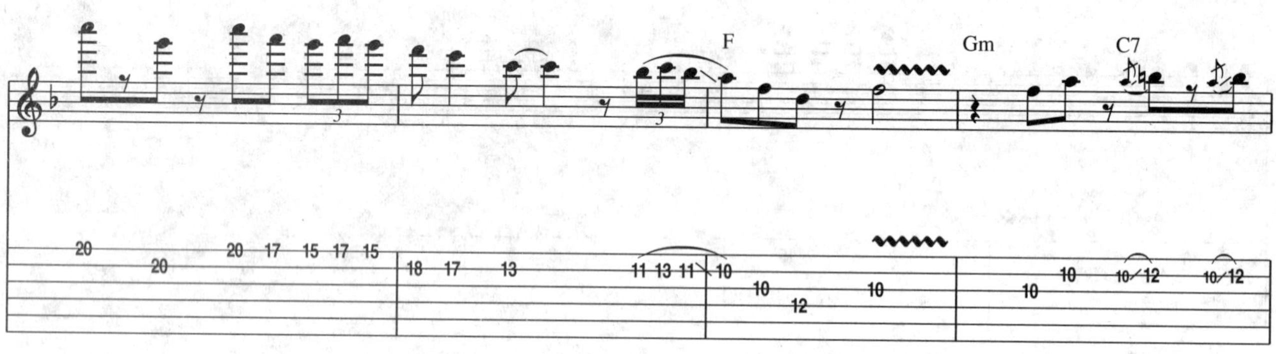

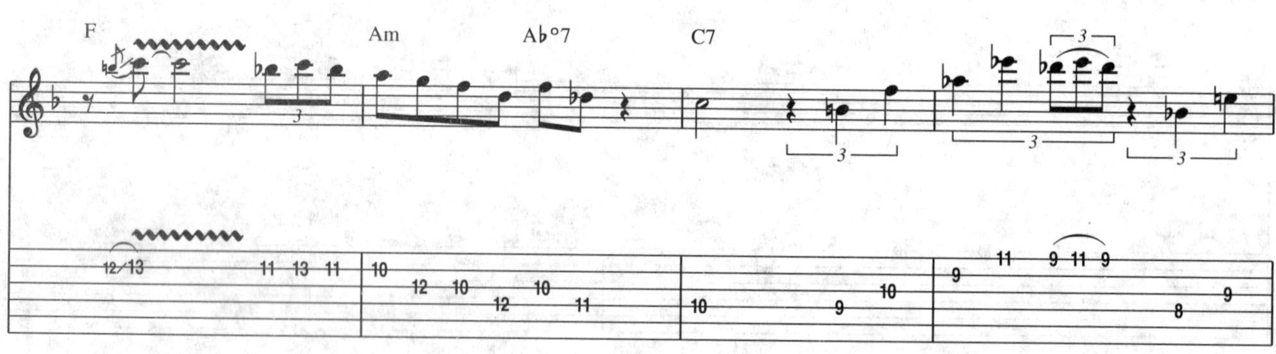

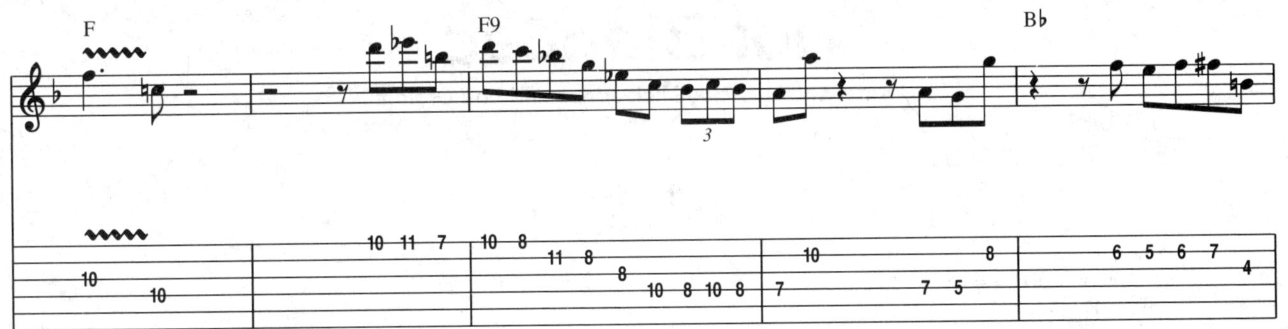
F
F9
B♭

G9
C7
Harm.
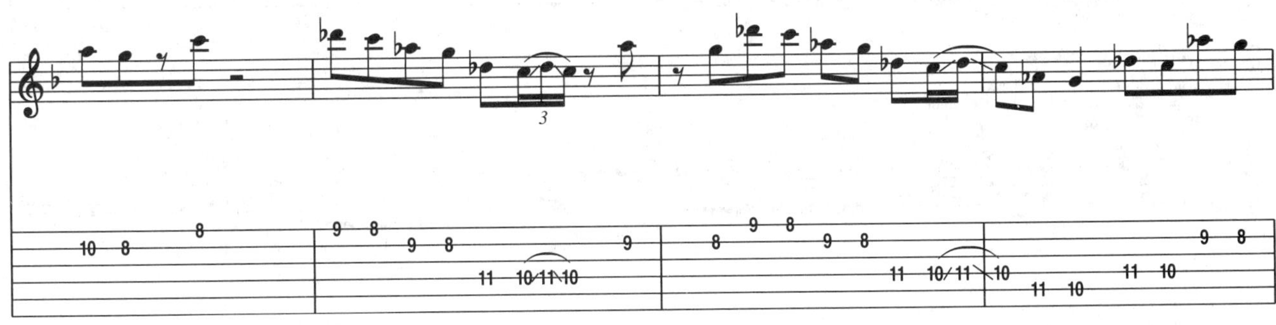
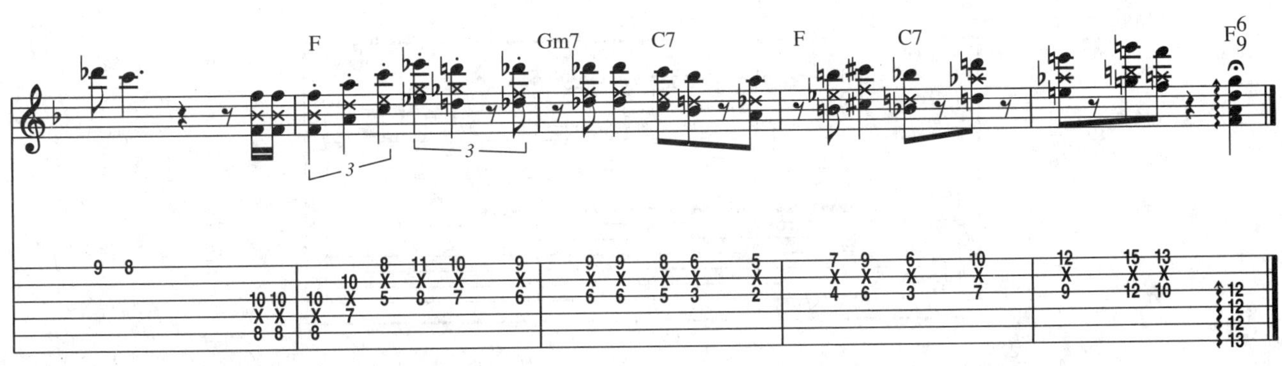
F
Gm7
C7
F
C7
F6/9

Hot Blooded

Words and Music by Mick Jones and Lou Gramm

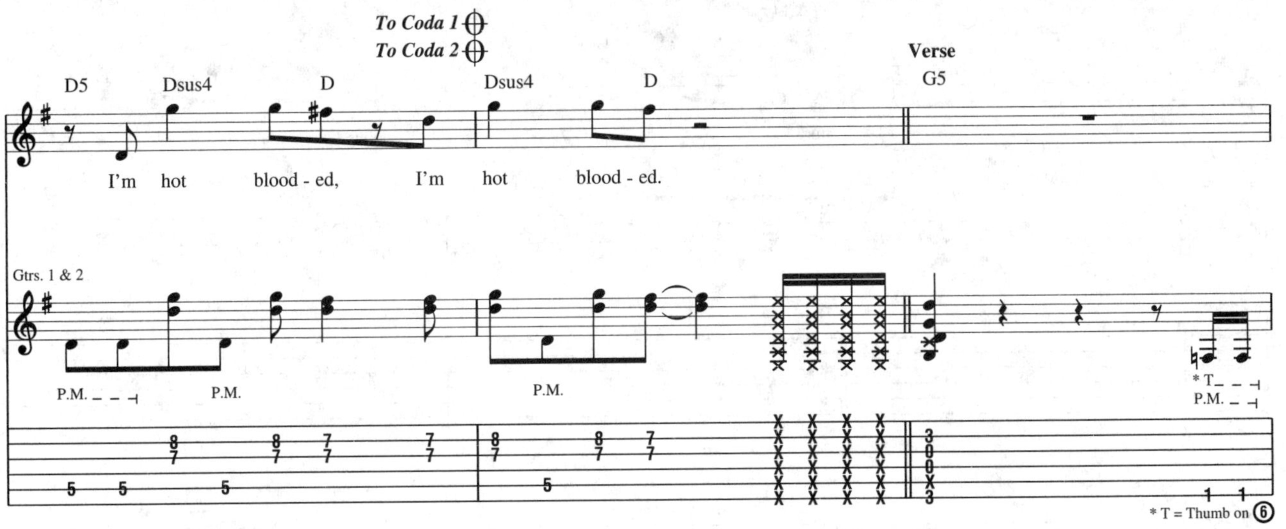
To Coda 1
To Coda 2
Verse
D5
Dsus4
D
Dsus4
D
G5
I'm hot blood - ed, I'm hot blood - ed.
Gtrs. 1 & 2
P.M.
P.M.
P.M.
* T
P.M.
* T = Thumb on ⑥

Fsus2
C5
G5
Fsus2
C5
1. You don't have to read my mind to know what I
Rhy. Fig. 2
End Rhy. Fig. 2
P.M.
T
P.M.
P.M.

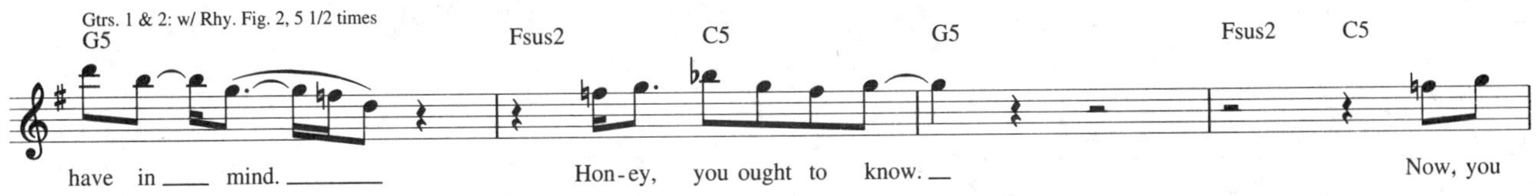
Gtrs. 1 & 2: w/ Rhy. Fig. 2, 5 1/2 times
G5
Fsus2
C5
G5
Fsus2
C5
have in mind. Hon-ey, you ought to know. Now, you

G5
Fsus2
C5
G5
Fsus2
C5
move so fine, let me lay it on the line. I

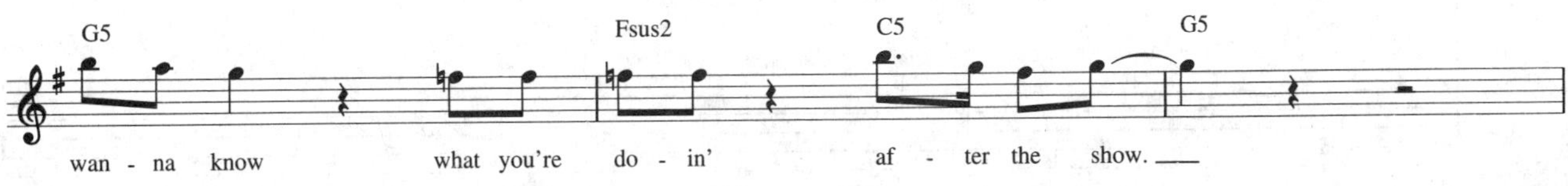
G5
Fsus2
C5
G5
wan - na know what you're do - in' af - ter the show.

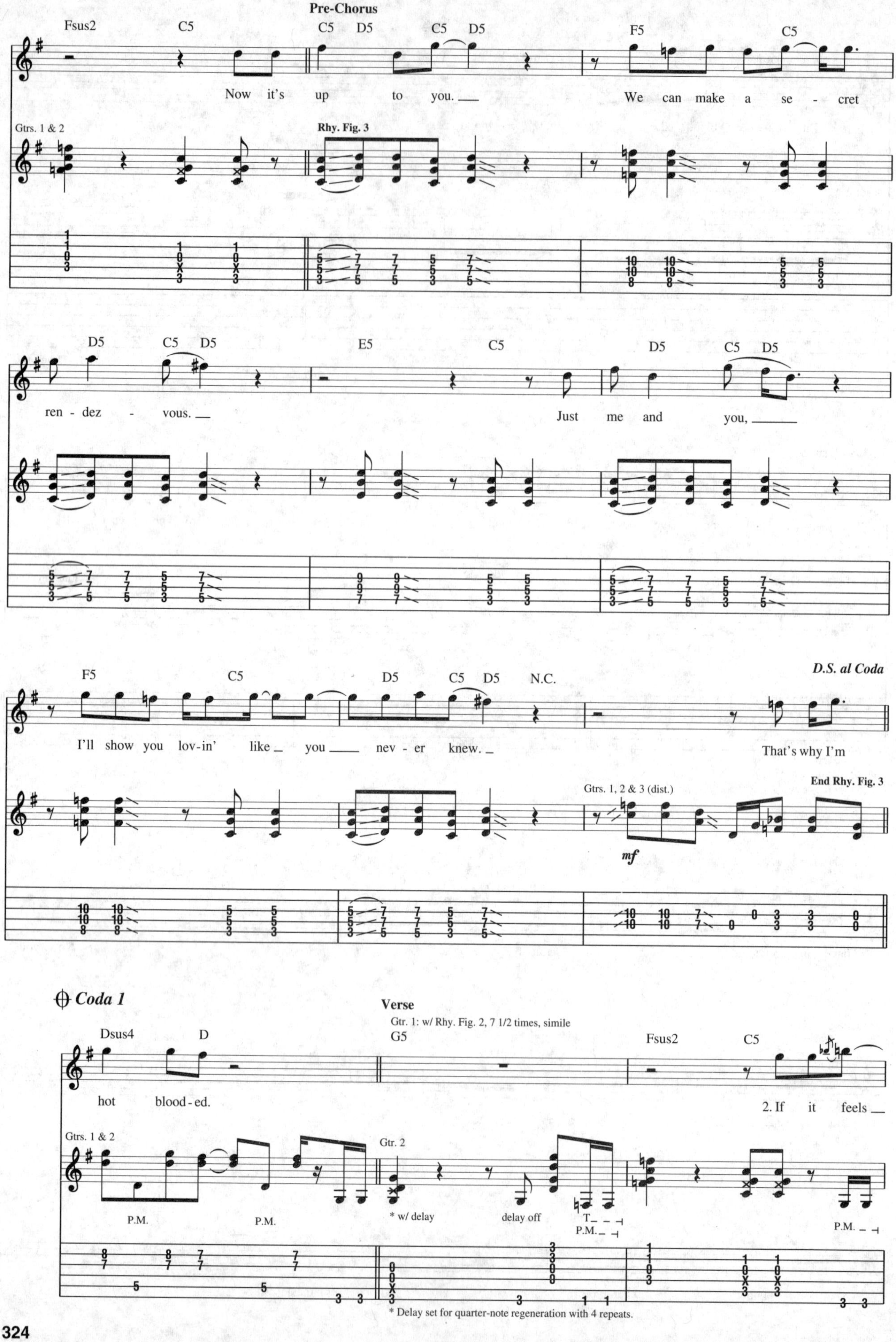

Pre-Chorus

Fsus2 C5 | C5 D5 C5 D5 | F5 C5

Now it's up to you. We can make a se - cret

Gtrs. 1 & 2

Rhy. Fig. 3

D5 C5 D5 | E5 C5 | D5 C5 D5

ren - dez - vous. Just me and you,

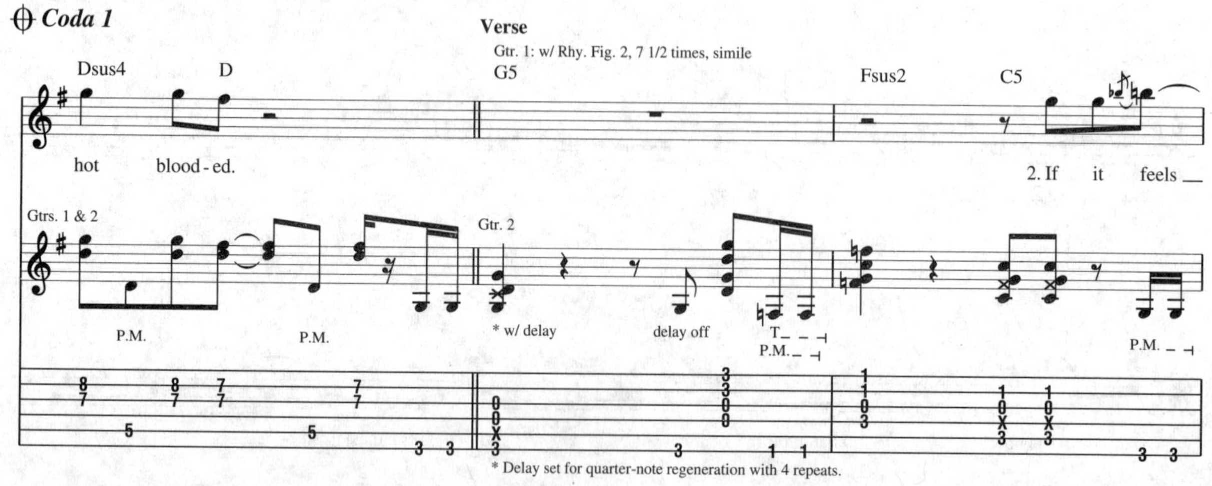

* Delay set for quarter-note regeneration with 4 repeats.

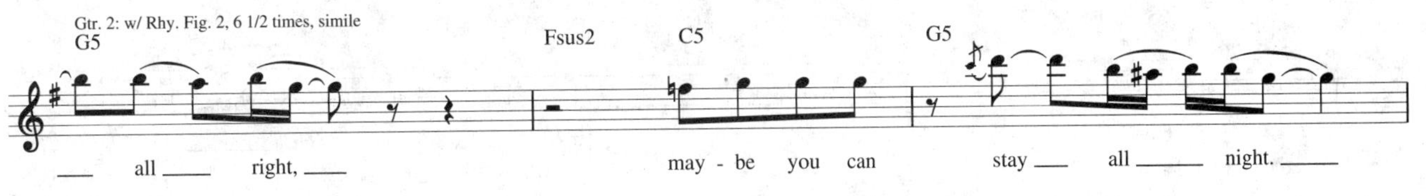
Gtr. 2: w/ Rhy. Fig. 2, 6 1/2 times, simile
G5
Fsus2
C5
G5
all right,
may - be you can
stay all night.

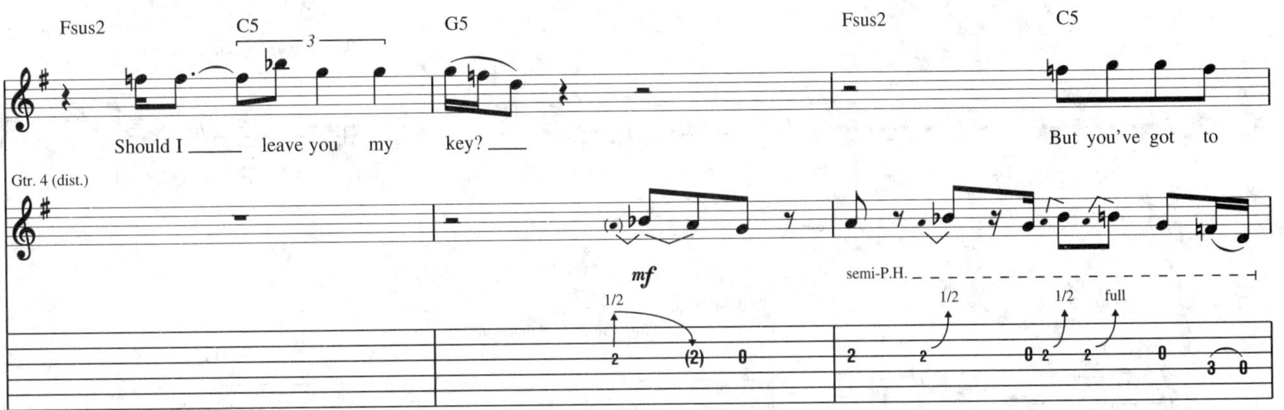
Fsus2
C5
G5
Fsus2
C5
Should I leave you my
key?
But you've got to
Gtr. 4 (dist.)
mf
semi-P.H.
1/2
1/2
1/2
full

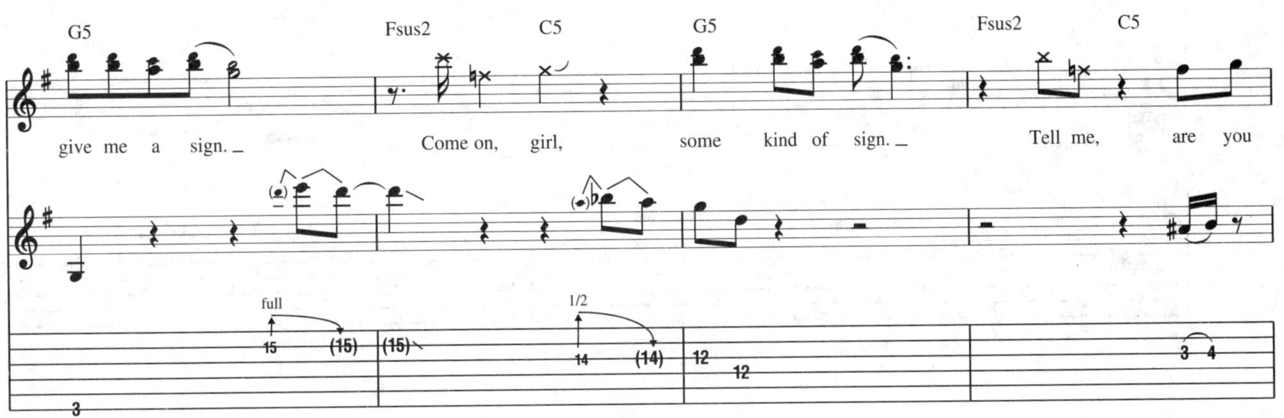
G5
Fsus2
C5
G5
Fsus2
C5
give me a sign.
Come on, girl,
some kind of sign.
Tell me, are you
full
1/2

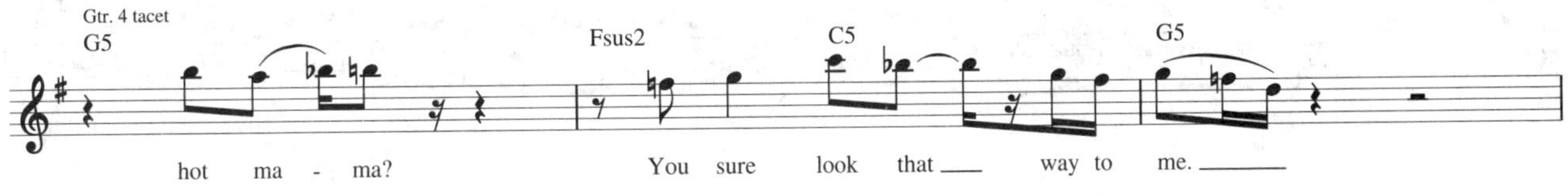
Gtr. 4 tacet
G5
Fsus2
C5
G5
hot ma - ma?
You sure look that way to
me.

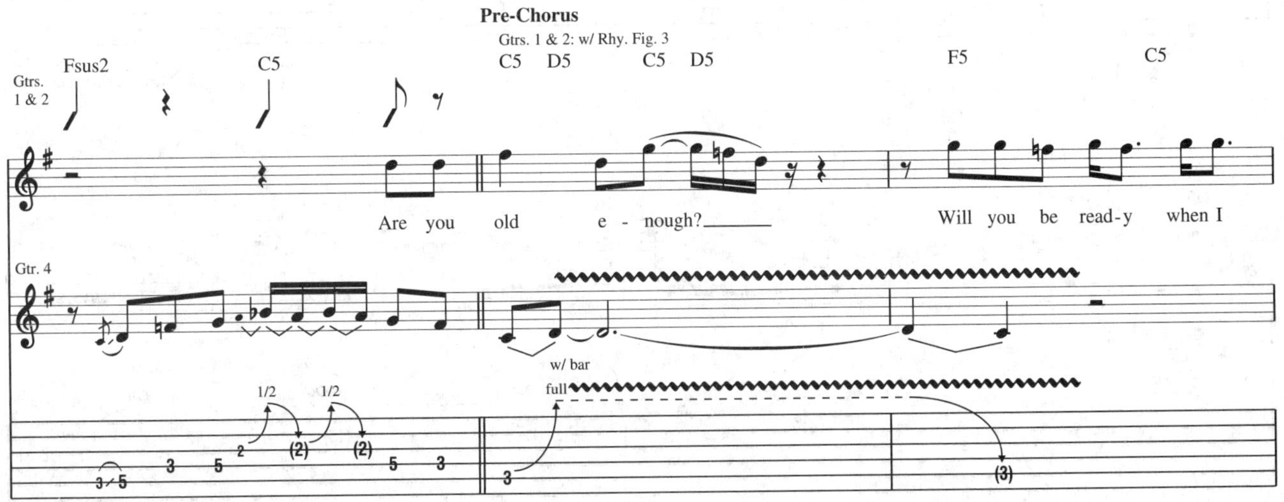
Pre-Chorus
Gtrs. 1 & 2: w/ Rhy. Fig. 3
Gtrs. 1 & 2
Fsus2
C5
C5 D5 C5 D5
F5
C5
Are you
old e - nough?
Will you be read-y when I
Gtr. 4
w/ bar
1/2
1/2
full

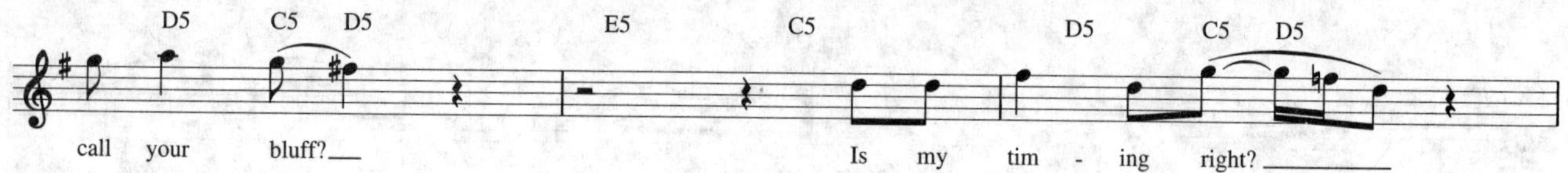
D5
C5
D5
E5
C5
D5
C5
D5
call your bluff?
Is my tim - ing right?

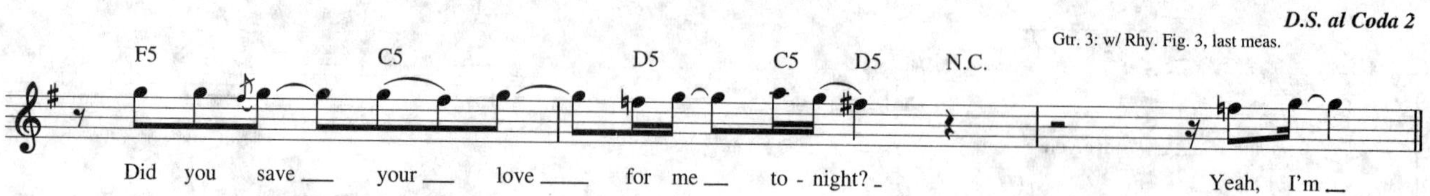
D.S. al Coda 2
Gtr. 3: w/ Rhy. Fig. 3, last meas.
F5
C5
D5
C5
D5
N.C.
Did you save your love for me to - night?
Yeah, I'm

Coda 2
Guitar Solo
Gtrs. 1 & 2: w/ Rhy. Fig. 2, 7 1/2 times
Dsus2
D
G5
Fsus2
C5
G5
hot blood-ed. I'm hot.
Gtrs. 1 & 2
Gtr. 4
P.M.
P.M.
full
full
full

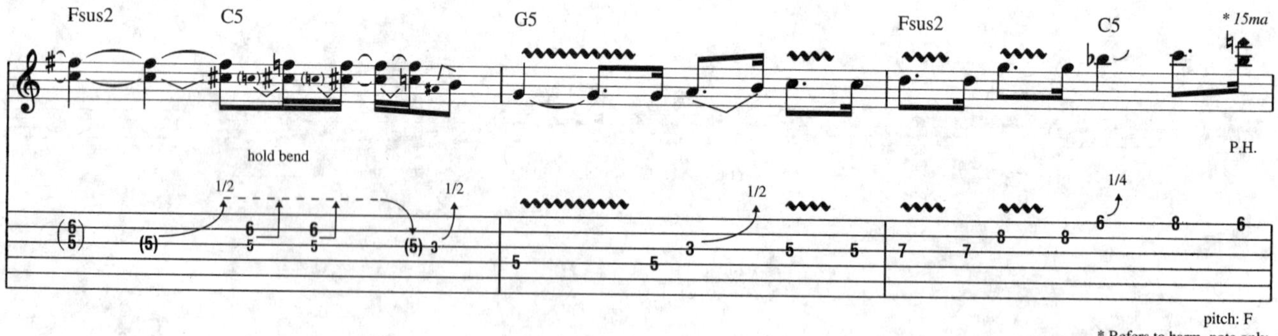
Fsus2
C5
G5
Fsus2
C5
* 15ma
hold bend
1/2
1/2
1/2
1/4
P.H.
pitch: F
* Refers to harm. note only.

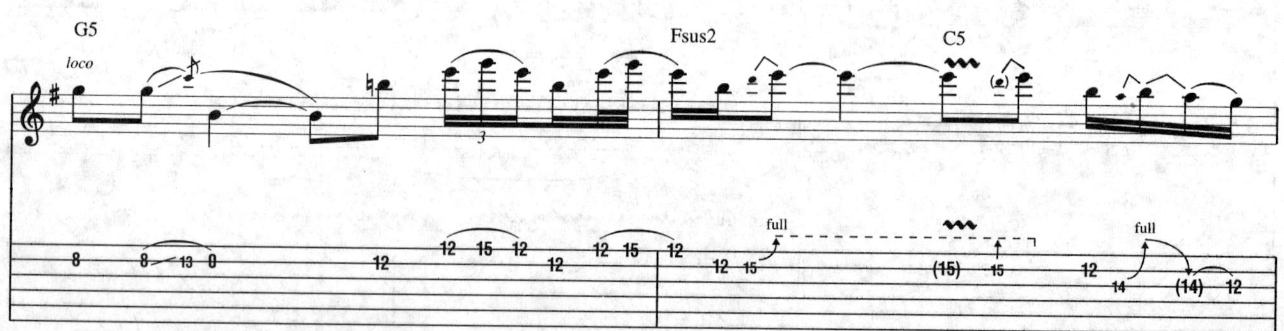
G5
loco
Fsus2
C5
full
full

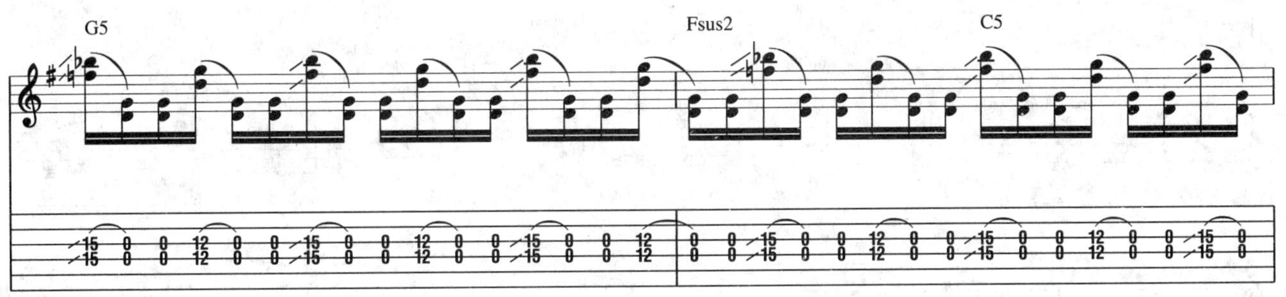
G5
Fsus2
C5

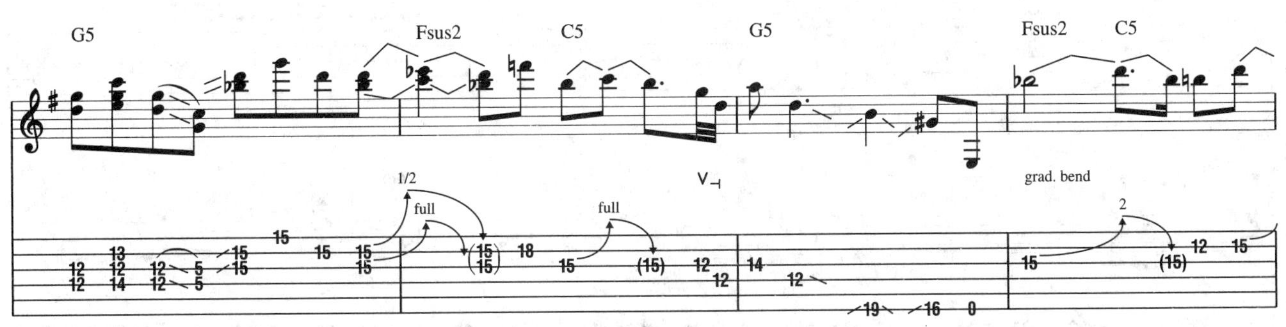
G5
Fsus2
C5
G5
Fsus2
C5
grad. bend

Pre-Chorus
Gtrs. 1 & 2: w/ Rhy. Fig. 3
G5
Fsus2
C5
C5 D5
C5 D5
F5
C5
Gtrs. 1 & 2
Now it's up to you.
Can we make a se - cret
Gtr. 4
rake
Harm.
w/ bar
grad. release
* hypothetical fret location

D5
C5 D5
E5
C5
D5
C5 D5
F5
C5
ren-dez - vous?
Oh.
Be - fore
we do
you'll have to get a - way from
w/ bar

Chorus
Gtrs. 1 & 2 : w/ Rhy. Fig. 1, 3 times
Gtr. 3: w/ Rhy. Fill 1, simile
Gtr. 3: w/ Rhy. Fig. 3, last meas.
D5 C5 D5 N.C.
G5 Gsus4 G C Csus4
you know who. Well, I'm hot blood-ed, check it and see.
1/2
G5 Gsus4 G C Csus4 G5 Gsus4 G
I got a fe - ver of a hun - dred and three. Come on, ba - by, do you
Gtr. 4 tacet
C Csus4 D5 Dsus4 D Dsus4 D
do more than dance? I'm hot blood-ed, I'm hot blood-ed.
Outro
Gtr. 1: w/ Rhy. Fig. 1, 3 times
G5 Gsus4 G
(Hot blood-ed.)
Rhy. Fig. 4
Gtrs. 1 & 2
End Rhy. Fig. 4
* Gtrs. 2 & 3
P.M.
* composite arrangement
C Csus4 G5 Gsus4 G C Csus4 G5 Gsus4 G
Ev - er - y night. You're look-ing so tight. Now you're
(Hot blood - ed.) (Hot blood-ed.)
P.M.

Gtr. 1: w/ Rhy. Fig. 4
C Csus4 D5 Dsus4 D Dsus4 D
driv - ing me wild.
I'm so hot for you, child.
(Hot blood - ed. Hot blood - ed.)
let ring
1/2
Begin Fade
Gtr. 1: w/ Rhy. Fig. 1, 3 times
G5 Gsus4 G C Csus4 G5 Gsus4 G C Csus4
I'm a lit-tle bit high.
You're a lit-tle bit shy.
(Hot blood-ed.)
(Hot blood-ed.)
P.M.
G5 Gsus4 G C Csus4
Gtr. 1: w/ Rhy. Fig. 4
D5 Dsus4 D
(Hot blood - ed.) You're mak - ing me sing
(Hot blood - ed.) for your
P.M.
let ring
Dsus4 D
Gtrs. 2 & 3 tacet
G5 Gsus4 G C Csus4
Fade Out
sweet, sweet thing.
(Hot blood - ed.)
Did you hear what I say?
Gtr. 1
let ring
P.M.
P.M.
P.M.

I Just Want to Celebrate

Words and Music by Nick Zesses and Dino Fekaris

Intro

Moderately ♩ = 88

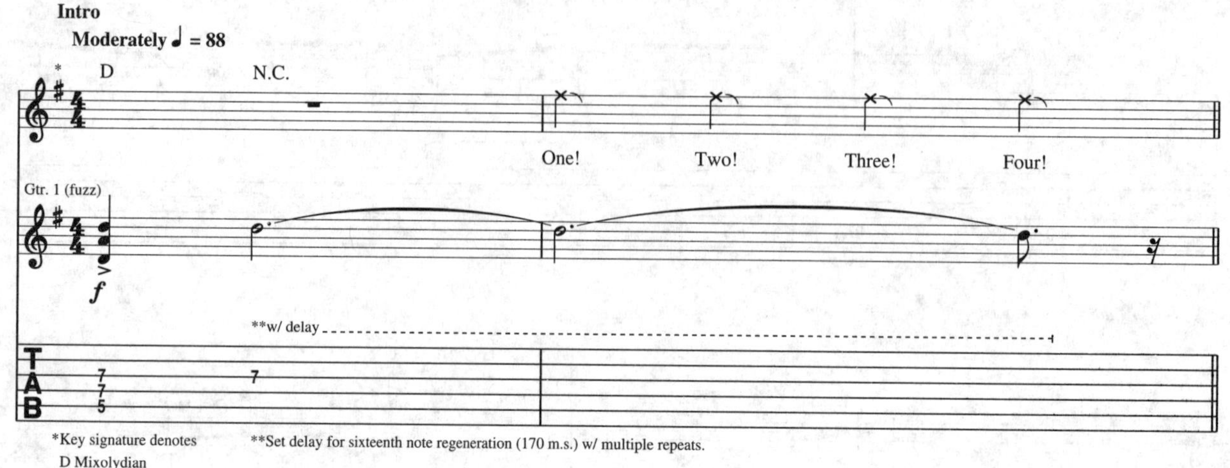

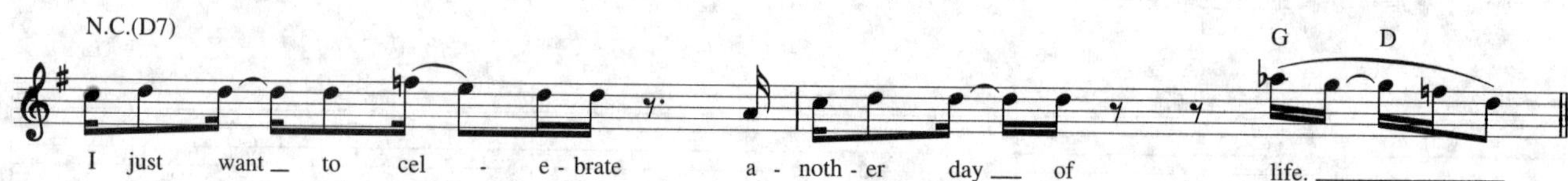

Verse

E
C5
G5
D5
turned the oth - er way and I car - ried on
an - y - how.
That's why I'm tell - in' you I
End Rhy. Fig. 2
1/2
Chorus
N.C.(D7)
G5
D5
just wan - na cel - e - brate, yeah yeah,
a - noth - er day of liv - in'.
Yeah,
Gtr. 1: w/ Rhy. Fig. 1, simile
N.C.(D7)
G
D
I just want to cel - e - brate
a - noth - er day of life.
Verse
Gtr. 1: w/ Rhy. Fig. 2, 1st 3 meas, simile
N.C.(D7)
G
D
N.C.(D7)
G
D
2. Had my hand on a dol - lar bill,
and the dol - lar bill blew a - way.
But the
E
C5
G5
D
sun is shin - in' down on me,
and it's here to stay.
That's why I'm tell - in you I
(Here to stay.)
Gtr. 1

Chorus
Gtr. 2 tacet, 2nd time
N.C.(D7)
Gtr. 2: w/ Fill 1, 2nd time
G
D
just want to cel - e - brate, yeah yeah, a - noth - er day of liv - in'. Yeah,
Rhy. Fig. 3

N.C.(D7)
G
D
I just want to cel - e - brate a - noth - er day of life.
End Rhy. Fig. 3

Bridge
N.C.(D7)
(G)
(D)
Do - in' it all gets you down, oh no.
Gtr. 1
1/4

Fill 1
Gtr. 2
mp
1/2
full
full
full
full
*Played behind the beat.

To Coda

(C/D)
Don't let it turn you a - round and a - round and a - round and a - round and a -
('Round, round, 'round.)
Gtr. 2 (fuzz)
f
w/ wah-wah
12
Gtr. 1
5
5 5 5 5 5 5 5 5

round.
3. Well, I
8va
3
full
full
full
full
(12)
10
X X 10
10
13 (13)
10 13 10 13 10 13 10 13 15 13 15 15 15 15 13
Verse
Gtr. 2 tacet
Gtr. 1: w/ Rhy. Fig. 2, simile
N.C.(D7)
G D
N.C.(D7)
G D
can't be both - ered with sor - row and I can't be both - ered with hate, no no. I'm

E
C5
G5
D
us - in' up my time by feel - in' fine
ev - 'ry day, yeah. That's why I'm tell - in you
(Ev' - ry day.)
Chorus
Gtr. 1: w/ Rhy. Fig. 3 simile
N.C.(D7)
G5
D
I just wan - na cel - e - brate. Oh yeah.
Gtr. 2
full
full
full
full
13 13 10 12 12 10 12
12 10 12 12 12 10 12 10 12 12 10 12 10
D.S. al Coda
N.C.(D7)
G
D
I just wan - na cel - e - brate a - noth - er day. Oh,
8va
hold bend
full
full
17 17 17 (17) 15 17 16 15 16 15 17 15 16 15 17
Coda
Gtr. 1 tacet
N.C.(C/D)
'round and 'round, 'round. 'Round.
N.C.
(drums)
Outro
N.C.(D)
I just wan - na
w/ Voc. ad. lib., till fade
cel - e - brate, cel - e - brate. I just wan - na cel - e - brate.
Play 3 Times and Fade
I just wan - na cel - e - brate.

I Love Rock 'N Roll

Words and Music by Alan Merrill and Jake Hooker

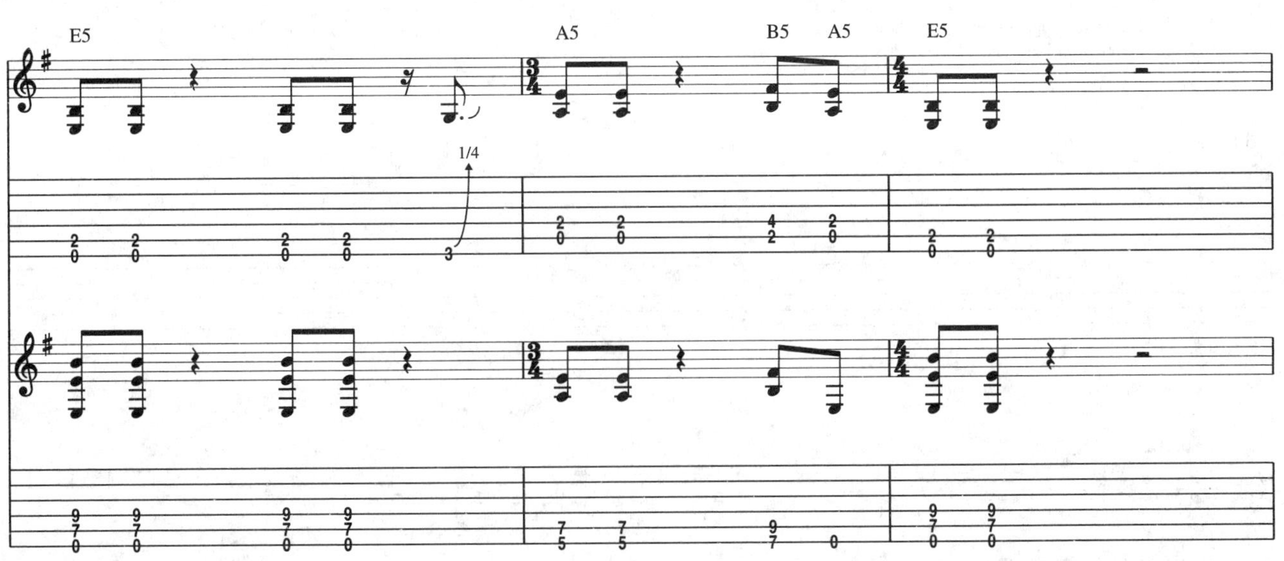

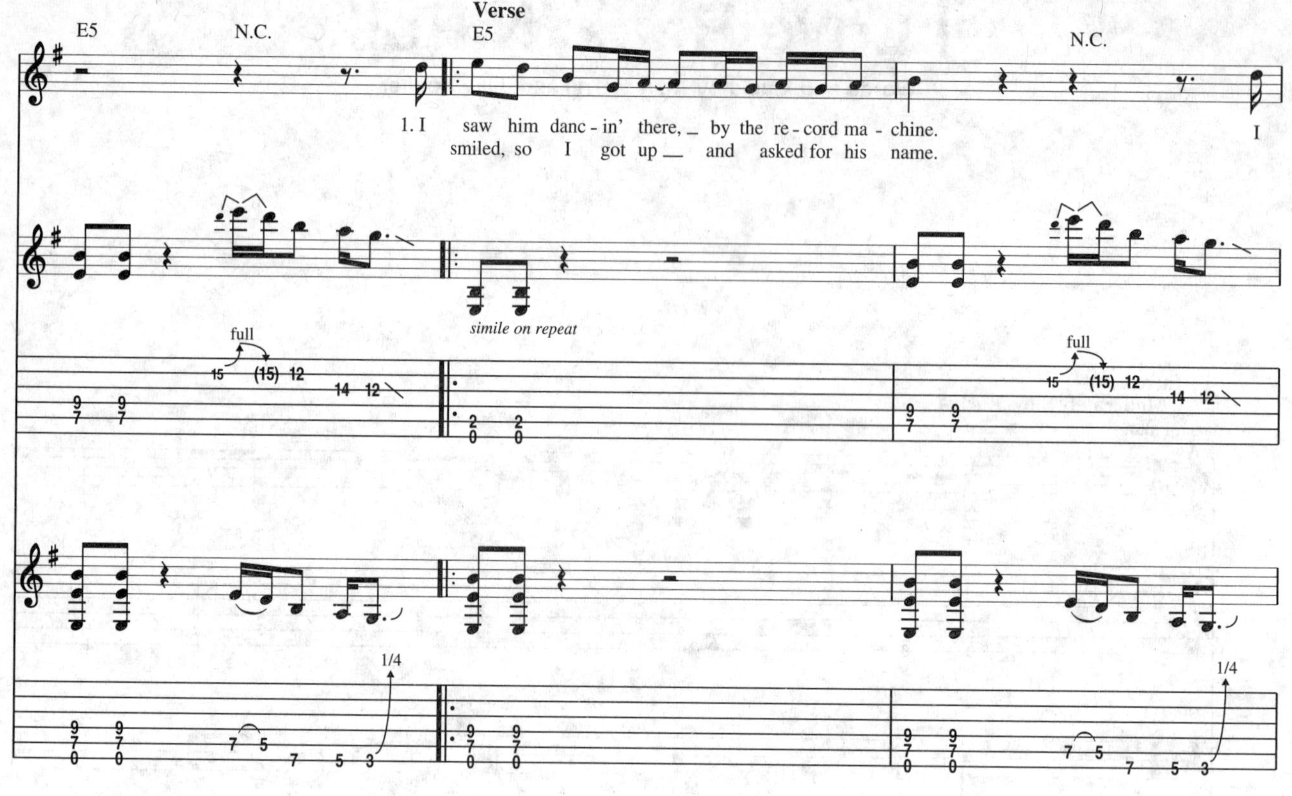
Verse
E5
N.C.
E5
N.C.
1. I saw him danc - in' there, by the re - cord ma - chine. I
smiled, so I got up and asked for his name.
simile on repeat
full
1/4

E5
B5
N.C.
A5
B5
knew he must have been a - bout sev - en - teen. The beat was go - in' strong,
"That don't mat-ter," he said, "'cause it's all the same." I said, "Can I take ya home where
full
1/4

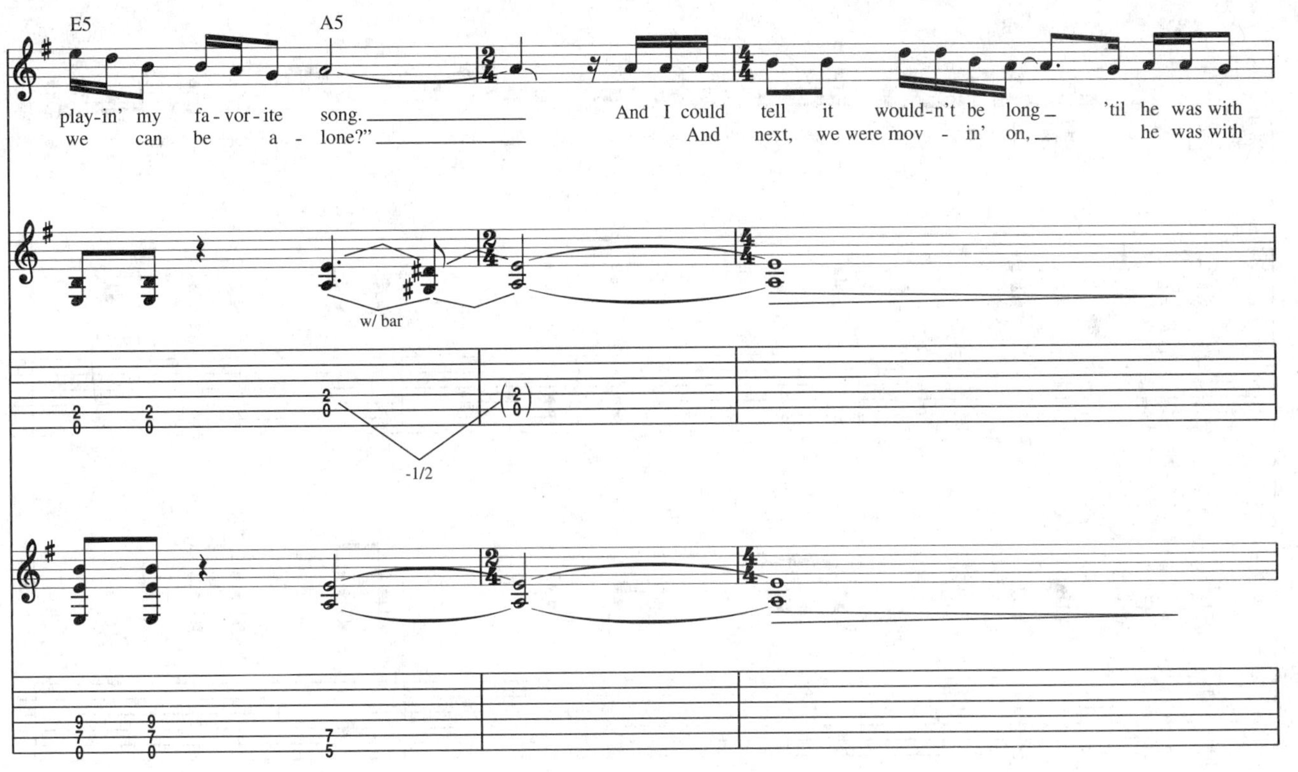
E5
A5
play-in' my fa-vor-ite song.
we can be a - lone?"
And I could tell it would-n't be long 'til he was with
And next, we were mov - in' on, he was with
w/ bar
-1/2

N.C.
B5
me, yeah, me! And I could tell it would-n't be long 'til he was with me, yeah, me, sing-in',
me, yeah, me! Next, we were mov - in' on, he was with me, yeah, me, sing-in',

Chorus

E5
A5
B5
E5
I love rock 'n' roll, so put an-oth-er dime in the juke-box, ba - by. I love rock 'n' roll, so
1/4
1/4

A5
B5
E5
N.C.
come and take your time and dance with me. Ow! 2. He
full
1/4

Guitar Solo/Pre-Chorus
Gtr. 3 (dist.)
E5
E7
N.C.
E5
w/ bar
full
1/2
Gtr. 1
Gtr. 2
1/4
B5
N.C.
A5
B5
E5
Said, "Can I take ya home where we can be a -
P.M.

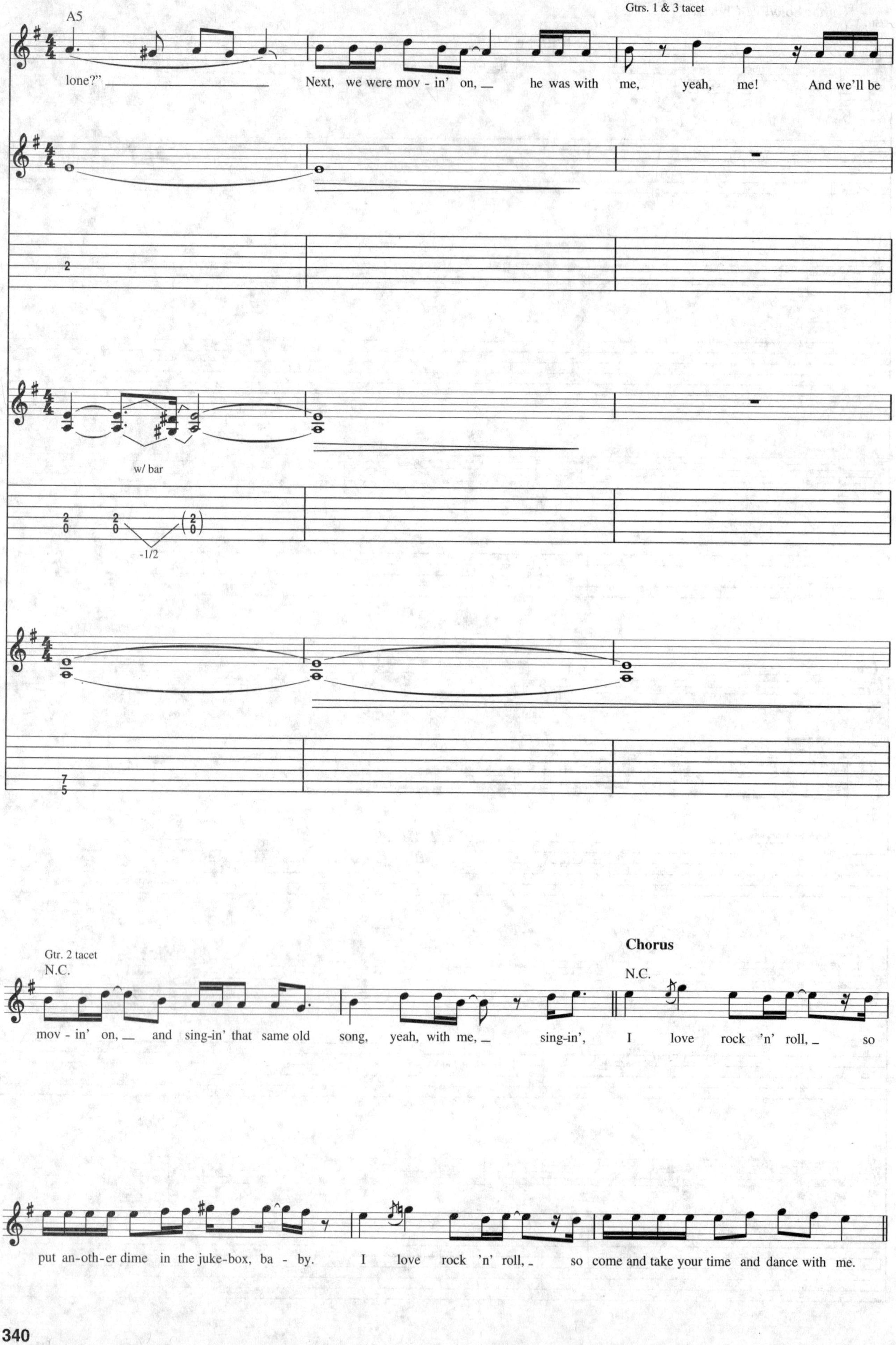

A5

Gtrs. 1 & 3 tacet

lone?" Next, we were mov - in' on, he was with me, yeah, me! And we'll be

w/ bar

-1/2

Outro-Chorus
E5
A5
B5
I love rock 'n' roll, so put an-oth-er dime in the juke-box, ba - by.
Gtr. 1
1/4
Gtr. 2
*Gtr. 3
*Play 3rd & 4th times only.
1., 2., 3.
4.
E5
A5
B5
A5
B5
E5
I love rock 'n' roll, so come and take your time and dance with
come and take your time and dance with me!
1/4

I Stand Alone

Words and Music by Sully Erna

Drop D tuning, down 1 step:
(low to high) C-G-C-F-A-D

Intro

Moderately slow  **= 84**

N.C.

Gtr. 1 (dist.)

f

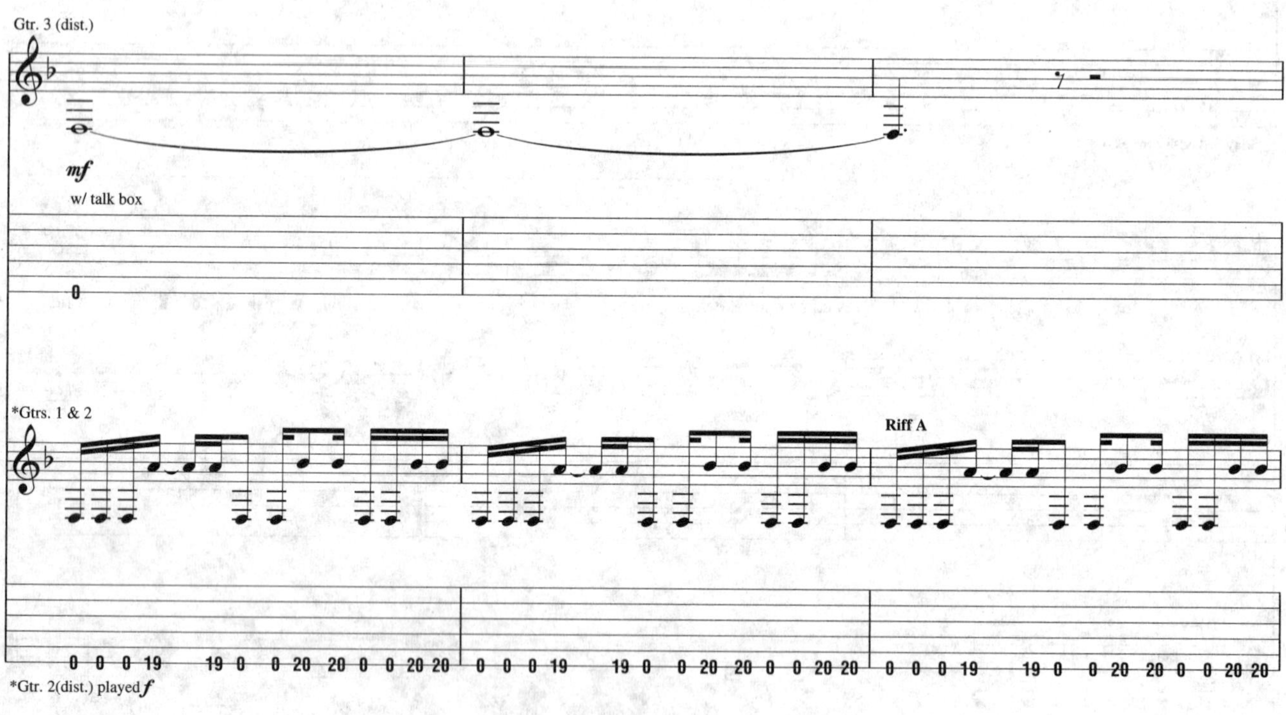

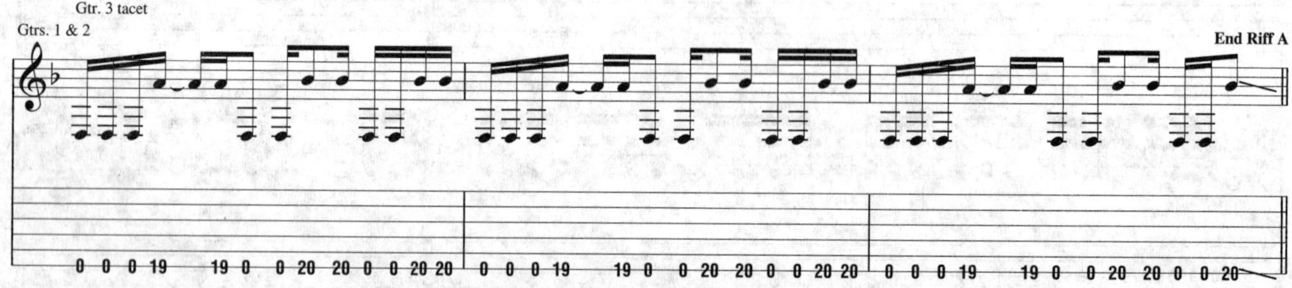

Verse
D
Ab5
D
G5 F5
1. I've told you this once be - fore, can't con - trol me.
Gtr. 1
Rhy. Fig. 1
P.M.
Gtr. 2
Rhy. Fig. 1A
D
Ab5
D
N.C.
If you try to take me down you're gon - na break.
End Rhy. Fig. 1
End Rhy. Fig. 1A
Gtrs. 1 & 2: w/ Rhy. Figs. 1 & 1A (1st 2 meas.)
D
Ab5
D
G5 F5
And I feel your ev - 'ry noth - ing that you're do - ing for me.

D
A♭5
A♭6/9
And I'm think - ing you ought to make your own way.
Gtr. 3
Rhy. Fig. 2
Gtr. 1
End Rhy. Fig. 2
P.M.
P.M.
Rhy. Fig. 2A
Gtr. 2
End Rhy. Fig. 2A
P.M.
P.M.
Chorus
Gtrs. 1 & 2: w/ Riff A
Gtr. 3 tacet
N.C.
I stand a - lone in - side. I stand a - lone.
Whispered: (I. I.)
*w/ echo set for half-note regeneration w/ 2 repeats.
Verse
Gtrs. 1 & 2: w/ Rhy. Fig. 1 (1 1/2 times)
D
A♭5
D
G5 F5
D
A♭5
2. You're al - ways hid - ing be - hind your so - called god - dess. So what? You don't think
D
N.C.
D
A♭5
D
G5 F5
that we can see your face? Res - ur - rect - ed back be - fore the fi - nal fall - ing.

Gtrs. 1 & 2: w/ Rhy. Figs. 1 & 1A (1st 2 meas.)
D
A♭5
D
G5
F5
And I'll nev - er rest un - til I can make my own
G5
B♭sus2
E♭5
way. I'm not a - fraid of fad - ing.
Gtr. 1
let ring
let ring
Gtr. 2
Chorus
Gtrs. 1 & 2: w/ Riff A (last 2 meas.)
N.C.
I stand a - lone. Feel - ing your
Whispered: (I.)
G5
B♭5
sting down in - side me, I'm not dy - ing for it.
Rhy. Fig. 3
Gtrs. 1 & 2
End Rhy. Fig. 3

Gtrs. 1 & 2: w/ Riff A (last 2 meas.)
N.C.
I
(I.)
stand a - lone.
Ev - er - y -

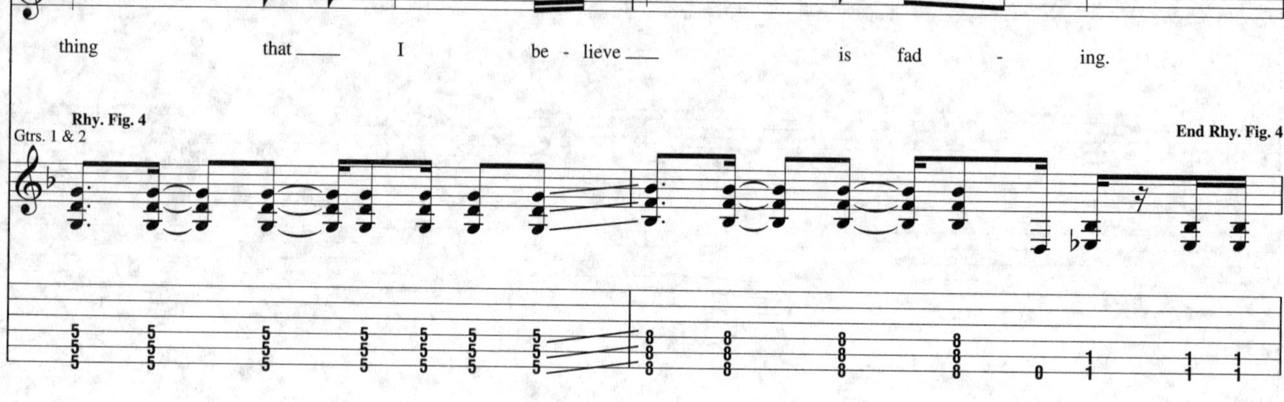
G5
B♭5
E♭5
thing that I be - lieve is fad - ing.
Rhy. Fig. 4
Gtrs. 1 & 2
End Rhy. Fig. 4

Gtrs. 1 & 2: w/ Riff A (1st 2 meas., 2 times)
N.C.
I stand a - lone in - side. I stand a - lone.
(I.
I.
I.)
*w/ echo set for half-note regeneration w/ 2 repeats.

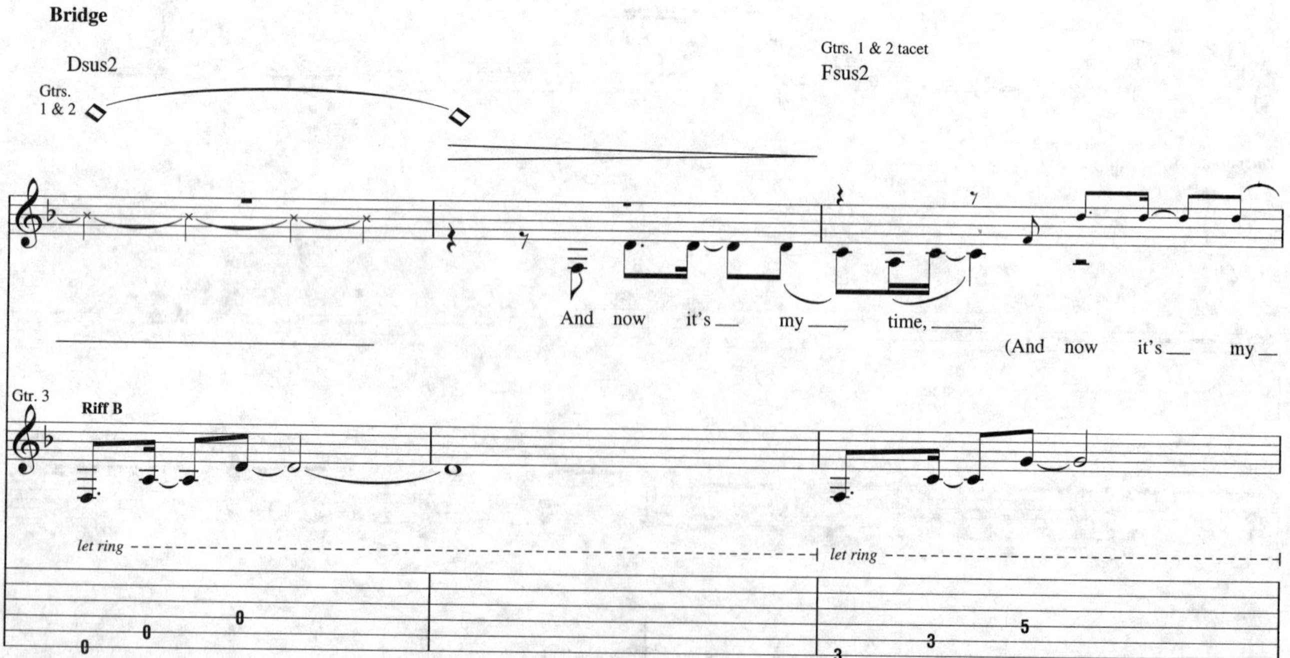
Bridge
Dsus2
Gtrs. 1 & 2
Gtrs. 1 & 2 tacet
Fsus2
And now it's my time,
(And now it's my
Gtr. 3
Riff B
let ring
let ring

Gtr. 3: w/ Riff B (3 times)
N.C.
D5
it's my time to dream,
time,
it's my time to dream,
dream of the
End Riff B
Gtr. 1
mf
P.S.
let ring
Gtr. 1 tacet
Fsus2
N.C.
skies.
dream of the skies.)
Make me be-
Dsus2
lieve that this place is-n't plagued by the poi-son in
Gtr. 2
mf
Gtr. 1
w/ amp tremolo
let ring

Fsus2
N.C.
me.
Help me de -
tremolo off
string noise
Gtr. 1 tacet
D5
cide if my fire will burn out be - fore you can
Gtr. 2
let ring
Fsus2
N.C.
breathe,
breathe in - to
Gtrs. 1 & 2

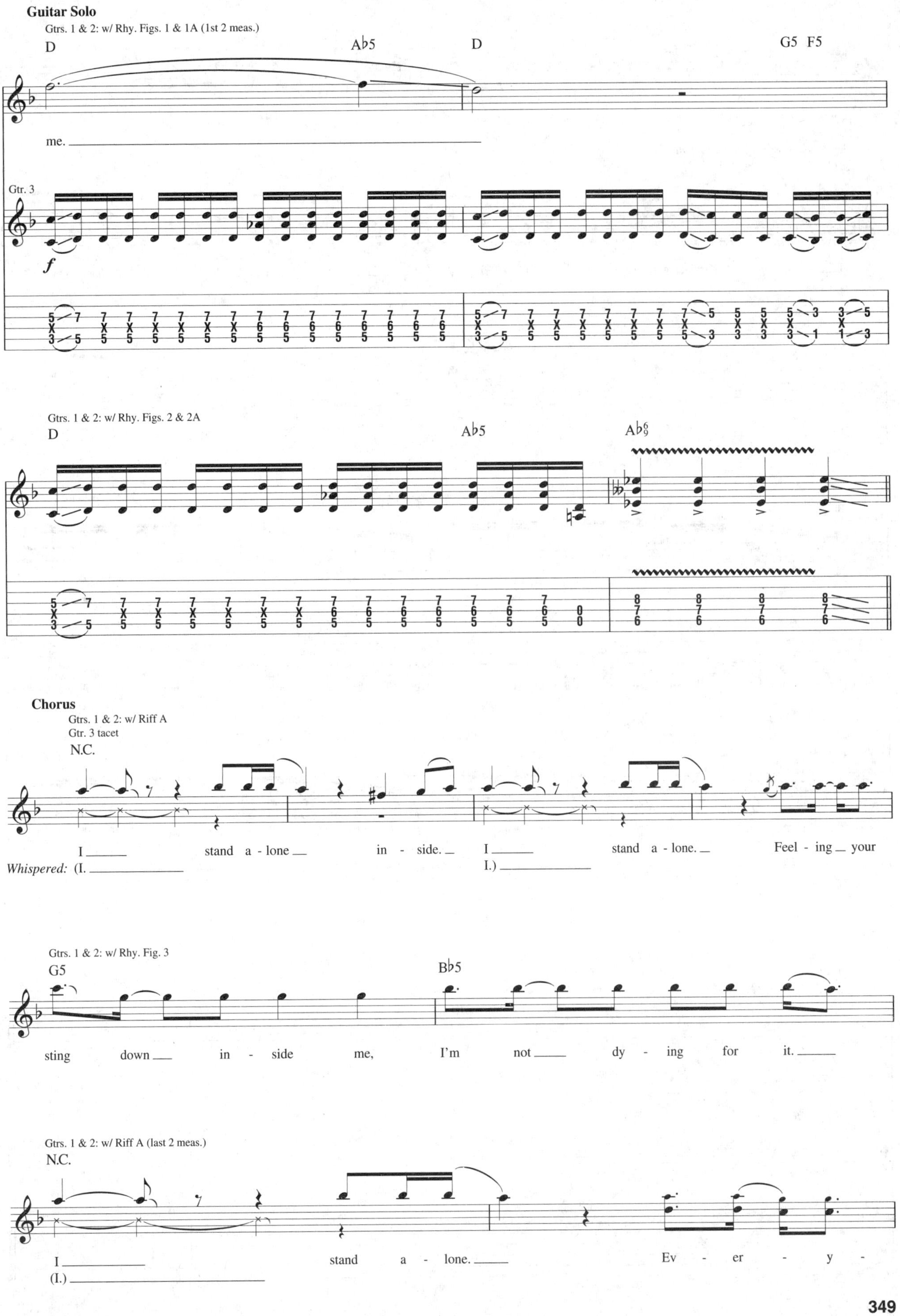
Guitar Solo
Gtrs. 1 & 2: w/ Rhy. Figs. 1 & 1A (1st 2 meas.)
D
A♭5
D
G5 F5
me.
Gtr. 3
f
Gtrs. 1 & 2: w/ Rhy. Figs. 2 & 2A
D
A♭5
A♭6/9
Chorus
Gtrs. 1 & 2: w/ Riff A
Gtr. 3 tacet
N.C.
I stand a - lone in - side. I stand a - lone. Feel - ing your
Whispered: (I. I.)
Gtrs. 1 & 2: w/ Rhy. Fig. 3
G5
B♭5
sting down in - side me, I'm not dy - ing for it.
Gtrs. 1 & 2: w/ Riff A (last 2 meas.)
N.C.
I stand a - lone. Ev - er - y -
(I.)

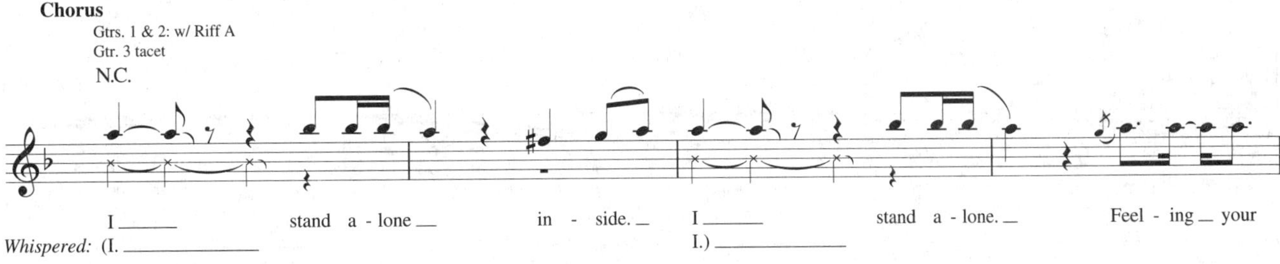

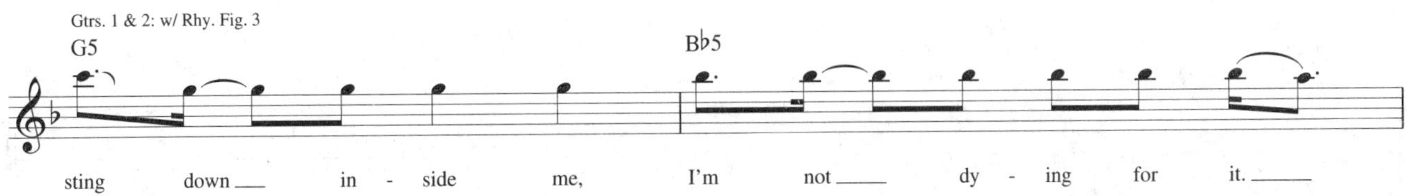

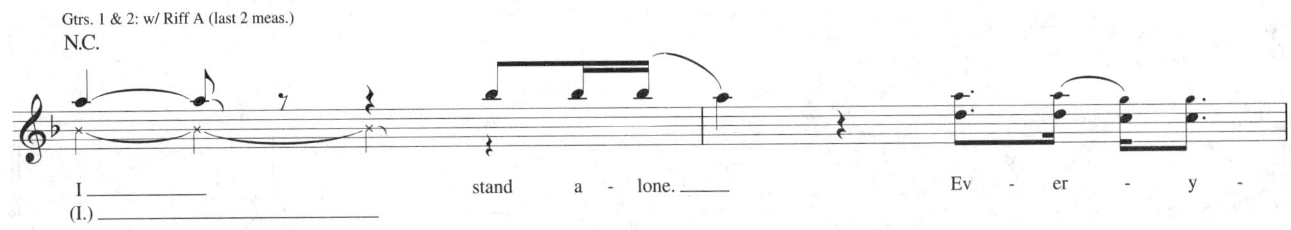

Gtrs. 1 & 2: w/ Rhy. Fig. 4
G5
B♭5
E♭5
thing that I be - lieve is fad - ing.
Gtrs. 1 & 2: w/ Riff A (1st 2 meas., 2 times)
N.C.
I stand a - lone in - side. I stand a - lone in - side.
(I. I.
I stand a - lone in - side.
I.
Riff C
Gtr. 1
End Riff C
Gtr. 2
Riff C1
End Riff C1
Gtrs. 1 & 2: w/ Riffs C & C1
I stand a - lone in - side.
I.)
Gtr. 3
mf

I'm Your Hoochie Coochie Man

Written by Willie Dixon

Chorus
D7
A7
Ev - 'ry - bod - y knows I'm here.
Well, you know I'm the Hoo - chie Coo - chie Man,
E7
1., 2.
D7
A7
E7
ev - 'ry - bod - y knows I'm here.
3.
D7 N.C.
A7
D7
A7 G7
G#7 A7
the whole round world knows I'm here.
1/4
1/4

The Impression That I Get

Words and Music by Dicky Barrett and Joe Gittleman

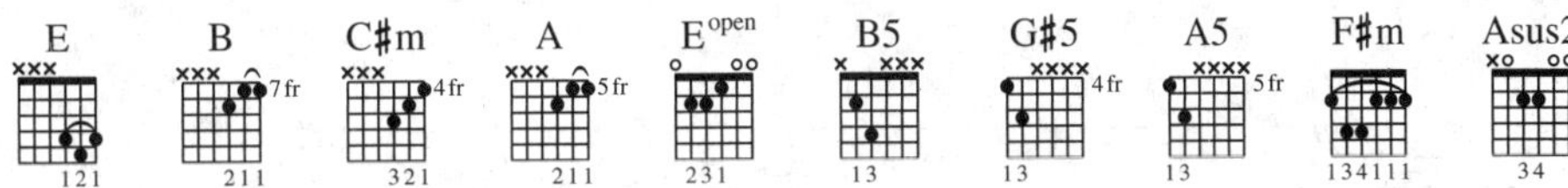

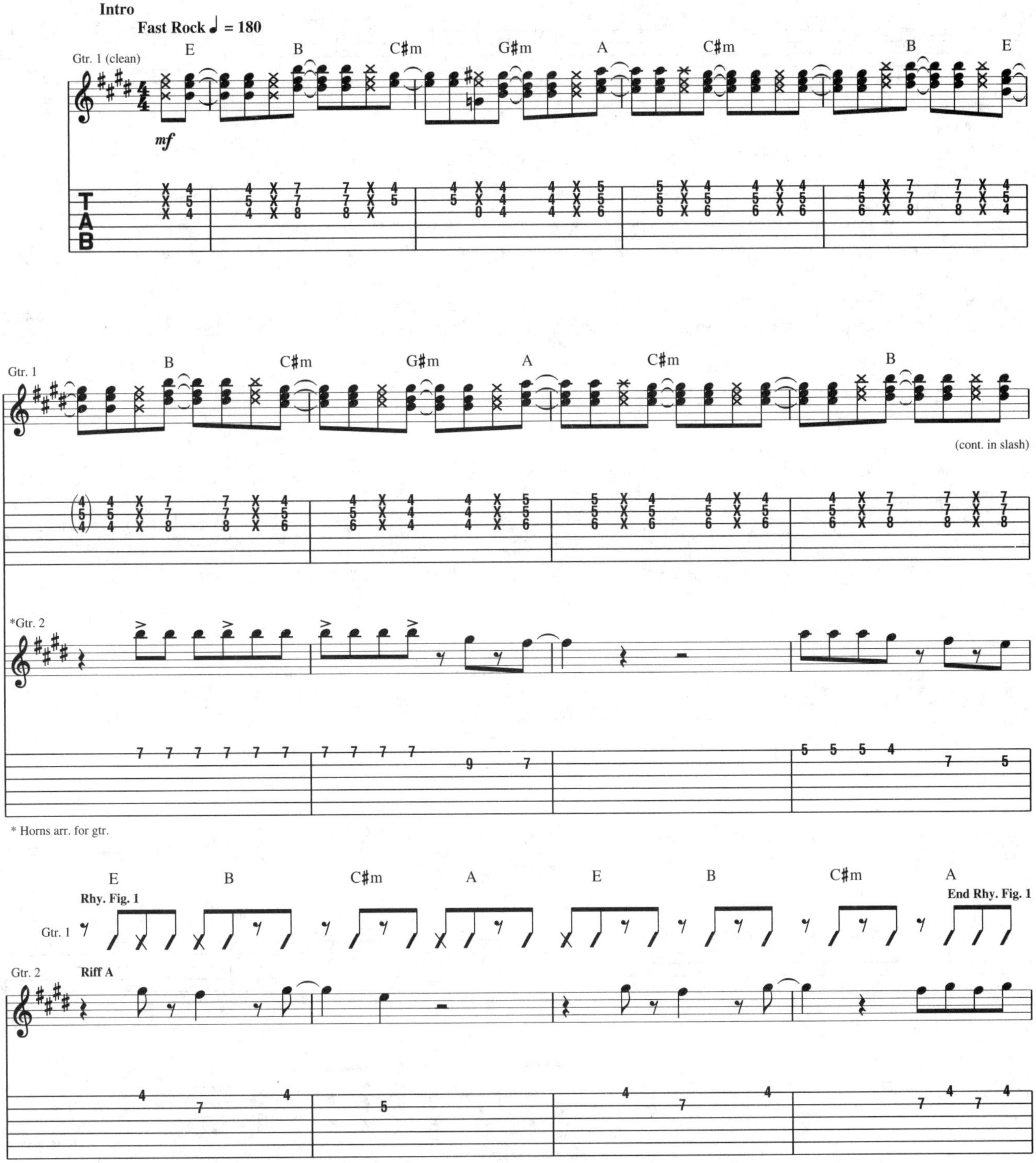

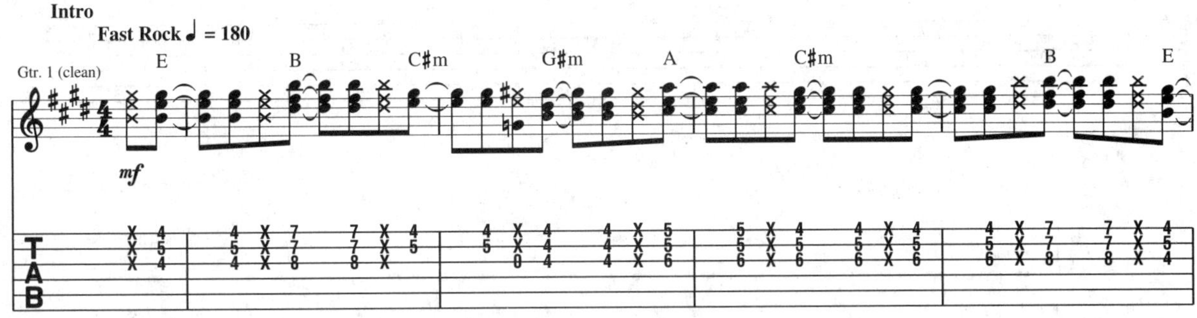

Gtr. 1

B C#m G#m A C#m B

(cont. in slash)

*Gtr. 2

* Horns arr. for gtr.

E B C#m A E B C#m A

Rhy. Fig. 1 — End Rhy. Fig. 1

Gtr. 1

Gtr. 2 Riff A

Verse

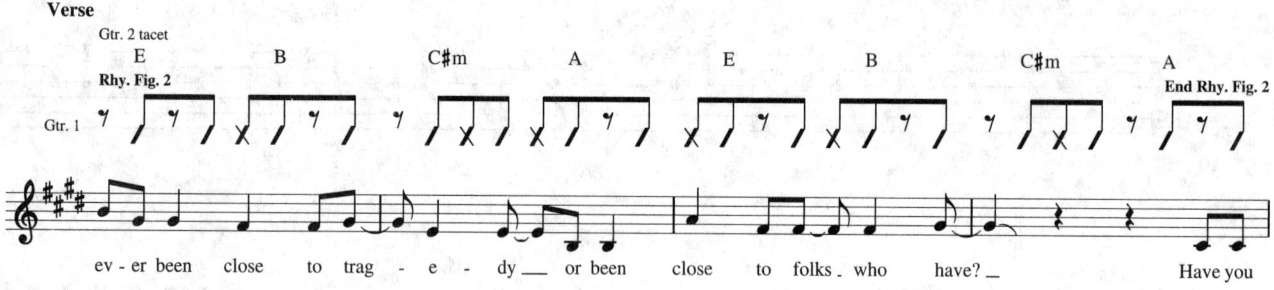

Pre-Chorus

Chorus
E open
B5
G♯5
Rhy. Fig. 4
Gtr. 3
nev - er had to knock on wood, but I know some - one who has,
Gtr. 1
Riff B
*let ring throughout
* next 16 meas.
A5
E open
which makes me won-der if I could. It makes me won-der if I've
B5
nev - er had to knock on wood. And I'm glad I have - n't yet,

G♯5
A5
End Rhy. Fig. 4
because I'm sure it is - n't good. That's the im - pres-sion that I get.
End Riff B
Interlude
Gtr. 1: w/ Rhy. Fig. 1, 2 times, simile
Gtr. 2: w/ Riff A
Gtr. 3 tacet
E B C♯m A E B C♯m A E B C♯m A E B C♯m A
2. Have you
Verse
*E B C♯m A E B C♯m A
ev - er had the odds stacked up so high you need a strength most don't pos - sess? Or has it
Gtr. 1
**slight P.M. throughout
* Chord symbols reflect implied tonality.
** next 8 meas.
E B C♯m A E B
Gtr. 3
P.S.
ev - er come down to do or die? You got to rise a - bove the rest.

Pre-Chorus
Gtr. 1: w/ Rhy. Fig. 3, simile
F#m
Asus2
F#m
Asus2
Gtr. 3
No.
Well,
I've
Chorus
Gtrs. 1 & 3: w/ Riff B & Rhy. Fig. 4, simile
E
B5
G#5
nev - er had to knock on wood,
but I know some - one who has
and I'm glad I have - n't yet
To Coda
A5
E
which makes me won - der if I could.
be - cause I'm sure it is - n't good.
It makes me won - der if I've
That's the im - pres - sion that I get.
Interlude
F#m
A5
F#m
A5
F#m
A5
E
Gtr. 3
Gtr. 1
Gtr. 3
divisi
Verse
Gtr. 3 tacet
E
B
C#m
G#m
A
C#m
B
E
3. I'm not a cow - ard, I've just nev - er been test - ed.
I'd like to think that if I was, I would pass.
Gtr. 1

D.S. al Coda
(take repeat)
B C♯m G♯m A C♯m B
Look at the test-ed and think, there, but for the grace go I. Might be a cow-ard, I'm a - fraid of what I might find out.
Gtr. 1
Gtr. 3
P.S.

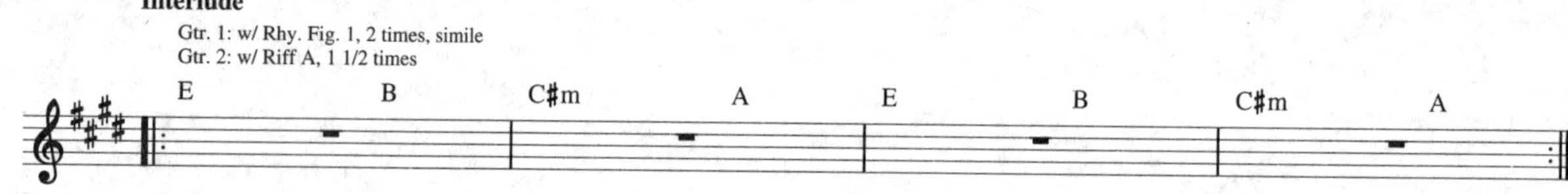
Coda
Interlude
Gtr. 1: w/ Rhy. Fig. 1, 2 times, simile
Gtr. 2: w/ Riff A, 1 1/2 times
E B C♯m A E B C♯m A

Gtr. 1
E B C♯m A E B C♯m A
*slight P.M. throughout
* next 8 meas.

Gtr. 1
E B C♯m A E B C♯m A
Gtr. 2

Outro
Gtrs. 1 & 2 tacet
N.C.(E)
(B)
I've nev - er had to, but I bet - ter knock on wood 'cause I know some - one who has
(A)
which makes me won - der if I could. It makes me won - der if I've...
Gtr. 1
p
(E)
(B)
Nev - er had to, but I bet - ter knock on wood 'cause I'm
pp
(A)
sure it is - n't good and I'm glad I have - n't yet.
(A)
That's the im - pres - sion that I get.
decresc.

Iron Man

Words and Music by Frank Iommi, John Osbourne, William Ward and Terence Butler

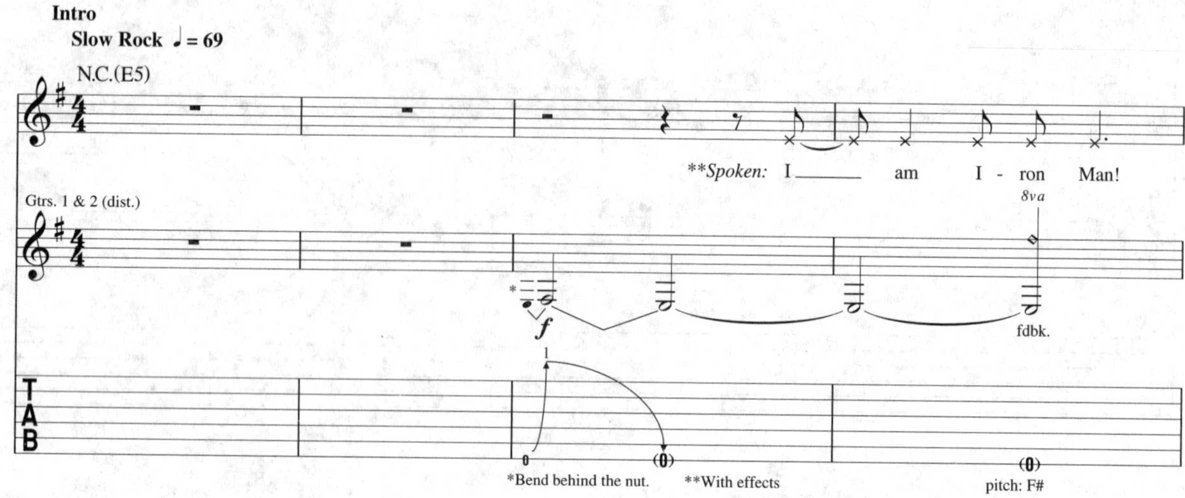

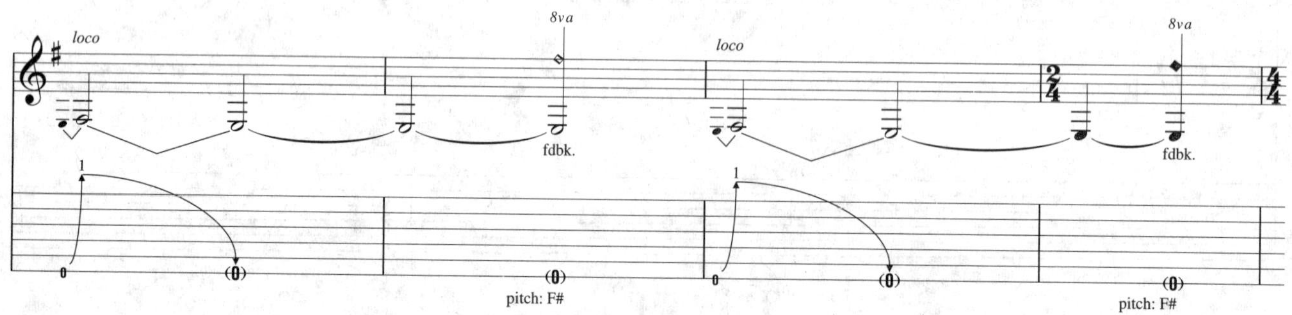

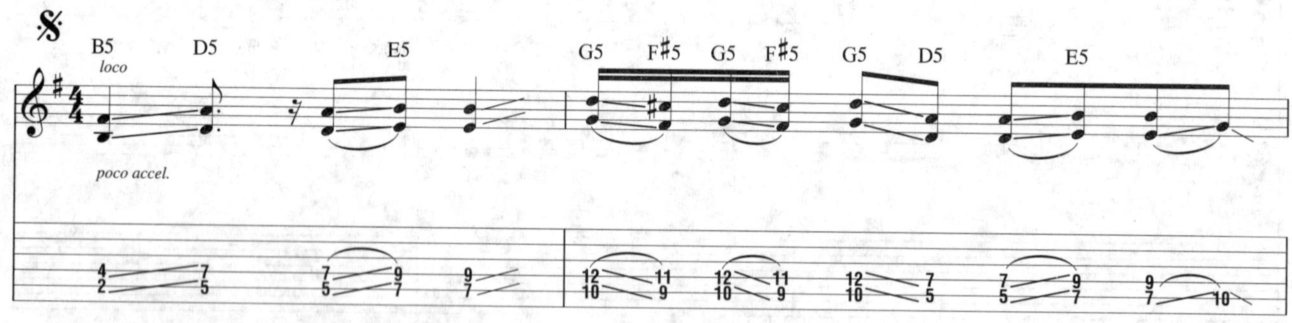

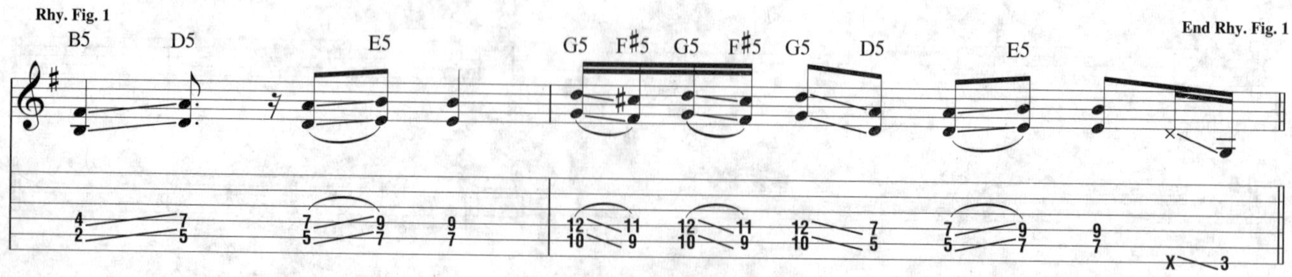

Verse
Slightly Faster ♩ = 76
N.C.(B5) (D5) (E5) (G5) (F♯5) (G5) (F♯5) (G5) (F♯5) (D5) (E5)
1. Has he lost his mind? Can he see or is he blind?
2. Is he live or dead? I see thoughts with - in his head.
3. Heav - y boots of lead, fills his vic - tims full of dread,
Riff A
End Riff A
Gtrs. 1 & 2: w/ Riff A
(B5) (D5) (E5) (G5) (F♯5) (G5) (F♯5) (G5) (D5) (E5)
Can he walk at all, or if he moves will he fall?
We'll just pass him there. Why should we e - ven care?
run - ning as fast as they can. I - ron Man lives a - gain!
1. Gtrs. 1 & 2: w/ Rhy. Fig. 1
B5 D5 E5 G5 F♯5 G5 F♯5 G5 D5 E5
2.
Interlude
Gtrs. 1 & 2
N.C.(B5) (A5) (B5)
simile on repeat
1/4
(A5) (B5) (A5)
To Coda
B5 D5 E5 G5 F♯5 G5 F♯5 G5 D5 E5

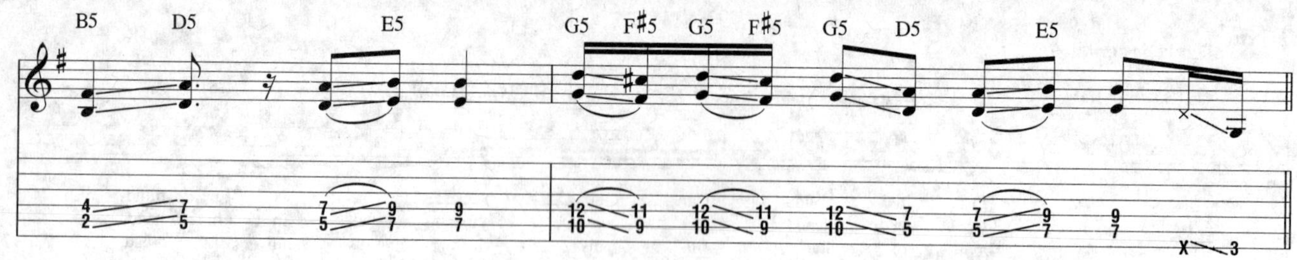

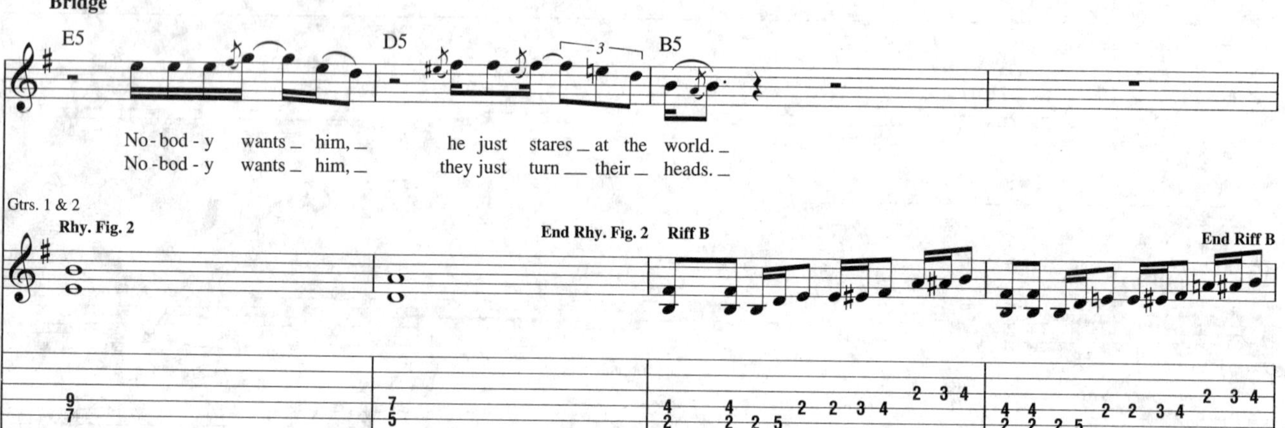

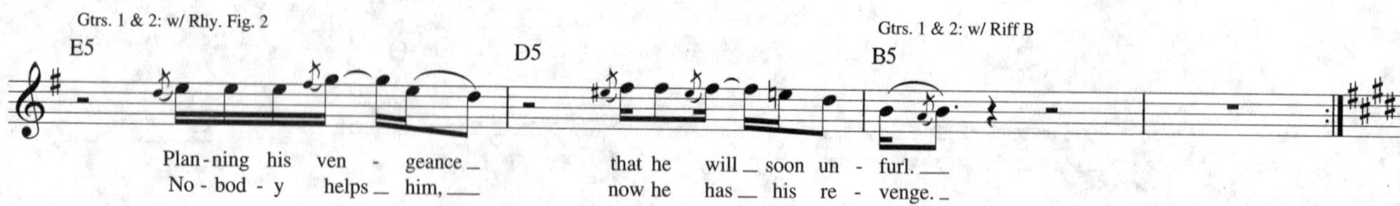

Interlude

Double - Time ♩ = 164

N.C. (C♯m)

Gtrs. 1 & 2 **Riff C** **End Riff C**

Guitar Solo

Interlude

Half - Time Feel ♩ = 76

Gtrs. 1 & 2: w/ Riff B, 2 times

D.S. al Coda
(take 2nd ending)

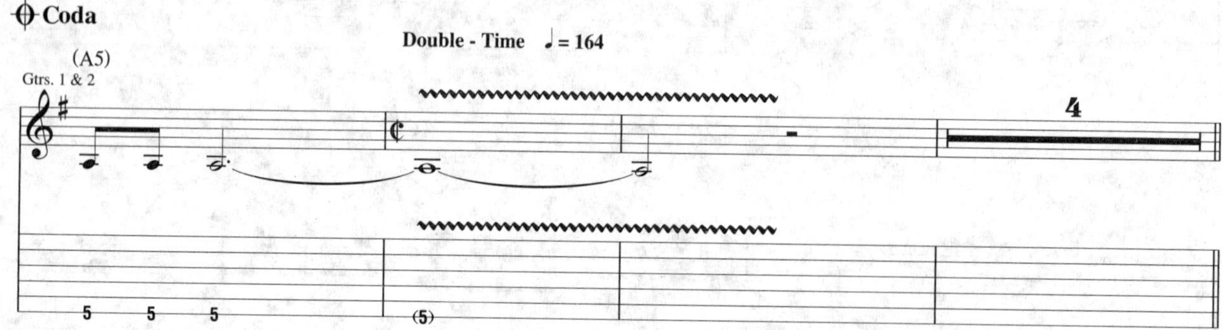

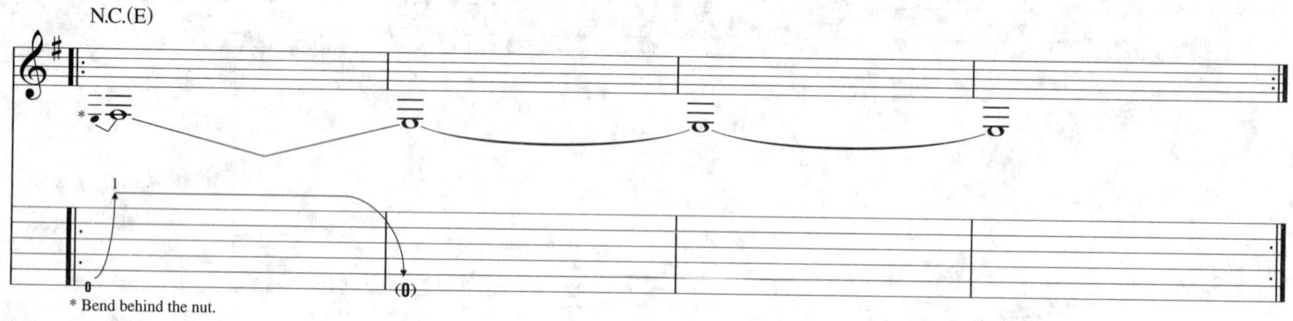

* Bend behind the nut.

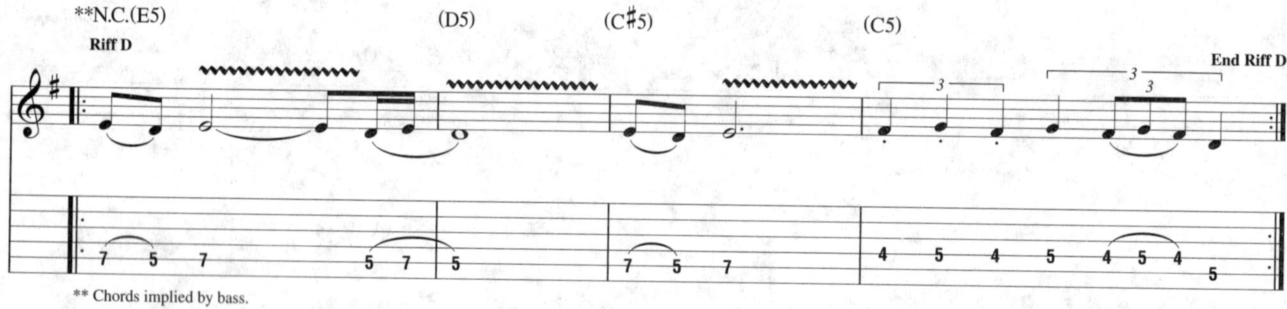

** Chords implied by bass.

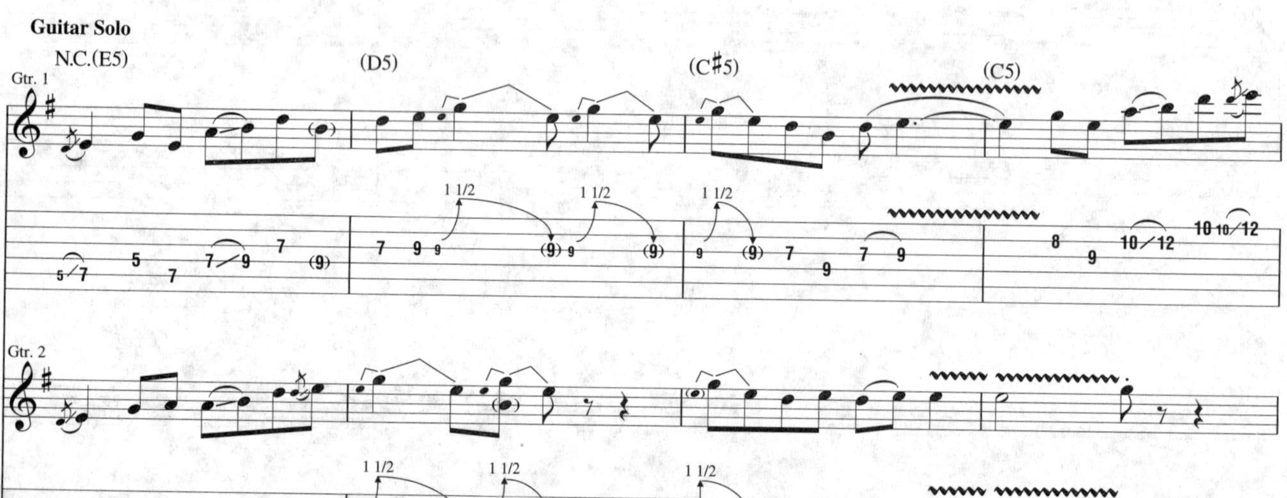

Outro

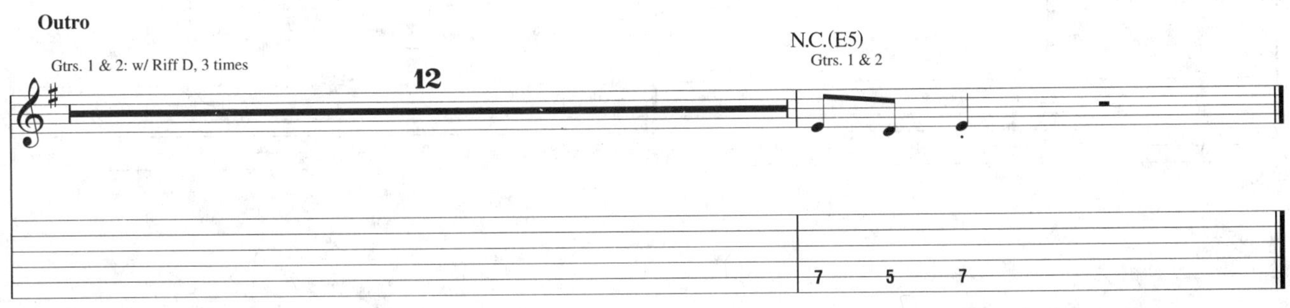

It Hurts Me Too

Words and Music by Mel London

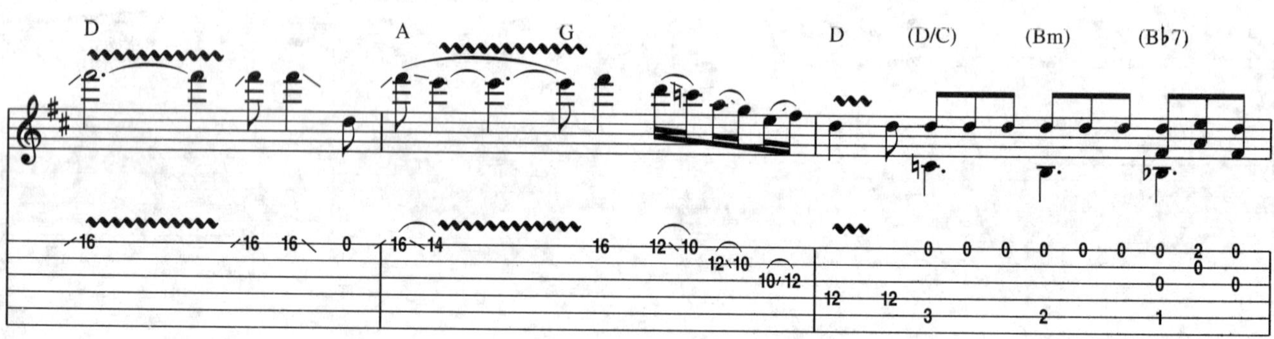

G5 G6 G5 G6
mind. Now, the man you love, he hurt you all the
less. Why make up be - hind him, and take his
you. But you love him, and stick to him like
down. No, I won't stand to see you pushed a -
To Coda
G5 G6 G5 G6 D A5 A6 G5 G6 G5
time. mess? glue. round.
But when things go wrong, so wrong with you, it hurts me
1., 2.
3.
D.S. al Coda
D A A
too.
2. You'll love him more,
3. He love an-oth-er
Coda
A5 A6 G5 D (D/C) (Bm) (B♭7) (D/A) D
you, it hurts me too.

Jessica

Written by Dickey Betts

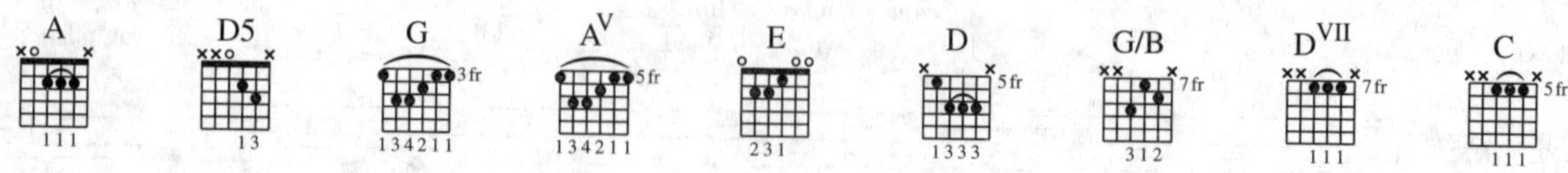

Intro

Uptempo Country Rock ♩ = 208

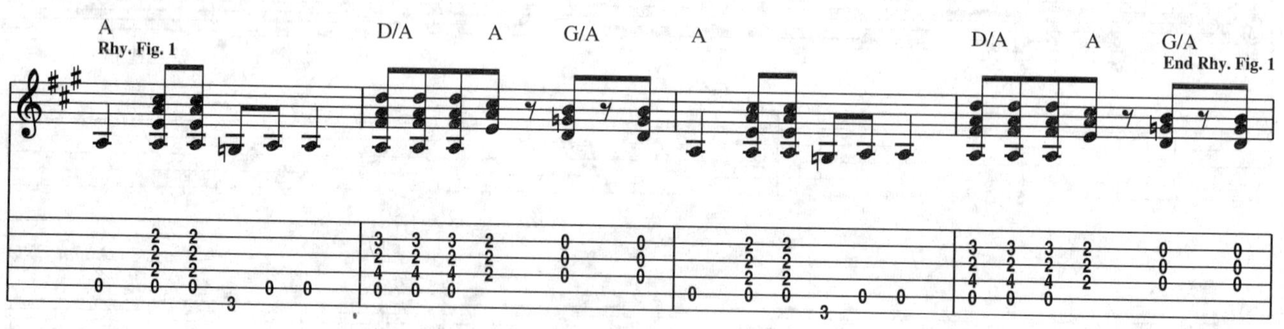

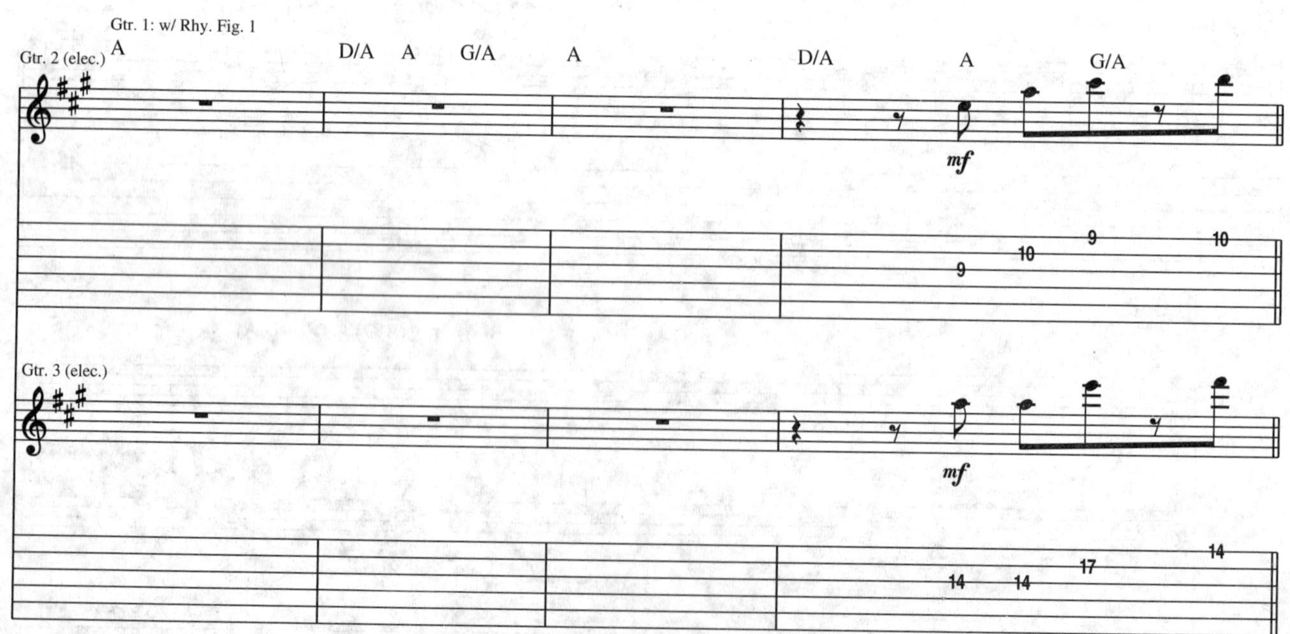

Chorus
Gtr. 1: w/ Rhy. Fig. 1, 3 times
A
D/A
A
G/A
A
D/A
A
G/A
full
full

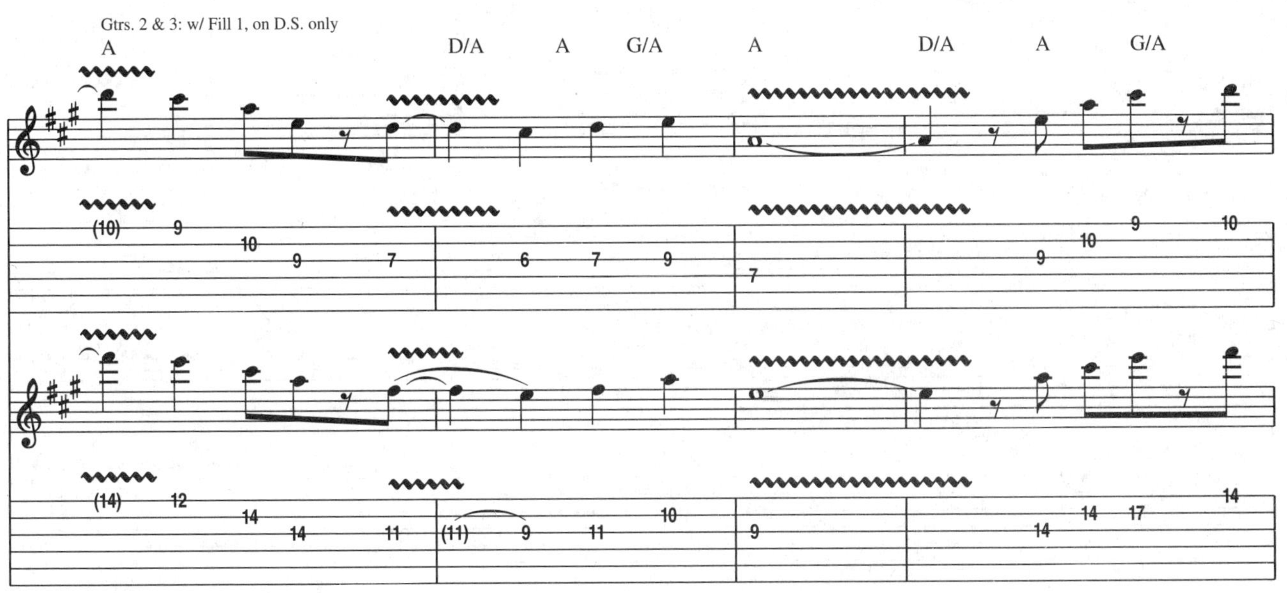
Gtrs. 2 & 3: w/ Fill 1, on D.S. only
A
D/A
A
G/A
A
D/A
A
G/A

Fill 1
Gtr. 2
Gtr. 3

1.
A
D/A
A
G/A
A
D/A
A
G/A
full
full
Gtr. 1: w/ Rhy. Fig. 1, 1st 3 meas. only
A
D/A
A
G/A
A
A
D5
Gtr. 1

2.
Gtr. 1: w/ Rhy. Fig. 1
A
D/A
A
G/A
To Coda
Bridge
Gtr. 3 tacet
G
Rhy. Fig. 2
Gtr. 1
sim.
Gtr. 2
* Strum bottom 3 stgs. only.

A
G
E
full full
Chorus
Gtr. 1: w/ Rhy. Fig. 1, 3 times
A
D/A
A
G/A
A
End Rhy. Fig. 2
Gtr. 2
full
full
Gtr. 3
D/A
A
G/A
A
D/A
A
G/A
A

D/A A G/A A D/A A G/A A

full full

Gtr. 1: w/ Rhy. Fig. 1, 1st 2 meas. only

D/A A G/A A D/A A G/A

Gtrs. 1 & 3 tacet

N.C.

Gtr. 2

*Gtr. 4

* Gtr. & piano arr. for one gtr.

1 1/2

Breakdown
Gtr. 1
A
D/A
A
D/A
A
Gtr. 2
hold bend
1/4
hold bend
1/4
A
Rhy. Fig. 3
D/A
A
D/A
A
End Rhy. Fig. 3
Riff A
End Riff A
hold bend
1/4
hold bend
1/4
Gtr. 1: w/ Rhy. Fig. 3
Gtr. 2: w/ Riff A
*Gtr. 5
A
D/A
A
D/A
A
* Piano arr. for gtr.
Gtr. 1: w/ Rhy. Fig. 3, 7 times
Gtr. 2: w/ Riff A, 7 times
A
D/A
A
D/A
A
play 7 times
let ring

Piano Solo
play 16 times
A
D/A
A
D/A
N.C.
Gtr. 1
Gtrs. 1 & 2
Guitar Solo
D
D
5fr
Rhy. Fig. 4
Gtr. 1
Gtr. 2
G/B
D^VII
C
End. Rhy. Fig. 4
Gtr. 1: w/ Rhy. Fig. 4, 49 times
D
full

G/B D^VII C D G/B D^VII C D
G/B D^VII C D G/B D^VII C D
G/B D^VII C D G/B D^VII C D G/B D^VII C
full
D G/B D^VII C D G/B D^VII C D
G/B D^VII C D G/B D^VII C D
G/B D^VII C D G/B D^VII C D
full
full

G/B
D^VII
C
D
full
3

G/B D^{VII} C D G/B D^{VII} C D G/B D^{VII} C
full
full
D G/B D^{VII} C D G/B D^{VII} C D
8va
full
G/B D^{VII} C D G/B D^{VII} C D G/B D^{VII} C
8va
full
D G/B D^{VII} C D G/B D^{VII} C
8va
full
full
D G/B D^{VII} C D G/B D^{VII} C
8va

loco
D
G/B
D^VII
C
Gtr. 1
G

G
D
D VII
G/B
D VII
C
D VII
G/B
D VII
C
D VII
Gtr. 1 tacet
Gtr. 2
N.C.(D)
Gtr. 3

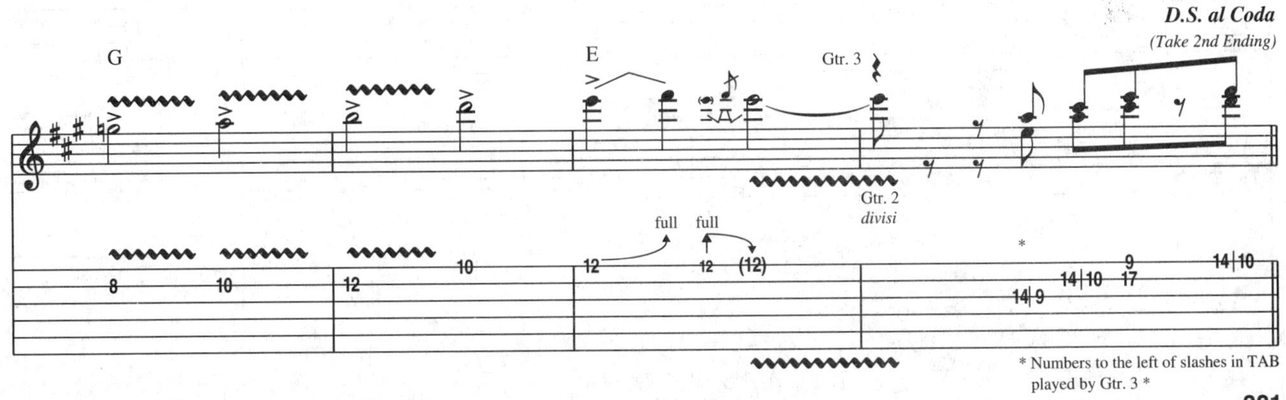

* Numbers to the left of slashes in TAB played by Gtr. 3 *

Coda
Gtr. 1: w/ Rhy. Fig. 1, 4 times
D/A
A
G/A
A
full
full
D/A
A
G/A
A

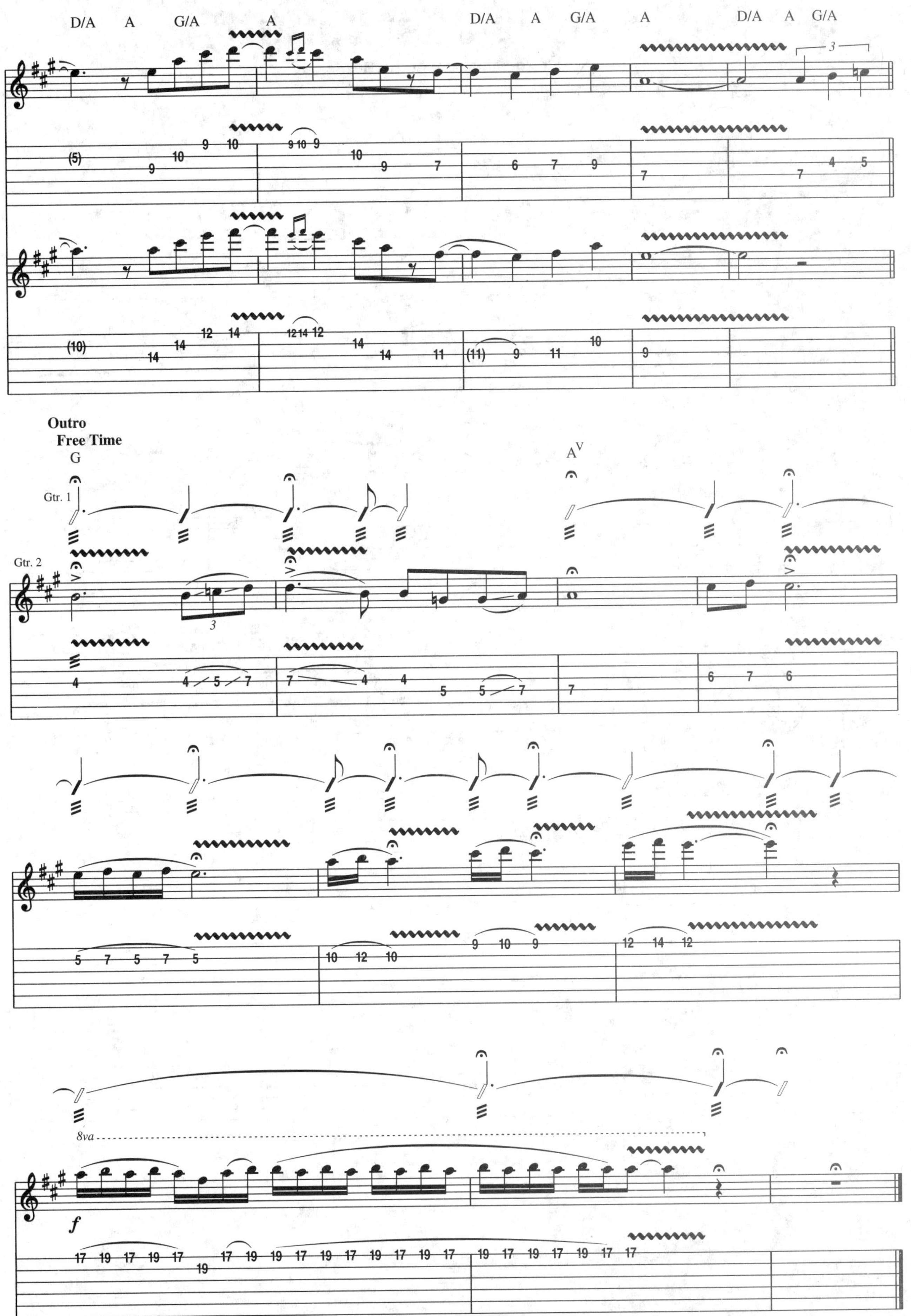

D/A A G/A A D/A A G/A A D/A A G/A
Outro
Free Time
G
Gtr. 1
Gtr. 2
A^{V}
8va

Jesus Is Just Alright

Words and Music by Arthur Reynolds

Lead Voc.: w/ Voc. Fill 2, 3rd time
Lead Voc.: w/ Voc. Fill 1, 2nd time
D/A
Am7
E7#9
F9
E7#9
with me,
Je - sus is just al - right.
End Rhy. Fig. 1
simile on repeats
Gtr. 1: w/ Rhy. Fig. 1, simile
Am
D/A
Am
I don't care what they may say,
I don't care what they may know.
I don't care what they
I don't care where they
To Coda 1
To Coda 2
E7#9
Am
D/A
Am7
may do.
may go.
I don't care what they may say.
I don't care what they may know.
Je - sus is just al - right,
C5
Am
E7#9
F9
whoa, yeah.
Je - sus is just al - right.
Gtr. 1
Chorus
Voc. Fill 1
End Voc. Fill 1
E7#9
Am
D/A
Whoa, ho, ho.
Do, do, do, do, do, do, do, do,

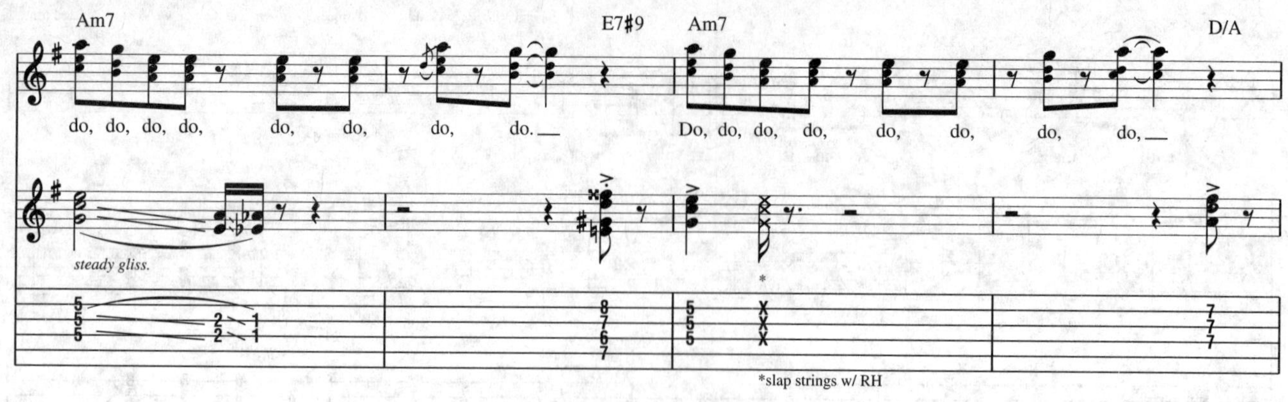

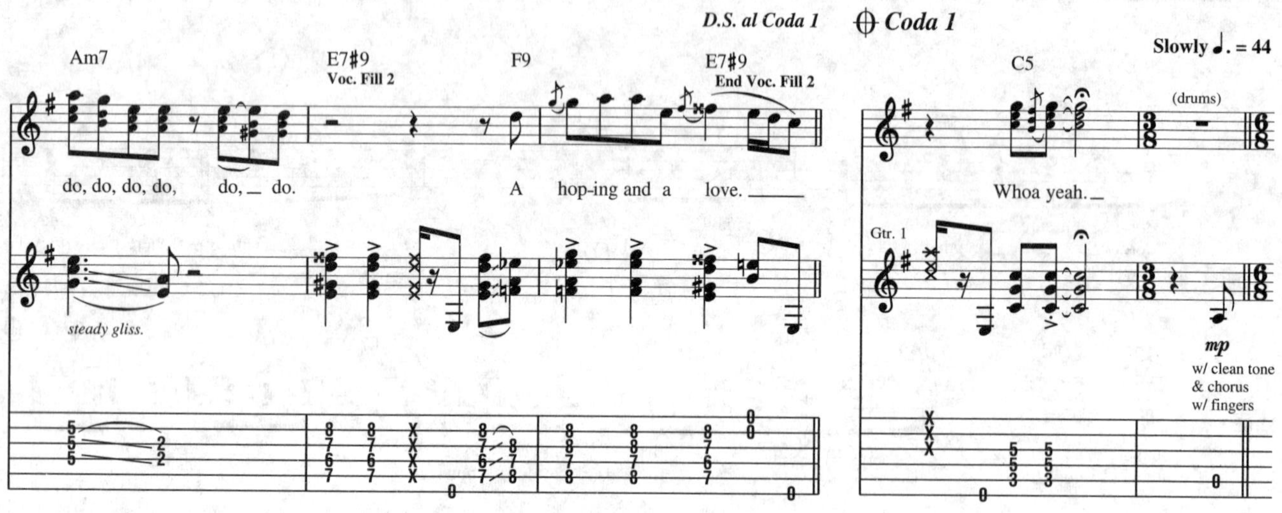

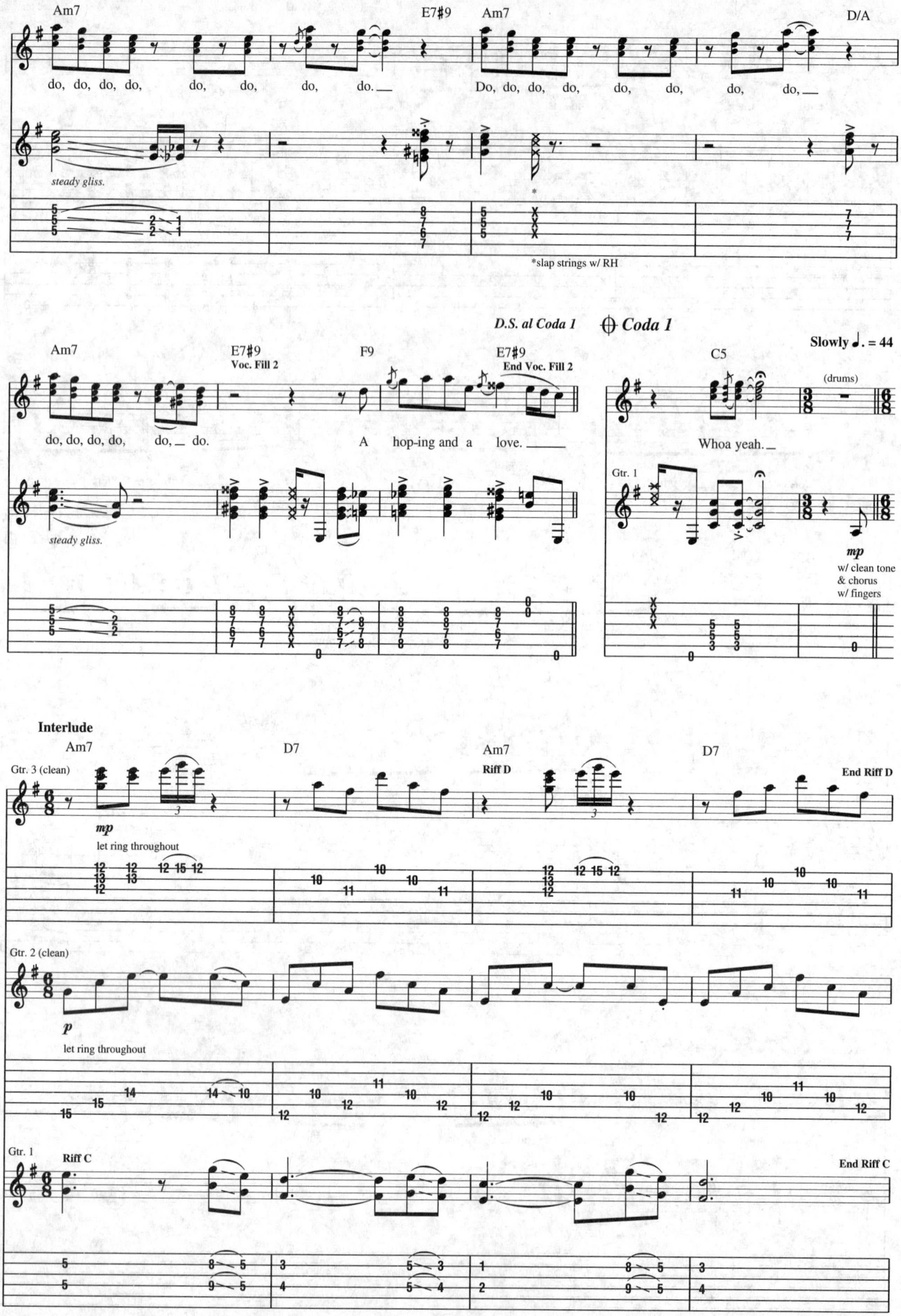
Am7
E7#9
Am7
D/A
do, do, do, do, do, do, do, do.
Do, do, do, do, do, do, do, do,
steady gliss.
*slap strings w/ RH
D.S. al Coda 1
Coda 1
Slowly ♩. = 44
Am7
E7#9
Voc. Fill 2
F9
E7#9
End Voc. Fill 2
C5
(drums)
do, do, do, do, do, do.
A hop-ing and a love.
Whoa yeah.
steady gliss.
Gtr. 1
mp
w/ clean tone
& chorus
w/ fingers
Interlude
Am7
D7
Am7
Riff D
D7
End Riff D
Gtr. 3 (clean)
mp
let ring throughout
Gtr. 2 (clean)
p
let ring throughout
Gtr. 1
Riff C
End Riff C

Gtr. 1: w/ Riff C, 1 3/4 times, simile
Gtr. 3: w/ Riff D, 7 1/2 times, simile
Am7
D7
Gtr. 2: w/ Riff E, 6 1/2 times, simile
Am7
Je - sus,
he's my
friend.
Gtr. 2
Riff E
End Riff E
Gtr. 4 (dist.)
mf
full
D7
Am7
D7
Am7
But Je - sus
well he's my
friend.
mp
mf
Gtr. 1: w/ Fill 1
D7
Gtr. 1: w/ Riff C, 1 3/4 times
Am
D7
He took me by the hand,
full
Am7
D7
Am7
D7
and lead me far
from this land.
Je - sus,
he's my
mp
mf
full
Fill 1
Gtr. 1

Guitar Solo

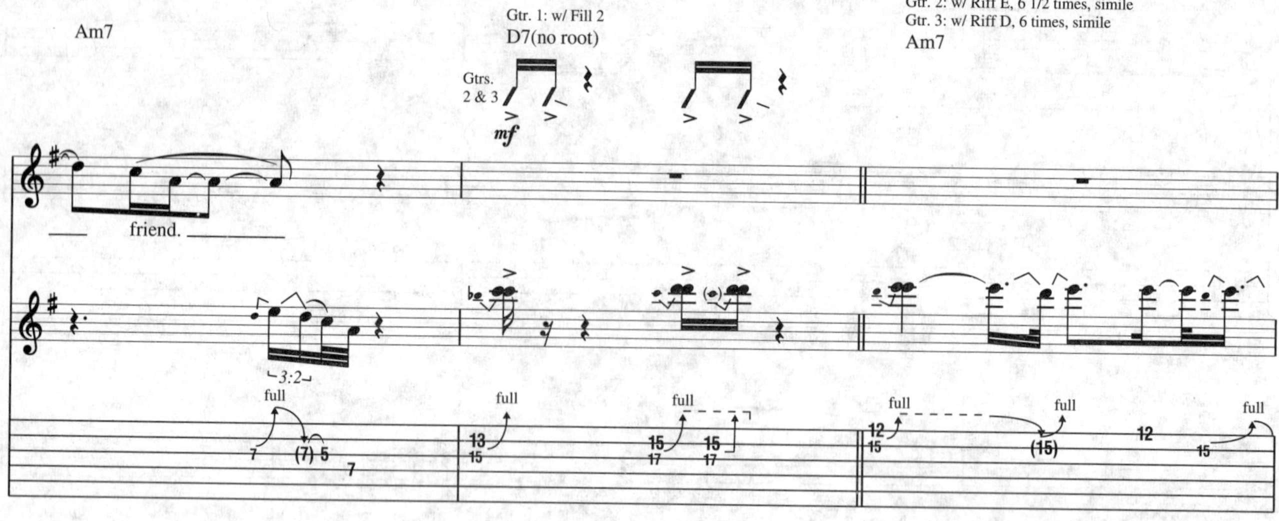
Gtr. 1: w/ Riff C, 1 3/4 times, simile
Gtr. 2: w/ Riff E, 6 1/2 times, simile
Gtr. 3: w/ Riff D, 6 times, simile
Am7
Gtr. 1: w/ Fill 2
D7(no root)
Gtrs. 2 & 3
mf
friend.
3:2
full

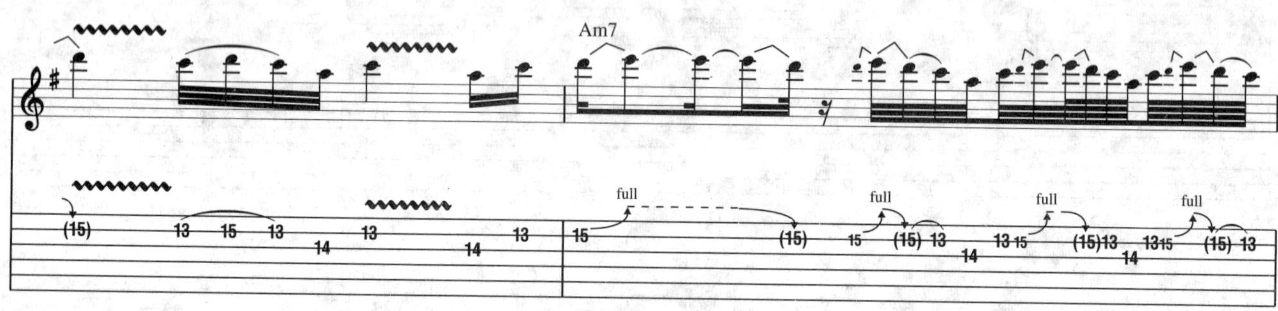
Am7
full

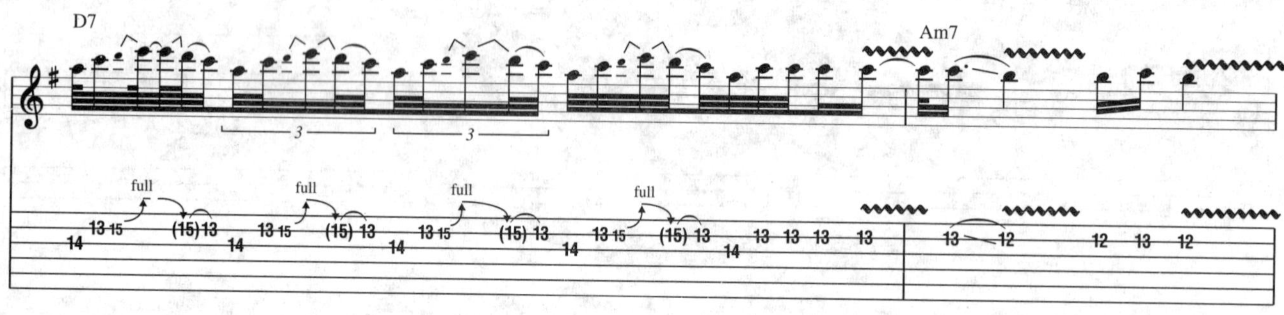
D7
Am7
full

D7
Am7
Gtr. 1: w/ Fill 1
Gtr. 4 tacet
Gtr. 1
full
1/2 full

Fill 2
Gtr. 1

Guitar Solo
A Tempo
Gtr. 3: w/ Fill 3
*Gtr. 1: w/ Riff A, 7 times
Am7
D7
Am7
Am
Gtr. 4
rit.
mp
*w/ dist.
mf
rake
full
1/4
3/4
D.S. al Coda 2
(take 1st lyrics)
Gtr. 1: w/ Riff B
8va
Em
1/2
Coda 2
C5
Whoa, yeah.
Fill 3
Gtr. 3

Kind Hearted Woman Blues

Words and Music by Robert Johnson

*Tune Down 1/2 Step; Capo II:

①=E♭ ④=D♭

②=B♭ ⑤=A♭

③=G♭ ⑥=E♭

**Symbols in parentheses represent chord names (implied tonality) respective to capoed guitar. Symbols above reflect harmony implied by vocals. Capoed fret is "0" in TAB.

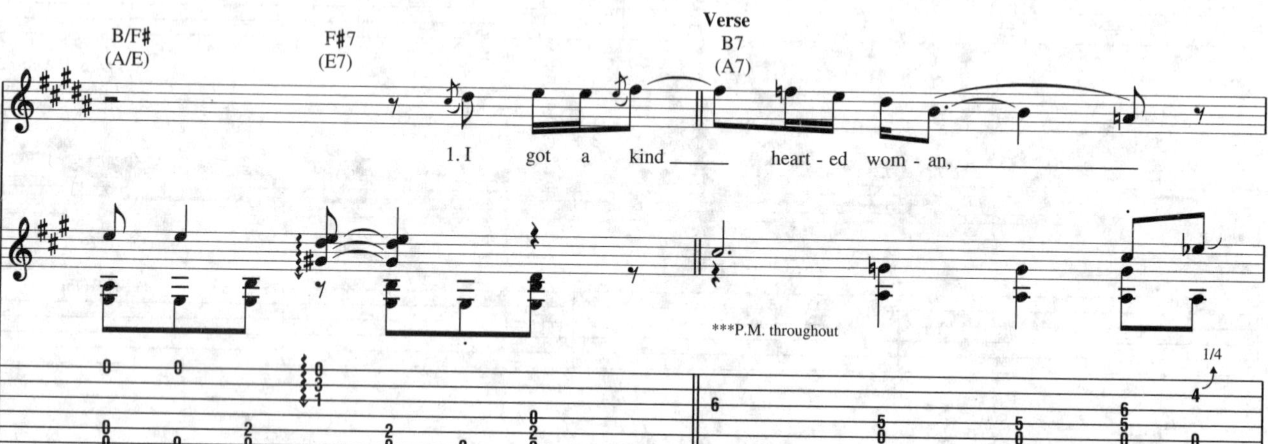

***downstemmed notes only, except during the Bridge

*Tunings were determined using the original 78s. To play along with the *Robert Johnson - The Complete Recordings* CD set, Capo III.

B7
(A7)
E7/G#
(D7/F#)
I got a kind heart-ed wom-an,
do an-y-thing'n this world for me.
B7
(A7)
B°7
(A°7)
B7
(A7)
F#7
(E7)
But these e-
E7/G#
(D7/F#)
vil heart-ed wom-en,
man, they will not let me be.
B
(A)
B7/A
(A7/G)
E/G#
(D/F#)
Em/G
(Dm/F)
B/F#
(A/E)
F#7
(E7)
Verse
B7
(A7)
2. I love my ba-by.
My ba-by don't love me.

B°7
(A°7)
B7
(A7)
B°7
(A°7)
B7
(A7)
E7/G#
(D7/F#)
I love my ba - by, oooh.
B7
(A7)
B°7
(A°7)
B7
(A7)
My ba - by don't love me.
I real - ly
F#7
(E7)
E7/B
(D7/A)
love that wom - an,
can't stand to leave her be.
B
(A)
B7/A
(A7/G)
E/G#
(D/F#)
Em/G
(Dm/F)
B/F#
(A/E)
F#7
(E7)
Bridge
B7
(A7)
A - ain't but the one thing

B°7
(A°7)
B7
(A7)
B°7
(A°7)
makes Mis - ter John - son drink. I's wor - ried 'bout how you treat me, ba - by.
B7
(A7)
B°7
(A°7)
B7
(A7)
E7/G#
(A7/F#)
I be - gin to think. Oh, babe, my life don't feel the same.
1/2
* P.M.
1/4
* Resume P.M. on downstem notes.
B7
(A7)
B°7
(A°7)
B7
(A7)
F#7
(E7)
You breaks my heart when you call
E7/B
(D7/A)
B
(A)
B7/A
(A7/G)
E/G#
(D/F#)
Em/G
(Dm/F)
B/F#
(A/E)
F#7
(E7)
Mis - ter So - and - So's name.

Guitar Solo
B7
(A7)
1/4

E7/G♯
(D7/F♯)
B7
(A7)

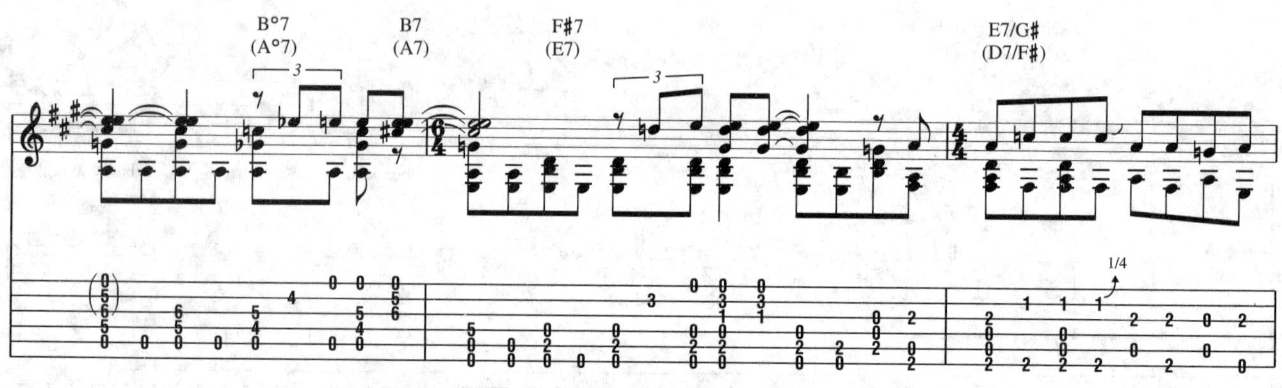
B°7
(A°7)
B7
(A7)
F♯7
(E7)
E7/G♯
(D7/F♯)
1/4

B5
(A5)
B7/A
(A7/G)
E/G♯
(D/F♯)
Em/G
(Dm/F)
B/F♯
(A/E)
F♯7
(E7)
Verse
B7
(A7)
3. She's a kind ___ heart-ed wom-an, ___

B°7
(A°7)
B7
(A7)
B°7
(A°7)
B7
(A7)
she stud-ies e - vil all the time.
She's a kind
E7/F♯
(D7/F♯)
heart - ed wom - an,
she stud - ies e - vil all the time.
B7
(A7)
B°7
(A°7)
B7
(A7)
F♯7
(E7)
You well's to kill me,
E7/G♯
(D7/A)
B
(A)
B7/A
(A7/G)
E/G♯
(D/F♯)
Em/G
(Dm/F)
F♯7
(E7)
B7
(A7)
as to have it on your mind.

Landslide

Words and Music by Stevie Nicks

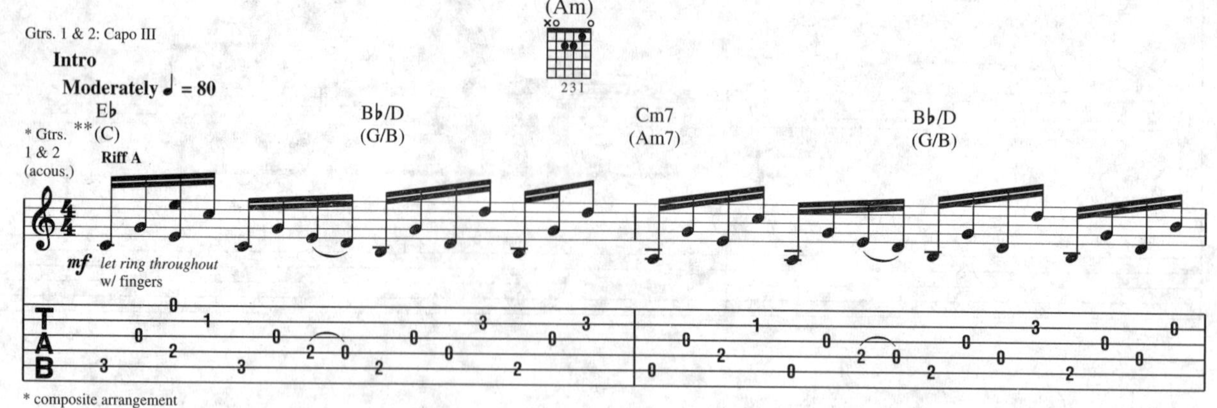

* composite arrangement

** Symbols in parentheses represent chord names respective capoed guitar. Symbols above reflect actual sounding chords. Capoed fret is "0" in tab. Chord symbols reflect implied harmony.

Eb (C) Bb/D (G/B) Cm7 (Am7) Bb/D (G/B)

End Riff A

Verse

Gtrs. 1 & 2: w/ Riff A (1 1/2 times)

Eb (C) Bb/D (G/B) Cm7 (Am7) Bb/D (G/B)

1. I took my love, took it down.
mir-ror in the sky, what is love? Can the child

Eb (C) Bb/D (G/B) Cm7 (Am7) Bb/D (G/B)

Climbed a moun - tain and I turned a - round. And I saw
with - in my heart rise a - bove? Can I sail

Eb (C) Bb/D (G/B Cm7 (Am7) Bb/D (G/B)

my re - flec - tion in the snow - cov - ered hills till the
through the chang - ing o - cean tides? Can I

Eb (C) Bb/D (G/B) 1. Cm7 (Am7) Bb/D (G/B)

land - slide brought me down.
han - dle the sea - sons of 2. Oh,

Gtrs. 1 & 2

2.
Cm7
(Am7)
B♭/D
(G/B)
E♭
(C)
B♭/D
(G/B)
my
life?
Gtr. 1
* Gtr. 2
* Two gtrs. arr. for one.
Mm.
Chorus
F7/A
(D7/F♯)
B♭
(G)
F/A
(D/F♯)
Well,
I've
been
a - fraid
of
chang -
Riff B
Riff B1

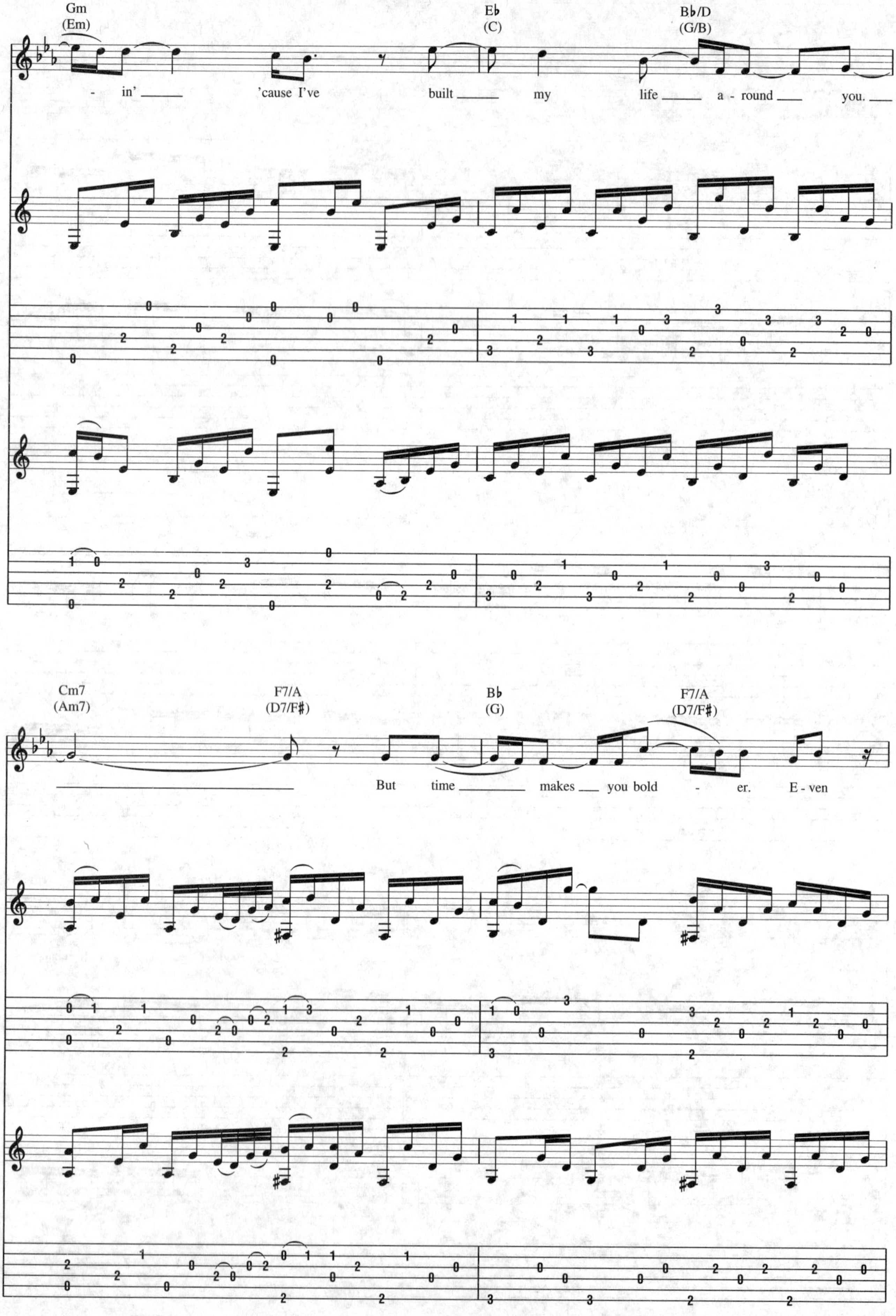

Gm (Em) | E♭ (C) | B♭/D (G/B)

-in' 'cause I've built my life a-round you.

Cm7 (Am7) | F7/A (D7/F♯) | B♭ (G) | F7/A (D7/F♯)

But time makes you bold-er. E-ven

Gm
(Em)
Eb
(C)
Bb/D
(G/B)
chil - dren get old - er and I'm get-tin' old - er too.
End Riff B
End Riff B1
Guitar Solo
Gtrs. 1 & 2: w/ Riff A (1 3/4 times)
Cm7
(Am7)
Bb/D
(G/B)
Eb
(C)
Bb/D
(G/B)
Cm7
(Am7)
Bb/D
(G/B)
Gtr. 3 (elec.)
mf
w/ clean tone
Gtr. 1
Gtr. 2

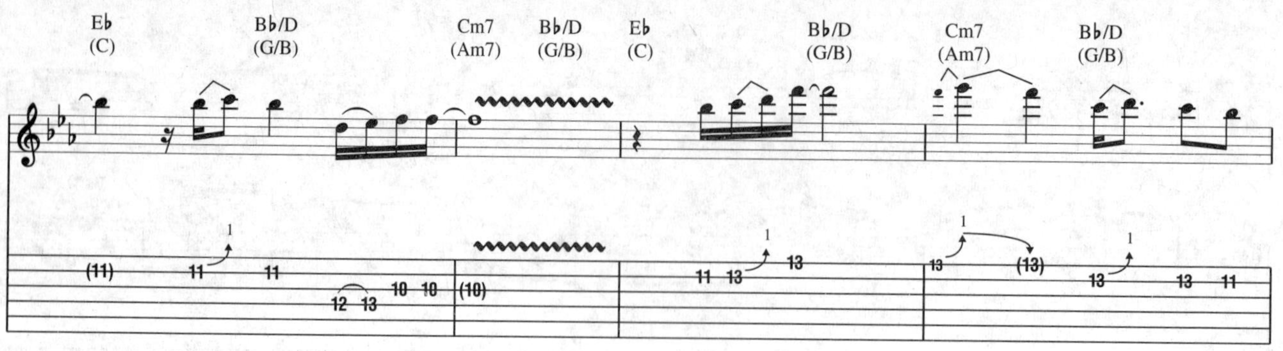
Eb
(C)
Bb/D
(G/B)
Cm7
(Am7)
Bb/D
(G/B)
Eb
(C)
Bb/D
(G/B)
Cm7
(Am7)
Bb/D
(G/B)
(11) 11 1 11 12 13 10 10 (10) 11 13 1 13 13 1 (13) 13 1 13 11

Gtr. 1: w/ Fill 1
Gtr. 2: w/ Fill 1A
Eb
(C)
Bb/D
(G/B)
Cm7
(Am7)
F7/A
(D7/F#)
Well, I've
p
hold bend
1
10 11 11 10 11 12 13 12 10 11 10 11 13 11 10 11 10 8 10 8 8 10 8

Chorus

Gtr. 1: w/ Riff B
Gtr. 2: w/ Riff B1
Bb
(G)
F/A
(D/F#)
Gm
(Em)
Eb
(C)
Bb/D
(G/B)
been a - fraid of chang - in' 'cause I've built my life a - round you.
hold bend
1
8 7 10 11 10 (10) 11 10

Fill 1
Gtr. 1
0 1 0 0 2 3 0 2 2 0 2 2 0 2 3 0

Fill 1A
Gtr. 2
0 1 1 0 0 0 2 0 2 0 0 2 2 1 0 2 0 0

Gtr. 3 tacet
Cm7 (Am7) F7/A (D7/F#) Bb (G) F7/A (D7/F#) Gm (Em)
But time makes you bold - er. E-ven chil - dren get old - er and I'm
Gtr. 2: w/ Riff A (3 times)
Eb (C) Bb/D (G/B) Cm7 (Am7) Bb/D (G/B)
get - tin' old - er too. Oh, I'm
Gtr. 1
Eb (C) Bb/D (G/B) Cm7 (Am7) Bb/D (G/B)
get - tin' old - er too. Ah,
p
Gtr. 1: w/ Riff A (2 times)
Eb (C) Bb/D (G/B) Cm7 (Am7) Bb/D (G/B) Eb (C) Bb/D (G/B)
take my love, take it down. Ah, climbed a moun - tain and turned a - round.
Cm7 (Am7) Bb/D (G/B) Cm7 (C) Bb/D (G/B)
And if you see my re - flec - tion in the snow -

Cm7
(Am7)
Bb/D
(G/B)
Eb
(C)
Bb/D
(G/B
Cm7
(Am7)
Bb/D
(G/B)
- covered hills, well, the land - slide 'll bring you down. And if you see
Gtr. 3
p
let ring throughout
hold bend

Gtrs. 1 & 2: w/ Riff A (1st meas.)
Eb
(C)
Bb/D
(G/B)
Gtrs. 1 & 2: w/ Fill 2
Cm7
(Am7)
Bb/D
(G/B)
Gtrs. 1 & 2: w/ Riff A (1st 3 meas.)
Eb
(C)
Bb/D
(G/B)
my re-flec - tion in the snow - cov-ered hills, well the land - slide 'll bring you down.
hold bend
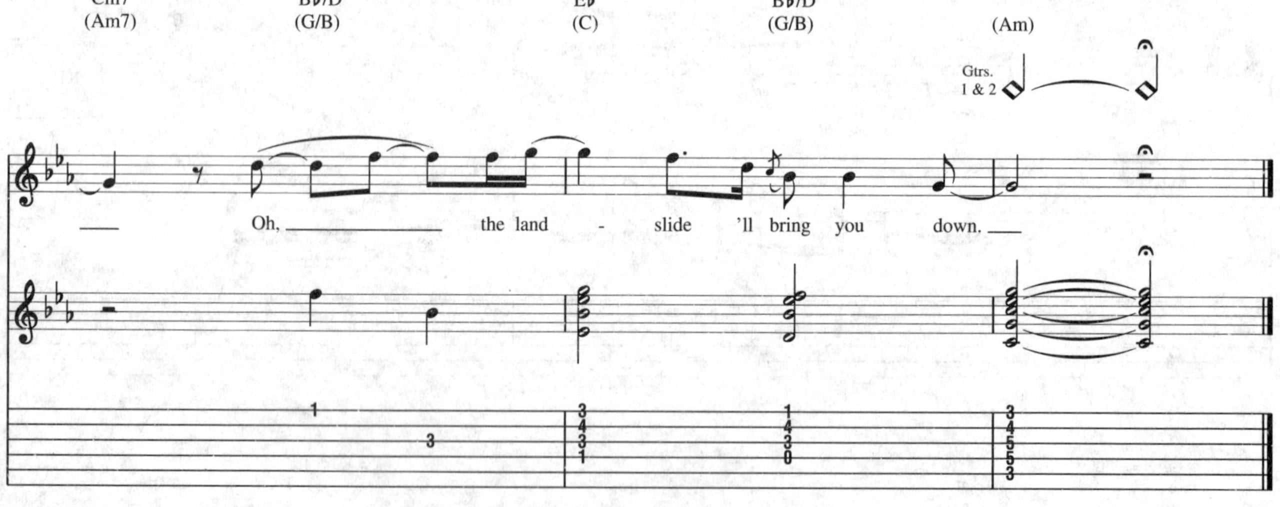
Cm7
(Am7)
Bb/D
(G/B)
Eb
(C)
Bb/D
(G/B)
(Am)
Gtrs. 1 & 2
Oh, the land - slide 'll bring you down.
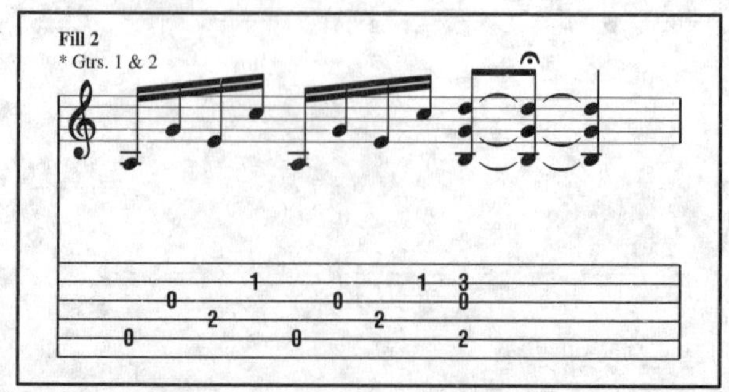
Fill 2
* Gtrs. 1 & 2

Layla

Words and Music by Eric Clapton and Jim Gordon

* Composite arr. Gtr. 6 mixed down on this recording. It is easier to hear on previous releases.

1.
2.

Verse
Gtrs. 2, 4, 5 & 6 tacet
D5
N.C.
C♯m
G♯m
C♯m7
Ah, what-'ll you do when you get lone - ly,
End Riff B
full
1/2
End Riff B1
Gtr. 3
Gtrs. 4 & 5
divisi
mf
End Riff B2

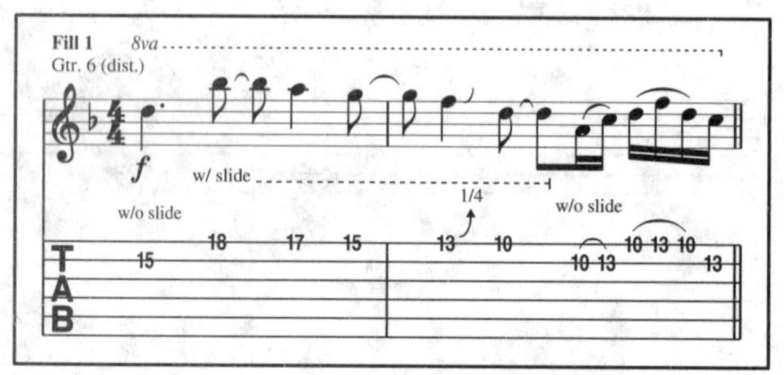

Fill 1
Gtr. 6 (dist.)
8va
f
w/ slide
w/o slide
1/4

Rhy. Fill 1
Gtr. 3

Rhy. Fill 2
Gtr. 2

Fill 2
Gtr. 6
8va
w/o slide
w/ slide

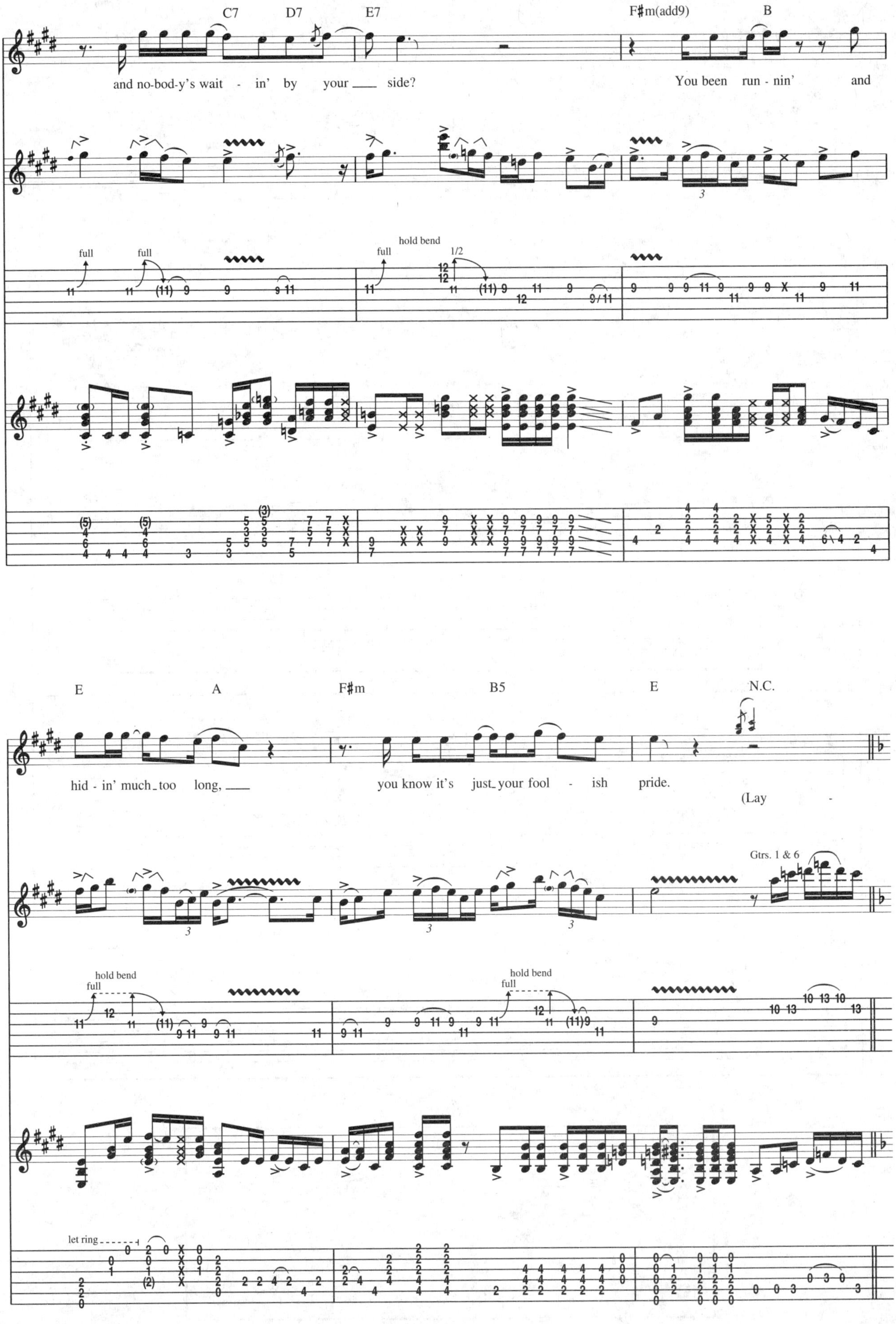

E A F♯m B5 E N.C.

hid - in' much too long, you know it's just your fool - ish pride.

(Lay -

Gtrs. 1 & 6

hold bend
full

let ring

Chorus
Gtrs. 1, 4 & 5: w/ Riffs B, B1 & B2, 1st & 2nd times;
w/ Riffs B, B1 & B2, 1st 7 meas, 3rd time
Gtr. 2: w/ Riff A, 3 times
Gtr. 3: w/ Rhy. Fig. 1, 3 times
Gtr. 6: w/ Fill 3, 1st time; w/ Riff B, 1st 4 meas, 2nd time;
w/ Riff B, 1st 2 meas., 3rd time
Gtr. 6: w/ Fill 5, 3rd time
D5 C5 B♭5 C5 D5 N.C. D5 C5 B♭5 C5
You got me on my knees.
I
la.
Lay - la.)

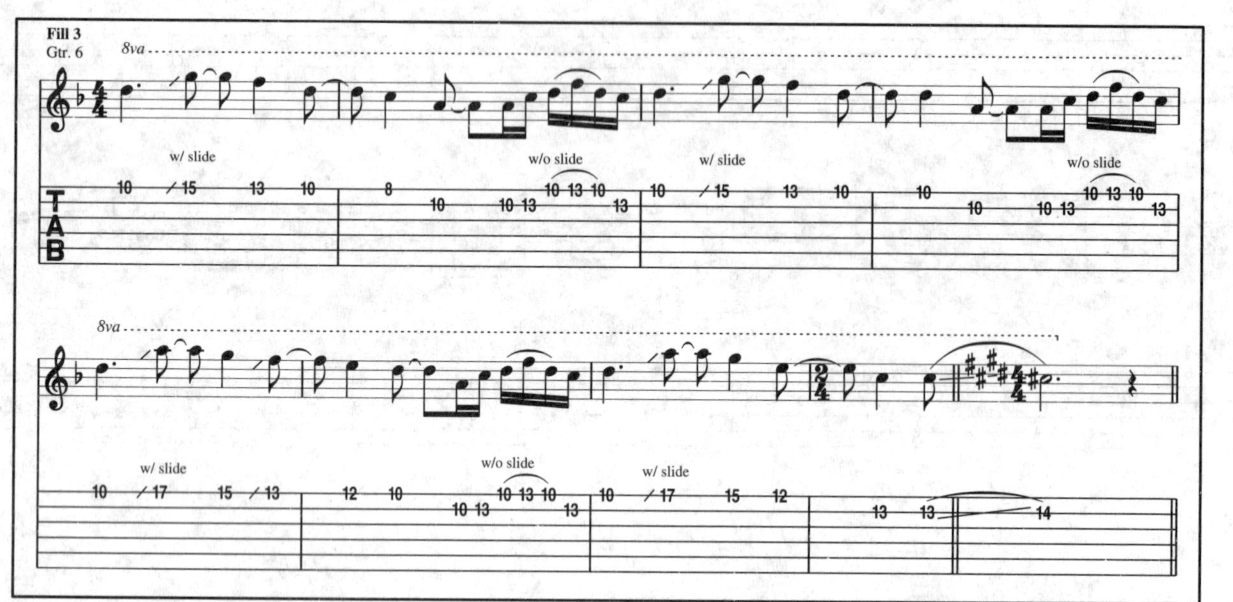
Fill 3
Gtr. 6
8va
w/ slide
w/o slide
w/ slide
w/o slide
w/ slide
w/o slide
w/ slide

Fill 5
Gtr. 6
8va
w/ slide
w/o slide
* position slide halfway between 17th & 18th frets
8va

Rhy. Fill 2
Gtr. 3

To Coda 2
To Coda 1
Gtr. 2: w/ Rhy. Fill 2, simile, 1st & 2nd times;
w/ Riff A, 1st meas., 3rd time
Gtr. 3: w/ Rhy. Fill 1, 1st & 2nd times;
w/ Rhy. Fig. 1, 3rd time
Gtr. 6: w/ Fill 1, simile, 2nd time
Gtr. 6: w/ Fill 4, 2nd time
D5 N.C. D5 C5 B♭5 C5 D5 N.C. D5 C5 B♭5 C5
beg you dar - lin' please, Lay - la, darlin' won't you ease my wor-ried mind.
Verse
Gtrs. 2, 4, 5 & 6 tacet
C♯m G♯m7 C♯m7 C7 D7
2. I tried to give you con - so-la - tion when your old man, he let you
Gtr. 1
mf
full
hold bend
Gtr. 3
Gtrs. 4 & 5 divisi
dim.
E F♯m B E A
down. Like a fool, I fell in love with you,
Fill 4
Gtr. 6
8va

D.S. al Coda 1
F#m
B
E
N.C.
you turned my whole world up - side down.
(Lay -
Gtrs. 1 & 6
full
full
Coda 1
Verse
Gtrs. 2, 4, 5 & 6 tacet
C#m7
G#m
C#m7
C7
D7
3. So make the best of the sit - u - a - tion,
be-fore I fin - n'ly go in -
Gtr. 1
1/2
full
1/2
1/2
full
Gtr. 3
Gtrs. 4 & 5
divisi
Gtr. 3

E
F♯m
B
- sane.
Please don't ___ say ___ we'll
full
hold bend
E
A
F♯m
B
nev - er find ___ a way, ___
and tell me all ___ my love's - in
full
hold bend

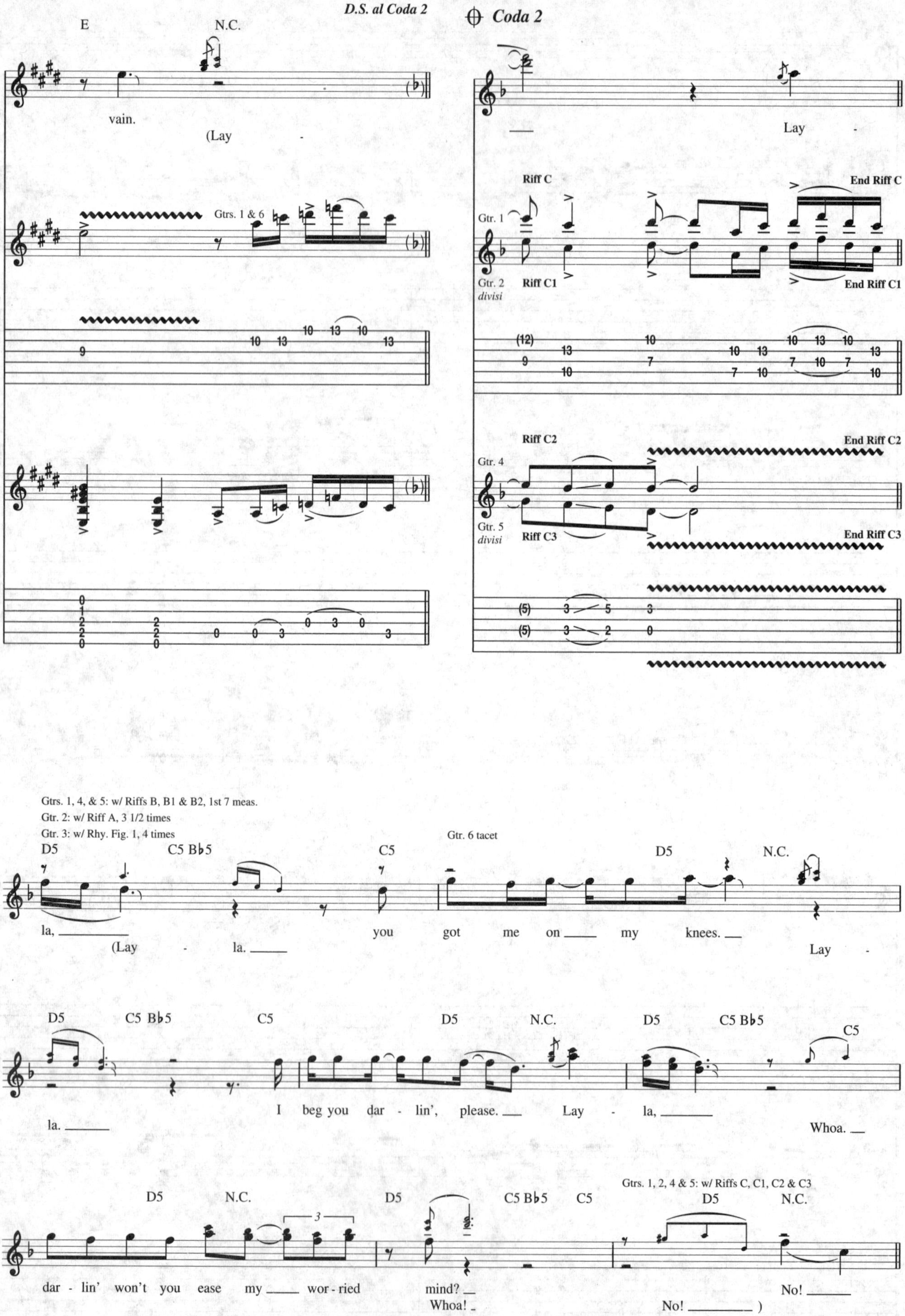

D.S. al Coda 2

Coda 2

E N.C.

vain.

(Lay -

Lay -

Gtrs. 1 & 6

Riff C End Riff C

Gtr. 1

Gtr. 2 *divisi* Riff C1 End Riff C1

Riff C2 End Riff C2

Gtr. 4

Gtr. 5 *divisi* Riff C3 End Riff C3

Guitar Solo

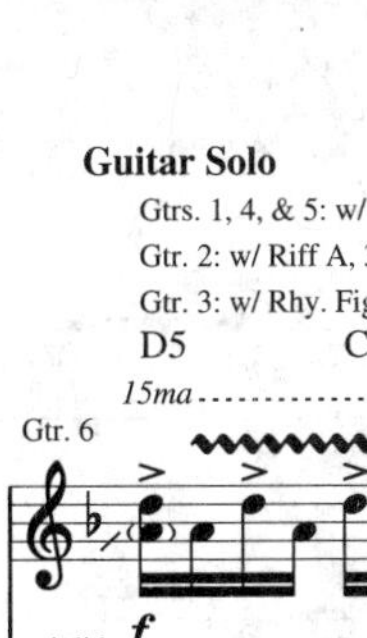

Gtrs. 1, 4, & 5: w/ Riffs B, B1 & B2, 1st 7 meas.
Gtr. 2: w/ Riff A, 3 1/2 times
Gtr. 3: w/ Rhy. Fig. 1, 11 1/2 times, simile

* TAB numbers based on location of notes beyond fretboard.

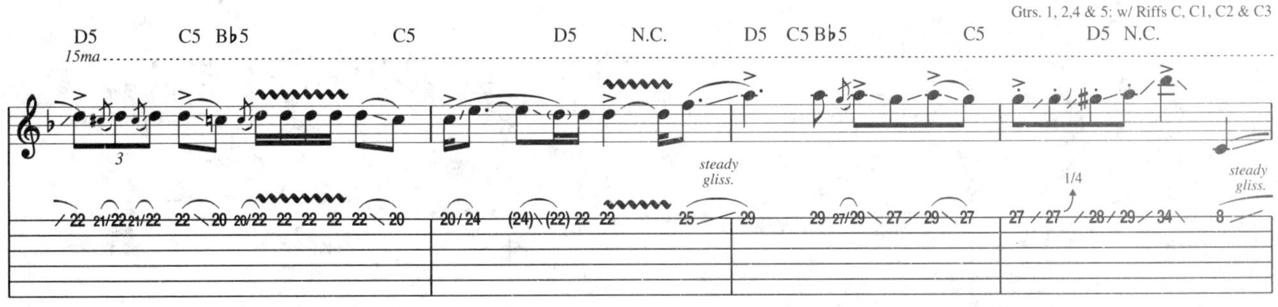

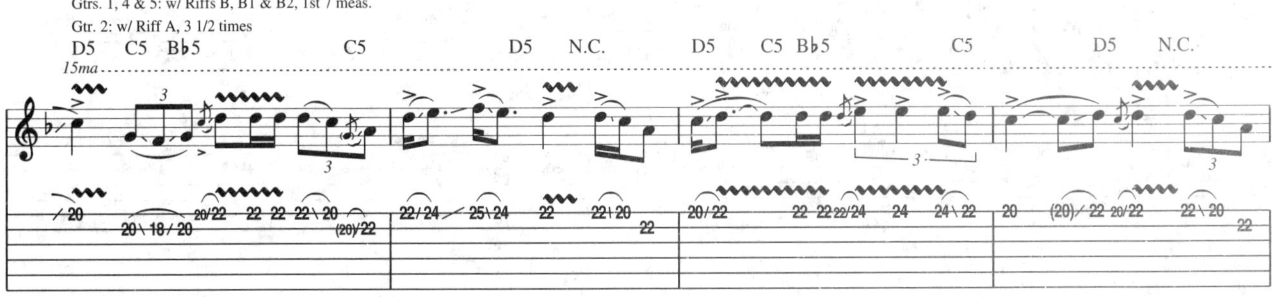

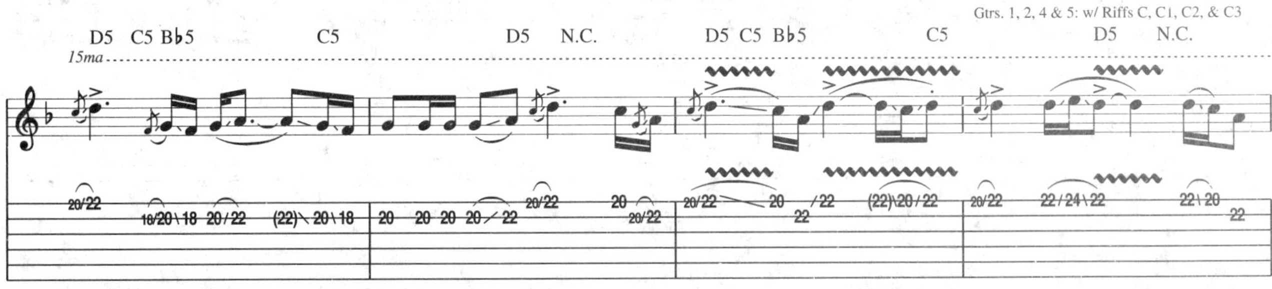

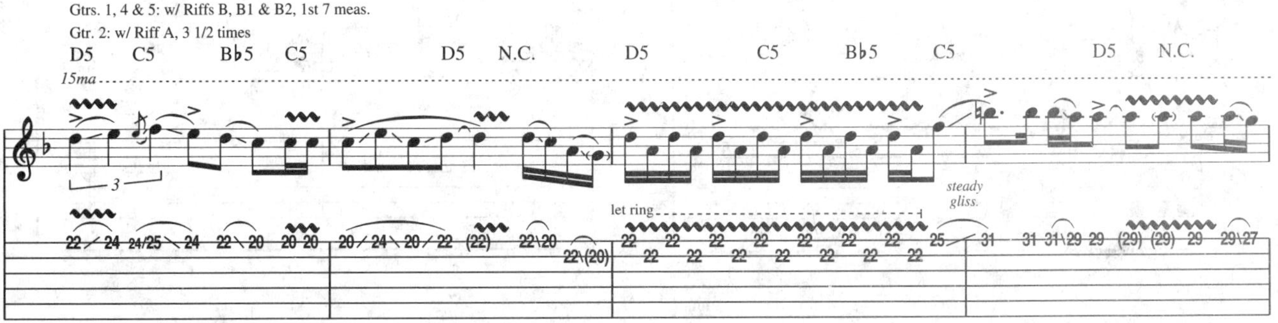

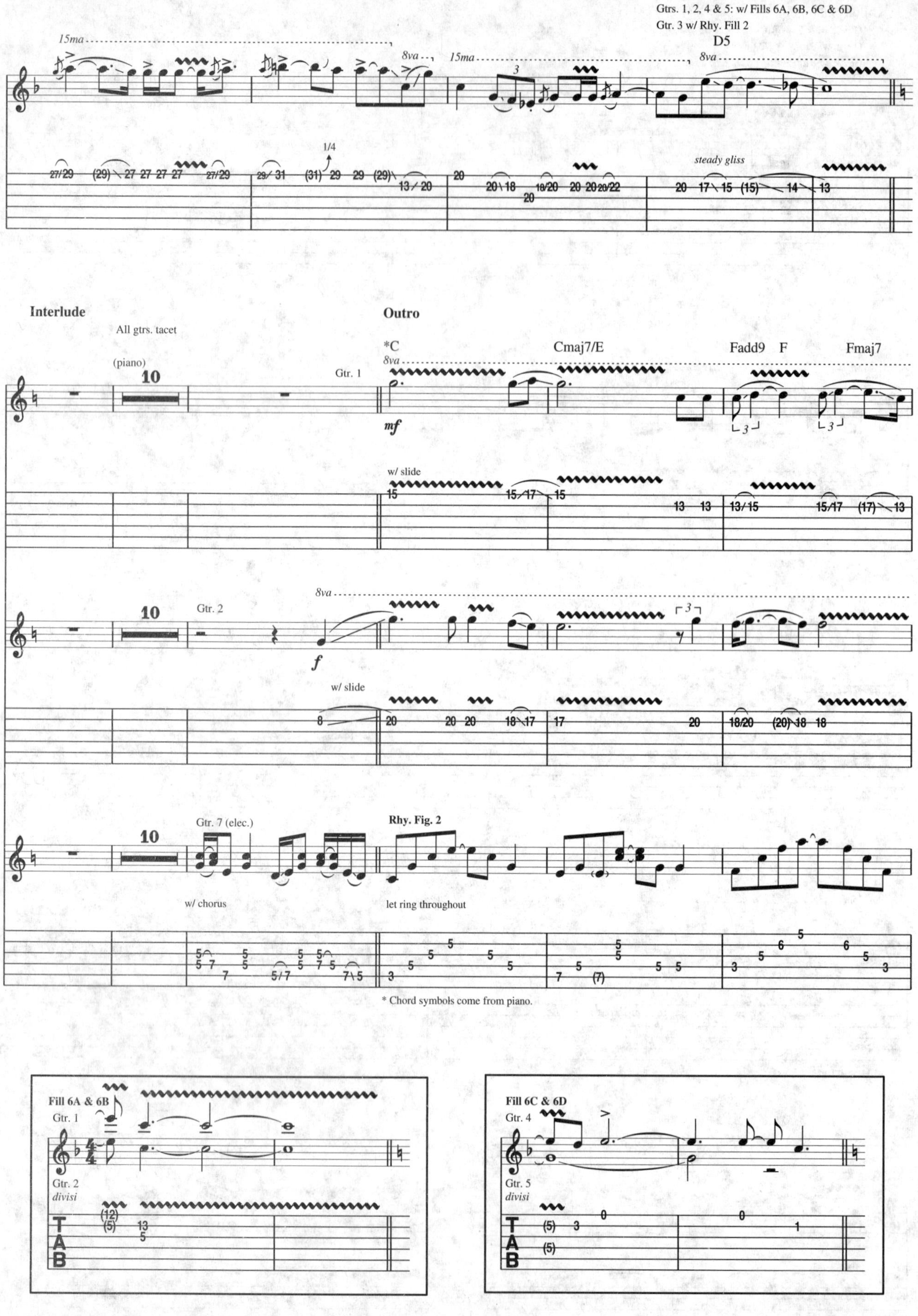

Gtrs. 1, 2, 4 & 5: w/ Fills 6A, 6B, 6C & 6D
Gtr. 3 w/ Rhy. Fill 2

Interlude

All gtrs. tacet

(piano)

Gtr. 1

Outro

*C Cmaj7/E Fadd9 F Fmaj7

8va

mf

w/ slide

Gtr. 2

8va

f

w/ slide

Gtr. 7 (elec.)

Rhy. Fig. 2

w/ chorus

let ring throughout

* Chord symbols come from piano.

F6 F B♭7 B♭7(♭5) B♭7 C

8va

loco

8va

P.M.

Gtr. 7: w/ Rhy. Fig. 2, 1st 5 meas., simile

C Cmaj7/E Fadd9 F Fmaj7

let ring

8va

End Rhy. Fig. 2

P.M.

P.M.

F6 F B♭7 B♭7(♭5) B♭7 C C/B

8va

Gtr. 7

Rhy. Fig. 3

Am Dsus4 Dm G Gsus4 C E7

8va

f

8va

mf

Am
D
loco
Gsus4
G
Gadd9
G5
8va
w/ slide
loco
End Rhy. Fig. 3
Gtr. 7: w/ Rhy. Fig. 2, 1st 4 meas., simile
C
C/E
Fadd9
F
Fmaj7
F6
F
Gtr. 7: w/ Rhy. Fig. 2, 3/4 time, simile
C
15ma
8va
w/ slide
C/E
Fadd9
F
Fmaj7
F6
F
B♭7
B♭7(♭5) B♭7
C
steady gliss.

Gtr. 7 w/ Rhy. Fig. 2, 1st meas.
Gtr. 7 w/ Rhy. Fill 3, simile
Gtr. 7 w/ Rhy. Fig. 2, 1st 7 meas., simile
C
Cmaj7/E
Fadd9
F
Fmaj7
8va
Gtr. 1
Gtr. 2
loco
Gtr. 8 (acous.)
Riff D
F6
F
B♭7
B♭7(♭5)
B♭7
C
Gtr. 7: w/ Rhy. Fill 4 (see next page)
End Riff D
Rhy. Fill 3
Gtr. 7

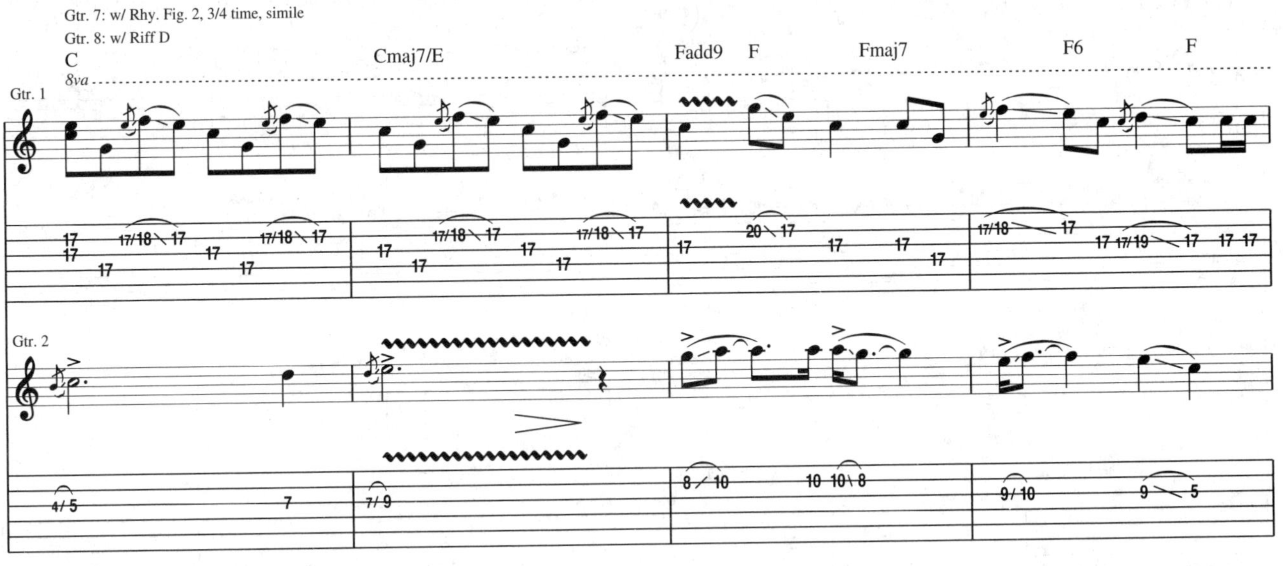
Gtr. 7: w/ Rhy. Fig. 2, 3/4 time, simile
Gtr. 8: w/ Riff D
C
Cmaj7/E
Fadd9
F
Fmaj7
F6
F
8va
Gtr. 1
Gtr. 2

Gtr. 7: w/ Rhy. Fill 5
Gtr. 7: w/ Rhy. Fig. 3, simile
Bb7
Bb7(b5) Bb7
C
8va

Rhy. Fill 4
Gtr. 7

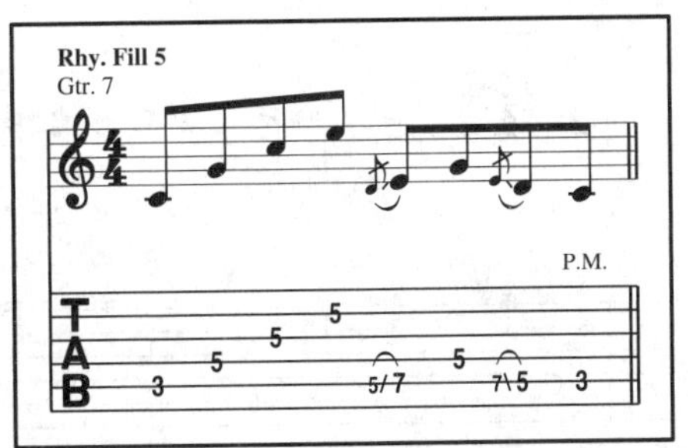
Rhy. Fill 5
Gtr. 7
P.M.

Am
Dsus4 Dm
G
Csus4
C
E7/B
8va
Gtr. 1
Gtr. 2
mp
semi-harm.
Gtr. 8
Gtr. 7: w/ Rhy. Fill 6 (see next page)
G
Gtr. 7: w/ Rhy. Fig. 2, 1st 4 meas., simile
C
C/E
Fadd9
F
Fmaj7
F6
F
steady gliss.
Rhy. Fig. 4
End Rhy. Fig. 4

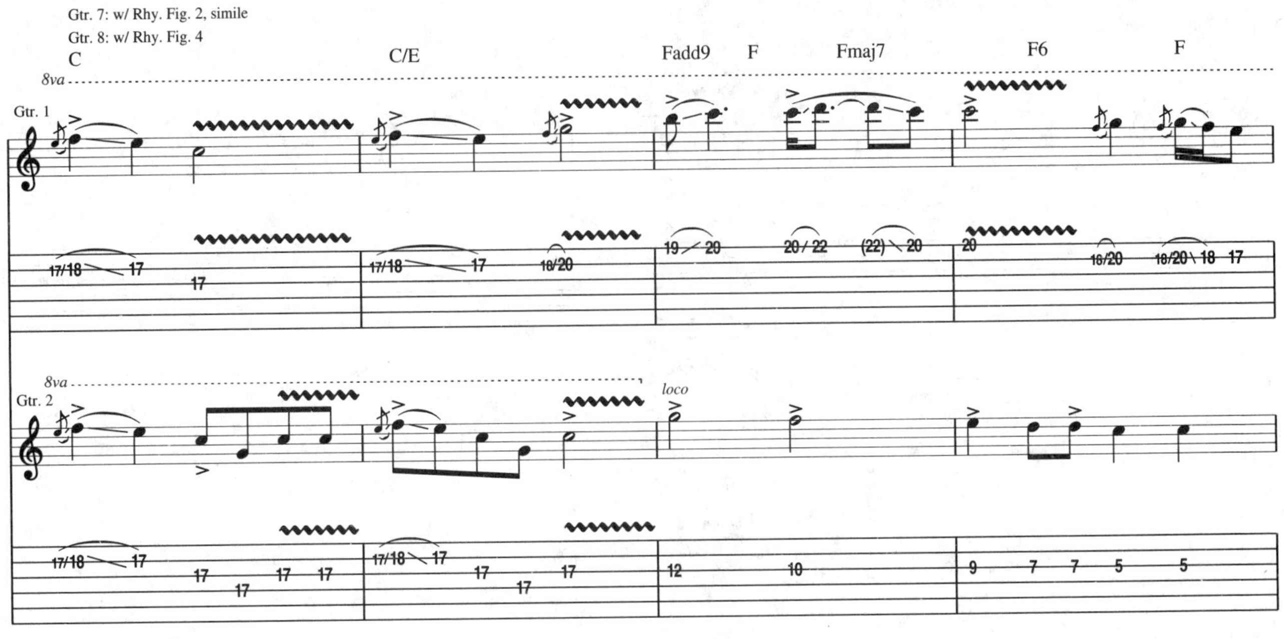

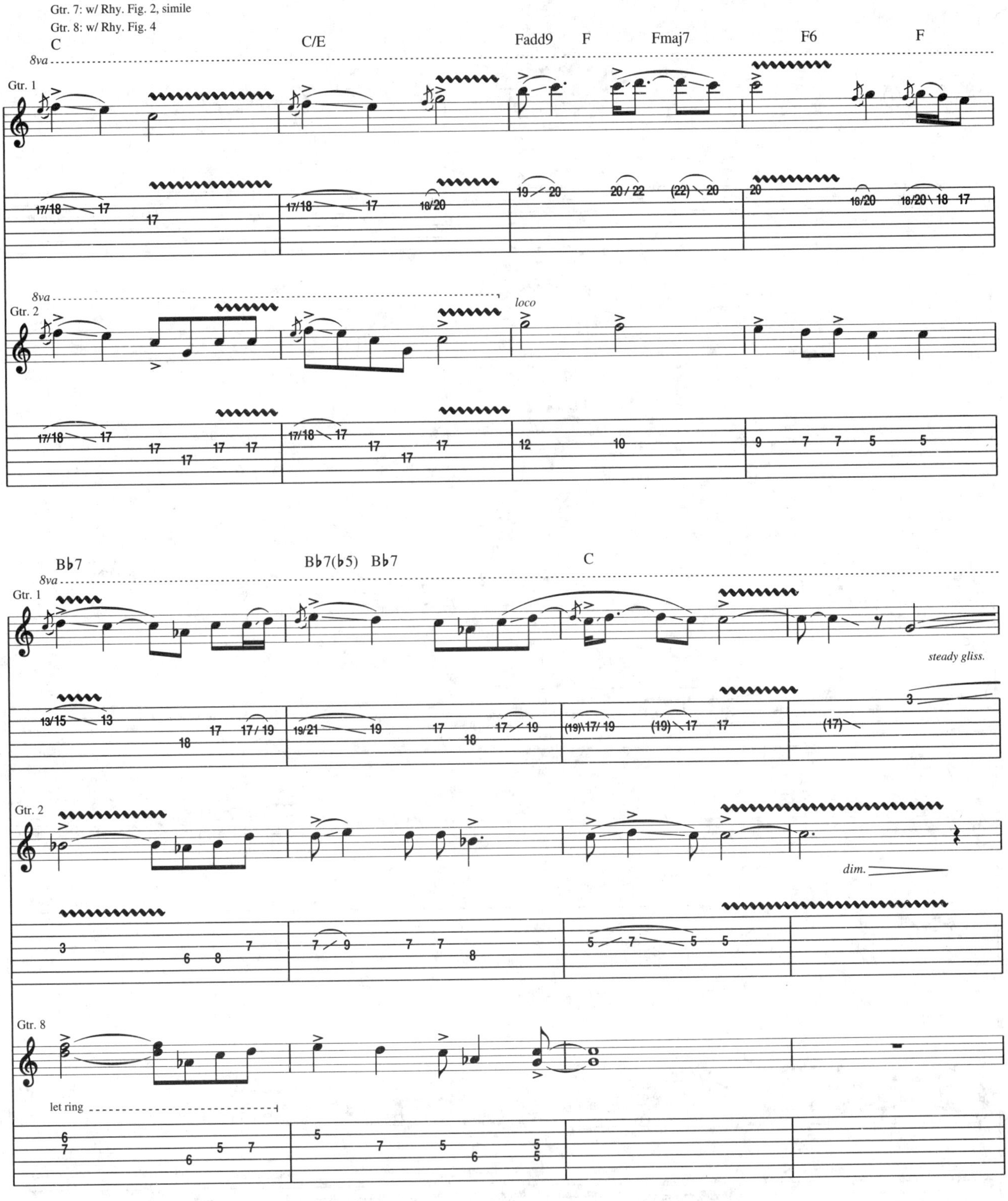

Bb7 Bb7(b5) Bb7 C

8va

Gtr. 1

steady gliss.

Gtr. 2

dim.

Gtr. 8

let ring

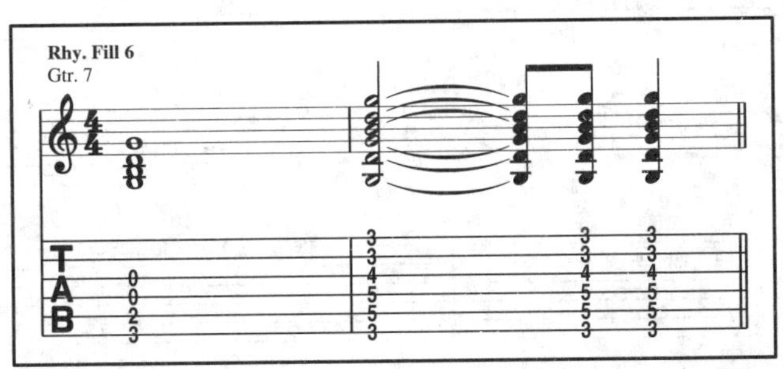

Gtr. 7: w/ Rhy. Fig. 2, 1st 4 meas., 5 times, simile
Gtr. 8: w/ Rhy. Fig. 4, 5 times
C
C/E
Fadd9 F
Fmaj7
F6
F
C
8va
mf
mf
C/E
Fadd9 F
Fmaj7
F6
F
C
C/E
Fadd9
F
Fmaj7
F6
F
C
C/E
Fadd9 F
Fmaj7
3

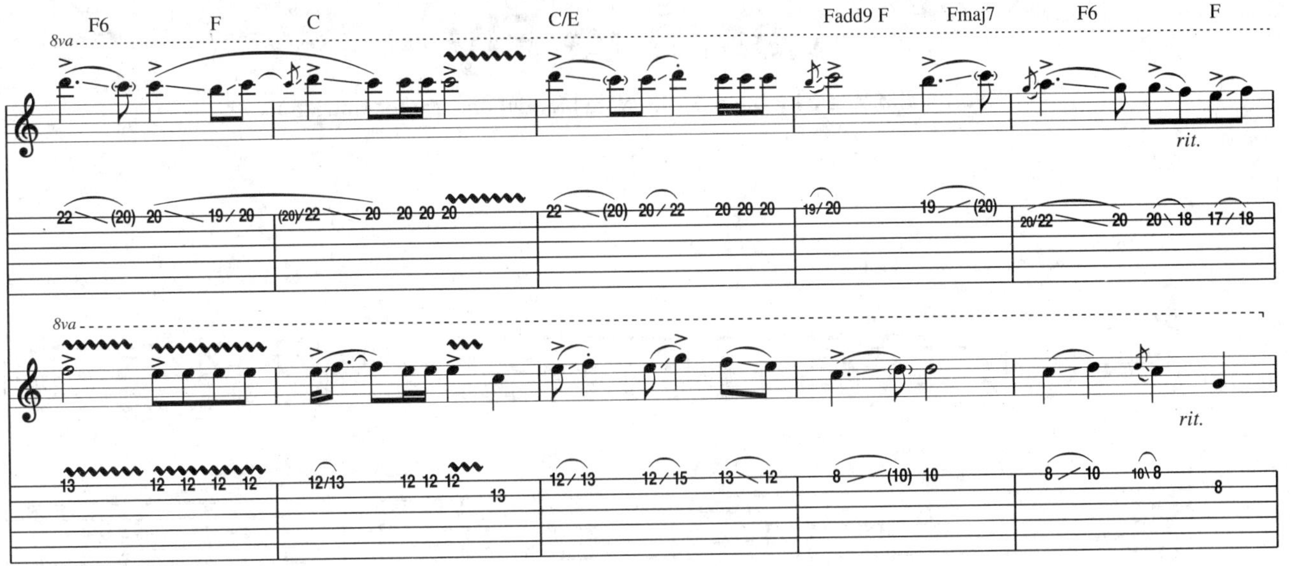

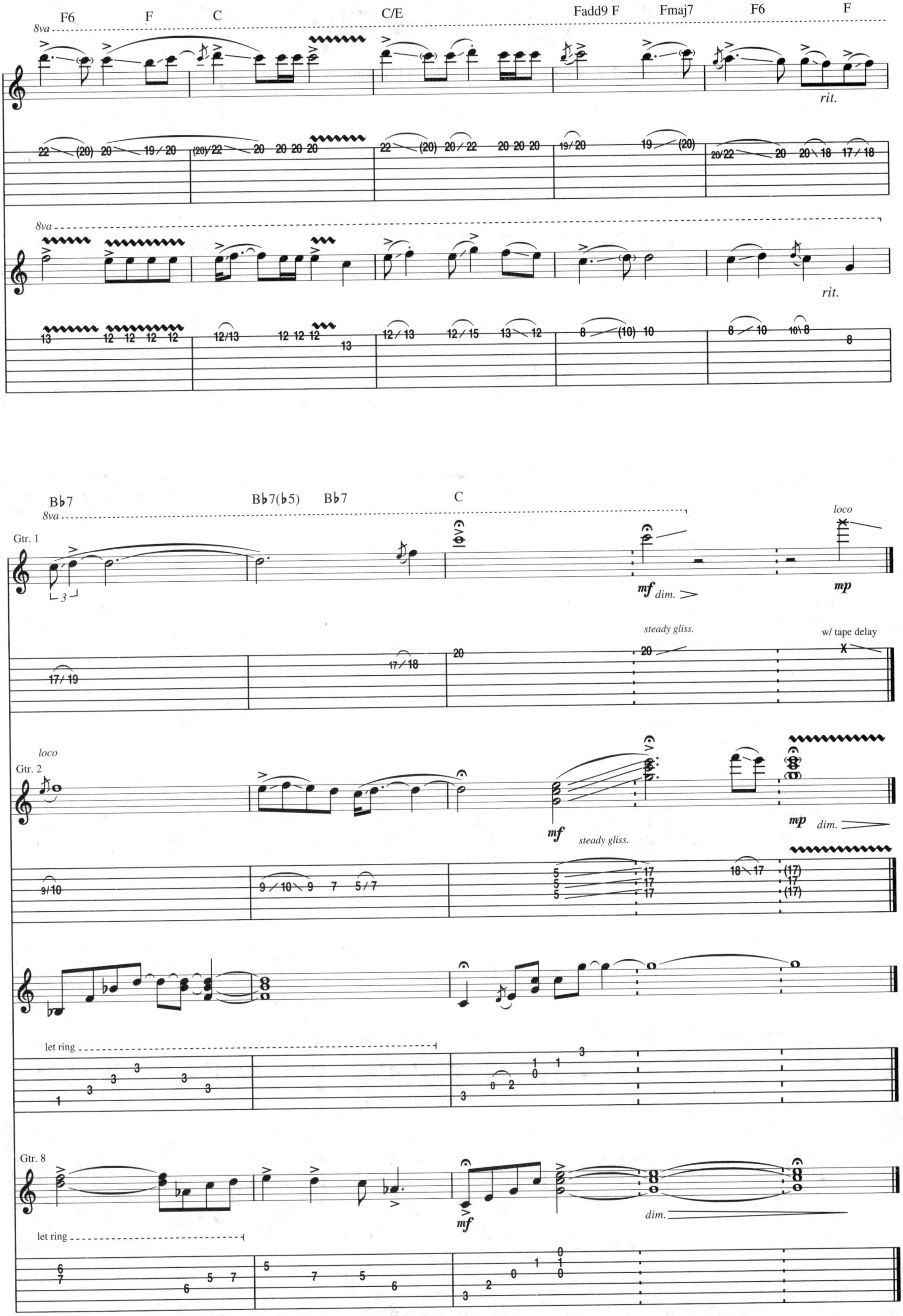
F6
F
C
C/E
Fadd9 F
Fmaj7
F6
F
8va
rit.
8va
rit.
Bb7
Bb7(b5)
Bb7
C
8va
Gtr. 1
loco
mf dim.
mp
steady gliss.
w/ tape delay
loco
Gtr. 2
mf
steady gliss.
mp dim.
let ring
Gtr. 8
mf
dim.
let ring

Learn to Fly

Words and Music by Dave Grohl, Nate Mendel and Taylor Hawkins

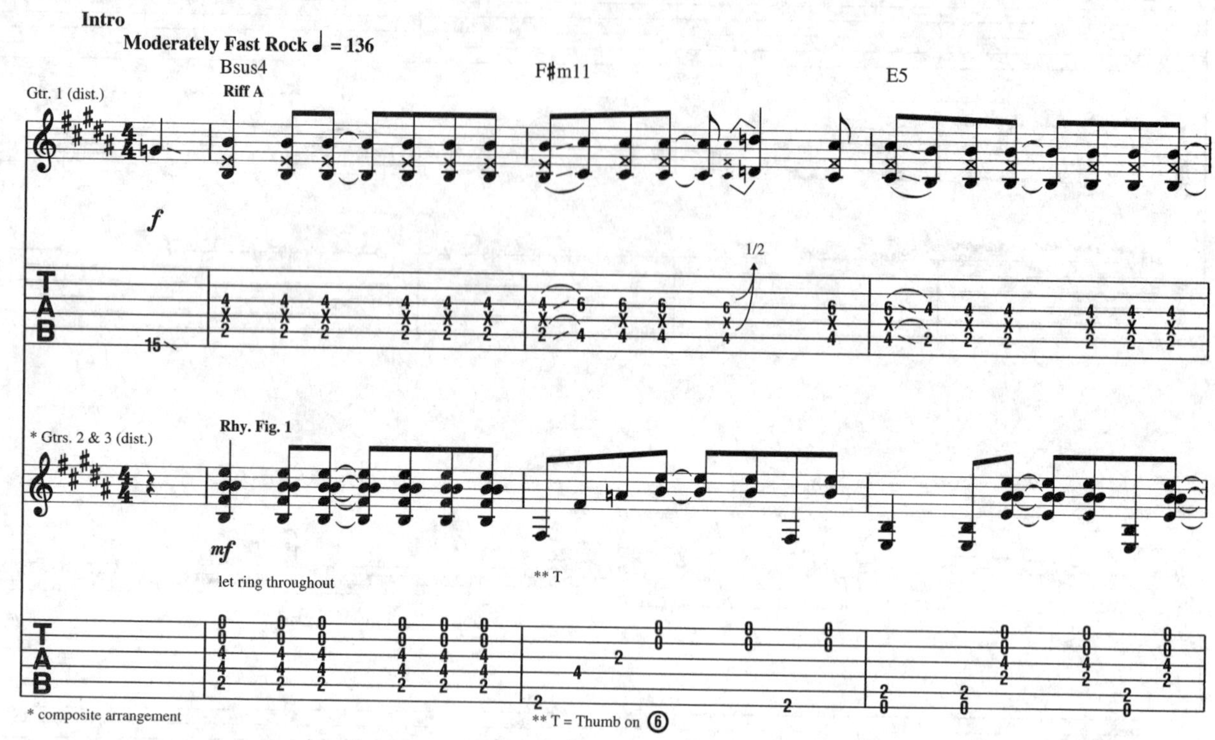

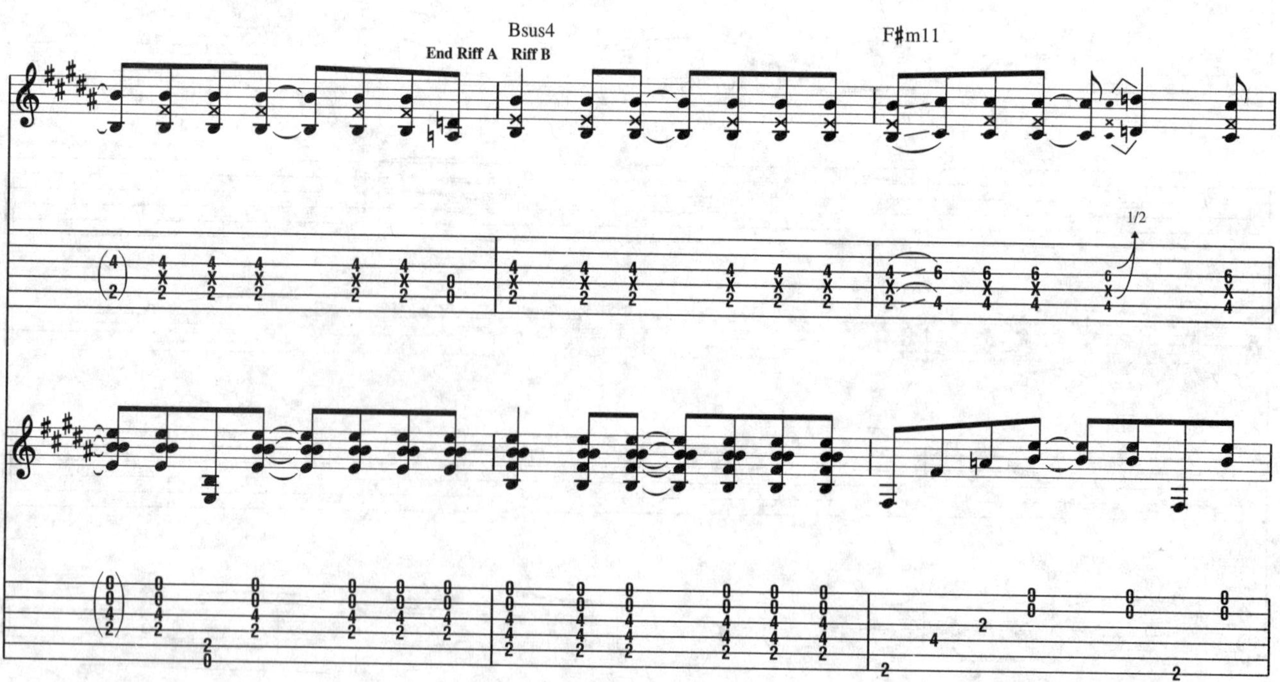

Verse
E5
Bsus2
1. Run and tell all of the an -
End Riff B
Fill 1
let ring
End Rhy. Fig. 1
Riff C
F#m11
E5
- gels, this could take all night.
End Fill 1
End Riff C
Gtrs. 2 & 3: w/ Riff C, 2 1/2 times, simile
Gtr. 1 tacet
Bsus2
F#m11
E5
Think - in' it in time will help me get things right.

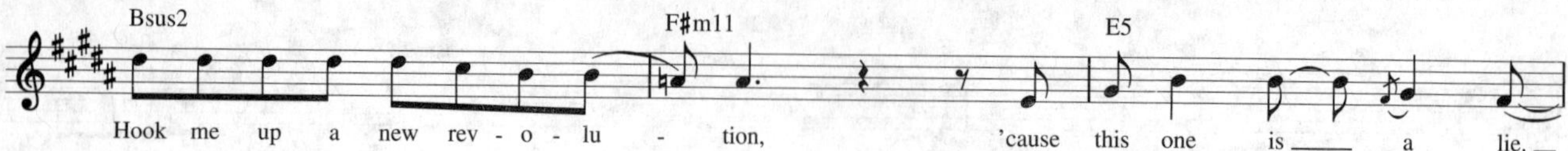
Bsus2
F#m11
E5
Hook me up a new rev - o - lu - tion, 'cause this one is a lie.

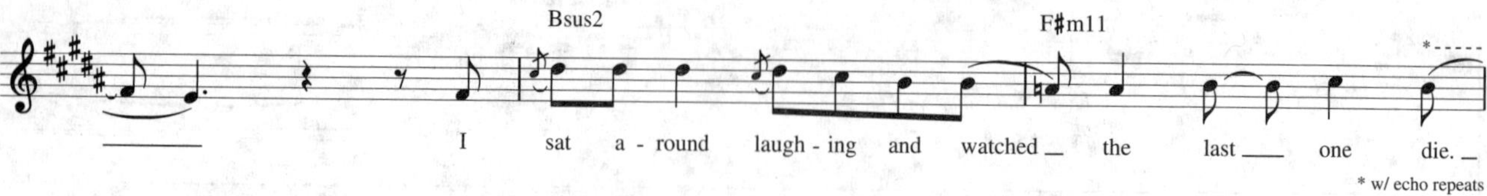
Bsus2
F#m11
I sat a - round laugh - ing and watched the last one die.
* w/ echo repeats

E5
Chorus
Gtr. 1: w/ Riff A, 3rd time
Bsus4
Yeah I'm look - in' to the sky to save
Gtrs. 2 & 3
Rhy. Fill 1
End Rhy. Fill 1
Rhy. Fig. 2

Gtr. 4: w/ Fill 2, 2nd & 3rd times, simile
F#m11
E5
me, look - in' for a sign of life. I'm
End Rhy. Fig. 2

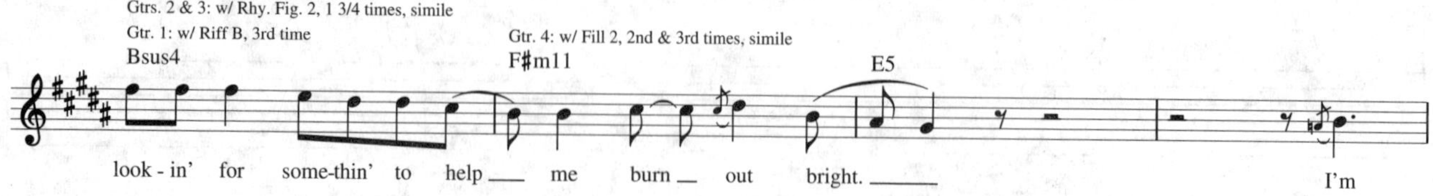
Gtrs. 2 & 3: w/ Rhy. Fig. 2, 1 3/4 times, simile
Gtr. 1: w/ Riff B, 3rd time
Bsus4
Gtr. 4: w/ Fill 2, 2nd & 3rd times, simile
F#m11
E5
look - in' for some-thin' to help me burn out bright. I'm

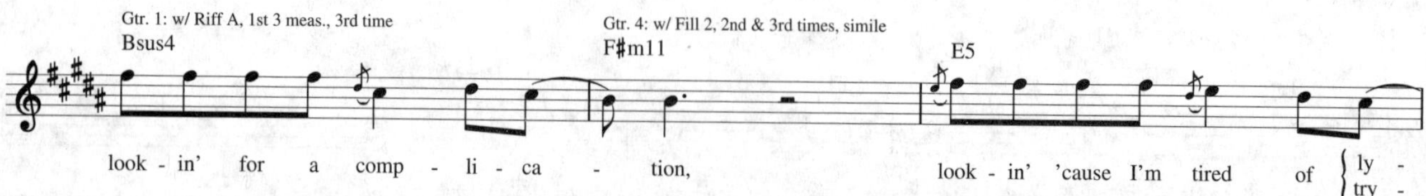
Gtr. 1: w/ Riff A, 1st 3 meas., 3rd time
Bsus4
Gtr. 4: w/ Fill 2, 2nd & 3rd times, simile
F#m11
E5
look - in' for a comp - li - ca - tion, look - in' 'cause I'm tired of ly - / try -

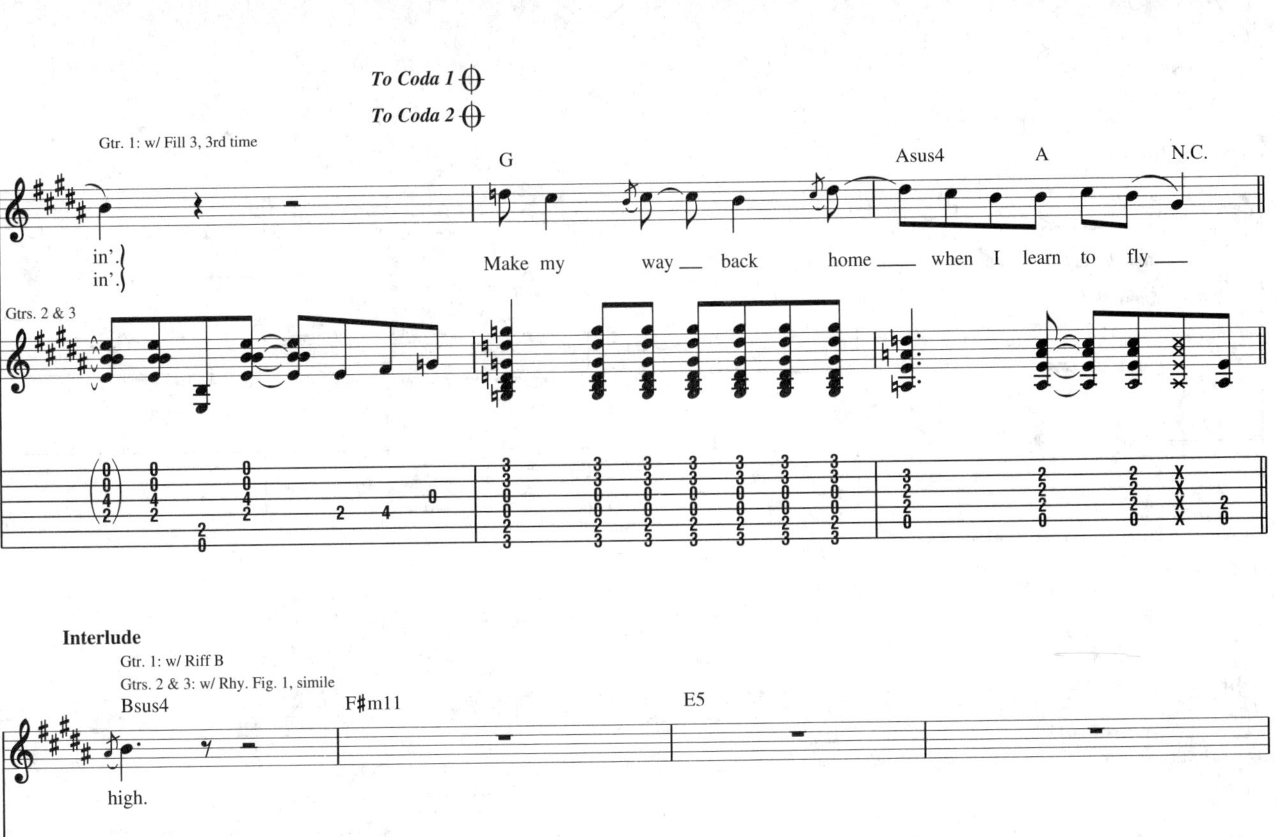
To Coda 1
To Coda 2
Gtr. 1: w/ Fill 3, 3rd time
G
Asus4
A
N.C.
in'.
in'.
Make my way back home when I learn to fly
Gtrs. 2 & 3

Interlude
Gtr. 1: w/ Riff B
Gtrs. 2 & 3: w/ Rhy. Fig. 1, simile
Bsus4
F♯m11
E5
high.
Gtr. 4 (slight dist.)
mp
Gtr. 1: w/ Riff A, simile
Bsus4
F♯m11
E5
2. I
Fill 2
End Fill 2

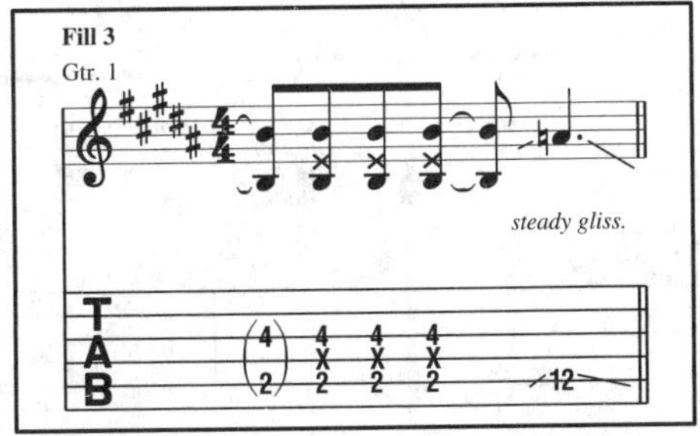
Fill 3
Gtr. 1
steady gliss.

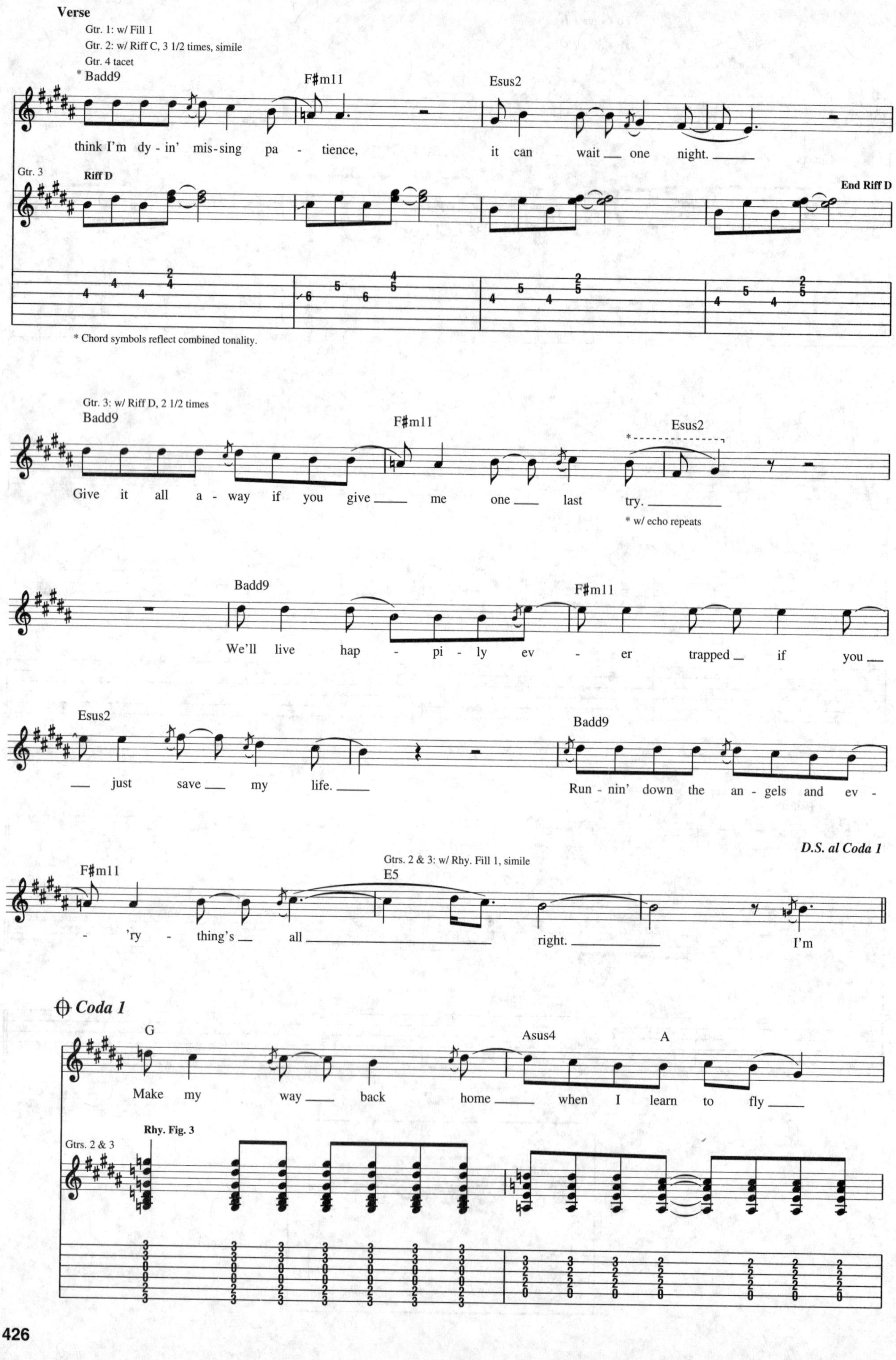
Verse
Gtr. 1: w/ Fill 1
Gtr. 2: w/ Riff C, 3 1/2 times, simile
Gtr. 4 tacet
* Badd9
F#m11
Esus2
think I'm dy - in' mis-sing pa - tience, it can wait one night.
Gtr. 3
Riff D
End Riff D
* Chord symbols reflect combined tonality.
Gtr. 3: w/ Riff D, 2 1/2 times
Badd9
F#m11
Esus2
Give it all a - way if you give me one last try.
* w/ echo repeats
Badd9
F#m11
We'll live hap - pi - ly ev - er trapped if you
Esus2
Badd9
just save my life. Run - nin' down the an - gels and ev -
F#m11
Gtrs. 2 & 3: w/ Rhy. Fill 1, simile
E5
D.S. al Coda 1
- 'ry - thing's all right. I'm
Coda 1
G
Asus4
A
Make my way back home when I learn to fly
Rhy. Fig. 3
Gtrs. 2 & 3

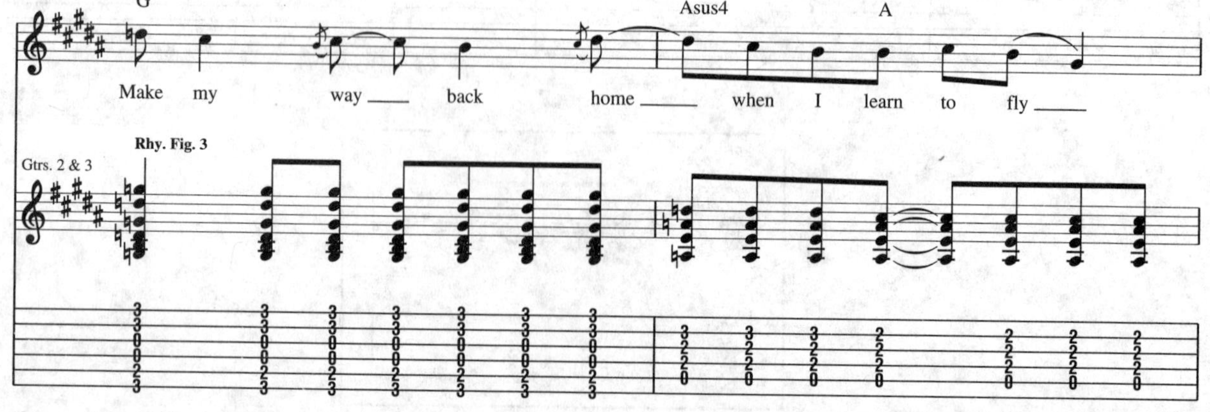

E
G
Asus4
A
high.
Make my way back home when I learn to...
End Rhy. Fig. 3
Bridge
Bsus4
G
D
Fly a - long with me, I can't quite make it a - lone
1.
2.
D.S. al Coda 2
E
D/F#
G
Asus4
A
Try to make this life my own.
my own.
I'm
Coda 2
Gtrs. 2 & 3: w/ Rhy. Fig. 3, 1st 2 meas.
G
Asus4
A
Make my way back home when I learn to...
Outro-Chorus
Gtr. 1: w/ Riff A, simile
Gtrs. 2 & 3: w/ Rhy. Fig. 2, 3 times, simile
Bsus4
Look - in' to the sky to save
Gtr. 4: w/ Fill 2, simile
F#m11
E5
me, look - in' for a sign of life.
I'm

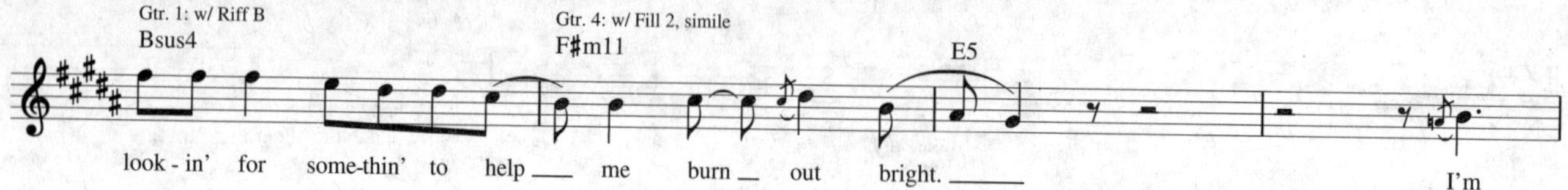
Gtr. 1: w/ Riff B
Bsus4
Gtr. 4: w/ Fill 2, simile
F♯m11
E5
look - in' for some-thin' to help me burn out bright. I'm

Gtr. 1: w/ Riff A
Bsus4
Gtr. 4: w/ Fill 2, simile
F♯m11
E5
look - in' for a comp - li - ca - tion, look - in' 'cause I'm tired of try -

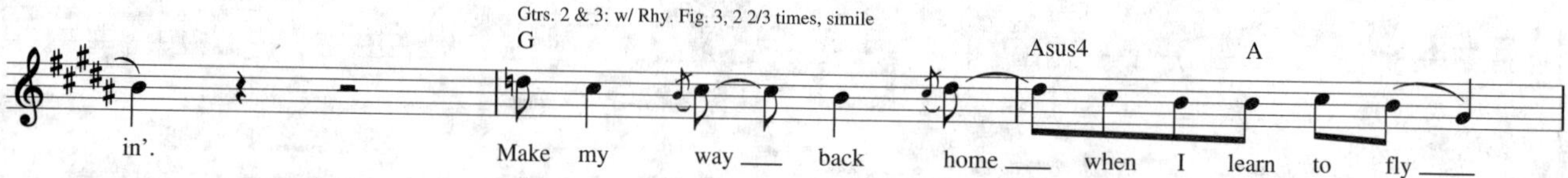
Gtrs. 2 & 3: w/ Rhy. Fig. 3, 2 2/3 times, simile
G
Asus4
A
in'. Make my way back home when I learn to fly

E
G
Asus4
A
high. Make my way back home when I learn to fly.

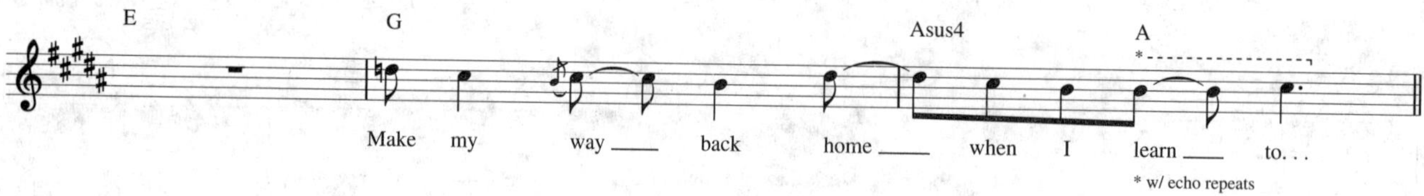
E
G
Asus4
A
Make my way back home when I learn to. . .
* w/ echo repeats

Outro

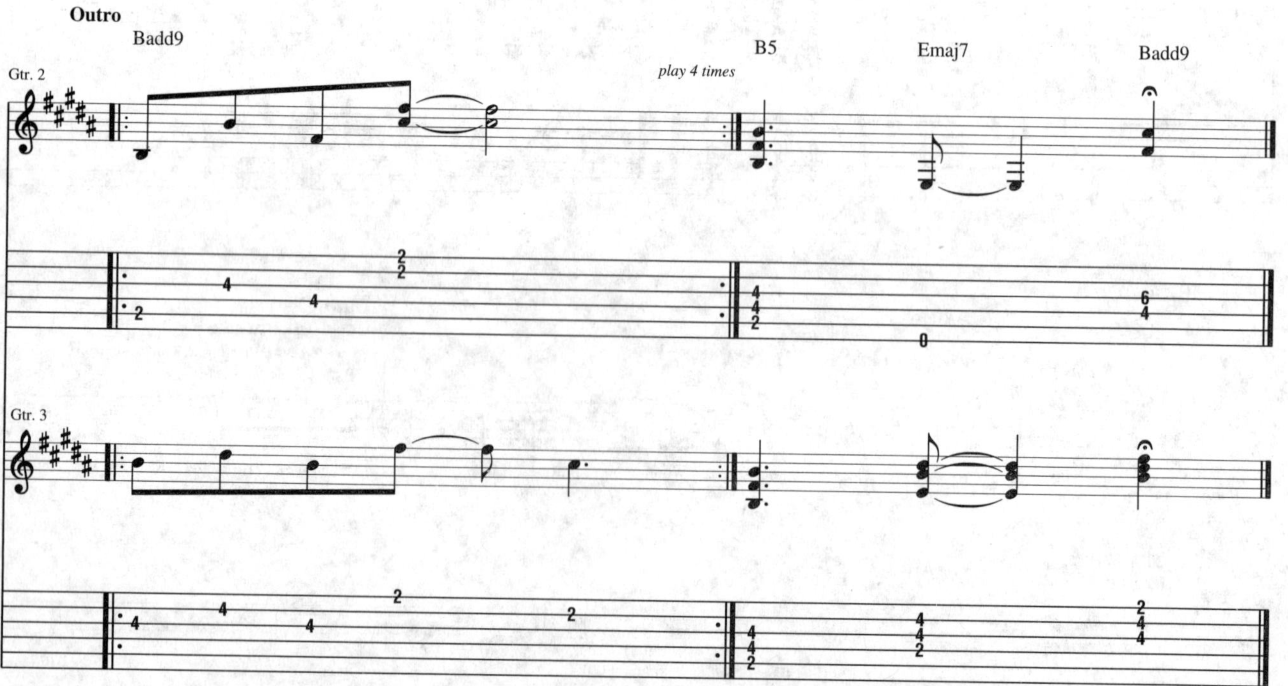
Badd9
B5
Emaj7
Badd9
Gtr. 2
play 4 times
Gtr. 3

Learning to Fly

Words and Music by Tom Petty and Jeff Lynne

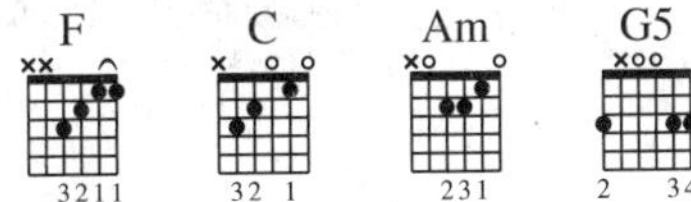

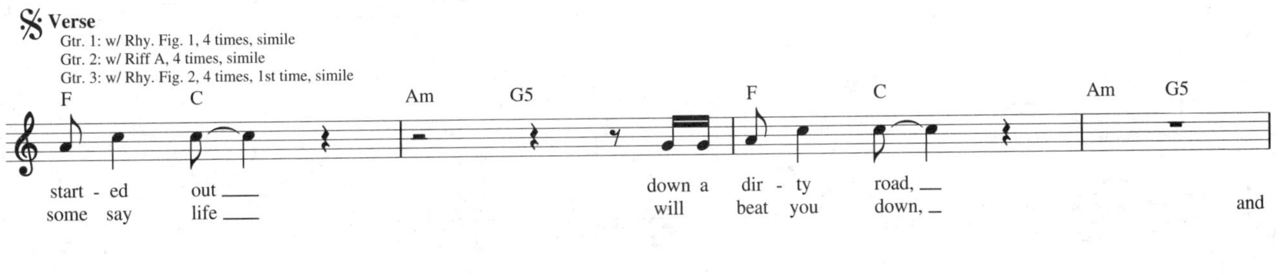

Gtr. 3: w/ Rhy. Fig. 2, 2 times, simile
2nd time, Bkgd. Voc.: w/ Voc. Fill 1, 4 times
F C Am G5 F C Am G5
sun went down _ as I crossed the hill. ___ And the
start - ed out ___ for God knows where. _ I
F C Am G5 F C
town lit up, the world got still. ___
guess I'll know when I get there. ___
Chorus
Gtr. 1: w/ Rhy. Fig. 1, 2 times, simile
Gtr. 2: w/ Riff A, 2 times, simile
Gtr. 3: w/ Rhy. Fig. 2, 2 times, simile
Am G5 F C Am G5 F C Am G5
I'm learn-ing to fly _ but I ain't got wings. _
a-round the clouds. _
Gtr. 4
(elec.) Riff B
mf
w/ clean tone & chorus
let ring
To Coda
F C Am G5 F C Am G5
Com - ing ___ down _ is the hard - est thing. _ 2. Well, the
What goes up ___ must come down. _
End Riff B
let ring
Verse
Gtr. 1: w/ Rhy. Fig. 1, 2 times, simile
Gtr. 2: w/ Riff A, 2 times, simile
Gtr. 3: w/ Rhy. Fig. 2, 2 times, simile
Gtr. 4 tacet
F C Am G5 F C Am G5
good old ___ days _ may not re - turn ___ and the
Voc. Fill 1
(Oo.) ___

Chorus

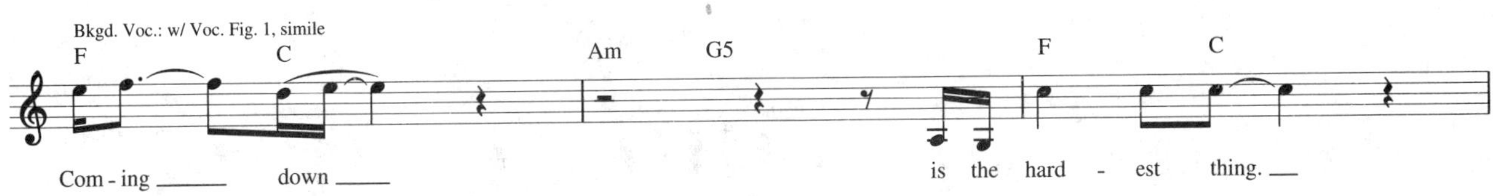

Guitar Solo

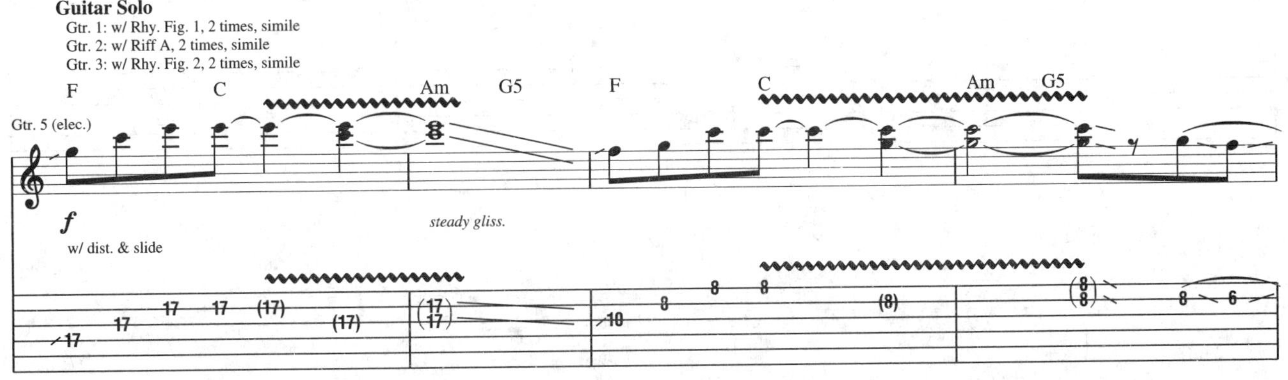

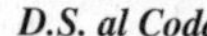
D.S. al Coda

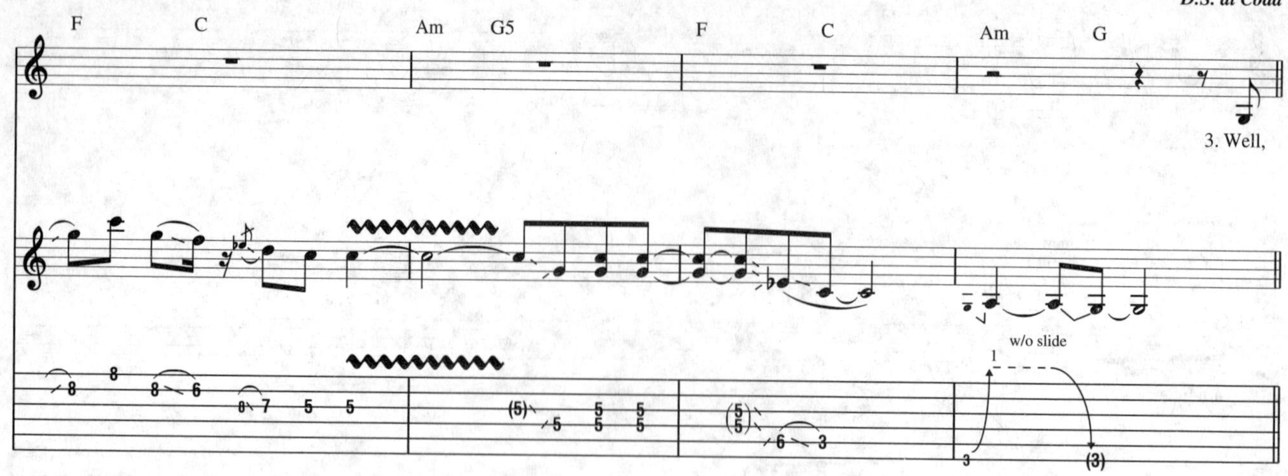
F
C
Am
G5
F
C
Am
G
3. Well,
w/o slide

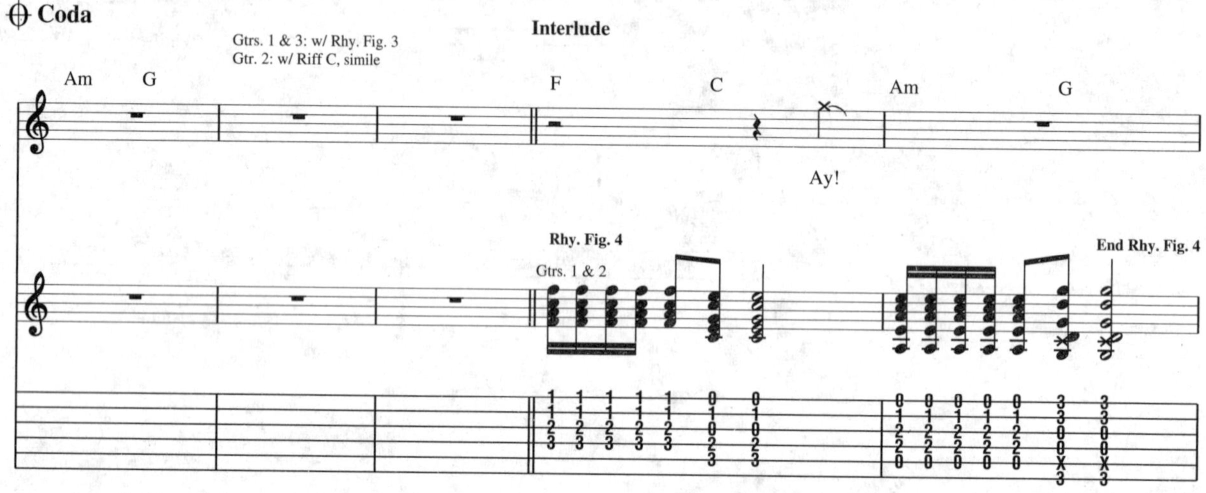
Coda
Interlude
Gtrs. 1 & 3: w/ Rhy. Fig. 3
Gtr. 2: w/ Riff C, simile
Am
G
F
C
Am
G
Ay!
Rhy. Fig. 4
Gtrs. 1 & 2
End Rhy. Fig. 4

Chorus
Bkgd. Voc.: w/ Voc. Fig. 1, 1st 3 meas.
Gtr. 1: w/ Rhy. Fig. 1, till fade
Gtr. 2: w/ Riff A, till fade
Gtr. 3: w/ Rhy. Fig. 2, till fade
Gtr. 5 tacet
Gtrs. 1 & 2:
w/ Rhy. Fig. 4
Gtr. 4: w/ Riff B, till fade
F
C
Am
G
F
C
Am
G
F
C
Am
G
I'm learn-ing to fly
but I ain't got wings.
Gtr. 5
Gtr. 6 (elec.)
mp
w/ clean tone
Riff D
End Riff D
P.M.

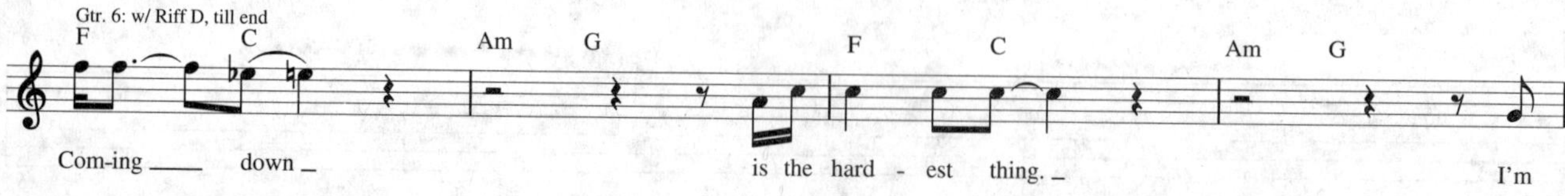
Gtr. 6: w/ Riff D, till end
F
C
Am
G
F
C
Am
G
Com-ing down
is the hard - est thing.
I'm

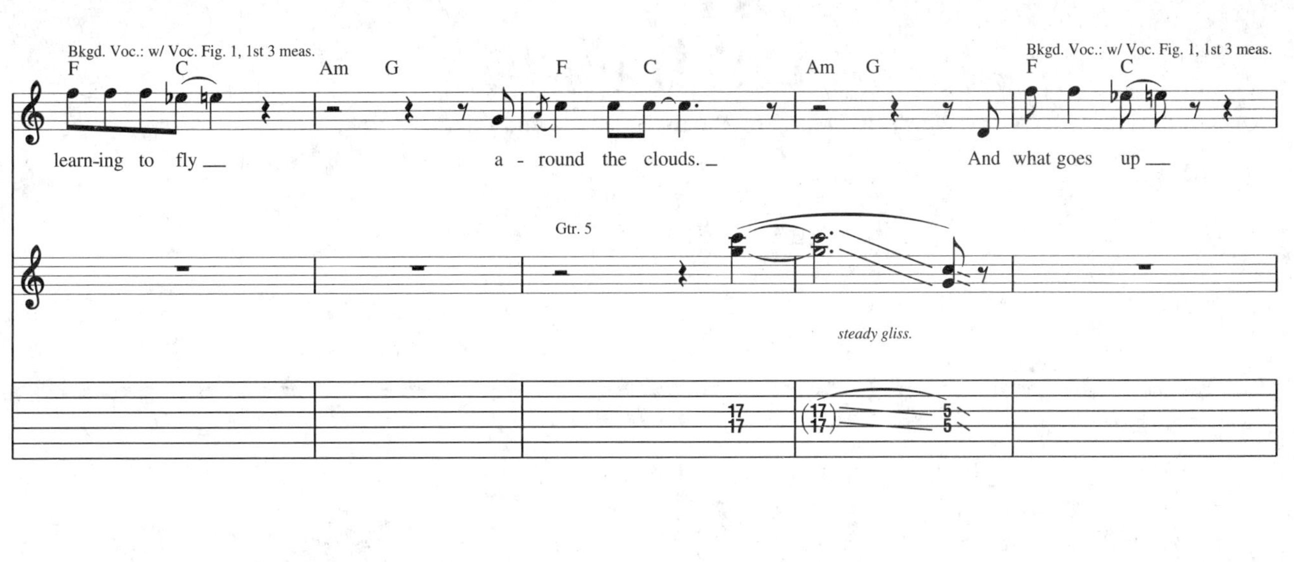
Bkgd. Voc.: w/ Voc. Fig. 1, 1st 3 meas.
F C Am G F C Am G F C
learn-ing to fly a - round the clouds. And what goes up
Gtr. 5
steady gliss.
17
17
(17)
(17)
5
5

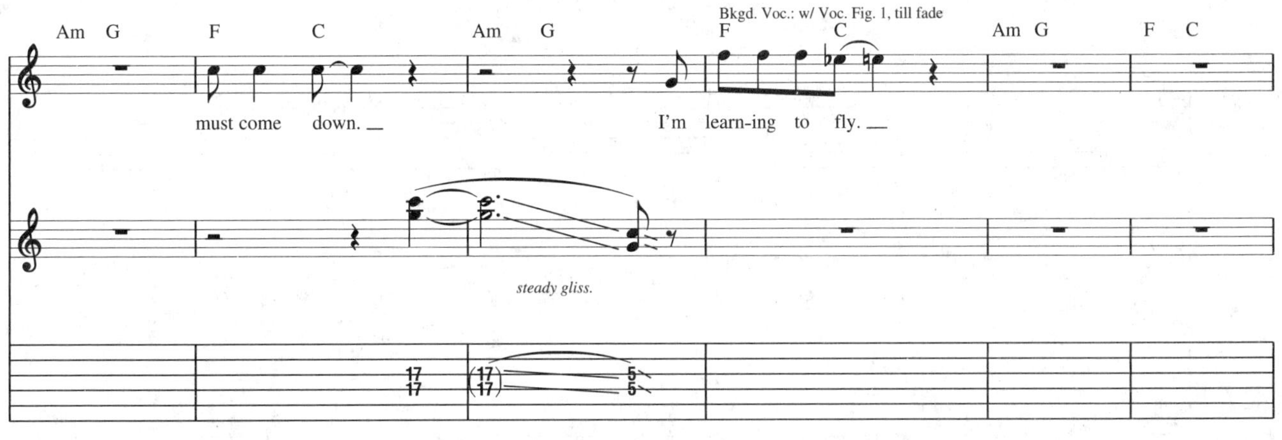
Bkgd. Voc.: w/ Voc. Fig. 1, till fade
Am G F C Am G F C Am G F C
must come down. I'm learn-ing to fly.
steady gliss.
17
17
(17)
(17)
5
5

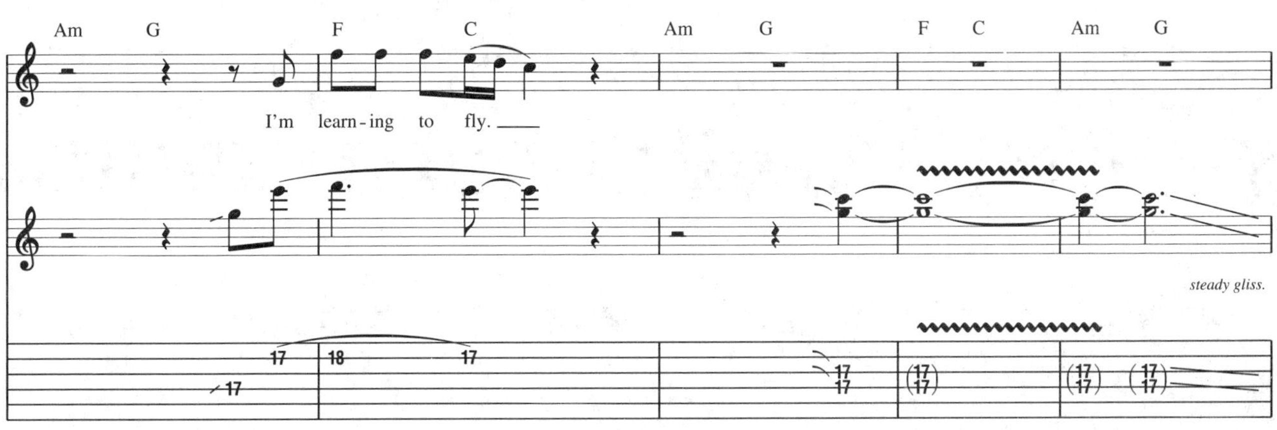
Am G F C Am G F C Am G
I'm learn-ing to fly.
steady gliss.
17
17 18 17
17
17
(17)
(17)
(17)
(17)
(17)
(17)

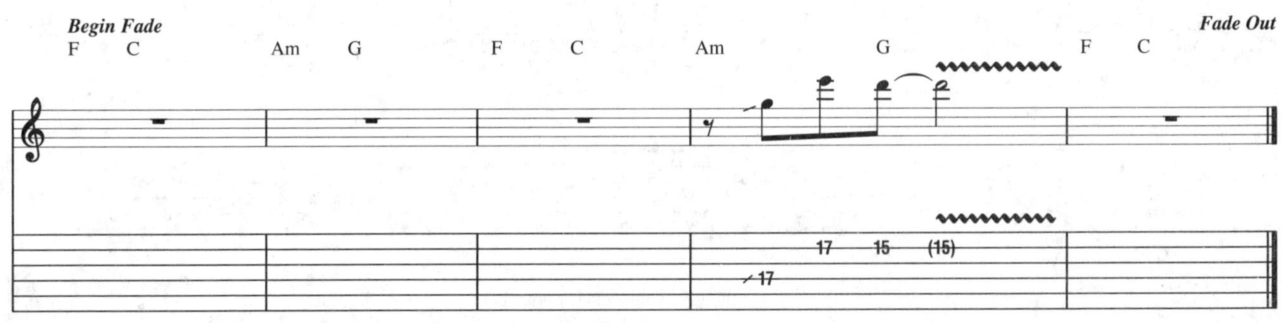
Begin Fade
Fade Out
F C Am G F C Am G F C
17
17 15 (15)

Let It Ride

Words and Music by Randy Bachman and Charles Turner

E
F#m7
Bm7
End Rhy. Fig. 1B
F#m7
End Rhy. Fig. 1
End Rhy. Rig. 1A
Gtrs. 1, 2 & 3: w/ Rhy. Figs. 1, 1A, & 1B
D/A
A
E
F#m7
Bm7
F#m7
Good - bye I lied. Don't cry. Would you let it ride?
D/A
A
E
F#m7
Bm7
Good - bye I lied. Don't cry. Would you let it ride?
Verse
N.C.
Gtrs. 1, 2 & 3
Rhy. Fig. 2
End Rhy. Fig. 2
Gtrs. 1, 2 & 3: w/ Rhy. Fig. 2, 3 1/2 times
1. You can see the morn - ing, but I can see the light.
2. Well my life is not com - plete, I nev - er see you smile.
Try, try, try to let it ride.
Try, try, try to let it ride.

Well, you've been out run - ning, I've ___ been wait - ing half the night. _
Ba - by you want the for - giv - ing kind, and that's just not my style.
3. I've been do - ing things worth while, and you've been cook - in' time.
Gtrs. 1, 2 & 3
F♯m
E
Try, try, try to let it ride. ___ And
Try, try, try to let it ride. ___
Try, try, try to let it ride. ___
Chorus
Gtrs. 1, 2 & 3: w/ Rhy. Figs. 1, 1A & 1B, simile
D/A
A
E
F♯m7
would you ___ cry ___ if I told you that ___ I lied ___ And would you
(You cry. ___ I lied. ___
Bm7
F♯m7
say good - bye? Or would you let it ride? ___ And
Don't cry. ___ Would you let it ride? ___)
D/A
A
E
F♯m7
would you ___ cry ___ if I told you that ___ I lied ___ And would you
(You cry. ___ I lied. ___
To Coda
Guitar Solo
Gtrs. 1, 2 & 3: w/ Rhy. Fig. 2, 5 times
N.C.
Bm7
say good - bye? Or would you let it ride? ___
Don't cry. ___ Would you let it ride? ___)
Gtr. 4
mf
slight dist.
1/2
full
1/4
full
full
full
full
full

D.S. al Coda

Coda

Interlude

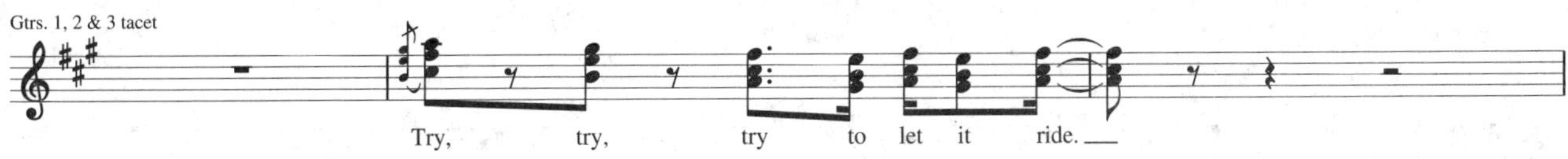

Gtrs. 3: w/ Rhy. Fig. 2
play 4 times
Try, try, try to let it ride.
Would you let it ride?
(sing on last repeat)
Gtr. 1
Gtr. 2

Gtrs. 1, 2 & 3: w/ Rhy. Fig. 2, 1 1/2 times
Would you let it ride?
Would you let it ride?
F#
4fr
Gtrs. 1, 2 & 3
Would you let it ride?

Outro

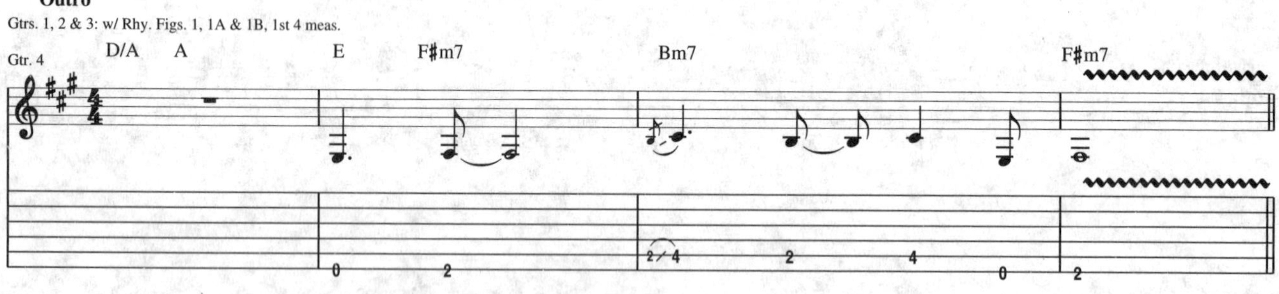
Gtrs. 1, 2 & 3: w/ Rhy. Figs. 1, 1A & 1B, 1st 4 meas.
Gtr. 4
D/A
A
E
F#m7
Bm7
F#m7

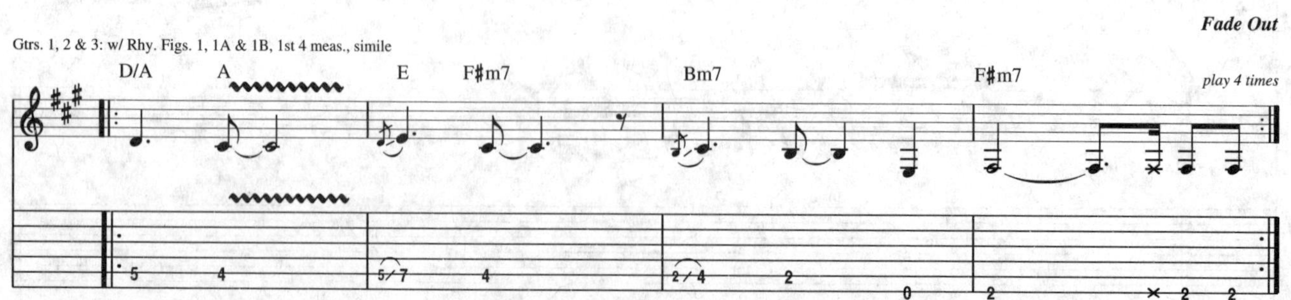
Gtrs. 1, 2 & 3: w/ Rhy. Figs. 1, 1A & 1B, 1st 4 meas., simile
Fade Out
play 4 times
D/A
A
E
F#m7
Bm7
F#m7

Lit Up

Words and Music by Joshua Todd Gruber, Keith Edward Nelson, Jonathan Brightman and Devon Glenn

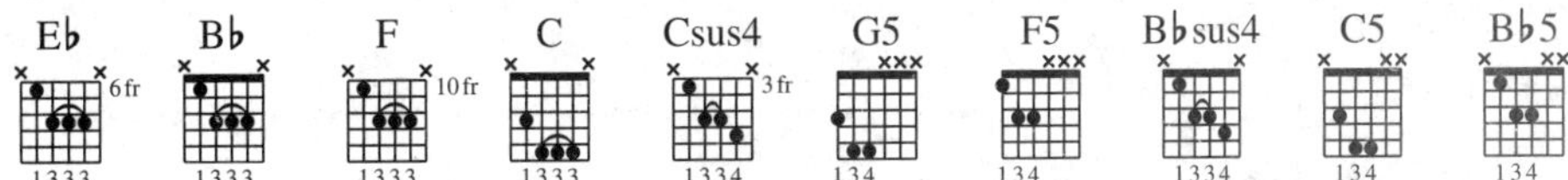

Gtr. 1; Open G Tuning:
①=D ④=D
②=B ⑤=G
③=G ⑥=D

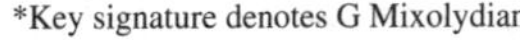

*Key signature denotes G Mixolydian.

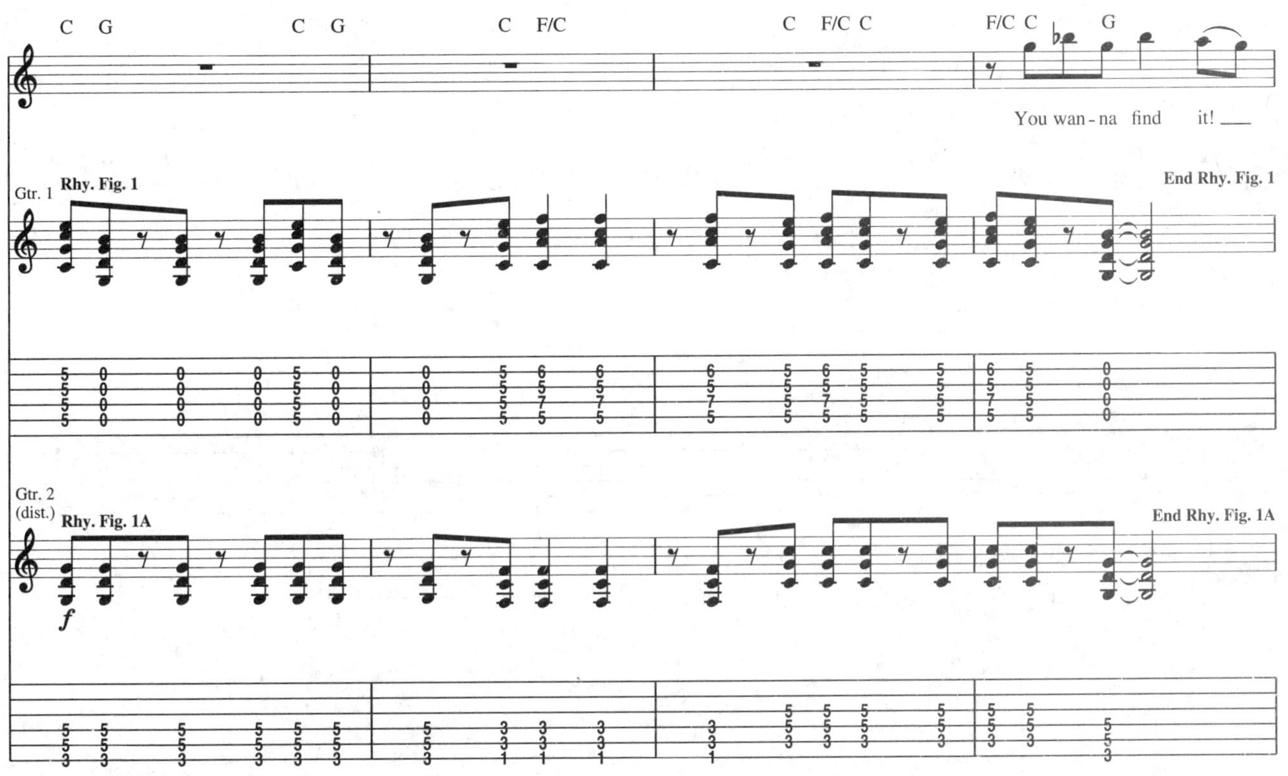

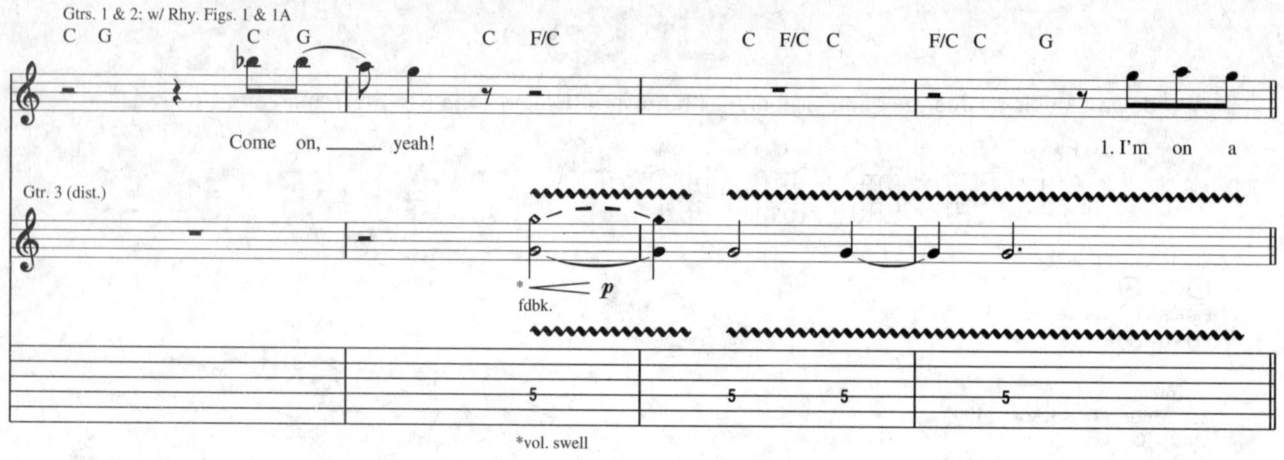

Verse

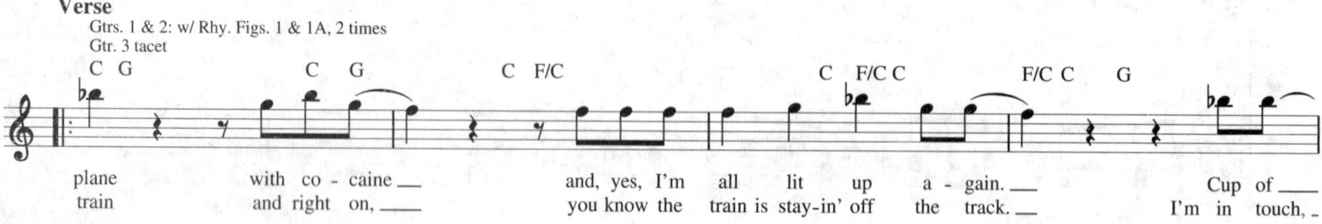

𝄋 Chorus

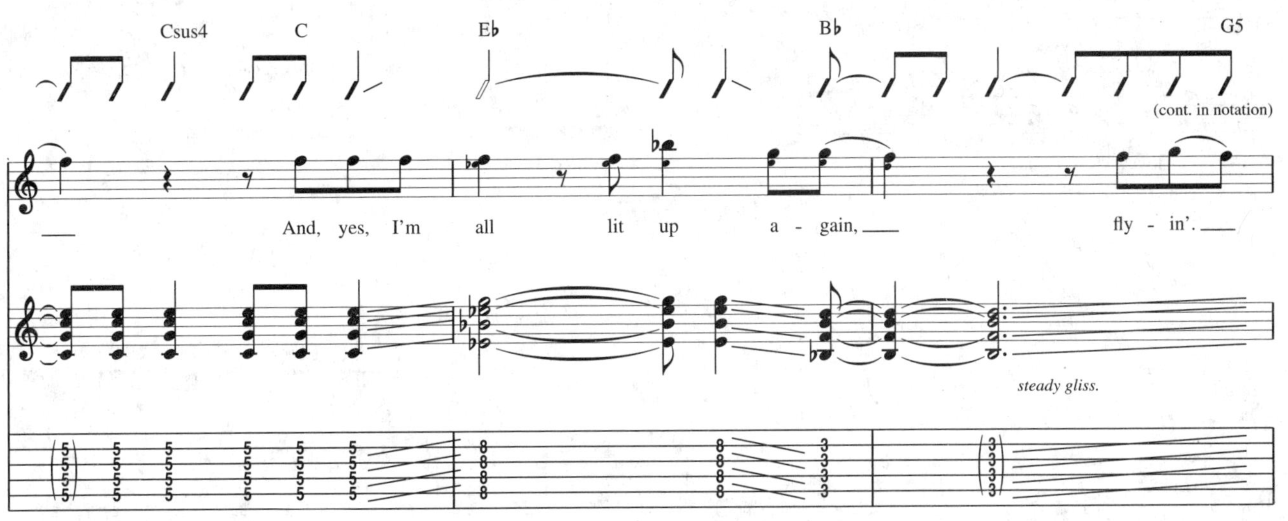

Csus4
C
Eb
Bb
G5
(cont. in notation)
And, yes, I'm all lit up a - gain, fly - in'.
steady gliss.

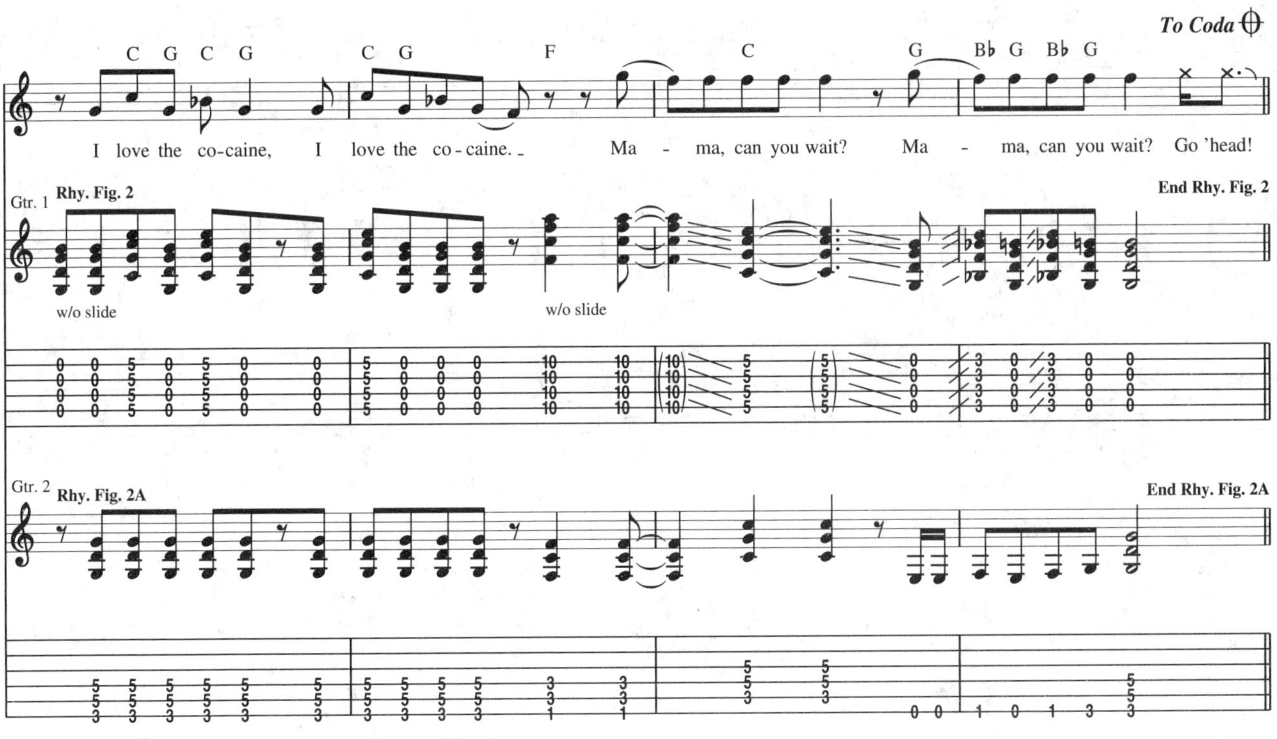

To Coda
C G C G
C G
F
C
G
Bb G Bb G
I love the co-caine, I love the co-caine. Ma - ma, can you wait? Ma - ma, can you wait? Go 'head!
Gtr. 1
Rhy. Fig. 2
End Rhy. Fig. 2
w/o slide
w/o slide
Gtr. 2
Rhy. Fig. 2A
End Rhy. Fig. 2A

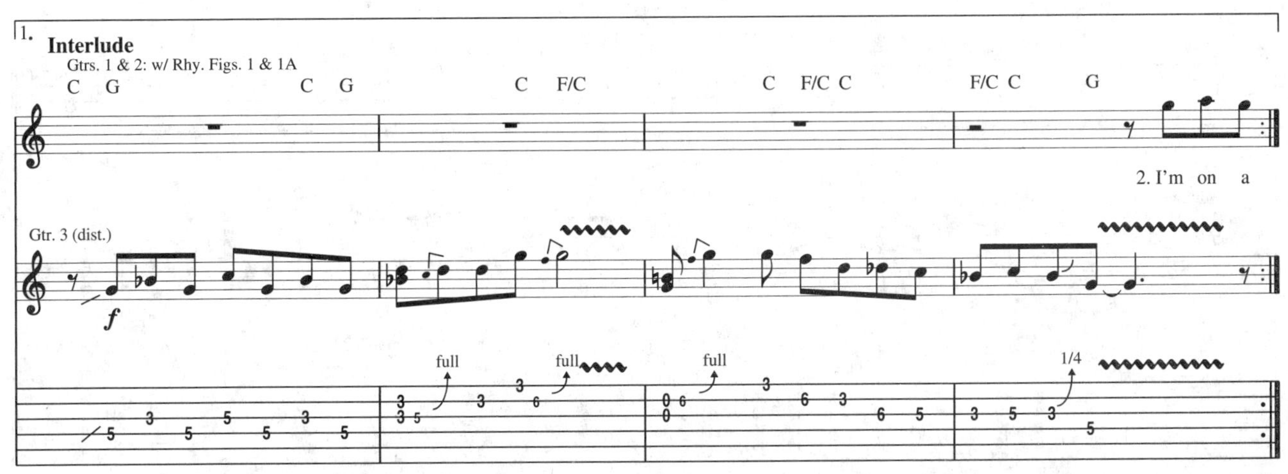

1.
Interlude
Gtrs. 1 & 2: w/ Rhy. Figs. 1 & 1A
C G
C G
C F/C
C F/C C
F/C C
G
2. I'm on a
Gtr. 3 (dist.)
f
full
full
full
1/4

2.
Gtrs. 1 & 2: w/ Rhy. Figs. 2 & 2A
C G C G
C G
F
C
G B♭ G B♭ G
I love the co-caine, I love the co-caine. Ma - ma, can you wait? Oh, can you wait long?

Guitar Solo

G5
F5
C
Csus4
C
B♭
B♭sus4
B♭
G5
Gtr. 2
Gtr. 3
hold bend
1/2
full
Gtr. 1
w/o slide

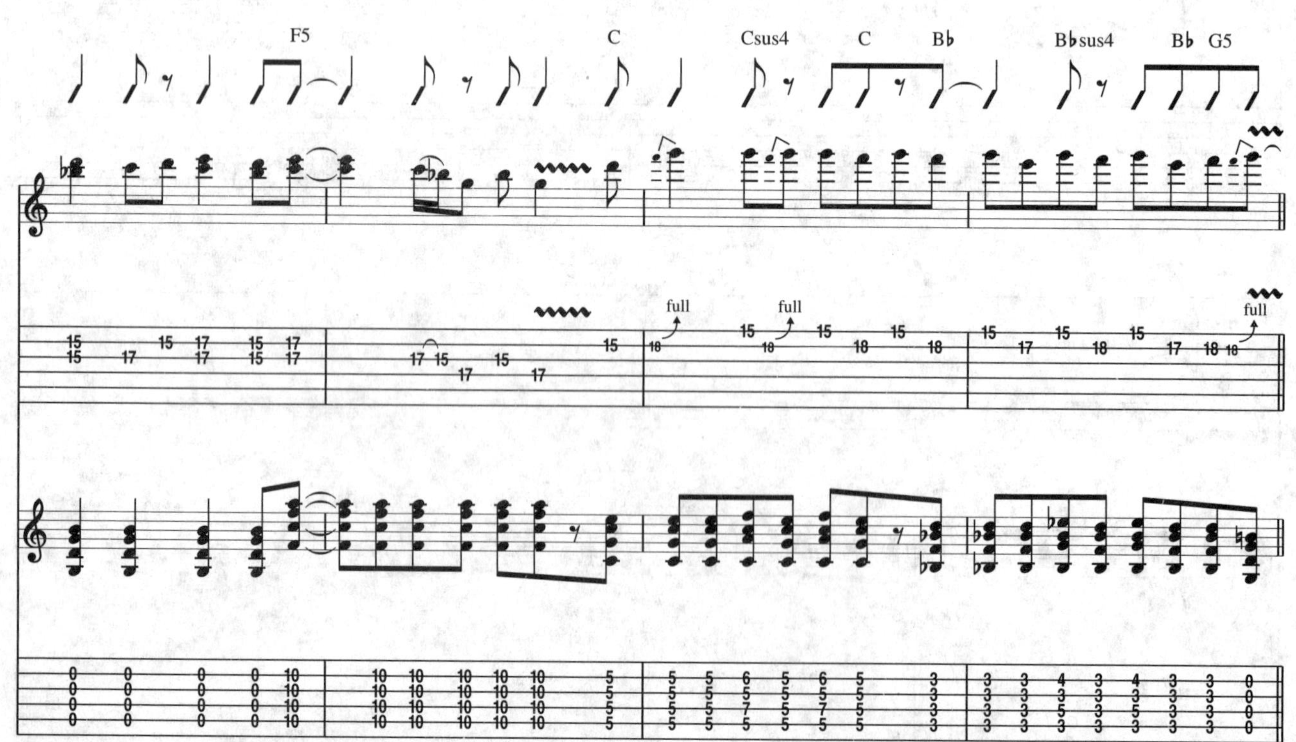
F5
C
Csus4
C
B♭
B♭sus4
B♭ G5
full
full
full

Bridge

Gtrs. 1, 2 & 3 tacet
N.C.(F)
(C)
(B♭)
You cracked the door for the cu - ri - ous girl 'cause she's wait - in', she's been wait - in'.
(G)
(F)
(C)
(B♭)
I chop a line for the fiend-in' man 'cause he wants one.
You know, you know you got to.
(G)
(F)
(C)
(B♭)
Can you feel it? Can you feel it to-night? Are you a - lone? Tell me, are you fuck-in' high?
Gtr. 1
D.S. al Coda
G5
F5
C5
B♭5
Gtr. 2
In a mo-ment you just so right. You're right, love. Are you right, love? are And, yes, I'm
Gtr. 1
w/ slide

Coda
Gtrs. 1 & 2: w/ Rhy. Figs. 2 & 2A
C G C G
C G
F
C
G Bb G Bb G
I love the co-caine, I love the co-caine. Ma - ma, can you wait? Oh, can you wait long?
Gtr. 3
15
Outro - Guitar Solo
Gtrs. 1 & 2: w/ Rhy. Figs. 1 & 1A, 3 times
C G C G C F/C C F/C C F/C C G
Oh, yeah!
1/2
full
19
C G C G C F/C C F/C C F/C C G
Don't wan-na fight you.
full
full
C G C G C F/C C F/C C F/C C G
Al - right, yeah!
Uh.

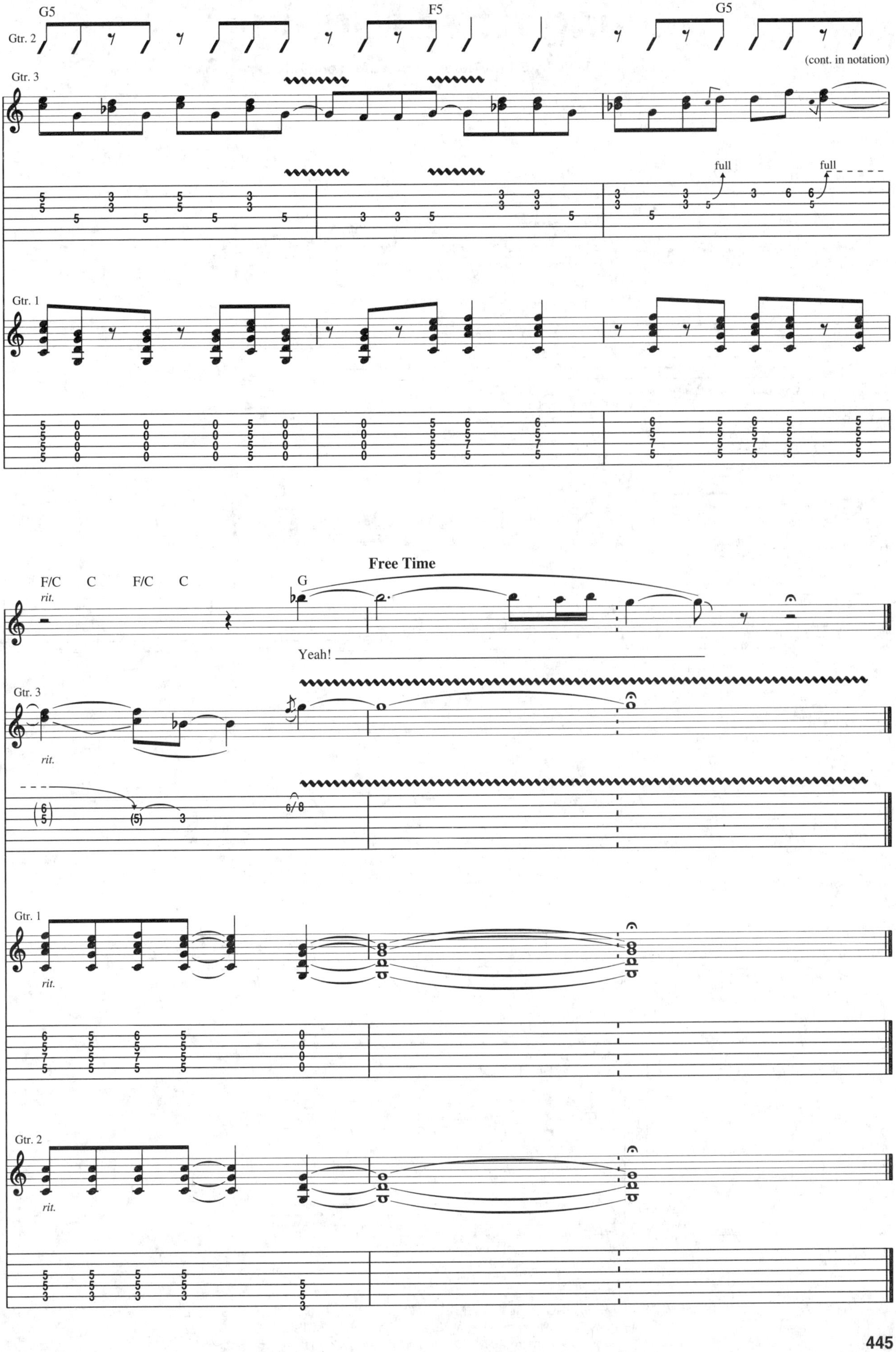

G5 F5 G5

Gtr. 2

(cont. in notation)

Gtr. 3

full full

Gtr. 1

F/C C F/C C

Free Time

G

rit.

Yeah! ___

Gtr. 3

rit.

Gtr. 1

rit.

Gtr. 2

rit.

Living After Midnight

Words and Music by Glenn Tipton, Rob Halford and K.K. Downing

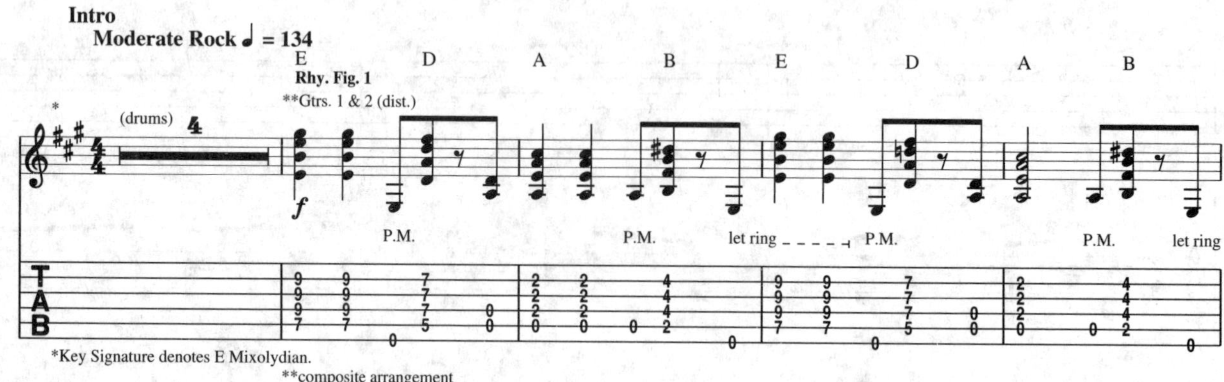

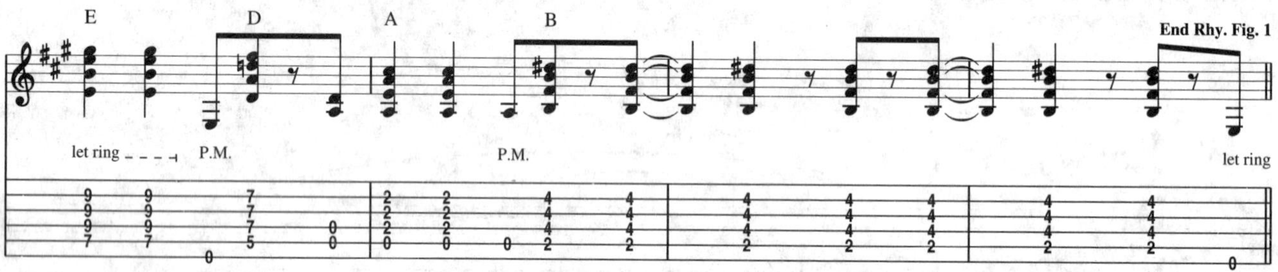

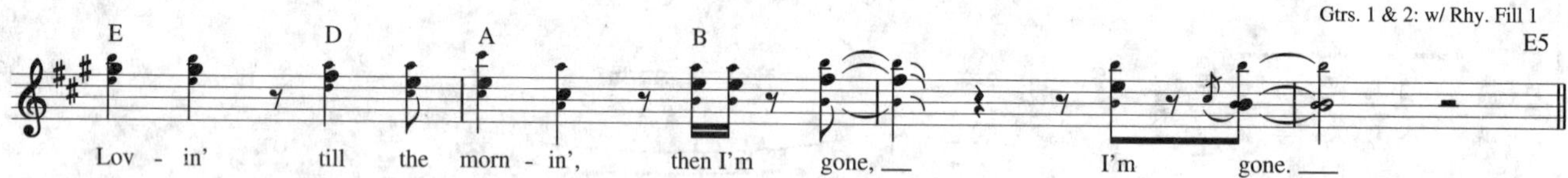

Verse
Gtr. 3: w/ Fill 1, 3rd time
E5
G5
E5
G5
E5
1. I took the cit - y 'bout - a one A. M. Load - ed, load - ed.
2. Got gleam-in' chrome re - flect-ing feel. Load - ed, load - ed.
3. The air's e - lec-tric, spark-in' pow-er. Load - ed, load - ed.
Gtrs. 1 & 2
P.M.
1/4
let ring
I'm all geared up to score a - gain. Load - ed, load - ed.
Read-y to take on ev - 'ry deal. Load - ed, load - ed.
I'm get-tin' hard - er by the hour. Load - ed, load - ed. I
G
Pre-Chorus
To Coda
G5 F#5
B5
D5
I come a-live in the ne - on lights. That's when I make my moves right.
My pulse is rac - in', hot to take. But this mo-tor's revved up, fit to break.
set my sights and then home in. The joint starts fly-'n' when I be - gin.
fdbk.
pitch: G
F#
Fill 1
Gtr. 3

Chorus

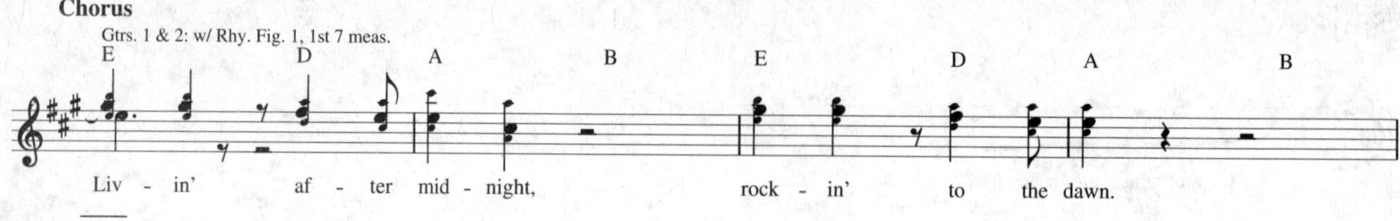

Bridge

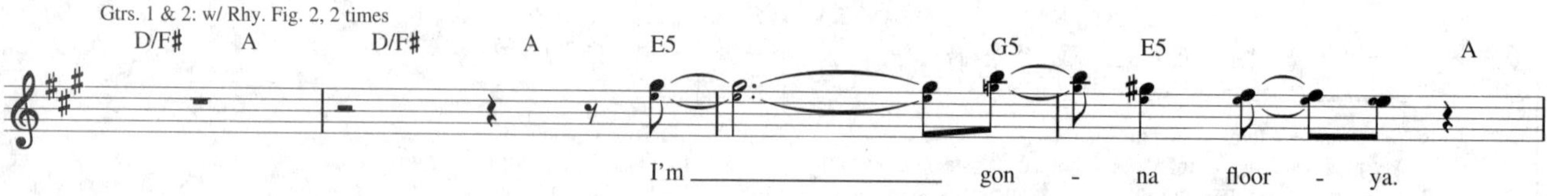

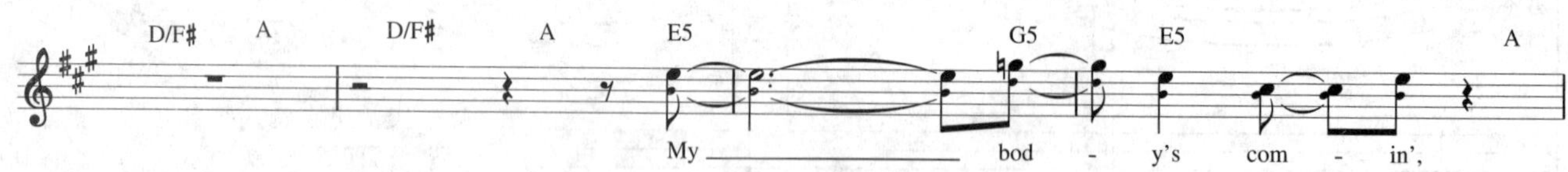

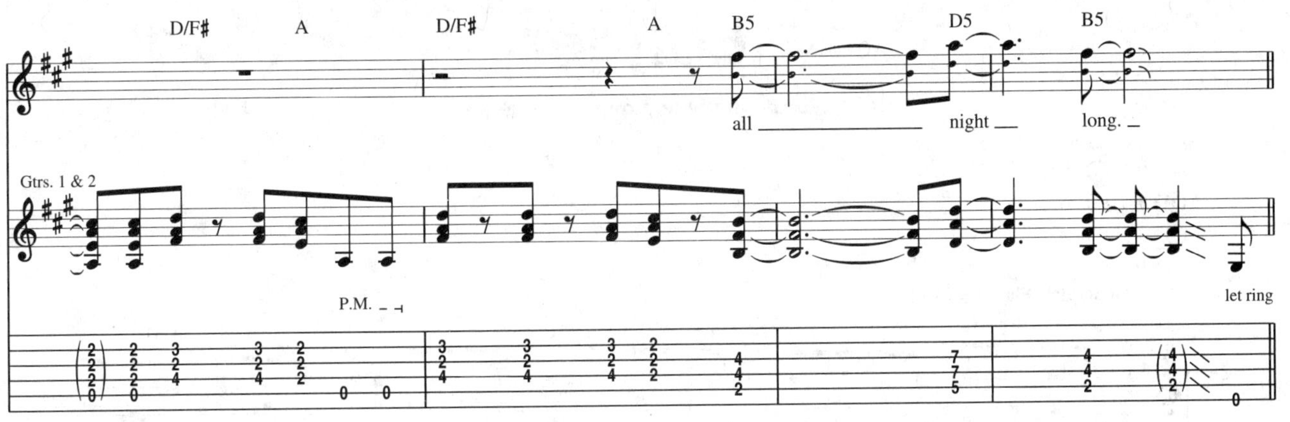
D/F# A D/F# A B5 D5 B5
all night long.
Gtrs. 1 & 2
P.M.
let ring

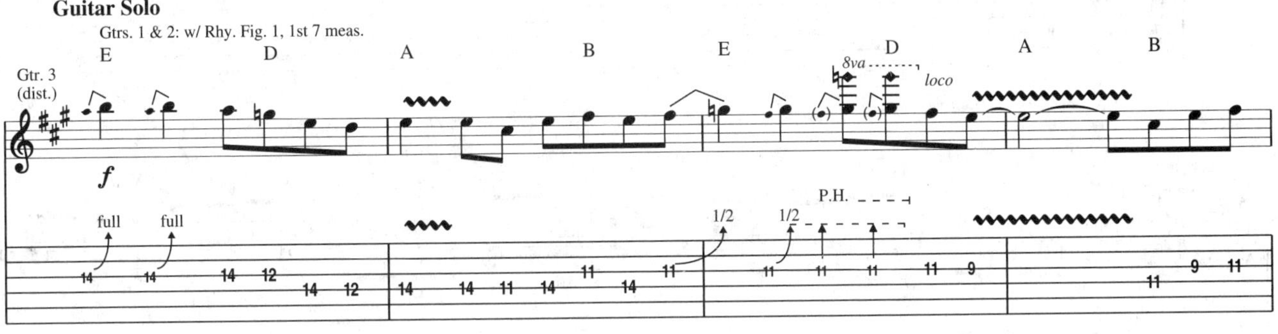
Guitar Solo
Gtrs. 1 & 2: w/ Rhy. Fig. 1, 1st 7 meas.
E D A B E D A B
Gtr. 3 (dist.)
8va
loco
f
full
full
1/2
1/2
P.H.

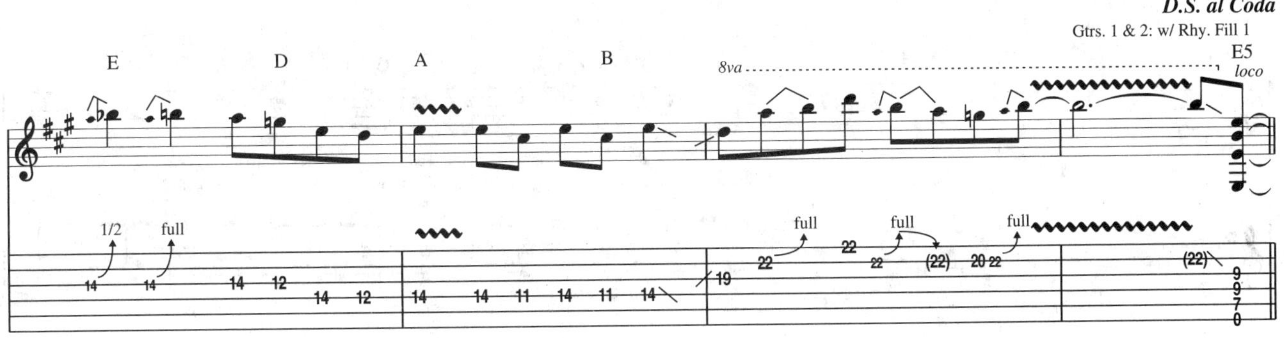
D.S. al Coda
Gtrs. 1 & 2: w/ Rhy. Fill 1
E D A B E5
8va
loco
1/2
full
full
full
full

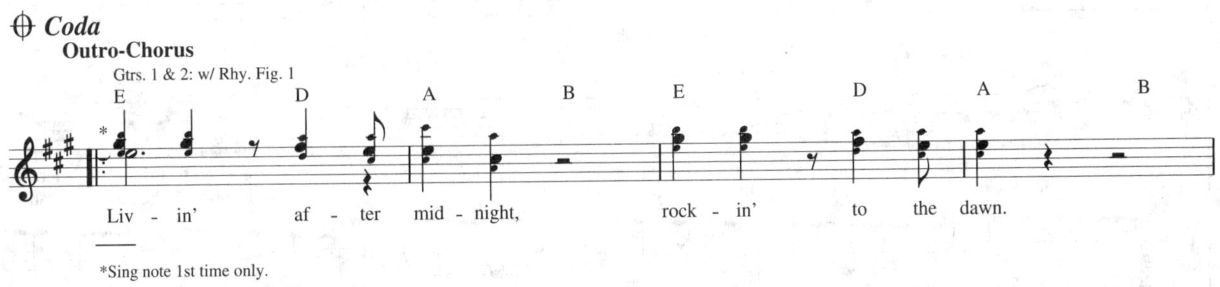
Coda
Outro-Chorus
Gtrs. 1 & 2: w/ Rhy. Fig. 1
E D A B E D A B
Liv - in' af - ter mid - night, rock - in' to the dawn.
*Sing note 1st time only.

Play 3 Times and Fade
E D A B
Lov - in' till the morn - in', then I'm gone, I'm gone.

Longer

Words and Music by Dan Fogelberg

1.
2.
Gmaj7/B
C
Bb
Am7
G
C/G
D/G
stars up in the heav-ens,
I've been in love with you.
for - est, pri-me - val,
I am in love with you.
End Riff A
Chorus
F/C
Eb/Bb
5:2
I'll bring
fire in the win - ters.
Riff B
You'll send
show-ers in the springs.
We'll fly
D7sus4
D7
Dm7
through the falls and sum-mers
with love on our wings.
End Riff B

Verse

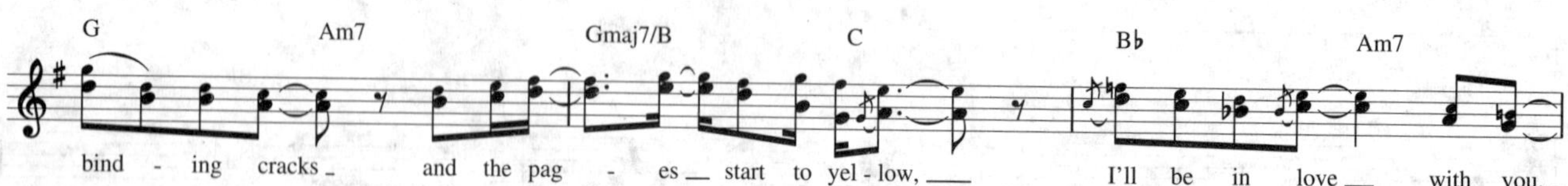

Trumpet Solo

* Trumpet arr. for gtr.

Verse
Gtr. 1: w/ Riff A
D7sus4
D7
Dm7
D7
G
Am7
4. Long - er than there've been

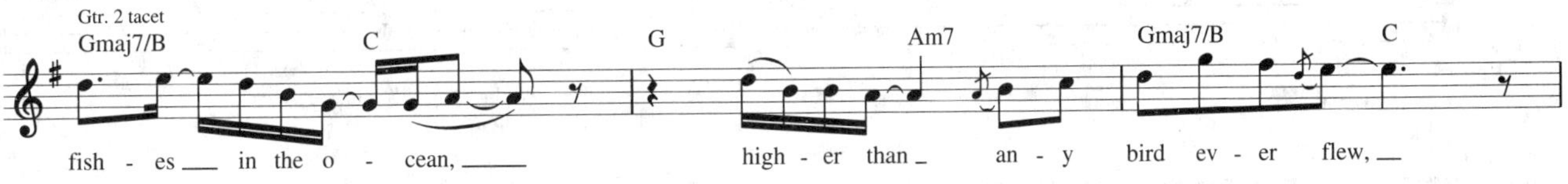
Gtr. 2 tacet
Gmaj7/B
C
G
Am7
Gmaj7/B
C
fish - es in the o - cean, high - er than an - y bird ev - er flew,

G
Am7
Gmaj7/B
C
B♭
Am7
long - er than there've been stars up in the heav - ens, I've been in love with you.

G
B♭
Am7
G
I am in love with you.
Gtr. 1

B♭
Am7

Loser

Words by Beck Hansen
Music by Beck Hansen and Karl Stephenson

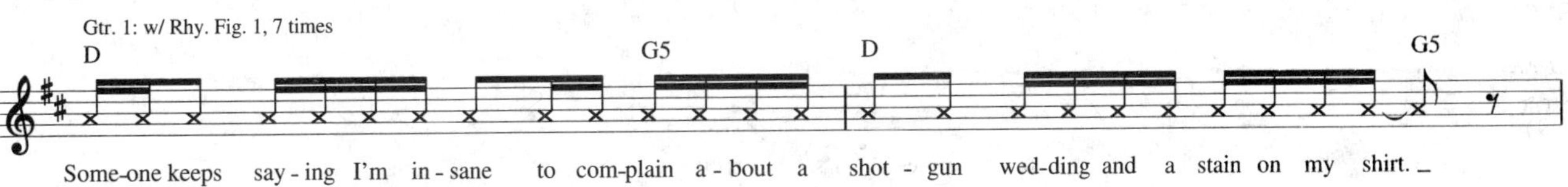
Gtr. 1: w/ Rhy. Fig. 1, 7 times
D G5 D G5
Some-one keeps say-ing I'm in-sane to com-plain a-bout a shot-gun wed-ding and a stain on my shirt.

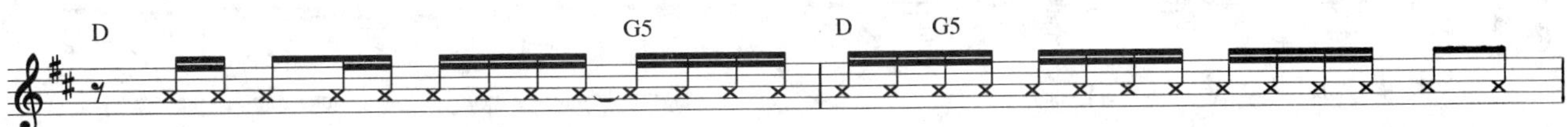
D G5 D G5
Don't be-lieve ev-'ry-thing that you breathe. You get a park-ing vi-o-la-tion and a mag-got on your sleeve. So

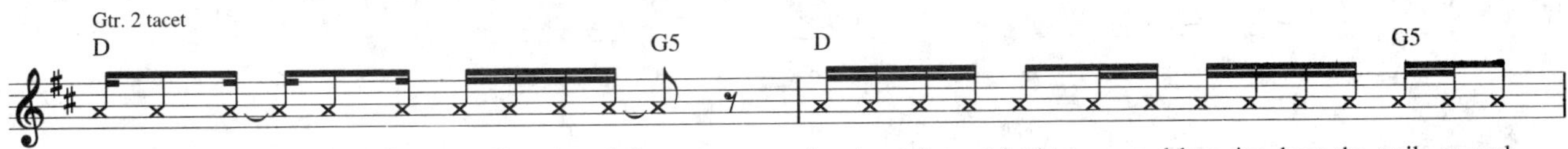
Gtr. 2 tacet
D G5 D G5
shave your face with some mace in the dark. Sav-ing all your food stamps and burn-ing down the trail-er park.

Chorus
Gtr. 1: w/ Rhy. Fill 2
Gtr. 1: w/ Rhy. Fig. 1, 8 times
Gtr. 2: w/ Riff A, 4 times
D G5 D D G5 D G5
Yo. Cut it. Soy un per-di-dor. I'm a
*w/ multi-tracked vocals on Chorus and Bridge sections

D G5 D G5 D G5
los-er, ba-by, so why don't you kill me? Soy un
Spoken: Double barrel buck shy.

D G5 D G5 D G5
per-di-dor. I'm a los-er, ba-by, so why don't you kill me?

Verse
Gtrs. 1 & 2 tacet
N.C.
2. Forc-es of e-vil and a bo-zo night-mare. Bent all the mu-sic with the pho-ny gas cham-ber, 'cause

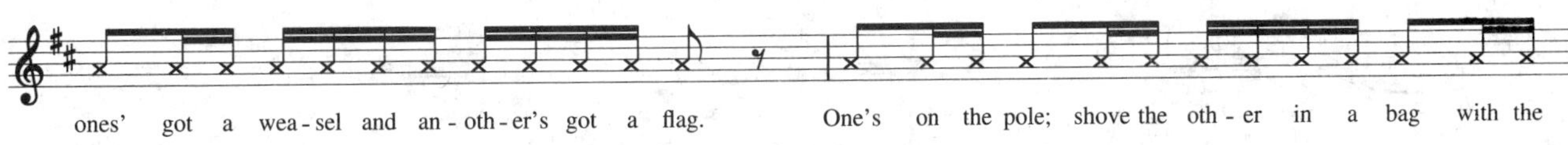
ones' got a wea-sel and an-oth-er's got a flag. One's on the pole; shove the oth-er in a bag with the

Rhy. Fill 2
Gtr. 1
T
A
B

Gtr. 1: w/ Rhy. Fig. 1, 4 times
D G5 D G5
re - run shows and the co - caine nose job, the day - time crap of the folk sing - er slob.
D G5 D G5
He hung him - self with a gui - tar string. A slab of tur - key neck, and its' hang - ing from a pi - geon wing.
Gtr. 1 tacet
N.C. (D7)
A - get right if you can't re - late. Trade the cash for the beef, for the bod - y, for the hate. And my
Gtr. 3
time is a piece of wax fall - in' on a ter - mite who's chok - in' on the splin - ters.
Gtr. 3
Chorus
Gtr. 1: w/ Rhy. Fig. 1, 7 times
Gtr. 2: w/ Riff A, 3 1/2 times
Gtr. 3 tacet
D G5 D G5 D G5 D G5
Soy un per - di - dor. I'm a los - er, ba - by, so why don't you kill me?
Spoken: Get crazy with the Cheez Whiz.
Gtr. 1: w/ Rhy. Fill 1
Gtr. 2: w/ Rhy. Fill 3
D G5 D G5 D G5 D
Soy un per - di - dor. I'm a lo - ser, ba - by, so why don't you kill me?
Spoken: Drive-by body pierce.
Rhy. Fill 3
Gtr. 2
T
A
B

Bridge
Gtrs. 1 & 2 tacet
N.C.
Yo, bring it on down. Soy.
Gtr. 1: w/ Rhy. Fig. 1, 7 times
w/ Bkgd. voc. ad Lib, next 4 meas.
D G5 D G5 D G5 D G5
Soy.
Gtr. 3
Gtr. 2: w/ Riff A, 1 1/2 times
Gtr. 1: w/ Rhy. Fill 4
Gtr. 2: w/ Rhy. Fill 5
D G5 D G5 D G5 D
Spoken: I'm a driver, I'm a winner. Things are gonna change. I can feel it.
Chorus
4th time, Begin Fade
Gtr. 1: w/ Rhy. Fig. 1, 4 times
Gtr. 2: w/ Riff A, 2 times
Gtr. 3 tacet
D G5 D G5 D G5 D G5
So, un per-di - dor. I'm a los-er, ba - by, so why don't you kill me?
Spoken: I can't believe it.
Outro
Gtr. 3: w/ Rhy. Fill 1
Gtr. 2: w/ Riff A, till fade
Gtr. 1 tacet
Repeat and Fade
N.C. (D)
don't you kill me? don't you kill me? don't you kill me?
Spoken: Uuuuuuuuuh. Spoken: Sprechen Sie Deutsch, baby? Spoken: You know what I'm sayin'?
Rhy. Fill 4
Gtr. 1
Rhy. Fill 5
Gtr. 2

Mama Kin

Words and Music by Steven Tyler

E5 B5 A5 A6 A5 A7 A6 E5
P.M.
P.M.
P.M.
E6 E5 E7 E6 E5 E6 E7 E6 A5 A6 A7 A5 A6 E5
*steady gliss.
P.M.
1/2
*Slide up ⑥ w/ middle finger while picking specified rhythm.
E6 (E5) E7 (E5) E6 A5 A6 A5 A7 A6 E5 E6 (E5) E7 E6 E5
1/4
1/2
1/2

E6
E7
E6
A5
A6
A7
A6
E5
E6
E7
E6
1/2
F#5
1/2
B5
B6
B7
B6
B5
1/2
1/4
B6
B5
B7
B6
G5
G#5
A5
A#5
B5
1/2
1/2
1/2
1/4
grad. bend
full

Gtr. 2 tacet
Gtr. 1
E5 B5 A5 E5 E6 E5 E7 E5 E6
P.M.
P.M.
P.M.
P.M.
Gtr. 1
E5 B5 A5 A6 A7 A6 E5 E6 E5 E7 E5 E6 E5
P.M.
Gtr. 2
E6 E7 E6 E5 E6 E7 E6 E5 E6 E7 E6
15ma
loco
P.H.
1/2
1/2
1/2
pitch: C♯
P.M.
P.M.

* ④ and ⑤ are muted by R.H.

E6 E7 E6 E5 B5 A5
Whole - earth lov - er, keep - in' un - der - cov - er, nev -
Rhy. Fig. 1
P.M.
Rhy. Fig. 1A
E5 E6 E5 E7 E5 E6 E5 E6 (E5) E7 E5 E6
- er know - in' where ya been.
P.M.
E5 B5 A5 E5
You've been fad - in', al - ways out par - ad - in'. Keep in touch with ma - ma kin.
P.M.

Pre-Chorus
E6 E5 E7 E5 E6 E5
E6 E5 E7 (E5) E6
A5 A6 (A5) A7 (A5) A6 E5
Well, you've al - ways got your tail on the wag,
End Rhy. Fig. 1
Rhy. Fig. 2
P.M.
End Rhy. Fig. 1A
Rhy. Fig. 2A
E6 E5 E7 (E5) E6
A5 A6 (A5) A7 A5 A6 E5
E6 E5 E7 (E5) E6 E5
shoot - in' fire from your mouth just like a drag - on.
P.M.
1/2
E6 E5 E7 E5 E6
A5 A6 (A5) A7 A5 A6 E5
E6 (E5) E7 E5 E6
You act like a per - pet - u - al drag. You
P.M.
P.M.
P.M.

F#5
B5
B6
B7
B6
B5
bet - ter check it out, 'cause some - day soon you'll have ta climb back on the wag - on.
End Rhy. Fig. 2
B6
B5
B7
B6
G5
G#5
A5
A#5
B5
don't pick
End Rhy. Fig. 2A
Verse
Gtrs. 1 & 2: w/ Rhy. Figs. 1 & 1A, simile
E5
B5
A5
E5
2. It ain't eas - y liv - in' like you wan - na. It's so hard to find peace of mind.
E6
E5
E7
E5
E6
E5
E6
E5
E7
E5
E6
E5
B5
Yes, it is. The way I see it, you

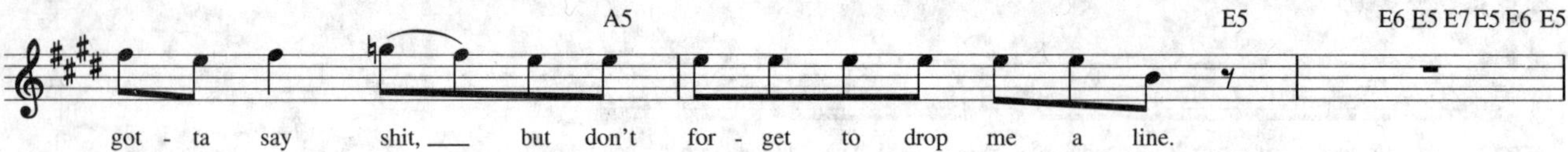

Pre-Chorus

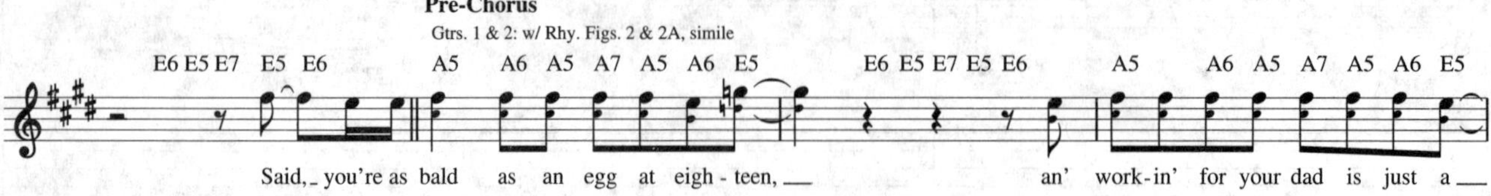

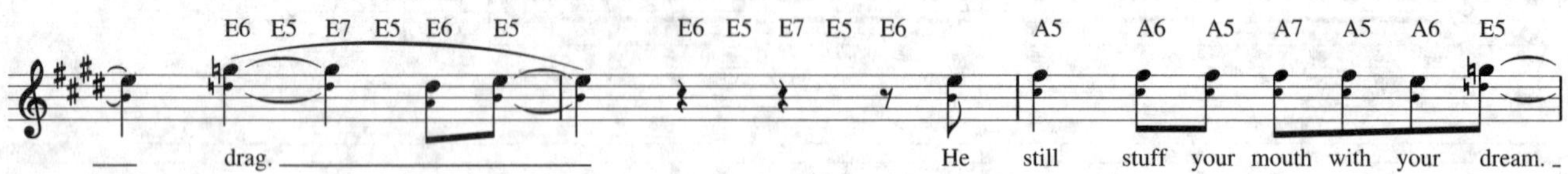

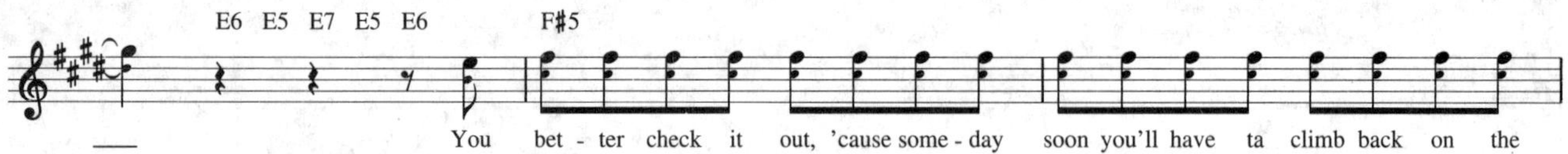

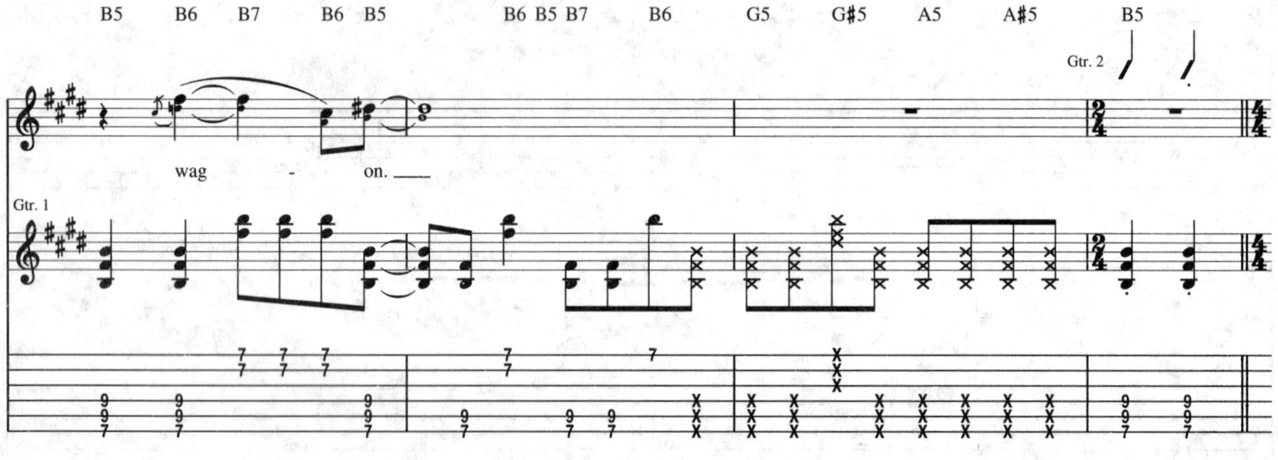

Chorus

E5
B5
E5
Liv - in' out your fan - ta - sy.
Sleep - in' late an'
B
E5
A5
G5
D5
B5
smok - in' tea. Mm, hmm.
Keep in touch with ma - ma kin.
Gtr. 1
Gtr. 2
Rhy. Fig. 3A
E5
A5
G5
D5
B5
E5
A5
Tell her where you gone 'n' been.
Liv - in' out your

G5 D5 B5 E5 A5 G5 D5

fan - ta - sy. Sleep - in' late an' smok - in' tea.

End Rhy. Fig. 3

End Rhy. Fig. 3A

C5 C6 C5 C6 C5 C6 C5 C6 B5 B6 B5 B6 B5 B6 B5 B6

Ah.

N.C.(A5)
(A7)
(A6)
(A5)
(A7)
(A6)
full
full
full
full

Verse
Gtrs. 1 & 2: w/ Rhy. Figs. 1 & 1A, simile
E5 B5 A5 E5 E6 E7 E6 E5
3. It ain't eas - y, liv - in' like you wan-na. And it's so hard ta find peace of mind. Yes, it

E6 E7 E6 E5 B5 A5 E5
is. The way I see it, you got - ta say shit, but don't for - get to drop me a line.

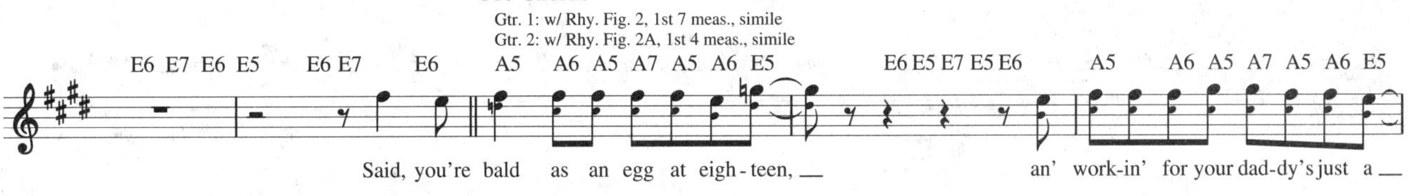
Pre-Chorus
Gtr. 1: w/ Rhy. Fig. 2, 1st 7 meas., simile
Gtr. 2: w/ Rhy. Fig. 2A, 1st 4 meas., simile
E6 E7 E6 E5 E6 E7 E6 A5 A6 A5 A7 A5 A6 E5 E6 E5 E7 E5 E6 A5 A6 A5 A7 A5 A6 E5
Said, you're bald as an egg at eigh - teen, an' work-in' for your dad-dy's just a

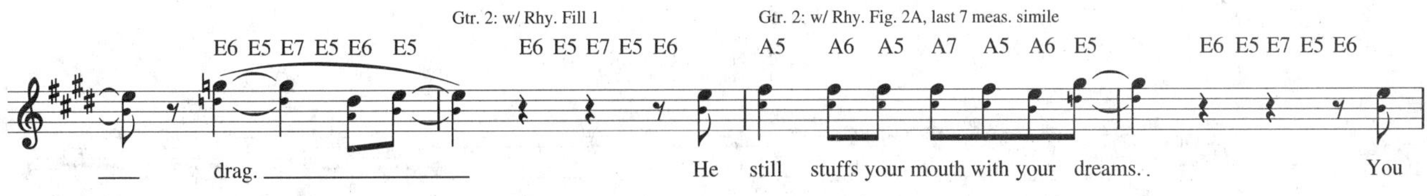
Gtr. 2: w/ Rhy. Fill 1
Gtr. 2: w/ Rhy. Fig. 2A, last 7 meas. simile
E6 E5 E7 E5 E6 E5 E6 E5 E7 E5 E6 A5 A6 A5 A7 A5 A6 E5 E6 E5 E7 E5 E6
drag. He still stuffs your mouth with your dreams. You

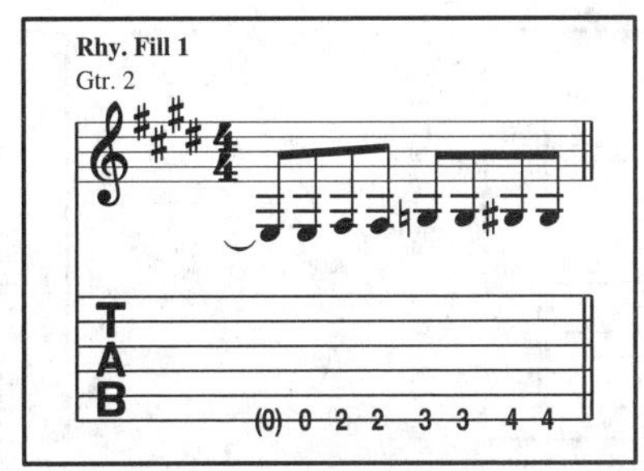
Rhy. Fill 1
Gtr. 2
T
A
B
(0) 0 2 2 3 3 4 4

F#5
bet - ter check it out, 'cause some - day soon you'll have ta climb back on the
Gtr. 1
Gtr. 3 tacet
Gtr. 2: w/ Rhy. Fill 2
B5 B6 B7 B6 B5 B6 B5 B7 B6 G5 G#5 A5 A#5 B5
wag - on.
Gtr. 3 (dist. - Perry)
mf w/ slide
Chorus
Gtr. 1: w/ Rhy. Fig. 3, 1st 6 meas., simile
E5 B5 E5
Keep in touch with ma - ma kin. Tell her where ya
B5 E5 B5
gone 'n' been. Liv - in' out your fan - ta - sy.
Gtr. 1: w/ Rhy. Fill 3
Gtr. 1: w/ Rhy. Fig. 3, last 8 meas., simile
Gtr. 2: w/ Rhy. Fig. 3A, simile
E5 B E5 A5
Sleep - in' late an' smok - in' tea. Mm, hmm. Keep in touch with
Rhy. Fill 2
Gtr. 2
Rhy. Fill 3
Gtr. 1

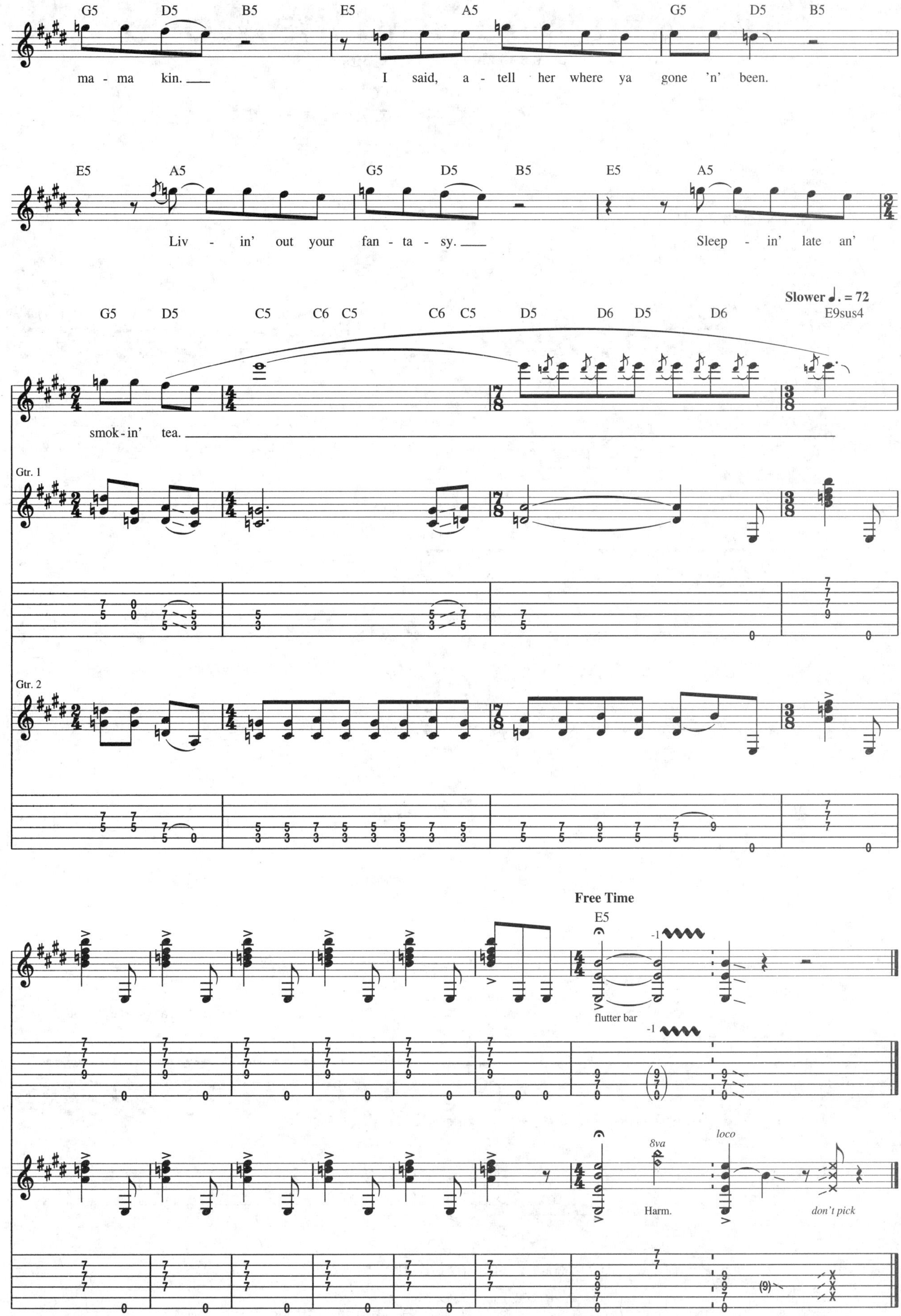

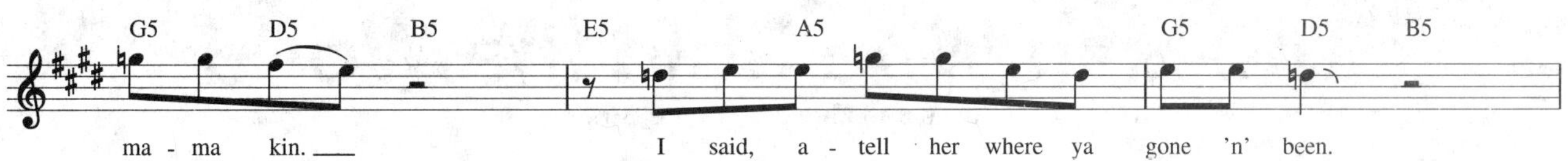

E5 A5 G5 D5 B5 E5 A5

Liv - in' out your fan - ta - sy. Sleep - in' late an'

Slower ♩. = 72

G5 D5 C5 C6 C5 C6 C5 D5 D6 D5 D6 E9sus4

smok - in' tea.

Gtr. 1

Gtr. 2

Free Time

E5

-1

flutter bar

8va

loco

Harm.

don't pick

The Man Who Sold the World

Words and Music by David Bowie

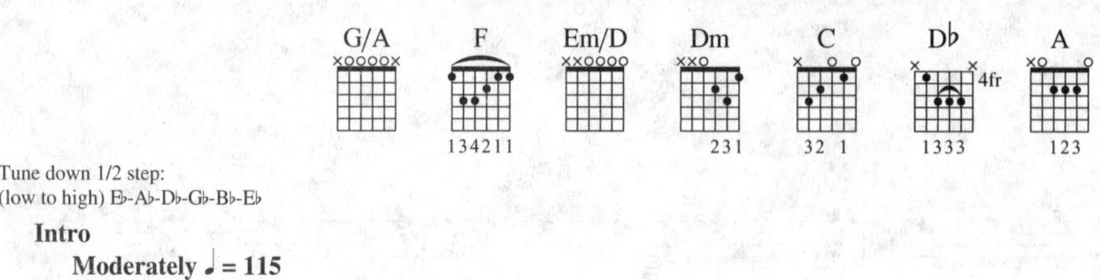

Tune down 1/2 step:
(low to high) E♭-A♭-D♭-G♭-B♭-E♭

Intro

Moderately ♩ = 115

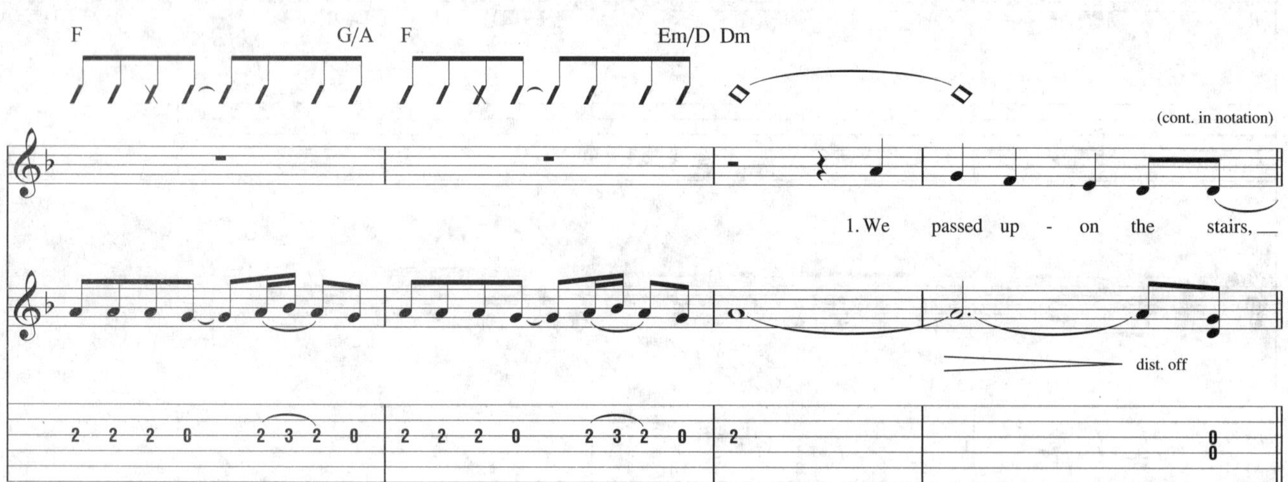

Verse

*Composite arrangement

A
F
he said I was his friend, which came as a sur - prise.
for years and years I roamed. I gazed a gaz - y stare.

C
A
I spoke in - to his eyes. I thought you died a
We walked a mil - lion hills. I must have died a

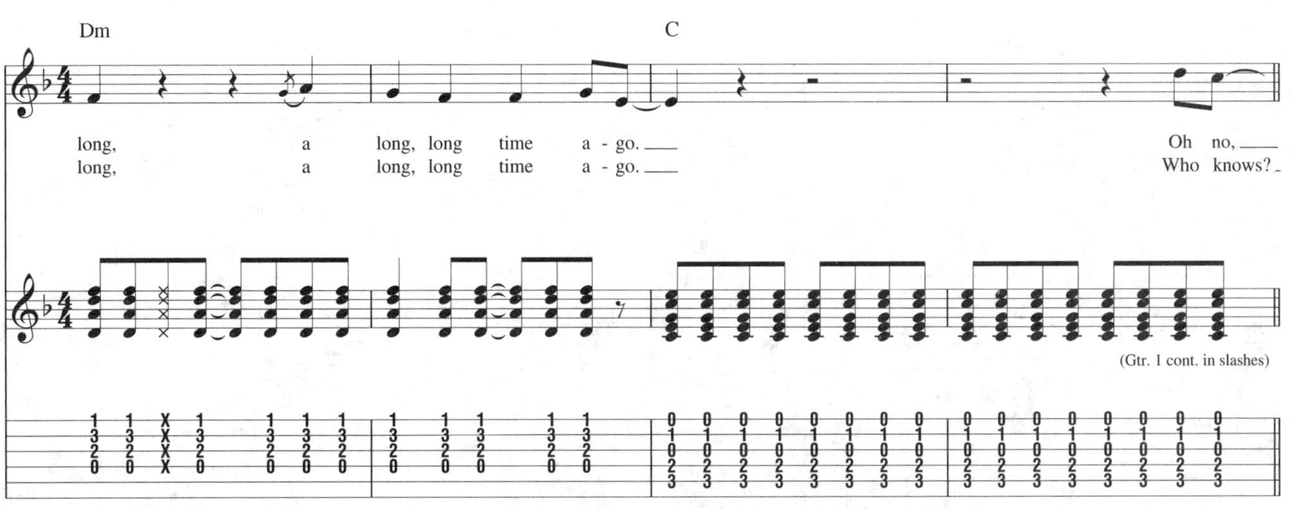
Dm
C
long, a long, long time a - go. Oh no,
long, a long, long time a - go. Who knows?
(Gtr. 1 cont. in slashes)

Chorus
C
G/A
F
G/A
D♭
G/A
Gtr. 1
1., 3. not me, we nev - er lost con - trol.
2. Not me. I nev - er lost con - trol.
Gtr. 2
F
G/A
C
G/A
F
G/A
(cont. in notation)
The face to face of a
You're face to face with the
1., 3.
1st & 3rd time, Gtr. 1: w/ Riff A
2nd time, Gtr. 1: w/ Riff A (1st 3 meas.)
D♭
A
Dm
man who sold the world.
man who sold the world.
Gtrs. 1 & 2
Gtr. 2

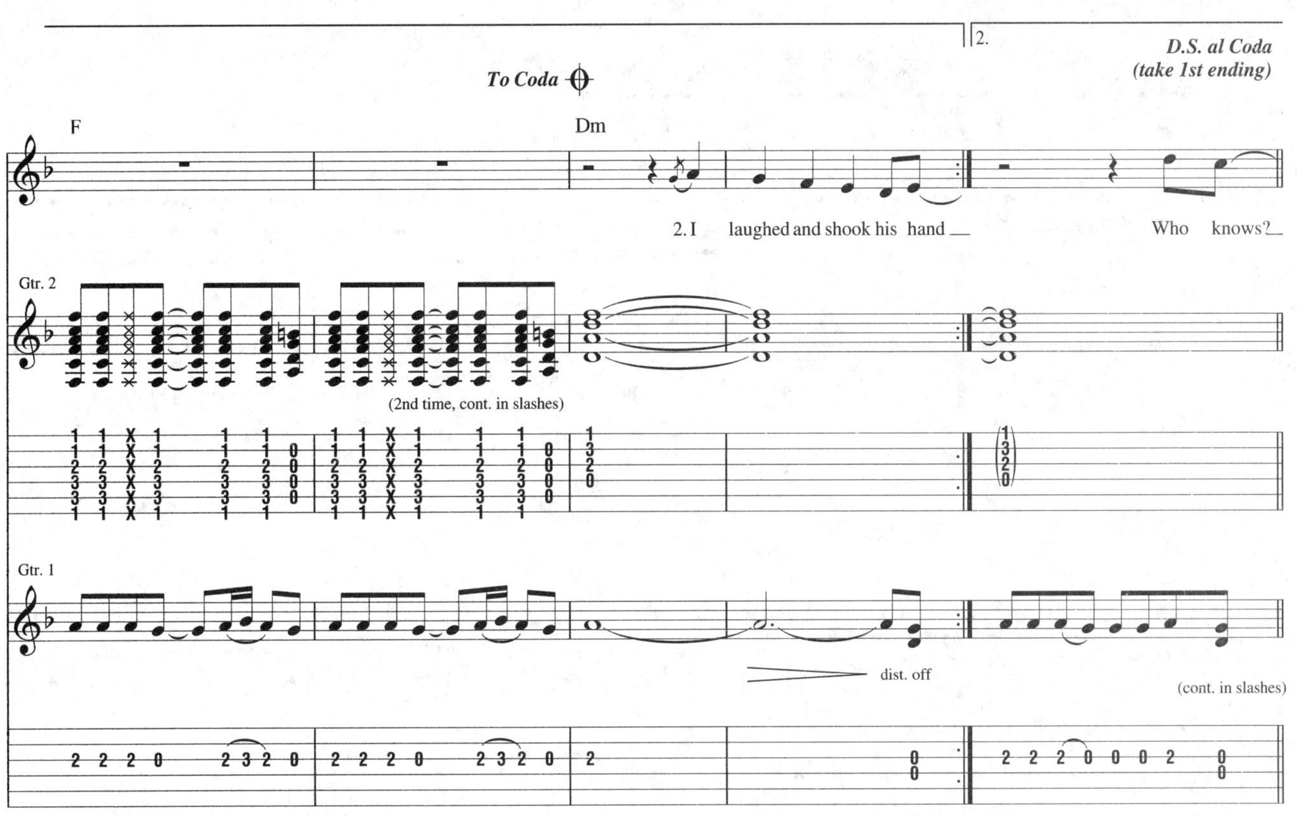

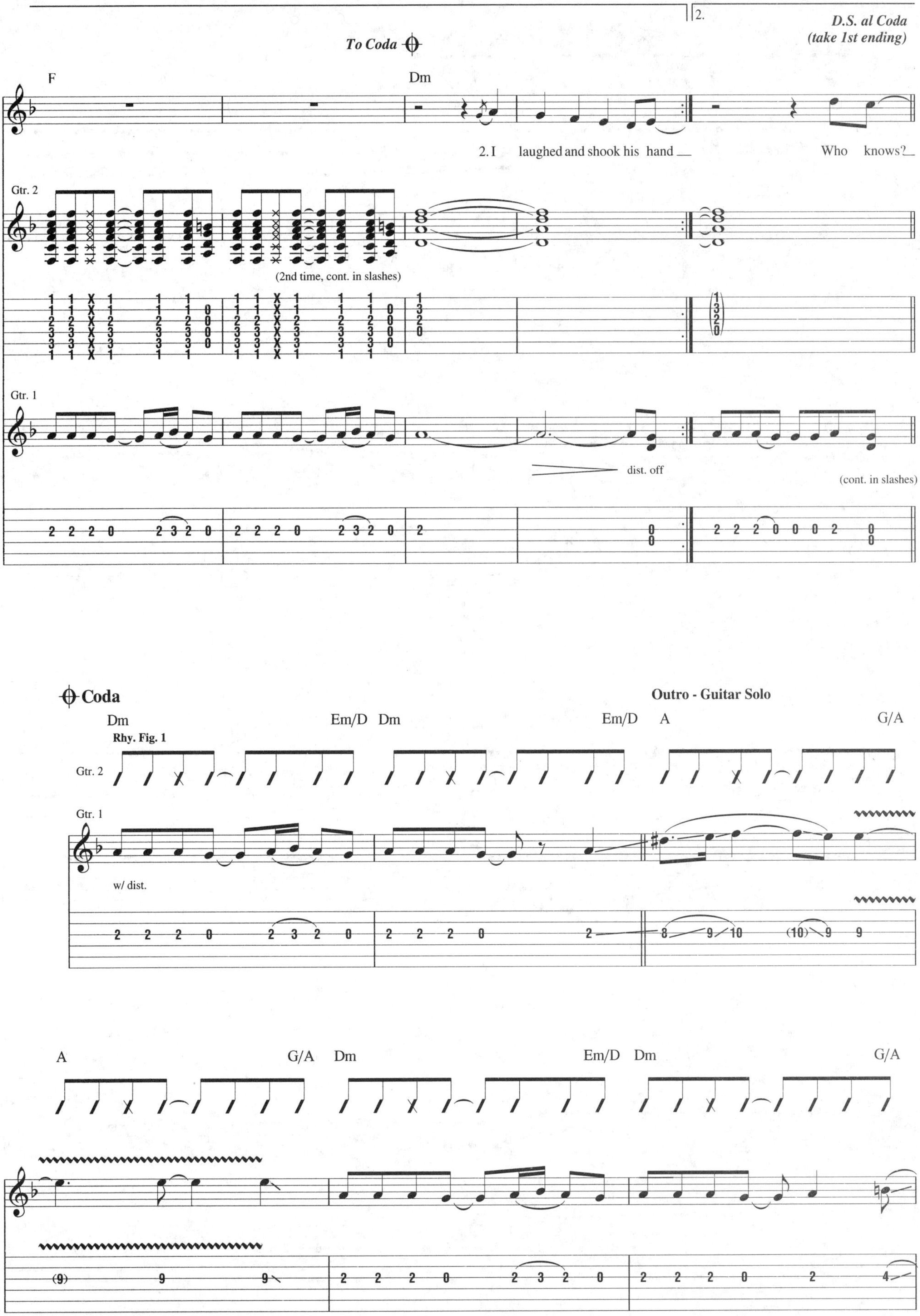

To Coda
2.
D.S. al Coda
(take 1st ending)
F
Dm
2. I laughed and shook his hand
Who knows?
Gtr. 2
(2nd time, cont. in slashes)
Gtr. 1
dist. off
(cont. in slashes)
Coda
Outro - Guitar Solo
Dm
Em/D
Dm
Em/D
A
G/A
Rhy. Fig. 1
Gtr. 2
Gtr. 1
w/ dist.
A
G/A
Dm
Em/D
Dm
G/A

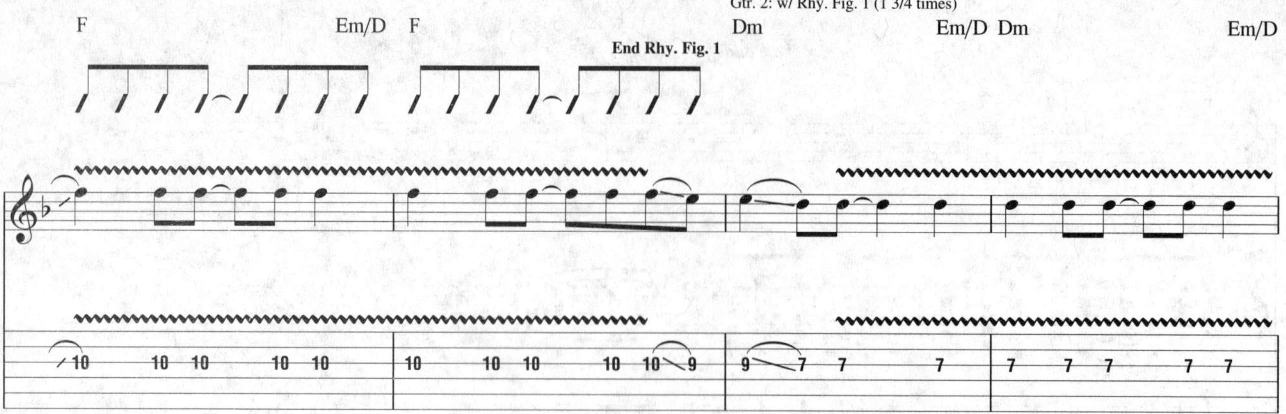
Gtr. 2: w/ Rhy. Fig. 1 (1 3/4 times)
F
Em/D
F
End Rhy. Fig. 1
Dm
Em/D
Dm
Em/D

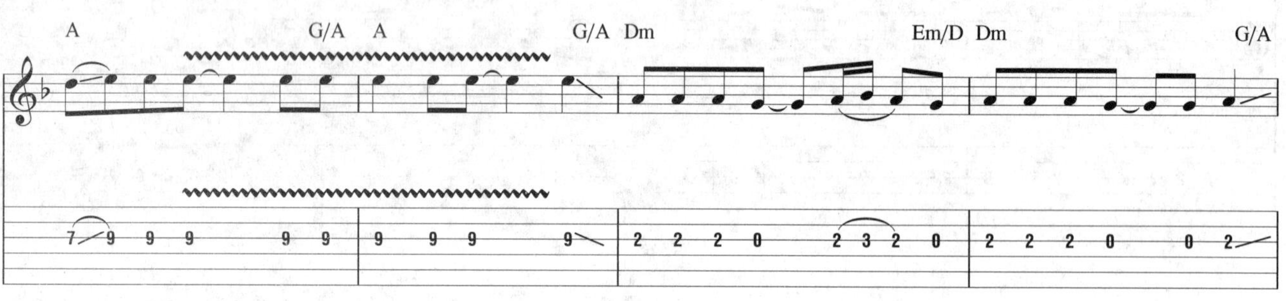
A
G/A
A
G/A
Dm
Em/D
Dm
G/A

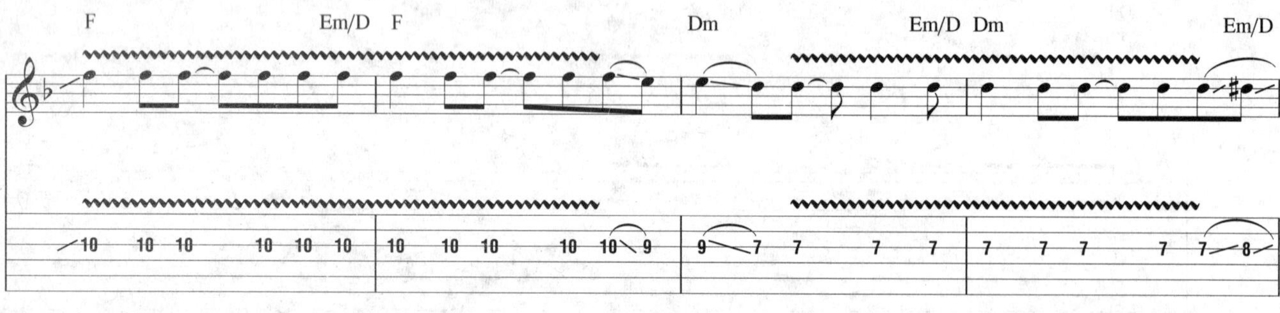
F
Em/D
F
Dm
Em/D
Dm
Em/D

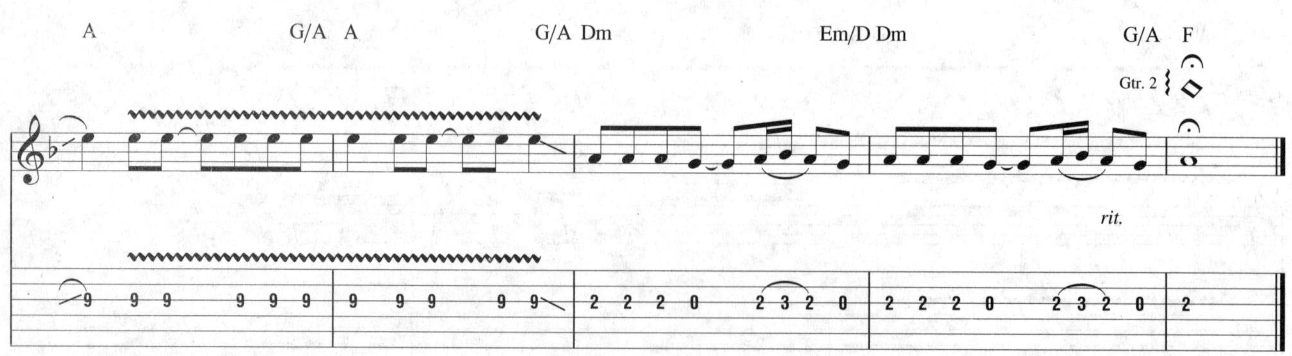
A
G/A
A
G/A
Dm
Em/D
Dm
G/A
F
Gtr. 2
rit.

Mannish Boy

Words and Music by McKinley Morganfield (Muddy Waters), M.R. London and Ellas McDaniel

(bass enters)
N.C.(B7)
Asus4
(w/full band accompaniment)
N.C. (B7)
E D
N.C. (B7)
E D
Oh wo, wo wo wo wo
rake
Verse
N.C.(B7)
E D
N.C.(B7)
E D
B
E D
wo wo hey. Hey! 1. When I was a young boy,
rake
full
N.C.(B7)
E D
N.C.(B7)
E D
N.C.(B7)
E D
right a-bout the age of five, I think, I had some-thin' in my pock-et, keep a lot of folk a-live.
N.C.(B7)
E6 D
N.C.(B7)
E D
N.C.(B7)
E D
Now I'm a man, age twen-ty one, you know, ba-by,
full
Chorus
N.C.(B7)
E D
N.C.(B7)
E D
N.C. (B7)
E D
we have a whole lots-a fun. 'Cause I'm a man, s-spelled m,
let ring

N.C.(B7) E D N.C.(B7) E D N.C.(B7) E D N.C.(B7) E D
A, child, N, boy That's what I am, am,
N.C.(B7) E D N.C.(B7) E D N.C.(B7)
now, now, I am.
Deh deh do deh deh do deh deh do deh do do do.
hold bend
rake
Deh deh do deh deh do deh deh do deh deh do.
B E D
N.C.(B7) E D N.C.(B7) E D N.C.(B7) E D6
Hey!
Verse
N.C.(B7) E D N.C. (B7) E D N.C. (B7) E D
2. All you pret-ty wom-en, stand in line. I'll make love to you

N.C.(B7)
E D
E6 D6
hour's time.
Line I shoot
will nev-er miss.
The way I make love,
you just can't re-sist.
Chorus
'Cause I'm a man,
spelled M,
A, child,
now,
N.
Call me,
you, child.
Na na na na na.
Do do do do do do do
do do do do do.
hold bend
full
1/2

Bm7
E6 N.C. (B)
Do do do do do do do do. Do do do.
hold bend
Bm7
E6
Bm7
E
B
Bm7
Eb/B
Bm7
Guitar Solo
N.C. (B7)
Ah ow wah. Aw aw wah. Wah wah oh wah wah.
(wah on)
Wah wah wah wow. Wahwahwah wah wah wah ow. Wah wah wah wah oh.
*E D N.C.(B7) E D N.C.(B7) E D
Wah wah wah wah, wah wah wah wah wah wah wah wah wah wah wah
let ring
*Chords derived from bass figure.

N.C.(B7)
E D
N.C.(B7)
E D
N.C.(B7)
E6 D
wah
wah.
mf
full
full
full
1/4
N.C.(B7)
E6 D B
Bridge
N.C.(E)
(D)
'Cause I'm a man, al -
cresc.
f
full
B7 Bm7
E7
D9
B9 F#
E
Dadd9
right.
*trem. pick lightly while sliding up
B
Eadd9
Dadd9
B
(bass break
rake
N.C.(B7)
(drum break
B7#9
N.C.
rake

(B7)
E D
N.C.(B7)
Guitar Solo
Yeah!
Gtr. 2
(w/fuzzface/octavia & univibe)
Gtr. 1
semi - harm
full
1/4
1/2
(wah on)

N.C.(B7)
E
D
N.C.(B7)
E
D
semi - harm
full
full
full
Bridge
B7♯9
E5
D5
N.C. (B)
'Cause I'm a man, child, you hear my... I said I'm a
Gtr. 1 (Gtr. 2 tacet)
E5
D5
A5 B5
E5
D5
man, hear me say - in'. Well, I'm a man,
sim.

A5 B5
E5
D5
A5 B5
hey, hey, hey. Said, I'm a man. Hey, ba - by.
(Band tacet)
A5 B5 D5 E5 N.C.(B)
(band re - enters)
B7#9
E D
Yeah.
N.C.(B7)
E D Bm7
E6/B Bm
E5 D5 Bm7
E6/B N.C.(B) E D
Verse
N.C.(B7)
E D N.C.(B7)
E D N.C.(B7)
E D
3. I'm go-in' down south, uh, to Kan-sas, too. Bring back my sec-ond cou-sin,
rake
rake
N.C.(B7)
E D N.C.(B7)
E D N.C. (B7)
E D
Lit-tle John the Con-que-roo. 'Cause I'm a man, the fun we have

N.C. (B7)
E D
N.C.(B7)
E D
N.C. (B7)
chas-in' rab - bits
in the sand,
now.
Hey, hey,
hey, yeah, hey.
Wo, hoo.
Hey, hey, hey, hey.
Hey!
P.M.
Outro
N.C.(B7)
E D
N.C.(B7)
E D
N.C.(B7)
E D
(wah on)
P.M.
semi - harm
N.C. (B7)
E D
Begin Fade
N.C.(B7)
1/2
1/4
8va
loco
Harm.
full
Fade Out

Mary Had a Little Lamb

Written by Buddy Guy

E7
B7
yeah. _
Ev - 'ry - where the child went,
And what a time did they have

A7
E7
1.
2.
the lamb, _ the lamb was sure to go, yeah.
that day at ___ school. _____
2. He fol - lowed her to school _ Uh.
Gtr. 1
full

Guitar Solo

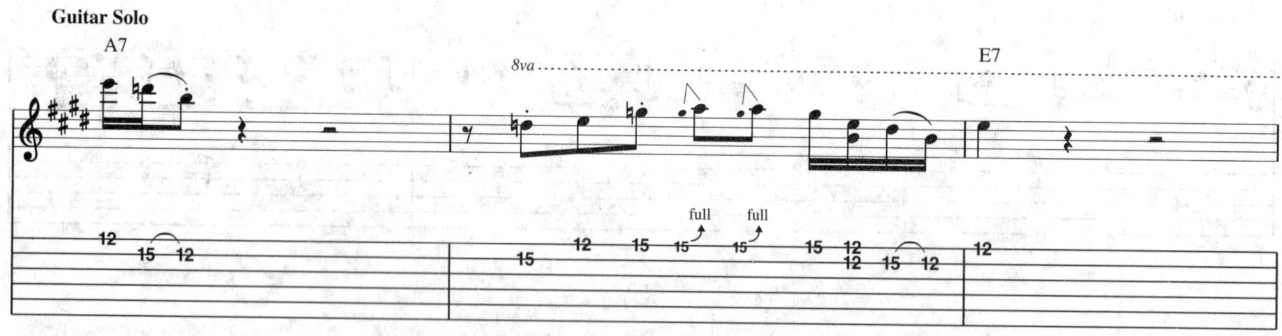
A7
8va
E7
full
full

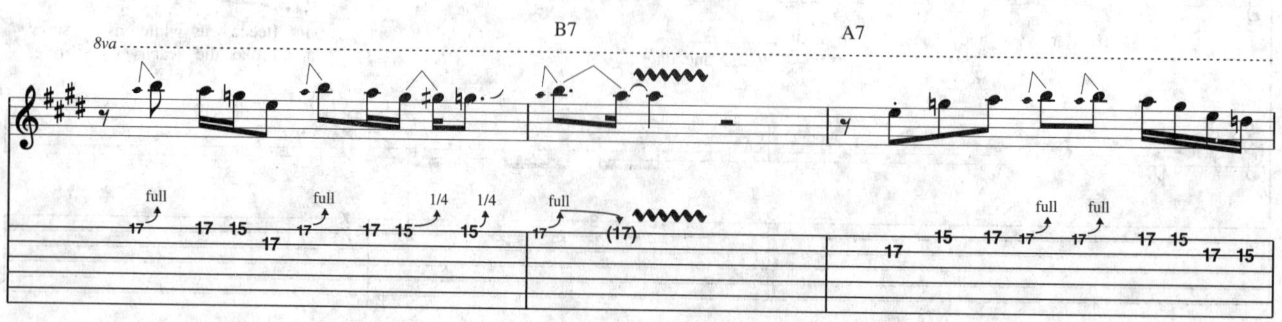
8va
B7
A7
full
full
1/4
1/4
full
full
full

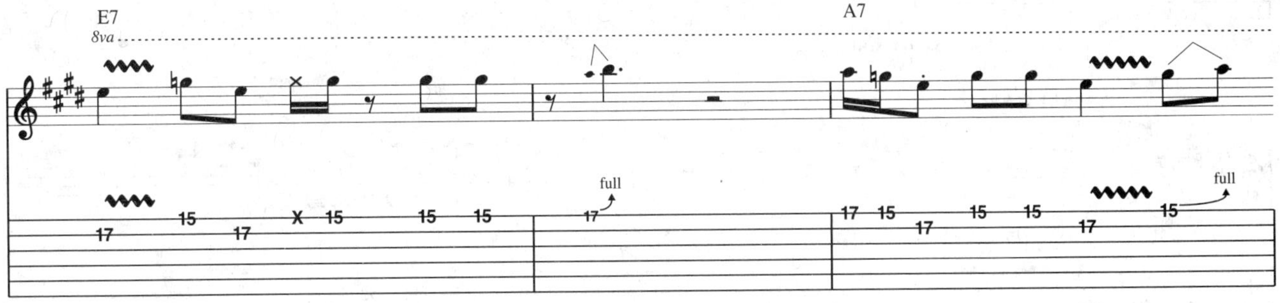
E7
8va
A7
full
full

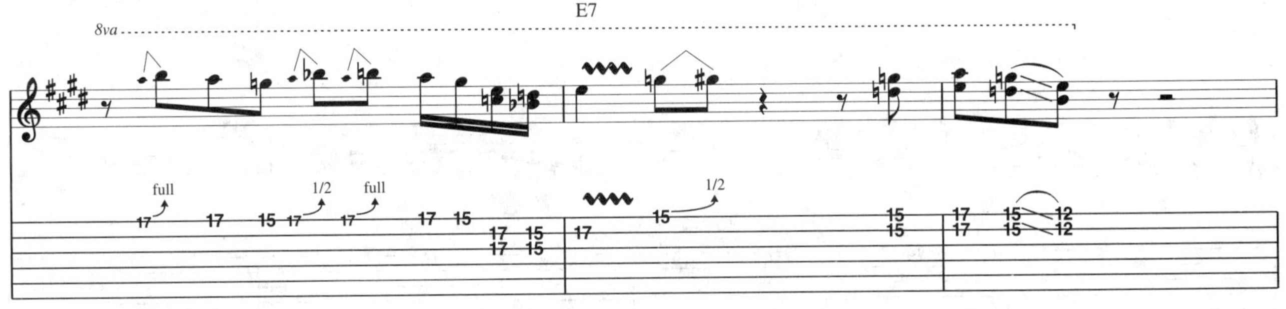
8va
E7
full
1/2
full
1/2

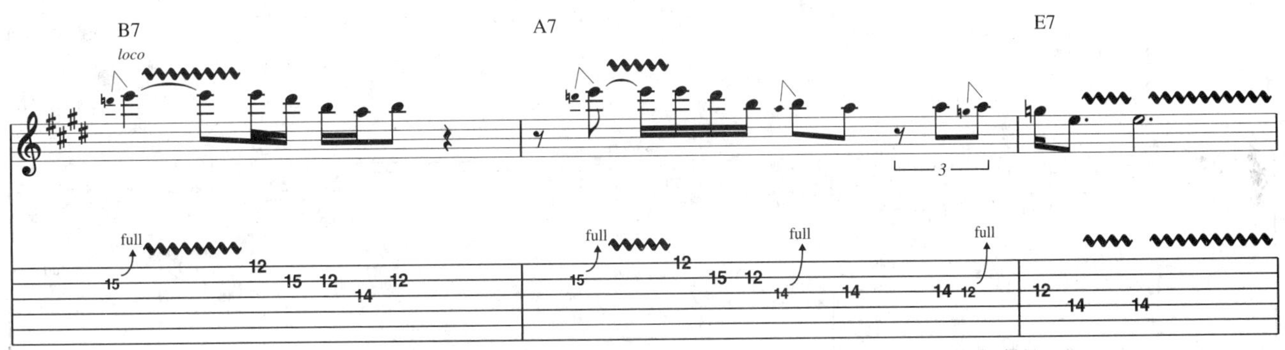
B7
loco
A7
E7
full
full
full
full

Verse
Gtr. 1 tacet
A7
3. Tis - ket, tas - ket, ba - by, al - right, a green and yel - low bas -
no, no, oo. No, no, no, no,
E7
- ket, now. I wrote a let - ter to my
yeah. No, no, no, no,
B7
ba - by,
no, yeah.
A7
and on my way I passed it, now.
No, no, no, no, no, no, yeah. Uh,
E7
Uh, uh, uh.
uh, uh, uh.
1.
4. No, no, no, no,

2.

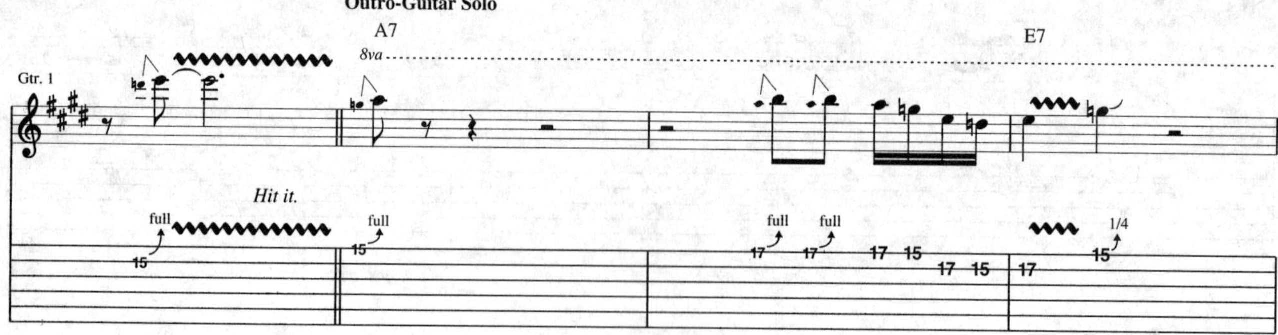
Outro-Guitar Solo
A7
E7
8va
Gtr. 1
Hit it.
full
full
full
full
1/4

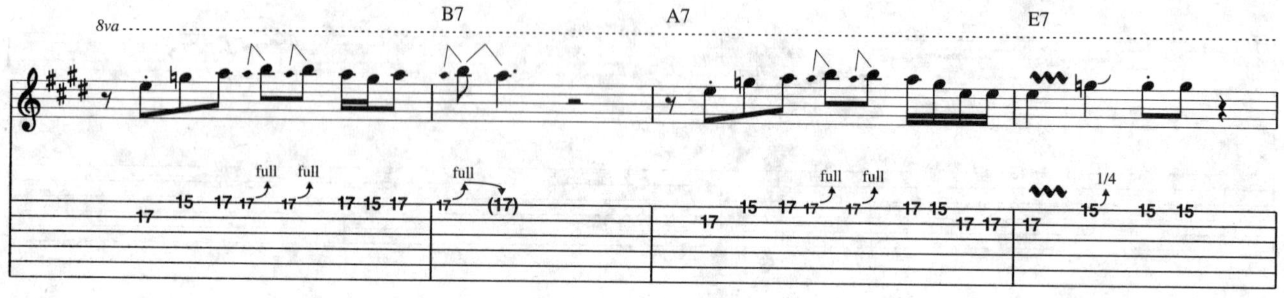
8va
B7
A7
E7
full
full
full
full
full
1/4

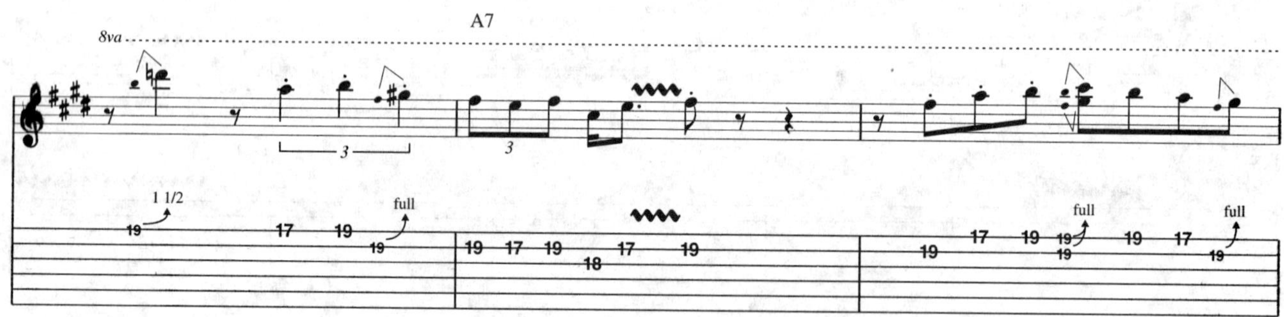
8va
A7
1 1/2
full
full
full

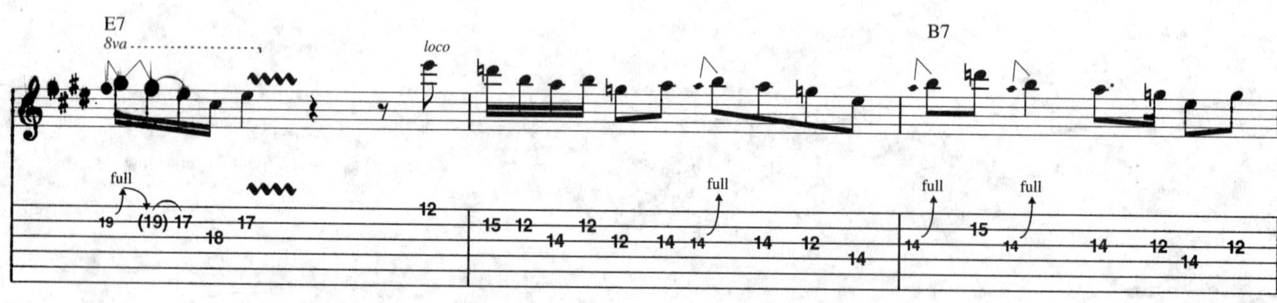
E7
8va
loco
B7
full
full
full
full

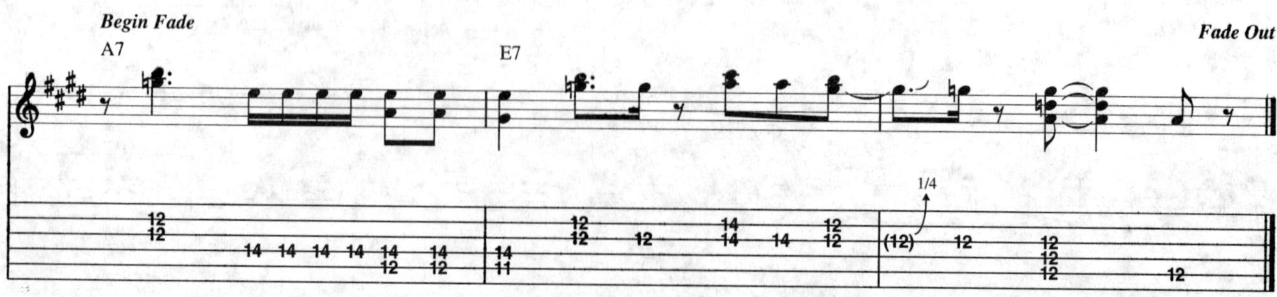
Begin Fade
A7
E7
Fade Out
1/4

Mississippi Queen

Words and Music by Leslie West, Felix Pappalardi, Corky Laing and David Rea

D5 E5
Mis - sis - sip - pi Queen,
D5 E5
she taught me ev - 'ry-thing.

Verse

G5 A5
1. Way down a-round Vicks-burg,
G5 A5
a-round Lou - i - si - an - a way,

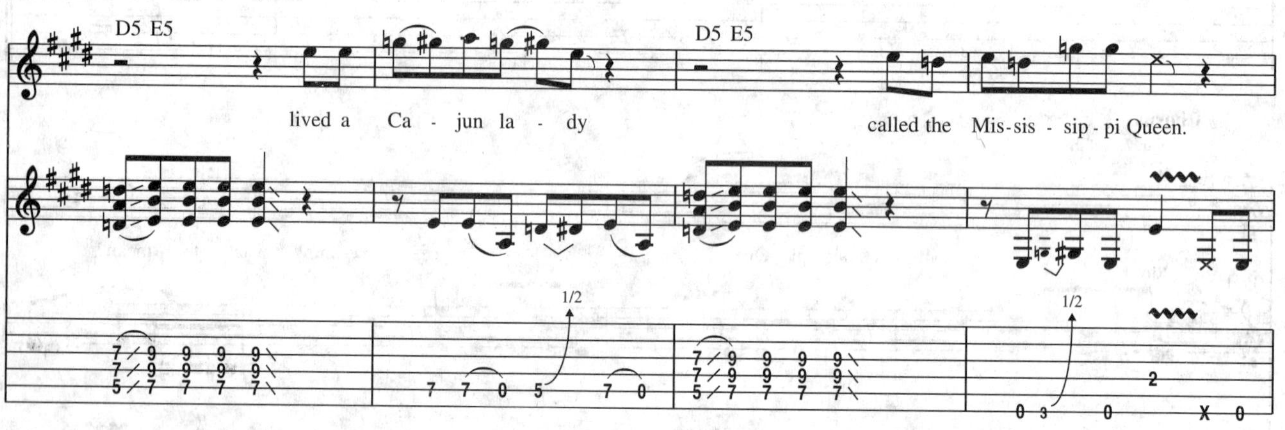
D5 E5
lived a Ca - jun la - dy
D5 E5
called the Mis-sis - sip - pi Queen.

A5 B5
You know she was a danc - er,
G5 A5
she moved bet - ter on wine. While the

N.C.(E5)
N.C.
rest of them dudes was a' get-tin' their kicks; bud-dy, beg your par-don I was get-tin' mine.
End Rhy. Fig. 1
* Top note vib. only.
Chorus
Gtr. 1: w/ Rhy. Fig .1
D5 E5
D5 E5
Mis - sis-sip-pi Queen, if you know what I mean.
Gtr. 2
full
hold bend
D5 E5
D5 E5
Mis-sis-sip - pi Queen, she taught me ev-'ry-thing.
full
1/2
Verse
G5 A5
G5 A5
2. This la - dy she asked me if I would be her man.

D5 E5
You know that I told her
D5 E5
I'd do what I can
full
full
full
full

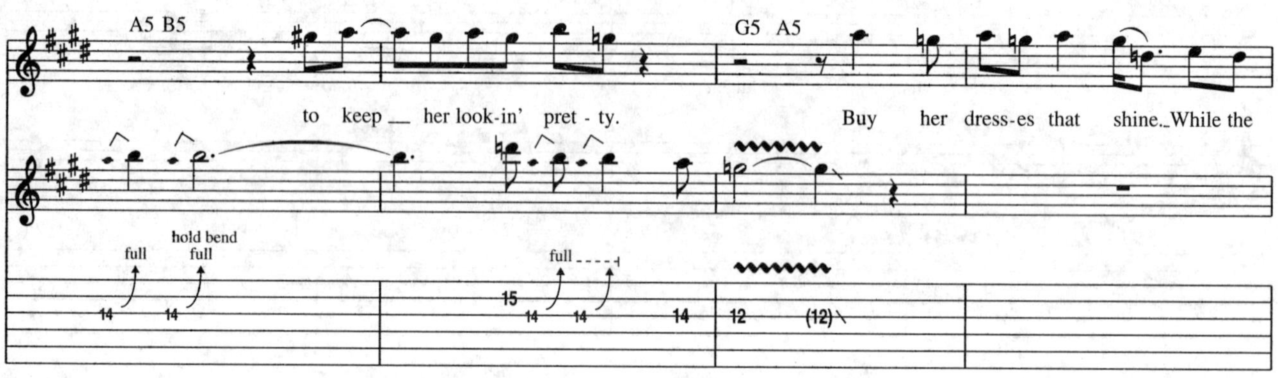
A5 B5
to keep her look-in' pret-ty.
G5 A5
Buy her dress-es that shine. While the
full
hold bend
full
full

N.C.(E5)
rest of them dudes was a' mak-in' their bread; bud-dy, beg your par-don I was los-in' mine.

Guitar Solo

Gtr. 1: w/ Rhy. Fig. 1, 1st 23 meas. only
D5 E5
D5 E5
D5 E5
Gtr. 2
8va
loco
full
hold bend
full
hold bend
full

D5 E5
G5 A5
full
1/2
1/2
full

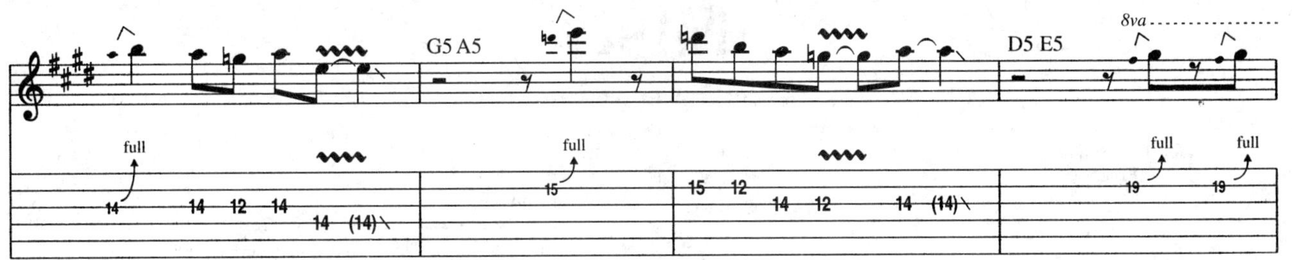

G5 A5
D5 E5
8va
full
15 12
14 12 14 (14)
19

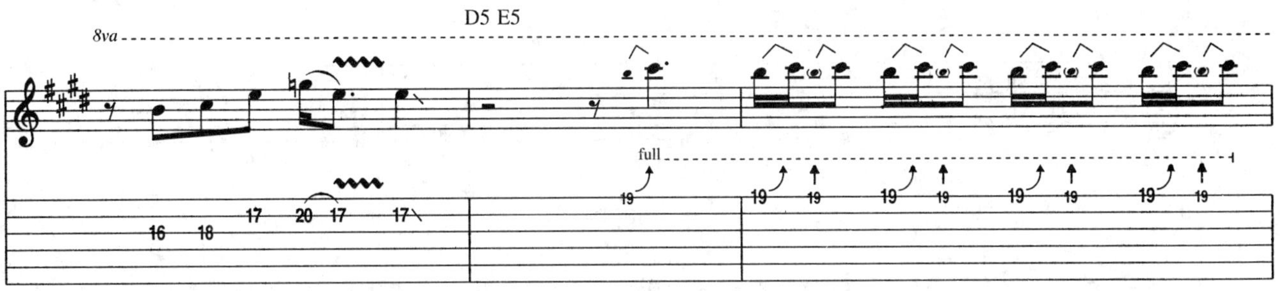

D5 E5
8va
full
16 18 17 20 17 17
19

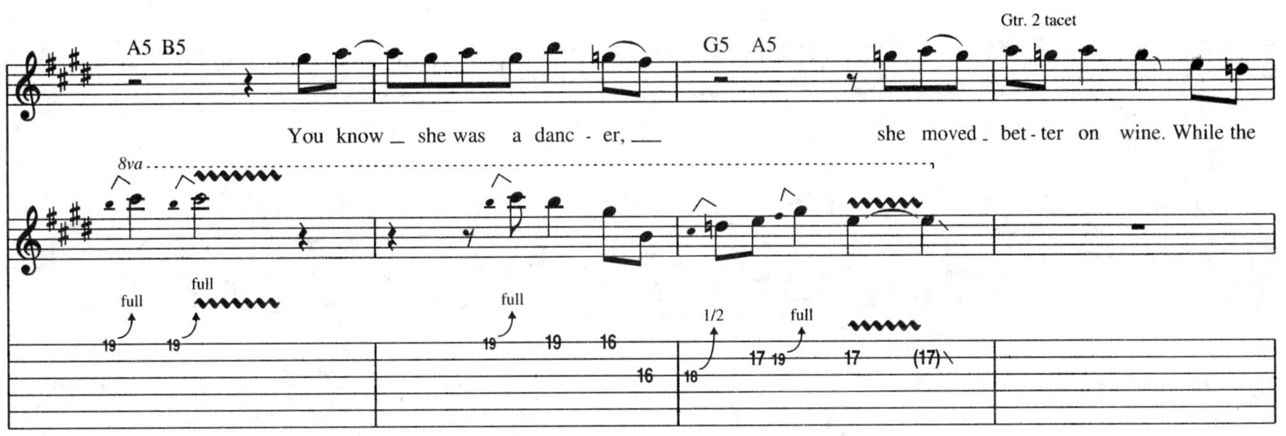

A5 B5
G5 A5
Gtr. 2 tacet
You know she was a danc - er,
she moved bet - ter on wine. While the
8va
full
1/2
19 19 16
16 18 17 19 17 (17)

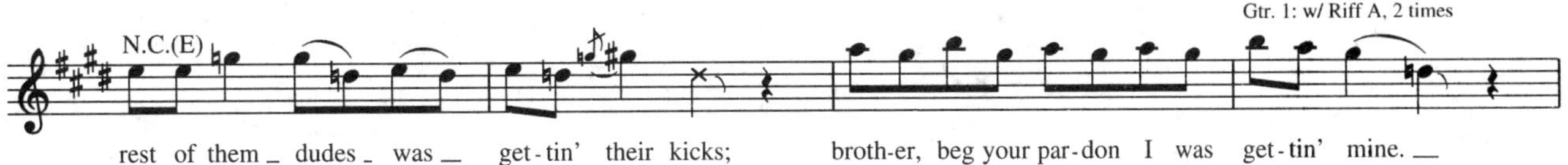

N.C.(E)
Gtr. 1: w/ Riff A, 2 times
rest of them dudes was get - tin' their kicks;
broth - er, beg your par - don I was get - tin' mine.

Gtr. 1: w/ Fill 2
Hey,
Mis - sis - sip - pi Queen.

Fill 2
Gtr. 1
5 7 5
7 (7)

Misty

Music by Erroll Garner

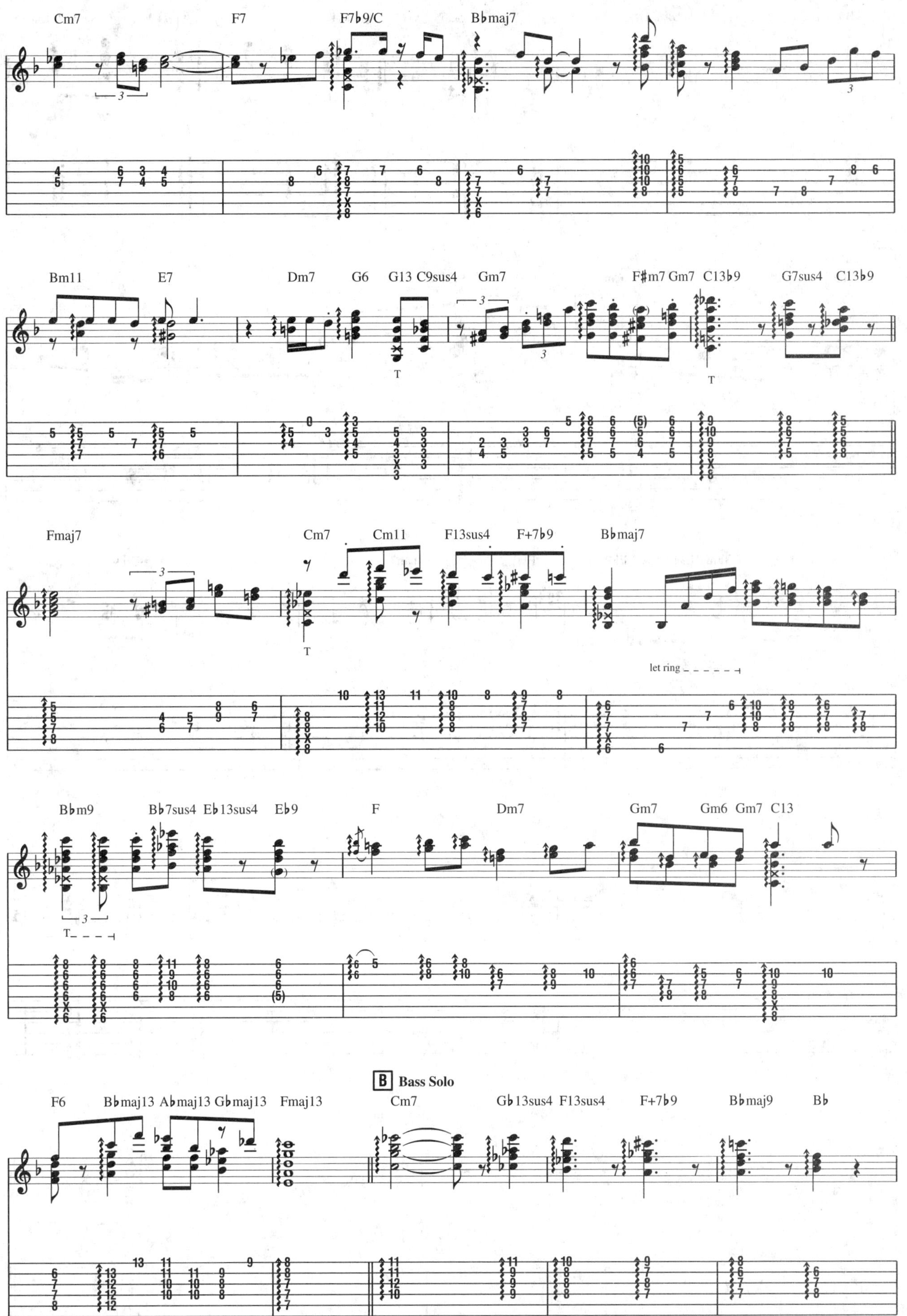
Cm7
F7
F7♭9/C
B♭maj7
Bm11
E7
Dm7
G6
G13 C9sus4
Gm7
F♯m7 Gm7
C13♭9
G7sus4
C13♭9
Fmaj7
Cm7
Cm11
F13sus4
F+7♭9
B♭maj7
let ring
B♭m9
B♭7sus4
E♭13sus4
E♭9
F
Dm7
Gm7
Gm6 Gm7 C13
B Bass Solo
F6
B♭maj13 A♭maj13 G♭maj13
Fmaj13
Cm7
G♭13sus4 F13sus4
F+7♭9
B♭maj9
B♭

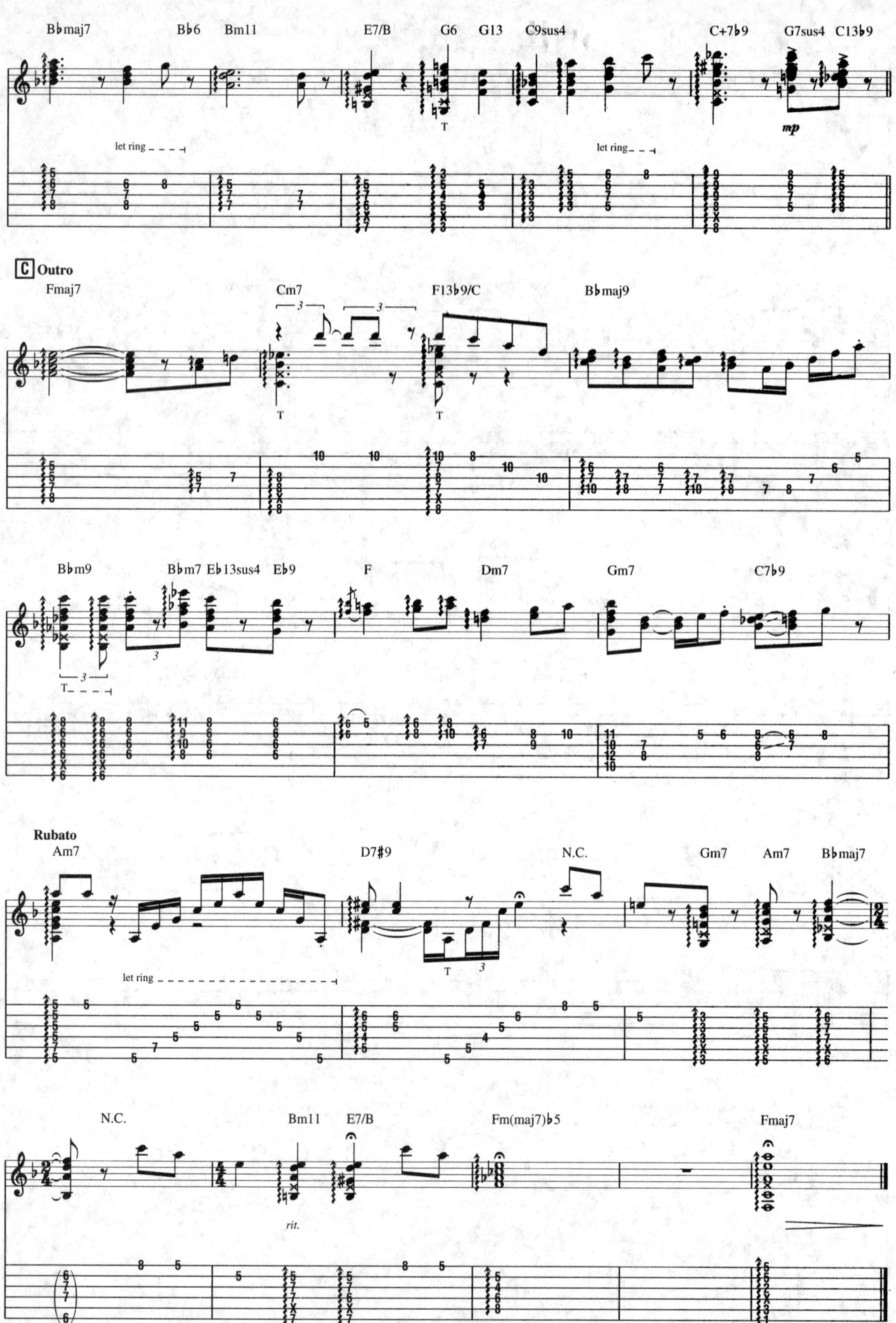

B♭maj7
B♭6
Bm11
E7/B
G6
G13
C9sus4
C+7♭9
G7sus4
C13♭9
let ring
let ring
mp
T
C Outro
Fmaj7
Cm7
F13♭9/C
B♭maj9
T
T
B♭m9
B♭m7
E♭13sus4
E♭9
F
Dm7
Gm7
C7♭9
T
Rubato
Am7
D7♯9
N.C.
Gm7
Am7
B♭maj7
let ring
T
N.C.
Bm11
E7/B
Fm(maj7)♭5
Fmaj7
rit.

Moonlight in Vermont

Words by John Blackburn
Music by Karl Suessdorf

* Chord symbols reflect implied tonality.

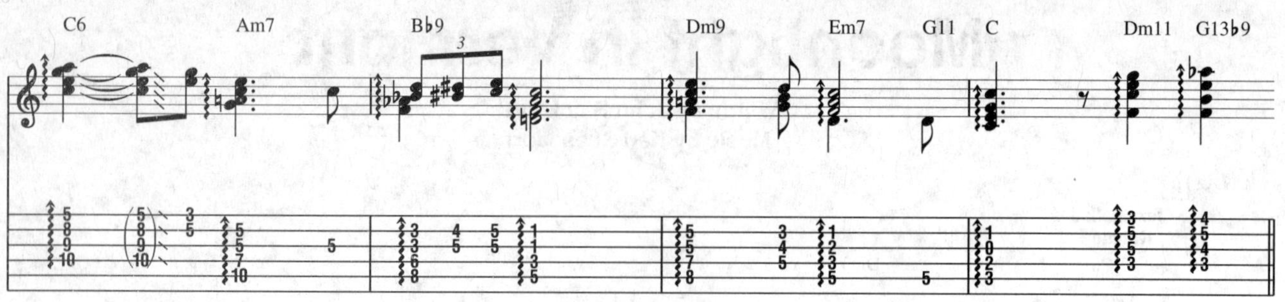
C6
Am7
B♭9
Dm9
Em7
G11
C
Dm11
G13♭9

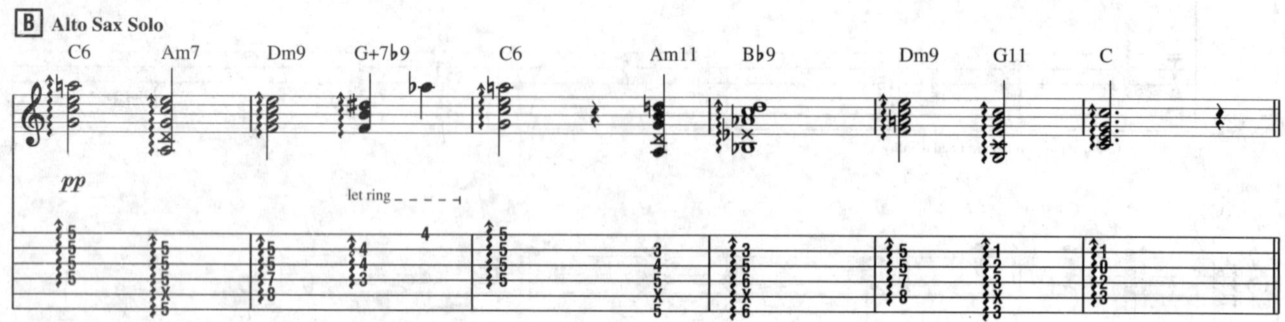
B Alto Sax Solo
C6
Am7
Dm9
G+7♭9
C6
Am11
B♭9
Dm9
G11
C
pp
let ring

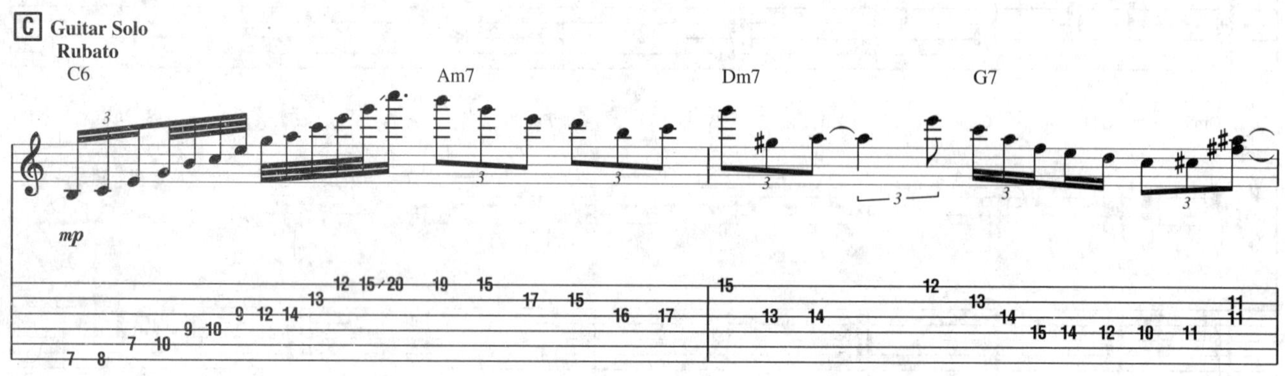
C Guitar Solo
Rubato
C6
Am7
Dm7
G7
mp

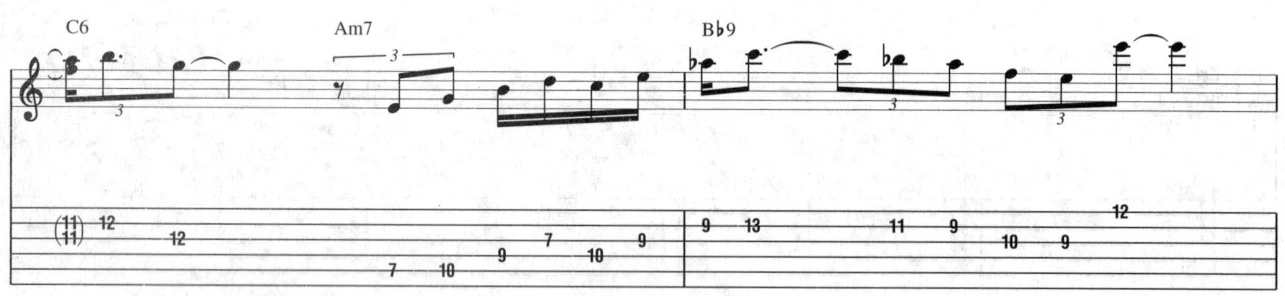
C6
Am7
B♭9

Dm9
G7♭9
C6

D Bass Solo
F♯m11
B7
Emaj7
C♯m7
F♯m9
B13♭9
8va
p
H.H.
let ring
E6/9
Gm11
C7
Fmaj7
Gm11
C+7♭9
15ma
* hypothetical fret location
F6/9
G13♭9 B♭13♭9 D♭13♭9 E13♭9 G13♭9
E
C6
Am7
Dm9
G13♭9
loco
C6
Am7
B♭9
Dm9
G13
C
N.C.
Dm9
D♭13♯11
Cmaj7
rit. poco a poco

Mr. Jones

Words by Adam Duritz
Music by Adam Duritz and David Bryson

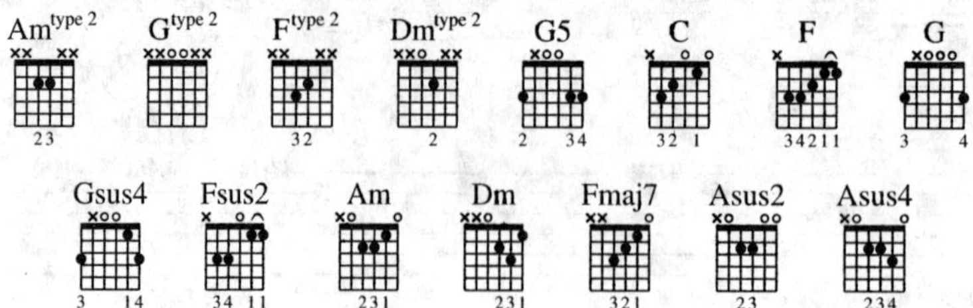

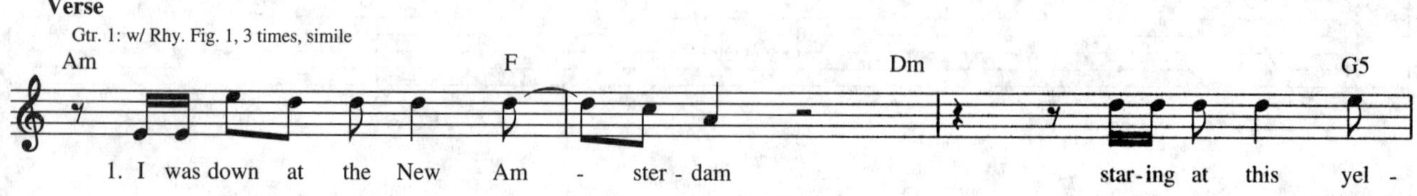

Gtr. 2: w/ Fill 1
Am
F
- haired flamen - co danc - er She dances while his fa -
Dm
G5
Am
ther plays gui - tar She's sud - den - ly beau - ti - ful We all
F
G5
Gtr. 2: w/ Fill 1
Am
want some - thing beau - ti - ful I wish I was beau - ti - ful. So come
(bass and drums in)
w/ Lead Voc. ad lib.
Am type 2
G type 2
F type 2
Dm type 2
Rhy. Fig. 2
Gtr. 3 (clean elec.)
mf
dance this si - lence down through the morn - ing
Gtr. 2: w/ Fill 2
End Rhy. Fig. 2
Fill 1
* Gtr. 2
mf
* w/light dist. and amp. vib.
Fill 2
Gtr. 2

Verse
Gtr. 1: w/ Rhy. Fig. 1, 1 7/8 times
Gtr. 3: w/ Rhy. Fig. 2, 1 7/8 times
Am
F
Dm
G5
Am
2. Cut up, Ma - ri - a! Show me some of them Span - ish dance - es
will paint my pic - ture Paint my - self in blue and red and black and gray

Gtr. 2: w/ Fill 1
F
G5
Am
Pass me a bot - tle, Mis - ter Jones
All of the beau - ti - ful col - ors are very very mean - ing - ful Gray

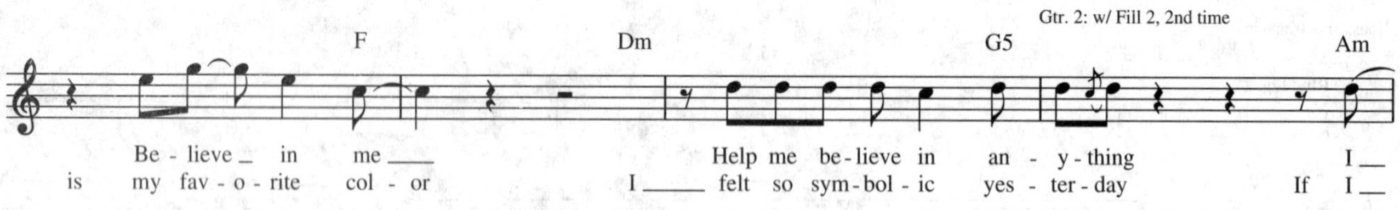
Gtr. 2: w/ Fill 2, 2nd time
F
Dm
G5
Am
Be - lieve in me Help me be - lieve in an - y - thing I
is my fav - o - rite col - or I felt so sym - bol - ic yes - ter - day If I

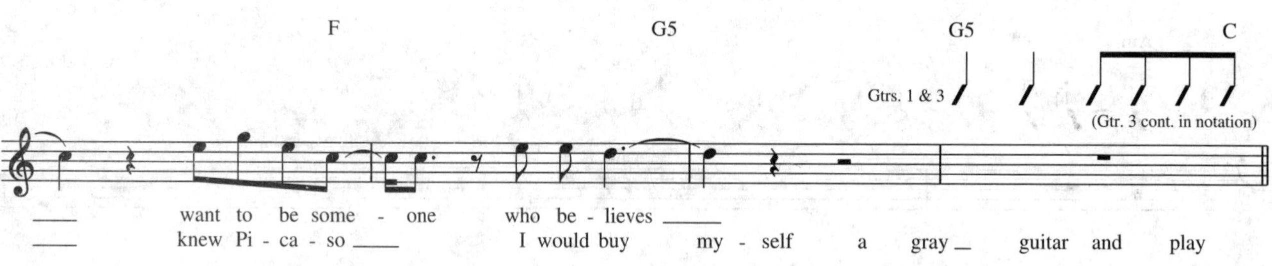
F
G5
G5
C
Gtrs. 1 & 3
(Gtr. 3 cont. in notation)
want to be some - one who be - lieves
knew Pi - ca - so I would buy my - self a gray guitar and play

Chorus
Bkgd. Voc.: w/ Voc. Fig. 1, 2nd & 3rd time
C
F
G
Rhy. Fig. 3
Gtr. 1
1. Mis - ter Jones and me tell each oth - er fair -
2., 3. See Additional Lyrics
Gtr. 3
Rhy. Fig. 3A
let ring

Gsus4 G C F Fsus2 F G
y tales
Stare at the beau - ti - ful wo - men
"She's look -
let ring
Gtr. 3: w/ Rhy. Fig. 3A
C F
ing at you. Ah, no, no, she's look - ing at me." Smil - ing in the bright
End Rhy. Fig. 3A
G Gsus4 G C
lights
Com - ing through in ster - e - o
When
To Coda
F G
End Rhy. Fig. 3
ev - ery - bod - y loves you,
you can nev - er be lone -
Bkgd. Voc. Fig. 1
sing 4 times
Hey, la, la. Hey, la, la. Yeah.

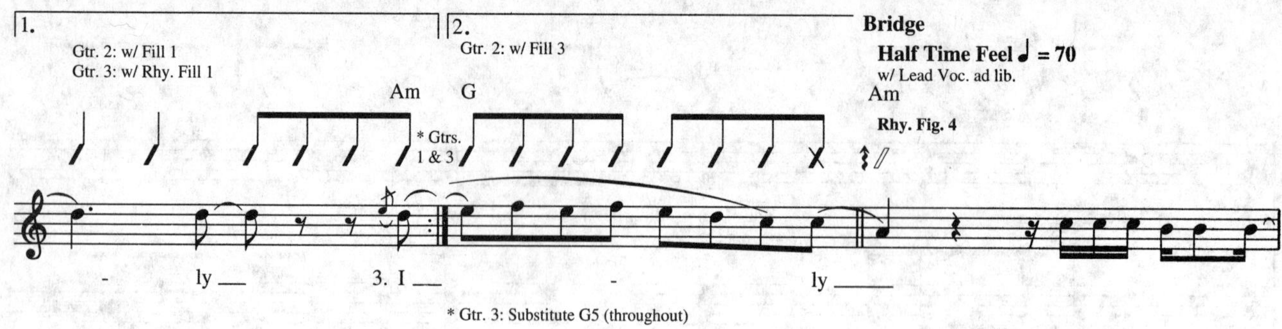
1.
2.
Bridge
Gtr. 2: w/ Fill 1
Gtr. 3: w/ Rhy. Fill 1
Gtr. 2: w/ Fill 3
Half Time Feel ♩ = 70
w/ Lead Voc. ad lib.
Am G
Am
* Gtrs. 1 & 3
Rhy. Fig. 4
- ly __ 3. I __ - ly ____
* Gtr. 3: Substitute G5 (throughout)

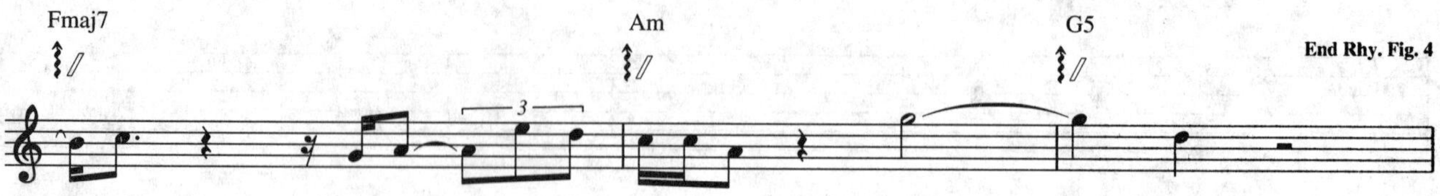
Fmaj7
Am
G5
End Rhy. Fig. 4
3

Gtrs. 1 & 3: w/ Rhy. Fig. 4
Gtr. 3: w/ Rhy. Fill 2
Am
Fmaj7
I want to be a li - on
Ev - ery - bod - y wants to pass __ as cats __

Rhy. Fill 1
Gtr. 3
let ring

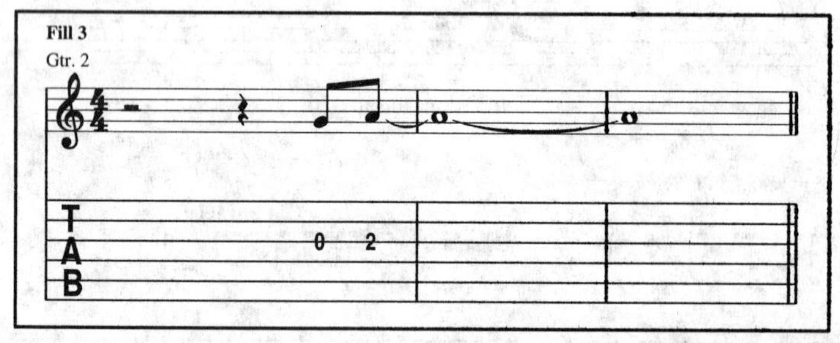
Fill 3
Gtr. 2

Rhy. Fill 2
Gtr. 3
(cont. in slash)
let ring

Am
G5
3
We all want to be big big stars, but we got dif-ferent rea - sons for that

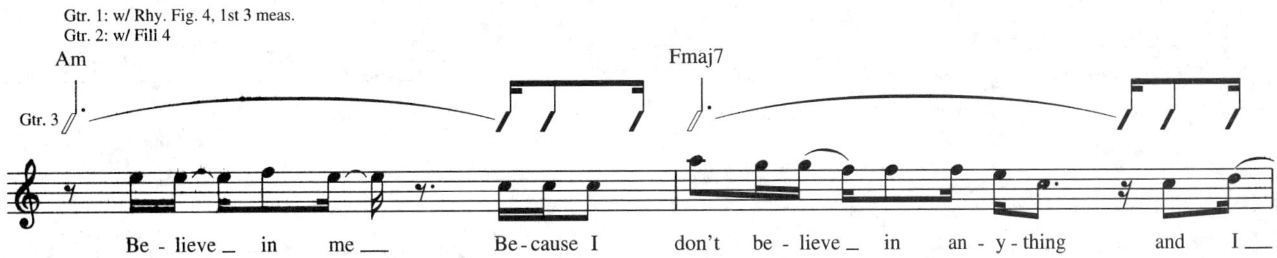
Gtr. 1: w/ Rhy. Fig. 4, 1st 3 meas.
Gtr. 2: w/ Fill 4
Am
Fmaj7
Gtr. 3
Be - lieve in me Be-cause I don't be - lieve in an - y - thing and I

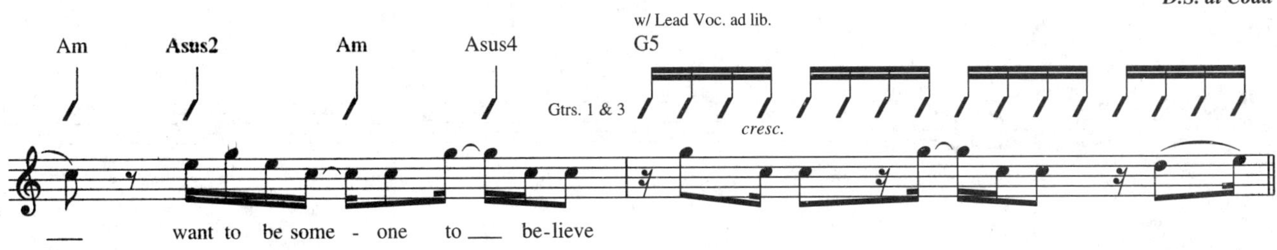
* D.S. al Coda
w/ Lead Voc. ad lib.
Am
Asus2
Am
Asus4
G5
Gtrs. 1 & 3
cresc.
want to be some - one to be-lieve
* Resume orig. tempo at 𝄋

Coda
Gtr. 3: w/ Rhy. Fill 3
Bkgd. Voc.: w/ Voc. Fig. 1
Gtr. 1: w/ Rhy. Fig. 3
Gtr. 3: w/ Rhy. Fig. 3A, 1 3/4 times
G
C
F
G
that's just a-bout as funk - y as you can be Mis - ter Jones and me

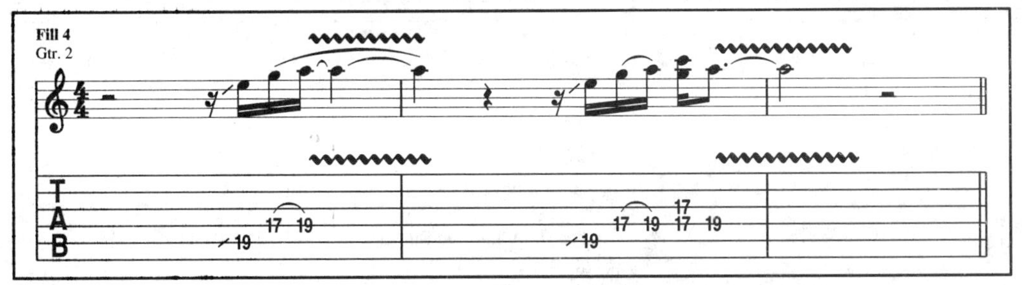
Fill 4
Gtr. 2
T
A
B
19 17 19
19 17 19 17 17 19

Rhy. Fill 3
Gtr. 3
T
A
B

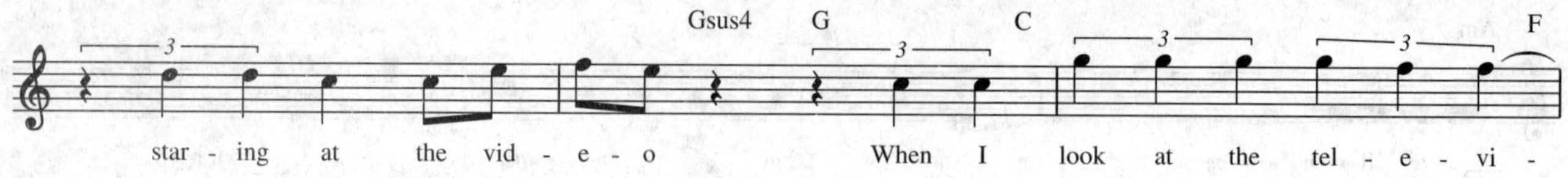

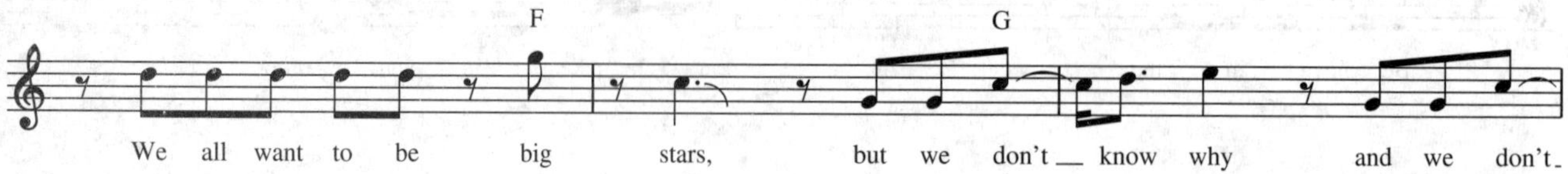

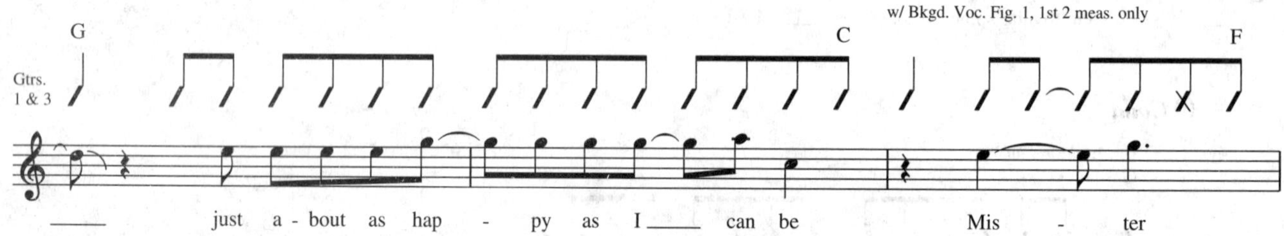

Additional Lyrics

2. Mr. Jones and me look into the future
   Stare at the beautiful women
   "She's looking at you.
   Uh, I don't think so. She's looking at me."
   Standing in the spotlight
   I bought myself a gray guitar
   When everybody loves me, I will never be lonely

3. Mr. Jones and me stumbling through the barrio
   Yeah we stare at the beautiful women
   "She's perfect for you, Man, there's got to be
   somebody for me."
   I wanna be Bob Dylan
   Mr. Jones wishes he was someone just a little more
   funky
   When everybody loves you, son, that's just about as
   funky as you can be

My Girl

Words and Music by William "Smokey" Robinson and Ronald White

Gtr. 1 tacet
*Cmaj7
Dm7
1.
G7
Dm7
G7
My girl,
(My girl.)
(My girl.)
talk-in' 'bout
my girl,
my girl.
2. I've got
Gtr. 2
sim.
* Chord symbols reflect overall tonality.
2.
Gtr. 2 tacet
G7
Dm7
G7
N.C.
(C)
Gtr. 1: w/ Riff A
my girl.
Oo.
Interlude
Gtrs. 1 & 2: w/ Riff B & Rhy. Fig. 1
C5
F
C5
F
(Hey, hey, hey.
Hey, hey, hey.)
Dm
G
Em
A
Gtr. 2
Oo,
yeah.
3. I don't
Verse
D5
G
D5
G
Rhy. Fig. 2
End Rhy. Fig. 2
Gtr. 2
need no mon - ey,
(Oo.)
for - tune, or fame.
I got
Gtr. 1
Riff C
End Riff C
Gtrs. 1 & 2: w/ Riff C & Rhy. Fig. 2
D5
G
D5
G
all the rich-es, ba - by,
(Oo,
one man can claim.
oo.)
Well,

Chorus

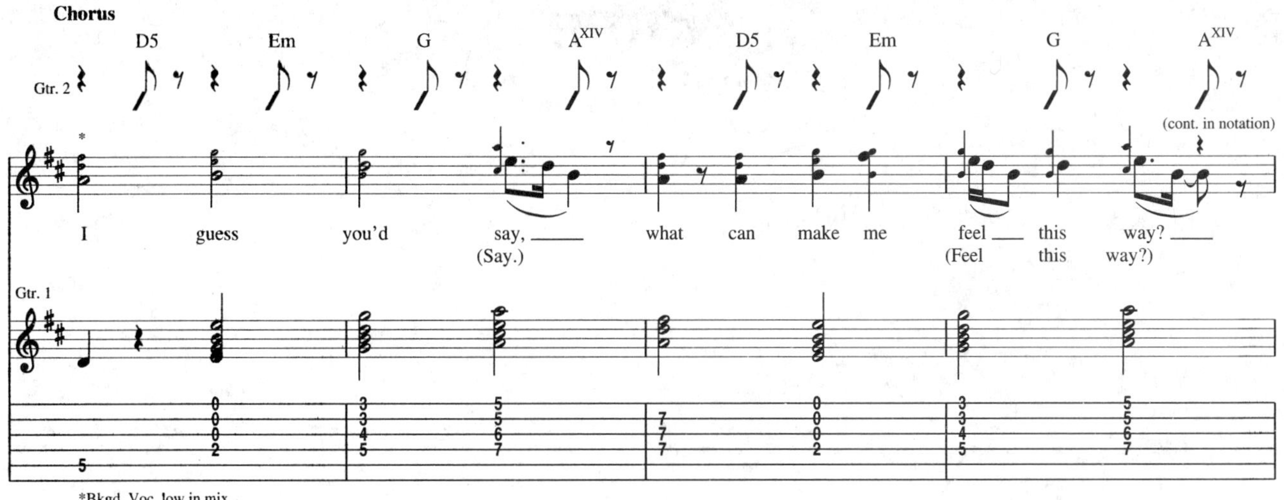

D5 Em G A^XIV D5 Em G A^XIV
Gtr. 2
(cont. in notation)
I guess you'd say, what can make me feel this way?
(Say.) (Feel this way?)
Gtr. 1
*Bkgd. Voc. low in mix

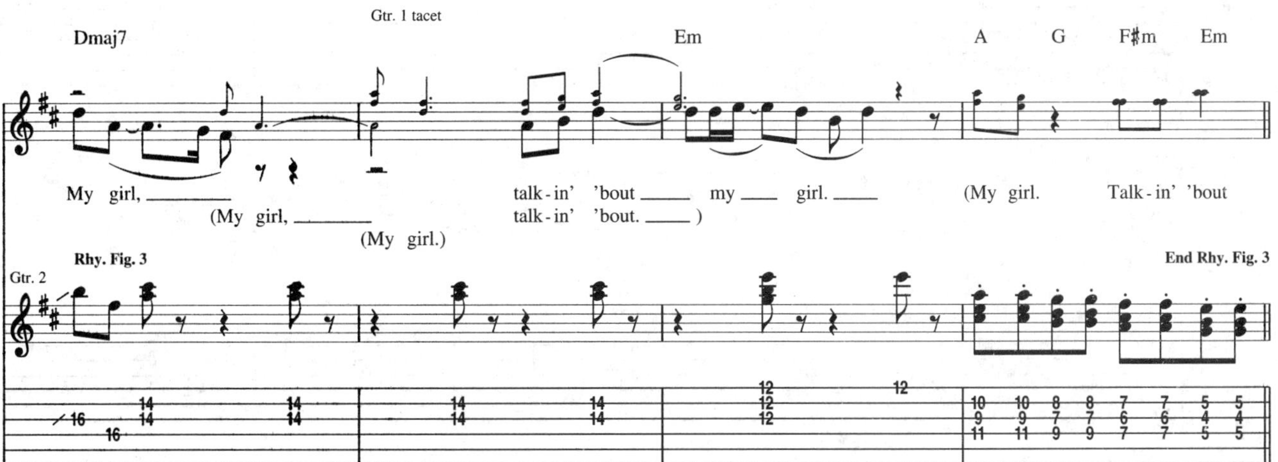

Gtr. 1 tacet
Dmaj7 Em A G F♯m Em
My girl, talk-in' 'bout my girl. (My girl. Talk-in' 'bout
(My girl, talk-in' 'bout.)
(My girl.)
Rhy. Fig. 3
Gtr. 2
End Rhy. Fig. 3

Gtr. 2: w/ Rhy. Fig. 3, 1 1/2 times
Dmaj7
my girl.) I got sun - shine on a cloud - y day with my
(Oo, oo. Whoa, whoa.

Begin Fade
Em A G F♯m Em
girl. I've e - ven got the month of May with
A - bout, talk - in' 'bout

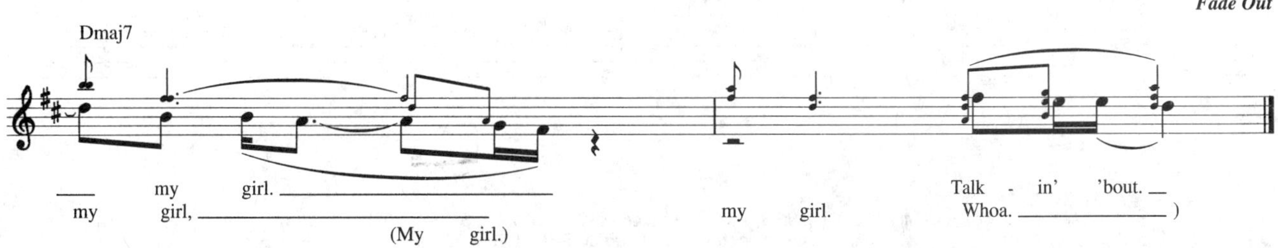

Fade Out
Dmaj7
my girl. Talk - in' 'bout.
my girl, my girl. Whoa.)
(My girl.)

Name

Words and Music by John Rzeznik

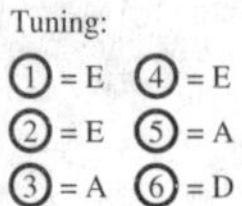

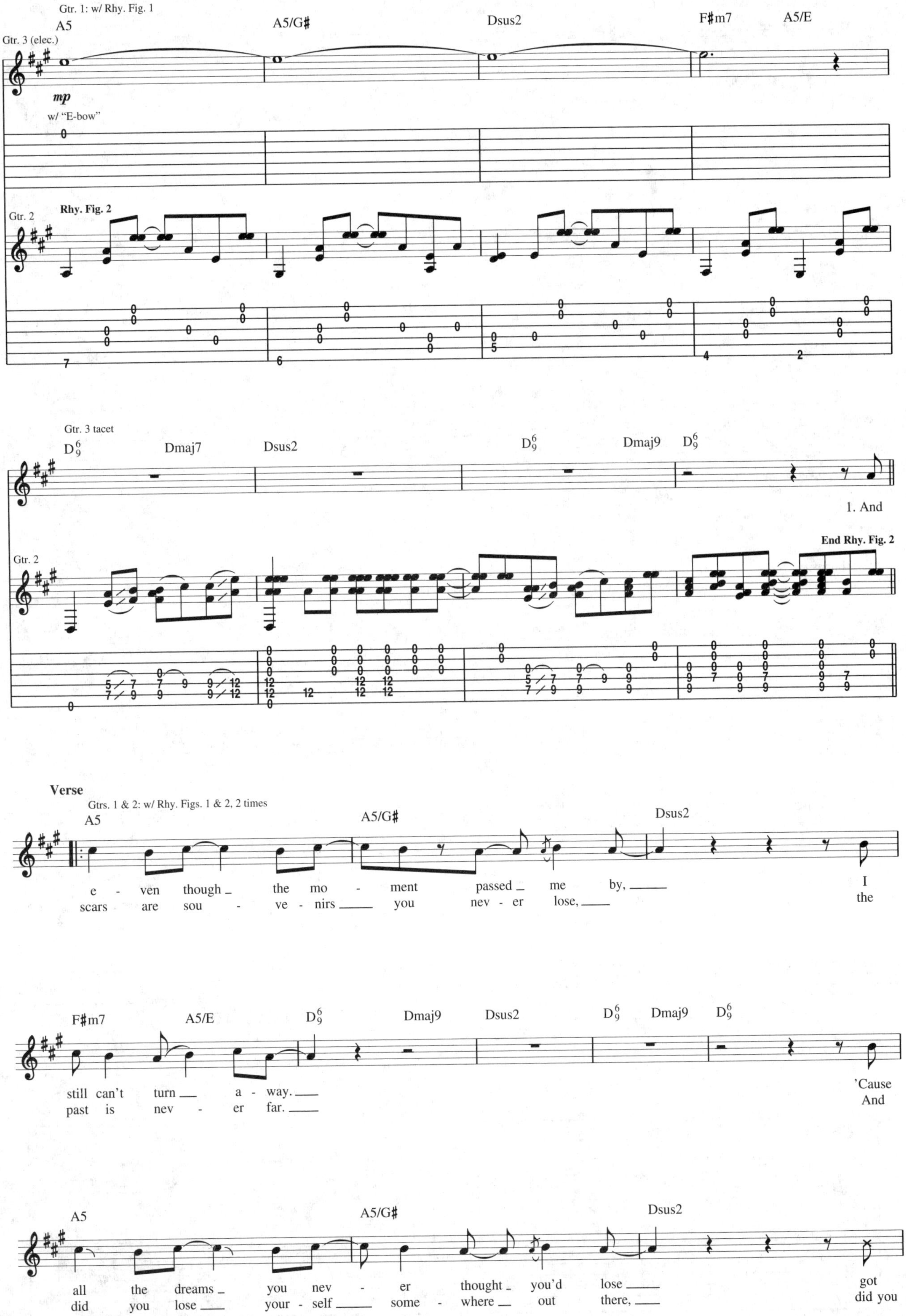

Gtr. 1: w/ Rhy. Fig. 1

A5 A5/G♯ Dsus2 F♯m7 A5/E

Gtr. 3 (elec.)

mp

w/ "E-bow"

Gtr. 2

Rhy. Fig. 2

Gtr. 3 tacet

D6/9 Dmaj7 Dsus2 D6/9 Dmaj9 D6/9

1. And

Gtr. 2

End Rhy. Fig. 2

Verse

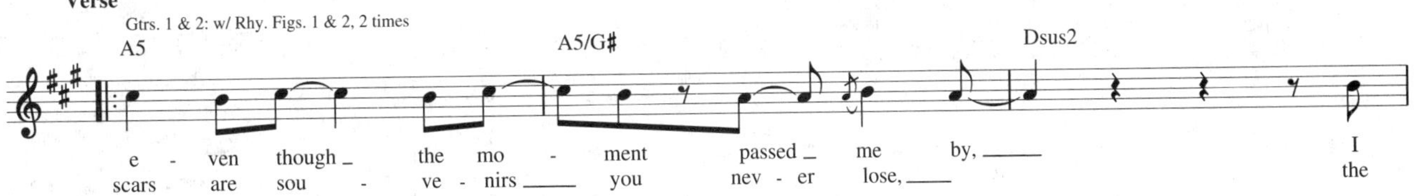

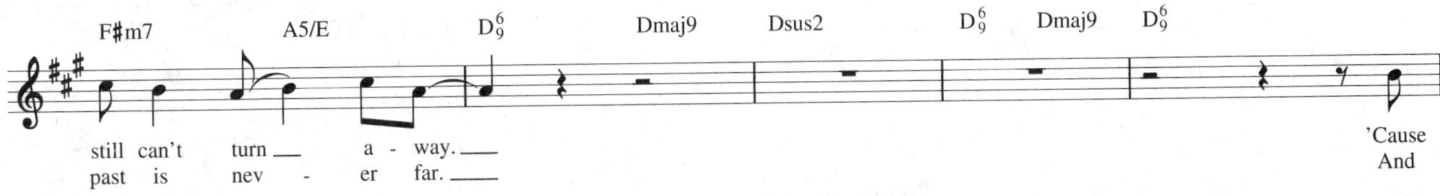

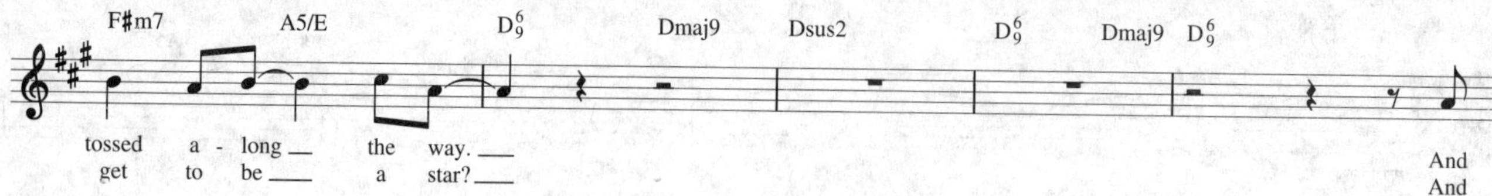

End Half-Time Feel

Gtr. 2: w/ Rhy. Fill 1, 1st time
Gtrs. 1 & 2: w/ Rhy. Fill 2, 2nd time

F#m7 A5/E D6/9 Dmaj9 Dsus2 D6/9 Dmaj9 D6/9

lost or thrown a - way. And
more than who we are? We

F#m7
Esus4
A/E
Dsus2
A/D
Dsus2
A
don't be - long to no one, that's a shame.
Re - runs all be - come our his - to - ry.
But if
A
F#m7
Esus4
A/E
Dsus2
you could hide be - side me may - be for a - while.
ti - red song keeps play - in' on a ti - red ra - di - o.
And
F#m7
Esus4
Dsus2
I won't tell no one your name.
And I won't tell 'em your

Half-Time Feel
A5
A5/G#
Dsus2
F#m7
A5/E
name.
I won't tell 'em your name.
D6/9
Dmaj9
Dsus2
D6/9
Dmaj9
D6/9
2. And
Gtr. 2: w/ Rhy. Fig. 2, 1st 7 meas.
Gtr. 1: w/ Rhy. Fig. 1
A
A5/G#
Dsus2
F#m7
A5/E
Mmm,
mmm,
mmm.
I won't tell 'em your name
D6/9
Dmaj9
Dsus2
D6/9
Dmaj9
Gtr. 2: w/ Rhy. Fill 1
D6/9
End Half-Time Feel
Ow!

Guitar Solo
F#m7
Esus4
Dsus2
Gtr. 2
f
let ring throughout
Gtr. 1
Rhy. Fig. 3
End Rhy. Fig. 3
Gtr. 1: w/ Rhy. Fig. 3, 4 1/2 times, simile
Gtr. 3 tacet
Gtr. 3
w/ "E-bow"
mf

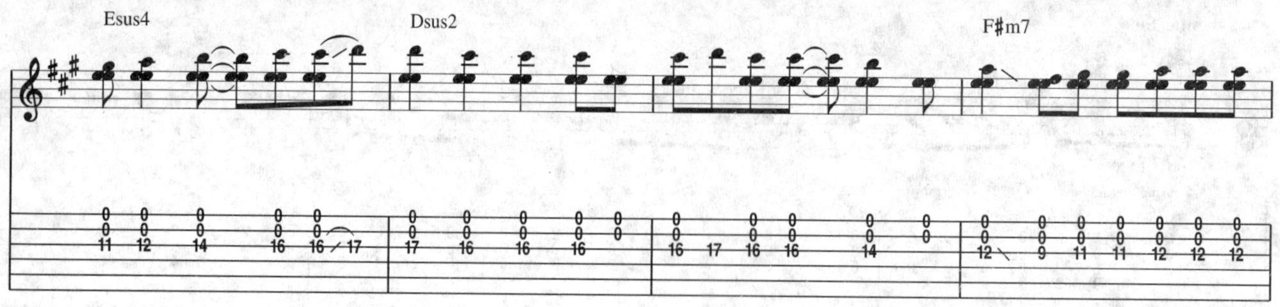
Esus4
Dsus2
F#m7

Esus4
Gtr. 3
Dsus2
F#m7
w/ out "E-Bow"
Gtr. 2

Gtr. 3 tacet
Esus4
Dsus2
Verse
Half-Time Feel
A5
3. I think a - bout
Gtr. 2
Gtr. 1

A5/G#
Dsus2
F#m7
A5/E
D6/9
Dmaj9
you all the time,
but I don't need the same.
Gtr. 3
Gtrs. 1 & 2
Gtr. 3 tacet
Dsus2
D6/9
Dmaj9
D6/9
A5
It's lone - ly where you are.
A5/G#
Dsus2
F#m7
A5/E
Dsus2
Come back down
and I won't tell 'em your name.
Dmaj9
D
A

No One Like You

Words and Music by Klaus Meine and Rudolf Schenker

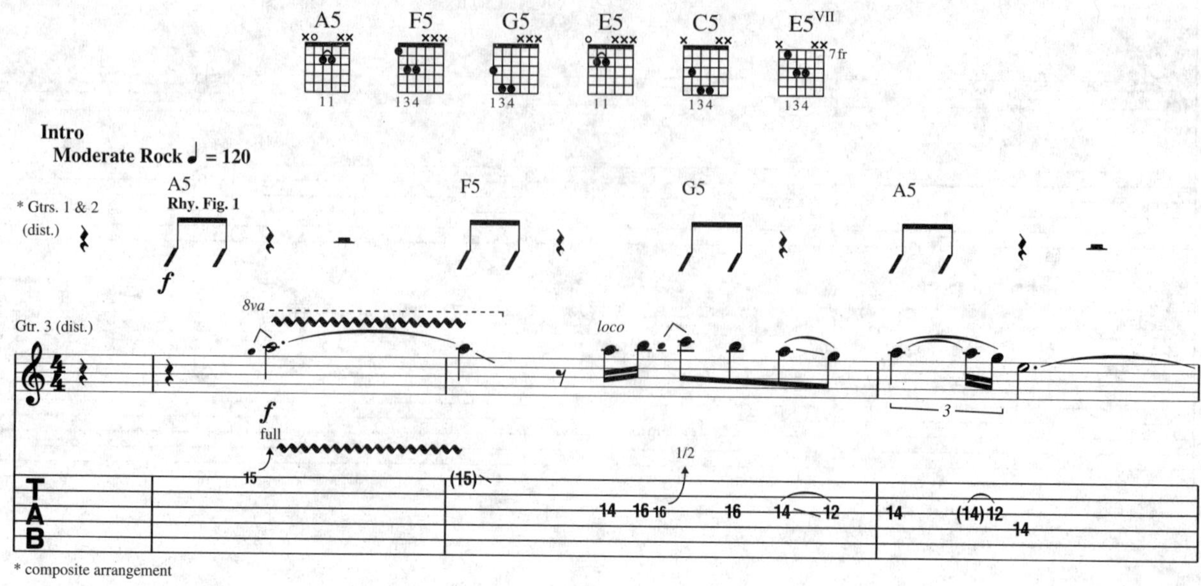

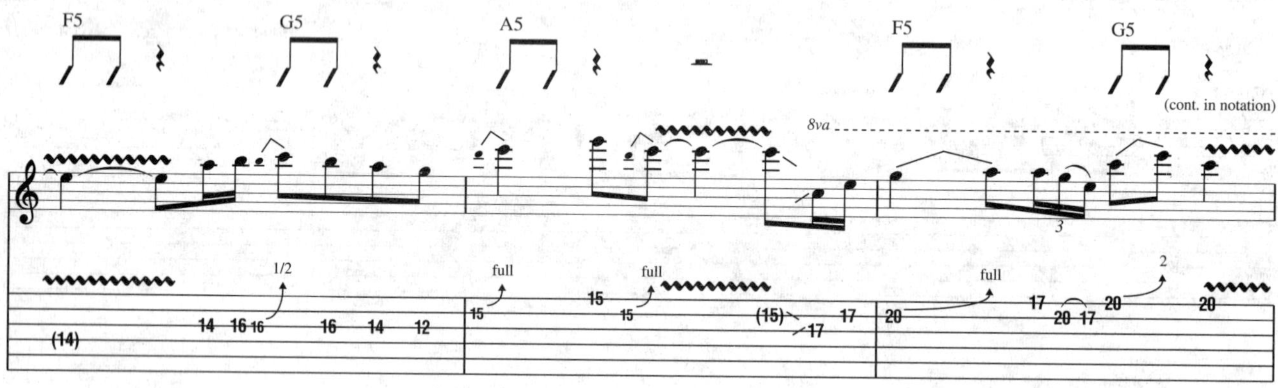

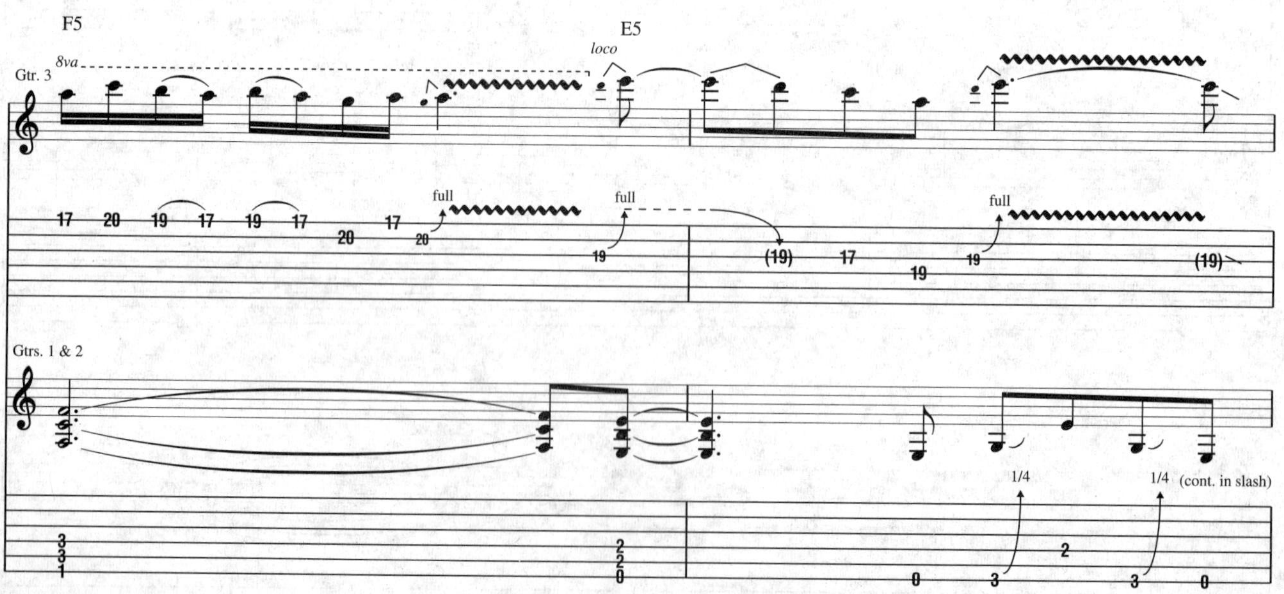

A5
F5
G5
A5
Gtrs. 1 & 2
8va
Gtr. 4 (dist.)
loco
f
full
Gtr. 3
full
1/2
F5
G5
A5
F5
G5
8va
full
2
1/2
F5
E5
End Rhy. Fig. 1
8va
loco
* dim.
(Gtr. 1 cont. in notation)
* Use volume control

* Chord symbols reflect implied tonality.

** doubled w/ acous. gtr. next 17 meas., 2nd time

* doubled w/ acous. gtr. next 13 meas., 1st time

Am
F
Am
It's get - ting hard - er now that I'm gone; if I
just im - ag - ine you'd come through this door; you'd take
F
C5
E5 VII
Gtr. 2
To Coda
had the choice I would stay.
all my sor - row a - way.
There's no one like
Gtr. 1
Gtr. 3
(cont. in slash)
semi-harm.
(1)
Chorus
* Gtrs. 1 & 2: w/ Rhy. Fig. 1, simile
Gtr. 3 tacet
A5
F5
G5
A5
you! I can't wait for the nights with you. I im - ag -
* w/ dist.
F5
G5
A5
F5
G5
- ine the things we do. I just wan - na be loved by you.

F5
E5
A5
No one like you!
I can't wait
Gtr. 3
fdbk.
full
full
Gtr. 3 tacet
G5
for the nights with you.
I im - ag - ine the things we do.
D.S. al Coda
I just wan - na be loved by you.
Coda
Chorus
* Gtrs. 1 & 2: w/ Rhy. Fig. 1, 1st 14 meas.
Gtr. 3 tacet
you.
* w/ dist.
I can't wait for the nights with you.
I im - ag -
- ine the things we do.
I just wan - na be loved by you.
Gtr. 3 Riff A
* End Riff A
semi-harm.
* Omit tie on recall

F5 G5 A5 F5 G5
for the nights with you. I im - ag - ine the things we do.
* 8va
loco
P.H.
full
* applies to harmonics only
* see previous footnote
A5 F5 G5 F5 E5
Rhy. Fig. 2
End Rhy. Fig. 2
Gtrs. 1 & 2
I just wan - na be loved by you.
semi-harm.
1/2
Guitar Solo
Gtrs. 1 & 2: w/ Rhy. Fig. 1, 1st 6 meas.
3/4
grad. bend
1 1/2

Gtrs. 1 & 2: w/ Rhy. Fig. 2
F5
E5
semi-harm.
grad. release
full
Gtrs. 1 & 2: w/ Rhy. Fig. 1, 1st 8 meas.
A5
F5
G5
* 8va
Gtr. 4
Gtr. 3
divisi
* refers to both gtrs.
** Gtr. 3 to left of slash in tab.
A5
Gtr. 4 tacet
F5
G5
A5
8va
Gtr. 3
F5
G5
F5
E5
P.H.
Chorus
Gtrs. 1 & 2: w/ Rhy. Fig. 1, 1st 15 meas.
A5
No one like you!
I can't wait
Gtr. 3 8va
loco
Gtr. 5 (dist.)
Riff B
End Riff B
P.M.
Gtr. 5: w/ Riff B, 5 times
Gtr. 3 tacet
F5
G5
A5
F5
G5
for the nights with you.
I im-ag-ine the things we do.

Gtr. 3: w/ Riff A, simile
A5
F5
G5
F5
E5
I just wan - na be loved by you.
No one like

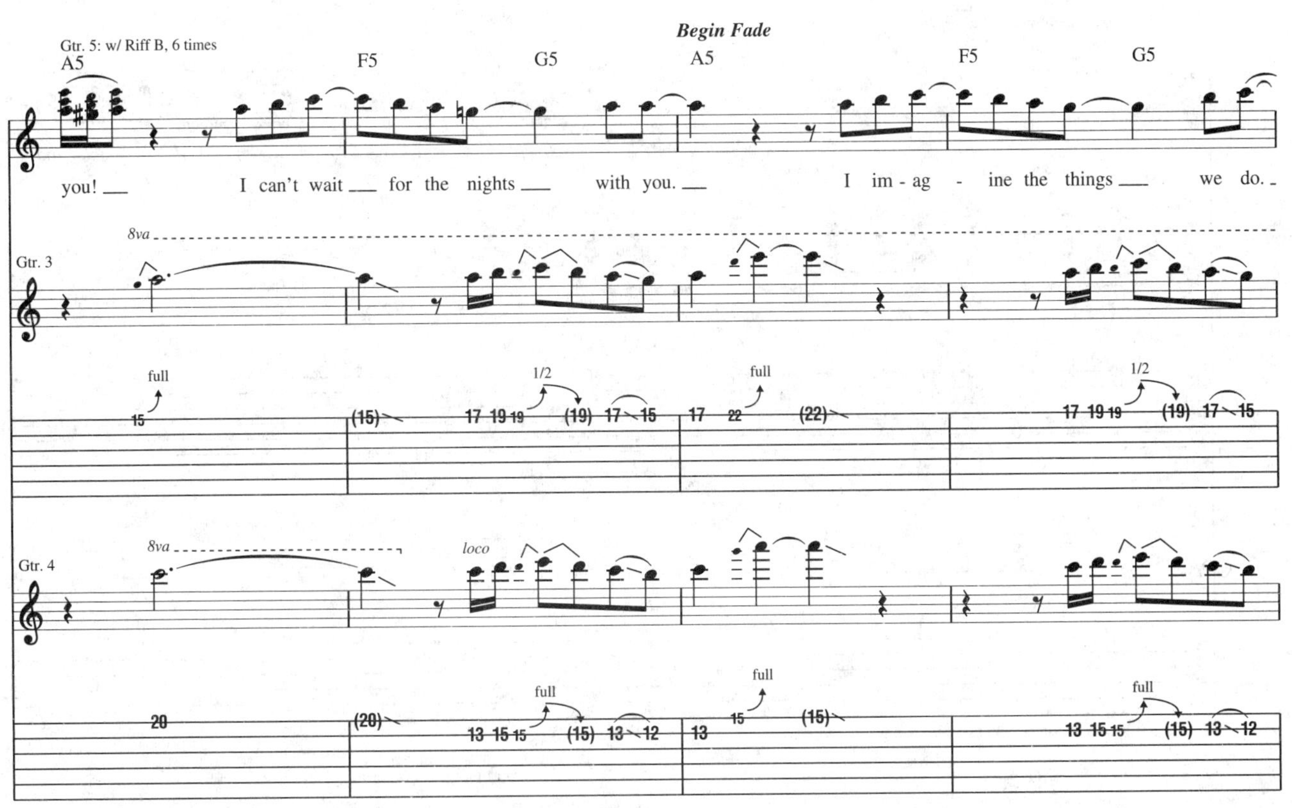
Begin Fade
Gtr. 5: w/ Riff B, 6 times
A5
F5
G5
A5
F5
G5
you! I can't wait for the nights with you. I im - ag - ine the things we do.
8va
Gtr. 3
full
1/2
full
1/2
Gtr. 4
8va
loco
full
full
full

Fade Out
A5
F5
G5
F5
E5
I just wan - na be loved by you!
8va
full
full
full
1/2
full
full

No Particular Place to Go

Words and Music by Chuck Berry

*Chord symbols reflect implied tonality.

C

I stole a kiss at the turn of a mile. My cu - ri - os - i - ty run-nin' wild.
The night was young and the moon was gold, so we both de - cid - ed to take a stroll.

G D

Cruis - in' and play-in' the ra - di - o
Can you i - mag - ine the way I felt?

G
with no par-tic-u-lar place to go
I could-n't un-fas-ten her safe-ty belt.
2. Rid - in' a-long in my au-to-mo -
4. Rid - in' a-long in my cal-a-boose,
End Rhy. Fig. 1
Verse
Gtr. 2: w/ Rhy. Fig. 1
G
bile,
I's anx-ious to tell her the way I feel.
still try-in' to get her belt a-loose.
Gtr. 1
C
So I told her soft-ly and sin-cere,
All the way home I held a grudge
and she leaned and whis-pered in my
for the safe-ty belt that would-n't budge.

G
D
ear.
Cud - dl - in' more and driv - in' slow
Cruis - in' and play - in' the ra - di - o

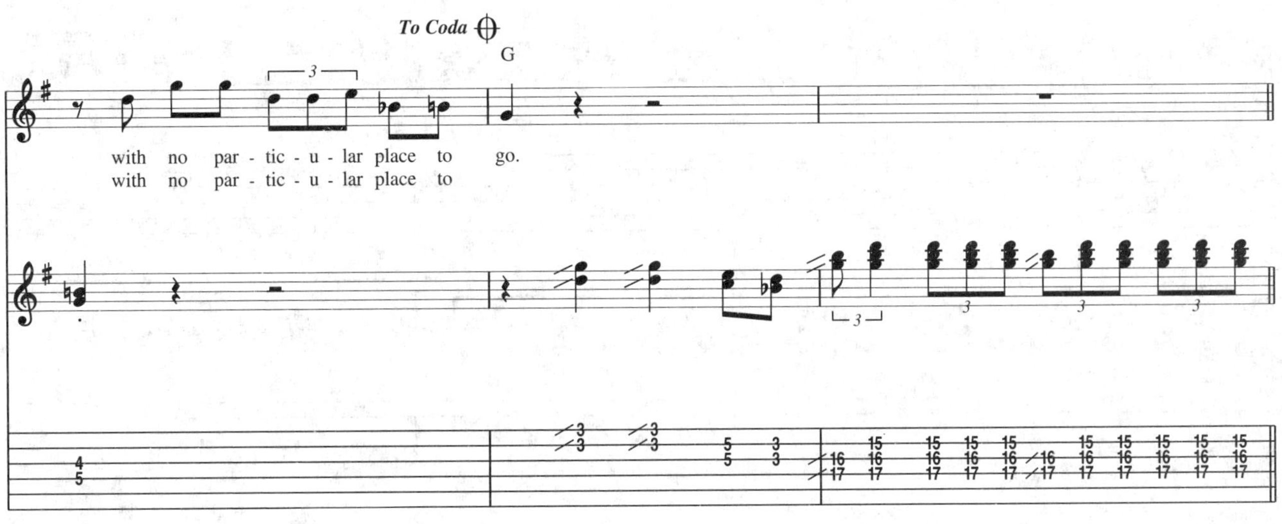
To Coda
G
with no par - tic - u - lar place to go.
with no par - tic - u - lar place to

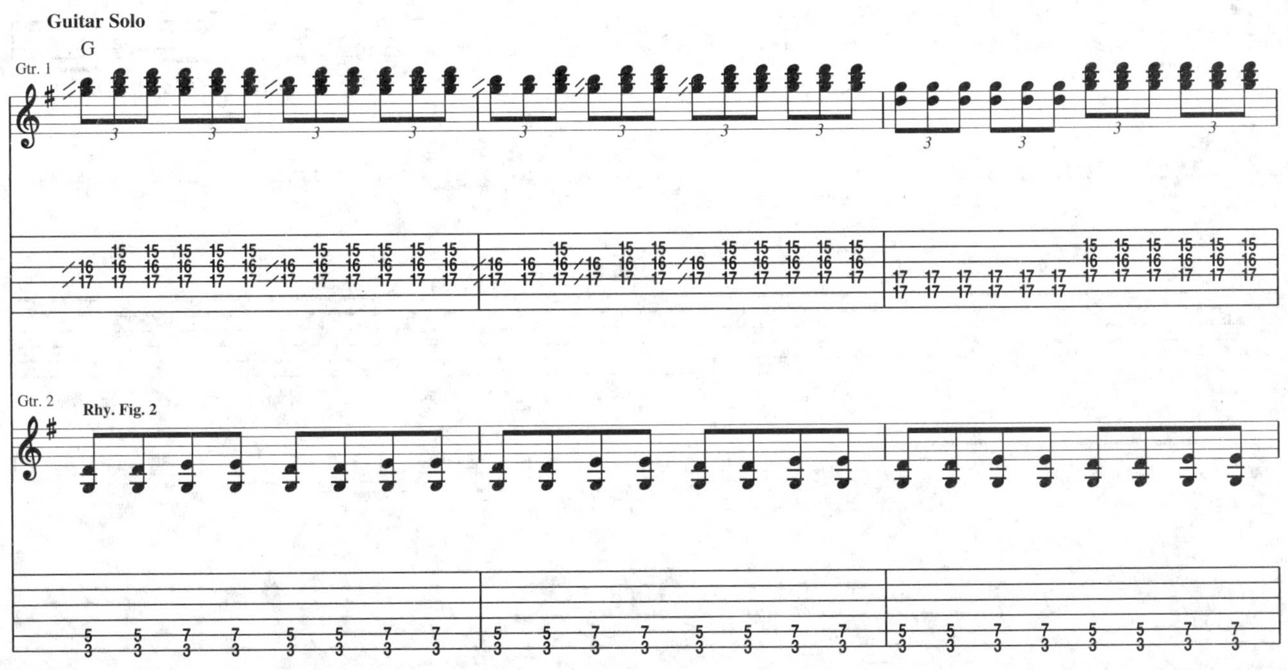
Guitar Solo
G
Gtr. 1
Gtr. 2
Rhy. Fig. 2

C
G
D
C
G
D.S. al Coda
3. No par - tic - u - lar place to
End Rhy. Fig. 2

Coda
Outro-Guitar Solo
Gtr. 2 w/ Rhy. Fig. 2
G
go.
C
D

Gtr. 2: w/ Rhy. Fig. 2, 1st 10 meas.
G
C
G
D
C
G
Gtr. 1
Ab7
G7
Gtr. 2

Oh, Pretty Woman

Words and Music by Roy Orbison and Bill Dees

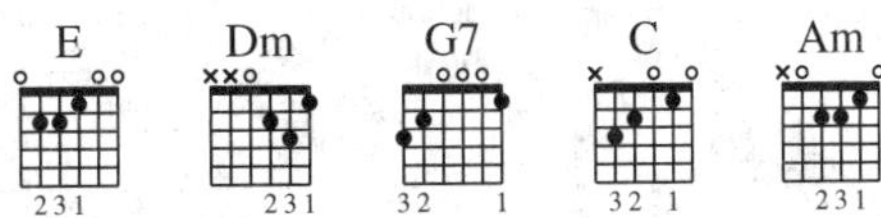

D
E
Rhy. Fig. 2
End Rhy. Fig. 2
Gtr. 1
wom - an,
wom - an,
I don't be - lieve you.
that you look love - ly
You're not the truth.
as can be.
No one could
Are you
End. Rhy. Fig. 1
Riff B
Gtr. 2
End Riff B
(Gtr. 1 cont. in slashes)

Gtrs. 1 & 2: w/ Rhy. Fig. 2 & Riff B
*Gtrs. 1 & 2: w/ Riff A
2nd time, Gtrs. 1 & 2: w/ Riff A (1st 3 meas.)
E7
1.
look as good as you.
lone - ly just like me?
Mer - cy!
Rrr!
2. Pret - ty
*mf
2.
Bridge
E
Dm
G7
Rhy. Fig. 3
Gtr. 1
Pret - ty wom - an, stop a - while.
Gtr. 2
Rhy. Fig. 3A
w/ amplifier vibrato

C
Am
Dm
End Rhy. Fig. 3
Pret - ty wom - an, talk a - while.
Pret - ty wom - an,
End Rhy. Fig. 3A

G7
C
give your smile to me.
let ring
Gtrs. 1 & 2: w/ Rhy. Figs. 3 & 3A
Dm
G7
C
Am
Pret - ty wom - an, yeah, yeah, yeah.
Pret - ty wom - an, look my way.
Dm
G7
C
Gtr. 1
(cont. in notation)
Pret - ty wom - an, say you'll stay with me
Gtr. 2
Gtr. 2 tacet
A
F♯m
Dm
E
'cause I need you. I'll treat you right.
Gtr. 1
A
F♯m
Dm
Come to me, ba - by. Be mine to -

Gtrs. 1 & 2: w/ Riff A
E7
Verse
Gtr. 1 w/ Rhy. Fig. 1
A
F♯m
night. 3. Pret - ty wom - an, don't walk on by. Pret - ty
A
F♯m
D
Gtrs. 1 & 2: w/ Rhy. Fill 1
Gtrs. 1 & 2: w/ Rhy. Fig. 2 & Riff B (5 1/2 times)
E
wom - an, don't make me cry. Pret - ty wom - an, don't walk a - way.
O - kay. If that's the way it must be, o - kay.
I guess I'll go on home, it's late. There'll be to - mor - row night, but
E
N.C.
E7
Gtr. 1
(cont. in notation)
wait. What do I see? Is she
Gtr. 2
Gtrs. 1 & 2
Gtrs. 1 & 2: w/ Riff A (1 1/2 times)
walk - in' back to me? Yeah, she's walk - in' back to me.
A5
N.C.
Oh, whoa, pret - ty wom - an.
Gtrs. 1 & 2
Rhy. Fill 1
Gtrs. 1 & 2

Oleo

By Sonny Rollins

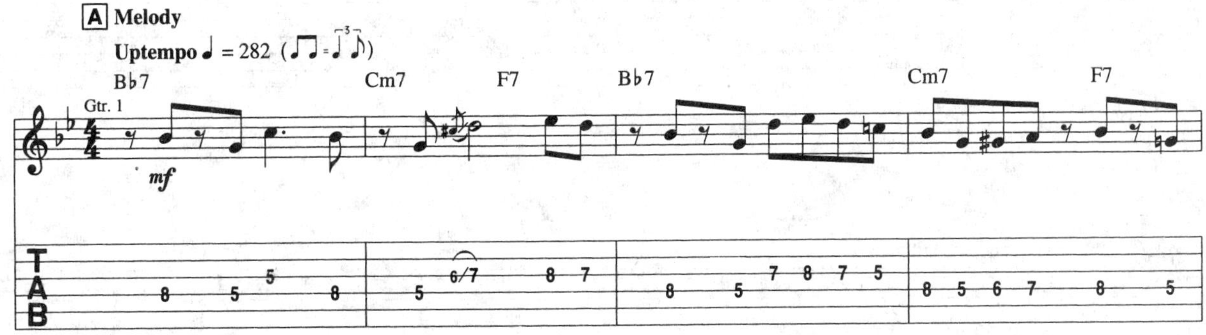

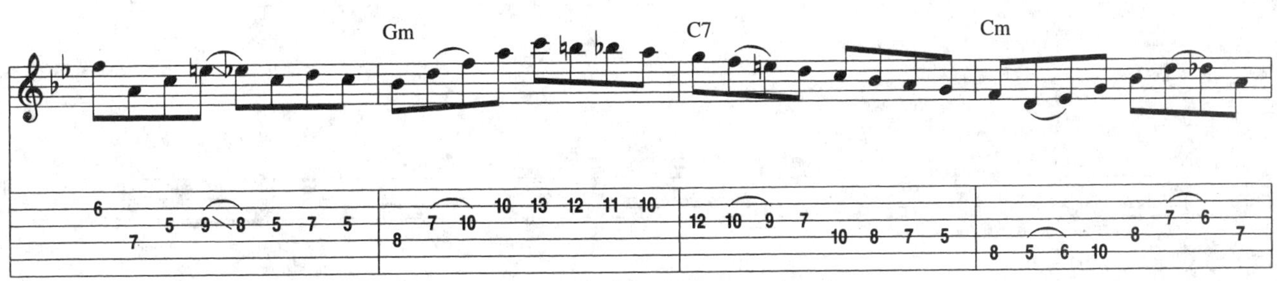

F7
B♭7
Cm7
F7
B♭7

Cm7
F7
B♭7
E♭7
B♭7

B Guitar Solo
F7
B♭7

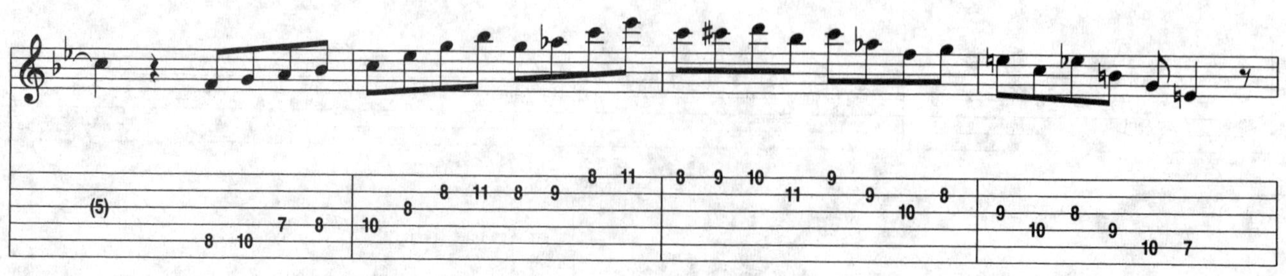

D7
G7

C7
F7

B♭7

B♭7

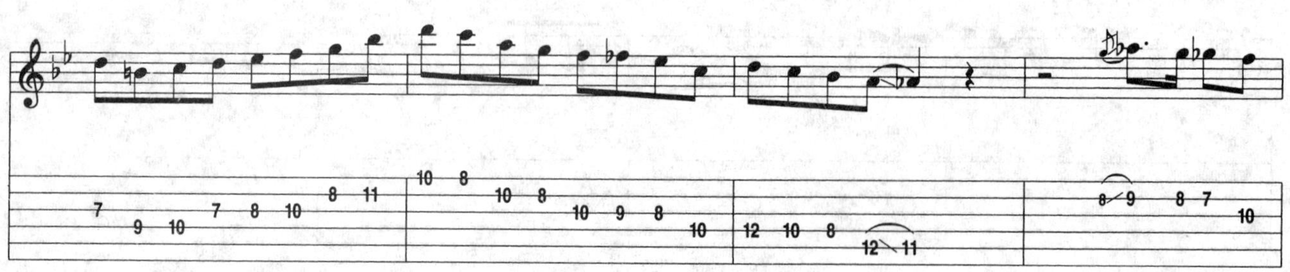

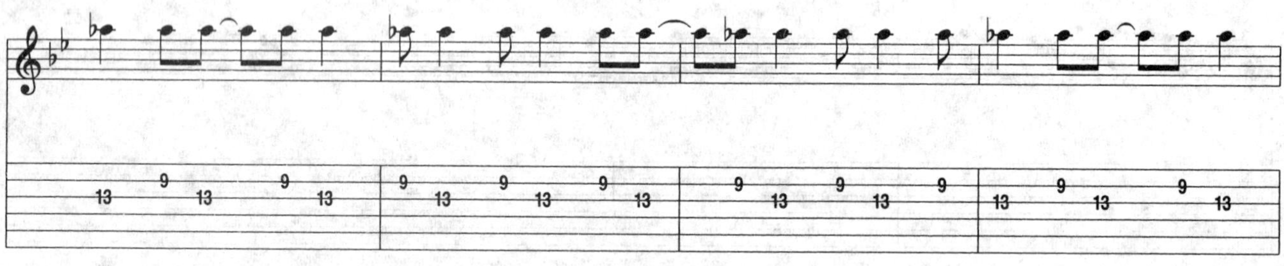

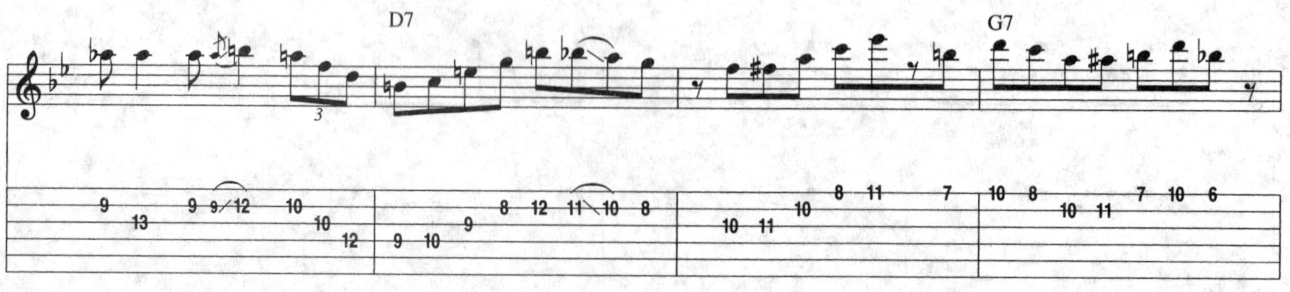
D7
G7

C7

F7

B♭7

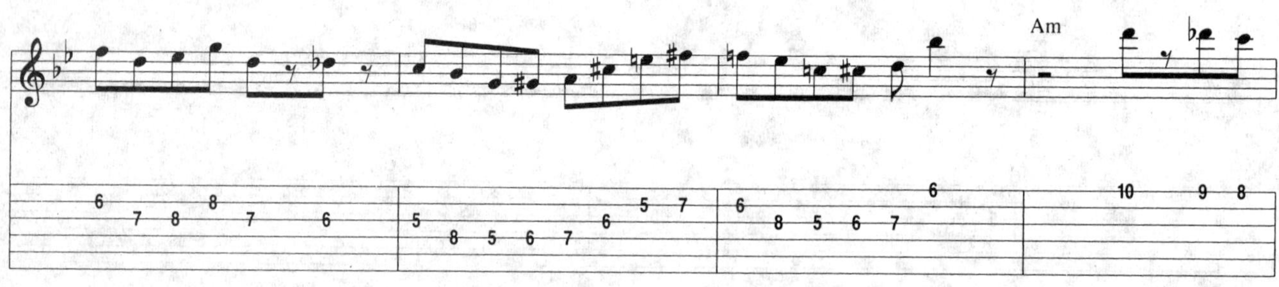
Am

D7
G7
C7

F7
B♭7

B♭7

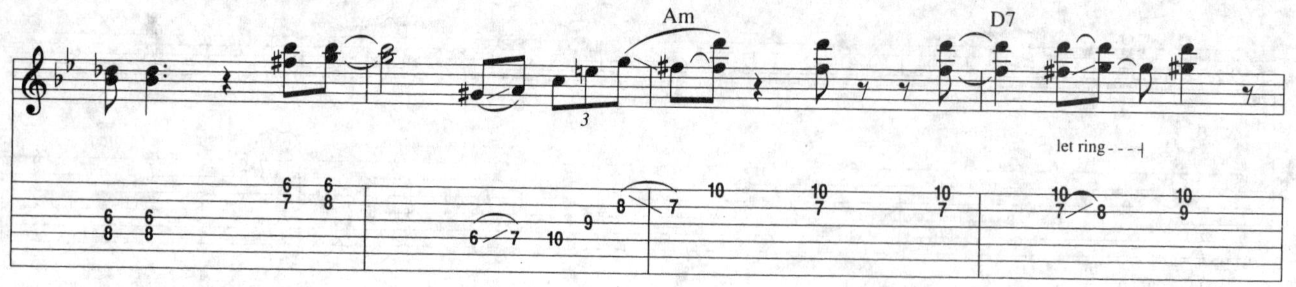
Am
D7
let ring

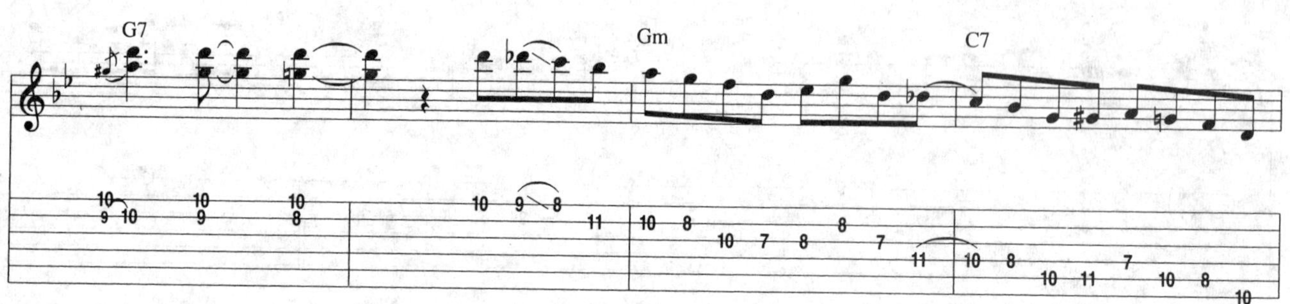
G7
Gm
C7

Cm
F7
B♭7

Owner of a Lonely Heart

Words and Music by Trevor Horn, Jon Anderson, Trevor Rabin and Chris Squire

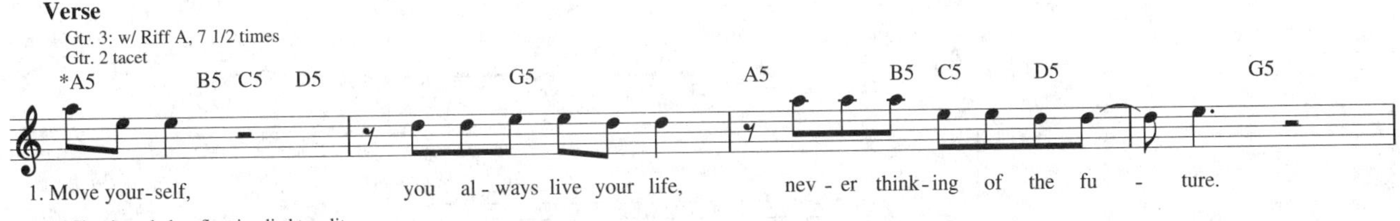

*Chord symbols reflect implied tonality

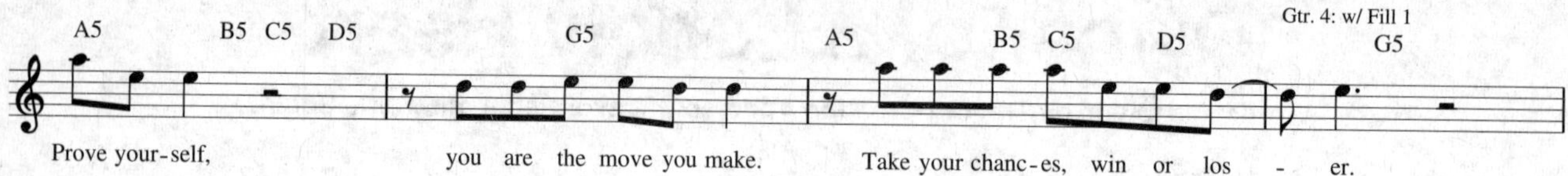

Gtr. 4: w/ Fill 1
A5 B5 C5 D5 G5 A5 B5 C5 D5 G5
Prove your-self, you are the move you make. Take your chanc-es, win or los - er.

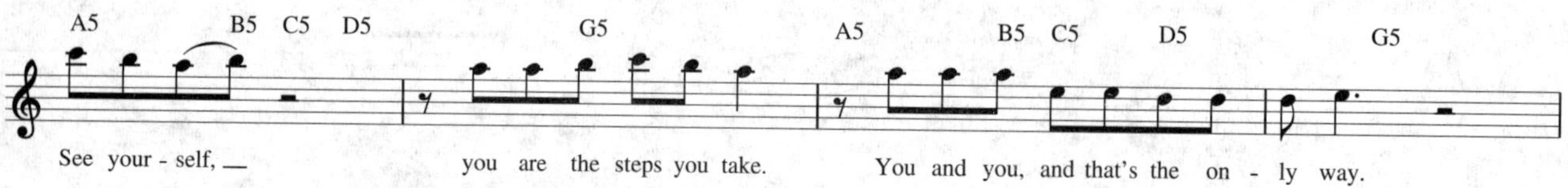

A5 B5 C5 D5 G5 A5 B5 C5 D5 G5
See your-self, you are the steps you take. You and you, and that's the on-ly way.

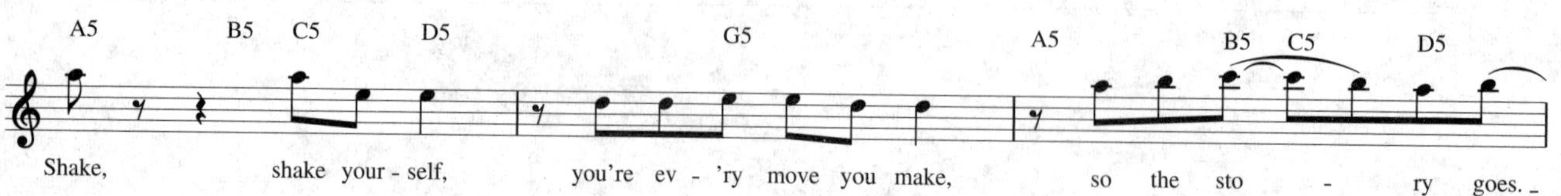

A5 B5 C5 D5 G5 A5 B5 C5 D5
Shake, shake your-self, you're ev-'ry move you make, so the sto - ry goes.

Chorus
G5 A5 B5 C5 D5 G5 A5 B5 C5 D5
Own-er of a lone-ly heart. Own-er of a lone-ly heart.
Gtr. 4
w/ chorus
Harm.
Gtr. 3
w/ chorus
P.M.
let ring

Fill 1
Gtr. 4 (clean)
mf

To Coda 1
To Coda 2
G5
A5
B5
C5
D5
G5
Own - er of a bro - ken heart.
(Oo, much bet - ter than a)
Harm.
Harm.
let ring
let ring
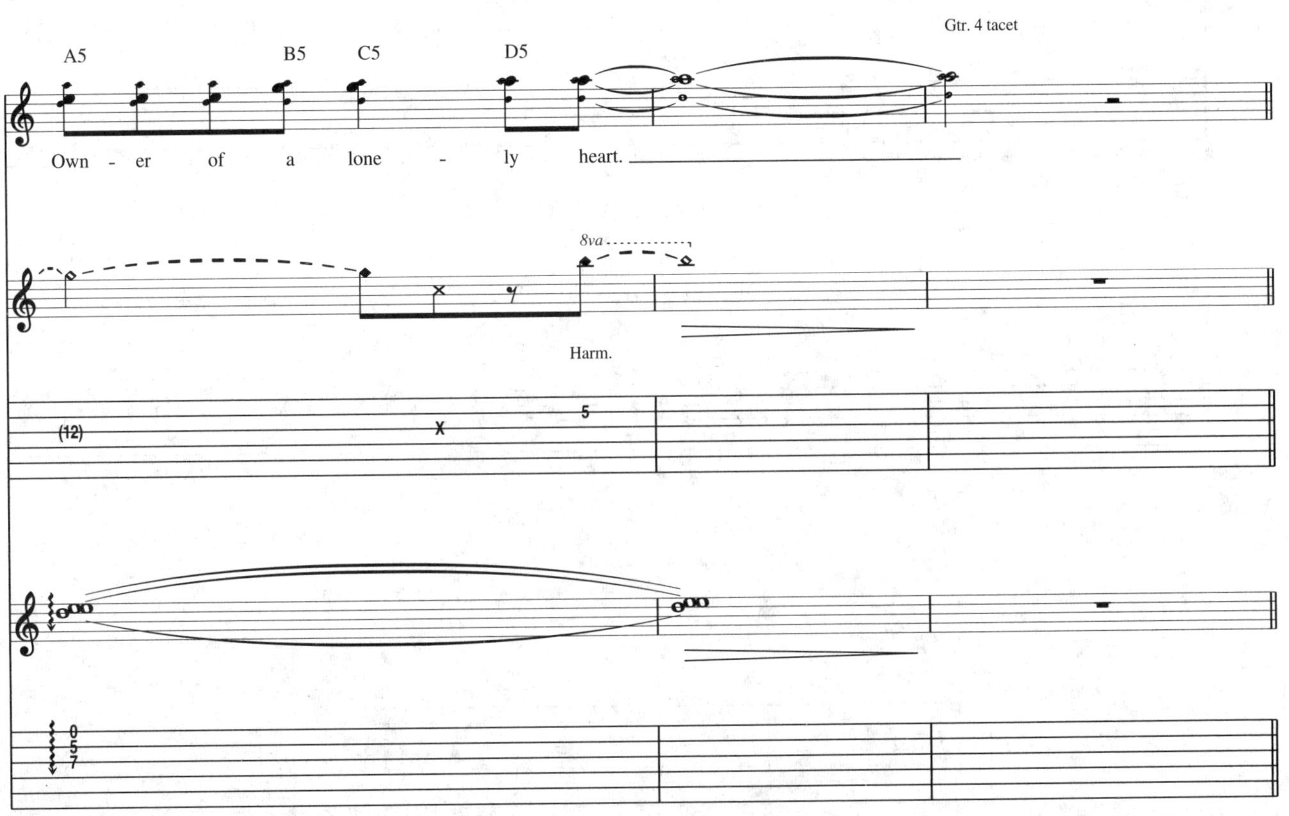
Gtr. 4 tacet
A5
B5
C5
D5
Own - er of a lone - ly heart.
8va
Harm.

Verse
Gtr. 2: w/ Rhy. Fig. 1
Gtr. 3: w/ Riff A, 8 times
A5 B5 C5 D5 G5
Gtr. 2: w/ Rhy. Fig. 1A
A5 B5 C5 D5 G5
2. Say you don't want to chance it, you've been hurt so be - fore.
Gtr. 2: w/ Rhy. Fig. 1
A5 B5 C5 D5 G5
Gtr. 2: w/ Rhy. Fig. 1A
A5 B5 C5 D5
Watch it, now, the ea-gle in the sky, how he dan-cin' one and on - ly.
Gtr. 2: w/ Rhy. Fig. 1
A5 B5 C5 D5 G5
Gtr. 2: w/ Rhy. Fig. 1A
A5 B5 C5 D5
You lose your-self, no, not for pit - y's sake. There's no real rea - son to be lone - ly.
Gtr. 2: w/ Rhy. Fig. 1, 2 times
A5 B5 C5 D5 G5 A5 B5 C5 D5 G5
D.S. al Coda
Be your - self, give your free will a chance. You've got to want to suc - ceed.
Coda 1
Bridge
A5 B5 C5 D5 A A C/A G/A
Own-er of a lone-ly heart.
Gtr. 4
chorus off
Gtr. 3
chorus off
Rhy. Fig. 1A
Gtr. 2

To Coda 3
A
C/A
G/A
Own - er of a lone - ly heart.
Rhy. Fig. 2A
End Rhy. Fig. 2A
Rhy. Fig. 2
End Rhy. Fig. 2
Gtrs. 3 & 4: w/ Rhy. Figs. 2 & 2A, 4 times
Af-ter my own in - de - ci - sion they con - fused me so. My love said,
Own - er of a lone - ly heart.
Asus4
"Nev-er ques-tion your will at all." In the end you've got to go, look be-fore you leap, and
Own - er of a lone-ly heart.
G♯13
E13 F13 F♯13 G13 G♯13
don't you hes - i - tate at all, no, no. Yow! Ah, ah, ah, ah, ah,
Guitar Solo
A5 B5 C5 D5 G5
yow!
Gtr. 5 (dist.)
*w/ harmonizer
*Set to harmonize one ocatve lower and a fifth above.

Gtr. 2: w/ Fill 2
A5
B5
C5
D5
8va
G5
F#5
loco
grad. release
full
Interlude
Gtr. 5 tacet
A7sus4
D/F#
Gsus2
play 3 times
D.S. al Coda 2
Gtr. 4
w/ chorus
let ring throughout
Gtr. 3
P.M.
Fill 2
Gtr. 2
w/ wah-wah
w/ bar

Coda 2
A5 B5 C5 D5 G5 A5 B5 C5 D5 G5 A5 B5 C5 D5
Own-er of the lone - ly heart.
Own-er of the lone - ly heart.
Own-er of the lone - ly heart.
Gtr. 4
Harm.
Harm.
Gtr. 3
let ring
let ring

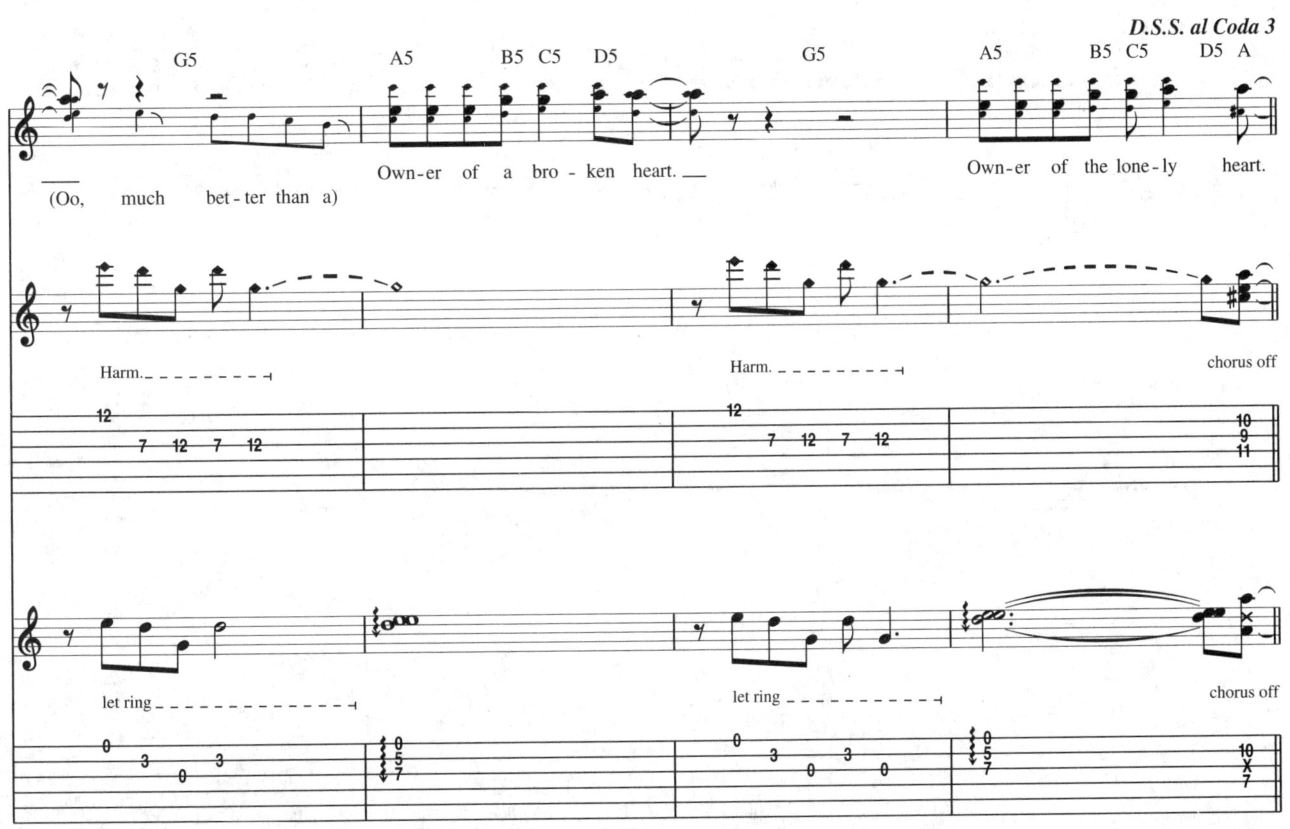
D.S.S. al Coda 3
G5 A5 B5 C5 D5 G5 A5 B5 C5 D5 A
(Oo, much bet-ter than a)
Own-er of a bro - ken heart.
Own-er of the lone-ly heart.
Harm.
Harm.
chorus off
let ring
let ring
chorus off

Coda 3

Gtrs. 3 & 4: w/ Rhy. Figs. 2 & 2A, 4 times
A
C/A
G/A
A
C/A
G/A
Soon-er or lat - er each con - clu - sion will de - cide the lone - ly heart.
Own - er of a lone - ly heart.

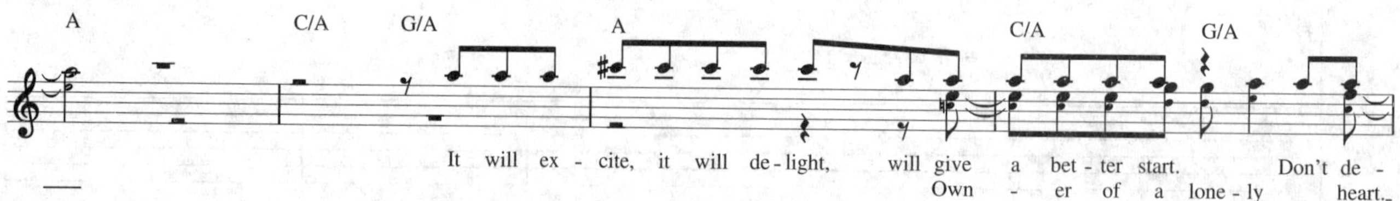
A
C/A
G/A
A
C/A
G/A
It will ex - cite, it will de - light, will give a bet - ter start. Don't de -
Own - er of a lone - ly heart.

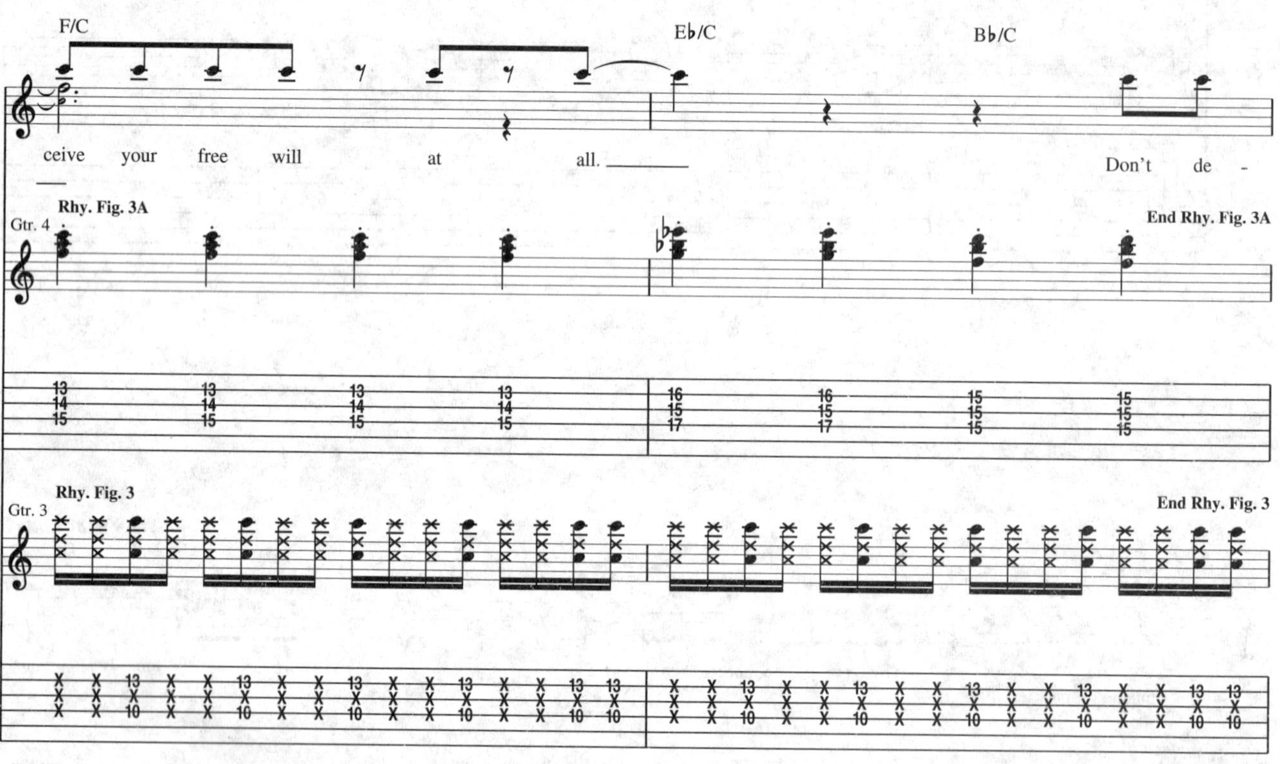
F/C
E♭/C
B♭/C
ceive your free will at all. Don't de -
Rhy. Fig. 3A
Gtr. 4
End Rhy. Fig. 3A
Rhy. Fig. 3
Gtr. 3
End Rhy. Fig. 3

Begin Fade
Gtrs. 3 & 4: w/ Rhy. Figs. 3 & 3A, till fade
w/ ad lib. Bkgd. Voc., till fade
F/C
E♭/C
B♭/C
F/C
ceive your free will at all. Don't de - ceive your free will at all.

Fade Out
E♭/C
B♭/C
F/C
E♭/C
B♭/C
Just re - ceive it. Just re - ceive it.

Papa's Got a Brand New Bag

Words and Music by James Brown

A7
E7
B
Pa - pa's got a brand _ new bag.
2. Come here ma -
End Rhy. Fig. 1
Verse
Gtr. 1: w/ Rhy. Fig. 1, simile
E
E7
E
- ma, _ and dig this cra - zy scene. _ It's not too _ fan -
A7
E
E7
E
- cy but it's _ fine _ and it's _ pret-ty clean. _ It ain't no
B7
A7
E7
B
drag. _ Pa - pa's got a brand _ new bag. 3. Do the
Bridge
Gtr. 1: w/ Rhy. Fig. 1, 1st 2 meas., 4 times
E
jerk. You do the fly. Don't _ play him cheap. Oh, you know he ain't shy. _ You're do-in' the
mon-key, the mashed po - ta - to. Jump back Jack. See you la - ter, _ al - li - ga - tor. _ 3. Come down so
Verse
Gtr. 1: w/ Rhy. Fig. 1, simile
E
far. _ Pa - pa's in the scene. _ He ain't too _ hip
A7
E
E7
E
now. _ Well, I can dig the new breed, _ uh. He ain't no
B7
A7
E7
B
drag. _ He's got a brand new bag. _ 4. Well, Pa -

Verse
E
E9
E
pa, you're do - in' the jerk. Pa - pa, you're do - in' the
Gr. 1
E7
E
A7
jerk. You're do - in' the twist just like this. He's do - in' the
Gtr. 1: w/ Rhy. Fig. 1, last 6 meas., simile
E
E7
B7
pipe ev - 'ry day and ev - 'ry night. The thing
A7
E7
B
like the boo - mer - ang. Hey. Come on.
Outro
Gtr. 1: w/ Rhy. Fig. 1, 1st 2 meas. till fade
E
Hey, hey. Come on. Hey, hey. Said you're up - tight.
Begin Fade
You're out of sight. Come on. See what
Fade Out
you know. Come on. See what you know. I just want you.

Paperback Writer

Words and Music by John Lennon and Paul McCartney

Chorus
D5
N.C.(A7)
writ - er.
Pa - per - back writ - er.
2. It's a
4. If you

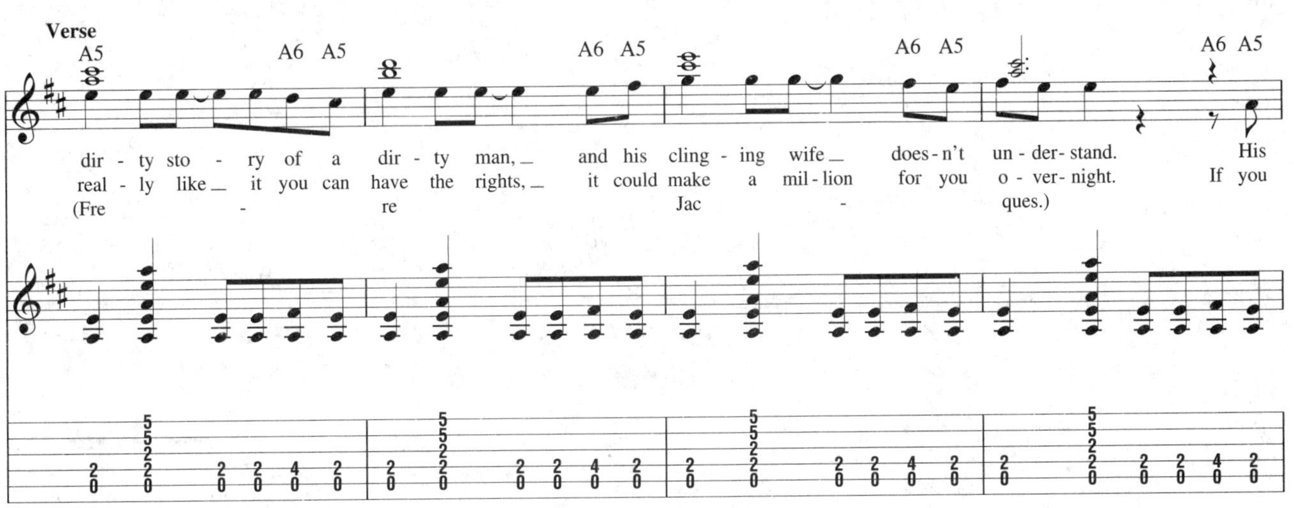
Verse
A5
A6 A5
A6 A5
A6 A5
A6 A5
dir - ty sto - ry of a dir - ty man, and his cling - ing wife does - n't un - der - stand. His
real - ly like it you can have the rights, it could make a mil - lion for you o - ver - night. If you
(Fre - re Jac - ques.)

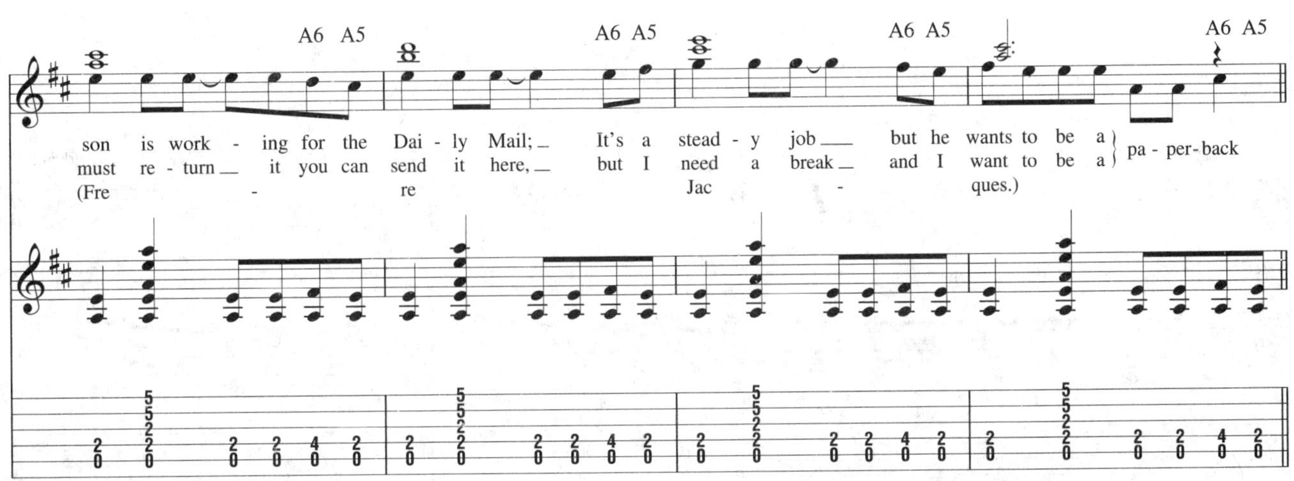
A6 A5
A6 A5
A6 A5
A6 A5
son is work - ing for the Dai - ly Mail; It's a stead - y job but he wants to be a
must re - turn it you can send it here, but I need a break and I want to be a
pa - per - back
(Fre - re Jac - ques.)

Chorus

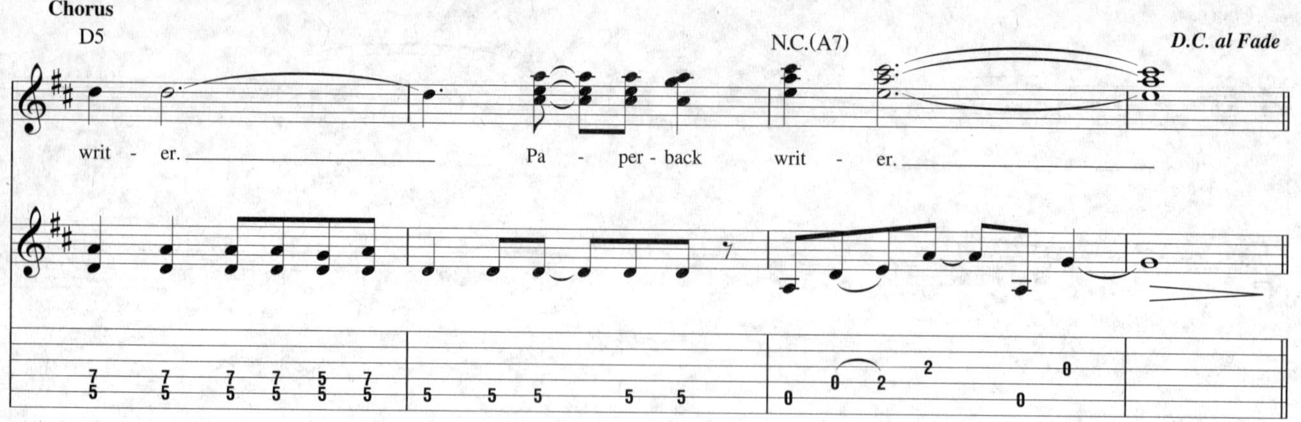

Bridge

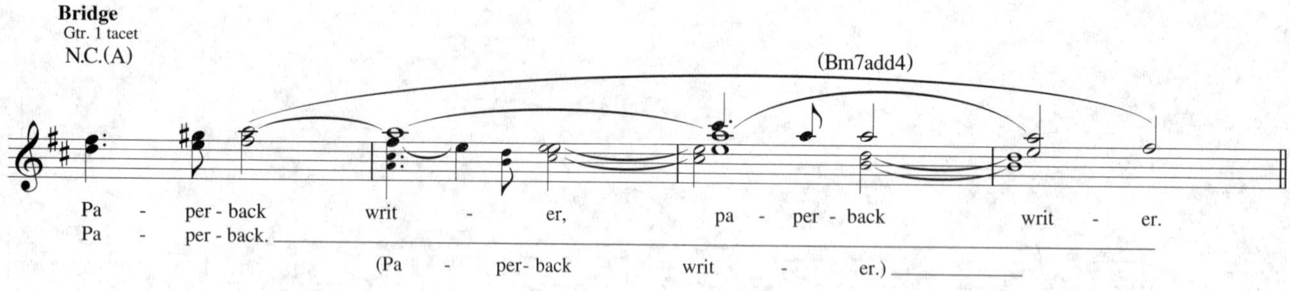

Breakdown

Outro

Paranoid

Words and Music by Anthony Iommi, John Osbourne, William Ward and Terence Butler

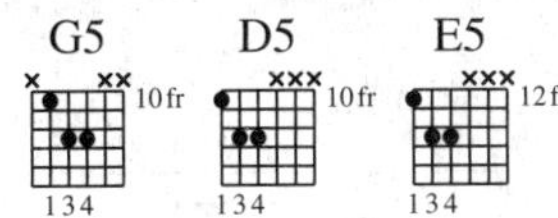

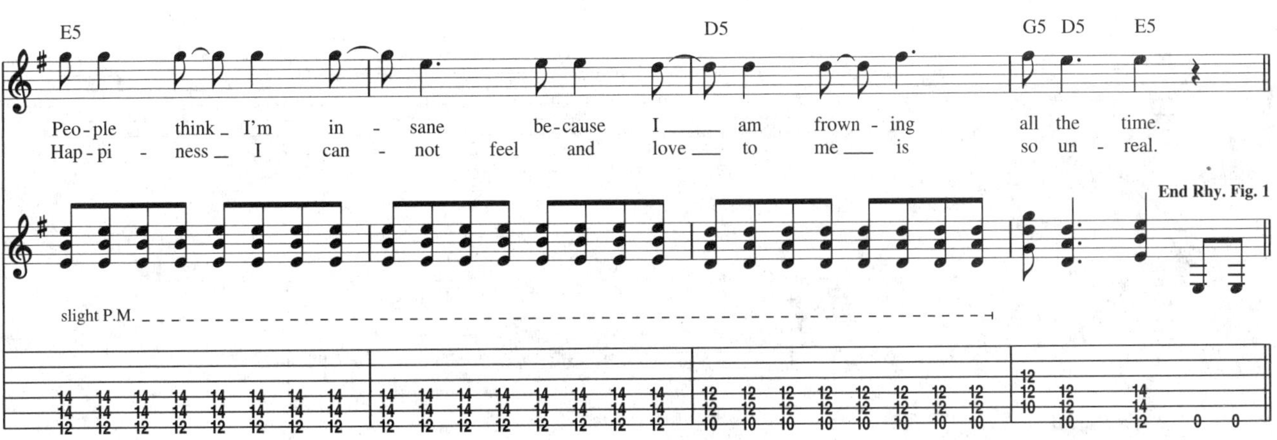

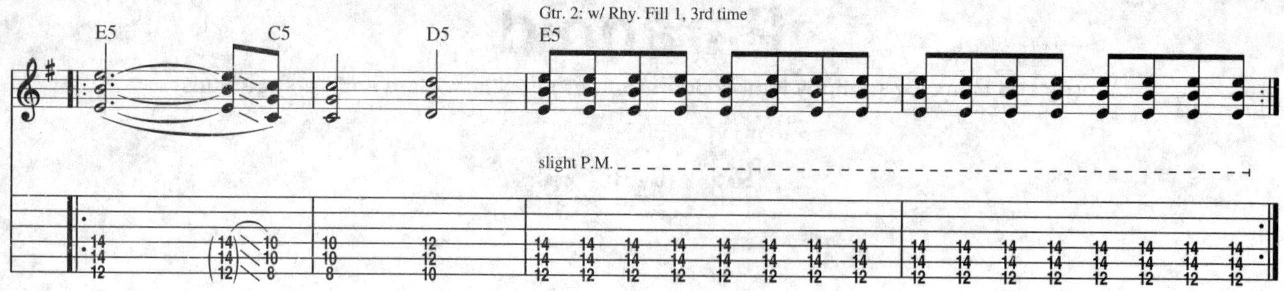
Gtr. 2: w/ Rhy. Fill 1, 3rd time
E5
C5
D5
E5
slight P.M.

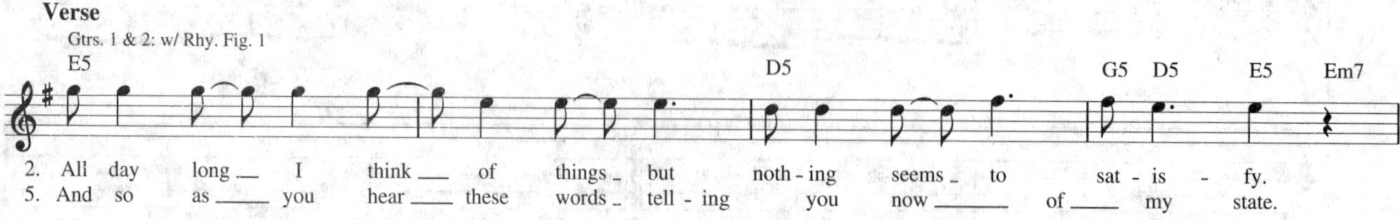
Verse
Gtrs. 1 & 2: w/ Rhy. Fig. 1
E5
D5
G5 D5
E5
Em7
2. All day long I think of things but noth-ing seems to sat-is-fy.
5. And so as you hear these words tell-ing you now of my state.

To Coda
E5
D5
G5 D5
E5
Think I'll lose my mind if I don't find some-thing to pass it by.
I tell you to en-joy life, I wish I could but it's too late.

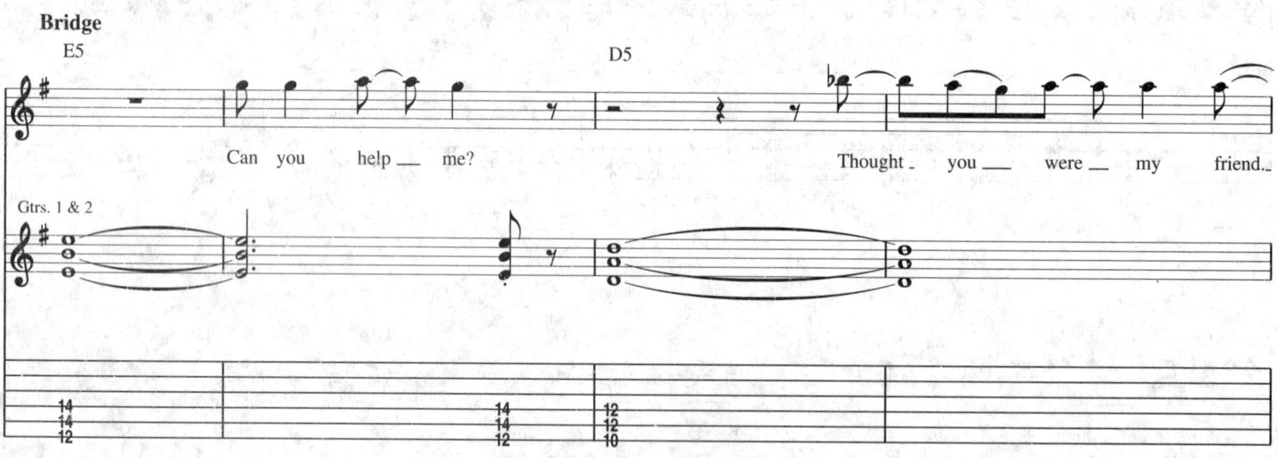
Bridge
E5
D5
Can you help me? Thought you were my friend.
Gtrs. 1 & 2

Rhy. Fill 1
Gtr. 2
P.M.
TAB

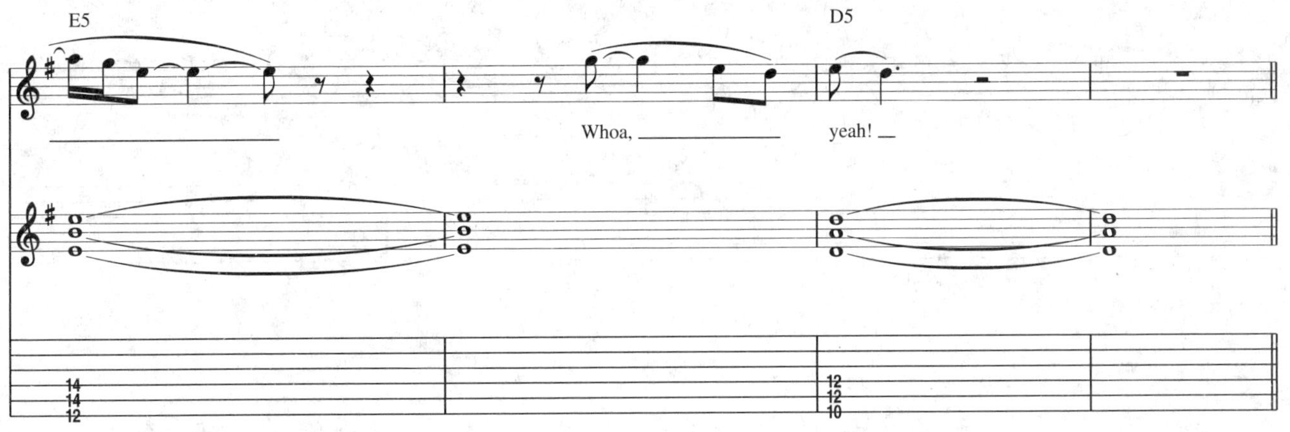

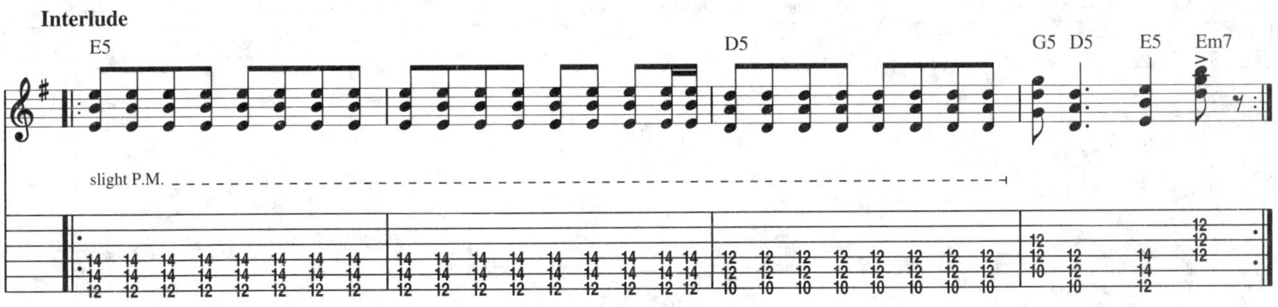

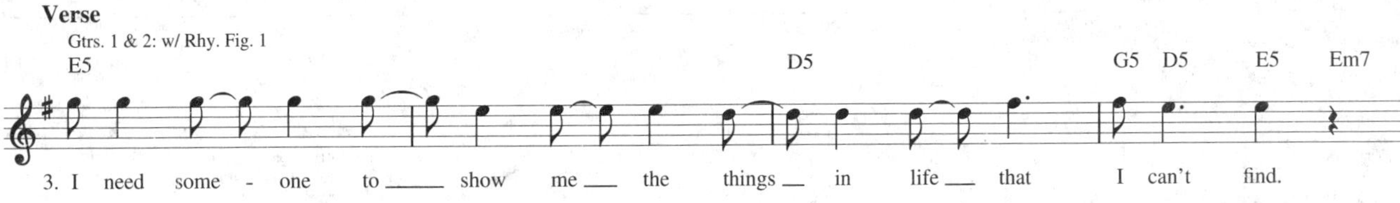

*With heavily distorted ring modulation effect in right channel.

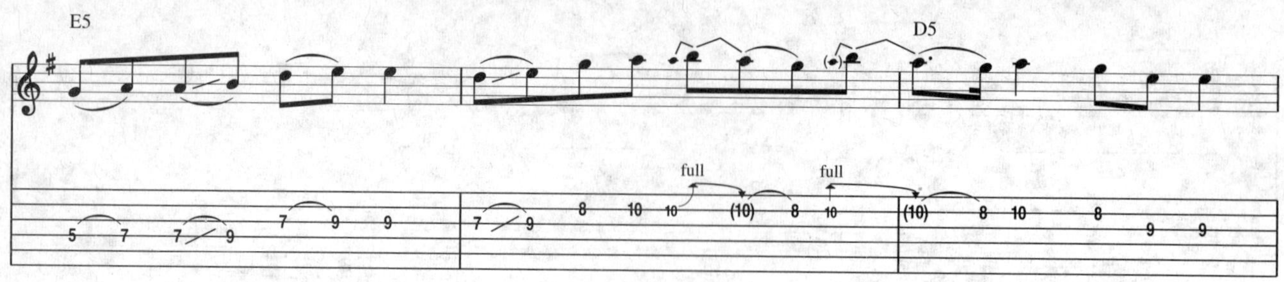
E5
D5
full
full

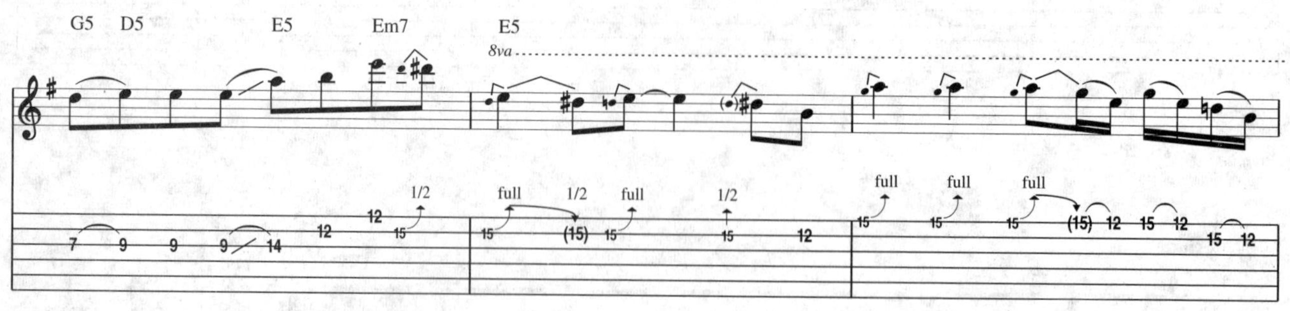
G5 D5 E5 Em7
E5
8va
1/2
full 1/2 full 1/2
full full full

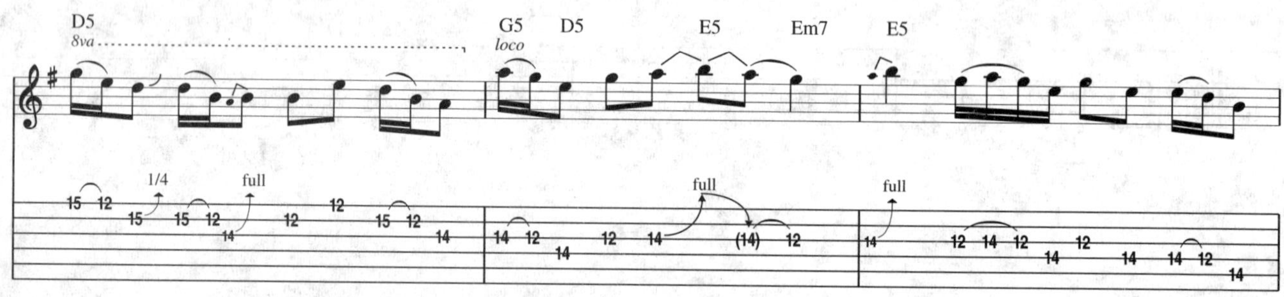
D5
8va
G5 D5 E5 Em7 E5
loco
1/4 full
full
full

Interlude
D.S. al Coda
Gtrs. 1 & 2: w/ Rhy. Fig. 1,
1st 4 meas., 2 times
D5
G5 D5 E5 Em7
8

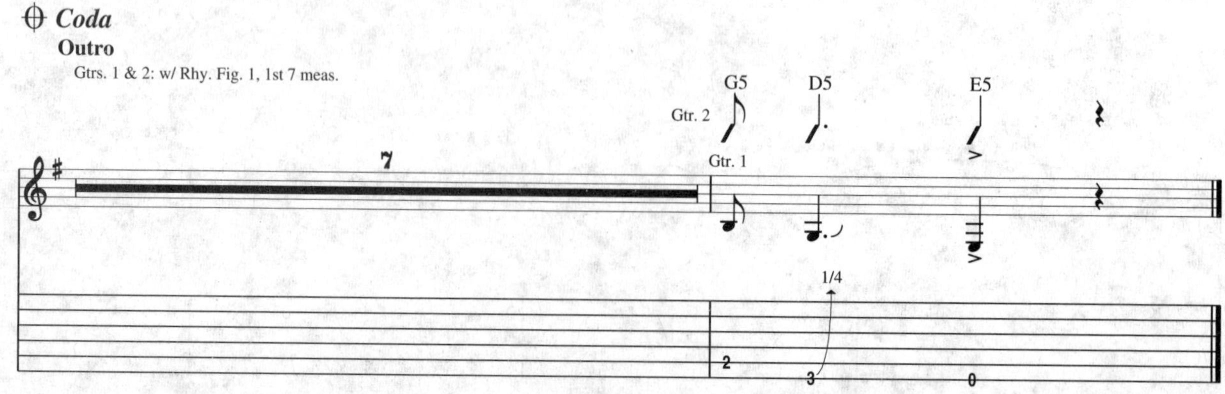
Coda
Outro
Gtrs. 1 & 2: w/ Rhy. Fig. 1, 1st 7 meas.
G5 D5 E5
Gtr. 2
Gtr. 1
7
1/4

Piece of My Heart

Words and Music by Bert Berns and Jerry Ragovoy

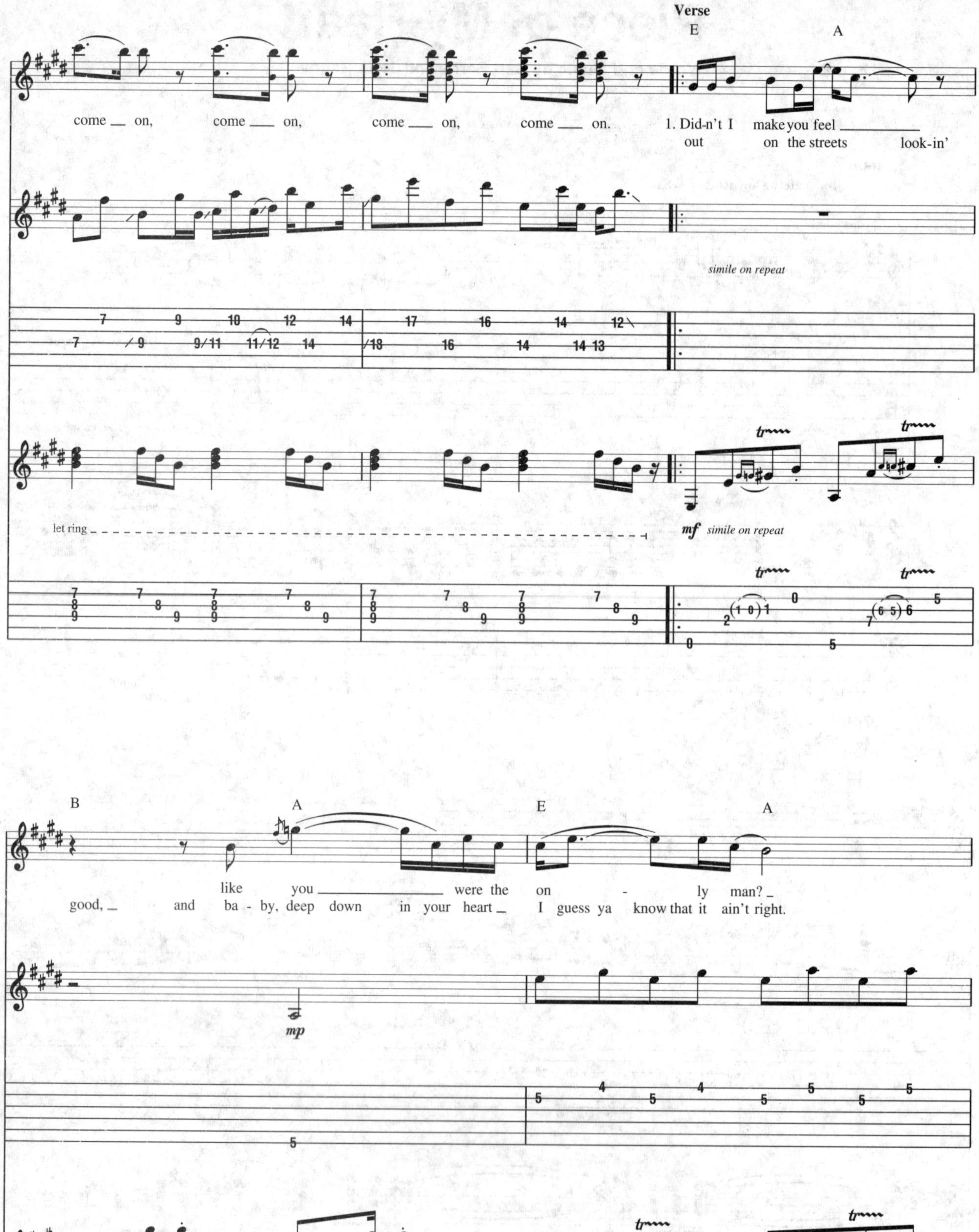

come __ on, come __ on, come __ on, come __ on.

Verse

E A

1. Did-n't I make you feel ____________
out on the streets look-in'

simile on repeat

let ring

mf *simile on repeat*

B A E A

Well, yeah, and did - n't I give you near - ly ev - 'ry-thing that a wom-an
Now, but now, but now, but now, but now, but now, but hear me when I cry at night.

tr tr

7 7 7 7 7 8 8 9 9 5 5 5 5 6 6 7 7 7 5
5 4 5 4 5 5 5 5

7 7 7 7 8 8 9 9 7 5 5 5 5 6 6 7 7 5
tr tr (1 0) 1 0 2 0 (6 5) 6 7 5 5

Pre-Chorus

B C♯m

3 3

pos - si - bly can? Hon - ey, you know I did. And each time I tell my - self that I,
Babe, and I cry all the time. But each time I tell my - self that I,
(Oh.

mf

f

B

D

when I think I've had e - nough. _ Oh, but I'm ___ gon - na show ya, ba - by, _____ that a

when I can't stand the pain. ___ But, when you hold me in ___ your arms, __________ I'm

___ Oh. ___________________________________

B

wom - an ___ can be tough. _ I want you to } come _____ on, come ______ on,

sing - ing once a - gain. ______________ I said

____)

let ring ------------------------------------

Chorus

E A B A

Voc. Fig. 1

come __ on, come ___ on {and / yeah} take it. Take an-oth-er lit-tle piece of my heart, _ now, ba - by. _____
(Take it. Oh, ______

Rhy. Fig. 1

f

P.M.

Rhy. Fig. 1A

let ring

let ring

E A B A

break it. Break an - oth - er lit - tle bit off my heart, __ now, dar - lin' yeah, ____ yeah, yeah, yeah. _
Oh, _________

P.M.

let ring

E A B B♭ A

End Voc. Fig. 1

have a...) Have an-oth-er lit-tle piece of my heart, __ now, ba - by. __ Well, you know you got _ it if it

End Rhy. Fig. 1

P.M.

End Rhy. Fig. 1A

1.

E F♯m E E A B A

makes you feel good, _ oh, yes in - deed. _ 2. You're

2.
Guitar Solo
F#m
A
B
F#m
8va
full
1 1/2
1/2
1/4
w/ bar
-1

A
B
C♯m
8va
loco
w/ bar
B
D
B
I need you to
come on, come on, come on, come on and
let ring

Chorus

E A B B♭

Have an - oth - er lit - tle piece of my heart, now, ba - by.

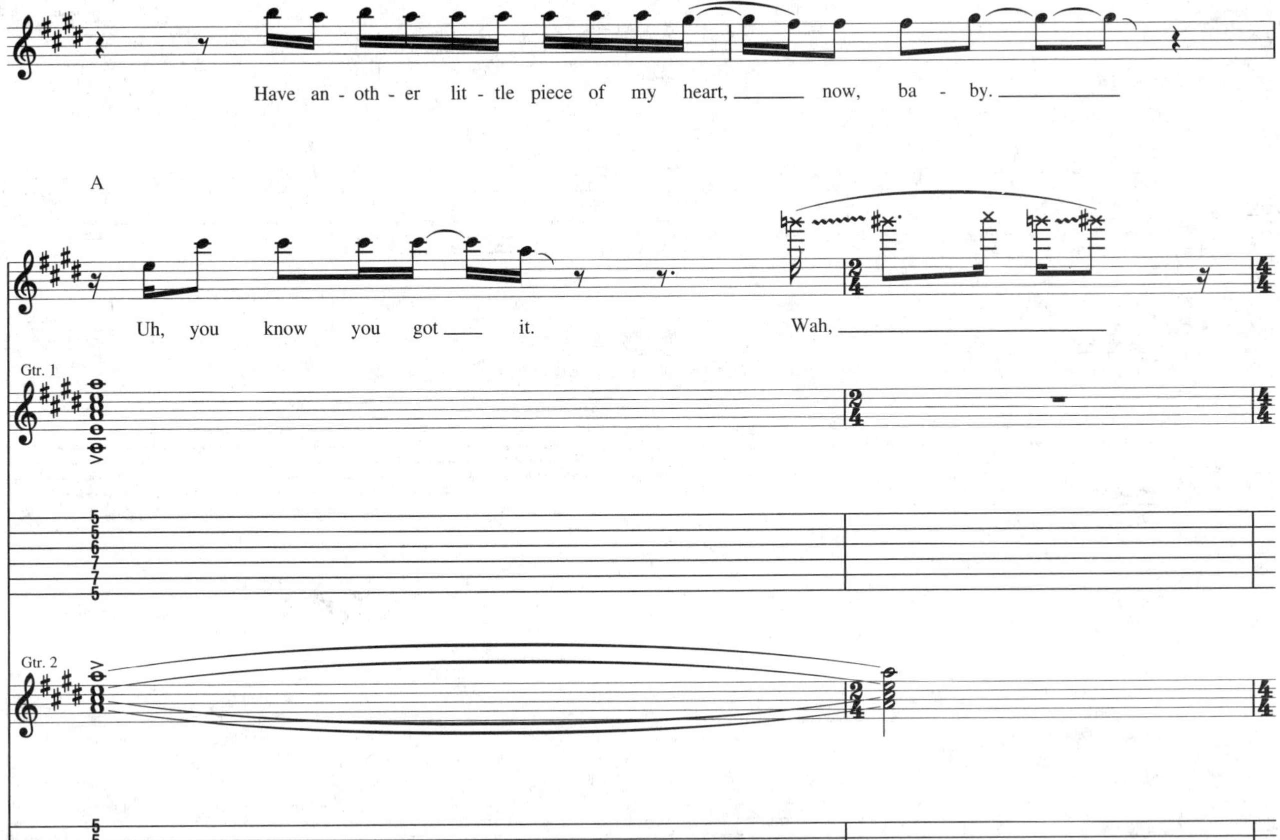

E
A
B
A
Break an - oth - er lit - tle bit off my heart, now, dar - lin', yeah, yeah, yeah.

E
A
B
B♭
Have an - oth - er lit - tle piece of my heart, now, ba - by.

A
E F♯mE
F♯m
Well, you know you got it, sure e-nough, it makes you feel good.
(...makes you feel good.)
Gtr. 1
grad. bend
full
Gtr. 2

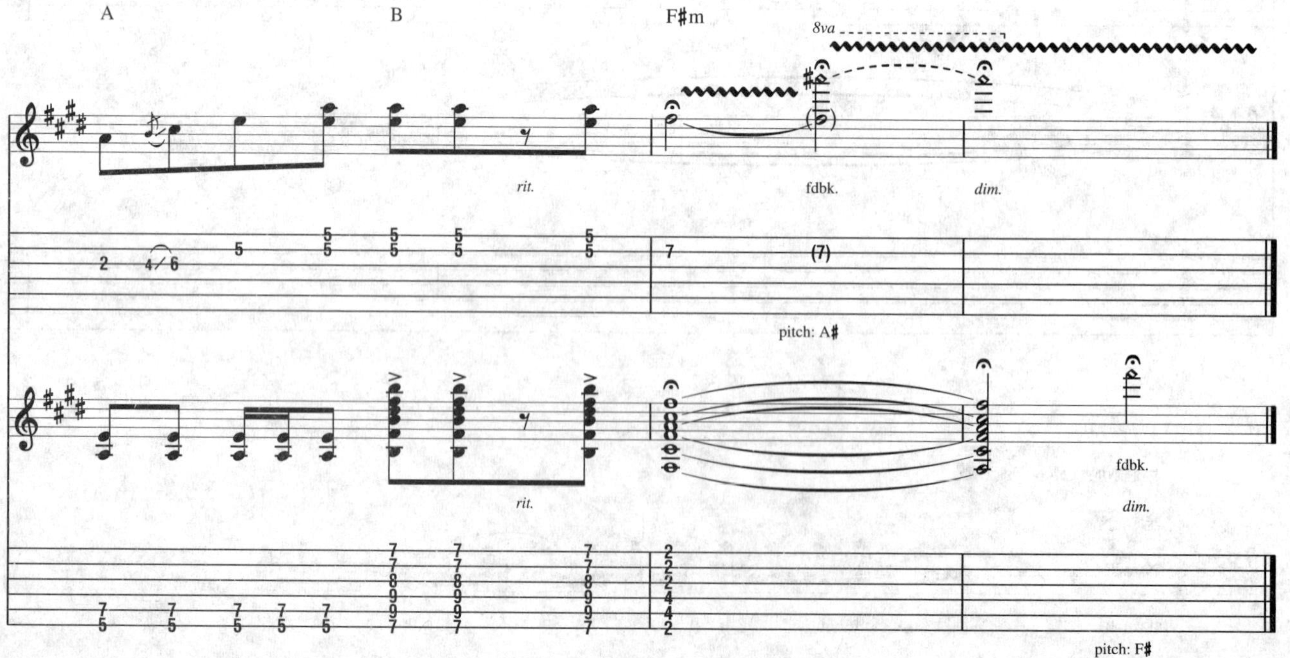
A
B
F♯m
8va
rit.
fdbk.
dim.
pitch: A♯
rit.
fdbk.
dim.
pitch: F♯

Pretty Fly (For a White Guy)

Words and Music by Dexter Holland

Chorus
B5 E#5 F#5 E#5 F#5 B5 E#5 F#5 E#5 F#5
don't de - bate. (He's a) play - er straight.
Gtr. 1
Rhy. Fig. 4
D5 A5 D5 E5 D5 A5 B5 E#5 F#5 E#5 F#5
You know he real - ly does - n't get it an - y - way. (He's) gon - na play the field and
End Rhy. Fig. 4
B5 E#5 F#5 E#5 F#5 D5 A5 D5 E5 D5/E E5 F5 E5 D5
keep it real. For you no way, for you no way. So if
Gtr. 1: w/ Rhy. Fig. 4
B5 E#5 F#5 E#5 F#5 B5 E#5 F#5 E#5 F#5
you don't rate, just o - ver - com - pen - sate. At least a
D5 A5 D5 E5 D5 A5
To Coda 2
you - 'll know you can al - ways go on Rik - ki Lake.

To Coda 1
Bridge
G5 D5 G5 A5 N.C.(E5) A5 B5 F#5 F5 E5 D5 E5 B5 N.C.
The world {needs / loves} wan - na be's, so hey, hey, do that brand new thing.
Gtr. 1
Interlude
Gtr. 1: w/ Rhy. Fig. 1, 3 times
B5 F#5 A5 B5 E5 D5 B5 F#5 A5
Give it to me, ba - by. Uh, huh, uh, huh. Give it to me, ba - by.
Gtr. 1: w/ Rhy. Fig. 2
D.S. al Coda
B5 E5 D5 B5 F#5 A5 B5 N.C.
Uh, huh, uh, huh. And all the girl - ies say I'm pret - ty fly... 2. He
(For a white guy.)
Coda 1
Verse
B5 N.C. (B5)
thing. 3. Now he's get - tin' a tat - too, yeah, he's get - tin' ink done. He
B5 A5
asked for a thir - teen but they drew a thir - ty - one. Friends say he's try - ing too hard and he's

B5
A5
B5
A5
B5
not quite hip but in his own mind he's the, he's the dop - est trip.
let ring
P.S.
Interlude
Gtr. 1: w/ Rhy. Fig. 1, 3 times
B5
F#5
A5
B5
E5
D5
B5
F#5
A5
Give it to me, ba - by. Uh, huh, uh, huh. Give it to me, ba - by.
D.S.S. al Coda 2
B5
E5
D5
B5
N.C.
B5
E5
D5
Uh, huh, uh, huh. U - no, dos, tres, quat - ro, cin - co, cin - co, seis.
So
Gtr. 1
Coda 2
Bridge
G5
D5
G5
A5
N.C.(E5) A5
G5
D5
G5
A5
N.C.(E5) A5
The world needs wan-na be's, ah. The world loves wan-na be's, ah.
Gtr. 1
G5
D5
G5
A5
N.C.(E5) A5
B5
F#5
F5
E5
D5
E5
B5
N.C.
(So) let's get some more wan-na be's and hey, hey, do that brand new thing.

Radar Love

Words and Music by George Kooymans and Barry Hay

Pre-Chorus
* E5
Voc. Fig. 1
B5
F#5
When she is lone - ly and the long - ing gets too much,
(Oo,
Gtr. 1
Rhy. Fig. 1
* Chord symbols reflect basic tonality.
E5
B5
A5/B
B5/C#
she sends a ca - ble com - ing in from a - bove.
oo.
let ring
C#5
B5/C#
Chorus
D
A5
End Voc. Fig. 1
Don't need a phone at all.
Ah.
)
We've got a thing, and that's a -
Gtr. 2 (slight dist.)
w/ slide
End Rhy. Fig. 1
Rhy. Fig. 2
Gtr. 1
let ring

* Lead Voc. dbld. one octave lower, next 16 meas.

Gtr. 1: w/ Riff B
Bren - da Lee ___ com - in' on strong. ___ The
road has got ___ me hyp - no - tized, ___ and I'm
Gtr. 1
14
14
16 14 16 16 14
16 14 16 16 14
(14)
(14)

spin - nin' in - to ___ a new ___ sun - rise. ___
2
2
4 2 4 4 2
4 2 4 4 2

Pre-Chorus
Bkgd. Voc.: w/ Voc. Fig. 1
Gtr. 1: w/ Rhy. Fig. 1, simile
E5
B5
When I ___ get lone - ly and I'm for sure I've had e - nough, _

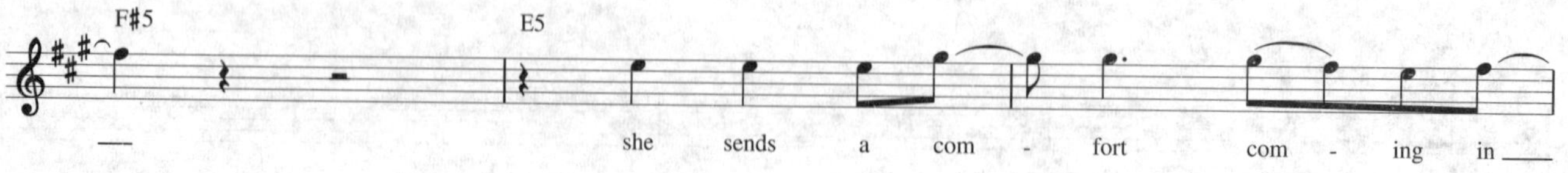
F#5
E5
— she sends a com - fort com - ing in ___

To Coda
B5
A5/B
B5/C#
C#5
B5/C#
— from a - bove. ___ We don't need no let - ter at all. ___

Chorus
Gtr. 1: w/ Rhy. Fig. 2
D
A5
E5
F#5
We've got a thing that's called ra - dar love.
Gtr. 2
D
A5
E5
N.C.
We've got a light in the sky. Ra - dar
Interlude
Gtrs. 1 & 2 tacet
(F#m7)
(bass & drums)
(bass, drums & synth.)
love.
Gtr. 3
(slight dist.)
* F#m7
play 3 times
** mf
simile on repeats
* Chord symbols reflect overall tonality.
** played mp on repeats

let ring
hold bend
full
full
hold bend
* w/ delay
full
w/o delay
* set for 1 sec.
full
full
** w/ delay
** Set for 1/2 sec., gradually decreasing delay time to zero.
let ring
let ring

8va
full
full
full

C♯5
loco
Gtr. 4
8va
w/ pick & fingers
w/ pick
1/2
1/2
full
1/2
Gtr. 1

Breakdown
Gtrs. 1 & 4 tacet
N.C.
(drums)
N.C.
Riff C
Gtrs. 1 & 4
End Riff C

Gtr. 4: w/ Riff C, 2 times
Gtr. 1
Gtrs. 1 & 4

Interlude
Gtrs. 1 & 4 tacet
N.C.(F#m7)
(bass)
Woo!
Verse
N.C.(F#m7)
3. No more speed, I'm al - most there.
Gtr. 2
mf
Gtr. 1
mf
full
full
Got - ta keep cool, now, got - ta take care.

Last car to pass, here I go!
And the line of cars drove
down real slow, whoa.
And the ra - di - o played that for -
* w/ delay
w/o delay
1 1/2
* set for 1 sec.
got - ten song.
Bren - da Lee, it's com-in' on strong.
full
full
full

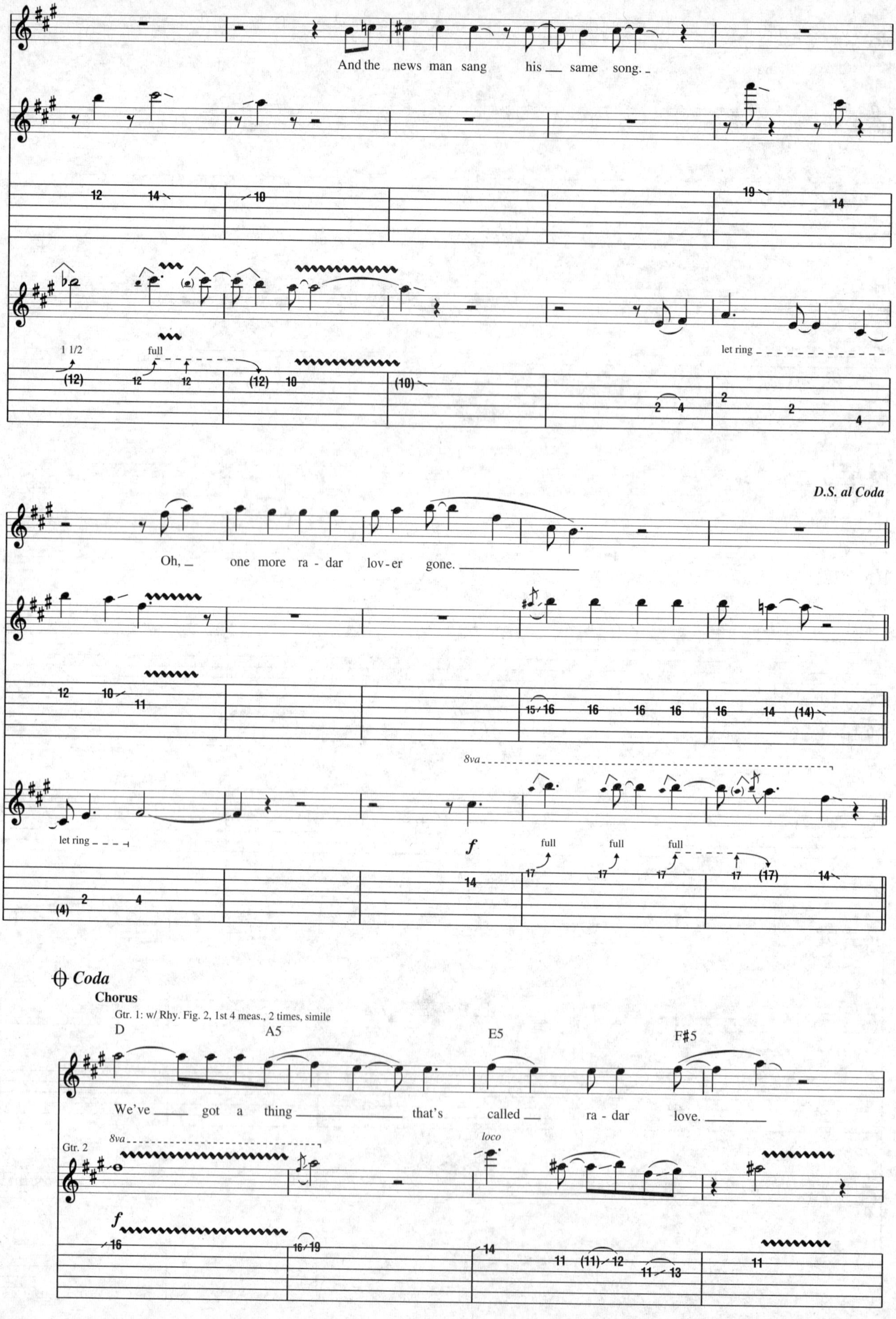

And the news man sang his __ same song. _

1 1/2 full

let ring

D.S. al Coda

Oh, _ one more ra - dar lov - er gone. ___

8va

let ring

f

full full full

𝄌 *Coda*

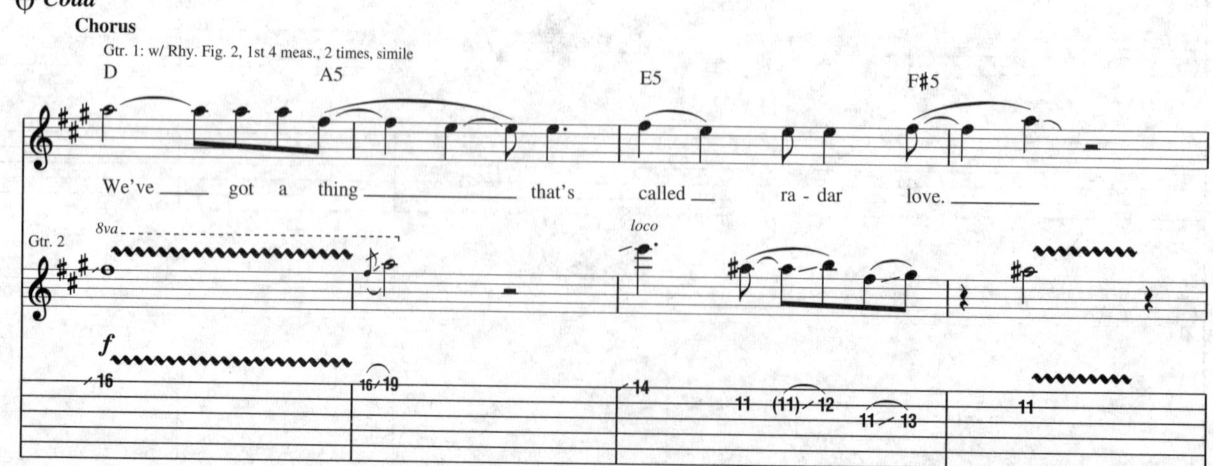

D
A5
E5
F♯5
We've got a light in the sky.
Gtr. 1: w/ Rhy. Fig. 2, simile
We've got a thing that's called a ra - dar love.
8va
We've got a thing that's called ra - dar love.
Gtr. 2 tacet
N.C.
Interlude
(F♯m7)
loco
Outro
F♯m7
(bass & drums)
Gtr. 1
mp
cresc.
play 4 times
f

Ramblin' Man

Words and Music by Dickey Betts

*Tune Up 1/2 Step:

① = E♯ ④ = D♯

② = B♯ ⑤ = A♯

③ = G♯ ⑥ = E♯

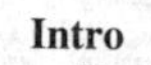

Intro

Fast Rock ♩ = 184

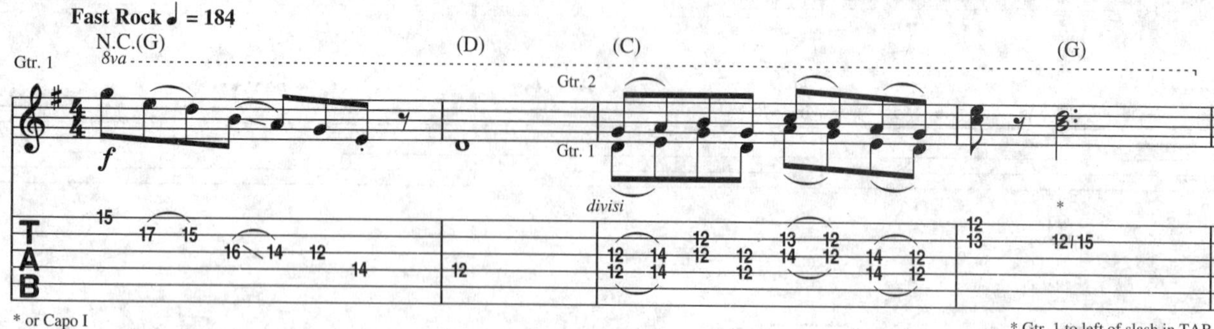

* or Capo I

* Gtr. 1 to left of slash in TAB.

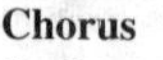

Chorus

Gtr. 2 tacet

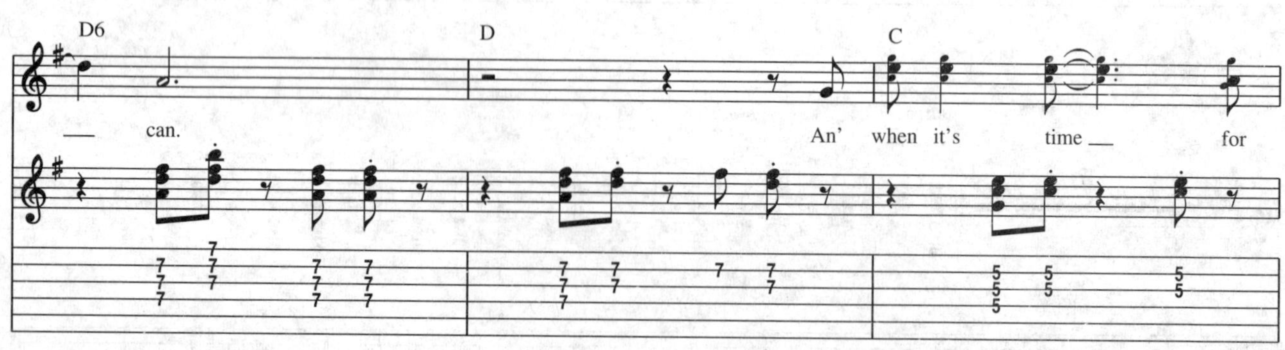

G
Em
C
leav - in' I hope you'll un - der - stand,
G
D6
G
that I was born a ram - blin' man.
End Rhy. Fig. 1
Verse
G
C6
1. Well, my fath - er was a gam - bler down in
2. on my way to New Or - leans this
mf
G
Geor - gia, and he wound up on the wrong
morn - in', and leav - in' out of
C6
D6
D
end of a gun. And
Nash - ville, Ten - nes - see. They're

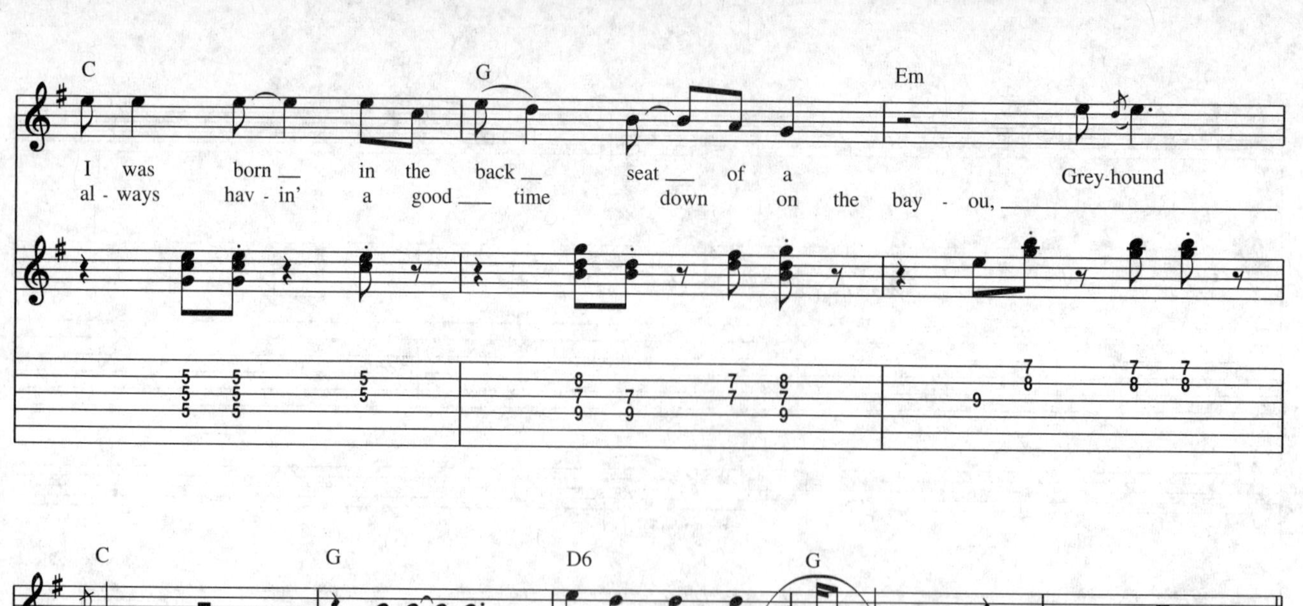

Chorus

Gtr. 1: w/Rhy. Fig. 1, simile

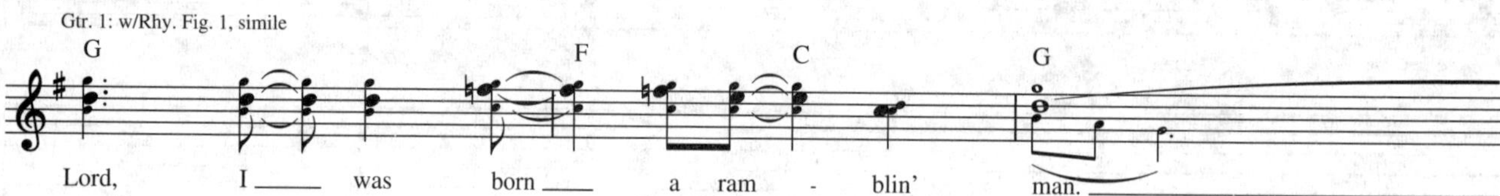

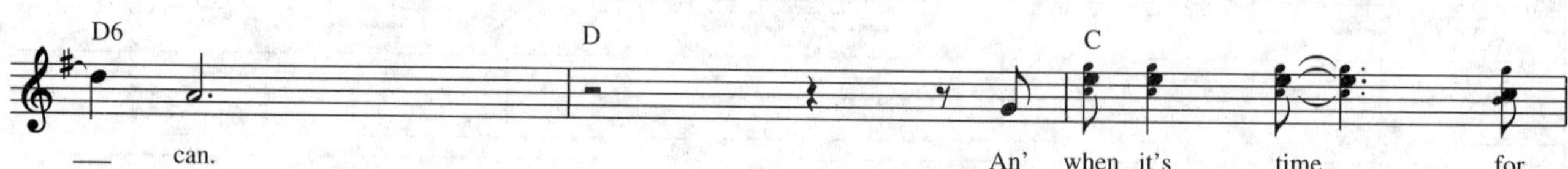

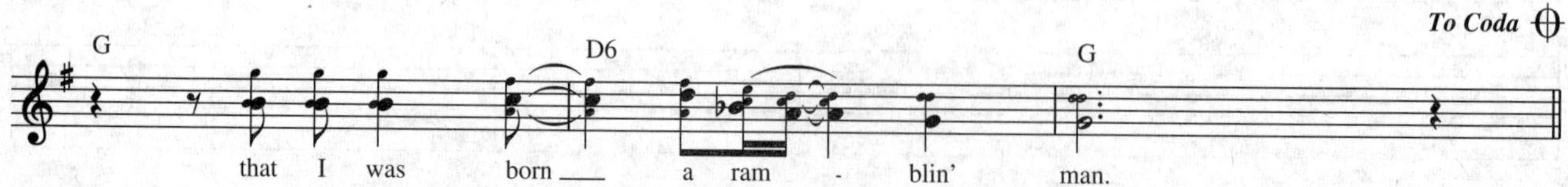

Interlude
Gtr. 2
D
N.C.
8va
loco
Piano
Gtr. 1
Gtr.1
divisi
Guitar Solo
Gtrs. 1 & 2 tacet
G
C
G
Gtr. 3
full
Al - right!
C
D
C
G
Em
C
1/2
D.S. al Coda
G
D
G
loco
2. I'm

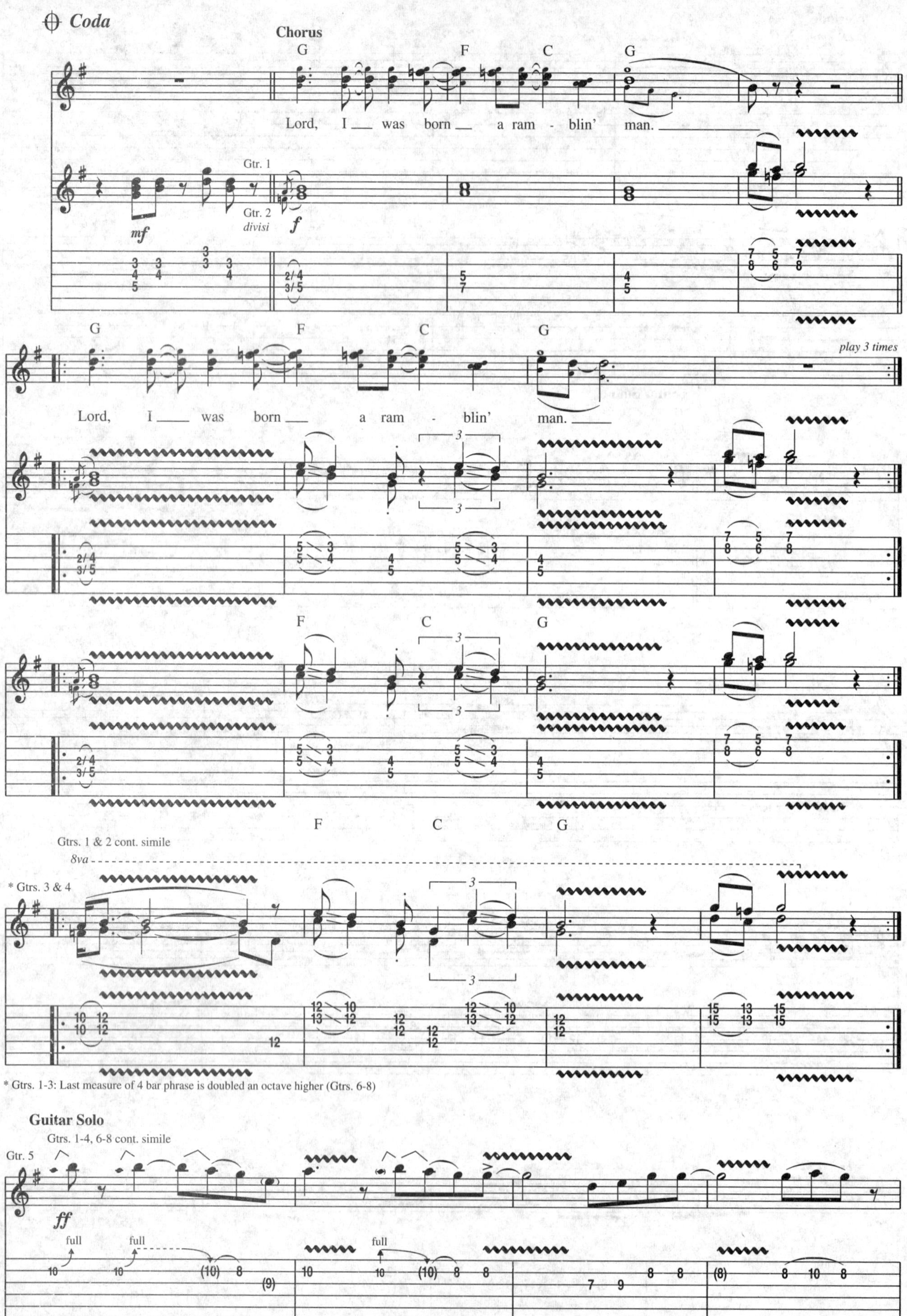

* Gtrs. 1-3: Last measure of 4 bar phrase is doubled an octave higher (Gtrs. 6-8)

F
C
G
full
(let bends ring à la pedal steel guitar)

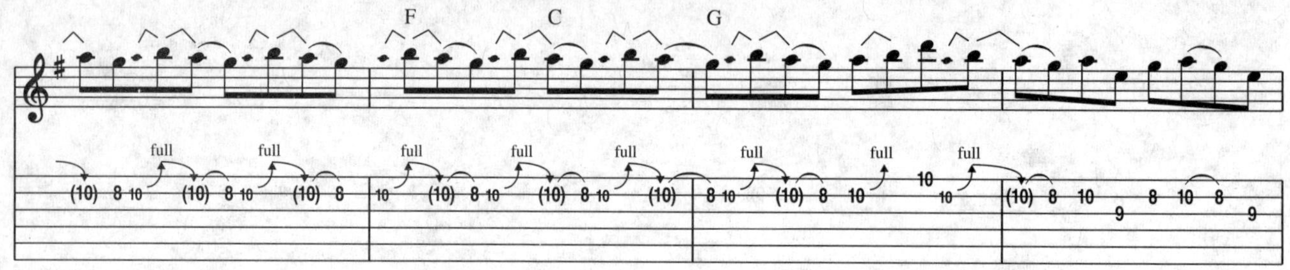
F
C
G
full
full
full
full
full
full
full
full
(10) 8 10 (10) 8 10 (10) 8
10 (10) 8 10 (10) 8 10 (10)
8 10 (10) 8 10 10 10
(10) 8 10 9 8 10 8 9

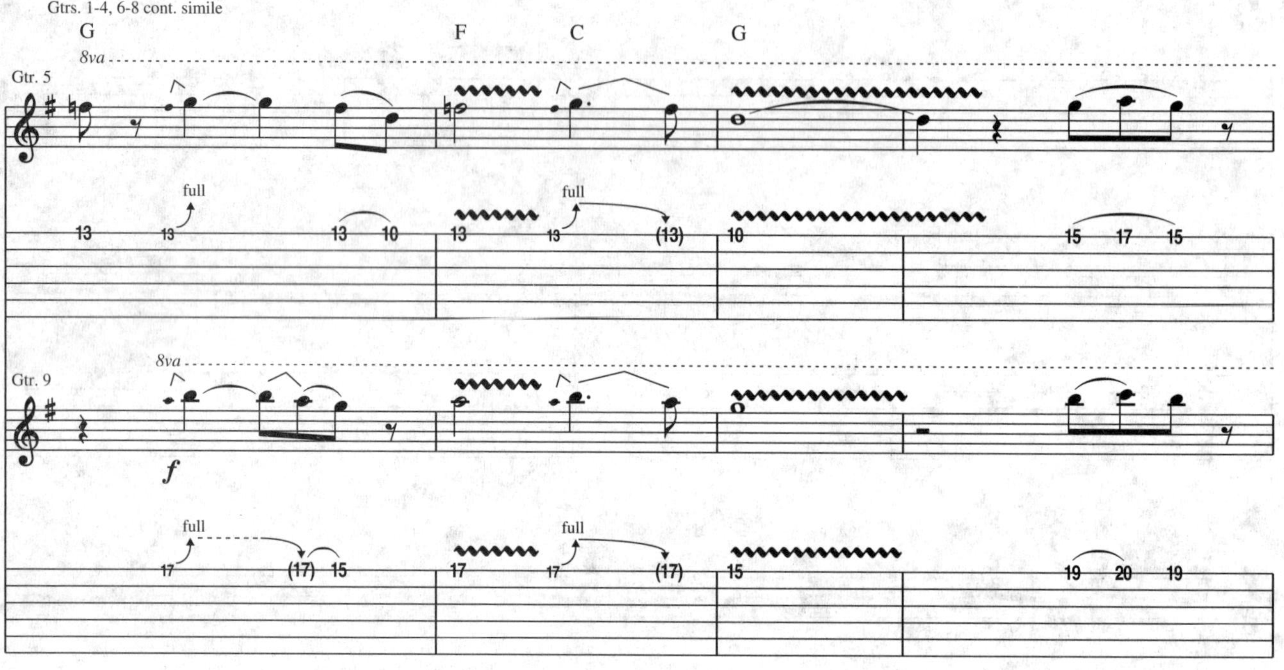
Gtrs. 1-4, 6-8 cont. simile
G
F
C
G
8va
Gtr. 5
full
13 13 13 10
full
13 13 (13)
10
15 17 15
8va
Gtr. 9
f
full
17 (17) 15
full
17 17 (17)
15
19 20 19

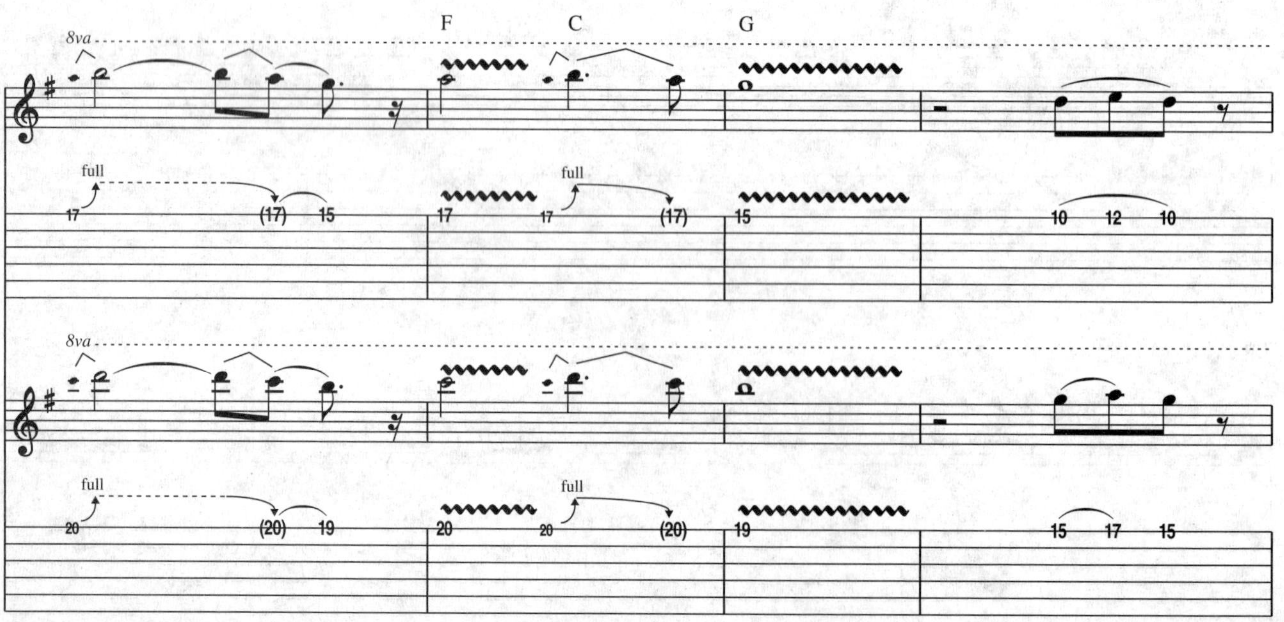
F
C
G
8va
full
17 (17) 15
full
17 17 (17)
15
10 12 10
8va
full
20 (20) 19
full
20 20 (20)
19
15 17 15

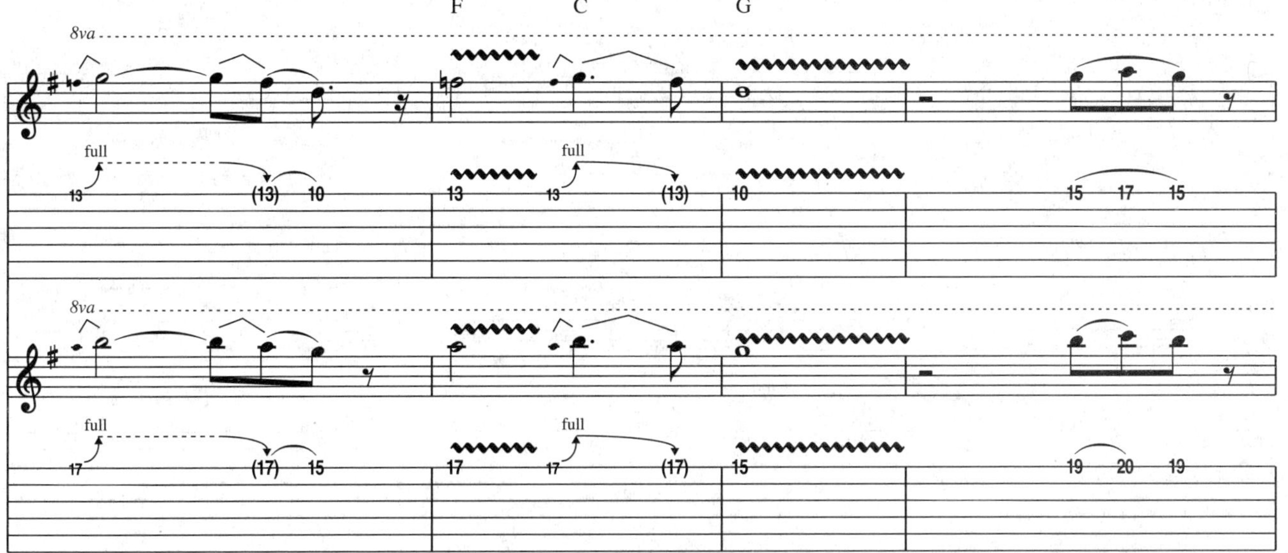
F
C
G
8va
full
full
8va
full
full

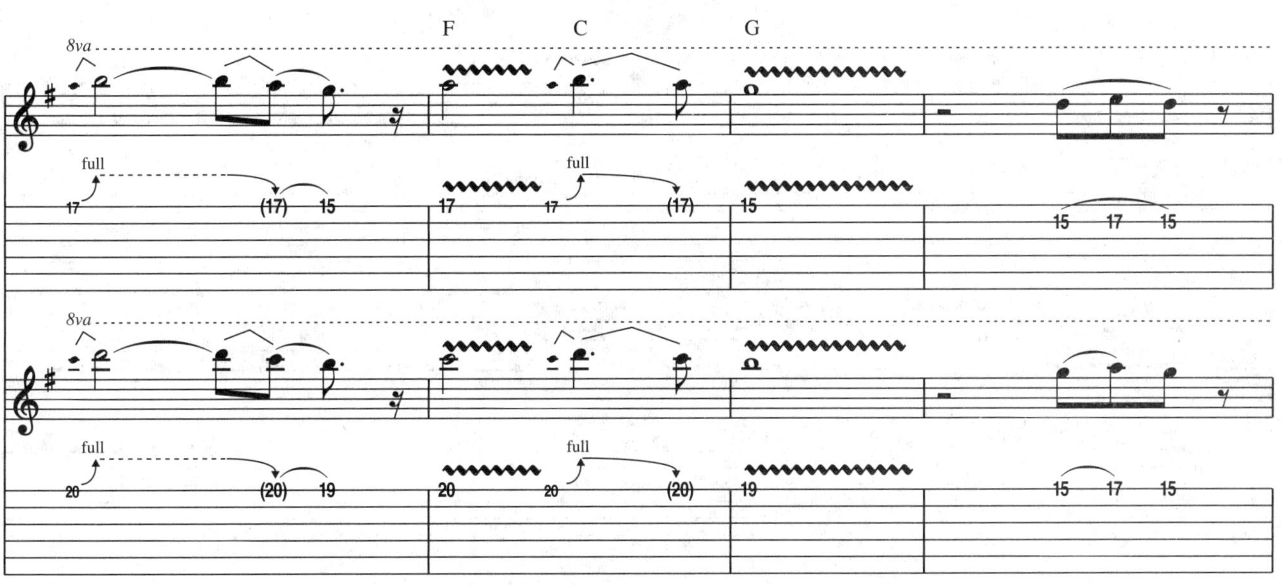
F
C
G
8va
full
full
8va
full
full

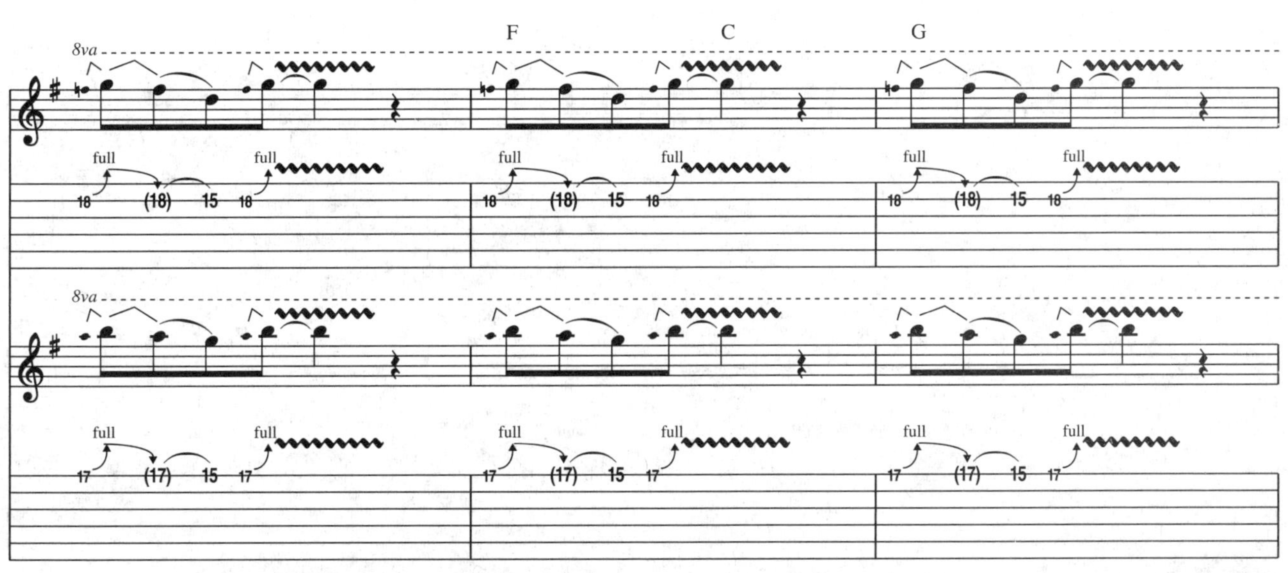
F
C
G
8va
full
full
full
full
full
full
8va
full
full
full
full
full
full

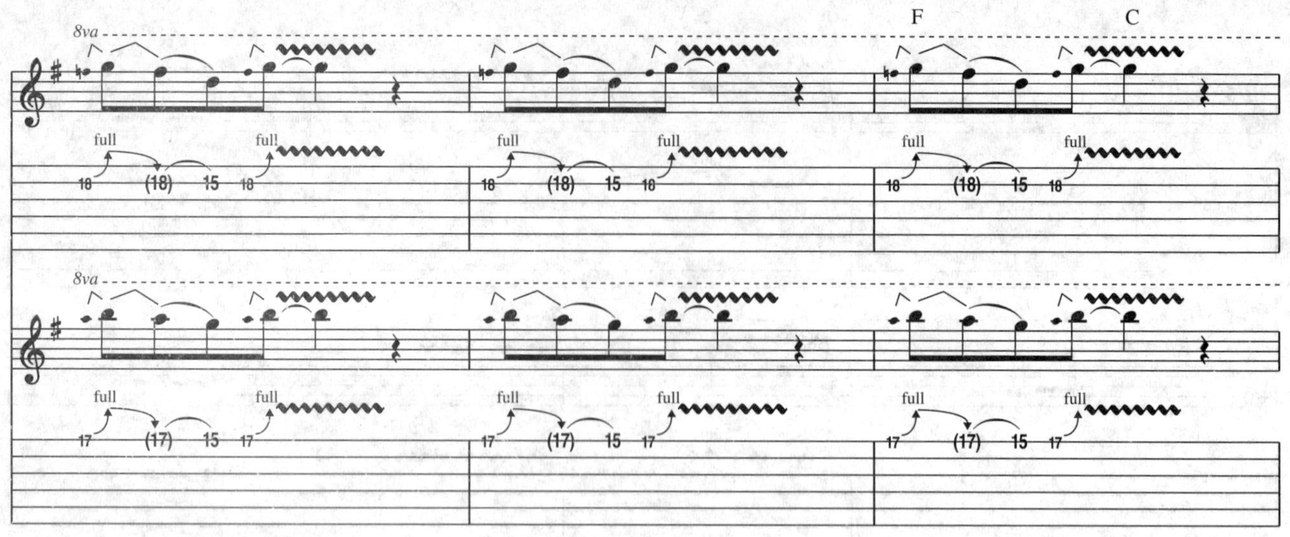
F
C
8va
full
18
(18)
15
17
(17)

G
8va
full
18
(18)
15
17
(17)

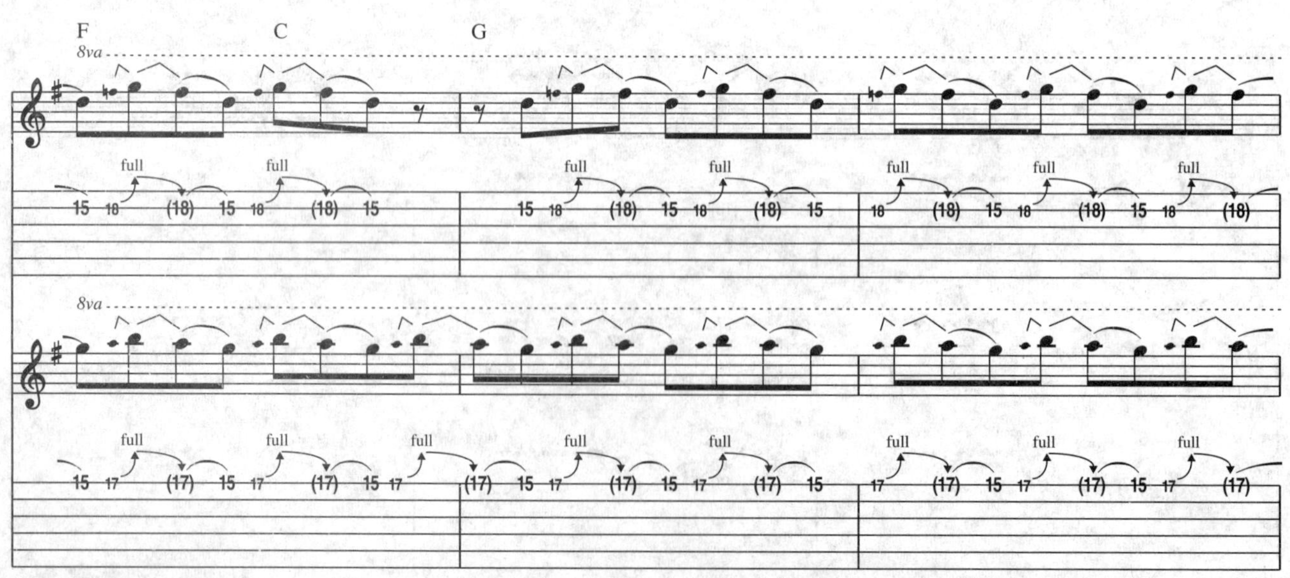
F
C
G
8va
full
18
(18)
15
17
(17)

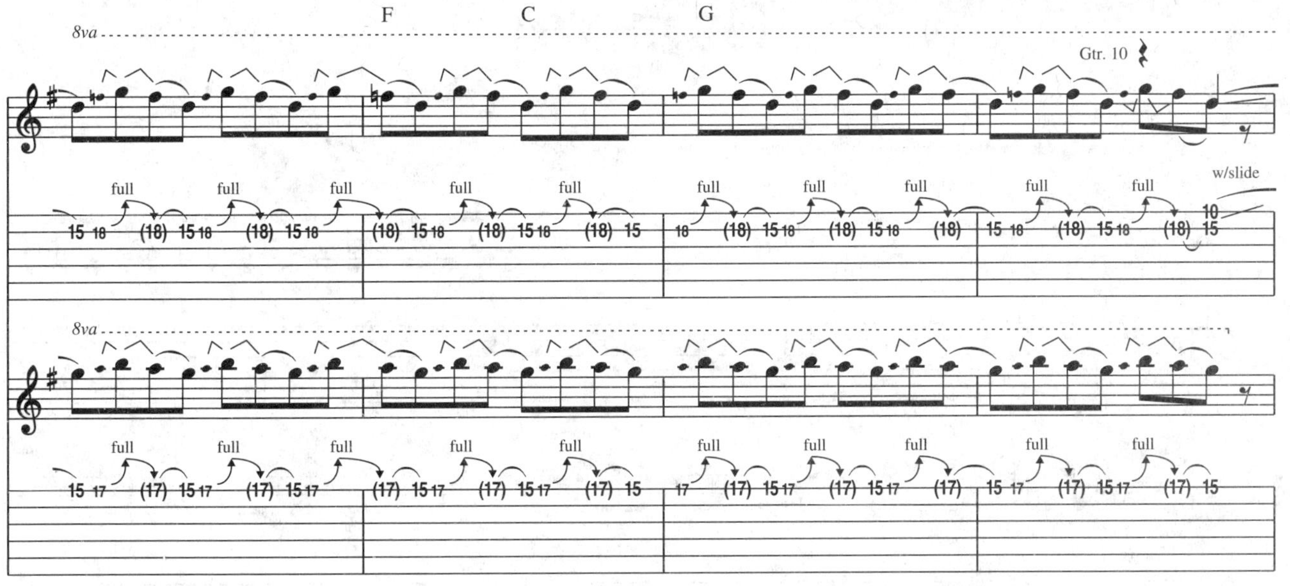

Gtrs. 5 & 9 tacet
(Gtrs. 1-4, 6-8 cont. simile)

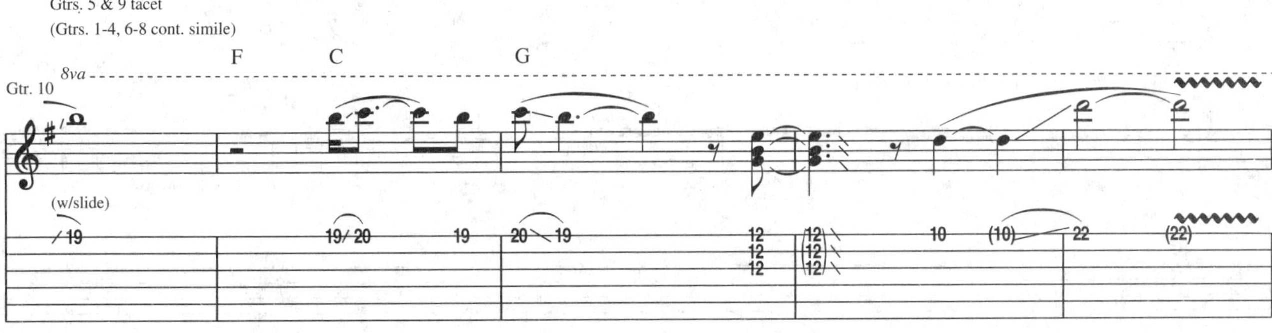

Begin Fade

Fade Out

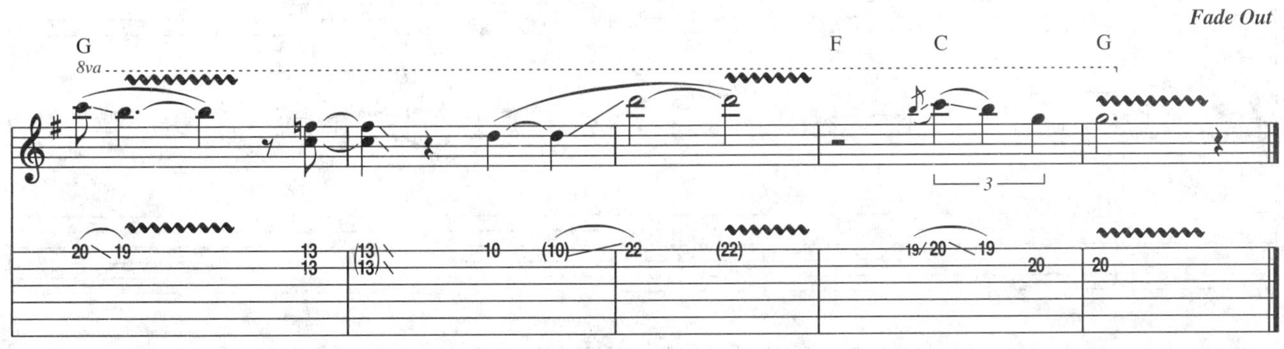

Ramrod

By Al Casey

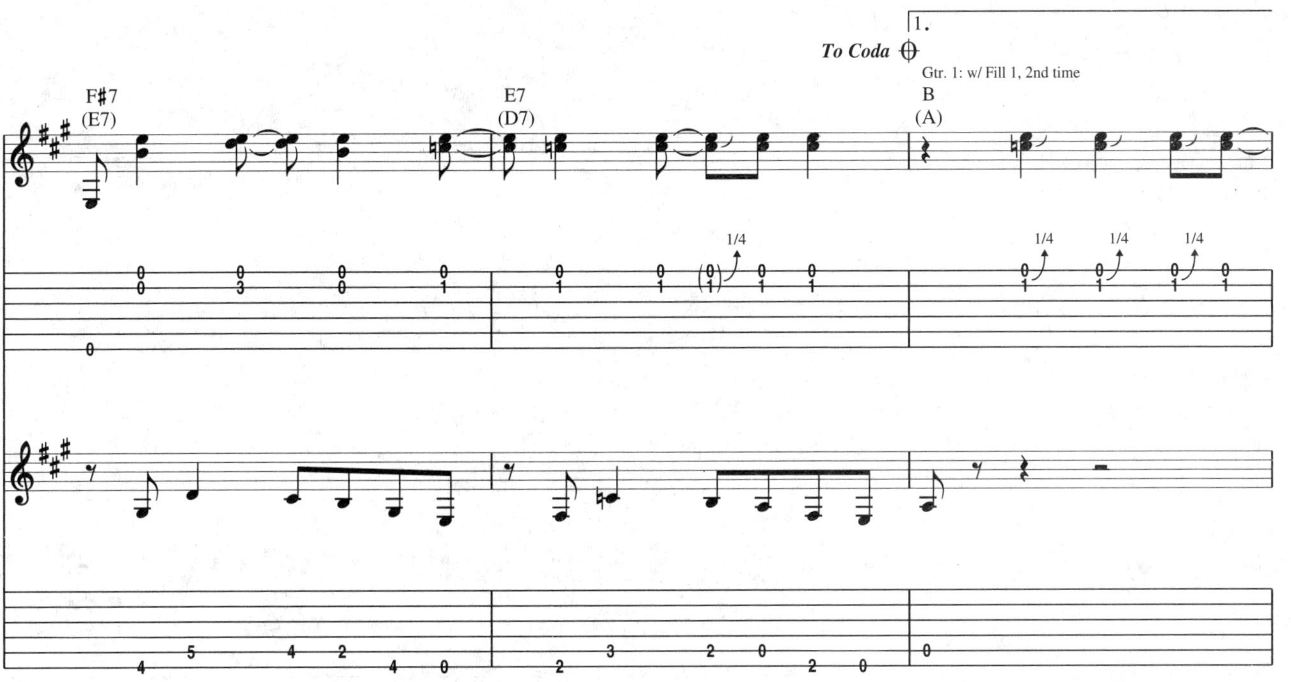

To Coda
1.
Gtr. 1: w/ Fill 1, 2nd time
F#7
(E7)
E7
(D7)
B
(A)
1/4

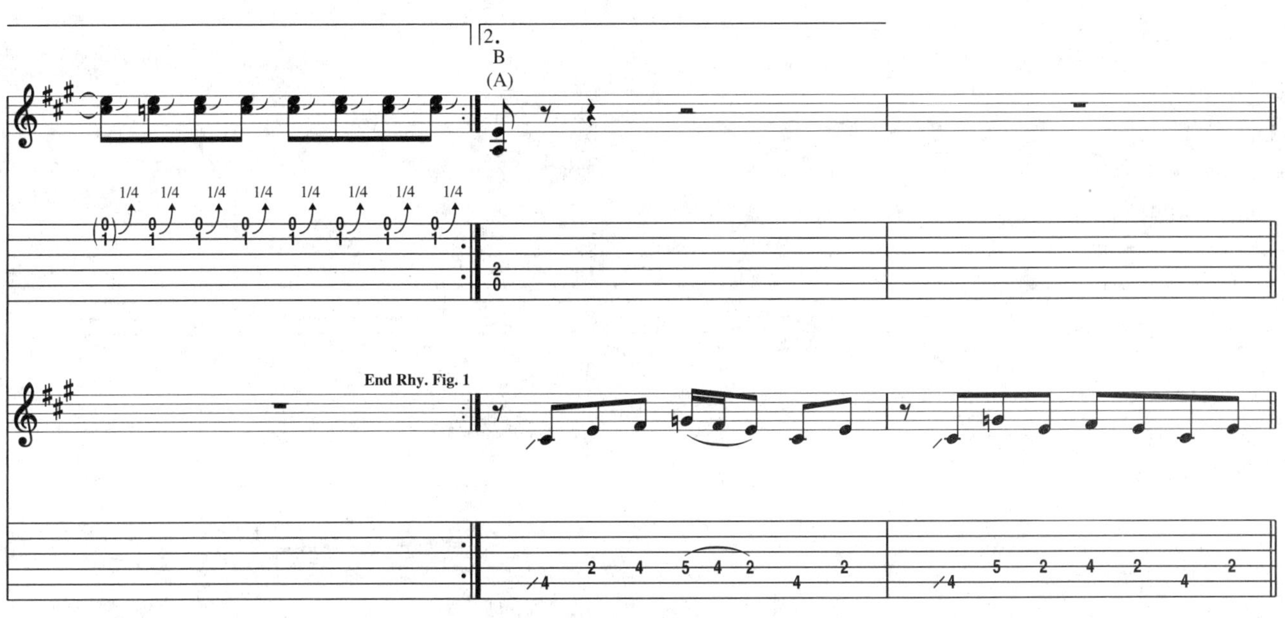

2.
B
(A)
1/4
End Rhy. Fig. 1

Fill 1
Gtr. 1
T
A
B

C
Gtr. 2: w/ Rhy. Fig. 1, simile
B7
(A7)
Gtr. 1

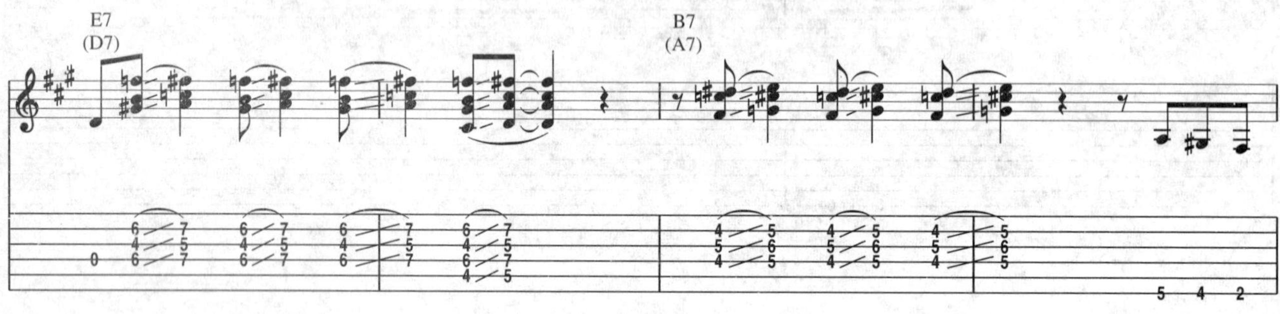
E7
(D7)
B7
(A7)

D.S. al Coda
(take repeat)
F#7
(E7)
E7
(D7)
B
(A)
1/4

Coda
Gtr. 1
rit.
1/2
Gtr. 2
rit.

Rebel, Rebel

Words and Music by David Bowie

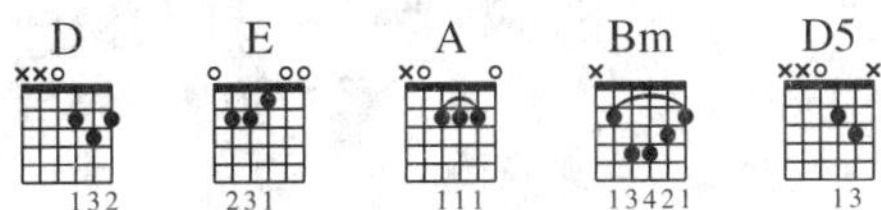

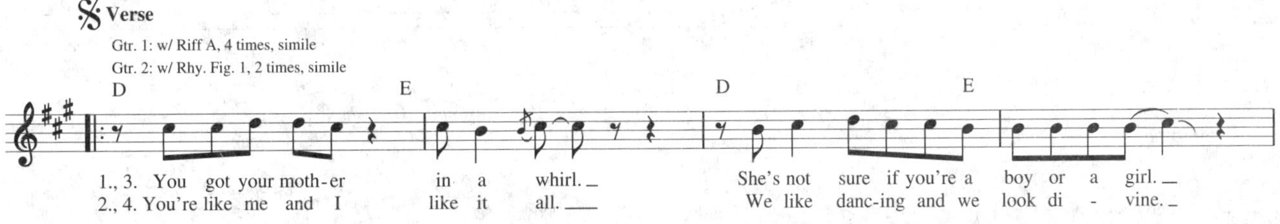

1., 3.
2., 4.
D
E
Hey, babe your hair's al - right.
Hey babe, let's go / stay out to - night.
You love bands when they're play-ing hard.
You want more and you want it fast.
Pre-Chorus
A
D
Bm
Gtr. 2
simile on repeat
They put you down, they say I'm wrong.
You tack - y thing, you put them on.
Gtr. 1
let ring
slight P.M.
Chorus
Gtr. 1: w/ Riff A, 2 times, simile
Gtr. 2: w/ Rhy. Fig. 1, 1 1/2 times
Re - bel, Re - bel, you've torn your dress.
Re - bel, Re - bel, your face in a mess.
Re - bel, Re - bel, how could they know?
Hot tramp, I love you so.
grad. bend
1/2
Interlude
Gtr. 2 tacet
(3rd time) To Coda
Dadd9
A E
Don't ya?
Gtr. 2: w/ Rhy. Fig. 1
Doo, doo, doo, doot,

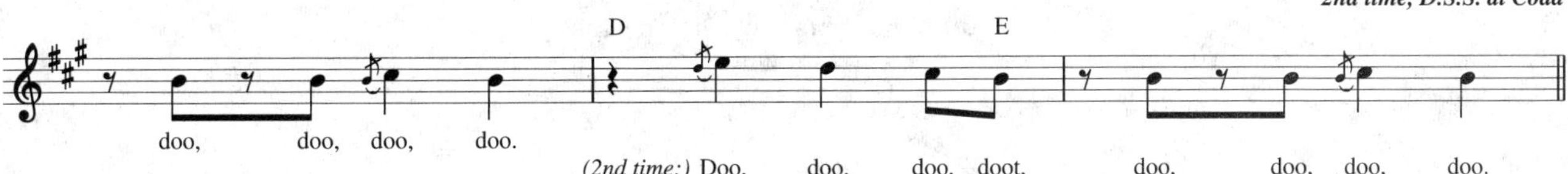

Additional Lyrics

2. You wanna be there when they count up the dudes
   And I love your dress.
   You're a juvenille success
   Because your face is a mess.

3. So, how could they know?
   I said, "How could they know?"
   So what you want to know?
   Calamity's child, chi-chile, chi-chile,
   Where you wanna go?

4. What can I do for you? Looks like I've been there too.
   Because you've torn your dress.
   And your face is a mess.
   Ooh, your face is a mess, oh, oh.

5. So how could they know?
   How could they know?

Rhiannon

Words and Music by Stevie Nicks

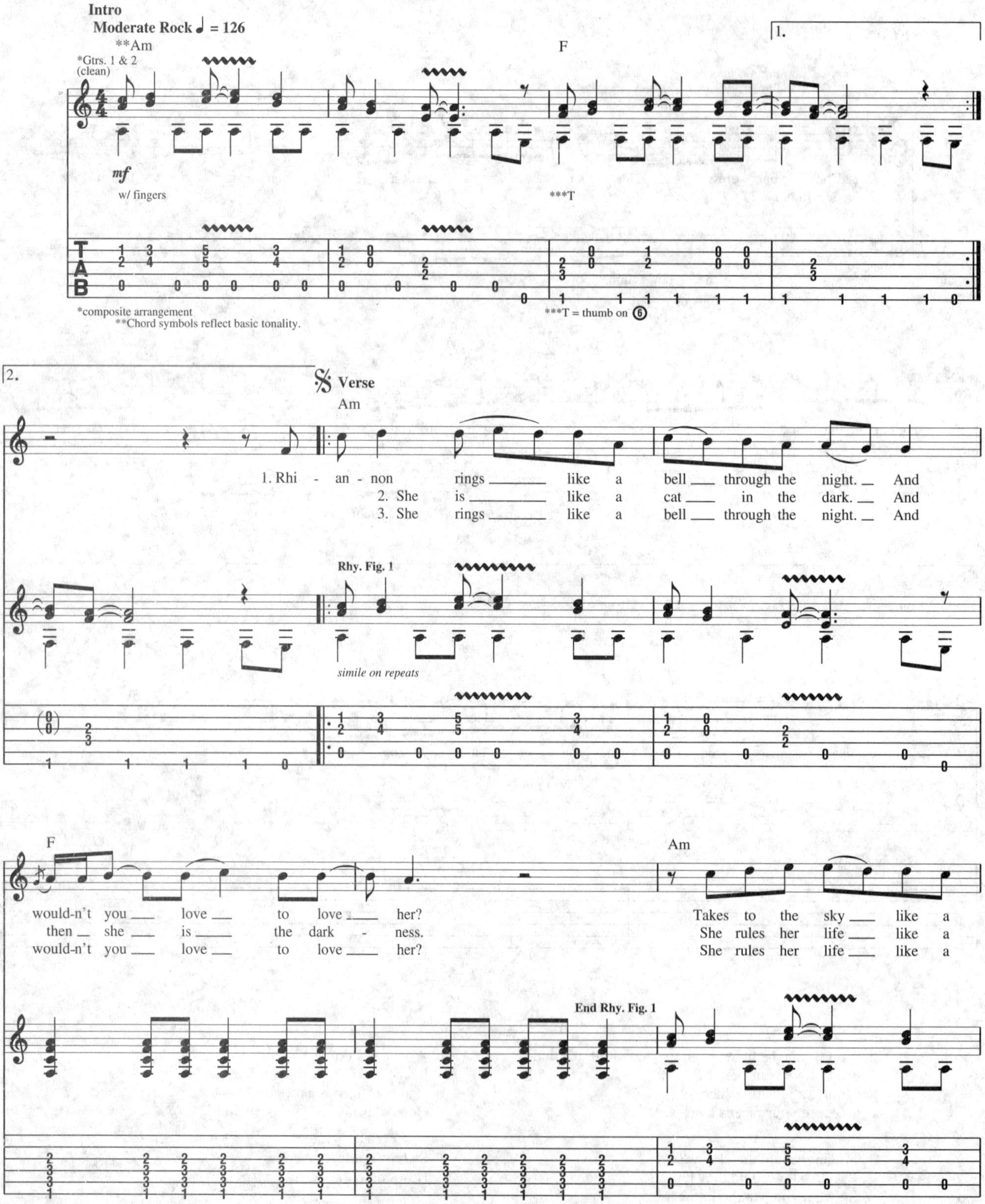

Intro
Moderate Rock ♩ = 126

**Am — F — 1.

*Gtrs. 1 & 2 (clean)

mf
w/ fingers

***T

*composite arrangement
**Chord symbols reflect basic tonality.
***T = thumb on ⑥

2. — 𝄋 Verse
Am

1. Rhi - an - non rings ___ like a bell ___ through the night. ___ And
2. She is ___ like a cat ___ in the dark. ___ And
3. She rings ___ like a bell ___ through the night. ___ And

Rhy. Fig. 1
simile on repeats

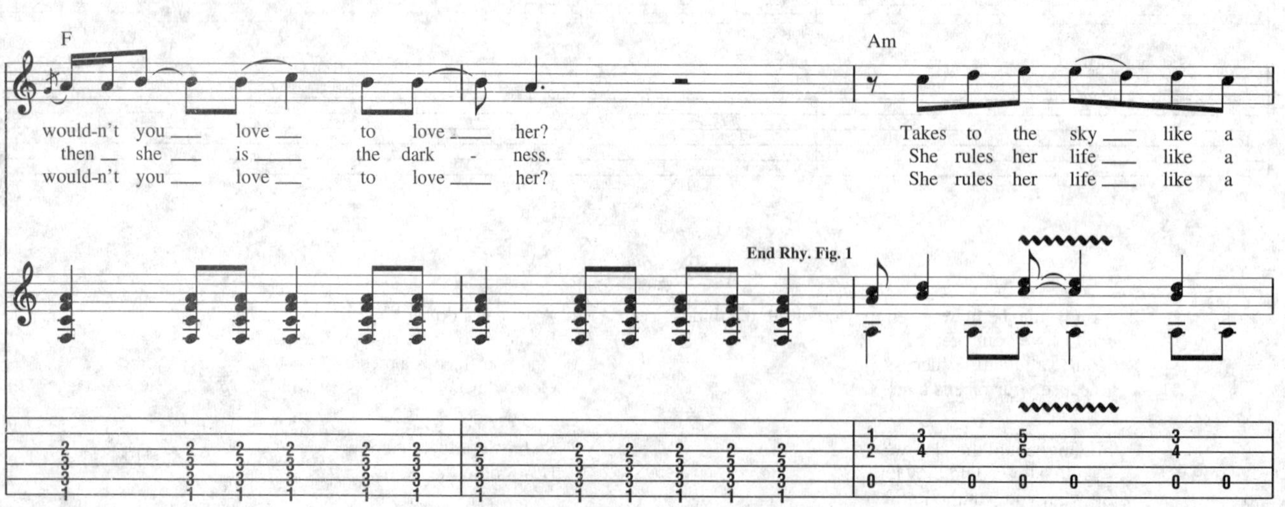

F
bird in flight. And who will be her lov - er?
fly - ing sky - lark. And when the sky is star - lets.
bird in flight. And who will be her lov - er?
Pre-Chorus
C
F
All your life you've nev - er seen a wom-an tak - en by the wind.
C
F
Would you stay if she prom - ised you heav-en? Will you ev - er win?
To Coda
Chorus
Gtrs. 1 & 2: w/ Rhy. Fig. 1, 4 times
Am
Will you ev - er win? Rhi -
Gtr. 3 (dist.)
mf

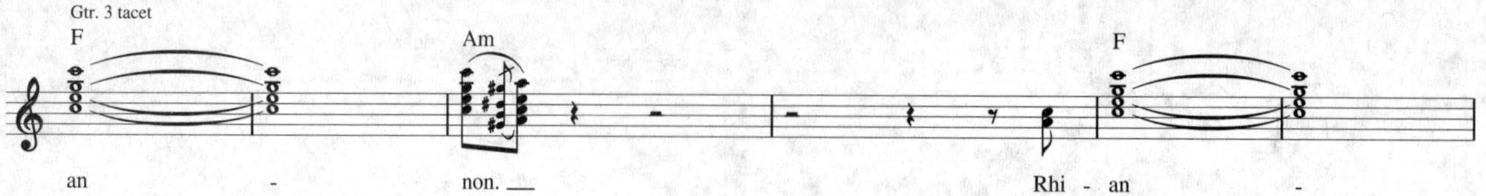
Gtr. 3 tacet
F
Am
F
an - non. Rhi - an -

Am
F
non. Rhi - an -
Gtr. 3
full

Gtr. 3 tacet
Am
F
- non. Rhi - an -

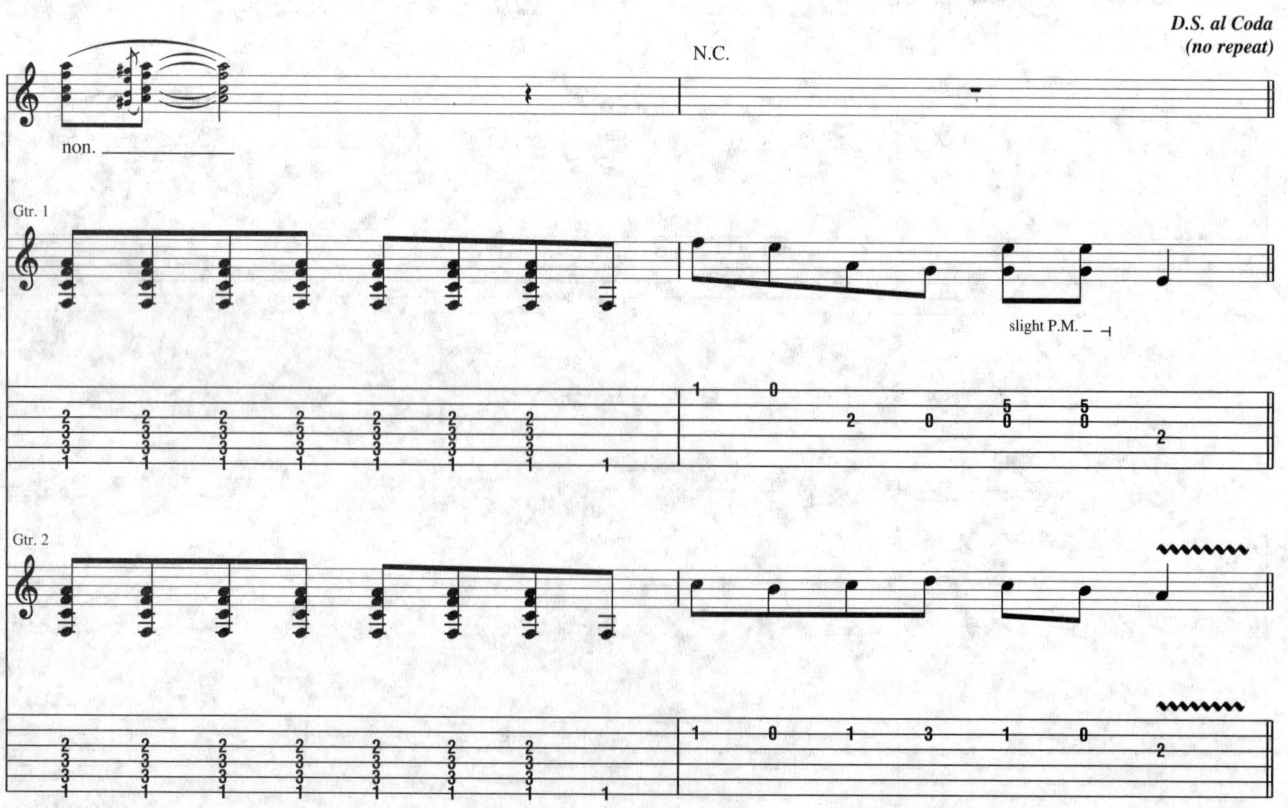
D.S. al Coda
(no repeat)
N.C.
non.
Gtr. 1
slight P.M.
Gtr. 2

Coda
Chorus
Gtr. 1: w/ Rhy. Fig. 1, 7 times
Gtr. 2: w/ Rhy. Fig. 1, 3 times
F
Am
Rhi -
Gtrs. 1 & 2
Gtr. 3
8va
full
Gtr. 3 tacet
F
Am
F
an - non. Rhi - an -
Am
Gtr. 3 tacet
F
non. Rhi - an -
Gtr. 3
8va
let ring
Am
F
Tak - en by, tak - en by the sky.
Sky.
non. (Oo.
Gtr. 2 Rhy. Fig. 2
End Rhy. Fig. 2
Gtr. 2: w/ Rhy. Fig. 2, 3 times, simile
Am
F
Tak - en by, tak - en by the sky.
Sky.
Gtr. 3
loco
mp

Outro-Guitar Solo

Gtrs. 1 & 2: w/ Rhy. Figs. 1 & 2, simile till fade

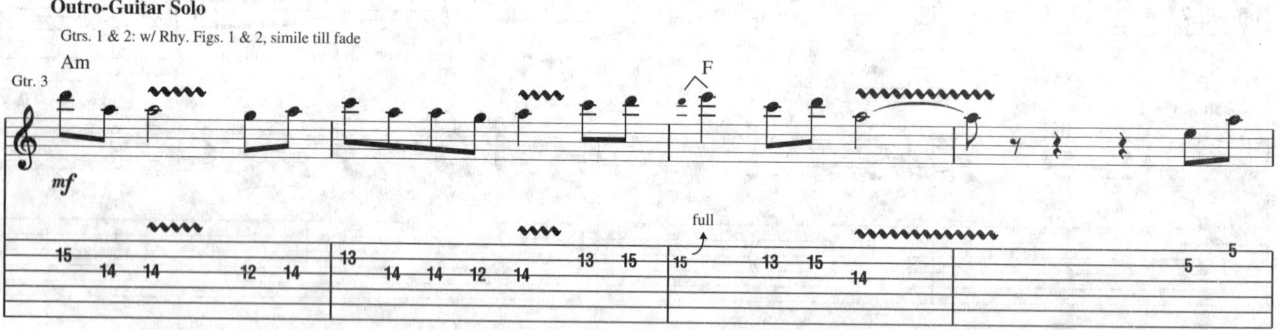

Am
F
1/4

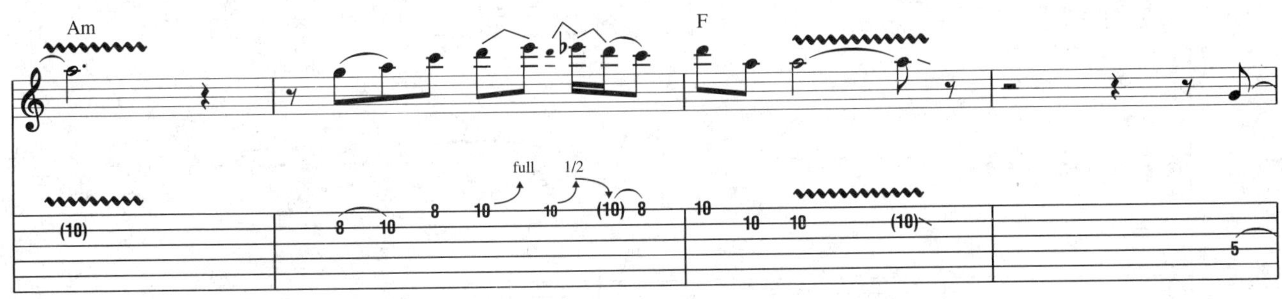
Am
F
full
1/2

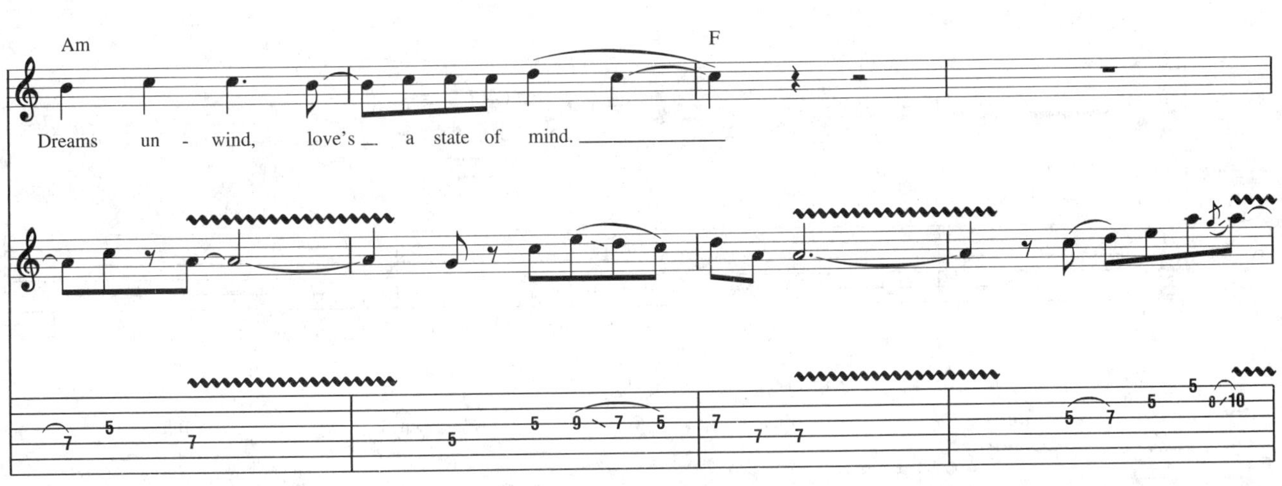
Am
F
Dreams un - wind, love's a state of mind.

Begin Fade
Am
F
Gtr. 3 tacet
Am
Fade Out
Dreams un - wind, love's a state of mind.
full
1/2

Ridin' the Storm Out

Words and Music by Gary Richrath

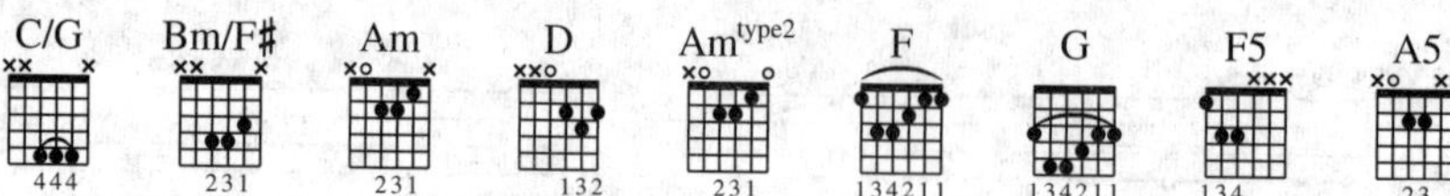

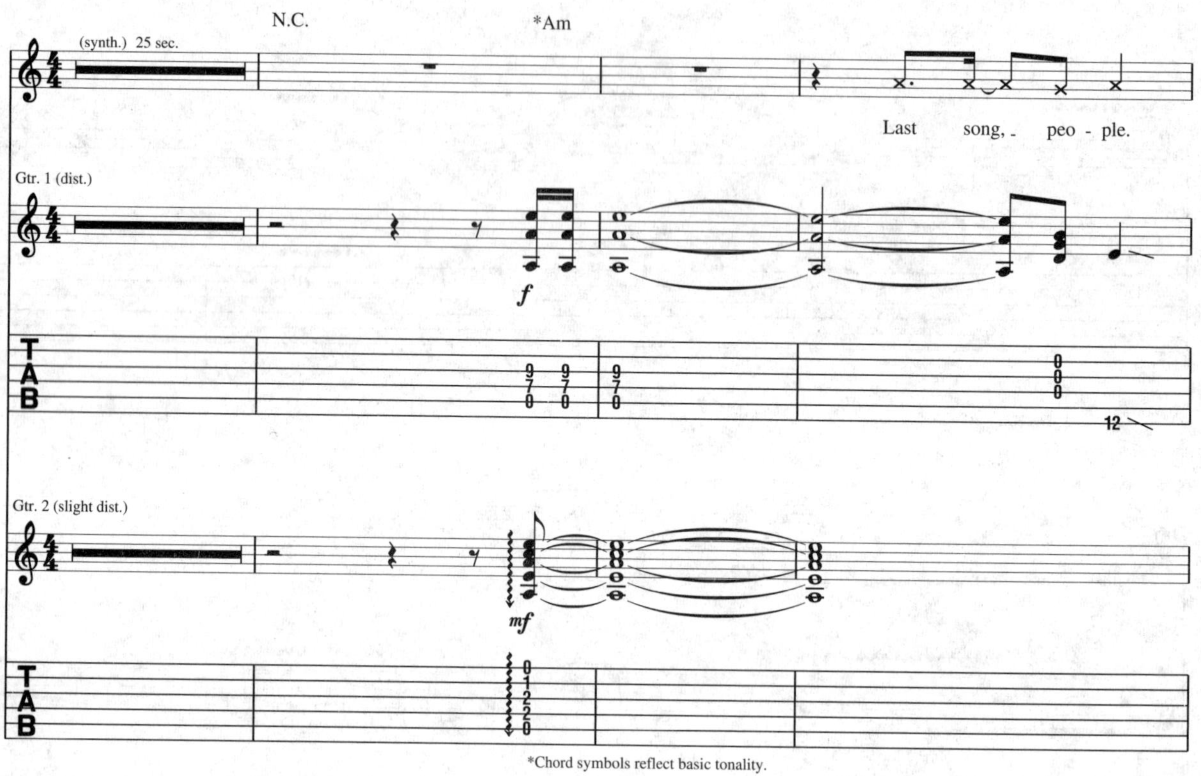

*Chord symbols reflect basic tonality.

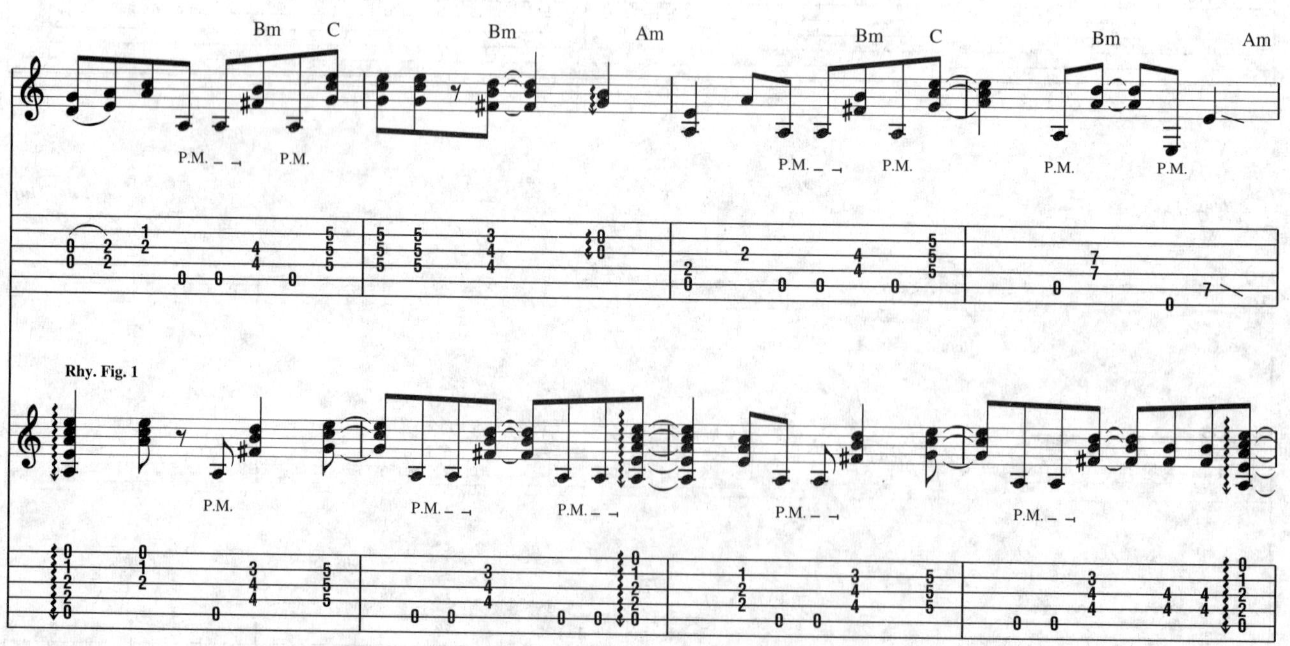

Bm C Bm Am Bm C Bm Am
P.M. P.M. P.M. P.M.
grad. release
full
End Rhy. Fig. 1
P.M. P.M.
Verse
Gtr. 2: w/ Rhy. Fig. 1, 1 5/8 times, simile
Bm C Bm Am Bm C Bm Am
1. Rid - in' the storm out, wait-in' for the thaw out on a full
Gtr. 1
Rhy. Fig. 2
End Rhy. Fig. 2
mf
let ring
Bm C Bm Am Bm C Bm Am
moon night in the Rock - y Mountain win - ter.
P.M. * P.M. P.M. P.M. f P.M.
* ghost note probably not intended
Bm C Bm Am Bm C Bm Am
Wine bot-tle's low watch - in' for the snow and
mf
P.M. P.M. P.M.

Bm C C/G Bm/F♯ Am
Rhy. Fig. 3
End Rhy. Fig. 3
Gtr. 2
think-in' a-bout what I've been mis-sin' in the cit - y.
And I'm
P.M. P.M. P.M. let ring P.M.
Pre-Chorus
D A D Am type 2 E G
open open 3fr
Rhy. Fig. 4
End Rhy. Fig. 4
(cont. in notation)
not mis-sin' a thing, watch-ing the full moon cross - ing the range.
steady gliss.
Chorus
F G Am G5 F5
Rid - in' the storm out.
Rid - in' the storm out.
*Gtrs. 1 & 2
Rhy. Fig. 5
* composite arrangement
Gtr. 2: w/ Rhy. Fig. 1, last 4 meas., simile
Bm C
End Rhy. Fig. 5
Gtr. 1

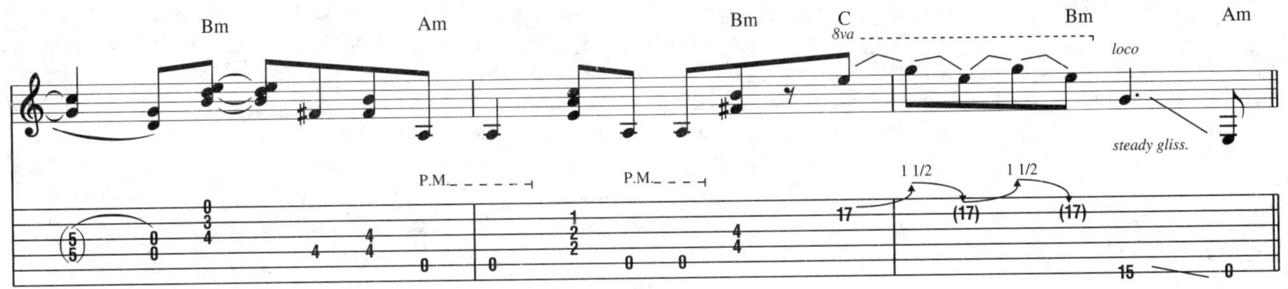
Bm
Am
Bm
C
8va
Bm
Am
loco
steady gliss.
P.M.
P.M.
1 1/2
1 1/2

Verse

Gtr. 2: w/ Rhy. Fig. 1, 1 5/8 times, simile
Am
Bm
C
Bm
Am
Bm
C
Bm
Am
2. La - dy be - side _ me,
well, she's a there to guide _ me. _
mf
P.M.

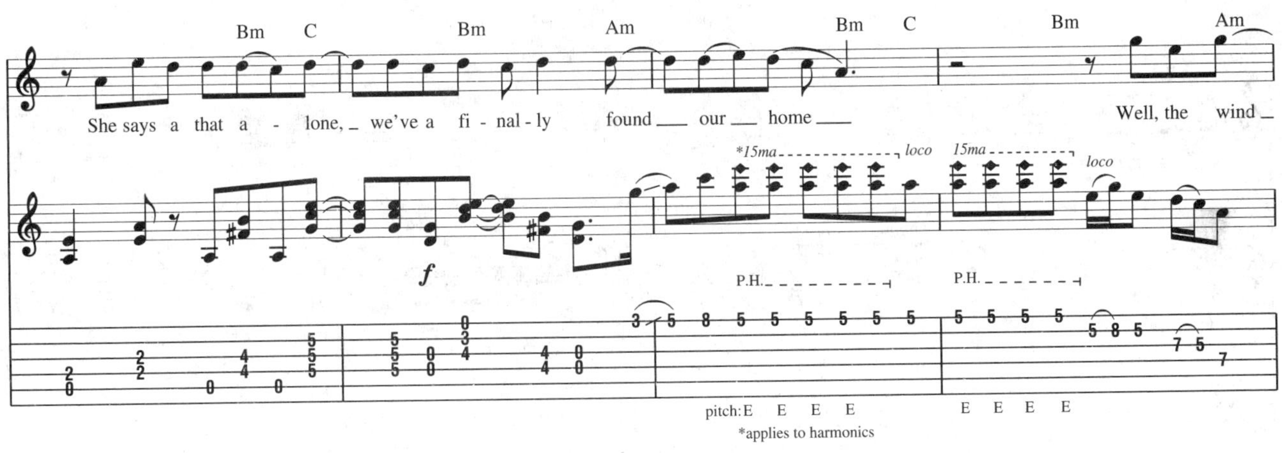
Bm
C
Bm
Am
Bm
C
Bm
Am
She says a that a - lone, _ we've a fi - nal - ly found _ our _ home _
Well, the wind _
*15ma
loco
15ma
loco
f
P.H.
P.H.
pitch: E E E E
E E E E
*applies to harmonics

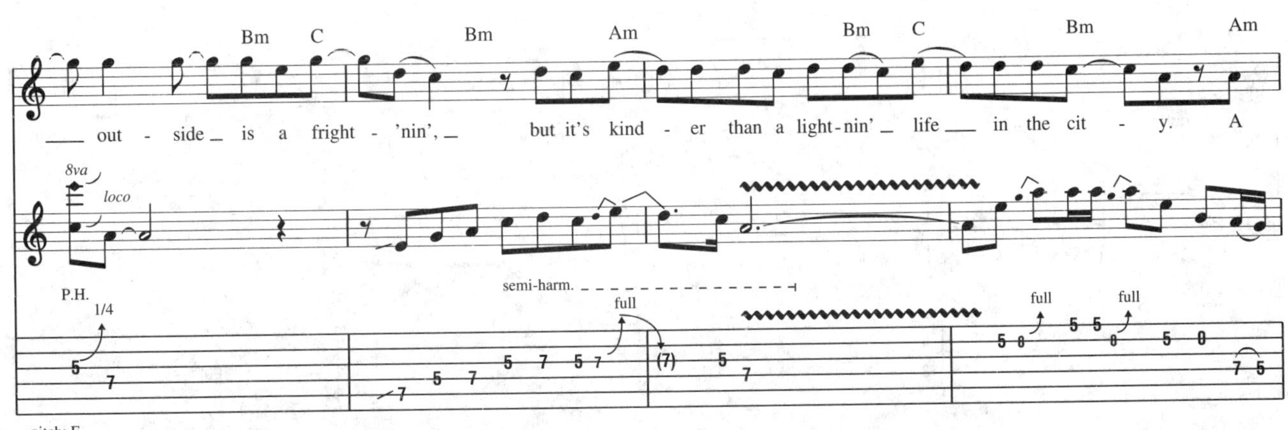
Bm
C
Bm
Am
Bm
C
Bm
Am
_ out - side _ is a fright - 'nin', _ but it's kind - er than a light-nin' _ life _ in the cit - y. A
8va
loco
semi-harm.
P.H.
1/4
full
full
full
pitch: E

Pre-Chorus

Chorus

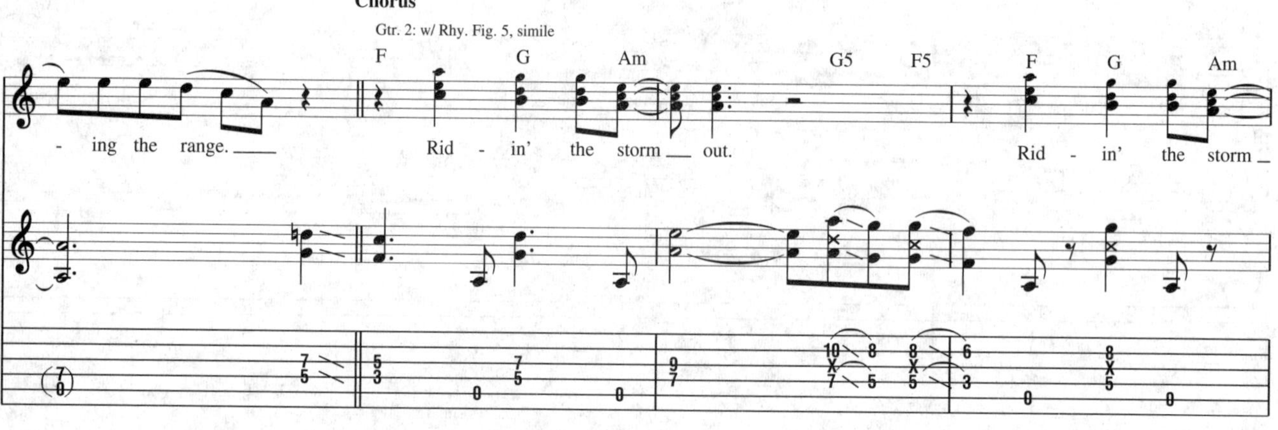

G6 Am G Am G6 A5 G
out. Whoa, yes, I am.
Gtr. 1
Gtr. 2
Guitar Solo
A5 N.C. A5 N.C.
full
G F G Am G F
8va
loco
full full full full

G
Am
G
F
8va
G
full
full
full
Am
G
F
G
A5
steady gliss.
full
Gtr. 2: w/ Rhy. Fig. 1, 1st 4 meas., simile
Bm
C
Bm
Am
loco
Bm
C
Bm
Am
Gtr. 1
1 1/2
1 1/2
1 1/2
full
Verse
Gtr. 1: w/ Rhy. Fig. 2, simile
Gtr. 2: w/ Rhy. Fig. 1, 1 5/8 times, simile
3. Rid - in' the storm out. I'm a - wait - in' for the thaw
out on a full moon night in the Rock - y Mountain kind a win -
mf
f

Bm C Bm Am Bm C
- ter. Oh, yeah. Wine bot - tle's low.
8va
full
Bm Am Bm C Bm Am
I'm a watch - in' for the snow. I'm
8va loco 8va loco
1 1/2 full full full 2 full full
Gtr. 2: w/ Rhy. Fig. 3, simile
Bm C C/G Bm/F# Am N.C.
think-in' a - bout what I've been a - mis - sin' in the cit - y. Oh, ho, ho, well, I'm
mf
P.M.
Pre-Chorus
Gtr. 2: w/ Rhy. Fig. 4, simile
D N.C. D Am
not mis-sin' a thing. I'm a watch - in' the full moon cross - in' the range.
8va loco
Harm.

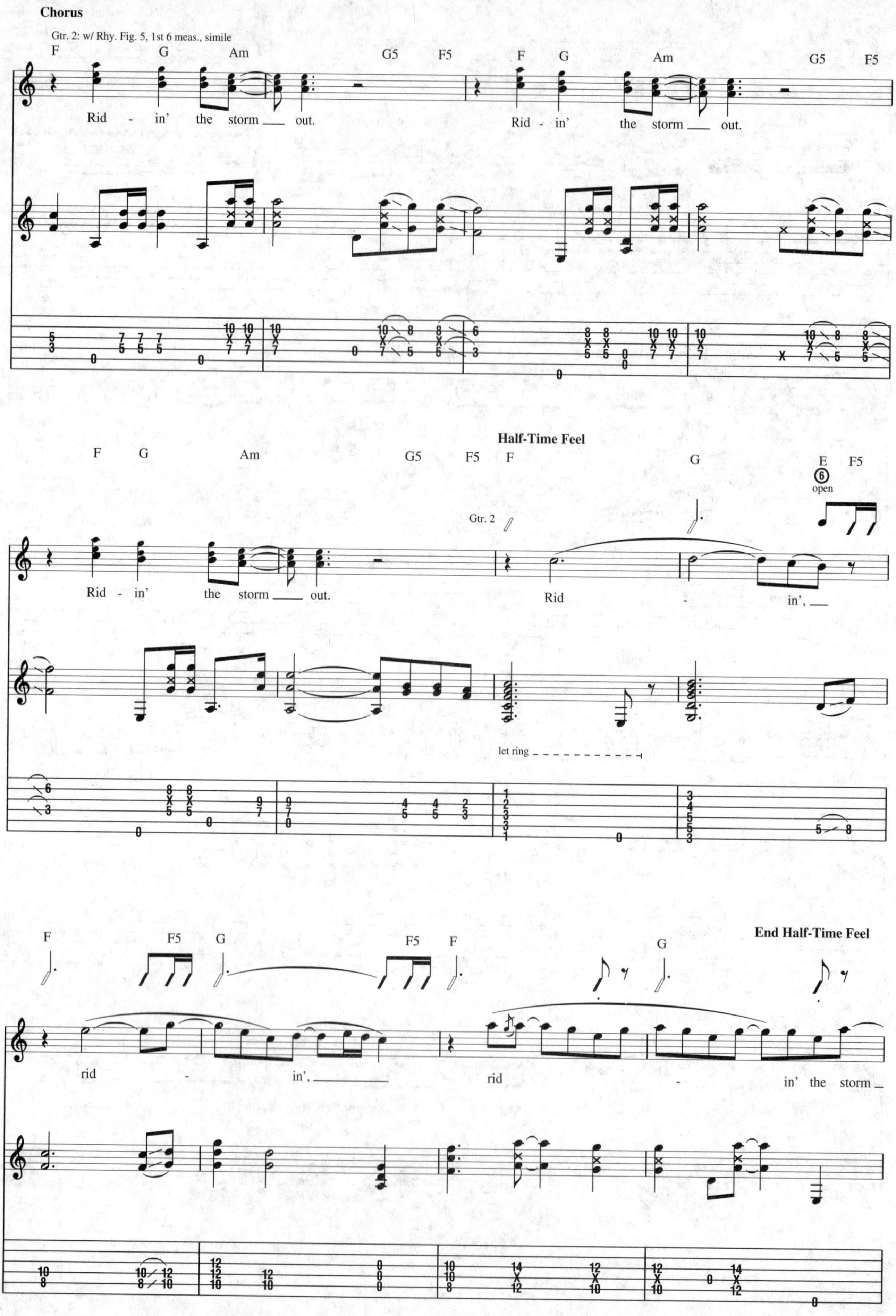

Chorus
Gtr. 2: w/ Rhy. Fig. 5, 1st 6 meas., simile
F G Am G5 F5 F G Am G5 F5
Rid - in' the storm out. Rid - in' the storm out.
F G Am G5 F5
Half-Time Feel
F G E F5
⑥ open
Gtr. 2
Rid - in' the storm out.
Rid - in',
let ring
F F5 G F5 F G
End Half-Time Feel
rid - in',
rid - in' the storm

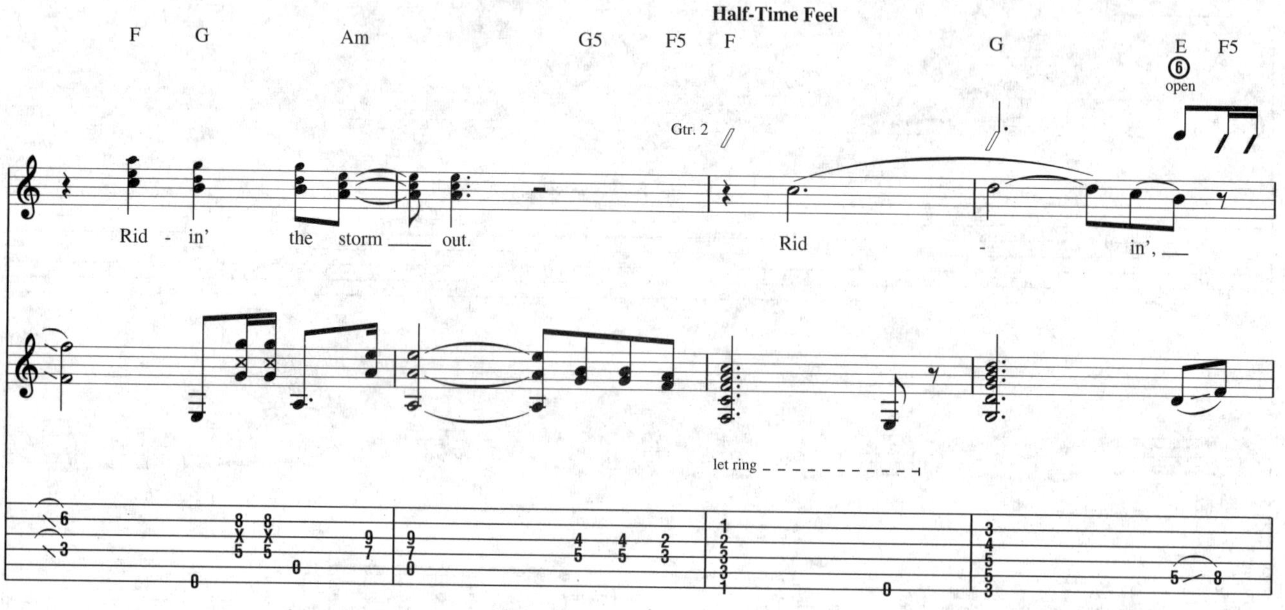

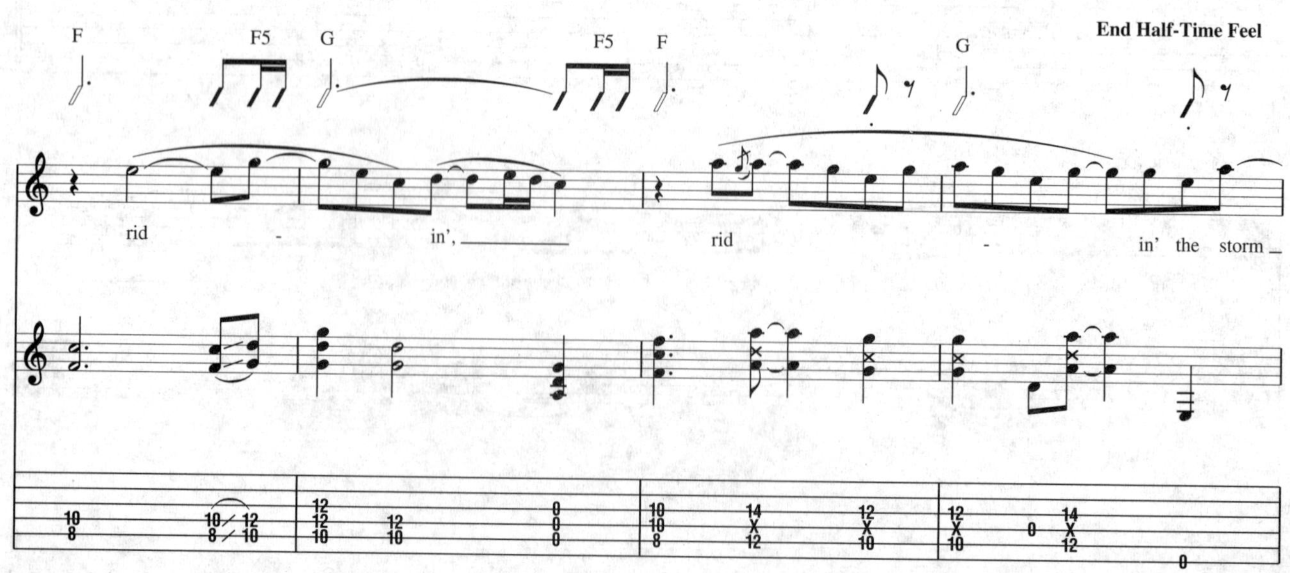

A5
Am
out.
Oh,
no.
Oh,
no.
Oh,
oh,
oh,
oh,
oh.
P.M.
Guitar Solo
Gtr. 2: w/ Rhy. Fig. 1, 4 times, simile
Gtr. 1
Am
Bm
C
Bm
Am
Bm
C
Bm
Am
1/2
8va
full

8va
Bm
C
loco
Am
full
1 1/2
steady gliss.
P.M.
let ring
Outro
Free Time
Gtr. 1
F
G
fdbk.
Gtr. 2
(cont. in slash)

Am type 2

Gtr. 2: w/ Rhy. Fig. 6, 4 times, simile

Rhy. Fig. 6

End Rhy. Fig. 6

Gtr. 2

Gtr. 1

let ring

full

Lord, ya' know I'm rid - in'. Lord, ya'

8va loco 8va loco 8va loco 8va

full full full

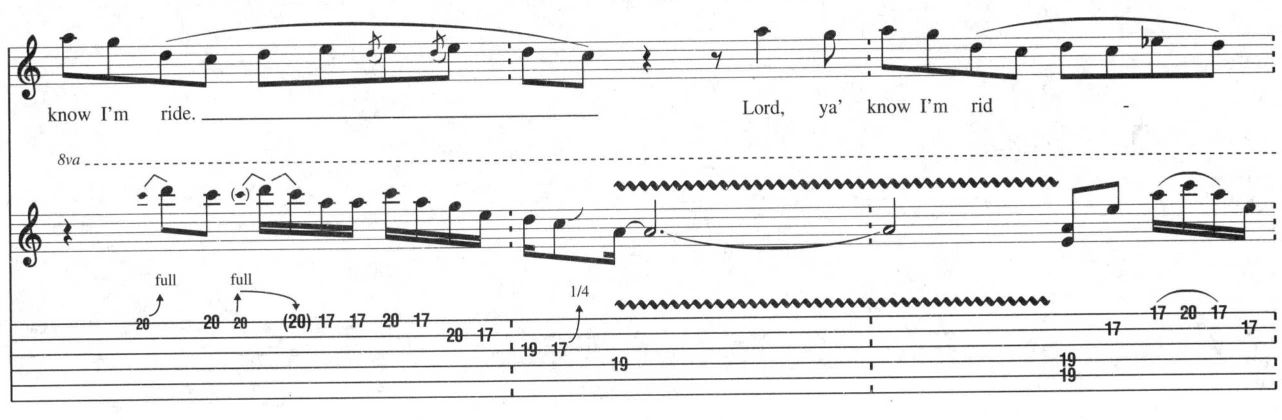

Rock and Roll Hoochie Koo

Words and Music by Rick Derringer

Verse

A5 C5 D5 C5

1. Could-n't stop mov-in' when it first took hold.

End Riff A

Rhy. Fig. 1

End Riff A1

Rhy. Fig. 1A

let ring

1/2

N.C. A5 C5 D5 C5 N.C.

It was a warm spring night at the old town hall. There was a

End Rhy. Fig. 1

full 1/2 full full 1/2

w/ bar

-1/2 -1/2

Gtr. 1: w/ Rhy. Fig. 1
A5
C5
D5
C5
N.C.
group called the Jok - ers, they were lay - in' it down.
To
Gtr. 2
w/ bar
A5
C5
D5
C5
N.C.
know I'm nev - er gon - na lose that funk - y sound.
End Rhy. Fig. 1A
w/ bar
Chorus
F5
G5
A5
N.C.
Voc. Fig. 1
F5
F6
F5
C5
G5
End Voc. Fig. 1
Rock and roll hooch - ie koo.
(Rock and roll hooch - ie koo.
Lord - y, ma - ma light my fuse.
Rhy. Fig. 2
Gtr. 1
8va
loco
Rhy. Fig. 2A
Gtr. 2
P.M.

A5 N.C. F5 G5

Light my fuse. Rock and roll hooch - ie koo.

8va loco

P.M.

A5 N.C. F5 F6 C5 G5 A5 N.C.

Drop on out an' spread the news.

Rock and roll hooch - ie koo.)

End Rhy. Fig. 2

8va loco

P.M.

1/4

End Rhy. Fig. 2A

P.M.

1/4

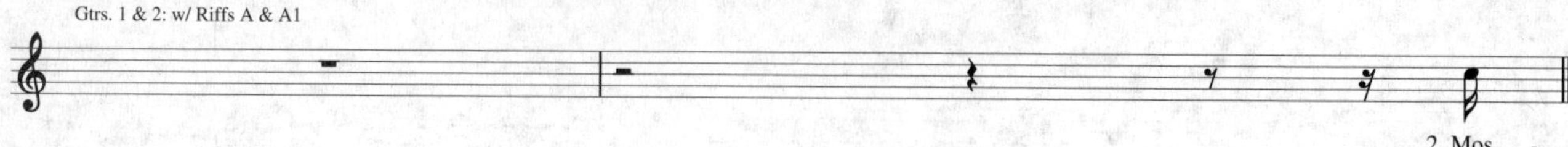
Gtrs. 1 & 2: w/ Riffs A & A1
2. Mos -

Verse
Gtr. 2: w/ Rhy. Fig. 1A, simile
A
C5
D5
C5
N.C.
qui - toes start - ed buz - zin' 'bout this __ time of year. ______
I'm
hope you all know _ what I'm talk - in' a - bout.
The way you
Gtr. 1
full
1/2
full

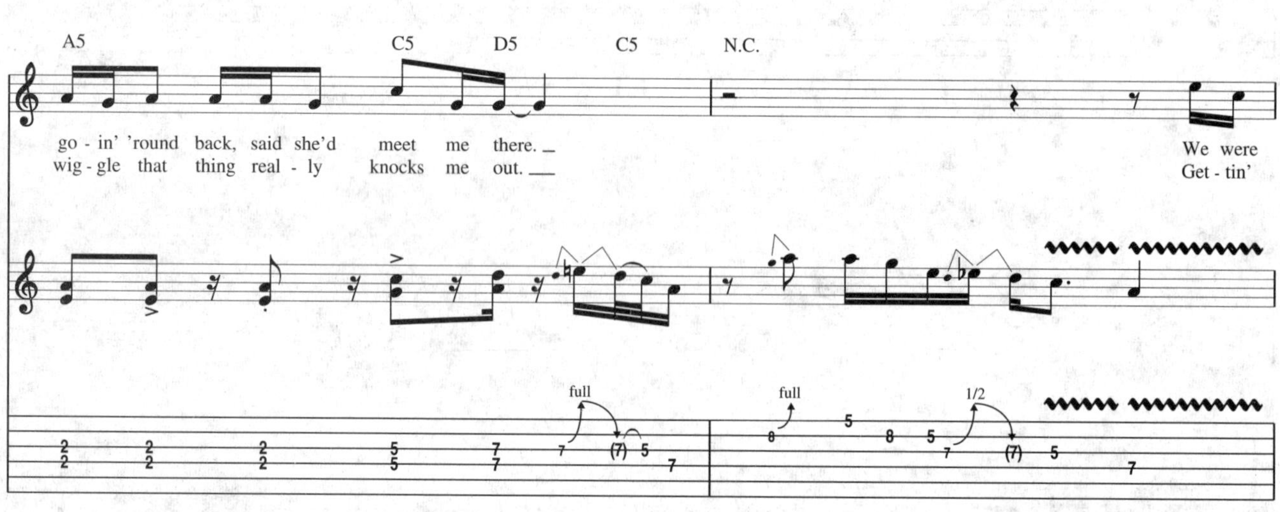
A5
C5
D5
C5
N.C.
go - in' 'round back, said she'd meet me there. _
We were
wig - gle that thing real - ly knocks me out. __
Get - tin'
full
full
1/2

A5
C5
D5
C5
N.C.
rol - lin' in the grass, it was be - hind the barn. ______
Well, my
high all the time, hope you all are too. ______
Come
full
1/2
full

Gtr. 1: w/ Fill 1, 2nd time
A5 C5 D5 C5 N.C.
ears start - ed ring - in' like a fire a - larm.
on lit - tle 'cuz, I'm gon - na do it to you.
full
full
1/2

Chorus
Gtrs. 1 & 2: w/ Rhy. Figs. 2 & 2A, simile
Bkgd. Voc.: w/ Voc. Fig. 1
F5 G5 A5 N.C.
Rock and roll hooch - ie koo.
F5 C5 G5 A5 N.C.
Lord - y, ma - ma light my fuse.

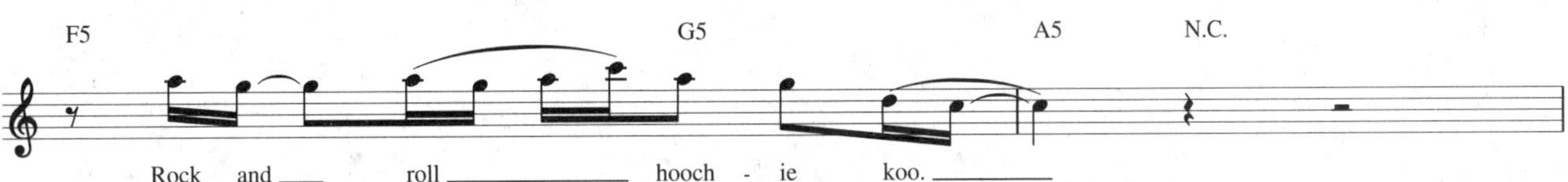
F5 G5 A5 N.C.
Rock and roll hooch - ie koo.

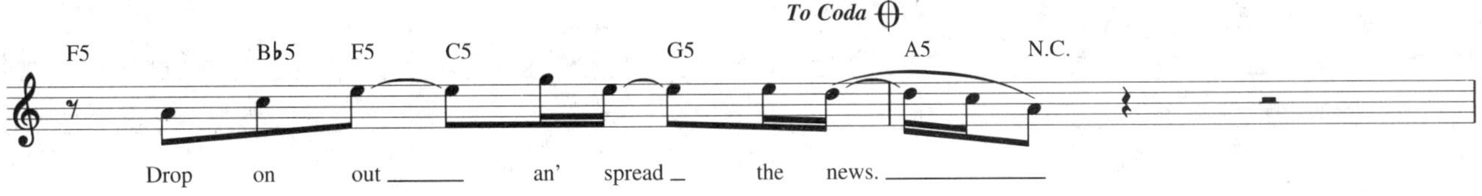
To Coda
F5 B♭5 F5 C5 G5 A5 N.C.
Drop on out an' spread the news.

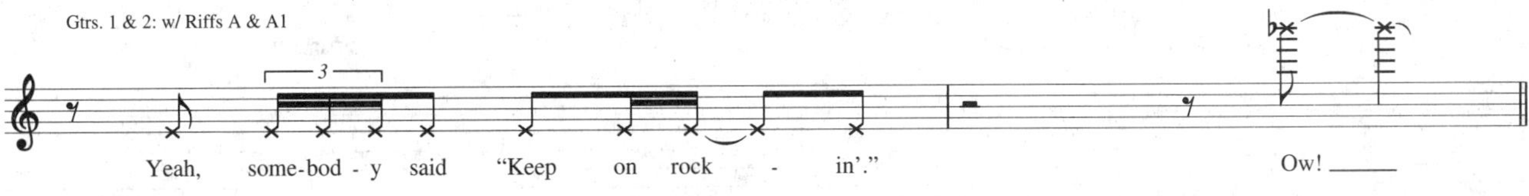
Gtrs. 1 & 2: w/ Riffs A & A1
Yeah, some-bod - y said "Keep on rock - in'."
Ow!

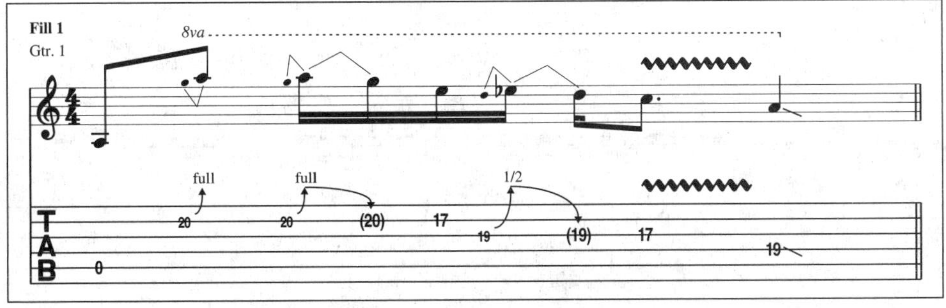
Fill 1
Gtr. 1
8va
full
full
1/2

Guitar Solo
A5
C5
D5
C5
A5
C5
D5
C5
Gtr. 1
full
full
full
full
1/4
1/4
Gtr. 2
Rhy. Fig. 3
End Rhy. Fig. 3
Gtr. 2: w/ Rhy. Fig. 3
6:4
8va
loco
1/2
1/2
Rhy. Fig. 3A
End Rhy. Fig. 3A
Gtr. 2: w/ Rhy. Fig. 3A, simile

Gtr. 1
A5
C
D
A5
C
D
let ring
full
Gtr. 2
1/4
A5
C
D
A5
C
D
full
1/4
A5
C
D
A5
C
D
full
1/4

D.S. al Coda
A5 C D A5 C D
3. I
1/4
1/4

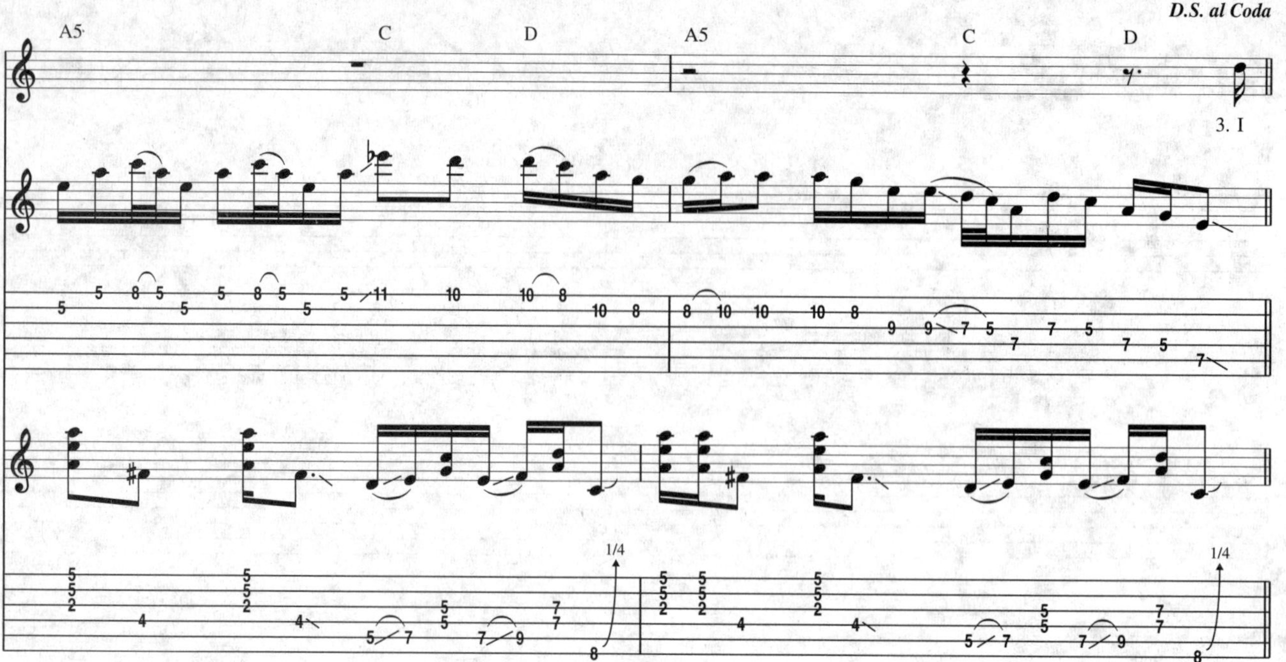

𝄌 *Coda*

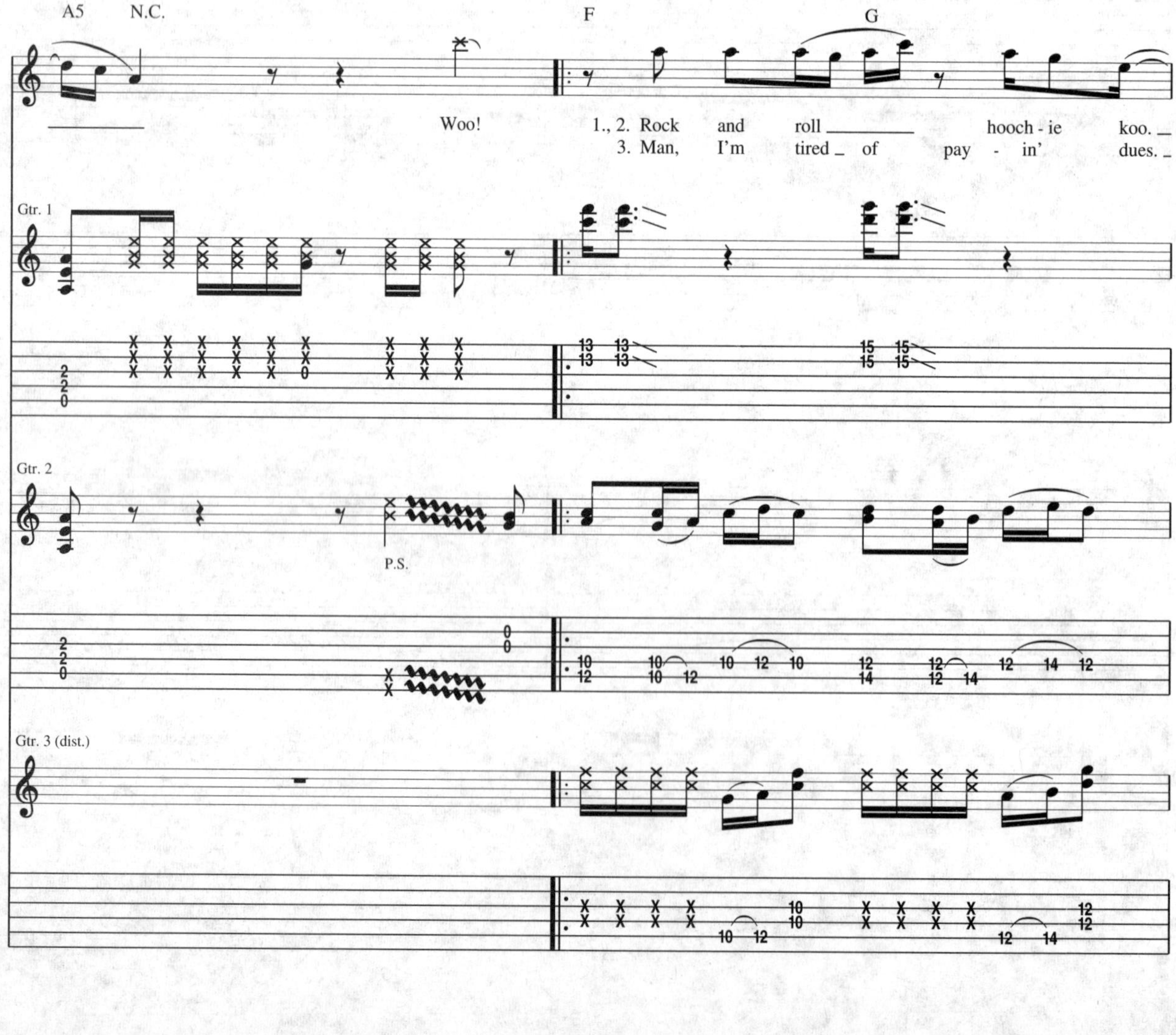
Outro-Chorus
A5 N.C. F G
Woo!
1., 2. Rock and roll hooch - ie koo.
3. Man, I'm tired of pay - in' dues.
Gtr. 1
Gtr. 2
P.S.
Gtr. 3 (dist.)

Bkgd. Voc.: w/ Voc. Fig. 1

A5 F5 C5 G5 A5

Bkgd. Voc.: w/ Voc. Fig. 1

play 3 times

Lord - y ma - ma, light my fuse.
Dropped on out and spread the news. Yeah.
Done said good-bye to all my blues.

P.M.

F5 G5 A5

Free Time

rit.

Lord - y ma - ma, light my fuse. Woo!

rit.

full 5:4 6:4

rit.

rit.

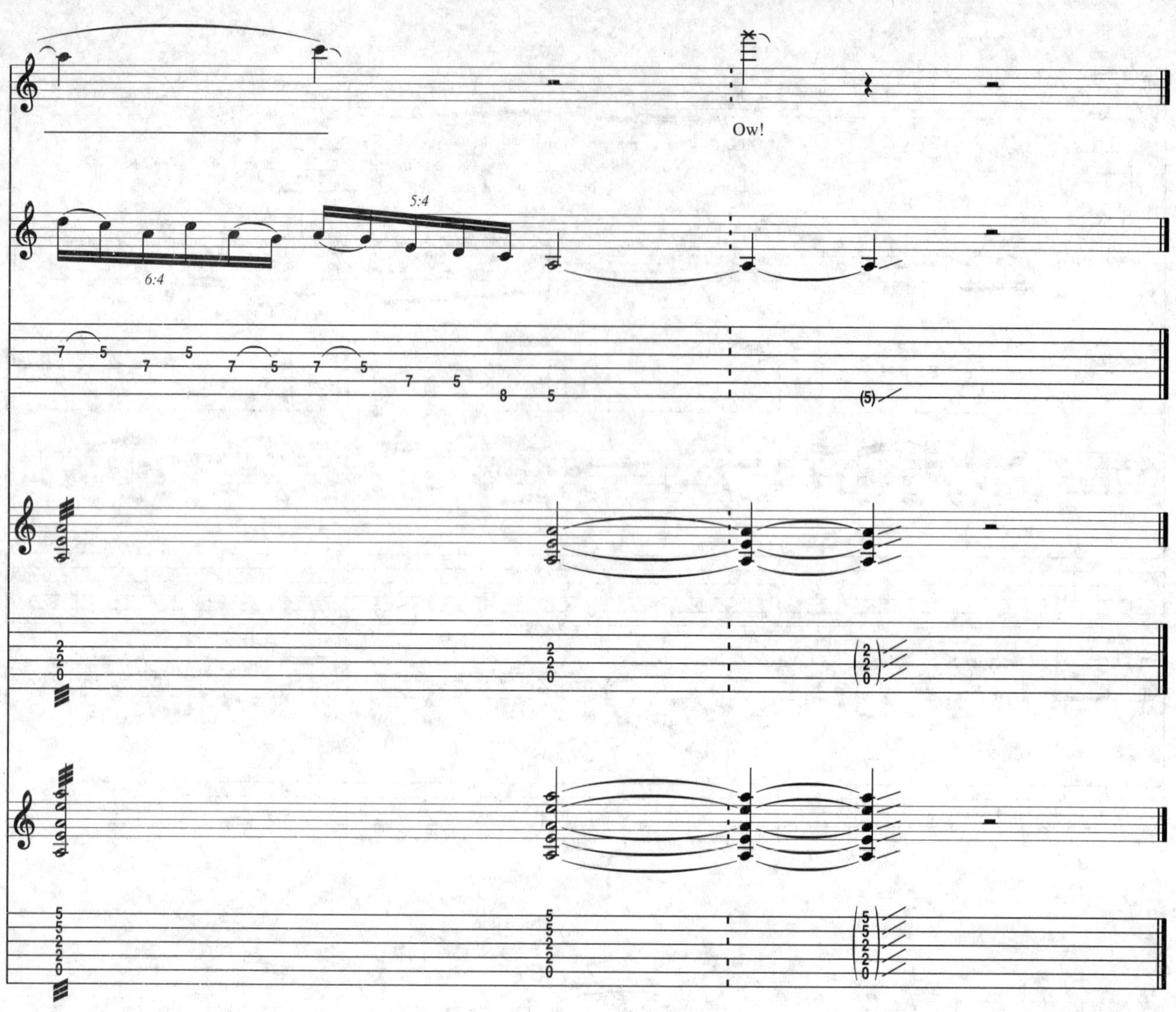
6:4
5:4
Ow!
7 5 7 5 7 5 7 5 7 5 8 5
(5)
2
2
0
2
2
0
5
5
2
2
2
0

Rock and Roll Never Forgets

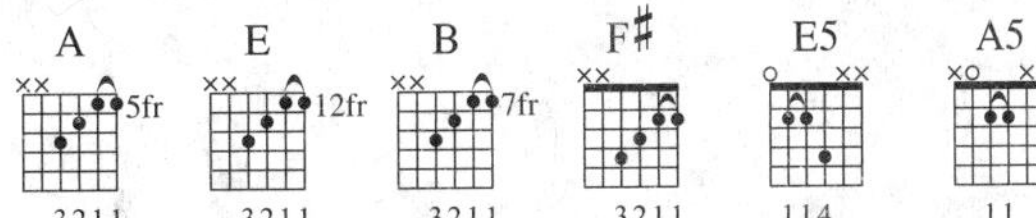

Intro

Moderately fast Rock ♩ = 148

*E5 A5

Gtr. 1 (slight dist.)

Riff A

f let ring

Gtr. 2 (dist.)

Rhy. Fig. 1

f

*Chord symbols reflect basic harmony.

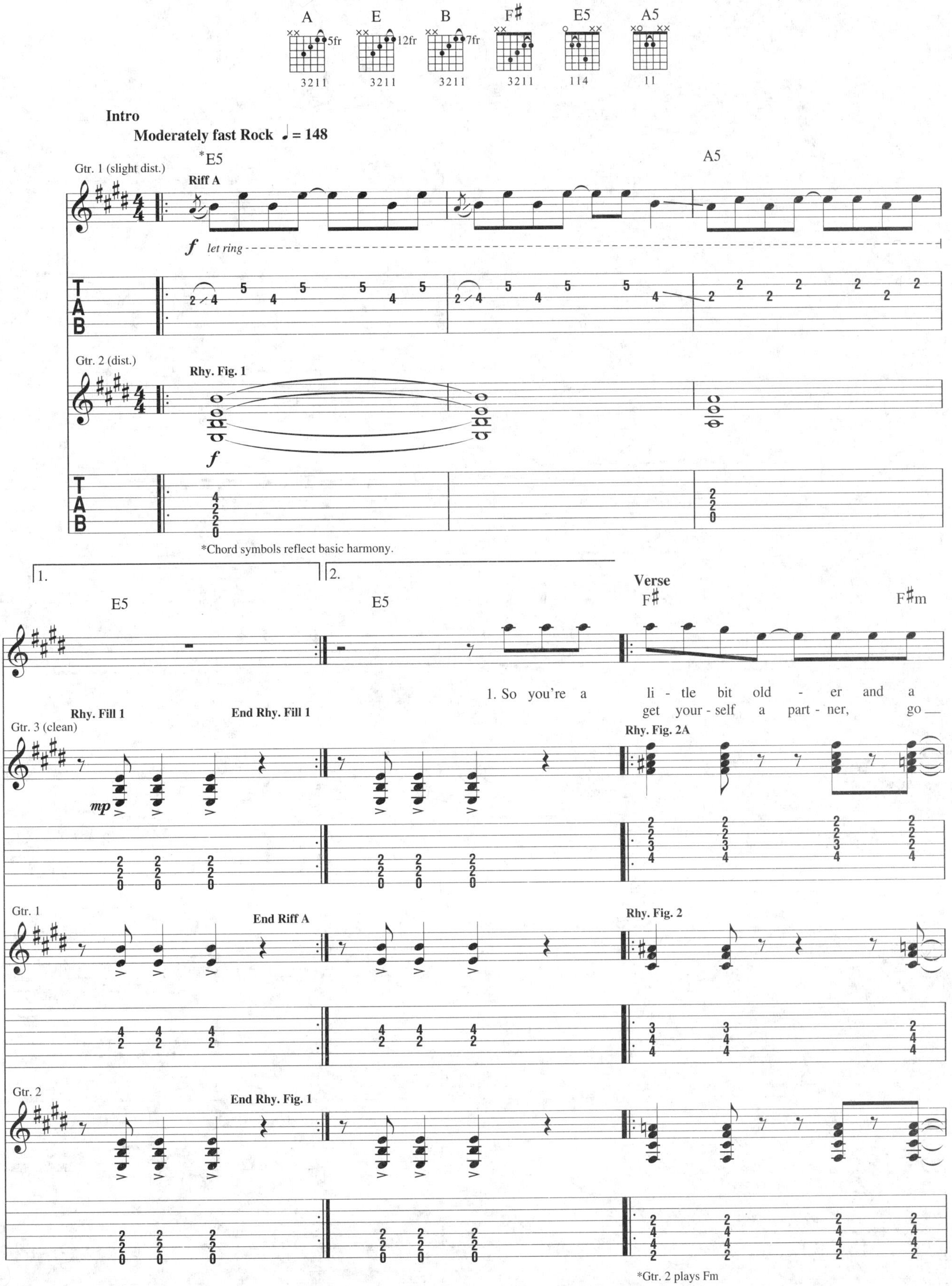

1. 2.

E5 E5

Verse

F♯ F♯m

1. So you're a li - tle bit old - er and a
get your - self a part - ner, go

Rhy. Fill 1 End Rhy. Fill 1

Gtr. 3 (clean)

Rhy. Fig. 2A

mp

Gtr. 1

End Riff A

Rhy. Fig. 2

Gtr. 2

End Rhy. Fig. 1

*Gtr. 2 plays Fm

E
F♯
lot less bold - er than you used to be. ___ So you
___ down to the con - cert or the lo - cal bar. ___ Check the
P.M.
F♯m
E
used to shake 'em down, but now ___ you stop and think a - bout your
lo - cal news - pa - pers, chanc - es are you won't have to go ___
P.M.

dig - ni - ty.
too far.
So, now
Yeah, the
End Rhy. Fig. 2A
(cont. in slashes)
End Rhy. Fig. 2
P.M.
P.M.
Pre-Chorus
A
E
A
Rhy. Fig. 3
Gtr. 3
sweet six - teen's turned thir - ty - one,
you
raf - ters will be ring - ing 'cause the beat's so strong,
the
sweet six - teen's turned thir - ty - one,
Gtr. 1
P.M.
Gtr. 2

E
A
get to feel - in' wear - y when the work day's done. Well, all
crowd will be sway - ing and sing - ing a - long. And all
feel a lit - tle ti - red, feel - ing un - der the gun. Well, all
P.M.
E
End Rhy. Fig. 3
you got to do is get up and in - to your kicks
you got to do is get in, in - to the mix
of Chuck's chil - dren are out there, play - ing his licks.
P.M.

B
Rhy. Fig. 4
End Rhy. Fig. 4
if you're in a fix.
if you need a fix.
Get in - to your kicks,
F♯
(cont. in notation)
Come
You can come
then come

Chorus
F#m
B
back, ba - by, rock and roll nev - er for - gets.
Gtr. 3
Rhy. Fig. 5B
Gtr. 1
Rhy. Fig. 5
P.M.
1/4
Gtr. 2
Rhy. Fig. 5A
1.
2.
To Coda
E
N.C.
E
N.C.
2. You bet - ter
Oo, the
End Rhy. Fig. 5B
End Rhy. Fig. 5
P.M.
End Rhy. Fig. 5A

Bridge

Gtr. 3: w/ Rhy. Fig. 3
A
E
A
E
band's still play - ing it loud and lean.
Lis - ten to the gui - tar play - er
Gtr. 1
Gtr. 2
A
E
mak - ing it scream.
All you got to do is just make that scene to - night.
Gtr. 3: w/ Rhy. Fig. 4 (2 times)
B
Hey, to - night!
Woo!

Guitar Solo
Gtrs. 1 & 3: w/ Rhy. Figs. 2 & 2A
F♯
F♯m
E
F♯
Gtr. 2
hold bend
let ring
let ring
D.S. al Coda
F♯m
E
A
Well, now
hold bend
Coda
Gtrs. 1, 2 & 3: w/ Rhy. Figs. 5, 5A & 5B (1st 3 meas.)
F♯m
B
Said you can come back, ba - by, rock
Rhy. Fill 2B
End Rhy. Fill 2B
Gtr. 3
Gtr. 1
Rhy. Fill 2
End Rhy. Fill 2
Gtr. 2
Rhy. Fill 2A
End Rhy. Fill 2A

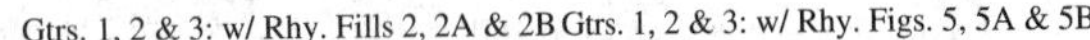
Gtrs. 1, 2 & 3: w/ Rhy. Fills 2, 2A & 2B Gtrs. 1, 2 & 3: w/ Rhy. Figs. 5, 5A & 5B

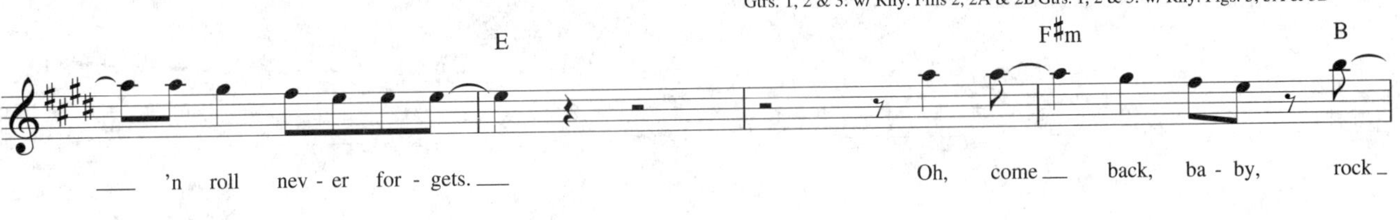
E
F#m
B
'n roll nev - er for - gets.
Oh, come back, ba - by, rock

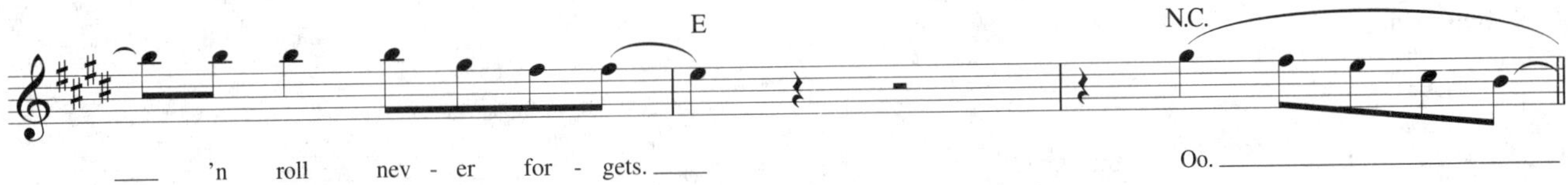
E
N.C.
'n roll nev - er for - gets.
Oo.

Interlude

Gtr. 1: w/ Riff A (2 times)
Gtr. 2: w/ Rhy. Fig. 1 (2 times)
Gtr. 3: w/ Rhy. Fill 1
E5
A5
E5
Oh, yeah.
Oh, yeah.

Gtr. 3: w/ Rhy. Fill 1
A5
E5
Ha.
Uh, huh.
Uh, huh,
nev - er for - gets.

E5
A5
E5
Rhy. Fig. 6B
End Rhy. Fig. 6B
Gtr. 3
Oh, no.
Oh, no.
Oh, nev - er for - gets.
Rhy. Fig. 6
End Rhy. Fig. 6
Gtr. 1
Gtr. 2
Rhy. Fig. 6A
End Rhy. Fig. 6A

Gtrs. 1, 2 & 3: w/ Rhy. Figs. 6, 6A & 6B

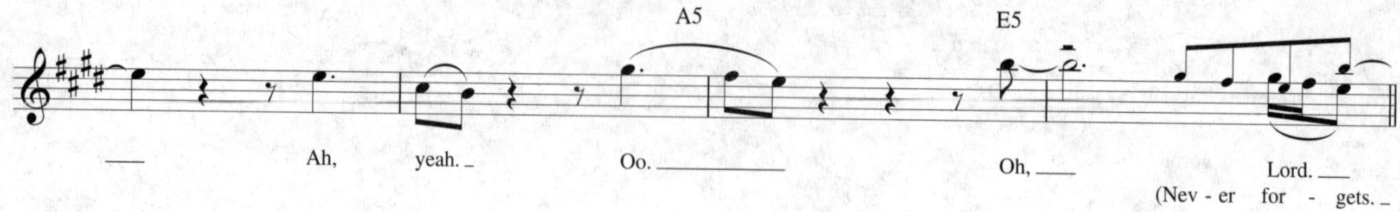

Outro-Guitar Solo

Gtrs. 1 & 3: w/ Rhy. Figs. 6 & 6B (till fade)

A5
E5
yeah.
Oo,
oo.
Ow!
Nev - er for - gets.)
let ring
hold bend
A5
E5
let ring
Nev - er, nev - er for - gets.
Oh,
no.
Oh,
A5
let ring
hold bend
no.
E5

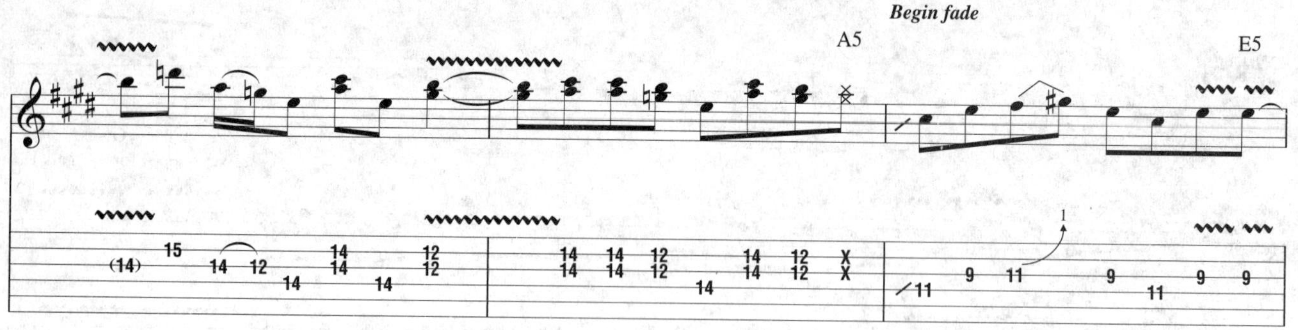
Begin fade
A5
E5
1
(14)
15
14
12
14
14
14
14
14
12
12
14
14
14
14
12
12
14
14
14
12
12
X
X
11
9
11
9
11
9
9

A5
1/2
(9)
9
11
9
13

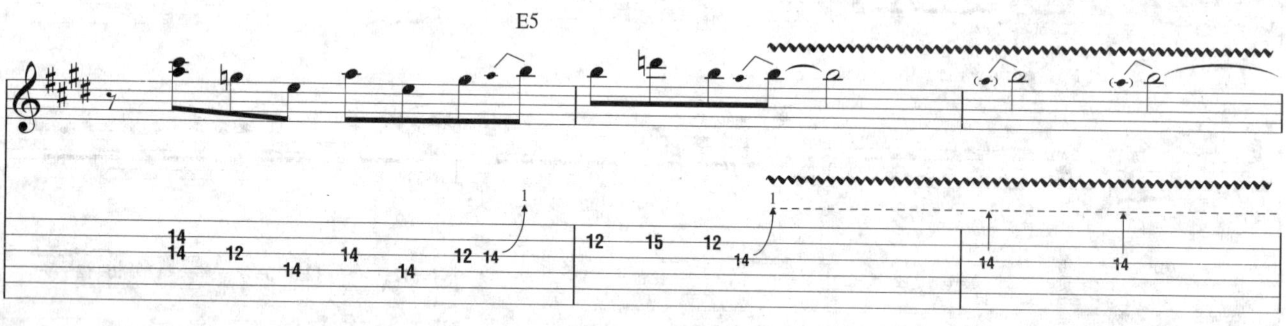
E5
1
1
14
14
12
14
14
14
12
14
12
15
12
14
14
14

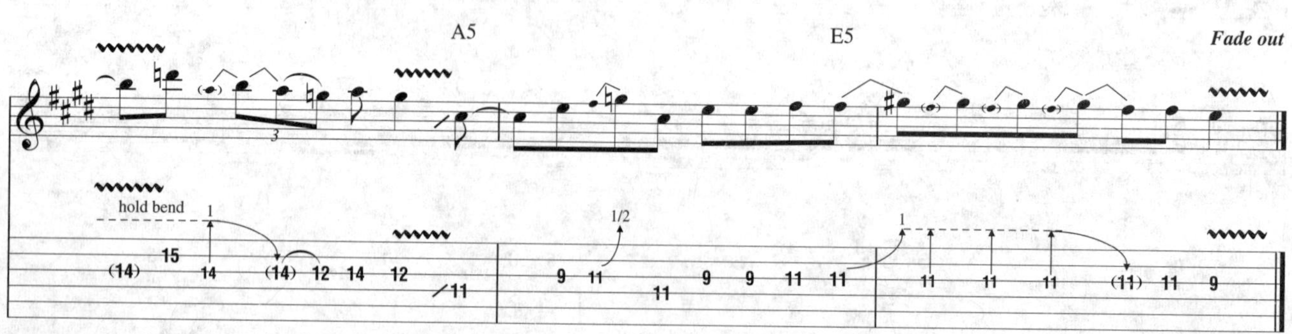
A5
E5
Fade out
hold bend
1
1/2
1
3
(14)
15
14
(14)
12
14
12
11
9
11
11
9
9
11
11
11
11
11
(11)
11
9

Rock Around the Clock

Words and Music by Max C. Freedman and Jimmy DeKnight

* Chord symbols reflect basic harmony.

**Vol. knob lowered about halfway.

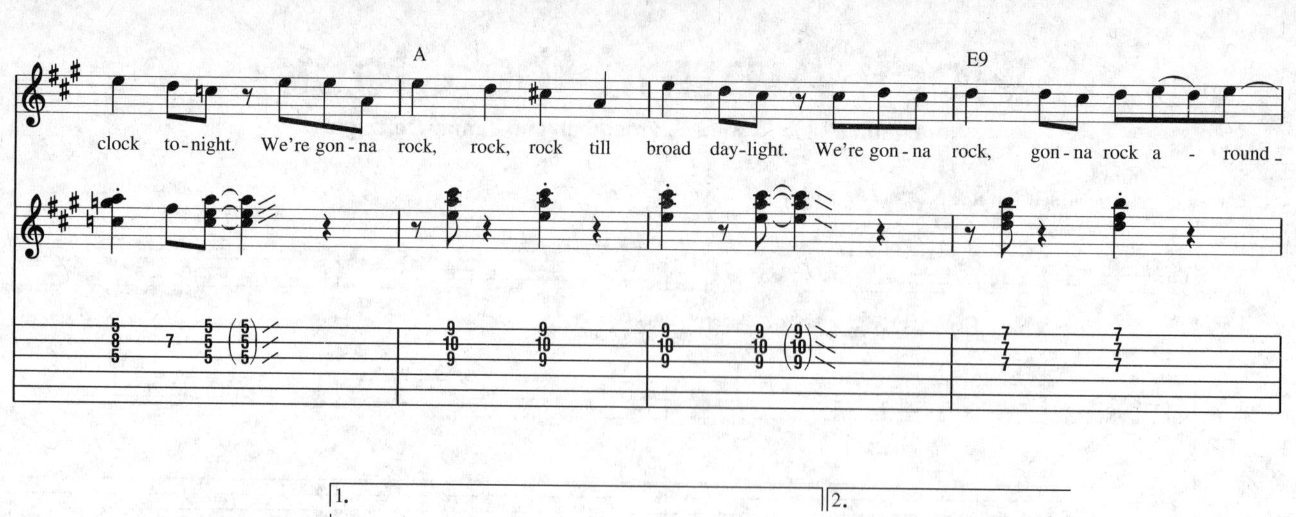
A
E9
clock to-night. We're gon-na rock, rock, rock till broad day-light. We're gon-na rock, gon-na rock a - round

1.
2.
4th time, To Coda
A
A
the clock to-night.
2. When the
4. When it's
*f
*Raise vol. knob to full.

Guitar Solo

A

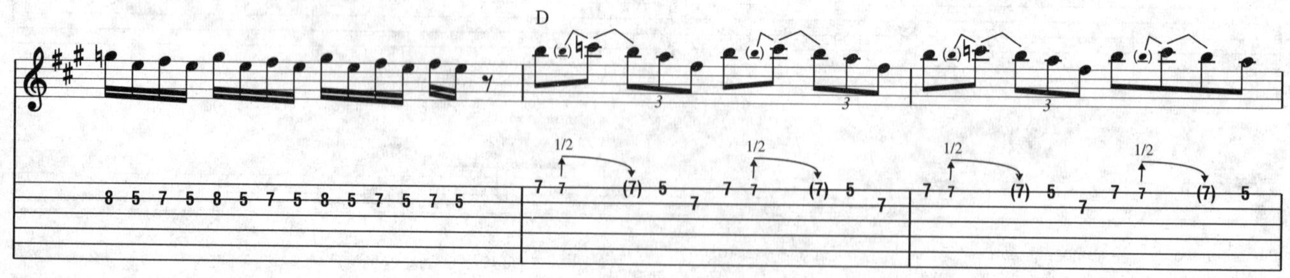
D
1/2

A
E7

D.S. al Coda
(take repeat)
A
3. When the
Coda
Interlude
A
A
*f
*As before
D9
A
E9
A
Verse
A
5. When the clock strikes twelve, we'll cool off then, start a
mf

Additional Lyrics

3. When the chimes ring five, six and seven,
We'll be right in seventh heaven.
We're gonna rock around the clock tonight.
We're gonna rock, rock, rock till broad daylight.
We're gonna rock, gonna rock around the clock tonight.

4. When it's eight, nine, ten, eleven too,
I'll be goin' strong and so will you.
We're gonna rock around the clock tonight.
We're gonna rock, rock, rock till broad daylight.
We're gonna rock, gonna rock around the clock tonight.

Run to the Hills

Words and Music by Steven Harris

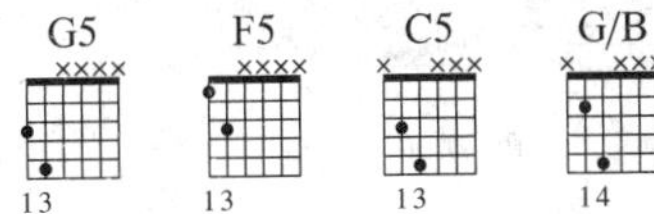

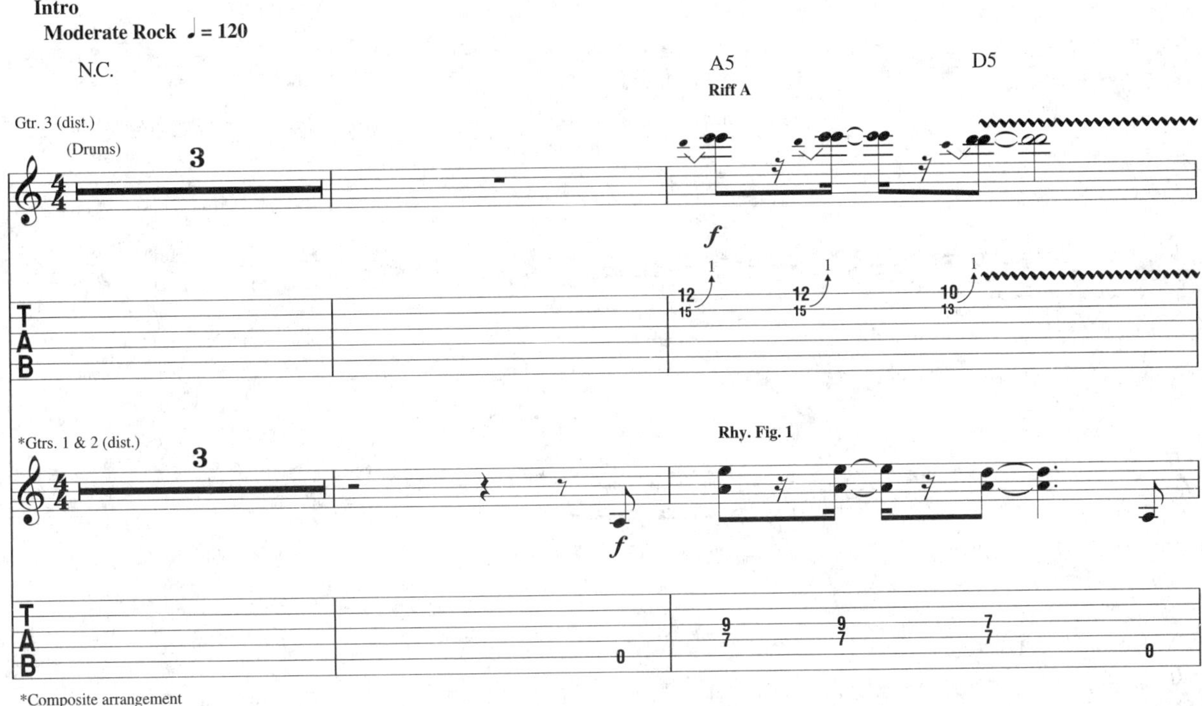

Verse
Gtrs. 1 & 2: w/ Rhy. Fig. 1 (3 3/4 times)
Gtr. 3: w/ Riff A (3 3/4 times)
A5 D5 A5 C5 D5
1. White man came a - cross the sea, he brought us pain and
G5 A5 D5 A5
mis - er - y. He killed our tribes, he killed our creed, he
C5 D5 G5 A5 D5
took our game for his own need. We fought him hard, we
A5 C5 D5 G5 A5
fought him well, out on the plains we gave him hell. But
D5 A5 C5 D5
man - y came, too much for Cree. Oh, will we ev - er
Interlude
Faster ♩ = 180
G5 D5 D5
be set free?
Gtr. 3
hold bend
w/ bar
Gtrs. 1 & 2
P.M.

Verse
1st time, Gtr. 3 tacet
D5
2. Rid - ing through dust clouds and bar - ren wastes,
3. Sol - dier blue in the bar - ren wastes,
w/ bar
P.M.
C5
G/B
C5
G/B
D5
gal - lop - ing hard on the plains.
hunt - ing and kill - ing's a game.
Chas - ing the red - skins
Rap - ing the wom - en and
Gtrs. 1 & 2
C5
G/B
C5
G/B
back to their holes, fight - ing them at their own game.
wast - ing the men, the on - ly good in - juns are tame.

A5
C5
F5
Mur - der for free - dom, a stab in the back, wom - en and chil - dren and
Sell - ing them whis - key and tak - ing their gold, en - slav - ing the young and de -
D5
Chorus
G5
Rhy. Fig. 2A
Gtr. 2
cow - ards at - tack.
stroy - ing the old.
Run
Gtr. 2
(Gtr. 2, cont. in slashes)
Gtr. 1
Rhy. Fig. 2
P.S.
P.M.
F5
to the hills,
P.M.
P.M.

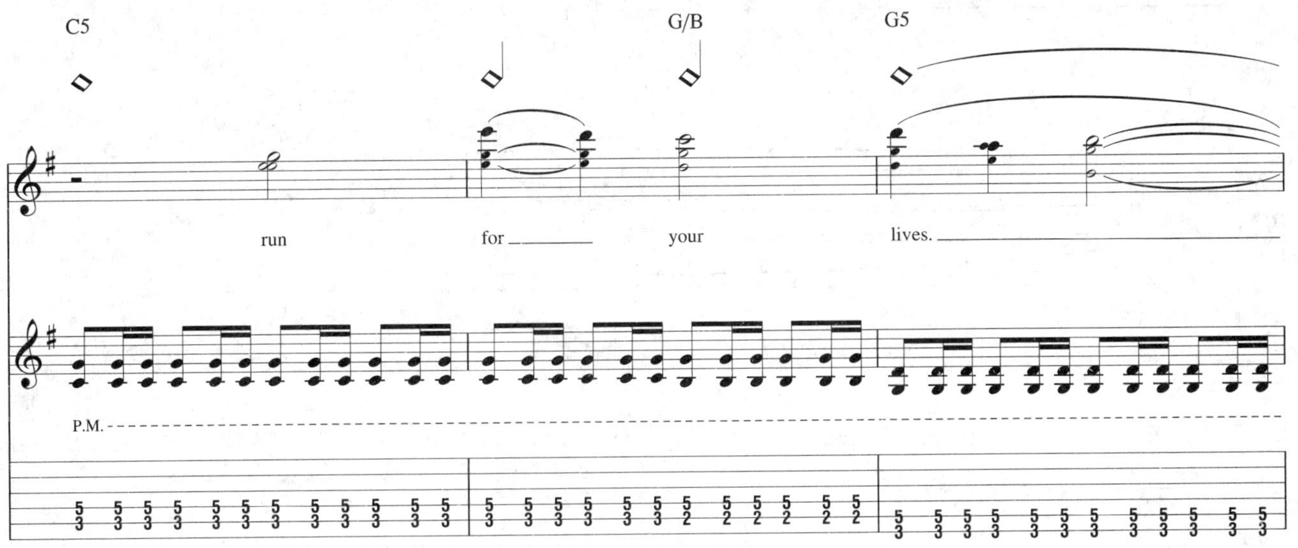

Gtrs. 1 & 2: w/ Rhy. Figs. 2 & 2A (1st 6 meas.)

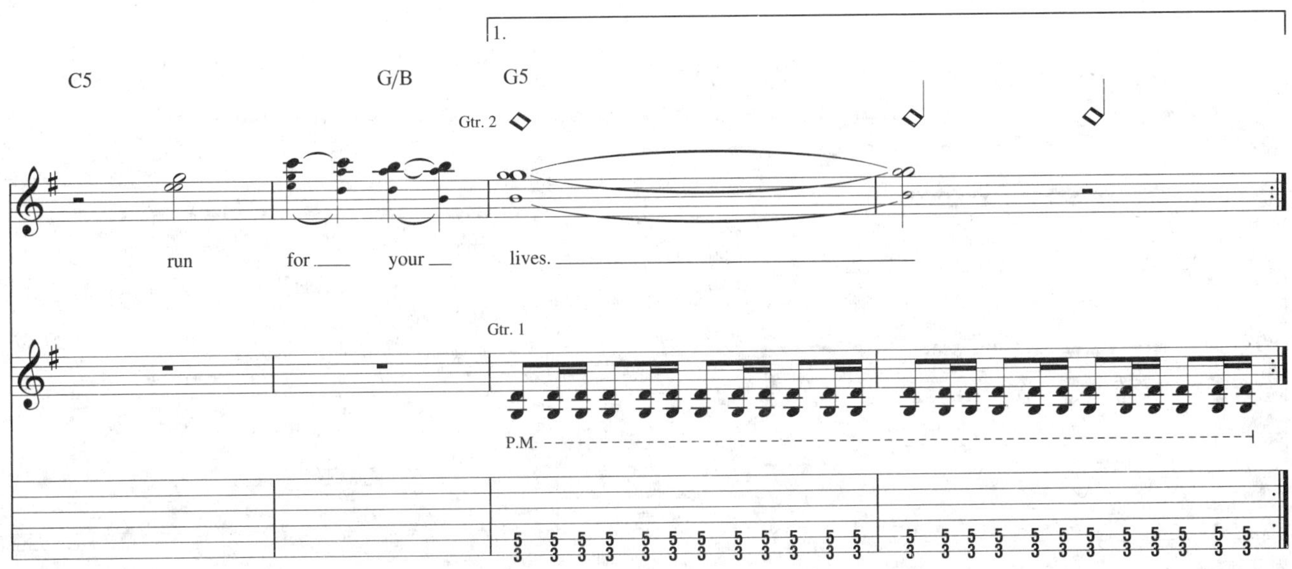

*Chord symbols reflect implied harmony.

Gtrs. 1 & 2: w/ Rhy. Fig. 3 (3 times)

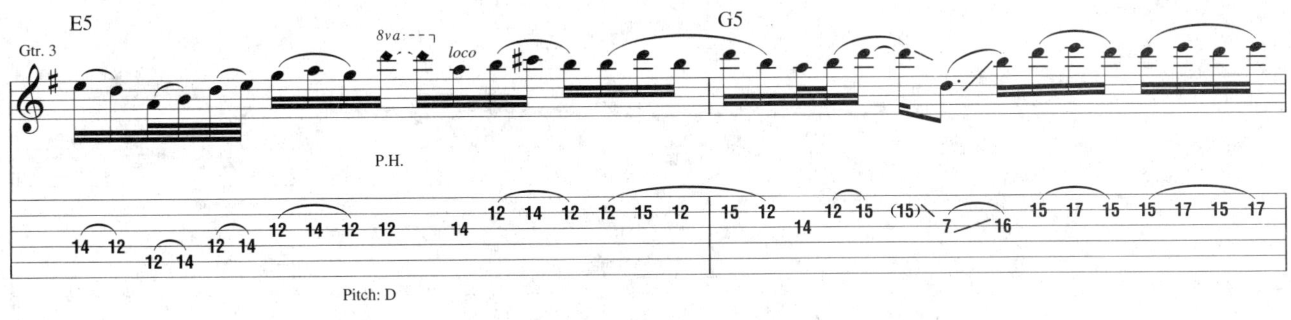
E5
G5
Gtr. 3
8va
loco
P.H.
Pitch: D

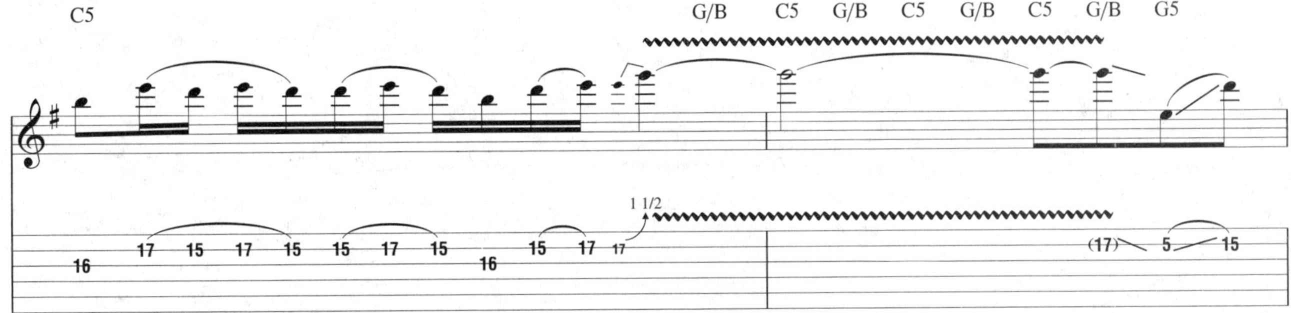
C5
G/B C5 G/B C5 G/B C5 G/B G5
1 1/2

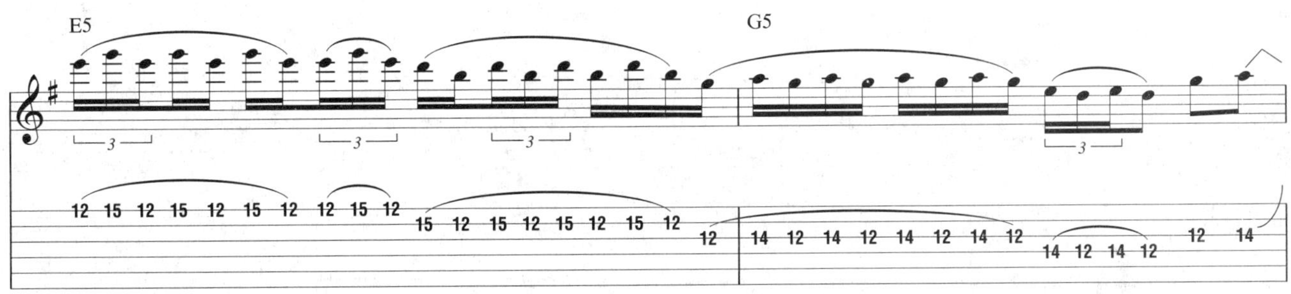
E5
G5

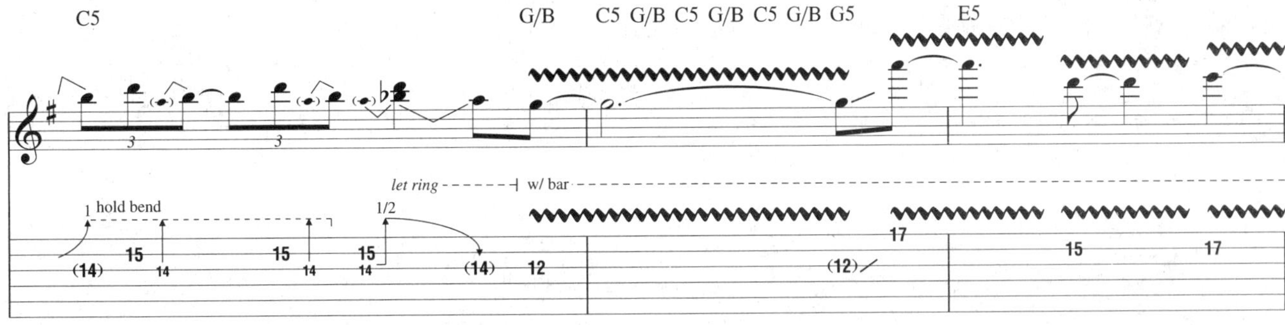
C5
G/B C5 G/B C5 G/B C5 G/B G5
E5
let ring
w/ bar
hold bend
1/2

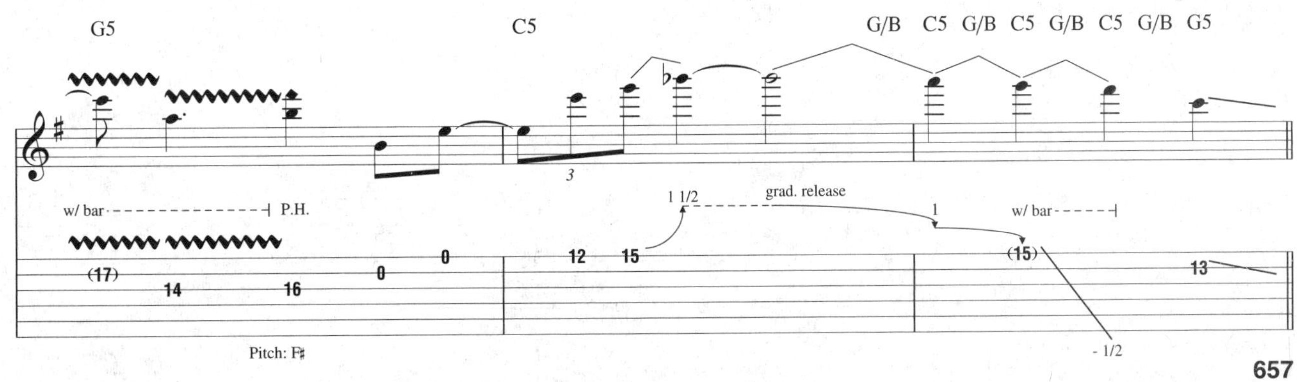
G5
C5
G/B C5 G/B C5 G/B C5 G/B G5
w/ bar
P.H.
1 1/2
grad. release
Pitch: F♯
- 1/2

Interlude

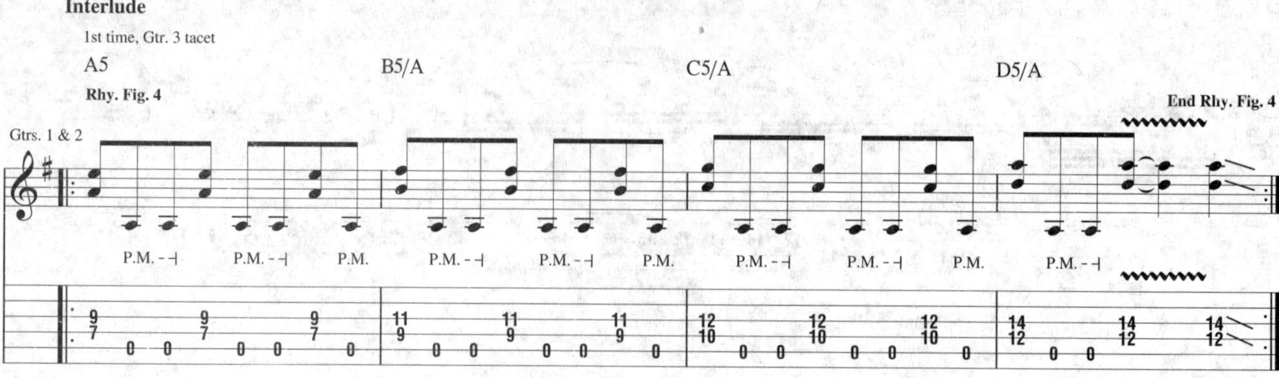

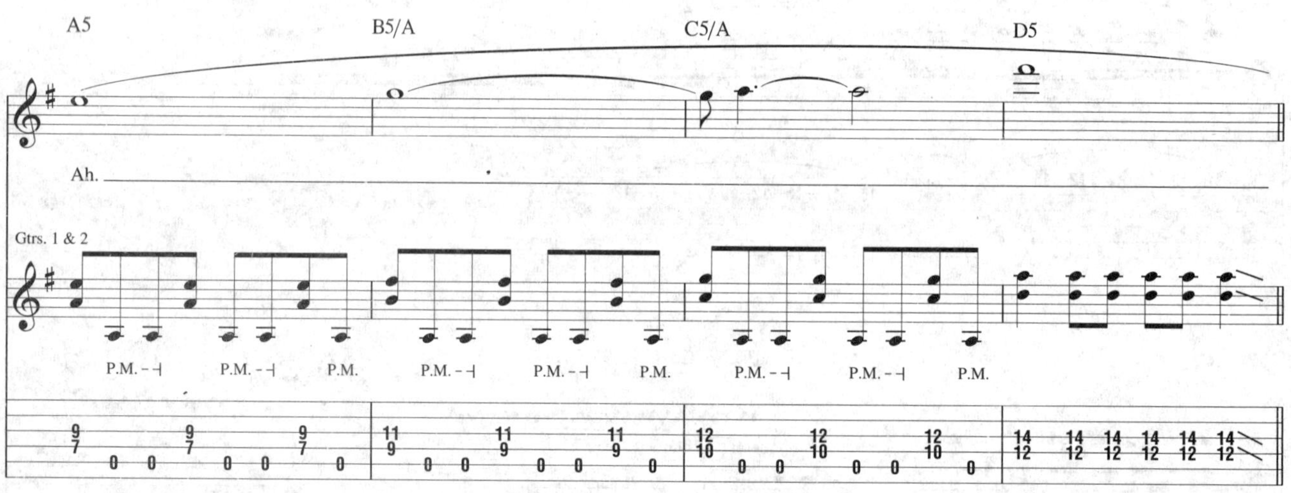

Outro-Chorus

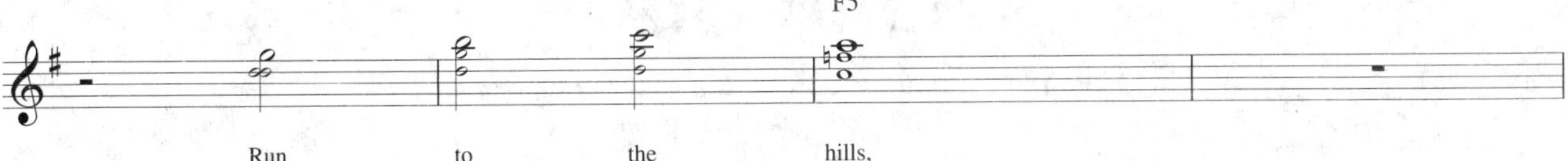
F5
Run to the hills,

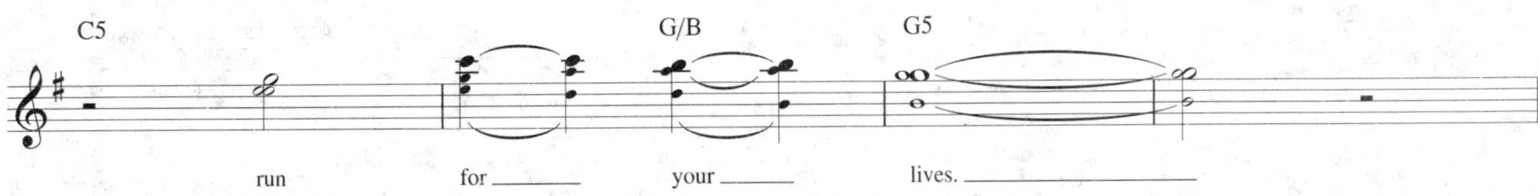
C5
G/B
G5
run for your lives.

F5
Run to the hills,

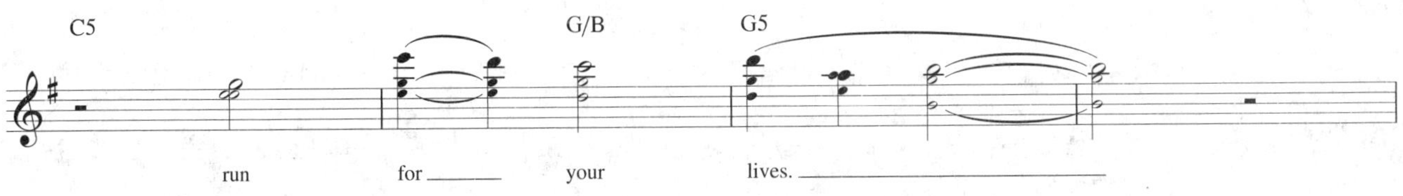
C5
G/B
G5
run for your lives.

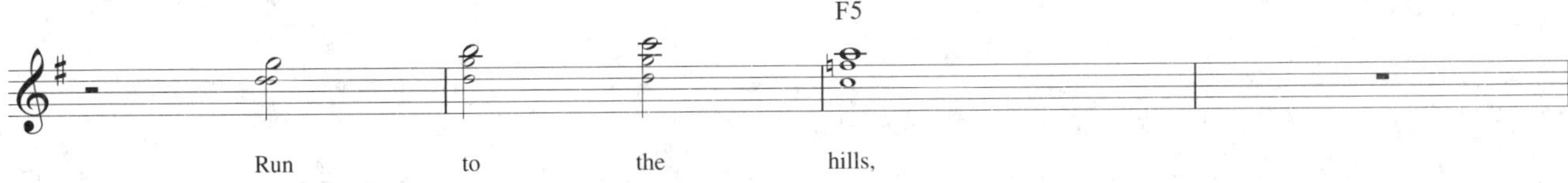
F5
Run to the hills,

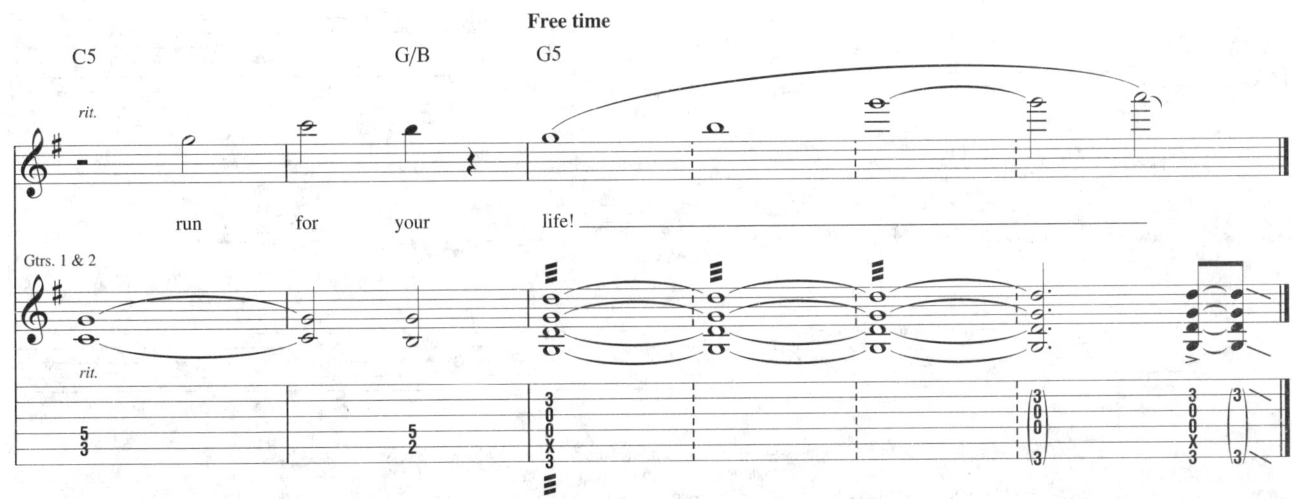
Free time
C5
G/B
G5
rit.
run for your life!
Gtrs. 1 & 2
rit.

Satin Doll

Words by Johnny Mercer and Billy Strayhorn
Music by Duke Ellington

Fmaj7
Gm7
C7
Am7sus4 Am7 Am9 D9
Am7sus4 Am7 Bm Am
Dm7
Em7
D#m7 Em7
A13
E7#9
Bb7 A7
A+7
Dm7
G13sus4
Dm9 Dm7sus4 Dm9 G13
let ring
Em7
A13sus4
Em7 Em7sus4 Em9
Am13
Eb9 D9
D13
Eb13 D13
Abm9
Db9
Db13 C6/9
N.C.
C Guitar Solo
Dm7
G7
Em7
A7
Am7
D7
Abm7
Db7
Cmaj7
A7
Dm7
p
mf

G7
Em7
A7
D7
D♭7
Cmaj7
Gm7
C7
Gm7
C7
Fmaj7
Am7
D7
Am7
D13
D♭13 Dm7
G7
Dm7
G13
Em7
A7
A+7
D7
D♭7
Cmaj7

*Played behind the beat.

Dm7
G7
Em7
let ring
A7
A7#5
D7
D13
Db7
Cmaj13
Em7
A7
Dm7
G7
Em7
A7
A+7
D7
Db7
Cmaj7
A7
Dm7
G7
Em7

A7
D7
D♭7
let ring
P.M.
Cmaj7
Gm7
C13
Fmaj 6/9
Am7
D7
Am7
D7
Dm7
G7
Dm7
G7
Em7
A7
D7
D♭11
C 6/9
B♭maj11
D Trade
Em7
A+7
A7
Dm7
G7
Em7
D♯m7
Em7
A7

D13
D♭7
Cmaj7
A7
A+7
Dm7
G7
Em7
D♯m7 Em7
A7
D13
D♭13
Cmaj6/9
Gm9
C13
Fmaj7
p
D+7
D13
D7
G7sus4
E7
A7
let ring
mf
Dm7
G7
E7♯9
E♭7♯9 E7♯9
A7
D13
p
D♭9
Cmaj7
Em7
A7
E Melody
Dm7
G13sus4
Dm7
G13
mf

Em7
A13
A13sus4
Em7
A13 A9♯5
D13
G7sus4 D13
A♭m9
D♭9
D♭13 C6/9
F13
E7♯9
let ring
A
Dm7
G13sus4
Dm7
G13
Em7
A13
A13sus4
Em7
A13 A9♯5
D9
D11 D9
A♭m9
G+7
D♭maj7 Cmaj7
Gm7
let ring
C7
Fmaj7
*Played ahead of the beat.
Am7
D7
G7

Dm7 G13 G13sus4 Dm7 G7 Em7 A13 A13sus4
Em7 A13 A+7 Am7 D13 G7sus4 D13 A♭m9 D♭9 D♭13 C6/9 E7♯5 E♭13 D7
D13 G7sus4 D13 A♭m9 D♭9 D♭13 C6/9 F13 E7♯9 A7
Free Time
D13 G7sus4 D13 A♭m9 D♭9 D♭13 C6/9 N.C.
rit.
C7
let ring

School's Out

Words and Music by Alice Cooper and Michael Bruce

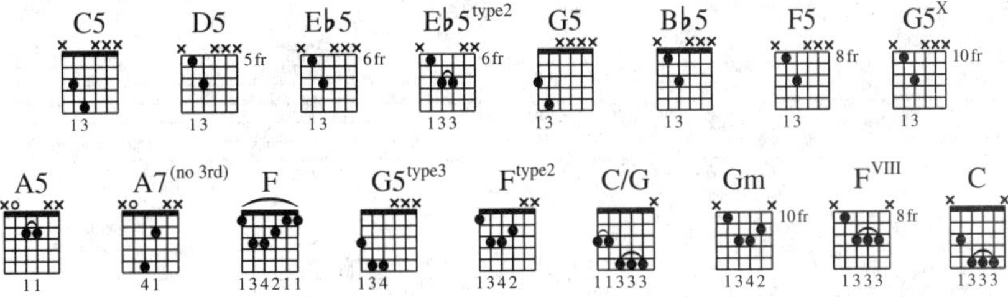

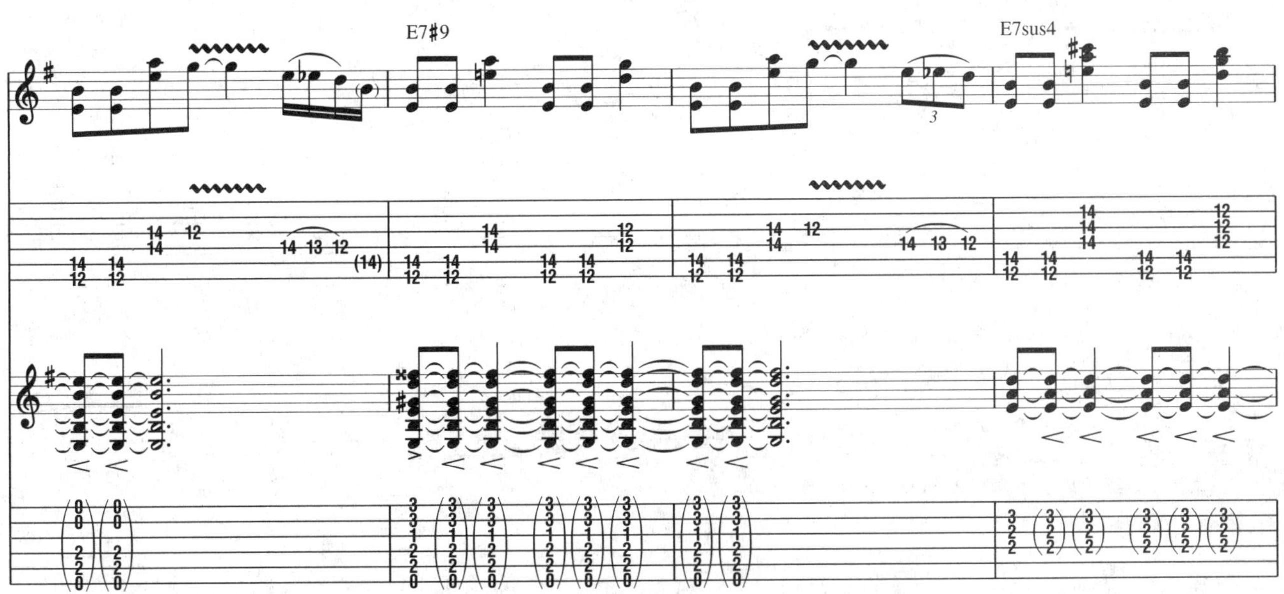

E5
A/E
E5
Em7
E5
A/E Em
E5
A/E
E5
Em7
Rhy. Fig. 1
End Rhy. Fig. 1
Rhy. Fig. 2

Verse

Gtr. 2: w/ Rhy. Fig. 2, 4 times
E5
A/E Em
E5
A/E
E5
Em7
E5
A/E Em
1. Well, we got no choice, all the girls
Rhy. Fig. 3
End Rhy. Fig. 3
End Rhy. Fig. 2

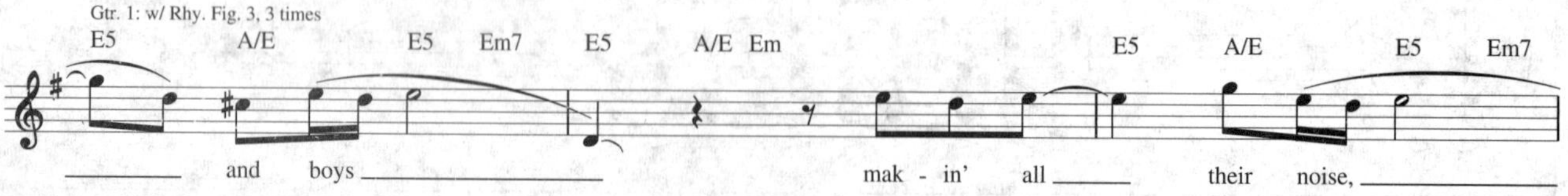

Gtr. 1: w/ Rhy. Fig. 3, 3 times
E5
A/E
E5
Em7
E5
A/E Em
E5
A/E
E5
Em7
and boys
mak - in' all their noise,

E5
A/E Em
E5
A/E
E5
Em7
E5
A/E Em
'cause they found new toys.
Well, we

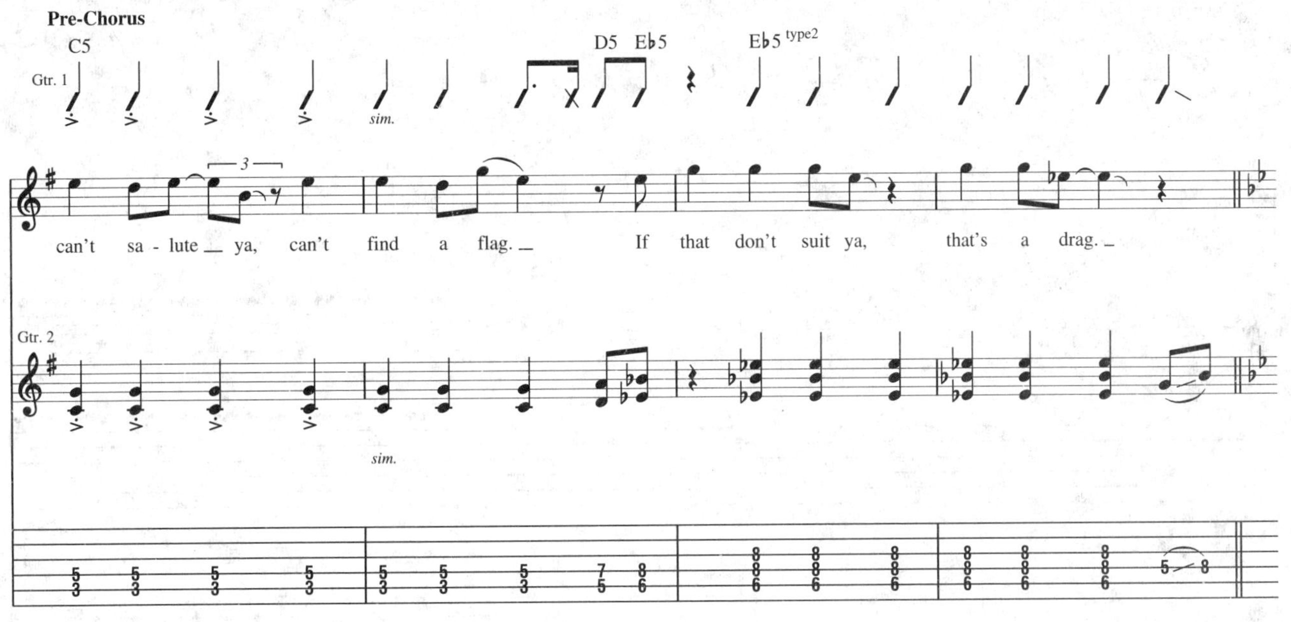

Pre-Chorus

C5
D5 Eb5
Eb5 type2
Gtr. 1
sim.
can't sa - lute ya, can't find a flag.
If that don't suit ya, that's a drag.
Gtr. 2
sim.

Chorus

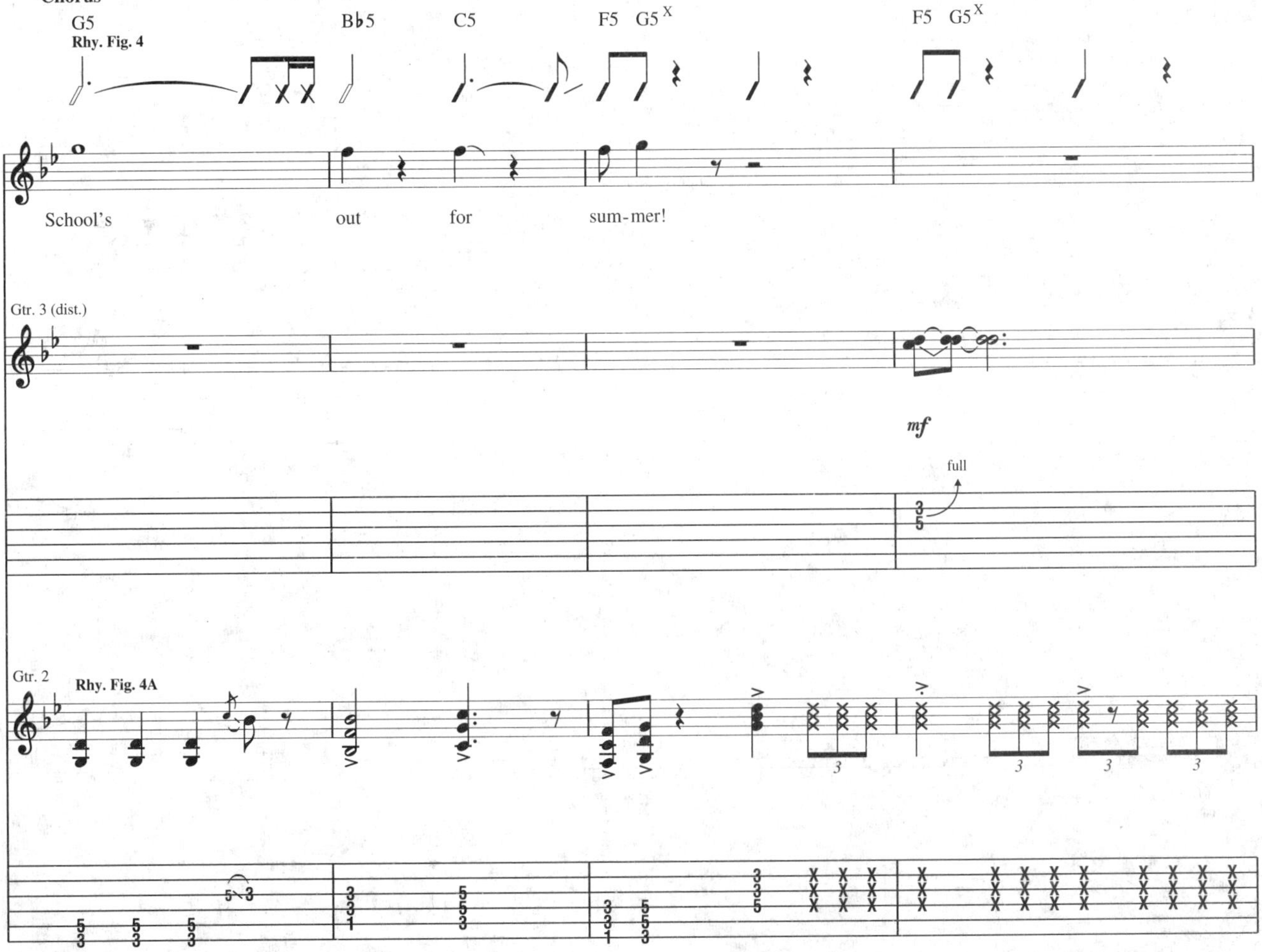
G5
Bb5
C5
F5 G5 X
F5 G5 X
Rhy. Fig. 4
School's out for sum-mer!
Gtr. 3 (dist.)
mf
full
Gtr. 2
Rhy. Fig. 4A

G5
B♭5
C5
F5 G5X
F5 G5X
End Rhy. Fig. 4
School's out for - ev - er!
full
End Rhy. Fig. 4A

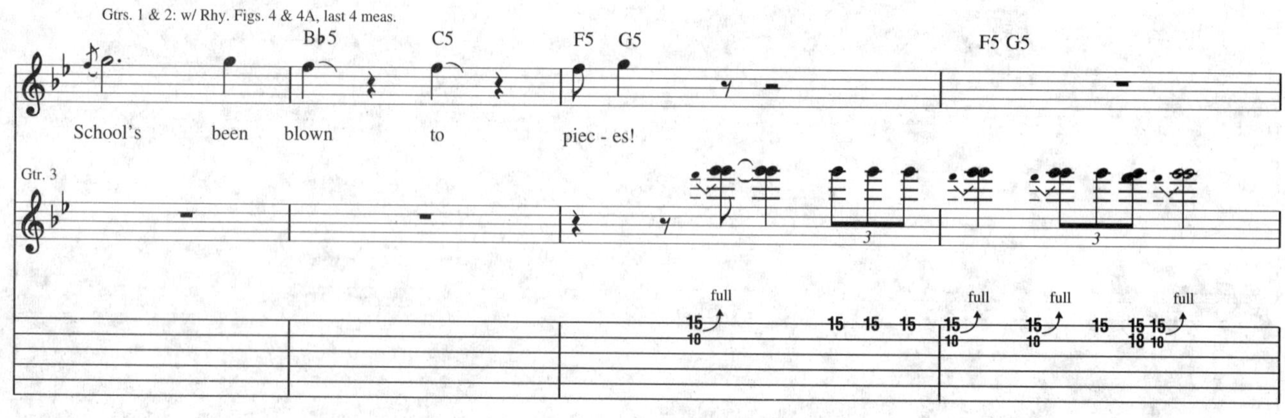
Gtrs. 1 & 2: w/ Rhy. Figs. 4 & 4A, last 4 meas.
B♭5
C5
F5 G5
F5 G5
School's been blown to piec - es!
Gtr. 3
full
full
full
full

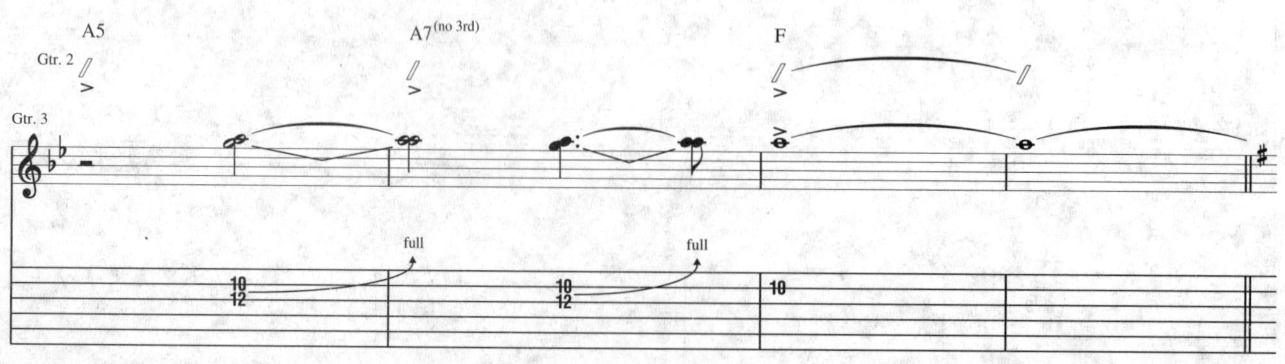
A5
A7(no 3rd)
F
Gtr. 2
Gtr. 3
full
full

Bridge

Gtr. 2 tacet

C Csus2#11 C Csus2#11 C Csus2#11 C Csus2#11

No more pen - cils, no more books,

Gtr. 3

fdbk.

(10) (10)

Rhy. Fig. 5

* Gtr. 4

mf

sim.

* Kybd. arr. for gtr.

Dsus 2/4 D D9 D Dsus 2/4 D

Gtr. 2

no more teach - er's dir - ty looks. Yeah!

(No more teach - er's dir - ty looks.)

(10)

End Rhy. Fig. 5

Guitar Solo
Gtr. 4 tacet
Gtr. 2: w/ Rhy. Fig. 1, 2 times
Gtr. 1: w/ Rhy. Fig. 6, 3 times
E5 A/E E5 Em E5 A/E Em E5 A/E E5 Em E5 A/E Em
Gtr. 3
full
fdbk.
Rhy. Fig. 6
End Rhy. Fig. 6
Gtr. 1
w/ bar
E5 A/E E5 Em E5 A/E E5 Em E5 A/E Em
2. Well, we got
Gtr. 3
Gtr. 2
Verse
Gtr. 1: w/ Rhy. Fig. 3, 4 times
Gtr. 2: w/ Rhy. Fig. 2, 3 1/2 times
Gtr. 3 tacet
E5 A/E E5 Em7 E5 A/E Em E5 A/E E5 Em7
no class, and we got no prin - ci - ples,
E5 A/E Em E5 A/E E5 Em7 E5 A/E Em E5 A/E E5 Em7
and we got no in - no-cence. We can't e - ven think of a word that rhymes!

Chorus
Gtrs. 1 & 2: w/ Rhy. Figs. 4 & 4A, simile
E5 A/E Em G5 B♭5 C5 F5 G5 F5 G5
School's out for sum-mer!
Gtr. 2
Gtr. 3
full
full
full
w/ bar
B♭5 C5 F5 G5 F5 G5
School's out for - ev - er! My
8va
full
full
full
full
w/ bar
Bridge
Gtrs. 1 & 2 tacet
Gtr. 4: w/ Rhy. Fig. 5, 1 3/4 times
G5 type 3 F type 2 C/G C Csus2♯11 C Csus2♯11
Gtrs. 1 & 2
school's been blown to piec - es! No more pen - cils,
loco
grad. bend
full
fdbk.
w/ children's laughter & talking
C Csus2♯11 C Csus2♯11 Dsus2/4 D D9 D Dsus2/4 D D9 D
no more books, no more teach - er's dir - ty looks.
grad. bend
1/2
full
Gtr. 3 tacet
C Csus2♯11 C Csus2♯11 C Csus2♯11 C Csus2♯11
Out for sum - mer, out till fall.

Chorus
Gtrs. 1 & 2: w/ Rhy. Figs. 4 & 4A, 1 1/2 times, simile
Dsus 2/4 D D9 D Dsus 2/4 D G5 B♭5 C5
We might not go back at all! School's out for
Gtr. 3
Gtr. 1
divisi
full
F5 G5 F5 G5 B♭5 C5
ev - er! School's out for
F5 G5 F5 G5 B♭5 C5 F5 G5
sum-mer! School's out with fe - ver!
8va
w/ bar
F5 G5 Gm F VIII C
w/ school bell
w/ children's cheers & tape effects
Gtr. 2
School's out com - plete - ly!
loco
grad. bend
fdbk.

Seven Come Eleven

By Benny Goodman and Charlie Christian

C Guitar Solo
N.C.(A♭7)
1/2
G7

C7
F7
Bb7
Eb7
N.C.(Ab7)
1/2
1/4
D Vibe Solo
play 8 times
8
play 4 times
D.S. al Coda
(take repeat)
Coda
E Clarinet Solo
31

Shake Me

Words and Music by Tom Keifer

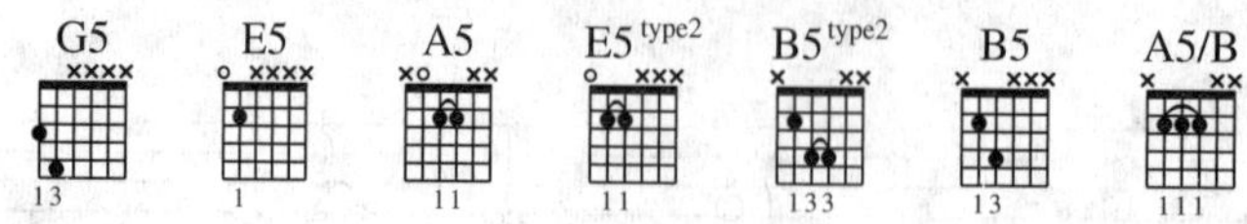

Intro

Moderate Rock ♩ = 135

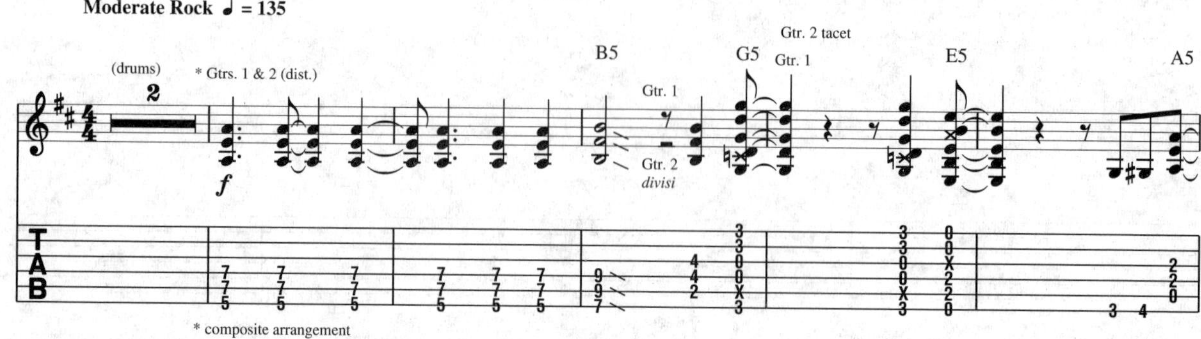

* composite arrangement

Verse

A5
E5
B5
G5
In the morn - in' we were still go - in' strong,
Now let me tell ya, it
Rhy. Fig. 2
P.M.
E5
A5
E5
B5
sure felt good.
First time I saw that girl I knew it would.
P.M.
P.M.
(cont. in slash)
G5
E5
G
G♯
E
A5
3fr
4fr
open
End Rhy. Fig. 2
Gtr. 2
P.M.
(cont. in notation)
Now let me tell ya, it sure felt right.
No pull - in' teeth she did - n't wan - na fight. She said,
Gtr. 1
Rhy. Fig. 3
End Rhy. Fig. 3
Chorus
B5
A5
E5
B5
E5
N.C.
"Shake me all night." She said, "Shake me, shake it don't break it ba - by.
Gtrs. 1 & 2
Rhy. Fig. 4
semi-harm.

B5
A5
E5
A5
F#5
B5
G5
Shake me all night." She said, "All night long."
End Rhy. Fig. 4
Gtr. 1
Gtr. 2
divisi
Gtr. 1: w/ Rhy. Fig. 1, 1st 3 meas.
Gtr. 2 tacet
E5
A5
E5 type2
B5 type2
Gtr. 2
All night long, ba - by.
Gtr. 3 (dist.)
f
w/ bar
1/2
-1
-1/2
Verse
Gtr. 1: w/ Rhy. Fig. 1, 3 times
Gtr. 2: w/ Rhy. Fig. 1, 2 times, simile
Gtr. 3 tacet
B5
G5
E5
A5
2. Screamed and scratched and rolled out of the bed, I nev - er real - ly got her
E5 B5
G5
E5
A5
out of my head. And now and then she makes those so - cial calls, gives me a squeeze, gets me

Gtr. 2: w/ Rhy. Fig. 2, simile
E5 B5 G5 E5
kick - in' the walls.
Now let me tell ya, it still feels tight,
A5 E5 B5 G5
Gtr. 1: w/ Rhy. Fig. 3
and we were sha - kin' af - ter ev - er - y bite.
I feel her com - in' in the
E5 A5 E5 A5 E5 A5 E5
mid-dle of the night,
scream-in' high - er.
Gtrs. 1 & 2
w/ delay repeats
Chorus
Gtrs. 1 & 2: w/ Rhy. Fig. 4
B5 A5 E5 B5 E5
"Shake me all night." She said, "Shake me, shake
N.C. B5 A5 E5
it don't break it ba - by. Shake me all night." She said,
To Coda
Bridge
B5 E5 N.C. A5 E5
"Shake me." Ooh, yeah. All night. Keep
Gtrs. 1 & 2
semi-harm.

* composite arrangement
** applies to harmonic only

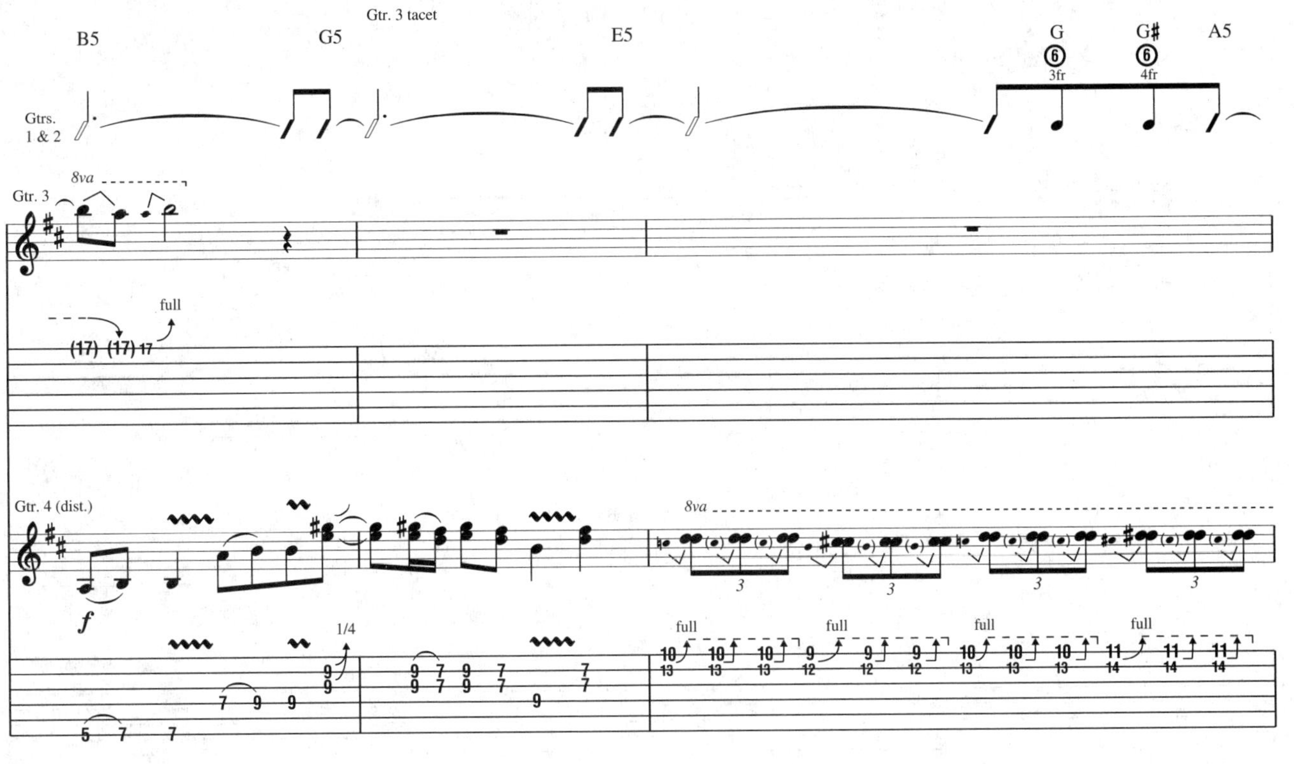
Gtr. 3 tacet
B5
G5
E5
G
3fr
G#
4fr
A5
Gtrs. 1 & 2
Gtr. 3
8va
full
Gtr. 4 (dist.)
1/4
full

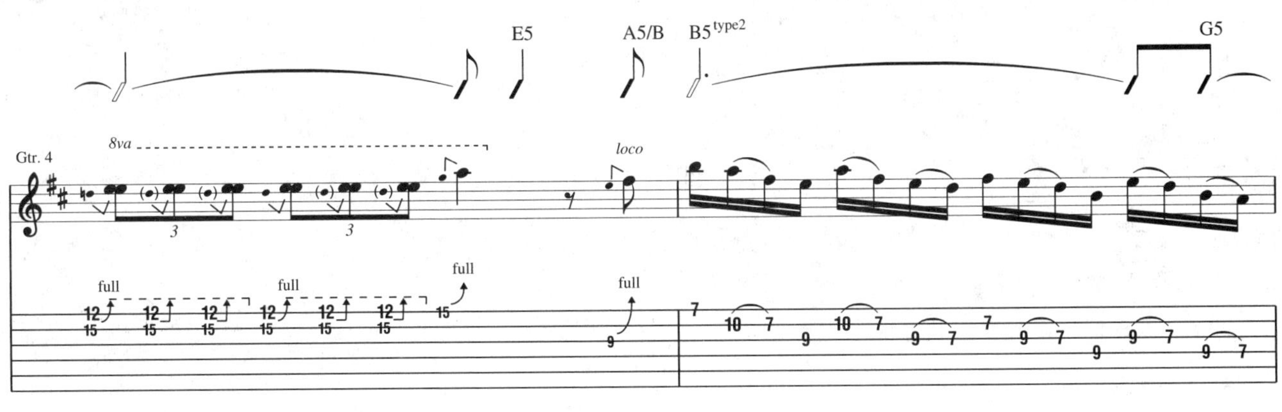
E5
A5/B
B5 type2
G5
Gtr. 4
8va
loco
full

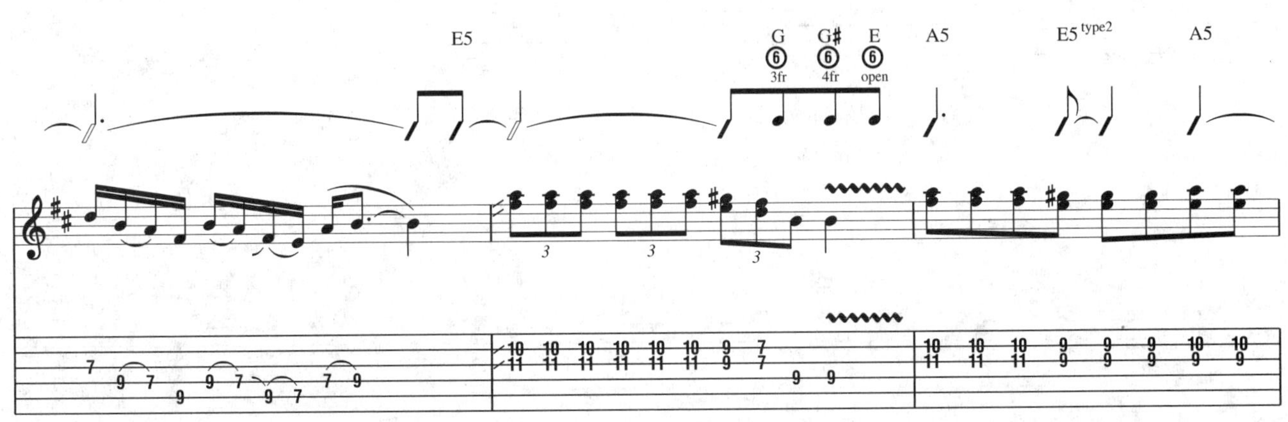
E5
G
3fr
G#
4fr
E
open
A5
E5 type2
A5

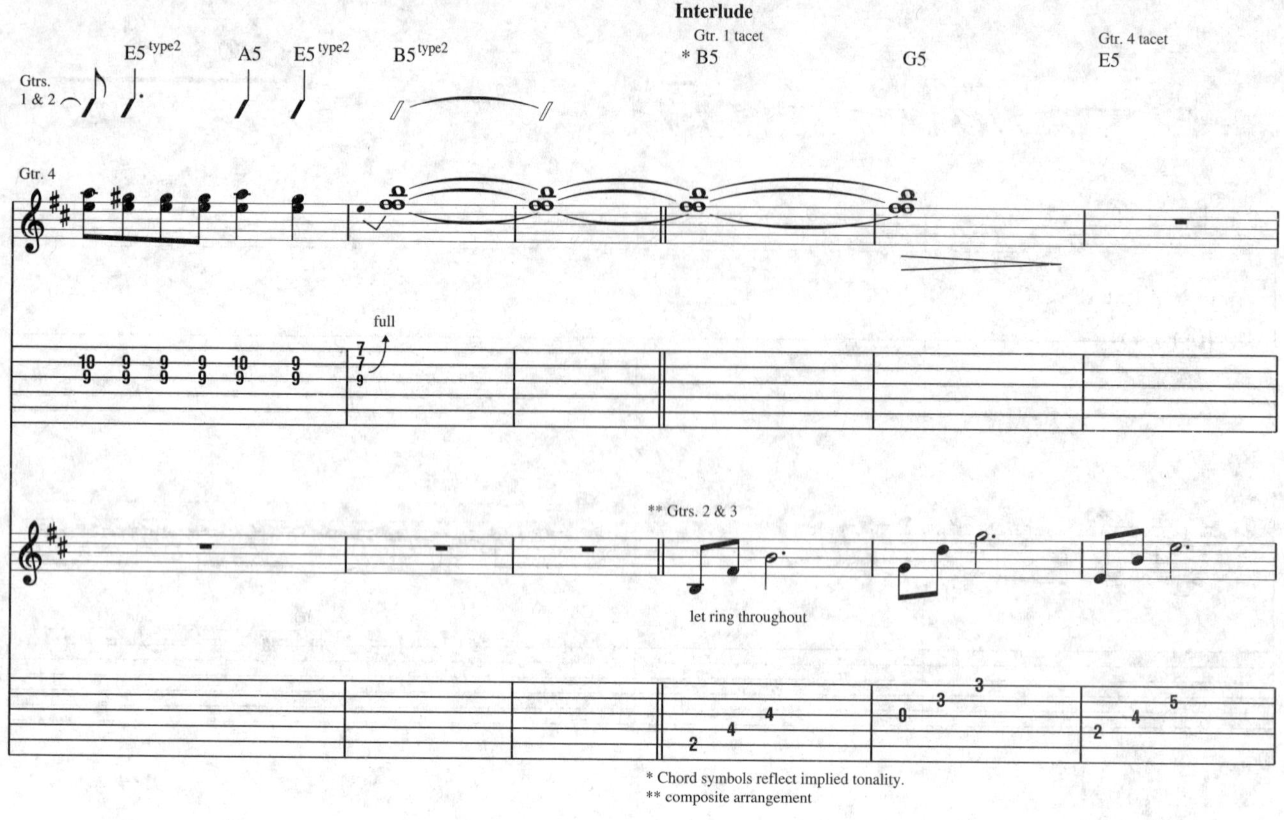

* Chord symbols reflect implied tonality.
** composite arrangement

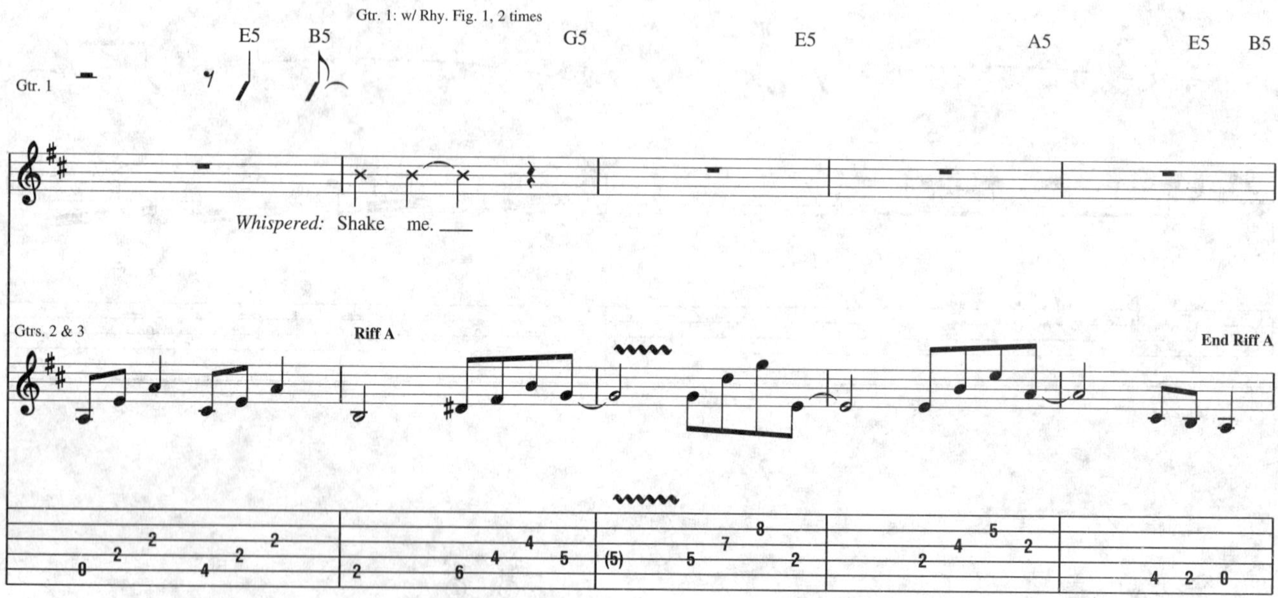

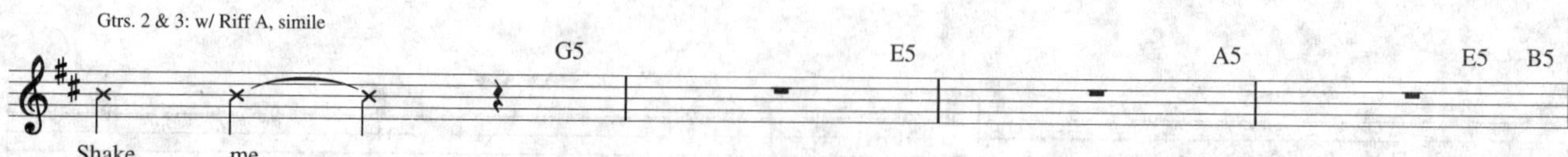

D.S. al Coda
Gtr. 1: w/ Rhy. Fig. 3
G5
E5
Gtr. 3 tacet
A5 E5 A5 E5 A5 E5
Shake me.
Shake me.
Gtrs. 2 & 3
Gtrs. 1 & 2
Coda
Outro-Guitar Solo
Gtrs. 1 & 2: w/ Rhy. Fig. 4, 1st 4 meas., 3 times
Begin Fade
N.C.
B5 A5 E5 B5 E5 N.C.
yeah.
Shake me.
(Shake me.) Yeah.
Gtr. 3
semi-harm.
1/4
B5 A5 E5 B5 E5 N.C.
(Shake me.) Ooh, b - b - ba - by, yeah, yeah. Shake me.
1/2
Fade Out
B5 A5 E5 B5 E5 N.C.
Ah,
Yeah.
(Shake me.)
(Shake me.)
full

Shining Star

Words and Music by Maurice White, Philip Bailey and Larry Dunn

E7#9
Yeah.
(Yeah,
Rhy. Fig. 1
End Rhy. Fig. 1

Gtr. 2: w/ Rhy. Fig. 1, simile
Hey.
Ha!
Gtr. 1
P.M.
1/4

Verse

Gtr. 2: w/ Rhy. Fig. 1, 6 times, simile
E7#9
1. When you wish up - on a star, your
*sim.
1/4
*next 12 meas.

dreams will take _ you ver - y far, ___ yeah. ___ When _
___ you wish _ up - on _ a dream, ___ life _
___ ain't al - ways what _ it seems, oh, yeah. _ What'd
___ you see _ on nights _ of clear? ___ Hey. ___ In _

Chorus

Interlude

Guitar Solo

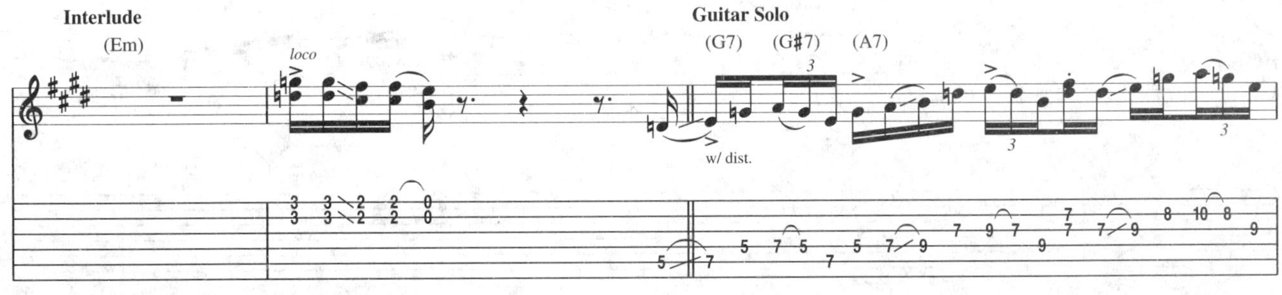

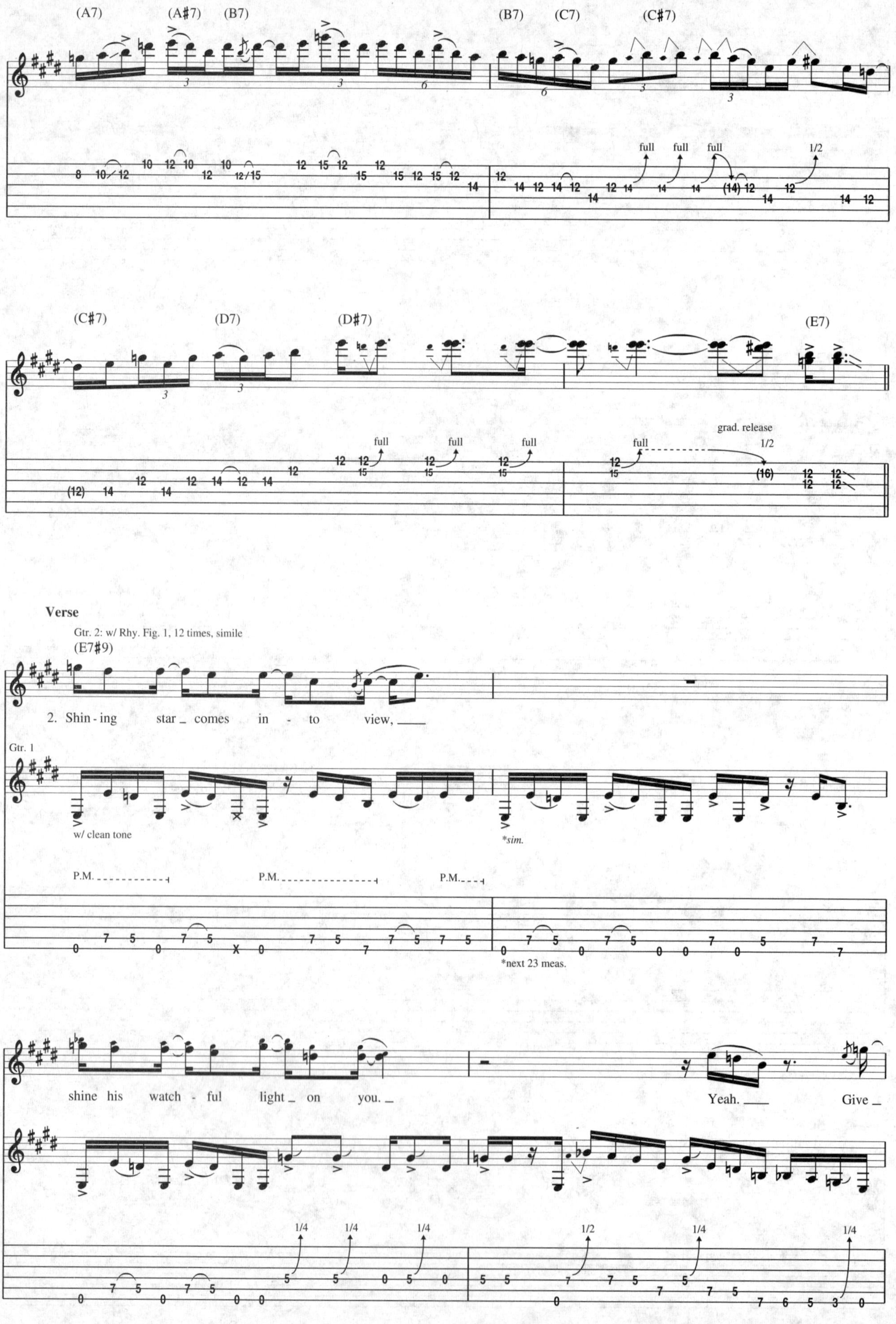

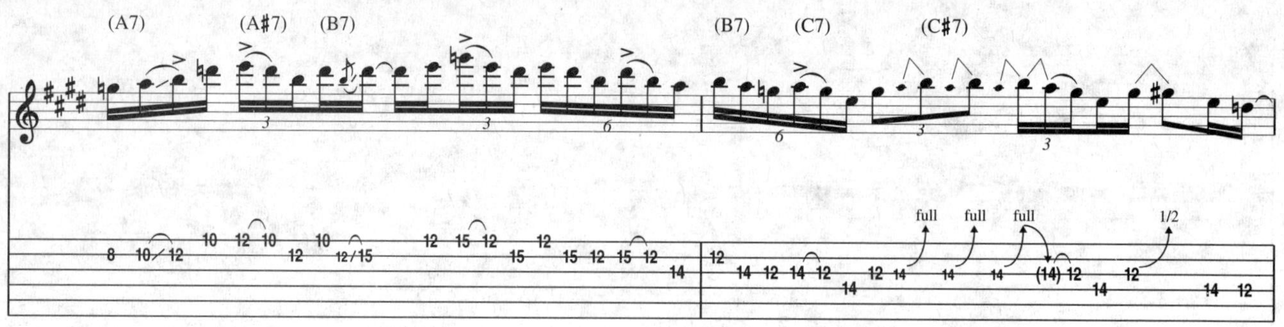

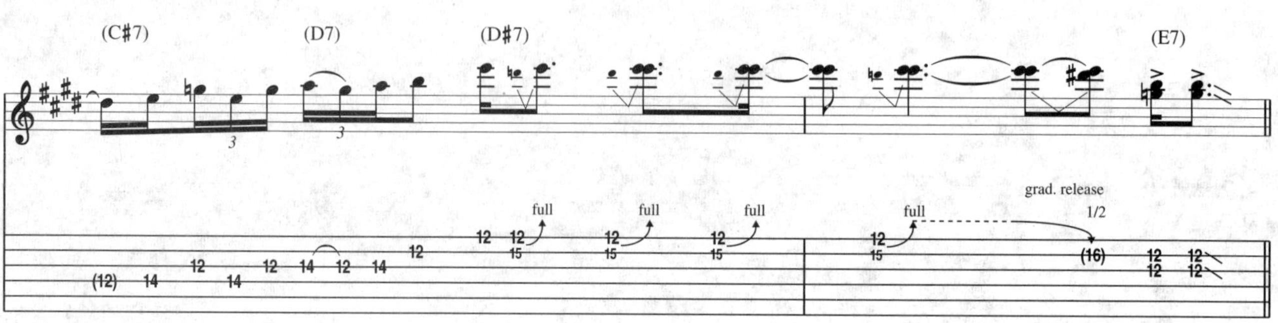

Verse

Gtr. 2: w/ Rhy. Fig. 1, 12 times, simile

(E7#9)

2. Shin - ing star _ comes in - to view, ____

Gtr. 1

w/ clean tone

*sim.

P.M.

*next 23 meas.

shine his watch - ful light _ on you. _ Yeah. __ Give _

you strength to car - ry on,
yeah,
yeah.
Make
your bod - y big and strong,
yeah.
Born
a man - child of the sun,
yeah,
yeah.
Saw
my work had just be - gun.
Yeah,
found

I had to stand a - lone, yeah. Yeah, bless
it now, I've got my own, oh, yeah. Oh, yeah. So if
you find your - self in need, why don't you
lis - ten to those words of heed? Be
1/4
1/2

a gi - ant grain of sand.
Words
1/2
1/4
of wis - dom, yes I can.
You're a
1/4
1/2
1/2
Chorus
Gtr. 2 tacet
N.C.(A7)
(D7)
Gtr. 1 tacet
(G7)
(C7) (B7)
(A7)
(D7)
shin - ing star,
no mat - ter who you are.
Shin - ing bright to see,
what you could
Gtr. 1
1/4
(G7)
(C7)
(A7)
(D7)
(G7)
(C7) (B7)
tru - ly be.
Your're a
shin - ing star,
no mat - ter who you are.
Shin - ing
1.
2.
(A7)
(D7)
(G7)
(E7)
(G7)
(C7)
bright to see,
what you could
tru - ly be.
You're a
tru - ly be.
Shin -
1., 2.
3.
(A7)
(D7)
(G7)
(C7)
(B7)
- ing star for you to see
what your life can tru - ly be.
Shin -
your life can tru - ly be.

Shout It Out Loud

Words and Music by Paul Stanley, Gene Simmons and Bob Ezrin

Gtr. 1: w/Rhy. Fill 1
A
D5
A
— to be re - mind - ed? Need ___ to be re - mind - ed.
— the par - ty start - ed. Get ___ the par - ty start - ed.
Pre Chorus
D5 D6 D5 D6 D5 D6 D5 D6 A5 A6 A5 N.C. E5
It does - n't mat - ter what you do or say. Just for - get ___ the things that you've been _ told._
Don't let 'em tell you that there's too much noise. They're too old ___ to real - ly un - der - stand._
Rhy. Fig. 2
Gtrs. 1 & 2, composite parts
Gtr. 2: w/Rhy. Fill 2
E6 N.C. D5 D6 D5 D6 D5 D6 D5 A5
We can't do it an - y oth - er way. Ev - ery - bod -
You'll still get row - dy with the girls and boys, 'cause it's time _
Rhy. Fill 1
Gtr. 1
Rhy. Fill 2
Gtr. 2

A6
A5 N.C. B
- y's got to rock and roll. Woa.
— for you to take a stand. Yeah.
End Rhy. Fig. 2
Chorus
B E B E B E B A B
Shout it, shout it, shout it out loud.
Rhy. Fig. 3
End Rhy. Fig. 3
1.
B E B E B E B A N.C. B
Shout it, shout it, shout it out loud.
2. If you
Guitar Solo
2.
Gtrs. 1 & 2: w/Rhy. Fig. 2
D5 D6 D5 D6 D5 D6 D5 D6 A5 A6 A5 N.C. E5
loud.
Gtr. 3
f (distortion)
full
1/2
full
1 1/2
P.H.

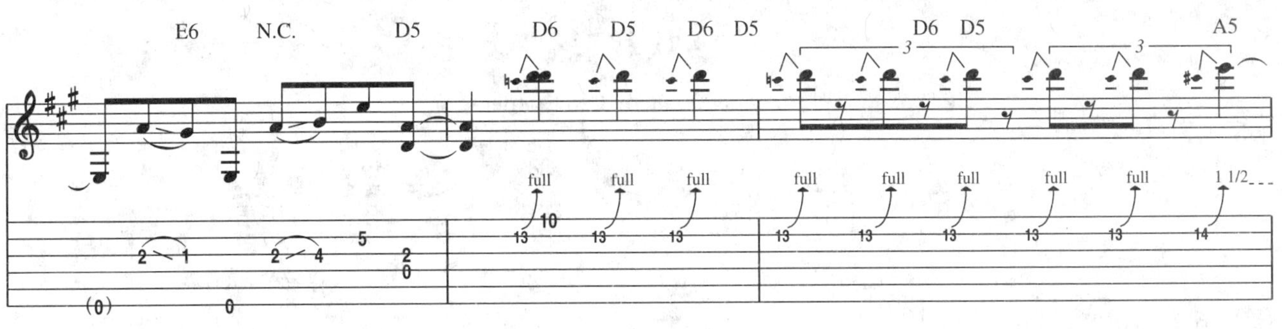

Breakdown
(Drums and Vocals)

Gtrs. 1 & 2: w/Rhy. Fig. 3

Chorus

Gtrs. 1 & 2: w/Rhy. Fig. 3

Signs

Words and Music by Les Emmerson

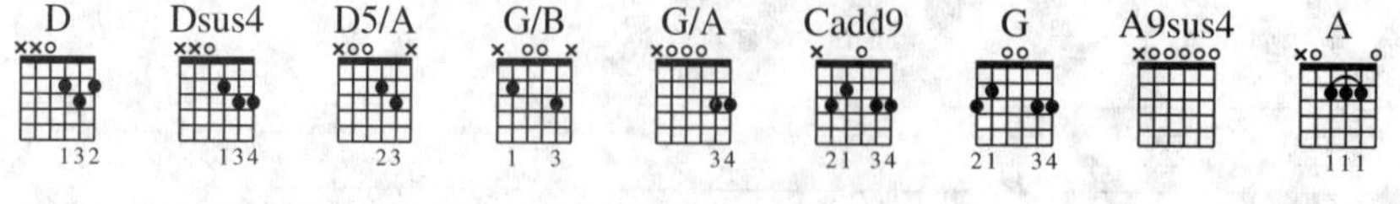

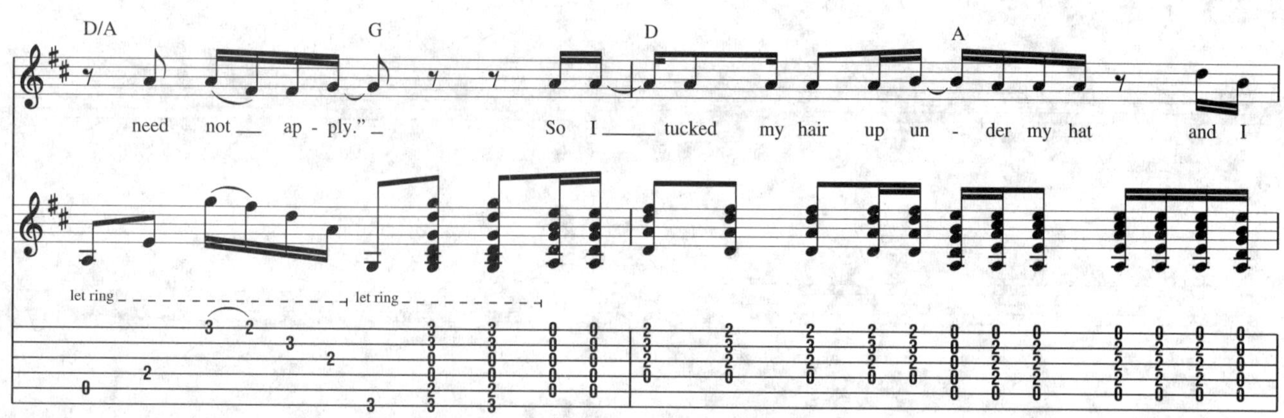

G
D
A
man, I think you'll do." Uh, so I took off my hat and said, "I-mag-ine that, huh,
Chorus
G
A
D
Cadd9
G
me a-work-ing for you." Oh. Signs, signs, ev - 'ry-where a sign fuck-
** Lead vocal is doubled next 4 meas.
To Coda
D
G
D
A
G5/A
- ing up the scen-er-y, break-ing my mind. Do this don't do that. Can't you read the sign?
1.
Cadd9
D
Dsus4 D
Dsus4 D
Dsus4 D
D5/A G5/A
Gtr. 1
(cont. in notation)
2. And the
Gtr. 2
(cont. in slash)

2.
Cadd9
D
Dsus4 D/F#
G
A
Oh.
Uh,
* T
* T = Thumb on 6
Bridge
A
G
D
Dsus4 D
Dadd4
say now, mis - ter, can't you read? You got to have a shirt and tie to get a seat.
let ring
D
A
G
A9sus4
You can't watch, no, you can't eat. You ain't sup - posed to
D
Dsus4 D
Dsus4 D
Dsus4 D
N.C.
be here. And the

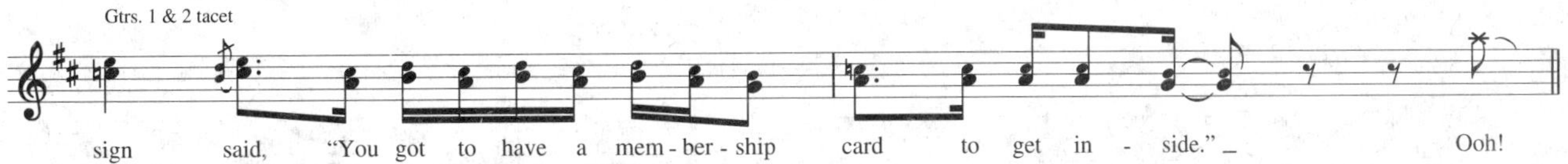
Gtrs. 1 & 2 tacet
sign said, "You got to have a mem - ber - ship card to get in - side." _ Ooh!

Guitar Solo

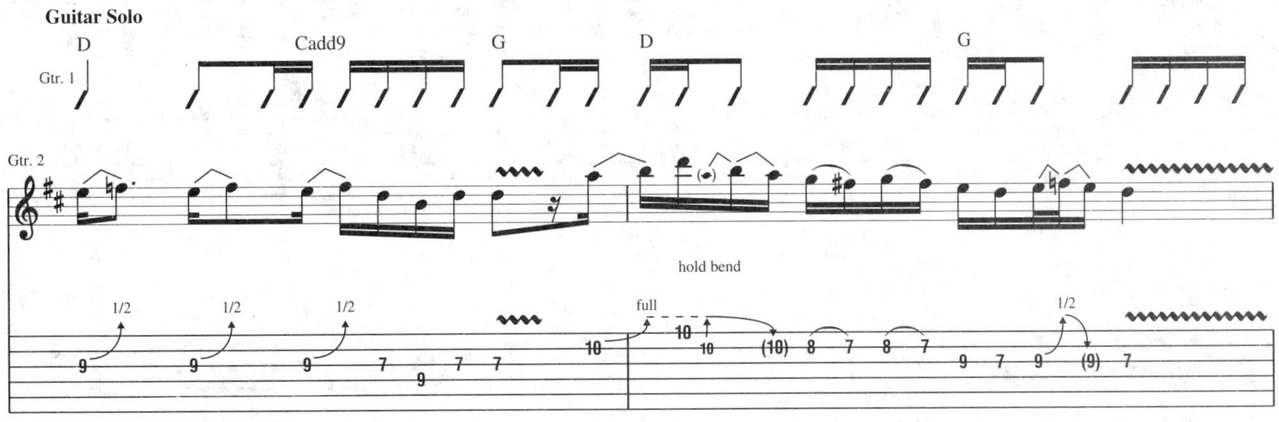
D
Cadd9
G
D
G
Gtr. 1
Gtr. 2
hold bend
1/2
full
1/2

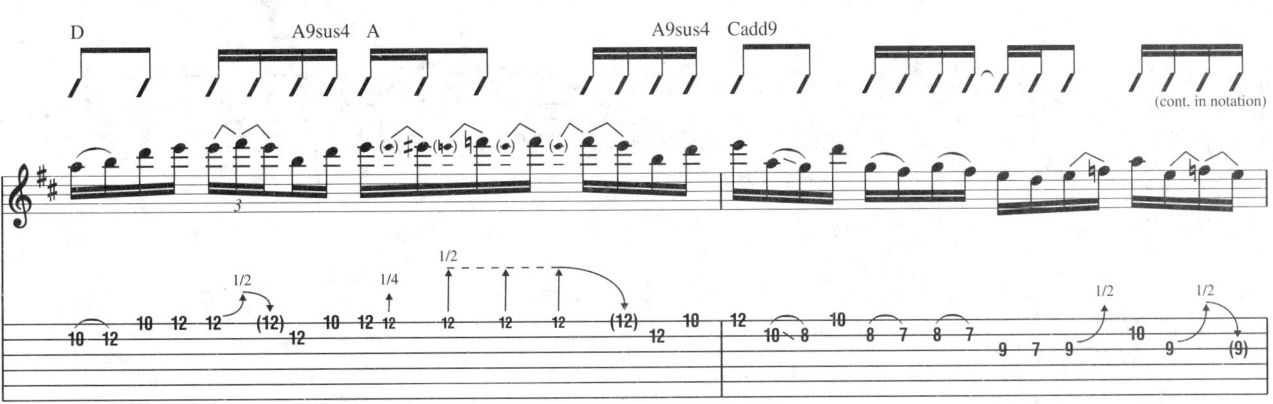
D
A9sus4
A
A9sus4
Cadd9
(cont. in notation)
1/2
1/4
1/2

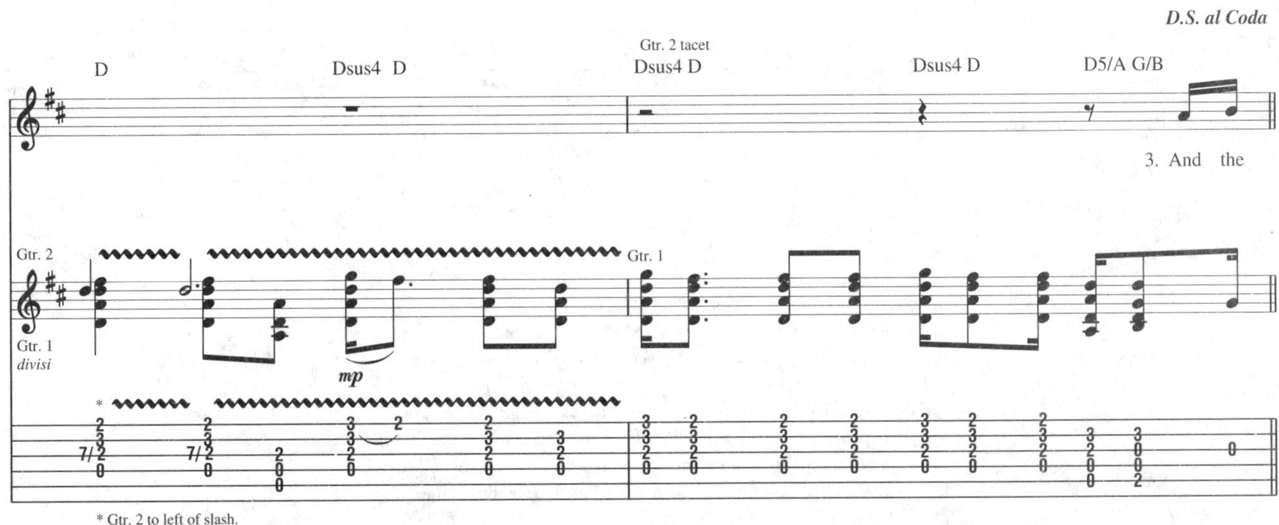
D.S. al Coda
Gtr. 2 tacet
D
Dsus4 D
Dsus4 D
Dsus4 D
D5/A G/B
3. And the
Gtr. 2
Gtr. 1
Gtr. 1
divisi
mp
* Gtr. 2 to left of slash.

Additional Lyrics

2. And the sign says, "Anybody caught trespassing will be shot on sight."
So I jumped the fence and yelled at the house, "Hey, what gives you the right
To put up a fence to keep me out or to keep Mother Nature in?"
If God was here he'd tell it to your face, "Man, you're some kinda sinner."

3. And the sign says, "Everybody welcome, come in and kneel down and pray."
And then they pass around the plate at the end of it all, and I didn't have a penny to pay.
So I got me a pen and paper, and I made up my own fuckin' sign.
I said, "Thank you, Lord, for thinkin' about me, I'm alive and doing fine."

Sir Duke

Words and Music by Stevie Wonder

B/D#
G#m/B
with an e - qual op - por - tu - ni - ty for all to
But here are some of mu - sic's pi - o - neers that time will
rake
G/B
F#/A#
F/A Fadd9/A F/A Fadd9/A F/A
(cont. in notation)
sing, dance and clap their hands. But just be -
not al - low us to for - get, now. For there's
Pre-Chorus
E9 Eb9 D9 Db9 D9 Eb9 E9
cause a rec - ord has a groove don't make it in the groove. But you can
Ba - sic, Mil - ler, Satch - mo, and the king of all, Sir Duke. And with a
Gtrs. 2 & 3
To Coda
Eb9 D9 Db9 D9 Eb9 E9 F9 F#9
tell right a - way at let - ter A when the peo - ple start to move.
voice like El - la's ring - ing out there's no way the band could lose.
(Gtr. 3 cont. in slash)

Chorus
B/D#
Rhy. Fig. 1A
Fm
Gtr. 3
P.M.
They can feel it all o - ver.
Rhy. Fig. 1
Gtr. 2
rake
P.M.
simile on repeat
sim.
Emaj7/D#
D#m
C#m
F#/A#
End Rhy. Fig. 1A
They can feel it all o - ver peo - ple.
End Rhy. Fig. 1
Gtrs. 2 & 3: w/ Rhy. Figs. 1 & 1A, simile
B
Fm
Emaj7
D#m
F#
They can feel it all o - ver.
They can feel it all o - ver peo - ple, go!
Interlude
N.C.
Riff A

18 16
18 16
18 16
18
16
16
18 16 18 16
18
16
18 16 18
16
18
16
18 16 18 16 14 16 14
16
14

D.S. al Coda
End Riff A
14 16 14 16 18 16 18 16 18 16 18 16
18 16 18 16 18 16 14 14

Coda

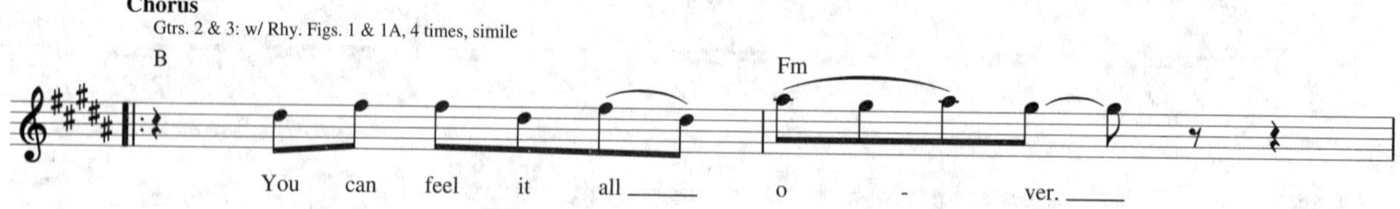
Chorus
Gtrs. 2 & 3: w/ Rhy. Figs. 1 & 1A, 4 times, simile
B
Fm
You can feel it all o - ver.

1., 2., 3.
4.
Emaj7
D#m
C#m
F#
C#m
F#
You can feel it all o - ver peo - ple. o - ver me, yeah, go, go!

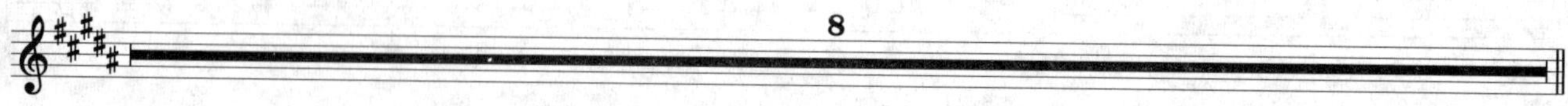
Interlude
Gtr. 2: w/ Riff A
8

Chorus
Gtrs. 2 & 3: w/ Rhy. Figs. 1 & 1A, 6 times, simile
Lead Voc. ad lib on repeats
B
Fm
You can feel it all o - ver.

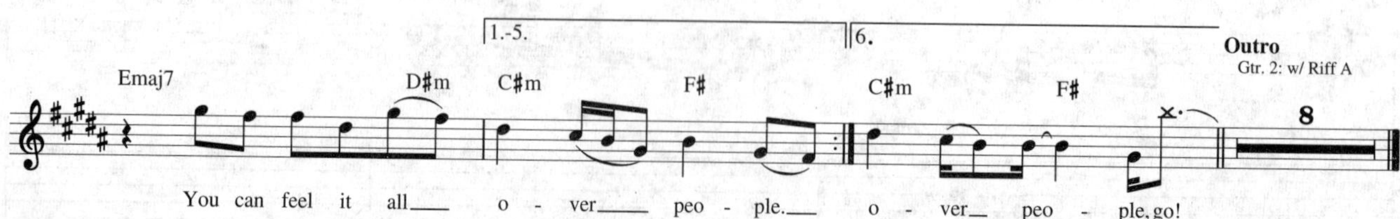
1.-5.
6.
Outro
Gtr. 2: w/ Riff A
Emaj7
D#m
C#m
F#
C#m
F#
8
You can feel it all o - ver peo - ple. o - ver peo - ple, go!

Sleepwalk

By Santo Farina, John Farina and Ann Farina

Fm
G7
C
Am
Fm
1.
G7
w/ pick & finger
mp
Gtr. 1: w/ Rhy. Fig. 2
C
Am
F
G7
2.
G7
8va
loco
Gtr. 2
mf
w/ pick
& finger
H.H.
w/ pick & fingers
C
F
C
C
F
Gtr. 1
Gtr. 2
Fm
C
C7
F
Fm

G7
G7#9
D
Gtr. 1: w/ Rhy. Fig. 1, 2 times
C
Am
Fm
G7
C
Gtr. 2
Am
Fm
G7
C
Am
Gtr. 1
rit.
rit.
Free Time
Fm
G7
G7#9
G+7b9
8va
H.H.
w/ pick & finger

Slither

Words and Music by Scott Weiland, Slash, Duff McKagan, Matt Sorum and Dave Kushner

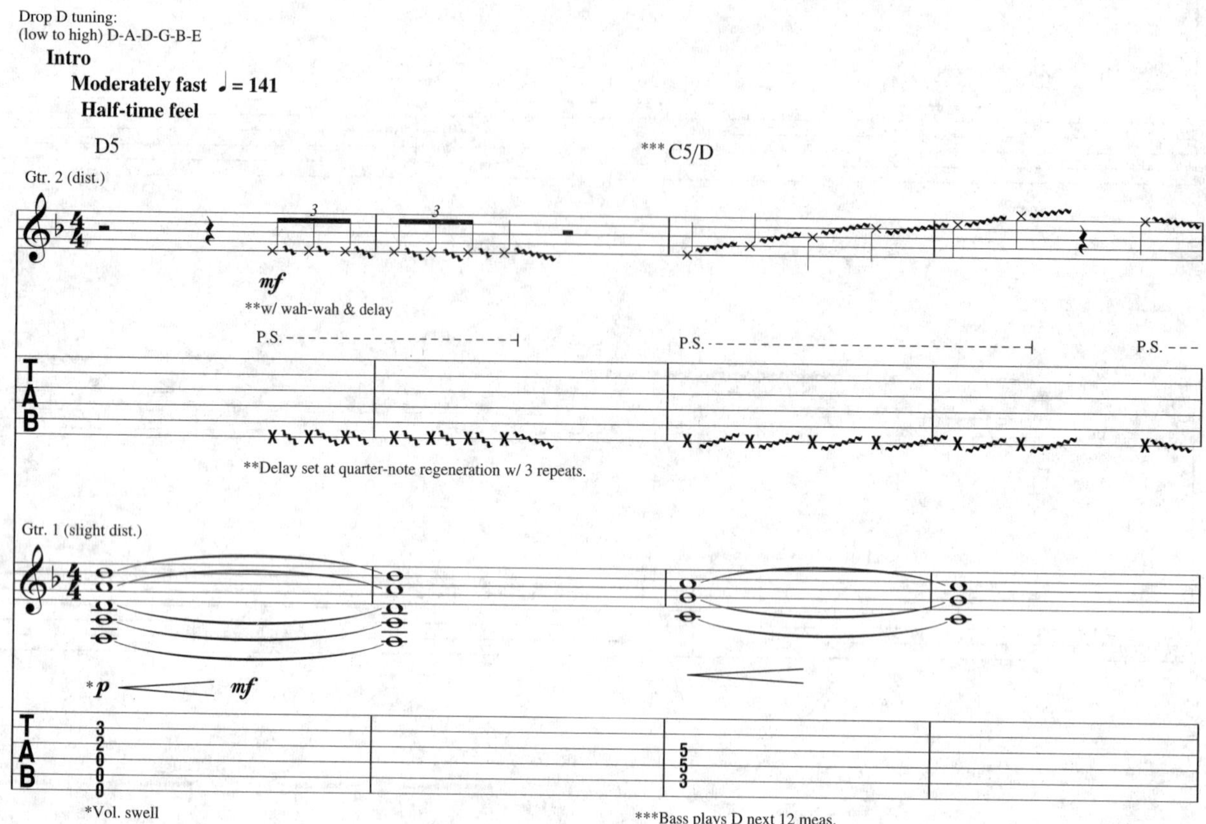

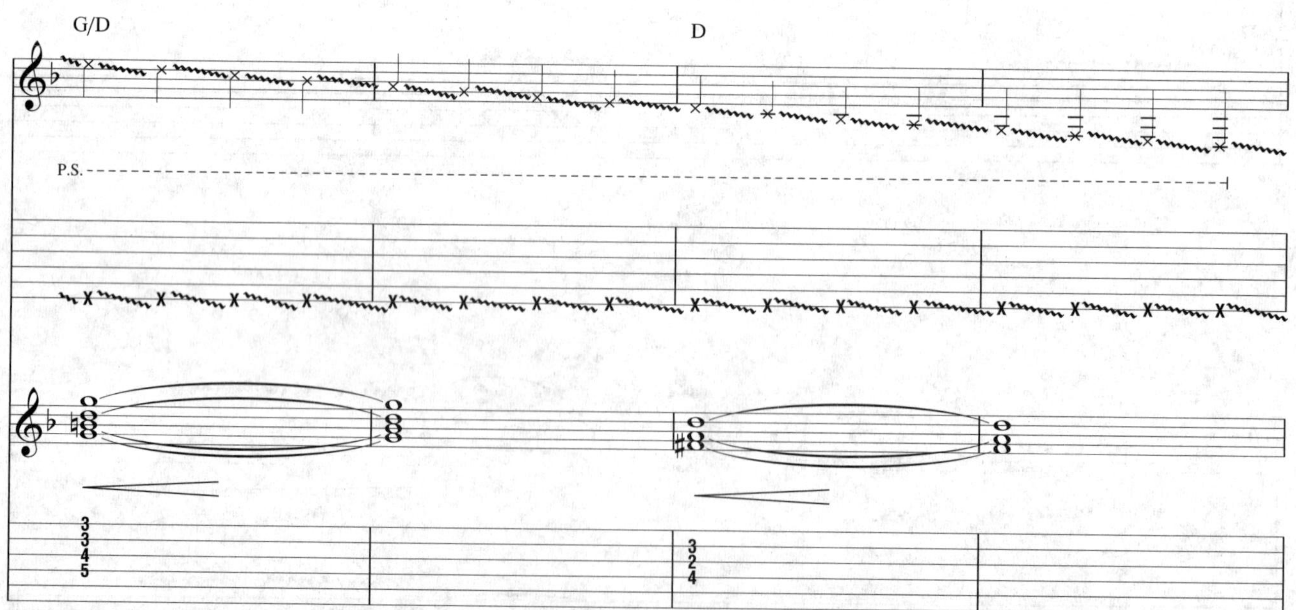

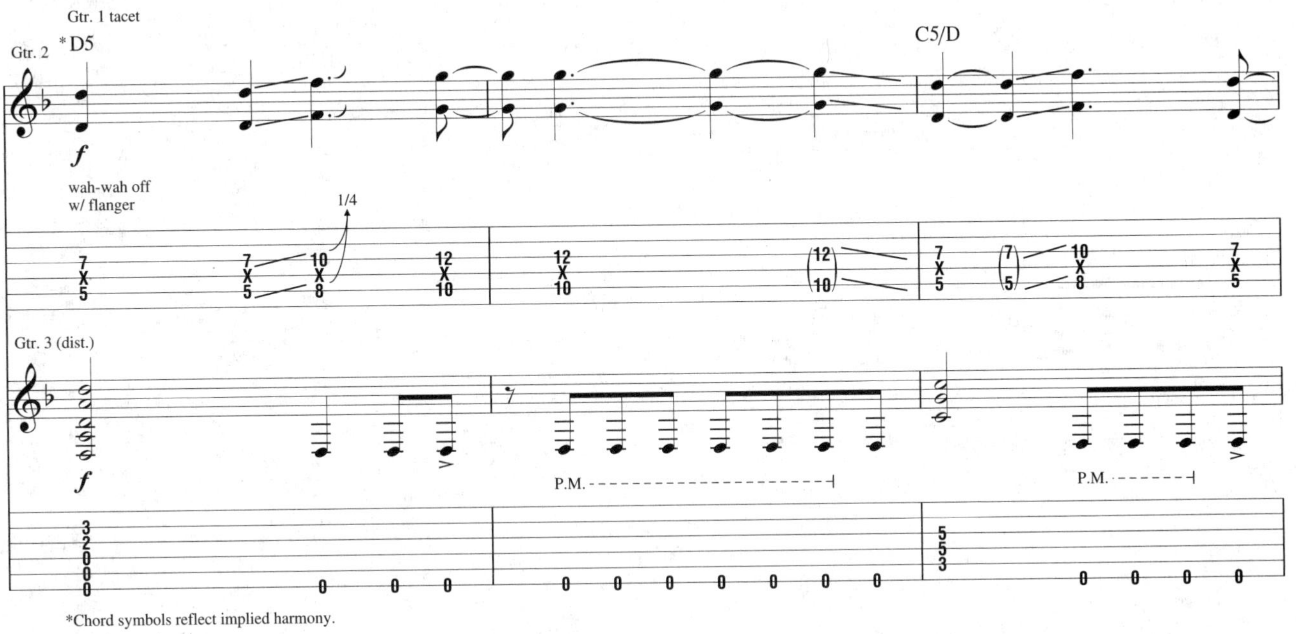

*Chord symbols reflect implied harmony.

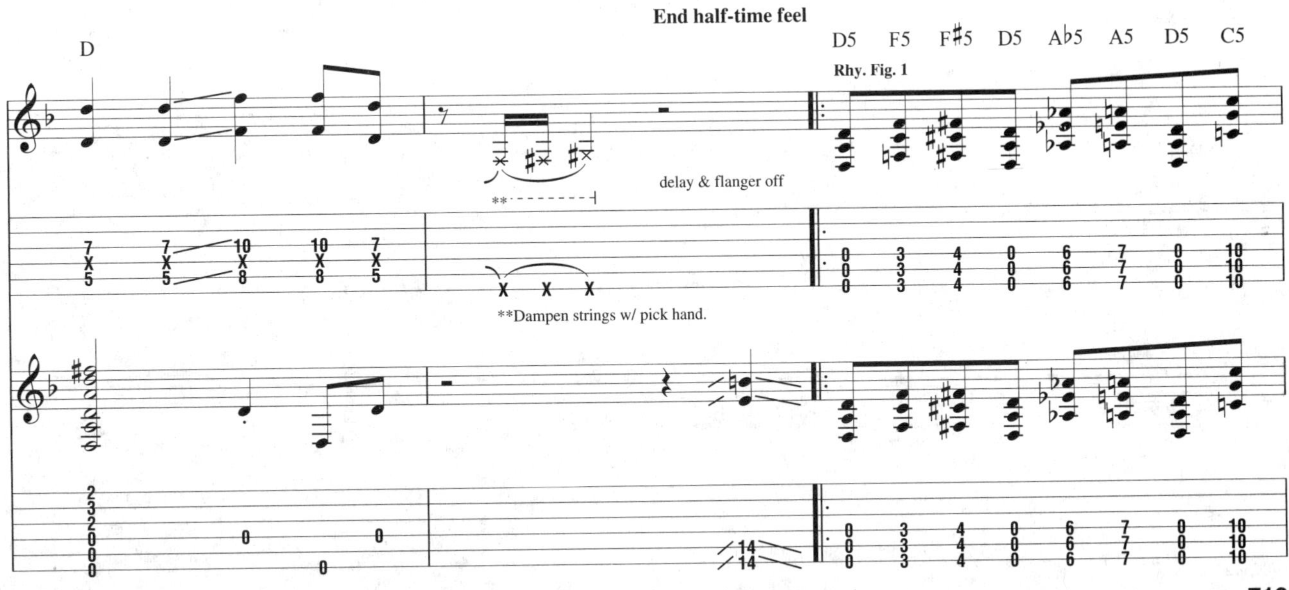

**Dampen strings w/ pick hand.

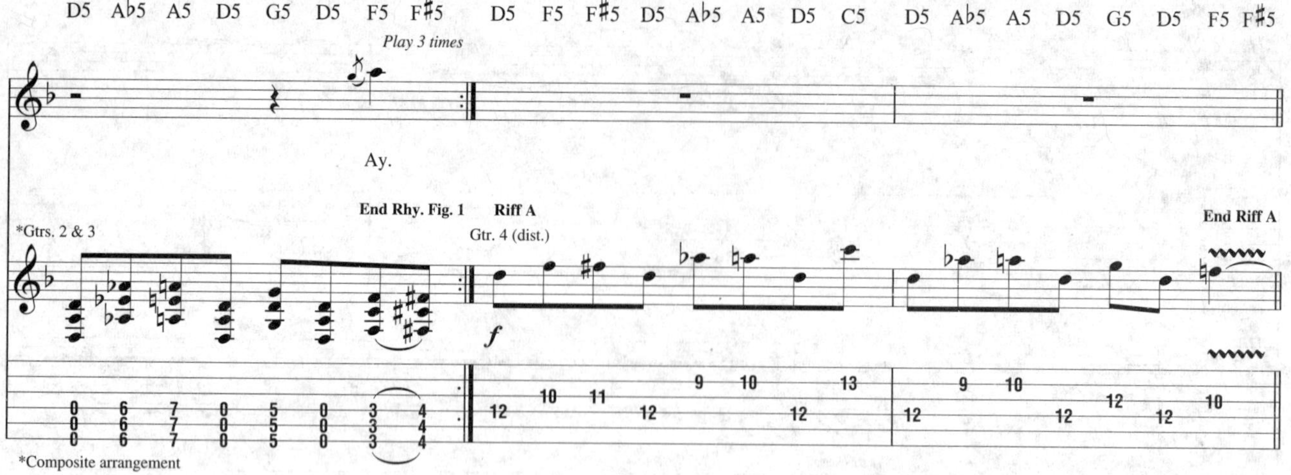

*Composite arrangement

2nd time, Gtr. 4: w/ Fill 1
Gtrs. 2 & 3: w/ Riff B
Gtr. 4 tacet
D5 F5 F♯5 D5 A♭5 A5 D5 C5 D5 A♭5 A5 D5 G5 D5 F5 F♯5 D5 F5 F♯5 D5 A♭5 A5 D5 C5
Al - ways keep me un -
Gtr. 4
Gtrs. 2 & 3
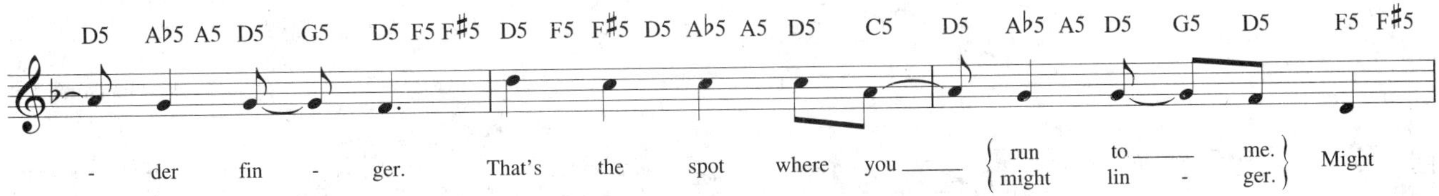
D5 A♭5 A5 D5 G5 D5 F5 F♯5 D5 F5 F♯5 D5 A♭5 A5 D5 C5 D5 A♭5 A5 D5 G5 D5 F5 F♯5
- der fin - ger. That's the spot where you run to me. Might
might lin - ger.

D5 F5 F♯5 D5 A♭5 A5 D5 C5 D5 A♭5 A5 D5 G5 D5 F5 F♯5 D5 F5 F♯5 D5 A♭5 A5 D5 C5 D5 A♭5 A5 D5 G5 D5 F5
see some type of pleas - ure in my mind.
(Ah.)
Gtrs. 2 & 3
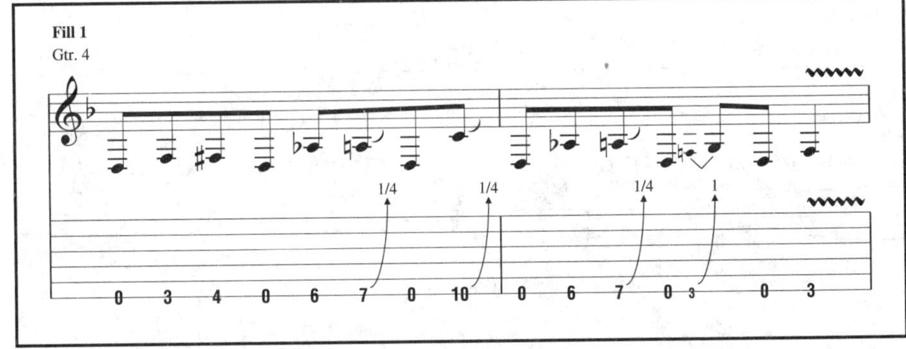
Fill 1
Gtr. 4

Chorus
Half-time feel
D5
Cadd9
Yeah, here comes the wa - ter. It comes to
Gtr. 4
Riff C
Rhy. Fig. 2
Gtrs. 2 & 3
G/B
D5
1.
End half-time feel
wash a - way the sins of you and I. This time you will
End Riff C
End Rhy. Fig. 2
Interlude
Gtrs. 2 & 3: w/ Rhy. Fig. 1 (4 times)
Gtr. 4 tacet
D5 F5 F♯5 D5 A♭5 A5 D5 C5 D5 A♭5 A5 D5 G5 D5 F5 F♯5 D5 F5 F♯5 D5 A♭5 A5 D5 C5 D5 A♭5 A5 D5 G5 D5 F5 F♯5
see. Ay, ay,

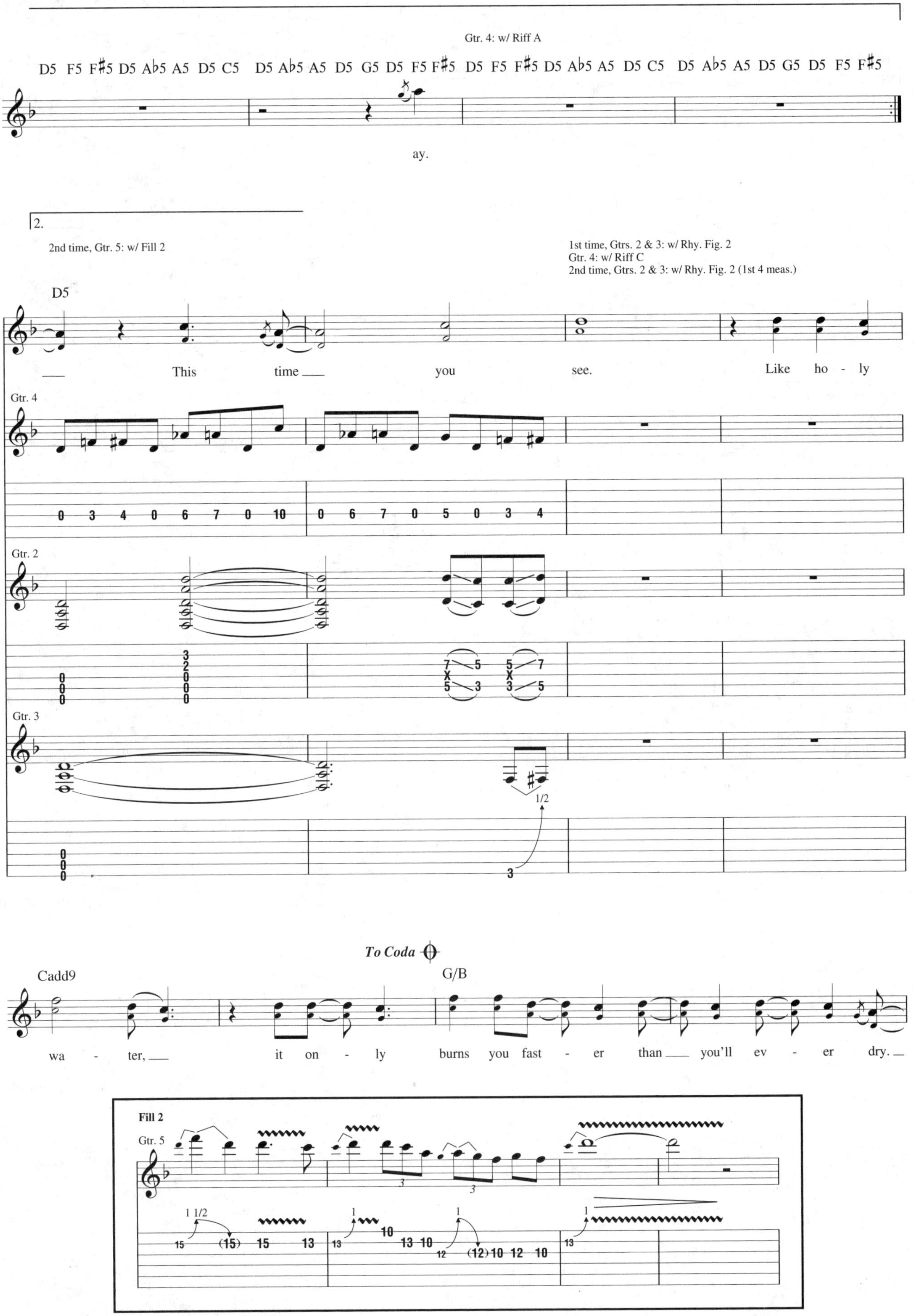

2.

2nd time, Gtr. 5: w/ Fill 2

1st time, Gtrs. 2 & 3: w/ Rhy. Fig. 2
Gtr. 4: w/ Riff C
2nd time, Gtrs. 2 & 3: w/ Rhy. Fig. 2 (1st 4 meas.)

D5

___ This time ___ you see. Like ho - ly

Gtr. 4

Gtr. 2

Gtr. 3

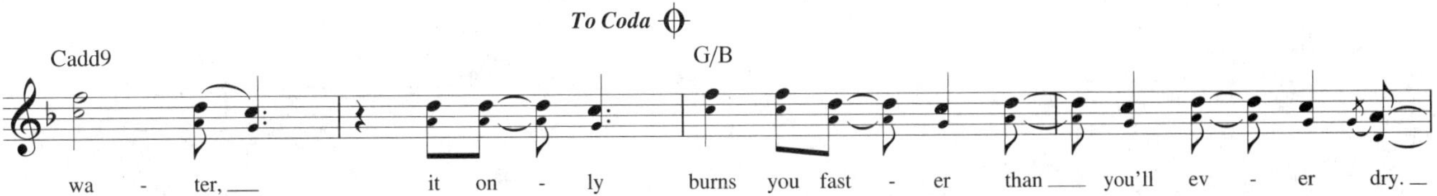

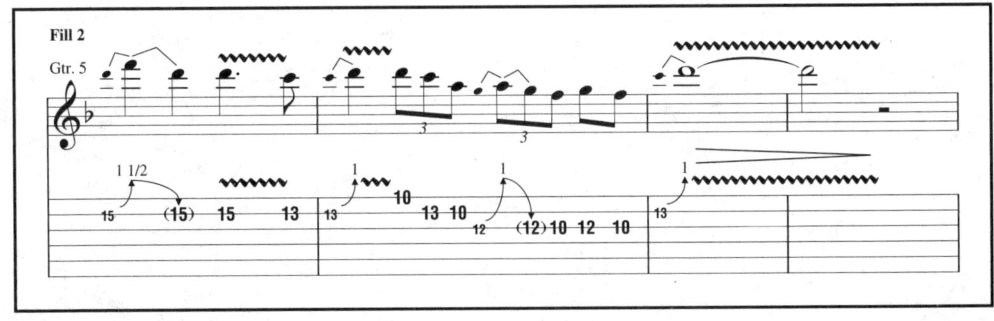

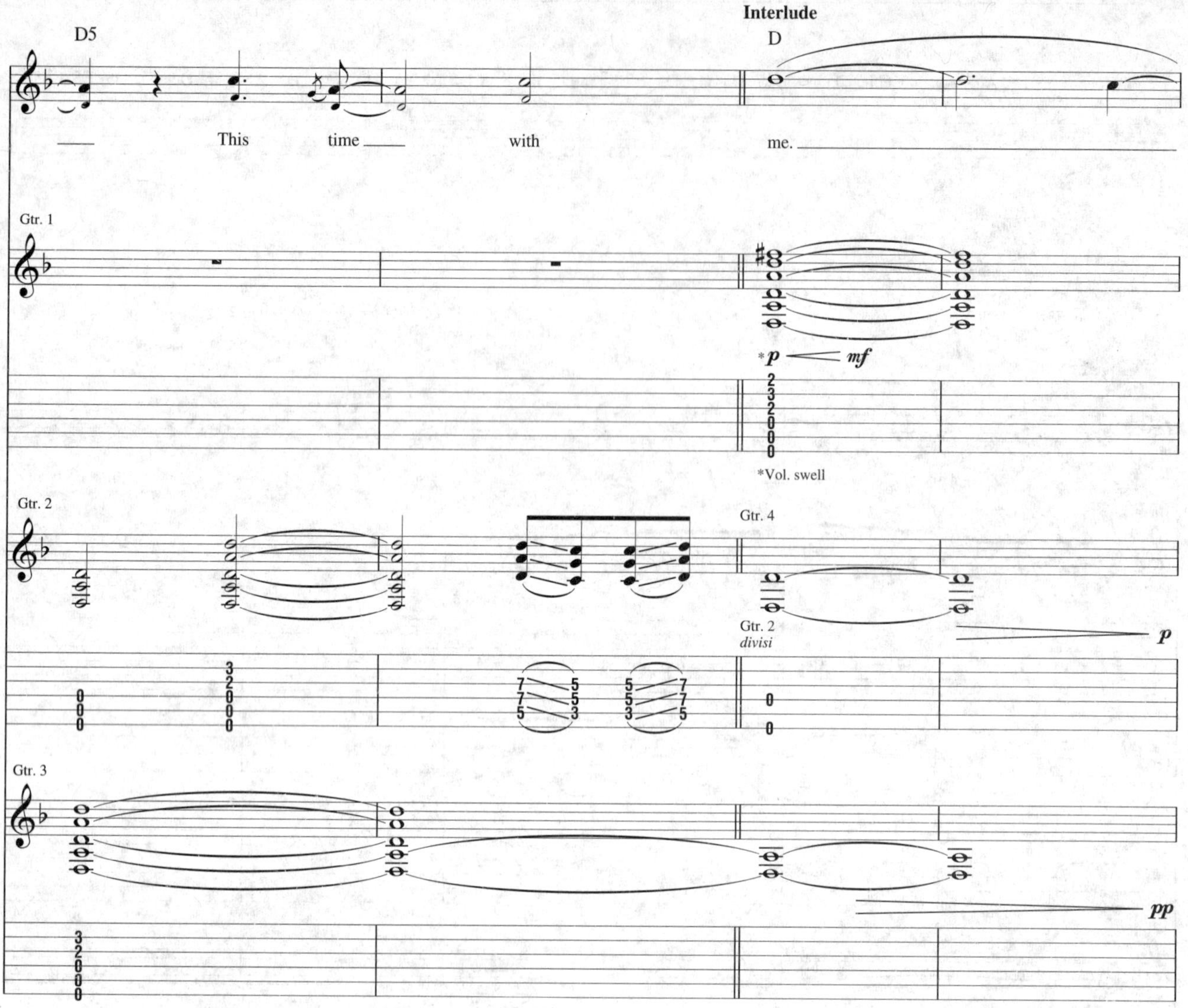

Interlude

D5

D

This time with me.

Gtr. 1

*p mf

2
3
2
0
0
0

*Vol. swell

Gtr. 2

3
2
0
0
0

0
0
0

7 5
7 5
5 3

5 7
5 7
3 5

Gtr. 4

Gtr. 2
divisi

0

0

p

Gtr. 3

3
2
0
0
0

pp

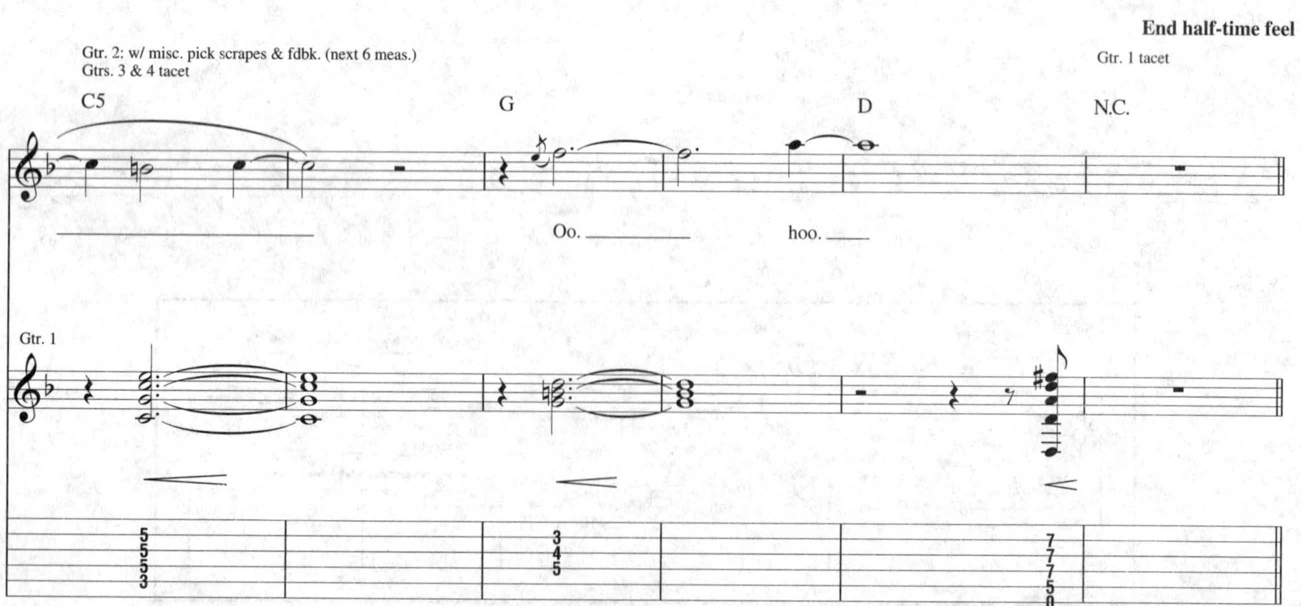

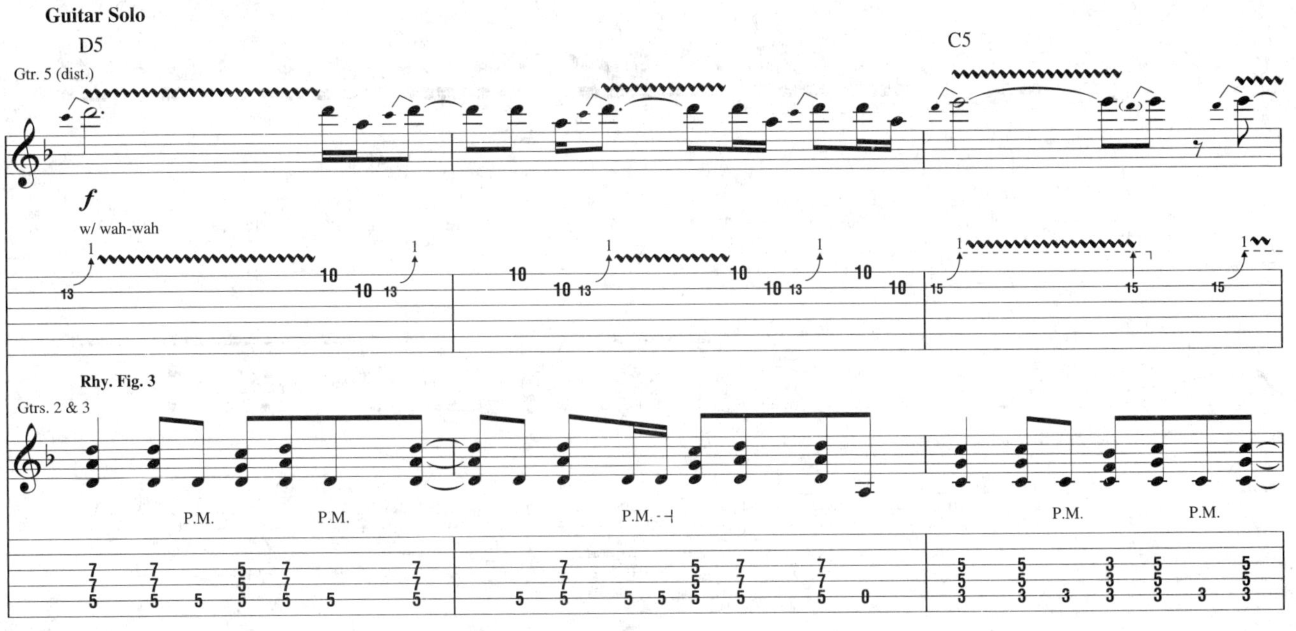

Guitar Solo
D5
C5
Gtr. 5 (dist.)
f
w/ wah-wah
Rhy. Fig. 3
Gtrs. 2 & 3
P.M.
P.M.
P.M.
P.M.
P.M.

G/B
Cadd9
8va
End Rhy. Fig. 3
P.M.
P.M.

D5
8va
loco
P.M.
P.M.
P.M.
let ring

Gtr. 3: w/ Rhy. Fig. 3
Gtr. 5
Gtr. 2

C5

G/B
Cadd9

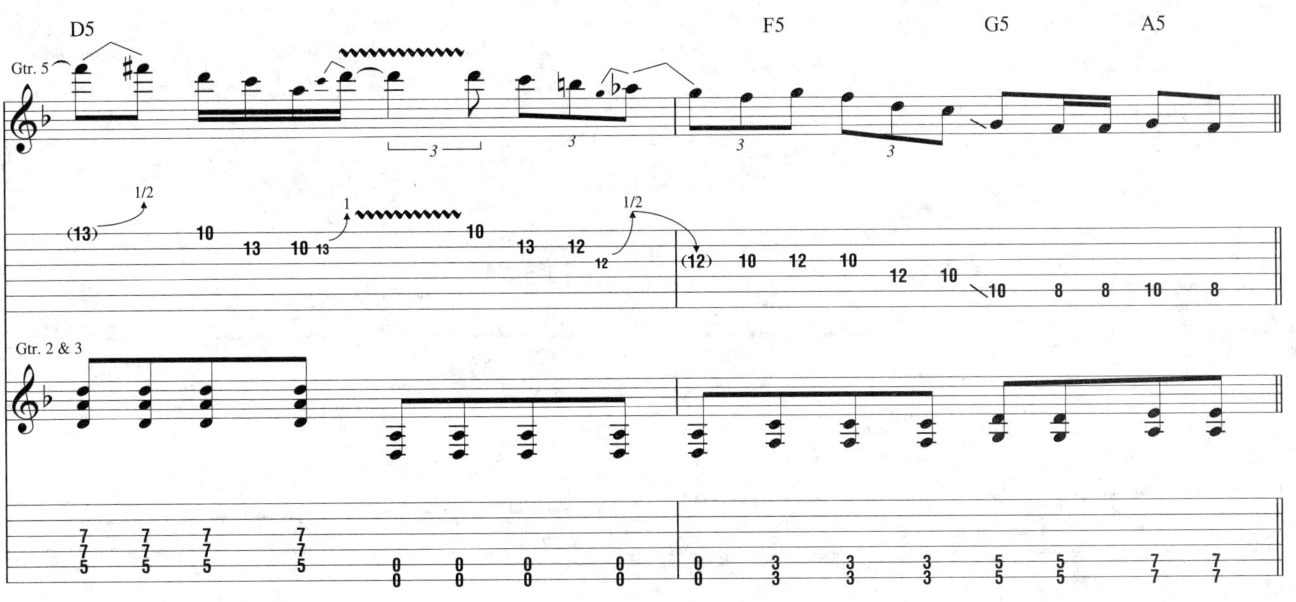
D5
F5
G5
A5
Gtr. 5
1/2
1
1/2
Gtr. 2 & 3

Verse

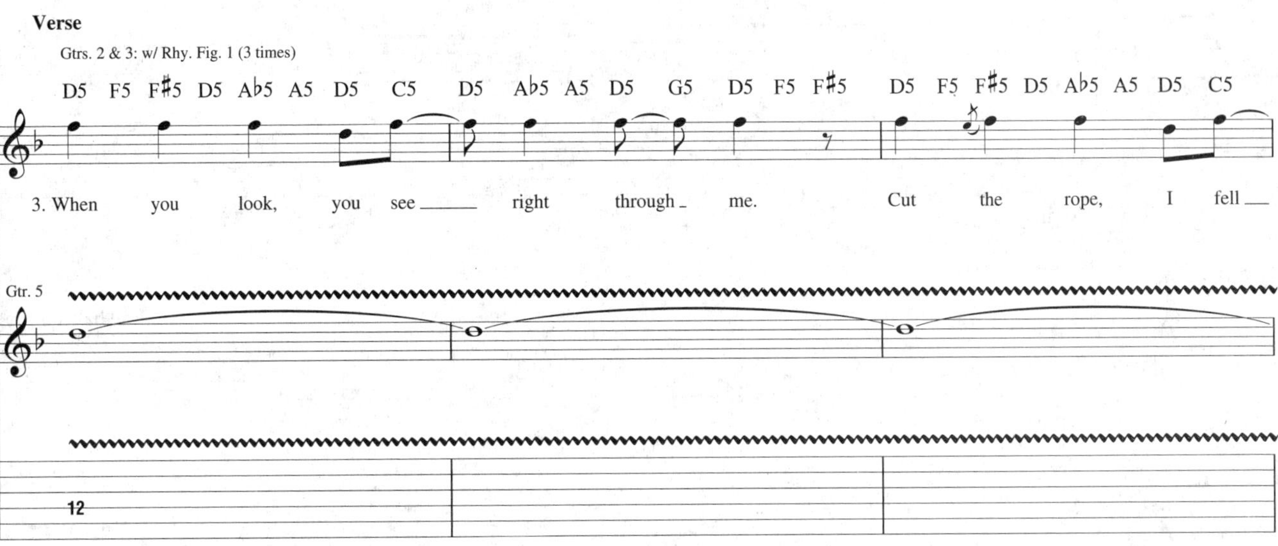
Gtrs. 2 & 3: w/ Rhy. Fig. 1 (3 times)
D5 F5 F♯5 D5 A♭5 A5 D5 C5 D5 A♭5 A5 D5 G5 D5 F5 F♯5 D5 F5 F♯5 D5 A♭5 A5 D5 C5
3. When you look, you see right through me. Cut the rope, I fell
Gtr. 5

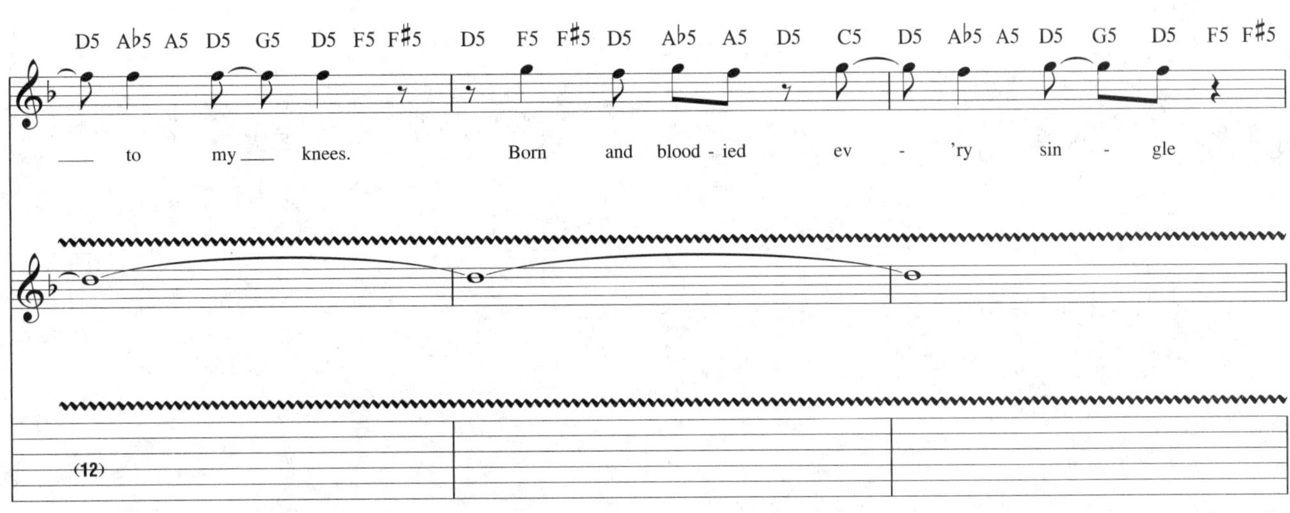
D5 A♭5 A5 D5 G5 D5 F5 F♯5 D5 F5 F♯5 D5 A♭5 A5 D5 C5 D5 A♭5 A5 D5 G5 D5 F5 F♯5
to my knees. Born and blood - ied ev - 'ry sin - gle

D.S. al Coda
(take 2nd ending)
D5 C5 D5 B5 C5 D5 A5 D5 A♭5 A5 D5 G5 D5 F5 F♯5
time.
Gtr. 5
Gtr. 4
Gtrs. 2 & 3
Coda
G/B D5
End half-time feel
burns you fast - er than you'll ev - er dry. This time with
8va
Gtr. 2
Gtr. 3

Outro

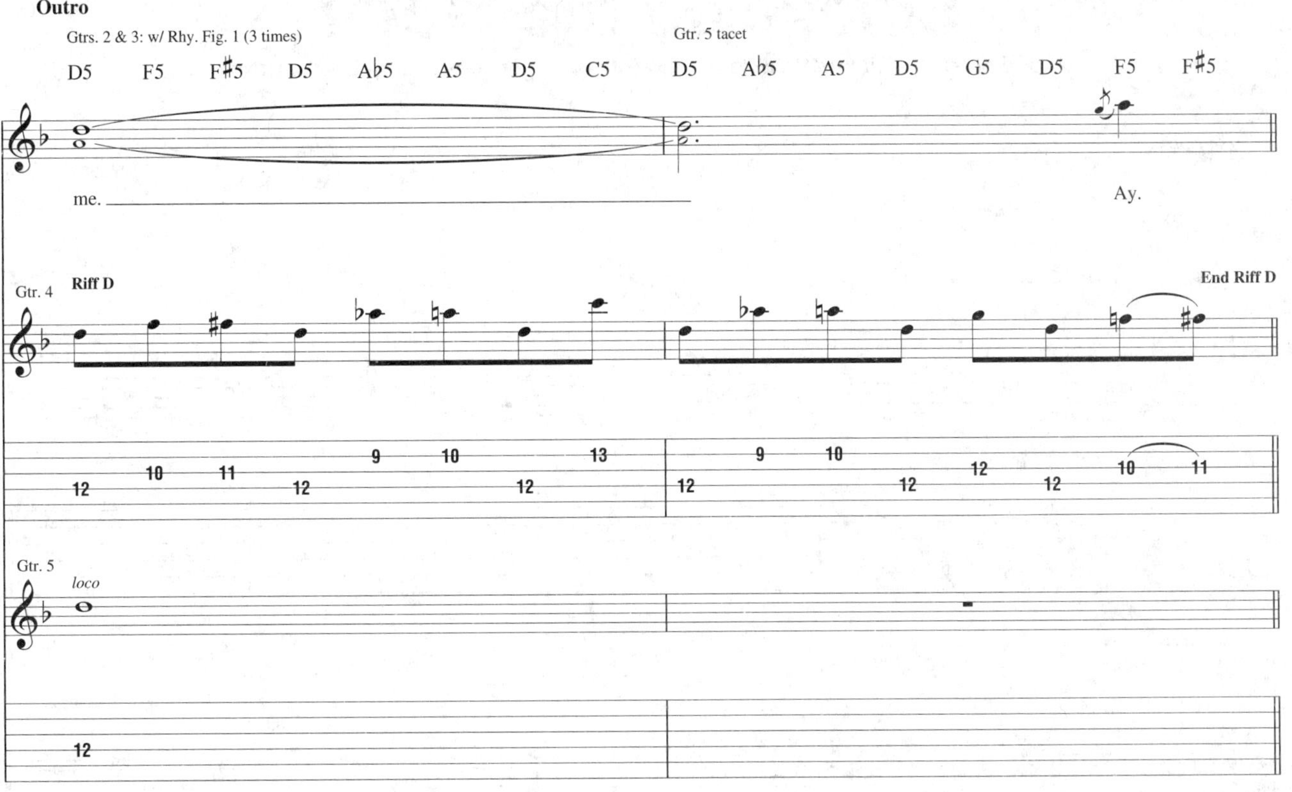
Gtrs. 2 & 3: w/ Rhy. Fig. 1 (3 times)
Gtr. 5 tacet
D5 F5 F♯5 D5 A♭5 A5 D5 C5 D5 A♭5 A5 D5 G5 D5 F5 F♯5
me.
Ay.
Gtr. 4
Riff D
End Riff D
Gtr. 5
loco

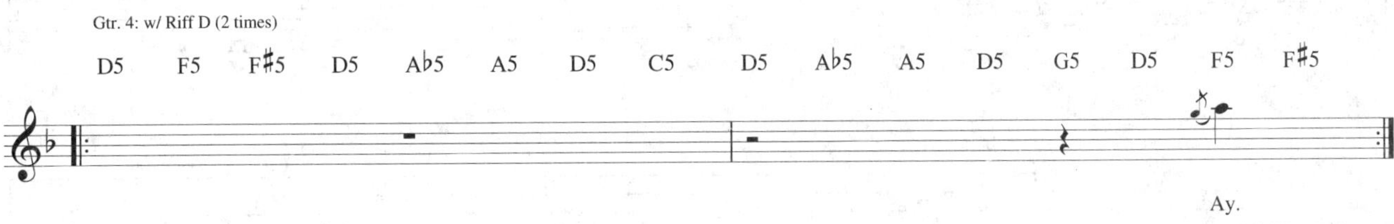
Gtr. 4: w/ Riff D (2 times)
D5 F5 F♯5 D5 A♭5 A5 D5 C5 D5 A♭5 A5 D5 G5 D5 F5 F♯5
Ay.

D5 C5 D5 B5 C5 D5 A5 D5 A♭5 A5 D5 G5 D5 F5 F♯5 D5 N.C.
Gtr. 4
Gtrs. 2 & 3

Smoke on the Water

Words and Music by Ritchie Blackmore, Ian Gillan, Roger Glover, Jon Lord and Ian Paice

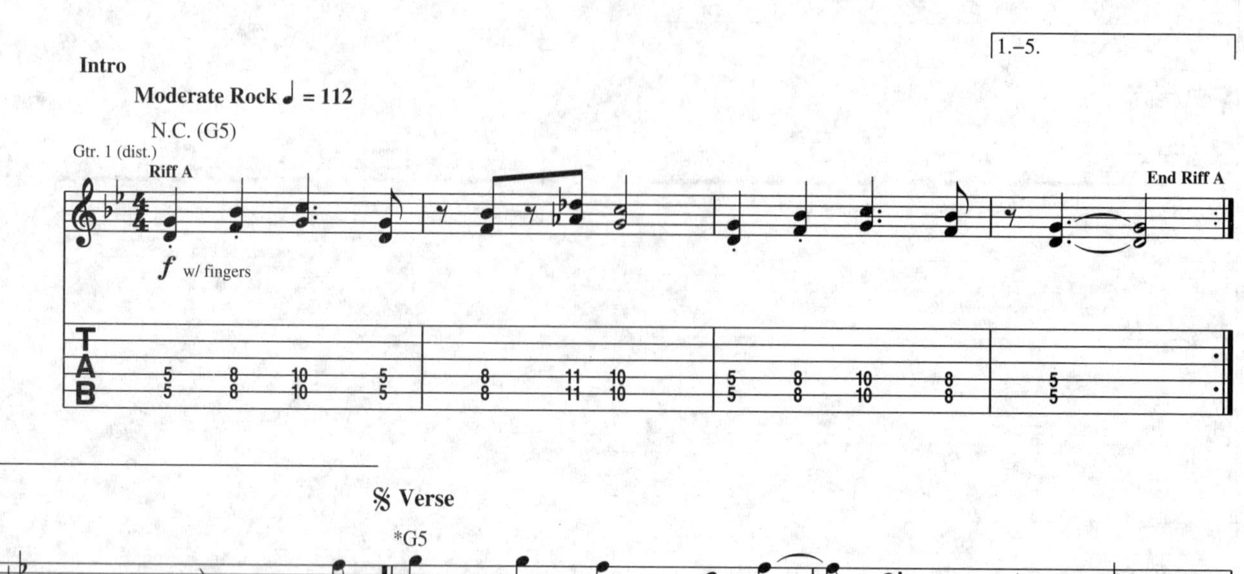

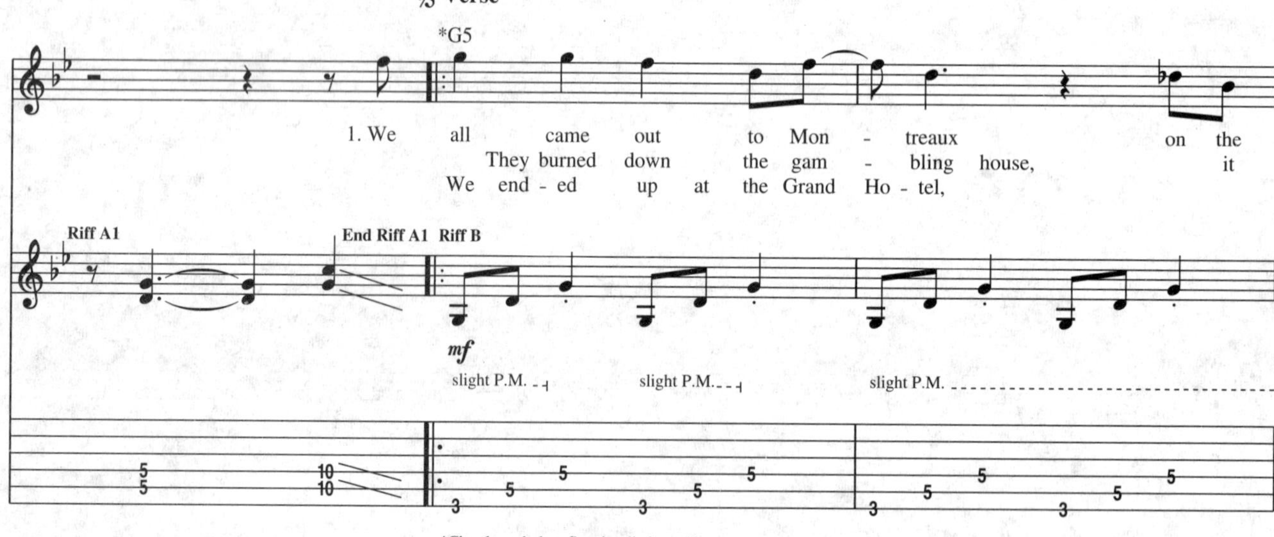

*Chord symbols reflect implied tonality.

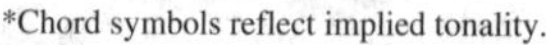

Gtr. 1: w/ Riff B, 3 times, simile

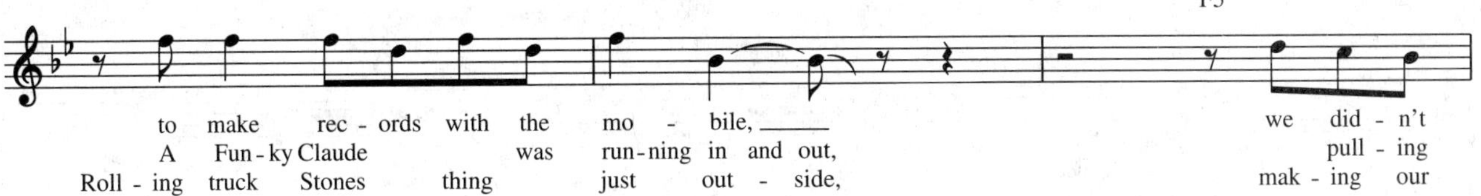

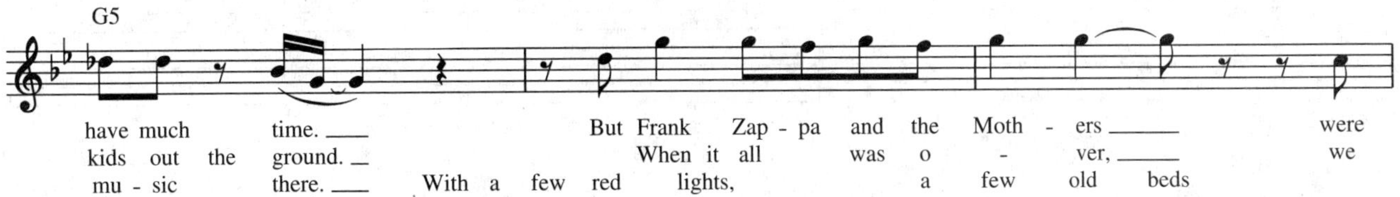

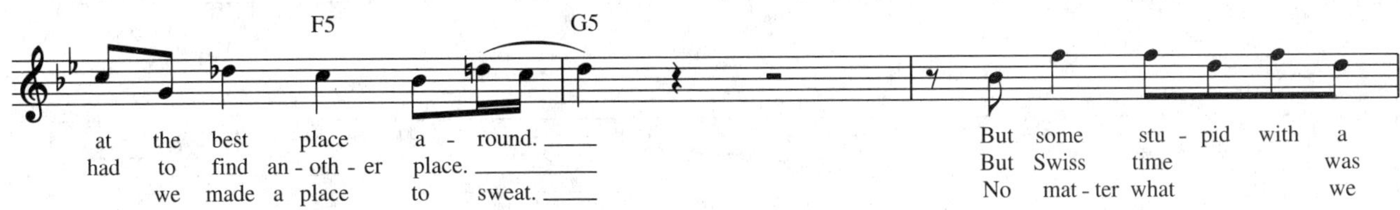

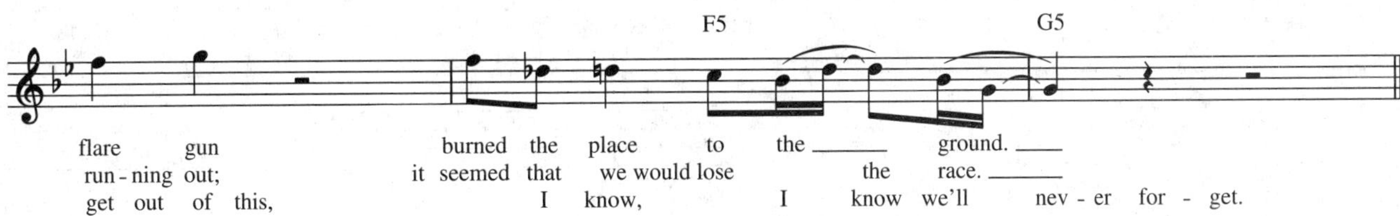

To Coda
1.
2.
Gtr. 1: w/ Riff A 1 3/4 times Gtr. 1: w/ Riff A1 Gtr. 1: w/ Riff A 1 3/4 times Gtr. 1: w/ Riff A1
C5
A♭5
N.C.(G5)
N.C.(G5)
Smoke on the wa - ter.
Gtr. 2 (dist.)
Guitar Solo
G5
Gtr. 2
C5
G5
full
1/4
1/2
Gtr. 1
slight P.M.
slight P.M.
C5
1/2
slight P.M.

G5
full
w/bar
-2 1/2
slight P.M.
C5
G5
full
1/2
full
slight P.M.
C5
G5
8va
1/2
full
slight P.M.

C5
8va
full
F5
loco
1/2
1/4
grad. bend
Gtr. 1: w/ Riff A, 1 3/4 times
N.C.(G5)
Gtr. 2
3/4
D.S. al Coda
Gtr. 2 tacet
Gtr. 1: w/ Riff A1

Coda

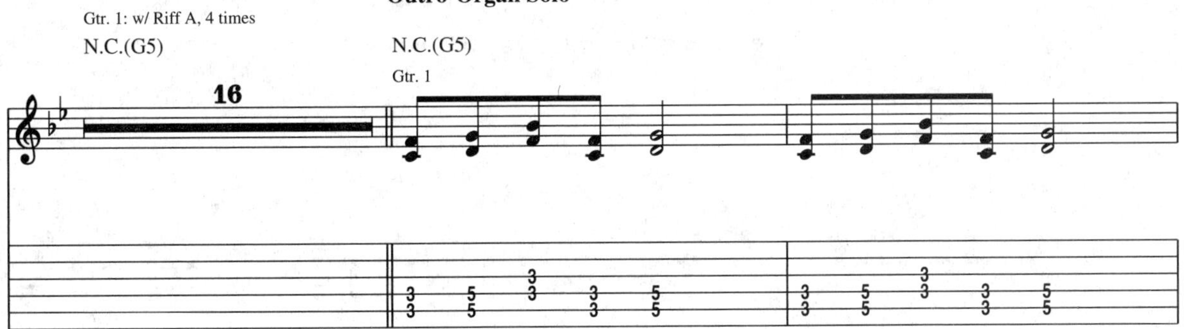
Outro-Organ Solo
Gr. 1: w/ Riff A, 4 times
N.C.(G5)
16
N.C.(G5)
Gtr. 1

Begin Fade

Fade Out

Snortin' Whiskey

Words and Music by Pat Travers and Pat Thrall

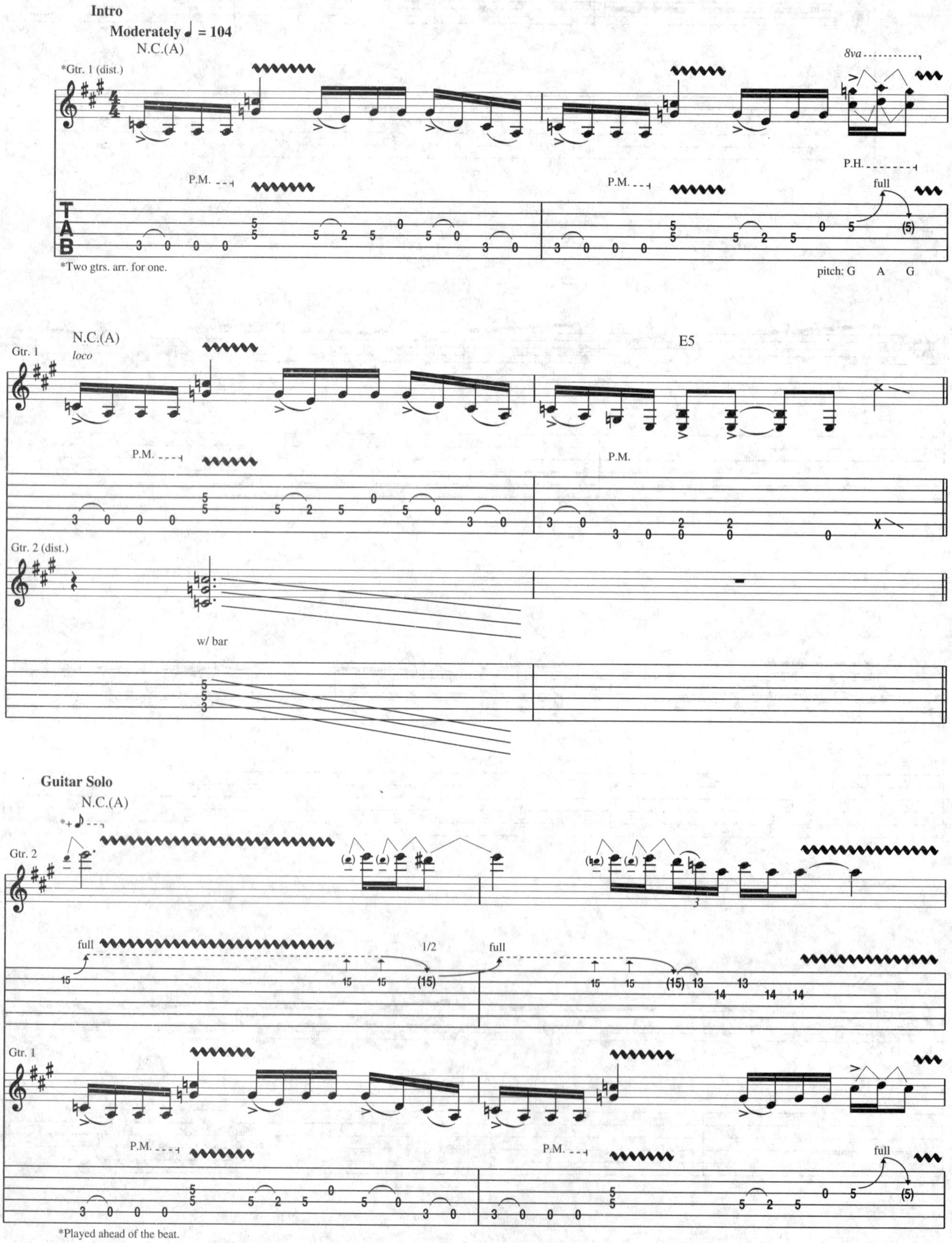
Intro
Moderately ♩ = 104
N.C.(A)
*Gtr. 1 (dist.)
8va
P.M.
P.H.
full
pitch: G A G
*Two gtrs. arr. for one.
N.C.(A)
Gtr. 1
loco
E5
P.M.
Gtr. 2 (dist.)
w/ bar
Guitar Solo
N.C.(A)
Gtr. 2
full
1/2
Gtr. 1
P.M.
full
*Played ahead of the beat.

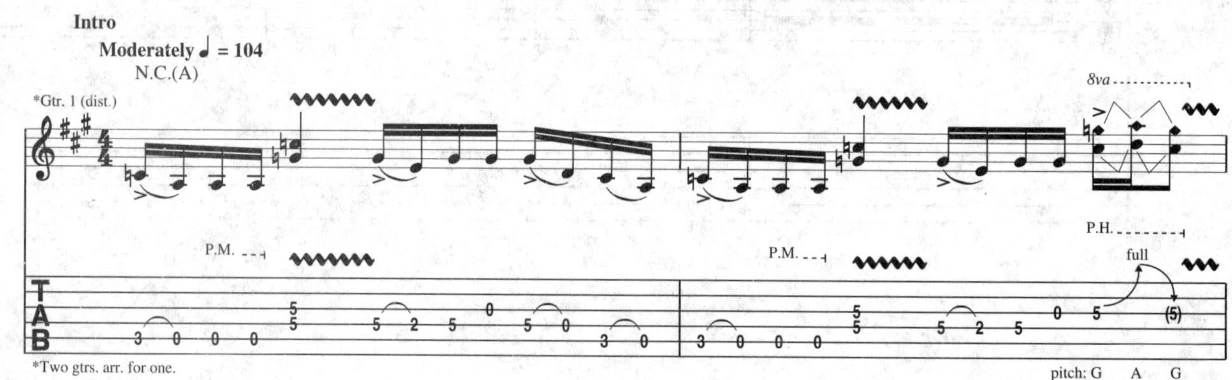

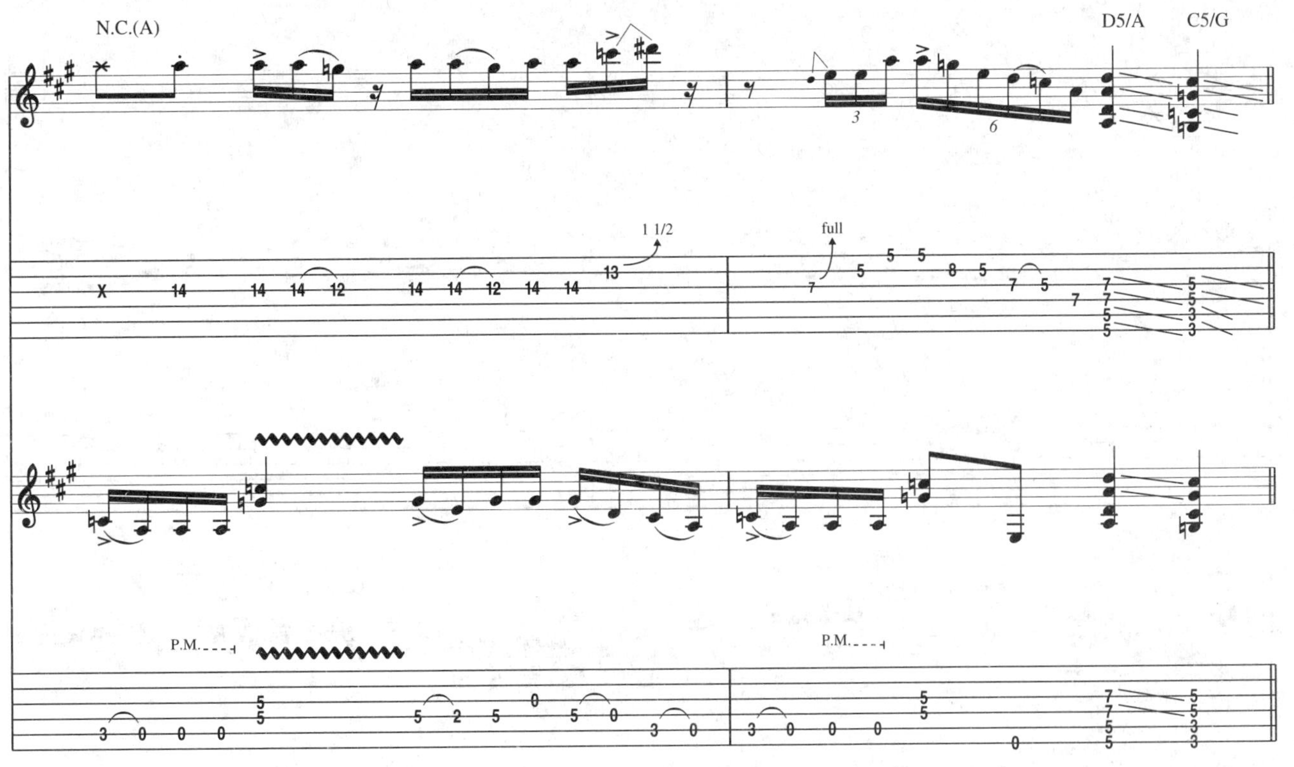

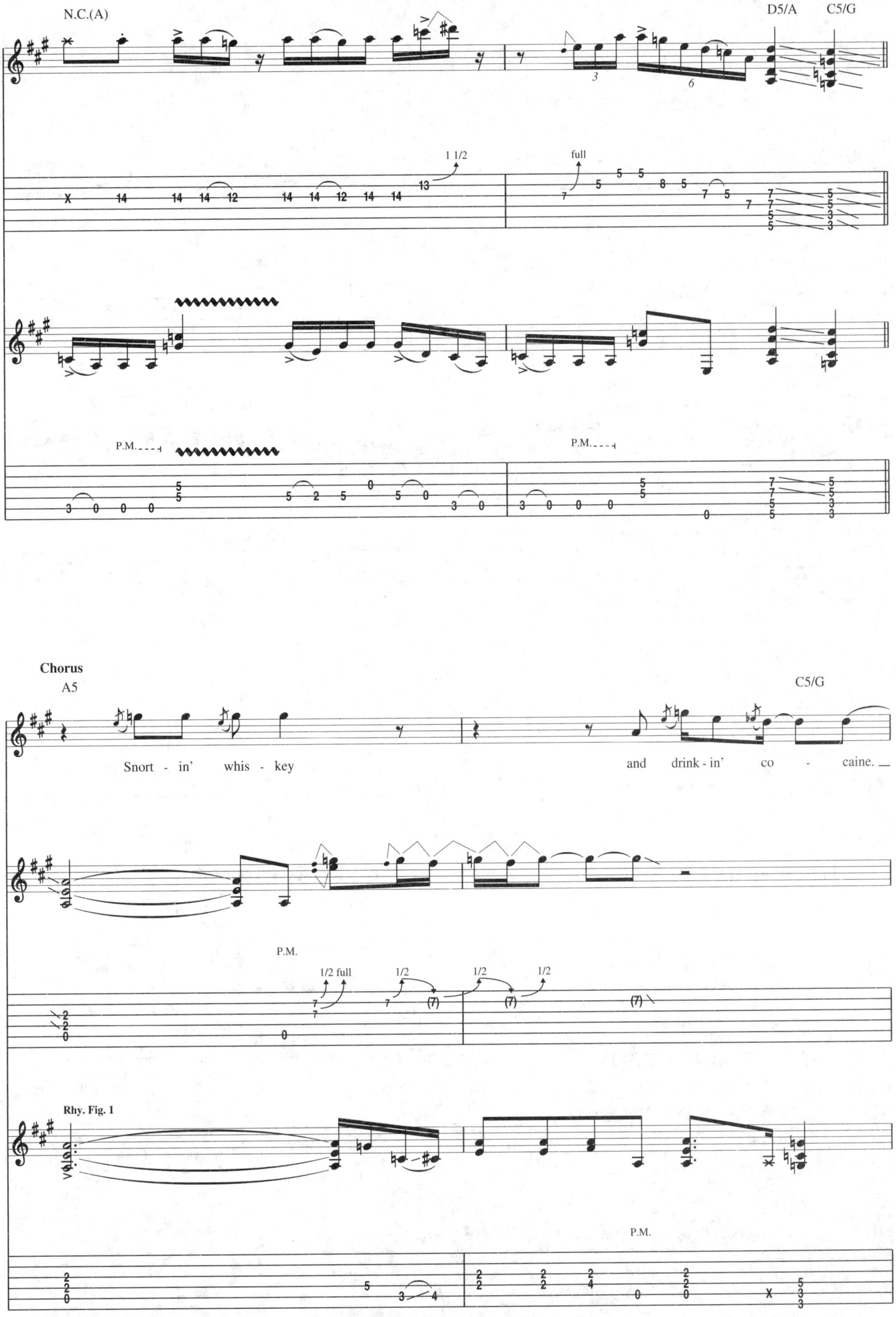

Chorus

A5

C5/G

Snort - in' whis - key and drink - in' co - caine.

P.M.

1/2 full 1/2 1/2 1/2

Rhy. Fig. 1

P.M.

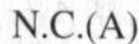

let ring
1/2 full full hold bend
1/2 full hold bend 1/2 full hold bend
let ring

P.M.
P.M.

C5 D5 C5/G

Been snort - in' whis - key and drink - in' co - caine.

full

P.M. P.M.

N.C.(A)

hold bend hold bend

full full full full

1/2 full full

P.M.

1/4 P.M. 1/4

E5 F#5 C/G G#5

Got this feel - in', gon - na drive that girl in - sane.

full full

let ring

N.C.(A)
E5
full
1/4
full
1/4
full
End Rhy. Fig. 1
P.M.

Verse

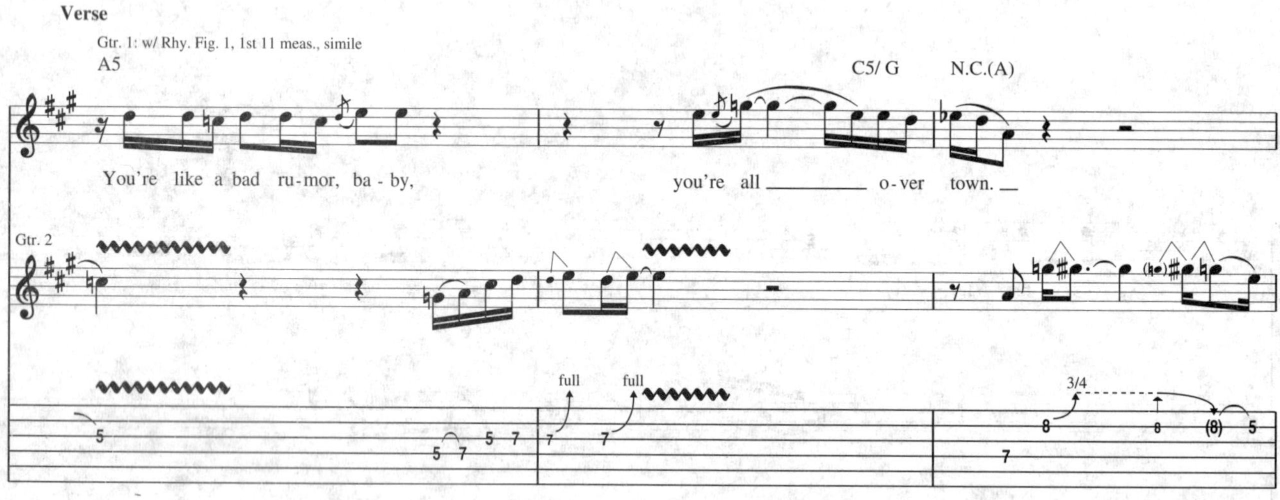
Gtr. 1: w/ Rhy. Fig. 1, 1st 11 meas., simile
A5
C5/ G
N.C.(A)
You're like a bad ru-mor, ba - by, you're all o-ver town.
Gtr. 2
full
full
3/4

C5
D5
C5/ G
You're like a bad ru-mor, ba - by, you're all o-ver
full

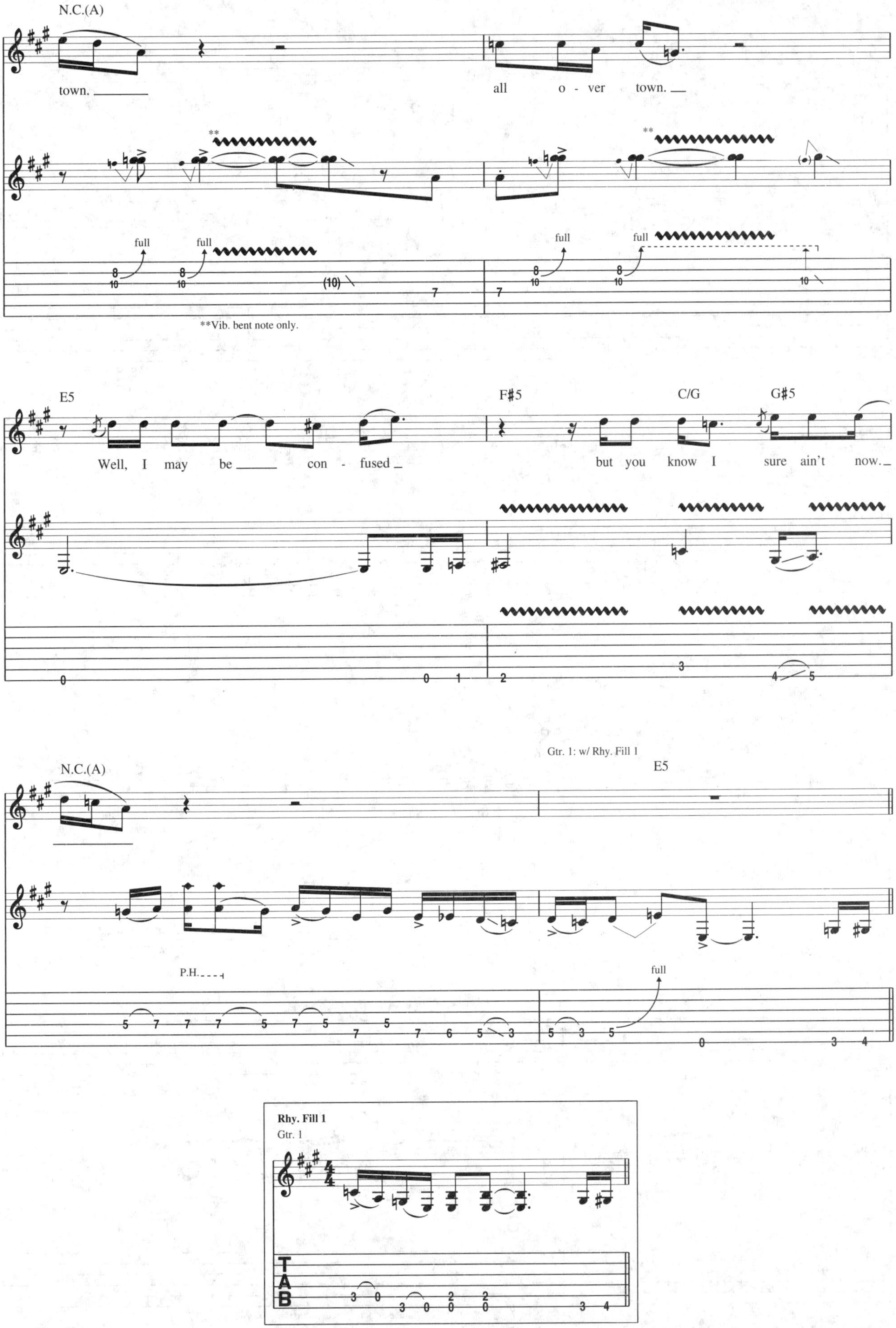

N.C.(A)

town. ___ all o - ver town. __

full full full full

**Vib. bent note only.

E5 F#5 C/G G#5

Well, I may be ___ con - fused _ but you know I sure ain't now. _

Gtr. 1: w/ Rhy. Fill 1

N.C.(A) E5

P.H.

full

Bridge

A5 G G# A

I'm a fast mov-er, ba-by, I can show you a-round. I've got so much co-caine,

Gtr. 2

Gtr. 1

C5/G B5/F# C5/G C#5/G# D5 C5/G

ain't nev-er com-in' down. Snort-in' whis-key, drink-in' co - caine.

Harm.

P.M.

*Shake neck by headstock to simulate vibrato.

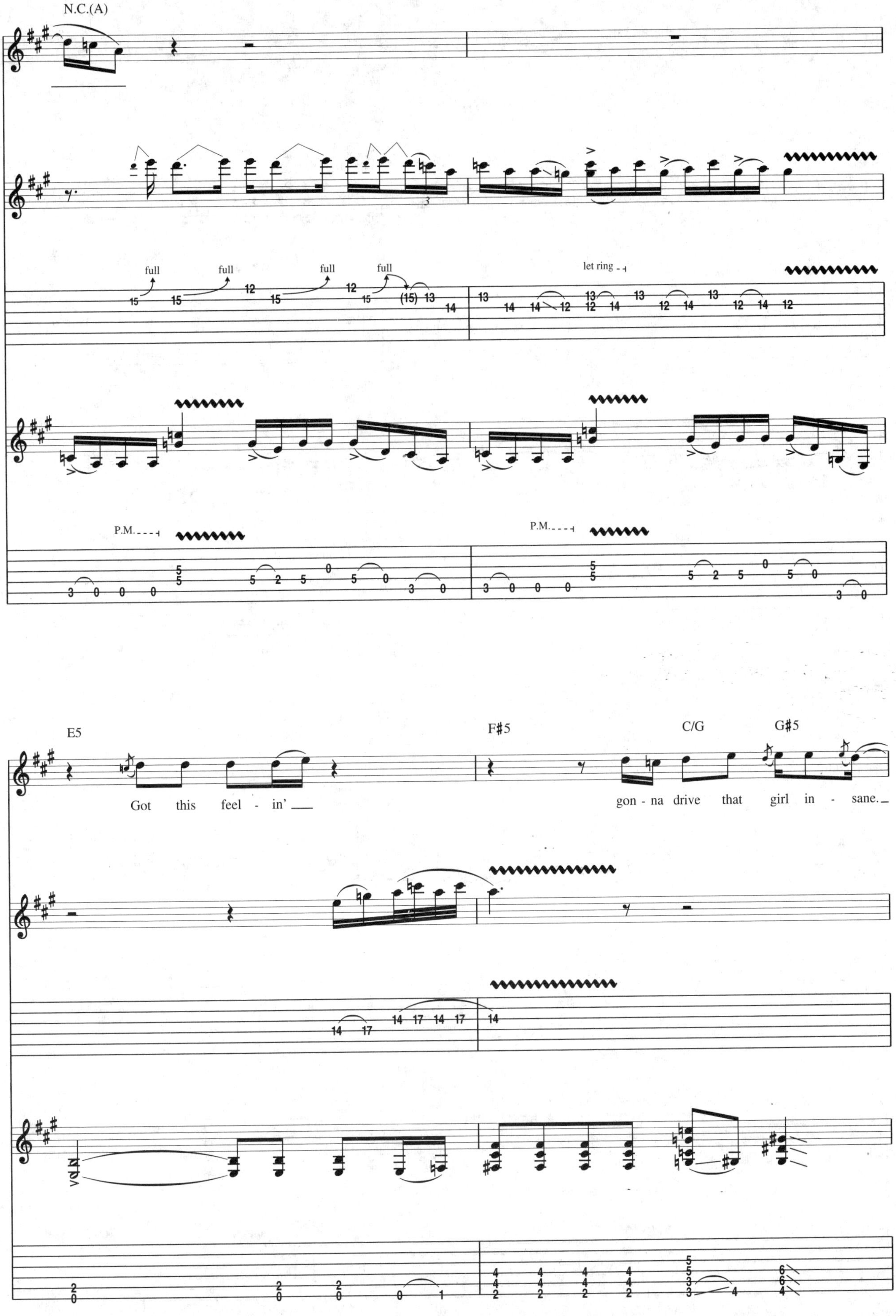

N.C.(A)

full full full full

let ring

P.M.

P.M.

E5 F#5 C/G G#5

Got this feel - in' gon - na drive that girl in - sane.

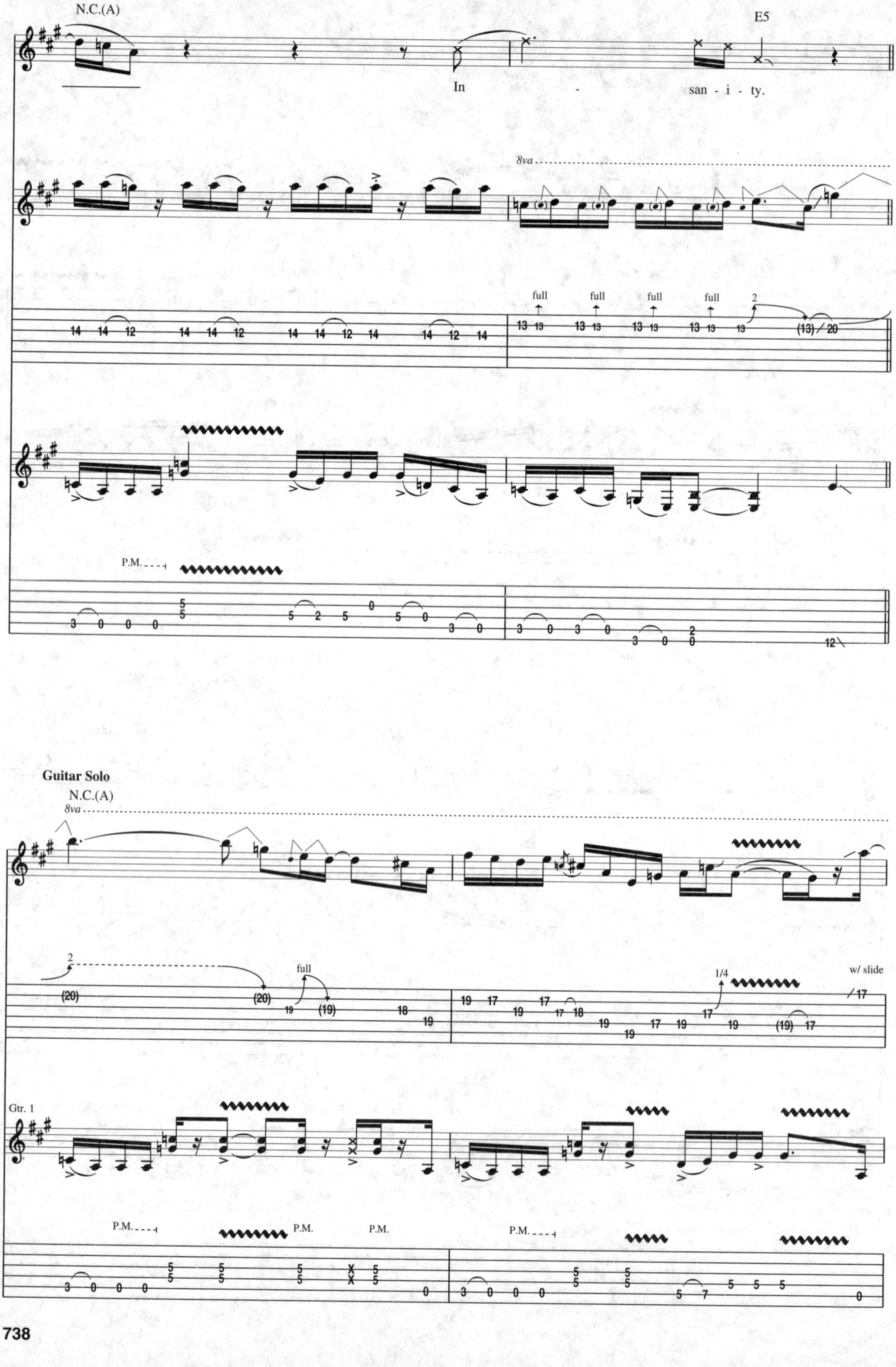

N.C.(A) E5

In - san - i - ty.

8va

full full full full 2

P.M.

8va
w/out slide
full
P.M.

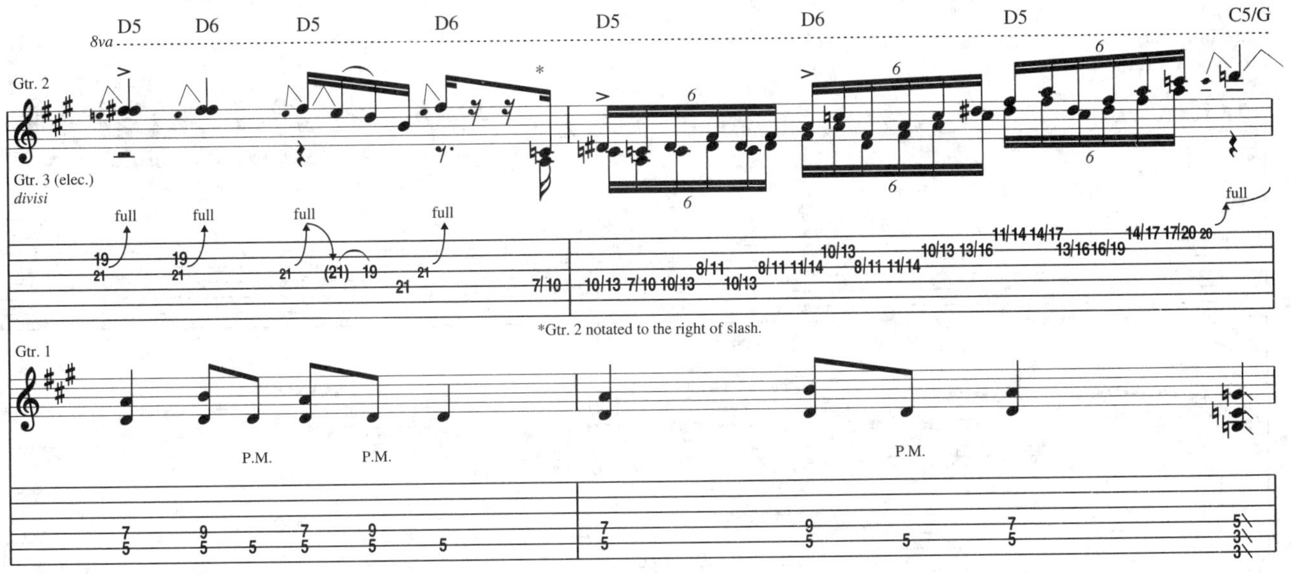
D5
D6
C5/G
8va
Gtr. 2
Gtr. 3 (elec.)
divisi
full
*Gtr. 2 notated to the right of slash.
Gtr. 1
P.M.

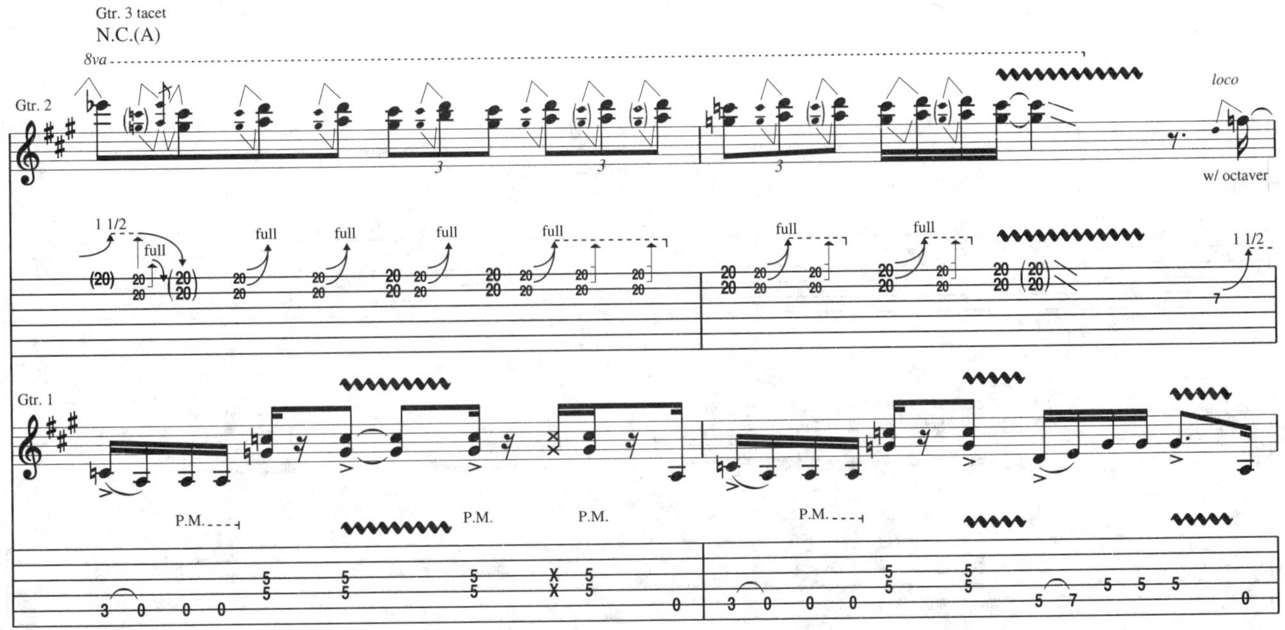
Gtr. 3 tacet
N.C.(A)
8va
Gtr. 2
loco
w/ octaver
1 1/2
full
Gtr. 1
P.M.

E5
F#5
C5/G
G#5
full
grad. release
1/2
w/out octaver
1 1/2
P.S.
let ring
Interlude
N.C.(F#5)
w/ clean tone & chorus
Rhy. Fig. 2
End Rhy. Fig. 2
Gtr. 1: w/ Rhy. Fig. 2, 2 1/2 times
Gtr. 2
P.M.
w/ clean tone & chorus

Guitar Solo
Gtr. 1: w/ Rhy. Fill 2
D5/A C5/G
Gtr. 2 tacet
N.C.(A)
Gtr. 1 (dist.)
w/ leslie effect
let ring
hold bend
full
P.M.
*Vib. bent note only.
Gtrs. 1 & 2
Chorus
Gtr. 1: w/ Rhy. Fig. 1, 1st 4 meas., simile
A5
C5/ G
Snort - in' whis - key, drink - in' co - caine.
8va
Gtr. 2
1/2
N.C.(A)
loco
P.H.
w/ slide
Rhy. Fill 2
Gtr. 1

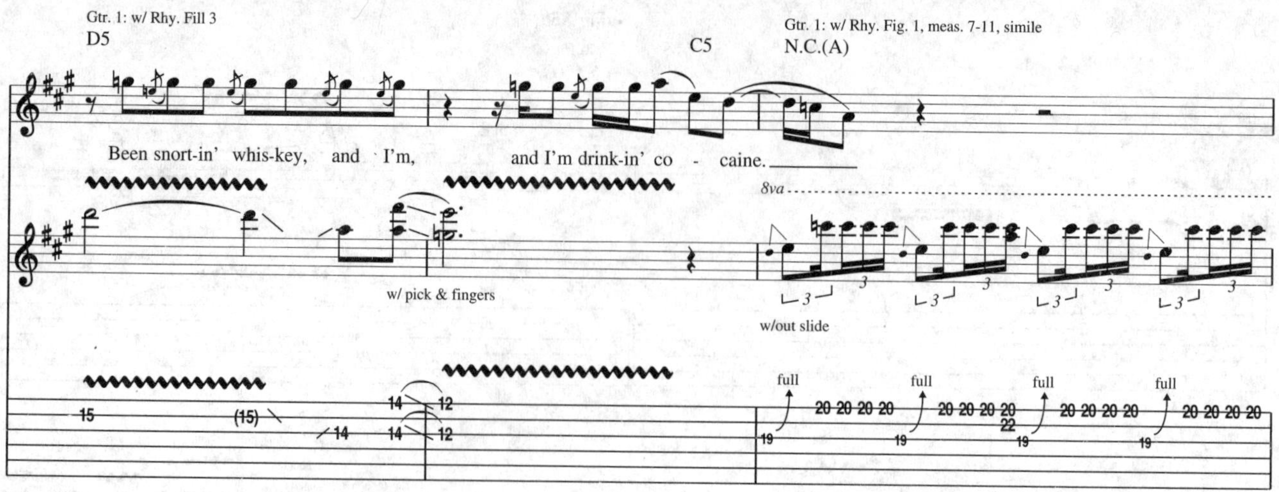
Gtr. 1: w/ Rhy. Fill 3
D5
C5
Gtr. 1: w/ Rhy. Fig. 1, meas. 7-11, simile
N.C.(A)
Been snort-in' whis-key, and I'm, and I'm drink-in' co - caine.
w/ pick & fingers
8va
w/out slide
full

E5
Got this feel - in',
8va
loco
fdbk.
full
1/2
3/4

F#5
C/G
G#5
N.C.(A)
I'm gon-na drive that girl in - sane.
full

Rhy. Fill 3
Gtr. 1
P.M.
P.M.
P.M.
P.M.
P.M.

E5

Got this feel - in',

Gtr. 2

full full full full full 1 1/2 full

Gtr. 1

P.M.

Something to Talk About

(Let's Give Them Something to Talk About)

Words and Music by Shirley Eikhard

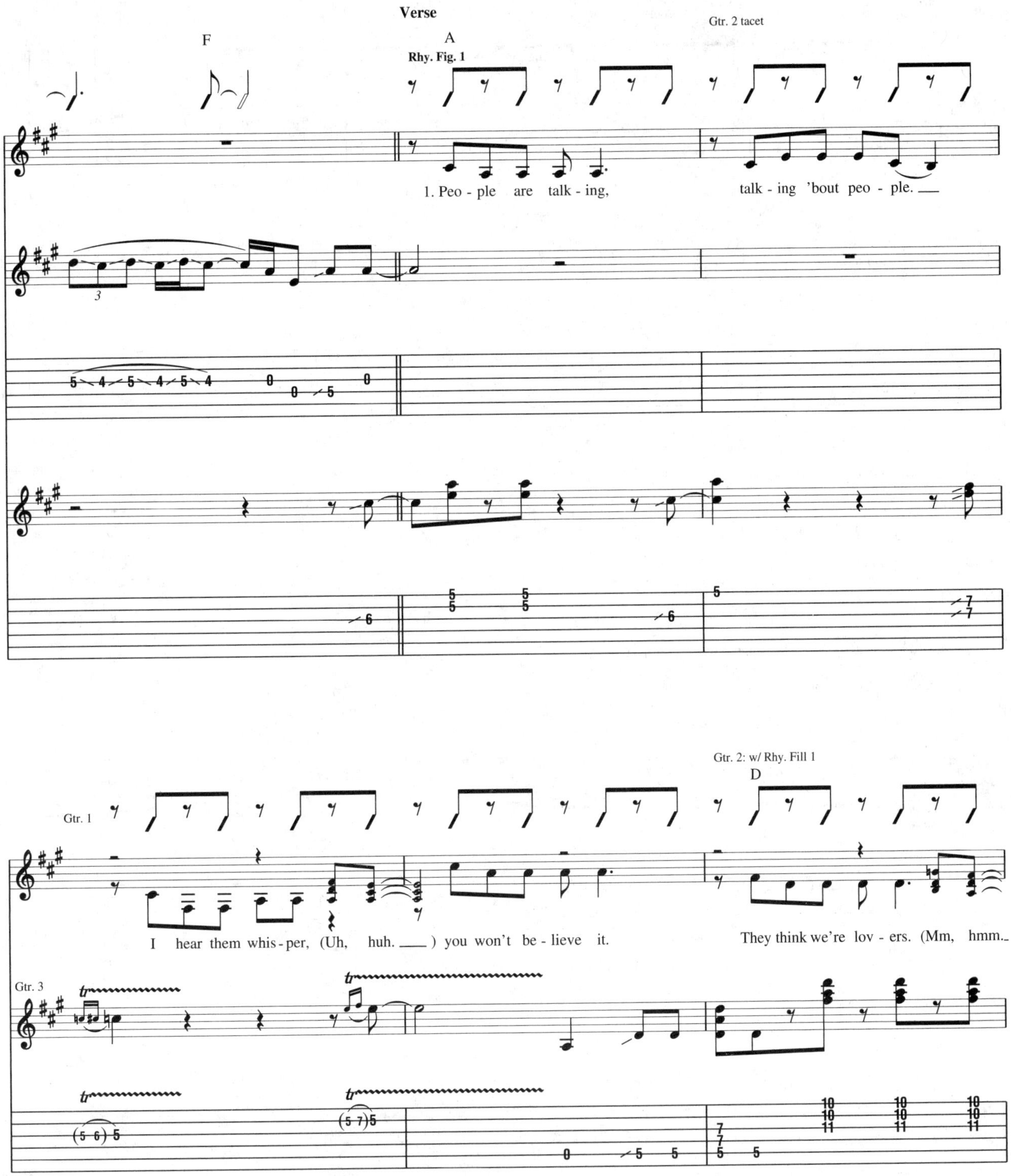

Verse

Gtr. 2 tacet

F

A

Rhy. Fig. 1

1. Peo - ple are talk - ing, talk - ing 'bout peo - ple.

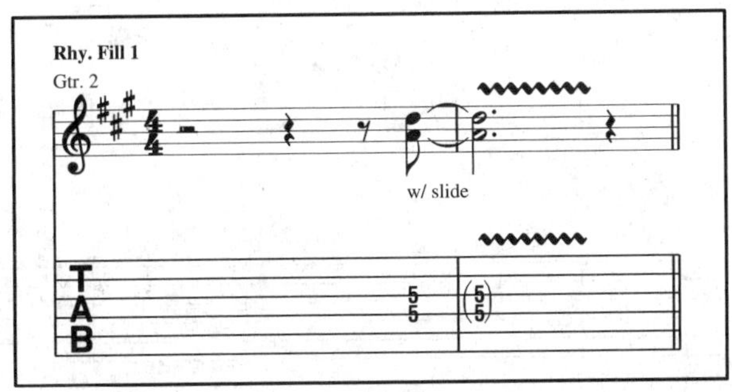

A
End Rhy. Fig. 1
) kept un - der - cov - er.
I just ig - nore it, but they keep say - ing we

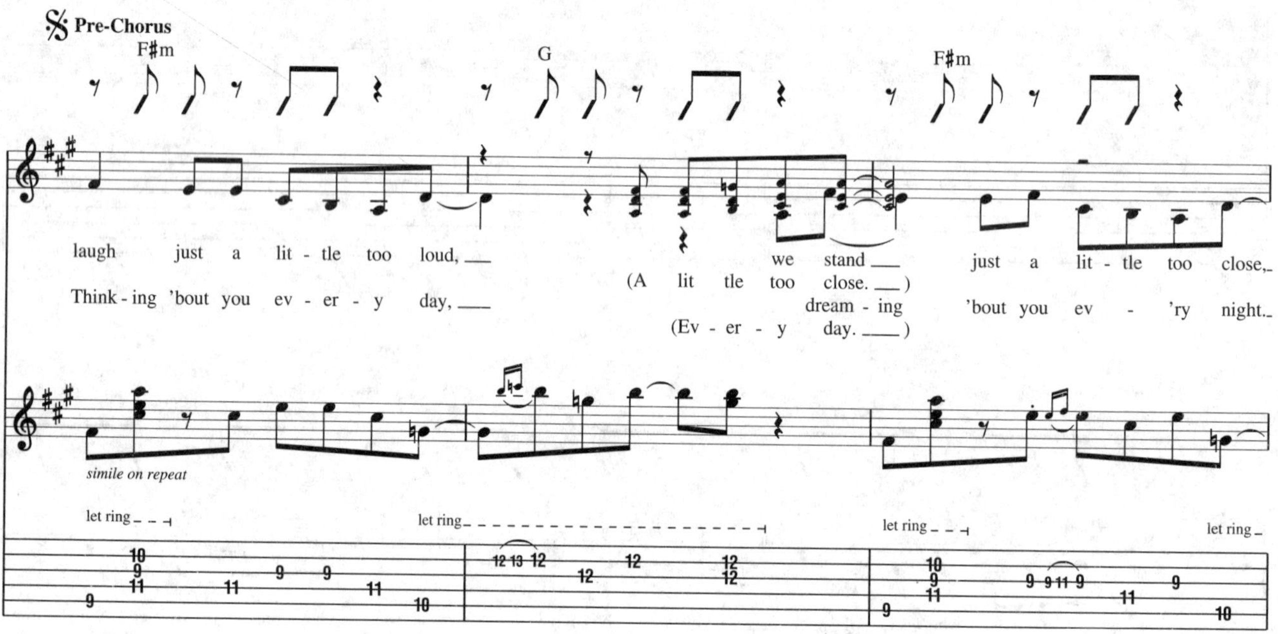
Pre-Chorus
F♯m
G
F♯m
laugh just a lit - tle too loud,
we stand
just a lit - tle too close,
(A lit tle too close.)
Think - ing 'bout you ev - er - y day,
dream - ing 'bout you ev - 'ry night.
(Ev - er - y day.)
simile on repeat
let ring

G
C
F
we stare just a lit - tle too long.
(Too close.)
I'm hop - ing that you feel the same way.
(Ev - er - y night.)
let ring

Chorus
Gtr. 1: w/ Rhy. Fill 2, 2nd time
E
A
Rhy. Fig. 2
May - be they're see - ing
Now that we know it, uh,
some - thing we don't, dar - ling.
let's real - ly show it dar - ing.
Let's give them some - thing to talk
Let's give them some - thing to talk
Rhy. Fig. 2A

E7
A
E7
a - bout.
(Some - thing to talk a - bout.)
Let's give them some - thing to talk a - bout.
(Some - thing to talk
a - bout,
(Some - thing to talk a - bout.)
a lit - tle mys - t'ry to fig - ure out.
(Some - thing to talk
w/ pick & middle finger
sim.

Rhy. Fill 2
Gtr. 1

Gtr. 3: w/ Rhy. Fill 3, 2nd time
A
E
F♯m
G
To Coda
D
End Rhy. Fig. 2
Let's give them some-thing to talk a - bout. How a - bout love?
a - bout. __)
Let's give them some-thing to talk a - bout. How a - bout love, __ love, __ love? __
a - bout. __)
End Rhy. Fig. 2A
let ring

F
Verse
Gtr. 1: w/ Rhy. Fig. 1
A
2. I feel so fool - ish, (Uh - huh. __) I nev - er no - ticed
Gtr. 3

Rhy. Fill 3
Gtr. 3

D
you'd act so ner-vous. (Uh - huh. ___) Could you be fall-ing for me? ___ It took a ru-mor (Mm, hmm. ___

D.S. al Coda
A
___) to make me won-der. ___ Now ___ I'm con-vinced I'm go - in' un - der.

Coda
Guitar Solo
Gtrs. 1 & 3: w/ Rhy. Figs. 2 & 2A, simile
F
A
E7
Rhy. Fill 4
End Rhy. Fill 4
*Rhy. Fill 4 A
Gtr. 3
End Rhy. Fill 4 A
Gtr. 2
Gtr. 2
divisi
w/ slide
* Rhy. Fill applies to Gtr. 3

A
E7
A
let ring

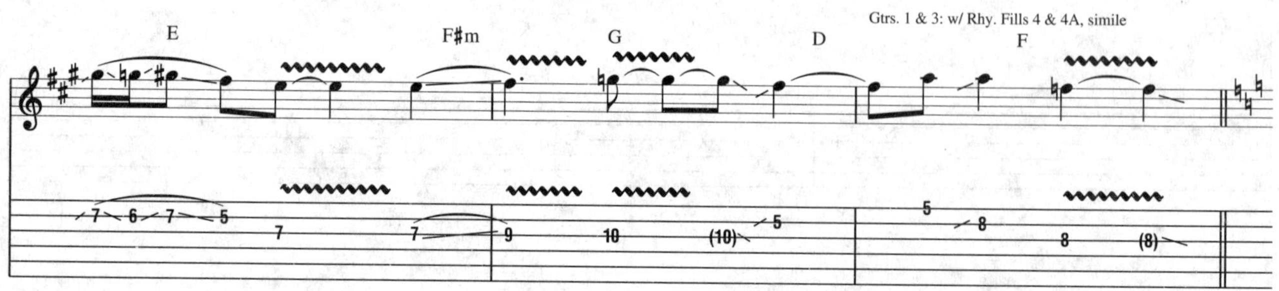
E
F#m
G
D
Gtrs. 1 & 3: w/ Rhy. Fills 4 & 4A, simile
F

Chorus

Gtr. 2 tacet
C
Let's give them some-thing to talk a - bout, babe,
a lit - tle mys - t'ry to fig -
Gtr. 1
1/2
Gtr. 3
1/2

Gtr. 1 tacet
Gsus4
G
Am
ure out.
Let's give them some-thing to talk a - bout.
How a - bout love?
(Love,
Gtr. 3
full

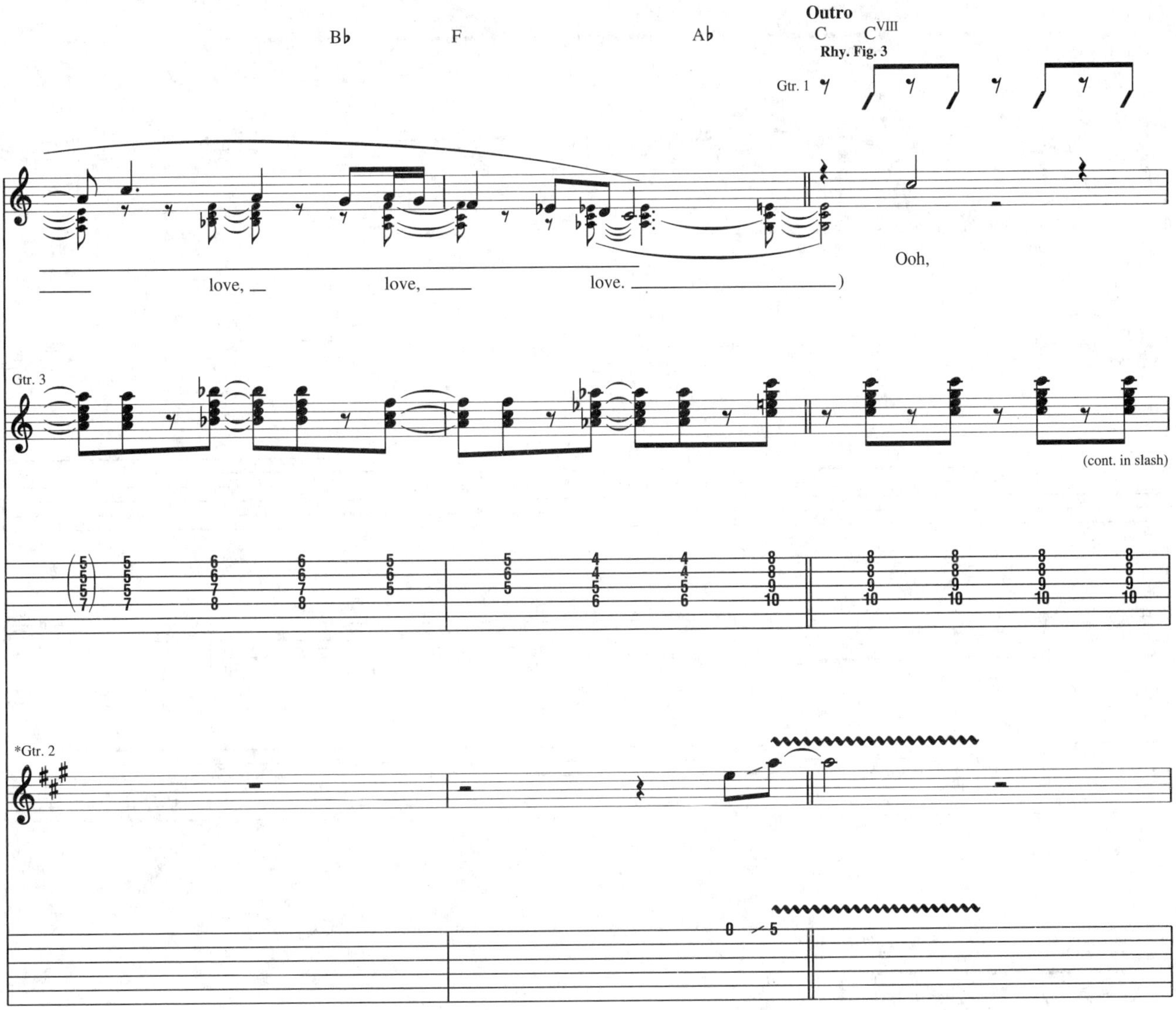
Outro
B♭
F
A♭
C
C^VIII
Rhy. Fig. 3
Gtr. 1
love,
love,
love.
)
Ooh,
Gtr. 3
(cont. in slash)
*Gtr. 2

* Capo III
Capoed fret is "0" in TAB.

G7
C^VIII
G7
Gtrs. 1 & 3
(Gtr. 3 cont. in notation)
lis - ten now, ba - by.
(Some - thing to talk a - bout.)
Well, a lit - tle mys - t'ry won't hurt.
(Some - thing to talk
Gtr. 2

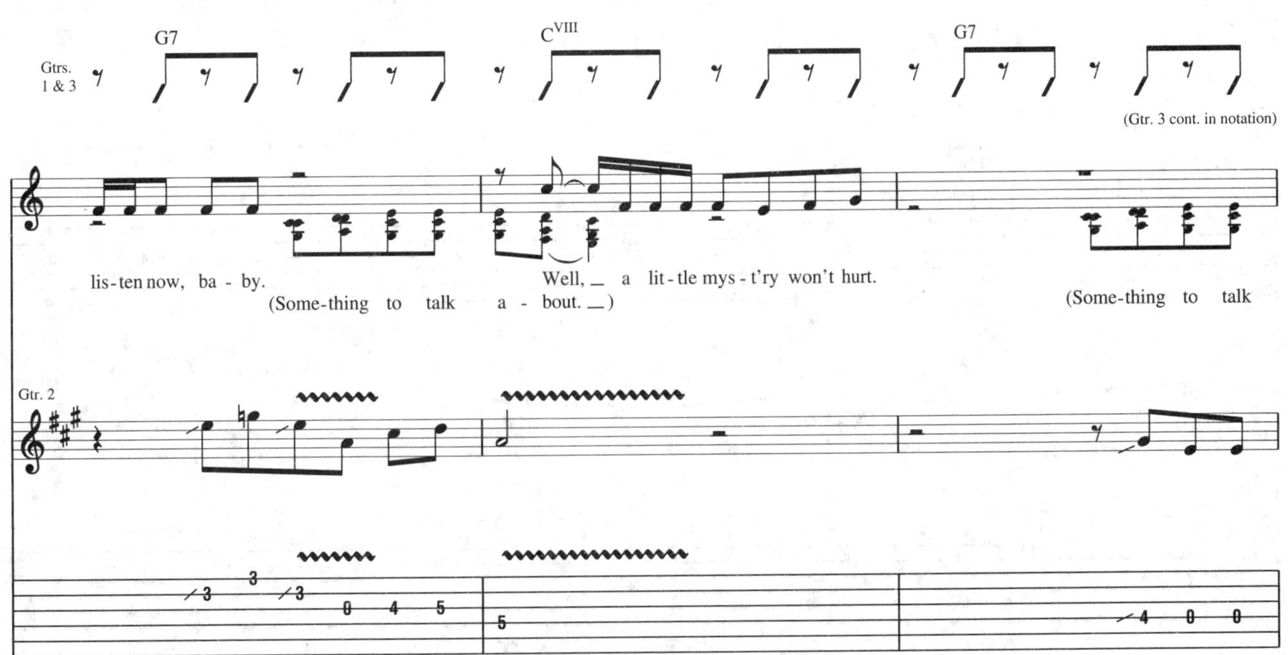

* Symbols in parentheses represent chord names respective to capoed guitar.
Symbols above reflect actual sounding chord.

Gtr. 3: w/ Rhy. Fig. 3, last 6 meas., simile
Begin Fade
C (A) G7 (E7) C (A) G (E)
Huv. Oh, oh. Oo hoo. How a - bout love,
Gtr. 2
8va
loco
Bb (G) F (D) Ab (F)
Gtr. 1: w/ Rhy. Fig. 3
Gtr. 3: w/ Rhy. Fill 5, 2 1/2 times, simile
C (A)
love, love?
G7 (E7) C (A) G7 (E7)
Bop, bop, deh, deh, A - uh, uh. Ah, ba, da, ba, da.
Gtr. 3: w/ Rhy. Fig. 3, last 3 meas.
Fade Out
C (A) G (E) Am (F#m) Bb (G) F (D) Ab (F)
Mm. How a - bout love, love?

Southern Cross

Words and Music by Stephen Stills, Richard Curtis and Michael Curtis

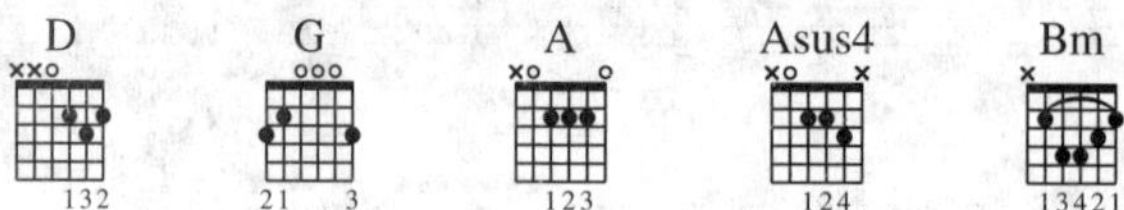

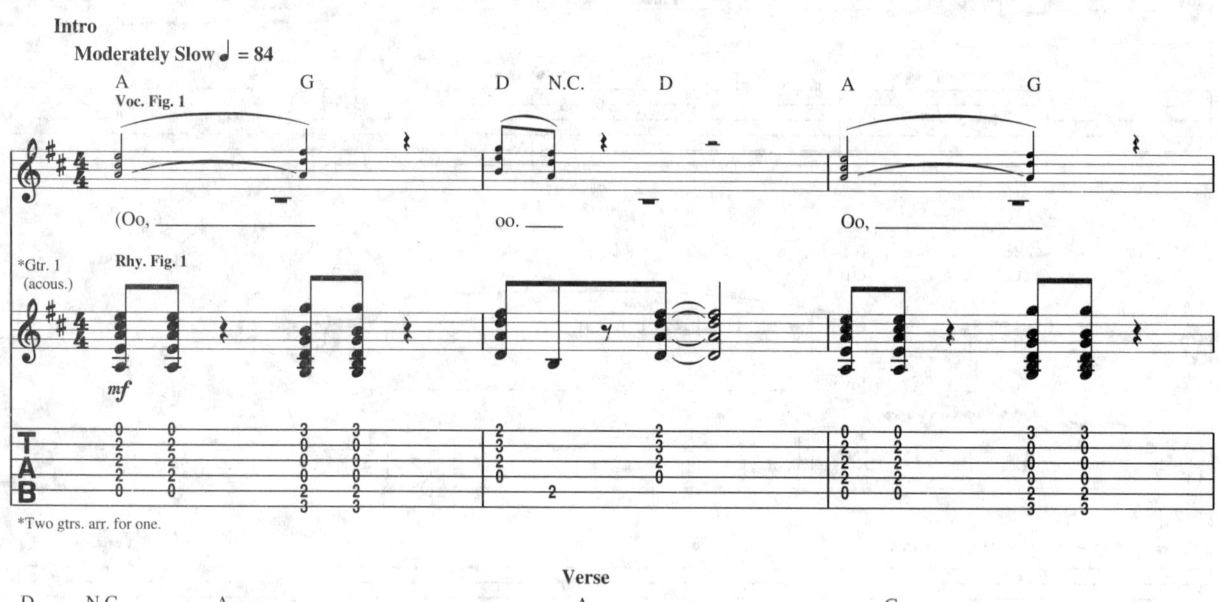

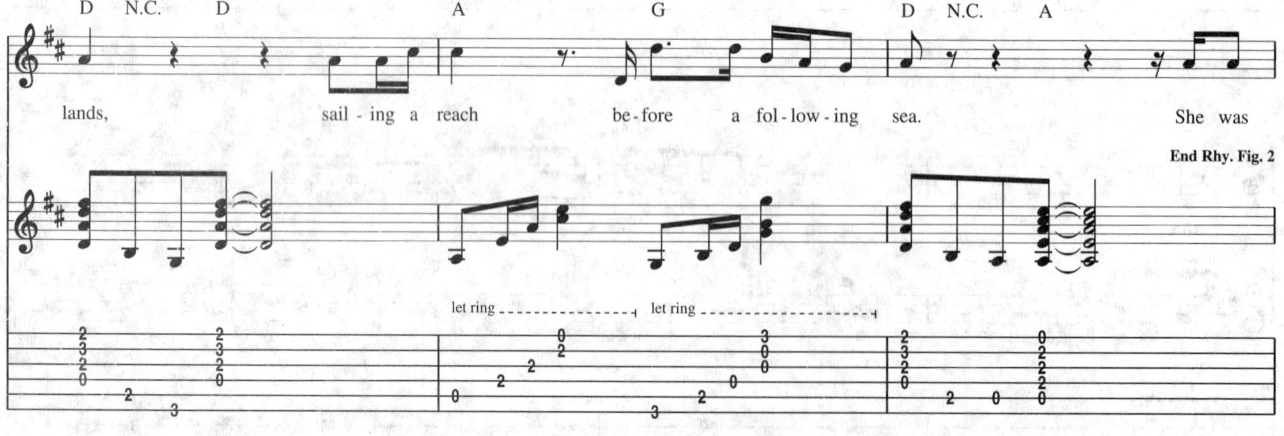

Gtr. 1: w/ Rhy. Fig. 2
G
D N.C. D
mak - ing for the trades on the out - side and the
A G D N.C. A
down - hill run to Pa - pe - e - te. 2. Off the wind
Verse
A G D N.C. D
on this head - ing lie the Mar - que - sas. We got
Rhy. Fig. 3
Gtr. 1
let ring
A G D N.C. A
eight - y feet of a wat - er - line nice - ly mak - ing way. In a
End Rhy. Fig. 3
let ring
G D N.C. D
nois - y bar in Av - a - lon I tried to call you, but on a
let ring

A G D Bm A
mid-night watch I re-al-ized why twice you ran a-way.___ Think _ a-bout...
let ring
let ring
Pre-Chorus
G D G A
Think a-bout how man-y times I have fa - all-en.
let ring
G D G A
Spir-its are us-ing me, larg-er voic-es ca-all-in'.
let ring
G D G
What heav-en brought you and me can-not be for-go-
let ring

A
A5
ot - ten.
I have been a -
Been a - round the world.
(cont. in slash)
Chorus
D G A Asus4 A D G A
Gtr. 1
f
round the world.
Look-in'.
Look - in' for that wom - an, girl
To Coda
Asus4 A D G A
who knows love can en - dure.
Who knows, she knows.
And you know it will.
*downstem Voc. sung 1st time
Gtr. 1: w/ Rhy. Fig. 1
G D N.C. D A G D N.C. A
Mm.
3. When you see
Verse
Gtr. 1: w/ Rhy. Fig. 2, simile
A G D N.C. D A G
the South - ern Cross for the first time,
you un - der - stand now why you come this
Gtr. 1: w/ Rhy. Fig. 2, 1st 3 meas.
D N.C. A G D N.C. D
way.
'Cause the truth you might be run - ning from is so small,
but it's as

*Three gtrs. arr. for one. One gtr. per string.

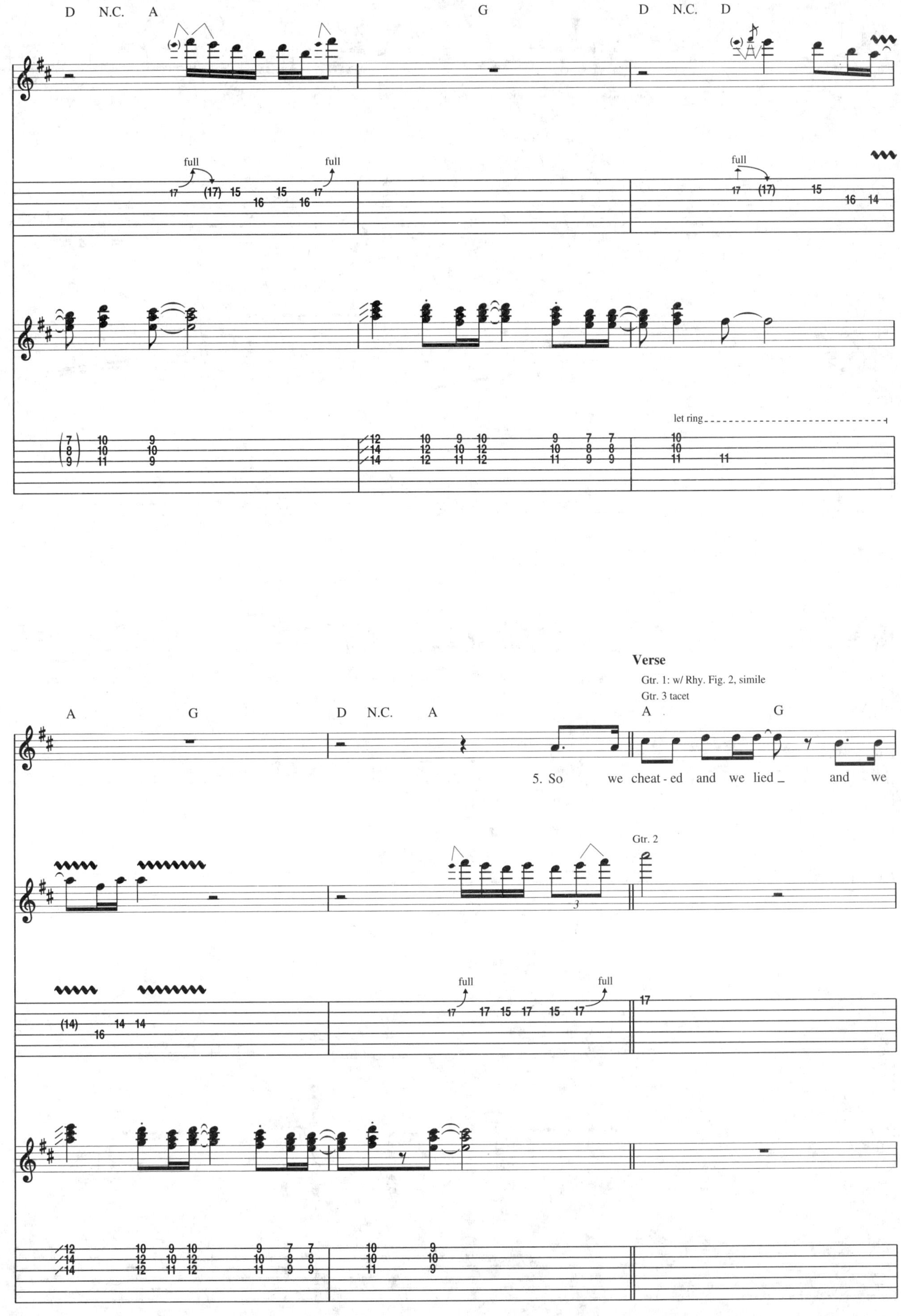

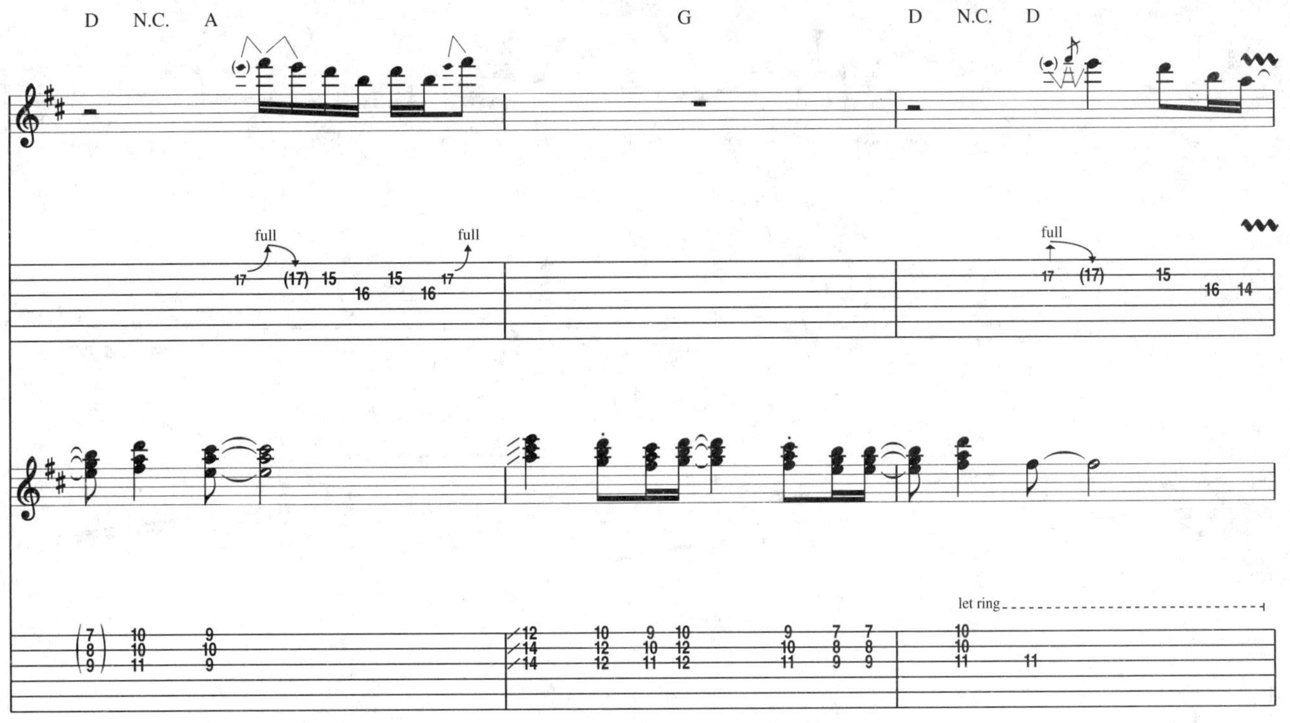

A G D N.C. A

Verse

Gtr. 1: w/ Rhy. Fig. 2, simile

Gtr. 3 tacet

A G

5. So we cheat - ed and we lied _ and we

Gtr. 2

full full

Gtr. 2 tacet
D N.C. D
A
G
D N.C. A
test - ed. And we nev - er failed to fail; it was the eas - i - est thing to do.

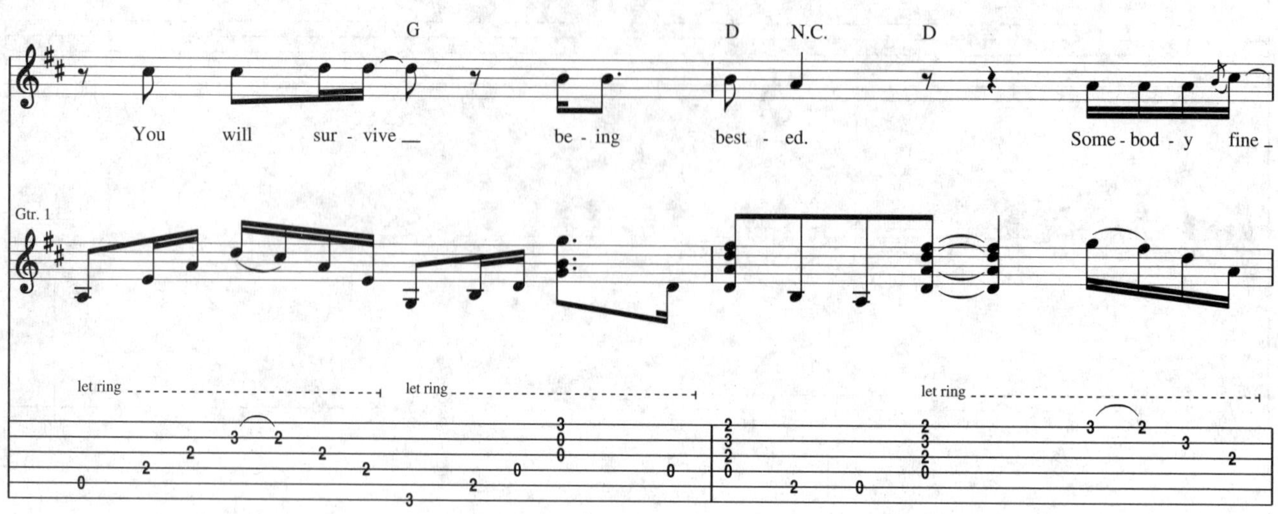
G
D N.C. D
You will sur - vive being best - ed. Some - bod - y fine
Gtr. 1
let ring
let ring
let ring

A
G
D
Bm
A
will come a - long, make me for - get a - bout lov - ing you at the South - ern
let ring
let ring

G
D N.C. D
A
G
D N.C. D
Cross.

The Space Between

Words and Music by David J. Matthews and Glen Ballard

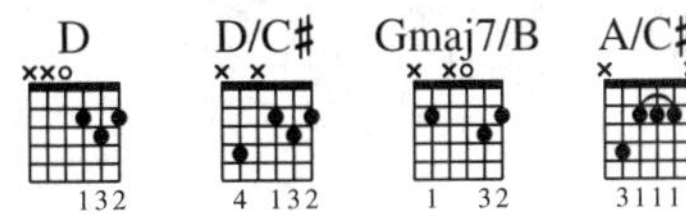

All gtrs.: Tune down 2 1/2 steps:
(low to high) B–E–A–D–F♯–B

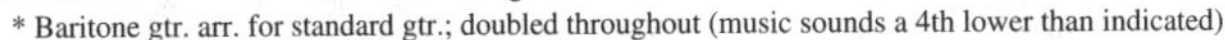
* Baritone gtr. arr. for standard gtr.; doubled throughout (music sounds a 4th lower than indicated).

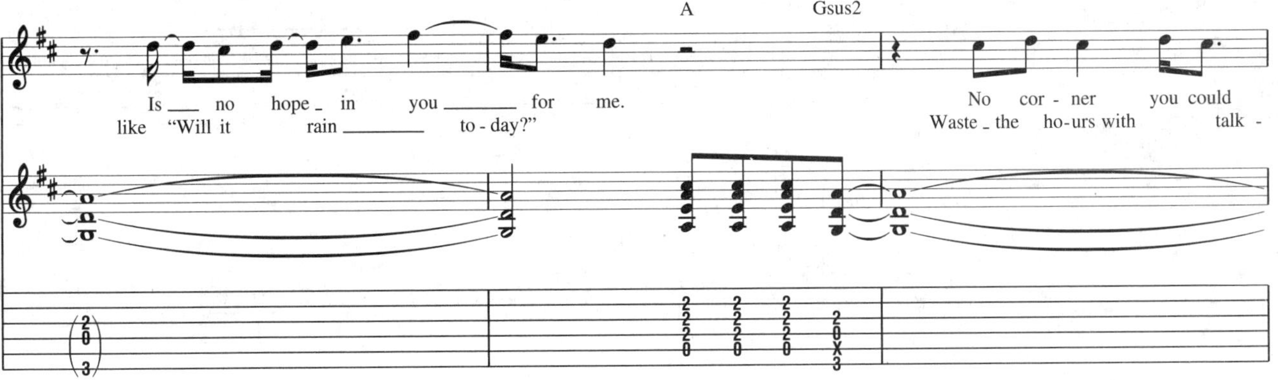

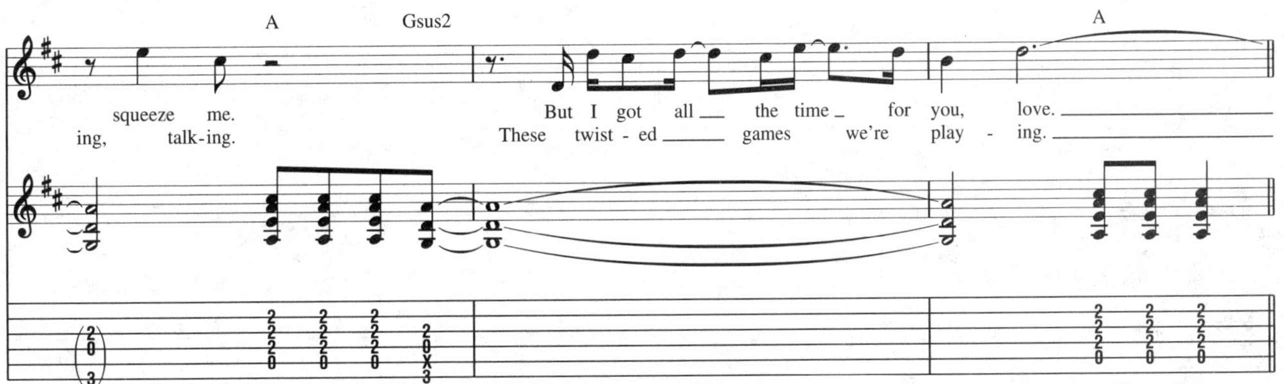

Chorus
Gtr. 1 tacet
D
Rhy. Fig. 1
D/C♯
Gmaj7/B
* Gtr. 2
mf
The space be - tween the tears we cry is the laugh -
We're strange al - lies with war - ring hearts. What a wi -
Riff A
Gtr. 3
8va
let ring
w/ chorus effect
* Kybds. arr. for gtr.
A/C♯
End Rhy. Fig. 1
ter, keeps us com - ing back for more.
ld - eyed beast you be.
The space be - tween the wick - ed lies
End Riff A
let ring sim.
Gmaj7/B
Gtrs. 2 & 3 tacet
A
Gsus2
we tell and hope to keep us safe from the pain.
But will I hold you a - gain?
loco
Gtr. 1
divisi
But will I hold you a - gain?
Will I hold...

Bridge
E5 D5 A/C♯ C5 B5 E5 D5 A/C♯
Look at us spin-ning out in the mad - ness of a roll - er coast - er.
You know you went off like the dev-il in a
Fill 1
End Fill 1
* Gtr. 4
Gtr. 1
* Sax arr. for gtr.

Gtr. 4: w/ Fill 1
C5 B5 E5 D5 A/C♯ C5 B♭5
church, in the mid-dle of a crowd - ed room.
All we can do, my love, is hope we don't take this ship down.
Gtr. 1

Chorus
Gtr. 2: w/ Rhy. Fig. 1 (6 times)
Gtr. 3: w/ Riff A (6 times)
Gtr. 1 & band tacet
D D/C♯ Gmaj7/B
The space be - tween where you smile and hide, that's where you'll find

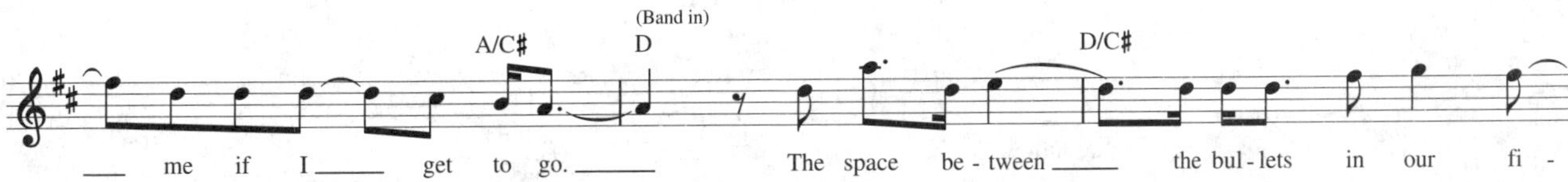
(Band in)
A/C♯ D D/C♯
me if I get to go.
The space be - tween the bul - lets in our fi -

Gmaj7/B
A/C#
D
- re fight is where I'll be hid - ing, wait - ing for you. The rain that falls
D/C#
Gmaj7/B
A/C#
splashed in your heart, ran like sad - ness down the win - dow in - to your
D
D/C#
Gmaj7/B
A/C#
room. The space be - tween our wick - ed lies is where we hope to keep safe from pain.
D
D/C#
Gmaj7/B
A/C#
D
Take my hand 'cause we're walk - ing out of here. Oh,
D/C#
Gmaj7/B
A/C#
oh. Right out of here, love, is all we need, dear.
Outro-Chorus
Gtr. 2: w/ Rhy. Fig. 1 (2 times)
Gtr. 3: w/ Riff A (2 times)
Band tacet
D
D/C#
Gmaj7/B
The space be - tween what's wrong and right is where you'll find
A/C#
D
D/C#
me hid - ing, wait - ing for you. The space be - tween your heart and
* Gtr. 5
Riff B
End Riff B
* Bass arr. for gtr.
Repeat and fade
Gtr. 5: w/ Riff B (2 times)
Gtr. 2: w/ Rhy. Fig. 1
Gtr. 3: w/ Riff A
Gtr. 5: w/ Riff B (4 times)
Gmaj7/B
A/C#
D
D/C#
Gmaj7/B
A/C#
mind is the space we'll fill with time. The space be - tween.

Start Me Up

Words and Music by Mick Jagger and Keith Richards

F Fsus2 F Fsus2 G5 B♭5 F/A B♭5 E F5 F C/E
6 open 6 1fr
if you start me up, I'll nev - er stop. __ If you start me up,
Gtr. 1

F5 C/E F5 G5 B♭5 F/A B♭5 Fsus2 F Fsus2
if you start me up, I'll nev - er stop. __ I'll be run-nin' hot, uh. __

F Fsus2 F Fsus2 G5 B♭5 A G C E F5 Fsus2
5 open 6 3fr 5 3fr 6 open
The job we're rig-gin' now don't blow my top. __ If you start me up, uh,

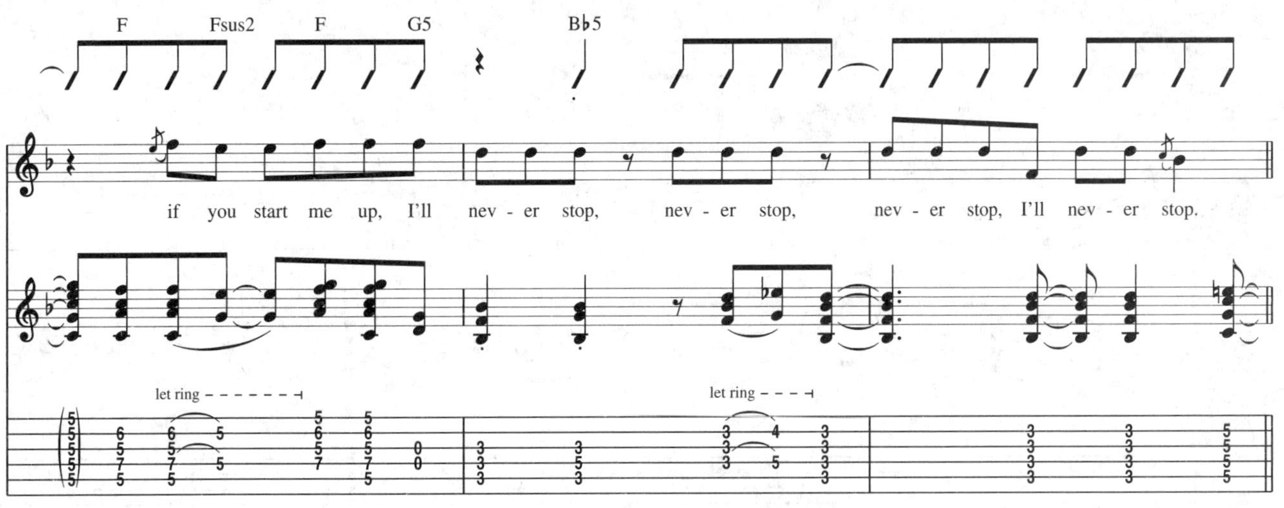
F Fsus2 F G5 B♭5
if you start me up, I'll nev - er stop, nev - er stop, nev - er stop, I'll nev - er stop.
let ring
let ring

Chorus

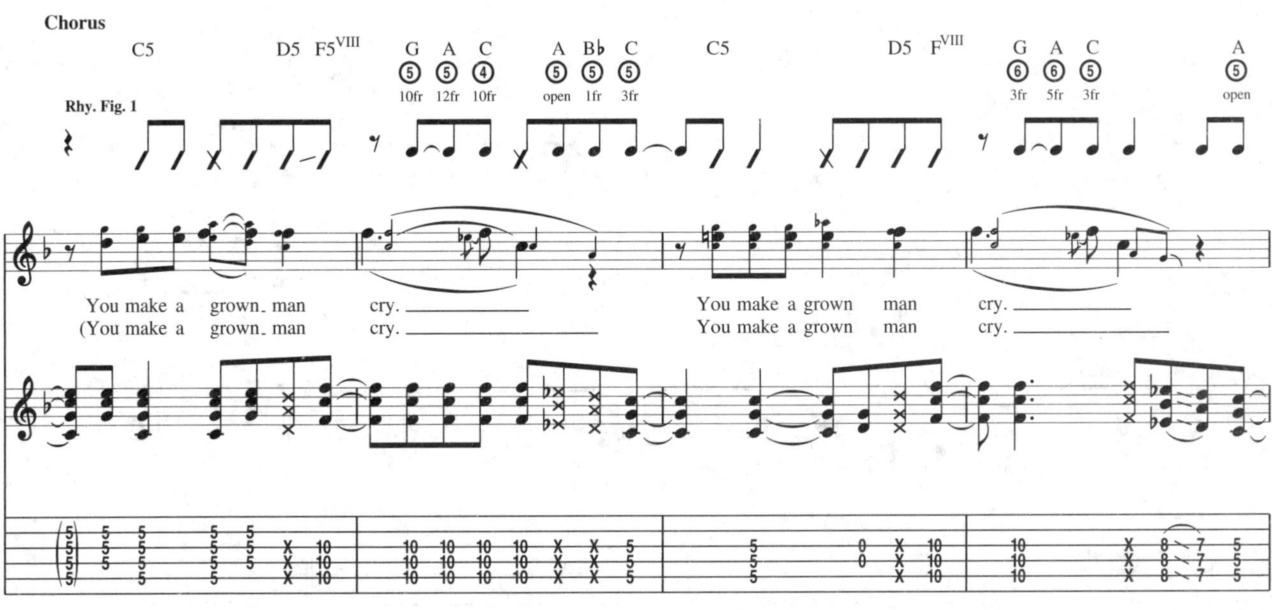
C5 D5 F5VIII G A C A B♭ C C5 D5 FVIII G A C A
10fr 12fr 10fr open 1fr 3fr 3fr 5fr 3fr open
Rhy. Fig. 1
You make a grown_ man cry.
(You make a grown_ man cry.
You make a grown man cry.
You make a grown man cry.

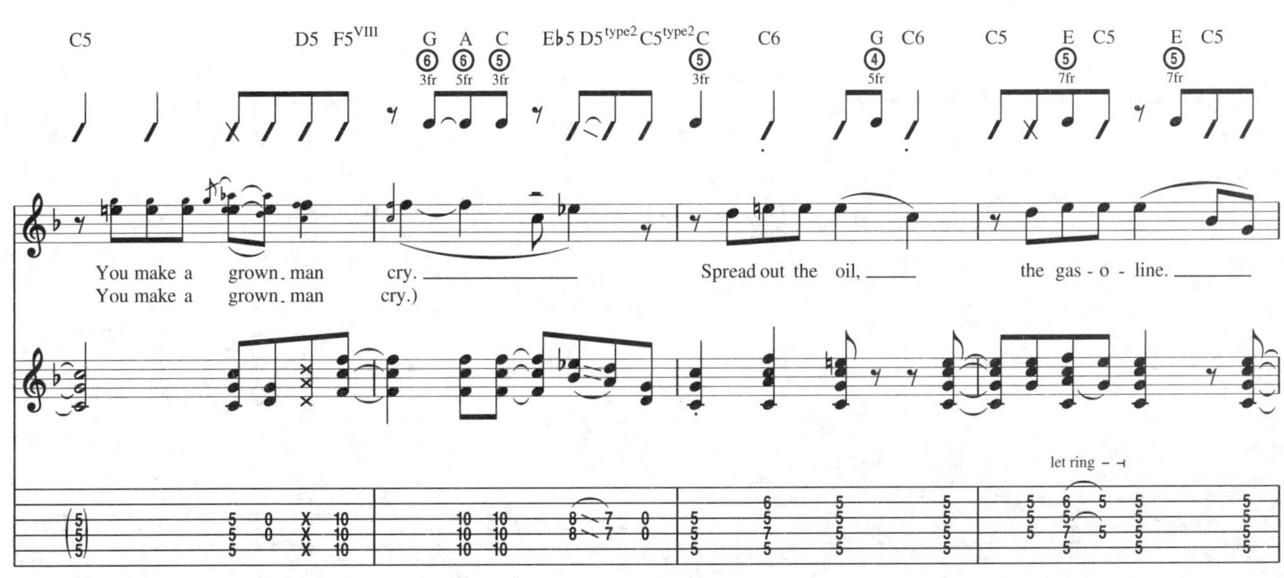
C5 D5 F5VIII G A C E♭5 D5type2 C5type2 C C6 G C6 C5 E C5 E C5
3fr 5fr 3fr 3fr 5fr 7fr 7fr
You make a grown_ man cry.
You make a grown_ man cry.)
Spread out the oil, the gas - o - line.
let ring

D G A C5 E♭5 D5type2 C A C5type2 Fsus2 F Fsus2
7fr 5fr 7fr 5fr 7fr
End Rhy. Fig. 1
I want a smooth ride in a mean, mean ma - chine.
let ring

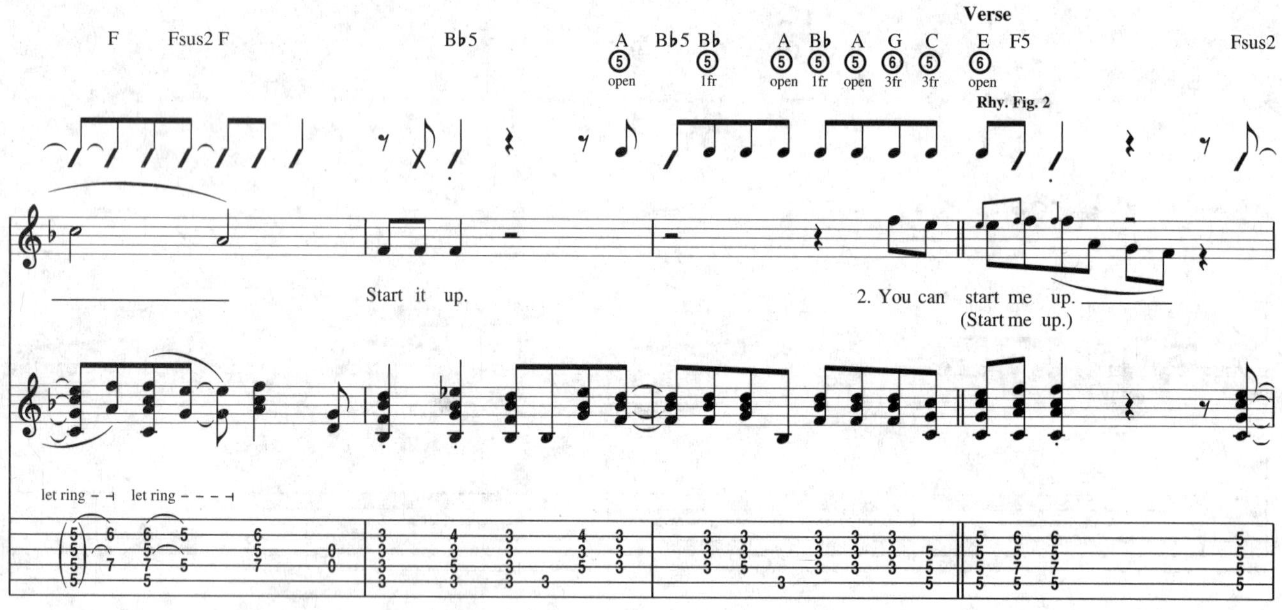

F Fsus2 F B♭5 A B♭5 B♭ A B♭ A G C E F5 Fsus2
Verse
open 1fr open 1fr open 3fr 3fr open
Rhy. Fig. 2
Start it up. 2. You can start me up.
(Start me up.)
let ring let ring

F Fsus2 F Fsus2 A B♭5 A G C
open open 3fr 3fr
Kick on the start - er, give it all you've got, you've got, you've got. I

E F5
6
open
F F5
6
1fr
B♭5 F B♭
4 3
3fr 3fr
F/A B♭5
End Rhy. Fig. 2
can com-pete with the rid - ers in the oth - er heats. If you
Gtr. 3 (elec.)
mf w/ clean tone
let ring
full
full
full
full
Gtr. 1
let ring
F5
B♭ B♭5
5
1fr
B♭5 A G E
5 5 6 6
1fr open 3fr open
rough it up, 'n' if you like it, you can start it up, start it up, start it up, start it up.
let ring
let ring
let ring

Chorus

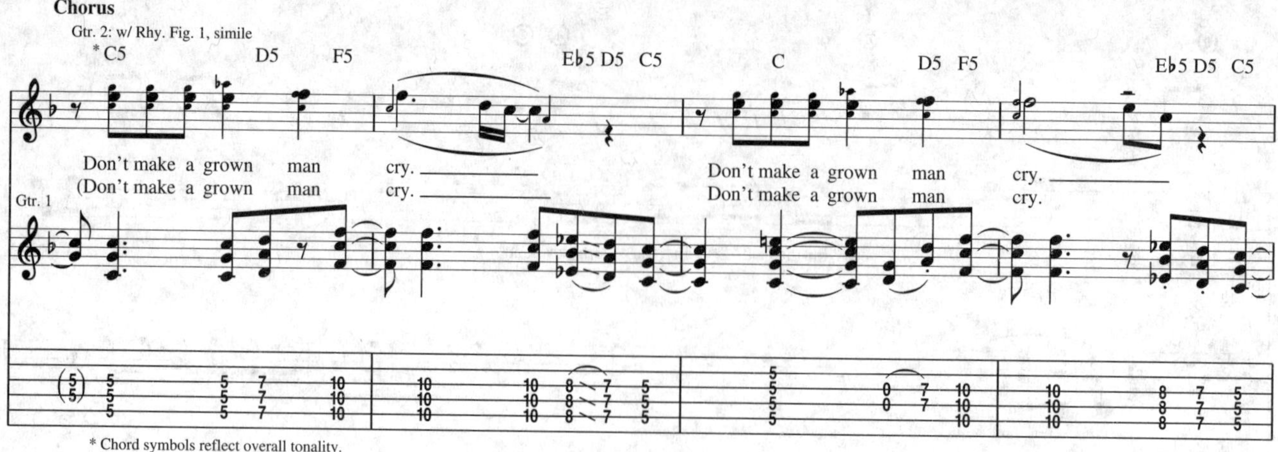

* Chord symbols reflect overall tonality.

Verse
Gtr. 2: w/ Rhy. Fig. 2, simile
Bb5 Bb6 Bb5 Bb6 Bb5 Bb Eb/Bb Bb C Fadd9/C C Fadd9/C F F/C
Start it up. 3. Mm, start me up. Now, give it
Bb5 Bb6 Bb5 Bb6 Bb5 Bb C F/C C F/C C5 F/C Bb5
all you've got, you've got to nev-er, nev-er, nev-er stop. Start it up. Whoo! Oh, ba-by, why don't ya
Chorus
Gtr. 2: w/ Rhy. Fig. 1, simile
Bb6 Bb5 Bb C5 D5 F5
start it up? Nev-er nev-er, nev-er. You make a grown man
(Start it up. Start it up. You make a grown man
Eb5 C5 G F5 Eb5
cry. You make a grown man cry.
cry. You make a grown man cry.

C5
G5
F5
Eb5 D5
G
C
F/C
C
F/C
C
You make a grown _ man cry.
You make a grown _ man cry.)
Ride like the wind at dou - ble speed.
Eb5
D5 C5
E
F5
C/E
F5
C/E
F5
open
Gtr. 2
I'll take you plac - es that you nev - er, nev - er seen.
Verse
Gtr. 2: w/ Rhy. Fill 2
Gtr. 2: w/ Rhy. Fig. 2, simile
F/A Bb5
Bb
Eb/Bb Bb5
C5
F/C
C
Fadd9/C C
F/C
3. Once you start it up,
let me tell you, we will
let ring
Rhy Fill 2
Gtr. 2

Bb5
Bb6
Bb5
Bb
C5
F/C
C
Fadd9/C
nev - er stop, we'll nev - er stop, we'll nev - er, nev - er, nev - er stop.
Start me up.
let ring
C F/C
Bb5
C5
Outro
Gtr. 2: w/ Rhy. Fig. 2, simile
C
Fadd9/C
We'll nev - er stop, nev - er stop.
You, you,
Gtr. 3
grad. bend
full
hold bend
Gtr. 1
let ring
F/C
C
F/C
Bb
Eb/Bb
Bb
C F/C
C
you made a grown man cry.
You,
full

Begin Fade

Gtr. 2: w/ Rhy. Fig. 2, 1st 5 meas., simile

F/C C F/C Bb Eb/Bb Bb C F/C C

you made a dead man come. You, you,

hold bend full full full full full

let ring

F/C C F/C Bb5 Bb6 Bb5 Bb6 Bb C Fadd9/C C

Fade Out

you made a dead man come. Yeah. And you, you,

full full full full 1/2 full full full full

let ring

Statesboro Blues

Words and Music by Willy McTell

even gliss.
* D7
G7
D7
even gliss.
Rhy. Fig. 1
semi-P.M. throughout
* Chord symbols outline general harmony throughout.
* Slide positioned halfway between 13th and 14th fret.
G7

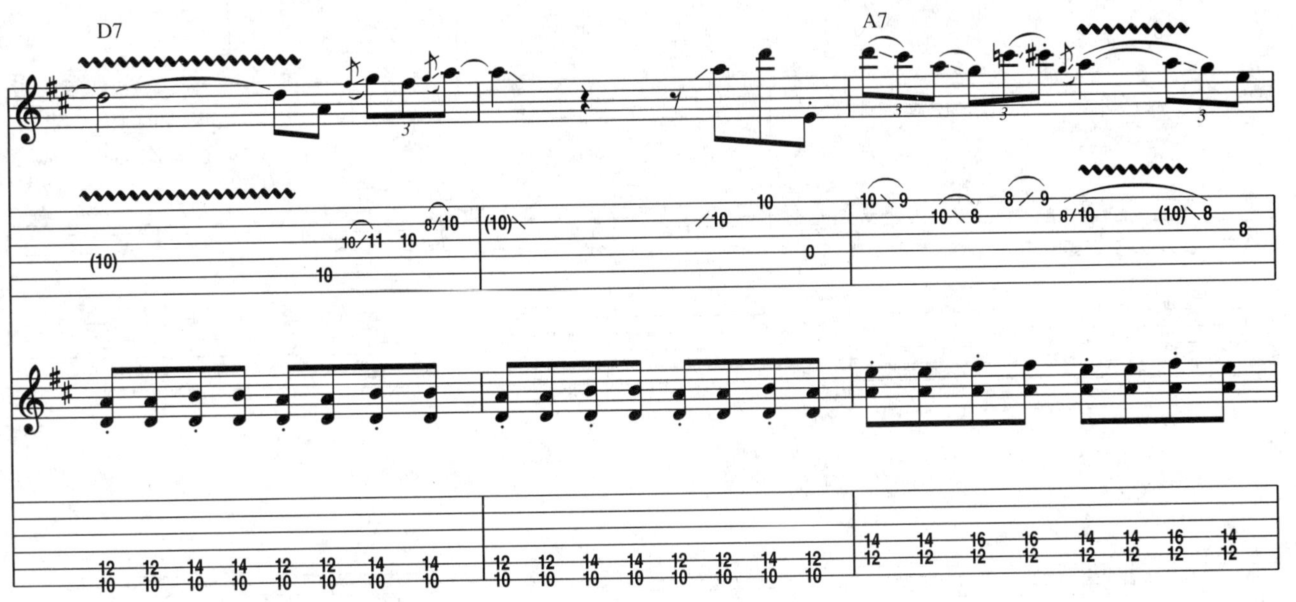
D7
A7

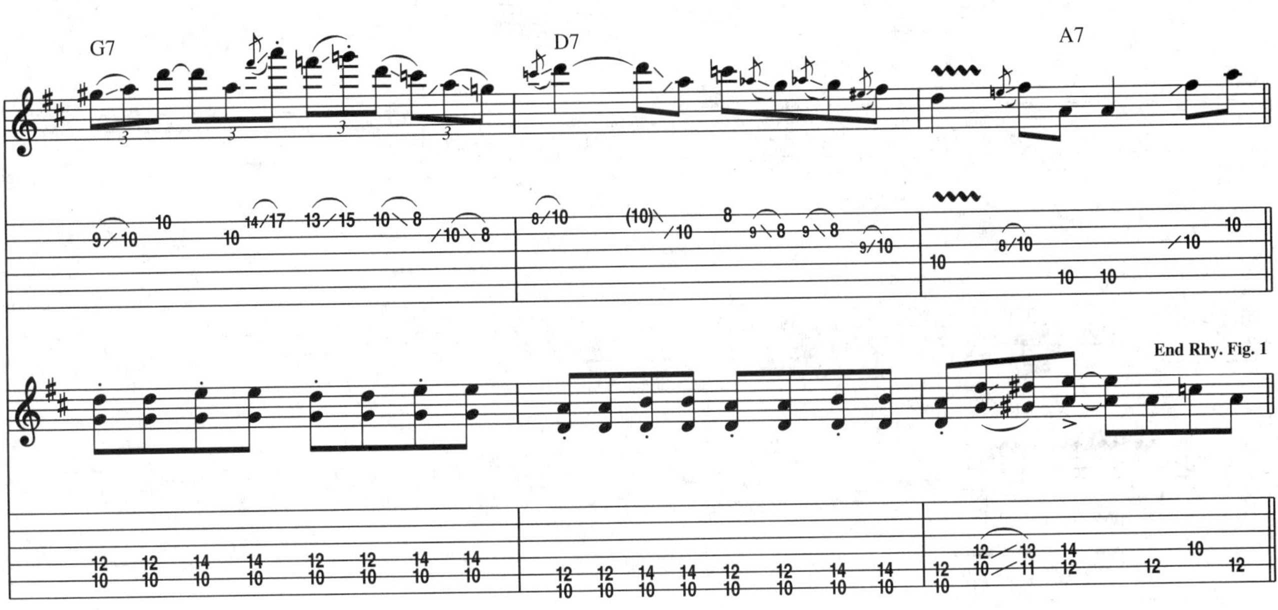
G7
D7
A7
End Rhy. Fig. 1

Verse
Gtr. 2: w/ Rhy. Fig. 1, simile
D7
G7
D7
1. Wake up, ma - ma, turn your lamp down low.
Gtr. 1
mf

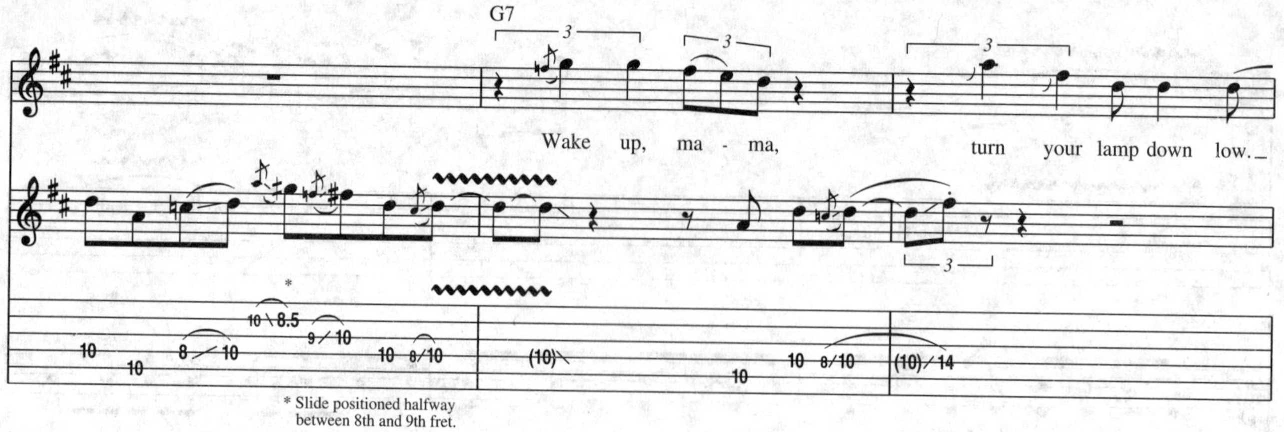
G7
Wake up, ma - ma, turn your lamp down low.
* Slide positioned halfway between 8th and 9th fret.

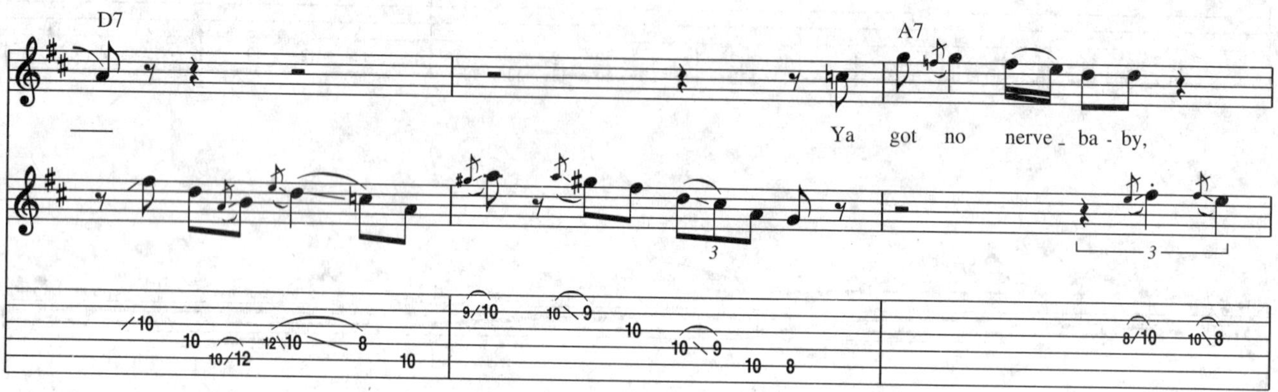
D7
A7
Ya got no nerve ba - by,

G7
D7
A7
ya turn Un-cle John from your door.

Verse
Gtr. 2: w/ Rhy. Fig. 1
D7
G7
D7
2. I woke up this morn - in' an' I had them States-bo - ro blues.
* Slide positioned halfway between 8th & 9th fret

G7
I woke up this morn - in' an' I had them States - bo - ro blues.

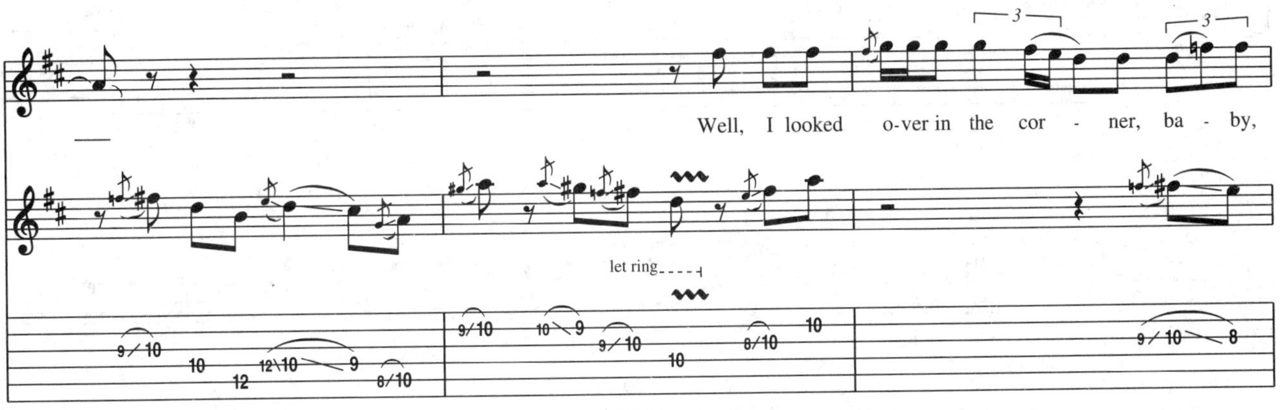
Well, I looked o - ver in the cor - ner, ba - by,
let ring

G7
D7
A7
your grand - pa seem to have them, too.
Oh!
mp
mf
f

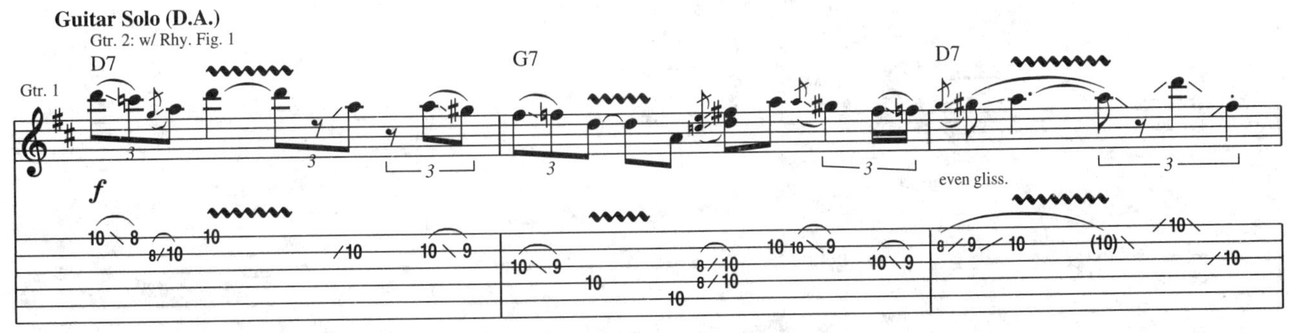
Guitar Solo (D.A.)
Gtr. 2: w/ Rhy. Fig. 1
D7
G7
D7
Gtr. 1
f
even gliss.

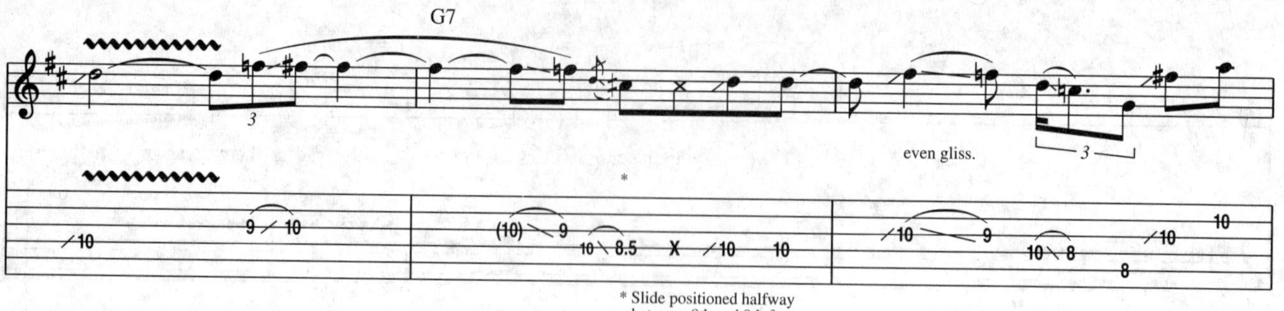
G7
even gliss.
* Slide positioned halfway between 8th and 9th fret.

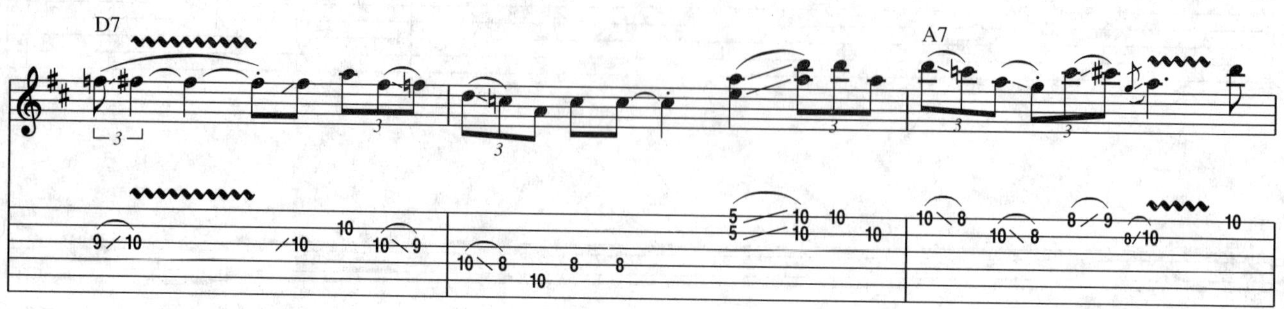
D7
A7

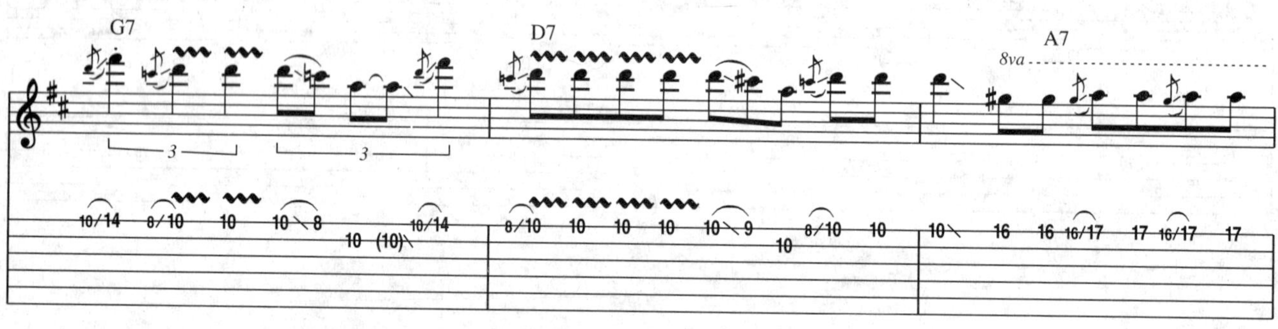
G7
D7
A7
8va

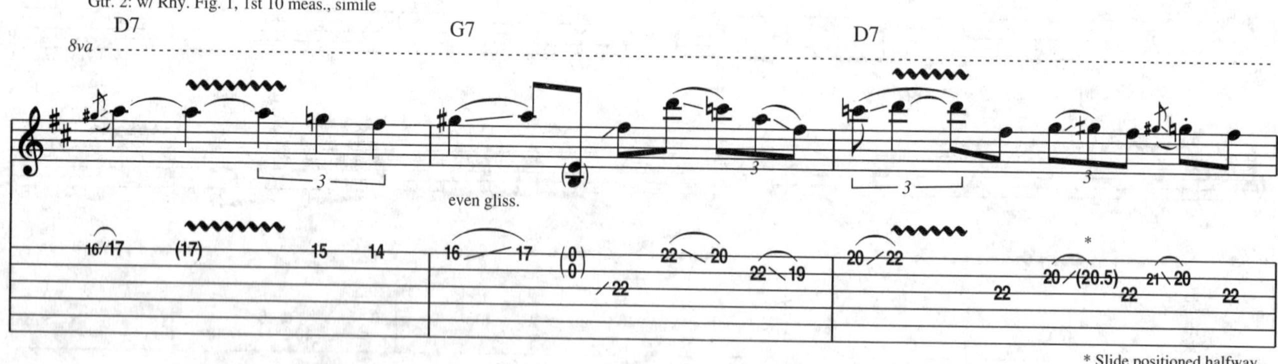
Gtr. 2: w/ Rhy. Fig. 1, 1st 10 meas., simile
D7
G7
D7
8va
even gliss.
* Slide positioned halfway between 20th and 21st fret.

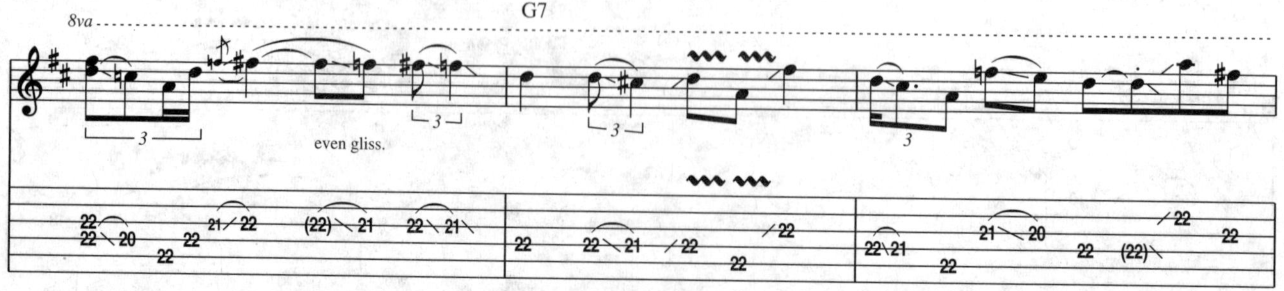
8va
G7
even gliss.

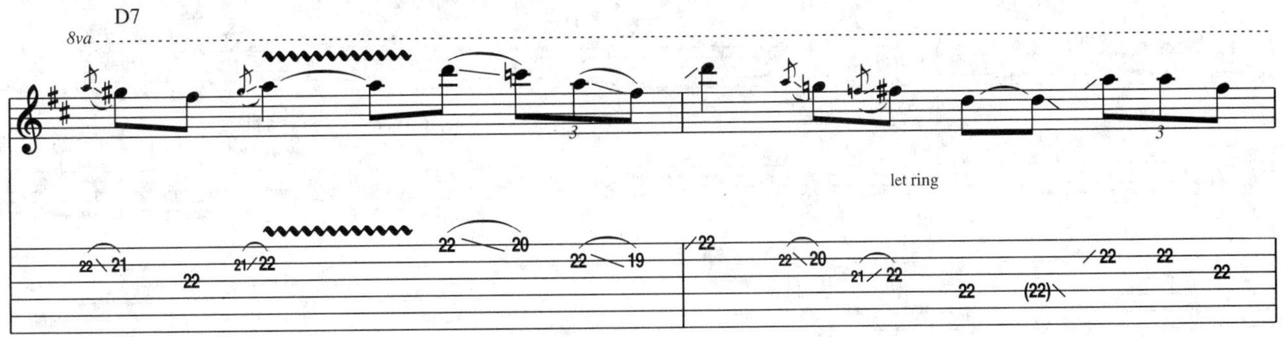

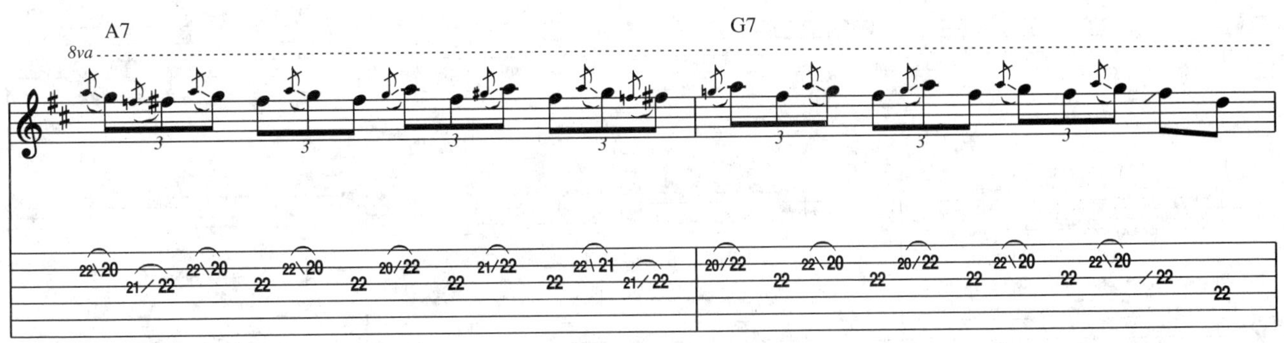

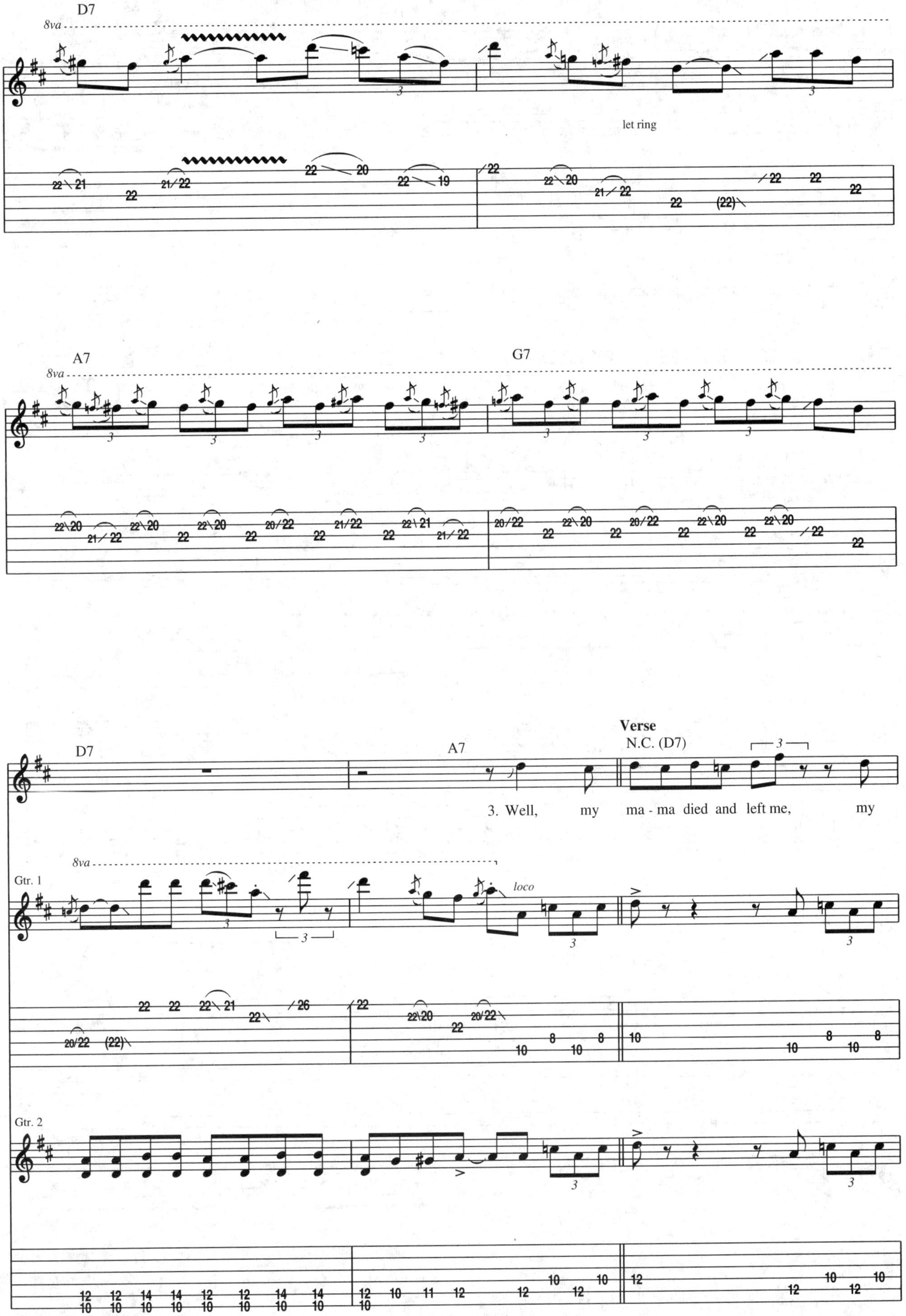

Verse

D7 A7 N.C. (D7)

3. Well, my ma - ma died and left me, my

Gtr. 1

8va

loco

Gtr. 2

pa - pa died and left me. I ain't good look-in', ba - by want some-one sweet and kind.
G7
(even ♪)
D7
I'm go-in' to the coun-try, ba - by, do you wan - na go?
dim.
* Slide positioned halfway between 8th and 9th fret.
A7
If you can't make it, ba - by,

G7
D7
(even ♪)
your sis - ter Lu - cille said she wan-na go.
Spoken: Well, I sho' nuff tell ya . . .
* Slide positioned halfway between 8th and 9th fret.
Guitar Solo (D.B.)
Gtr. 2
even bend
full
Gtr. 1
Rhy. Fig. 2
w/out slide
1/2

D7
8va
A7
let ring
hold bend
full
G7
loco
End Rhy. Fig. 2
Gtr. 1: w/ Rhy. Fig. 2
Gtr. 2
even bend
1/2
(even
1/4

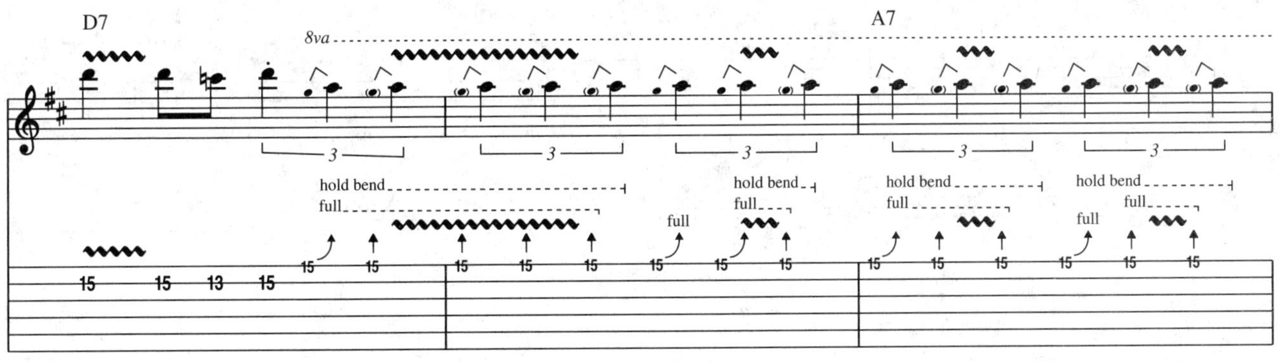
D7
A7
8va
hold bend
full
full

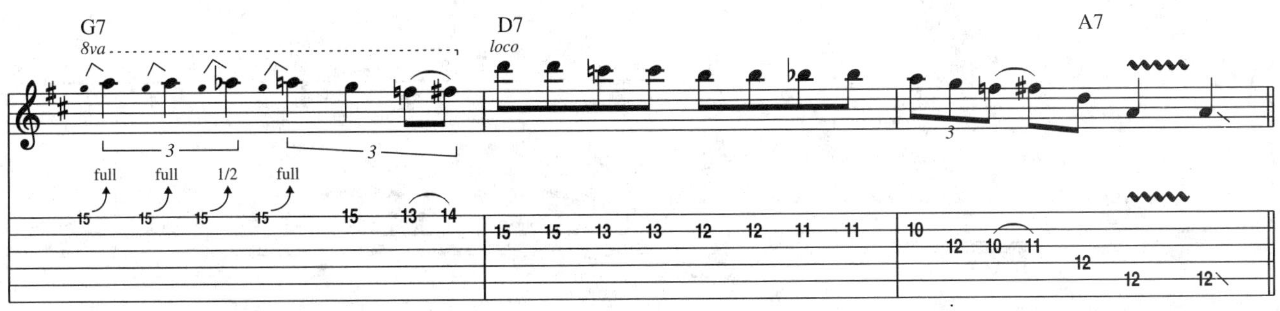
G7
8va
D7
loco
A7
full
full
1/2
full

Verse

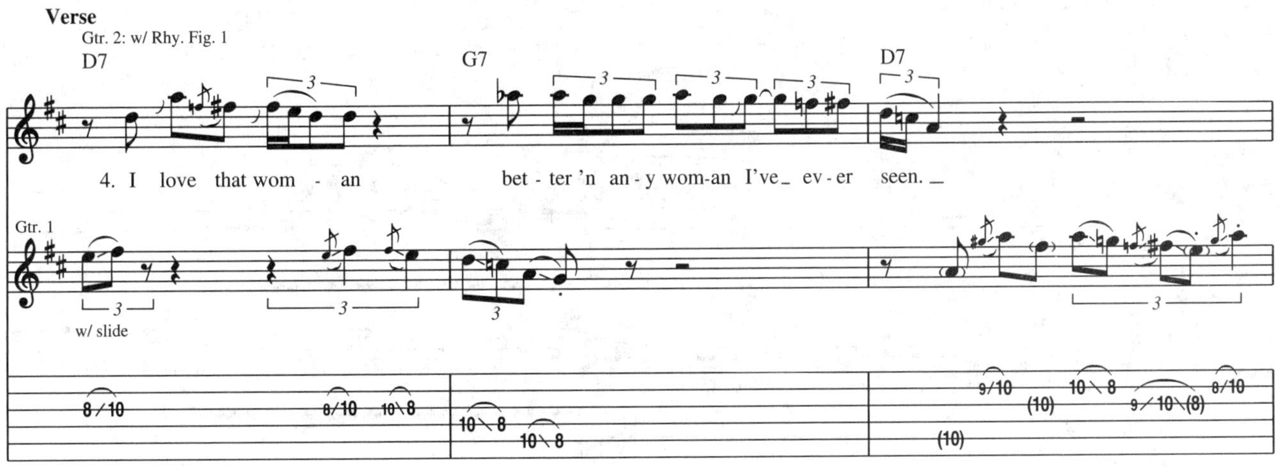
Gtr. 2: w/ Rhy. Fig. 1
D7
G7
D7
4. I love that wom - an bet - ter 'n an - y wom-an I've ev - er seen.
Gtr. 1
w/ slide

G7
Well I love that wom - an, bet - ter 'n an - y wom - an I've ev - er
8va

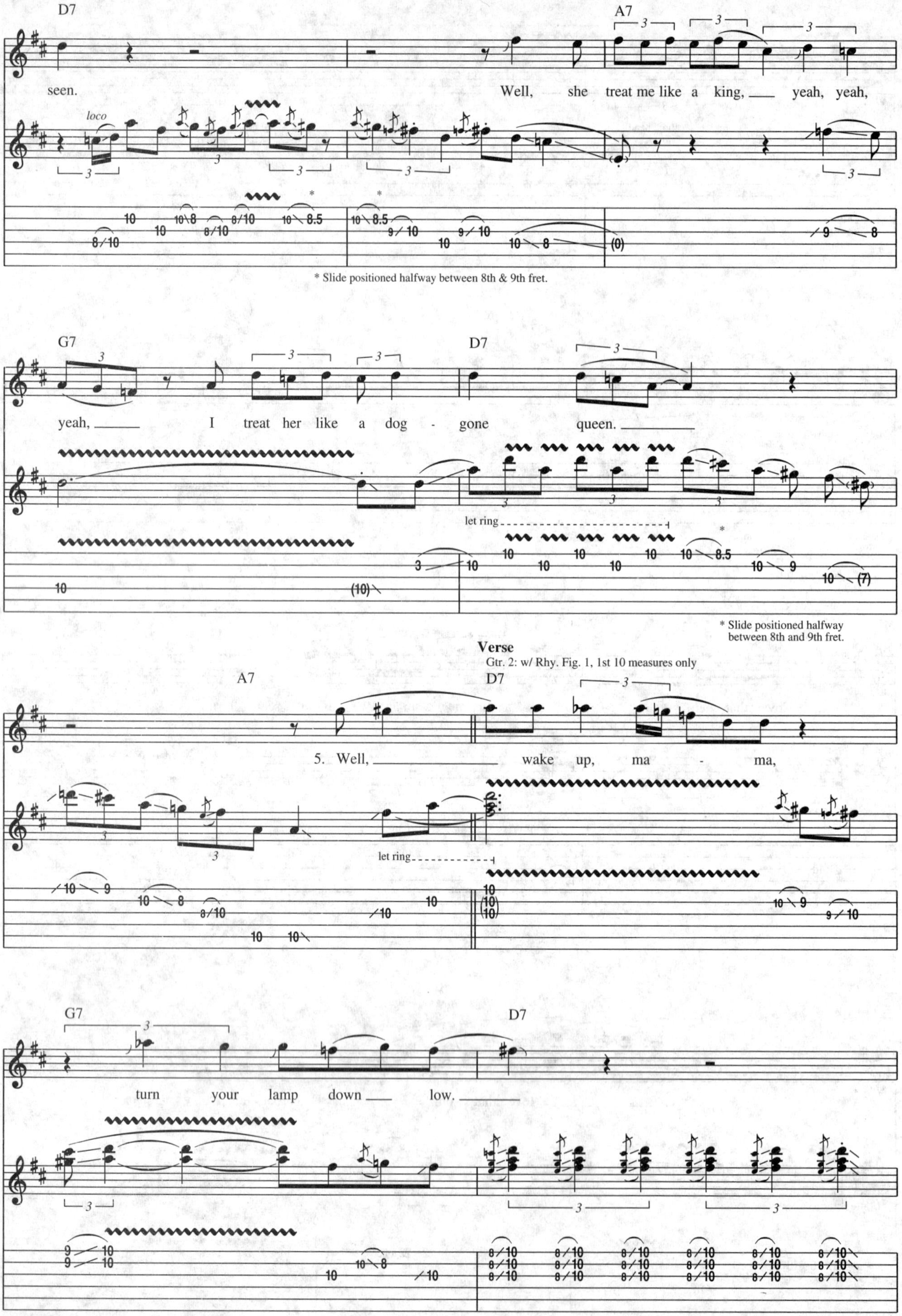

* Slide positioned halfway between 8th & 9th fret.

G7
D7
yeah, I treat her like a dog - gone queen.
let ring
* Slide positioned halfway between 8th and 9th fret.

Verse

Gtr. 2: w/ Rhy. Fig. 1, 1st 10 measures only

A7
D7
5. Well, wake up, ma - ma,
let ring

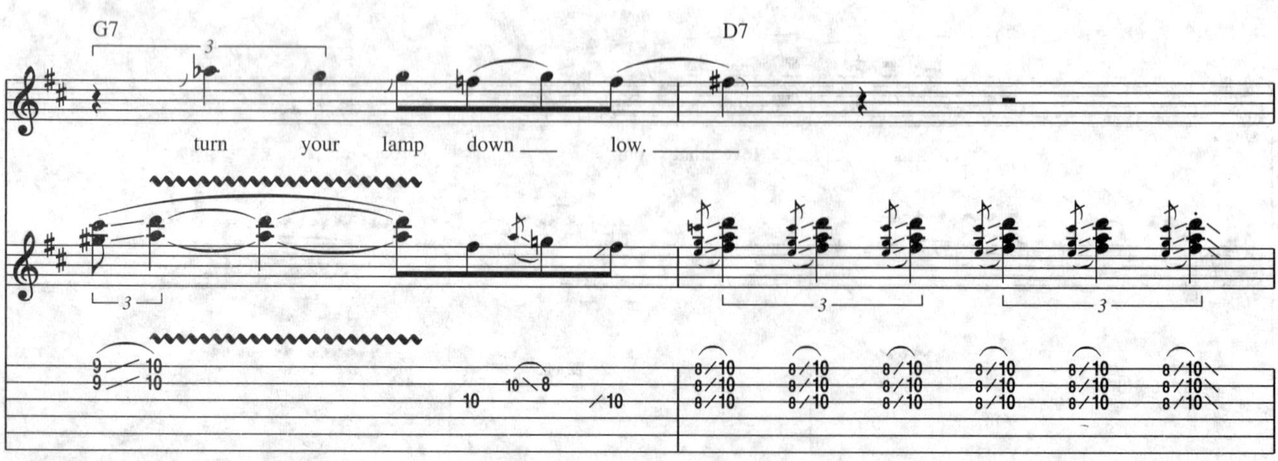

G7
Wake _ up, ma - ma, well turn your lamp down low. _
8va
loco
* Slide positioned halfway between 8th and 9th fret.
D7
Ya
* Slide positioned halfway between 8th and 9th fret.
A7
got no _ love, _ ba - by,
G7
ya turn Un - cle John _ from your
8va
loco
D7
C#6 D6
on cue:
door. _
yeah. _
Gtr. 1
let ring
Gtr. 2
* Slide positioned halfway between 8th and 9th fret.

Stray Cat Strut

Words and Music by Brian Setzer

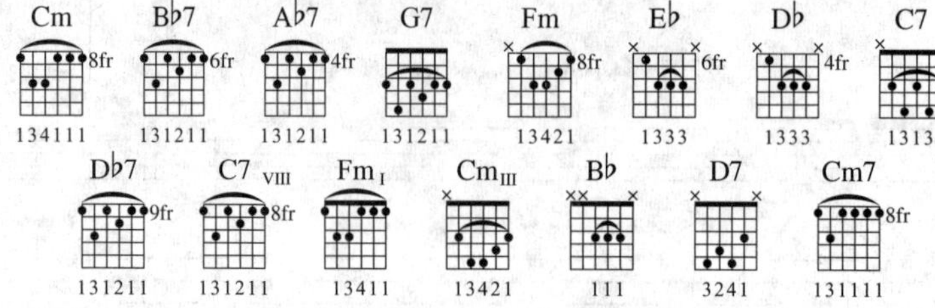

Intro

Moderately ♩ = 132

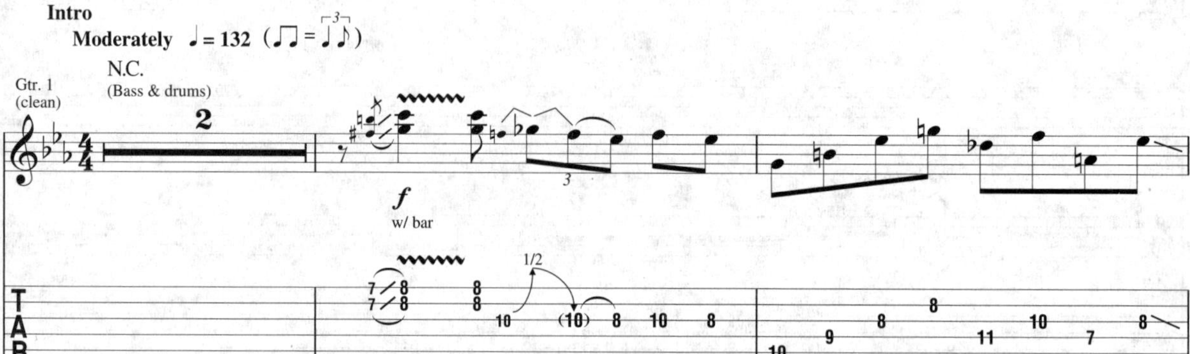

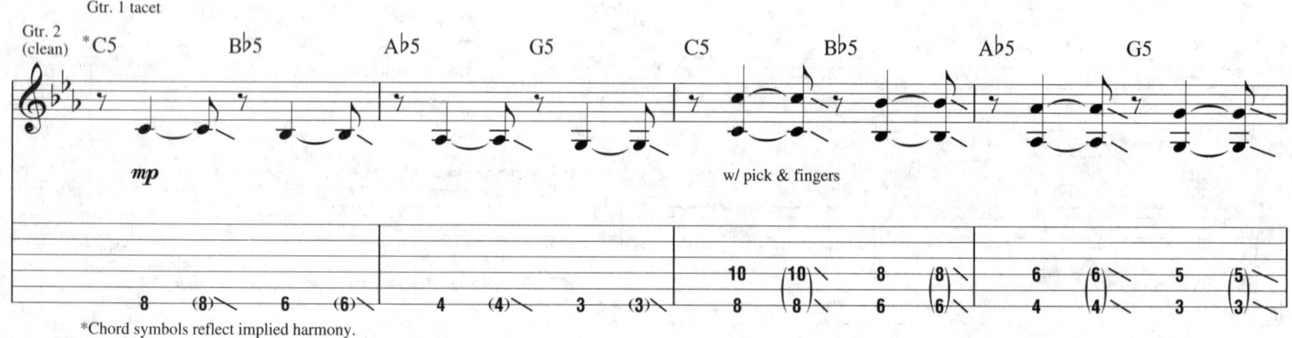

*Chord symbols reflect implied harmony.

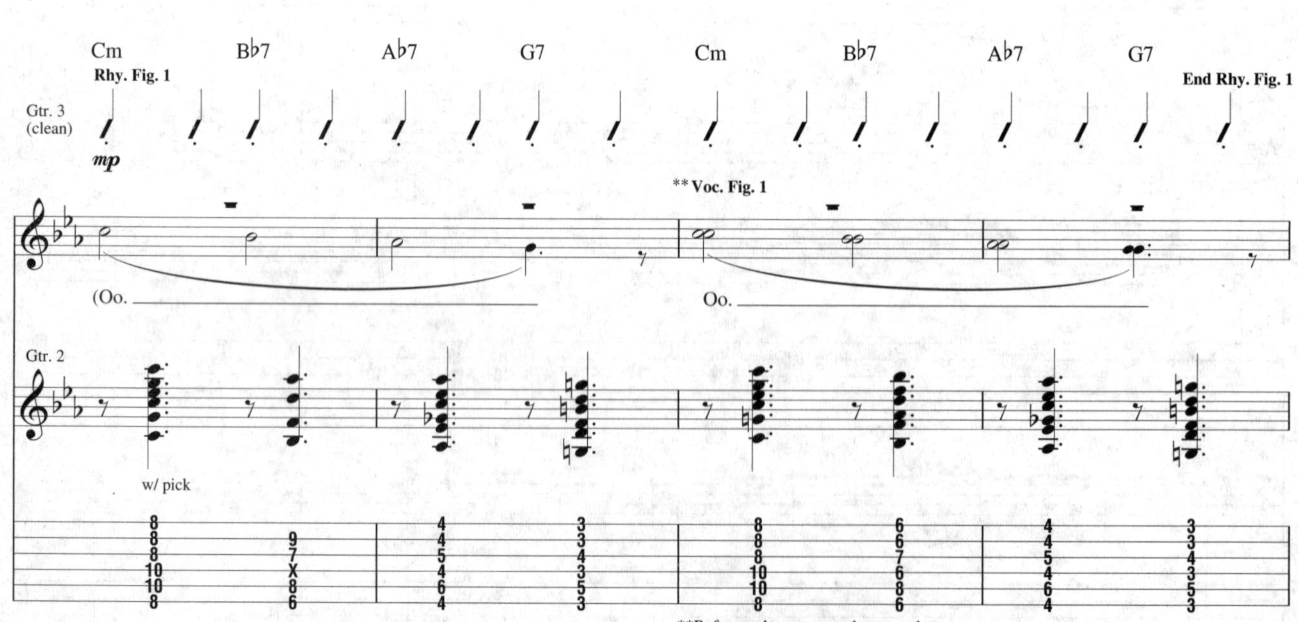

**Refers to downstemmed notes only.

Gtr. 3: w/ Rhy. Fig. 1
Cm
B♭7
A♭7
G7
Cm
B♭7
A♭7
G7
Cm
End Voc. Fig. 1
1. Black
Oo.
Oo.)
Gtr. 2
Verse
Gtr. 3: w/ Rhy. Fig. 1 (2 1/2 times)
and or - ange stray cat sit - tin' on a fence.
Ain't
let ring
got e-nough dough to pay the rent.
I'm
Rhy. Fig. 2

Cm
B♭7
A♭7
G7
Cm N.C.
Rhy. Fill 1
End Rhy. Fill 1
Gtr. 3
flat broke but I don't care,
I strut right by with my tail in the air.
Gtr. 2
End Rhy. Fig. 2
let ring
Chorus
Fm
E♭
D♭
C7
Fm
E♭
D♭7
C7VIII
Stray cat strut, I'm a...
I'm a fe - line Cas - a - no - va.
Get a
(La - dies' cat.
Hey! Man, that's sad.)
Fm
E♭
D♭7
C7VIII
Fm N.C.
Gtr. 2 tacet
shoe thrown at me from a mean old man.
Get my din - ner from a gar - bage can.

Interlude

Guitar Solo

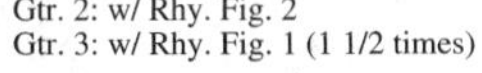

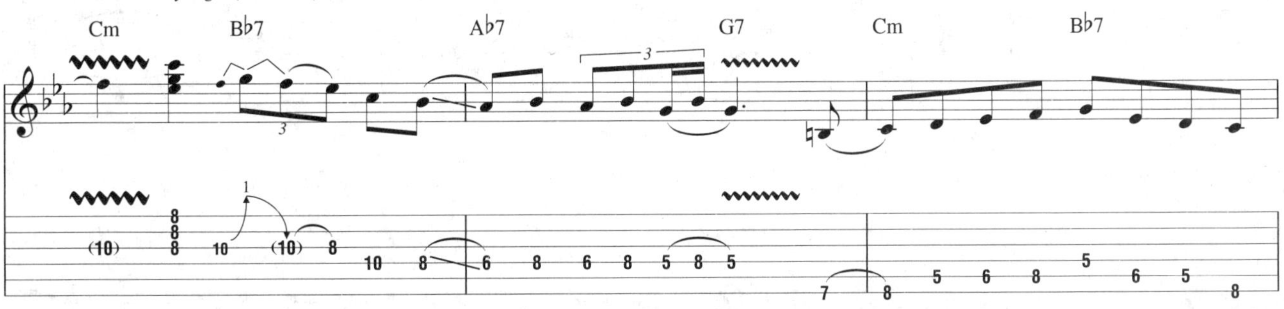

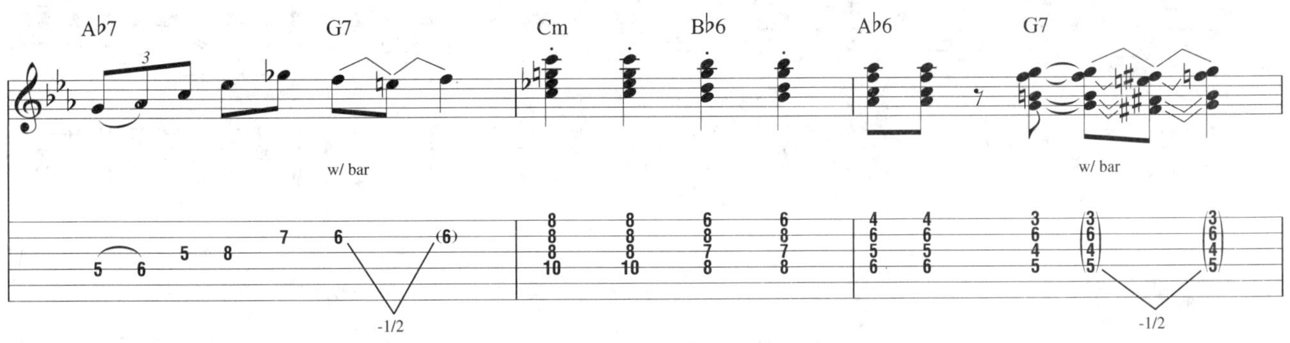

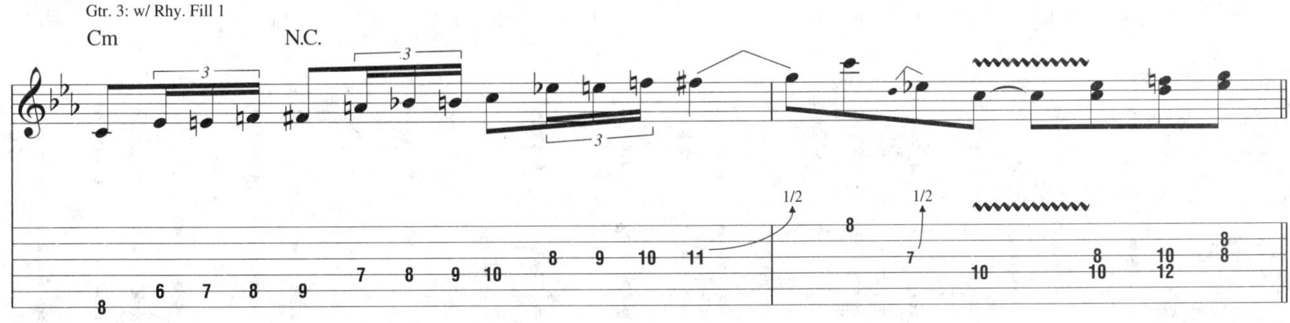

Bridge
Gtr. 1 tacet
Fm
Fm I
Cm III
B♭
Gtr. 3
I don't both - er chas - in' mice a - round. _ Whoa, no! _ I
Gtr. 1
Gtr. 2
Fm I
D7
G7
slink down the al - ley, look - in' for a fight, howl - in' to the moon light on a hot sum - mer night. _ 2. Sing -
Verse
Bkgd. Voc.: w/ Voc. Fig. 1
Gtr. 3: w/ Rhy. Fig. 1 (1 1/2 times)
Cm
B♭7
A♭7
G7
- in' the blues _ while the la - dy cats cry, "Wild _ stray cat, you're a real _ gone _ guy." I
Rhy. Fig. 3

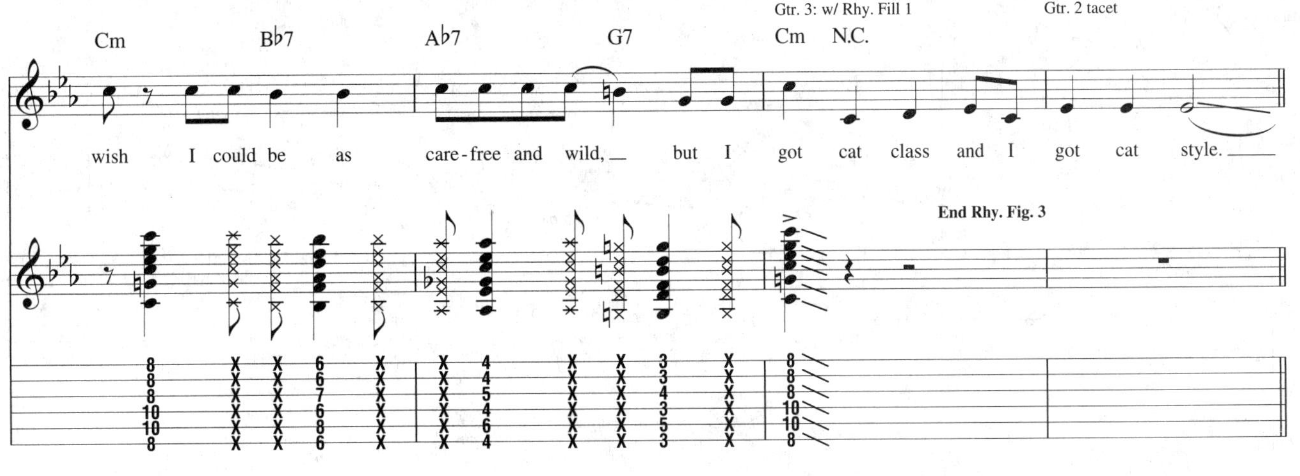
Gtr. 3: w/ Rhy. Fill 1
Gtr. 2 tacet
Cm
B♭7
A♭7
G7
Cm N.C.
wish I could be as care-free and wild, but I got cat class and I got cat style.
End Rhy. Fig. 3

Interlude

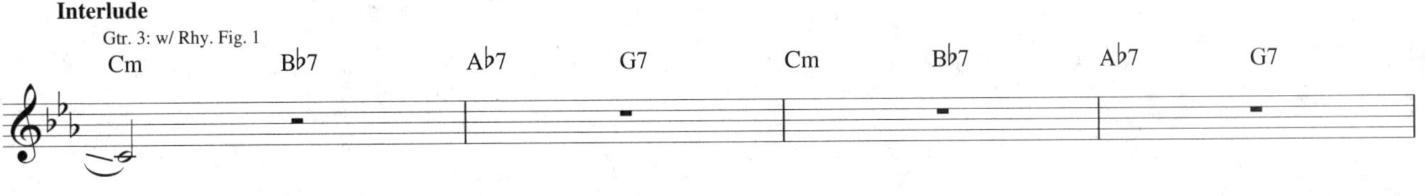
Gtr. 3: w/ Rhy. Fig. 1
Cm
B♭7
A♭7
G7
Cm
B♭7
A♭7
G7

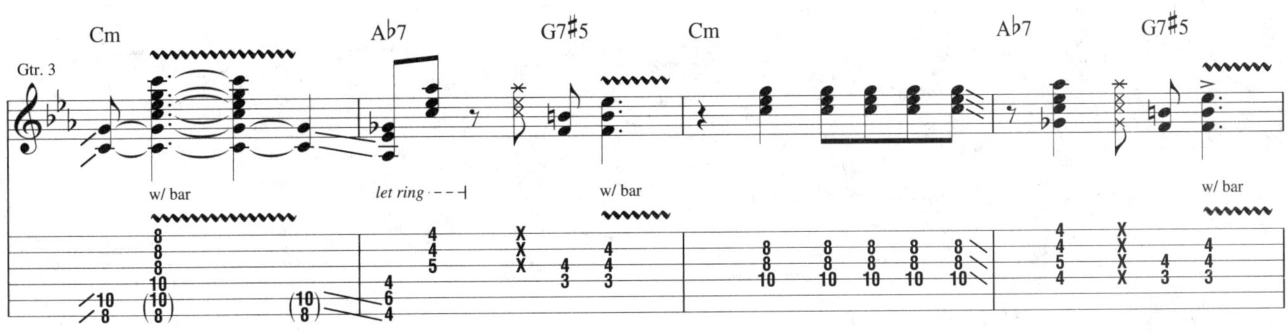
Cm
A♭7
G7♯5
Cm
A♭7
G7♯5
Gtr. 3
w/ bar
let ring
w/ bar
w/ bar

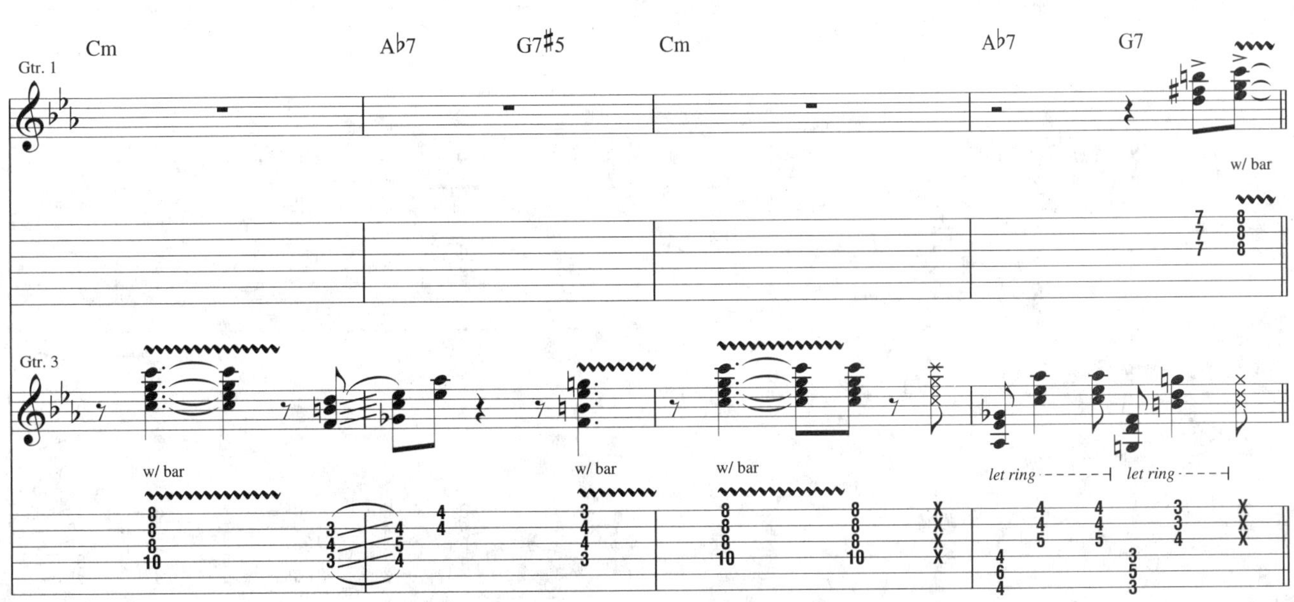
Cm
A♭7
G7♯5
Cm
A♭7
G7
Gtr. 1
w/ bar
Gtr. 3
w/ bar
w/ bar
w/ bar
let ring
let ring

Guitar Solo

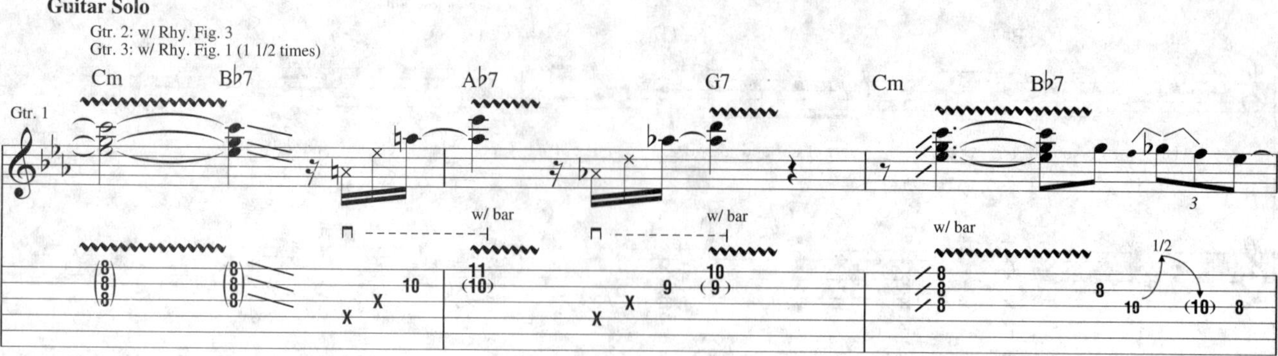

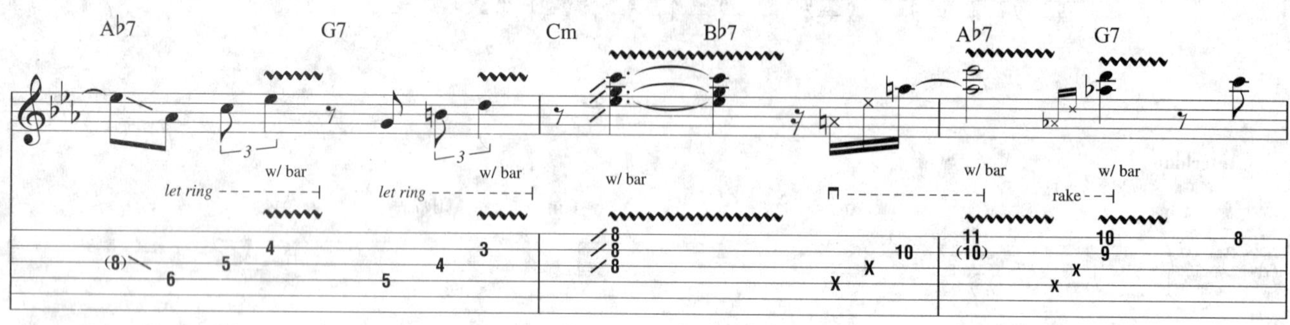

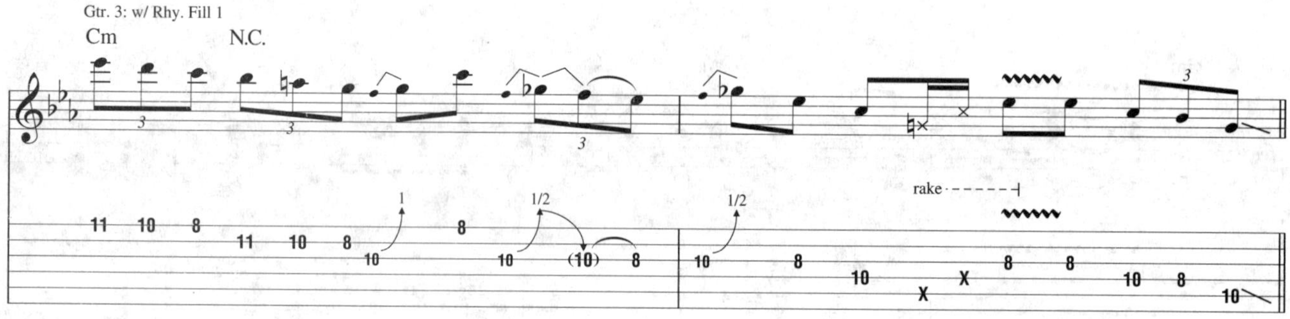

Bridge

Fm
D7
G7
Gtr. 3
slink down the al - ley, look - in' for a fight, howl - in' to the moon-light on a hot sum - mer night. 3. Sing -
Gtr. 2
let ring
w/ pick & fingers
let ring
w/ pick
let ring
Verse
Bkgd. Voc.: w/ Voc. Fig. 1
Gtr. 2: w/ Rhy. Fig. 3 (1st 5 meas.)
Gtr. 3: w/ Rhy. Fig. 1 (1 1/2 times)
Cm
B♭7
A♭7
G7
- in the blues while the la - dy cats cry, "Wild stray cat, you're a real gone guy." I
Outro
Gtr. 3: w/ Rhy. Fill 1
Cm N.C.
N.C.
(Bass & drums)
wish I could be as care-free and wild, but I got cat class and I got cat style.
Gtr. 2
Cm7
Gtr. 3
rit.
Yow!
Gtr. 2
1/2
1/4
rit.

The Stumble

By Freddie King and Sonny Thompson

A5
Bb(b5)
E5/B
C#5
F#5
B5
1/2
1/4
B
Gtr. 2: w/ Rhy. Fig. 1, simile
E5
A6
End Rhy. Fig. 1
Gtr. 1
full
E6
P.M.
B6

C
Gtr. 2: w/ Rhy. Fig. 1, 1st 8 meas.
E5 A5 E5 A5 A6 A5 A6 A5 A6 A5 A6 A5
let ring
let ring
1/4

E5 E6 E5 E6 E5 E6 E5 E6 E5 A5 A6 A5 A6 A5 A6 A5 A6 A5
let ring
let ring
1/4

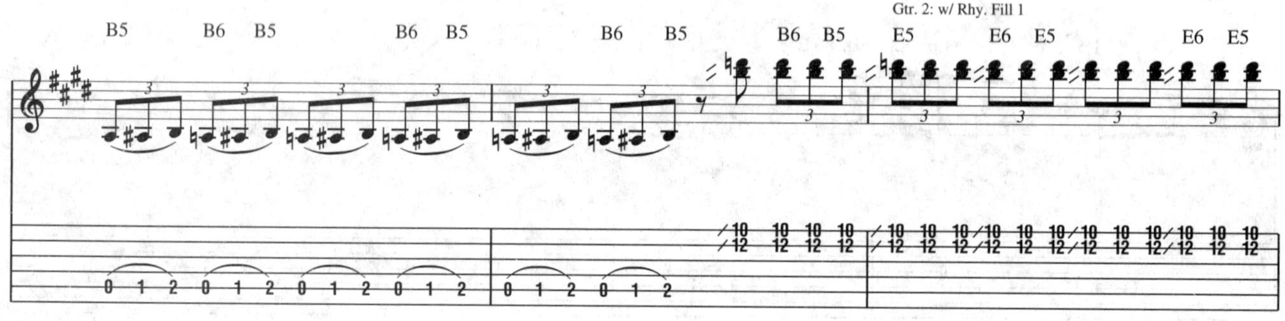
Gtr. 2: w/ Rhy. Fill 1
B5 B6 B5 B6 B5 B6 B5 B6 B5 E5 E6 E5 E6 E5

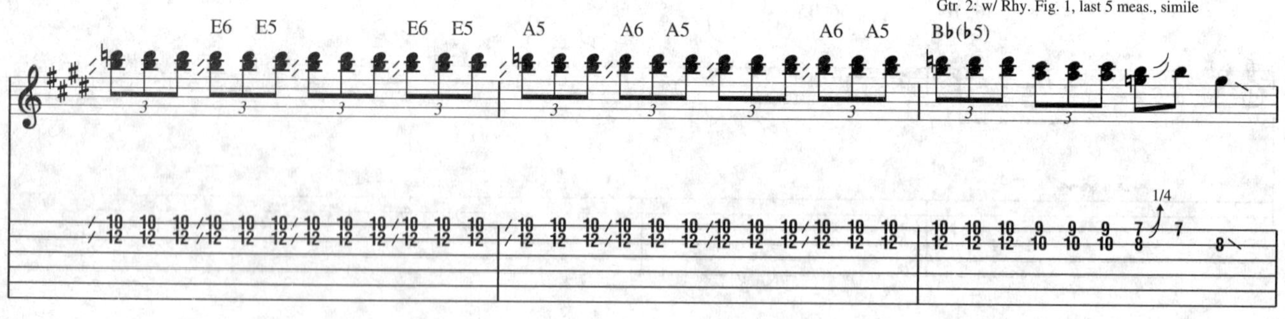
Gtr. 2: w/ Rhy. Fig. 1, last 5 meas., simile
E6 E5 E6 E5 A5 A6 A5 A6 A5 B♭(♭5)
1/4

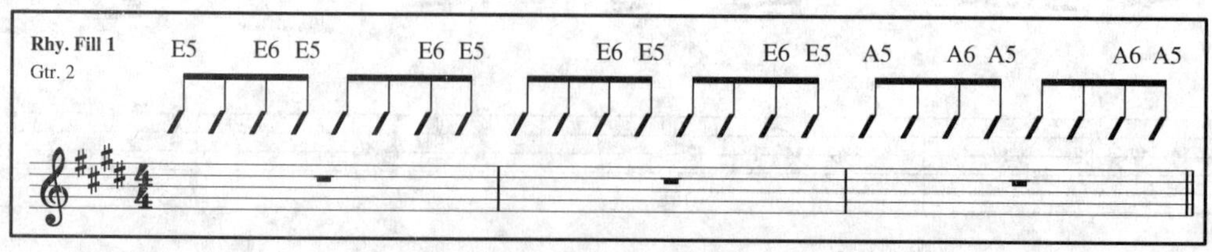
Rhy. Fill 1
Gtr. 2
E5 E6 E5 E6 E5 E6 E5 E6 E5 A5 A6 A5 A6 A5

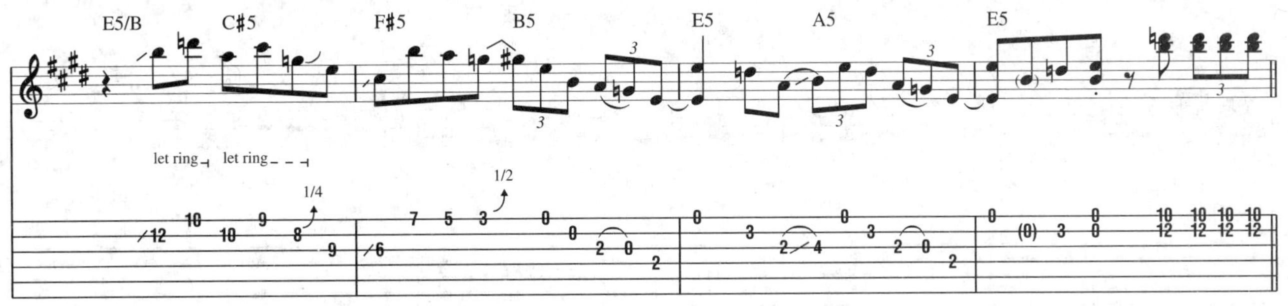
E5/B
C♯5
F♯5
B5
E5
A5
E5
let ring
let ring
1/4
1/2

D
Gtr. 2: w/ Rhy. Fig. 1, 1st 6 meas.
A5
A6 A5
A6 A5
A6 A5
A6 A5
E5 E6 E5
E6 E5
E6 E5
E6 E5
let ring
1/4

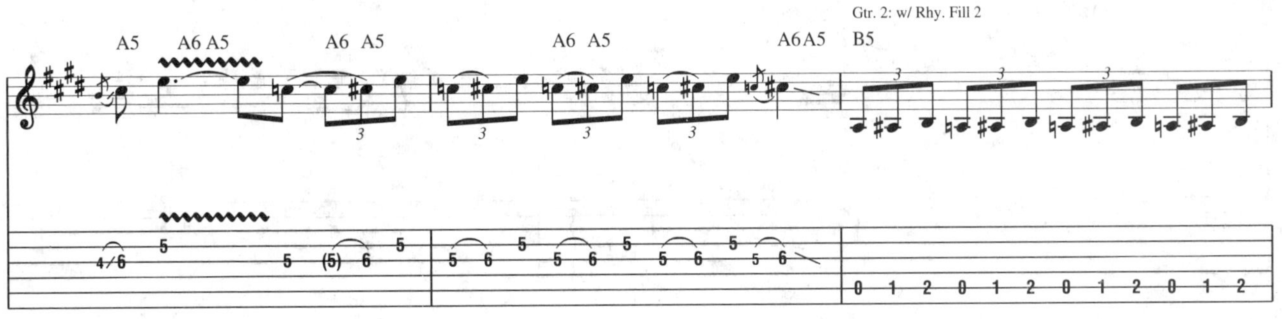
Gtr. 2: w/ Rhy. Fill 2
A5
A6 A5
A6 A5
A6 A5
A6 A5
B5

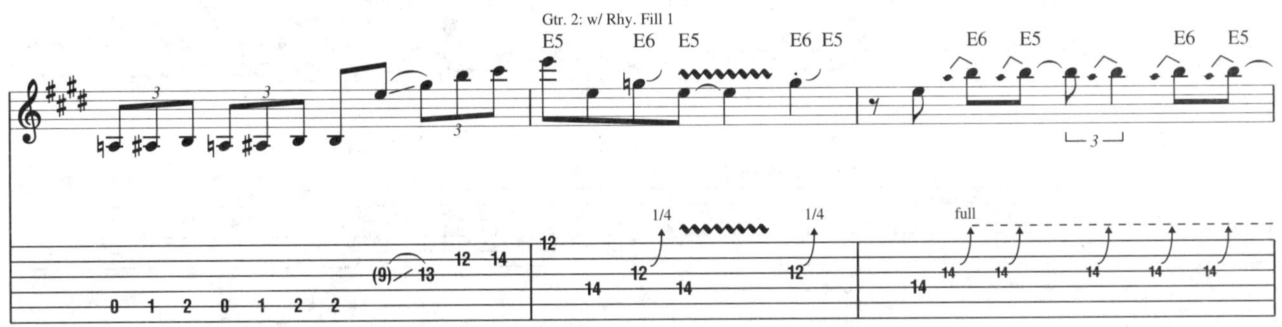
Gtr. 2: w/ Rhy. Fill 1
E5
E6 E5
E6 E5
E6 E5
E6 E5
1/4
full

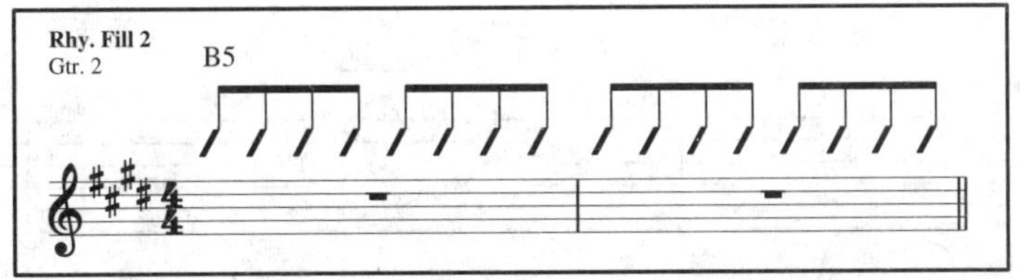
Rhy. Fill 2
Gtr. 2
B5

Gtr. 2: w/ Rhy. Fig. 1, last 5 meas., simile
A5
A6 A5
A6 A5
B♭(♭5)
E5/B
C♯5
full
F♯5
B5
E5
A5
E5
E
Gtr. 2: w/ Rhy. Fig. 1, simile
A5 A6 A5 A6 A5
A6 A5
A6 A5
E5
E6 E5
E6 E5
E6 E5
E6 E5
A5 A6 A5
A6 A5
P.M.
1/4
A6 A5
A6 A5
B5 B6 B5
B6 B5
B6 B5
B6 B5
E5
A5
B♭(♭5)

E5/B C#5 F#5 B5 E5 A5 E5
let ring

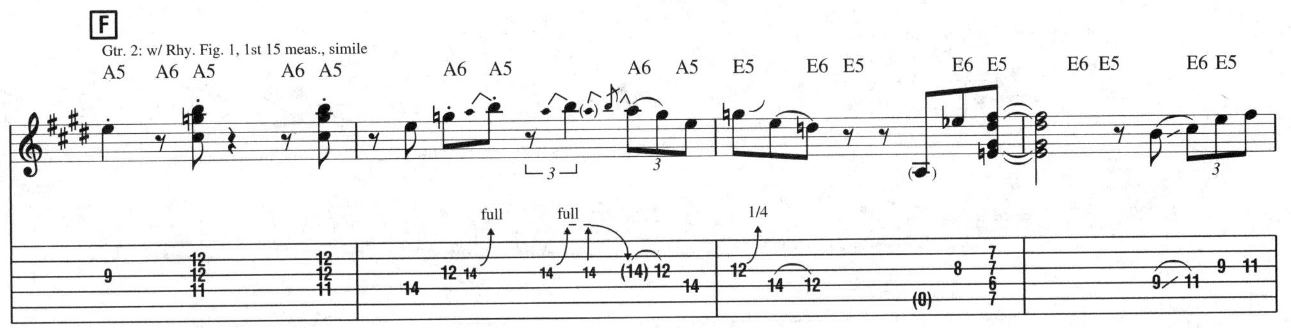
F
Gtr. 2: w/ Rhy. Fig. 1, 1st 15 meas., simile
A5 A6 A5 A6 A5 A6 A5 A6 A5 E5 E6 E5 E6 E5 E6 E5 E6 E5
full
full
1/4

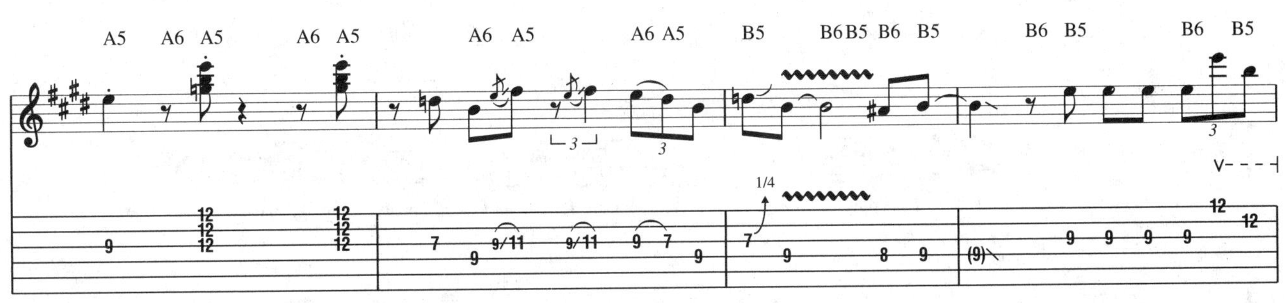
A5 A6 A5 A6 A5 A6 A5 A6 A5 B5 B6 B5 B6 B5 B6 B5 B6 B5
1/4

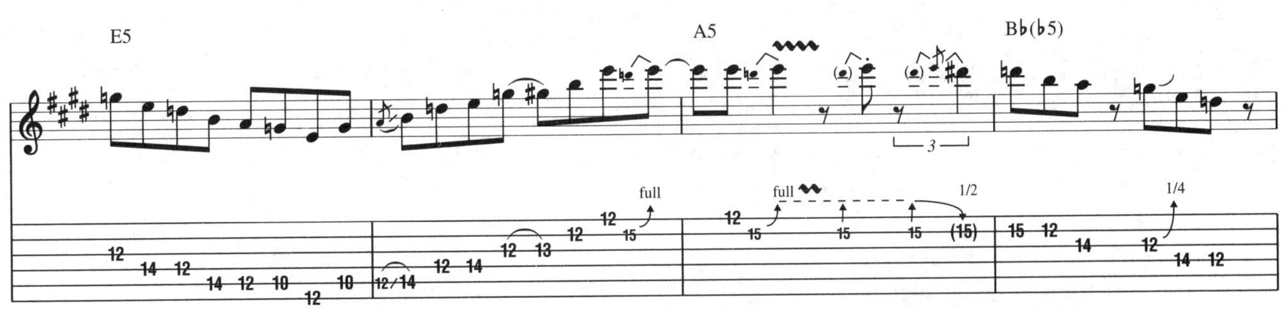
E5 A5 Bb(b5)
full
full
1/2
1/4

E5/B C#5 F#5 B5 E5 A5 E5
Gtr. 2
Gtr. 1

Sunday Bloody Sunday

Words by Bono and The Edge
Music by U2

Verse
Gtr. 1: w/ Rhy. Fig. 1, simile
B5 D5 G
night!
2. Bro - ken bot - tles un - der chil - dren's feet,
) 3. And the bat - tle's just be - gun,
Gtr. 1: w/ Riff A, 1 1/2 times, simile
Bm D G6 Bm D
bod - ies strewn a - cross the dead - end street.
there's man - y lost, but tell me who has won?
But I won't heed the bat - tle
The trench - es dug with - in our
G6 Bm D
call. It puts my back up, puts my back up a - gainst the wall.
hearts, and moth - ers' chil - dren, broth - ers, sis - ters torn a - part.
Chorus
Gtr. 1: w/ Riff A, simile
Bm D G6
Sun - day blood - y Sun - day.
Sun - day, blood - y Sun - day.
1. N.C.(F) (Em7) (D) (F) (Em7)
Sun - day blood - y Sun - day.
Sun - day. blood - y Sun - day.
Gtr. 1
Harm.
w/ bar
Interlude
Gtr. 1: w/ Rhy. Fig. 1, 2 times, simile
2. D
Oh, let's go!
How long,
*Gtrs. 1 & 2
* composite arrangement
Em D Em
how long must we sing this song? How long, how long?
'Cause to -
(Ah.

Gtr. 1: w/ Rhy. Fig. 1, 4 times, simile
Gtr. 2 tacet
B5 D5 G B5 D5 G
night we can be as one, to - night! To -
Ah. Ah.)
Bkgd. Voc.: w/ Voc. Fig. 1
B5 D5 G B5 D5 G
night, to - night. To - night, to - night.
Sun - day, blood - y Sun - day. Sun - day, blood - y Sun - day. Oh, let's go!
Guitar Solo
Gtrs. 1 & 2
N.C.(B5) (D5) (G) (B5) (D5)
(G) (B5) (D5) (G)
Chorus
(B5) (D5) (G) N.C.(B5) (D5) (G)
Wipe the tears from
Gtr. 1: w/ Rhy. Fig. 1, 5 times, simile
Gtr. 2 tacet
B5 D5 G B5 D5 G
your eyes. Wipe your tears a - way. I'll wipe your tears
B5 D5 G B5 D5
a - way. I'll wipe your tears a - way.
Sun - day, blood - y Sun -
Voc. Fig. 1
(Ah. Ah.

G
B5
D5
G
I'll wipe your blood - shot eyes.
- day.
Sun - day, bloody - y Sun - day.
N.C.(F)
(Em7)
(D)
(F)
(Em7)
(D)
Sun - day, blood - y Sun - day,
ah.
Sun - day, blood - y Sun - day.
Gtr. 1
Harm.
(F)
(Em7)
(D)
(F)
(Em7)
(D)
Sun - day, blood - y Sun - day,
ah.
Yeah. let's go!
Sun - day, blood - y Sun - day.
Harm.
Violin Solo
Gtr. 1: w/ Rhy. Fig. 1, 2 times, simile
Verse
Gtr. 1: w/ Rhy. Fig. 1, 8 times, simile
B5
D5
G
B5
D5
4. And it's true we are im - mune,
when fact is fic - tion and T
G
B5
D5
G
V re - al - i - ty.
And to - day the mil - lions cry,
Sun - day, blood - y Sun - day.
* Vocals fade in gradually.
B5
D5
G
B5
D5
we eat and drink while to - mor - row they die.
The real bat - tle yet be - gun,
Sun - day, blood - y Sun - day.
Sun - day, blood - y Sun -
G
B5
D5
G
B5
D5
to claim the vi - t'ry Je - sus won
on
Sun -
- day.
Sun - day, blood - y Sun - day.
Sun - day, blood - y Sun -
G
B5
D5
G
Bm7
Gtr. 1
- day.
- day.
Sun - day, blood - y Sun - day.

Sunshine of Your Love

Words and Music by Jack Bruce, Pete Brown and Eric Clapton

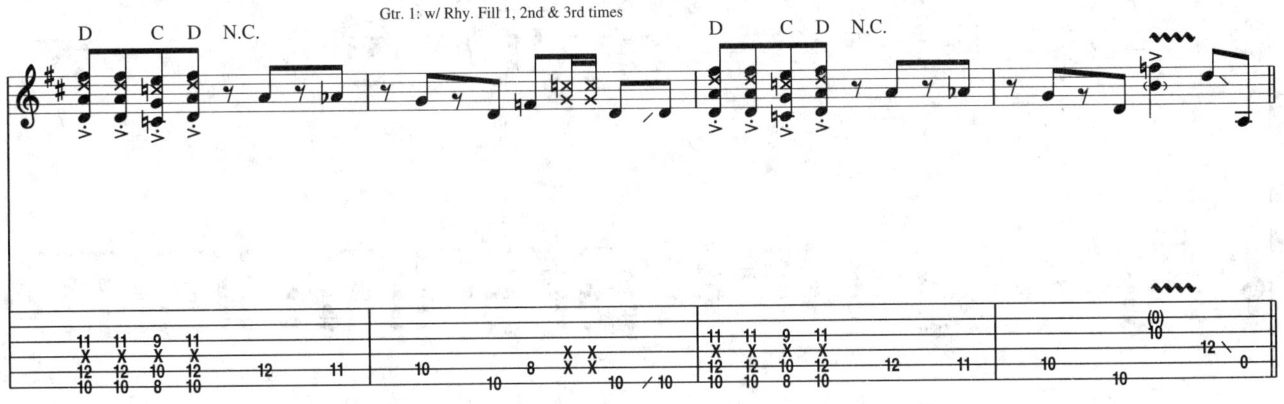
To Coda
Gtr. 1: w/ Rhy. Fill 1, 2nd & 3rd times
D
C
D
N.C.
D
C
D
N.C.

Chorus
A
C
G
A
C
G
I've been wait - ing so long
to be where I'm go - ing
Rhy. Fig. 2
End Rhy. Fig. 2

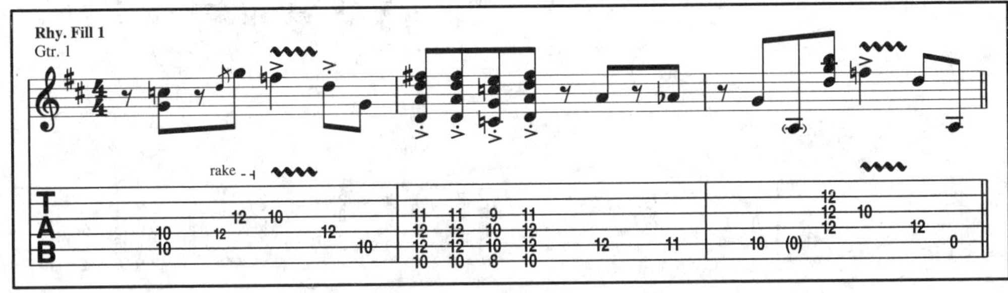
Rhy. Fill 1
Gtr. 1
rake

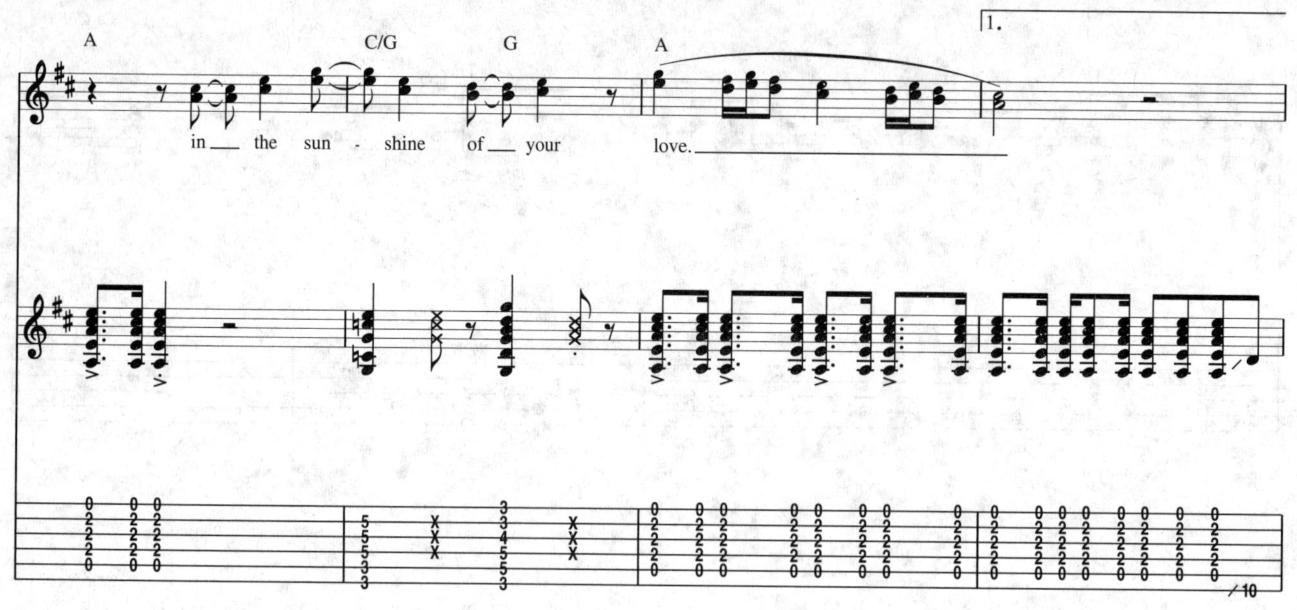

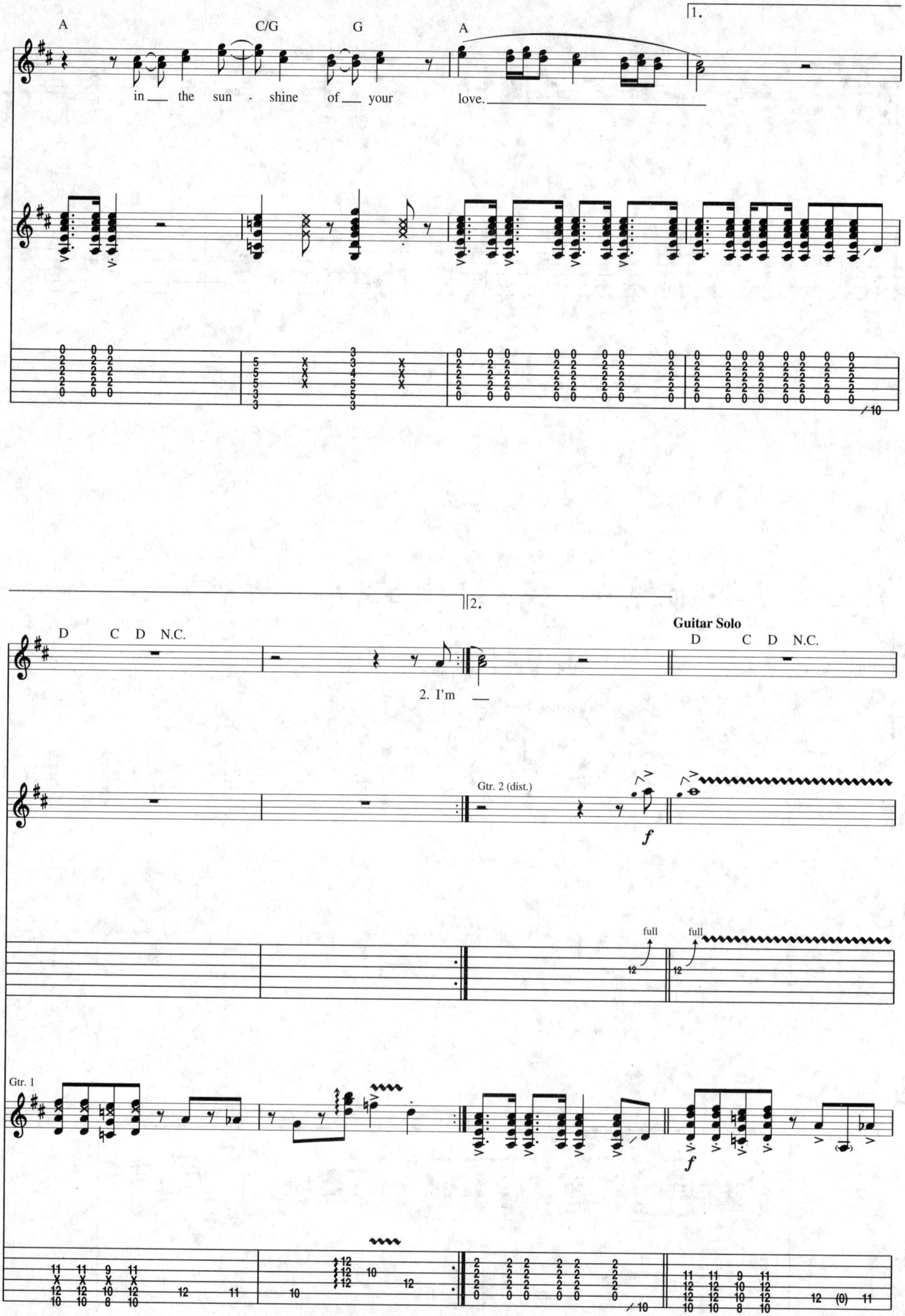
1.
A
C/G
G
A
in the sun - shine of your love.
2.
D C D N.C.
2. I'm
Guitar Solo
D C D N.C.
Gtr. 2 (dist.)
f
full
full
Gtr. 1
f

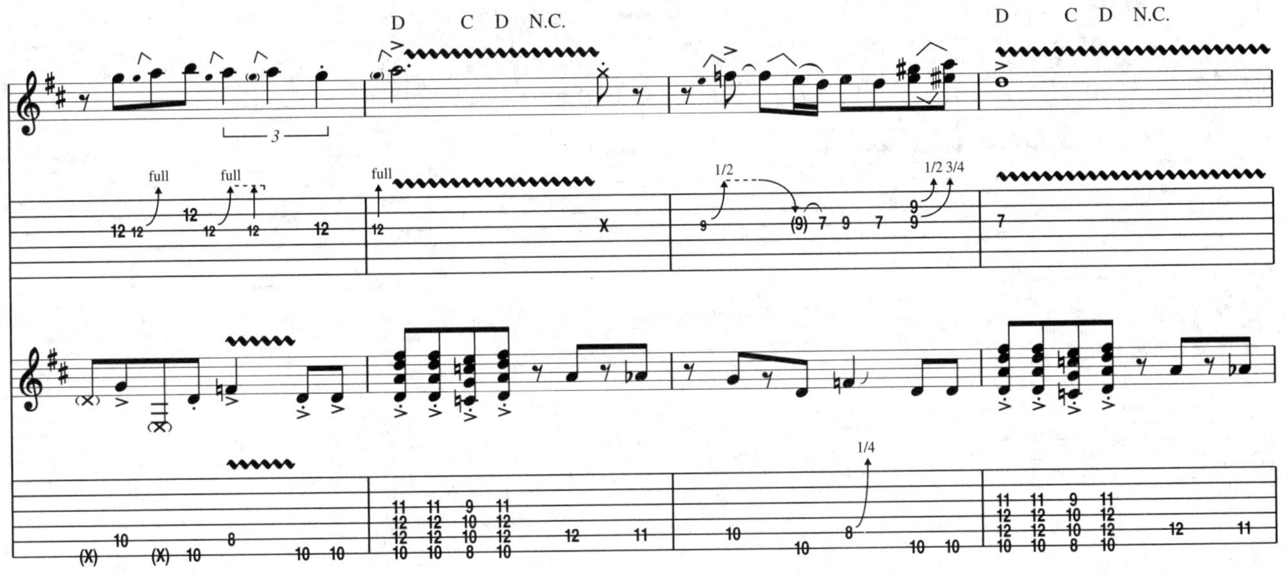
D C D N.C.
D C D N.C.
full
full
full
1/2
1/2 3/4
1/4

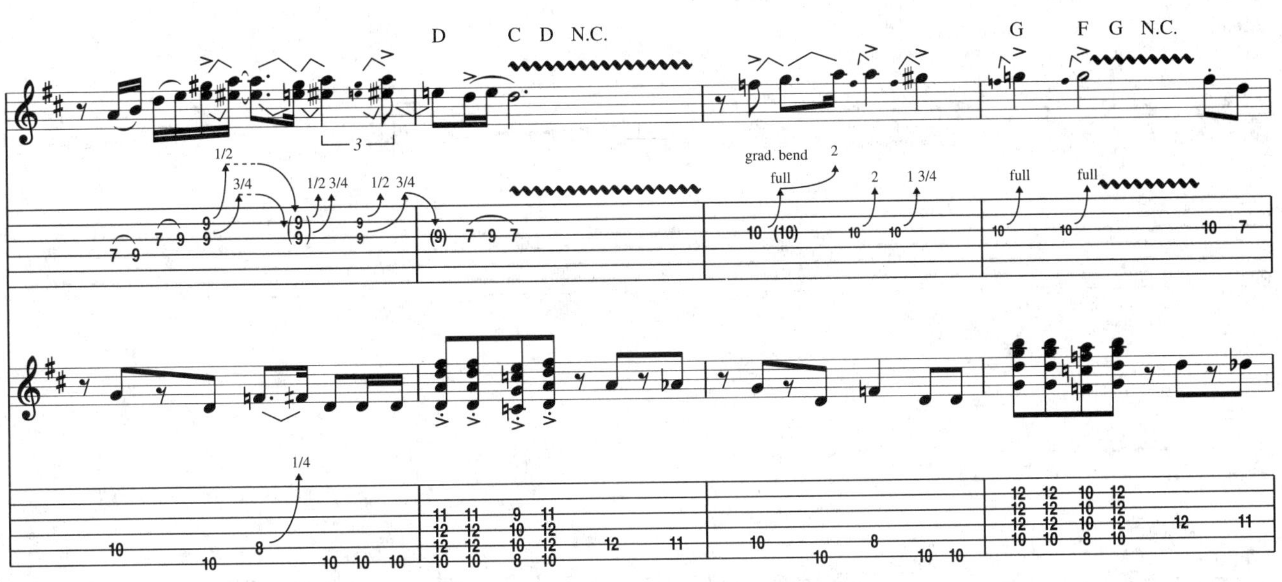
D C D N.C.
G F G N.C.
1/2
3/4
1/2 3/4
1/2 3/4
grad. bend
full
2
2
1 3/4
full
full
1/4

G F G N.C.
full
full
1/2
full
1 1/2
full
rake

D
C
D
N.C.
(cont. in slash)
G
D
F
D
10fr
10fr
8fr
10fr
Gtr. 1
Gtr. 2
A
C/G
G
1/2
full
C
P.M.
(cont. in notation)

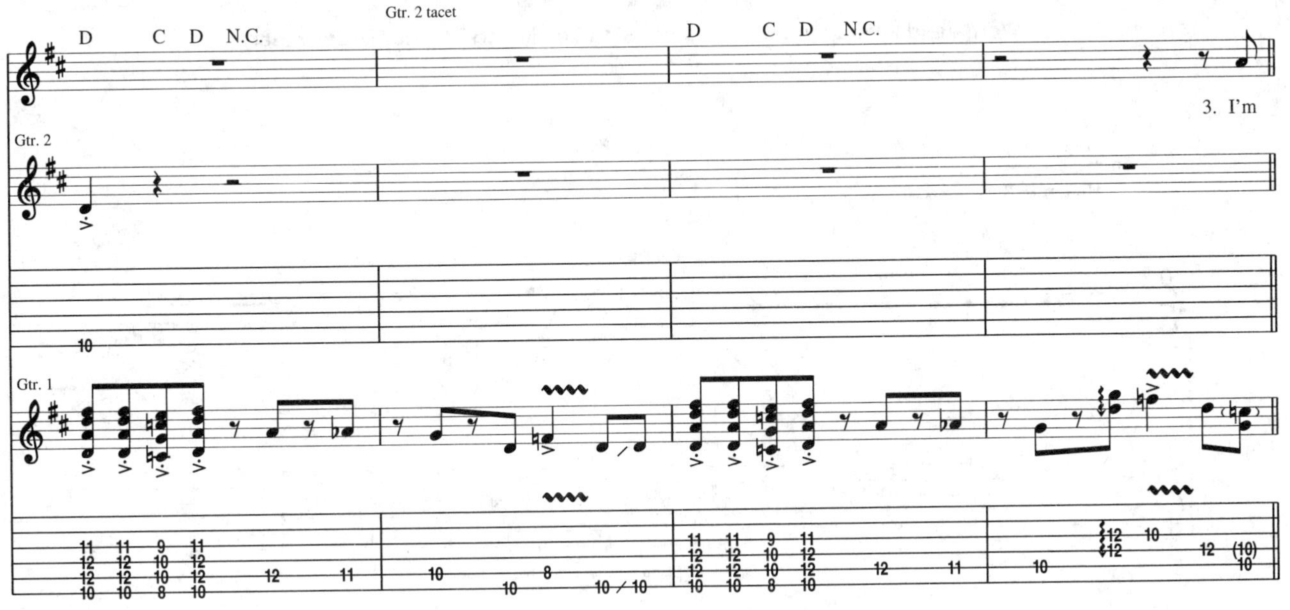
D.S. al Coda
(2nd lyrics)
Gtr. 2 tacet
D C D N.C.
3. I'm
Gtr. 2
Gtr. 1

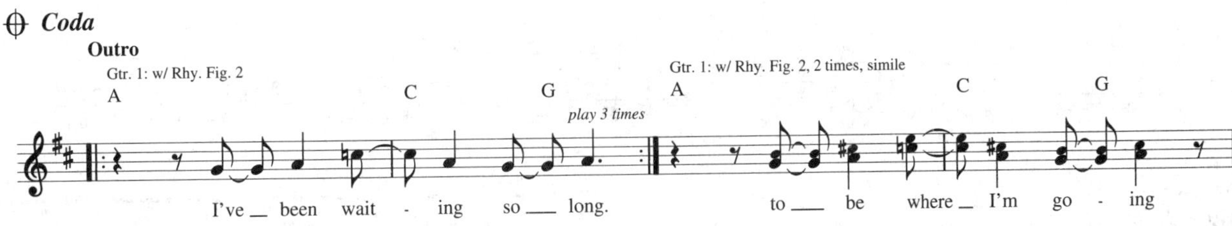
Coda
Outro
Gtr. 1: w/ Rhy. Fig. 2
A C G
play 3 times
Gtr. 1: w/ Rhy. Fig. 2, 2 times, simile
I've been wait - ing so long. to be where I'm go - ing

A C G A
in the sun - shine of your love.
Gtr. 1

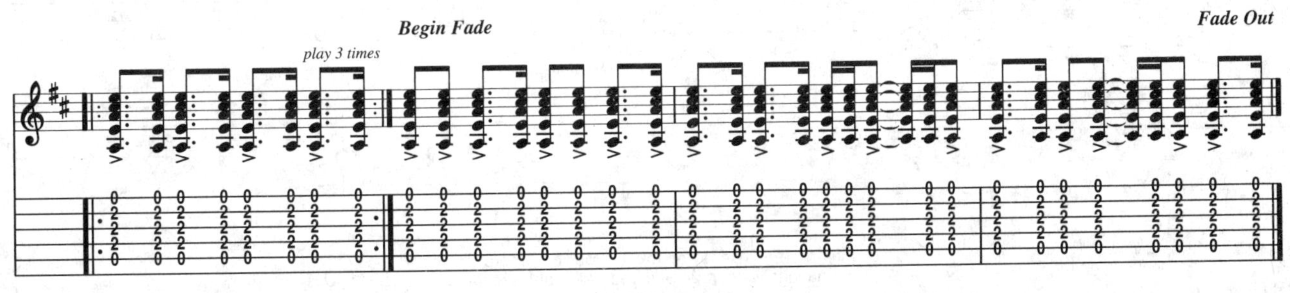
Begin Fade
play 3 times
Fade Out

Susie-Q

Words and Music by Dale Hawkins, Stan Lewis and Eleanor Broadwater

A C B
Oh, Su - sie - Q, ba - by I love you, Su - sie - Q.
Well, say that you'll be true and nev - er leave me blue, Su - sie - Q.
Gtr. 1
Rhy. Fig. 3
End Rhy. Fig. 3
Gtr. 2
Gtr. 2: w/ Rhy. Fig. 1 (3 times)
Gtr. 1: w/ Rhy. Fig. 2
E
Like the way you walk. I like the way you talk.
Well, say that you'll be mine. Well, say that you'll be mine.
End Rhy. Fig. 2
To Coda 2
To Coda 1
Gtr. 2: w/ Rhy. Fig. 3
Gtr. 2: w/ Rhy. Fig. 1
I like the way you walk, I like the way you talk, Su - sie - Q.
Well, say that you'll be mine, ba - by, all the time, Su - sie - Q.
Guitar Solo
Gtr. 2: w/ Rhy. Fig. 1 (2 times)
w/ dist.
w/ bar

Gtr. 2: w/ Rhy. Fig. 3
A
C
B
Gtr. 2: w/ Rhy. Fig. 1 (3 times)
E
15ma
loco
w/ bar
P.H.
Pitch: A B♭ C♯ D
Gtr. 1
Gtr. 3 (dist.)
pp
w/ fast amp tremolo
Gtr. 2: w/ Rhy. Fig. 2
A
C
B
Gtr. 2: w/ Rhy. Fig. 1
E
mp
Interlude
Gtr. 1: w/ Riff A (3 times)
E
Gtr. 3
ff
gradually slow down tremolo
p
tremolo off

D.S. al Coda 1

Coda 1

Guitar Solo

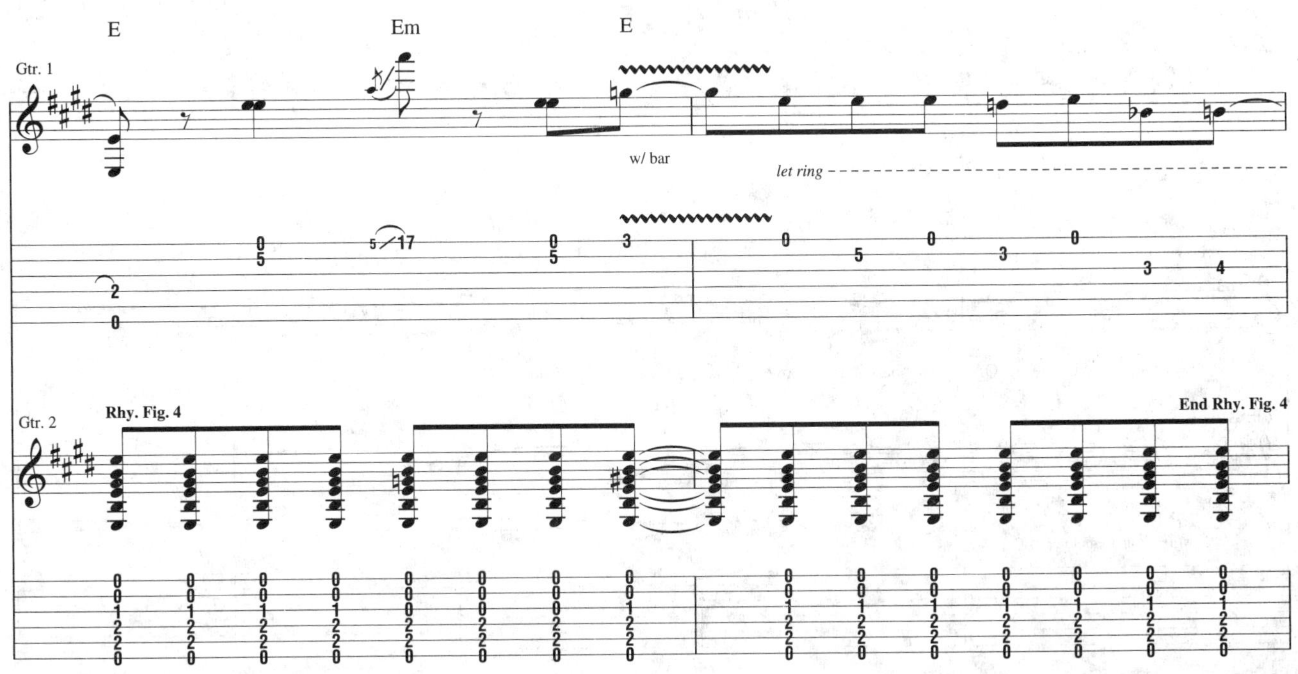

Gtr. 2: w/ Rhy. Fig. 4 (3 times)
Em
E
Em
E
(Oo,
oo,
oo,
oo,
Gtr. 1
let ring
w/ bar
let ring
w/ bar
w/ bar
let ring
w/ bar
Em
E
Gtr. 2: w/ Rhy. Fig. 1 (2 times)
E7
oo,
oo,
oo.)
let ring
w/ bar
w/ bar
Interlude
D.S. al Coda 2
Gtr. 1: w/ Riff A (3 times)
Gtr. 1: w/ Riff B
E
3. Oh, Su - sie - Q.
Coda 2
Gtr. 1: w/ Rhy. Fig. 2
Gtr. 2: w/ Rhy. Fig. 1 (2 times)
E
Oh, Su - sie - Q.
Oh, Su - sie - Q.
Gtr. 2: w/ Rhy. Fig. 3
A
C
B
Gtr. 2: w/ Rhy. Fig. 1
E
Oh, Su - sie - Q, ba - by, I love you, Su - sie - Q.
Gtr. 3
pp
w/ fast amp tremolo
p
grad. bend

Outro-Solo

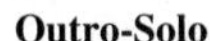

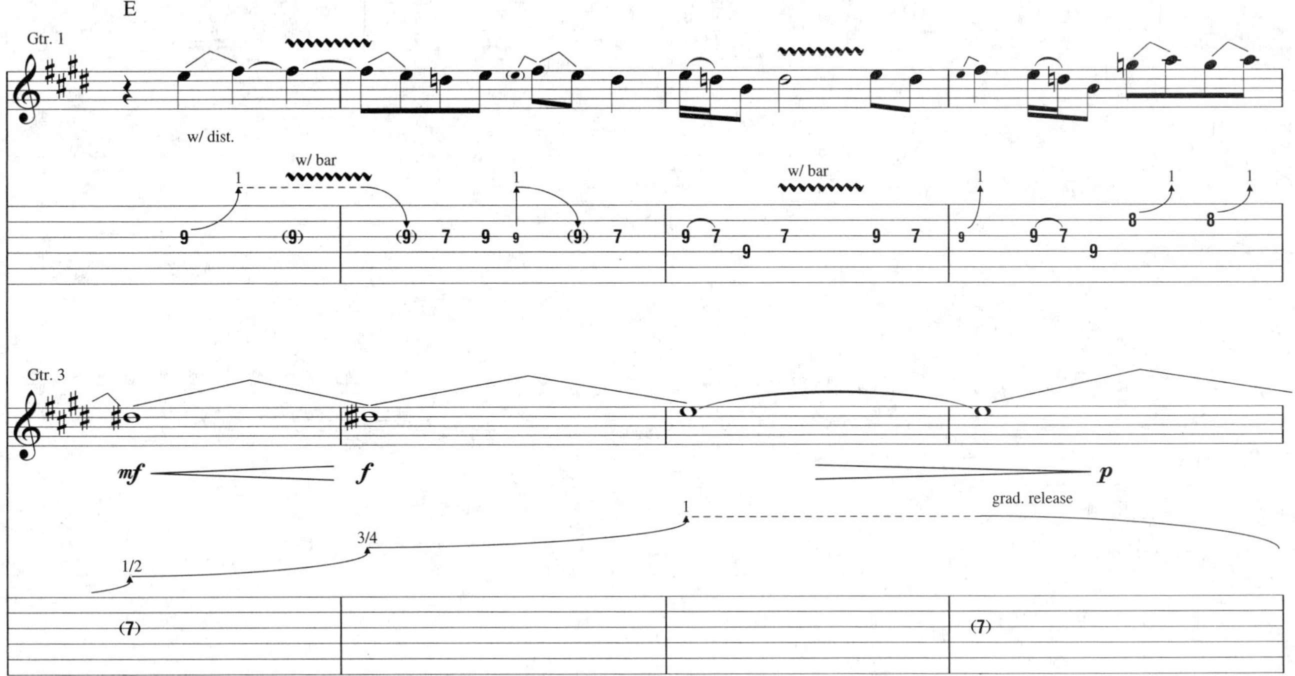
Gtr. 2: w/ Rhy. Fig. 1 (till fade)
E
Gtr. 1
w/ dist.
w/ bar
w/ bar
Gtr. 3
mf
f
p
grad. release
1/2
3/4
1

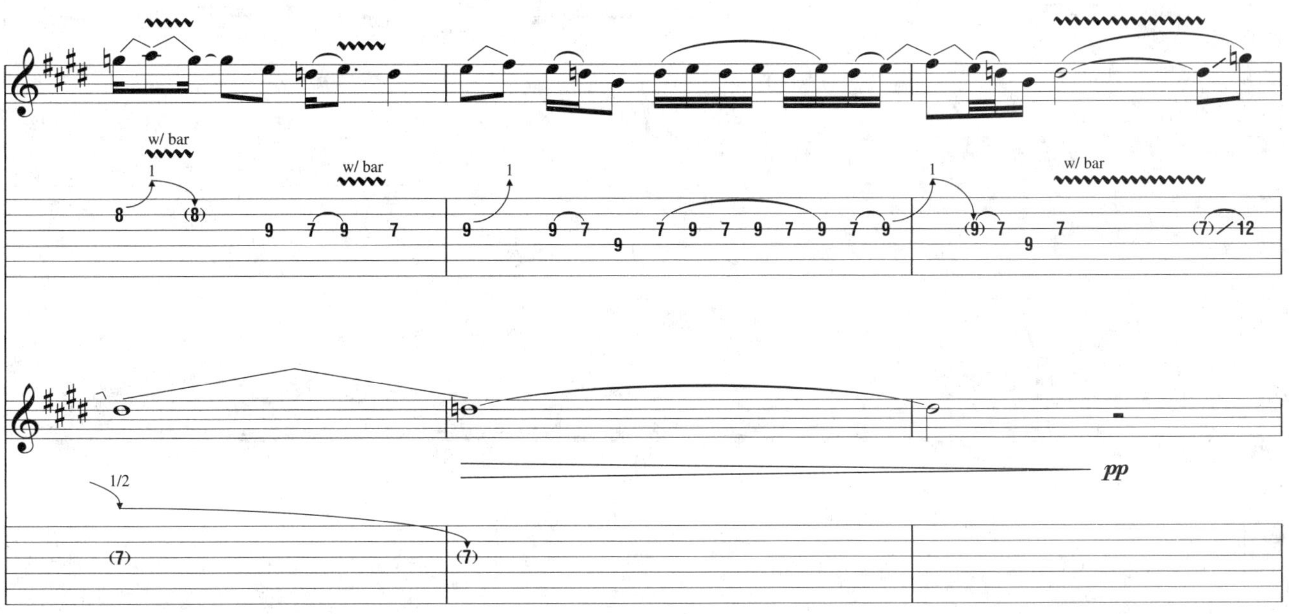
w/ bar
w/ bar
w/ bar
1/2
pp

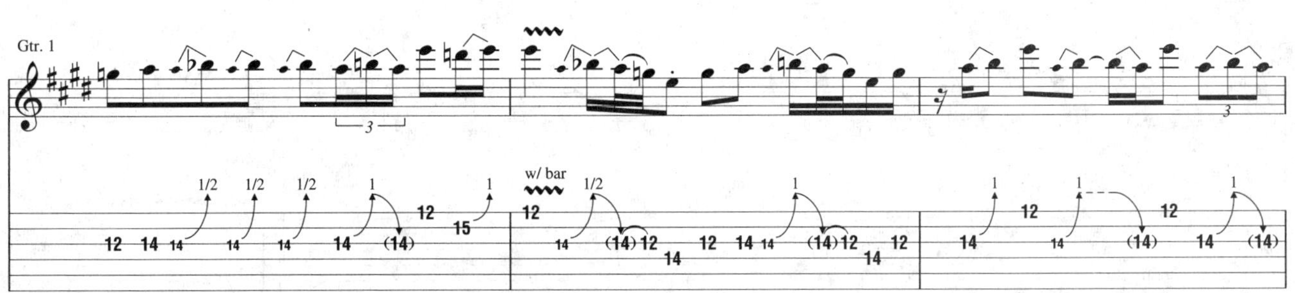
Gtr. 3 tacet
Gtr. 1
w/ bar

Gtr. 3: w/ fdbk., amp tremolo & vol. swells (till fade)

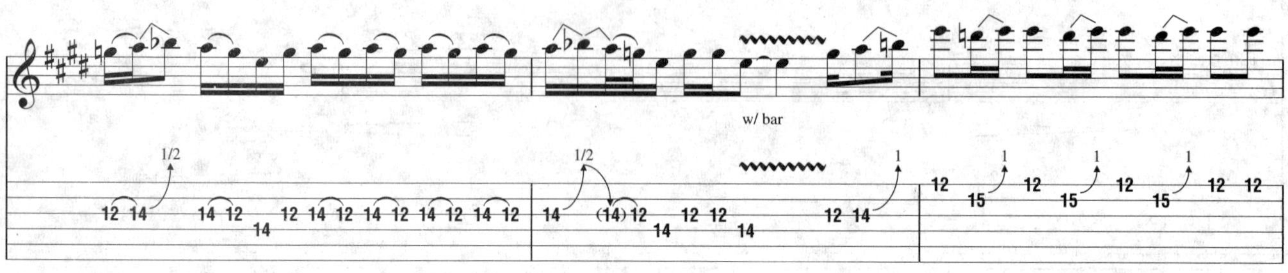

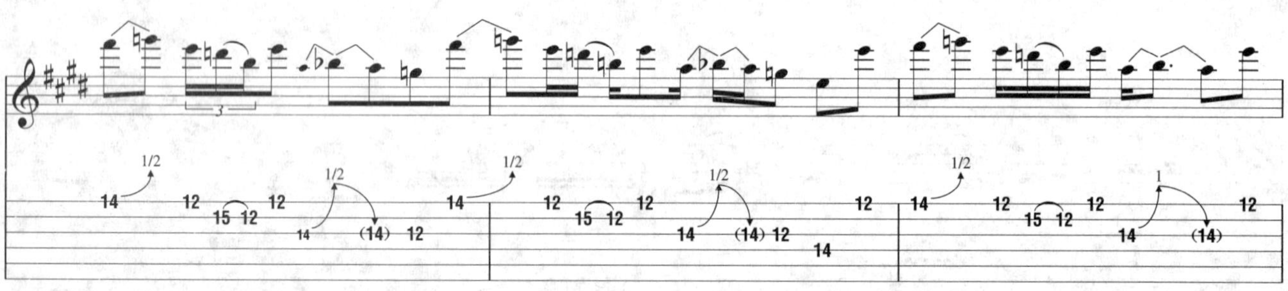

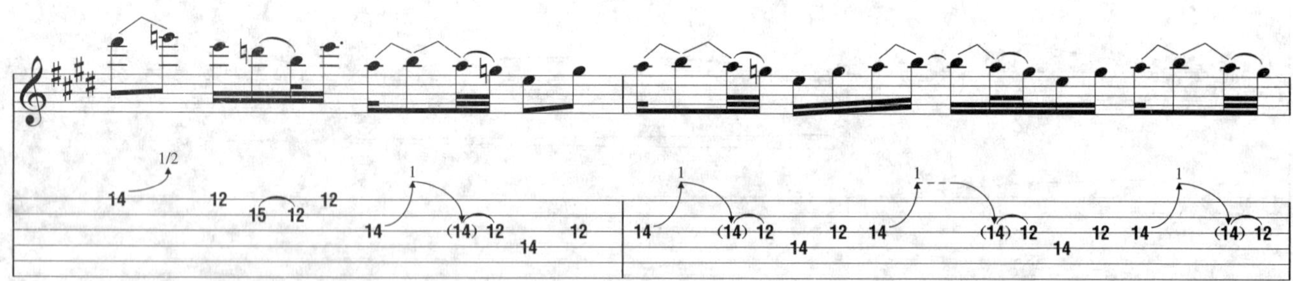

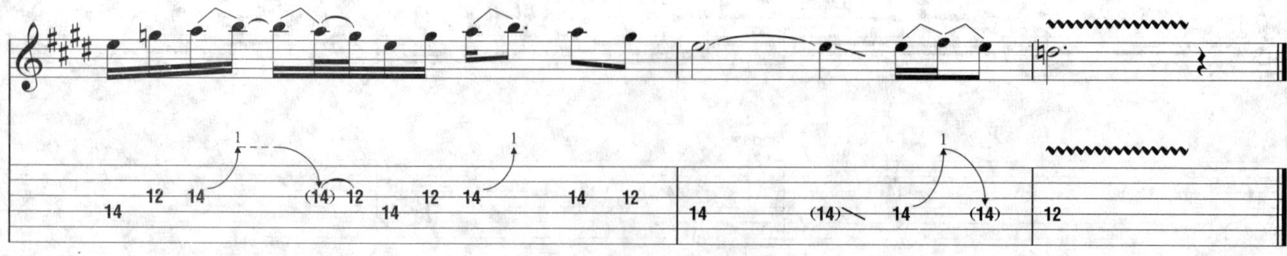

Sweet Child o' Mine

Words and Music by W. Axl Rose, Slash, Izzy Stradlin', Duff McKagan and Steven Adler

G
Gtr. 1: w/ Fill 1
D
Dsus4 D
End Rhy. Fig. 2
(cont. in slash)
Verse
Gtr. 2: w/ Rhy. Fig. 1
Gtrs. 1 & 3 tacet
D
C
Gtr. 3
1. She's got a smile that it seems to me re - minds me of child - hood mem - o - ries, where ev - 'ry - thing was as fresh as the bright blue sky.
2. She's got eyes of the blu - est skies, as if they thought of rain. I'd hate to look in to those eyes and see an ounce of pain. Her
Gtr. 4
(clean elec.)
G
D
Gtr. 2: w/ Rhy. Fig. 1, first 7 meas.
Cadd9
Now and then when I see her face she takes me a - way to that spe - cial place, and if I
hair re - minds me of a warm safe place where as a child I'd hide, and
w/ chorus
Fill 1
Gtr. 1
TAB

G
D
Dsus4 D Dsus2 D
Gtr. 2
stared _ too _ long, I'll prob - 'ly break down and cry. ______
pray for the thun - der and the rain ______ to qui - et - ly pass ____ me by. ______
Chorus
Gtr. 1: w/ Fill 2, 3rd time
A5
Rhy. Fig. 3
B5 C5
D
Dsus4 D Dsus2 D
End Rhy. Fig. 3
Whoa, whoa, _ whoa, _ sweet child o' mine. _____
*Gtr. 1
*On D.S., double Gtr. 2
To Coda
A5
B5 C5
D
Whoa, oh, _ oh, oh, ____ sweet love o' mine. __
Fill 2
Gtr. 1
1/2
1/4

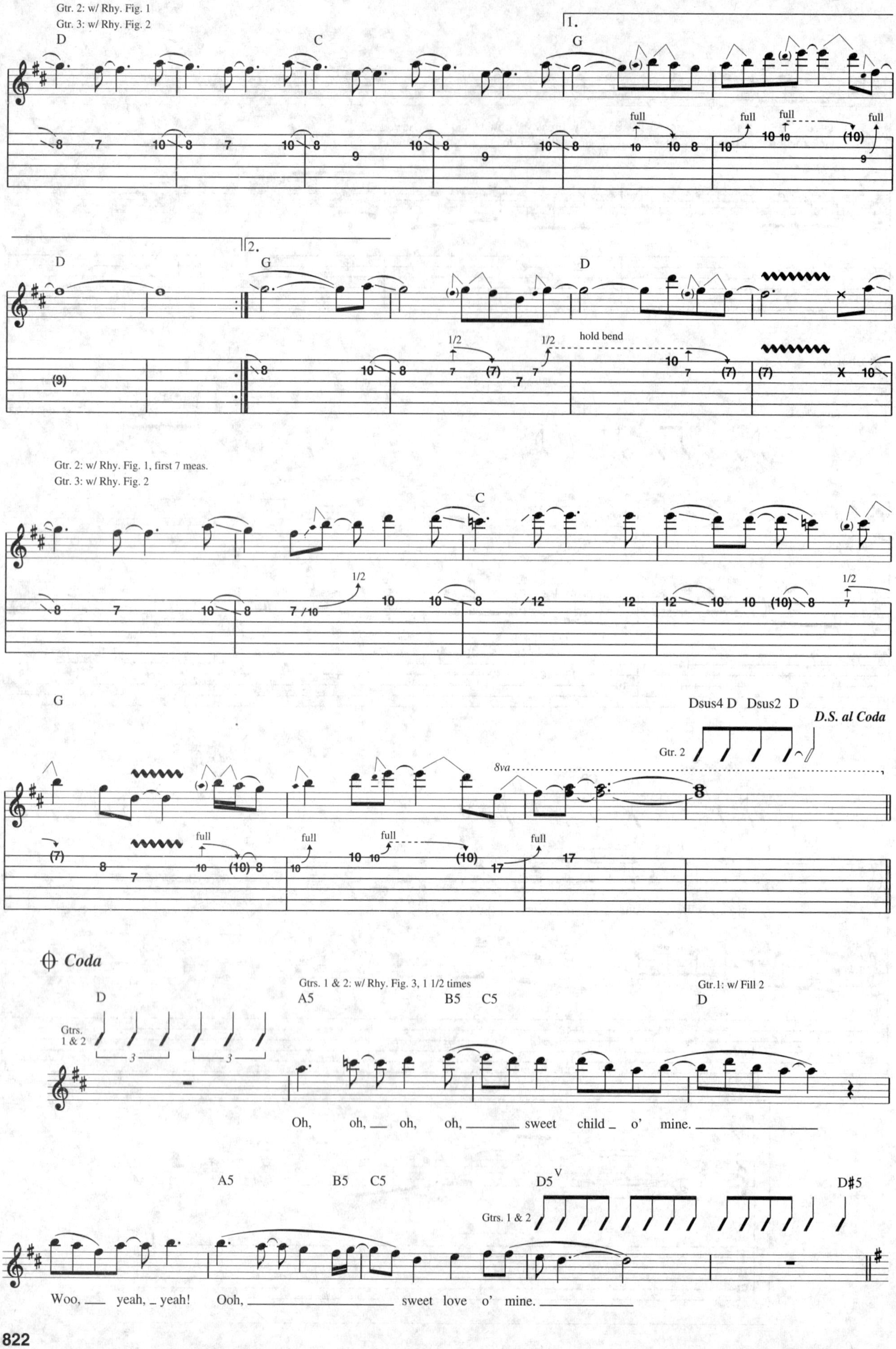

Gtr. 2: w/ Rhy. Fig. 1
Gtr. 3: w/ Rhy. Fig. 2

D C 1. G

D 2. G D

Gtr. 2: w/ Rhy. Fig. 1, first 7 meas.
Gtr. 3: w/ Rhy. Fig. 2

C

G Dsus4 D Dsus2 D *D.S. al Coda*

Gtr. 2

8va

Guitar Solo
Em
C
B7
Am
8va
loco
Gtr. 1
full
full
full
Gtr. 4
Rhy. Fig. 4
End Rhy. Fig. 4

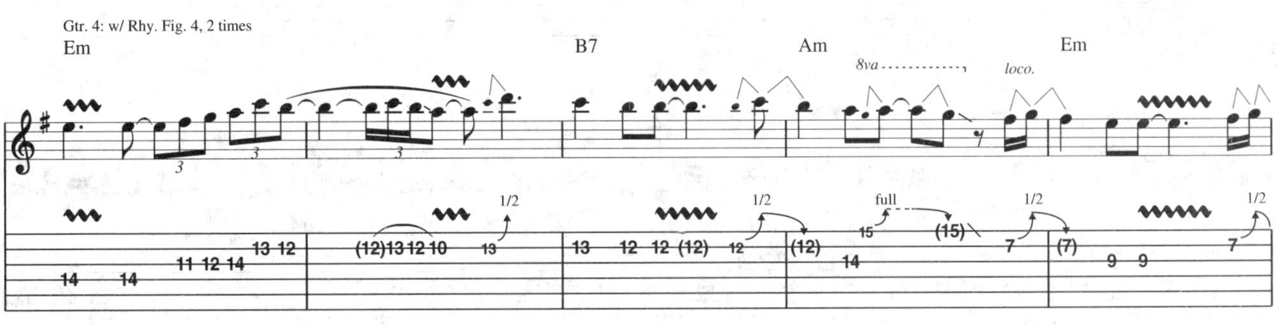
Gtr. 4: w/ Rhy. Fig. 4, 2 times
Em
B7
Am
8va
loco.
Em
1/2
1/2
full
1/2
1/2

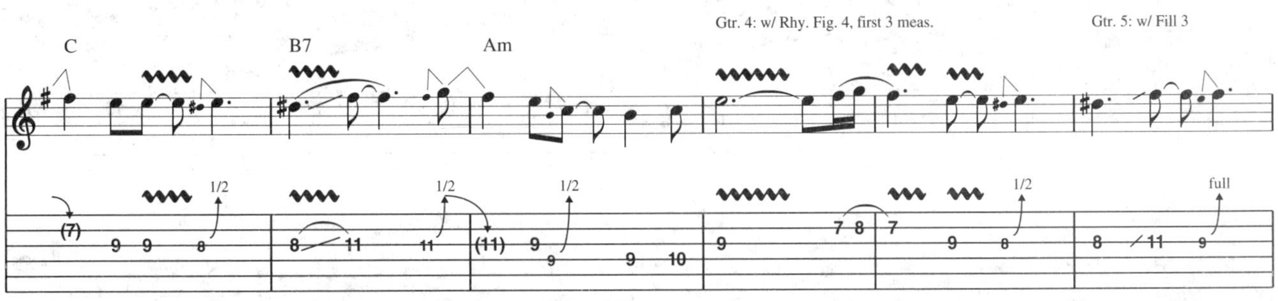
C
B7
Am
Gtr. 4: w/ Rhy. Fig. 4, first 3 meas.
Gtr. 5: w/ Fill 3
1/2
1/2
1/2
1/2
full

Fill 3
Gtr. 5
8va
w/ wah - wah
full
full
full
T
A
B

Gtr. 4: w/ Rhy. Fill 1
A5
G
F♯
Em
E
F♯
G5
3fr
2fr
Rhy. Fig. 5
open
2fr
Gtr. 2
P.M.
8va
Gtr. 5
w/ wah-wah
full
full
A5
B5
C5
D5
G5
End Rhy. Fig. 5
Gtr. 2: w/ Rhy. Fig. 5, 3 times
Em
G5
8va
loco
full
1/2
A5
B5
C5
D5
G5
E5
hold bend
full
1/4
G5
A5
B5
C5
D5
G5
8va
1/4
Em
G5
8va
full
Rhy. Fill 1
Gtr. 4

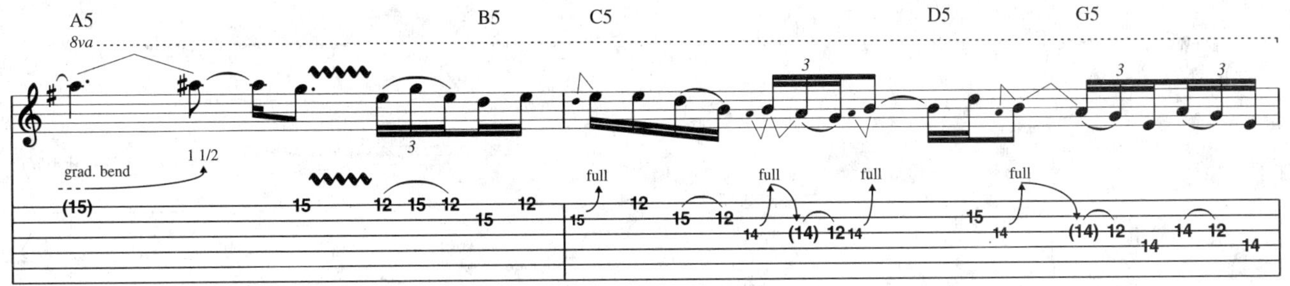

Gtr. 2: w/ Rhy. Fig. 6, 2 times

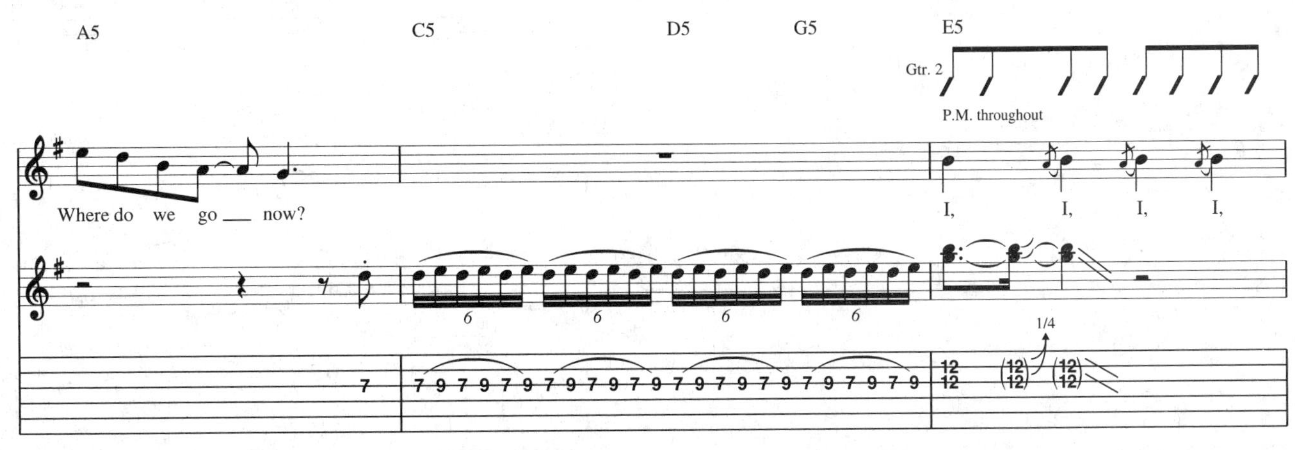

G5
A5
C5
D5V
G5III
I,
I,
I,
I,
Where do we go now,
now?
8va
full
full
15
(15)
12
14
(14)
12
18
17
18
17
17
22
E5
E
6
open
F#
6
2fr
G5
A5
B5
Rhy. Fig. 7
8va
Where do we go?
Ah.
Where do we go now?
full
(22)
22
22
22
22
22
(22)
17
17
(17)
17
(17)
17
C5
D5V
G5III
End Rhy. Fig. 7
Gtr. 2: w/ Rhy. Fig. 7
E5
G5
When do we go?
loco
grad. bend
1/2
A5
C5
D5
G5
Where do we go now?

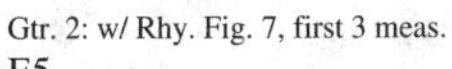
Gtr. 2: w/ Rhy. Fig. 7, first 3 meas.
E5

G5
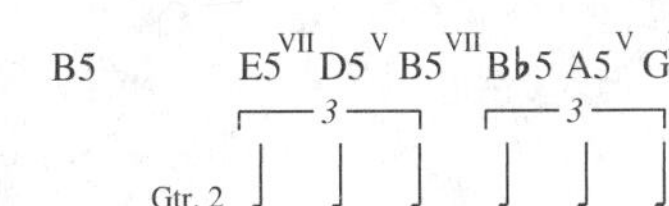
A5
B5
Gtr. 2
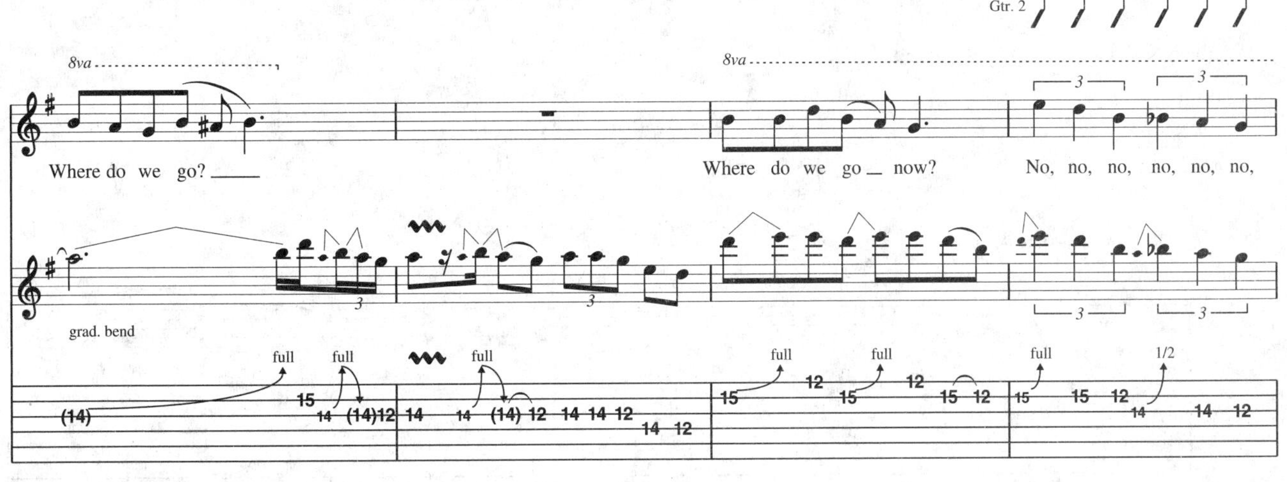
Where do we go?
Where do we go now?
No, no, no, no, no, no,
grad. bend
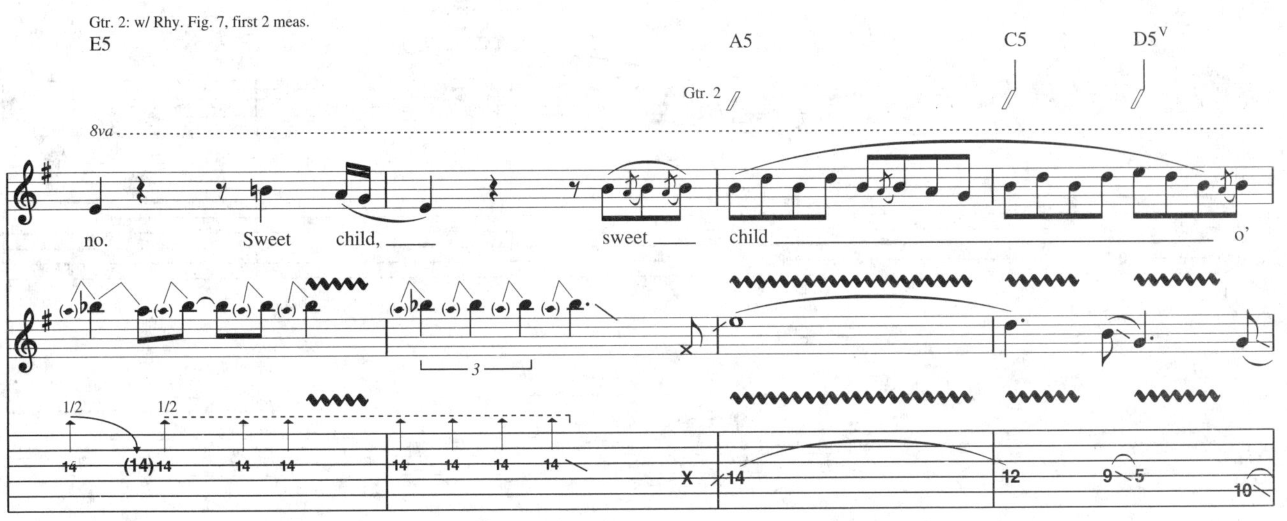
Gtr. 2: w/ Rhy. Fig. 7, first 2 meas.
E5
A5
C5
Gtr. 2
no. Sweet child, sweet child o'
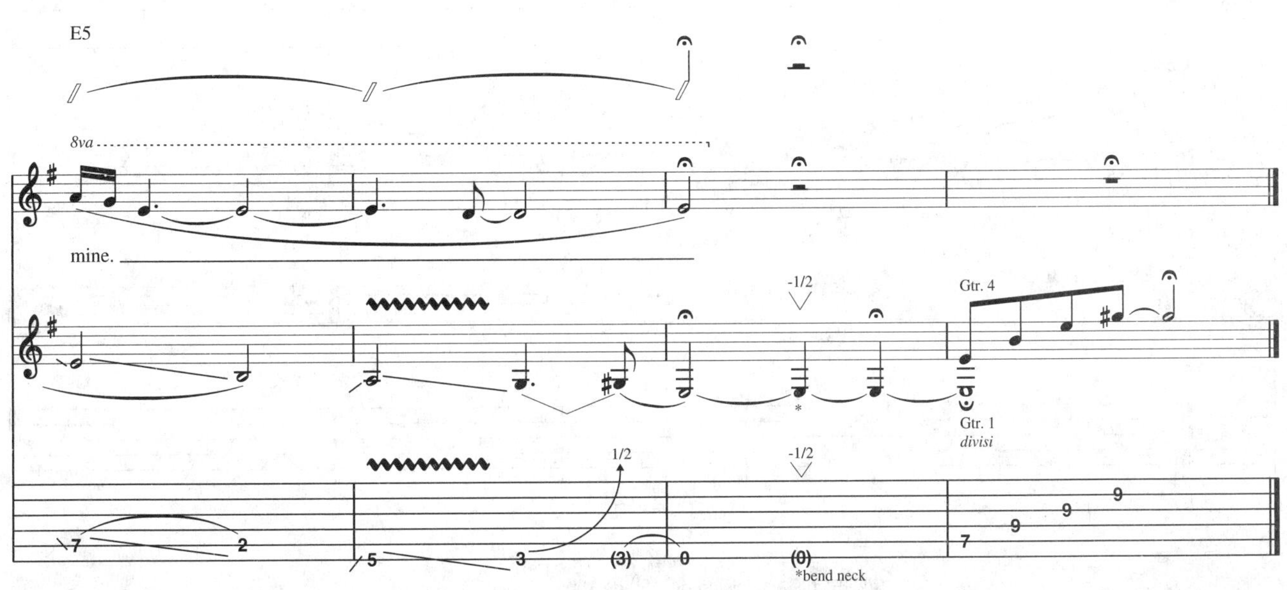
E5
mine.
Gtr. 4
Gtr. 1
divisi
*bend neck

Sweet Emotion

Words and Music by Steven Tyler and Tom Hamilton

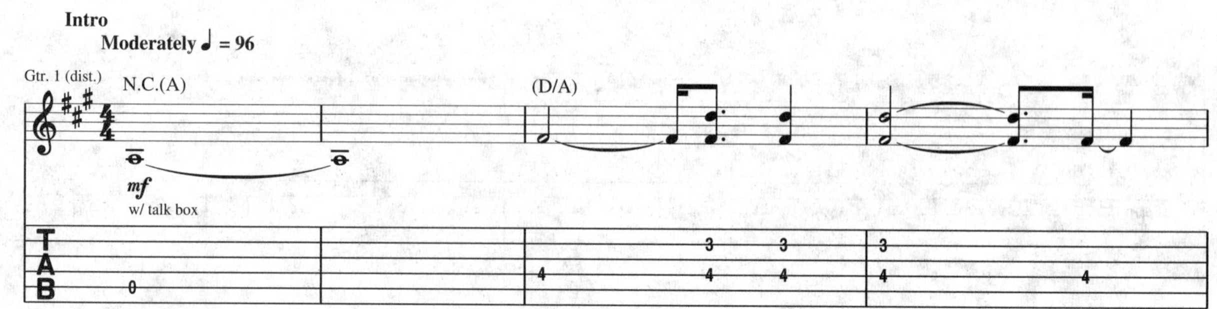

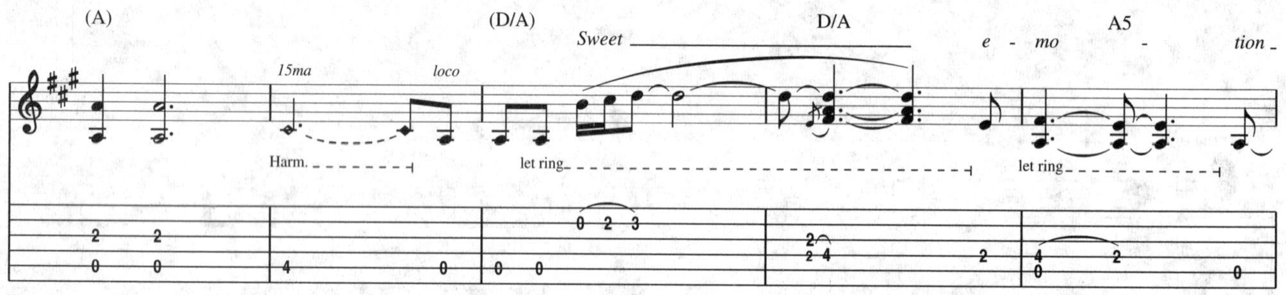

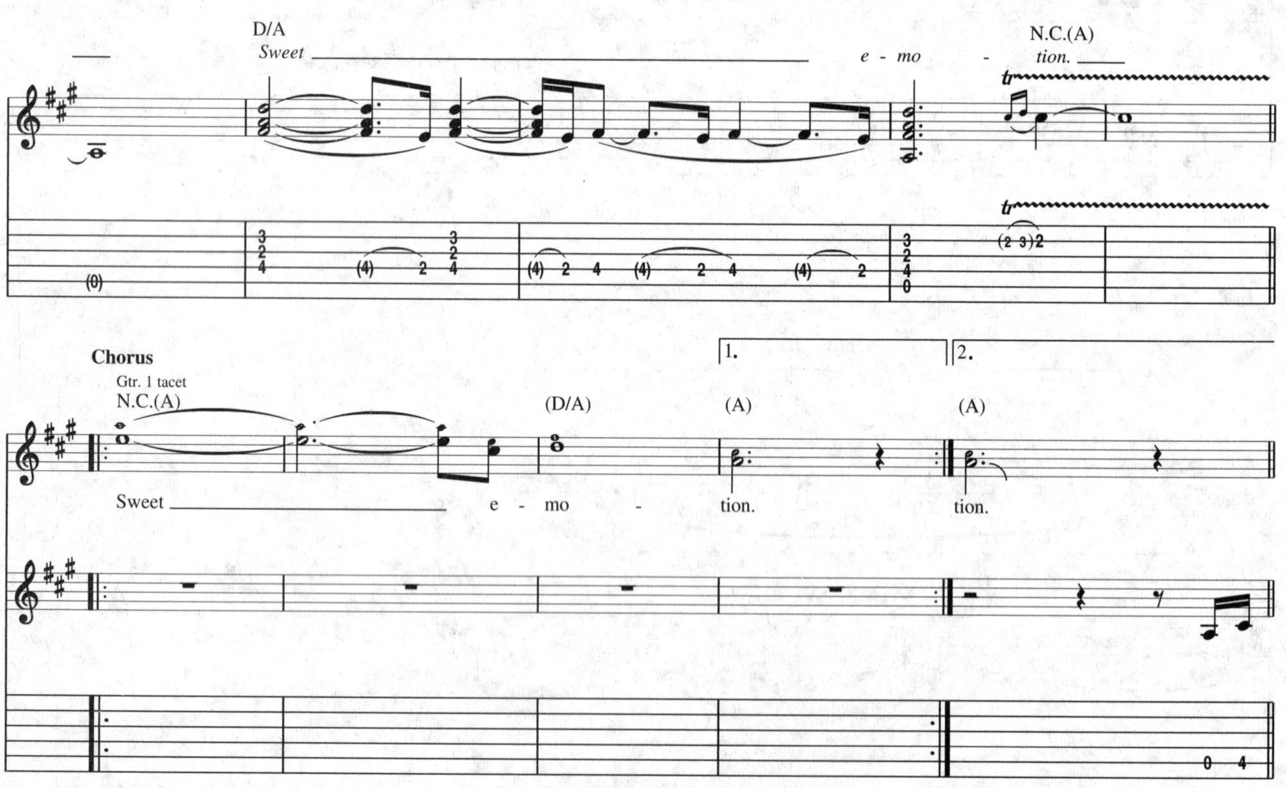

Verse
Gtr. 1: w/ Fill 1, 1st time; w/ Fill 2, 2nd time
A5
D A A5
Talk a - bout things and no - bod - y cares, you're
pulled in - to town in a po - lice car, you're
Gtr. 2 (dist.)
mf
Gtr. 1 tacet
D A
wear - in' out things that no - bod - y wears. You're
dad - dy said I took you just a lit - tle too far. You're
Riff A
End Riff A
Gtr. 2: w/ Riff A, 2 times
call - in' my name, but I got - ta make clear, I
tell - in' her things but your girl - friend lied, you
can't say, ba - by, where I'll be in a year.
can't catch me 'cause the rab - bit done died. Yes it did!
Interlude
*Gtrs. 1 & 2
N.C.
*composite arr.
Fill 1
Gtr. 1
let ring
Fill 2
Gtr. 1
let ring

2. Some
4. You
Gtr. 2
Gtr. 1
divisi
Verse
Gtr. 2: w/ Riff A, 4 times
D A
sweet - talk - in' ma - ma with a face like a gent said my
stand in the front just - a shak - in' yo ass, I'll
get up and go must - 've got up and went. Well, I
take you back - stage you can drink from my glass. I'm
got good news, she's a real good li - ar, 'cause my
talk-in' 'bout some - thin' you can sure un - der - stand, 'cause a
back - stage boo - gie, set yo' pants on fire.
month on the road and I'll be eat - in' from your hand.
Interlude
Gtrs. 1 & 2
N.C.

Gtr. 2
Gtr. 1
To Coda
Chorus
N.C.(A)
Sweet
e -
Gtr. 1
let ring
Gtr. 2
(D/A)
(A)
mo -
tion
let ring

Sweet
e -
let ring
(D/A)
(A)
D.S. al Coda
mo
-
tion.
3. I
let ring
Coda
Gtr. 2
N.C.
Gtr. 1
divisi
Gtr. 2 tacet
Gtr. 1
8va
grad. bend
fdbk.
1 1/2
full
1/2
pitch: F♯

Outro
Gtr. 1
E
loco
E7
let ring
Gtr. 3 (dist.)
Riff B1
End Riff B1
mf
w/ talk box
full
full
Gtr. 2
Riff B
End Riff B
Guitar Solo
Gtrs. 2 & 3: w/ Riffs B & B1, 4 times
E5
Gtr. 1
1/4
full
full
1/2
full
1/4
full
1/4
full
1/2
full
full

Begin Fade
Gtr. 2: w/ Riff B, till fade
G
4
5fr
Gtr. 3
full
Gtr. 3: w/ Riff B1, till fade
1/2
let ring
Fade Out

Sweet Little Angel

Words and Music by B.B. King and Jules Bihari

G♭7
G7
G♭7
sweet 'lil an - gel.
I love the way she
4:3
4:3
full
D♭maj7
E♭m7
Fm7
Em7
spreads her wings.
Yes,
5:3
full
E♭m7
G♭7
when she spreads her wings a-round me,
I gets joy and ev-'ry -
3
D♭
E♭m7
G♭/A♭
A♭7
thing.
2. I
4:3
4:3
4:3
full
full
1/4

Verse
Gtr. 1: w/ Fill 1, 2nd time
Db7
Gb7
asked my ba - by for a nick-el
and she gave me a twen-ty dol-lar bill.
my ba - by should quit me,
Lord, I do be - lieve
full
Gtr. 1: w/ Fill 2, 2nd time
Db
Db7
4:3
Yes, asked my ba -
I would die.
Yes, if
full
full
1/4
Gb7
G7
Gb7
- by for a nick-el
and she gave me a twen-ty dol-lar bill.
my ba - by should quit me,
Lord, I do be - lieve I would
Fill 1
Gtr. 1
Fill 2
Gtr. 1

Dbmaj7
Ebm7
Fm7
Em7
die.
Yes, you know I asked
Yes,
5:3
4:3
full
1/4
To Coda
Ebm7
Gb7
her for a lit-tle drink o' liq-uor,
if you don't love me, lit-tle an-gel,
and she gave me a
4:3
full
Db
Ebm7
Gb/Ab
Ab7
whis-key still.
4:3
4:3
mf
full
full
Guitar Solo
Db
Gb7
Db
1/2
full
full

Db7
Gb7
G7
8va
loco
1/4
full
Dbmaj7
Ebm7
Fm7
Em7
4:3
D.S. al Coda
Db
Gb/Ab
Ab7
3. Hey, if
Coda
Free Time
N.C.
please, tell me the rea-son why.
Gb
D13 Db7

Take a Picture

Words and Music by Richard Patrick

Asus2
A
Asus4
Rhy. Fig. 1
Gtr. 2
Rhy. Fig. 1A
Gtr. 3
(12-str. acous.)
let ring
D6/9sus4
D6/9add4
End Rhy. Fig. 1
End Rhy. Fig. 1A
Gtrs. 2 & 3: w/ Rhy. Figs. 1 & 1A, simile
1. A -
Verse
Gtrs. 2 & 3: w/ Rhy. Figs. 1 & 1A, 6 times
Gtr. 1: w/ Riff B, 6 times, 2nd time
wake on my air - plane, a - wake on my air - plane, my skin is bare, my
2. I don't be - lieve in, I don't be - lieve in your sanc - ti - ty,

D6/9sus4 D6/9add4 Asus2 A Asus2 Asus4 A Asus2
skin is theirs. A - wake on my air - plane, a - wake on my air - plane, my
your pri - va - cy. I don't be - lieve in, I don't be - lieve in
D6/9sus4 D6/9add4 D6/9sus4 D6/9add4 Asus2 A
skin is bare, my skin is theirs, ah. I
sanc - ti - ty or hy - poc - ri - sy. Can ev - 'ry - one a - gree that
Asus2 Asus4 A Asus2 D6/9sus4 D6/9add4 D6/9sus4 D6/9add4 Asus2 A
feel like a new - born. And I
no one should be left a - lone? Could ev - ry - one a - gree that
Asus2 Asus4 A Asus2 D6/9sus4 D6/9add4 D6/9sus4 D6/9add4
feel like a new - born. A -
they should not be left a - lone? Yeah. And
Asus2 A Asus2 Asus4 A Asus2 D6/9sus4 D6/9add4
wake on my air - plane, a - wake on my air - plane, I
I feel like a new - born.
Gtr. 1: w/ Riff A
D6/9sus4 D6/9add4 Asus2 A Asus2 Asus4 A Asus2 D6/9sus4 D6/9add4
feel so real.
And I feel like a new - born,
Chorus
Gtr. 1: w/ Rhy. Fig. 3, 2nd time
D6/9sus4 D6/9add4 Asus2 Dsus2
Rhy. Fig. 2
Gtrs. 2 & 3
simile on repeats
kick - ing and scream - ing. Could you take my pic - ture? 'Cuz
Rhy. Fig. 3
Gtr. 1
play 4 times
T
A
B

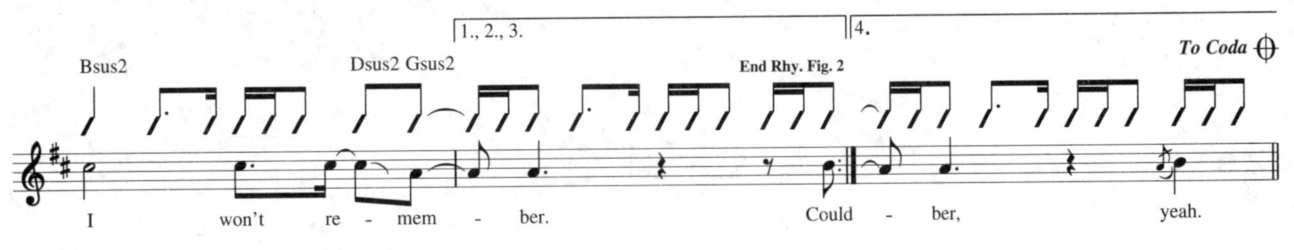
1., 2., 3.
4.
To Coda
Bsus2
Dsus2 Gsus2
End Rhy. Fig. 2
I won't re - mem - ber.
Could - ber, yeah.

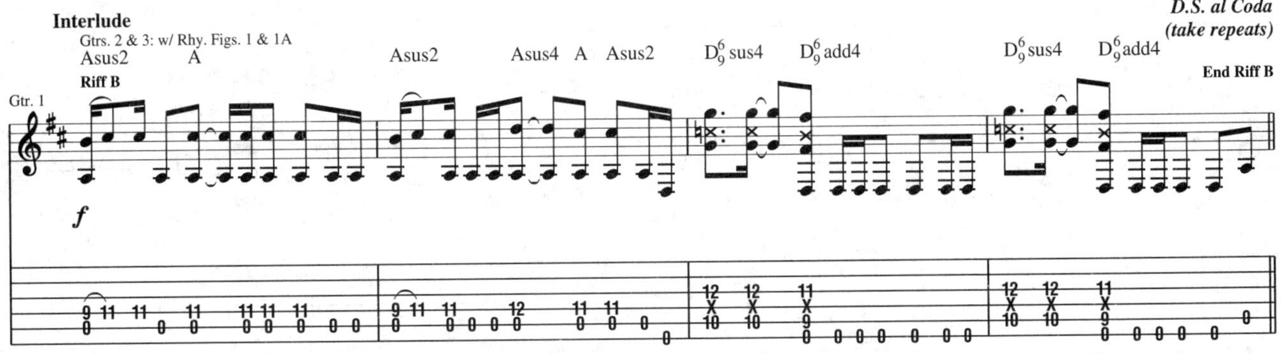
Interlude
D.S. al Coda
(take repeats)
Gtrs. 2 & 3: w/ Rhy. Figs. 1 & 1A
Asus2 A Asus2 Asus4 A Asus2 D6/9sus4 D6/9add4 D6/9sus4 D6/9add4
Riff B
End Riff B
Gtr. 1
f

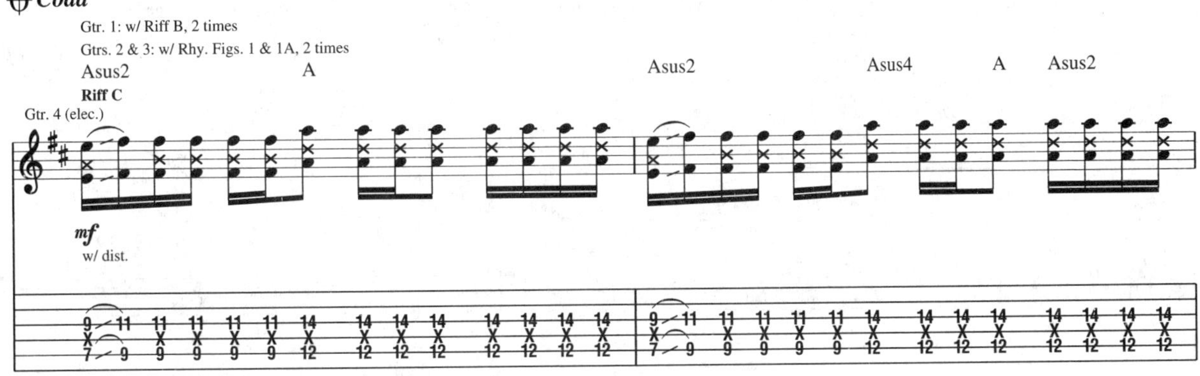
Coda
Gtr. 1: w/ Riff B, 2 times
Gtrs. 2 & 3: w/ Rhy. Figs. 1 & 1A, 2 times
Asus2 A Asus2 Asus4 A Asus2
Riff C
Gtr. 4 (elec.)
mf
w/ dist.

D6/9sus4 D6/9add4 D6/9sus4 D6/9add4 Asus2 A

Asus2 Asus4 A Asus2 D6/9sus4 D6/9add4 D6/9sus4 D6/9add4
End Riff C

Bridge

Gtr. 1: w/ Riff B, 2 times
Gtrs. 2 & 3: w/ Rhy. Figs. 1 & 1A, 2 times
Gtr. 4: w/Riff C, simile

Asus2 A Asus2 Asus4 A Asus4 D^6_9sus4 D^6_9add4

Hey dad, what do you think a - bout __ your son now? ________

1.
D^6_9sus4 D^6_9add4

Oh. ________

2.
D^6_9sus4 D^6_9add4

Outro-Chorus

Gtrs. 1, 2 & 3: w/ Rhy. Figs. 2 & 3, 6 times

Asus2 Dsus2

Could you take my __ pic - ____ ture? _____

Bsus2 Dsus2 Gsus2

'Cause I won't re - mem - ber.

1., -5.
Could

6.
- ber. Yeah.

Outro

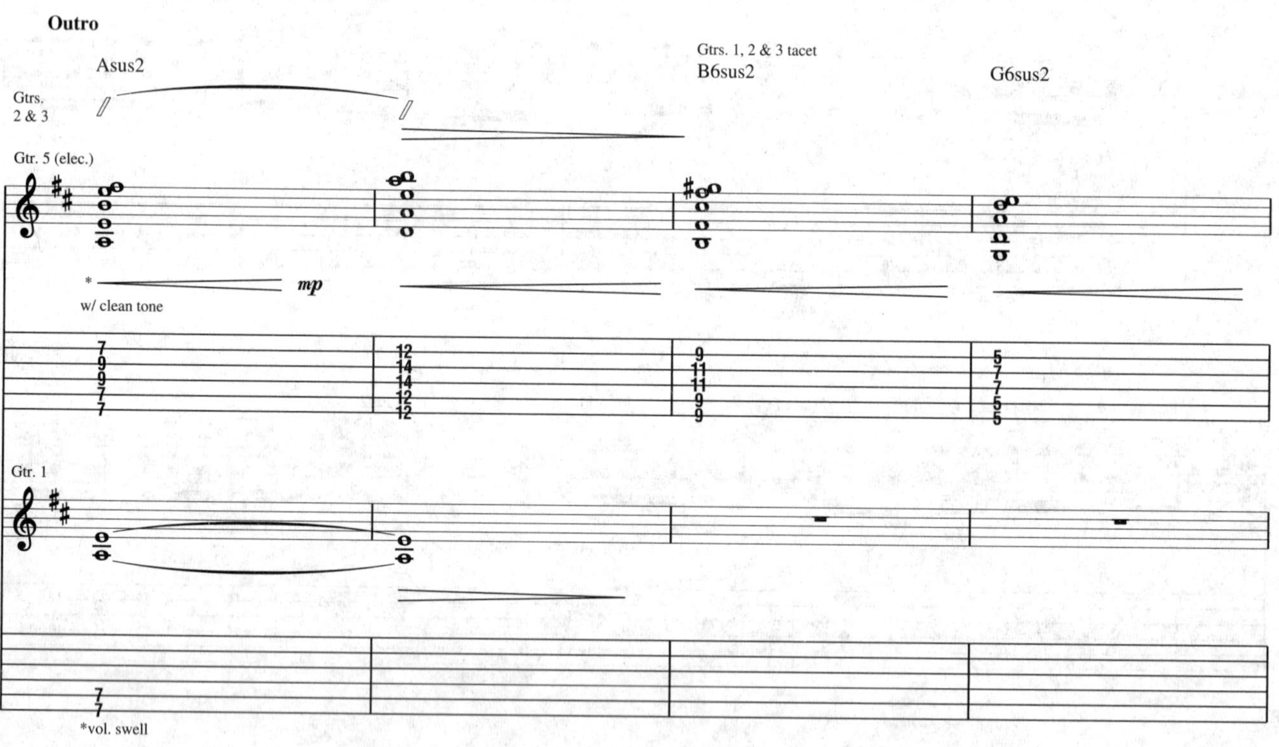

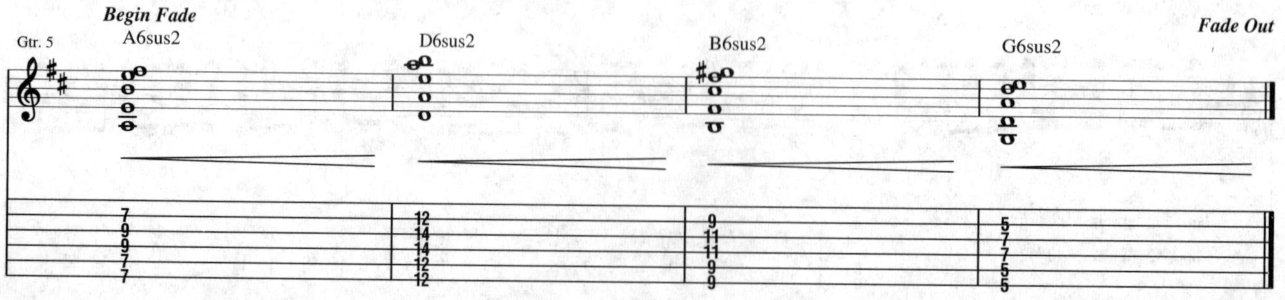

Takin' Care of Business

Words and Music by Randy Bachman

B♭6 B♭5 F5 F6 F5 C5 C6 C5 C6 C5
They
(cont. in slash)
Verse
C5 C6 C5 B♭5 B♭ B♭6 B♭ B♭5 F5 F F6 F F5 F6 C5
Rhy. Fig. 1
Gtrs. 1 & 2
Gtr. 2: w/ Fill 1, 3rd time
P.M.
1., 3. get up ev - 'ry morn - ing from the a - larm clock's warn - ing. Take the eight fif - teen in - to the
2. eas - y as fish - ing you could be a mu - si - cian, if you could make sounds loud and
End Rhy. Fig. 1
Gtrs. 1 & 2: w/ Rhy. Fig. 1, 3 times, simile
C6 C5 C6 C5 C6 C5 B♭5 B♭6 B♭5
cit - y. There's a whis - tle up a - bove and peo - ple push - ing, peo - ple shov - ing, and the
mel - low. Get a sec - ond hand gui - tar, chanc - es are you'll go far if you
Gtr. 2: w/ Fill 2, 3rd time
F5 F6 F5 F6 C5 C6 C5 C6 C5 C6 C5 B♭5
girls who try to look pret - ty. And if your train's on time you can
get in with the right bunch of fel - lows. Peo - ple see you hav - ing fun just a -
Fill 1
Gtr. 2
full
Fill 2
Gtr. 2
1/2

Bb6 Bb5 F5 F6 F5 F6 C5 C6 C5 C6 C5
get to work by nine and start your slav - ing job to get your pay. If you
ly - ing in the sun. Tell them that you like it this way. It's the
Gtr. 2: w/ Fill 3, 3rd time
C6 C5 Bb5 Bb6 Bb5 F5 F6 F5 F6 C5
ev - er get an - noyed, look at me, I'm self em - ployed. I love to work at noth - ing all day.
work that we a - void and we're all self em - ployed. We love to work at noth - ing all day.
Chorus
Gtr. 2: w/ Fill 4, 3rd time
C6 C5 C6 C5 C5 Bb5 Eb Bb5 F5
Rhy. Fig. 2
Gtr. 1
And I've been tak - ing care of busi - ness ev - 'ry day. Tak -
And we've been tak - ing care of busi - ness ev - 'ry day. Tak -
Gtr. 2
F6 F5 C5 C6 C5
End Rhy. Fig. 2
- ing care of busi - ness ev - 'ry way. I've been tak -
- ing care of busi - ness ev - 'ry way. We've been tak -
Fill 3
Gtr. 2
full full full 1/2 full full full full full full full
Fill 4
Gtr. 2
full full full full full full full

Gtr. 1: w/ Rhy. Fig. 2
Gtr. 2: w/ Fill 5, 3rd time
C5
Bb5
Eb
Bb5
F5
F6
F5
C5
- ing care of busi - ness, it's all mine. Tak - ing care of busi - ness and
- ing care of busi - ness, it's all mine. Tak - ing care of busi - ness and
To Coda
1. Interlude
Gtr. 2: w/ Rhy. Fill 1, 2nd time
Gtr. 1: w/ Rhy. Fig. 1, 2 times, simile
C6
C5
Bb6
work - ing o - ver - time, work out.
work - ing o - ver - time.
1/2
full
let ring
2. There's work
Fill 5
Gtr. 2
Rhy. Fill 1
T
A
B

2. Guitar Solo
Gtr. 1: w/ Rhy. Fig. 1, 2 times, simile
Gtr. 2
C6 C5 Bb5 Bb6 Bb5 F5 F6 F5 F6 C5
C6 C5 C6 C5 C6 C5 Bb5 Bb6 Bb5
8va
let ring
full
F5 F6 F5 F6 C5 C6 C5 C6 C5
Interlude
C5
Gtr. 1
Whoa!
Gtrs. 1 & 2 tacet
Al - right. Ow.
Gtrs. 1 & 2
C
Bridge
F Eb Bb C F Eb Bb C
Gtrs. 1, 2 & 3
Take good
F Eb Bb C F Eb
care of my busi - ness, when I'm a - way, ev - 'ry day.

Guitar Solo
Gtr. 3 tacet
B♭
C
8fr
C5 C6
C5
B♭5
B♭6
B♭5
P.M.
Gtr. 1: w/ Rhy. Fig. 1, 2 times, simile
(Gtr. 2 cont. in notation)
Whoa.
Gtr. 2
full
1/4
F5
F6
F5
F6
F5
C6
C5
C6
C5
C6
C5
B♭5
1/2
B♭6
B♭5
F5
F6
F5
F6
F5
C6
C5
D.S. al Coda
C6
C5
They
Coda
Breakdown
Gtr. 1 tacet
N.C.
Gtr. 2 tacet
Gtr. 2
Tak -
- ing care of busi - ness.
Whoa.
Tak - ing care of busi - ness.

C
Bb
F
Gtrs. 1 & 2
Gtrs. 1 & 2: w/ Rhy. Fill 2, 2nd time
1. Tak - ing care of busi - ness, ev - 'ry day. Tak -
2. - ing care of busi - ness, it's all mine. Tak -
C
- ing care of busi - ness ev - 'ry way. Tak -
- ing care of busi - ness, work - ing o - ver - time.
Outro
Gtr. 1: w/ Rhy. Fig. 2, 2 times, simile
C5
Bb5
Eb
Bb5
F5
F6
F5
C5
Tak - ing care of busi - ness. Tak - ing care of busi - ness.
*Gtr. 2
full
*2nd time ad. lib.
C6 C5
Bb5
Eb
Bb5
F5
We've been tak - ing care of busi - ness. We've been tak -
1/2
F6
F5
C5
C6 C5
Fade Out
- ing care of busi - ness. Tak -
Rhy. Fill 2
Gtrs. 1 & 2
T
A
B

Teach Your Children

Words and Music by Graham Nash

Drop D tuning:
(low to high) D-A-D-G-B-E

* Steel gtr. arr. for gtr.
** Two gtrs. arr. for one.

D
Dsus2
D
A
that you can live by.
And
End Rhy. Fig. 2
Gtr. 2: w/ Rhy. Fig. 2, simile
G5
so, be - come your - self be - cause the past
is just a good - bye.
Gtr. 1
let ring
full
* vol. swell
Chorus
Gtr. 2: w/ Rhy. Fig. 2, 2 1/2 times, simile
Teach your chil - dren well. Their fa - ther's
hell did slow - ly go by. And
1/2

D
Dsus2
D
G5
feed them on your dreams. The one they
let ring
hold bend
full
D
Dsus2
D
A
picks the one you'll know by.
Don't you ev - er ask them why.
If they told you, you would
Bm
Gtr. 1
cry. So just look at them and sigh
Gtr. 2
Rhy. Fig. 3

Gtr. 2: w/ Rhy. Fig. 1, simile

G5 A D Dsus2 D G5

and know they love you.

let ring let ring let ring

full hold bend full full hold bend

End Rhy. Fig. 3

D Dsus2 D A

2. And

Gtr. 1

let ring let ring

full full full full full full full full

* vol. swells

A
D
Dsus2
D
by.
And so, please help
them with your
must be free to teach your chil - dren what
full
1/2
1/2
full

G5
D
Dsus2
D
youth.
They seek the truth
be - fore they can
you be - lieve in? Make a world that
let ring
full
hold bend
full
hold bend
let ring
w/ bar
full
- 1/4

Chorus
Gtr. 2: w/ Rhy. Fig. 2, 2 1/2 times, simile
A
D
Dsus2
D
G5
die.
Teach
your par - ents well.
Their chil - dren's
we can live in.)
8va
hold bend
full
full
let ring
full
hold bend
let ring
full

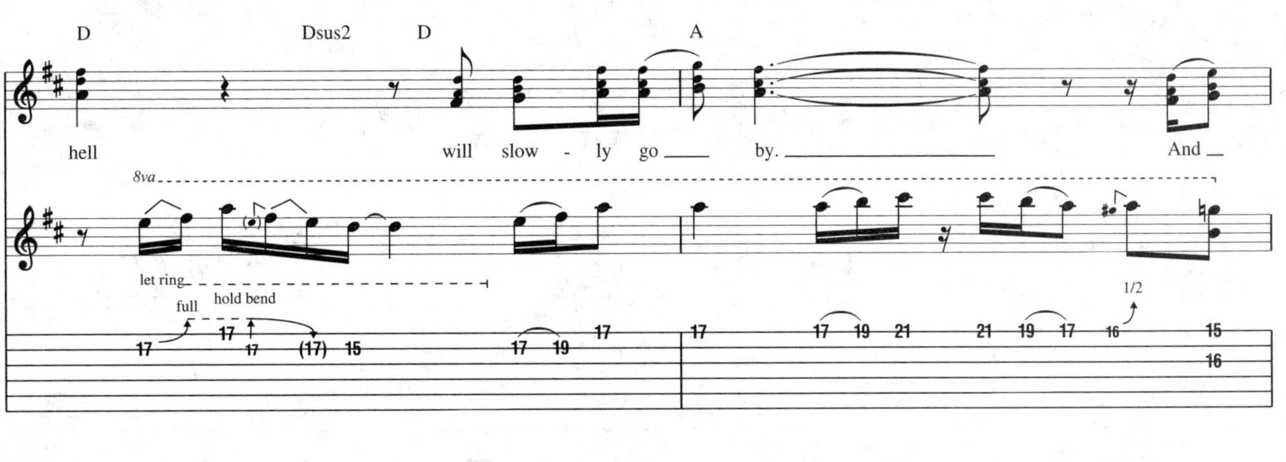
D
Dsus2
D
A
hell will slow - ly go by. And
8va
let ring
full
hold bend
1/2

D
Dsus2
D
G5
feed them on your dreams. The one they
loco
full
let ring
let ring
full
full
full

D
Dsus2
D
A
picks the one you'll know by.
full
full
hold bend
full
hold bend

D
Dsus2
D
G5
Don't you ev - er ask them why. If they told you, you would
let ring
full
let ring
full
full
hold bend
full

Gtr. 2: w/ Rhy. Fig. 3, simile
D
Bm
G5
A
cry. So just look at them_ and sigh. and know they
let ring
full
D
G5
love you.
8va
loco
Gtr. 1
w/ bar
- 1/2
Gtr. 2
w/ pick & fingers
w/ pick
D
A
D
A
D/A
P.M.
let ring
hold bend

Tears in Heaven

Words and Music by Eric Clapton and Will Jennings

A7/E
F♯7
F♯7sus4
F♯/A♯
Bm7
and car - ry on, 'cause I know I don't be - long
through night and day 'cause I know I just can't stay
D/E
To Coda
A
E/G♯
F♯m7
F♯m7/E
1.
D/F♯
E7sus4 E7
here in hea - ven.
here in hea - ven.
A
2.
D/F♯
E7sus4 E7
A
Bridge
C
G/B
Am
Time can bring ya down,
D/F♯
G
D/F♯
Em
D/F♯ G
C
G/B
Am
time can bend your knees.
Time can break your heart,

D/F♯
G
D/F♯
E
A/E
E7
have ya beg - gin' please,
beg - gin' please.
Interlude
A
E/G♯
F♯m7
F♯m7/E
D/F♯
A
E
A/E
E7
A
E/G♯
F♯m7
F♯m7/E
D/F♯
A
E
A/E
E7
Chorus
F♯m7
C♯/E♯
A7/E
Be - yond the door
there's peace, I'm sure,

F#7
G#m
F#/A#
Bm7
D/E
and I know there'll be no more tears in hea - ven.
A
E/G#
F#m7
F#m7/E
D/F#
E7sus4
E7
Verse
3. Would you know my name
if I saw you in hea - ven?
A/E
E
E7
Would you be the same

D.S. al Coda
F♯m7/E
D/F♯
A/E
E
A/E
E7
if I saw you in hea - ven?
Coda
A
E/G♯
F♯m7
F♯m7/E
ven.
'Cause I
Bm7
D/E
A
E/G♯
F♯m
know I don't be - long here in hea - ven.
Freely
F♯m/E
D/F♯
E7sus4
E7
A
rit.
let ring

This Masquerade

Words and Music by Leon Russell

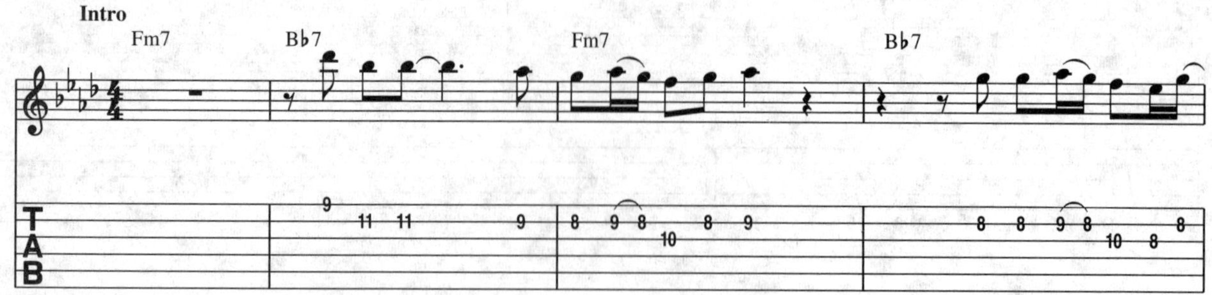

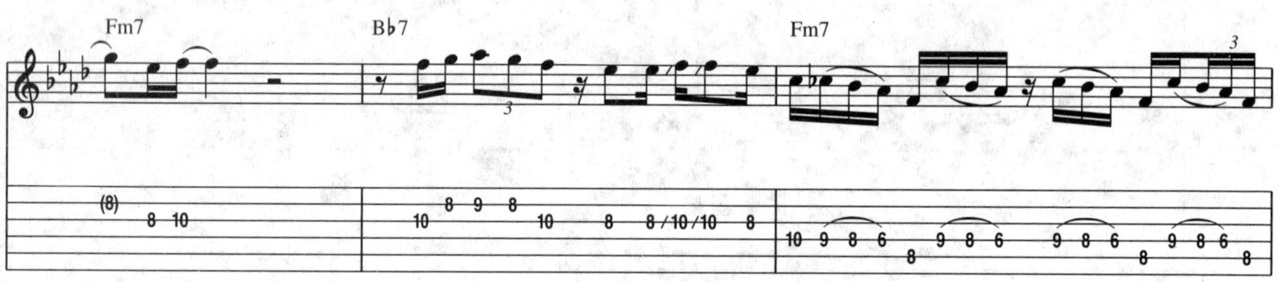

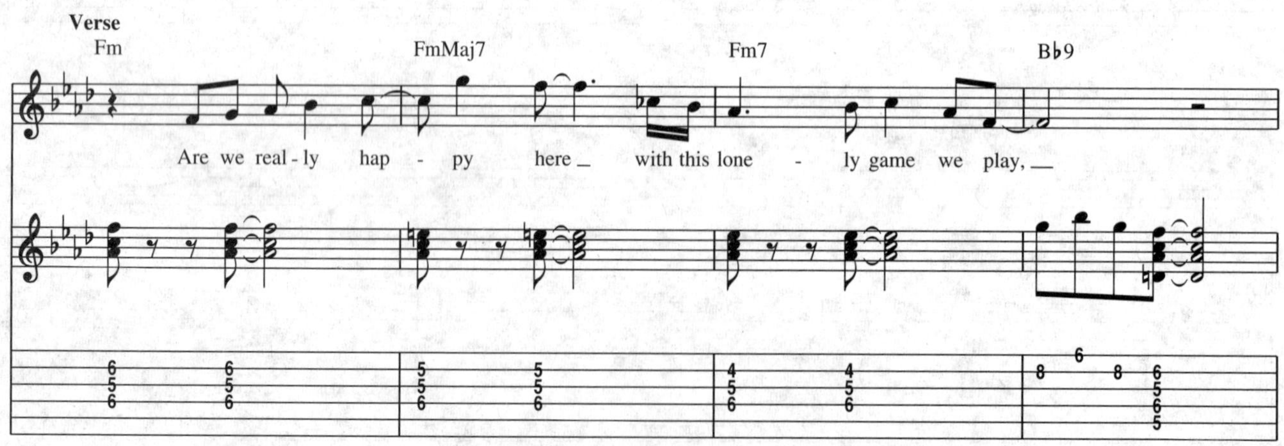

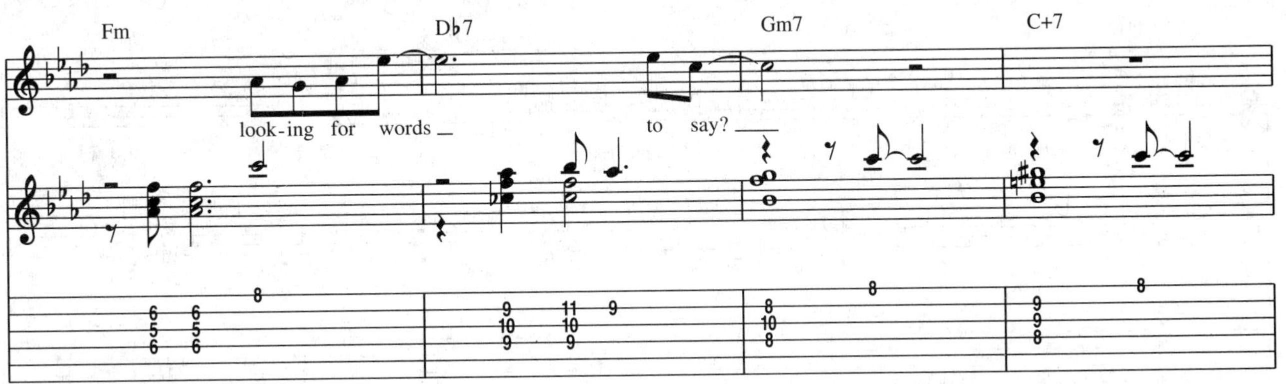
Fm
D♭7
Gm7
C+7
look-ing for words _ to say? _

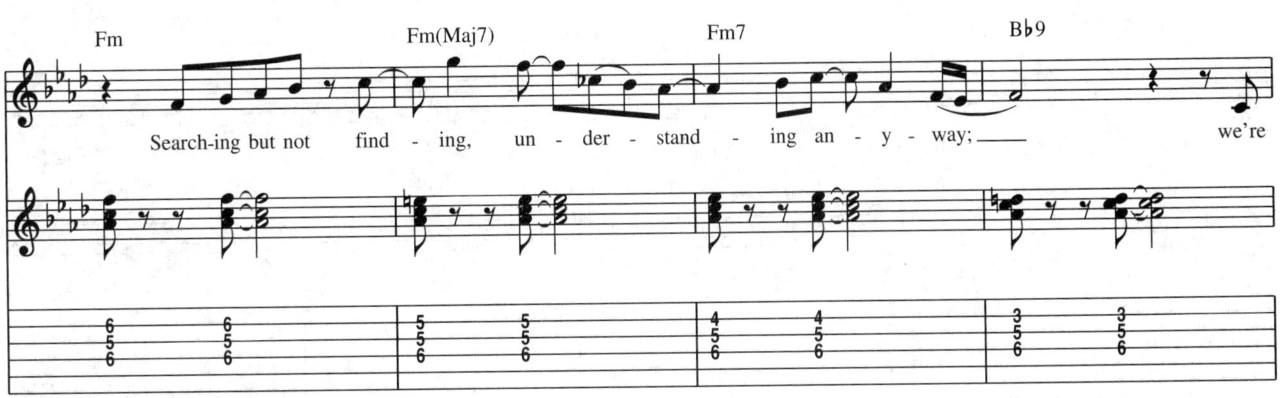
Fm
Fm(Maj7)
Fm7
B♭9
Search-ing but not find - ing, un - der - stand - ing an - y - way; _ we're

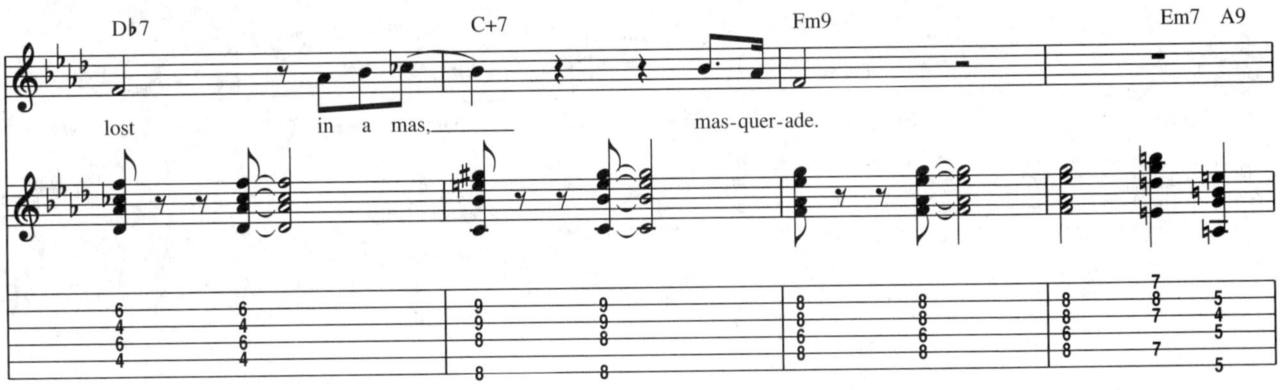
D♭7
C+7
Fm9
Em7 A9
lost in a mas, _ mas-quer-ade.

Bridge
E♭m7
A♭7(♭9)
D♭maj9
B♭+7
B♭+7(♭9)
Both a-fraid to say _ we're just _ too far _ a - way _

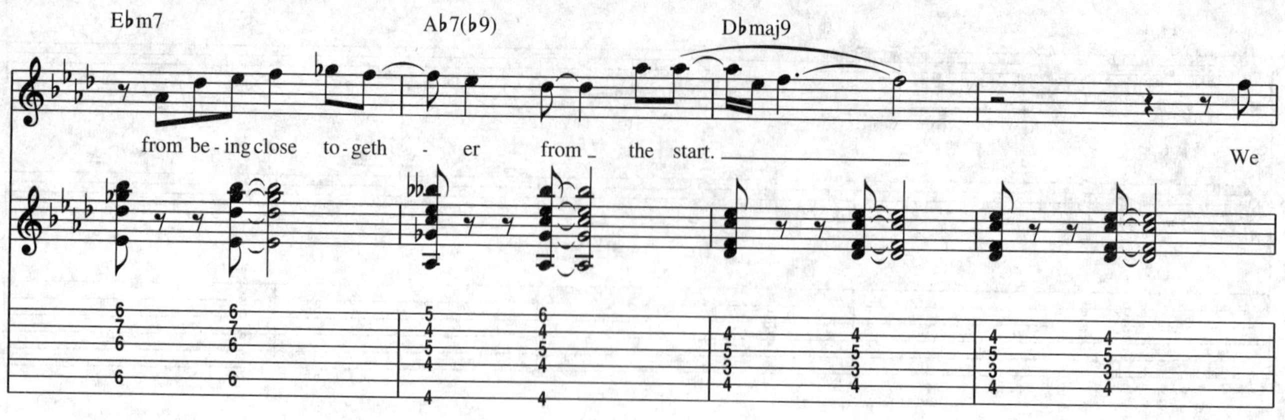
E♭m7
A♭7(♭9)
D♭maj9
from be-ing close to-geth - er from the start.
We

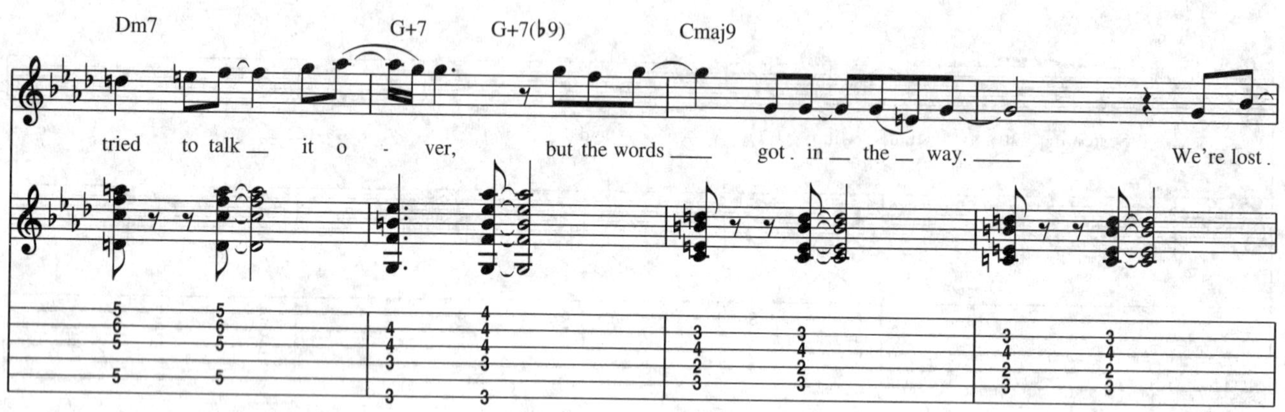
Dm7
G+7
G+7(♭9)
Cmaj9
tried to talk it o - ver, but the words got in the way.
We're lost

Gm7
G7
G+7
C7
Gm7
C7
C+7
inside this lone - ly game we play.

Verse

Fm
FmMaj7
Fm7
B♭9
Thoughts of leav-ing dis - ap - pear ev-'ry time I see your eyes.

Fm
D♭7
Gm7
No mat - ter how hard
I try

C+7
C+7(♭9)
Fm
FmMaj7
to un - der - stand the rea - sons that we

To Coda
Fm7
B♭9
D♭7
car - ry on this way,
we're lost
in the mas -

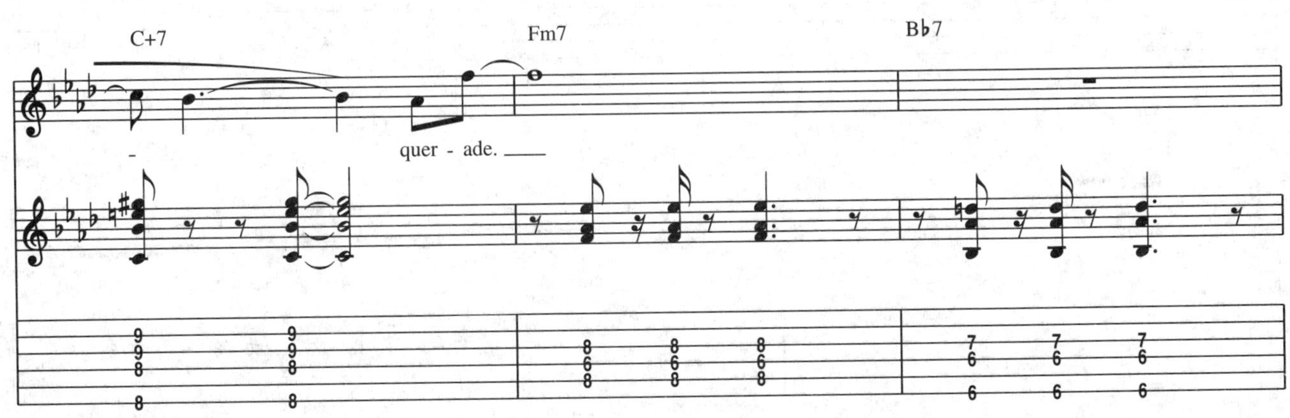
C+7
Fm7
B♭7
- quer - ade.

Guitar Solo
Fm7
Bb7
Fm7
Bb7
Fm7
Bb7
Fm7
Bb7
Fm7
Bb7
Fm7
Bb7
Fm7
Bb7
Fm7
Bb7
1/2

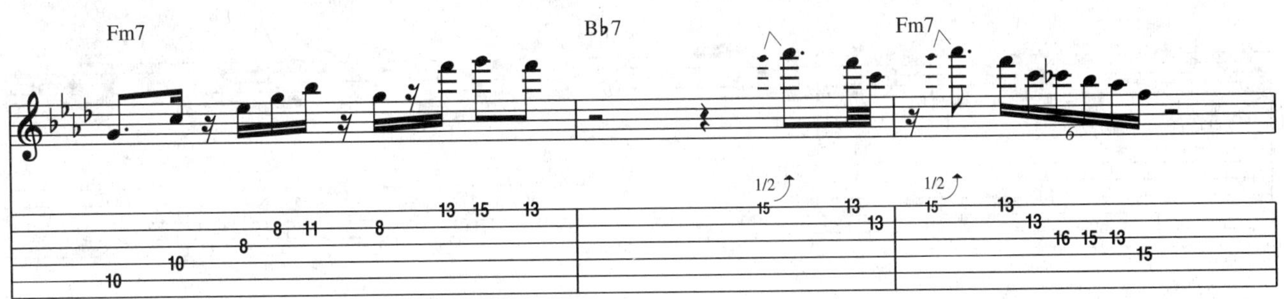
Fm7
B♭7
Fm7
1/2
1/2

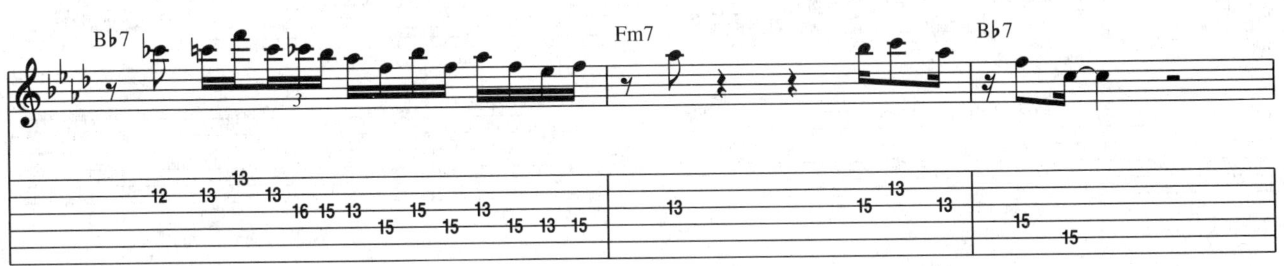
B♭7
Fm7
B♭7

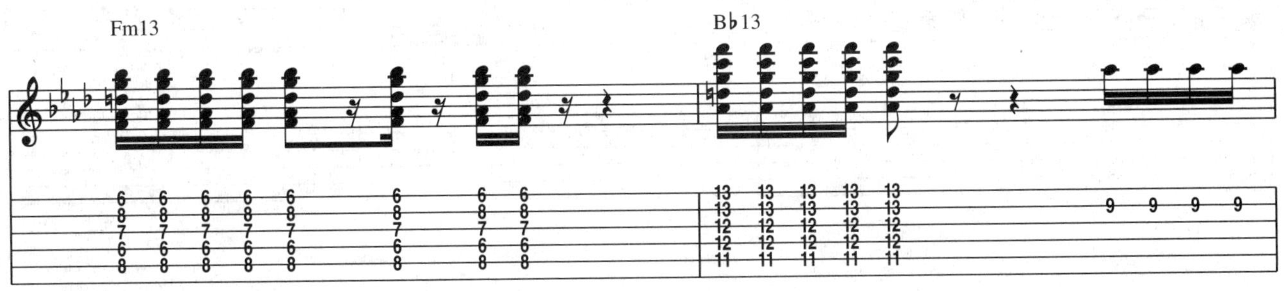
Fm13
B♭13

Fm7
B♭7

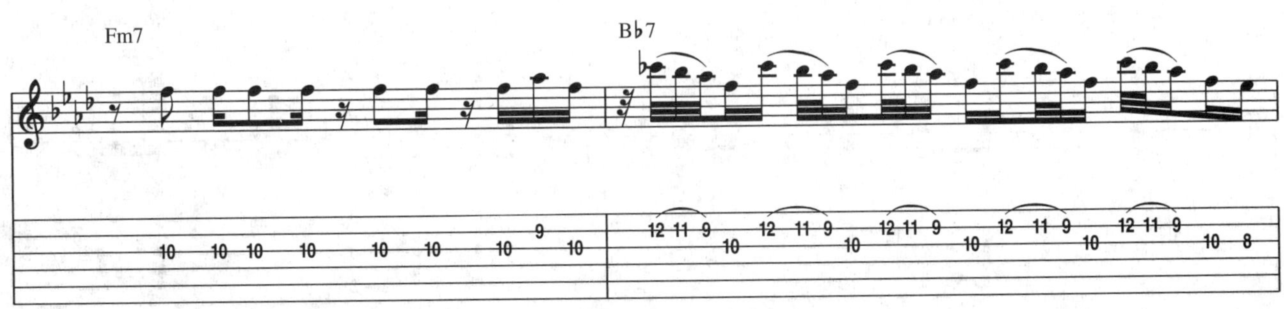
Fm7
B♭7

Fm7
B♭7

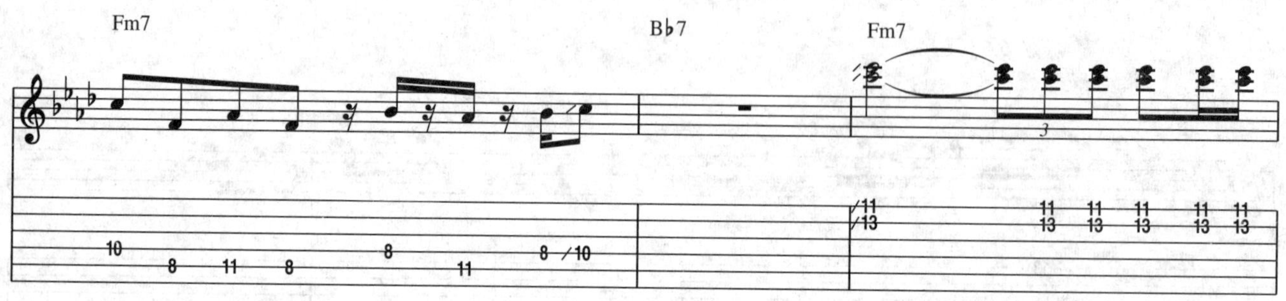
Fm7
B♭7
Fm7

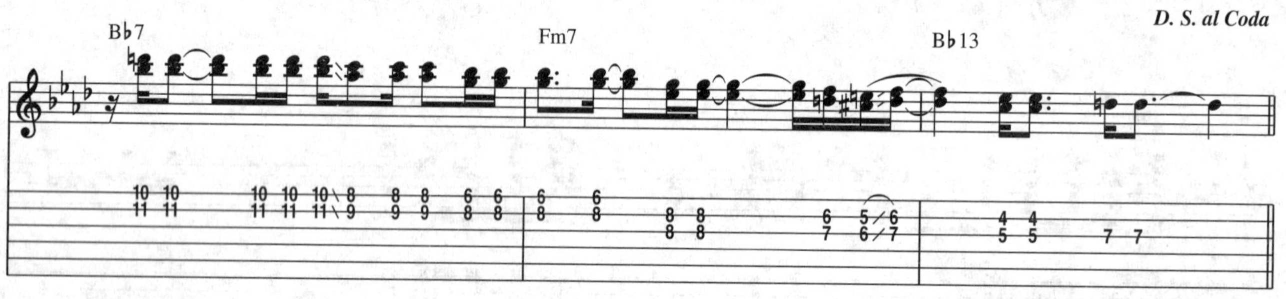
D. S. al Coda
B♭7
Fm7
B♭13

Coda
C+7
Fm7
B♭7
B♭13
quer - ade.

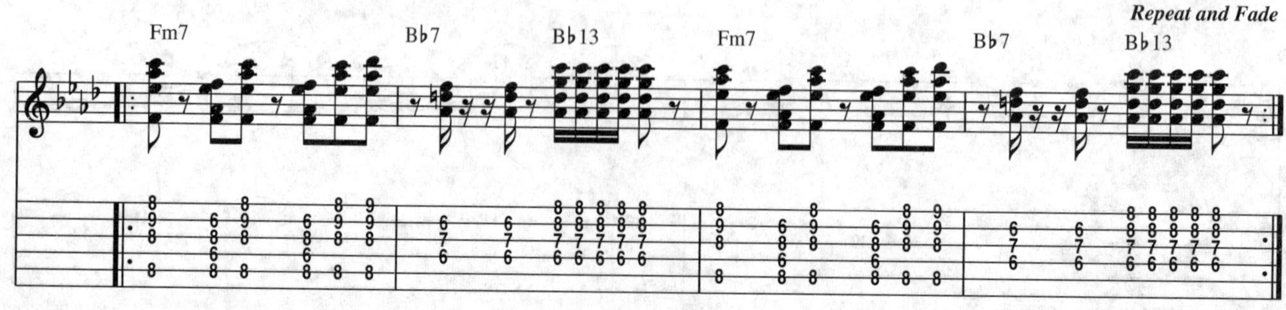
Repeat and Fade
Fm7
B♭7
B♭13
Fm7
B♭7
B♭13

Til I Hear It from You

Words and Music by Jesse Valenzuela, Robin Wilson and Marshall Crenshaw

E A

first I'd laugh, but now it's sink - in' in fast,
Who gets what they say? It's like - ly they're

let ring

let ring

let ring

*Sing harmony 2nd time only.

F♯m7add4 C♯m E

whatever they sold me. Well, ba - by, } I don't wan - na
just jeal - ous and jad - ed. Well, may - by }

let ring

(Gtr. II cont. in slashes)

let ring

let ring

sl.

let ring

sl.

Chorus
D
E
D
Gtr. II
take advice from fools.
I'll just figure ev-'ry-thing is cool
E
Rhy. Fig. 2A
A
A/G♯
until I hear it from you.
Rhy. Fig. 2
let ring
1st & 2nd times w/Bkgd. Voc. Fill 1
3rd time w/Bkgd. Voc. Fill 2
F♯m
E
Dsus2
1.
(end Rhy. Fig. 2A)
(end Rhy. Fig. 2)
Bkgd. Voc. Fill 1
Hear it from you.
Bkgd. Voc. Fill 2
Hear it from you.

2.
w/last bar of Rhy. Figs. 2 & 2A
w/Rhy. Figs. 2 & 2A
1st time w/Bkgd. Voc. Fill 1
2nd time w/Bkgd. Voc. Fill 2
To Coda
A
A/G♯
F♯m
E
Dsus2
Un - til I hear it from you.
Bridge
w/Rhy. Fill 1
B7add4
Gtr. I
I can't let it get me off, or break up my train of thought.
Gtr. II
sl.
let ring
P
As far as I know, noth - ing's wrong until I hear it from
G
Rhy. Fill 1 (Gtr. I)
let ring

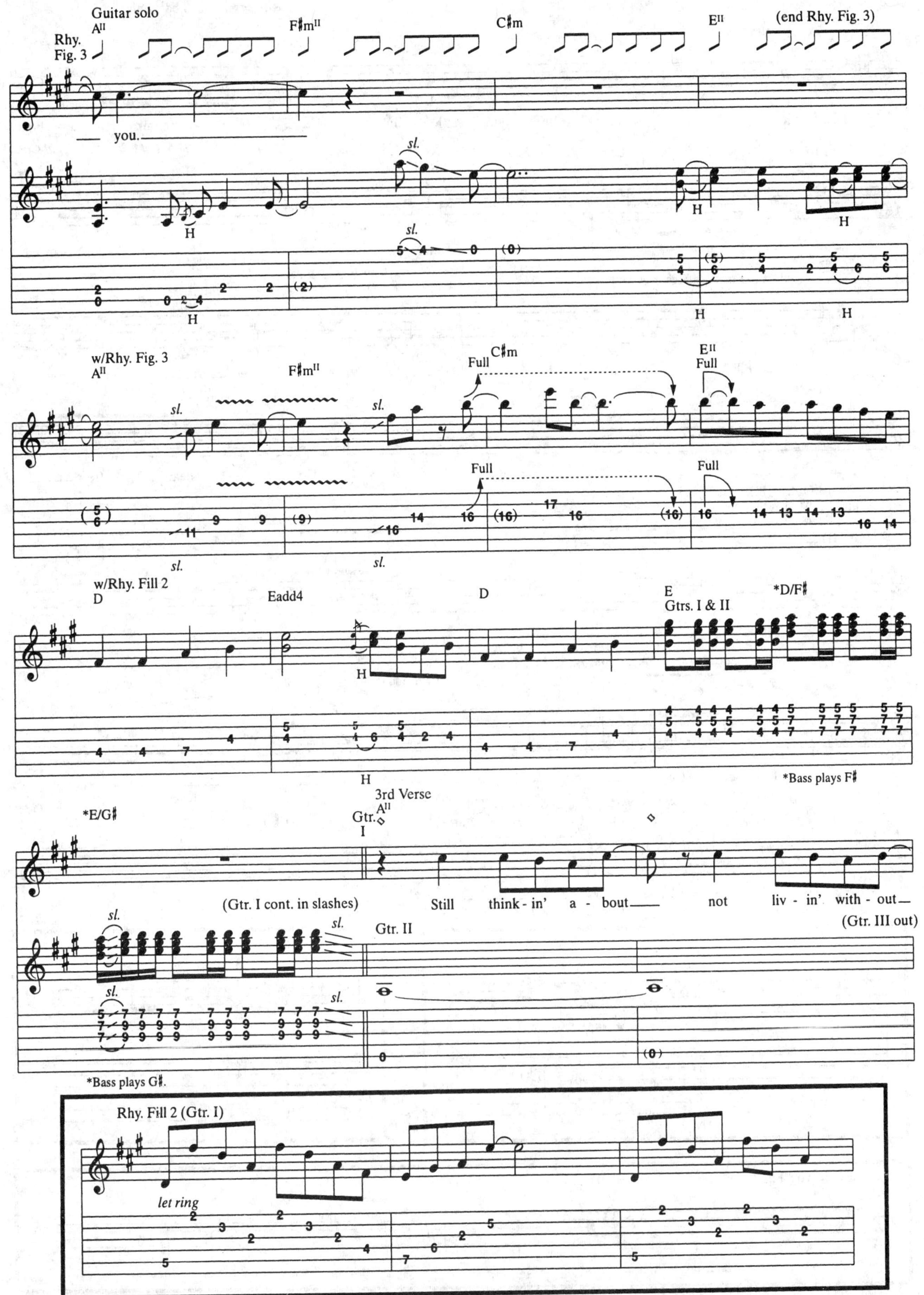
Guitar solo
Rhy. Fig. 3
A[II]
F♯m[II]
C♯m
E[II]
(end Rhy. Fig. 3)
you.
sl.
H
w/Rhy. Fig. 3
Full
Full
w/Rhy. Fill 2
D
Eadd4
E
Gtrs. I & II
*D/F♯
*Bass plays F♯
*E/G♯
3rd Verse
Gtr. I
(Gtr. I cont. in slashes)
Still think - in' a - bout not liv - in' with - out
(Gtr. III out)
Gtr. II
*Bass plays G♯.
Rhy. Fill 2 (Gtr. I)
let ring

w/Rhy. Fig. 1 (1st 3 bars only)
C♯m
E^II
A5
— it. Out - side look - in' in. — Til we're talk - in' a - bout
F♯m7
C♯m
Gtr. I
E^II
D.S. (take 2nd ending) al Coda
— not step-pin' a - round — it. Well, may - be I don't wan-na
Coda
(w/last bar of Rhy. Figs. 2 & 2A)
w/Rhy. Figs. 2 & 2A
A
A/G♯
w/Bkgd. Voc. Fill 2
Un - til I hear — it from — you. —
F♯m
E
Dsus2
Un - til I hear it from —
Outro
w/Rhy. Fig. 3
Rhy. Fig. 3A (Gtr. II)
A
F♯m7add4
w/Fill 1
C♯m
— you, — oh — no. —
E
(end Rhy. Fig. 3A)
w/Rhy. Figs. 3 & 3A and Bkgd. Voc. Fig. 1
A
F♯m7add4
C♯m
Un-til I hear it from — you, — ooh. —
w/Rhy. Figs. 3 & 3A and Fill 2
E
A
F♯m7add4
C♯m
E
Repeat and fade
Un-til I hear it from — you. —
(Sing 1st time only)
Fill 1 (Gtr. III)
H
H
Fill 2 (Gtr. III)
Repeat and fade
Bkgd. Voc. Fig. 1
Won't take ad - vice — from fools. —
I'll fig-ure ev-'ry - thing — is cool. —

Time

Words and Music by Roger Waters, Nicholas Mason, David Gilmour and Rick Wright

E F#m

frit - ter and waste _ the hours _ in an off - hand way. ___

A

Kick-ing a - round _ on a piece of ___ ground ___ in your home _ town,

P.M.

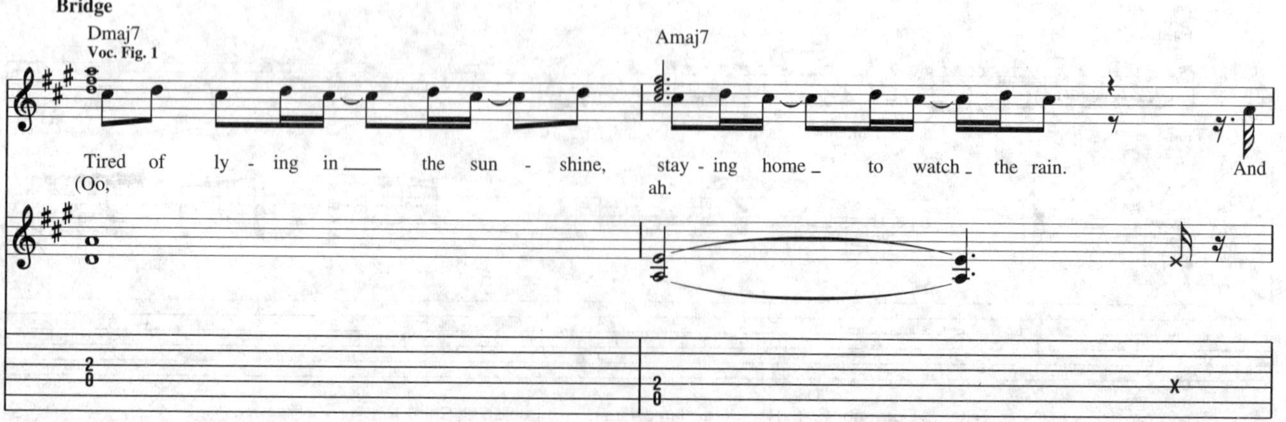

Dmaj7
Amaj7
you are young and life is long and there is time to kill to - day.
Oo,
ah.
Dmaj7
C♯m
And then one day you find, ten years have got be - hind you.
Oo,
oo.
Bm
End Voc. Fig. 1
E
No one told you when to run. You missed the start - ing gun.
Oo,
oh, ah,
Guitar Solo
F♯m
A
ah.)
Gtr. 2
(dist.)
w/ delay
grad. bend
Gtr. 1

E
F#m
A
let ring
8va
loco
Harm.
grad. release
string noise
* Harmonic located between 2nd & 3rd frets.

A
8va
hold bend
let ring
E
F#m
w/ bar

E
F♯m
8va
P.M.

Interlude

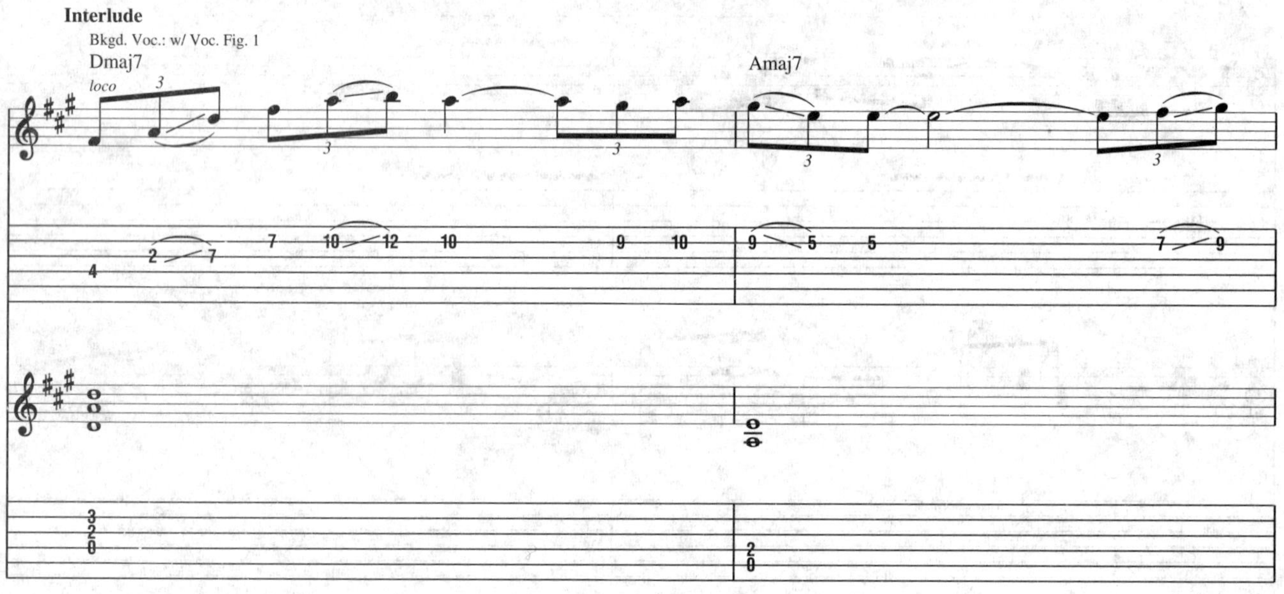
Bkgd. Voc.: w/ Voc. Fig. 1
Dmaj7
loco
Amaj7

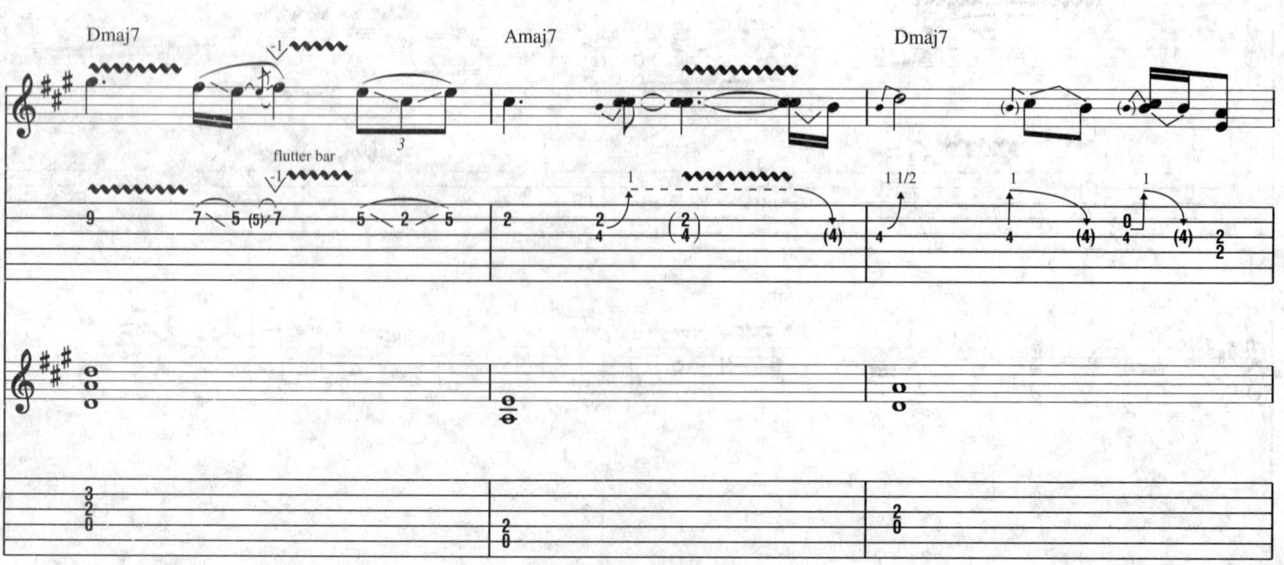
Dmaj7
Amaj7
Dmaj7
flutter bar

C#m Bm E

2. And you run.
(Oh, ah,

Verse

Gtr. 2 tacet

F#m A

you run to catch up with the sun but it's sink - ing. (and)
ah.)

let ring

E
F♯m
racing around to come up behind you again. The
Gtr. 1
let ring
A
sun is the same in a relative way, but you're older,
let ring
E
F♯m
shorter of breath, and one day closer to death.
Bridge
Dmaj7
Amaj7
Ev'ry year is getting shorter, never seem to find the time.
(Oo,
ah.
(Yeah,

Dmaj7
Amaj7
Plans that ei - ther come to naught or half a page. of scrib-bled lines.
Oo, ah.
Oh.
mf
p
mf
Dmaj7
C#m
Hang - ing on in qui - et des - par - a - tion is the Eng - lish way. The
Oo, ah.
Oh.)
Bm
Bm7
F
rit.
time is gone, the song is o - ver. Thought I'd some - thing more to say.
Oo, oo, oo,
rit.
rit.

Breathe (Reprise)

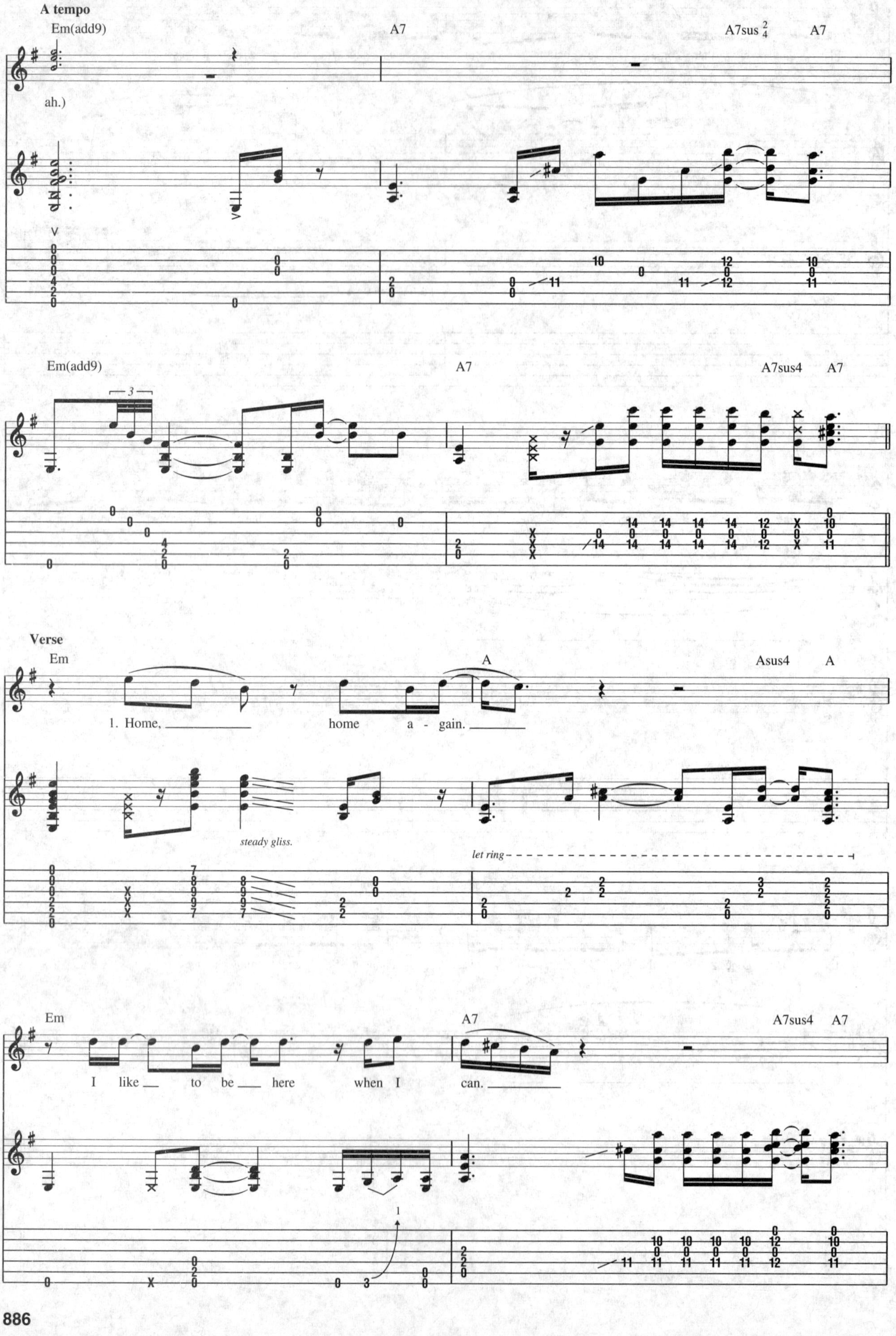

A tempo

Em(add9) A7 A7sus $\frac{2}{4}$ A7

ah.)

Em(add9) A7 A7sus4 A7

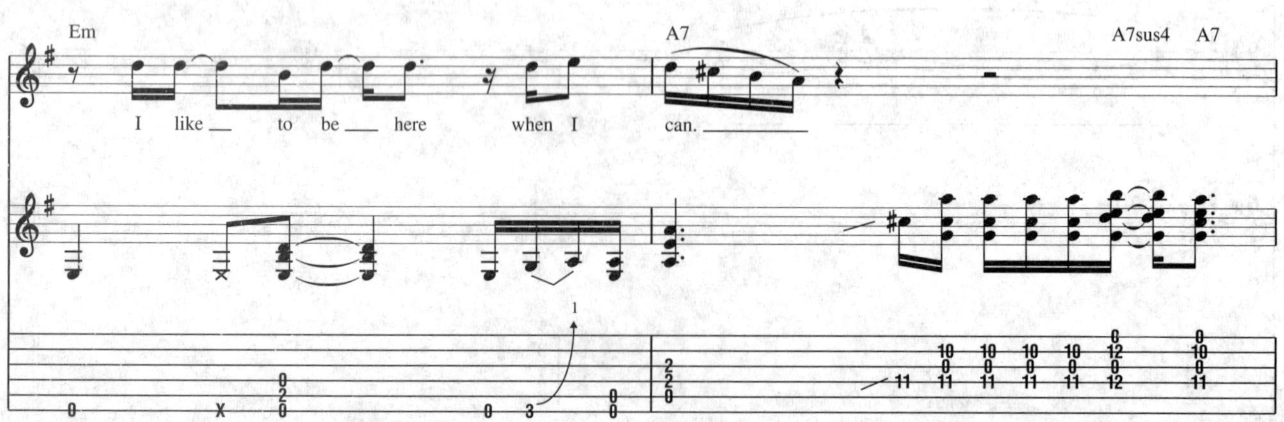

Em(add9)
A
A6sus4
A
A7sus2/4
And when I come home cold and tired, it's
let ring
Em
A
Asus4
A
good to warm my bones beside the fire.
let ring
Cmaj7
Bm
Far away across the field, the tolling of the iron bell
Segue into
"The Great Gig in the Sky"
Fmaj7
G7
D7#9
D7♭9
Bm
rit.
calls the faithful to their knees to hear the softly spoken magic spell.
let ring
rit.

Time for Me to Fly

Words and Music by Kevin Cronin

Gtr. 1: w/ Rhy. Fig. 2, simile
Aadd4
swal - lowed my pride for you, I lived and lied for you, but a
Gadd9
D Gadd9/D D Gadd9/D D
you still make me feel like a thief. You got me
Aadd4
Gadd9
D
steal - in' your love a - way 'cause a you nev - er give it.
Gtr. 1
Rhy. Fig. 3
Aadd4
Gadd9
D
Peel - in' the years a - way and a we can't re - live it. Oh,
Gadd9
D
Gadd9
D
I make you laugh and a you make me cry.

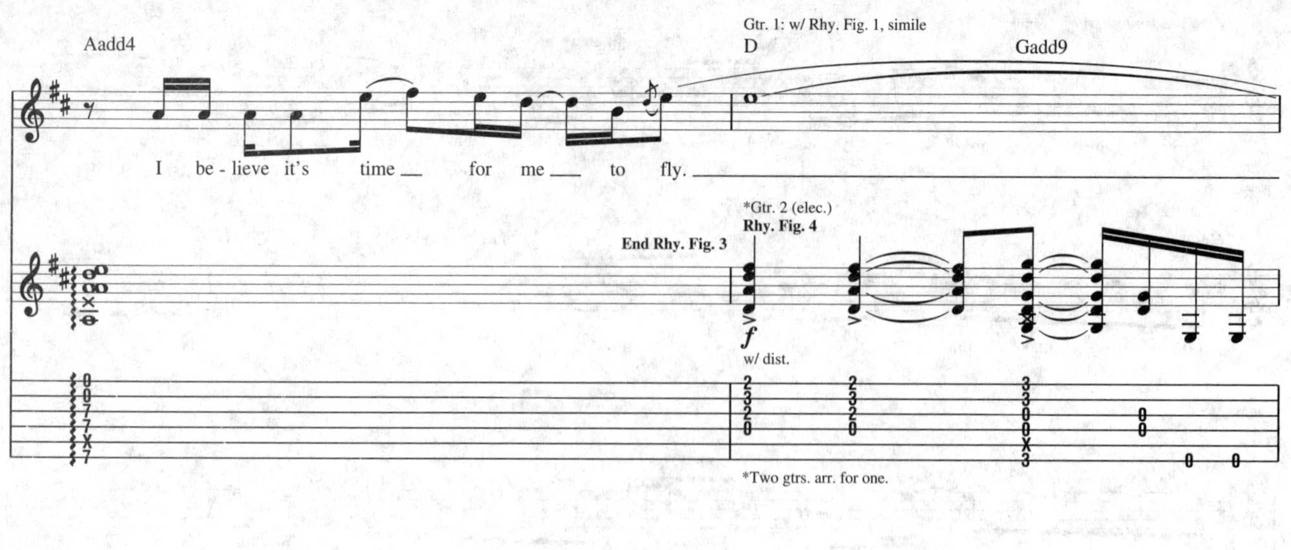

Aadd4
Gtr. 1: w/ Rhy. Fig. 1, simile
D
Gadd9
I be - lieve it's time for me to fly.
*Gtr. 2 (elec.)
Rhy. Fig. 4
End Rhy. Fig. 3
w/ dist.
*Two gtrs. arr. for one.

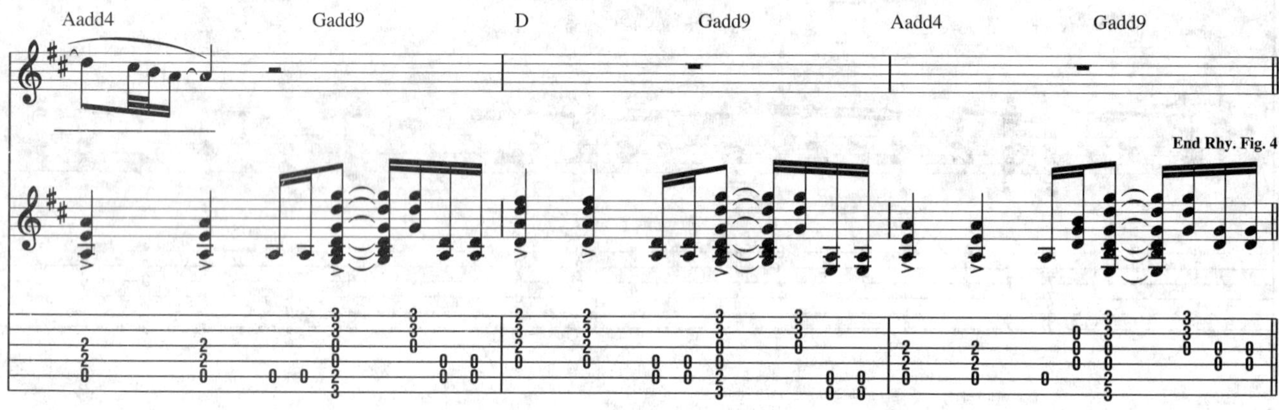

Aadd4
Gadd9
D
Gadd9
Aadd4
Gadd9
End Rhy. Fig. 4

Verse
Gtr. 1: w/ Rhy. Fig. 2, 2 times, simile
D
Aadd4
2. You said we'd work it out. You said that you had no doubt, that
Rhy. Fig. 5

Gadd9
D
Gadd9/D
D
Gadd9/D
D
deep down we were real - ly in love. Oh, but
End Rhy. Fig. 5

Gtr. 2: w/ Rhy. Fig. 5, simile
Aadd4
I'm tired of hold - in' on to a feel - in' I know is gone.
Gadd9
D Gadd9/D D Gadd9/D D
I do be - lieve that I've had e - nough. I've had e -
Gtr. 1: w/ Rhy. Fig. 3
Aadd4 Gadd9 D Aadd4
nough of the false - ness of a worn out re - la - tion. E - nough of the jeal - ous - y and the
Gtr. 2
Gadd9 D Gadd9 D Gadd9 D
in - tol - er - a - tion. Oh, I make you laugh and a you make me cry.
Aadd4 D Gadd9 D
Gtr. 1
I be - lieve it's time for me to fly. (Time for me to fly.
21

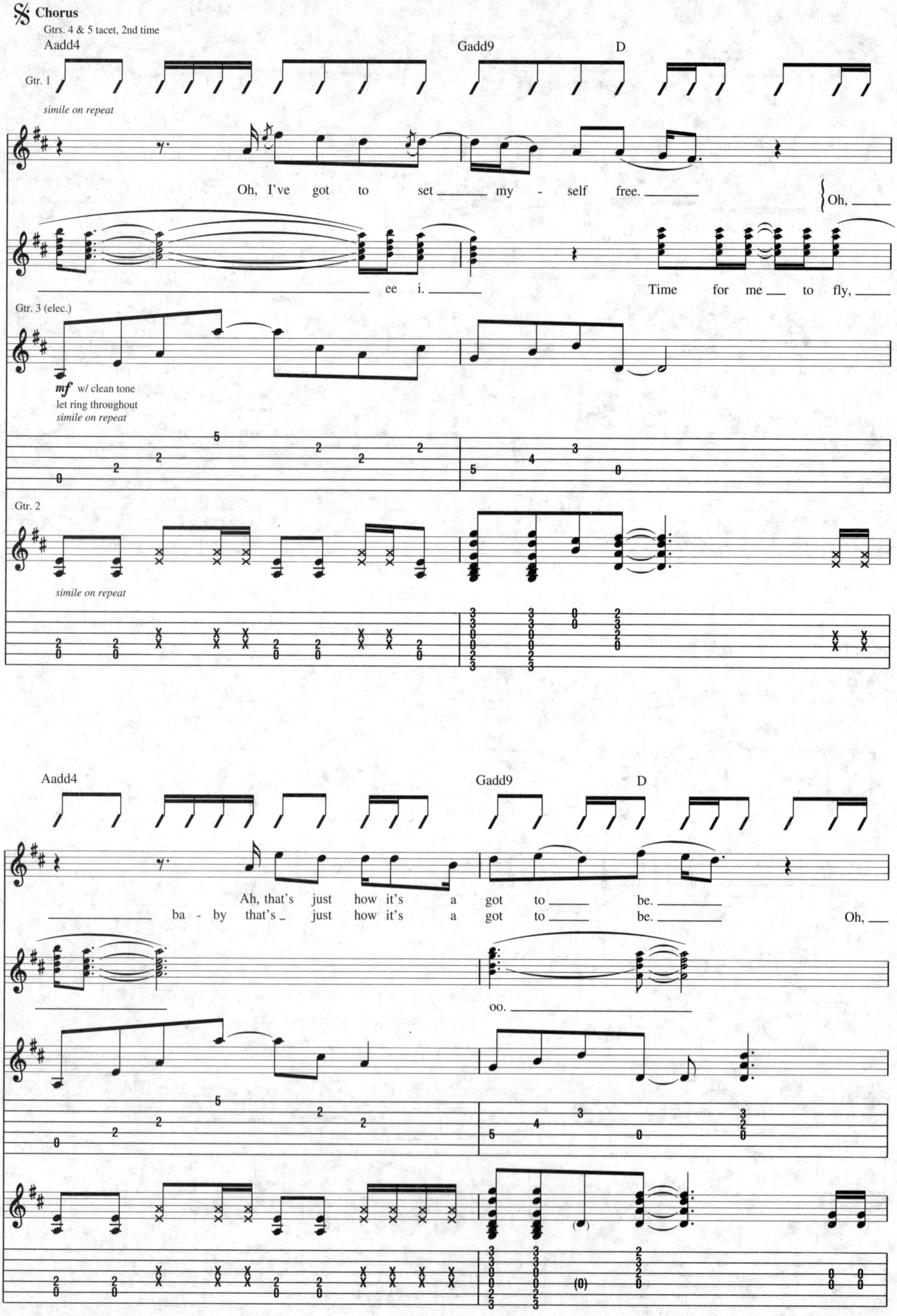

Chorus

Gtrs. 4 & 5 tacet, 2nd time

Aadd4 | Gadd9 D

Gtr. 1

simile on repeat

Oh, I've got to set my - self free. Oh,

ee i. Time for me to fly,

Gtr. 3 (elec.)

mf w/ clean tone

let ring throughout

simile on repeat

0 2 2 5 2 2 2 | 5 4 3 0

Gtr. 2

simile on repeat

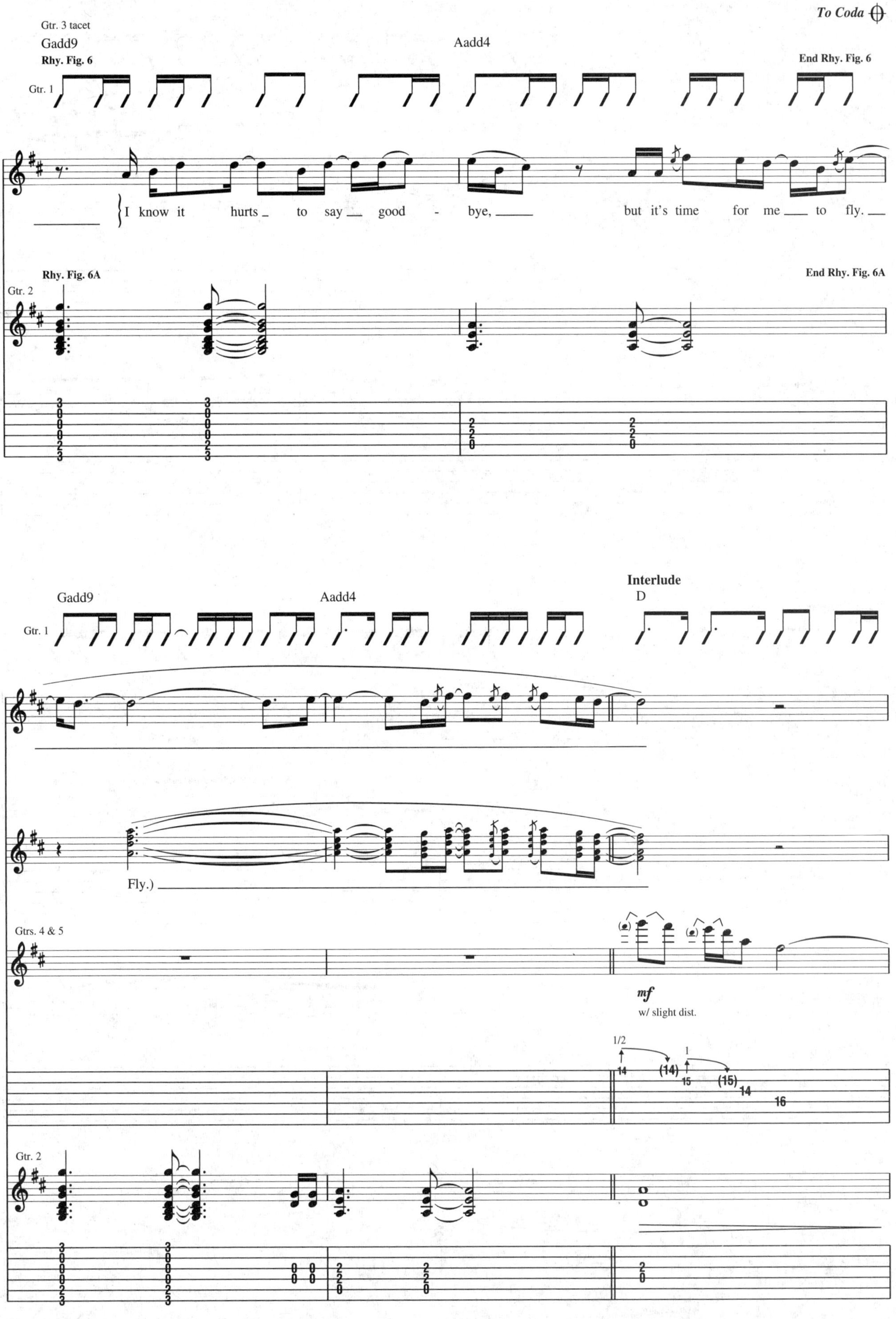

Gadd9 Aadd4

Interlude

D

Gtr. 1

Fly.)

Gtrs. 4 & 5

mf

w/ slight dist.

1/2 1

Gtr. 2

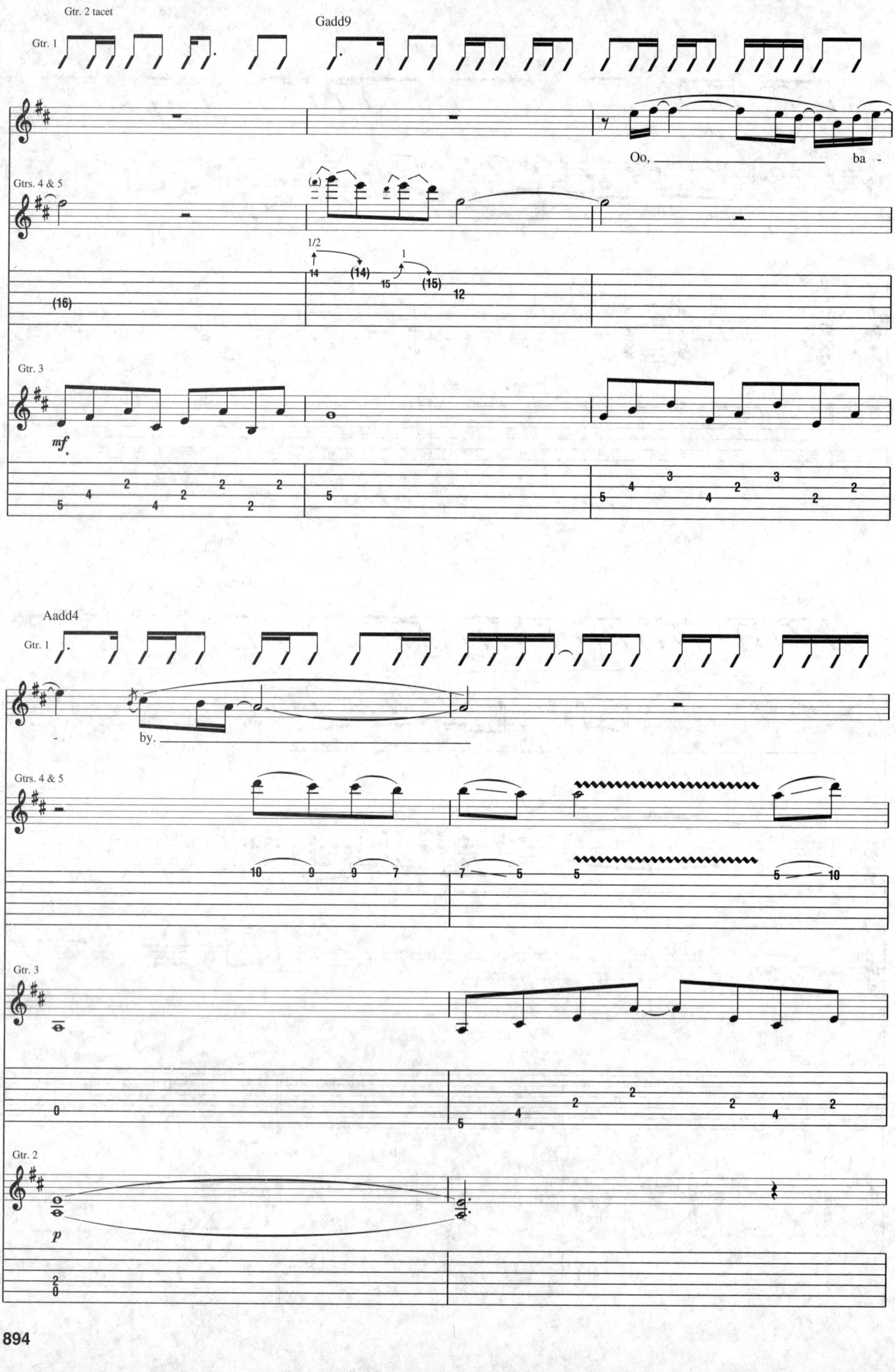

Aadd4

Gtr. 1

- by.

Gtrs. 4 & 5

Gtr. 3

Gtr. 2

p

D.S. al Coda
D
Well, don't you know it's time for me to fly.
8va
Gtr. 4
Gtr. 5
divisi
1/2 1/2
mf
f
Coda
Gtr. 1: w/ Rhy. Fig. 6, 2 times, simile
Gtr. 2: w/ Rhy. Fig. 6A, 1 1/2 times, simile
Gadd9
Aadd4
It's time for me to fly,
Ah,
ah.
Gadd9
A5
ee i ee i.
It's time for me to fly.
Gtr. 2

Gtrs. 1 & 2: w/ Rhy. Figs. 1 & 4, 1 1/2 times, simile
D
Gadd9
Aadd4
Gadd9
D
Gadd9
It's time for me to fly.
Oo.)
(It's time for me to fly.
It's time for me to fly.

Aadd4
Gadd9
D
Gadd9
It's time for me to fly,
babe.)
It's time for me to fly.

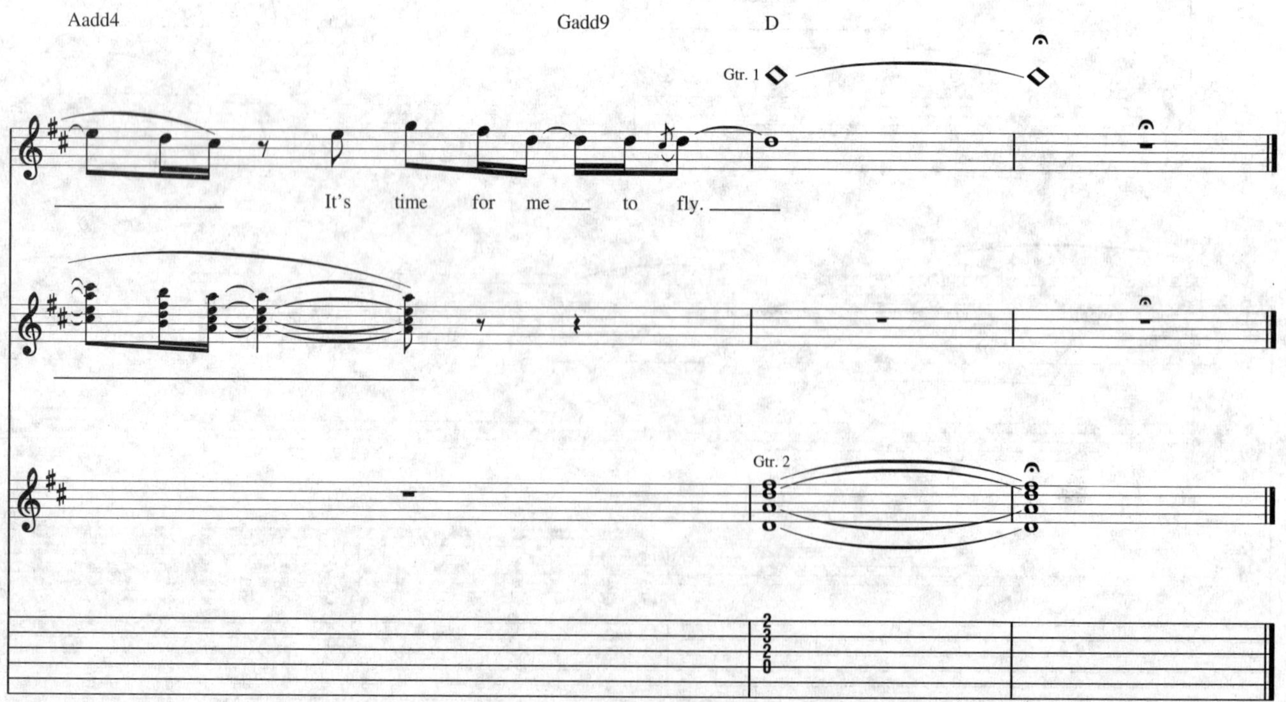
Aadd4
Gadd9
D
Gtr. 1
It's time for me to fly.
Gtr. 2
2
3
2
0

Time in a Bottle

Words and Music by Jim Croce

*Symbols in parentheses represent chord names respective to capoed guitar. Symbols above reflect actual sounding chord. Capoed fret is "0" in tab.

Verse

A Tempo

Dm (Am) Dm/C♯ (Am/G♯) Dm/C (Am/G) Dm/B (Am/F♯)

I could save time in a bot - tle, the
I could make days last for - ev - er, if
I had a box just for wish - es and

Gm6/B♭ (Dm6/F) A7 (E7)

first thing that I'd like to do is to
words could make wish - es come true, I'd
dreams that had nev - er come true, the

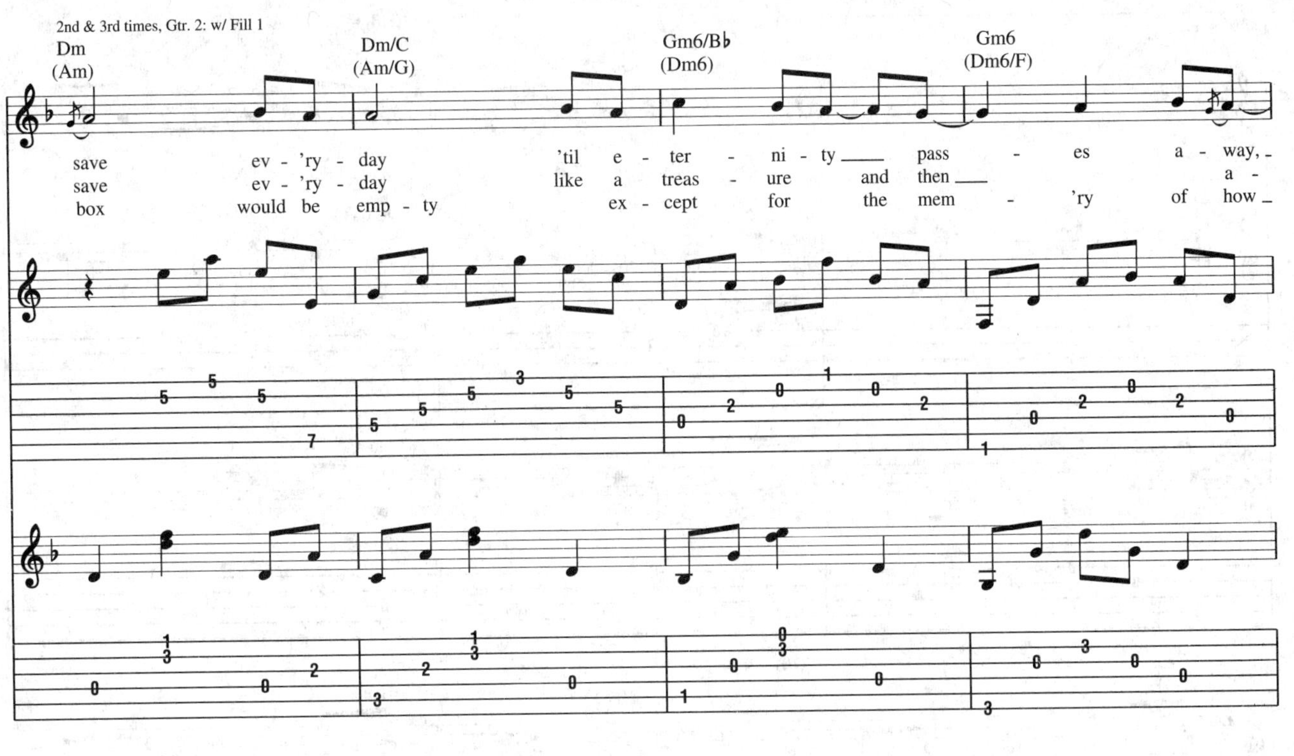

2nd & 3rd times, Gtr. 2: w/ Fill 1
Dm
(Am)
Dm/C
(Am/G)
Gm6/B♭
(Dm6)
Gm6
(Dm6/F)
save ev - 'ry - day 'til e - ter - ni - ty pass - es a - way,
save ev - 'ry - day like a treas - ure and then a -
box would be emp - ty ex - cept for the mem - 'ry of how

2nd & 3rd times, Gtr. 2: w/ Fill 2
Dm/F
(Am)
Gm
(Dm)
1.
A7
(E7)
just to spend them with you.
gain, I would spend them with you.
they were an - swered by you.
2. If

Fill 1
Gtr. 2

Fill 2
Gtr. 2

2.
A7
(E7)
Bridge
D
(A)
But there nev - er seems to
Riff A1
Riff A
D/C#
(A/G#)
D/B
(A/F#)
D/A
(A/E)
be e - nough time to do the things you want to do once you
G6
(D6/F#)
Dadd9/F#
(Aadd9/E)
Em7
(Bm7)
A
(E)
find them.
I've
End Riff A1
End Riff A

Gtrs. 1 & 2: w/ Riffs A & A1
D
(A)
D/C♯
(A/G♯)
Bm7
(A/F♯)
looked a - round e - nough to know that you're the one I

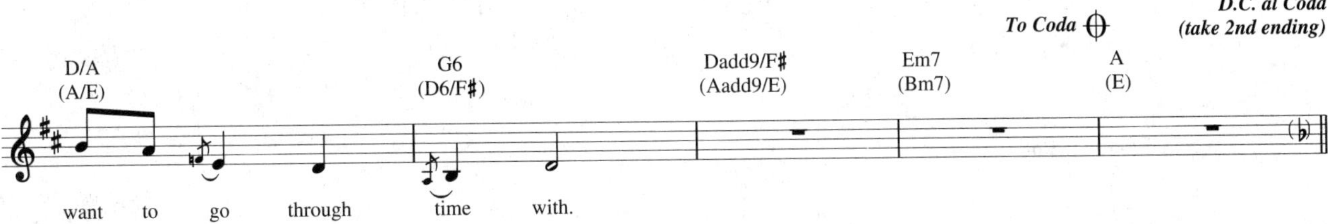
To Coda
D.C. al Coda
(take 2nd ending)
D/A
(A/E)
G6
(D6/F♯)
Dadd9/F♯
(Aadd9/E)
Em7
(Bm7)
A
(E)
want to go through time with.

Coda
A
(E)
Outro
Dm(add9)
Am(add9)
Gtr. 2
Harm.
Gtr. 1
Harm.

Harm.
Harm.
Harm.
Harm.

Today

Words and Music by Billy Corgan

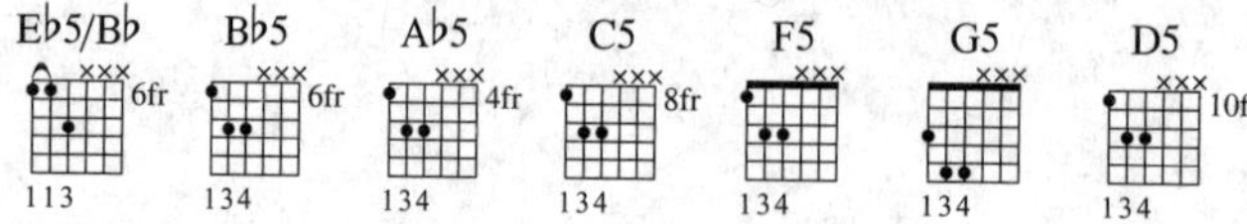

Intro

Moderate Rock ♩ = 84

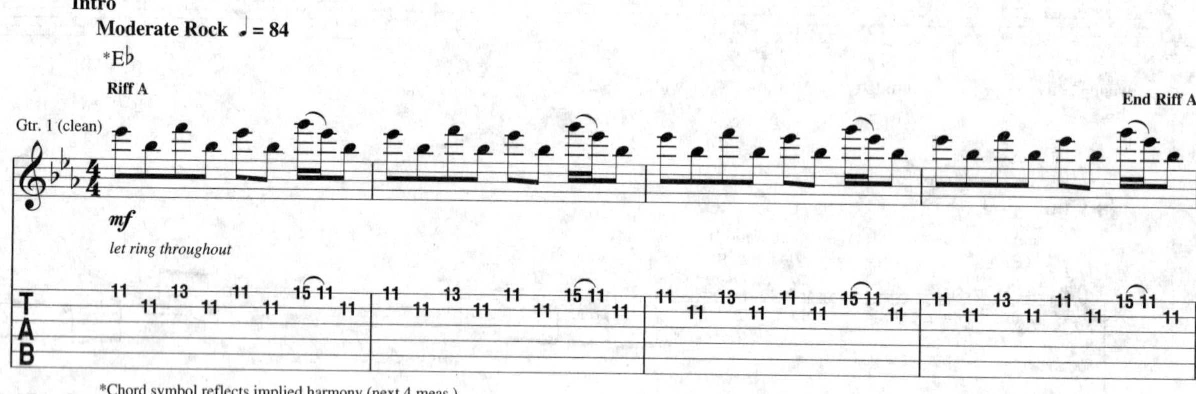

*Chord symbol reflects implied harmony (next 4 meas.).

**Doubled throughout

Eb5/Bb
Bb5
E
C5
E
Ab5
Bb5 Eb5/Bb
Bb5
E
Ab5
Bb5
open
let ring
8va
*fdbk
Gtr. 1
Gtr. 2
divisi
*Microphonic fdbk., not caused by string vibration.
Verse
Gtrs. 1 - 4 tacet
Eb5/Bb
Bb
Ab
1. To - day is the great - est day I've ev - er known.
Rhy. Fig. 1
Gtr. 5 (slight dist.)
mp
let ring throughout
Eb/Bb
Bb
Ab
Ebsus2/Bb
Bb
Can't live for to - mor - row, to - mor - row's much too long. I'll burn my eyes

A♭
E♭sus2/B♭
B♭
B C
out
be - fore I get out.
End Rhy. Fig. 1

Bridge

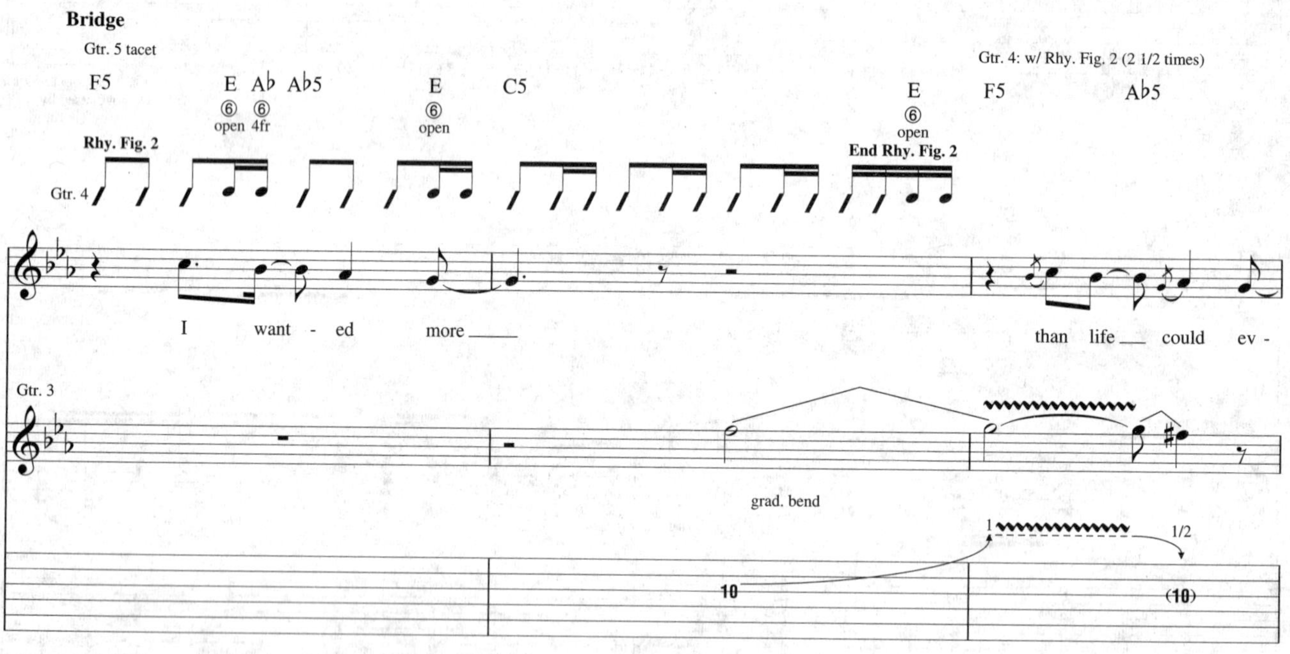
Gtr. 5 tacet
F5
E A♭ A♭5
⑥ ⑥
open 4fr
E
⑥
open
C5
Gtr. 4: w/ Rhy. Fig. 2 (2 1/2 times)
E
⑥
open
F5
A♭5
Rhy. Fig. 2
End Rhy. Fig. 2
Gtr. 4
I want - ed more
than life could ev -
Gtr. 3
grad. bend
1
1/2

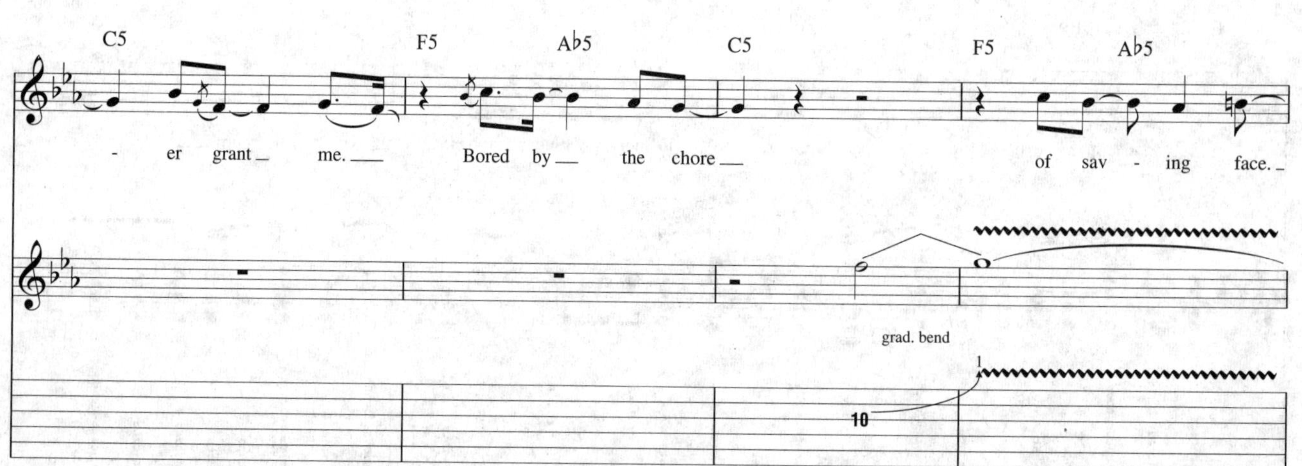
C5
F5
A♭5
C5
F5
A♭5
- er grant me.
Bored by the chore
of sav - ing face.
grad. bend
1

Verse
Gtrs. 3 & 4 tacet
Gtr. 5: w/ Rhy. Fig. 1
G5
E D D5
open 10fr
Gtr. 4
E♭5/B♭
B♭
A♭
2. To - day is the great - est day I've nev - er known.
Gtr. 3
Gtr. 1

E♭/B♭
B♭
A♭
E♭sus2/B♭
B♭
Can't wait for to - mor - row, I might not have that long.
I'll tear my heart

A♭
E♭sus2/B♭
B♭
B C
out
be - fore I get out.

Bridge
Gtr. 1 tacet
F5 A♭5 E♭5/B♭ B♭5
Gtr. 4: w/ Rhy. Fig. 3 (2 1/2 times)
F5 A♭5
Pink rib - bon scars ___ that nev - er for - get. ___ I tried _ so hard _
Gtr. 4
Rhy. Fig. 3
End Rhy. Fig. 3
E♭5/B♭ B♭5 F5 A♭5 E♭5/B♭ B♭5 F5 A♭5
___ to cleanse _ these re - grets. ___ My an - gel wings ___ were bruised _ and re - strained. _ My bel - ly stings. ___
Chorus
G5 D5 E♭5/B♭ B♭5 E♭5/B♭ A♭5 G5
___ To - day ___ is, ___ to - day ___ is, ___
Gtr. 3
Riff B
End Riff B
mp
*w/ octaver & wah-wah as filter
1/2
Gtr. 4
*Octaver set for one octave below.
Gtr. 3: w/ Riff B (3 times)
E♭5/B♭ B♭5 E♭5/B♭ A♭5 G5 E♭5/B♭ B♭5
to - day ___ is, ___ the great - est day, ee, yeah, ___ ee, oo. ___
Gtr 4
(cont. in slashes)

C5
E
Ab5
Bb5
Eb5/Bb
Bb5
E
C5
⑥ open
Gtr. 4
Oo, ay, ah,
oo.
Gtr. 3
octaver off
1/2
Bridge
Gtr. 4: w/ Rhy. Fig. 2 (3 times)
F5
Ab5
I want to turn you on.
wah-wah off
grad. bend
fdbk.
I want to turn you...

Outro
Gtr. 2: w/ Riff A (2 times)
Gtr. 3 tacet
Gtr. 4: w/ Rhy. Fig. 4 (2 1/2 times)
E♭5/B♭ B♭5 E C5 E A♭5 B♭5 E♭5/B♭ B♭5
Rhy. Fig. 4
open
End Rhy. Fig. 4
To - day is the great - est, to - day is the great -
(Yeah, yeah, yeah.)
*w/ dist.

C5 A♭5 B♭5 E♭5/B♭ B♭5 C5 A♭5 B♭5
- est day. To - day is the great - est day that
Gtr. 3
wah-wah off
w/ wah-wah

Gtr. 3 tacet
E♭5/B♭ B♭5 C5 E A♭5 B♭5 E♭5/B♭
open
I have ev - er real - ly known.
Gtr. 2

Tube Snake Boogie

Words and Music by Billy F Gibbons, Dusty Hill and Frank Beard

Intro

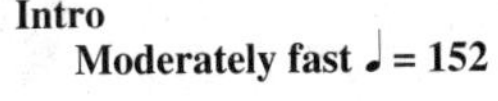

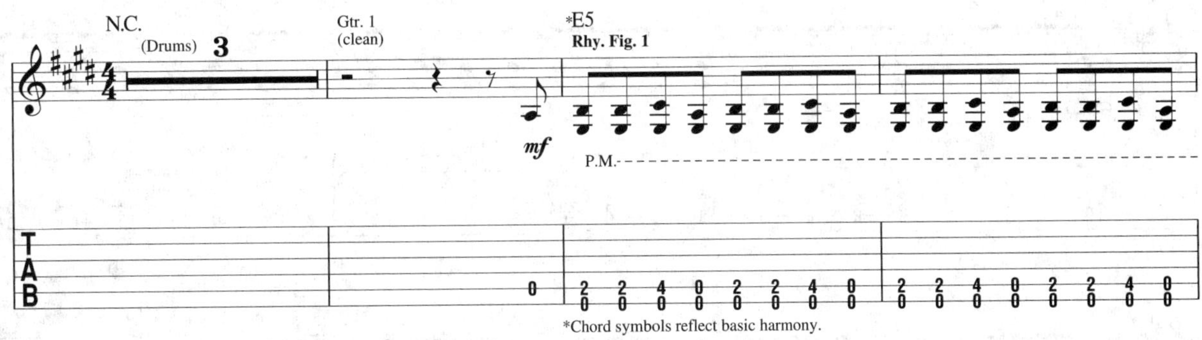

*Chord symbols reflect basic harmony.

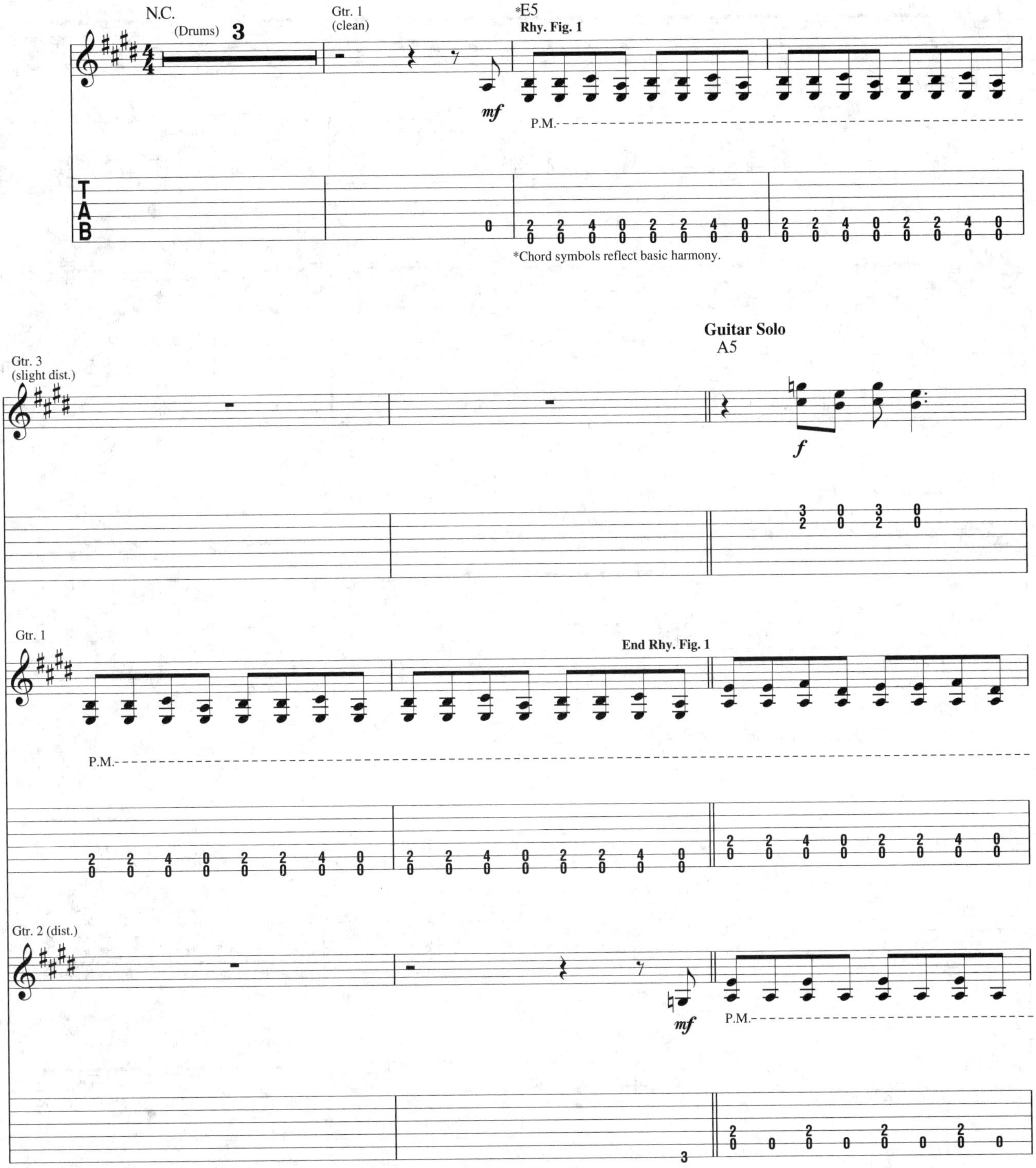

Guitar Solo

A5

Gtr. 3 (slight dist.)

f

Gtr. 1

End Rhy. Fig. 1

P.M.

Gtr. 2 (dist.)

mf

P.M.

let ring
P.H.
P.M.
P.M.
Gtr. 3
Gtrs. 1 & 2: w/ Rhy. Fig. 1
E5
1/2
1
1/2
Gtr. 3
B5
A5
let ring
1/4
Rhy. Fig. 2
Gtrs. 1 & 2
P.M.

*Chord symbols reflect combined harmony.

Gtrs. 1 & 2: w/ Rhy. Fig. 2
B5
Bsus2/4
B
Asus2/4
A
Gtr. 3 tacet
E5
B7#9
boo - gie lit - tle ba - by,
boo - gie woo - gie ba - by,
boo - gie woo - gie all night long.
Gtr. 3
End Rhy. Fig. 4
Guitar Solo
Gtrs. 1 & 2: w/ Rhy. Fig. 3
Gtr. 3
E5
w/ dist.
let ring
F#5
G5
G#5
A5
E5
let ring
Gtrs. 1 & 2: w/ Rhy. Fig. 2 (1st meas.)
B5
let ring
Gtr. 3
A5
E5
let ring
N.C.
grad. bend
let ring
Gtrs. 1 & 2
P.M.

Gtrs. 1 & 2: w/ Rhy. Fig. 3
Gtr. 3
E5
F#5
G5
G#5
grad. bend
semi-harm.
1/4
A5
E5
let ring
Gtrs. 1 & 2: w/ Rhy. Fig. 2
B5
A5
E5
B7#9
1/2
Verse
Gtr. 3 tacet
N.C.
3. I got a gal, she lives on the hill.
She won't do it but her
Gtrs. 1 & 2: w/ Rhy. Fig. 3 (last 4 meas.)
Gtr. 3: w/ Rhy. Fig. 4
A5
A
A
sis - ter will. When she boo - gie, she do the
E5
E
E
Gtrs. 1 & 2: w/ Rhy. Fig. 2
B5
B
tube snake boo - gie. Well, now boo - gie lit - tle ba - by,
A
E5
B7#9
boo - gie woo - gie all night long. Blow your top, blow your top.
(Blow your top.)

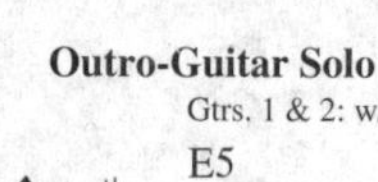
Outro-Guitar Solo

Gtrs. 1 & 2: w/ Rhy. Fig. 3
E5
F♯5
G5
G♯5
Gtr. 3
let ring
let ring

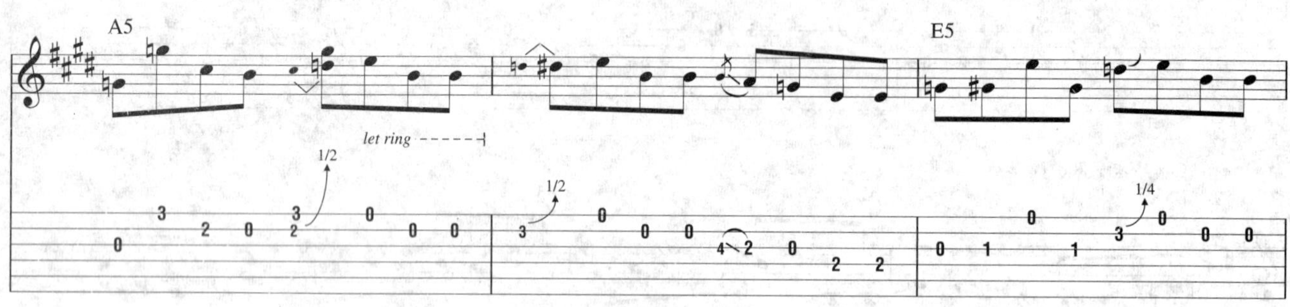
A5
E5
let ring
1/2
1/2
1/4

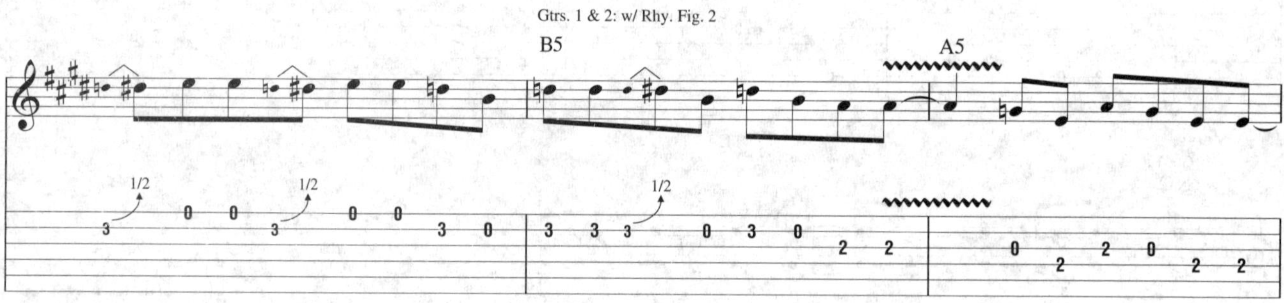
Gtrs. 1 & 2: w/ Rhy. Fig. 2
B5
A5
1/2
1/2
1/2

Gtrs. 1 & 2: w/ Rhy. Fig. 3
E5
B7♯9
E5
1/2
1/2

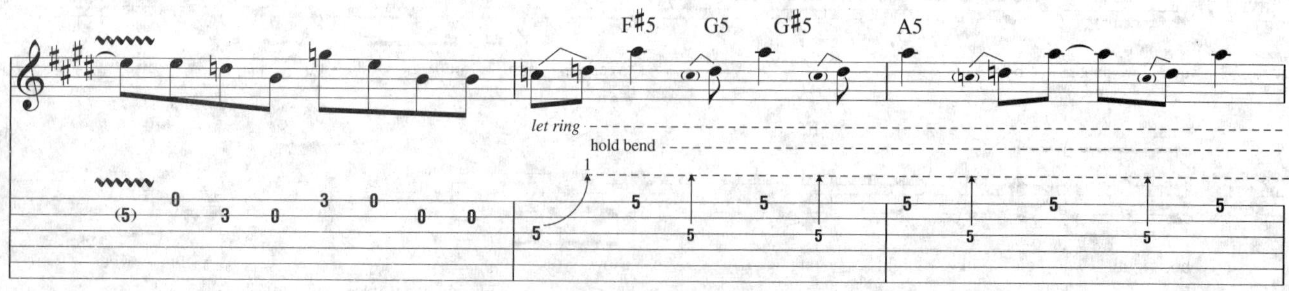
F♯5
G5
G♯5
A5
let ring
hold bend
1

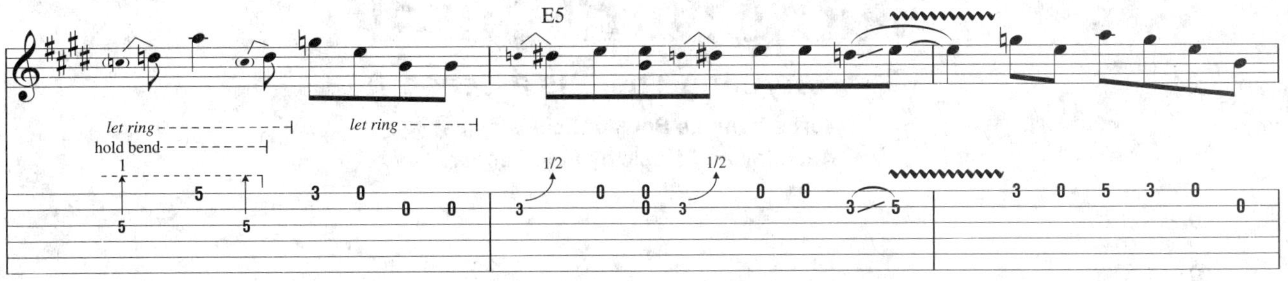
E5
let ring
hold bend
let ring
1
1/2
1/2

Gtrs. 1 & 2: w/ Rhy. Fig. 2
B5
A5
E5
1/4

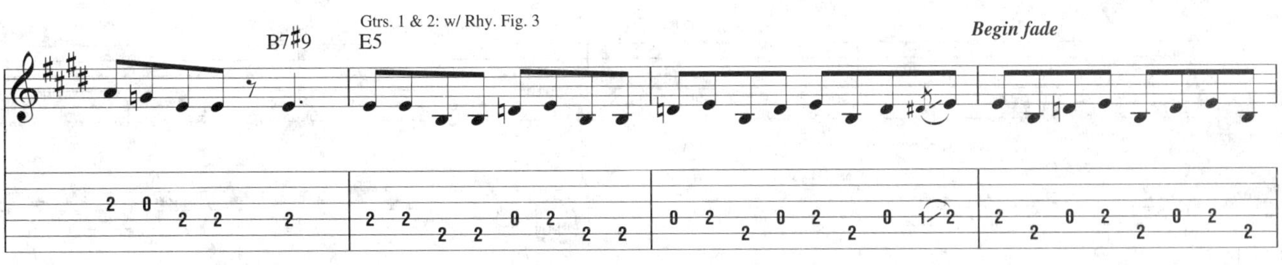
Gtrs. 1 & 2: w/ Rhy. Fig. 3
B7♯9
E5
Begin fade

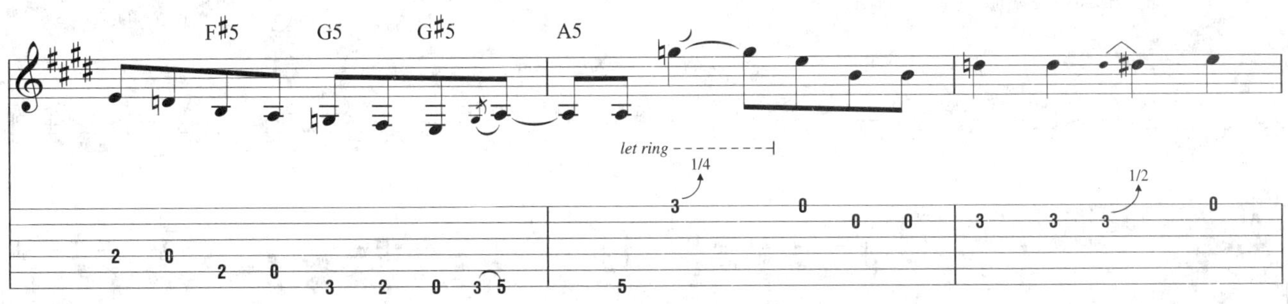
F♯5
G5
G♯5
A5
let ring
1/4
1/2

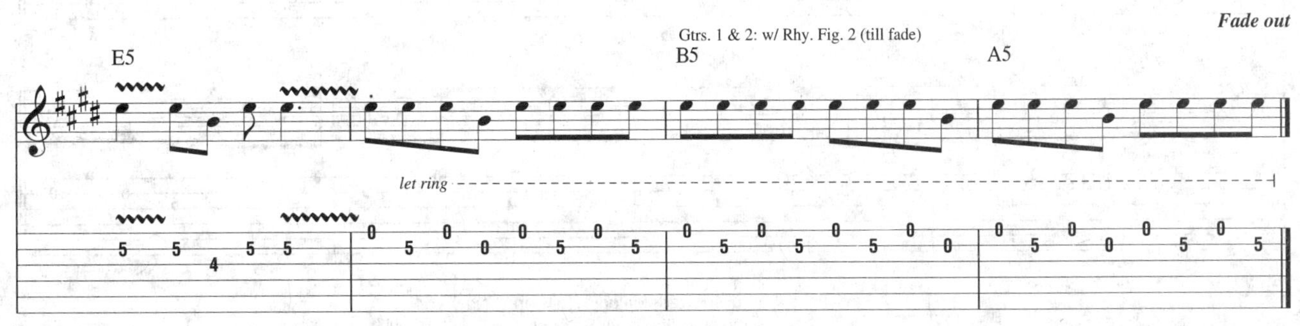
Fade out
Gtrs. 1 & 2: w/ Rhy. Fig. 2 (till fade)
E5
B5
A5
let ring

Turn! Turn! Turn!

(To Everything There Is a Season)

Words from the Book of Ecclesiastes
Adaption and Music by Pete Seeger

Gtr. 2; Drop D Tuning:
①= E ④= D
②= B ⑤= A
③= G ⑥= D

Intro

Moderate Folk-Rock ♩ = 120

* Chord symbols reflect combined tonality.

*Vocs. doubled throughout

Chorus
D6/9
G6
D6/9/F#
Asus2/E
Em7
D
G6
D6/9/F#
thing turn, turn, turn, there is a sea - son turn, turn,
*Gtrs. 1 & 3
Gtr. 2
Rhy. Fig. 2
P.M.
*composite arrangement
Asus2/E
Em7
G6
D6/9/F#
Em
A
Asus4
D
Dsus4
D
turn, and a time to ev'ry pur-pose un - der Heav - en.

Verse
D G5 A A7 D Dsus4 A A7
1. A time to be born, a time _ to die. A time to plant, a time _ to
2. A time to build up, a time to break down. A time to dance, a time _ to
3. A time of love, a time _ of hate. A time of war, a time _ of
4. A time to gain, a time _ to lose. A time to rend, a time _ to
Rhy. Fig. 3
D Dsus4 A A7 D Em7 G6 D6/9/F#
reap. A time to kill, a time _ to heal. A time to laugh, _ a
mourn. A time to cast a - way stones. A time to gath - er
peace. A time you may em - brace. A time to re - frain
sow. A time for love, a time _ for hate. A time for peace, _ I

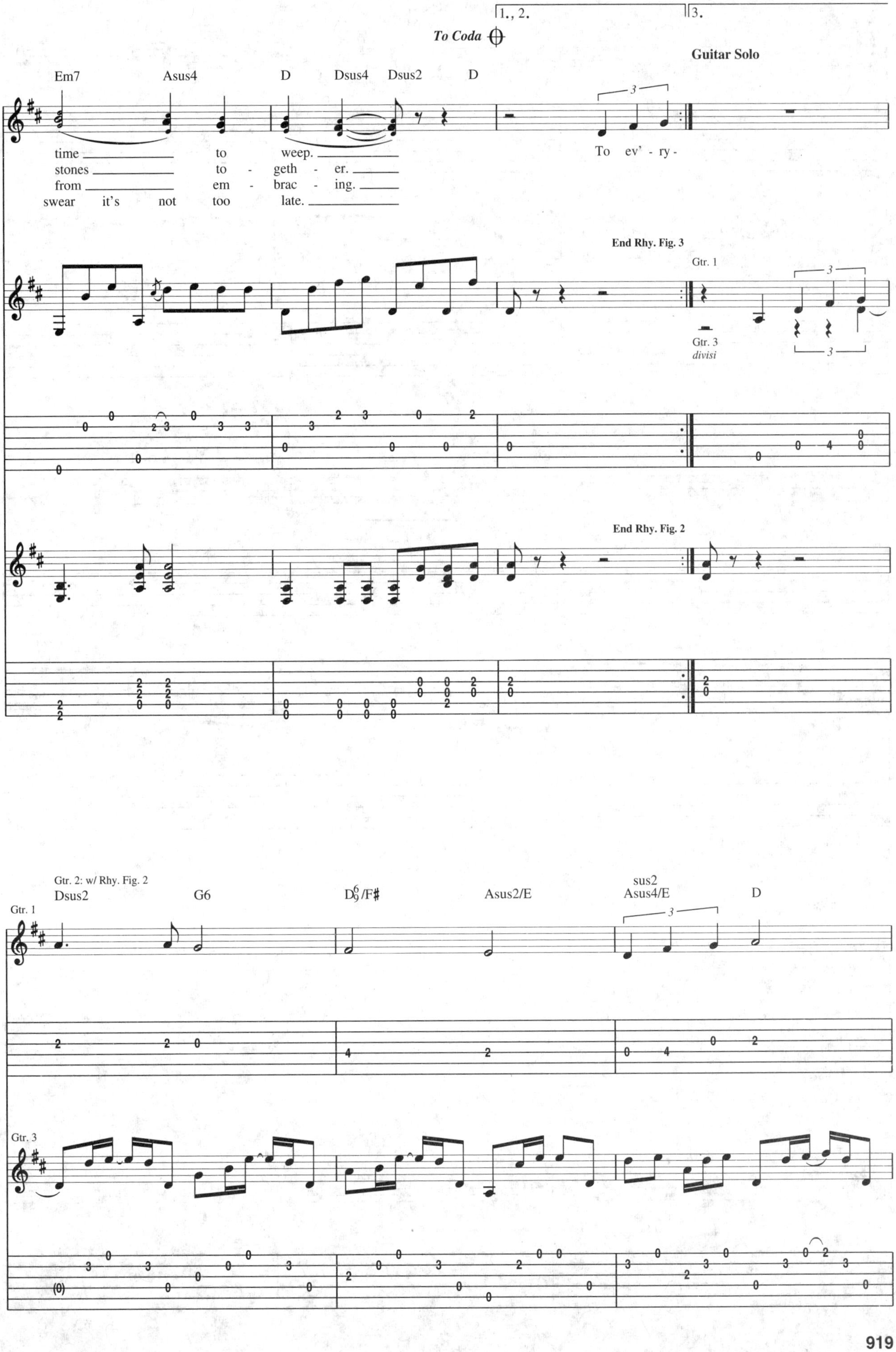

1., 2. | 3.

To Coda ⊕

Guitar Solo

Em7 Asus4 D Dsus4 Dsus2 D

time ______ to weep. ______ To ev' - ry -

stones ______ to - geth - er. ______

from ______ em - brac - ing. ______

swear it's not too late. ______

End Rhy. Fig. 3

Gtr. 1

Gtr. 3 *divisi*

End Rhy. Fig. 2

G6
D^6_9/F#
Asus2/E
sus2
Asus4/E
G6
D^6_9/F#
Em7
Asus4
D
Dsus4
Dsus2
D
D
Dsus4
Dsus2
Gtr. 3: w/ Rhy. Fig. 3, simile
A
A7
D
Dsus4
A
A7
D
Dsus4
A
A7
D
Em7

G6 D$^6_9$/F♯ Em7 Asus4 D Dsus2 Dsus4 D

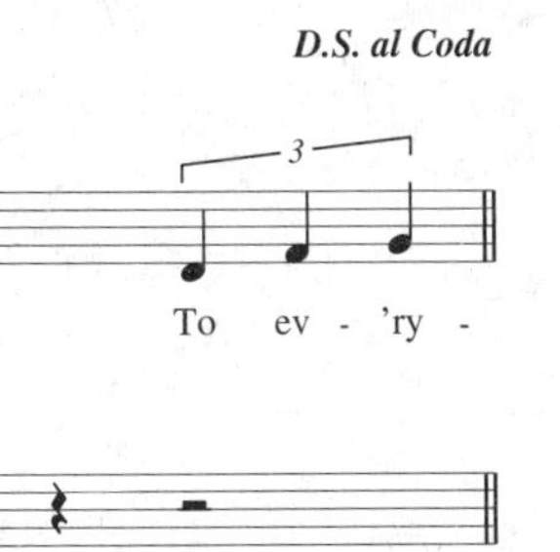

𝄌 *Coda*

Outro

Gtrs. 2 & 3: w/ Rhy. Figs. 1 & 1A, till fade, simile

Dsus2 G6 F♯m11 Em Bm/D A

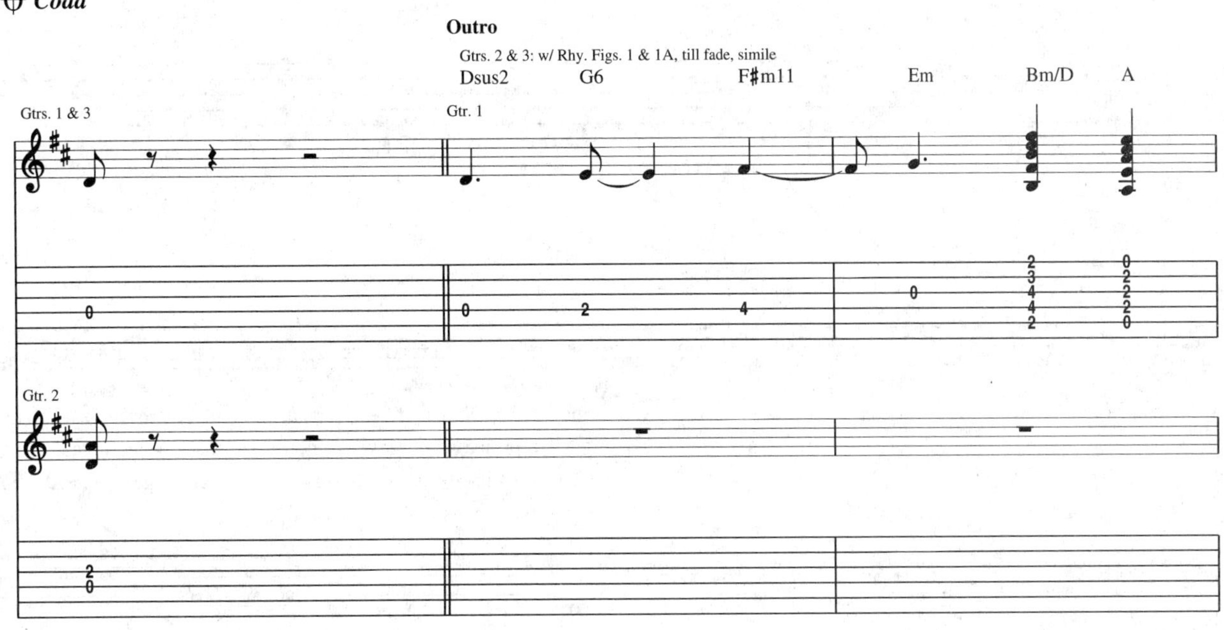

Begin Fade

Dsus4 G6 F♯m11 Em Bm/D A Dsus4 G6 F♯m11 Em Bm/D A

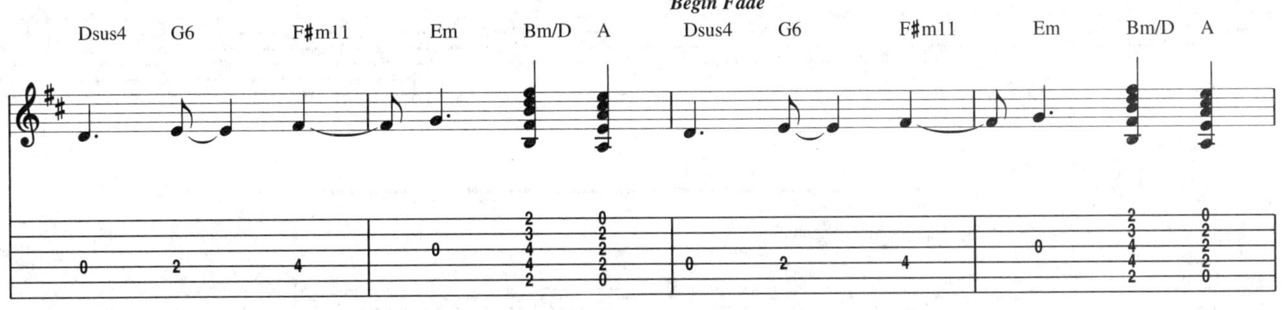

Fade Out

Dsus4 G6 F♯m11 Em Bm/D A Dsus4 G6 F♯m11 Em Bm/D A

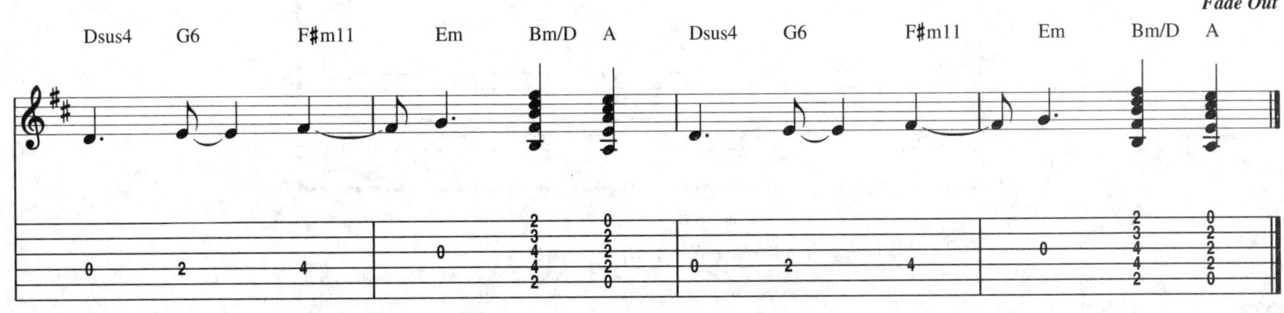

Two Princes

Words and Music by Spin Doctors

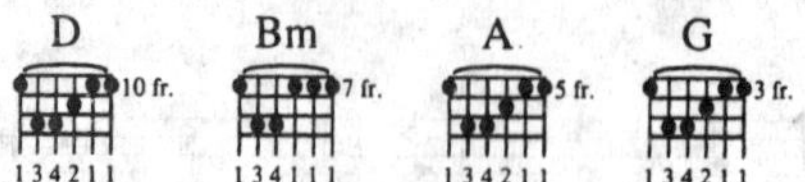

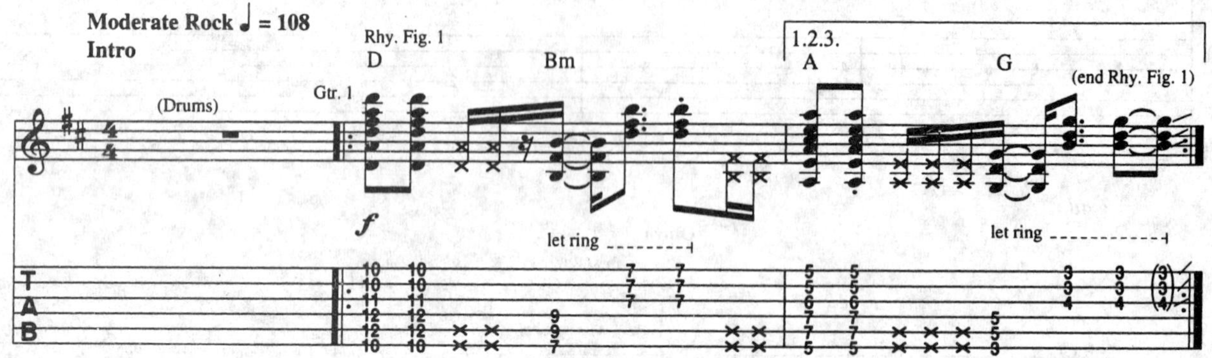

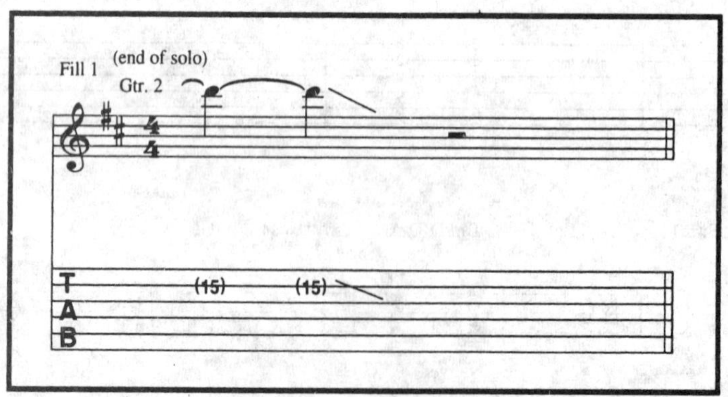

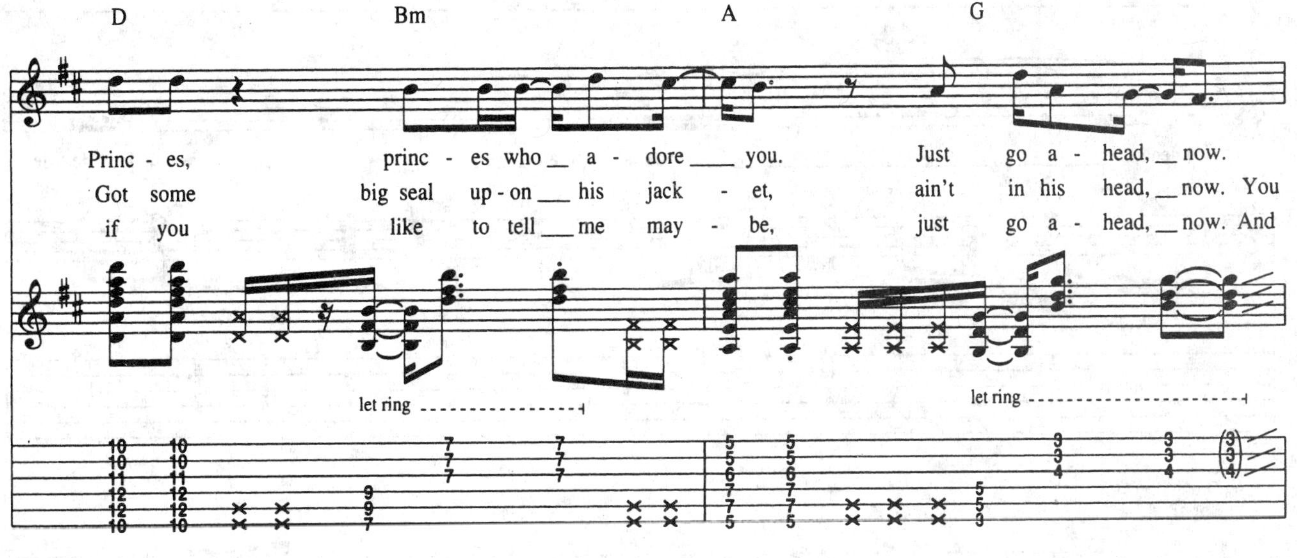
D
Bm
A
G
Princ - es, princ - es who __ a - dore ____ you. Just go a - head, __ now.
Got some big seal up - on __ his jack - et, ain't in his head, __ now. You
if you like to tell __ me may - be, just go a - head, __ now. And
let ring
let ring

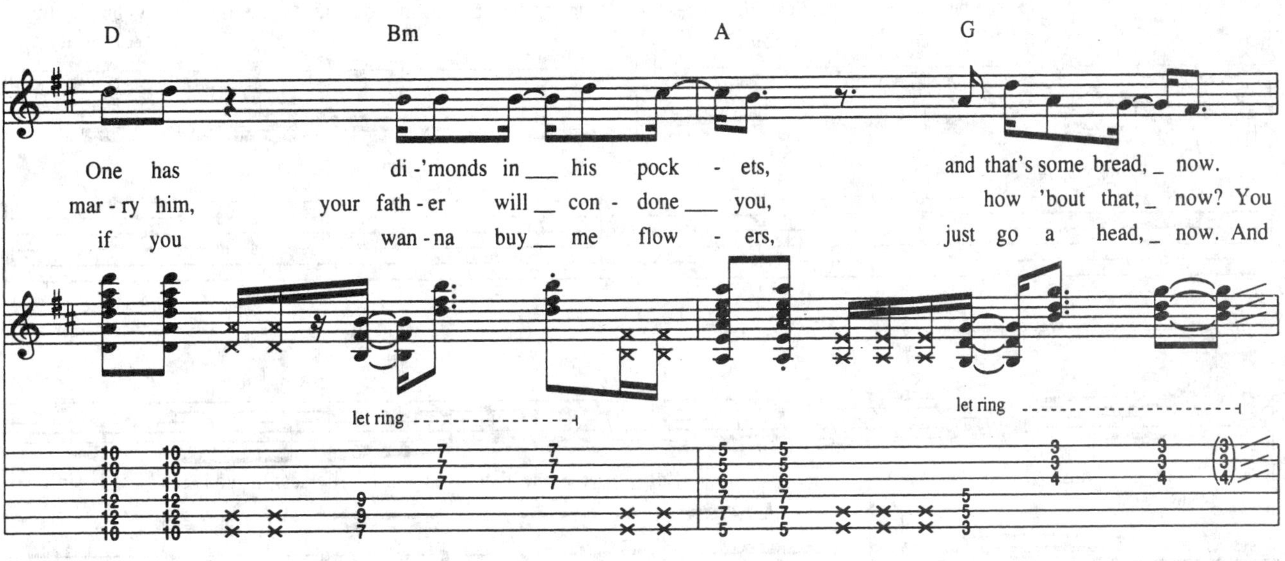
D
Bm
A
G
One has di - 'monds in __ his pock - ets, and that's some bread, _ now.
mar - ry him, your fath - er will __ con - done ___ you, how 'bout that, _ now? You
if you wan - na buy __ me flow - ers, just go a head, _ now. And
let ring
let ring

D
Bm
A
G
3rd time to Coda I
This one, said he wants to buy __ you rock - ets, ain't in his head, _ now.
mar - ry me, your fath - er will __ dis - own ___ you, he'll eat his hat, __ now.
if you like to talk __ for hours, ____ just go a - head, __ now.
let ring
let ring

1.
D
Bm7
A
G
Yeah, yeah, yeah. De de de
Rhy. Fig. 2
let ring
D
Bm7
A
G
dit. D-be, be be de. Be-dee-dl-y de-bu du-bu du-bu du-bu du-bu du-bu du-bu du-bu.
(end Rhy. Fig. 2)
let ring
2.
G
D
G
Mar-ry him or mar-ry me. I'm the one that loves you ba-by, can't you see? I ain't
Rhy. Fig. 3
A
2nd time to Coda II
got no fu-ture or fam-'ly tree, but I know what a prince and lov-er ought to be.
(end Rhy. Fig. 3)

D. S. al Coda I
Coda I
Guitar Solo
D
Bm
Gtr. 1
Gtr. 2
I know what a prince and lov - er ought to be. __ Said. . .
A
G
full
1/2
w/Rhy. Fig. 3 (Gtr. 1)
hold bend

A
hold bend
hold bend
let ring
full
full
full
Gtr. 1
A
D. S. (take 2nd ending) al Coda II
Said. . .
(cont. in Fill 1)
hold bend
let ring
let ring
full
full
1/2
full
1/2
full
Coda II
A
C5
A5
N.C.
D
N.C.
I know what a prince and lov - er ought to be.
Said if you want to call _ me ba -
(Gtr. tacet)
1/4
by, just go a - head, _ now. And if you like to tell _ me may - be, just go a - head _ now. And
if you wan - na buy _ me flow - ers, just go a - head, _ now. And if you like to talk _ for hours, _
w/Rhy. Fig. 2 (2 times)
D
Bm7
A
G
just go a - head, _ now. And if you want to call _ me ba - by, just go a - head, _ now. And

D Bm7 A G D Bm7
if you like to tell __ me may - be, just go a - head, _ now. And if you like to buy _ me flow -
A G D Bm7 A G
ers, just go a - head, __ now. And if you like to talk __ for hours, ____ just go a - head, __now.
D Bm A G
w/Rhy. Fig. 1 (4 times)
If you want to call me ___ ba - by, just go a - head, __ now.
D Bm A G
And if you'd like to tell ___ me ___ may - be, just go a - head, ___ now.
D Bm A G D Bm
If you want to buy me flow - ers, just go a - head, __ now. And if you like to talk for hours, _
A G D Bm7 A G
w/Rhy. Fig. 2 (2 times)
__ just go a - head, _ now. Oh, ____ ba - by. Oh, _
(Just go a - head, _ now.)
D Bm7 A G D Bm7
____ oh, ____ just, just go a - head, ___ now. Oh, ____ your __ maj -
(Just go a - head, ___now.)
A G D Bm7
es - ty, ____ come on __ for - get ___ the king ___ and
(Just go a - head, __ now.)
A G D Bm7 A G
Repeat and fade
w/Rhy. Fig. 1
(cont. Lead voc. ad lib)
mar - ry me. ____ (Just go a - head, __ now.)
(Just go a - head, __ now.)

Unchained

Words and Music by David Lee Roth, Edward Van Halen, Alex Van Halen and Michael Anthony

Gtr. 1: Drop D tuning, down 1/2 step:
(low to high) D♭-A♭-D♭-G♭-B♭-E♭

Gtr. 2: Tune down 1/2 step:
(low to high) E♭-A♭-D♭-G♭-B♭-E♭

Intro

Moderate Rock ♩ = 138

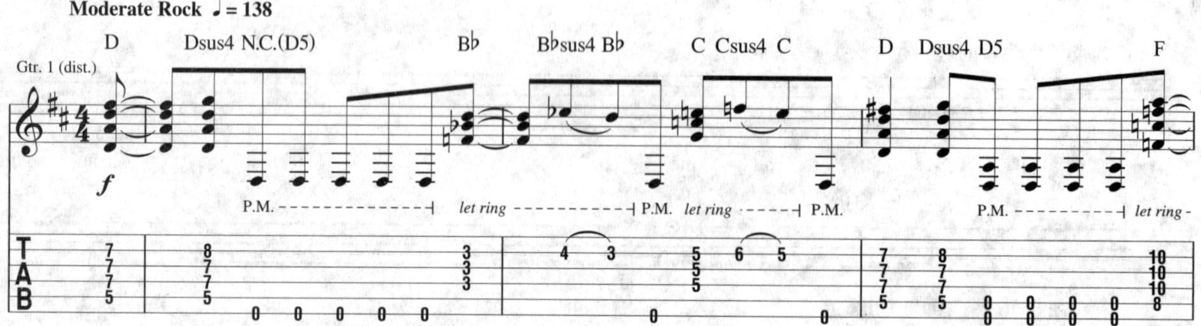

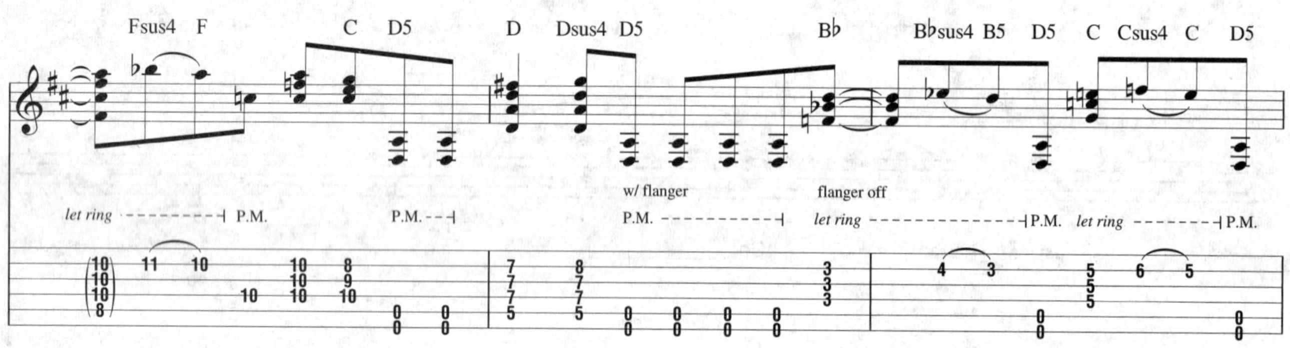

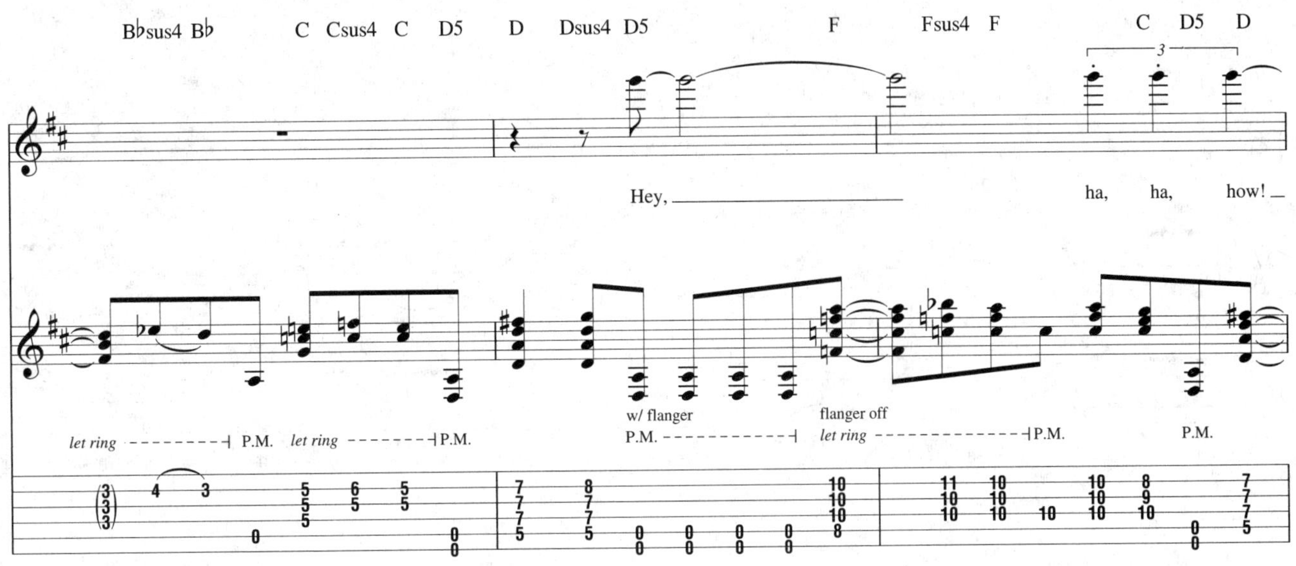

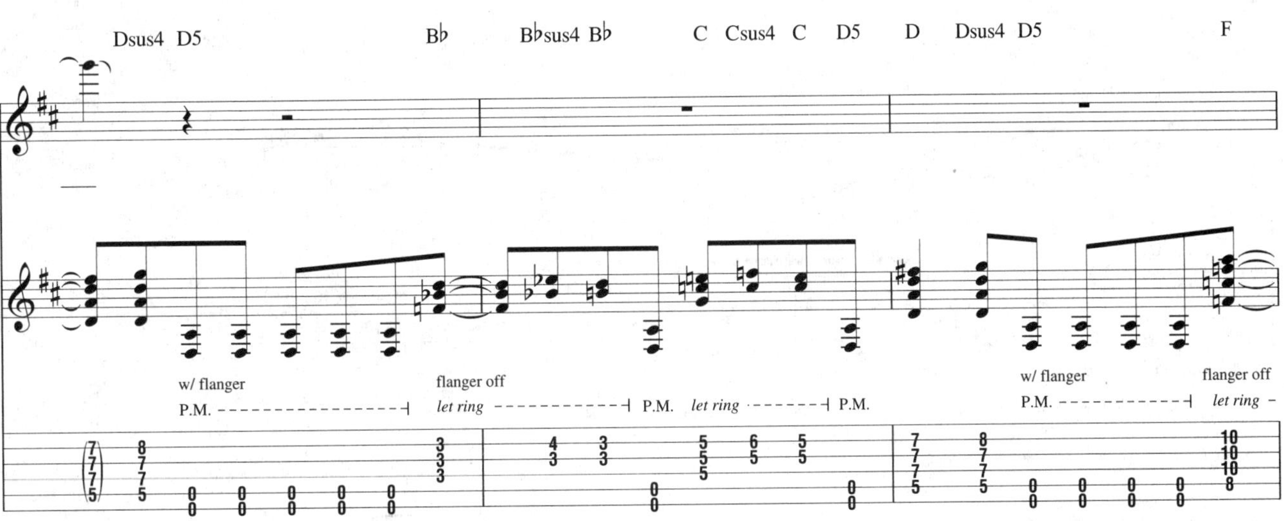

*Chord symbols reflect implied harmony (next 8 meas.).

2nd time, Gtr. 1: w/ Fill 1
F C D7(no3rd) B♭
then I don't care where I'm go - in'. Here's to your
this is my chance to fly. May - be e -
P.M.
P.M.
1/4
P.M.
P.M.
1/4

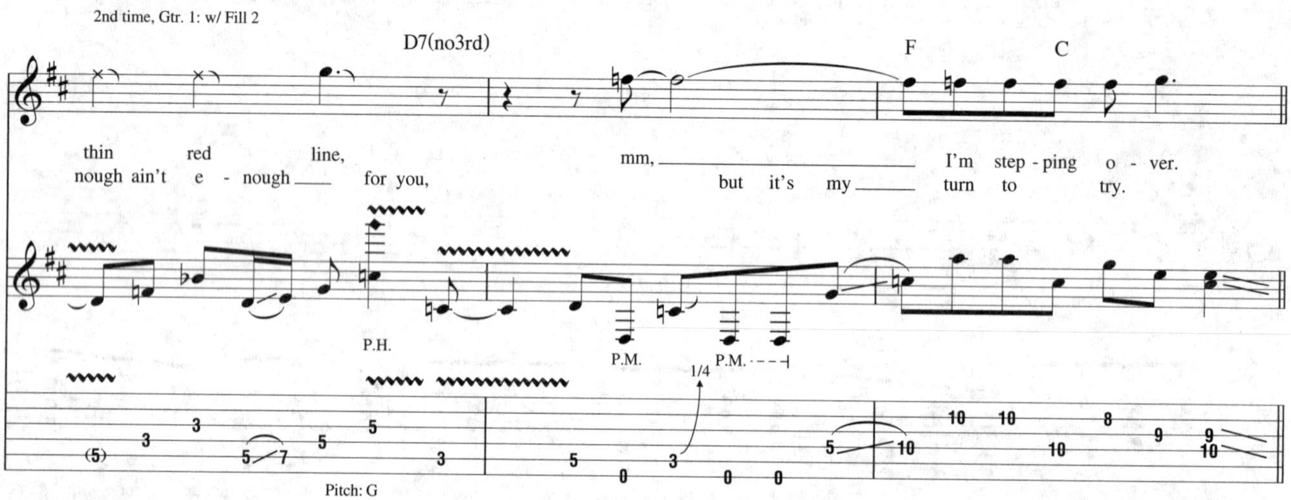
2nd time, Gtr. 1: w/ Fill 2
D7(no3rd) F C
thin red line, mm, I'm step - ping o - ver.
nough ain't e - nough for you, but it's my turn to try.
P.H.
P.M.
P.M.
1/4
Pitch: G

Pre-Chorus
G5 F5 G5 F5 G5 F5 G5 F5
All: Thought you'd nev - er miss me till I got a fat cit - y ad - dress.
Harm.
Harm.
Harm.
Harm.
Pitch: D
Fill 1
Gtr. 1
P.M.
Fill 2
Gtr. 1
P.H.
Pitch: G D

A5
G5
A5
G5
A5
G5
A5
Non - stop talk - er, what a rock - er. Blue - eyed mur - der in a
Harm.
Harm.
Harm.
Harm.
Chorus
A♭5
G5
F5
D
Dsus4
D5
B♭
B♭sus4
B♭
C
Csus4
C
D5
size five dress. Change, nothin' stays the same. Un - chained,
w/ flanger
P.M.
flanger off
let ring
P.M.
let ring
P.M.
D
Dsus4
N.C.(D5)
F
Fsus4
F
C
D
Dsus4
D5
B♭
and ya hit the ground runnin'. Change, ain't noth - in'
w/ flanger
P.M.
flanger off
let ring
P.M.
w/ flanger
P.M.
flanger off
B♭sus4
B♭
D5
C
Csus4
C
D5
D
Dsus4
D5
F
Fsus4
F
C
D7(no3rd)
1.
stays the same. Un - chained, yeah, ya hit the ground run - nin'.
2. I know
let ring
P.M.
let ring
P.M.
w/ flanger
P.M.
flanger off
let ring
P.M.

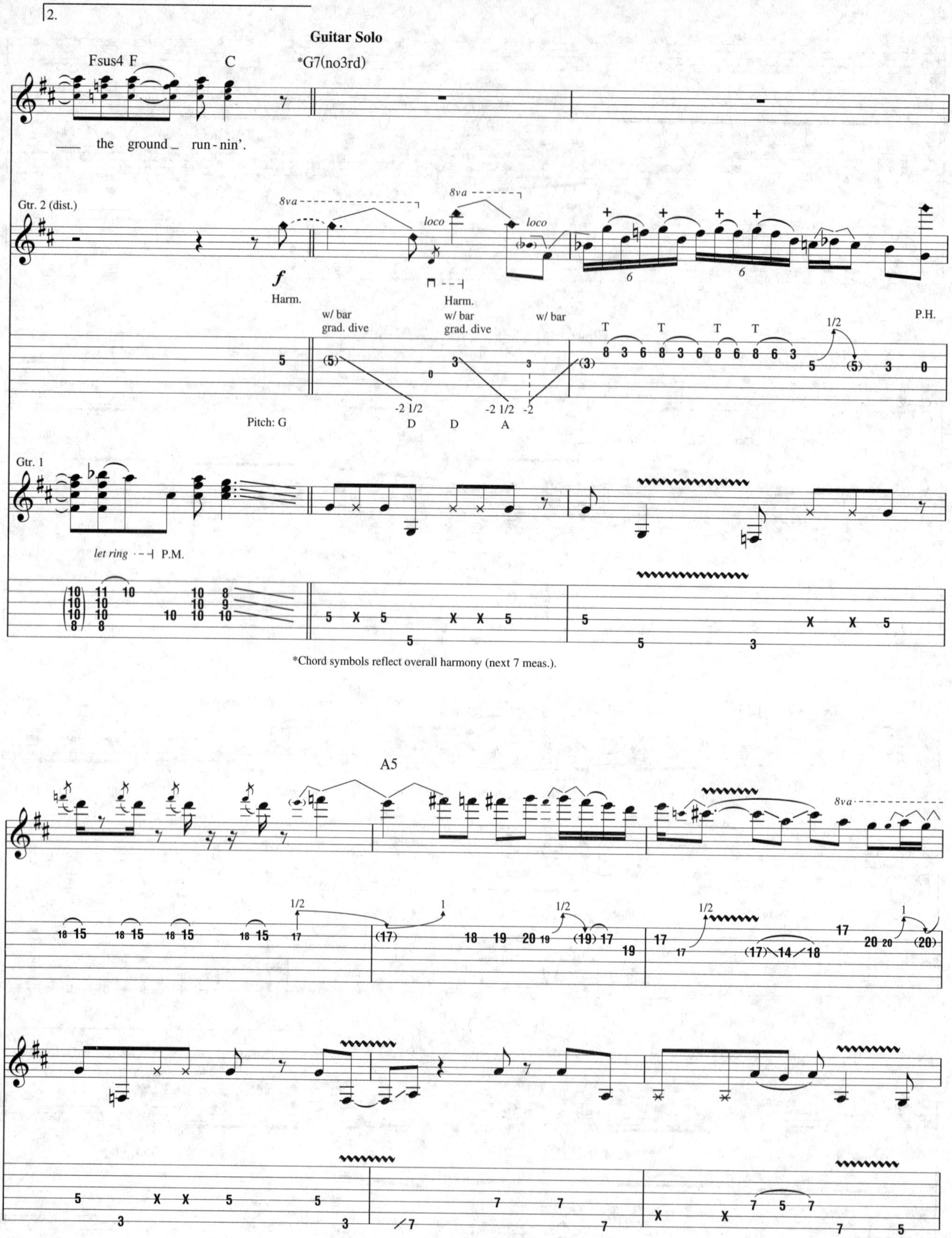

Guitar Solo

Fsus4 F C *G7(no3rd)

the ground run - nin'.

Gr. 2 (dist.)

8va loco 8va loco

f

Harm. Harm.

w/ bar grad. dive w/ bar grad. dive w/ bar

P.H.

Pitch: G D D A

Gtr. 1

let ring P.M.

*Chord symbols reflect overall harmony (next 7 meas.).

Chorus
A5 A♭5 G5 F5 D D5 B♭
Change, noth - in'
8va
w/ flanger
flanger off
w/ flanger
flanger off
P.M.
Gtr. 2 tacet
B♭sus4 B♭ D5 C Csus4 C D5 D Dsus4 D5 F Fsus4 F C D5
stays the same. Un - chained, yeah, ya hit the ground run - nin'. Change,
Gtr. 1
let ring P.M. let ring P.M. P.M. let ring P.M. P.M.
D Dsus4 D5 B♭ B♭sus4 B♭ D5 C Csus4 C D5 D Dsus4 D5 F
ain't noth - in' stays the same. Un - chained, yeah, ya hit
P.M. let ring P.M. let ring P.M. P.M.

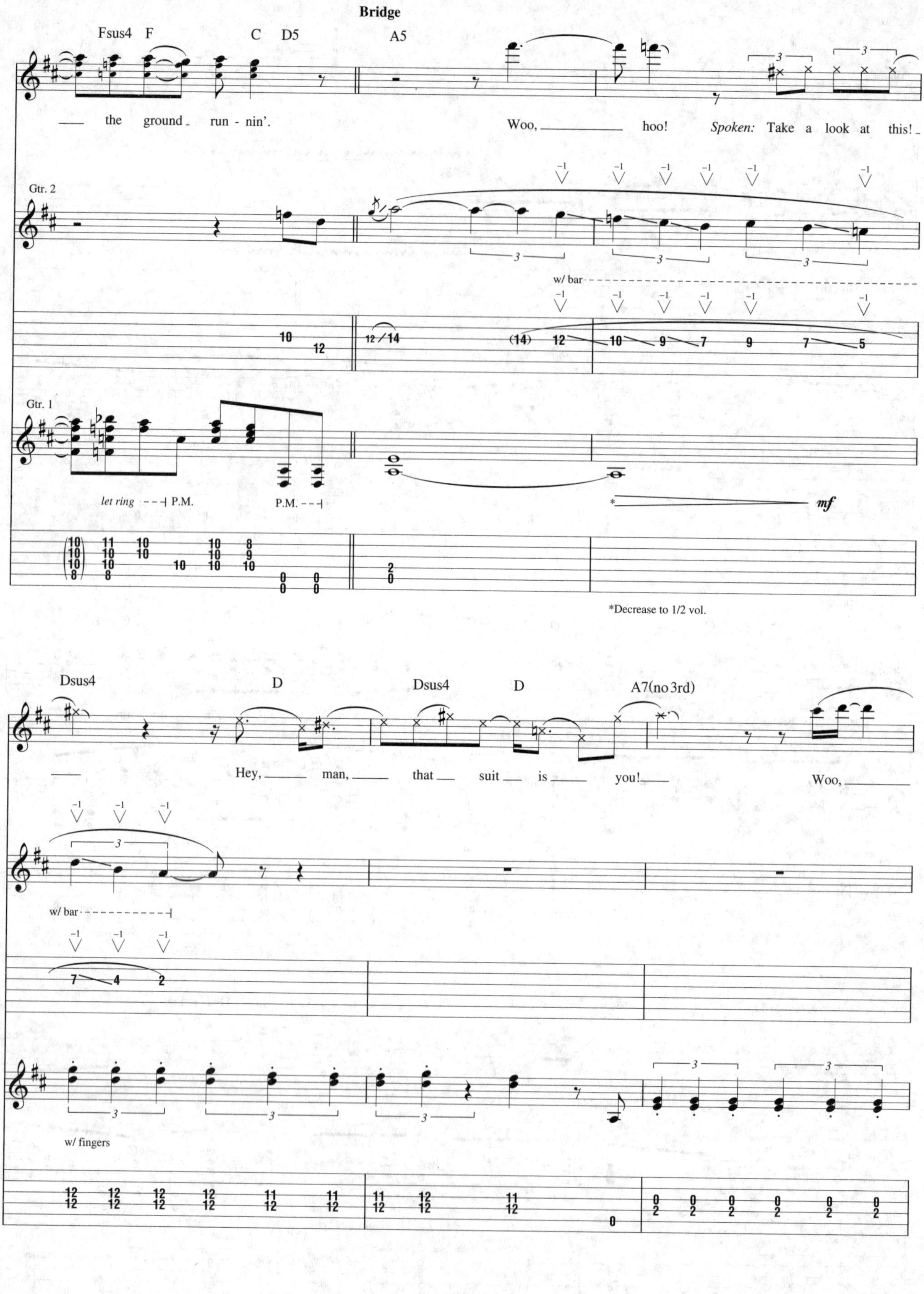

Bridge

Fsus4 F C D5 A5

— the ground - run - nin'. Woo, — hoo! *Spoken:* Take a look at this! -

Gtr. 2

w/ bar

Gtr. 1

let ring P.M. P.M.

mf

*Decrease to 1/2 vol.

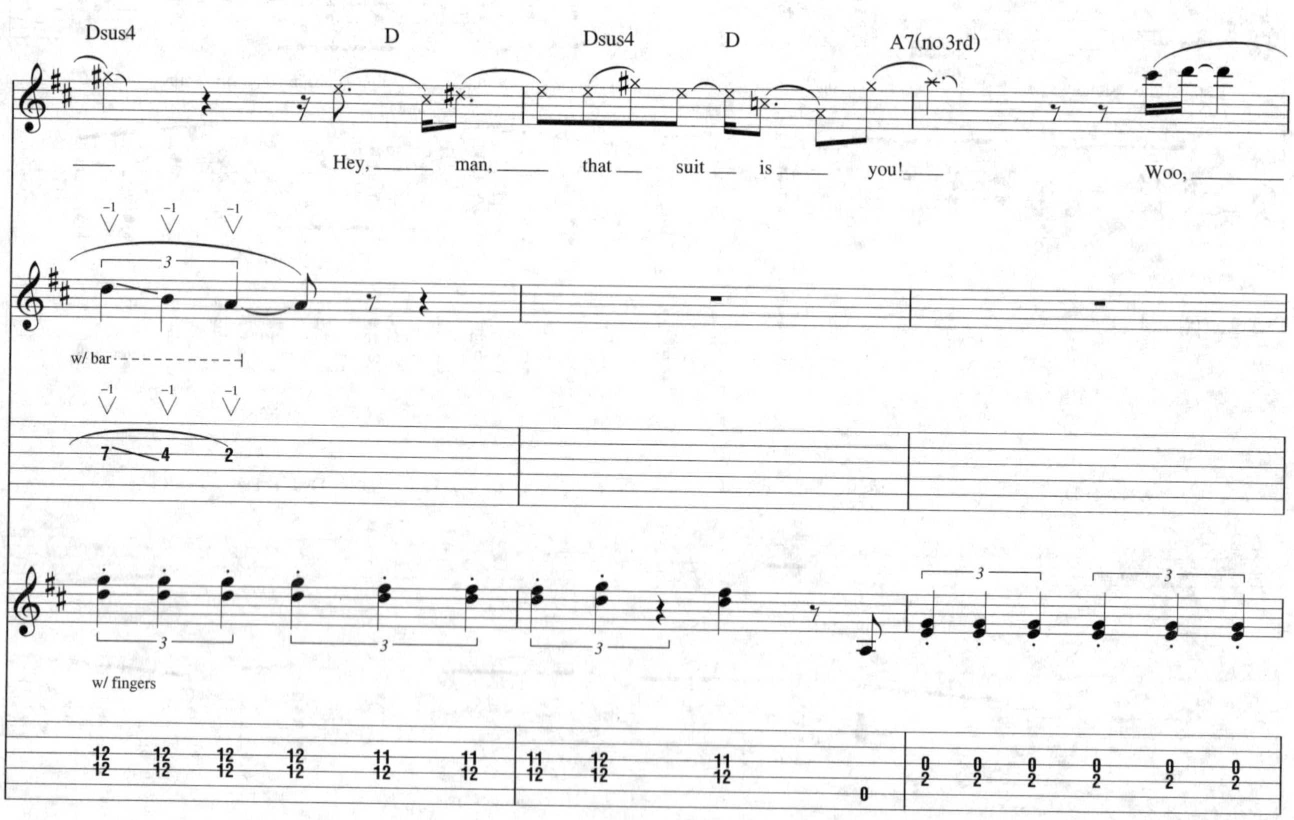

A5
A7
wee! You'll get some leg to-night for sure!
Tell us how you
D
Dsus4
D
A7(no 3rd)
A5
do, woo, hoo, hoo!
Spoken: Come on, Dave, gim-mie a break.
Heh, heh, heh,
8va
loco
T.H.

D
heh, one break, com - in' up! Change,
P.S. P.S. P.S.
w/ pick
P.M.
*Vol. swell

Chorus

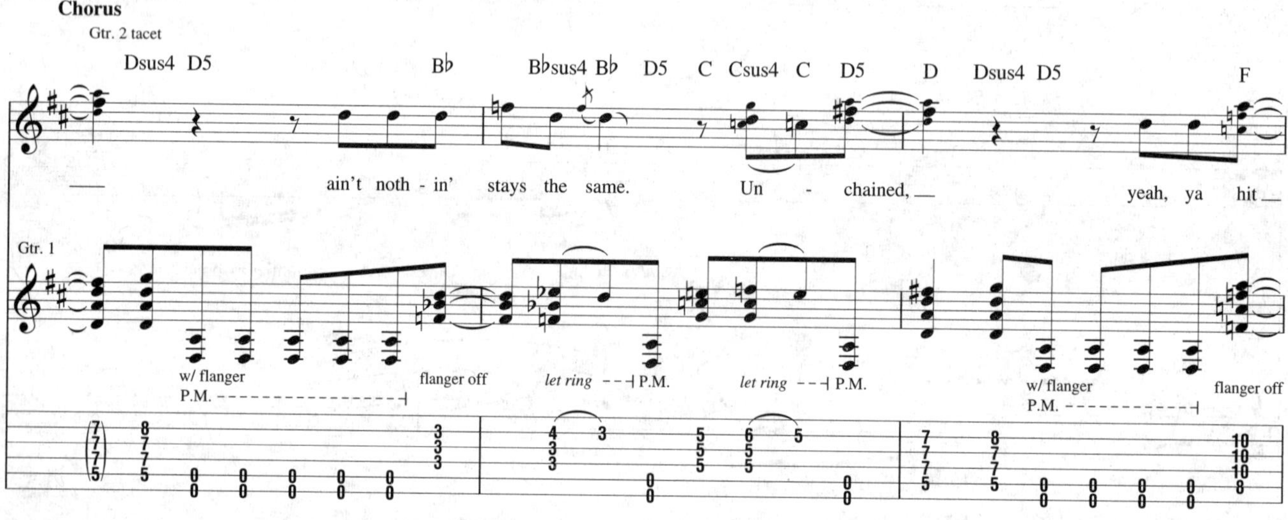
Gtr. 2 tacet
Dsus4 D5 B♭ B♭sus4 B♭ D5 C Csus4 C D5 D Dsus4 D5 F
ain't noth - in' stays the same. Un - chained, yeah, ya hit
Gtr. 1
w/ flanger
P.M.
flanger off
let ring
P.M.
let ring
P.M.
w/ flanger
P.M.
flanger off

Fsus4 F C D5 D Dsus4 D5 B♭ B♭sus4 B♭ D5 C Csus4 C D5
the ground run - nin'. Change, ain't noth - in' stays the same. Un - chained,
let ring
P.M.
P.M.
w/ flanger
P.M.
flanger off
let ring
P.M.
let ring
P.M.

D Dsus4 D5 F Fsus4 F C D Dsus4 D5 B♭

yeah, ya hit the ground run - nin'. Change, ain't noth - in'

Gtr. 2

Gtr. 1

w/ flanger flanger off let ring P.M. P.M. P.M.

P.M.

B♭sus4 B♭ D5 C Csus4 C D5 D Dsus4 D5 F Fsus4 F C D5

stays the same. Un - chained, yeah, ya hit the ground run - nin'. Change,

let ring P.M. let ring P.M. w/ flanger flanger off let ring P.M. P.M.

P.M.

D Dsus4 D5 B♭ B♭sus4 B♭ D5 C Csus4 C D5 D Dsus4 D5
ain't noth - in' stays the same. _
Un - chained. _
P.M.
let ring
F C F C Fsus4 F C D
Free time
N.C.
w/ bar
-3 1/2
slack
*pp
*Decrease to 3/4 vol.
**Strum w/ R.H. pinky.

Unskinny Bop

Words and Music by Bobby Dall, Brett Michaels, Bruce Johannesson and Rikki Rockett

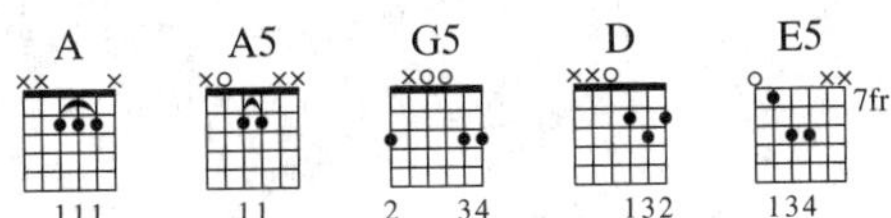

Tune down 1/2 step:
(low to high) E♭-A♭-D♭-G♭-B♭-E♭

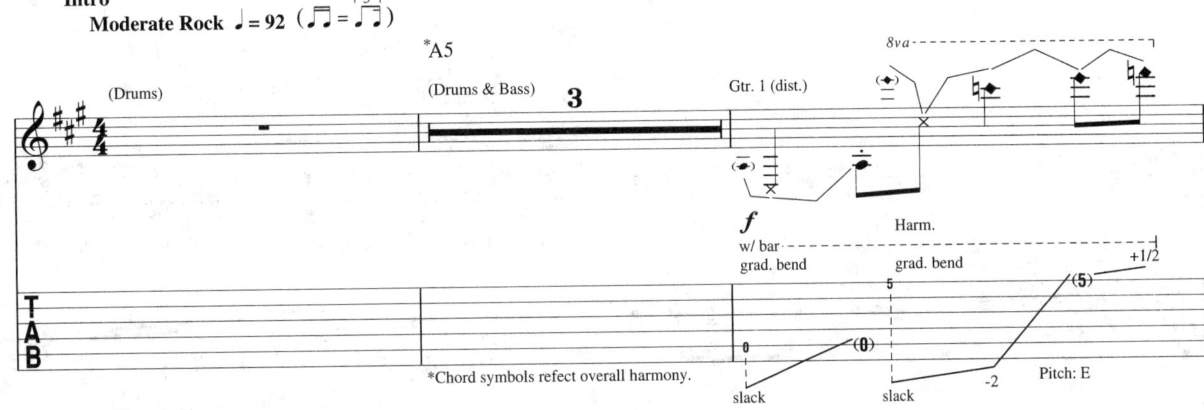

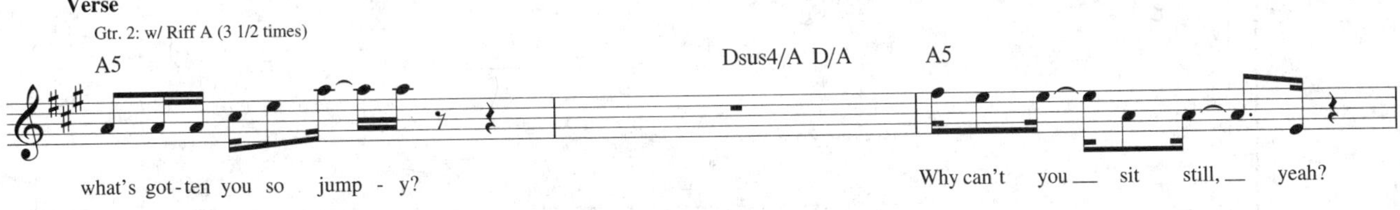

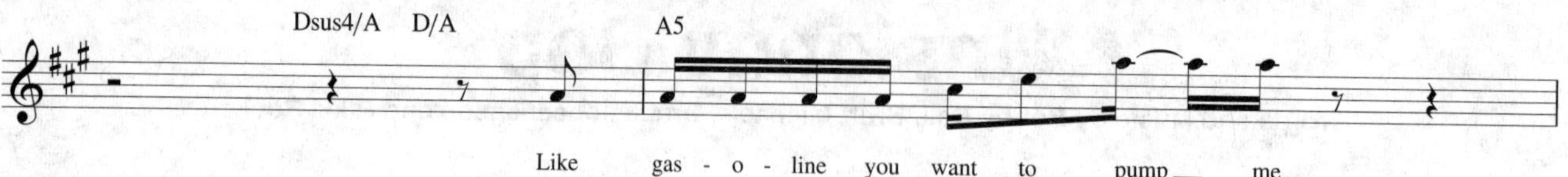
Dsus4/A
D/A
A5
Like gas - o - line you want to pump me

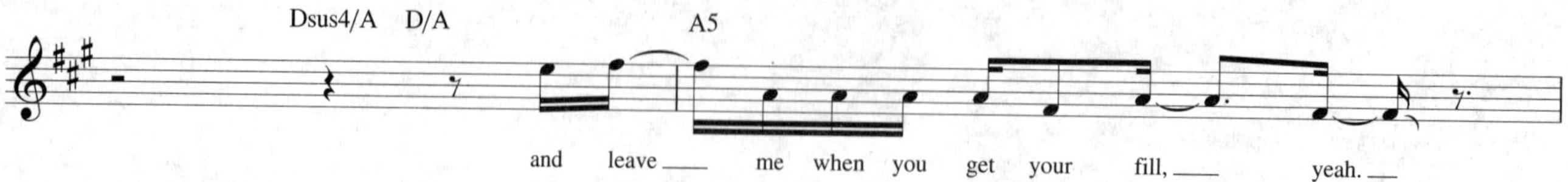
Dsus4/A
D/A
A5
and leave me when you get your fill, yeah.

Pre-Chorus
Dsus4/A
D/A
E5
G5
Ev - 'ry time I touch you, uh, you get hot.
Gtr. 2
P.M.
1/4
1/2

2nd time, Gtr. 1: w/ Fill 1
E5
G5
E5
G5
I want to make love, you nev - er stop.
Come up for air, you pull me to the floor.
P.M.
P.H.
Pitch: B
1/2

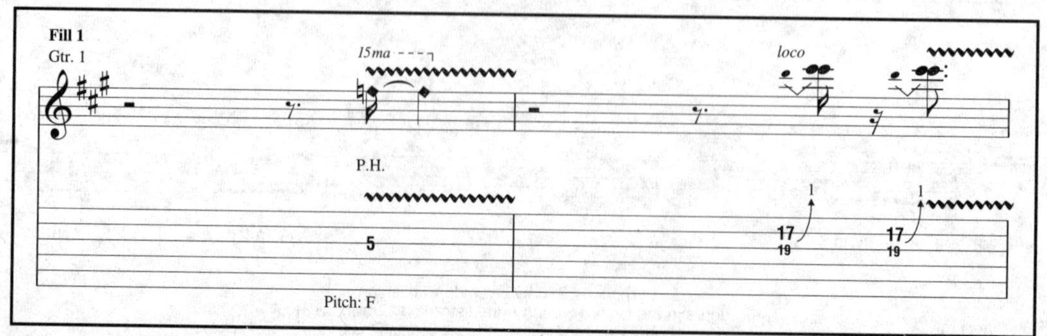
Fill 1
Gtr. 1
15ma
loco
P.H.
Pitch: F

𝄋𝄋 Chorus

E5 G5 A

What's been go - ing on in that head of yours? Just

Voc. Fig. 1

(Un - skin - ny bop,

Gtr. 2

Riff B

P.M. P.M. P.H.

Pitch: D

*Gtr. 3

Riff B1

*Kybd. arr. for gtr.

Gtr. 3: w/ Riff B1 (2 times)

G5 D A

blows me a - way, yeah.

oo. Un - skin - ny bop, bop,

End Riff B

P.H.

Pitch: A B A

End Riff B1

mf

G5
D
A
All night and day, yeah. She
oo. Un - skin - ny bop, bop, bop, bop.
Gtr. 2
15ma
loco
P.H.
P.H.
Pitch: G♯ F♯

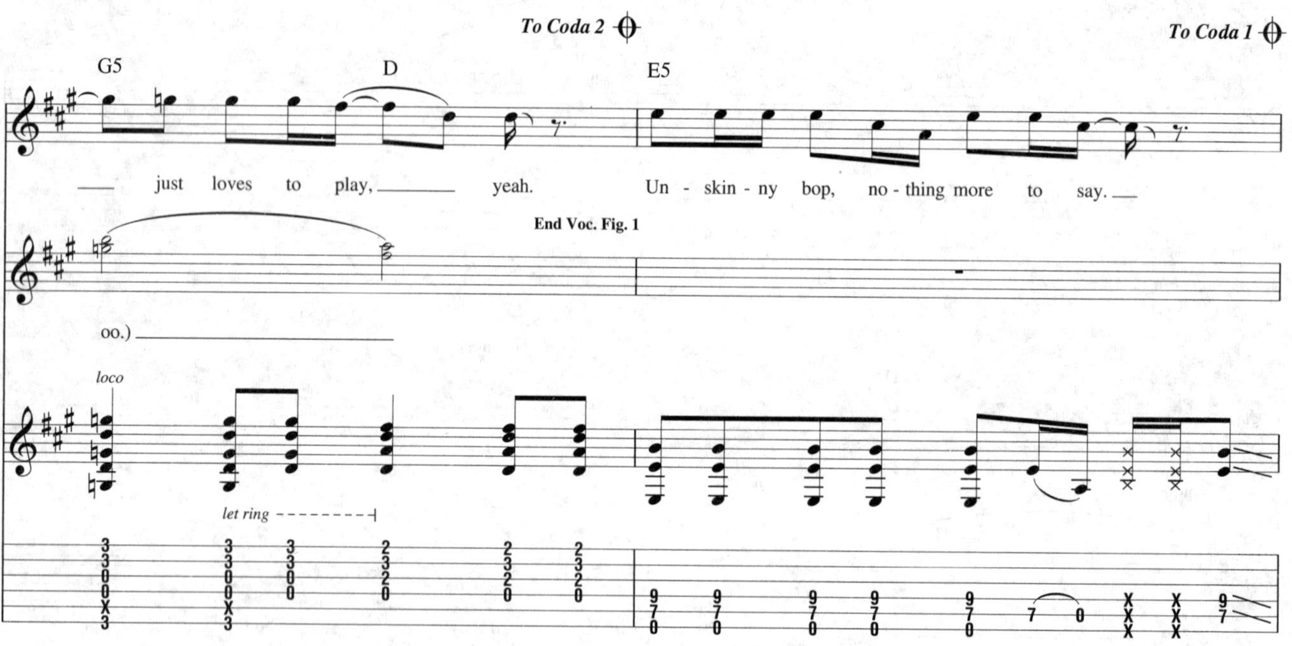
To Coda 2
To Coda 1
G5
D
E5
just loves to play, yeah. Un - skin - ny bop, no - thing more to say.
End Voc. Fig. 1
oo.)
loco
let ring

Verse
Gtr. 2: w/ Riff A (4 times)
F♯5 E5 G5 E5 G♯5 E5 A5
A
2. Look at me so fun - ny.
Rhy. Fig. 1
Gtr. 4 (slight dist.)
mf

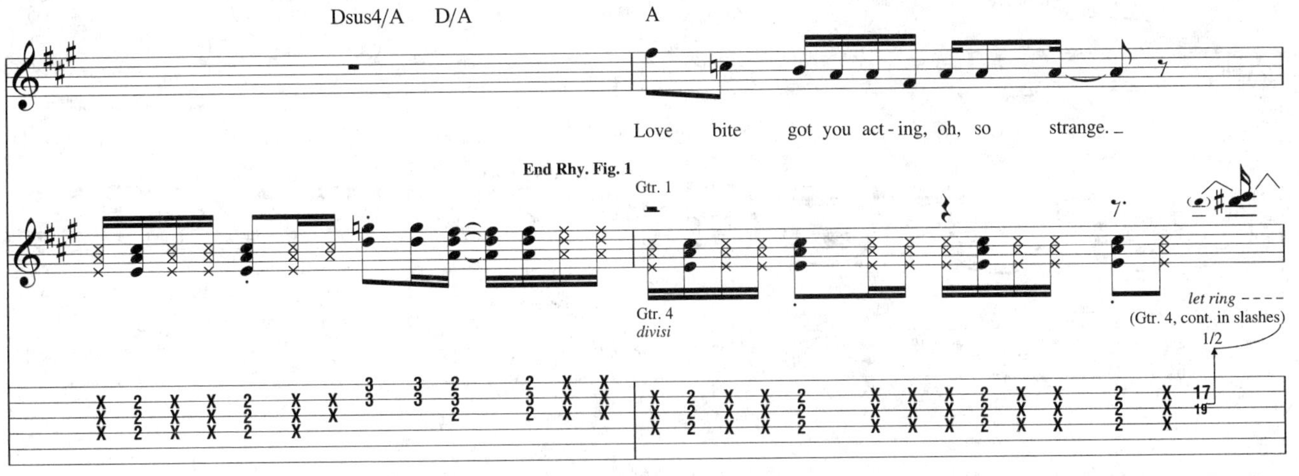
Dsus4/A D/A
A
Love bite got you act - ing, oh, so strange.
End Rhy. Fig. 1
Gtr. 1
Gtr. 4
divisi
let ring
(Gtr. 4, cont. in slashes)
1/2

Gtr. 1 tacet
Gtr. 4: w/ Rhy. Fig 1 (2 times)
A
Gtr. 4
You got too man - y bees in your hon - ey.
Gtr. 1
let ring

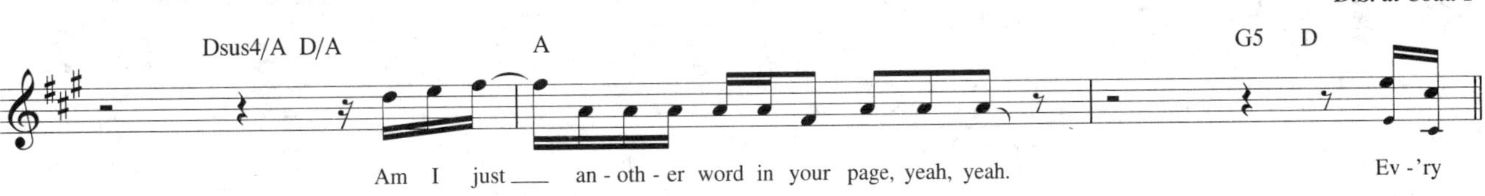
D.S. al Coda 1
Dsus4/A D/A
A
G5 D
Am I just an - oth - er word in your page, yeah, yeah.
Ev - 'ry

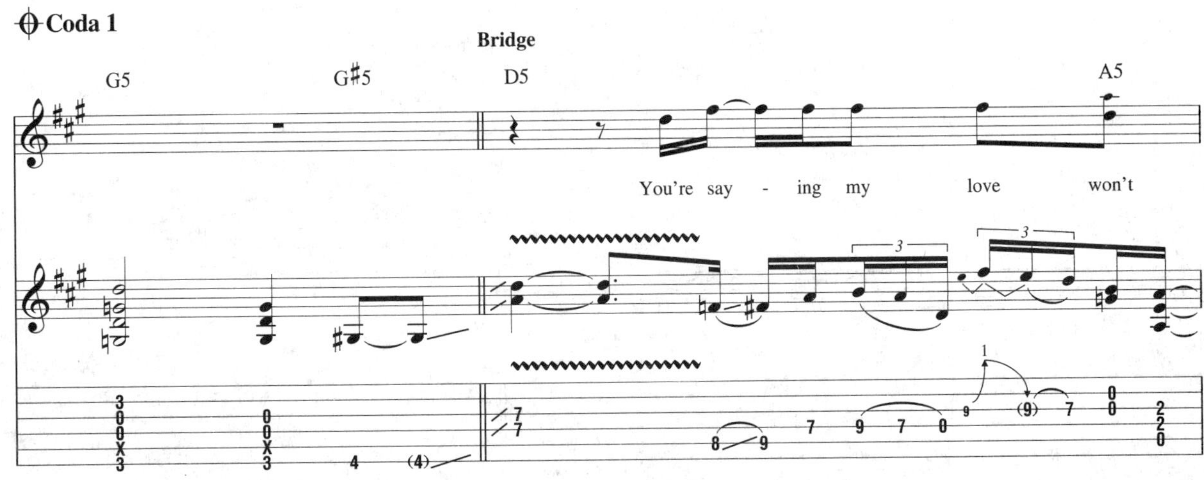
Coda 1
Bridge
G5
G♯5
D5
A5
You're say - ing my love won't

D/A
A
D5
A5
do ya. That ain't love writ - ten
D/A
A
D5
A5
on your face. Well, hon - ey, I can see right
A7(no3rd)/G
E5
E6
E5
E6
E7
through ya. Yeah, who's rid - ing who at the end of the race.
F♯5
E5
G5
E5
G♯5
E5
A5
Guitar Solo
A5
Rhy. Fig. 2
Gtr. 2
Gtr. 1
8va
loco
(cont. in slashes)
P.H.

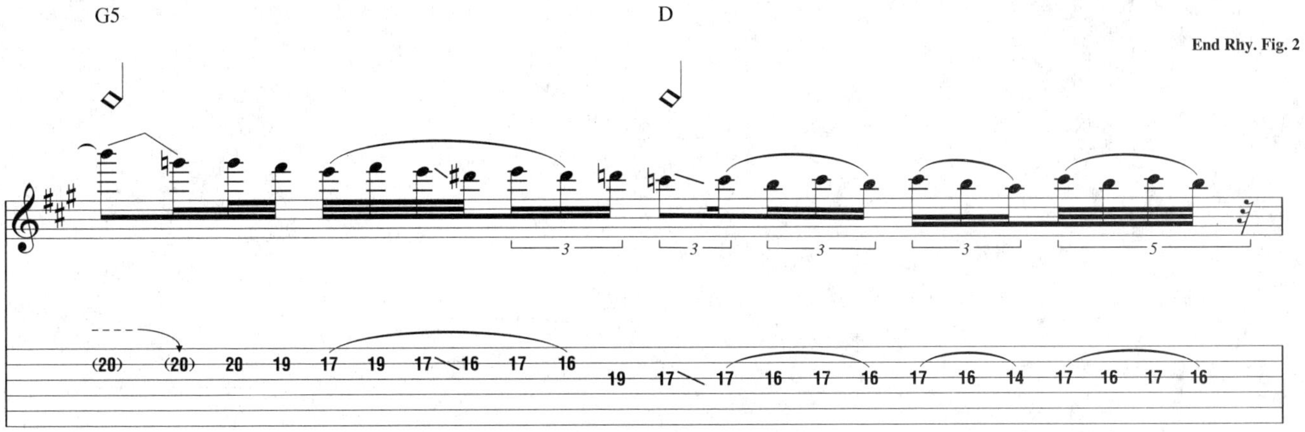
G5
D
End Rhy. Fig. 2

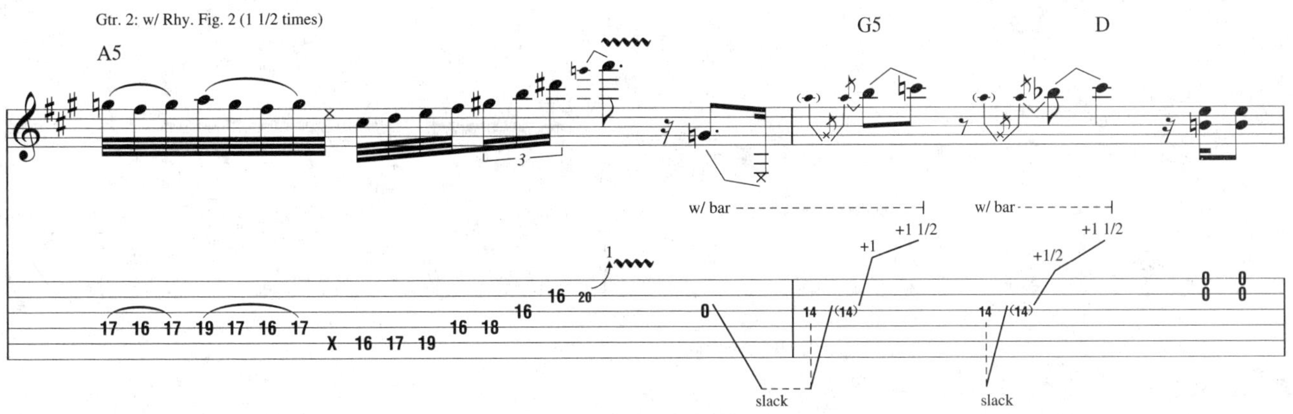
Gtr. 2: w/ Rhy. Fig. 2 (1 1/2 times)
A5
G5
D
w/ bar
w/ bar
+1
+1 1/2
+1/2
+1 1/2
slack
slack

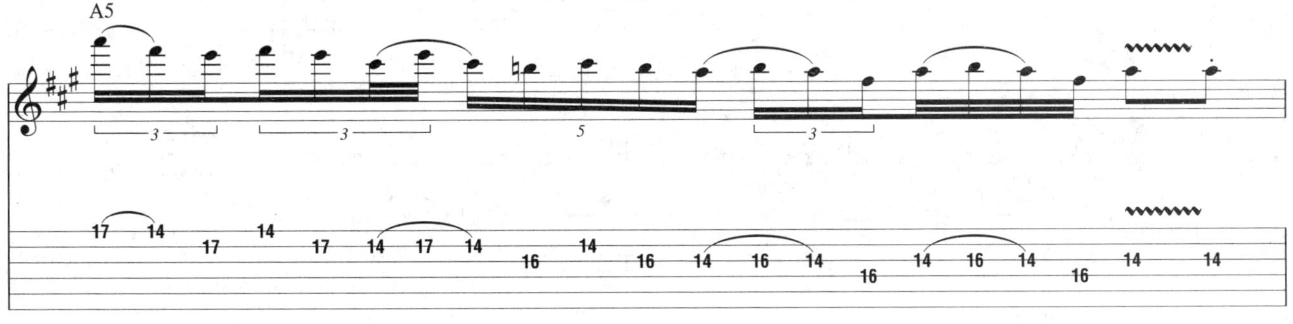
A5

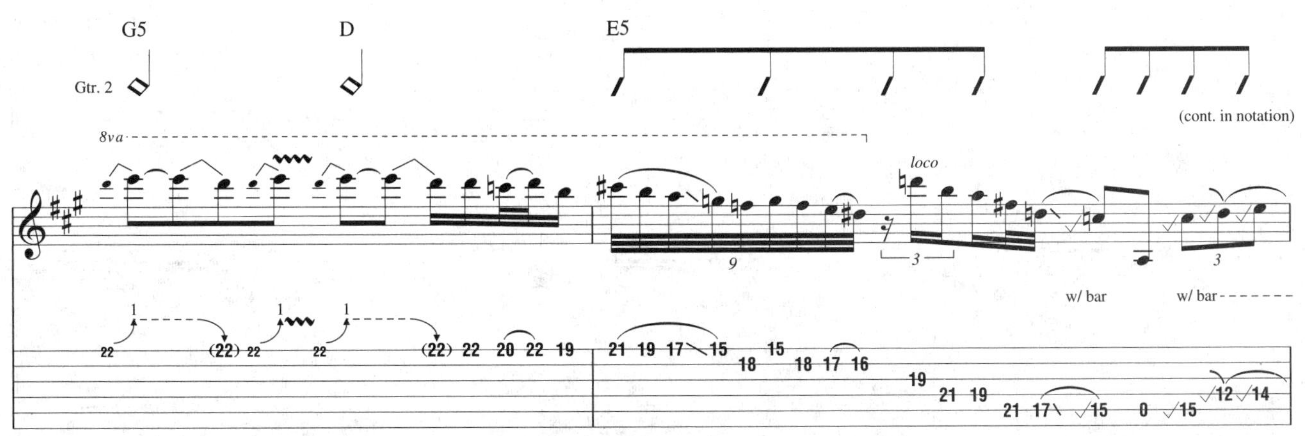
G5
D
E5
Gtr. 2
(cont. in notation)
8va
loco
w/ bar
w/ bar

Interlude

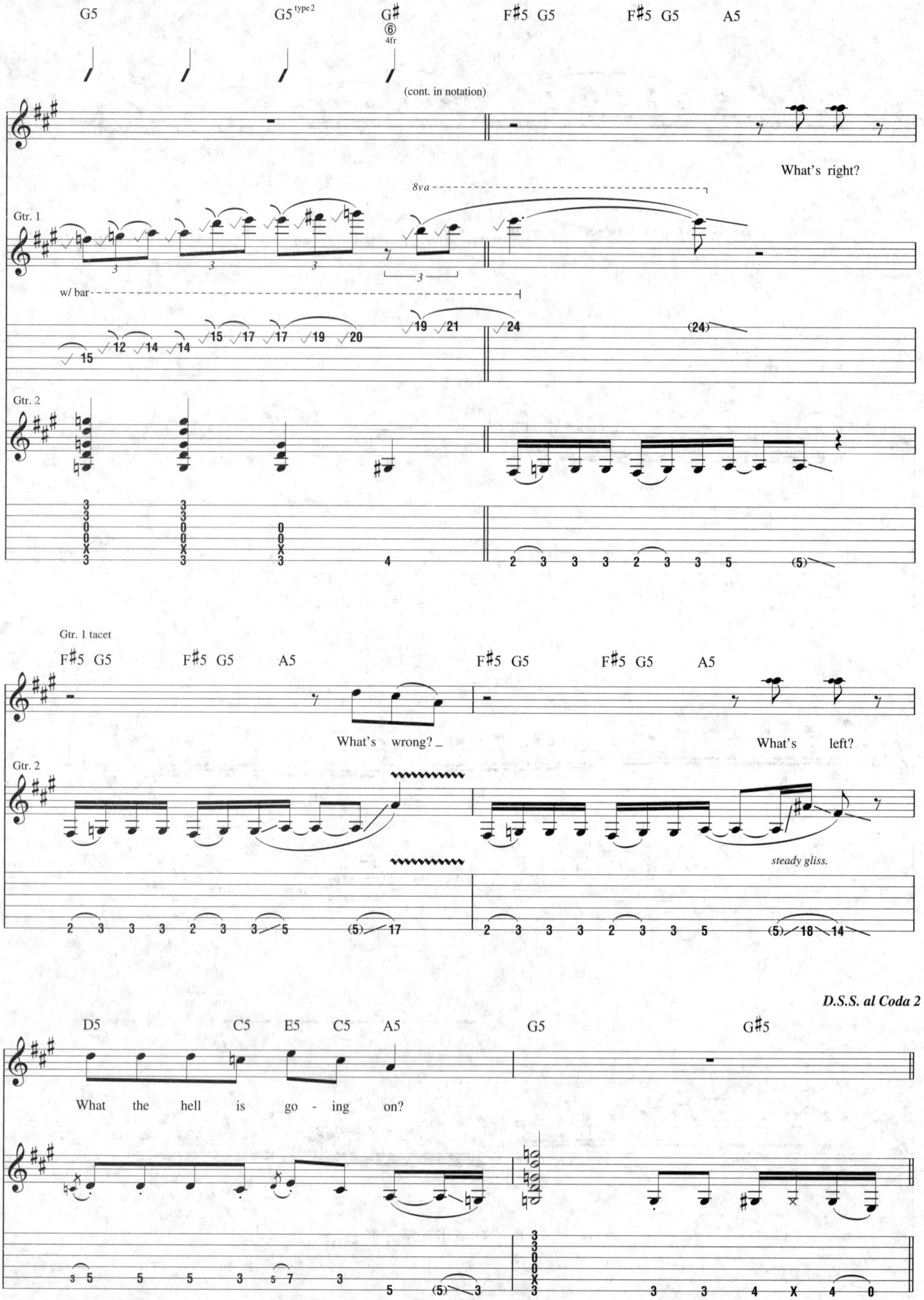

G5 G5 type 2 G# ⑥ 4fr F#5 G5 F#5 G5 A5

(cont. in notation)

What's right?

8va

Gtr. 1

w/ bar

Gtr. 2

D.S.S. al Coda 2

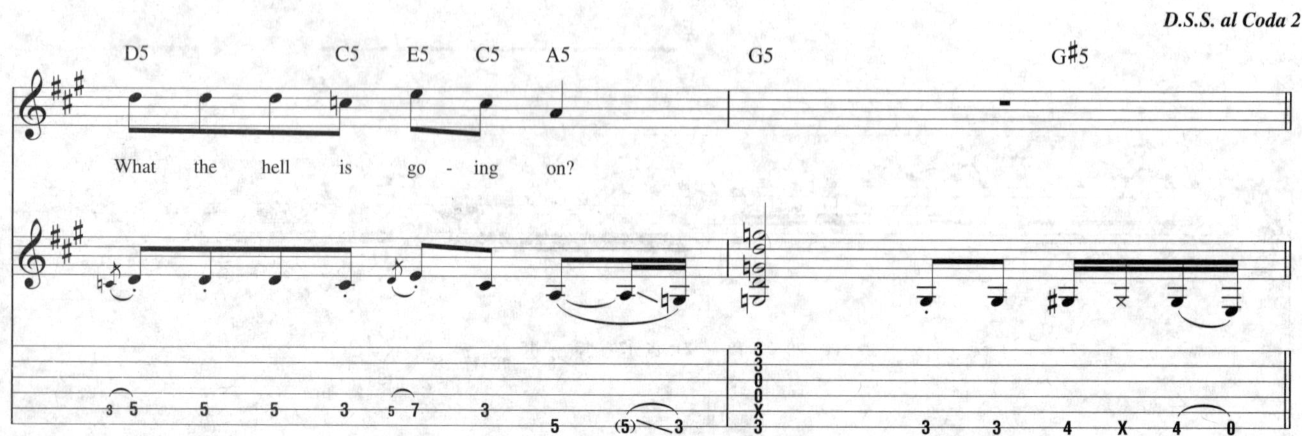

Coda 2

Gtr. 3: w/ Riff B1 (till fade)
A
(Come up for air, you pull me to the floor.)
8va
loco
P.H.
hold bend

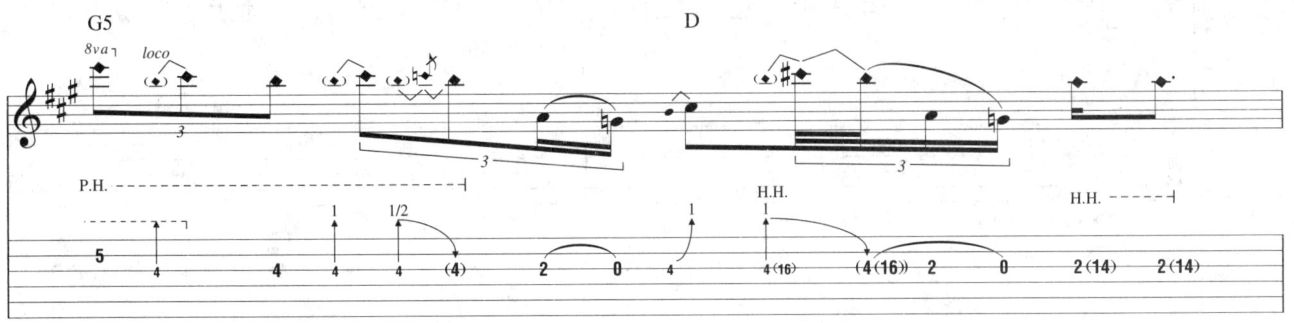
G5
D
8va
loco
P.H.
H.H.

Bkgd. Voc: w/ Voc. Fig. 1 (till fade)
A
G5
D
Look good, look good, look good, look good, look good, look.

Begin fade
Gtr. 2: w/ Riff B, simile (till fade)
A
G5
D
A
All night and day, yeah. Look
Fade out
G5
D
A
G5
D
A
good, look good, look good, look good, look.

Wait and Bleed

Words and Music by M. Shawn Crahan, Paul Gray, Nathan Jordison and Corey Taylor

D5
N.C.
Gtr. 1
Gtr. 2
Rhy. Fill 1
End Rhy. Fill 1
Verse
Good-bye!
1. I wipe it off on tile, the light is bright-er this
Gtrs. 1 & 2
Rhy. Fig. 1
* Gtrs. 1 & 2
End Rhy. Fig. 1
Eb5 Gb5 Eb5
P.M.
* composite arrangement
Gtrs. 1 & 2: w/ Rhy. Fig. 1, 7 times
time. Ev - 'ry - thing is three - D blas - phe - my. My eyes are red and gold,
the hair is stand - ing staight up. This is not the way I pic - tured me.

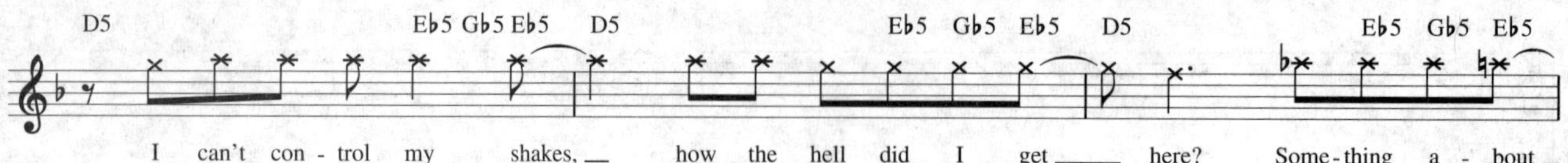
D5
Eb5 Gb5 Eb5
D5
Eb5 Gb5 Eb5
D5
Eb5 Gb5 Eb5
I can't con - trol my shakes, how the hell did I get here? Some - thing a - bout

D5
Eb5 Gb5 Eb5
D5
Eb5 Gb5 Eb5
D5
Eb5 Gb5 Eb5
this, so ver - y wrong… I have to laugh out loud, I wish I did - n't like

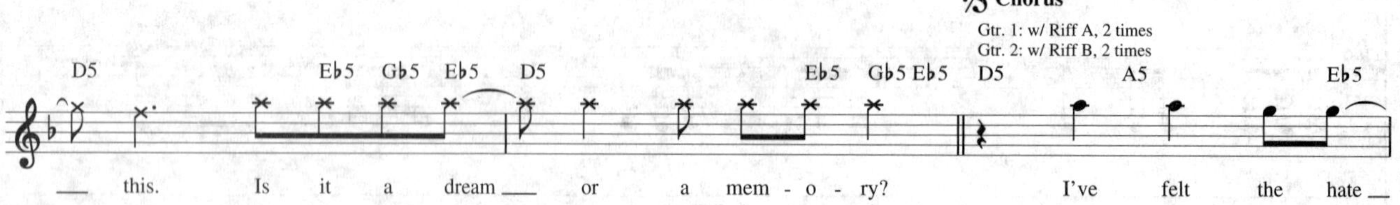
Chorus
Gtr. 1: w/ Riff A, 2 times
Gtr. 2: w/ Riff B, 2 times
D5
Eb5 Gb5 Eb5
D5
Eb5 Gb5 Eb5
D5
A5
Eb5
this. Is it a dream or a mem - o - ry? I've felt the hate

Bb5
D5
A5
Eb5
Bb5
D5
A5
Eb5
rise up in me… Kneel down and clear the stone of leaves… I wan - der out

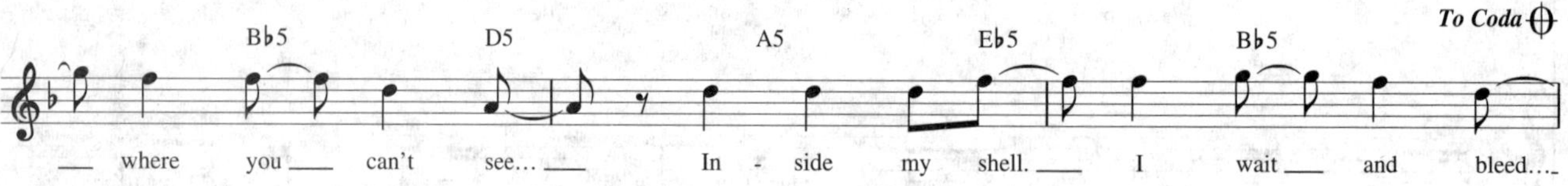
To Coda
Bb5
D5
A5
Eb5
Bb5
where you can't see… In - side my shell. I wait and bleed…

D5
Eb5 Gb5 Eb5
D5
Eb5 Gb5 Eb5
D5
N.C.
2. Get out - ta my
Gtrs. 1 & 2
P.M.
P.M.

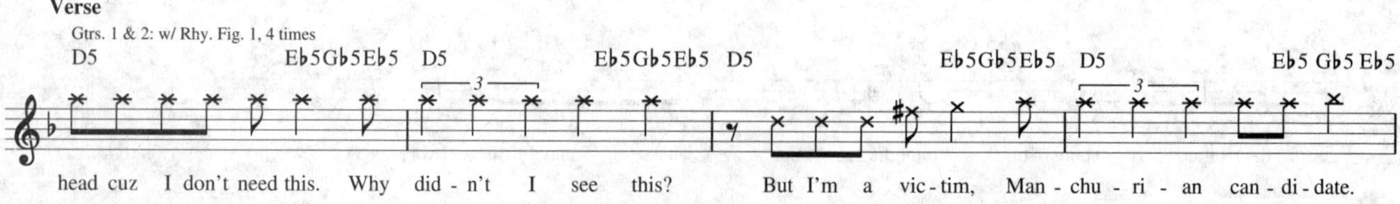
Verse
Gtrs. 1 & 2: w/ Rhy. Fig. 1, 4 times
D5
Eb5Gb5Eb5
D5
Eb5Gb5Eb5
D5
Eb5Gb5Eb5
D5
Eb5 Gb5 Eb5
head cuz I don't need this. Why did - n't I see this? But I'm a vic - tim, Man - chu - ri - an can - di - date.

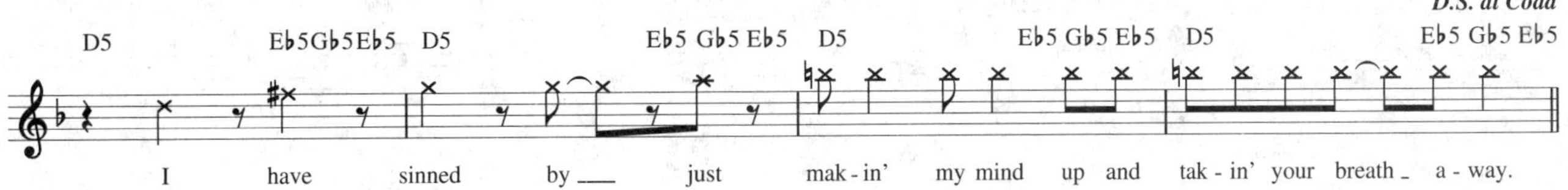
D.S. al Coda
D5
Eb5Gb5Eb5
D5
Eb5 Gb5 Eb5
D5
Eb5 Gb5 Eb5
D5
Eb5 Gb5 Eb5
I have sinned by ___ just mak - in' my mind up and tak - in' your breath _ a - way.

Coda
Gtr. 1: w/ Riff A
D5
A5
Eb5
Bb5
D5
A5
Eb5
Bb5
___ I've felt the hate ___ rise up ___ in me… ___ Kneel down and clear ___ the stone _ of leaves….
Gtr. 2
Riff C
End Riff C

Gtr. 2: w/ Riff C, simile
D5
A5
Eb5
Bb5
D5
Bb5
Eb5
N.C.
___ I wan - der out ___ where you _ can't see… ___ in - side my shell, ___ I wait _ and bleed? ___
Gtr. 1

Interlude
Gtr. 2 tacet
N.C.
P.M.
1/2

D5
N.C.
D5
N.C.
Good - bye!
Riff D
Gtrs. 1 & 2
End Riff D
P.M.
1/2
P.M.
P.M.
P.M.
P.M.
P.M.
Bridge
Gtrs. 1 & 2: w/ Riff D
Gtrs. 1 & 2: w/ Riff D, 3 times
You have - n't learned a thing. I have - n't changed a thing. My
flesh was in my bones. The pain was al - ways free. You have - n't learned a thing. I have - n't changed a thing. My
flesh was in my bones. The pain was al - ways free!
Chorus
D5
A5
E♭5
I've felt the hate
Gtrs. 1 & 2
Rhy. Fig. 2
P.M.
P.M.
P.M.
* Lead Voc. dbld.
rise up in me… Kneel down and clear the stone of leaves…
End Rhy. Fig. 2

Gtrs. 1 & 2: w/ Rhy. Fig. 2
D5 A5 Eb5 D5 A5 Eb5
I wan - der out where you can't see... In - side my shell, I wait and bleed...
Gtr. 1: w/ Rhy. Fig. 2, 2 times
Gtr. 2: w/ Riff C, 2 times, simile
D5 A5 Eb5 D5 A5 Eb5
I've felt the hate rise up in me... Kneel down and clear the stone of leaves...
D5 A5 Eb5 D5 A5 Eb5
I wan - der out where you can't see... In - side my shell, I wait and bleed!
Gtr. 2: w/ Rhy. Fill 1
D5 N.C. D5
Outro
D5 Eb5 Gb5 Eb5
Uh!
Gtr. 1
Gtrs. 1 & 2
D5 Eb5 Gb5 Eb5 D5 Eb5 Gb5 Eb5 D5 Eb5 Gb5 Eb5
And it waits for you!
D5 Eb5 Gb5 Eb5 D5 Eb5 Gb5 Eb5 D5 Eb5 Gb5 Eb5 D5

Wake Up Little Susie

Words and Music by Boudleaux Bryant and Felice Bryant

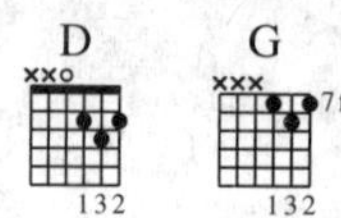

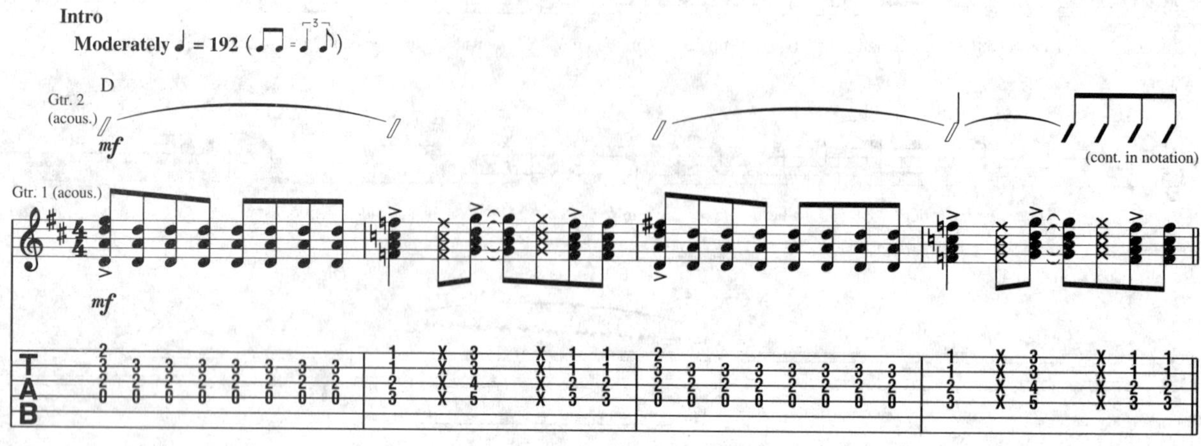

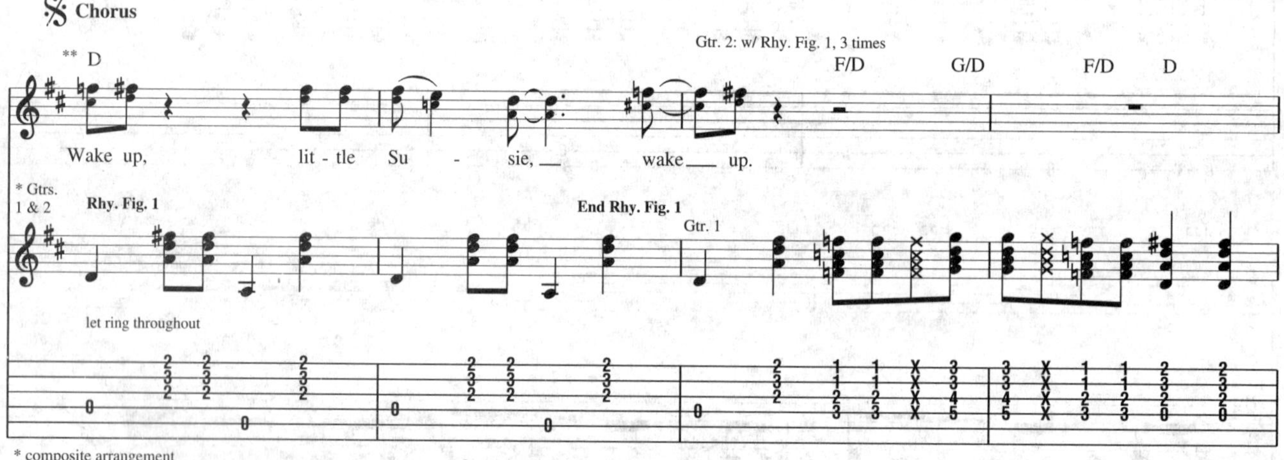

* composite arrangement

** Chord symbols reflect overall tonality.

Gtr. 3: w/ Rhy. Fill 1

Rhy. Fill 1

Gtr. 3 (elec.)

End Rhy. Fill 1

mf w/ clean tone

both went sound a - sleep. Wake up, little Su - sie, and weep. The mov -
mov - ie was-n't so hot, it did - n't have much of a plot. We fell

Gtrs. 1 & 2

D G D G D G

- ie's o - ver, it's four o - clock and we're in trou - ble deep.
a - sleep, our goose is cooked, our rep - u - ta - tion is shot.

Wake up, lit - tle

A G A

Su - sie. Wake up, lit - tle Su - sie. Well,

Gtr. 3

simile on repeat

Gtrs. 1 & 2

Verse
A
E7
A
E7
A
what-'re we gon-na tell your ma - ma? What-'re we gon-na tell your pa?
rake

Gtr. 3 tacet
E7
A
N.C.
What-'re we gon-na tell our friends when they say, "Ooh, la,
Gtrs. 1 & 2

To Coda
D
A7
D
la?" Wake up, lit-tle Su - sie. Wake up, lit-tle Su - sie.

Bridge

A7 D

Well, I told your ma - ma that you'd be in by ten.

Gtr. 3

P.M. slight P.M. slight P.M. slight P.M.

Gtrs. 1 & 2

D7 G

Well, Su - sie, ba - by, looks like we goofed a - gain.

P.M. P.M. P.M.

A7
G
A7
Wake up, little Susie. Wake up, little Susie,
P.M.
let ring
Gtr. 3 tacet
N.C.
Gtr. 2: w/ Rhy. Fig. 1, 2 times
D
F/D
G/D
F/D
D
F/D
G/D
F/D
D.S. al Coda
We got - ta go home
Gtrs. 1 & 2
Gtr. 1
Coda
A7
D
A7
D
Wake up, little Susie. Wake up, little Susie.
D
F/D
G/D
D
F/D
G/D
D
F/D
G/D
F/D
Play 2 Times and Fade

Walk This Way

Words and Music by Steven Tyler and Joe Perry

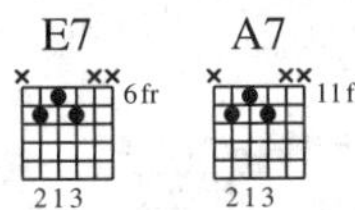

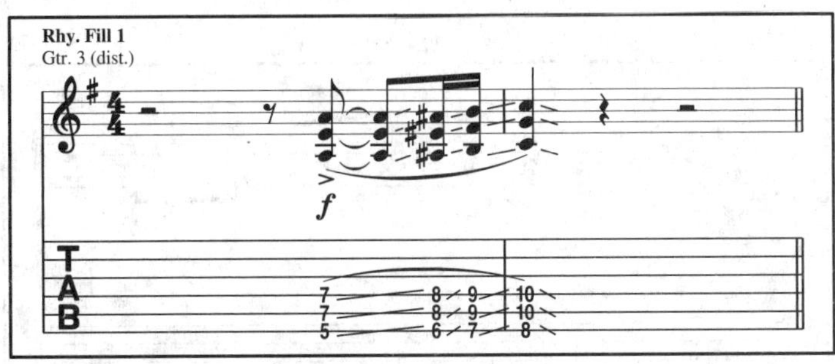

ain't seen noth-in' till you're down on a muf-fin and you're sure to be a-chang-in' your ways." I met a
three young la-dies in the school gym lock-er when I no-ticed they was look-in' at me. I was a
P.M.
Gtr. 3: w/ Rhy. Fill 2, 2nd time
cheer - lead - er, was a real young bleed-er all the times I could rem - i - nisce, 'cause the
high school los-er, nev-er made it with a la-dy 'til the boys told me some-thin' I missed, then my
Rhy. Fig. 2
P.M.
A5
best things in lov-in' with a sis-ter and a cou-sin on-ly start-ed with a lit-tle kiss, a-like this!
next door neigh-bor with a daugh-ter had a fav-or so I gave her just a lit-tle kiss a-like this!
End Rhy. Fig. 2
P.M.
Rhy. Fill 2
Gtr. 3

Interlude
Gtr. 1: w/ Riff A, 2nd time
N.C.(E5)
Gtr. 1
Gtr. 2 divisi
P.M.
Gtr. 3: w/ Rhy. Fill 1
Gtrs. 1 & 2
A5
P.M.
Verse
Gtrs. 1 & 2: w/ Rhy. Fig. 1, 3 times, simile
N.C.(C7)
2., 4. See - saw swing-in' with the boys in the school and your feet fly - in' up in the air, I sing,
"Hey did - dle did - dle" with your kit - ty in the mid - dle of the swing like you did - n't care. So I
took a big chance at the high school dance with a miss - y who was read - y to play, was a
* Sing harmony 1st time only.
Riff A
Gtr. 1
P.M.
P.M.

P.M.

To Coda
me she was fool-in' 'cause she knew what she was do-in'
and I know'd love was here to stay __ when she told me to...
when she told me how to walk this way. _ She told __ me to...
Gtrs. 1 & 2
P.M.
Chorus
C7
F7
C7
(Walk this __ way, __ talk this __ way, __ walk this __ way, __
Gtr. 1
Gtr. 2
F7
Guitar Solo
Gtrs. 1 & 2: w/ Rhy. Fig. 2
N.C.(C7)
walk this __ way. __)
Uh, just gim-me a kiss.
Gtr. 3
1/2
full

A5
A-like this!
full
1/2
full
Interlude
N.C.(E5)
Oo.
Gtr. 1
Gtr. 2
divisi
P.M.
Gtr. 3: w/ Rhy. Fill 1
D.S. al Coda
A5
Uh.
Gtrs. 1 & 2
P.M.
Coda
Chorus
C7
F7
(Walk this way,
talk this way,
Gtr. 1
Gtr. 2

C7
F7
C7
talk this way,
walk this way,
talk this way,
F7
C7
F7
talk this way,
walk this way,
talk this way.)
Uh, just gim-me a kiss.

Guitar Solo
Gtrs. 1 & 2: w/ Rhy. Fig. 2
N.C.(C7)
Gtr. 3
1/2
A5
Like this!
Guitar Solo
Gtrs. 1 & 2: w/ Riff B, till fade
Gtr. 3 N.C.(E5)
A5
N.C.(E5)
w/ bar
full
1 1/2
-1/2
Riff B
Gtrs. 1 & 2

Gtr. 4
(dist.)
E7
A7
mf
full
1/2
8va
loco

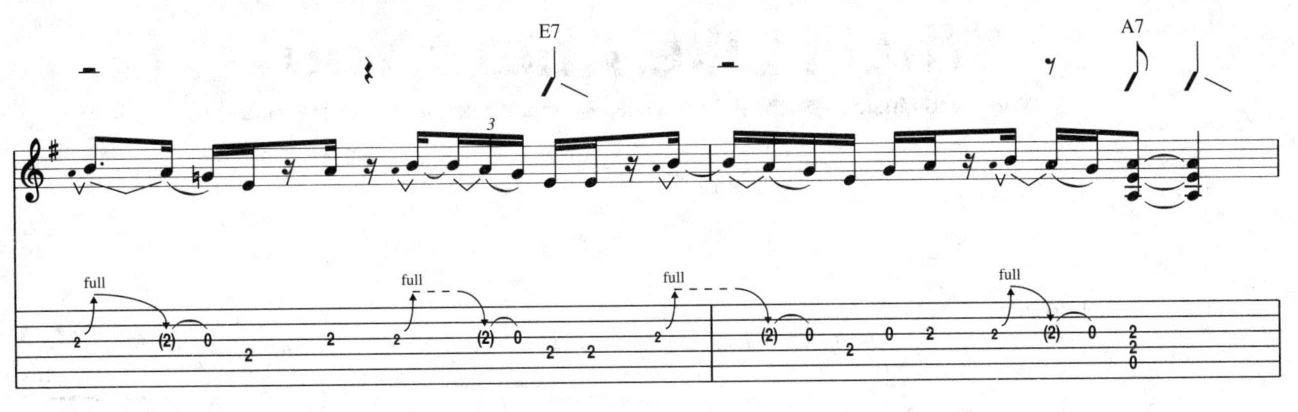
E7
A7
full
full
full
full

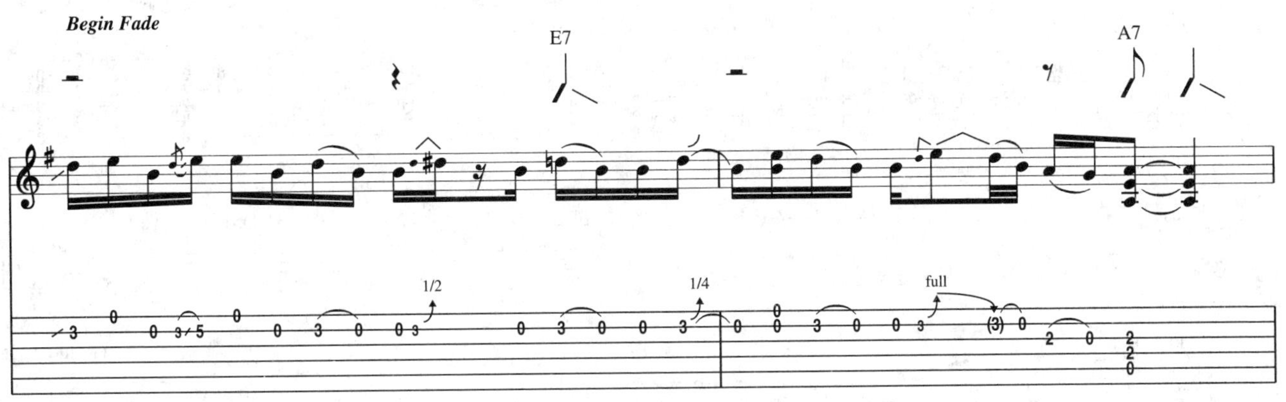
Begin Fade
E7
A7
1/2
1/4
full

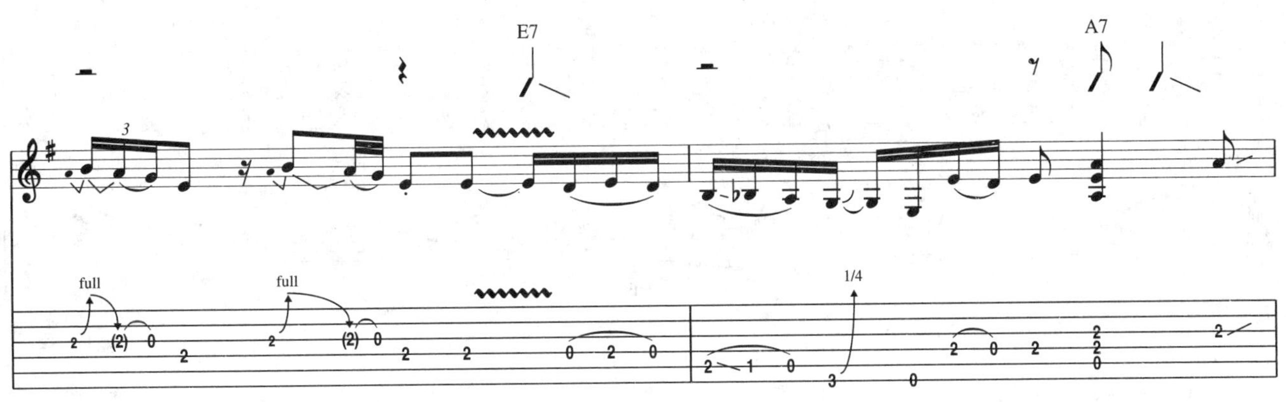
E7
A7
full
full
1/4

E7
A7
Fade Out
E7
let ring
full
full
full
full
full

What I Like About You

Words and Music by Michael Skill, Wally Palamarchuk and James Marinos

*Chord symbols reflect basic harmony.

Gtrs. 1 & 2: w/ Rhy. Figs. 3 & 3A
E A D/F♯ Asus4 A E A D/F♯ A
Uh, huh. 1. What I like a - bout
Verse
Gtrs. 1 & 2: w/ Rhy. Figs. 3 & 3A (2 times)
E A D/F♯ Asus4 A E A D/F♯ A
you, you hold me tight.
E A D/F♯ Asus4 A E A D/F♯ A
Tell me I'm the on - ly one, wan - na come o - ver to - night. Yeah.
Chorus
*Gtrs. 1 & 2: w/ Rhy. Figs. 3 & 3A (2 times)
E A D/F♯ Asus4 A E A D/F♯ A
Keep on whis - per - in' in my ear. Tell me all the things that I wan - na hear 'cause it's true,
(Ah. Ah. That's
*w/ strumming variations ad lib. throughout song
E A D/F♯ Asus4 A E A D/F♯ A
that's what I like a - bout you. 2. What I like a - bout
what I like. That's what I like.)
Verse
Gtrs. 1 & 2: w/ Rhy. Figs. 3 & 3A (2 times)
E A D/F♯ Asus4 A E A D/F♯ A
you, you real - ly know how to dance. When you go
you, you keep me warm at night.
E A D/F♯ Asus4 A E A D/F♯ A
up - town, jump a - round, think a - bout true ro - mance. Yeah.
Nev - er wan - na let you go, know you make me feel al - right. Yeah.
Chorus
1st time, Gtr. 1: w/ Rhy. Fig. 3 (2 times)
1st time, Gtr. 2: w/ Rhy. Fig. 3A (2 3/4 times)
2nd time, Gtrs. 1 & 2: w/ Rhy. Figs. 3 & 3A (5 times)
E A D/F♯ Asus4 A E A D/F♯ A
Keep on whis - per - in' in my ear. Tell me all the things that I wan - na hear 'cause it's true,
(Ah. Ah. That's

To Coda
E A D/F♯ Asus4 A E A D/F♯ A
that's what I like a - bout you. That's what I like a - bout
what I like a - bout you. That's what I like a - bout you. That's
E A D/F♯ Asus4 A E A *D/F♯ G5
Gtr. 2
(cont. in notation)
you. That's what I like a - bout you. Wow!
what I like a - bout you. That's what I like.)
Gtr. 1
*See top of first page of song for chord diagrams pertaining to rhythm slashes.
Guitar Solo
G5 D5 G5
Gtrs. 1 & 2
A5 A D/F♯ A B/F♯
E/G♯ B/F♯ B
let ring
Hey!
(Hey!)

Harmonica Solo

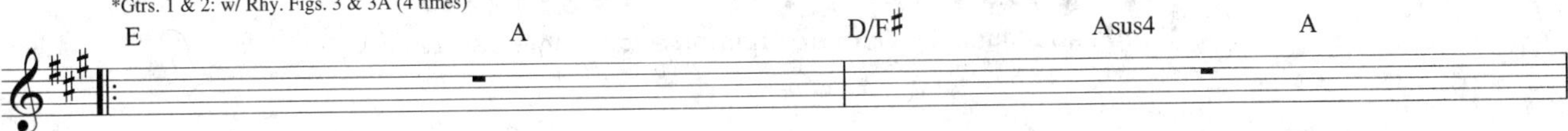
*Gtrs. 1 & 2: w/ Rhy. Figs. 3 & 3A (4 times)
E A D/F♯ Asus4 A
*4th time, Gtr. 2 plays f

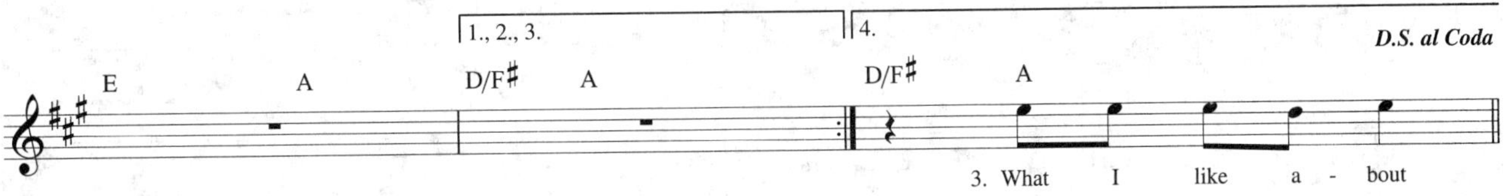
1., 2., 3.
4.
D.S. al Coda
E A D/F♯ A D/F♯ A
3. What I like a - bout

Coda
E A D/F♯ Asus4 A E A D/F♯ A
you. That's what I like a - bout you. Whispered: That's what I like a - bout
what I like a - bout you. That's what I like a - bout you. That's

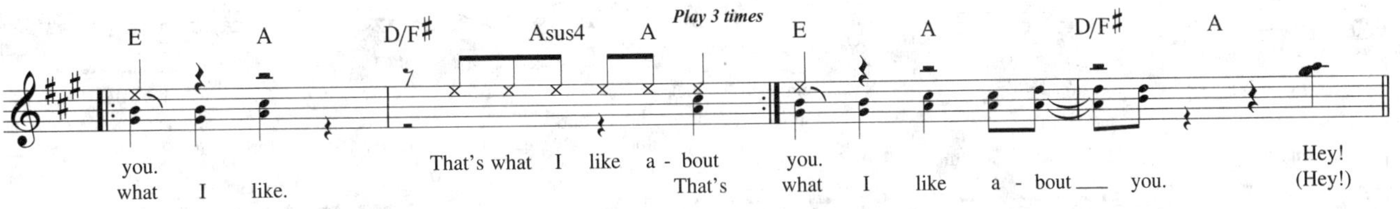
Play 3 times
E A D/F♯ Asus4 A E A D/F♯ A
you. That's what I like a - bout you. Hey!
what I like. That's what I like a - bout you. (Hey!)

Outro

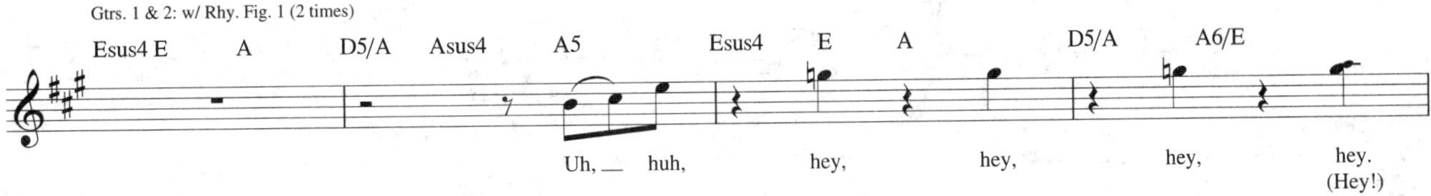
Gtrs. 1 & 2: w/ Rhy. Fig. 1 (2 times)
Esus4 E A D5/A Asus4 A5 Esus4 E A D5/A A6/E
Uh, huh, hey, hey, hey, hey.
(Hey!)

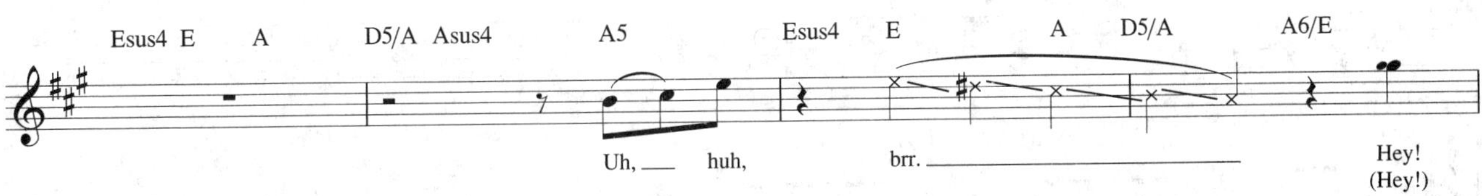
Esus4 E A D5/A Asus4 A5 Esus4 E A D5/A A6/E
Uh, huh, brr. Hey!
(Hey!)

Gtrs. 1 & 2: w/ Rhy. Fig. 2
Esus4 E A D5/A Asus4/E A5 Esus4 E A D5 A6/E A5
Uh, huh. Hey!
(Hey!)

What's Your Name

Words and Music by Gary Rossington and Ronnie Van Zant

A

I found my lim - o driv - er, "Mis -
It seems that one of the crew had a
I got six hun - dred miles to ride

End Rhy. Fig. 1A

End Rhy. Fig. 1

E

- ter, take us to the show."
go with a one of the guests, ah, yes.
to do one more show, oh, no.

A

I done
Well, the
Can I

w/ pick & fingers

3rd time, Gtr. 3: w/ Rhy. Fig. 3 (1st 2 meas.)
G
made some plans for later on to-night.
po-lice said we can't drink in the bar, what a shame.
get you a tax-i home? It sure was grand.
P.M.
G A E A
I'll find a lit-tle queen and I know I can treat her right.
Won't 'cha come up-stairs, girl, and have a drink of cham-
When I come back here next year I wan-na see you a-gain.

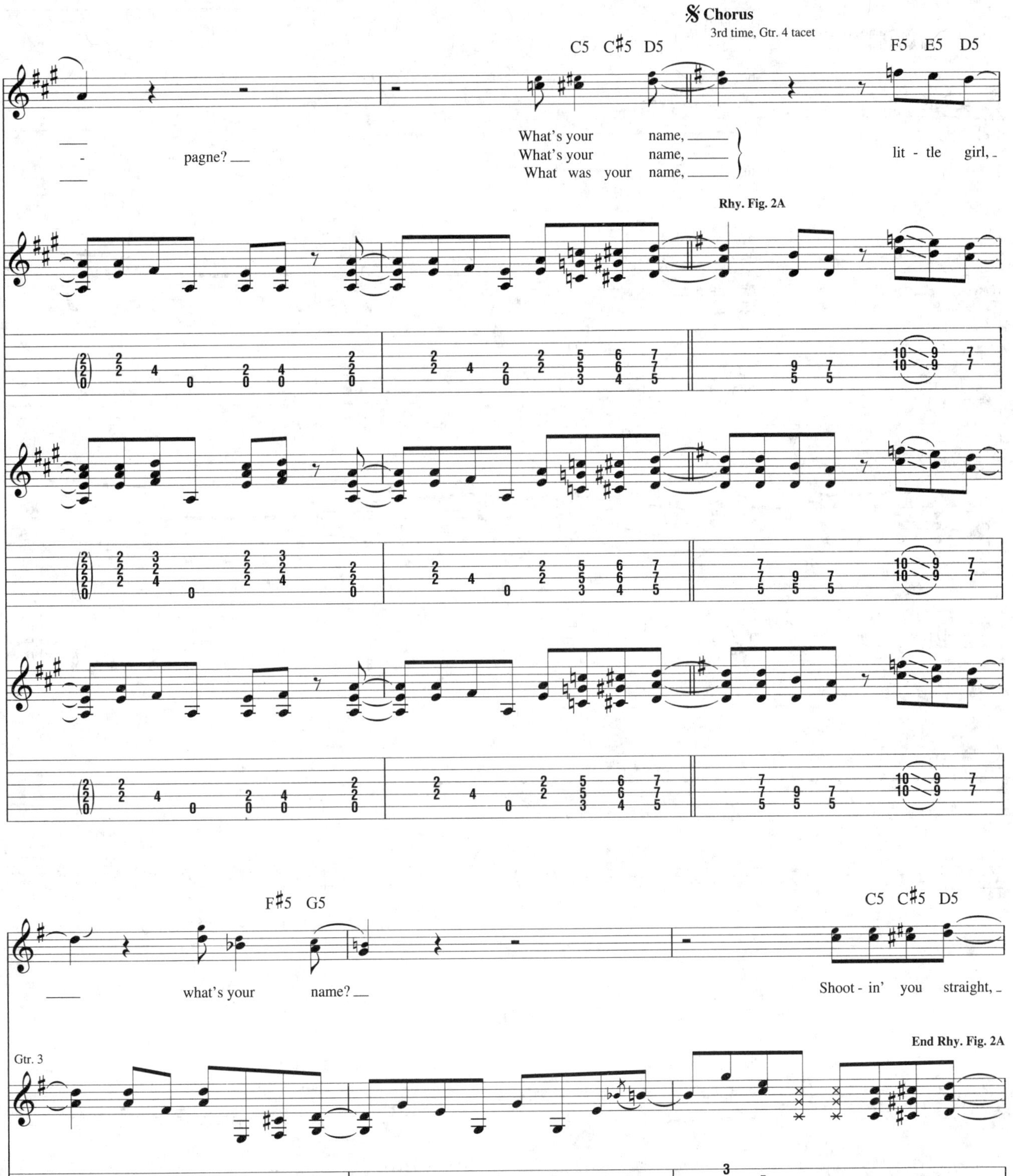

𝄋 Chorus

3rd time, Gtr. 4 tacet

C5 C♯5 D5 F5 E5 D5

- pagne? What's your name, What's your name, What was your name, lit - tle girl,

Rhy. Fig. 2A

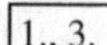
1., 3.

2nd & 4th times, Gtrs. 1 & 2: w/ Rhy. Fig. 2 (2 1/2 times)
2nd & 4th times, Gtr. 3: w/ Rhy. Fig. 2A (2 1/2 times)
F5 E5 D5
F♯5 G5
G
lit - tle girl,
1., 3. won't 'cha do the same?
2., 4. well, there ain't no shame.

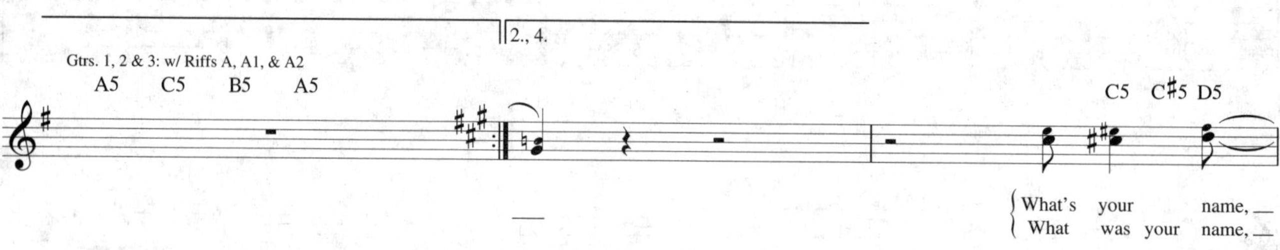
Gtrs. 1, 2 & 3: w/ Riffs A, A1, & A2
A5 C5 B5 A5
2., 4.
C5 C♯5 D5
What's your name,
What was your name,

F5 E5 D5
F♯5 G5
lit - tle girl,
what's your name?

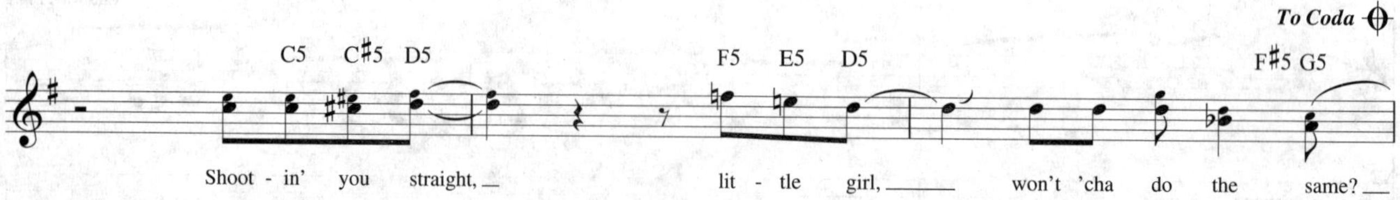
To Coda
C5 C♯5 D5
F5 E5 D5
F♯5 G5
Shoot - in' you straight,
lit - tle girl,
won't 'cha do the same?

Guitar Solo
Gtrs. 1 & 2: w/ Rhy. Figs. 1 & 1A (1 3/4 times)
G
A
Oh,
yeah!
Gtr. 4 (dist.)
let ring
Gtr. 3
Rhy. Fig. 3
Gtrs. 1 & 2
Gtr. 4
G
A
let ring
Gtr. 3
End Rhy. Fig. 3
Gtr. 3: w/ Rhy. Fig. 3 (1st 3 meas.)
Gtr. 4
G
A

Gtr. 4
G
Gtr. 3
Gtr. 2
Gtr. 1
F♯m
G
A
let ring
1 1/2

D.S. al Coda
(take repeat)

C G A C5 C♯5 D5

What's your name,

Coda

Whew!

Gtr. 3

Gtr. 2

Gtr. 1

When the Children Cry

Words and Music by Mike Tramp and Vito Bratta

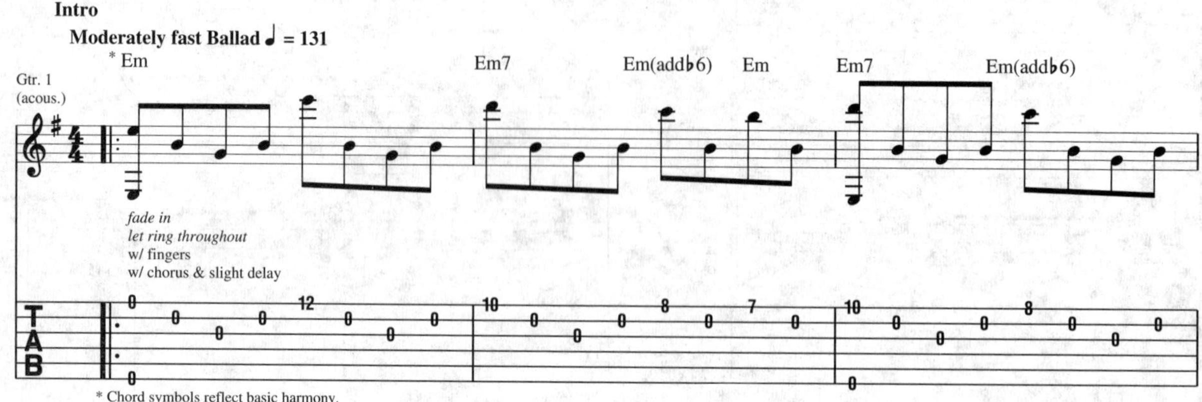

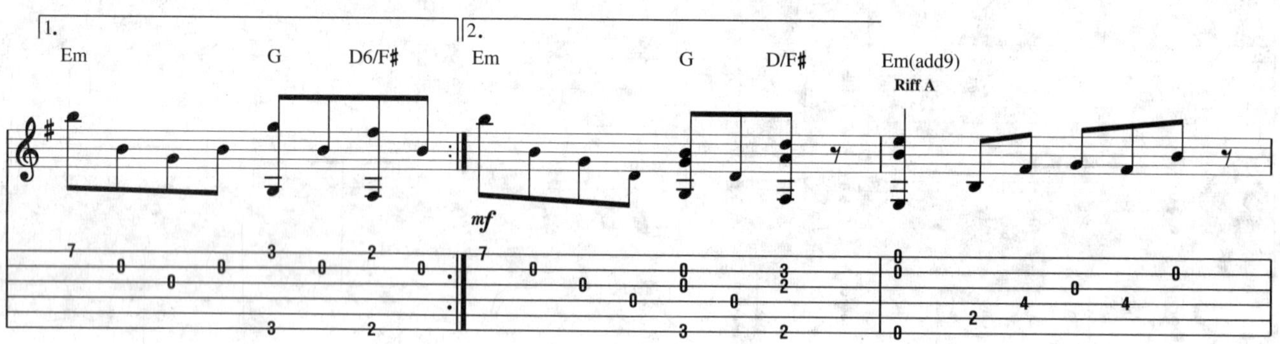

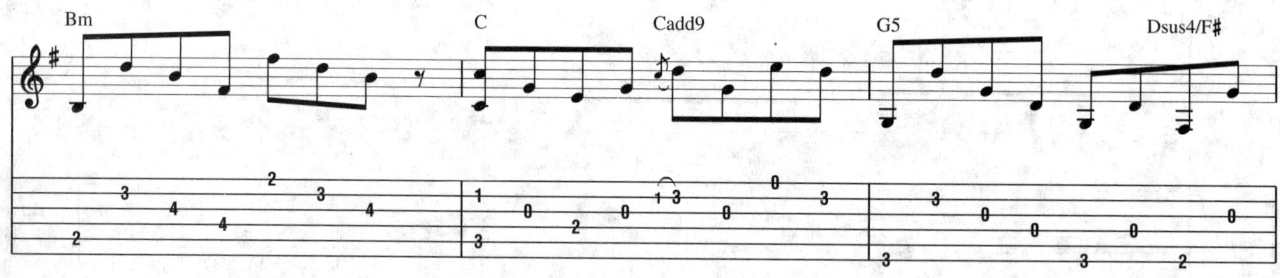

Verse
D
G
1. Lit - tle child
End Riff A
Riff B
Harm.
rit.

D/F#
Em
Bm7
dry your cry - ing eyes.

C
Cadd9
G5
Dsus4/F#
Em(add9)
D
How can I ex - plain the fear you feel in - side?
End Riff B

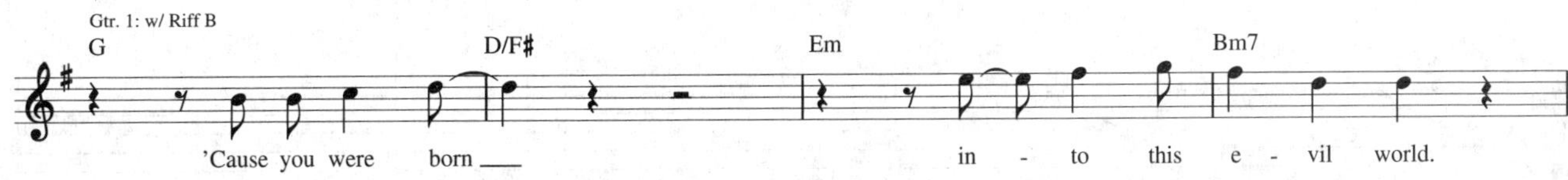
Gtr. 1: w/ Riff B
G
D/F#
Em
Bm7
'Cause you were born in - to this e - vil world.

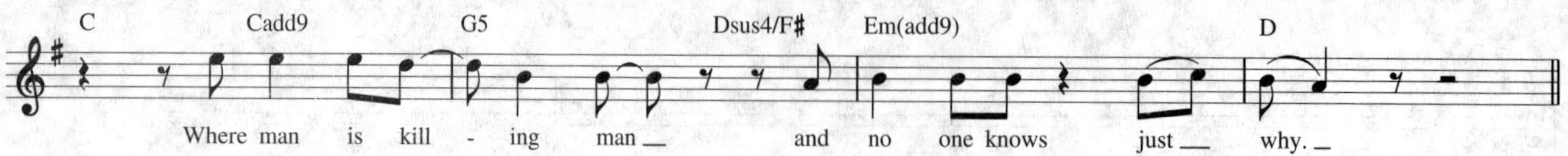
C
Cadd9
G5
Dsus4/F♯
Em(add9)
D
Where man is kill - ing man __ and no one knows just __ why. _

Pre-Chorus
C
Bm
Em(add9)
What have we be - come? _ Just __ look what we __
No more pres - i - dents. _ And all ___ the wars _
Riff C

Bm
C
Cadd9
G5
Dsus4/F♯
___ have done. _ All that we've __ de - stroyed _
___ will end. __ One u - nit - ed world __

To Coda
Em(add9)
D
Dsus4
D
you must build a - gain. ________
un - der God. ____
When the
End Riff C

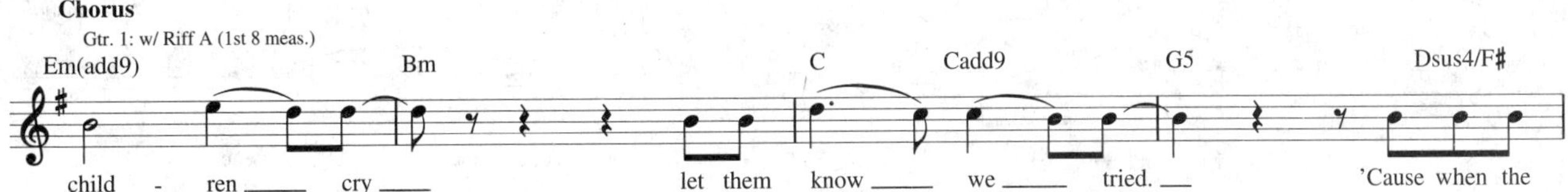

Chorus
Gtr. 1: w/ Riff A (1st 8 meas.)
Em(add9) Bm C Cadd9 G5 Dsus4/F♯
child - ren cry let them know we tried. 'Cause when the

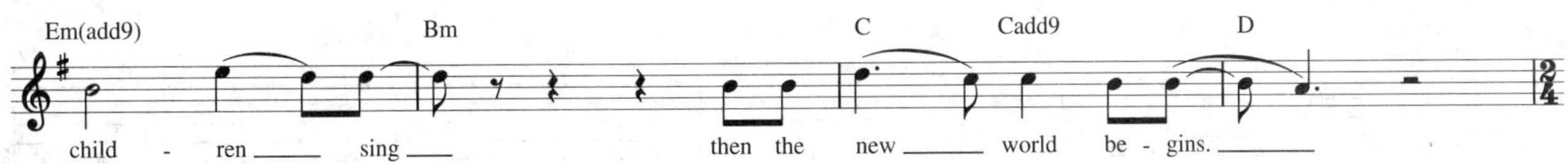

Em(add9) Bm C Cadd9 D
child - ren sing then the new world be - gins.

Verse
Gtr. 1: w/ Riff B (2 times)
G D/F♯ Em
2. Lit - tle child you must
Gtr. 1
Riff B1
Gtr. 2 (elec.)
mp
w/ dist., compression & delay

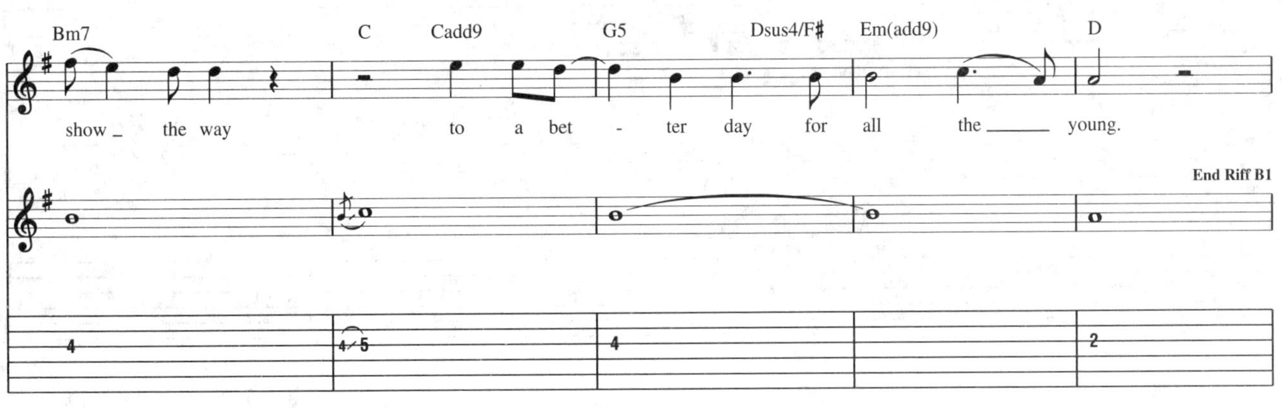

Bm7 C Cadd9 G5 Dsus4/F♯ Em(add9) D
show the way to a bet - ter day for all the young.
End Riff B1

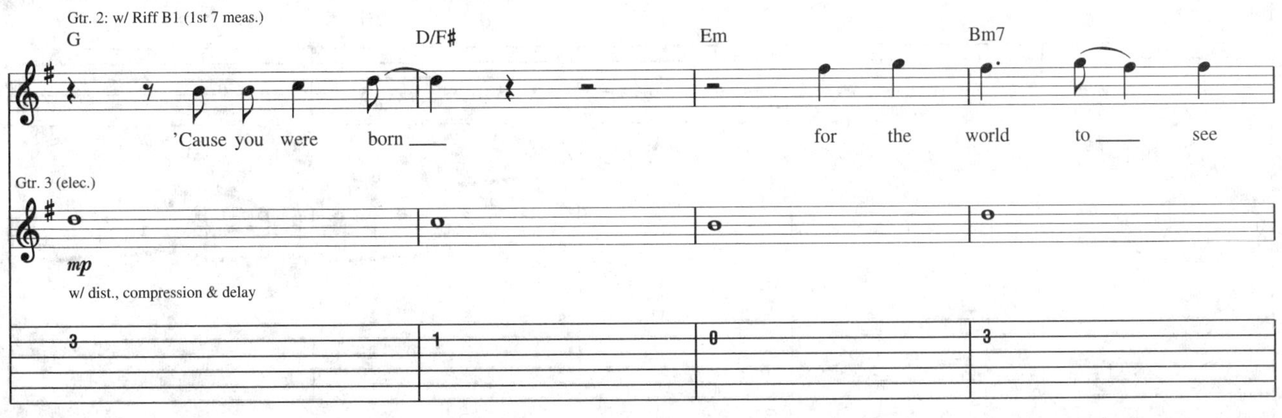

Gtr. 2: w/ Riff B1 (1st 7 meas.)
G D/F♯ Em Bm7
'Cause you were born for the world to see
Gtr. 3 (elec.)
mp
w/ dist., compression & delay

D.S. al Coda
C
Cadd9
G5
Dsus4/F#
Em(add9)
D
that we all can live with love and peace.
Coda
Chorus
Gtr. 1: w/ Riff A (1st 7 meas.)
Em(add9)
Bm
C
Cadd9
G5
Dsus4/F#
child - ren cry let them know we tried. 'Cause when the
Gtr. 3
Riff A1
Gtr. 2
Riff A2
divisi
Em(add9)
Bm
C
Cadd9
D
Dsus4
D
child - ren sing then the new world be - gins.
Gtr. 4 (elec.)
w/ dist.
Gtr. 3
End Riff A1
Gtr. 2
End Riff A2
Gtr. 1

Guitar Solo

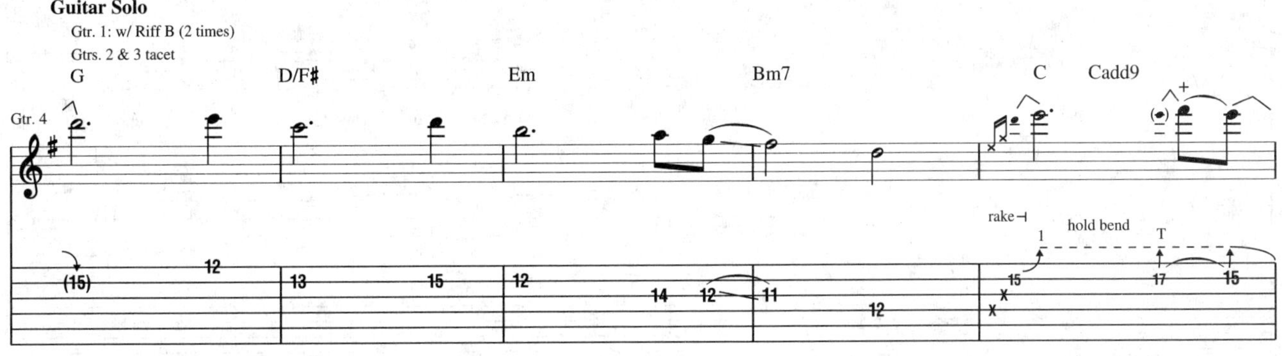

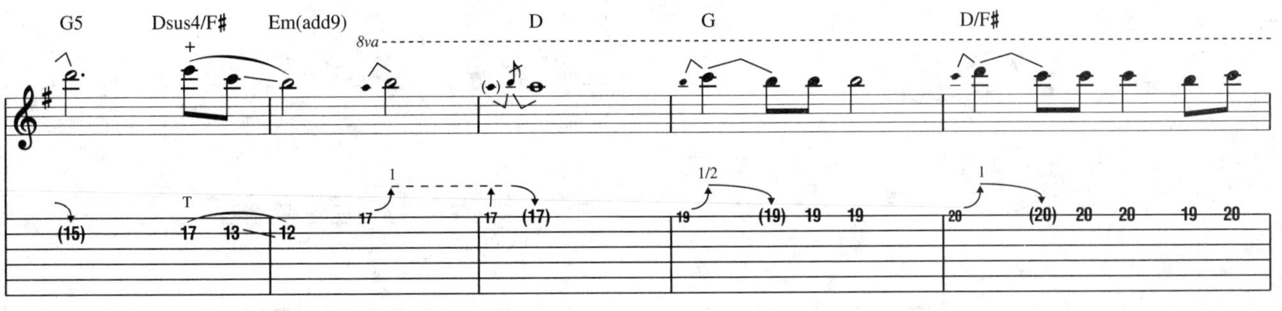

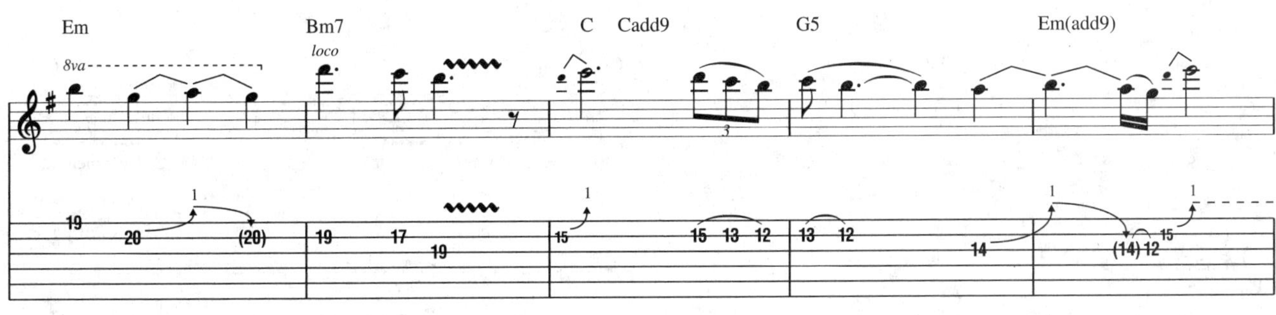

Pre-Chorus

Gtr. 1: w/ Riff C
C
Bm
Em(add9)
Bm
No more pres - i - dents.
And all the wars will end.
Gtr. 4
8va
loco
* vol. swells
C
Cadd9
G5
Dsus4/F♯
Gtr. 4 tacet
Em(add9)
D
Dsus4
D
One u - nit - ed world un - der God.
When the
Chorus
Gtrs. 1, 2 & 3: w/ Riffs A, A1 & A2 (1st 7 meas.)
Em(add9)
Bm
C
Cadd9
G5
Dsus4/F♯
child - ren cry let them know we tried. 'Cause when the
Gtrs. 1, 2 & 3: w/ Fills 1, 1A & 1B
child - ren fight let them know it ain't right. When the
Gtrs. 1, 2 & 3: w/ Riffs A, A1 & A2
child - ren pray let them know the way. 'Cause when the
('Cause when the
child - ren sing then the new world be - gins.
child - ren sing then the new world be - gins.)
rit.
Fill 1
Gtr. 1
Fill 1B
Gtr. 3
Gtr. 2
divisi
Fill 1A

Wild Thing

Words and Music by Chip Taylor

Verse
Gtr. 2: w/ Fill 1, 2nd time
Gtr. 2 tacet
A
Gsus4 A Gsus4 A
Gsus4 A Gsus4
1. Wild thing, I think I love you,
2. Wild thing, I think you move me,
but I wan-na know for sure.
A
Gsus4 A Gsus4 A
So, come on and hold me tight.
I love you.
You move me.
To Coda
Pre-Chorus
A D E D A D E D
Chorus
Gtr. 1: w/ Rhy. Fig. 1, 1st 7 meas.
A D E D A D
Wild thing, you make my heart sing.
E D A D E D A D
You make ev - 'ry - thing groov - y.
Wild thing.
Fill 1
Gtr. 2
8va

Recorder Solo
Gtr. 1: w/ Rhy. Fill 1
Gtr. 1: w/ Rhy. Fig. 1
E A D E D A D E D
*Gtr. 2
8va
*Recorder arr. for gtr.
D.S. al Coda
A D E D A D E Gsus4 A Gsus4
Coda
E
Outro-Chorus
Gtr. 1: w/ Rhy. Fig. 1, 1st 2 meas., till fade
A D E D A D E D A D
Wild thing, you make my heart sing. You make ev - 'ry-thing groov - y.
E D A D E D A D
Wild thing. Come on, come on wild thing.
Begin Fade
Fade Out
E D A D E D A D
Shake it, shake it, wild thing. I love you, wild thing.
Rhy. Fill 1
Gtr. 1

Wonderwall

Words and Music by Noel Gallagher

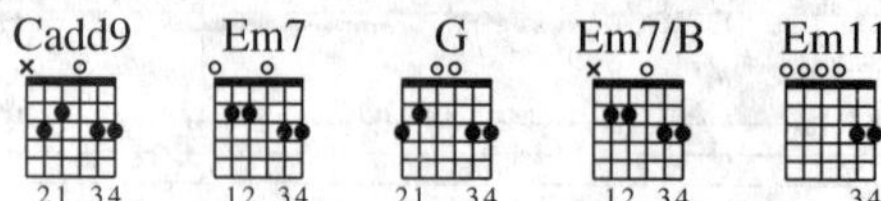

Capo II

Intro

Moderately ♩ = 87

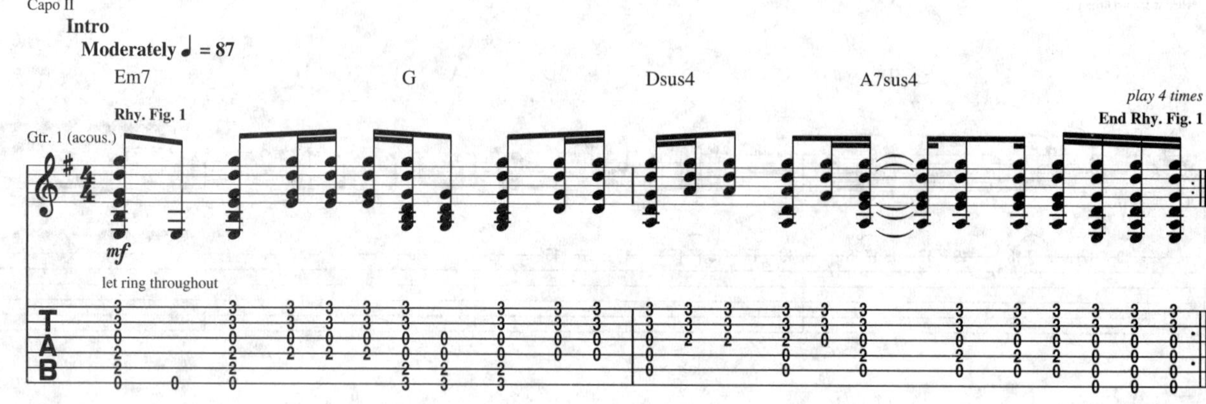

Verse

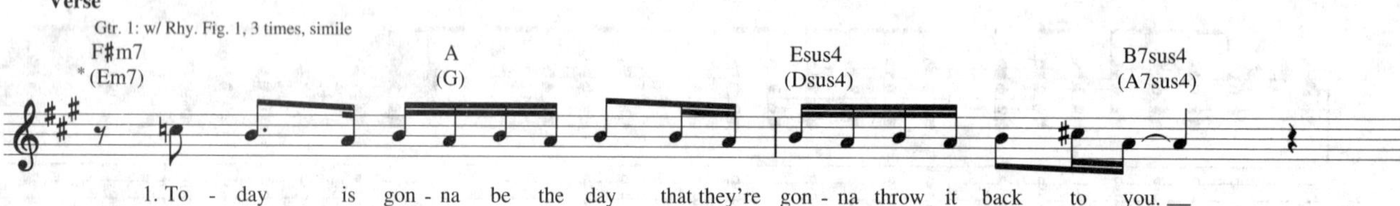

* Symbols in parentheses represent chord names respective to capoed guitars. Symbols above reflect actual sounding chords.

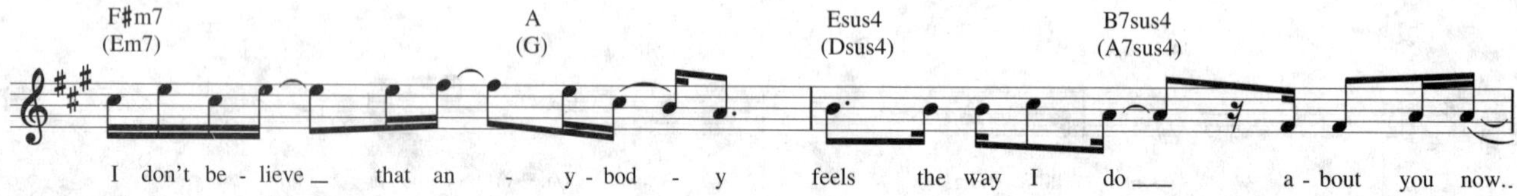

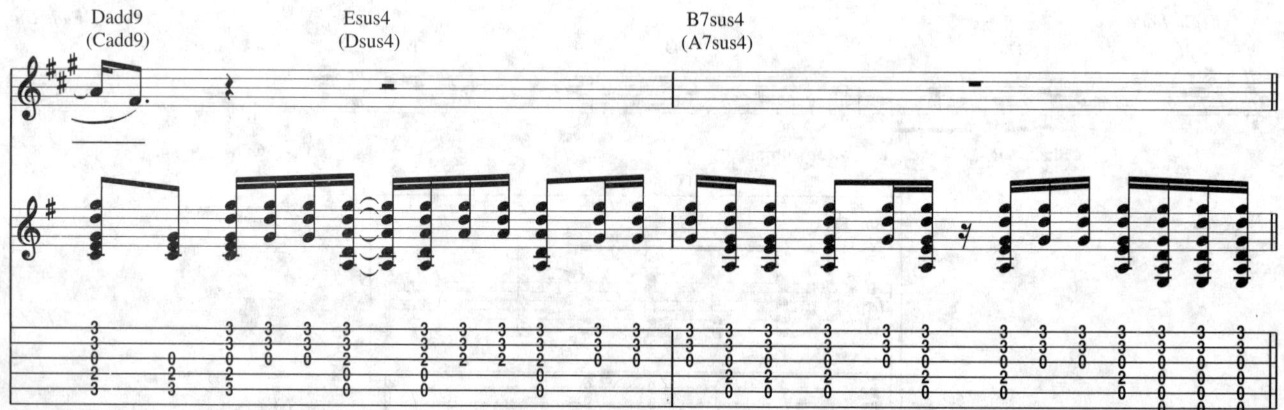

Verse
Gtr. 1: w/ Rhy. Fig. 1, 4 times, simile
F#m7
(Em7)
A
(G)
Esus4
(Dsus4)
B7sus4
(A7sus4)
2. Back - beat, the word is on the street that the fire in your heart is out.
3. To - day was gon - na be the day, but they'll nev - er throw it back to you.
I'm sure you've heard it all be - fore, but you nev - er real - ly had a doubt.
By now you should have some - how re - al - ized what you're not to do.
I don't be - lieve that an - y - bod - y feels the way I do a - bout you now.
And all
And all
Pre-Chorus
*D
(C)
E
(D)
the roads we have to walk are wind - ing, and all
the roads that lead you there were wind - ing, and all
Gtrs. 1 & 2 (clean)
mf
let ring throughout
* Chord symbols reflect overall tonality.
the lights that lead us there are blind - ing.
the lights that light the way are blind - ing.

D
(C)
E
(D)
A
(G)
E/G♯
(D/F♯)
F♯m7
(Em7)
A
(G)
There are man - y things that I would like to say to you, but I don't know how.

B7sus4
(A7sus4)
Be-cause
I said
(cont. in slash)

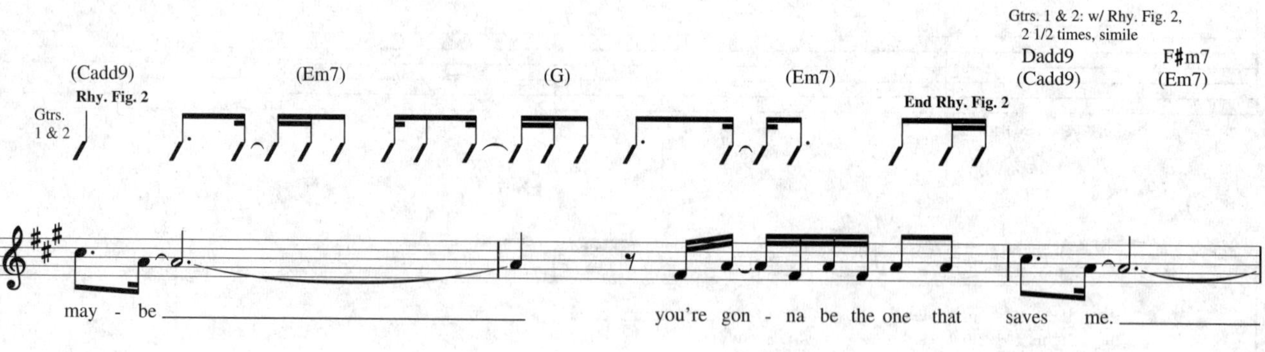
Gtrs. 1 & 2: w/ Rhy. Fig. 2,
2 1/2 times, simile
(Cadd9)
Rhy. Fig. 2
Gtrs.
1 & 2
(Em7)
(G)
(Em7)
End Rhy. Fig. 2
Dadd9
(Cadd9)
F♯m7
(Em7)
may - be
you're gon - na be the one that saves me.

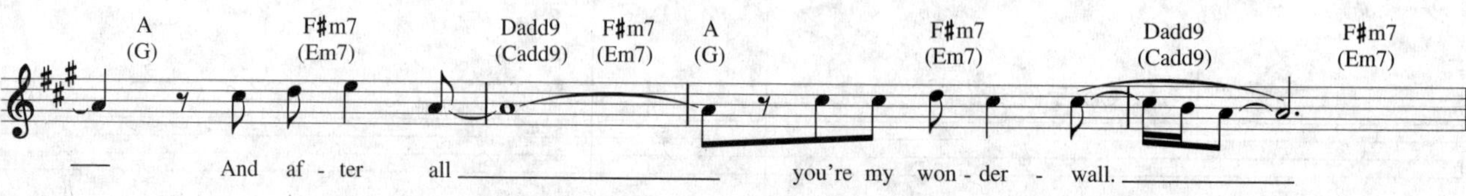
A
(G)
F♯m7
(Em7)
Dadd9
(Cadd9)
F♯m7
(Em7)
A
(G)
F♯m7
(Em7)
Dadd9
(Cadd9)
F♯m7
(Em7)
And af - ter all
you're my won - der - wall.

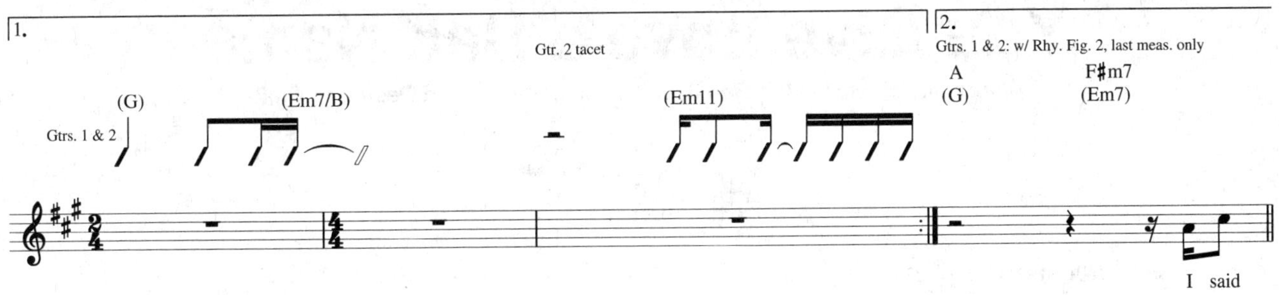
1.
Gtr. 2 tacet
2.
Gtrs. 1 & 2: w/ Rhy. Fig. 2, last meas. only
(G)
(Em7/B)
(Em11)
A
(G)
F#m7
(Em7)
Gtrs. 1 & 2
I said

Chorus

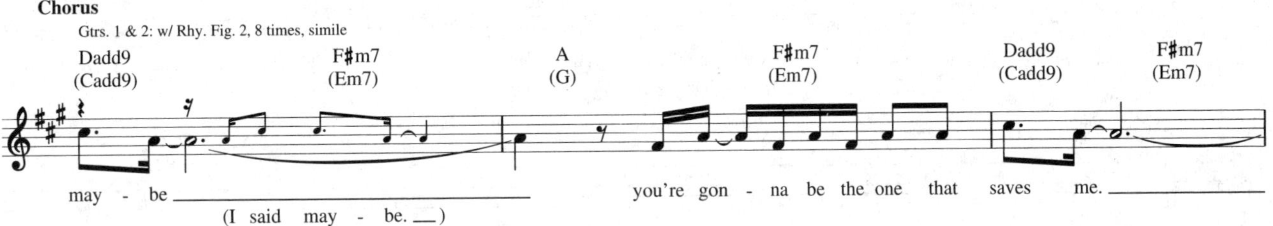
Gtrs. 1 & 2: w/ Rhy. Fig. 2, 8 times, simile
Dadd9
(Cadd9)
F#m7
(Em7)
A
(G)
F#m7
(Em7)
Dadd9
(Cadd9)
F#m7
(Em7)
may - be
(I said may - be.)
you're gon - na be the one that saves me.

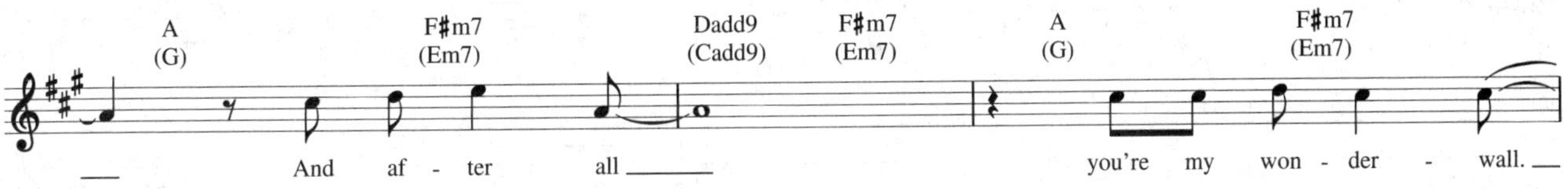
A
(G)
F#m7
(Em7)
Dadd9
(Cadd9)
F#m7
(Em7)
A
(G)
F#m7
(Em7)
And af - ter all
you're my won - der - wall.

Dadd9
(Cadd9)
F#m7
(Em7)
A
(G)
F#m7
(Em7)
Dadd9
(Cadd9)
F#m7
(Em7)
I said may - be
(I said may - be.)

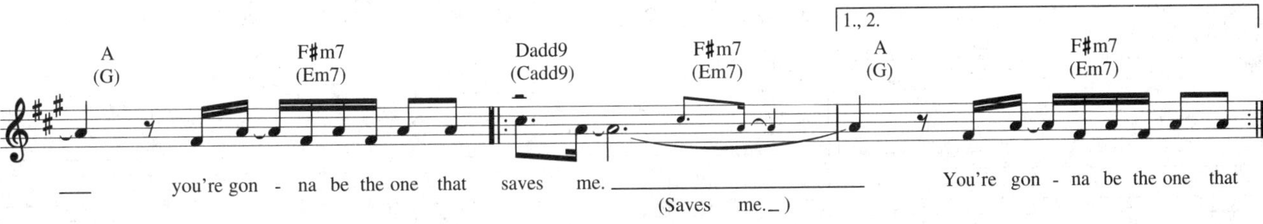
1., 2.
A
(G)
F#m7
(Em7)
Dadd9
(Cadd9)
F#m7
(Em7)
A
(G)
F#m7
(Em7)
you're gon - na be the one that saves me.
(Saves me.)
You're gon - na be the one that

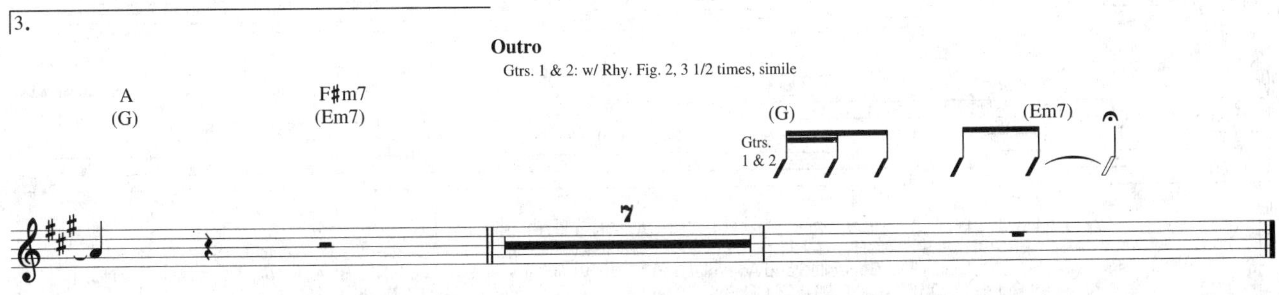
3.
Outro
Gtrs. 1 & 2: w/ Rhy. Fig. 2, 3 1/2 times, simile
A
(G)
F#m7
(Em7)
(G)
(Em7)
Gtrs. 1 & 2
7

You Give Love a Bad Name

Words and Music by Jon Bon Jovi, Richie Sambora and Desmond Child

Verse

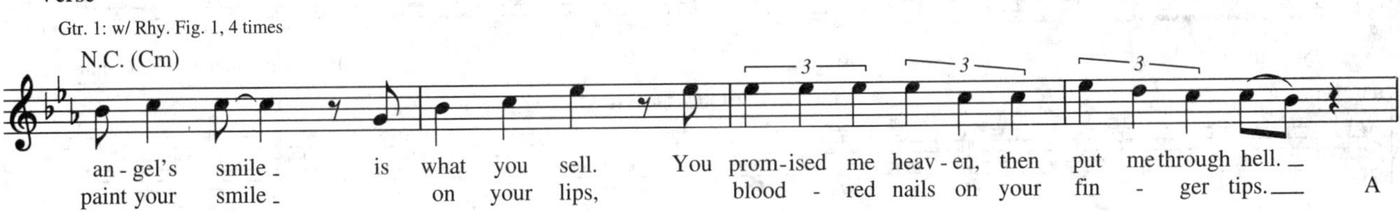

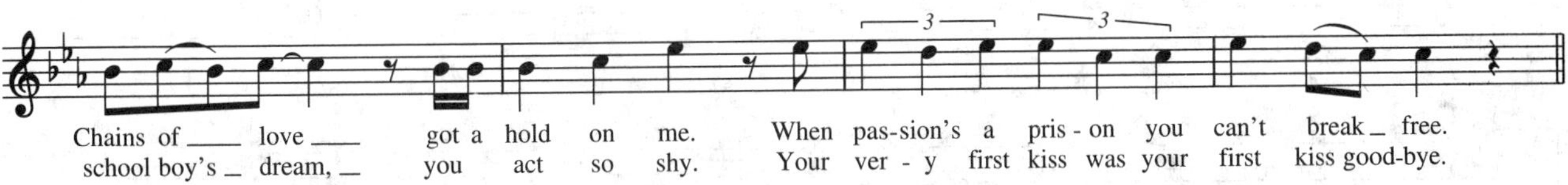

Pre-Chorus

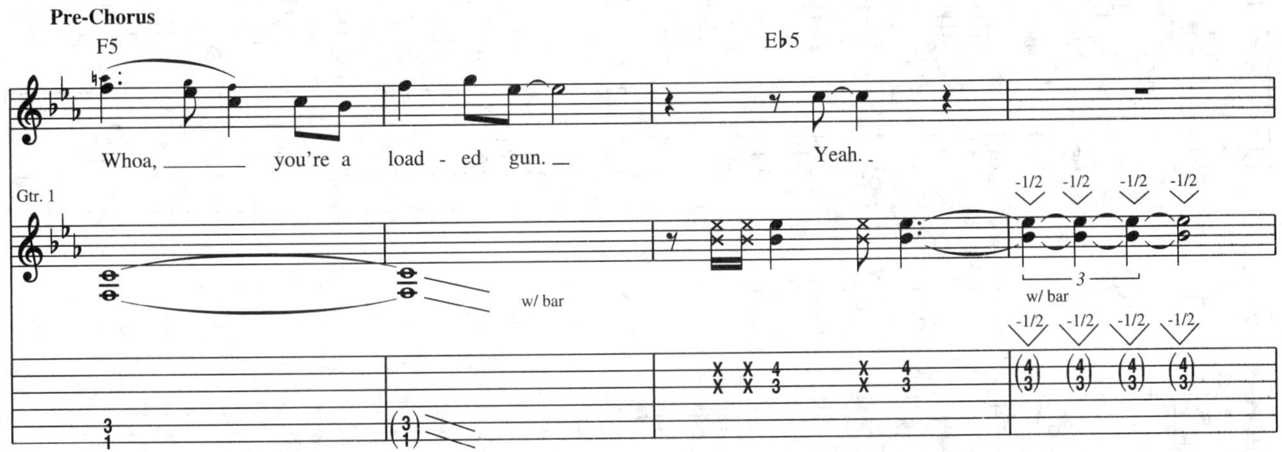

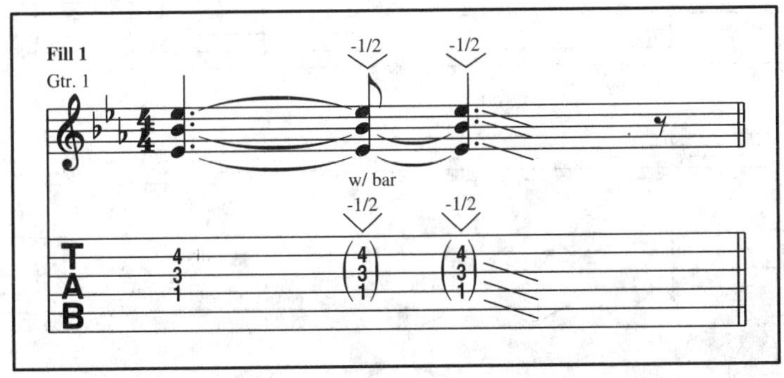

Bb5
N.C.(Bb)
Oh, there's no-where to run. No one can save me, the dam-age is done.
8va
loco
P.H.
w/ bar
P.H.
w/ bar
pitch: D
Chorus
C5
Ab5
C5
Bb5
C5
Ab5
Bb5
Eb5
C5
Shot through the heart, and you're to blame. You give love a bad name, bad name. I
Rhy. Fig. 2
End Rhy. Fig. 2
play my part, and you play your game. You give love a bad name, bad name. And
you give love a bad name.
1.
2.
* Gtr. 2
Harm.
* w/ harmonizer

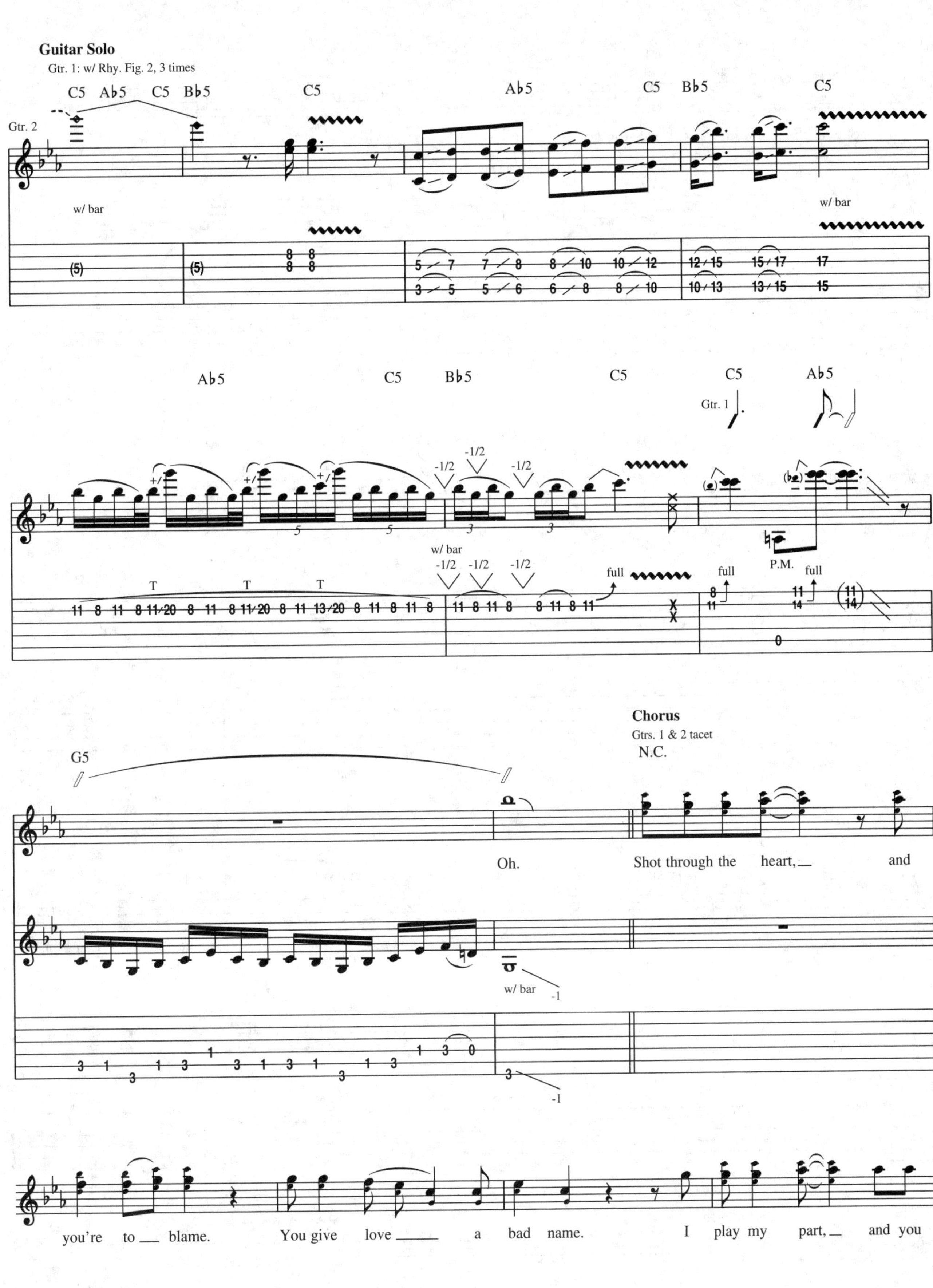
Guitar Solo
Gtr. 1: w/ Rhy. Fig. 2, 3 times
C5 A♭5 C5 B♭5
C5
A♭5
C5 B♭5
C5
Gtr. 2
w/ bar
w/ bar
A♭5
C5 B♭5
C5
C5
A♭5
Gtr. 1
w/ bar
full
full
full
P.M.
G5
Chorus
Gtrs. 1 & 2 tacet
N.C.
Oh.
Shot through the heart, and
w/ bar
you're to blame. You give love a bad name. I play my part, and you
play your game. You give love a bad name, bad name.

*w/ harmonizer

You Shook Me

Written by Willie Dixon and J.B. Lenoir

A7
E7
me ba - by,
you shook me all night long.
steady gliss.
w/o slide

1.
To Coda
Gtr. 1: w/ Fill 2, 3rd time
B7
A7
You shook me so hard baby,
ba - by, ba - by, please come
w/ slide

E7
B7
home.
2. I have a bird
w/o slide

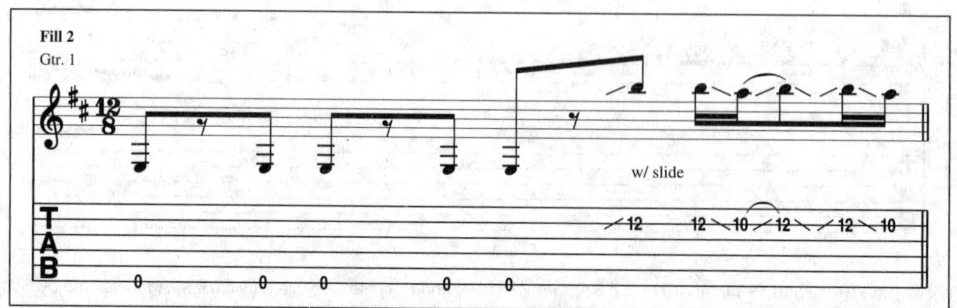
Fill 2
Gtr. 1
w/ slide

2.
B7
A7
bird, won't do noth - in', oh, oh, oh,
8va
E7
B7
with - out a dia - mond ring
8va
loco
Organ Solo
E7
E5
E6
E5
E6
E5
w/o slide
E6
E5
A5
A6
A5
A6
A5
G5
E5
E6
E5
B7
let ring

A7
E
Am
A#°
E7
B7
let ring
Harmonica Solo
E5
E6
A5
G5
A
G
B7
Gtr. 2
(fuzz)
E7
f
w/ slide
& reverb
w/o slide
Gtr. 1
Oh,
yeah.
(cont. in slash)

Guitar Solo

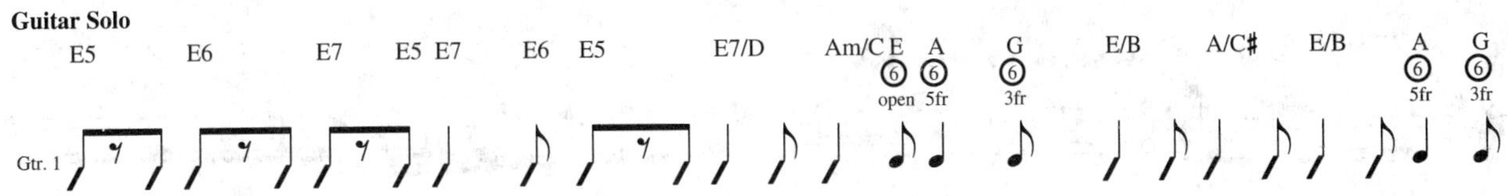
E5
E6
E7
E5 E7
E6 E5
E7/D
Am/C
E
A
G
open
5fr
3fr
E/B
A/C♯
E/B
A
G
5fr
3fr
Gtr. 1

8va
Gtr. 2
w/ slide
w/o slide
w/ slide
w/o slide
w/ slide

E7 type2
E5
A5

8va
w/o slide
full

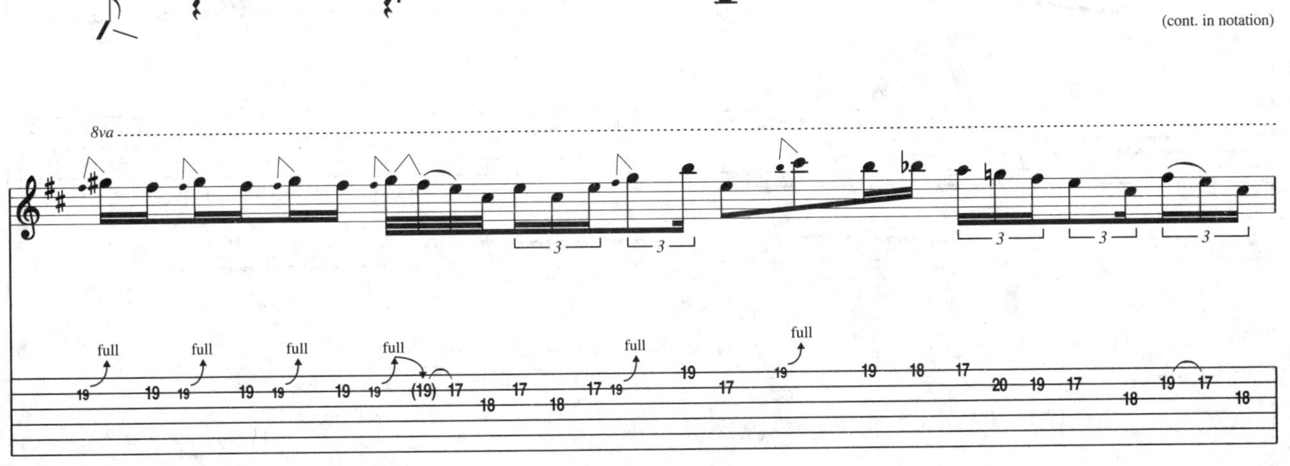
(cont. in notation)
8va
full

E5
8va
E6
E5
Gtr. 2
full
full
full
full
full
Gtr. 1
E6
E5
B7
8va
full
let ring
A7
loco
full
full
full
full
let ring

D.S. al Coda

Coda

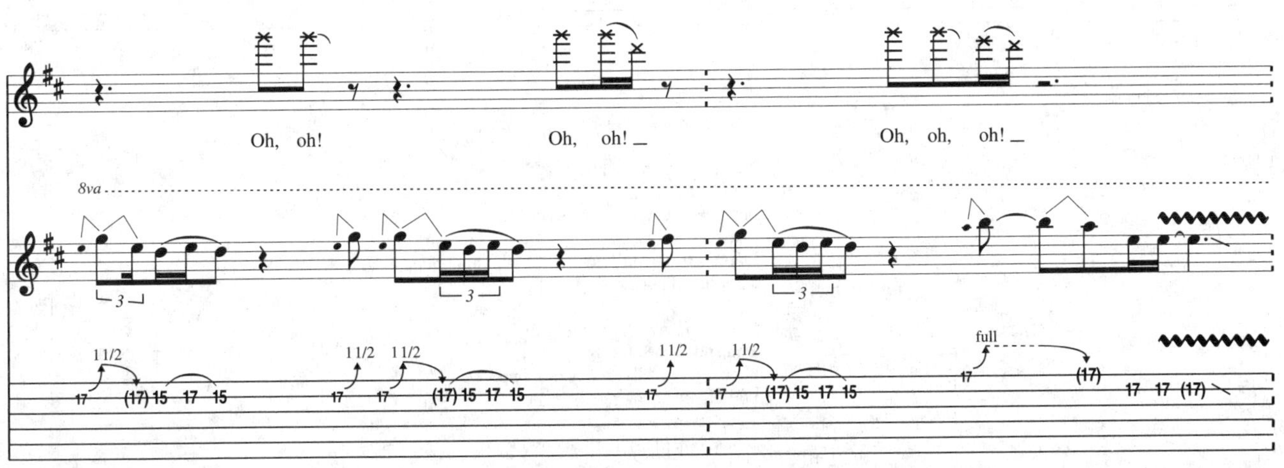

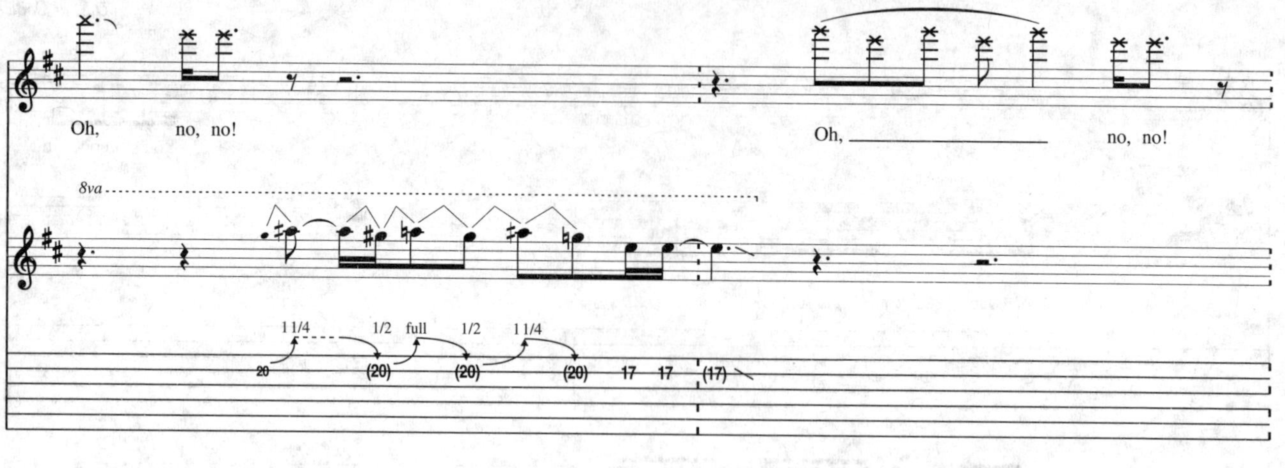

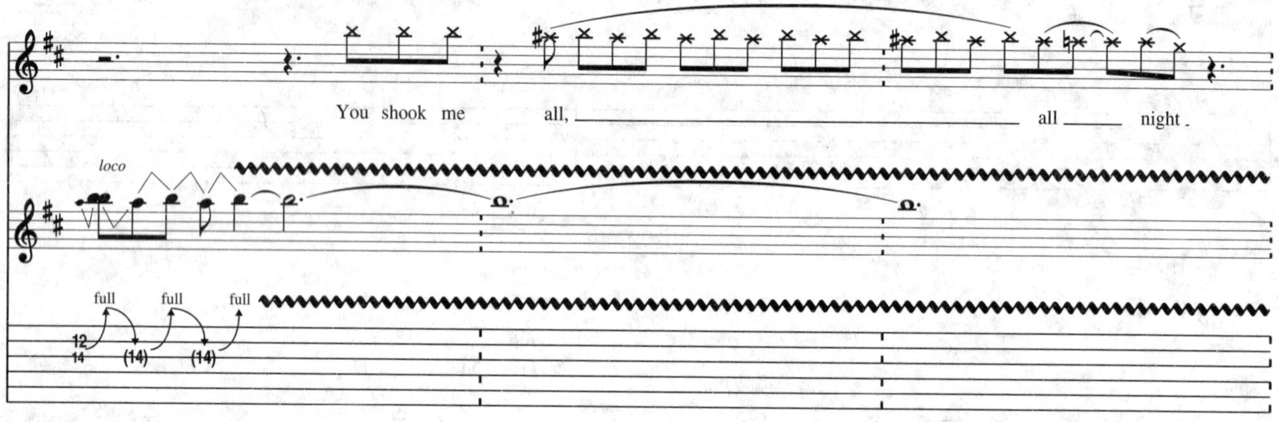

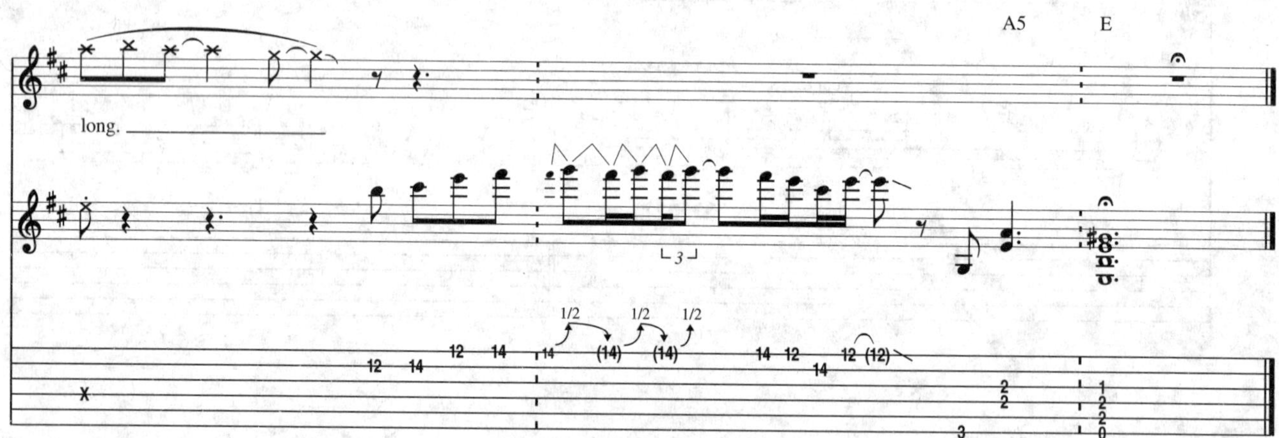

Additional Lyrics

2. I have a bird that whistles and
I have birds that sing.
I have a bird that whistles and
I have birds that sing.
I have a bird won't do nothin; oh, oh, oh, oh,
without a diamond ring.

3. You know you shook me, babe,
You shook me all night long.
I know you really, really did, babe.
I think you shook me, baby,
You shook me all night long.
You shook me so hard, baby, I know.

You Were Meant for Me

Lyrics by Jewel Kilcher
Music by Jewel Kilcher and Steve Poltz

Tune Down 1/2 Step:
(low to high) Eb-Ab-Db-Gb-Bb-Eb

Gtr. 1: w/ Riff A, simile
Csus2
G6/B
C
I break the yolks and make a smile - y face.
I kind - a like it in my

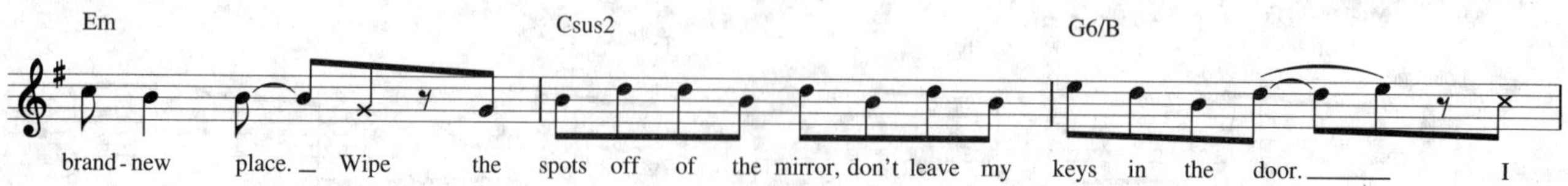
Em
Csus2
G6/B
brand - new place. Wipe the spots off of the mirror, don't leave my keys in the door. I

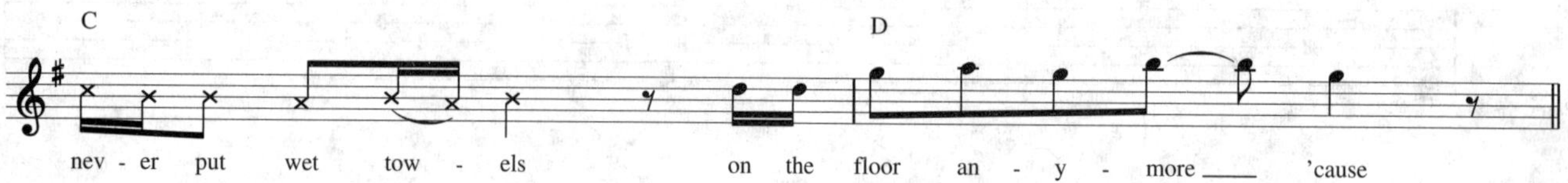
C
D
nev - er put wet tow - els on the floor an - y - more 'cause

Chorus
C
D
G
G5/F#
Em
dreams last so long, e - ven af - ter you're gone.

C
D
G5
G5/F#
Em
I know that you love me and soon you will see you were

To Coda
1.
C
D
Em
meant for me and I was meant for you.
8va
loco
Harm.
2.
Em
Bridge
Am7
you.
I go a-bout my bus-'ness, I'm
D
Bm
D
C
* C/B
do-ing fine. Be-sides, a what would I say if I had you on the line.
* bass plays B
D.C. al Coda
A Tempo
Am7
D
Bm/F#
rit.
Em
Same old sto-ry, not much to say. Hearts are bro-ken ev-'ry day.
rit.

Additional Lyrics

2. I called my momma, she was out for a walk.
Consoled a cup of coffee but it didn't wanna talk.
So I picked up the paper, it was more bad news;
More hearts being broken or people being used.
Put on my coat in the pouring rain.
I saw a movie, it just wasn't the same
'Cause it was happy, oh, I was sad
And it made me miss you, oh, so bad 'cause...

3. I brush my teeth, I put the cap back on.
I know you hate it when I leave the light on.
I pick a book up and then I turn the sheets down
And then I take a deep breath and a good look around.
Put on my PJs and hop into bed.
I'm half alive but I feel mostly dead.
I try and tell myself it'll all be alright.
I just shouldn't think anymore tonight 'cause...

You've Got a Friend

Words and Music by Carole King

*Symbols in parentheses represent chord names respective to capoed guitar. Symbols above reflect actual sounding chord. Capoed fret is "0" in TAB.

Bm7
(Am7)
E7sus4
(D7sus4)
A
(G)
Asus4
(Gsus4)
A
(G)
noth-ing, whoa, noth-ing is go - ing right,

G#m7
(F#m7)
C#7
(B7)
C#7sus4
(B7sus4)
C#7
(B7)
F#m
(Em)
C#7
(B7)
F#m7
(Em7)
close your eyes and think of me, and soon I will be there to

Bm7
(Am7)

C♯m7
(Bm7)

E7sus4
(D7sus4)

bright-en up e - ven your dark - est night. You just call

Chorus

A
(G)

Amaj7
(Gmaj7)

Dmaj7
(Cmaj7)

Bm7
(Am7)

E7sus4
(D7sus4)

out my name, and you know wher-ev - er I am, I'll come run -

A
(G)
Amaj7
(Gmaj7)
E7sus4
(D7sus4)
- ning, oh _ yeah, babe, _ to see you a - gain. __

A
(G)
Amaj7
(Gmaj7)
D
(C)
F#m7
(Em7)
Win-ter, spring, sum-mer or fall, __ now, all you got to do _ is __ call, __ and I'll

Dmaj7
(Cmaj7)
C♯m7
(Bm7)
D/E
(C/D)
E7sus4
(D7sus4)
A
(G)
D
(C)
be there, yeah, yeah, yeah. You've got a friend.

Verse
A
(G)
G♯m7
(F♯m7)
C♯7sus4
(B7sus4)
C♯7
(B7)
F♯m
(Em)
Gtr. 2 tacet
C♯7
(B7)
C♯7/G♯
(B7/F♯)
C♯7
(B7)
2. If the sky above you should turn

F♯m
(Em)
C♯7
(B7)
F♯m
(Em)
F♯m7
(Em7)
Bm7
(Am7)
E7sus4
(D7sus4)
— dark — and full of clouds, — and that old North wind — should be - gin to blow, —
Gtr. 1
A
(G)
Asus4
(Gsus4)
A
(G)
G♯m7
(F♯m7)
C♯7
(B7)
C♯7sus4
(B7sus4)
C♯7
(B7)
keep your head — to - geth - er and
Gtr. 2
Gtr. 1
F♯m7
(Em)
C♯7
(B7)
F♯m
(Em)
F♯m7
(Em7)
Bm7
(Am7)
C♯m7
(Bm7)
call my name — out loud, — now. — Soon I'll be knock - in' up - on your door. —

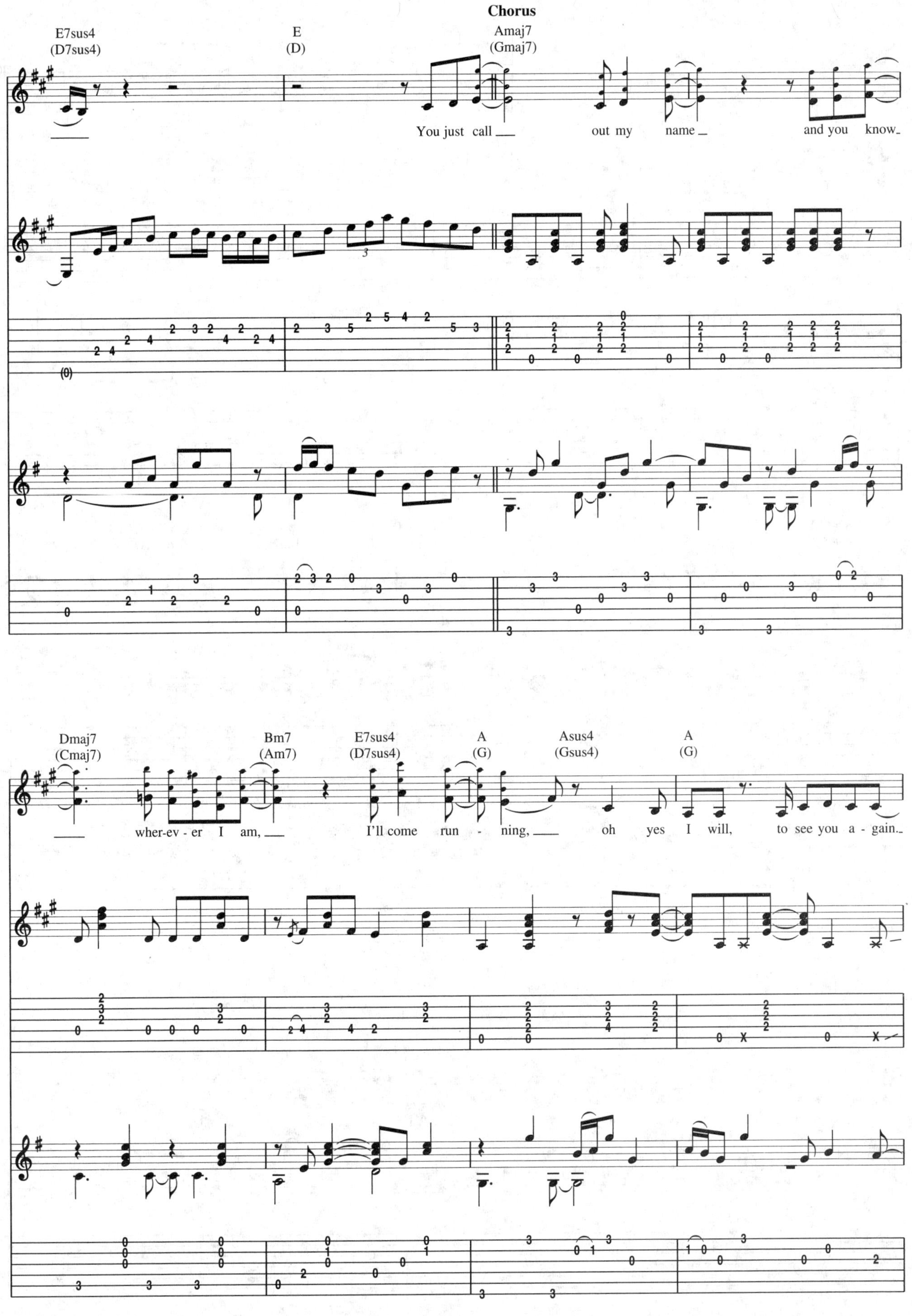

Chorus

E7sus4 (D7sus4) E (D) Amaj7 (Gmaj7)

You just call ___ out my name ___ and you know_

E7sus4
(D7sus4)
A
(G)
Amaj7
(Gmaj7)
Win-ter, spring, sum-mer or fall, yeah,
Dmaj7
(Cmaj7)
F#m7
(Em7)
Dmaj7
(Cmaj7)
C#m7
(Bm7)
Bm7
(Am7)
D/E
(C/D)
E7sus4
(D7sus4)
all you got to do is call,
and I'll be there,
yeah, yeah,
yeah.
Hey, ain't
Bridge
Gtr. 2 tacet
D/G
(C/F)
G
(F)
D
(C)
A
(G)
Asus4
(Gsus4)
Amaj7
(Gmaj7)
it good to know
that you've got a friend
when peo-ple can be so
cold?
They'll
Gtr. 1

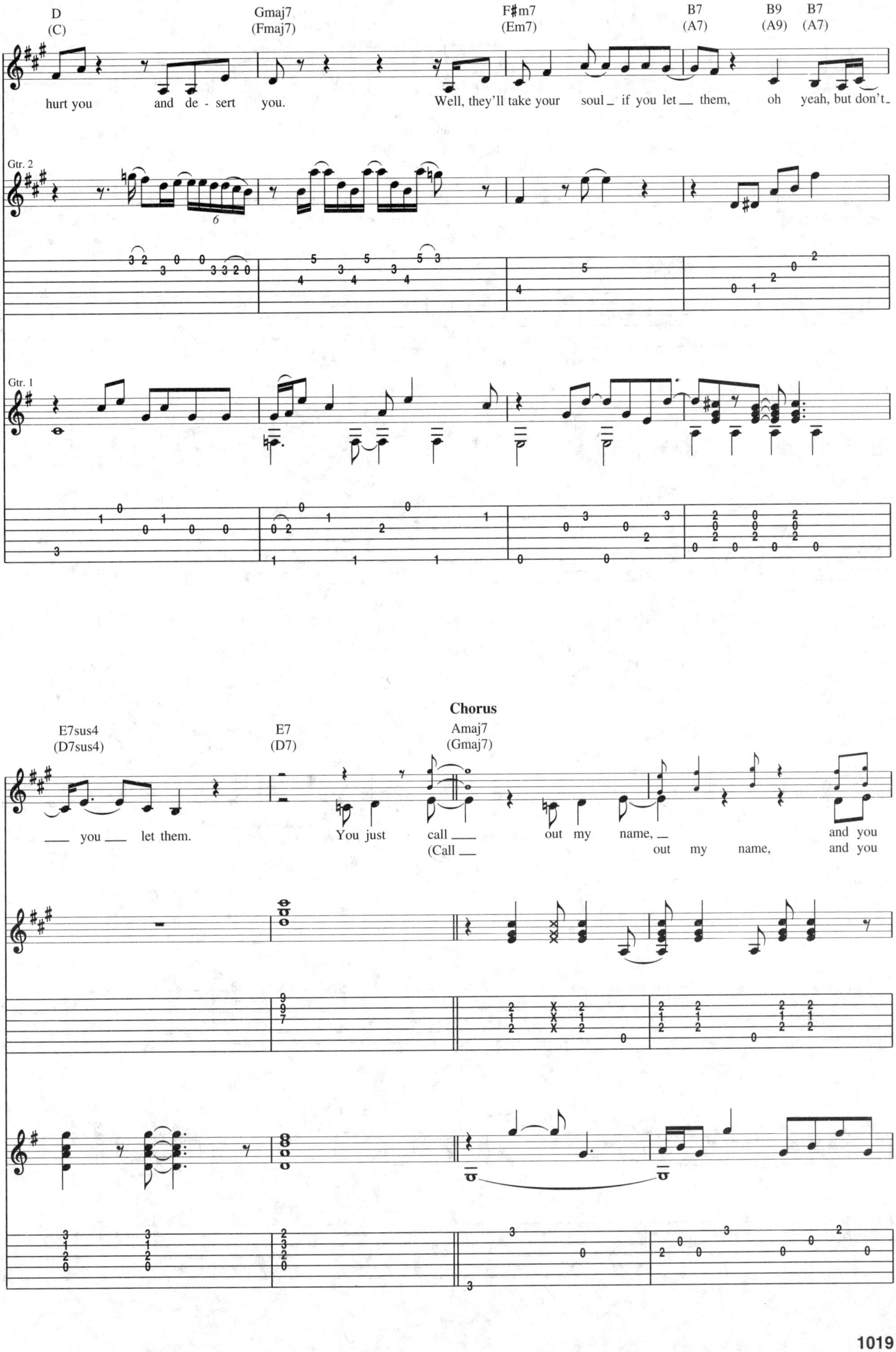

Chorus

E7sus4 (D7sus4) E7 (D7) Amaj7 (Gmaj7)

you let them. You just call out my name, and you

(Call out my name, and you

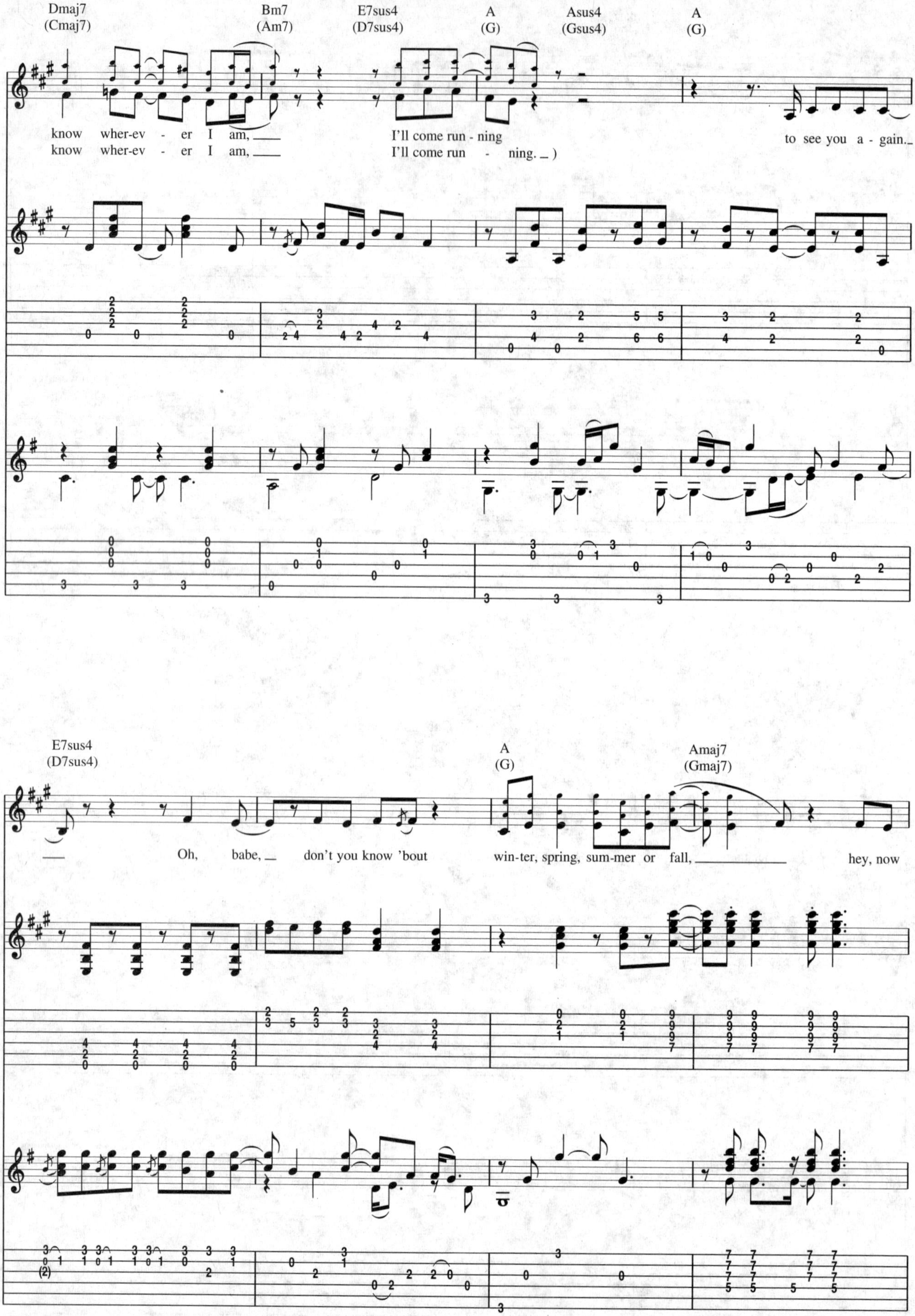

Dmaj7 (Cmaj7) Bm7 (Am7) E7sus4 (D7sus4) A (G) Asus4 (Gsus4) A (G)

know wher-ev - er I am, I'll come run - ning to see you a - gain.
know wher-ev - er I am, I'll come run - ning.)

Dmaj7
(Cmaj7)
F#m7
(Em7)
Dmaj7
(Cmaj7)
C#m7
(Bm7)
Bm7
(Am7)
all you've got to do is call.
Lord, I'll be there, yes I will.

Outro
E7sus4
(C/D)
(D7sus4)
A
(G)
D
(C)
You've got a friend.
You've got a

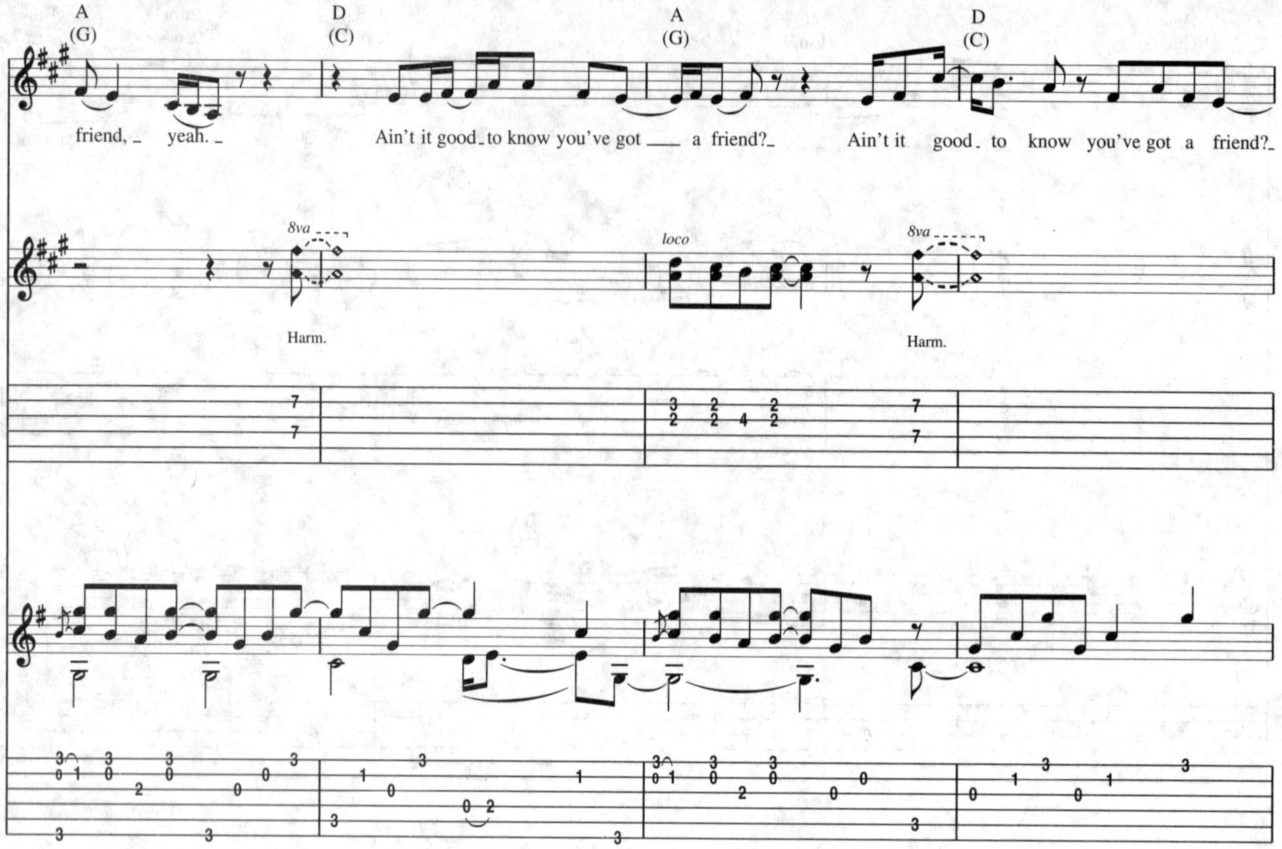
A
(G)
D
(C)
A
(G)
D
(C)
friend, yeah.
Ain't it good to know you've got a friend?
Ain't it good to know you've got a friend?
8va
Harm.
loco
8va
Harm.

A
(G)
D
(C)
A
(G)
Oh, yeah, yeah. You've got a friend.
loco
8va
Harm.
loco

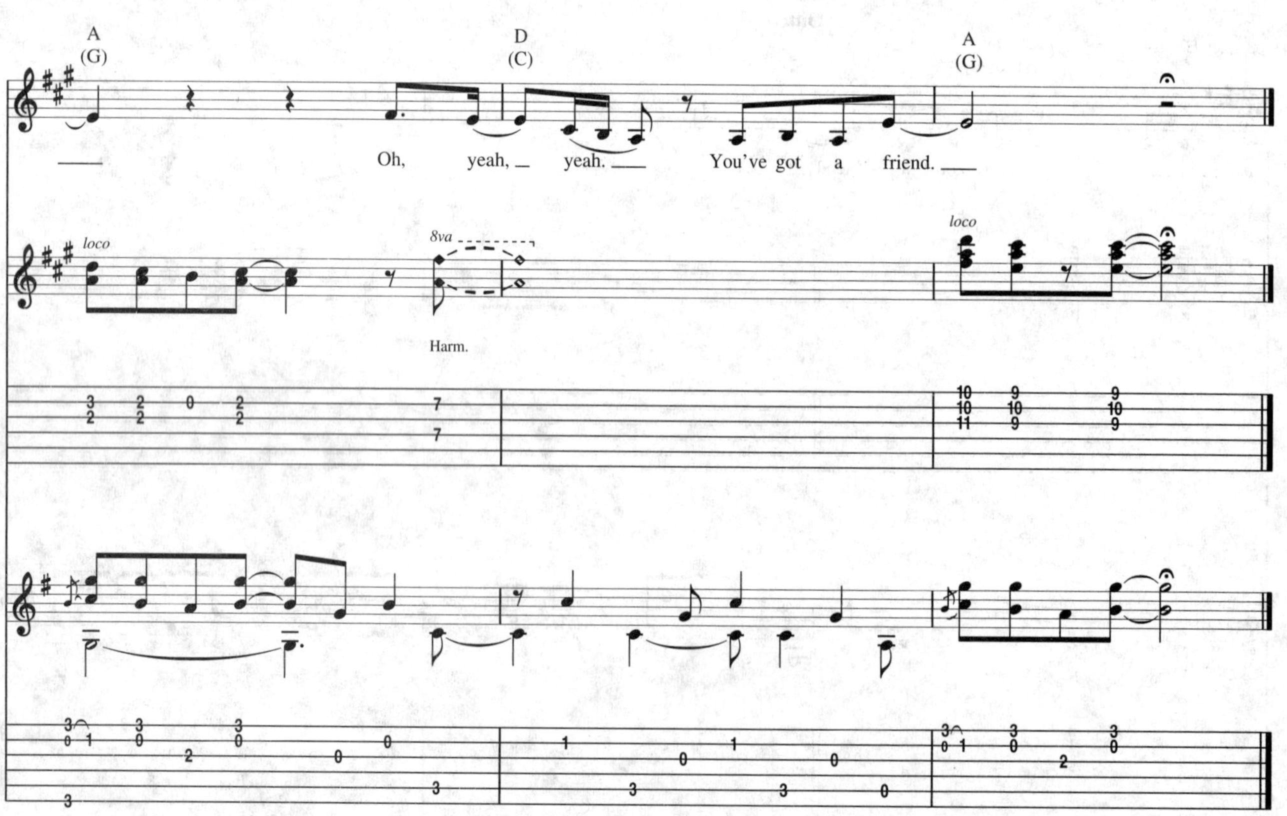

Guitar Notation Legend

Guitar music can be notated three different ways: on a *musical staff*, in *tablature*, and in *rhythm slashes*.

RHYTHM SLASHES are written above the staff. Strum chords in the rhythm indicated. Use the chord diagrams found at the top of the first page of the transcription for the appropriate chord voicings. Round noteheads indicate single notes.

THE MUSICAL STAFF shows pitches and rhythms and is divided by bar lines into measures. Pitches are named after the first seven letters of the alphabet.

TABLATURE graphically represents the guitar fingerboard. Each horizontal line represents a string, and each number represents a fret.

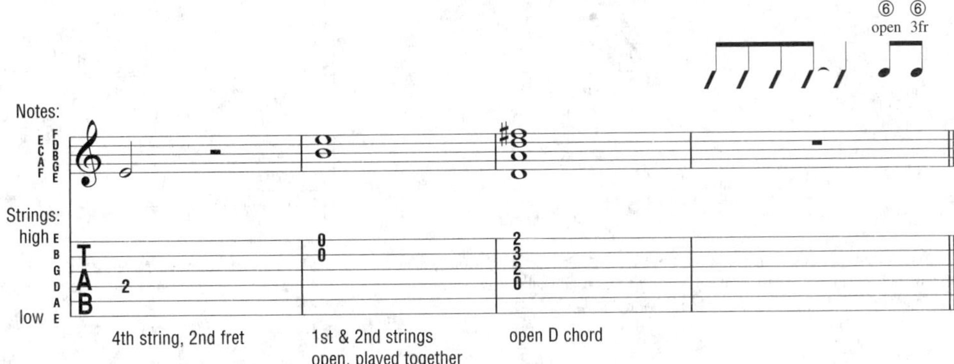

Definitions for Special Guitar Notation

HALF-STEP BEND: Strike the note and bend up 1/2 step.

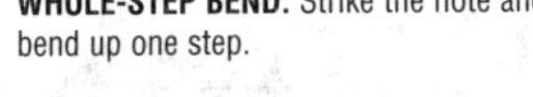

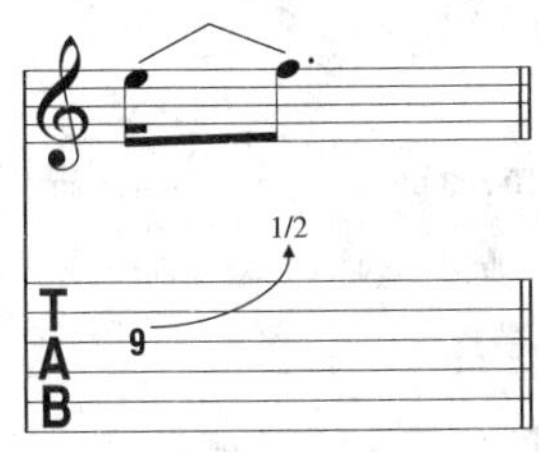

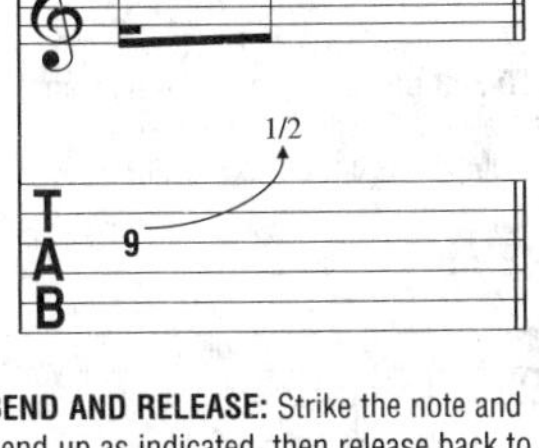

WHOLE-STEP BEND: Strike the note and bend up one step.

GRACE NOTE BEND: Strike the note and immediately bend up as indicated.

SLIGHT (MICROTONE) BEND: Strike the note and bend up 1/4 step.

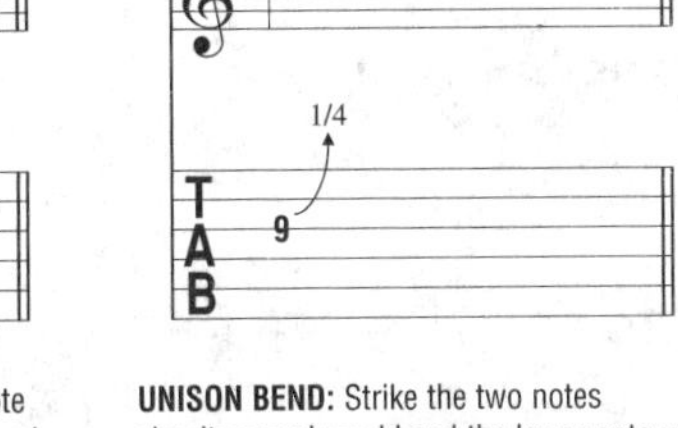

BEND AND RELEASE: Strike the note and bend up as indicated, then release back to the original note. Only the first note is struck.

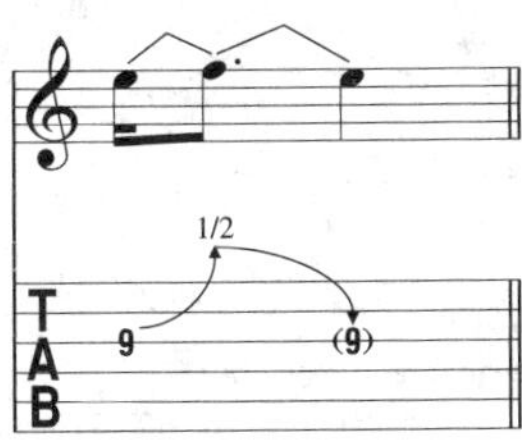

PRE-BEND: Bend the note as indicated, then strike it.

PRE-BEND AND RELEASE: Bend the note as indicated. Strike it and release the bend back to the original note.

UNISON BEND: Strike the two notes simultaneously and bend the lower note up to the pitch of the higher.

VIBRATO: The string is vibrated by rapidly bending and releasing the note with the fretting hand.

WIDE VIBRATO: The pitch is varied to a greater degree by vibrating with the fretting hand.

HAMMER-ON: Strike the first (lower) note with one finger, then sound the higher note (on the same string) with another finger by fretting it without picking.

PULL-OFF: Place both fingers on the notes to be sounded. Strike the first note and without picking, pull the finger off to sound the second (lower) note.

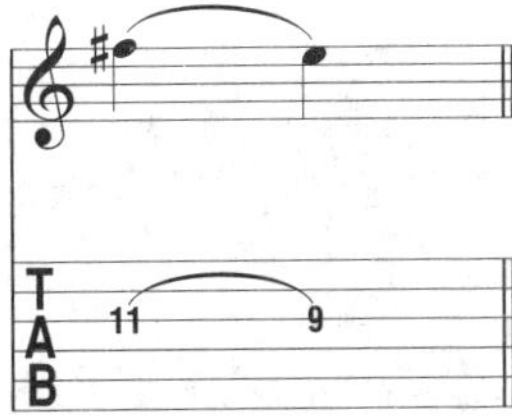

LEGATO SLIDE: Strike the first note and then slide the same fret-hand finger up or down to the second note. The second note is not struck.

SHIFT SLIDE: Same as legato slide, except the second note is struck.

TRILL: Very rapidly alternate between the notes indicated by continuously hammering on and pulling off.

TAPPING: Hammer ("tap") the fret indicated with the pick-hand index or middle finger and pull off to the note fretted by the fret hand.

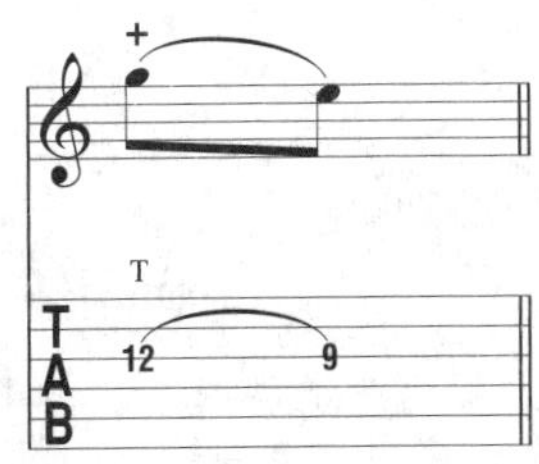

NATURAL HARMONIC: Strike the note while the fret-hand lightly touches the string directly over the fret indicated.

PINCH HARMONIC: The note is fretted normally and a harmonic is produced by adding the edge of the thumb or the tip of the index finger of the pick hand to the normal pick attack.

HARP HARMONIC: The note is fretted normally and a harmonic is produced by gently resting the pick hand's index finger directly above the indicated fret (in parentheses) while the pick hand's thumb or pick assists by plucking the appropriate string.

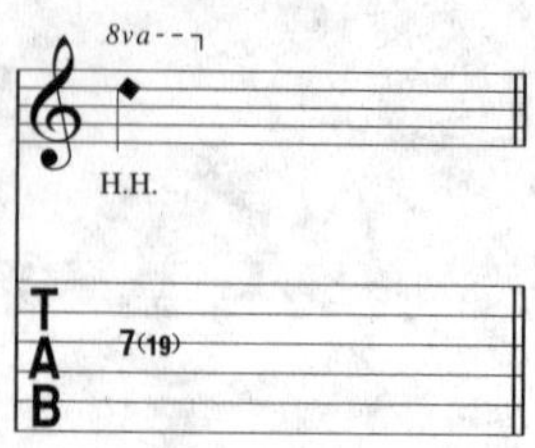

PICK SCRAPE: The edge of the pick is rubbed down (or up) the string, producing a scratchy sound.

MUFFLED STRINGS: A percussive sound is produced by laying the fret hand across the string(s) without depressing, and striking them with the pick hand.

PALM MUTING: The note is partially muted by the pick hand lightly touching the string(s) just before the bridge.

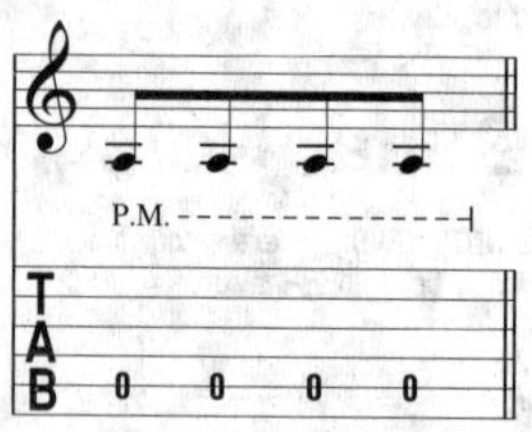

RAKE: Drag the pick across the strings indicated with a single motion.

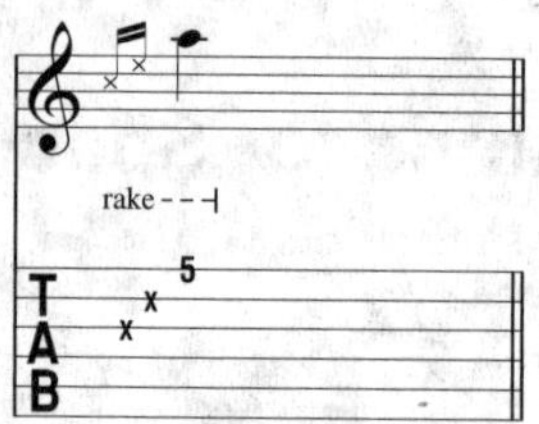

TREMOLO PICKING: The note is picked as rapidly and continuously as possible.

ARPEGGIATE: Play the notes of the chord indicated by quickly rolling them from bottom to top.

VIBRATO BAR DIVE AND RETURN: The pitch of the note or chord is dropped a specified number of steps (in rhythm), then returned to the original pitch.

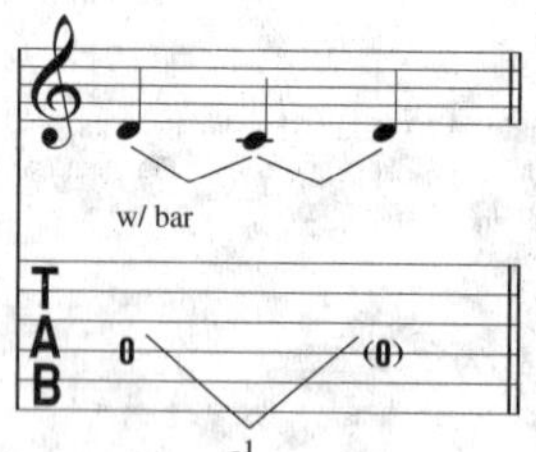

VIBRATO BAR SCOOP: Depress the bar just before striking the note, then quickly release the bar.

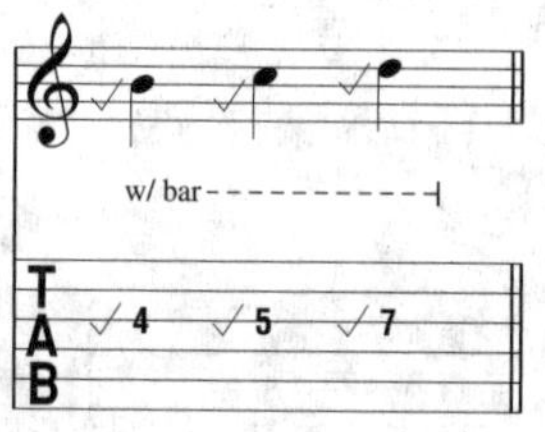

VIBRATO BAR DIP: Strike the note and then immediately drop a specified number of steps, then release back to the original pitch.

Additional Musical Definitions

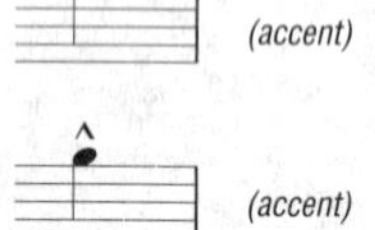 *(accent)* • Accentuate note (play it louder).

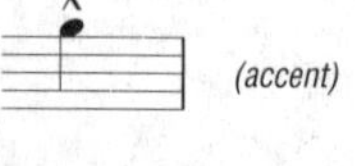 *(accent)* • Accentuate note with great intensity.

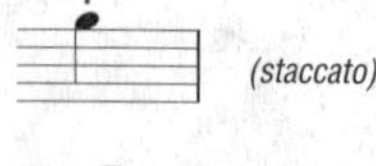 *(staccato)* • Play the note short.

⊓ • Downstroke

V • Upstroke

D.S. al Coda • Go back to the sign (𝄋), then play until the measure marked "***To Coda,***" then skip to the section labelled "**Coda.**"

D.C. al Fine • Go back to the beginning of the song and play until the measure marked "***Fine***" (end).

Rhy. Fig. • Label used to recall a recurring accompaniment pattern (usually chordal).

Riff • Label used to recall composed, melodic lines (usually single notes) which recur.

Fill • Label used to identify a brief melodic figure which is to be inserted into the arrangement.

Rhy. Fill • A chordal version of a Fill.

tacet • Instrument is silent (drops out).

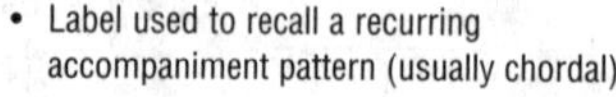

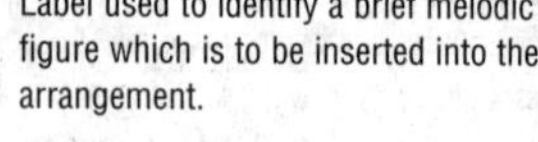 • Repeat measures between signs.

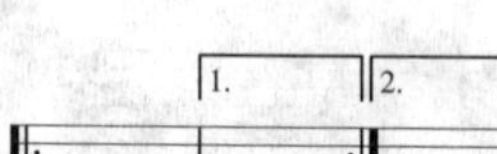

• When a repeated section has different endings, play the first ending only the first time and the second ending only the second time.

NOTE: Tablature numbers in parentheses mean:
1. The note is being sustained over a system (note in standard notation is tied), or
2. The note is sustained, but a new articulation (such as a hammer-on, pull-off, slide or vibrato) begins, or
3. The note is a barely audible "ghost" note (note in standard notation is also in parentheses).